Handbook of Bullying in Schools

The *Handbook of Bullying in Schools: An International Perspective* provides a comprehensive review and analysis of what is known about the worldwide bullying phenomena. It is the first volume to systematically review and integrate what is known about how cultural and regional issues affect bullying behavior and its prevention. It draws on insights from scholars around the world to advance our understanding of:

- Theoretical and empirical foundations for understanding bullying
- Assessment and measurement of bullying
- Research-based prevention and intervention methods

Key features include the following:

Comprehensive—41 chapters bring together conceptual, methodological, and preventive findings from this loosely coupled field of study, thereby providing a long-needed centerpiece around which the field can continue to grow in an organized and interdisciplinary manner.

International Focus—Approximately 40% of the chapters deal with bullying assessment, prevention, and intervention efforts outside the USA.

Chapter Structure—To provide continuity, chapter authors follow a common chapter structure: overview, conceptual foundations, specific issues or programs, and a review of current research and future research needs.

Implications for Practice—A critical component of each chapter is a summary table outlining practical applications of the foregoing research.

Expertise—The editors and contributors include leading researchers, teachers, and authors in the bullying field, most of whom are deeply connected to organizations studying bullying around the world.

Shane R. Jimerson, Ph.D., is a Professor at the University of California, Santa Barbara.

Susan M. Swearer, Ph.D., is an Associate Professor at the University of Nebraska-Lincoln.

Dorothy L. Espelage, Ph.D., is a Professor at the University of Illinois, Urbana-Champaign.

Handbook of Bullying in Schools

An International Perspective

Edited by

Shane R. Jimerson
Susan M. Swearer
Dorothy L. Espelage

Routledge
Taylor & Francis Group

NEW YORK AND LONDON

First published 2010
by Routledge
270 Madison Ave, New York, NY 10016

Simultaneously published in the UK
by Routledge
2 Park Square, Milton Park, Abingdon, Oxon OX14 4RN

Routledge is an imprint of the Taylor & Francis Group, an informa business

Typeset in Minion by EvS Communication Networx, Inc.
Printed and bound in the United States of America on acid-free paper by Edwards Brothers, Inc.

Library of Congress Cataloging in Publication Data
Handbook of bullying in schools ; an international perspective / edited by Shane R. Jimerson, Susan M. Swearer, and Dorothy L. Espelage.
p. cm.
Includes bibliographical references and index.
1. Bullying in schools—Handbooks, manuals, etc. I. Jimerson, Shane R. II. Swearer, Susan M. III. Espelage, Dorothy L. (Dorothy Lynn)
LB3013.3.H343 2009
371.5'8—dc22
2009034689

ISBN 10: 0-8058-6392-3 (hbk)
ISBN 10: 0-8058-6393-1 (pbk)
ISBN 10: 0-203-86496-4 (ebk)

ISBN 13: 978-0-8058-6392-5 (hbk)
ISBN 13: 978-0-8058-6393-2 (pbk)
ISBN 13: 978-0-203-86496-8 (ebk)

Dedicated to

our families and special persons who remind us of the importance of our efforts and make us smile everyday:

Gavin & Taite Jimerson
Kathryn O'Brien
Catherine & Alexandra Napolitano
Scott Napolitano
MacKenzie Hardesty
Ray Musleh

and to the professionals who engage in activities to prevent bullying, as well as the scholars who advance our understanding of bullying, including conceptual foundations, appropriate measurements, and the development and evaluation of bullying prevention programs. It is our hope that the contributions of scholars from around the world will provide invaluable insights and serve as a catalyst for future scholarship that will advance our collective understanding and efforts to promote healthy peer relationships.

Contents

1

International Scholarship Advances Science and Practice Addressing Bullying in Schools

SHANE R. JIMERSON, SUSAN M. SWEARER, AND DOROTHY L. ESPELAGE

Bullying is commonly defined as repeated aggressive behavior in which there is an imbalance of power or strength between the two parties (Nansel et al., 2001; Olweus, 1993). Bullying behaviors may be direct or overt (e.g., hitting, kicking, name-calling, or taunting) or more subtle or indirect in nature (e.g., rumor-spreading, social exclusion, friendship manipulation, or cyberbullying; Espelage & Swearer, 2004; Olweus, 1993; Rigby, 2002). Notably, bullying has been documented and studied in countries around the world (e.g., Australia, Belgium, Brazil, Canada, China, Denmark, England, Finland, France, Germany, Greece, Ireland, Italy, Latvia, Lithuania, Japan, Netherlands, New Zealand, Norway, Portugal, Scotland, South Africa, South Korea, Sweden, Switzerland, Turkey, and the United States). To date, studies in all countries in which bullying has been investigated, have revealed the presence of bullying. Indeed, the study of bullying at school is decidedly international, with seminal scholarship originating in Sweden, Norway, England, Japan, and Australia.

Recent literature has focused explicitly on considering international perspectives on interventions to address bullying in schools (Smith, Pepler, & Rigby, 2004; Ttofi, Farrington, & Baldry, 2008). Scholars have also attempted to understand the phenomenon of bullying through cross-national studies. For example, Smith, Cowie, Olafsson, and Liefooghe (2002) examined the meaning of bullying in 14 different countries to explore how the use of specific terms (e.g., bullying, teasing, harassment, hitting, excluding) may affect estimates of the prevalence of bullying. Despite the recent increase in the amount of research addressing bullying, much remains to be discovered and understood regarding assessment and measurement of bullying, as well as how to design and implement of effective prevention and intervention programs. Considering the extant research that has emerged during the past four decades from around the world, the *Handbook of Bullying in Schools* provides an unprecedented compendium of information and insights from leading scholars around the world.

International Interest in Bullying

Research has revealed that students around the world regularly report witnessing and experiencing bullying (Eslea et al., 2003). Although bullying among children and youth is not a recent phenomenon, it has received increased attention internationally during the past several decades.

For instance, in Australia, it is estimated that 1 child in 6 is subjected to bullying on a weekly basis (Rigby, 2002). Previous studies in Norway and Sweden found that 15% of students reported being involved in bully/victim problems at least 2–3 times per month (Olweus, 1993). Studies in the United States have yielded slightly higher rates of bullying, ranging from a low of 10% for "extreme victims" of bullying (Perry, Kusel, & Perry, 1988) to a high of 75% who reported being bullied at least one time during their school years (Hoover, Oliver, & Thomson, 1993). In a nationally representative study of American students in Grades 6 through 10, Nansel and colleagues (2001) reported that 17% had been bullied with some regularity (several times or more within the semester) and 19% had bullied others.

Bullying is not a part of normative development for children and adolescents and should be considered a precursor to more serious aggressive behaviors (Nansel et al., 2001). It is also clear that bullying can contribute to an environment of fear and intimidation in schools (Ericson, 2001). Furthermore, the culmination of more than a decade of research indicates that bullying may seriously affect the psychosocial functioning, academic work, and the health of children who are targeted (Limber, 2006; Swearer et al., 2001). The persistent prevalence and deleterious consequences associated with bullying have resulted in numerous countries around the world developing national initiatives to address bullying (examples listed in Table 1.1).

Recent Meta-Analyses of International Scholarship Addressing Bullying

A recent meta-analysis (Ttofi et al., 2008; sponsored by The Swedish National Council for Crime Prevention) includes the results of a systematic review of 59 reports describing evaluations of 30 school-based bullying prevention and intervention programs implemented and studied around the world. The meta-analysis included four types of research design: (a) randomized experiments; (b) experimental-control comparisons with before and after measures of bullying; (c) other experimental-control comparisons; and (d) age-cohort designs, where students of a specific age after the intervention were compared with students of the same age in the same school before the intervention. Studies considered for inclusion in the meta-analysis included research

Table 1.1 Examples of National Initiatives to Address Bullying and Website Resources

Australian Bullying. No Way
　　http://www.bullyingnoway.com.au
Australia "National Safe Schools Framework"
　　http://www.nssf.com.au >
Canada, Promoting Relationships and Eliminating Violence
　　http://www.prevnet.ca
European Commission CONNECT project on Violence in Schools
　　http://www.gold.ac.uk/connect
International Observatory on School Violence
　　http://www.ijvs.org
New Zealand, No Bully - Kia-Kaha
　　http://www.police.govt.nz/service/yes/nobully/
South Australia, "Bullying, Out of Bounds"
　　http://www.decs.sa.gov.au/schlstaff/pages/bullying
United States Department of Education
　　http://www.ed.gov/admins/lead/safety/training/bullying/index.html
United States Department of Health & Human Services - Stop Bullying Now
　　http://stopbullyingnow.hrsa.gov/index.asp?area=main
Substance Abuse and Mental Health Services Administration
　　http://mentalhealth.samhsa.gov/15plus/aboutbullying.asp
　　http://www.sshs.samhsa.gov/initiative/resources.aspx

from Australia, Austria, Belgium, Canada, Czechoslovakia, Cyprus, Denmark, England and Wales, Finland, France, Germany, Greece, Iceland, Ireland, Israel, Italy, Luxembourg, Japan, Malta, New Zealand, Northern Ireland, Norway, Portugal, Scotland, Spain, Sweden, Switzerland, The Netherlands, and the United States. The effect sizes regarding impact on bullying ranged from .77 to 2.52, with a weighted mean of 1.43. Statistical significance varied across the four types of research design, with 1 out of 9 of the randomized experiments yielding significant effect sizes; 6 out of 9 of the before-after experimental control yielding significant effect sizes; 2 out of 4 other experimental control yielding significant effect sizes; and 6 out of 6 of the studies using age-cohort designs yielding significant effect sizes.

Based on the results of the meta-analysis, Ttofi and colleagues (2008) concluded that 12 anti-bullying programs were clearly effective in reducing bullying and victimization: Andreou, Didaskalou, and Vlachou (2007), Ertesvag and Vaaland (2007), Evers, Prochaska, Van Marter, Johnson, and Prochaska (2007), Melton et al. (1998), Olweus/Bergen 2, Olweus/Bergen 1, Olweus/Oslo 1, Olweus/New National, Olweus/Oslo 2, Raskauskas (2007), Salmivalli, Kaukiainen, and Voeten (2005), and Salmivalli, Karna, and Poskiparta (this volume). Moreover, analyses of a systematic coding of program elements revealed the most important program elements associated with a decrease in *bullying* were: parent training, improved playground supervision, disciplinary methods, school conferences, information for parents, classroom rules, classroom management, and videos. The most important program elements associated with a decrease in *victimization* were videos, disciplinary methods, work with peers, parent training, cooperative group work, and playground supervision.

Furthermore, the findings from this recent meta-analysis raise several questions that Ttofi and colleagues (2008) propose. For example; "Why do results vary across different countries? Why do results vary by research design? Why do programs appear to work better with older children? Why are larger and more recent studies less effective than smaller-scale and older studies? Why do results vary with the outcome measure of bullying or victimization?" (p. 73).

Based on their meta-analysis of results included in 59 reports from 1983–2008, Ttofi and colleagues (2008) concluded that, "overall, school-based anti-bullying programs are effective in reducing bullying and victimization. The results indicated that bullying and victimization were reduced by about 17–23% in experimental schools compared with control schools" (p. 6). However, it is not clear whether this reduction results in clinically (versus statistically) meaningful changes that improve student's perceptions of school safety and prevent further bullying and/or peer victimization over the long haul. The authors also highlight that studies in Norway yielded more favorable results, relative to the studies in the United States.

Another recent meta-analysis, including 16 studies (published between 1994–2003) from 6 countries, of studies focusing on a broad range of interventions to address bullying, found that the majority of the outcomes revealed no meaningful change, either positive or negative (Merrell, Guelder, Ross, & Isava, 2008). Merrell and colleagues also highlighted that school bullying intervention programs are more likely to influence knowledge, attitudes, and self-perceptions, rather than actual bullying behaviors. Given that changes in attitudes need to occur prior to behavioral changes, these findings suggest that the programs as delivered might be too low of a dose and future work should consider how dose and implementation level impacts outcomes.

An examination of dosage issues and treatment fidelity in bullying prevention and intervention programming is vital. Ttofi and colleagues (2008) highlighted that the total number of program components (dose) and the duration and intensity of the programming for students and teachers were significantly linked to reductions in bullying behavior. In a recent study examining teacher adherence to anti-bullying programming, dose effects were also found (Biggs, Vernberg, Twemlow, Fonagy, & Dill, 2008). Results from the implementation of the Creating a Peaceful School Learning Environment (CAPSLE) program found that the greater number of program components delivered and teacher treatment adherence were both associated with helping peers, greater empathy, and less aggressive bystander behavior among elementary-school students. Treatment fidelity is a critical, yet understudied component of bullying prevention and intervention programming.

These recent studies serve as a reminder of the importance of considering scholarship from around the world, and considering the multitude of variables associated with applied research. Additionally, different types of analyses are necessary to understand the effects associated with bullying programming at individual, peer, school, family, and community levels. These studies also highlight the importance of research design, conceptual foundations, assessment, and measurement used in the empirical work to advance our understanding of "what works" in bullying prevention and intervention programming. Whereas much has been learned about bullying over the past 30 years, we still have a long way to go in order to reduce bullying behaviors in schools across the world.

Handbook of Bullying in Schools

Collectively, the chapters in this volume offer an international analysis of the bullying phenomena, which provides a foundation (conceptually, empirically, and practically) for implementing and examining prevention and intervention programs to reduce bullying behaviors. Recent scholarship has increasingly focused on understanding and preventing bullying. However, despite this recent focus on elucidating correlates and sequelae of bullying behaviors, less is known about how culture and regional issues might affect these behaviors. Thus, the *Handbook of Bullying in Schools* advances the knowledge and understanding of bullying by incorporating valuable information from scholars and practitioners around the world. The information included in the chapters provides fundamental information of interest to scholars, practitioners, and other professionals.

This handbook is intentionally designed to share insights from scholarship around the world, to advance our collective understanding of: (a) theoretical and empirical foundations for understanding bullying, (b) assessment and measurement of bullying, and (c) research-based prevention and intervention for bullying. Leading scholars and practitioners from numerous countries provide information about their attempts to prevent bullying, which in many cases includes innovative approaches to theory, assessment, and intervention. The following provides a brief description of the information that is included in each section of the handbook.

Theoretical and Empirical Foundations for Understanding Bullying Each of the chapters in this section provides important information regarding conceptual foundations related to specific issues, reviews relevant scholarship, and also identifies areas where future research is needed. The information included in this section is essential in establishing a solid foundation for engaging in research as well as implementing bullying prevention and intervention programs around the world.

Assessment and Measurement of Bullying Each chapter in this section identifies and discusses important aspects related to assessing and measuring bullying. Reviewing previous research, including measures used, and identifying convergence and discrepancies as well as related implications are each invaluable in advancing both the science and practice regarding bullying.

Research-Based Prevention and Intervention for Bullying Chapters in this section provide a brief overview of numerous efforts around the globe to implement prevention and intervention programs to address bullying. Authors detail the conceptual foundations underlying the particular programs, delineate the specific strategies incorporated in the program, report results of research related to the effectiveness of the strategies, and identify limitations and areas of need for further scholarship.

In developing the contents of this handbook, it was essential to emphasize an appropriate balance of both breadth and depth, thus, providing information on numerous facets of school bullying. A specific goal of this volume is to spark a comprehensive international discourse of bullying prevention and intervention efforts. A particularly important component included in each chapter is a conclusion or summary table delineating *implications for practice*. It is anticipated that the scholarship emerging during the next decade will build upon the information included here.

References

Andreou, E., Didaskalou, E., & Vlachou, A. (2007). Evaluating the effectiveness of a curriculum-based anti-bullying intervention program in Greek primary schools. *Educational Psychology, 27*, 693–711.

Biggs, B. K., Vernberg, E. M., Twemlow, S. W., Fonagy, P., & Dill, E. J. (2008). Teacher adherence and its relation to teacher attitudes and student outcomes in an elementary school-based violence prevention program. *School Psychology Review, 37*, 533–549.

Ericson, N. (2001). *Addressing the problem of juvenile bullying*. US Department of Justice, no. 27. Washington, DC: U.S. Government Printing Office.

Ertesvag, S. K., & Vaaland, G. S. (2007). Prevention and reduction of behavioural problems in school: An evaluation of the Respect program. *Educational Psychology, 27*, 713–736.

Eslea, M., Menesini, E., Morita, Y., O'Moore, M., Mora-Merchán, J. A., Pereira, B., et al. (2003). Friendship and loneliness among bullies and victims: Data from seven countries. *Aggressive Behavior, 30*, 71–83.

Espelage, D. L., & Swearer, S. M. (2004). *Bullying in American schools: A social-ecological perspective on prevention and intervention*. Mahwah, NJ: Erlbaum.

Evers, K. E., Prochaska, J. O., Van Marter, D. F., Johnson, J. L., & Prochaska, J. M. (2007). Transtheoretical-based bullying prevention effectiveness trials in middle schools and high schools. *Educational Research, 49*, 397–414.

Hoover, J. H., Oliver, R., & Thomson, K. (1993). Perceived victimization by school bullies: New research and future directions. *Journal of Humanistic Education and Development, 32*, 76–84.

Limber, S. P. (2006). The Olweus bullying prevention program: An overview of its implementation and research basis. In S. R. Jimerson & M. J. Furlong (Eds.), *The handbook of school violence and school safety: From research to practice* (293–308). Mahwah, NJ: Erlbaum.

Melton, G. B., Limber, S. P., Flerx, V., Nation, M., Osgood, W., Chambers, J., et al. (1998). *Violence among rural youth*. Washington, DC: U.S. Department of Justice, Office of Justice Programs, Office of Juvenile Justice and Delinquency Prevention.

Merrell, K. W., Guelder, B. A., Ross, S. W., & Isava, D. M. (2008). How effective are school bullying intervention programs? A meta-analysis of intervention research. *School Psychology Quarterly, 23*, 26–42.

Nansel, T. R., Overpeck, M., Pilla, R. S., Ruan, W. J., Simons-Morton, B., & Scheidt, P. (2001). Bullying behaviors among US youth: Prevalence and association with psychosocial adjustment. *Journal of the American Medical Association, 285*, 2094–2100.

Olweus, D. (1993). *Bullying at school: What we know and what we can do*. Cambridge, MA: Blackwell.

Perry, D. G., Kusel, S. J., & Perry, C. L. (1988). Victims of peer aggression. *Developmental Psychology, 24*, 807–814.

Raskauskas, J. (2007). *Evaluation of the Kia Kaha anti-bullying programme for students in years 5–8*. Wellington: New Zealand Police.

Rigby, K. (2002). *New perspectives on bullying*. London: Jessica Kingsley.

Salmivalli, C., Kaukiainen, A., Voeten, M. (2005). Anti-bullying intervention: Implementation and outcome. *British Journal of Educational Psychology, 75*, 465–487.

Smith, P. K., Cowie, H., Olafsson, R. F., & Liefooghe, A. P. D. (2002). Definitions of bullying: A comparison of terms used, and age and gender differences, in a 14-country international comparison. *Child Development, 73*, 1119–1133.

Smith, P. K., Pepler, D., & Rigby, K. (Eds.). (2004). *Bullying in schools: How successful can interventions be?* New York: Cambridge University Press.

Swearer, S., Song, S., Cary, P. T., Eagle, J. W., & Mickelson, W. T. (2001). Psychosocial correlates in bullying and victimization: The relationship between depression, anxiety, and bully/victim status. In R. A. Geffner & M. Loring (Eds.), *Bullying behavior: Current issues, research, and interventions* (pp. 95–121). Binghamton, NY: Haworth Press.

Ttofi, M. M., Farrington, D. P., & Baldry, A. C. (2008). *Effectiveness of programmes to reduce school bullying: A systematic review.* The Swedish National Council for Crime Prevention. Retrieved January 9, 2009, from http://www.bra.se/extra/faq/?module_instance=2&action=question_show&id=474&category_id=9

Section I
Foundations for Understanding Bullying

2

Understanding and Researching Bullying
Some Critical Issues

DAN OLWEUS

The Beginnings

A strong societal interest in the phenomenon of peer harassment or victimization/bullying first started in Sweden in the late 1960s and early 1970s under the designation "mobbning" or "mobbing" (Heinemann, 1969, 1972; Olweus, 1973). The term was introduced into the public Swedish debate by a school physician, P.-P. Heinemann, in the context of racial discrimination (Heinemann, 1969). Heinemann had borrowed the term "mobbing" from the Swedish version of a book on aggression written by the well-known Austrian ethologist, Konrad Lorenz (1963, 1968). In ethology, the word mobbing is used to describe a collective attack by a group of animals on an animal of another species, which is usually larger and a natural enemy of the group. In Lorenz's book (1968), mobbing was also used to characterize the action of a school class or a group of soldiers ganging up against a deviating individual.

The term "mob" has been used for quite some time in social psychology (Lindzey, 1954), and to some extent by the general public in English-speaking countries, to describe a relatively large group of individuals—a crowd or a mass of people—joined in a common activity or goal. As a rule, the mob has been formed by accident, is loosely organized, and exists only for a short time. In the social psychological literature, distinctions have been made between several types of mobs, including the aggressive mob (the lynch mob), the panic-stricken mob (the flight mob), and the acquisitive mob (the hoarding mob). Members of the mob usually experience strong emotions, and the behavior and reactions of the mob are considered to be fairly irrational (see Lindzey, 1954).

At an early point in this debate, I expressed doubts about the suitability of the term, as used in ethology/social psychology, to describe the kind of peer harassment that occurred in school settings (Olweus, 1973, 1978). Generally, with my background in aggression research (e.g., Olweus, 1969, 1972), I felt that the connotations implied in the concept of mobbing could easily lead to inappropriate expectations about the phenomenon of bullying and to certain aspects of the problem being overlooked as exemplified in the next paragraph.

One particular point of concern with the term related to the relative importance of the group versus its individual members. The notion that school mobbing is a matter of collective aggression by a relatively homogeneous group did in my view obscure the relative contributions made by individual members. More specifically, the role of particularly active perpetrators or bullies could easily be lost sight of within this group framework. In this context, I also questioned how often the kind of all-against-one situations implied in mobbing actually occur in school. If harassment by a small group or by a single individual were the more frequent type in schools, the concept of mobbing might result, for example, in teachers having difficulty identifying the phenomenon of bullying in their classrooms. In addition, the concept of mobbing will almost automatically place responsibility for potential problems with the recipient of the collective aggression, the victim, who is seen as irritating or provoking the majority of ordinary students in one way or another.

Use of the concept of mobbing might also lead to an overemphasis on temporary and situationally determined circumstances: "The mob, suddenly and unpredictably, seized by the mood of the moment, turns on a single individual, who for some reason or other has attracted the group's irritation and hostility" (Olweus, 1978, p. 5). Although I believed that such temporary emotional outbreaks from a group of school children could occur, I considered it more important to direct attention to another kind of possible situation, in which an individual student is exposed to aggression systematically and over longer periods of time—whether from another individual, a small group, or a whole class (Olweus, 1973, 1978, p. 5).

An additional problem was that, at that time, there existed basically no empirical research data to shed light on the many issues and concerns involved in the general debate about the bullying phenomenon. Against this background, in the early1970s, I initiated in Sweden (I am a native Swede, who has lived in Norway for more than 35 years) what now appears to be the first systematic research project on bullying by peers. Results from this project were first published as a book in Swedish in 1973 (Olweus, 1973). In 1978, a somewhat expanded version of this book appeared in the United States under the title *Aggression in the Schools: Bullies and Whipping Boys* (Olweus, 1978). A key aim of this research was to sketch a first outline of the anatomy of peer harassment in schools and to seek empirical answers to at least some of the key questions that had been in focus in the public Swedish debate.

Taking a retrospective perspective, I think it is fair to say that this project and later research (e.g., Olweus, 1978, 1993, 1994; Farrington, 1993) have shown that several of my early concerns were justified. For example, there is no doubt that students in a class vary markedly in their degree of aggressiveness and that these individual differences tend to be quite stable over time, often over several years, if no systematic intervention is introduced (Olweus, 1977, 1979).

Similarly, the research clearly shows that a relatively small number of students in a class are usually much more actively engaged in peer harassment or bullying than others, who are not directly involved in bullying at all or only in more or less marginal roles (Olweus, 1993, 2001). Reports from bullied students indicate that they are most often mainly bullied by a small group of two or three students (Olweus & Solberg, 1998), often with a negative leader. In addition, a considerable proportion of the victims, some 25–35%, report that they are mainly bullied by a single student (Olweus, 1988; Olweus & Solberg, 1998). Data from researchers in England, Holland, and Japan, participating in the same cross-national project on bully/victim problems, indicate that this is largely true also in other ethnic contexts with (partly) different cultural backgrounds and traditions (Junger-Tas & Kesteren, 1998; Morita & Soeda, 1998; Smith et al., 1999). Further, these and other (e.g., Rigby & Slee, 1991) data also show that a considerable proportion of the students in a class have a relatively negative attitude toward bullying and would like to do, or actually try to do (according to self-reports), something to help the victim.

This research-based picture of peer harassment in schools is very different from what is generally implied in the social psychological or ethological concepts of mobbing. Also, the use of the term "mobbing" (and derivatives of it) by Scandinavians has certainly come to deviate from both the scientific and the ordinary English root meaning of the term. This is particularly evident when we hear a (Scandinavian) student saying "he/she mobbed me today." Obviously, the word mobbing has gradually, and, in part on the basis of highly publicized research findings, acquired a new meaning in Scandinavian everyday language, loosely implying relatively systematic, repetitive harassment of an individual (or possibly a group) by one or more other individuals (usually but not necessarily by a peer/peers). This new meaning of the word is well established in Norway, Sweden, and Denmark, and in my view, there are no grounds for trying to change this usage.

At the same time, it was clear at an early stage that, for an English-speaking audience, the terms "mob" and "mobbing" are not very useful in describing the phenomenon of bullying; they typically elicit associations in the direction of the social psychological/ethological concepts and the original meaning of the word mob. On the basis of experiences along these lines, I tended to use the term bully/victim (or whipping boy) problems (instead of, or in addition to, mobbing) in my early writings in English (e.g., Olweus, 1978). Currently, the terms "bullying" or "bully/victim problems" seem to have gained general international acceptance (in English-speaking countries) to denote the kind of peer harassment we Scandinavians, somewhat inappropriately from a linguistic point of view, call mobbing.

Definition of Bullying

At the time of initiation of my first research project on bullying, it was not possible, or even desirable, to set forth a very stringent definition of peer harassment or bullying. However, the need for a relatively clear and circumscribed definition became urgent in connection with the government-initiated campaign against bullying in Norway in 1983 (Olweus, 1986, 1993). Specifically, an important part of this campaign was a nationwide registration of bully/victim problems by means of a student questionnaire that I developed. The basic definition of bullying or peer victimization underlying the construction of the questionnaire was the following: A student is being bullied or victimized when he or she is exposed, repeatedly and over time, to negative actions on the part of one or more other students. This definition emphasized intentionally negative or aggressive acts that are carried out repeatedly and over time. It was further specified that in bullying there is a certain imbalance of power or strength. The student who is exposed to negative actions has difficulty defending himself or herself (for further details, see, Olweus 1993, 1999a). Use of the three criteria of intention, repetitiveness, and imbalance of power for classification of a behavior as bullying seems now to be well accepted among both researchers and practitioners (e.g., Smith & Brain, 2000).

As defined above, bullying is a subset of aggression or aggressive behavior, which, in turn, is generally defined as "behavior intended to inflict injury or discomfort upon another individual" (Olweus, 1972; Berkowitz, 1993). Bullying is thus aggressive behavior with certain special characteristics such as repetitiveness and an asymmetric power relationship. The relation between the concepts of bullying, aggression, and violence is discussed in more detail in another context (Olweus, 1999a).

Measuring Bully/Victim Problems with the Olweus Bullying Questionnaire (OBQ)

In my first research project on bullying comprising some 900 boys who were 13- to 15-year-olds at the first time of measurement, I used a combination of teacher nominations and peer ratings to classify students as victims (whipping boys), bullies, and control boys (Olweus, 1973, 1978). The project also used a number of other data sources including self-reports, mother reports, stress hormone data, projective techniques, and psycho-physiological measurements. Although a number of self-report items related to bullying and victimization were included in the project, they were not used in the classification of the students into the various bully/victim categories. However, extensive experience with the questionnaire I developed in the context of the nation-wide 1983 campaign against bullying and the associated intervention project from 1983 to 1985 (Olweus, 1991, 2005), convinced me that a carefully constructed questionnaire can be an excellent tool for the measurement of bully/victim problems.

Although the basic definition of bullying (involving the three criteria listed above) has been retained unchanged, the "definition" presented to the students in a revised version of the questionnaire, the *Revised Olweus Bullying Questionnaire* (in earlier writings, often referred to as the *Olweus Bully/Victim Questionnaire*; Olweus, 1996, 2007), has been somewhat expanded. In the latest version of the questionnaire (Olweus, 2007), this definition reads as follows:

> *We say a student is being bullied when another student, or several other students,*
> - say mean and hurtful things or make fun of him or her or call him or her mean and hurtful names
> - completely ignore or exclude him or her from their group of friends or leave him or her out of things on purpose
> - hit, kick, push, shove around, or lock him or her inside a room
> - tell lies or spread false rumors about him or her or send mean notes and try to make other students dislike him or her
> - and other hurtful things like that.

When we talk about bullying, these things happen *repeatedly*, and it is *difficult for the student being bullied to defend himself or herself.* We also call it bullying when a student is teased repeatedly in a mean and hurtful way. But we *do not call it bullying* when the teasing is done in a friendly and playful way. Also, it is *not bullying* when two students of about the same strength or power argue or fight (Olweus, 2007, p. 2).

After a general or global question about being bullied in the past couple of months (or bullying other students in a different section of the questionnaire), taking all possible forms of bullying into account, the students are asked to respond to questions about nine specific forms of bullying they may have been exposed to. These various forms of bullying comprise direct physical and verbal (including racial and sexual) harassment, threatening, and coercive behaviors, as well as more indirect or relational ways of harassment in the form of intentional social isolation, having rumors spread, and manipulation of friendship relationships (cf. Björkqvist, Lagerspetz, & Kaukiainen, 1992; Crick & Grotpeter, 1995; Underwood, 2003). There are also some questions on the questionnaire about digital or cyber bullying.

The questionnaire can be and has been administered in both anonymous (e.g., Olweus, 2005) and confidential mode (e.g., Olweus, 1991; Solberg & Olweus, 2003). In the anonymous mode, the students only provide information about their own classroom, grade, gender, and school. In the confidential mode, they also report their names which are then hidden through a code system. In the latter case, individual students can be followed over time. Depending on the research question, this may be less important in certain intervention designs (Olweus, 2005).

To make the measuring instrument more sensitive to change, most of the questions refer to a specific reference period, "the past couple of months." To call the students' attention to the fact that they should assess their situation and reactions during this relatively short period and not some longer or undefined time period, the reference period is explicitly mentioned in a number of question texts (e.g., "How often have you been bullied at school in the past couple of months?") and usually in at least one of the response alternatives to a question. For most of the questions, the response alternatives are frequency alternatives and they are made as concrete as possible (e.g., "I have not been bullied at school in the past couple of months," "it has only happened once or twice," "2 or 3 times a month," "about once a week," and "several times a week"). Such specific response alternatives were preferred to alternatives such as "often" or "seldom" which lend themselves to more subjective interpretation and provide more error variance in the measurement.

The questionnaire also contains several questions about the reactions of "others" to bullying, as perceived by the respondents, that is, the behavior and attitudes of teachers, peers, and parents. These questions provide important information about the school's efforts to counteract bullying and in which areas additional efforts may be particularly needed.

Overview of the Remaining Chapter

With this introduction as a general background, I will now continue with the main themes of my chapter. First, I focus on the issue of power imbalance as one defining characteristic of bullying, after which I make a number of comparisons between the two most common methods of measuring bullying/victimization: peer nominations and self-reports as exemplified by the OBQ. After a presentation of the measurement goals of the two methods and a fairly detailed discussion of why a direct correspondence between them cannot be expected, the methods are compared with regard to prevalence estimation and the measurement of change. The chapter ends with a report on a large-scale empirical study of possible gender differences in the area of bullying, taking into account perpetrator and victim perspectives as well as bullying by same- and cross-gender peers. This self-report study focuses on the question: "Are girls just as aggressive as boys?"

My key aim with this chapter is to elucidate some problems in the field, in particular problems with the peer nomination method, which have not been analyzed nor discussed enough (Espelage, Mebane, & Swearer, 2004; see also Ladd & Kochenderfer-Ladd, 2002; and Underwood, Galen, & Paquette, 2001 for interesting discussions of some of the issues) and to provide empirical data on some of these issues. Hopefully, this chapter will contribute to fruitful discussions with and among the many researchers who invest their time and efforts in bullying research and intervention work.

Is the Power Imbalance Important?

In the Olweus Bully/Victim Questionnaire, the power imbalance implied in bullying is introduced through the definition presented to the students. One way of getting at least a rough impression of the extent to which this aspect of the definition is perceived by the students in responding to the questionnaire is to examine the psychological and social adjustment of the victim group as defined by the questionnaire.

In most current empirical analyses, this victim group consists of two subgroups, usually named submissive/passive victims or victims only and provocative/aggressive victims or bully-victims (Olweus, 1978; Solberg & Olweus, 2003; Solberg, Olweus, & Endresen, 2007a). Typically, students who have responded that they have been bullied at least "2 or 3 times a month" in the past couple of months have been classified as victims. The students in this overall group of victims have been further differentiated through their responses to the global question about bullying other students. Those students who have responded that they have also bullied other students "2 or 3 times a month" or more, are classified as bully-victims or provocative victims.

Students who have responded that they have not bullied other students (not at all or only once or twice) are categorized as victims only or submissive/passive victims.

In a number of studies, the submissive/passive victim/victims only have been described as anxious, depressed with negative self-views, socially isolated, and generally non-aggressive (e.g., Olweus, 1993; Hawker & Boulton, 2000). These results strongly suggest that students with such characteristics have been the "underdogs" or victims in interpersonal interactions or relationships characterized by an imbalance of power.

It is somewhat less clear what should be expected with regard to the usually considerably smaller group of provocative victims/bully-victims (Solberg et al., 2007a). However, it is natural to expect that these students, in similarity with the submissive victims, would display elevated levels of internalizing problems and social isolation if they have been the targets of regular bullying by more powerful peers. This is also what has been found in empirical research (Olweus, 1993, 2001; Solberg, Olweus, & Endresen, 2007b). However, this group of students can also be expected to display a good deal of externalizing problems, since they report bullying other students as well, but this is of less relevance from the power imbalance perspective.

Overall, the psychological and social characteristics of these two victim groups are consistent with the assumption that the students have roughly understood the definition of bullying with its emphasis on the power imbalance and responded to the questionnaire in agreement with such an understanding.

In a recent paper, three English researchers have taken a more direct approach to the power imbalance issue (Hunter, Boyle, & Warden, 2007). In their study of approximately 1,400 students in the 8- to 13-year-old range the researchers asked the participants to indicate via self-report how often they had been exposed to a number of aggressive behaviors in the past two weeks. In addition, the participants were asked to indicate if the aggressor(s) in question was more "powerful" as reflected in greater physical strength, higher popularity, or a situation in which the perpetrator was part of a group. In this way, the researchers could identify a relatively large group of students (named peer-victimized students) who had been exposed to recurrent aggression and from this group they separated out a group of students who had been aggressed against in interactions or a relationship characterized by at least one form of power imbalance. Students in the latter group who comprised approximately 40% of the peer-victimized group (and 12% of the whole sample) were named victims of bullying. When comparing these two groups of aggressed against/victimized students, they found several theoretically meaningful differences. The victims of bullying perceived significantly more threat and less control over their situation in addition to being more depressed, engaging in more wishful thinking, and seeking more social support than the other group. In conclusion, the authors emphasized the importance of making a difference between peer-victimized students and bullied students with the presence of a power imbalance as the differentiating criterion. The results of this study clearly suggest that, from the perspective of the targeted students, bullying is a more serious and hurtful form of peer aggression.

These studies and conceptual arguments strongly underscore the importance of differentiating between being bullied, in the context of a power-imbalanced relationship, and being exposed to (recurrent) aggressive acts. In the latter case, it is actually doubtful if one, without further analyses, can regard and name the exposed students as victims. One reason for the importance of differentiating between these two groups of "victims" is that some students who themselves initiate many aggressive interactions are likely to be exposed to aggressive acts from their opponents also when they are clearly the "winners" of the aggressive interaction. These students will then correctly report that they have been exposed to aggressive acts and as a consequence be included in the total group of victims (and bully-victims). However, such students are not likely to have much in common with students who have been exposed to the aggressive acts in the context of a bullying relationship with a clear power imbalance (Hunter et al., 2007).

To classify such aggressive students as "victims" would result in greater heterogeneity of this group in terms of psychological and social adjustment: It may include both Victims Only, Bully-Victims, and Bullies Only. It would also increase the overlap between bullies and victims as well as the correlation between victimization and aggression/bullying variables in dimensional analyses, possibly leading to unfortunate conclusions to the effect that bullies and victims are largely the same students and have (relatively) similar characteristics (see Solberg et al., 2007a).

In the foregoing discussion, the power imbalance was explicitly introduced in the definition of bullying or directly measured. It should be acknowledged, however, that the power imbalance can also be introduced indirectly through the wording of the descriptors employed in some commonly used peer nomination techniques. Examples include formulations like "Who gets pushed around by other kids?" "Who is put down and made fun of?" "He/she gets beat up by other kids" which formulations suggest that the target student has difficulty defending him or herself. In several of these techniques, however, the descriptors used to measure "the opposite side of the coin" often reflects generally aggressive behavior ("Who starts a fight over nothing?" "He/she calls others mean names.") rather than bullying behavior specifically. In a recent paper (Solberg et al., 2007a), we have named this approach the "aggression line" in partial contrast to the "bullying line" in which there is an emphasis on the power imbalance.

Victims of bullying are likely to overlap in part with and can be seen as a subgroup of peer-victimized students with special characteristics. Similarly, students who bully others are likely to overlap in part with and can be seen as a subgroup of aggressive students with special characteristics. Although there is a good deal of overlap between the subgroups generated within the aggression line and the bullying line, there are very likely also some important distinguishing characteristics. There is obviously a need for more empirical studies to inform us about the character and importance of these distinctions. At this point in time, it is essential to be clear about these likely differences, to be more precise in describing and interpreting the results of our studies, and not to use the relevant terms as synonymous without empirical support. With regard to the latter point, authors should be careful not to present results as applying to bullying when they actually have measured victimization and general aggression (also see Hunter et al., 2007).

Self-Report and Peer Reports of Bully/Victim Problems

The two most common methods for measuring bully/victim problems or related concepts are self-report and some form of peer report. Sometimes these methods are pitted against one another and some authors have expressed a clear preference for one of the methods. Others have claimed that both methods provide valuable but incomplete information and that the best thing may be to combine information from both data sources. Still others (Juvonen, Nishina, & Graham, 2001) have been more specific in arguing that the two methods tap different constructs: subjective self-views and social reputation. According to Juvonen et al., both methods may provide valid and useful information but for different purposes. They also caution against uncritically aggregating data from the two sources which may actually result in the masking of important associations.

To get a better understanding of the relation between these methods and their characteristics, is important to take a closer look at the kind of information they provide or aim to provide and also to specify in some detail for what purpose(s) the measurements will be used. Although peer nominations and self-report may serve other functions, for this analysis I have chosen the following three goals all of which may be considered important: (a) measurement of relatively stable individual differences on the relevant dimensions and the selection of extreme groups of involved students (e.g., victims only, bullies only, bully-victims, and non-involved students); (b) prevalence estimation; and (c) measurement of change. In the context of the first goal, I will also examine the degree of correspondence or convergence between data derived from peer and self-reports and highlight some differences which are likely to reduce the expected correspondence. I will largely restrict my choice of methods to my own questionnaire, the OBQ, and to peer nominations. Both these methods are in frequent use. I am also focusing primarily on measurement with students in the age range 10 to 16 years (typically grades 4–10).

In previous sections a good deal of information was provided on the measurement of bully/victim problems with the questionnaire. Therefore, a few words about the peer nomination method of which there are several relatively similar versions is warranted.

Peer Nominations

In a typical peer nomination procedure, students are presented with a roster of the names (and possibly pictures) of their classmates and asked to nominate a fixed number, often three, or an unlimited number of usually same-gender peers in their classroom or grade who fit one or several descriptions of victimization/being bullied and aggression/bullying other students (Who is the kid who …; He/she is picked on … Find the names of three classmates who …). The number or percentage of nominations received is used as the student's score on the relevant dimension. The scores are often standardized within gender, grade, and/or classroom.

Peer nominations can be seen as a special form of rating (Guilford, 1954). By their very nature, peer nominations (or ratings) are aimed at measuring relatively stable, enduring characteristics such as typical behavior patterns that the nominees display or are exposed to (Cronbach, 1970; Guilford, 1954). As detailed by Cairns and Green (1979), in making ratings (nominations) the raters (nominators) usually have to perform a number of complex cognitive operations in which they abstract and integrate a whole series of action patterns, usually with implicit reference to a comparison group of children in the same sex-age range and circumstances. In this way, the raters/nominators are likely to control for or "discount(s) situational, relational, ephemeral sources of variation that may be responsible for the observed behavior" (p. 212).

In terms of generalizability theory (Cronbach, Gleser, Nanda, & Rajaratnam, 1972), the explicit or implicit goal of such nominations is usually to maximize the "person variance component" in relation to the total variance. This will increase the reliability of the measurement which is calculated as the person variance component divided by the total variance (e.g., Cronbach, 1970). This goal is often emphasized by the way the descriptors are formulated (above) including use of the present tense (Who is such and such?). If the nominators have a reasonable level of agreement in their nominations, the aggregate or sum of the nominations will be a highly reliable measure. This suggests that the nominated students are well differentiated on the key dimensions of interest (but see below). In particular, such a sum score (possibly transformed) means that the method permits reliable selection of extreme groups of students who are nominated as being bullied/victimized and/or as bullying/being aggressive against other students.

The aim of the OBQ is also to measure relatively stable individual-differentiating characteristics. However, in contrast with peer nominations, each student is directly assessed (that is, assesses himself or herself) on a graded response scale with regard to how well he/she fits the descriptors (questions) in the questionnaire. With its repeated reference to the time frame of "the past couple of months," the OBQ is clearly designed to measure less stable characteristics than typical peer nominations. The two global questions which have been found to contain much valid information (e.g., Solberg & Olweus, 2003; Solberg et al., 2007b), aim to provide individual overall estimates of being bullied and bullying other students (taking all possible forms of bullying into account) and seem to be well suited for such a purpose and for the selection of extreme groups of involved students. It is also possible to sum or aggregate the students' scores on the various forms of being bullied/bullying others (verbal, physical, indirect/relational, sexual, racial, bullying etc.), and thereby arrive at highly reliable mean scores, usually with internal consistency coefficients in the .80–.90 range (Olweus, 2006; Kyriakides, Kaloyirou, & Lindsay, 2006).

In sum, important goals in using peer nominations as well as the OBQ are to measure relatively stable individual-differentiating characteristics in being bullied and bullying/aggressing against other students and to select distinct extreme groups of bullied and bullying students. With this discussion as a background and the difference with regard to the reference period being assessed in mind, it is of interest to take a look at the degree of correspondence between data derived from self and peer reports, as documented in empirical studies.

Correspondence Between Self-Report and Peer Reports

There has been no systematic review of studies that have used both the OBQ and some form of peer nominations. For the purposes of the present discussion, I will therefore rely on an unpublished meta-analysis presented at the Society for Research on Child Development symposium in Tampa, Florida, by Card in 2003. Card's careful analysis included 21 studies of the correlation between self and peer reports of victimization. Some of the studies included had used the OBQ. The peer reports were both nominations and ratings. Because of this heterogeneity, these data do not match exactly the purposes of the present analysis, but they will nevertheless provide an empirically based impression of the degree of correspondence that has been typically reported.

The average correlation across the 21 studies was 0.37. Considering the fact that the studies included in the meta-analysis were of varying quality and several of them were not particularly designed to maximize correspondence between data from the two sources, this is a respectable result. This correlation is clearly higher than the average association between self- and peer data reported in a well-known meta-analysis of cross-informant reports on child behavior problems ($r = .26$; Achenbach, McConaughy, & Howell, 1987). This suggests that to be victimized/bullied is something that can be more easily observed and assessed than some other child behavior problems. Still, one may wonder why the average correlation was not larger.

Factors Contributing to Lack of Correspondence

In reflecting on this issue, it becomes obvious that, given the design of the instruments and the way data are typically treated in the two methods, there are a number of reasons why a very close correspondence cannot be expected. Some of these possible reasons are briefly discussed in the following paragraphs.

First, a good deal of bullying is of a subtle and somewhat secretive nature which may be difficult for peers to observe but is clearly perceived by the targeted student and accordingly, likely to be reported in the OBQ (cf. Cairns & Cairns, 1986). This may be especially true for situations where the bullying is mainly executed by a single student, which happens relatively frequently (Olweus, 1988). In such cases, the peer group may have little knowledge about what actually goes on, in particular since many victims of bullying typically do not tell anybody about their experience (Olweus, 1993).

Second, in the OBQ the students report on the frequency with which they have been bullied/bullied other students whereas the peer nomination method measures frequency of nominations of "extreme students," not the frequency or seriousness of the implicated behaviors. It may be reasonable to assume that a score of many, or a high proportion of, nominations which more "extreme" individuals will receive, actually reflects some frequency/seriousness (and maybe degree of visibility) dimension, at least roughly. However, for less extreme individuals, it is not self-evident that an average number of nominations, for example, directly translate into an average level or frequency/seriousness of problem behaviors. Also, in many peer nomination studies a considerable proportion of students receive no nominations at all (e.g., Espelage, Holt, & Henkel, 2003) and individuals with "zero scores" cannot without further analyses be assumed to have identical low levels of the characteristic in question. This lack of discrimination among non-extreme students will very likely reduce the correlation between peer and self-reports. In addition, it can be shown that the variance and distribution of nominations for a classroom (or grade) are substantially influenced by the number of nominators (classroom size) and the degree of inter-nominator agreement. As a consequence, also behaviorally fairly non-extreme students may well be selected into the extreme group (for example, students with a standard score +1 above the mean) from relatively smaller classrooms and/or classrooms with poor internominator-agreement (typically with smaller variance). The effects of such mechanisms, which are not well described and understood, are also likely to reduce correspondence with self-report data.

Third, as has been documented in our studies (Olweus, 1993, 1999b), a good deal of bullying is carried out by older students towards younger ones, in particular in the lower grades (4–6). To be bullied by older students will be captured in the key questions in the OBQ but is less likely to be registered in the peer nominations which typically only refer to students in the nominators' own classroom or grade.

Fourth, as has also been documented in our studies (Olweus, 1993, 1999b), a good deal of bullied girls report that they are mainly bullied by boys. Such cross-gender bullying will be captured in the key questions in the OBQ but probably not in peer nominations that are restricted to same-gender nominees (which is a fairly common restriction). In particular, girls bullied by boys and boys bullying girls may not be well identified under peer nomination conditions.

Fifth, the common practice of statistically standardizing peer nominations within classroom, gender, and/or grade will often result in the removal of meaningful between-classroom/gender/grade variance. To illustrate, if there is a marked difference in the number/proportion of nominations of bullying (extreme) students for Grade 4 and Grade 5 and these data are standardized within grade, this means that this developmental difference is effectively eliminated. The two distributions of standardized nominations will have the same mean values and standard deviations in spite of the fact that one grade has a much higher level of problems with bullying. As a related consequence, the most extreme students in each grade will receive roughly similar standardized values even if the extreme students in the most aggressive grade have received larger numbers/higher proportions of nominations. Since such differences in the level of problems are likely to be captured in self-reports, also the practice of standardizing may reduce the degree of correspondence between self and peer reports. Results similar to those achieved through statistical standardization are likely to obtained by procedurally restricting nominations to students of the same category (classroom/gender/grade) in combination with use of a fixed number of nominations (e.g., "Find the three same-gender peers in the class who fit the description…").

At the same time, it should be noted that the practice of standardization may not be a great problem from the perspective of correspondence, if correlations between self-reports and peer nominations are calculated separately for girls and boys within classrooms for different grades and then averaged (maybe weighted by group size). This is not regularly done, however, and the likely disturbing effects of statistical and procedural standardizing should be given more consideration and be investigated much more thoroughly than has been done so far.

A more general comment on the reliability of peer nominations also seems warranted. The typically high reliability of many peer nomination dimensions is often regarded as an indication of the validity of the measure. In considering this issue, it is important to remember that the high reliabilities are obtained though summation of the nominations of many nominators. Behind a good reliability estimate of 0.80 for nominations in a classroom of 15 boys (and 15 girls), for example, the average inter-nominator agreement is only 0.20 (using the Spearman-Brown formula "backwards"). If the students are allowed to make cross-gender nominations, the average inter-nominator agreement (among the 30 nominators) behind a reliability coefficient of 0.80 would be as low as 0.12. It is highly questionable if a variable with such a low inter-nominator agreement really measures what it is intended to measure. In standard psychometric textbooks (Cronbach, 1970; Guilford, 1954), it is generally emphasized that to obtain valid nominations/ratings, it is important that the dimensions to be rated are well defined and the nominators/raters know the persons to be nominated/rated well and have observed them in many relevant situations. When the inter-nominator agreement is as low as 0.10–0.20, this is not likely to be the case and it not unreasonable to assume that some kind of general rejection and dislike dimension is an important component of the nomination variable obtained. Such a variable may well correlate substantially with other peer nomination variables of rejection and the like but may not relate strongly to self-reports on relevant specific behaviors/situations.

Summing up the discussion about the correspondence between data from the two methods, a number of studies have obviously found a good deal of overlap, as indicated by the average correlation of 0.37 (Card, 2003). This is a good sign since some degree of overlap or convergence is to be expected. A more detailed examination reveals, however, that there are also clear differences in what the two methods are likely to measure and in how the raw data are used or "transformed" to generate the variables of interest. As detailed in the various points above, it is obvious that several of the reasons why the association between self-reports and peer reports is not stronger than what has been reported so far, are linked to characteristics of the peer nomination method.

Considering the usually painful and somewhat subjective nature of being bullied, it is natural to maintain that the students themselves, rather than their peers, are likely to be the best informants on such experiences at least by the time they have reached the age of 10 or so (see Ladd & Kochenderfer-Ladd, 2002). There may, of course, be some bullied students who are not willing or able to acknowledge even to themselves that they are bullied. There may also be some students who for one reason or another provide erratic or misleading answers. But, by and large, it is definitely our experience with the OBQ that the majority of students take the task of answering the questionnaire quite seriously and tend to respond accordingly.

With regard to bullying other students, one cannot completely rule out the possibility that there is some degree of underreporting, at least for some forms of bullying. At the same time, we have been surprised to find quite marked associations with other self-reports on rule-breaking and antisocial behaviors (Solberg & Olweus, 2003; Bendixen & Olweus, 1999; Solberg et al., 2007b), suggesting that students are largely candid in their reporting also of socially undesirable or condemned behaviors. This impression is supported by reviews of self-reports used in delinquency research (e.g., Farrington, 2001).

With an acceptable level of inter-nominator agreement and a large enough group of nominators, peer nomination data are likely to provide reasonably adequate measures of relatively stable, individual-differentiating bully/victim characteristics, at least as regards more visible or "public" forms of bullying and the more extreme students in the peer group. It is likely that the strength of the typical peer nomination method may be more in the identification of distinct extreme groups than in creating distributions of students roughly arranged/ranked according to frequency or seriousness on the problematic behavior dimensions.

Against this background, it is obvious that peer nomination data cannot be considered some kind of "gold standard" or "ultimate criterion" of the validity of self-reports on bully/victim problems. Given the points discussed, it may seem more natural to switch perspective and raise the question: To what extent can peer nomination data predict self-reports of bully/victim problems and in what ways can such peer nominations be improved to increase the degree of correspondence between the two sources of data? Such a shift of focus of course does not imply that self-report data on bullying problems cannot be made more comprehensive and reliable, for example by aggregating across different forms of bullying, by incorporating information about how long the bullying has lasted and the number of students who have participated in the bullying. It should be emphasized that the previous discussion and conclusions apply to the OBQ, in particular, and cannot be generalized without further analyses to other self-report instruments with possibly different formats and characteristics.

Prevalence Estimation

It is often important for school, political, or administrative decision makers to get an estimate of the level of bully/victim problems in a school or organization (Solberg & Olweus, 2003). A suitable measure can be "a period prevalence estimate" which may be expressed as the proportion or percentage of individuals in the unit of interest who have been exposed to bullying behavior by other individuals (or have bullied other individuals) with some defined frequency within a specified time period (Olweus, 1989; Solberg & Olweus, 2003, p. 240). Such a measure has a clear meaning or interpretation, can be easily reproduced by different researchers, and permits meaningful comparisons between groups and time points.

Both conceptual arguments and empirical research indicate that single variables/items with well-defined response alternatives such as the global questions in the OBQ are suitable for prevalence estimation (e.g., "2 or 3 times a month" or possibly "about once a week" as possible cutoff points; Solberg & Olweus, 2003). Such a prevalence estimate is equal to the mean of the dichotomized distribution (0/1). Also a sum/mean (composite) score derived by summation/averaging across various forms of bullying can function reasonably well. However, since such composite scores can be generated in a number of different ways, they are typically somewhat more abstract and general than an estimate derived from a single variable/item.

There are several problems with peer nominations for the purpose of prevalence estimation. First, as mentioned, the peer nomination method does not directly provide information about the frequency of specific behaviors or conditions but rather the number/proportion of nominations for some kind of problem behavior that students receive. The link between number/proportion of nominations and the frequency/seriousness of the behaviors of interest is not well researched or understood. And because the focus is on the (three or more) extreme students and not every student in the class has been assessed on a graded scale, it is not clear what an average peer nomination value or prevalence estimate actually measures or represents.

A related problem with peer nominations is linked to the fact that the procedures used to arrive at a cutoff point for classifying a student as a "victim" or "bully" are often quite complex, difficult to reproduce, and more or less arbitrary. The prevalence estimates arrived at in a particular study are likely to depend on a number of factors including the number of students/nominators in the classroom, the degree of consensus among nominators, if the number of nominations are fixed or unlimited, if and how the nominations are standardized, and so on. All of this will make it difficult, if not impossible, for different researchers to reproduce the differentiating criterion employed in a particular study and arrive at prevalence estimates which have basically the same meaning.

In addition, the decision rules used in choosing a relevant cutoff point often seem to be made post hoc and are often somewhat arbitrary. Why does one researcher use a distance of, for example, one standard deviation above the mean as a cutoff point whereas another uses a 0.50 standard deviation? Or why should a researcher require that, say, 20% rather than 35% of the classmates have made certain nominations in order to classify a student as a victim? There may exist some statistical/psychometric and possibly substantive considerations behind such decisions, but from a prevalence perspective, the end result is likely to be quite different depending on which choices are made along the road. Often, the rationale for choosing one alternative rather than another is not discussed at all.

The potential problems of statistical or procedural standardization examined in the previous section of this chapter come into play even more markedly in the context of prevalence estimation. In particular, if the peer nominations are standardized within gender or grade/age group, this will remove or considerably reduce the variance that many developmental psychologists and educators are or should be particularly interested in studying. Also, within-classroom standardization is likely to remove or reduce potentially interesting and valid between-classroom variance (in addition to removing/reducing between-grade variance) which may be explored in multi-level analyses (Raudenbush & Bryk, 2002), for example. Generally, with the practice of standardizing within one or more categories/factors and the interpretative problems mentioned in the first point above, it becomes extremely difficult to know what is actually measured and compared in the final analysis. This is likely to hamper meaningful analyses of group differences in prevalence estimates and developmental changes over time. A consequence of the previous arguments is that prevalence estimates derived from common peer nomination methods and often involving some form of standardization must be regarded as largely arbitrary.

There seem to be two major reasons for standardizing nominations: (a) to adjust for different numbers of nominators in different classrooms/grades/nominator groups and (b) to try to make scores on different peer nomination variables, maybe measured in different metric, (more) comparable by expressing them in standard deviation units. Although standardization may be beneficial in some respects, it is clear, in the context of prevalence estimation and in the measurement of change (see below) which also usually implies prevalence comparisons between different grade/age groups and time points, that this practice has some very undesirable effects. Unfortunately, it seems that use of standardized peer nominations for the purpose of prevalence estimation has become something of a convention in the field. It is very important that researchers take a more critical look at this practice.

By suggesting that researchers should adopt a critical view of standardized peer nominations, I do not want to imply that peer nomination data based on nominations of extreme students may not be of some value for a comparison of the relative sizes of different subgroups (e.g., victims only, bullies only, bully-victims) or of their characteristics for example. However, the critical points raised here relate in particular to the size of the group(s) of involved/not-involved students, how the basic cutoff point is determined, its meaning and reproducibility.

Summing up, most peer nomination variants are not well designed for prevalence estimation and many of them use some kind of standardization which is likely to further complicate matters. Prevalence estimates derived from common peer nomination methods do not have a clear meaning, are difficult or impossible to reproduce precisely, and rely on the use of more or less arbitrary cutoff points. Such estimates are poorly designed for comparisons of prevalence estimates across groups and time points. There seem to be few such problems with self-report data derived from the OBQ.

Measurement of Change

Both peer nominations and the OBQ may be used for the measurement of possible effects of anti-bullying interventions, which is to measure change. How do these two methods compare in that regard?

As pointed out in an earlier section, both methods aim to measure relatively stable individual-differentiating characteristics. However, this goal is achieved in different ways in the two methods which is of major importance with regard to their capacity for measuring change.

The very nature of the peer nomination procedure, which in some ways is a kind of "guess who" situation-finding the students who fit a certain description will tend to discount possible changes in the level of problems over time. Even if the overall level of problems has decreased substantially in a school after an intervention, many bullying students nominated 1 year or maybe 6 months before will most likely be nominated again as bullying other students. This is simply because they still are the students who fit the descriptions best even if most of them have considerably reduced their bullying behavior at follow-up. The same will probably apply to students who have been bullied. To a certain extent at least, peer nominations reflect the individual students' social reputations, as argued by Juvonen et al. (2001), and reputations usually do not change quickly.

The effects of such mechanisms are likely to be accentuated if the students are given instructions to nominate a fixed number of peers, instructions that most students will want to comply with. As previously pointed out, such a format will tend to serve as a kind of standardization within classroom/grade/time point and will largely reduce or eliminate possibilities for registering change. Use of statistical standardization will have similar effects, as explained in previous sections.

In contrast, the self-report questionnaire measures mostly painful subjective experiences of being bullied and if clear changes in the levels of harassment occur, this is likely to be quickly registered by the targeted student. Similarly, also students who bully other students will tend to note if their behavior is questioned, blocked or confronted by teachers or peers, and maybe reported to parents.

Another important difference is that in the questions of the OBQ, it is repeatedly emphasized that the responses concern "the past couple of months." The absence of such a reference period in peer nomination methods reinforces the focus on stable or typical behavior patterns or situations.

In this context, it is natural to call attention to the often overlooked difference between psychometric and "edumetric" tests or measures (Carver, 1974; Lipsey, 1983). The main goal of psychometric tests is to measure relatively stable individual-differentiating characteristics whereas the main purpose of edumetric tests is to register change when real change has occurred. Many of the considerations that are used in assessing the quality of a psychometric test are largely irrelevant with regard to an edumetric test. The main validity criterion for such a test is the degree to which it can differentiate between a control condition and an intervention condition in which real change is expected or known to have occurred (and, conversely, not to differentiate, when no real change has taken place). The ability of the test to reflect reliable differences across age (growth or gain) is another meaningful criterion (Carver, 1974).

From this perspective, it is obvious that the typical peer nomination technique aims to be a psychometric "test," while the OBQ has both a psychometric and edumetric orientation. And as documented in a number of studies, items or scales from the OBQ have shown quite marked differences in the expected direction between control and intervention conditions (e.g., Olweus, 1991, 2005). There seem to be very few studies where peer nominations have been able to document positive effects of an intervention. Also, meaningful age and gender differences have been consistently registered with the OBQ in many large-scale studies (Olweus, 1993; Solberg et al., 2007a; Smith, Madsen, & Moody, 1999).

From a somewhat different perspective, typical peer nomination methods aim largely to measure "trait" variance, whereas the OBQ has documented sensitivity to both "trait" and "state" variance.

According to the analyses presented in the previous sections, common peer nomination methods are poorly suited for both prevalence estimation and the measurement of change. Such methods may have certain strength in the selection of extreme groups of students such as victims only, bullies only and bully-victims, at least with regard to more visible or "public" forms of bullying. There are, however, considerable interpretative problems with this methodology when it is used for the measurement of stable, individual-differentiating bully/victim characteristics for a whole sample or population. Use of statistical or procedural standardization usually complicates matters further.

Generally, it seems that the value of peer nominations in the area of bully/victim and related research has been somewhat exaggerated and the problems associated with the methodology correspondingly underrated. There is simply a strong need for much more methodological groundwork to find out if at all, and in which cases how, common peer nomination methods can be meaningfully used for prevalence estimation and the study of developmental changes including comparisons of prevalence estimates or mean values across groups and time.

In drawing these conclusions, I have disregarded the possible ethical problems associated with use of peer nominations for socially undesirable behavior patterns including "like least–nominations." In several countries, including the Scandinavian countries and Australia, many research projects with such peer nominations very likely would be rejected for ethical reasons by the research evaluation committees. Future research should also examine this issue in more detail.

Are Girls as Aggressive as Boys?

It is usually reported that boys are more aggressive than girls (for an overview, see Coie & Dodge, 1998). However, this conclusion has been called into question by research which began to be published in the late 1980s and the 1990s. This research came from Finland with a focus on indirect aggression (e.g., Björkqvist, Lagerspetz, & Kaukiainen, 1992; Lagerspetz, Björkqvist, & Peltonen, 1988) and somewhat later from the United States with reference to relational aggression (e.g., Crick & Grotpeter, 1995; Crick et al., 1999). In particular, both research groups have argued that the conclusion about boys' higher levels of aggression is likely to be a consequence of the fact that the aggressive behaviors typically studied in research have been direct physical and maybe verbal forms. Further, if the definition and operationalization of aggression were broadened to include more indirect and subtle forms, this might well result in a different conclusion. Relatedly, even stronger formulations, made by both the Finnish and the US research groups, have stated that girls are just as aggressive as boys. Examples are: "… the claim that human males are more aggressive than females appears to be false" (Björkqvist, Österman, & Lagerspetz, 1994, p. 28), and "… the previously described studies provide strong evidence that gender differences in aggression are minimal (or nonexistent) when both physical and relational forms of aggression are considered" (Crick et al., 1999, p. 99). Although these authors also have expressed themselves more cautiously in later contexts, the view created by these early findings and statements seems still to be quite common.

Although different terms are used, it is obvious that indirect and relational aggression (and also the term "social aggression"; Cairns, Cairns, Neckerman, Ferguson, & Gariepy, 1989; Galen and Underwood, 1997) cover much the same phenomena (see Björkqvist, 2001; Underwood, 2003). The key components seem to be intentional social exclusion, spreading of rumors, and manipulation of friendship relationships. To avoid the discussion of which term is most appropriate, the term, "indirect/relational aggression/bullying" will be used as a summary label in this chapter.

The "Early" Studies of Indirect and Relational Aggression

What is then the empirical evidence for the statement that girls are as aggressive as boys? Although Björkqvist and colleagues in their early studies found that girls by and large scored higher than boys on peer-rated items of indirect forms of aggression (e.g., Björkqvist et al., 1992), and Crick and colleagues obtained similar results with regard to relational aggression (e.g., Crick & Grotpeter, 1995; Crick et al., 1999), results from later studies have been inconsistent (for reviews, see Espelage et al., 2004; Underwood, 2003). The evidence available thus far is obviously not conclusive. Before presenting my own results on this issue, I want to take a critical look at the early research which lead up to the suggestion that the common conclusion about gender differences in aggression might have to be revised.

The Björkqvist group constructed a kind of peer rating technique (although they themselves named it peer nominations; Björkqvist et al., 1992, p. 119) in which the students rated all of their classmates of the same gender on a four-point scale (from 0 = "not at all" to 3 = "very much") on several variables with an aggressive content. These variables included items of physical aggression ("hits," "kicks"), direct verbal aggression ("yells," "calls the other names"), and indirect aggression ("tells bad or false stories," "says to others: let's not be with him/her"). The format of the technique was: "What does he/she do *when angry* with another boy/girl in the class?" (italics added).

My misgivings about this procedure concern the extent to which it actually measures prevalence/levels of aggressive behavior. The reason for this doubt is that the rater instructions state as a prerequisite that the student is (should be) angry. In my view, the results are then likely to primarily index typical or preferred modes of anger expression by girls and boys rather than measuring how often the various behaviors actually occur in the two genders. It is not the same thing to ask "How often does student X display this particular behavior when angry?" (as the Björkqvist group does) and "How often does student X display this particular behavior?"

In addition, it has been documented that boys, by and large, are more easily emotionally aroused (i.e., quick to anger) than girls (e.g., Knight, Guthrie, Page, & Fabes, 2002; Zillman, 1979), and by using anger as a prerequisite in the rating procedure, possible gender differences in prevalence or levels of aggression are likely to be reduced or eliminated and maybe even reversed. Through this procedure boys and girls are hypothetically placed on an equal footing with regard to degree of anger arousal. This is actually a kind of procedural counterpart to "covariance adjustment" and addresses the question: "How would the girls have reacted *if* they had had the same level of anger arousal as the boys?"

Furthermore, it must be recognized that, given the instructions, the rating task must in many cases have been fairly difficult when the raters had to rate students whom they had never or seldom seen angry. It is difficult to know for sure what strategy the raters actually employed in such cases but probably they chose to rely on some guessing or hypothesizing about what would have happened if the student being rated had been angry. Such guessing very likely would have been influenced by sex stereotypes about typical boy and girl reactions. Thus, since there are more non-angered girls than boys in an average classroom, this would be more of a problem for girl raters, which might have affected the rating outcome in "favor" of the girls.

All in all, there are some problems and ambiguities with the measurement procedure used in the Björkqvist et al. (1992) study, which should caution against strong conclusions. It is possible that the main results of the study tell us that when or if girls are angry, then they would react with more indirect aggression than boys but they don't tell us that girls actually do this more often than boys "under normal circumstances." It is interesting to note that another, more recent Finnish study (Salmivalli & Kaukiainen, 2005) using the Bjorkvist et al. instrument did not replicate the earlier findings: *"Across age groups, boys used all three types of aggression* [physical, verbal, and indirect] *more than girls"* (p. 160; italics in original).

There are actually some similar problems with the Crick and Grotpeter methodology. Also in these studies, being angry is used as a prerequisite in some (two or three out of four or five) of the peer nomination items used to measure relational aggression (Crick & Grotpeter, 1995; Crick, 1996). *"When mad* [italics added]. gets even by keeping the person from being in their group of friends" is an example (Crick & Grotpeter, 1995, p. 713). Even though the anger prerequisite is not included in the two remaining items, it is not unreasonable to assume that this condition has been present in the minds of the nominators also for these items. It is possible, however, that the complicating effect of use of this prerequisite is less marked with this peer nomination instrument since the goal is to nominate the three most extreme students rather than to rate all same-gender peers (including non-angry students) as was done in the Björkqvist et al. research.

At the same time, the focus on extreme students immediately raises the issue discussed above of whether the number/proportions of nominations can be considered an estimate of the average level of problems in the total groups of boys and girls, an estimate that can be used for meaningful gender and other comparisons across groups and times. Considering the complexities involved in generating a peer nomination variable (pointed out above), it is difficult to know what is actually reflected in the significant gender difference in relational aggression (in "favor" of the girls) reported by Crick and Grotpeter, for example (1995, p. 716). (Here, it is also worth mention that the prerequisite of anger does not seem to have been included in the items on direct physical aggression which might also have affected the results in favor of the girls.) In addition, it seems that the behavioral basis for drawing general conclusions about the relative aggressiveness of the two genders, with one dimension of direct physical aggression and one dimension of relational aggression, is too narrow. There are thus some problems also with the Crick and Grotpeter technique for the measurement of relational (and other) aggression which need to be investigated in much greater detail.

The critical analysis presented in the previous paragraphs is not meant to devalue or reduce the importance of the research of these authors. This research has been important in directing attention to more subtle and less visible forms of aggression, which no doubt exist and needs to be more thoroughly investigated and understood. At the same time, it is essential to analyze critically how results have been obtained and not to jump to premature conclusions which may turn out to be "false leads" in the long run (cf. Underwood et al., 2001). We certainly also need more empirical data on the topic that can inform our research and increase our understanding.

An Empirical Study Examining Bullying and Gender

In a number of our recent studies, we have collected self-report data via the OBQ on several different forms of bullying other students, including both typical direct and indirect/relational forms in a reasonably "fixed" context, the school environment. The results from these studies comprising more than 40,000 students have generally been quite consistent. For ease of reading,

I will focus on one of these studies of some 16,380 girls and boys about evenly distributed over the grade range of 4 through 10 (modal ages 10 through 16; Olweus, 2005; Solberg & Olweus, 2003).

The OBQ also provides information about students who have been bullied and if they have been mainly bullied by girls, boys, or a combination of boys and girls. This information permits separate analyses of girls mainly bullied by girls and boys mainly bullied by boys, that is, analyses of same-gender bullying from the perspective of the victims. These analyses give useful information about the kinds and prevalence of various forms of bullying used within each gender. In addition, the data will also shed light on the extent to which there is cross-gender bullying, with girls being bullied by boys and boys being bullied by girls.

The students in this sample were drawn from 143 elementary and junior high schools across Norway who took the questionnaire in the spring of 2003 in the context of a new nationwide initiative against bullying in Norwegian schools (Olweus, 2005), some 4 months before introduction of the Olweus Bullying Prevention Program (OBPP) in the schools. The levels of bully/victim problems in this sample were largely representative of the national level of such problems.

In the following analyses we focus on aggressive behavior patterns of an often very mean and malicious kind, which are quite common in our schools (Nansel et al., 2001; Olweus, 1993; Solberg et al., 2007a). Much bullying can be seen as a form of proactive aggression (see Coie and Dodge, 1998) with a good deal of self-initiated behavior on the part of the bullying students. However, many bullying students are also easily angered (high on reactive aggression; e.g., Olweus, 1978, 1993). It would seem that the behavior patterns implicated in bullying are very relevant when we want to examine whether or not girls and boys are equally aggressive. The questions for measuring bullying behavior/being bullied are not contingent on some prerequisite like anger (but preceded by the general definition of bullying).

Table 2.1 and Figure 2.1 depict the results in terms of dichotomized prevalence data that is, the percentage of students who have responded "2 or 3 times a month" or more on the various questions. As explained in Solberg and Olweus (2003), "2 or 3 times a month" is a suitable cutoff point for many purposes. However, a number of the analyses have also been carried out on the

Table 2.1 Percentage of Students Who Reported on Various Forms of Bullying Other Students and Being Bullied by Same-Gender and Cross-Gender Peers

	Lower grades (4-7)		Higher grades (8-10)	
	Girls	Boys	Girls	Boys
Global				
Bullying other students	2.8	7.0	3.5	9.0
Being bullied by same-gender peers	1.8	7.2	1.1	5.7
Being bullied by cross-gender peers	5.2	1.0	3.1	0.4
Verbal				
Bullying other students	2.0	4.6	2.0	7.9
Being bullied by same-gender peers	1.7	6.4	0.9	5.4
Being bullied by cross-gender peers	4.2	0.9	3.2	0.5
Isolation				
Bullying other students	1.6	1.9	2.8	3.8
Being bullied by same-gender peers	1.8	2.5	1.1	1.6
Being bullied by cross-gender peers	1.9	0.5	0.6	0.3
Rumors				
Bullying other students	0.7	0.9	0.7	2.1
Being bullied by same-gender peers	1.7	2.6	1.4	2.0
Being bullied by cross-gender peers	1.7	0.6	1.0	0.4

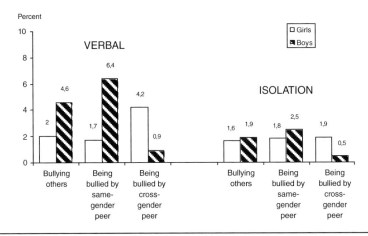

Figure 2.1 Gender differences in bullying other students and being bullied by same-gender and cross-gender peers. Direct verbal and indirect/relational (isolation) forms of bullying. Grades 4–7 (n for bullying other students; girls = 5396, boys = 5755).

same questions with the cutoff point of "only once or twice" with very much the same results (but generally higher percentage values). The same is true when the whole 5-point scale is used. Given the large size of the sample, most of the analyses of theoretical interest are highly significant but, for ease of exposition, such data are not reported in the present context.

The main findings broken down by grade level, 4–7 and 8–10 (which is natural division in Norwegian schools) are presented in Table 2.1. A selection of the results is displayed in Figure 2.1. Results are presented for four main variables: (a) Bullying–global ("How often have you taken part in bullying another student(s) at school in the past couple of months"?); (b) Bullying–verbal ("I called another student(s) mean names, made fun of or teased him or her in hurtful way"); (c) Bullying–isolation ("I kept him or her out of things on purpose, excluded him or her from my group of friends or completely ignored him or her"); and (d) Bullying–rumors ("I spread false rumors about him or her and tried to make others dislike him or her"). The basic contents of the questions/statements on indirect/relational bullying/aggression are very similar to formulations used in the measurement of indirect and relational aggression by Björkqvist el al. (1992) and Crick and Grotpeter (1995), respectively.

The variables in Table 2.1 represent both self-reported bullying behavior, that is, reports from the perspective of the perpetrators (first row in each set), and self-reports on being bullied by other students, that is, data from the perspective of the targeted students (second and third rows in each set). To illustrate, the first row of data in Table 2.1 shows the percentage of girls and boys in lower and higher grades, respectively, who have reported on the global question that they have bullied other students "2 or 3 times a month" or more often (2.8% and 3.5% for girls and 7.0 % and 9.0% for boys). The next row presents the percentage of students who have been bullied (globally) by same-gender peers, that is, girls being mainly bullied by girls (1.8% for lower grades and 1.1% for higher grades), and boys being mainly bullied by boys (7.2% for lower grades, and 5.7% for higher grades). The third row displays the percentage of students who have been bullied (globally) by cross-gender peers, that is, girls being mainly bullied by boys (5.2% for lower grades and 3.1% for higher grades), and boys being mainly bullied by girls (1.0% for lower grades and 0.4% for higher grades). The data for the other main variables have the same structure.

The results for one direct form of bullying, Bullying-verbal, and one indirect/relational form, Bullying-isolation, for students in grades 4–7 are presented in Figure 2.1. Bars number 1, 3, and 6 represent verbal bullying where girls have been the perpetrators and bars number 2, 4, and 5 represent verbal bullying with boys as perpetrators. Parallel data for indirect/relational bullying in the form of social isolation are presented in the bars on the right-hand side of the figure: Bars number 7, 9, and 12 with girls as perpetrators, and bars number 8, 10, and 11 with boys as perpetrators.

What Are the Main Conclusions from These Data?

The data for self-reported bullying behavior in Table 2.1 (first row in each group of variables) indicate that boys report higher levels of bullying other students on all variables for both lower and higher grades. The gender difference is very pronounced for global and verbal bullying and less marked for the indirect/relational forms. However, also for the two indirect/relational variables, boys have higher scores than girls and for the upper grades there are fairly clear differences (3.8% vs. 2.8% for isolation and 2.1 vs. 0.7% for rumors). The second row of data in each group of variables shows prevalence data for students being bullied by same-gender peers. Generally, the gender differences from the victim perspective parallel the findings for bullying other students. On all variables, boys mainly bullied by boys have higher values than girls mainly bullied by girls, although the differences between the genders are again less marked for the two indirect/relational variables.

Informative data are also contained in the third rows of the table, concerning students bullied by cross-gender peers. Looking at the Bullying–verbal variable for lower grades, for example, and comparing the percentage of girls bullied by boys (third row: 4.2%; bar number 5 in Figure 2.1) with the percentage for girls bullied by girls (second row: 1.7%; bar number 3 in Figure 2.1), it is obvious that girls are bullied verbally by many more boys than girls, for this variable and grade level, 229 boys versus 93 girls. Expressed in another way, only about 17% of all bullied girls in grades 4–7 have been verbally bullied mainly by girls whereas 42% have been mainly bullied by boys (and the rest mainly by girls and boys in combination). Paralleling these results, 59% of bullied boys have been mainly bullied by other boys and only 9% by girls. Roughly similar results are obtained for higher grades and for the Bullying–global variable.

In examining the two remaining variables, a considerable proportion of girls have been exposed to indirect/relational forms of aggression by boys, that is, through social isolation and rumor spreading. According to the girl victims, they are exposed to such bullying to approximately the same degree by girls and by boys (1.8 % vs. 1.9% for Bullying–isolation and lower grades; bars number 9 and 11 in Figure 2.1; 1.1% and 0.6% for higher grades, for example) In addition, boys use this form of bullying with similar or somewhat higher frequency in relation to other boys (2.5% and 1.6% for the lower and higher grades, respectively; for girls bullying girls, corresponding figures are 1.8% and 1.1%). Similar results are obtained for Bullying–rumors (2.6% and 2.0% for boys, lower and higher grades; for girls, corresponding figures are 1.7% and 1.4%).

Although the numbers/percentages for same-gender and cross-gender bullying students cannot be directly added (because of possible double-tallying of boys, in particular, who may bully both boys and girls), the conclusion drawn on basis of the two latter sets of data is that boys are also involved in indirect/relational bullying of other students to the same or an even greater extent than girls. At the same time, although we do not find a reversal of the gender pattern for any of the variables studied, the difference is clearly less marked for indirect/relational forms of bullying/aggression than for more direct forms. This is partly in line with the findings from Björkqvist et al. (1992) and Crick et al. (1999).

The basic issue can also be assessed with reference to the global being-bullied question which is designed to provide an overall estimate of the total "volume" of being bullied, taking all possible forms of bullying into account.(in our empirical analyses, all nine different forms of bullying measured in the OBQ correlate substantially with the global variable). In most of our previous research, we have found relatively small gender differences in being bullied globally (e.g., Olweus, 1993; Solberg et al., 2007a; a finding that was replicated in the present sample where the prevalence rate is 10.7% for girls and 11.8% for boys. However, our more detailed analyses have shown that these percentages are generated in very different ways. Of the bullied girls, only about 16% report that they have been mainly bullied (globally) by other girls whereas 46% have been mainly bullied by boys. At the same time, of bullied boys 63% have been mainly bullied by other boys and only 7% by girls.

On the basis of these data, we can obtain an estimate of the total number or volume of victims who have been exposed to some form of bullying by students of either gender. Translated into numbers, the total number of male and female victims (bullied mainly by girls or by boys, and disregarding students bullied by both girls and boys) is 1,123 and of that total, 932 or 83% have been mainly bullied by one or more boys, whereas only 191 or 17% have been mainly bullied by one or more girls. Many more victims are thus bullied by boys than by girls. (Cross-gender aggression/bullying have been largely neglected in peer nomination research. Results showing that a considerable proportion of bullied girls are mainly bullied by boys have been previously reported [Olweus, 1993], but these results have not been frequently cited in the bullying literature; see Rodkin and Berger, in press, for an exception.)

Although these data do not permit exact estimation of the number of girls and boys who have actually carried out the bullying (again due to possible double-tallying), they can be used as an estimate of the relative involvement in the bullying of other students by either gender. These figures derived from the victim perspective are in general agreement with the data on self-reported bullying behavior (global) presented in the first row in the first panel of Table 2.1.

Getting back to the basic question of whether girls are just as aggressive as boys, the data presented covering both direct and indirect/relational forms of bullying/aggression, perpetrator and victim perspectives, and same-gender and cross-gender relationships, clearly do not support such a conclusion. Taken together, these analyses show very convincingly, that the male gender is the more aggressive gender, at least as regards the kinds of largely self-initiated behavior patterns involved in bullying which must considered to be of particular relevance for an evaluation of this issue. The data also show that boys use indirect/relational forms of aggression to about the same or even greater extent than girls. Although girls overall use less aggression than boys as measured globally (taking all forms of bullying into account) as well as with a selection of direct and indirect/relational variables, they are more inclined, in relative terms, to use indirect forms of aggression than boys. But girls also use direct verbal forms of aggression/bullying (see Table 2.1 and Figure 2.1). On the basis of these results, there are no good grounds for designating indirect/relational forms of aggression as a special "female form of aggression," other than possibly in the relative sense just mentioned.

Overall, the results obtained from a large sample using the OBQ clearly contradict the statement that girls and boys are equally aggressive. When considering this issue, we should also not forget that girls typically score much higher than boys on most variables of social competence and prosocial behavior, variables which tend to correlate negatively with aggressive behavior.

Some Conclusions and Key Messages

In this chapter it has been argued that researchers who want to study/measure "bullying" should use/provide their participants with a clear definition of the phenomenon. Such a definition should include reference to a power imbalance between the individual exposed and his or her perpetrator(s), in addition to intentionality of the behavior and some repetitiveness. Both conceptual arguments and some recent empirical research underscore the importance of differentiating between being bullied according to such a definition (in the context of a power-imbalanced relationship) and being exposed to (recurrent) aggressive acts without such a specification. In particular, bullying is a more serious and hurtful form of peer aggression. Researchers should also be careful not to present results as applying to bullying when they have actually measured "victimization" generally defined as exposure to aggressive acts (without reference to a power imbalance) by one or more other individuals.

A key theme of this chapter has been to point out and exemplify a number of problems and weaknesses of common peer nomination techniques for the measurement of bully/victim (and many other) problems. These weaknesses come into play both with regard to prevalence estimation, the study of change, and measurement of relatively stable, individual differences and, to a somewhat lesser degree, the selection of extreme groups of involved students (e.g., victims only, bullies only, bully-victims, and non-involved students). In this regard, it is also cautioned against uncritical use of statistical or procedural standardization of peer nominations which is likely to remove or considerably reduce meaningful between gender/classroom/grade variance. It is further concluded that prevalence estimates derived from common peer nomination methods do not have a clear meaning, are difficult or impossible to reproduce precisely, and rely on the use of more or less arbitrary cutoff points. Such estimates are poorly designed for comparisons of prevalence estimates across groups and time points.

Another section examines the degree of correlation or correspondence between data on the same individuals derived from peer nominations and self-reports. Although a meta-analysis of 21 studies has reported a relatively respectable average cross-informant correlation of 0.37, the question is raised why the correlation was not larger. It is shown that several of the reasons why the association between self-reports and peer reports is not stronger, are linked to characteristics of the peer nomination method. The common view of peer nominations as the "gold standard" or "ultimate criterion" of the validity of self-reports is rejected. Many of the problems with peer nomination data are escaped when using a well-constructed questionnaire such as the OBQ. It

Table 2.2 Understanding and Researching Bullying: Summary of Implications for Practice

Those who study/measure "bullying" or bully/victim problems should use/provide their participants with a clear definition of the phenomenon. Such a definition should include reference to a power imbalance between the individual exposed and his or her perpetrator(s), in addition to intentionality of the behavior and some repetitiveness. Not including power imbalance in the definition may lead to the unfortunate conclusion that bullies and victims are largely the same students and have similar characteristics.

Common peer nomination techniques have several weaknesses that make them poorly suited for both prevalence estimation, the study of change, and the measurement of relatively stable, individual differences. Use of statistical or procedural (with a fixed number of nominations) standardization within gender/classrooms/schools often complicates matters further. The possible strengths of these methods may lie in the selection of extreme groups of students such as victims only, bullies only, bully-victims, at least with regard to more visible or "public" forms of bullying. However, there is little reason to regard peer nominations as some kind of "gold standard" or "ultimate criterion" for the measurement of bully/victim problems. Much more methodological groundwork is needed to understand if at all, and in which cases how, common peer nomination methods can be meaningfully used for prevalence estimation and the study of change. Several of the problems with peer nomination data can be escaped by using a well-constructed questionnaire.

A final section is focused on the claims made by both Finnish and US researchers that boys and girls are equally aggressive when indirect/relational forms of aggression/bullying are taken into account. Results from a large-scale empirical Norwegian study with the Olweus Bullying Questionnaire (OBQ) and data covering both direct and indirect/relational forms of bullying/aggression, perpetrator and victim perspectives, and same-gender and cross-gender relationships, clearly do not support a conclusion about no gender difference. Taken together, the data show very convincingly that males are the more aggressive gender.

is generally concluded that there is a strong need for much more methodological groundwork to find out if at all, and in which cases how, common peer nomination methods can be meaningfully used for prevalence estimation and the study of change.

A final section discusses some methodological weaknesses of "early" Finnish and U.S. studies of gender differences which have argued that boys and girls are equally aggressive when indirect/relational forms of aggression/bullying are taken into account. The ways these studies have measured aggressive behavior suggest that they are likely to primarily index typical or preferred modes of anger expression by girls and boys rather than measure how often the various behaviors actually occur in the two genders. The results from a large-scale empirical Norwegian study with the OBQ (n = 16,380) with data covering both direct and indirect/relational forms of bullying/aggression, perpetrator and victim perspectives, and same-gender and cross-gender relationships, clearly do not support a conclusion about no gender difference. As an illustration, the total number of male and female victims bullied mainly by girls or by boys was estimated at 1,123 and of them 932 or 83% had been mainly bullied by one or more boys, whereas only 191 or 17% had been mainly bullied by one or more girls. It was also found that boys used indirect/relational forms of aggression to about the same or even greater extent than girls. Taken together, these analyses show very convincingly, that the male gender is the more aggressive gender.

References

Achenbach, T. M., McConaughy, S. H., & Howell, C. T. (1987). Child/adolescent behavioral and emotional problems: Implications of cross-informant correlations for situational specificity. *Psychological Bulletin, 101*, 213–232.

Bendixen, M., & Olweus, D. (1999). Measuring antisocial behavior in early adolescence and adolescence: Psychometric properties and substantive findings. *Criminal Behaviour and Mental Health, 9*, 323–354.

Berkowitz, L. (1993). *Aggression. Its causes, consequences, and control.* New York: McGraw-Hill.

Björkqvist, K. (2001). Different names, same issue. *Social Development, 10*, 272–274.

Björkqvist, K., Lagerspetz, K. M. J., & Kaukiainen, A. (1992). Do girls manipulate and boys fight? Developmental trends in regard to direct and indirect aggression. *Aggressive Behavior, 18*, 117–127.

Björkqvist, K., Osterman, K., & Lagerspetz, K. M. J. (1994). Sex differences in covert aggression among adults. *Aggressive Behavior, 20*, 27–33.

Cairns, R. B., & Green, J. A. (1979). How to assess personality and social patterns: Ratings or observations? In R. B. Cairns (Ed.), *The analysis of social interactions. Methods, issues, and illustrations* (pp. 209–226). Hillsdale, NJ: Erlbaum.

Cairns, R. B., & Cairns, B. D. (1986). The developmental-interactional view of social behavior: Four issues of adolescent aggression. In D. Olweus, J. Block, & M. Radke-Yarrow (Eds.), *Development of antisocial and prosocial behavior.* New York: Academic Press.

Cairns, R. B., Cairns, B. D., Neckerman, H. J., Ferguson, L. L., & Gariepy, J. (1989). Growth and aggression: 1. Childhood to early adolescence. *Developmental Psychology, 25*, 320–330.

Card, N. (2003, April). *Victims of peer aggression: A meta-analytic review.* Paper presented at the biennal meeting of the Society for Research in Child Development, Tampa, FL.

Carver, R. P. (1974). Two dimensions of tests: psychometric and edumetric. *American Psychologist, 29*, 512–518.

Crick, N. R. (1996). The role of relational aggression, overt aggression, and prosocial behavior in the prediction of children's future social adjustment. *Child Development, 67*, 2317–2327.

Crick, N. R., & Grotpeter, J. K. (1995). Relational aggression, gender, and social-psychological adjustment. *Child Development, 66*, 710–722.

Crick, N. R., Wellman, N. E., Casas, J. F., O'Brien, M. A., Nelson, D. A., Grotpeter, J. K., & Markon, K. (1999). Childhood aggression and gender. A new look at an old problem. *Nebraska Symposium on Motivation*, 75–141.

Coie, J. D., & Dodge, K.A. (1998). Aggression and antisocial behavior. In N. Eisenberg (Ed.), *Handbook of child psychology* (Vol. 3, pp. 779–862). New York: Wiley.

Cronbach, L. J. (1970). *Essentials of psychological testing.* New York: Harper and Row.

Cronbach, L. J., Gleser, G. C., Nanda, H., & Rajaratnam, N. (1972). *The dependability of behavioral measurements.* New York: Wiley.

Espelage, D. L., Holt, M. K., & Henkel, R. R. (2003). Examination of peer group contextual effects on aggression during early adolescence. *Child Development, 74*, 205–220.

Espelage, D. L., Mebane, S. E., & Swearer, S. M. (2004). Gender differences in bullying: Moving beyond mean level differences. In D. L. Espelage & S. M. Swearer (Eds.), *Bullying in American schools* (pp. 15–35). Mahwah, NJ: Erlbaum.

Farrington, D. P. (1993). Understanding and preventing bullying. In M. Tonry (Ed.), *Crime and justice: A review of research* (Vol. 17, pp. 348–458). Chicago: University of Chicago Press.

Farrington, D. P. (2001). *What has been learned from self-reports about criminal careers and the causes of offending?* Retrieved DATE, from The University of Cambridge, Institute of Criminology: www.homeoffice.gov.uk/rds/pdfs/Farrington.pdf

Galen, B. R., & Underwood, M. K. (1997). A developmental investigation of social aggression among children. *Developmental Psychology, 33*, 589–600.

Guilford, J. P. (1954). *Psychometric methods.* New York: MaGraw-Hill.

Hawker, D. S .J., & Boulton, M. J. (2000). Twenty years' research on peer victimization and psychosocial maladjustment: A meta-analytic review of cross-sectional studies. *Journal of Child Psychology and Psychiatry and Allied Disciplines, 41*, 441–455.

Heinemann, P.-P. (1969). Apartheid. *Liberal debatt*, 3–14.

Heinemann, P.-P. (1972). *Gruppvåld bland barn och vuxna* [Group violence among children and adults]. Stockholm: Natur och kultur.

Hunter, S. C. , Boyle, J. M. E., & Warden, D. (2007). Perceptions and correlates of peer-victimization and bullying. *British Journal of Educational Psychology, 77*, 797–810.

Junger-Tas, J., & Kesteren, J. V. (1998) *Cross-cultural study of bully/victim problems in school: Final report for the Netherlands to the Japanese Ministry of Education.* Tokyo: Japanese Ministry of Education.

Juvonen, J., Nishina, A., & Graham, S. (2001). Self-views versus peer perceptions of victim status among early adolescents. In J. Juvonen, & S. Graham (Eds.), *Peer harassment in school* (pp. 105–124). New York: Guilford.

Knight, G. P., Guthrie, I. K., Page, M. C., & Fabes, R. A. (2002). Emotional arousal and gender differences in aggression: A meta-analysis. *Aggressive behavior, 28*, 366–393.

Kyriakides, L., Kaloyirou, C., & Lindsay, G. (2006). An analysis of the Revised Olweus Bully/Victim Questionnaire using the Rasch measurement model. *British Journal of Educational Psychology, 76*, 781–801.

Ladd, G. W., & Kochenderfer-Ladd, B. (2002). Identifying victims of peer aggresion from early to middle childhood: Analysis of cross-informant data for concordance, estimation of relational adjustment, prevalence of victimization, and characteristics of identified victims. *Psychological Assessment, 14*, 74–96.

Lagerspetz, K. M. J., Björkqvist, K., & Peltonen, T. (1988). Is indirect aggression typical of females? Gender differences in 11- to 12-year-old children. *Aggressive Behavior, 14*, 403–414.

Lindzey, G. (Ed.). (1954). *Handbook of social psychology* (Vol. 1). Cambridge, MA: Addison-Wesley.

Lipsey, M. W. (1983). A scheme for assessing measurement sensitivity in program evaluation and other applied research. *Psychological Bulletin, 94*, 152–165.

Lorenz, K. (1963). *Das sogenannte Böse.* [The so-called evil]. Vienna: Borotha-Schoeler.

Lorenz, K. (1968). *Aggression: Dess bakgrund och natur* [Aggression: Its background and nature]. Stockholm: Norstedt & Söner.

Morita, Y., & Soeda, H. (1998). *Cross-cultural study of bully/victim problems in school: Final report for the Netherlands to the Japanese Ministry of Education.* Tokyo: Japanese Ministry of Education.

Nansel, T.R ., Overpeck, M., Pilla, R. S., Ruan, W. J., Simons-Morton, B., & Scheidt, P. (2001). Bullying behaviors among US youth. Prevalence and association with psychosocial adjustment. *Journal of the American Medical Association, 285*, 2094–2100.

Lindzey, G. (Ed.). (1954). *Handbook of social psychology.* Cambridge, MA: Addison-Wesley.

Olweus, D. (1969). *Prediction of aggression.* Stockholm: Skandinaviska testförlaget.

Olweus, D. (1972). Personality and aggression. *Nebraska Symposium on Motivation, 20*, 261–321.

Olweus, D. (1973). *Hackkycklingar och översittare. Forskning om skolmobbning* [Hack Chicks and a bully. Research on school bullying]. Stockholm: Almqvist & Wicksell.

Olweus, D. (1977). Aggression and peer acceptance in adolescent boys: Two short-term longitudinal studies of ratings. *Child Development, 48*, 1301–1313.

Olweus, D. (1978). *Aggression in the schools. Bullies and whipping boys.* Washington, DC: Hemisphere Press (Wiley).

Olweus, D. (1979). Stability of aggressive reaction patterns in males: A review. *Psychological Bulletin, 86*, 852–875.

Olweus, D. (1986). *The Olweus Bully/Victim Questionnaire.* Mimeo. Bergen, Norway: Research Center for Health Promotion, University of Bergen.

Olweus, D. (1988). Det går att minska mobbning i skolan [It is possible to reduce bullying at school]. *Psykologtidningen, s*, 10–15.

Olweus, D. (1989). Prevalence and incidence in the study of antisocial behavior: Definitions and measurement. In M. Klein (Ed.), *Cross-national research in self-reported crime and delinquency* (pp. 187–201). Dordrecht, The Netherlands: Kluwer.

Olweus, D. (1991). Bully/victim problems among schoolchildren: Basic facts and effects of a school based intervention program. In D. Pepler and K. Rubin (Eds.), *The development and treatment of childhood aggression* (pp. 411–448). Hillsdale, NJ: Erlbaum.

Olweus, D. (1993). *Bullying at school: What we know and what we can do.* Oxford, UK: Blackwell.

Olweus, D. (1994). Annotation: Bullying at school: Basic facts and effects of a school based intervention program. *Journal of Child Psychology and Psychiatry, 35,* 1171–1190.

Olweus, D. (1996). *The revised Olweus Bully/Victim Questionnaire.* Mimeo. Bergen, Norway: Research Center for Health Promotion (HEMIL), University of Bergen, N-5015 Bergen, Norway.

Olweus, D. (1999a). Sweden. In P. K. Smith, Y. Morita, J. Junger-Tas, D. Olweus, R. Catalano, & P. Slee (Eds.), *The nature of school bullying: A cross-national perspective* (pp. 7–27). London: Routledge.

Olweus, D. (1999b). Norway. In P. K. Smith, Y. Morita, J. Junger-Tas, D. Olweus, R. Catalano, & P. Slee (Eds.), *The nature of school bullying: A cross-national perspective* (pp. 28–48). London: Routledge.

Olweus, D. (2001). Peer harassment. A critical analysis and some important issues. In J. Juvonen & S. Graham (Eds.), *Peer harassment in school* (pp. 3–20). New York: Guilford.

Olweus, D. (2005). A useful evaluation design, and effects of the Olweus Bullying Prevention Program. *Psychology, Crime & Law, 11,* 389–402.

Olweus, D. (2006). *Brief psychometric information on the Olweus Bullying Questionnaire.* Unpublished manuscript.

Olweus, D. (2007). *The Olweus Bullying Questionnaire.* Center City, MN: Hazelden.

Olweus, D., & Solberg, M. (1998). Cross-cultural study of bully/victim problems in school: Final report for Norway to Japanese Ministry of Education. In Y. Morita & H. Soeda (Eds.), *School bullying around the world.* Tokyo: Japanese Ministry of Education.

Raudenbush, S. W., & Bryk, A. S. (2002). *Hierarchical linear models.* Thousand Oaks, CA: Sage.

Rigby, K., & Slee, P. (1991). Bullying among Australian school children: reported behaviour and attitudes to victims. *Journal of Social Psychology, 131,* 615–627.

Rodkin, P. C., & Berger, C. (in press). Who bullies whom? Social status asymmetries by victim gender. *International Journal of Behavioral Development.*

Salmivalli, C., & Kaukiainen, A. (2005). "Female aggression" revisited: Variable and person-centered approaches to studying gender differences in different types of aggression. *Aggressive Behavior, 30,* 158–163.

Smith, P. K., & Brain, P. (2000). Bullying in schools: Lessons from two decades of research. *Aggressive Behavior, 26,* 1–9.

Smith, P. K., Madsen, K. C., & Moody, J. C. (1999). What causes the age decline in being bullied at school? Toward a developmental analysis of risks of being bullied. *Educational Research, 41,* 267–285.

Smith, P. K., Morita, Y., Junger-Tas, J., Olweus, D., Catalano, R., & Slee, P. (Eds.). (1999). *The nature of school bullying: A cross-national perspective.* London: Routledge.

Solberg, M., & Olweus, D. (2003). Prevalence estimation of school bullying with The Olweus Bully/Victim Questionnaire. *Aggressive Behavior, 29,* 239–268.

Solberg, M., Olweus, D., & Endresen, I. M. (2007a). Bullies and victims at school: Are they the same children? *British Journal of Educational Psychology, 77,* 441–464.

Solberg, M., Olweus, D., & Endresen, I. M. (2007b). *Bullies, victims, and bully-victims: How deviant are they and how different?* Unpublished manuscript.

Underwood, M. (2003). *Social aggression among girls.* New York: Guilford.

Underwood, M., Galen, B., & Paquette, J. (2001). Top ten challenges for understanding gender and aggression in children: Why can't we just go along? *Social Development, 10,* 248–266.

Zillman, D. (1979). *Hostility and aggression.* Hillsdale, NJ: Erlbaum.

3

Comparative and Cross-Cultural Research on School Bullying

ROSALIND MURRAY-HARVEY, PHILLIP T. SLEE, AND MITSURU TAKI

Overview

The comparative and cross-cultural research covered in this chapter spans 10 years of collaborative endeavor initiated in 1996 by the National Institute for Educational and Policy Research (NIER) in Tokyo, Japan. Since 1996, collaborations among researchers across continents have progressively grown, sparked by interest in sharing their own research and practice in order to better understand the relevant contexts in which issues around bullying are investigated in contexts beyond their own.

There is no doubt that school bullying and research into its nature, effects and prevention is now a global endeavor (Juvonen & Graham, 2001; Ohsako, 1997; Smith et al., 1999). This chapter describes the evolving international linkages made over the last decade in the Pacific Rim region regarding the issue of bullying. A considerable amount of research has been initiated in these countries including Australia (Slee, 2005), New Zealand (Sullivan, 2000), Japan (Morita, Soeda, Soeda, & Taki, 1999), Korea (Sim, as cited in Slee, Ma, Sim, Taki, & Sullivan, 2003), China (Ma, as cited in Slee et al., 2003), Canada (Hymel, Rocke Henderson, & Bonanno, 2005; Pepler, Craig, O'Connell, Atlas, & Charach, 2004), and the United States (Swearer & Espelage, 2004).

Interest into research on bullying, and into the development of policy and prevention programs in these countries has generated high levels of national and government funding support, in Japan primarily from NIER and Ministry of Education, Culture, Sports, and Technology (MEXT) and in Australia from the Australian Research Council (ARC).

Early Collaborative Work

In Japan, early research into the phenomenon of ijime (bullying) was conducted by Morita and his research group (Morita et al., 1999). In 1996 the Japanese Minister of Education issued a directive to study school bullying primarily as a result of a number of suicides directly linked to bullying. The appeal highlighted that bullying was a significant violation of human rights and was not to be condoned (Yano, 2005).

In Australia the earliest published studies on bullying were conducted by Rigby and Slee (1991, 1993). Not long after, in 1994, an Australian Federal Senate inquiry into school violence was conducted and the subsequent report "Sticks and Stones" (Commonwealth Government, 1994) identified bullying as a significant school problem.

The independent research being conducted in Japan and Australia, and other countries (The Netherlands, United Kingdom, United States, and Norway, to name a few) came together in 1996 when NIER and MEXT hosted two international research symposia on educational reform to inform the issue of school bullying in Japan. One outcome of the 1996 symposia was a collaborative, longitudinal, Japanese-Australian study. This comparative work was the foundation for the growing interest in conducting cross-cultural research across a number of Pacific-Rim countries.

Conceptual Foundations

The following quote from an adolescent student touches on key personal and relationship aspects of school bullying:

> Bullying and harassment is a big issue teachers and parents should do something about it. Lots of kids tell teachers and counselors but a lot of students don't tell anyone. I have been bullied but I haven't told anyone. I've thought about it but haven't got the courage. Teachers and counselors should be more inviting. (13-year-old male)

Shared understanding about issues of mutual concern related to bullying that have emerged through research collaboration is a feature of the work reviewed in this chapter. Although some of the countries are highly similar in terms of social and economic development, there are differences in the manner in which children are socialized and educated. As a result of these social and educational differences, cross-cultural research suggests that bullying is manifested in different ways. As well, there are variations across countries in the extent to which there has been a national focus on assessing and addressing bullying. There are also varying cultural interpretations related to the underlying dynamics of bullying across countries and these will be addressed in the chapter with reference to a number of completed and ongoing studies.

Multiple Perspectives on Bullying

The early Japanese-Australian collaborations focused on investigations that permitted comparisons across these two countries, not only to determine the prevalence of bullying and victimization but also with an interest in examining individual characteristics of bullies and victims, mainly from a psycho-pathological perspective. More recently the shift in research has been towards examining bullying from a social systems perspective—one that takes into account that bullying occurs within a social context and is not merely the manifestation of deviant behavior. A number of researchers (Dixon, Smith, & Jenks, 2006; Pepler et al., 2004; Slee, 2001; Swearer & Doll, 2001) have described the application of systems thinking to the understanding of school bullying.

Bullying Is a Complex Construct

Bullying is a complex phenomenon that needs to be understood as a construct and not merely portrayed as a simple act of aggression or violence. The Japanese-Australian research data, gathered via surveys of over 5,000 Japanese and over 3,000 Australian students in 2001, determined through confirmatory factor analysis (CFA) that the bullying survey items, selected as representations of four different types of bullying behavior, all contributed strongly to that construct. The CFA indices of fit for the Bullying subscale are CFI = 0.98, RMSEA = 0.14, SRMR = 0.05, and WRMR = 3.09 for the Australian data and CFI = 1.00, RMSEA = 0.00, SRMR = 0.01, and WRMR = 0.29 for the Japanese data. The weighted omega coefficients indicate high reliability of the subscales, calculated as 0.88 for Australia and 0.83 for Japan. Thus, bullying is represented, in Japan and Australia by all four behaviors, including not only the most overt (hitting, kicking, pushing) acts that most regularly portray the 'bully' in western contexts, but equally, if not more strongly, the more covert and subtle (ignoring, excluding) acts. A similar pattern was found for victimization; that is, our CFA identified all four types of victimization as powerful indicators of victimization. The CFA indices of fit for the Victimization subscale are CFI = 0.96, RMSEA = 0.19, SRMR = 0.07, and WRMR = 4.27 for the Australian data and CFI = 0.99, RMSEA = 0.02, SRMR = 0.01, and WRMR = 0.83 for the Japanese data. The weighted omega coefficients indicate high reliability of the subscales, calculated as 0.86 for Australia and 0.84 for Japan.

The complexity of the bullying-victimization relationship is also highlighted through research that identifies their inter-connectedness. Haynie et al. (2001) found that more than half of the bullies in their study also reported being victimized. Ma (2001) also identified a reciprocal relationship between bully and victim. The consistently high correlations between these constructs, revealed in our own research, lends further support to the notion of a "bully-victim" cycle and the danger of presenting stereotypical views of individuals as either bullies or victims.

Description of the Specific Issues

Definitions of Bullying across Cultures

A greater understanding of how different countries define and describe bullying is warranted as it has significant implications for conducting cross-cultural research (Slee et al., 2003). As Smith, Kanetsuna, and Koo (2006) argued, "While some researchers emphasise or even assume the essential commonality of 'bullying' across different cultures, others very strongly assert that bullying in England, ijime in Japan and wang-ta in Korea are fundamentally different" (p. 4). Our own research confirms Smith et al's observation in a context that also includes China where Ma (as cited in Slee et al., 2003) notes that "Bullying is called 'qifu' or 'qiwu' in Chinese and it means much the same as in Western culture ... (slap, punch, hit, threaten, extort, isolate, mock, call bad names, and so on) in order to upset or hurt" (pp. 428–429). Maharaj, Tie, and Ryba (2000) contend that bullying is a socio-culturally benign term that contributes to the "perception that violent and intimidatory behaviour amongst school pupils is an individual activity" (p. 9). This, according to Cassidy (2000) defines bullying as a psychological and behavioral construct which fails to recognize the social construction of relationships. Yoneyama and Naito (2003) drew researchers' attention to the need to investigate bullying within its social context, including "the nature of academic instruction, classroom management and discipline, and the nature of social interaction" (p. 316).

Taki's (2001) research highlights variations in how bullying is defined. The accepted Western understanding of bullying is that it is a particularly destructive form of aggression, defined as a physical, verbal, or psychological attack or intimidation that is intended to cause fear, distress, or harm to the victim, and where the intimidation involves an imbalance of power in favor of the perpetrator. Distinguishing features of this broadly accepted Western definition are an imbalance of power and repetition over time.

In the Japanese context, Taki (2001) has emphasized that Western and Japanese definitions of bullying differ with Japanese bullying (ijime) regarded as socially manipulative behavior within a group-interaction process, where persons in a dominant position aim to cause mental and/ or physical suffering to another member of the group (see also Smith, Cowie, Olafsson, & Liefooghe, 2002, for a detailed discussion of definitions). Although the defining features of ijime appear to be similar in many respects to Western definitions, Taki has identified two significant differences.

First, for the Japanese, bullying incorporates the idea of a dominant position that is determined by an in group-interaction process. This does not infer either a physical power or an asymmetric power relationship. It suggests that the victim interacts with bullies, often in the same group or classroom, and is forced into an unequal power relation with the bullies. The idea of the power imbalance within a relationship is strongly emphasized by Taki who notes that bullying in Japanese schools is done by ordinary [sic] children (Taki, 2001). Second, bullying in Japan emphasizes mental/emotional anguish over and above physical force which arises out of group processes and interactions.

Comparative research to date has highlighted a Western interpretation of bullying as more direct in nature compared to the ijime reported by Japanese students (Slee, 2003). Yokoyu (2003) and Treml (2001) have both noted that ijime (as reported amongst secondary school students) is difficult to detect because it is frequently subtle and indirect. Nevertheless, the perpetrators usually intend to inflict harm on the victims mentally even when it does not involve physical means.

Our research (Murray-Harvey, Slee, Saebel, & Taki, 2001) in Australian schools suggests that indirect (e.g., social) bullying is well entrenched and is typically under-reported. Research in non-Western contexts (Maharaj et al., 2000) highlights the need for a shift from conceptualizing bullying as the pathological behavior of deviant individuals towards conceptualizing bullying in socio-cultural terms. This is exemplified in our research where social bullying is now a better understood phenomenon through cross-cultural research.

Example/Application

Application to Policy and Practice

The research collaboration has already produced a number of practical and policy initiatives. One such outcome has been the proliferation of peer support programs in schools. Cowie (2003) notes that "Peer support interventions harness young people's potential to assume a helpful role to tackling interpersonal problems in the peer group" (p. 89). For example, in Australia, Japan and Korea, peer support programs are widespread in schools (Kwak, as cited in Yano, 2005; Taki, 2002). As well, intervention programs to address school bullying have been identified, translated, and evaluated in Japanese schools (Taki, 1997). In Australia, the National SAFE Schools Framework (Ministerial Council on Education, Employment, Training and Youth Affairs [MCEETYA] Student Learning and Support Services Taskforce, 2003) has set in place procedures for providing a safe learning environment. Schools are now being asked to develop anti-bullying policies, grievance procedures, and intervention programs so that students can learn in a safe and positive school environment.

Relevant Research

In early Japanese-Australian research conducted between 2000 and 2001 (see Murray-Harvey et al., 2001), consideration was given to issues of prevalence of bullying and victimization in both countries by surveying students in 18 schools (primary and secondary) in Tokyo (n = 5518) and 22 schools (primary and secondary) in Adelaide, Australia (n = 3145). To achieve this, Taki's

(2001) survey instrument was collaboratively adapted to include 57 common items. With the assistance of a Japanese interpreter, adjustments were made to the items by back translation to account for the different nuances in meaning between the two languages.

The procedure for administration of the "Your Life at School" surveys was discussed by researchers from the two countries and dates set so that surveys were administered at the same stage in each country's respective academic years. This involved a research assistant associated with the project in each country visiting the schools and supervising the administration and collection of the questionnaires. The eight bullying and victimization items referred to in this chapter are described in the next section.

In relation to victimization, students were asked to indicate on a 4-point Likert scale which was coded 1 = never; 2 = once or twice; 3 = 2–3 times per month; 4 = more than once a week, whether "this term how often have you been bullied at school by (a) isolated, ignored, called names; (b) picked on by others; (c) pushed, hit, kicked on purpose (jokingly); (d) robbed, kicked, hit harshly (on purpose)." The term "jokingly" is used to capture the subtle difference between bullying that is masked by ambiguous action (e.g., bumping into someone) and bullying that is intentionally hurtful (e.g., a direct push).

The bullying items were similarly constructed with students being asked whether "this term how often have you bullied someone at school by (a) isolating, ignoring, calling them names; (b) picking on others; (c) pushing, hitting, kicking on purpose (jokingly); (d) stealing, kicking, hitting harshly (on purpose)."

Data from both Japanese and Australian surveys were entered into a common data base. Bullying and victimization prevalence data from this initial comparative study are displayed in Table 3.1.

From the prevalence data shown in Table 3.1, it can be seen that in Australia victimization (being pushed, hit, kicked on purpose, jokingly) is a result of more direct and overt actions of others than it is in Japan. With regard to bullying, Japanese students more frequently bully by isolating, ignoring or name-calling than do Australian students whose bullying behavior is characteristically more direct and physical. Consideration was also given to possible gender influences between countries and is presented in Table 3.2. More detailed analyses were undertaken to test for significant differences between countries and between males and females. For these analyses the effect sizes were calculated using the Cramer V statistic.

Table 3.1 Frequency (Percentage) of Self-Reported Victimization and Bullying among Australian and Japanese School Students in Grades 5–10

Survey item	Australia			Japan		
	Often	Sometimes	Never	Often	Sometimes	Never
Victimization						
Isolated, ignored, called names	12.2	32.5	55.3	18.0	27.0	55.0
Picked on by others	10.1	27.0	62.9	7.8	16.7	75.5
Pushed, hit, kicked on purpose (jokingly)	13.2	31.3	55.5	11.5	14.3	74.2
Robbed, kicked, hit harshly (on purpose)	3.4	9.7	86.9	4.0	6.3	89.7
Bullying						
Isolating, ignoring, or calling them names	9.2	36.7	54.1	17.2	32.3	50.5
Picking on others	7.1	27.8	65.1	3.8	10.9	85.3
Pushing, hitting, kicking on purpose (jokingly)	11.6	28.0	60.4	5.6	11.0	83.4
Stealing, kicking, hitting harshly (on purpose)	2.5	5.6	91.9	1.7	3.0	95.3

Table 3.2 Frequency (Percentage) of Self-Reported Victimization and Bullying for Australian and Japanese Male and Female School Students in Grades 5–10

Survey item	Male			Female		
	Often	Sometimes	Never	Often	Sometimes	Never
Victimization:						
Isolated, ignored, called names:						
Australia	13.0	30.8	56.1	11.6	33.8	54.7
Japan	16.6	23.9	59.5	19.5	30.4	50.2
Picked on by others:						
Australia	11.2	27.5	61.3	9.1	26.7	64.2
Japan	10.5	18.5	71.0	4.9	14.8	80.3
Pushed, hit, kicked on purpose (jokingly):						
Australia	16.3	33.1	50.6	10.7	29.9	59.4
Japan	13.9	17.2	68.9	9.0	11.3	79.7
Robbed, kicked, hit harshly (on purpose)						
Australia	4.9	12.9	82.3	2.2	7.2	90.7
Japan	5.3	7.2	87.5	2.6	5.4	92.0
Bullying:						
Isolating, ignoring, or calling them names						
Australia	11.2	39.9	48.9	7.7	34.2	58.1
Japan	14.6	29.1	56.3	20.0	35.6	44.4
Picking on others						
Australia	9.8	31.0	59.3	5.0	25.2	69.8
Japan	6.1	15.2	78.8	1.4	6.5	92.1
Pushing, hitting, kicking on purpose (jokingly)						
Australia	15.3	28.4	56.3	8.8	27.6	63.5
Japan	8.4	15.5	76.1	2.6	6.2	91.2
Stealing, kicking, hitting harshly (on purpose)						
Australia	4.1	8.5	87.3	1.3	3.3	95.5
Japan	2.6	4.2	93.2	0.6	1.8	97.6

Table 3.2 shows that victimization occurs among boys at higher levels in Australia by being pushed, hit, or kicked on purpose (jokingly) than it does in Japan. The pattern of victimization for girls in both countries is similar. Victimization that involves being picked on is more prevalent for Australian girls than it is for Japanese girls. With regard to bullying, Australian students (both boys and girls) overall engage in the most direct form of bullying by pushing, hitting, kicking on purpose (jokingly) compared with Japanese boys and girls, with Japanese girls rarely engaging in this type of bullying and instead using isolating, ignoring or name-calling.

While isolating, ignoring or calling names is more prevalent in Japan ($p < .001$, ES = .11), with Japanese females engaging in this type of bullying significantly more than other types ($p < .001$, ES = .17), the effect sizes indicate that the differences between countries are not marked. Australian students engage more than Japanese students in the other types of bullying, namely *picking on others* ($p < .001$, ES = .23) and *pushing, hitting, kicking* either "lightheartedly" ($p < .001$, ES = .25) indicating small effect sizes for these two types of bullying, or "harshly" ($p <$

.001, ES = .07); with the low effect size for this type of bullying indicating a trivial difference between countries. The bullying reflected in behaviors involving isolating, ignoring or calling names has become the focus of more recent research (Crick et al., 1999; Owens, Shute, & Slee, 2004; Underwood, 2003).

Following up on the significant findings for isolating, ignoring or name-calling victimization and bullying, (i.e., social bullying) attention was then given to possible developmental patterns by examining prevalence from the school years 5 through 10. The frequency of self-reported victimization by school year across the two countries is shown in Figure 3.1.

Figure 3.1 illustrates that across year levels 5 to 9, Japanese students report more victimization by being isolated, ignored and called names than Australian students. For Japanese students, the rates are highest in grades 5, 6, and 7. For Australian students the rates are highest in grade 7, which is consistent with research reported by Rigby and Slee (1999). These comparative figures suggest that self-reported victimization is highest in both countries in the upper primary years of school.

In relation to self-reported social bullying, Japanese students report more isolating, ignoring and name-calling behaviors than their Australian counterparts across all year levels. In Japan this type of bullying occurs most in grade 9 (Junior High) and in Australia it occurs most in grade 7 (Upper Primary). Differences among the two countries in relation to developmental trends continues to be an area of research interest and are likely to be an important factor in determining where resources and interventions are distributed.

Although Japan and Australia are highly similar in relation to nationwide levels of social and economic development, the different cultural contexts between the two countries suggests that cross-cultural comparisons will improve understanding of students' overall well-being at school Spanning the years of research between Japan and Australia, data gathered from the "Your Life at School" survey has also been examined using path analysis (Murray-Harvey & Slee, 2007) to further understand the factors that either have an impact on school bullying, or are impacted on, by bullying.

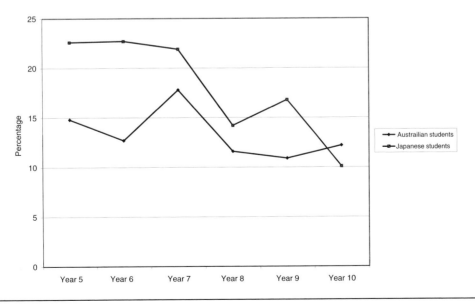

Figure 3.1 Victimization by isolating and ignoring among grade 5–10 school students in Australia and Japan.

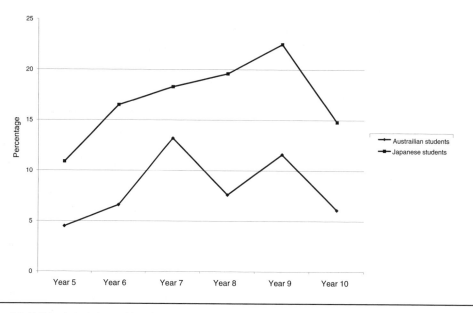

Figure 3.2 Bullying by isolating and ignoring among grade 5–10 school students in Australia and Japan.

Correlations, as presented in Table 3.3, have been found between bullying and a range of variables indicative of (a) students' psychological health (apathy, depression, aggression, and somatic symptoms); (b) sources of stress and support (peers, teachers, parents); (c) academic performance; and (d) feelings of belonging to school (Murray-Harvey & Slee, 2006).

Path analyses have been even more revealing in showing that when parents, teachers, or peers are perceived as stressors in students' lives these stressors are highly predictive of both bullying behavior and feeling victimized. We have become acutely aware, through examining the inter-relationships among these variables, of the role played, not only by peers (classmates) as sources of stress (and conversely as sources of support) but also of the role played by teachers and families, either to exacerbate or moderate (through their support), the impact of stresses in students' lives at school (Murray-Harvey & Slee, 2007). Path analysis also revealed a strong association between victimization and students' psychological health (Murray-Harvey & Slee, 2006).

Table 3.3 Correlations between Stressors and Support, Psychological Health, Academic Performance, and Belonging to School

	Stressor	Support	Poor Psychological Health	Academic Performance	School Belonging	Victimization
Stressor						
Support	−365					
Poor Psychological Health	550	−329				
Academic. Performance	−482	270	−511			
School Belonging	−377	445	−459	291		
Victimization	481	−132	335	−203	−241	
Bullying	370	−166	270	−219	−209	394

Note. Only correlations > 0.10 reported; decimal points omitted.

Pacific-Rim Research Project

While the survey content varied across the participating countries (Australia, Canada, Japan, Korea, and the United States), a common set of core questions regarding student experiences of being victimized and bullying others were included in all surveys. The example of social bullying shown here illustrates a variable for which there was found to be general consensus in relation to defining the phenomenon of bullying among the Pacific Rim research group (Taki et al., 2006).

Trends in reported experiences with social bullying and victimization across a sample of Grade 5 (age 10–11) students in the five countries (*n* = approx. 1500) are illustrated in Figures 3.3 and 3.4, which show the frequency of bullying and victimization, and Figures 3.5 and 3.6, which depict the frequency in relation to gender. The category "Sometimes" indicates students' reports that they have been bullied (socially), or engage in bullying (socially) once or twice a month.

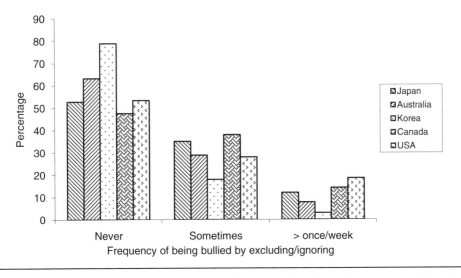

Figure 3.3 Frequency of victimization among Japanese, Australian, Korean, Canadian, and American Grade 5 students.

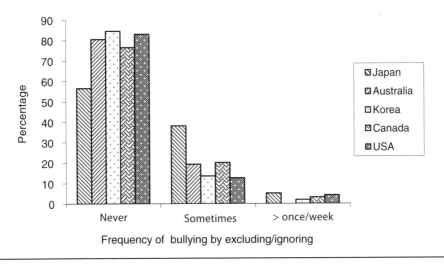

Figure 3.4 Frequency of social bullying among Japanese, Australian, Korean, Canadian, and American Grade 5 students.

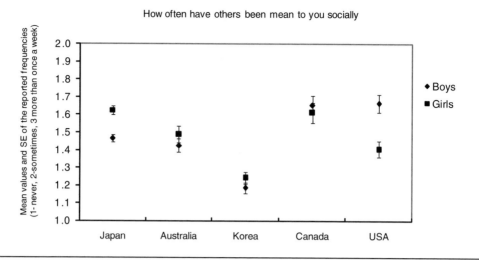

Figure 3.5 Social victimizaiton by exclusion and rumors across five countries.

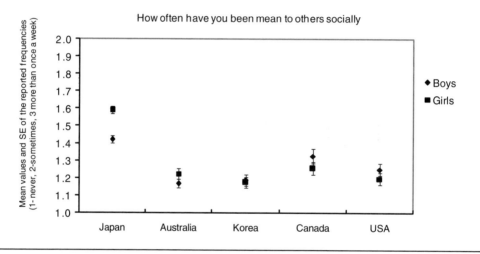

Figure 3.6 Social bullying by exclusion and rumors across five countries.

Across countries, the highest rates of reported bullying through social aggression were reported by students in Japan and the lowest by students in Korea. For boys and girls, rates of social bullying were highest in Japan ($p < .001$, ES = .14 for boys and ES = .22 for girls) and rates were not markedly different across Australia, Canada and the United States.

For both boys and girls, the lowest rates of social victimization were reported by students in Korea, significantly lower than all other countries ($p < .001$, ES = .14 for both boys and girls). For boys, similar, lower rates of social victimization were reported by students in Japan and Australia compared with U.S. and Canadian boys who reported the highest rates of social victimization. For girls, again the lowest rates were reported in Korea and the highest rates reported by girls from Japan and Canada.

Table 3.4 Summary Table of Implications for Practice

Comparative Research	Implications for Practice
Murray-Harvey & Slee (2006)	The harmful effects on student wellbeing of indirect, relational (social) bullying and the need to respond to and not ignore it
Owens , Daly, & Slee (2005)	The need to consider gender in relation to the development of intervention programs because boys and girls bully and bully others in different ways
Rigby & Slee (1999) Alsaker (2004)	Early intervention is warranted based on evidence that high levels of bullying occur in primary schools
Pepler et al., (2004)	A whole-school approach is needed to address bullying. Bullying is more than individual deviant behavior; it requires action on the part of teachers, parents, students, and the school community
Murray-Harvey & Slee (2006)	Clarifying definitions of bullying and victimization has highlighted the different types of bullying to include social as well as physical and verbal bullying
Murray-Harvey & Slee (2006)	Bullying is a relationship issue

Directions for Future Research

As described in this chapter, comparative research involving the Pacific Rim countries has resulted in a deeper appreciation of the efforts such countries have made in understanding and addressing the issue of school bullying. Japan has a long research history associated with the study of bullying and the Pacific Rim collaboration has deepened and enriched knowledge regarding the complexity of the bullying dynamic. In particular, the exchange of research involving Australia, Canada, China, Korea, and the United States has impacted program and policy development.

Opportunities exist to further this collaboration through joint research efforts that more broadly define bullying within its community context, along with research that permits examination of how teachers in classrooms across countries identify and deal with the more indirect types of bullying. A related research issue is the extent to which pre-service teacher education programs can alert teachers to the prevalence and severity of bullying in schools and improve understanding of effective programs and strategies that have been developed to address the issue. No data exist on whether some countries undertake this task more effectively than others and while the success of a program or strategy in one country cannot be assumed to translate into effective practice in another context, there is much to be learned from shared knowledge, through comparative research, of the way bullying is perceived, perpetrated, and managed.

References

Alsaker, F. D. (2004). Bernese programme against victimisation in kindergarten and elementary school. In P. K. Smith, D. Pepler, & K. Rigby (Eds.), *Bullying in schools: How successful can interventions be?* (pp. 289–307). London: Cambridge University Press.

Cassidy, T. (2000, December). *Challenging the bully: Towards an optimistic future.* Paper presented at the annual conference of the Australian Association for Research in Education, Sydney, Australia.

Commonwealth Government. (1994). *"Sticks and Stones": Report on violence in Australian Schools.* Canberra: Australian Government Publishing Service.

Cowie, H. (2003, May). Peer support: How young people themselves challenge school bullying. Paper presented at the Oxford Kobe Education Seminar, *Measures to reduce bullying in schools* (pp. 88–96). Kobe, Japan: Kobe Institute.

Crick, N. R., Wellman, N. E., Casas, J. F., O'Brien, M. A., Nelson, D. A., Grotpeter, J. K., et al. (1999). Childhood aggression and gender: A new look at an old problem. In D. Bernstein (Ed.), *Nebraska Symposium on Motivation: Vol. 45. Gender and motivation* (pp. 75–141). Lincoln: University of Nebraska Press.

Dixon, R., Smith, P. K., & Jenks, C. (2006). Using systemic thinking to inform research on bullying. In K. Österman & K. Björkqvist (Eds.), *Proceedings of the XVI World meeting of the International Society for Research on Aggression*: Vol. 8. *Contemporary research on aggression* (pp. 78–85). Vasa, Sweden: The Faculty of Social and Caring Science.

Haynie, D. L., Nansel, T., Eitel, P., Crump, A. D., Saylor, K., Yu, K., & Simons-Morton, B. (2001). Bullies, victims, and bully/victims: Distinct groups of at-risk youth. *Journal of Early Adolescence, 21,* 29–49.

Hymel, S., Rocke Henderson, N., & Bonanno, R. (2005). Moral disengagement: A framework for understanding bullying among adolescents. *Journal of Social Sciences, Special Issue, 8,* 1–11.

Juvonen, J., & Graham, S. (Eds.). (2001). *School-based peer harassment: The plight of the vulnerable and victimized.* New York: Guilford.

Ma, X. (2001). Bullying and being bullied: To what extent are bullies also victims? *American Educational Research Journal, 3,* 351–357.

Maharaj, A., Tie, W., & Ryba, A. (2000). Deconstructing bullying in Aotearoa/New Zealand: Disclosing its liberal and colonial connections. *Journal of Educational Studies, 35*(1), 9–24.

Ministerial Council on Education, Employment, Training and Youth Affairs (MCEETYA) Student Learning and Support Services Taskforce. (2003). *National safe schools framework.* Retrieved June 1, 2007, from http://www.dest. gov.au/sectors/school_education/publications_resources/profiles/national_safe_schools_framework.htm

Morita, Y., Soeda, H., Soeda, K., & Taki, M. (1999). Japan. In P. K. Smith, Y. Morita, J. Junger-Tas, D. Olweus, R. Catalano, & P. T. Slee (Eds.), *The nature of school bullying. A cross-national perspective* (pp. 309–323). London: Routledge.

Murray-Harvey, R., & Slee, P. T. (December 2006). Australian and Japanese school students' experiences of school bullying and victimization: associations with stress, support and school belonging. *The International Journal on Violence in Schools.* Retrieved June 1, 2007, from http://www.ijvs.org/1-6053-Article.php?id=28&tarticle=0

Murray-Harvey, R., & Slee, P. T. (2007). Supportive and stressful relationships with teachers, peers and family and their influence on students' social/emotional and academic experience of school. *Australian Journal of Guidance and Counselling, 7*(2), 126–147.

Murray-Harvey, R., Slee, P. T., Saebel, J., & Taki, M. (2001). *Life at school in Australia and Japan: The impact of stress and support on bullying and adaptation to school.* Paper presented at the annual conference of the Australian Association for Research in Education (AARE), Fremantle, Australia. Retrieved May 31, 2007, from http://www. aare.edu.au/01pap/mur01081.htm

Ohsako, T. (Ed.). (1997). *Violence at school: Global issues and interventions.* Paris: UNESCO International Bureau of Education.

Owens, L., Shute, R., & Slee, P. T. (2004). Girls' aggressive behavior. *The Prevention Researcher, 11*(3), 9–12.

Owens, L., Daly, A., & Slee, P. (2005). Sex and age differences in victimization and conflict resolution among adolescents in a South Australian school. *Aggressive Behavior, 31,* 1–12.

Pepler, D., Craig, W., O'Connell, P., Atlas, R., & Charach, A. (2004). Making a difference in bullying: Evaluation of a systemic school-based program in Canada. In P. K. Smith, D. Pepler, & K. Rigby (Eds.), *Bullying in schools: How successful can interventions be?* (pp. 125–141). London: Cambridge University Press.

Rigby, K., & Slee, P. T. (1991). Bullying among Australian school children: Reported behaviour and attitude toward victims. *Journal of Social Psychology, 131,* 615–627.

Rigby, K., & Slee, P. T. (1993). Children's attitudes towards victims. In D. P. Tattum (Ed.), *Understanding and managing bullying* (pp. 119–133). London: Heinemann Books.

Rigby, K., & Slee, P. T. (1999). Australia. In P. K. Smith., Y. Morita., J. Junger-Tas., D. Olweus., R. Catalano, & P. T. Slee. (Eds.), *The nature of school bullying. A cross-national perspective* (pp. 324–440). London: Routledge.

Slee, P. T. (2001). The PEACE Pack: A program for reducing bullying in our schools. Flinders University, Adelaide, Australia.

Slee, P. T. (2003, May). School bullying in Australia: Developments in understanding and intervention initiatives. Paper presented at the Oxford Kobe Education Seminar, *Measures to reduce bullying in schools.* Kobe, Japan: Kobe Institute.

Slee, P. T. (2005). Bullying in Australia. In M. Tsuchiya & P. Smith (Eds.), *Eliminating bullying in schools — Japan and the world* (pp. 65–72). Kyoto, Japan: Minerva.

Slee, P. T., Ma, L., Sim, H., Taki, M., Sullivan, K. (2003). School bullying in five countries in the Asia-Pacific Region. In J. Keeves & R. Watanabe (Eds.), *The Handbook on Educational Research in the Asia Pacific Region* (pp. 425–439). Dordrecht: Kluwer Academic.

Smith, P., Morita, J., Junger-Tas, D., Olweus, D., Catalano, R., & Slee, P. T. (1999). *The nature of school bullying. A cross-national perspective.* London: Routledge.

Smith, P. K., Cowie, H., Olafsson, R. F., & Liefooghe, A. P. D. (2002). Definitions of bullying: A comparison of terms, uses, and age and gender differences, in a fourteen-country international comparison, *Child Development, 73,* 1119–1133.

Smith, P. K., Kanetsuna, T., & Koo, H. (2006). Cross-national comparison of 'bullying' and related terms: Western and eastern perspectives. In K. Österman & K. Björkqvist (Eds.), *Proceedings of the XVI World meeting of the International Society for Research on Aggression*: Vol. 8. *Contemporary research on aggression* (pp. 3–10). Vasa, Sweden: The Faculty of Social and Caring Science.

Sullivan, K. (2000). *The anti-bullying handbook*. Auckland, NZ: Oxford University Press.

Swearer, S. M., & Doll, B. (2001). Bullying in schools: An ecological framework. *Journal of Emotional Abuse, 2,* 7–23.

Swearer. S. M., & Espelage, D. L. (2004). A social-ecological framework of bullying among youth. In D. L. Espelage & S. M. Swearer (Eds.), *Bullying in American schools. A social-ecological perspective on prevention and intervention* (pp. 1–12). Mahwah, NJ: Erlbaum.

Taki, M. (1997). *The P.E.A.C.E. Pack. A Japanese translation*. Tokyo: Jiji-tsushin.

Taki, M. (2001). Relation among bullying, stress and stressor: A follow-up survey using panel data and a comparative survey between Japan and Australia. *Japanese Society*, 5, 25–41.

Taki, M (2002). *Changing schools by Japanese peer support — practical methods*. Tokyo: Kaneko Shobo.

Taki, M., Sim, H., Pepler, D., Hymel, S., Slee, P., Murray-Harvey, R., & Swearer, S. (2006, July). *Bullying Research Involving 5 Pacific Rim Countries*. Symposium conducted at the 19th Biennial Meeting of the International Society for the Study of Behavioural Development (ISSBD), Melbourne. Australia.

Treml, J. N. (2001). Bullying as a social malady in contemporary Japan. *International Social Work, 44,* 107–117.

Underwood, M. K. (2003). *Social aggression among girls*. New York: Guilford.

Yano, S. (2005, March). *Foreword. Director General*. International symposium on education reform 2005 (pp. 3–6). The National Institute of Educational Policy Research (NIER). Unpublished symposium.

Yokoyu, S. (2003, May). *Bullying and developmental psychology clinics focusing around how to work on trauma and recovery from bullying*. Paper presented at the Oxford Kobe Education Seminar, Measures to reduce bullying in schools (pp. 49–65). Kobe, Japan: Kobe Institute.

Yoneyama, S., & Naito, A. (2003). Problems with the paradigm: The school as a factor in understanding bullying (with special reference to Japan). *British Journal of Sociology of Education, 24*(3), 315–330.

4

Creating a Positive School Climate and Developing Social Competence

PAMELA ORPINAS AND ARTHUR M. HORNE

School bullying is a multifaceted problem. Although all bullying acts have in common the intent to hurt others, behaviors vary widely in severity and type, from demeaning looks to spreading malicious rumors to physically assaulting others. Similarly, the motives for bullying peers are diverse; Dagley (2000), for example, highlighted four motives: attention, revenge, power, or inadequacy. In consequence, the deterrence of school bullying requires a comprehensive model that examines a wide array of school and student characteristics needed to prevent and reduce bullying. Orpinas and Horne (2006) developed the School Social Competence Development and Bullying Prevention Model to provide an organized, comprehensive view of the critical components necessary for bullying prevention. The model has two components (see Figure 4.1). The outer circle reflects the school, and calls attention to eight characteristics that promote a positive school climate. The students are at the center, and the model highlights specific skills and cognitions that the school can focus on at the individual student level. This chapter describes the school and student components of the model. The chapter concludes by examining characteristics of a successful implementation.

School Social Competence Development and Bullying Prevention Model: The School Component

The fundamental component to reduce school bullying is to create a positive school climate that fosters caring behaviors. An environment where people spend a significant amount of their time (e.g., workplace, school) affects their psyche and their behavior. An organization's climate encompasses values, communication and management styles, rules and regulations, ethical practices, reinforcement of caring behaviors, support for academic excellence, and characteristics of the physical environment. A school with a positive climate is inviting, and students and teachers feel energized to perform at their best. Such an environment will increase the sense of connectedness to peers and belonging to the school, and students will perform better academically; thus, reducing the likelihood of aggressive behaviors (Eisenberg, Neumark-Sztainer, & Perry, 2003; Orpinas, Horne, & Staniszewski, 2003; Resnick et al., 1997). Unfortunately, some schools are managed like correctional facilities: a place of fear and threats that lacks caring and respect for

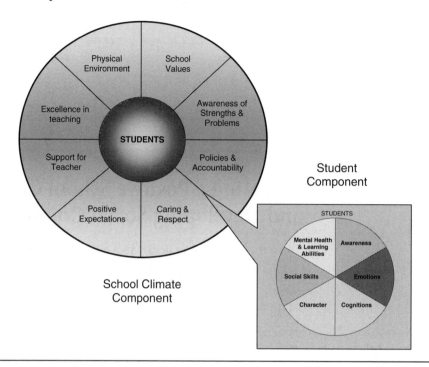

Figure 4.1 School Social Competence Development and Bullying Prevention Model (Orpinas & Horne, 2006).

students. Students would certainly want to avoid such an environment—thus, increasing the dropout rate—and they would learn to respond in kind, that is, by being aggressive.

The school component of the Social Competence Development model highlights eight critical areas for promoting a positive school climate and reducing bullying: (a) excellence in teaching, (b) school values, (c) awareness of strengths and problems, (d) policies and accountability, (e) caring and respect, (f) positive expectations, (g) teacher support, and (h) physical environment characteristics.

Excellence in Teaching

Students' academic performance is the first and most important goal of schools. Strong teaching skills, carefully prepared lessons, and an ability to motivate students will increase academic performance, reduce behavioral problems in the classroom, and promote a positive classroom climate (Hein, 2004; Pianta, 1999; Pierce, 1994). Research supports the need for promoting both positive behavior and academic performance (Caprara, Barbaranelli, Pastorelli, Bandura, & Zimbardo, 2000); when students behave in class, more time is allowed for teaching. However, teachers frequently struggle between the demands to cover the academic content of their class and the need to promote social skills.

Excellence in teaching includes mastery of the subject matter, as well as mastery of classroom process and dynamics. Teachers well-trained in the subject matter still have difficulties with classroom learning if they do not master teaching strategies as well. Not only do teachers need to teach with exercising respect and dignity, they must also understand the learning styles of their students and direct the classroom in a manner that facilitates understanding and application, rather than rote learning. For example, cooperative learning groups engage students with varying levels of knowledge to work together on academic tasks. The cooperative learning approach improves academic achievement and race relations, and promotes positive attitudes toward school, yet this educational strategy is not universally used (U.S. Department of Health and Human Services, 2001).

School Values

The school philosophy provides the framework to develop a positive school climate and prevent bullying (Horne, Orpinas, Newman-Carlson, & Bartolomucci, 2004; Orpinas, Horne, & Multisite Violence Prevention Project, 2004; Sullivan, 2000). The School Social Competence Model highlights three values that apply to educators and students: (a) all children can learn; (b) all people in the school community deserve to be treated with respect and dignity; and (c) violence, aggression, and bullying are not acceptable in school. To generate interest and support for these or other values, teachers and other members of the school community should participate in the process of defining the school's values (Bosworth, 2000; Orpinas et al., 2003). These values are the basis for creating the school's rules and consequences (Curwin & Mendler, 1997). While educators always initially endorse these three values, they may not embrace them in their practice. So it is important that these values are not seen as simply "read and agree" statements, but that the school actually spends time developing an awareness of their importance and provides examples of how easily educators can violate them.

Awareness of Strengths and Problems

No school is perfect, and the awareness of problems to solve and of strengths to capitalize on is the basis for change. Surveys of students, parents, and educators, as well as qualitative assessments (e.g., focus groups, interviews of key persons), can provide the necessary information to identify problems, define solutions, and guide the implementation of those solutions. During this process of examining strengths and areas that need improvement, educators should scrutinize their own attitudes, which may be supporting bullying or, at a minimum, not doing enough to stop it (e.g., "bullying is just a normal part of childhood," "bullies help kids who seem weaker by pushing them to learn to stand up for themselves," or "it is best to ignore bullying incidents"; Orpinas & Horne, 2006). Conducting an evaluation to learn of shortcomings is often an unpopular or threatening experience, particularly for administrators, and is often avoided. Yet without identifying specific areas of difficulty, the school will have great difficulty identifying how to improve.

Policies and Accountability

Policies for the prevention of bullying and other problems, as well as the accountability of the offenders, are essential for maintaining a positive school climate. However, to achieve this positive climate, administrators cannot develop policies through an autocratic process. All members of the school community should participate in the decision-making process for developing policies. In particular, school administrators must support the overall process of enhancing the school climate and solving discipline problems. Teacher input is most valuable in this process, as they have daily contact with students. School staff (e.g., custodians, bus drivers, and lunchroom workers) should also provide their unique perspective on how to achieve those goals. Meetings with parents through school-sponsored gatherings can enhance their understanding and support for school policies and goals. Additionally, policies, rules, and consequences should be based on the school's values, and should promote responsibility rather than blind obedience.

Curwin and Mendler (1999) compared these two models: responsibility versus obedience. The goal of the obedience model is for students to obey their teacher and follow the rules. In this model, punishments—such as being suspended or writing 100 times "I will not bully others"—are imposed on children, and students learn to avoid the potential punishing teacher or they learn not to be caught. Conversely, the goal of the responsibility model is to make students accountable for their choices. When students make bad decisions, educators help the students learn from the outcome and repair the damage to the victims. Under the responsibility model, a student who is caught bullying others might be asked to apologize to the victims and develop a plan to behave differently in future similar situations. The emphasis of these consequences is to repair the damage, reconnect the bully to peers and school, and solve the problem, rather than simply "paying back" for what was done.

Caring and Respect

Educators who value and actively demonstrate caring, respect, and a positive rapport with students will create an environment in which students behave appropriately because they care about each other, rather than because they fear the consequences (Hein, 2004). Specific strategies that may help to create this environment are:

1. Planning activities that increase connectedness among students and between students and teachers: Teachers can increase connectedness by promoting cooperation rather than competition, emphasizing democratic decision making, and providing opportunities for meaningful decision making.
2. Modeling respect with other teachers and with students: Educators should avoid behaviors that are demeaning such as shouting at students or using sarcastic or patronizing language. Rather, knowing students' names, using a positive language, and complimenting students for their efforts can foster a respectful environment.
3. Mastering positive approaches to discipline: Most teachers are familiar with the subject they teach, but frequently leave the profession because they are not able to handle discipline problems. Mastering strategies to prevent conflict in the classroom can help to create a positive climate, reduce bullying, and increase teaching effectiveness (Lewis, Sugai, & Colvin, 1998).
4. Celebrating classroom diversity: Beyond "tolerating" diversity, schools that create a positive climate "celebrate" diversity and genuinely promote understanding and appreciation for different cultural groups.

Positive Expectations

Whether it is a self-fulfilling prophecy, a perceptual bias, or an accurate perception, educators' expectations of their students may influence their own behavior toward the students and consequently the students' behavior in school (Kolb & Jussim, 1994; Rosenthal, 1994; Trouilloud, Sarrazin, Martinek, & Guillet, 2002). Teachers who believe that certain students will not learn, may spend less time with those students and provide less feedback on their work or teach more simplistic materials, thus, fulfilling their own expectations that the student is not up to par. Conversely, teachers' positive expectations may help to create an encouraging classroom climate that facilitates learning and achievement. The importance of maintaining positive expectations also applies to the relationship between administrators and teachers.

Teacher Support

Teachers play a key role in creating a positive school climate, but the daily stress and barrage of demands placed on them may hinder this process. Teachers need support and time from their administration to plan their lessons, meet with colleagues to solve problems, and attend skills-development workshops. Support group sessions can help teachers learn new skills and apply them in the classroom (Orpinas et al., 2004; Shapiro, Dupaul, Bradley, & Bailey, 1996). In our studies of teacher exhaustion, we have found that teachers experiencing greater levels of burnout also perceive students as demonstrating greater levels of aggression and misconduct in the classroom, and they generally have lower expectations for a student's success. Thus, a teacher's ability to maintain positive expectations for learning and behavior are influenced by the teacher's emotional state (Horne, Orpinas, & Multisite Violence Prevention Project, 2005).

Physical Environment

Although relationships among people are most important in creating a positive school climate, a safe, clean, and aesthetically pleasant physical environment can help support that positive climate. Not all schools can be new or offer the latest in equipment and physical niceties, but they can be maintained in such a manner that they are clean, physically attractive, and safe. Our experience in working with many schools over the past decade is that the way in which the physical environment is maintained and operated is a clear statement about the pride and satisfaction teachers, administrators, and students have for their school. Additionally, in positive schools, school walls are used to highlight teachers' and students' successes in all academic subjects, as well as arts and sports (Valentine, Clark, Hackmann, & Petzko, 2004).

School Social Competence Development and Bullying Prevention Model: The Student Component

The previous section describes the characteristics of a positive school environment. To reduce bullying, it is equally important to enhance students' social competence (Welsh, Parke, Widaman, & O'Neil, 2001). Students need social skills to develop friendships, solve conflicts without violence, have meaningful interactions with adults, plan for the future, and resist peer pressure. The student component of the School Social Competence Development and Bullying Prevention Model highlights six areas: (a) awareness, (b) emotions, (c) cognitions, (d) character, (e) social skills, and (f) mental health and learning abilities (Orpinas & Horne, 2006). These six areas are closely related; for example, whether a child expresses anger as rage or transforms anger into a constructive argument for social change depends on cognitive attributes, personal values, level of social skills, and mental health characteristics. Further, these manifestations of anger are strongly influenced by the quality of the environment: "One can plant good seeds into a pot of fertile soil or a pot of rocks and have very different outcomes, even if the original seeds were identical" (Bosworth, Orpinas, & Hein, 2009, p. 231). In spite of this caveat explaining the interconnectedness of these individual characteristics, for organizational purposes, we will describe each area separately.

Awareness

Most bullying prevention curricula start by increasing awareness of the problem (e.g., Newman, Horne, & Bartolomucci, 2000). Frequently, students, as well as their teachers, identify physical bullying as unacceptable, but fewer may recognize teasing, name-calling, rumors, or social isolation as unacceptable bullying behaviors. In this phase, students learn to recognize the characteristics of physical, verbal, and relational bullying. Students also become aware of the behaviors of bystanders who are part of the solution (e.g., ask for help, diffuse the problem, invite victims to join in play or workgroups) and those who are part of the problem (e.g., instigate fights, reinforce bullying by watching or laughing, pass demeaning rumors, or do nothing to stop the bullying). Ideally, the school will develop a common vocabulary, so that all teachers and students can define and recognize bullying behaviors. Awareness activities can be drawn from lesson plans provided by existing prevention programs, but they can also be integrated into existing history, English, or social sciences classes.

Emotions

Students' emotions are at the heart of the bullying problem. Goleman (1995) highlighted the importance of emotions—he coined the term "emotional intelligence"—in people's everyday lives. Emotional intelligence, as opposed to cognitive intelligence, comprises an array of personal skills for handling emotions and social situations: recognize one's and other people's feelings, delay gratification, control impulses, develop an optimistic view of life, persist on achieving a goal, and motivate oneself, just to name a few. The discussion that follows addresses one of the most important elements of emotional intelligence: how to identify and handle one's own emotions, how to recognize other people's emotions, and how to maintain a positive outlook of life. Orpinas and Horne (2006) highlighted three positive emotions that are particularly relevant to bullying prevention: (a) calmness, (b) optimism, and (c) connectedness to peers and school, as well as their counterparts: anger, pessimism, and disconnectedness. These negative emotions can destroy relationships and strain academic achievement.

Anger is a normal reaction to being treated aggressively, disrespectfully, or unfairly. Many children, particularly those living in violent neighborhoods or with neglectful parents, have valid reasons to be angry. And many children report being angry: A survey of over 9,000 middle school students in Texas showed that over half had been angry most of the day at least once during the week prior to the survey (unpublished data from the Students for Peace Project, Orpinas et al., 2000). Although it is understandable that some youth may be angry, students should learn that, no matter how angry they are, expressing anger by being physically or verbally aggressive towards others is not acceptable. Teachers can teach students a number of strategies to recognize anger and to manage it, such as: identify the physical manifestations of anger (e.g., body tension, increased heartbeat); be familiar with a wide array of emotions, as some children may confuse anger with fear or shame; increase awareness of situations that trigger anger; develop strategies to handle triggers of anger; reframe thoughts that lead to anger by using a cognitive strategy, such as the A-to-E Process of Thought and Action (Figure 4.2); apply relaxation techniques; or transform anger into compassion.

To develop a sense of optimism—another aspect of emotional intelligence—is as important to reduce bullying is also important to reduce bullying. Children may hold a pessimistic view of life for many reasons, including temperament, negative family situations, school problems, or negative cognitions, all of which can lead to depressive feelings. Depression is associated with aggression (Eisenberg, Neumark-Sztainer, & Story, 2003) and with substance use (Kelder et al., 2001). Teachers may help students to develop more positive attributions that enhance optimism and positive expectations within the school culture by providing opportunities for success, encouraging them to do their best, and helping students understand how attributions shape behavior (Orpinas et al., 2006; Seligman, Reivich, Jaycox, & Gillham, 1995).

The A-to-E Process of Thought and Action

A   Antecedent, the situation or event that occurred

B   Beliefs, thoughts, or attributions about the event or people associated with the event

C   Consistent affect, how one feels about the situation based upon his or her beliefs

D   Doing, the consequent response to the antecedent event — typically influenced by one's beliefs and consistent affect

E   External outcome, the consequence(s) of one's response

Figure 4.2 The A-to-E Process of Thought and Action. From: Orpinas, P. & Horne, A. M. (2006). *Bullying prevention: Creating a positive school climate and developing social competence.* Washington, D.C.: American Psychological Association. Reproduced with permission.

Students who feel connected to peers, school, and family are more likely to feel good about themselves, have positive relationships, and perform better academically. Most important for this chapter, connectedness reduces aggression and victimization (Bollmer, Milich, Harris, & Maras, 2005; Fox & Boulton, 2005; Simons-Morton, Crump, Haynie, & Saylor, 1999). School administrators and teachers can increase connectedness by maintaining a positive relationship with students, appreciating and complimenting students' successes and efforts, and providing opportunities for students get to know each other, as well as opportunities for students to compliment each other.

Cognitions

To develop social competence and prevent bullying, a cognitive strategy to handle the cognitive aspects of attributions and to solve conflicts can be very helpful, if not indispensable. The A-to-E Process of Thought and Action (Figure 4.2)—developed based on the work of cognitive psychologists, such as Ellis (1962), Beck (1972), and Maultsby (1984)—exemplifies a method to examine how an external event (e.g., Dianna passes a nasty rumor about Martin) leads to specific thoughts (e.g., Martin believes that Dianna is a bully, and she should pay for creating this rumor), and these thoughts are responsible for Martin's emotions (e.g., anger, frustration). Consistent with these emotions, Martin decides to act (e.g., insult or create another malicious rumor), which may lead to an external consequence (e.g., being suspended, being ganged up by Dianna's friends). By changing the thoughts, students can learn to change the resulting emotions, actions, and consequences.

Another cognitive aspect important to bullying prevention is learning to solve conflicts peacefully. Some students have a "natural" talent to solve conflicts without resorting to violence, most likely learned at home by observation of their parents. However, for many students, solving conflicts is a skill to be learned, and they need a step-by-step method. The process to solve conflicts generally follows these steps: calm down, identify the problem and the goal, generate solutions, anticipate possible consequences of those solutions, choose a solution and implement it, and evaluate the results. Some curricula provide an acronym to help students follow the steps, such as STOPP (**S**top and calm down, **T**hink about the problem and goals, **O**pt for solutions that are possible, **P**lan for possible consequences and do it, **P**lan working? Evaluate the outcomes; Horne, Bartolomucci, & Newman-Carlson, 2003) or SCIDDLE (**S**top, **C**alm down, **I**dentify the problem and your feelings about it, **D**ecide among your choices, **D**o it, **L**ook back, and **E**valuate; Meyer, Allison, Reese, Gay, & Multisite Violence Prevention Project., 2004).

Character

Beyond teaching emotional, cognitive, and behavioral techniques, bullying prevention should include character education. Some children know that bullying is wrong and have the social skills to interact with others in positive ways, but still opt to bully others. The discipline of character education uses a variety of strategies to help students act based on moral and ethical values (e.g., Lickona, 1991; Rusnak, 1998). A number of training programs directed toward reducing aggression include empathy training as an important element, for when students understand their peers, both behaviorally and emotionally, they are less likely to be injurious to the fellow students (Goldstein, 1999).

Social Skills

Beyond conflict resolution skills, general social and academic skills are necessary to develop social competency. Some children may bully others or be the targets of bullying because they lack emotional management skills (e.g., self-control, calm down), skills that show respect and concern for others (e.g., be polite, give compliments), verbal communication skills (e.g., engaging in conversation, being polite when interrupting), or listening skills (e.g., maintain eye contact). Academic skills (e.g., time management, study skills) are also necessary to perform well at school and prevent bullying, as some children may opt to bully to cover up their lack of academic performance.

Mental Health and Learning Abilities

Some bullying problems will not be solved by merely creating a positive school climate or teaching students social skills. Some children who bully others will require medical or psychological treatment. Students with learning disabilities will also need special resources (academic and otherwise), as they may be at special risk for being the being bullies or victims.

Implementation of a Comprehensive Model

The process of successfully implementing the School Social Competence Development and Bullying Prevention Model does not differ substantively from the implementation of other comprehensive prevention programs. Although implementation research lags behind studies identifying successful programs (Fixsen, Naoom, Blase, Friedman, & Wallace, 2005), we would like to highlight three elements that most researchers and practitioners agree are critical to a successful implementation.

The first element is commitment. Prevention programs, particularly comprehensive models of prevention, are not implemented in a vacuum. The school context will play a fundamental role in the intensity, length, and comprehensiveness of the implementation. Foremost, the school administration must be committed to create a positive school climate and to deter bullying (Orpinas et al., 1996). Administrators can garner resources, provide training, mobilize interest, create consensus among the different stakeholders of the school community, and clarify mechanisms for institutionalizing change (Adelman & Taylor, 2003). Teachers' understanding and commitment are also essential. To implement the model, teachers often need to change current practices of dealing with students, attend professional development workshops and support groups, and be at the forefront of implementation. Once school stakeholder have committed to create a positive school climate and develop students' social skills, a strategy to preventing bullying and other forms of aggression.

not include a specific curriculum, depending on the diagnosis of achers.

different behaviors and have different causes, a comprehensive vise the best prevention program.

ssential component of effective bully prevention strategies. Other pport a positive school climate, increasing awareness of strengths tion-focused approach, developing policies that increase onment of caring and respect, having positive expectations of all d creating a physical that promotes pride in the school.

need to include specific training on increasing awareness of the ng emotions, and developing a moral code that includes treating

from administration and staff, diligent diagnosis of the problem, ent bullying, as well as adequate allocation of time and funding.

move forward the implementation process is to assemble a team of stakeholders who will provide leadership.

The second element is assessment of the problem. Bullying problems may stem from many diverse causes, such as gang problems, social norms that support dating violence, or poor engagement in the school academic program. Thus, the school needs to identify the problem, that is, examine the prevalence of different types of bullying and possible risk and protective factors. The evaluation may include teacher, parent, and student surveys, as well as focus groups or interviews with key parties. As described in one of the school components of the model, teachers and administrators may engage in the process of assessing strengths and areas in need of improvement at the school level.

The third element is careful implementation. Based on the assessment, the school bullying prevention team can propose to the school community general and specific goals and a plan of action to achieve those goals. The implementation may require additional training for different parties and additional resources. Evaluation is not only important to identify the problem, but also to examine whether the strategies selected for change are implemented as planned (process evaluation) and whether the expected outcomes are being achieved (outcome evaluation). Regular reviews of what is working and what is failing will provide feedback to improve implementation. Changing the school climate is much more than a "quick fix" approach and, thus, schools may decide to tackle the problem in steps. For example, one school decided to develop a comprehensive strategy to reduce name-calling and put-downs (Orpinas et al., 2003), which resulted in an overall reduction of aggression.

To conclude, changing the school climate and preventing bullying is a process that requires commitment, diligent diagnosis of the problem, and careful implementation of strategies to prevent bullying (Table 4.1). Ongoing evaluation gives direction to improve implementation and modify less successful strategies or adapt to changes in the school environment. Administrators must avoid being like Sisyphus,[1] to repeat year after year the same activities that produce no accomplishments.

Note

1. The gods had condemned Sisyphus to ceaselessly rolling a rock to the top of a mountain, whence the stone would fall back of its own weight. They had thought with some reason that there is no more dreadful punishment than futile and hopeless labor. Albert Camus, *The Myth of Sisyphus and Other Essays.*

References

Adelman, H. S., & Taylor, L. (2003). On sustainability of project innovations as systemic change. *Journal of Educational and Psychological Consultation, 14,* 1–25.

Beck, A. T. (1972). *Depression: Causes and treatment.* Philadelphia: University of Pennsylvania Press.

Bollmer, J. M., Milich, R., Harris, M. J., & Maras, M. A. (2005). A friend in need — The role of friendship quality as a protective factor in peer victimization and bullying. *Journal of Interpersonal Violence, 20,* 701–712.

Bosworth, K. (2000). *Protective schools: Linking drug abuse prevention with student success.* Tucson: University of Arizona, College of Education.

Bosworth, K., Orpinas, P., & Hein, K. (2009). Development of a positive school climate. In M. Kenny, A. M. Horne, P. Orpinas, & L. Reese (Eds.), *Realizing social justice: The challenge of preventive interventions* (pp. 229–248). Washington, DC: American Psychological Association.

Camus, A. (1991). *The myth of Sisyphus and other essays* (Trans. Justin OBrien). New York: Vintage Books.

Caprara, G. V., Barbaranelli, C., Pastorelli, C., Bandura, A., & Zimbardo, P. G. (2000). Prosocial foundations of children's academic achievement. *Psychological Science, 11,* 302–306.

Curwin, R. L., & Mendler, A. N. (1997). *As tough as necessary: Countering violence, aggression, and hostility in our schools.* Alexandria, VA: Association for Supervision and Curriculum Development.

Curwin, R. L., & Mendler, A. N. (1999). *Discipline with dignity.* Alexandria, VA: Association for Supervision and Curriculum Development.

Dagley, J. C. (2000). Adlerian family therapy. In A.M. Horne & J. L. Passmore (Eds.), *Family counseling and therapy* (3rd ed., pp. 366–419). Itasca, IL: F.E. Peacock.

Eisenberg, M. E., Neumark-Sztainer, D., & Perry, C. L. (2003). Peer harassment, school connectedness, and academic achievement. *Journal of School Health, 73,* 311–316.

Eisenberg, M. E., Neumark-Sztainer, D., & Story, M. (2003). Associations of weight-based teasing and emotional well-being among adolescents. *Archives of Pediatrics & Adolescent Medicine, 157,* 733–738.

Ellis, A. (1962). *Reason and emotion in psychotherapy.* (2nd ed.) New York: L. Stuart.

Fixsen, D. L., Naoom, S. F., Blase, K. A., Friedman, R. M., & Wallace, F. (2005). *Implementation research: A synthesis of the literature.* Tampa:, University of South Florida, Louis de la Parte Florida Mental Health Institute, The National Implementation Research Network (FMHI Publication #231).

Fox, C. L., & Boulton, M. J. (2005). The social skills problems of victims of bullying: Self, peer and teacher perceptions. *British Journal of Educational Psychology, 75,* 313–328.

Goldstein, A. P. (1999). *The Prepare Curriculum: Teaching prosocial competencies* (rev. ed.) Champaign, Ill.: Research Press.

Goleman, D. (1995). *Emotional intelligence.* New York: Bantam Books.

Hein, K. (2004). Preventing aggression in the classroom: A case study of extraordinary teachers (Doctoral Dissertation, University of Georgia).

Horne, A. M., Bartolomucci, C. L., & Newman-Carlson, D. (2003). *Bully busters: A teacher's manual for helping bullies, victims, and bystanders (grades K-5).* Champaign, IL: Research Press.

Horne, A. M., Orpinas, P., & Multisite Violence Prevention Project. (2005). *Teacher burnout: Is it the person, the perceived environment, or the "real" environment?* Poster presentation accepted at the 113th Annual Convention of the American Psychological Association Washington, DC.

Horne, A. M., Orpinas, P., Newman-Carlson, D., & Bartolomucci, C. (2004). Elementary school Bully Busters program: Understanding why children bully and what to do about it. In D. L. Espelage & S. M. Swearer (Eds.), *Bullying in American schools: A social-ecological perspective on prevention and intervention* (pp. 297–325). Mahwah, NJ: Erlbaum.

Kelder, S. H., Murray, N. G., Orpinas, P., Prokhorov, A., McReynolds, L., Zhang, Q., et al. (2001). Depression and substance use in minority middle-school students. *American Journal of Public Health, 91,* 761–766.

Kolb, K., & Jussim, L. (1994). Teacher expectations and underachieving gifted children. *Roeper Review, 17,* 26–31.

Lewis, T. J., Sugai, G., & Colvin, G. (1998). Reducing problem behavior through a school-wide system of effective behavioral support: Investigation of a school-wide social skills training program and contextual interventions. *School Psychology Review, 27,* 446–459.

Lickona, T. (1991). *Educating for character: How our schools can teach respect and responsibility.* New York: Bantam Books.

Maultsby, M. C. (1984). *Rational behavior therapy.* Englewood Cliffs, NJ: Prentice-Hall.

Meyer, A. L., Allison, K. W., Reese, L. R. E., Gay, F. N., & Multisite Violence Prevention Project. (2004). Choosing to be violence free in middle school — The student component of the GREAT schools and families universal program. *American Journal of Preventive Medicine, 26,* 20–28.

Newman, D. A., Horne, A. M., & Bartolomucci, C. L. (2000). *Bully Busters: A teacher's manual for helping bullies, victims, and bystanders.* Champaign, IL: Research Press.

Orpinas, P., & Horne, A. M. (2006). *Bullying prevention: Creating a positive school climate and developing social competence*. Washington, DC: American Psychological Association.

Orpinas, P., Horne, A. M., & Multisite Violence Prevention Project. (2004). A teacher-focused approach to prevent and reduce students' aggressive behavior — The GREAT Teacher Program. *American Journal of Preventive Medicine, 26*, 29–38.

Orpinas, P., Horne, A. M., & Staniszewski, D. (2003). School bullying: Changing the problem by changing the school. *School Psychology Review, 32*, 431–444.

Orpinas, P., Kelder, S., Frankowski, R., Murray, N., Zhang, Q., & McAlister, A. (2000). Outcome evaluation of a multi-component violence-prevention program for middle schools: the Students for Peace project. *Health Education Research, 15*, 45–58.

Orpinas, P., Kelder, S., Murray, N., Fourney, A., Conroy, J., McReynolds, L., et al. (1996). Critical issues in implementing a comprehensive violence prevention program for middle schools: Translating theory into practice. *Education and Urban Society, 28*, 456–472.

Pianta, R. C. (1999). *Enhancing relationships between children and teachers*. Washington, DC: American Psychological Association.

Pierce, C. (1994). Importance of classroom climate for at-risk learners. *Journal of Educational Research, 88*, 37–42.

Resnick, M. D., Bearman, P. S., Blum, R. W., Bauman, K. E., Harris, K. M., Jones, J., et al. (1997). Protecting adolescents from harm — Findings from the National Longitudinal Study on Adolescent Health. *Jama-Journal of the American Medical Association, 278*, 823–832.

Rosenthal, R. (1994). Interpersonal expectancy effects — A 30-year perspective. *Current Directions in Psychological Science, 3*, 176–179.

Rusnak, T. (1998). *An integrated approach to character education*. Thousand Oaks, CA: Corwin.

Seligman, M. E. P., Reivich, K., Jaycox, L., & Gillham, J. (1995). *The optimistic child: A proven program to safeguard children against depression and build lifelong resiliency*. New York: Harper Perennial.

Shapiro, E. S., DuPaul, G. J., Bradley, K. L., & Bailey, L. T. (1996). A school-based consultation program for service delivery to middle school students with attention-deficit/hyperactivity disorder. *Journal of Emotional and Behavioral Disorders, 4*, 73–81.

Simons-Morton, B. G., Crump, A. D., Haynie, D. L., & Saylor, K. E. (1999). Student-school bonding and adolescent problem behavior. *Health Education Research, 14*, 99–107.

Sullivan, K. (2000). *The anti-bullying handbook*. Auckland, New Zealand: Oxford University Press.

Trouilloud, D. O., Sarrazin, P. G., Martinek, T. J., & Guillet, E. (2002). The influence of teacher expectations on student achievement in physical education classes: Pygmalion revisited. *European Journal of Social Psychology, 32*, 591–607.

U.S. Department of Health and Human Services (2001). *Youth violence: A report of the Surgeon General*. Rockville, MD: U.S. Department of Health and Human Services; Centers for Disease Control and Prevention, National Center for Injury Prevention; Substance Abuse and Mental Health Services Administration, Center for Mental Health Services; and National Institutes of Health, National Institute of Mental Health.

Valentine, J. W., Clark, D. C., Hackmann, D. G., & Petzko, V. N. (2004). *Leadership for highly successful middle level schools: A national study of leadership in middle level schools* (vol. II). Reston, VA: National Association of Secondary School Principals.

Welsh, M., Parke, R., Widaman, K., & O'Neil, R. (2001). Linkages between children's social and academic competence: A longitudinal analysis. *Journal of School Psychology, 39*, 463–482.

5

A Social-Ecological Model for Bullying Prevention and Intervention

Understanding the Impact of Adults in the Social Ecology of Youngsters

DOROTHY L. ESPELAGE AND SUSAN M. SWEARER

The phenomena of bullying and victimization do not occur in isolation and do not typically occur between a "bully" and a "victim." In fact, these phenomena are complicated social exchanges among individuals, peer groups, and their broader social environment (Swearer & Espelage, 2004). A social-ecological framework has been the basis of much of our understanding of human behavior, pioneered by Kurt Lewin's classic formula ($B = f(P, E)$), which illustrates that behavior is the function of the individual's interactions with his or her environment (Lewin, 1936). For youngsters, their environment is dramatically shaped by their parents and caregivers, and, when they are school-age, by the adults in their school environment. In fact, for the first 18+ years of a human's life, adults shape and influence the social ecology in which children and adolescents develop.

The interaction of individuals within their broader social context has a strong history in psychology, sociology, anthropology, and ethology. In the 1960s Konrad Lorenz wrote *On Aggression* (1967) where he postulated that aggressive behaviors are heritable with their etiology in Darwinian natural selection. Ethologists have studied aggressive behavior in animals and this work has been extrapolated by sociologists, anthropologists, and psychologists to the study of human behavior with the question of interest being, "why do humans engage in aggressive behavior?" It is beyond the scope of this chapter to address the multitude of mediating and moderating variables in the development and expression of aggressive behavior; however, what is known is that the variables that influence the etiology and the expression of aggressive behavior span individual, peer, family, school, community, and cultural domains.

Social Ecological Theory

Bronfenbrenner's classic ecological framework (1979) illustrates the intersecting systemic influences that affect human behavior. The elements of this ecological environment comprise the microsystem or the immediate social environment (e.g., roles, relationships, and activities); the mesosystem or social environment impacting development indirectly (e.g., parental employment setting; school administration issues; peer group in school); the exosystem that includes events that affect the individual (e.g., parents' friends; activities of teachers at school); and macrosystems, which refers to consistencies in the micro-, meso-, and exo-systems (e.g., socioeconomic status) that exist in the culture as a whole. While Bronfenbrenner's social-ecological framework illustrates the intricacy of human behavior, it is more difficult to empirically examine this complexity, particularly at the macrosystem level. Given the complexity of these reciprocal influences, a major methodological challenge is how to empirically examine these interacting relationships.

Empirical examination of the social-ecological as proposed by Bronfenbrenner is a daunting task. He writes, "A transforming experiment involves the systemic alteration and restructuring of existing ecological systems in ways that challenge the forms of social organization, belief systems, and lifestyles prevailing in a particular culture or subculture" (p. 41). How these "transforming experiments" are developed and tested is the challenge facing bullying and victimization researchers.

Applications of the Social-Ecological Model to Bullying Behavior

Social-ecological models have been used to study school violence (Khoury-Kassabri, Benbenishty, Astor, & Zeira, 2004), and this ecological conceptualization of human behavior has been extended to bullying and peer victimization (Garbarino, 2001; Newman, Horne, & Bartolomucci, 2000; Olweus, 1993; Swearer & Doll, 2001; Swearer & Espelage, 2004). Theory and research support the hypothesis that bullying and peer victimization are reciprocally influenced by the individual, family, peer group, school, community, and society.

The peer context has consistently been highlighted as important in understanding bullying perpetration and victimization. Several theories dominate the literature, including the homophily hypothesis (Cairns & Cairns, 1994; Espelage, Holt, & Henkel, 2003), attraction theory (Bukowski, Sippola, & Newcomb, 2000), and dominance theory (Pellegrini, 2002). The current study in this chapter assesses the association between bullying involvement and positive peer involvement along with familial, school, and neighborhood variables. The decision to include this variable was based on the research on deviancy training, a process by which values supportive of aggression are fostered, and youth ultimately engage in problematic behaviors such as substance use and delinquency (Dishion & Owen, 2002).

In a recent study testing the social ecological model in explaining engagement in bullying behaviors, multinomial logistic regression was used to examine the influence of peer attitudes toward bullying, school climate factors, neighborhood contextual variables, and individual negative affect on bullying perpetration and victimization rates (Swearer et al., 2006). Although the entire model was not significant in the analyses, favorable peer attitudes toward bullying and negative school climate were strongly associated with bullying perpetration.

Applications of Adult Influence on Bullying Among School-Aged Youth

Although much of the bullying and victimization reported by children and adolescents occurs in the schools, researchers have recently begun to examine the early developmental processes such as family socialization that could contribute to negative peer group outcomes. In considering the impact of family relationships on bullying, three areas of research will be reviewed in this section including the role of attachment style, parenting style, and social support.

Attachment and Bullying Attachment theory posits that the relations between a caregiver and child functions as a model for the child's relationships with others. Thus, a child with an insecure attachment learns to expect inconsistent and insensitive interactions with others, where as a child with a secure attachment style comes to expect consistent and sensitive interactions (Bowlby, 1969). In a widely cited study, Troy and Sroufe (1987) found that children who had insecure, anxious-avoidant, or anxious-resistant attachments at the age of 18 months were more likely than children with secure attachments to become involved in bullying at the age of four and five years. Thinking specifically about victims, Perry, Hodges, and Egan (2001) acknowledged that anxious/resistant children tend to cry easily, be manifestly anxious, and are hesitant to explore—all characteristics found to encourage victimization. Furthermore, Perry et al. (2001) pointed out that the self-concepts of resistantly attached children often include feelings of low self-worth, helplessness, and incompetence, again attributes often targeted by bullies.

Parenting and Bullying   In addition to one's attachment style functioning as a template for future relationships, parenting style or child-rearing behaviors also serve as models upon which children base their expectations of future interactions with others. With respect to the family context, much more is known about families of children and adolescents who bully others than families of children who are chronically victimized (Finnegan, Hodges, & Perry, 1998; Rodkin & Hodges, 2003). Olweus (1993) found that caregivers of boys who develop an aggressive reaction pattern tend to lack involvement and warmth, use "power assertive" practices such as physical punishment and violent emotional outbursts, and demonstrate a permissive attitude with regards to their child exhibiting aggressive behaviors. Bowers, Smith, and Binney (1994) confirmed this finding, emphasizing the high need for power among family members of bullies.

Generally speaking, for bullies, victims, or both, these children have been found to have authoritarian parents (Baldry & Farrington, 2000). However, studies such as the one conducted by Bowers and colleagues (1994) suggest that differences in parenting style can be further delineated. For instance, parents of bully-victims have characteristics demonstrative of the indifferent-uninvolved style. Specifically, bully-victims reported not only troubled relationships characterized by low warmth and abusive and inconsistent discipline, but also neglect and lacking in support. In light of findings that bullying, or antisocial behavior in general, tends to occur when parents are absent or unaware of what their child is doing, Olweus (1993) also highlighted the importance of parents monitoring their children's activities outside of school and with whom they associate. Additionally, high marital conflict between parents has also been found to influence the child's construal of aggressive behavior (Olweus, 1993).

McFayden-Ketchum, Bates, Dodge, and Pettit (1996) found that parents can also contribute to a decrease in children's aggression over time; aggressive children who experienced affectionate mother-child relationships showed a significant decrease in their aggressive-disruptive behaviors. Furthermore, these positive parental connections appeared to buffer the long-term negative consequences of aggression.

In contrast to the lack of warmth and involvement often demonstrated in families of bullies, victims' families have been characterized by over-involved and overprotective mothers (Bowers et al., 1994; Olweus, 1993). Olweus (1993) theorized that though victimized boys reported more positive relationships with their mothers than other boys, mothers functioning as overly controlling could inhibit their child's development of self-confidence, independence, and the ability to assert oneself. Development of such attributes is essential to foster positive peer relations. In summarizing the literature on victims' parents, Duncan (2004) also noted that fathers of victims have been found to be critical and distant.

Interestingly, a different pattern has been found in the parental relationships of female victims, such that while victimized boys tend to have overly protective mothers, girls who are victimized report a more negative attitude toward their mothers than do non-victims (Rigby,

1993). Finnegan and colleagues (1998) also noted this difference; victimization was associated with perceived maternal over-protectiveness for boys, but for girls, victimization was associated with perceived maternal rejection. Girls described hostile mothers that would threaten abandonment when they misbehaved. Finnegan et al. (1998) theorized that the enmeshed relationships between males and their mothers undermine one's autonomy that is necessary to establish and maintain status in the peer group. For females, the hostile and rejecting parenting style of mothers hinders the development of connectedness and leads to internalized symptoms such as depression or anxiety, putting one at risk of victimization.

One area shown to increase the risk of both bullying and victimization in children is that of maltreatment by parents, including physical, sexual and emotional abuse, and neglect (Shields & Cicchetti, 2001). Shields and Cicchetti (2001) propose that maltreatment fostered emotional dysregulation that was transferred to interactions with the peer group. Relatedly, Schwartz, Dodge, Petit, and Bates (1997) found that aggressive victims were often frequently exposed to violence in the home as an object of physical abuse and that though non-victimized aggressive boys did not show the same experience of physical abuse, they received higher ratings for exposure to aggressive role models.

Social Support and Bullying Another area of investigation related to potential influences of the family context includes studies on perceived social support. In a study of predominately Hispanic middle school students, those classified as bullies and bully-victims indicated receiving substantially less social support from parents than those students in the comparison or control group (Demaray & Malecki, 2003). Additionally, the researchers investigated the differences in perceptions of the importance of social support among the four groups and found the bully-victim and victim groups rated total social support as more important relative to the bully and comparison groups. In summary, a major theme that emerged from the ratings across groups is that generally speaking, victims and bully-victims reported less frequency of perceived social support but yet gave more weight to the importance of such support relative to other groups. Given the clearly established association between levels of social support and healthy outcomes, the implications of these findings are troublesome; the kids at greatest risk for negative outcomes who strongly value social support are reporting that they are not receiving it. Similarly, Rigby (2000) found that both the experience of peer victimization and low levels of perceived social support contributed significantly to lower overall well-being in a sample of 845 school-age children. Social support not only occurs within families and peer groups, social support occurs in classrooms (Doll, Zucker, & Brehm, 2004).

Importance of Adults in the Social-Ecology of Youngsters

The school context influences either engagement in bullying and/or positive social interactions. With respect to school climate, it appears that less tangible characteristics of schools (e.g., emotional climate) are associated with better academic and social outcomes for students (Kasen, Berenson, Cohen, & Johnson, 2004) and are similarly related to bullying. School climate is particularly important to consider because it is the adults in the school environment that set the tone of the milieu in the school. If teachers are engaged and supportive of students, then students will thrive with that support. However, if teachers are disengaged, this is associated with concomitant increases in bullying rates among middle school students (Kasen et al., 2004), in particular at locations such as playgrounds and lunchrooms (Craig & Pepler, 1997) where students often report feeling unsafe and afraid (Astor, Meyer, & Pitner, 2001). Classroom practices and teachers' attitudes are also components of school climate that contribute to bullying prevalence. Aggression varies from classroom to classroom, and in some instances aggression is supported (Rodkin & Hodges, 2003). Bullying tends to be less prevalent in classrooms in which most children are included in activities (Newman, Murray, & Lussier, 2001), teachers display warmth and responsiveness to children (Olweus & Limber, 1999), and teachers respond quickly and effectively to bullying incidents (Olweus, 1993). Furthermore, Hoover and Hazler (1994) note that when school personnel tolerate, ignore, or dismiss bullying behaviors they are conveying implicit messages about their support for bullying. Clearly, the adults in the social ecology of youngsters have an influence on engagement in bullying perpetration.

Unfortunately, the extant literature has examined the influence of multiple contexts of bullying and victimization in isolation and rarely examines these contexts in tandem. Thus, we include here a study of the influence of families, peers, schools, and neighborhoods on the frequency of bullying perpetration and victimization to demonstrate the importance of focusing on more than individual and peer predictors of these behaviors.

Methods

Participants

Participants were 6,612 middle school students and 14,467 high school students from a midwestern county from 38 middle and high schools. Students completed a modified Dane County Youth Survey (Koenig, Espelage, & Biendseil, 2005) during fall of 2008. The sample consisted of 49.7% males and 50.3% females. With respect to race, 78.6% of the respondents identified themselves as White, 5.4% identified as Biracial, 4.8% identified as Asian, 4.8% identified as Black, and 3.6% identified as Hispanic. The mean age of these students was 13.90 years. Socioeconomic levels varied across the schools, with free-reduced lunch eligibility ranging from 17% to 49%. Waiver of active consent was approved by the institutional review board.

Measures

The measures on the 2008 Dane County Youth Survey have been developed and validated over the last 8 years from data collected in 2000 and 2005. These surveys, including the 2008 version, were conducted to provide extensive information on the opinions, behavior, attitudes, and needs of students. The surveys included specific information on the self-reported victimization, substance use, sexual behavior, and quality of relationships with parents, peers, and schools among students in grades 7 through 12. Data from the 2008 Dane County Youth Survey were subjected to an exploratory factor analyses (EFA) and then subjected to confirmatory factor analyses (CFA) to provide evidence of construct validity. In addition to these measures, the University of Illinois Bully and Victim scales were included (Espelage & Holt, 2001).

Study Variables

Demographic Variables   Self-reports of sex, grade, and race, and free/reduced lunch were elicited to determine demographic characteristics of the students. Students were also asked if they had a parent that had ever been in prison or jail and were asked if their parents or family members were in a gang.

Self-Reported Bullying and Victimization   The University of Illinois Aggression Scales (Espelage & Holt, 2001) assessed the occurrence of bullying perpetration and victimization by peers. For all items, students were asked to indicate how often in the past 30 days they have engaged in a specified behavior. Response options included 0 (**never**), 1 (**1 or 2 times**), 2 (**3 or 4 times**), 3 (**5 or 6 times**), and 4 (**7 or more times**). A principal axis factor analysis and a confirmatory factor analysis across multiple studies support the bullying perpetration and victimization subscales as distinct factors (Espelage & Holt, 2001; Espelage, Holt, & Henkel, 2003).

The *Bullying* Scale contains 9 items that assess bullying behaviors including teasing, social exclusion, name-calling, and rumor spreading (e.g., "I teased other students" and "I upset other students for the fun of it"). Higher scores indicate higher self-reported bullying. Factor loadings in the development sample for the 9 items ranged from .52 through .75 and accounted for 31% of the variance. Espelage and Holt (2001) found a coefficient alpha of .87 and the Bullying Scale was found to be strongly correlated ($r = .65$) with the Youth Self-Report Aggression Scale (Achenbach, 1991), suggesting convergent validity. This scale was also found to converge with peer nomination data (Espelage et al., 2003). The Bullying Scale was not significantly correlated with the Victimization Scale ($r = .12$), providing evidence of discriminant validity. For the present study, an alpha coefficient of .90 was found.

The *Victimization* Scale contains 4 items assessing victimization by peers (e.g., "Other students called me names" and "I got hit and pushed by other students"). Higher scores indicate more self-reported victimization. Factor loadings ranged from .55 through .92, which accounted for 6% of the variance, and an alpha coefficient of .88 was obtained (Espelage & Holt, 2001). In the present study, an alpha coefficient of .86 was found.

Parental Factors

Thirteen items from the 2008 Dane County Youth Survey assessed parental factors. An EFA with Maximum Likelihood method of extraction and a Varimax rotation was used for these 13 items. Examination of the scree plot suggested that a majority of the variance was accounted for by two factors. Factor 1 pertained to aspects of family life that place a child at-risk for behavioral and emotional difficulties, including family violence and parental alcohol and drug use. This factor had an eigen value of 4.39 accounting for 34% of the total variance. Factor 2 included items that assessed supportive and caring parenting and monitoring and had an eigenvalue of 1.32 and accounted for 10% of the total variance. Confirmatory factor analysis indicated that a two-factor solution provided a strong fit for the data (RMSEA = .02; GFI, AGFI, CFI = .96). These two scales are described in more detail below.

Negative Home Life   This seven-item scale asks the extent to which students agree or disagree with each statement. Response options range from 0 (**Strongly Disagree**) through 3 (**Strongly Agree**). Four items relate to family sexual or physical violence: "My parents and I physically fight"; "My parents physically fight with each other"; "A parent kicked you or hit you with their hand/fist or with an object leaving bruises or bumps"; and "An adult touched you in a sexual way or forced you to touch him/her in a sexual way that made you feel unsafe or hurt you in anyway." Two items relate to parental alcohol and drug use: "My parent/s uses/use illegal drugs at least once a week" and "My parent/s gets/get drunk at lease once a week." The final item asked how much the student agreed/disagreed with the following "Sometimes things feel so bad at home I want to run away." Factor loadings ranged from .42 through .81 in the exploratory factor analysis and the alpha coefficient was .79.

Positive Parenting   This six-item scale asks the extent to which the students agree or disagree with each statement about their parent/s. Three items relate to monitoring or behavioral management: "My parents set clear rules about what I can and cannot do"; "My parents have consequences if I break rules"; and "My parents usually know where I am when I go out." Three items assess communication and caring: "My parents encourage me to do my best"; "My parents love and support me"; and "My parents have talked with me about my future plans." Factor loadings ranged from .57 through .71 in the exploratory factor analysis, and the alpha coefficient was .83.

School Factors

Eleven items from the 2008 Dane County Youth Survey assessed perceptions of school and school engagement. An EFA with Maximum Likelihood method of extraction and a Varimax rotation was used for these 11 items. Examination of the scree plot suggested that a majority of the variance was accounted for by two factors. Factor 1 pertained to perceptions of belonging to school and engagement. This factor had an eigenvalue of 2.67 accounting for 34% of the total variance. Factor 2 included items that assessed how many times they saw gangs, drugs, and violence in their school in the last year that had an eigen value of 1.78 and accounted for 23% of the total variance. Confirmatory factor analysis indicated that a two-factor solution provided a strong fit for the data (RMSEA = .04; GFI, AGFI, CFI = .97). These two scales are described in more detail below.

School Climate and Engagement   This six-item scale asks the extent to which students agree or disagree with each statement. Response options range from 0 (***Strongly Disagree***) through 3 (***Strongly Agree***). Two items relate to perceptions of teachers and fairness: "Teachers and other adults at school treat me fairly" and "The rules and expectations are clearly explained at my school." Three items assess school connectedness: "I usually enjoy going to school"; "There are adults I can talk to at school if I have a problem"; and "I feel like I belong at this school." One final item assesses future educational goals: "It is important to me that I graduate from school." Factor loadings ranged from .49 through .77 in the exploratory factor analysis and the alpha coefficient was .82.

School-Level Delinquency   This five-item scale asks students how many times in the last year they have seen the following things at their school: students using drugs or alcohol; gang activity; students smoking cigarettes; students physically fighting; and students with weapons. Response options include 0 (***never***), 1 (***1 or 2 times***), 2 (***3 or 4 times***), 3 (***5 or 6 times***), and 4 (***7 or more times***). Factor loadings range from .59 through .71 in the exploratory factor analysis and the alpha coefficient was .77.

Other Variables

Alcohol and Drug Use   An EFA with Maximum Likelihood method of extraction and a Varimax rotation was used for this 14-item scale. Examination of the scree plot suggested that one factor accounted for 92% of the variance with an eigen value of 14.74. Ten of the fourteen items asked students to think about the last 12 months, and indicated how often they: used nonprescription drugs to get high, used prescription drugs to get high, used other illegal drugs, used steroids to get high, used inhalants, used snuff or chewing tobacco, drank hard liquor, drank wine or beer, smoked cigarettes, and used marijuana. Response options include 0 (never), 1 (1 or 2 times in last month), 2 (1 to 3 times per month), 3 (1 to 3 times per week), 4 (4 to 6 times per week), and 5 (daily). Four items asked how often the students used illegal drugs, drank more than 5 alcoholic beverages in a row, attended school after drinking alcohol or using marijuana, and drank hard liquor in the past 30 days. Response options include 0 (never), 1 (1 to 2 times), 2 (3 to 5 times), 3

(6 to 9 times), 4 (10 to 19 times), 5 (20 to 29 times), and 6 (everyday). Factor loadings ranged from .94 through .98 in the exploratory factor analysis and the alpha coefficient was .98.

Positive Peers   Two items were used to assess positive peer influence. Students are asked how much they agree or disagree with "Most of my friends DO NOT drink or do drugs" and "Most of my friends DO NOT smoke cigarettes or chew tobacco." Response options range from 0 (Strongly Disagree) through 3 (Strongly Agree). The two items were significantly correlated (r = .76, p < .001).

Neighborhood Safety   Three items were used to assess perceptions of neighborhood. Students are asked how much they agree or disagree with "Generally, my neighborhood is a safe place to live"; "Adults in my neighborhood know me"; and "Usually I can count on the police if I am having a problem or need help." Response options range from 0 (Strongly Disagree) through 3 (Strongly Agree). An alpha coefficient of .86 was found.

Results

Demographic Differences on Bullying Perpetration and Victimization

Sex, grade, and race differences on study measures were examined to determine whether analyses needed to be conducted separately for these groups. A multivariate analysis of variance (MANOVA) was conducted with sex, grade, and race as independent variables with bullying and victimization as dependent variables. On the bullying and victimization scales, significant effects were found but effect size data suggested that all of these differences were small (sex Wilks' λ = .99, p < .001, η^2 = .001; grade Wilks' λ = .99, p < .001, η^2 = .003; race Wilks' λ = .98, p < .001, η^2 = .009). No significant two-way or three-way interactions were found.

   Next, differences on bullying and victimization scales were evaluated for students who reported having a parent that had ever been in jail or prison and those that did not. Data indicated that 3,298 students (16%) reported that "one or more of their parents/guardians had ever been in jail or prison." A multivariate analysis of variance (MANOVA) was conducted with jail status as independent variable (yes, no) and bullying and victimization as dependent variables. On the bullying and victimization scales, a significant effect was found for jail status (Wilks' λ = .95, p < .001, η^2 = .04). Univariate tests indicated significant effects for both bullying and victimization (Fs = 477.35, 216.60, p < .001, η^2s = .04, .02). Students who reported a parent being in jail or prison reported significantly more bullying (M = .55; SD = .81) and victimization (M = .56; SD = .84) in comparison to students who reported that their parent had never been in jail or prison (bullying M = .26; SD = .44; victimization M = .33; SD = .58).

   Finally, differences on bullying and victimization scales were evaluated for students who reported that one or more of their family members (excluding themselves) were involved in a street gang. Data indicated that 1,217 students (6%) reported that a family member is involved in a street gang. A multivariate analysis of variance (MANOVA) was conducted with gang status as independent variable (yes, no) and bullying and victimization as dependent variables. On the bullying and victimization scales, a significant effect was found for gang status (Wilks' λ = .91, p < .001, η^2 = .04). Univariate tests indicated significant effects for both bullying and victimization (Fs = 935.62, 332.49, p < .001, η^2s = .08, .03). Students who reported a parent or family member being a member of a gang reported significantly more bullying (M = .82; SD = 1.02) and victimization (M = .71; SD = 1.02) in comparison to students who reported that they did not have a parent or family member involved in a gang (bullying M = .26; SD = .42; victimization M = .35; SD = .58).

Predicting Bullying Perpetration

Correlation and regression analyses were employed to assess the associations between family, peer, school, and neighborhood variables and bullying perpetration. Correlational analyses indicated that victimization was strongly associated with bullying perpetration (r = .65, p < .001), indicating a considerable overlap between bullying perpetration and victimization. Greater bullying perpetration was also significantly associated with a negative family environment (r = .35; p < .001) and school-level delinquency (drug use, fighting; r = .41; p < .001); and less bullying perpetration was associated with more positive parenting (r = −.27; p < .001), positive peers (r = .31; p < .001), greater neighborhood safety (r = .31; p < .001), and greater school engagement (r = −.26; p < .001). Alcohol and drug use was modestly associated with bullying perpetration (r = .14, p < .01).

Regression analyses predicting bullying perpetration yielded a model that explained 36% of the variance in bullying perpetration. Because sex was a significant predictor (β = −.10; *p* < .001), with boys reporting more bullying perpetration, regression models were run separately for boys and girls. For boys, the family, peer, school, and neighborhood predictors accounted for 39% of the bullying perpetration. The strongest predictors of bullying perpetration were greater school level delinquency (β = .39, *p* < .001), greater negative family environment (β = .23, *p* < .01), followed by less school engagement (β = −.09, *p* < .001) and less positive peers (*r* = −.10; *p* < .001). For girls, the family, peer, school, and neighborhood predictors explained 31% of the variance. The strongest predictors of bullying perpetration were greater school level delinquency (β = .29, *p* < .001), greater negative family environment (β = .17, *p* < .01), followed by less school engagement (β = −.14, *p* < .001) and less positive peers (*r* = −.10; *p* < .001). Positive parenting and perceptions of neighborhood safety did not emerge as significant predictors of bullying perpetration for boys or girls. Grade and alcohol and drug use were not significant predictors either.

Predicting Bullying Victimization

Correlation and regression analyses were employed to assess the associations between family, peer, school, and neighborhood variables and peer victimization. Correlational analyses indicated that victimization was significantly associated with a negative family environment (r = .28; p < .001) and school-level delinquency (drug use, fighting; r = .25; p < .001); and less victimization was associated with more positive parenting (r = −.16; p < .001), great perceptions of neighborhood safety (r = .22; p < .001), greater school engagement (r = −.20; p < .001), and positive peers (r = .14; p < .001). Alcohol and drug use was not associated with victimization (r = .02, p > .05).

Regression analyses predicting peer victimization yielded a model that explained 16% of the variance in victimization. Because sex was a significant predictor (β = −.09; *p* < .001), with boys reporting more bullying victimization, regression models were run separately for boys and girls. For boys, the family, peer, school, and neighborhood predictors accounted for 17% of the victimization. The strongest predictors of bullying perpetration were greater school level delinquency (β = .23, *p* < .001), greater negative family environment (β = .21, *p* < .001), followed by less school engagement (β = −.09, *p* < .01) and less neighborhood safety perceptions (β = −.10; *p* < .01). For girls, the family, peer, school, and neighborhood predictors explained 13% of the variance. The strongest predictors of victimization were greater school level delinquency (β = .18, *p* < .001), greater negative family environment (β = .21, *p* < .01), followed by less school engagement (β = −.10, *p* < .001). Positive parenting, grade, and positive peers were not significant predictors of bullying victimization for boys or girls.

Conclusions and Implications for Practice

Despite both empirical (Hawley, Little, & Rodkin, 2007; Khoury-Kassabri, Benbenishty, Astor, & Zeira, 2004) and theoretical (Goldstein & Segall, 1983; Lorenz, 1967) evidence that the development of aggressive and bullying behavior is influenced by the social ecology, few studies have examined the influence of adults on youth from a social-ecological perspective. Clearly, both adults in the home, adults in the community, and teachers and administrators in the schools have a dramatic impact on youth. Despite the impact that adults have on youth engagement in bullying perpetration and victimization, empirical work has fallen short of examining parental, school, and teacher variables on engagement in bullying and victimization.

The data reported in this chapter suggest that the social ecology is important for understanding engagement in bullying. A large part of a student's social ecology includes the school. Typically, students are in school for six to nine hours per day. The adults (teachers, school administrators, school mental health professionals, school health professionals, school resource officers, school support staff) in the school set the tone for school functioning. Teacher engagement and teacher attitudes have been found to be vital for reducing bullying perpetration (Biggs, Vernberg, Twemlow, Fonagy, & Dill, 2008). Investment in the school by the adults in the school helps create the conditions to engage students. Conversely, when adults are not invested in the school, conditions are created whereby students disengage and are not connected to their school. Results presented in this chapter illustrate the influence that school engagement plays in bullying perpetration and victimization.

As Bronfenbrenner (1979) articulated, there is a reciprocal influence between the different levels of the social ecology. Based on previous empirical work and on the results from this chapter, Figure 5.1 is used to illustrate this reciprocity. To illustrate this model a case study is provided below.

Jack, a Caucasian eighth grader attends a rural school where funds are limited, and there are many pressing needs in the community. There is a high rate of mobility in the community, and one source of industry in the community is methamphetamine production. Jack's father, a meth addict, has been in-and-out-prison. His mother works three jobs to try to support her three children. While their rent is affordable, they also live in one of the worst areas of town. Jack struggles with depression and anger, as does his mother, who often self-medicates with alcohol. Jack is a quiet student who does not act out in school. As such, he was not seen as a student who needed help. The students who are successful at Jack's school are the athletes and the bright students. Jack reports, "If you're not athletic and not smart, you're a nobody." Jack had played football in elementary school, however his parents could not afford to enroll him in the youth sports program and given the stresses in their family, no one could drive him to the games. Jack wasn't particularly athletic, so he decided to stop playing football. The students who do not fit in the mainstream culture at this school are marginalized and typically turn to delinquent peer groups. Gang involvement in this community is also related to the methamphetamine industry. Local law enforcement can barely keep up with the crime and other needs in the community. In the middle of the eighth grade, Jack, who became the primary caregiver in his home when his father was back in jail, started drinking and hanging out with a delinquent peer group. His grades dropped and he started skipping school. Additionally, Jack and his friends would pick on and harass kids as they walked home from school. Jack came to the attention of the school counselor after his third referral for bullying behavior.

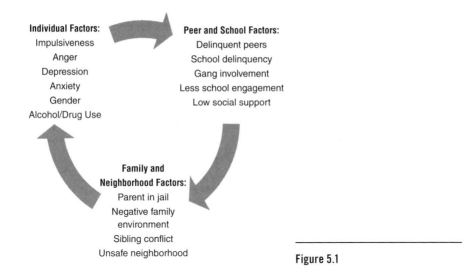

Individual Factors:
Impulsiveness
Anger
Depression
Anxiety
Gender
Alcohol/Drug Use

Peer and School Factors:
Delinquent peers
School delinquency
Gang involvement
Less school engagement
Low social support

Family and Neighborhood Factors:
Parent in jail
Negative family environment
Sibling conflict
Unsafe neighborhood

Figure 5.1

As illustrated in this case example, there are many factors that contributed to Jack's disengagement from school and his engagement in bullying behavior. The social ecology in which youth function provides fruitful directions for research. Future research on bullying perpetration and peer victimization should consider these reciprocal mechanisms and should include the examination of adult influences in the social ecology of youngsters.

References

Achenbach, T.M. (1991). *Manual for the Youth Self-Report and 1991 Profile.* Burlington, VT: University of Vermont Department of Psychiatry.

Astor, R. A., Meyer, H. A., & Pitner, R. O. (2001). Elementary and middle school students' perceptions of violence-prone school subcontexts. *Elementary School Journal, 101,* 511–528.

Baldry, A. C., & Farrington, D. P. (2000). Bullies and delinquents: Personal characteristics and parental styles. *Journal of Community and Applied Social Psychology, 10,* 17–31.

Biggs, B. K., Vernberg, E. M., Twemlow, S. W., Fonagy, P., & Dill, E. J. (2008). Teacher adherence and its relation to teacher attitudes and student outcomes in an elementary school-based violence prevention program. *School Psychology Review, 37,* 533–549.

Bowers, L., Smith, P. K., & Binney, V. (1994). Perceived family relationships of bullies, victims and bully/victims in middle childhood. *Journal of Social and Personal Relationships, 11*(2), 215–232.

Bowlby. J. (1969). *Attachment and loss: Volume 1.* New York: Penguin Books.

Bronfenbrenner, U. (1979). *The ecology of human development: Experiments by nature and design.* Cambridge, MA: Harvard University Press.

Bukowski, W. M., Sippola, L. K., & Newcomb, A. F. (2000). Variations in patterns of attraction to same- and other-sex peers during early adolescence. *Developmental Psychology, 36,* 147–154.

Cairns, R. B., & Cairns, B. D. (1994). *Lifelines and risks: Pathways of youth in our time.* Cambridge, England: Cambridge University Press.

Craig, W. M., & Pepler, D. J. (1997). Observations of bullying and victimization in the school yard. *Canadian Journal of School Psychology, 13*(2), 41–59.

Demaray, M. K., & Malecki, C. K. (2003). Perceptions of the frequency and importance of social support by students classified as victims, bullies and bully/victims in an urban middle school. *School Psychology Review, 32*(3), 471–489.

Dishion, T. J., & Owen, L. D. (2002). A longitudinal analysis of friendships and substance use: Bidirectional influence from adolescence to adulthood. *Developmental Psychology, 28*(4), 480–491.

Doll, B., Zucker, S., & Brehm, K. (2004). *Resilient classrooms: Creating healthy environments for learning.* New York: Guilford.

Duncan, R. D. (2004). The impact of family relationships on school bullies and their victims. In D. L. Espelage & S. M. Swearer (Eds.), *Bullying in American schools: A social-ecological perspective on prevention and intervention* (pp. 227–244). Mahwah, NJ: Erlbaum.

Espelage, D. L., & Holt, M. L. (2001). Bullying and victimization during early adolescence: Peer influences and psychosocial correlates. *Journal of Emotional Abuse, 2*(3), 123–142.

Espelage, D. L., Holt, M. K., & Henkel, R. R. (2003). Examination of peer-group contextual effects on aggression during early adolescence. *Child Development, 74*(1), 205–220.

Finnegan, R. A., Hodges, E. V., & Perry, D. G. (1998). Victimization by peers: Associations with children's reports of mother-child interaction. *Journal of personality and social psychology, 75*(4), 1076–1086.

Garbarino, J. (2001). An ecological perspective on the effects of violence on children. *Journal of Community Psychology, 29,* 361–378.

Goldstein, A. P., & Segall, M. H. (Eds.). (1983). *Aggression in global perspective.* New York: Pergamon Press.

Hawley, P. H., Little, T. D., & Rodkin, P. C. (Eds.). (2007). *Aggression and adaptation: The bright side to bad behavior.* Mahwah, NJ: Erlbaum.

Hoover, J. H., & Hazler, R. J. (1994). Bullies and victims. *Elementary School Guidance and Counseling, 25,* 212–220.

Kasen, S., Berenson, K., Cohen, P., & Johnson, J. G. (2004). The effects of school climate on changes in aggressive and other behaviors related to bullying. In D. L. Espelage & S. M. Swearer (Eds.), *Bullying in American schools: A social-ecological perspective on prevention and intervention* (pp. 187–210). Mahwah, NJ: Erlbaum.

Khoury-Kassabri, M., Benbenishty, R., Astor, R. A., & Zeira, A. (2004). The contributions of community, family, and school variables to student victimization. *Journal American Journal of Community Psychology, 34,* 187–204.

Koenig, B., Espelage, D. L., & Biendseil, R. (2005). *The Dane County youth assessment.* Unpublished report. Madison, WI: The Dane County Youth Commission.

Lewin, K. (1936). *Problems of topological psychology.* New York: McGraw-Hill.

Lorenz, K. (1967). *On aggression.* New York: Bantam.

McFadyen-Ketchum, S. A., Bates, J. E., Dodge, K. A., & Pettit, G. S. (1996). Patterns of change in early childhood aggressive-disruptive behavior: Gender differences in predictions from early coercive and affectionate mother-child interactions. *Child Development, 67*(5), 2417–2433.

Newman, D. A., Horne, A. M., & Bartolomucci, C. L. (2000). *Bully busters: A teacher's manual for helping bullies, victims, and bystanders.* Champaign, IL: Research Press.

Newman, R. S., Murray, B., & Lussier, C. (2001). Confrontation with aggressive peers at school: Students' reluctance to seek help from the teacher. *Journal of Educational Psychology, 93*(2), 398–410.

Olweus, D. (1993). Bully/victim problems among schoolchildren: Long-term consequences and an effective intervention program. In S. Hodgins (Ed.), *Mental disorder and crime* (pp. 317–349). Thousand Oaks, CA: Sage.

Olweus, D., Limber, S., & Mihalic, S. (1999). *The Bullying-Prevention Program: Blueprints for violence prevention.* Boulder, CO: Center for the Study and Prevention of Violence.

Pellegrini, A. D. (2002). Affiliative and aggressive dimensions of dominance and possible functions during early adolescence. *Aggression & Violent Behavior, 7,* 21–31.

Perry, D. G., Hodges, E. V., & Egan, S. K. (2001). Determinants of chronic victimization by peers: A review and a new model of family influence. In J. Junoven & S. Graham (Eds.), *Peer harassment in School: The plight of the vulnerable and victimized* (pp. 73–104). New York: Guilford.

Rigby, K. (1993) School children's perceptions of their families and parents as a function of peer relations. *Journal of Genetic Psychology, 154*(4), 501–514.

Rigby, K. (2000). Effects of peer victimization in schools and perceived social support on adolescent well-being. *Journal of Adolescence, 23*(1), 57–68.

Rodkin, P. C., & Hodges, E. V. (2003). Bullies and victims in the peer ecology: Four questions for psychologists and school professionals. *School Psychology Review, 32*(3), 384–400.

Schwartz, D., Dodge, K. A., Pettit, G. S., & Bates, J. E. (1997). The early socialization of aggressive victims of bullying. *Child Development, 68*(4), 665–675.

Shields, A., & Cicchetti, D. (2001). Parental maltreatment and emotion dysregulation as risk factors for bullying and victimization in middle childhood. *Journal of Clinical Child Psychology, 30*(3), 349–363.

Swearer, S. M., & Doll, B. (2001). Bullying in schools: An ecological framework. *Journal of Emotional Abuse, 2,* 7–23.

Swearer, S. M., & Espelage, D. L. (2004). A social-ecological framework of bullying among youth. In D. L. Espelage & S. M. Swearer (Eds.), *Bullying in American schools: A social-ecological perspective on prevention and intervention* (pp. 1–12). Mahwah, NJ: Erlbaum.

Swearer, S. M., Peugh, J., Espelage, D. L., Siebecker, A. B., Kingsbury, W. L., & Bevins, K. S. (2006). A socioecological model for bullying prevention and intervention in early adolescence: An exploratory examination. In S. R. Jimerson & M. Furlong (Eds.), *Handbook of school violence and school safety: From research to practice* (pp. 257–273). Mahwah, NJ: Erlbaum.

Troy, M., & Sroufe, L. A. (1987). Victimization among preschoolers: Role of attachment relationship history. *Journal of the American Academy of Child and Adolescent Psychiatry, 26,* 166–172.

6

The Etiological Cast to the Role of the Bystander in the Social Architecture of Bullying and Violence in Schools and Communities

STUART W. TWEMLOW, PETER FONAGY, AND FRANK C. SACCO

> At every quarterly examination a gold medal was given to the best writer. When the first medal was offered, it produced rather a general contention than an emulation and diffused a spirit of envy, jealousy, and discord through the whole school; boys who were bosom friends before became fierce contentious rivals, and when the prize was adjudged became implacable enemies. Those who were advanced decried the weaker performances; each wished his opponent's abilities less than his own, and they used all their little arts to misrepresent and abuse each other's performances.
>
> —Robert Coram, *Political Inquiries* (1791)

Clearly, bullying has been a fixture in schools for a long time. The epigraph documents school bullying in a way of particular relevance to this chapter: although Coram highlights the destructive interaction between boys who were bosom friends and became "contentious rivals," the problem seems to relate to the apparently innocuous effort by the school to promote excellence by offering a medal for writing. Though characteristic of the bystander role as defined in this paper, the school's effort does not imply any deliberate or malicious intent on the part of teachers and other members of the community to promote bullying, although some of the bystanders' actions seem at times self-serving and deliberate. The point is that the potential negative social impact of creating healthy competition based on interpersonal relationships should be considered from the outset by school administration.

The purpose of this chapter is to investigate bystander roles often occupied or assumed by teachers and students that create a social architecture for school bullying and violence not usually addressed by traditional school anti-bullying and antiviolence programs. The theoretical and practical experimental approach to the problem with school violence and bullying is to some degree radically different than many programs that target bullying and the bullies' victim, and/or create mental health approaches to address such bullying within the school climate. Our hypotheses, which were tested in a randomized trial was that attention to the audience for the bullying, that is the bystander architecture of the school, will ameliorate and change the bullying far more effectively than any medicalized approach using psychiatric interventions.

We also will define the role of the bystander from both a psychodynamic perspective and from the scant literature on the role of the bystander in school bullying and violence and then present data and case vignettes to illustrate the prevalence of bullying of students by teachers as perceived by other teachers, including a case vignette describing the potentially avoidable murder of a teacher by a student. The failure of policy makers to adequately deal with this problem propels them into an abdicating bystander role, which we propose has an important impetus in the etiology of school violence. This chapter finishes with a summary of potential areas for future research, including innovative approaches to community violence suggested by this work.

Redefining Bullying From the Bystander Perspective

In *Webster's Encyclopedic Unabridged Dictionary* (1996), the bystander is defined as "a person present but not involved; an onlooker" (p. 165). Synonyms include viewer, observer, witness, and passerby. The argument detailed in this chapter is that the social context—rooted in the Latin word, *contextus*, "a joining together"—situates the bystander in an unavoidably active role created, in the case of school violence, by the victim/victimizer interaction. Thus, it follows that being passive is not possible from this perspective. From this perspective, the victim, victimizer, and bystander roles are considered to be co-created and dialectally defined, and in these roles, mentalizing (i.e., self-awareness, self-agency, reflectiveness, and accurate assessment of the mental states of self and other people) is impaired.

Fonagy's (2001) concept of mentalizing takes an Hegelian perspective that points out that the individual defines himself through social feedback from interactions with others. Thus over time the individual's "theory of the mind" of self and others is continuously modified by feedback from interaction with others. In the case of the infant, for example, if the caretaker gives feedback in an empathic, constructive, and accurate manner, the child develops a theory of mind of others that can process reality in a healthy and adaptive fashion. If pathological feedback is received, the mind of the child may develop in distorted ways, manifested in overt and covert psychopathology in adult life including a loss of a sense of connection to the other who can thus be hurt with greater impunity. When an individual is not recognized in the mind of the other, there is a loss of mentalization and without a sense of connection to the other, a potential crucible for violence emerges: the other becomes dehumanized and can thus be hurt with greater impunity.

In summary we define the bystander role as an active role with a variety of manifestations, in which an individual or group indirectly and repeatedly participates in a victimization process as a member of the social system. Bystanding may either facilitate or ameliorate victimization. The bystander is propelled into the role by dint of their interaction with the victim and victimizer, and the ongoing interaction can be activated in a helpful or harmful direction. The various aspects of the dialectic and trialectic views of bullying are summarized in Table 6.1.

Previous work (Twemlow, Fonagy, & Sacco, 2001) proposed that a "power dynamic" fuels the victim-victimizer-bystander interaction disrupting mentalization through the impact of conscious and unconscious coercion on individuals and groups. The roles of bully, victim, and bystander can be seen from this perspective as representing a dissociating process; the victim is dissociated from the school community as "not us" by the bully on behalf of the bystanding community. The community bystander role could be described as an abdicating one. Abdication then is avoidance of acknowledgement of the role in the bullying process by the abdicating bystander, who projects the blame onto others. From this vantage point, interventions in a school setting must focus on the transformation of the bystander into a committed community member/witness. Our interventions were aimed at promoting recognition within the large

Table 6.1 Redefining Bullying: Implications for Practice

Dyadic	Triadic
* Victim-victimizer primary focus	* Social context of bully-victim-bystander (focus on bystander)
* Individual's role as bully or victim is seen as fixed	* Bully-Victim-Bystander roles co-created and in flux (always changing)
* Audience is passive observer	* Audience has an active role in violence
* Purely external/social definition	* Stress the role of unconscious power dynamics & processes
* Bully-Victim are behavioral roles	* Bully-Victim-Bystanders have complex combinations of roles and unconscious affiliations
* Focus is on behavioral change	* Focus is on Mentalizing , defined as the capacity to reflect, empathize, control feelings and set boundaries for oneself.
* Intervention targets individuals	* Intervention aimed at climate

school group of the dissociated element (represented by the victim), as a part of themselves about which they are anxious and the recognition of the dissociating process (represented by the bully) as a defensive action for which the bystanders are in part responsible. A peaceful school learning environment is thus restored when the fragmenting effect of the dissociation process is interrupted by first understanding that the dissociating process is a largely unconscious effort to deal with the anxiety felt by all in response to a dysfunctional, coercive, and disconnected social system. Individuals thus enlightened must then act with the support of all to change how coercive power dynamics are managed in the system as a whole. Dissociation is a violent process, and the goal of any intervention is the transformation of brute power into passionate statement and respectful communication. This requires a clear conceptualization of the group's task from a perspective that does not permit scapegoating, empowers bystanders into a helpful altruistic role, and does not overemphasize therapeutic efforts with the victim or victimizer. Symptomatic behavior, such as violence and bullying within such a system is, from this perspective, a consultation-in-action to the authority structure of the administrative system. That is, the symptom is not merely a problem to solve but a dysfunctional solution or adaptation, which keeps a larger more painful and more meaningful problem unseen. The abdicating bystander projects blame on the victim and victimizer as sufficient cause of the problem of school violence and bullying. Several bystander roles are summarized in Table 6.2. Approaches to school and community violence that place sole attention on correcting pathological bystanding roles and/or bully and victim roles, ignore what we believe is an important, if not critical part of the solution: to activate the helpful and often altruistic bystander role.

Who are helpful bystanders? Any individual in the school environment may occupy the role (e.g., teachers, students, support staff, volunteers, parents). They are often natural leaders being helpful, in a way that is not self-centered. Helpful bystanders do not seek the limelight, but instead gain pleasure in the act of being helpful. They often are idealistic, in a realistic, less driven sense. In schools and communities they rarely occupy traditional elected leadership roles, such as class president or committee chairman; they may doubt their own leadership skills, and need encouragement to emerge. Such individuals often turn to others with their problems—instead of directing and advising, they tend to listen and mentalize. Shirley Patterson's (Patterson, Memmott, Brennan, & Germain, 1992) work with natural helpers in community settings summarizes some of the features of this role. Seelig and Rosof (2001) have identified several pathological

Table 6.2 Bystanding Roles

Type	Mentalization	Subjective State	Role in the System
Bully (aggressive) bystander	Collapse of mentalization	Excitement, often Sado-masochistic	Establishes a way to set up victimization within the school community
Puppet-master variant[1] of Bully bystander	Authentic empathy and reflectiveness collapses capable of logical planning and non-feeling empathy.	Arrogant grandiose sense of powerfulness	Committed to violent outcomes, achieved by conscious manipulation
Victim (Passive) bystander	Collapse of mentalization	Fearful, apathetic, helpless	Passively and fearfully drawn into victimization process
Avoidant bystander	Mentalization preserved by denial	Defensive euphoria. An individual action	Facilitates victimization by denial of personal responsibility
Abdicating bystander	Mentalization preserved by projection and projective identification	Outraged at the "poor" performance of others. An agency of group action	Abdicated responsibility by scapegoating
Sham bystander	Mentalization preserved	Uses conscious largely verbal manipulation. Deliberate and calm	Neither victim nor victimizer role is authentic but is adopted for personal political reasons
Alter Ego Bystander	Mentalization preserved	Wants to be an important member of the most popular group in the climate and will use verbal manipulation to achieve those ends	This individual is either a victim or victimizer often acting as a body guard for the leader of the most popular group in the school, thus achieving a work related role for that group
Altruistic Bystander	Mentalization enhanced	Compassionate, helpful	Mature and effective use of individual and group

Notes: 1. In one of the recent school shootings a boy set up a shooting that occurred at a school dance, taking few pains to hide the plan and recruiting a resentful victim bystander into the role of killer, the puppet-master bystander did not attend the dance, but came later to observe the murders at the prearranged time (Twemlow, 2003).

variants of altruism in which the motivation for such helpfulness may be psychotic grandiosity, sadomasochism, and milder forms of neurotic conflict. In schools and communities, pathological motivations are often self-eliminating over time since the stresses of being continuously helpful often activate the underlying pathology. To our knowledge, there is no evidence-based method by which such altruistic bystanders can be identified, but, in a school setting, aware staff, especially counselors and social workers, can use clinical skills to help. Table 6.3 offers a clinical characterization of pathological and healthy charisma, which we have found very helpful in assessing altruistic helpfulness (Peter Olsson, MD, personal communication).

Although this is not the forum for detailed consideration of the research literature on altruism, there is convincing evidence that altruism is a fundamental drive or impulse in human and several other species (Shapiro & Gabbard, 1994) not merely a derivative, and can thus potentially be harnessed in the service of ameliorating violence. Such pragmatic forms of altruism, although lacking the mysticism and selflessness of well known forms of it in religious and spiritual leaders, focus on benefit to the community as a whole, not a theory, ideal, or deity. The quality of commitment to the community as a whole often serves as an inspiring model for others, often catalyzing unexpected and dramatic change in the system as a whole, although little systematic research has been done on catalyzing major change in social systems with small interventions.

Table 6.3 Characteristics of the Natural Leader and the Narcissistic Leader

Natural Leader

1) Non-cutting sense of humor that connects and empathizes with peers to encourage their autonomy and participation
2) Sanguine ability to empathize with peers in a way that helps Self and others
3) Creativity applied to leadership that promotes creativity in group projects and in individual group members
4) Personal needs are met by benevolent reaching-out to challenge the peer group to connect with their community via helpful projects and activities
5) This leader reaches out to foster and mentor positive leaders in younger grade level children modeling future leaders

Narcissistic Leader

1) Cutting, sarcastic, cold-aloof humor that puts-down or victimizes peers.
2) Empathy that largely promotes the Self above others and eventually at their expense or harm.
3) Creativity that promotes destructive sub-groups that cause isolation or alienation from the larger group.
4) Narcissistic leader's personal needs or psychopathology is deepened by efforts to dominate the peer group.
5) This type of leader bullies or puts-down younger aspiring leaders so as to maintain his or her fiefdom.

Some workers have collected anecdotes and derived a theory (e.g., the tipping phenomenon of Gladwell, 2000). In our experience in a violent secondary school in Jamaica a remarkable system-wide restoration of order began as a sort of epidemic of helpful bystanding seemingly created by a playful chant, the idea of a police officer helping in the altruistic bystander role. In an effort to get boys to be more tidy, a chant of "tuck your shirt in" was employed, which rapidly inspired songs, jokes, even a mini-craze to be tidy. In the space of a few days, there was hardly an untidy child in the school, and incidentally, fewer incidents of violence also.

Thus a helpful altruistic bystander might embody the following characteristics we found in a mostly unlikely place: a highly corrupt police force in Jamaica where an unusual group of senior police officers (more than 10 years in the police force) volunteered for training as an add-on to their usual police work. These police officers worked for poverty level wages under conditions that few United States police officers would tolerate. The project is elaborated in (Twemlow & Sacco, 1996) and the personal qualities of these altruistic peacemakers are summarized below:

1. Being more altruistic than egoistic
2. Awareness of, and takes responsibility for, community problems
3. Willingness to take physical risks for peace and not easily frightened
4. Relationship-oriented and humanistic
5. Self-motivated and a motivator of others
6. Alert, strong, and positive
7. Self-rewarding with low need for praise
8. Personally well organized
9. Advocate and protector of the vulnerable and disempowered
10. Able to see potential in all people
11. Low in sadism
12. An enthusiastic advocate, committed and understanding of the "cause"

Viewed from the perspective of the bystander, contemporary definitions of bullying need revision. Leaders of research into school bullying like Peter Smith in England (Smith & Ananiclouk, 2003) and Dan Olweus in Norway (Olweus, 1999) define bullying in dyadic terms. Thus defined, bullying is repetitive, harmful, produces gain for the bully, and involves an imbalance of strength where the bully is dominant and victim experience trouble defending themselves. Physical harm is usually of less concern than the insults, ostracizing, teasing, social isolation, and humiliation that cause much of the harm. In contrast, we suggest that bullying be newly defined in triadic terms, as an interaction effect between bully, victim, and bystander in which the responses of each directly effect the harmfulness of the outcome. The bully does not act as an individual, as, for example, in a private vendetta, but becomes, in part, an agent of the bystanding audience, and perhaps even intensifies the harm. From our clinical experience (Twemlow, 2000; Twemlow et al., 2001), we have found that bullies usually fantasize about the impact their actions will have on the bystander even if the bystanding audience is not physically present, along with states of mind suggesting prominent grandiose, sadomasochistic, and voyeuristic elements. To recontextualize traditional definitions in triadic terms, bullying is the repeated exposure of an individual to negative interactions directly or indirectly inflicted by one or more dominant persons. The harm may be caused through direct physical or psychological means and/or indirectly through encouragement of the process or avoidance by the bystander. How is this bystander role enacted? The following case vignette will illustrate.

Case Study I: Pathological Bystander Roles[1]

Children's selection of friends, allies, and comfort groups mirrors the organizational and cultural settings of their schools, neighborhoods, and major community groups, as the case described below illustrates.

The school at hand was a large K-8 school that served a very poor minority neighborhood in an East Coast city, with criminal activity near the school, trash on school property, often in the form of discarded needles, and pedophiles cruising the perimeter. We were asked to assess the school's need for a violence prevention program. The students had spent a long winter essentially shut in the school buildings. The school principal had assured us that the school had few bullying problems. Moments after entering the lunchroom, one boy knocked out another in the culmination of a long process of verbal abuse of the boy's mother. After the principal hastily settled this matter, a school counselor rushed up in rage after a student had pelted her in the chest with full milk cartons. The principal was an outstanding individual with idealistic concepts for her school and worked under very difficult conditions. These included an atmosphere of punishment and threat in the form of a school policy that penalized school administrators for poor student academic performance and disciplinary problems. The avoidant bystander role of the principal is not always based on denial in the strict sense, but a need for self-preservation attended by the wistful hope that nothing terrible will happen if one takes a positive attitude. Emphasis on the positive is a common technique used by teachers.

In the incident that followed several days later, during the first outside recess of the spring, two sixth grade students engaged in a fight in front of 125 peers who interlocked arms and cheered on the fight. When one of the fighters was knocked to the ground, 10 students continued punching the downed victim. The victim suffered serious facial damage from a ring worn by one of the students bullying him, a "dirty trick" similar to those seen on the World Wrestling Federation television show, proudly announced by one of the bullies.

Teachers were unable to intervene in the fight for more than 90 seconds because of the tightness of the audience of bystander children with arms interlocked around the combatants. Although students had been talking about the upcoming fight throughout the day, teachers were not aware of the brewing problem. The whole peer grade became invested in one side or another and excitement built up throughout the day.

Bystanders were active in fanning the flames of the violent act, beginning with the ride in the school bus. The two kids were matched up by rumor and innuendo, not actual personal conflict (i.e., this fight was staged by the bystanders through a peer group fantasy enacted in the fight).

Selected Literature Review of the Role of the Bystander in School Conflict

The recent spate of school shootings has placed bystanders squarely in the public eye (Twemlow, Fonagy, Sacco, & Vernberg, 2002), with articles highlighting the inaction or aborted actions of students, teachers, and parents who were aware of fellow student threats but did not act out of denial (avoidant bystanding) or fears that they would be targeted for tattling on peers (the conspiracy of silence). In some California schools, bystanders who did not report a shooter's previous threats were considered in need of protection (Cable News Network, 2001). On a more positive note, several high schools encourage bystanders to help prevent or stop violence by providing confidential or anonymous online and phone-line reporting (Education World, 2000; Sarkar, 2000).

Until recently, bystander behavior has largely been overlooked in the literature on victimization, although it appears that the role of the bystander is an important determinant of chronic victimization. Bystanders in the school environment are those who witness bullying and other acts of violence but are not themselves acting in the role of bully or victim (Twemlow, Sacco, & Williams, 1996). Bystander behaviors may perpetuate bully-victim patterns. For example, when passively allowing bullying to occur, or encouraging bullying by actually participating in the exclusion of others (O'Connell, Pepler, & Craig, 1999). Henry and colleagues (2000) showed that teachers who openly discouraged the use of aggression had students who were less likely to show the usual developmental increases in aggressive behavior over time. Slee (1993) showed that teachers who did not intervene in bullying often had students who would not help victims. The effectiveness of programs aimed at promoting helpful bystanding is clearly dependent on teacher modeling, as our own research has shown (Hazler, Miller, Carney, & Green, 2001). One study (Kupersmidt, 1999) of the ability of teachers and counselors to differentiate between bullying and other forms of conflict, noted that both had a rather poor understanding of bullying. Teachers often rated all physical conflict as bullying and underrated verbal, social, and emotional abuse. Kupersmidt (1999) looked at whether teachers could identify bullies and victims and found that they were more likely to accurately do so in elementary rather than middle school. Haundaumadi and Pateraki (2001), in a study of Greek children, reported that teachers and students felt that teachers rarely talked about bullying and children tended to speak more to their parents about such problems. This indicated that in Greece, as in the United States, if a child cannot handle the problem on their own, they may be perceived as a wimp, and therefore bullied. Interventions, thus, must address the social climate, particularly the complicated peer group interactions, in order to effectively deal with the problem. These factors are influenced by teacher training and the awareness of children's psychological needs and subjective states (Cohen, 1999). In a Finnish study (Salmivalli, 1995) of several hundred children, bystander roles were categorized into several groups: defenders of the victim, bystander from our perspective, assistant to the bully, reinforcer of the bully, and outsider. Boys were found to be more closely associated with the role of bully, reinforcer, and assistant, and girls with the roles of defender and outsider.. In other studies passive bystanders were found to reinforce the bully by providing a consenting audience, which sent the implicit message that aggression is acceptable (O'Connell, Pepler & Craig, 1999; Olweus, 1993). Child bystanders are often effective in trying to stop bullying (Craig & Pepler, 1997; O'Connell, Pepler, & Craig, 1999). Bystanders have been found to be less likely to help when they observe others doing nothing (the norm of nonintervention; Pilivm, Dovidio, Gaertner, & Clark, 1982). When adults intervene in response to bullying, lower levels of aggressive bystanding were found in elementary schools (Vernberg, Jacobs, Twemlow, Sacco, & Fonagy, 2000). Although this was not found in junior high school. Zerger (1996) reported that adolescents who believed that one should intervene in bullying, did predict bystander helping and that the opposite feeling that one should not intervene and that aggression is legitimate were related to joining in bullying. Cowie (2000) studied gender differences, suggesting that part of the difficulty in targeting boys into helpful roles results from the fact that they are more likely to drop out of these interventions because of their macho values, especially as the social modeled concept of masculinity develops.

Teachers' Perceptions of Other Teachers Who Bully Students

Previous research has identified yet another piece of this complicated bystanding puzzle: a study of teachers' perceptions of other teachers who bully students (Twemlow, Fonagy, Sacco, & Brethour, 2006) reports on 116 teachers from seven elementary schools who completed an anonymous questionnaire reflecting their feelings and perceptions about their own experiences of bullying and how they perceived their colleagues over the years. Forty-five percent of this sample of teachers admitted to having bullied a student and many recognized that the roles of bully, victim, and bystander are roles and not moral indictments or diagnoses and usually become damaging only if repeated frequently and if the roles become fixed. In this study, teachers' openness to seeing and admitting bullying suggests that efforts to prevent bullying by training teachers to recognize and deal with it both in themselves, students, and colleagues may be quite helpful. This study showed that few if any teachers perceived a current school policy or training experience that might help them handle a particular problem. Teachers who displayed a tendency to bully students also reported having been bullied when they were students in school, and were far more likely to report seeing other students bullied by teachers. They also reported having been bullied by students inside and outside the classroom. Lack of administrative support, lack of training in discipline techniques, overcrowded classrooms, and being envious of smarter students were found to be elements that were part of the pattern of these bullying teachers. A principle component factor analysis was performed on the data and rotated using a varimax procedure. The resulting screen plot showed two factors that together accounted for 52% of the variance. Factor one accounted for 34% of the variance (sadistic bully factor), and factor two accounting for 18% (bully-victim factor). Sadistic teachers tended to humiliate students, act spitefully, and seemed to enjoy hurting students' feelings. The bully-victim teacher is frequently absent, fails to set limits, lets other people handle his/her problems, and tends to see lack of training in discipline techniques as the primary cause their behavior, acting in many ways as an abdicating bystander by blaming others for their problems. Such teachers often explode in a rage and react in a bullying fashion when they have "reached their limit."

This research addresses a very sensitive area that we suggest compounds the problem of bullying and violence in schools and pulls the school and surrounding community into abdicating bystander roles. It is our experience that many principals are aware of teachers who have a tendency to bully students often do not place certain students with certain teachers, but are reluctant to talk about this due to fear of aggravating teacher unions and difficulty recruiting good teachers. Thus administrators and school policy makers have been slow to directly address the issue. Children can see teachers as bystanders when another teacher bullies a student and the problem is not addressed. Bullying teachers "force" loyalty in their colleagues, who may personally abhor their actions, but teachers who complain are often shunned as being anti-labor. Few positive alternatives exist for a teacher who wants to stop another teacher from bullying a student, and frankly few alternatives exist for parents who are often scapegoated and often expend significant sums of money on attorneys in pursuit of protection for their children. The matter is further complicated by the increase in bullying of teachers by parents in the guise of protecting their children. Teacher unions may actually hurt the larger body of teachers it represents by protecting the few who bully while ignoring the impact those teachers have on other teachers and on their students. This loyalty conflict forces the non-bullying teacher into the passive (victim bystander) role, propels the school administration into an abdicating bystander role. Facing these problems in an effort to deal with them may encourage better trained teachers and more creative and peaceful school learning environments.

Case Study II: The Abdicating Bystander Role of the School and Community in the Murder of a School Teacher

On December 5, 2001, an African American family life counselor and minister was stabbed to death by a 17-year-old student in front of two teachers and eight students, the first recorded case of the murder of a teacher by a student in Massachusetts. The student is now serving a life sentence for second-degree murder with the possibility of parole after 15 years. The murder took place in an alternative school designed for adolescents with behavior disorders. Information described below for this case was taken from police reports of the eye-witnesses to the murder as well as the clinical case record of the student convicted of murder.

The murderer was a young man who had been shuttled between living with his mother, grandfather, and with friends, transient situations resulting from a conflict with his mother. At the time of the murder, he had been on probation for stabbing his mother. Reports indicate that he felt overburdened and devalued by his family, specifically by his duty to care for his two younger siblings. He was also resentful and angry at what he experienced as a devaluation of his social status by his mother by what he felt was her publicly shaming him by calling his friends to apprise them of what she saw as his manipulations. In this incident, which was eerily similar to his stabbing of the teacher, he used a small blade to lash out against his mother: life events seemed to create a pattern of fear-based response against perceived shame and humiliation in this boy, a response called "injustice collection" in the recent school homicide literature (e.g., Twemlow et al., 2002).

Reports also indicate that the boy worked with counseling services to try to repair his relationship with his mother. He also participated in individual psychotherapy as well as case management efforts by state agencies, probation personnel, and private sector therapists to motivate a process to reconnect him to a more positive relationship with his mother. In fact, the murdered teacher was trying to find a place for him to stay because of these conflicts. The boy had repeated and prolonged absenteeism, was disconnected from any positive environment in the school, and expressed a feeling of being picked on and regularly provoked by his teachers and peers. His past history of psychiatric disorder was relatively insignificant, although there was a single experience of trauma due to kidnapping when he was about 7 years old, which resulted in the development of night terrors. His father was functionally absent, a street criminal and visible to him in that role from time to time. His mother was a hard working and overburdened social service worker. He experienced her as an exhausted victim of the system, and there were regular fights with his stepfather. He was often unkempt with poor bodily hygiene, which was the reason he gave for wearing his hood, concerned about how others would see him. He noted to his therapist on one occasion that he "had to fight in order not to be seem as weak by other kids." He spoke regularly of the victim, whom he felt was accusing him of things he did not do.

The lethal interaction began after the boy entered the classroom. Just prior, in the hallway, the victim had asked the boy to remove his hood. The boy remarked to two other students that he was sick of "the same old thing every day."

One of the students described the lethal incident: "We were going to sit down at our desks when I heard the student and the teacher arguing by the teachers desks, which is near the hallway door. I heard the teacher ask the student again if he would "just take the hood off." The student told the teacher that wanted to be left alone. The teacher moved as if he was about to touch the student and the student told him not to. The teacher said something like "what is that going to solve or do." The students then said again, "don't touch me." The teacher then said something that I couldn't hear. I then heard the student say, "You ain't going to leave me alone about it." The student then took off his coat that had the hood underneath. When the student took his coat off it looked like he wanted to fight the teacher. The teacher looked like he was squaring off too. The student then shrugged his shoulders a few times and brought his hands up in front. The teacher then made a fake left at the student. He came close but didn't hit the student. At this time, they both started going at it. They were both throwing punches. Punches were landed by both of them." The teacher was fatally stabbed in the abdomen in blows that looked to the audience like punches, and initially, the teacher seemed unaware that he had been seriously injured. He left the classroom and various people asked him if he was OK, to which he replied that he was, until finally the school nurse noted he was "covered in blood from his shirt to his shoes." CPR failed, and he was dead on arrival at a local hospital.

In a follow-up discussion between Frank Sacco and a White woman who was a classmate of the murdered teacher, some of his feelings on the night before the murder were explored. He had been in a class of primarily White females, learning about theories of counseling, and he was considered a popular member of the class because he was naturally good with children. The teacher of the class was distant and considered rather unforgiving. In the course of the teaching, she became critical of the murdered teacher because he didn't seem to appreciate her views of the theories that she was describing. She said to him, "You are not getting this and if you don't start learning you are not going to make a good counselor." This went on through out the class because he was unable to grasp the basis of the theory. "You need to study the theories more effectively."

The class members didn't remember her being abusive to others in the class, but after the class room they all gathered around, supporting him. The interviewee said, "I thought maybe you could see it in his face that he felt like crap. You know because he had been put down in front of the class, and I think he was thinking that it was true, that he wasn't good at his job, or what he hoped to be his job as a counselor." She had indicated to him that he might not pass the class. After his murder the following day, the same teacher did the debriefing in a cold but supportive way. Not much was discussed, and the class went on to study statistics.

In this tragic example, the murdered teacher had been put in a complicated, undefined role, a role the students did not fully understand. They called him a "security guard or counselor." He had been made into a victim of total insecurity about his specific role in the classroom. The school administration, school board, and people in the community the school served, collectively assigned this role to the teacher, and in doing so functioned as abdicating bystanders. The teacher was of imposing stature and had been recruited to monitor behavior problems as well as to counsel and teach students. It is often assumed that a big strong individual with the authority of a teacher may know how to handle these complicated and contradictory roles, but he was not trained for the dangers of such a situation and especially in how to activate a helpful bystanding role for himself.

Innovative Approaches to School and Community Violence

Can parents become so aggravated over sports that they may commit murder? It happens periodically. One such case occurred in Cambridge, Massachusetts: The father of an ice hockey player, beat to death the father of another boy on July 5, 2000, after they argued about rough play in a hockey practice. The jury found the man guilty of voluntary manslaughter, with a sentence of 8–12 years.

There is a general agreement that parents are behaving less well at their children's sports games, and we have seen the same parental loss of control occur in schools intensely committed to forensics and debate. Bullying of their children often occurs, into roles as highly skilled sports or debate experts, that perhaps the parent wanted at one time to fulfill when younger. As a karate teacher, more than once Stuart Twemlow had to speak to a father who berated his child, often a young child who cried in a fight when they were hit. It is as if the fathers forget their role. Strangely, stimulating a group to remain free of trouble created by power differentials may be a lot easier that it was thought to be. One example was a school-promoted karate tournament in which 300 people attended from a 5 state region. The only difference in this tournament was that every 30 minutes we meditated on the importance of thinking of the other person before acting, and remembering those who have given their lives in the service of others, in an effort to appeal both to the sacrificial aspect of altruism and the common aspect of altruism present even in bad people. That tournament is discussed to this day, it finished 2 hours ahead of time, there was not a single conflict about a fight or demonstration, and there were no fights or disagreements even in the children's division.

Although it is beyond the scope of this chapter to explore in detail the complicated problem of violence in the community at large, studies of violence in schools provide a potentially useful microcosm for understanding surrounding community violence. Schools have often failed to realize that education also depends on the social and emotional climate surrounding learning as evidenced by the largely behavioral training of school teachers with little emphasis on normal and pathological development, unless the teacher elects for specialized training. Given this narrow focus on intellectual training it is not surprising that coercive power dynamics are not given sufficient attention. One result of this limited focus is that community leaders can scapegoat agencies those who have been delegated the responsibility to educate children and to provide a safe learning environment, such as teachers and law enforcement officers. Without sophisticated awareness of pathological bystanding roles, problem children can be unnecessarily "evacuated" into the medical or criminal justice system and special classrooms and schools as aberrant or sick. Such an action causes considerable expense for the community and does not address the universal responsibility of everyone in the community for how schools function, an abdicating bystander role as we have defined it, dramatically illustrated in the case of the murder of the teacher. Since education is not just a right or a service, it is a defining necessity for a healthy society, addressing the social and emotional needs of children is an imperative of even greater importance than attention to structural issues in the school climate, such as the use of increasing security surveillance and increased presence of law enforcement. The work of Sampson and others (Sampson & Ramedenbush, 1997) on the collective efficacy of communities in the Chicago area is a helpful model. Collective efficacy is defined as social cohesion among neighbors combined with a willingness to intervene on behalf of the common good. Their large scale studies showed very strong evidence of a link between that factor and reduced violence in over 300 Chicago neighborhoods.

Figure 6.1 represents a summary model for the social and psychological factors that we believe are in a dialectical, co-created relationship with each other. Helpful (altruistic) bystanding will promote mentalization, and vice versa. In such a community, social affiliation and the needs of the group as a whole are of dominant concern (i.e., an individual sees personal needs as interdependent with the needs of others). The Peaceful Schools Project described in this chapter addresses these two elements in a primary prevention and secondary prevention approach to school violence. Coercive and humiliating power dynamics (defined as the conscious and

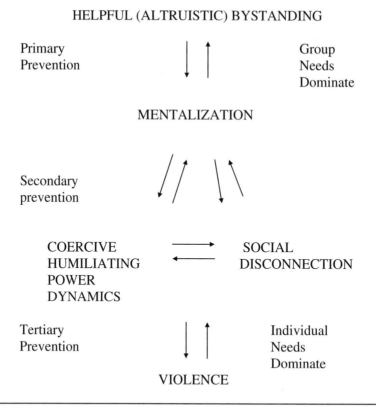

HELPFUL (ALTRUISTIC) BYSTANDING

Primary
Prevention

Group
Needs
Dominate

MENTALIZATION

Secondary
prevention

COERCIVE
HUMILIATING
POWER
DYNAMICS

SOCIAL
DISCONNECTION

Tertiary
Prevention

Individual
Needs
Dominate

VIOLENCE

Figure 6.1 A socio-psychodynamic model of community health.

unconscious use of force and humiliation by individuals and groups against other individuals and groups) and social disconnection (the feeling of being actively separated from a social group in the community) are two other factors that the research of Sampson and others, including Felton Earls, in social sciences research have related to violence and other forms of community disruption. Such factors create a social crucible of at-risk groups of individuals who may be violence prone, inviting a secondary prevention approach to such problems. These communities consist of individuals or small groups fighting for their own survival and the needs of the larger community are often ignored or forgotten. When coercive power dynamics and social disconnection become a fixed modus operandi of a social group, outbreaks of lethal violence occur; such has been hypothesized in the adolescent homicide perpetrators in the spate of murders in schools in the 1990s. Treating such children and their victims is a tertiary prevention action to address a collapsing and fragmented community.

This research suggests a testable model for producing social harmony in our communities and for improving the learning environment in schools, by connecting all stakeholders as passionate and committed members of the community rather than remaining bystanders in fragmented, self-centered sub groups. From this perspective then, connected and mentalizing people make safer communities. Approaches to school violence will be a fundamental failure, if they exclude the community in which the violence occurs.

The school must be acknowledged as an intricate part of the surrounding community. Busing affects this, since children bussed from external areas have trouble identifying with the connectedness at the school. This is one illustration of the many changes the communities will have to make to create schools that do not set up a situation for violence and bullying. Individual expert treatment of bullies and bullies victims will have short-term benefits, but no long term effect on the climate of the school. The randomized trial reported in chapter 26 (this volume), has shown that it is possible to change the school environment into one conducive to academic excellence, rather than bullying and other social games. After the intervention, I entered the first school and thought it had been closed for the afternoon, because it was so quiet. This previously extremely disruptive school, with attempted rapes, high suspensions, and poor academic achievement, is now clean, comfortable, and very quiet; the classes and classrooms are properly conducted and beautifully decorated. The climate allows the schools' play equipment to be used without significant destructiveness, and the school has academic excellence among black students, whose academic performance now exceeds white students, through the effect of the impact of social climate and the reduction of racial prejudice, without, incidentally, a single reference to prejudice during the training period.

This and other exciting ideas for further research have emerged from these studies over the past 14 years. We hope that others will pick up on these and other new theoretical approaches.

Acknowledgment

A modified version of this chapter was read at Scientific Approaches to Youth Violence Prevention, a conference of the New York Academy of Sciences April 23 through 26, 2004, and published in *Annals New York Academy of Sciences* (2004), *1036*, 215–232. Research supported by the Menninger Department of Psychiatry Baylor College of Medicine, Houston Texas and Foundation grants for the Peaceful Schools and Communities Project of the Child and Family Program Menninger Clinic, Houston, Texas.

Notes

1. Data for this case relied on the first hand descriptions by the school counselor in this school.

References

Cable News Network (CNN). (2001). *District bars students who allegedly heard of shooters plans.* Retrieved from http://www.cnn.com/2001/us/03/08/shooting.studnts.knew/index.html

Cohen, J. (Ed.). (1999). *Educating minds and hearts: Social emotional learning and the passage into adolescence.* New York: Teacher College Press.

Cowie, H. (2000). Bystander or standing by: Gender issues in coping with bullying in English schools. *Aggressive Behavior, 26,* 85–97.

Craig, W., & Pepler, D. (1997). Observations of bullying and victimization in the school yard. *Canadian Journal of School Psychology, 13,* 41–59.

Education World. (2000). Anonymity spurs students to report potential violence. Retrieved from http://www.educationworld.com/a_admin/admin202.html

Fonagy, P. (2001). *Attachment theory and psychoanalysis.* New York: Other Press.

Gladwell, M. (2000). *The tipping point.* New York: Little Brown.

Haundaumadi, A., & Pateraki, L. (2001). Bullying and bullies in Greek elementary schools: Pupils attitudes and teachers'/parents' awareness. *Educational Review, 53*(1), 19–27.

Hazler, R., Miller, D., Carney, J., & Green, S. (2001). Adult recognition of school bullying situations. *Educational Research, 43*(7), 133–147.

Henry, D., Guerra, N., Huesmann, R., Tolan, P., Van Acker, R. & Enron, L. (2000). Normative influences on aggression in urban elementary school classrooms. *American Journal of Community Psychology, 28,* 59–81.

Kupersmidt, S. (1999). Factor Influencing Teacher Identification of Peer Bullies and Victims. *School Psychology Review, 28*(3), 505–518.

O'Connell, P., Pepler, D., & Craig, W. (1999). Peer Involvement in bullying: Insights and challenges for Intervention. *Journal of Adolescence, 22,* 437–452.

Olweus, D. (1993). *Bullying at school: What we know and what we can do.* Cambridge, MA: Blackwell.

Olweus, D. (1999). In P. K. Smith, Y. Morita, J. Junger-Tas, D. Olweus, P. Catalano, & P. Slee (Eds.), *The nature of school bullying: A cross national perspective* (pp. 7–27). London: Routledge.

Patterson, S., Memmott, J., Brennan, E., & Germain, C. (1992). Patterns of natural helping in rural areas: implications for social work research. *Social Work Research and Abstract. 28*, 22–28.

Pilivm, J., Dovidio, J., Gaertner, S., & Clark, R. (1982). Responsive bystanders: The process of intervention. In V. Derlega & J. Grzelak (Eds.), *Cooperation and helping behavior: Theories and research* (pp. 279–304). New York: Academic Press.

Salmivalli, C. (1995). Bullies, victims and those others: Bullying as a groups process. *Psylzologia, 30*(5), 364–372.

Sampson, R., & Ramedenbush, S. (1997). Neighborhoods and violent crime: A multilevel study of collective efficacy. *Science, 277*(5328), 918–925.

Sarkar, D. (2000). Georgia taps web for school safety. Retrieved from http://www.fcw.com/civic/articles/2000/0821/web-georgia-08-23-00.asp

Seelig, B., & Rosof, L. (2001). Normal and pathological altruism. *Journal American Psychoanalytic Association, 49*(3), 934–959.

Shapiro, Y., & Gabbard, G. (1994). A reconsideration of altruism from an evolutionary and psychodynamic perspective. *Ethics and Behavior, 4*(1), 23–42.

Slee, P. (1993). Bullying: A preliminary Investigation of its nature and the effects of social cognition. *Early Child Development and Care, 87*, 47–57.

Smith, P., & Ananiclou, K. (2003). The nature of school bullying and the effectiveness of school-based interventions. *Journal of Applied Psychoanalytic Studies, 5*(2), 189–209.

Twemlow, S. (2000). The roots of violence: Converging psychoanalytic explanatory models for power struggles and violence in schools. *The Psychoanalytic Quarterly. LXIX*(4), 741–785.

Twemlow, S., Fonagy, P., & Sacco, F. (2001). A social systems — power dynamic approach for preventing school violence. In M. Shafii & S. Shafii (Eds.), *School violence: Contributing factors, management and prevention* (pp. 273–289). Washington DC: American Psychiatric Press.

Twemlow, S., Fonagy, P., Sacco, F., & Brethour, J. (2006). Teachers who bully students a hidden trauma. *International Journal of Social Psychiatry, 52*(3), 187–198.

Twemlow, S., Fonagy, P., Sacco, F., Gies, M., Evans, R., & Ewbank, R. (2001). Creating a Peaceful School Learning Environment: A Controlled Study of an Elementary School Intervention to Reduce Violence. *American Journal of Psychiatry, 158*, 808–810.

Twemlow S., Fonagy P., Sacco F., & Vernberg E. (2002). Assessing adolescents who threaten homicide in schools. *American Journal Psychoanalysis, 62*(3), 213–235.

Twemlow, S., & Sacco, F. (1996). Peacekeeping and peacemaking: The conceptual foundations of a plan to reduce violence and improve the quality of life in a midsized community in Jamacia. *Psychiatry: 59*, 156–174.

Twemlow, S., Sacco, F., & Williams, P. (1996). A clinical and interactionist perspective on the bully-victim-bystander relationship. *Bulletin of the Menninger Clinic, 60*, 296–313.

Vernberg, E., Jacobs, A., Twemlow, S., Sacco, F., & Fonagy, P. (2009). Submitted for publication. Victimization and violence-related cognitions. E. Vernberg (Chair), *Violence against peers: Developmental inevitability or unacceptable risk?* Symposium at Annual Meeting American Psychological Association, Washington, DC.

Zerger, A. (1996). *Bystanders and attitudes about violence during early adolescence.* Unpublished masters thesis, University of Kansas, Lawrence.

Social Behavior and Peer Relationships of Victims, Bully-Victims, and Bullies in Kindergarten

FRANCOISE D. ALSAKER AND EVELINE GUTZWILLER-HELFENFINGER

Overview of Bullying Among Younger Students

Given the paucity of studies addressing bully/victim problems in kindergarten, we want to succinctly address the similarity of the phenomenon among kindergarten and school-aged youth. Then, we will address the issue of social behavior and peer relations of children in the roles of victims, bully-victims, and bullies as compared to non-involved children. Doing so, we will discuss the resemblance of findings for kindergarten and school children and argue for the implementation of differentiated prevention programs.

Conceptual Foundations

Earlier studies have shown that bullying/victimization already occurs in preschool and kindergarten (Alsaker, 1993; Alsaker & Valkanover, 2001; Kochenderfer & Ladd, 1996). However, studies addressing the issue of victimization at this age are still extremely rare, and the validity of the classification into the roles defined for school-aged children is sometimes questioned. In fact, there is nothing in the agreed-upon definition of bullying—as systematic and repeated aggressive behavior directed against specific children and including an imbalance of power between the aggressors and their victims (Rigby, Smith, & Pepler, 2004; Olweus, 1993)—that speaks against the involvement of kindergarten children in bullying. Nevertheless, at this age conflicts often escalate in aggressive exchanges, and one of the challenges of assessing bully/victim problems in kindergarten is to discriminate between victimization and various other aggressive acts (Alsaker & Valkanover, 2001). Therefore, efforts must be made to train children and teachers to make this distinction.

In our own research, for example, we spend time with each child explaining different types of aggressive behavior (using drawings), including indirect forms such as exclusion from the group or rumors. Then, we ask the children to tell us some episodes, and discuss with them which of these were bullying situations. This procedure gives several opportunities to correct the children's own interpretations if necessary (Alsaker, 2003; Alsaker & Valkanover, 2001). Subsequently, children are asked to pick out the photographs of peers who bully other children and to indicate their victims. This procedure was developed because we noticed very early

(Alsaker, 1993) that kindergarten children had great difficulty in identifying victims without first identifying the perpetrators of the bullying acts. Thus, this temporal assessment procedure has proved important with this age group. Also, it is important to note that kindergarten children nominate themselves far more often as targets of peers' bullying than as bullying others (Alsaker & Valkanover, 2001; Kochenderfer & Ladd, 1996). Furthermore, it is very difficult to obtain information about the frequency of episodes even on self-experienced episodes—in children this age. Therefore, we strongly recommend the use of peer-nominations to assess the children's perspective.

Teachers' ratings in kindergarten yield high concordance with peer nominations, and there is now some consensus regarding their validity (Alsaker & Valkanover, 2001; Griffin & Gross, 2004; Ladd & Kochenderfer-Ladd, 2002). Actually, Perren and Alsaker (2006) reported that only 5.5% of the children could not be categorized as involved or not involved in bully/victim problems due to major non-agreements between teachers' answers and peer nominations. Training teachers to detect bullying before completing questionnaires seems to help reduce inflated rates of bully-victims and of children who cannot be classified (Alsaker & Nägele, 2008).

Another issue that has been discussed concerning bullying in kindergarten is whether children that age are able to display and be aware of indirect forms of aggressive behavior. This is an important issue, since indirect forms of aggressive behavior are central to bully/victim problems in school-aged children. In fact, several studies have found social or relational aggression to be part of kindergarten children's repertoire of aggressive acts (Crick et al., 2006; Monks, Smith, & Swettenham, 2005). Assessing indirect victimization in terms of exclusion from the group (Olweus tradition), Alsaker (1993; Alsaker & Nägele, 2008; Alsaker & Valkanover, 2001) found that both teachers and children report this kind of behavior. Also in Kochenderfer and Ladd's study (1997) both girls and boys did report on indirect aggressive acts. Indeed, kindergarten teachers report many experiences with subtle and relational aggressive acts among the children, although both physical and verbal aggressive behaviors are more common at this age (Alsaker, 2003). Our recent study among 1090 kindergarten children yielded a very interesting finding in this context: Bullies used significantly more frequently exclusion when they bullied others (63% endorsed exclusion) than the aggressive victims did (31%; Alsaker, 2007). Therefore, indirect forms of bullying should definitely be considered when assessing bullying behaviors in kindergarten.

Using a cut-off point of "at least once a week" for teacher ratings and a combination of teacher ratings and peer nominations, Alsaker and Nägele (2008) concluded that the prevalence of passive victims (6%) and bullies (10%) was comparable to figures obtained in school children, even if many school studies report somewhat lower percentages of bullies. Even after the above-mentioned training for teachers (before completing questionnaires), bully-victims were overrepresented (7%) as compared to studies involving older children. It seems realistic to assume that a certain number of those children who were nominated as bullying others and as being victimized were primarily often involved in rough-and-tumble (Pellegrini, 1993) conflicts with peers. However, as we will show in the present chapter, children categorized as bully-victims did differ from all other children in many ways. Thus, even if the prevalence seems somewhat inflated, the findings provide much support for the validity of this categorization. In conclusion, we might infer that studies conducted in kindergarten confirm that bullying is part of kindergarten children's daily life, and that it concerns at least as many children as it does among school-aged students.

Considering bullying as an interaction pattern unfolding within the specific social context in which it occurs (Pepler, Craig, & O'Connell, 1999), it is well established that individual behavior can only be one of many variables involved in this group process. All children in the group can influence this process by intervening and helping the victim, supporting the bully, or choosing to ignore what they witness (Salmivalli, Lagerspetz, Björkqvist, Österman, & Kaukiainen 1996). However, earlier studies have revealed that bullies are clever in choosing victims who do not represent a danger to them (Perry, Perry, & Boldizar, 1990) and that victims seem to lack skills that could protect them from these bullies (Egan & Perry, 1998). Accordingly, there may be factors associated with the victims' social behavior in the group, which make them vulnerable to victimization. First, victims might, for example, be too submissive, or they may behave in ways that would prevent other children from helping them. Second, there might be factors associated with bullies' behavior (beside intimidation) that could motivate peers to assist them and not the victim.

Most studies have found victimization and rejection by peers (in terms of sociometric status) to be highly correlated (Salmivalli & Isaacs, 2005). Ladd and Troop-Gordon (2003) reported rejection to be predictive of later victimization and victimization of later peer rejection. Victims as well as bully-victims were also found to have few friends who might protect them from being victimized (Hodges, Boivin, Vitaro, & Bukowski, 1999; Schwartz, Dodge, Pettit, & Bates, 2000). Unfortunately, passive and aggressive victims have not always been differentiated, and most studies were conducted using school age samples.

Knowledge of victims', bully-victims' and bullies' social behavior in the group and their peer relationships in kindergarten may add to our understanding of processes involved in bullying and help us develop more effective prevention programs. In the next section, we turn to the many facets of social behavior that may represent a risk for becoming the target of bullying, protect children from victimization, maintain bullies' behavior, and reinforce witnesses' not responding to bullying acts. Afterwards, we address victims', bully-victims', and bullies' peer relations in terms of being liked and of reciprocal friendships in the kindergarten class.

Social Behavior of Children Involved in Bully/Victim Patterns

Some authors have suggested that victims reinforce the bullies because they do not defend themselves, withdraw, or even cry easily (Olweus, 1978; Perry, Willard, & Perry, 1990). Perry, Perry, and Kennedy (1992) proposed to view aggressive victims as "ineffectual aggressors" who have difficulties regulating their affect and who easily become over-aroused. Schwartz, Dodge, Pettit, and Bates (1997) suggested that victimization is a consequence of the aggressive victim's irritability. In this section, we will address positive and negative facets of behavior in the peer group and present results from a large and representative study on victimization in kindergarten in Switzerland.

Pathways to Victimization

Pathways to Victimization (PTV) is a longitudinal project including information from children, teachers, and parents. In the present chapter, findings from the first wave of data collection will be reported.

Sixty-seven kindergartens in the Canton of Berne, Switzerland, were selected on the basis of a series of criteria, such as region, urban or rural areas, size of the community, or socio-economic factors. School authorities, teachers, and parents were asked for the permission to conduct the study. The final sample is composed of 1,090 children (96% of the drawn sample); 48% of children are girls, between 5 and 7.5 years. Children were interviewed by trained students, and teachers filled out a comprehensive questionnaire on each child, including behavior in the peer group, various behavioral and personality characteristics as well as emotional well-being. In the present chapter, teachers' reports are used as our main source of information concerning the classification of children involved in bully/victim problems. To calculate the bully-victim status of a child an eight-item questionnaire for teachers was used, assessing victimization and bullying separately (Alsaker & Valkanover, 2001; Perren & Alsaker, 2006). Children were categorized as being a bully or a victim if the specific events were observed at least once a week. When nothing else is reported, results were significant at least at the .05 alpha level. In all analyses, possible interactions between victimization and gender were tested. As mentioned above, 6% of children were observed to be victimized at least once a week without bullying other children themselves, and were categorized as passive victims. Twelve percent of children bullied peers at least once a week, without being bullied; accordingly, they were categorized as bullies. Seven percent of children bullied others and were victimized at least once a week; they were classified as aggressive victims. Twenty percent of children did sometimes bully peers or were sometimes bullied (not categorized); and finally, 55% of children were not involved in the bullying dynamic.

Aggressive Behavior

Bullies and aggressive victims have one a priori characteristic in common: they behave more aggressively than other children, and they do so consistently. Hence, this is one of the criteria to be met when these roles are operationalized. However, the two roles seem to differ in terms of the type of aggression displayed. Bullies are supposed to be more instrumental, whereas aggressive victims seem to use aggressive behavior reactively (Pellegrini et al., 1999). Aggressive victims have also been found to show more aggressive behavior (Perren & Alsaker, 2006) and more oppositional defiant behavior (Kokkinos & Panayiotou, 2004) than bullies. In fact, Salmivalli and Nieminen (2002) reported school-aged aggressive victims to be the most aggressive children of all, both in terms of proactive and reactive aggression. In our earlier kindergarten study, teachers reported that aggressive victims used physical aggression more often than bullies, whereas these two groups of aggressive children did not differ from another as to other forms of aggression (Perren & Alsaker, 2006).

Beside the specific items on bullying, teachers in the PTV study answered three items about open aggressive behaviors that are often used in the literature, which tap fighting, biting, and destroying things (see Ladd & Profilet, 1996). The results were as expected. Both in girls and in boys, aggressive victims were found to be the most physically aggressive children, that is, they were even significantly more aggressive than the bullies ($F_{overall}$ = 126.95, p < .0001; Post-hoc Bonferroni test, p < .0001, $M_{bully-victims}$ = 2.7, $M_{bullies}$ = 2; on a scale from 1 to 4, as a matter of comparison $M_{non-involved}$ = 1.3).

Similar results were obtained using a scale on oppositional and dysregulated behavior (temper tantrums, conflicts with the teacher, not following orders). Aggressive victims were reported as being the most oppositional children, even more so than bullies, who in turn showed more of these behaviors than both passive victims and non-involved children ($F_{overall}$ = 65.89, p < .0001; Post-hoc Bonferroni test, p = .003, $M_{bully-victims}$ = 2.36, $M_{bullies}$ = 2.05. Furthermore, Alsaker and Nägele (2008) reported aggressive victims to have the highest scores on all problems that could be associated with ADHD or at least with a lack of behavioral regulation (impulsivity, hyperactivity, inattention). This finding corresponds well to results for school-age children. Additionally, bullies used exclusion more frequently than physical aggression to bully peers, and they did so more often than bully-victims (63% vs. 31%). Only 30% of bullies used physical means at least once a week, while this was the case for 75% of aggressive victims. Aggressive victims also destroyed other children's property significantly more often than bullies (25% vs. 8%). Bullies and bully-victims did not differ in terms of verbal aggression (around 65% used it frequently in both groups).

In sum, results from kindergarten are consistent with studies on older children: Bullies have a broader repertoire of aggressive behavior, including social aggression, whereas bully-victims use much more physical means and seem to be dysregulated. We therefore suggest that exactly this combination of dysregulated and physical aggressive behavior may put children at risk for retaliation that could develop into systematic bullying and decrease peers' motivation to defend them when they are attacked by bullies. Probably, many children would consider bullies' acts as understandable and as a type of revenge. Furthermore, their highly aggressive behavior may also hide their actual status as victimized children in the eyes of adults.

Prosocial and Cooperative Behavior

Studies conducted with older children have shown that victims display less prosocial behavior than non-involved peers (Johnson et al., 2002; Toblin, Schwartz, Gorman, & Abou-ezzeddine, 2005). Perren and Alsaker (2006) reported passive victims in kindergarten to be as prosocial as their non-involved peers in terms of helping and comforting peers when needed and sharing their belongings with others, and to be more prosocial than bullies and aggressive victims. Passive victims were also found to be rather cooperative, but less so than non-involved children. In the PTV study, victims did not differ from bullies, and both were found to be more prosocial and cooperative than bully-victims, but not as much as non-involved peers (Alsaker, 2007). The latter results correspond to findings from studies on school-aged children and provide a picture of passive victims as being rather prosocial (with scores over the arithmetic mean of the scales) but less prosocial than non-involved peers.

These results might indicate that victims become less prosocial and cooperative when they experience being victimized over time. They may become aware of bullies and other peers abusing their inclination to share and help. They may also simply learn not to be prosocial because their prosocial acts are not rewarded (extinction). One limitation to this assertion is that the results presented are from cross-sectional data, involving different children at different ages. Therefore, we do not know whether the less prosocial older victims have actually experienced victimization over time or not. It might also be the case that less cooperative and prosocial school aged children are at higher risk of being victimized. Only longitudinal data from kindergarten through elementary school can elucidate this question.

Withdrawal and Shy Behavior

The construct of withdrawal is multifaceted, and withdrawing behavior may be caused or motivated by many factors. It would be beyond the scope of the present chapter to address these issues. However, in this section we will examine different facets of social behavior associated with shy-inhibited behavior and reticence to social contact. This behavioral approach is chosen because we think that the way children behave in the group matters more to other children than the motivation of that behavior. Peers judge what they see and experience.

Asendorpf (1998) reported that correlations between shy-inhibited behavior and rejection by peers increased from kindergarten through school. Rubin, LeMare, and Lollis (1990) reported corresponding results as to withdrawn behavior from second through fourth grade. These findings could be interpreted as the result of a vicious circle including shy or withdrawn behavior and negative experiences in the peer group. They may also indicate that, as children get older, withdrawn behavior is increasingly perceived as non-normative and is sanctioned with rejection by peers. Finally, children who withdraw from group activities, for example, may just not be attractive to many peers. These findings are related to sociometric rejection and not to bullying.

Nevertheless, as mentioned earlier, rejection and victimization are closely related, and results indicate that shy children are at risk for victimization.

Passive victims at different ages have been shown to withdraw from peers to a greater extent than other children (Olweus, 1978; Perren & Alsaker, 2006). In kindergarten, passive victims did not initiate contact with peers as often as others and seemed to enjoy other peers' company less than other children. Also in the PTV study, passive victims had the highest scores on withdrawal. That is, they often played alone and actively withdrew from peers. Furthermore, girls categorized as passive victims were described as showing little interest in their peers. Passive victims were rated by the teachers as being rather shy, whereas aggressive victims were not. Interestingly, although the finding regarding victims is true for both genders, non-involved boys were reported to be almost as shy as male passive victims. Moreover, Alsaker (1993) found that victimized children in day-care centers said they were afraid of their peers. In sum, in all studies, children who were categorized as passive victims seemed to feel very insecure in social situations with peers.

These associations could be expected, but until we have results from longitudinal studies we can only speculate whether children who display shy or inhibited behavior in the peer group are at risk of becoming victimized, or if victimized children become very insecure and learn not to trust peers and to withdraw from them. One thing is certain: shyness does not cause victimization. However, since bullies prefer easy targets, shy children might actually be perceived as perfect victims.

Assertiveness

As already noted, Egan and Perry (1998) proposed that victims might lack skills that could protect them from attacks by their peers, specifically assertiveness. Results from the earlier Bernese study support this hypothesis. Victims were lowest on setting limits to peers' demands (Perren & Alsaker, 2006). In the PTV study, the most remarkable result was that bullies showed the highest level of assertiveness as compared to all other children. The findings for passive victims were qualified by an interaction with gender. In girls, passive victims were reported to be significantly less assertive than all other children, whereas male passive victims did not differ from non-involved boys and aggressive victims. Independent of gender, aggressive victims did not lack assertiveness. However, their assertiveness does not seem to protect them from assaults by their peers. In fact, only non-aggressive assertiveness seems to function as a protective factor against victimization (Perry, Hodges, & Egan, 2001). That is, aggressive victims are almost certainly unable to differentiate between assertiveness and aggression, whereas bullies probably are able to make this differentiation.

In the earlier Bernese kindergarten study, children were also asked to tell how the victims of aggressive acts did react in these specific situations. Passive victims did not differ from non-involved children. Thirty percent of those children were reported by their peers to use physical retaliation in such situations. Also, 50% of passive victims said they would try to defend themselves. Therefore, we might conclude that some victims may try to defend themselves but do not seem to be effective enough (Alsaker, 2003). Observational studies of victims in various difficult social situations would probably help us understand to which extent they lack assertiveness or why they are not efficient when trying to stop attacks or when setting limits. We should also bear in mind that, even if retaliation has been shown to bring ongoing attacks to an end, it has also been shown to increase victims' risk of being victimized in the long term (Schwartz, Dodge, & Coie, 1993).

Leadership

Leadership at kindergarten age or also in school-aged children is often linked to play activities. As could be expected on the basis of the findings regarding withdrawal and shy behavior, in both Swiss kindergarten studies passive victims scored lower than the other children on leadership, (i.e., taking initiative in the peer group, proposing activities, etc.). On the other hand, bullies scored higher on leadership than all other children. Aggressive victims were in between and did not differ from non-involved children (Alsaker 2003, 2007).

The results presented so far show that the social portrayal of school-aged victims, bully-victims, and bullies can be replicated to a large extent with kindergarten children. We now turn to the integration of these children in the peer group, in terms of reciprocal friendships and acceptance by peers.

Peer Relations of Children Involved in Bully/Victim Patterns

Friendships

Among the various social relationships humans entertain, friendships are of major importance, giving meaning to social experience and playing a central role in (and for) a person's social functioning. Although friendships are a significant part of social life at all ages, their form, functions, and intensity vary according to a person's age (Hartup, 1992). During the preschool and school years (and later on), friendships are significant for children's individual and social development and adjustment (e.g., Bukowski, 2001; Erdley, Nangle, Newman, & Carpenter, 2001; Hay, Payne, & Chadwick, 2004).

The most basic characteristics of friendships are reciprocity and commitment. And in the preschool and early elementary school years, the main themes are affiliation and common interests as expressed in expectations centering on common pursuits and concrete reciprocities (Hartup, 1992). Moreover, friendships are "voluntary, intimate, dynamic relationships founded on cooperation and trust" (Gifford-Smith & Brownell, 2003, p. 248). Friendships are egalitarian relationships, as they are symmetrically (horizontally) structured and thus constitute a very specific developmental context for children (Bukowski, 2001).

Apart from ensuring continuing interaction, friendships serve various functions. Friendships are (a) contexts where basic social skills can be acquired or elaborated; (b) information sources for acquiring knowledge about the self, others, and the world; (c) emotional and cognitive resources; and (d) forerunners of subsequent (mutual and intimate) relationships (Hartup, 1992). Additionally, friendships satisfy individuals' need for intimacy and a sense of belonging (Barr, 1997; Sullivan, 1953). With respect to the emotional and cognitive resources that friendships offer, Bukowski (2001) emphasizes their protective power against victimization. Therefore, having a close friend may actually protect children who are characteristically at risk for peer victimization (e.g., Hodges et al., 1999; Hodges, Malone, & Perry, 1997; Pellegrini, Bartini, & Brooks, 1999).

To be able to establish and maintain friendship, children must acquire and retain very specific skills. During the preschool and early elementary school years, such friendship skills include participation (getting started, paying attention); cooperation (e.g., taking turns, sharing); communication (talking, listening); and validation support (being friendly, looking at the other person, giving a smile, offering help; Oden & Asher, 1997). Already at preschool age, children can have stable, enduring friendships (e.g., Howes, 1988).

What about the friendships of bullies, bully-victims, and victims? As previously mentioned, having a friend reduces the risk of being victimized for vulnerable children, (i.e., children in whom both individual [behavioral difficulties] and social risk factors [peer rejection] are combined; Hodges et al., 1999). Whereas both bully-victims and victims have few friends (e.g., Boulton & Underwood, 1992; Ray, Cohen, Secrist, & Duncan, 1997), it seems that some aggressive children can have friends (Cairns, Carins, Neckermann, Gest, & Gariépy, 1988) and that especially male bullies have large friendship networks (Boulton, 1999). These findings were confirmed by Perren and Alsaker's study on kindergarten children (2006). They found that both bully-victims and victims had fewer friends than non-involved children, whereas bullies had as many friends as non-involved children. Also, results based on peer-nominations in the PTV study indicated that passive and aggressive victims had significantly fewer reciprocal friends than bullies and non-involved children. A possible explanation of this finding is that victims lack the skills to maintain friendships over time. Accordingly, Champion, Vernberg, and Shipman (2003) found that passive victims had more conflicts within their friendships, while the study of Goldbaum, Craig, Pepler, and Connolly (2003) revealed that victims reported that their friendships were marked by less affection and trust. However, victims' lack of friendship should not be unilaterally attributed to their own behaviors. It is probable that other children refrain from befriending victims for fear of being victimized themselves (Perren & Alsaker, 2006; Hodges et al., 1997). Actually, in the PTV study, both passive and aggressive victims were reported by teachers to have difficulties finding friends, whereas bullies and non-involved children had no such problems.

Acceptance in the Group: How Well Liked are Victims, Bully-Victims, and Bullies?

When discussing the relationship between friendship and bullying/victimization, another important social construct, that of social acceptance, must be considered. Although it is based on social relationships between children, social acceptance does not denote those relationships per se, but a child's position or prestige within the peer group, respectively. Therefore, popularity is the construct most often contrasted with friendship and is viewed as a general, unilateral, group-oriented construct which represents the peer group's view towards an individual (Bukowski & Hoza, 1989). Although it is often assumed that popularity and friendship influence each other, several studies indicate that the two constructs are independent. Thus, unpopular children can have a best friend whereas not all popular children have a best friend (e.g., Bukowski & Hoza, 1989; Howes, 1990).

Regarding a child's risk for psychological disorders, peer acceptance plays an important role: on the one hand, because peer acceptance may buffer the risk for disorders, and, on the other hand, because children with disorders are in danger of being rejected by their peers (Hay et al., 2004). Moreover, as children's prosocial behavior, aggressiveness, as well as shyness influence their acceptance within the peer group (Newcomb, Bukowski, & Pattee, 1993), prosocial behavior helps children gain acceptance with peers, and the lack of prosocial behavior predicts children's rejection. Additionally, highly aggressive or very shy children are not well liked by their peers (Hay et al., 2004).

What about passive victims', aggressive victims', and bullies' acceptance by their peers? Several studies indicate that both passive and aggressive victims are less liked than bullies and non-involved children (e.g., Alsaker, 2003; Boulton & Smith, 1994). In our studies, we used a cardboard bus to assess how well-liked children were by their peers in kindergarten.

Using photographs of all children in the class, children are asked to nominate up to six peers they would take with them on a bus trip. Nominations are transformed into percentages of possible nominations in the group. In the PTV study, bullies and non-involved children received 39% of possible positive nominations on average, whereas passive and aggressive victims received significantly less nominations (24% and 28%, respectively). This finding replicates an earlier finding in kindergarten (Perren & Alsaker, 2006) and fits well with earlier studies in school age samples.

That aggressive victims, as compared to bullies and non-involved children, are not very well accepted by their peers may be a reflection of their high level of aggressive and otherwise dysregulated behavior. However, the results regarding passive victims remain puzzling. Until now, there are no findings to our knowledge that can explain why victims should be less liked by their peers than other children do. The findings reported above concerning passive victims' withdrawal and shyness, their lower ability to assert themselves in the group, and to set limits may all be regarded as factors leading to a low status in the peer group. This lower status may make them generally less attractive or salient to their peers, and thus they are less often chosen in sociometric tests. Additionally, this low status makes them more vulnerable to victimization, which in turn adds to their poor status, an explanation supported by Ladd and Tropp-Gordon's (2003) findings.

In sum, the findings on reciprocal friendships and acceptance in the peer group clearly indicate that risk factors for victimization are not located within the individual only, but that individual and group factors interact. As already mentioned, peers may be afraid of becoming victims themselves when associating with victims. Moreover, it is generally more rewarding for an individual's self-concept to identify with the leaders and winners rather than with the followers and losers. As a consequence, peers may not be overly motivated to help a child they do not like very much when that child is victimized.

Bullies' high acceptance in the peer group also needs further investigation. The results in kindergarten children correspond well with Boulton and Smith's (1994) findings. Bullies are leaders, they take initiative to activities, they can set limits, and they are not extremely aggressive and apparently not unpredictable. They are a clear danger to some children but not to all. Also, as stated by Sutton, Smith, and Swettenham (1999), bullies with well-developed social-cognitive skills may be able to manipulate peers' attitudes towards themselves. As already mentioned, bullies often use social aggression (exclusion) as opposed to openly aggressive behavior, and they seem to be rather clever in terms of social cognitive skills (Baumgartner & Alsaker, 2008). Furthermore, as aggressive children already cluster together in kindergarten (Perren & Alsaker, 2006), part of the positive nominations bullies receive may stem from other aggressive peers. In sum, all involved children seem to be trapped in roles they cannot escape (victims and bully-victims) or roles they are reinforced to maintain (bullies).

Conclusions

Bullying is a social phenomenon that requires both the presence of aggressive children in the group and the passivity of other children and adults in order to develop into a chronic pattern. On the other hand, some individual characteristics seem to increase children's vulnerability to becoming victimized. The differential results regarding passive victims', aggressive victims' and bullies' behavior in the peer group may shed some light on early risk factors of victimization and factors that may maintain bullying patterns. It seems clear that children who lack assertiveness, cannot set limits to their peers' demands, and who tend to withdraw are at risk for being victimized. First, they represent easy targets for bullies, and second, they may not be socially attractive or salient enough to other peers to incite them to intervene against the bullying. Also, the fact that they are not well integrated in the group, as they are not well liked, have difficulties finding friends, and actually have fewer reciprocal friends, adds to their vulnerability.

However, we have to keep in mind, that bullying is characterized by unfairness and imbalance; that bullies seldom act alone; and thus, that victims have few or no chances to defend themselves effectively. Therefore, even children who feel secure in other social contexts may become insecure, less prosocial, and even withdraw in order to minimize the risk of being maltreated in a specific group of peers. Additionally, if a child is rather shy from the outset, experiences of harassment will add to his or her insecurity.

In regard to bully-victims, the results from kindergarten studies confirm other findings concerning their highly aggressive behavior. Specifically, their physical aggressiveness combined with their poor emotional and behavioral regulation presents a risk for their becoming victimized. These children may appear fairly unpredictable and disturbing in the eyes of their peers. In addition, they are less cooperative and prosocial than others, and it is rather obvious that peers will not intervene to protect them and could even easily be influenced to assist the bullies. These children should be considered a high-risk group.

The general similarity or at least correspondence of results comparing school aged children (usually aged between 10 and 16) and kindergarten children aged 5 through 7 is impressing. Especially when we consider the fact that the data differ with respect to the source of information and the procedures used (self-report, teachers' reports, peer-nominations). The reliability of the findings indicates that bullying as we know it from research with school-aged children really *does* exist in kindergarten. Even the percentages of passive victims are highly similar. To sum up, what both types of victims seem to lack is (a) efficient, non-aggressive assertive behavior and (b) social support from peers who would refuse to take part in bullying and/or who could stop the bullying peers efficiently.

The presented findings suggest that the most important difference between bullies and aggressive victims consists in their respective ability or inability to control their physical aggression. Bullies' use of social aggression suggests that they have rather well-developed social understanding, including knowledge about norms and when to break norms or not. In other words, aggressive victims seem to rather inefficient and possibly dysregulated aggressors, as proposed by Perry et al. (1992), whereas bullies are rather controlled and efficient aggressors (see Sutton et al., 1999).

Regrettably, the findings on social behavior and peer relations of victims, bully-victims, and bullies show that there is no reason to believe that victims might be capable of bringing the situation to an end, or that peers would intervene against bullying, or that bullies would stop by themselves. All findings indicate that the situation is highly reinforcing for bullies and that they themselves, like the victims, are prisoners in a role they cannot escape without the consent and assistance from peers and adults.

Future Research in Kindergarten

As more precise knowledge on early risk and protective factors may contribute to the improvement of prevention programs, there are some issues that would deserve more attention in kindergarten. All findings confirm that aggressive victims must be regarded as being different from passive victims and other aggressive children, (i.e., bullies). This differentiation must occur in kindergarten studies. Currently, longitudinal studies are being conducted in different countries (including the PTV study). We need analyses of the pathways to and from victimization to disentangle the multifaceted causal pathways and the many consequences of victimization on children's psychosocial well-being. Moreover, observational studies both in children's naturalistic contexts and in experimental situations are needed, for example, to tell us more about the adequate and inadequate forms of self-assertiveness.

Table 7.1 Summary Table of Implications for Practice, the Early Detection of Vulnerable Children, and for Further Refinements of Prevention Programs

- Bullying is already a problem in kindergarten. Prevention must start at an early age.
- Children can hardly escape from their roles within the bullying dynamic. However, it is often hard to convince teachers to invest time in solving bullying problems. Therefore, prevention and intervention against victimization have to become compulsory elements of teachers training programs.
- Children displaying highly aggressive or otherwise dysregulated behavior at kindergarten entry are at a high risk of remaining very aggressive and becoming victimized. They can rapidly be marginalized and in the long-term turn into delinquent and violent adolescents. These children can, almost certainly, draw only limited benefit from general anti-bullying programs addressing the whole group. Bully-victims should be given an opportunity to learn to control their behavior. In such cases, individual counseling of the teacher and some treatment or support for the child and his parents are needed.
- Prevention programs must take the differences between all involved children into account. Even if bullies are aggressive, they are different from bully-victims, and they clearly do not need the same training in social skills as their victimized peers (Baumgartner & Alsaker, 2008).
- Passive victims were found to be more submissive, more withdrawn, and less sociable than others. This indicates that they may need some special training, especially in terms of assertiveness, to be able to cope with the complex and often rough peer situations.
- We have emphasized the significance of peer relationships as a factor maintaining the bullying pattern. Actually, bullying can only be solved when the whole group (adults and students) is involved. More emphasis should be placed on involving non-involved children in intervention efforts. They are social, prosocial, not aggressive, know how to set limits, and therefore represent an important resource against bullying and victimization.

The differences we found between the groups of children involved in bully/victim problems are of great significance both for the early detection of vulnerable children and for further refinements of prevention programs (implications for practice are described in Table 7.1). In conclusion, bullying and victimization are part of children's everyday life already in kindergarten. Children themselves cannot resolve these problems, and it is the responsibility of adults to ensure that children can learn and develop in a healthy social environment.

References

Alsaker, F. D. (1993). Isolement et maltraitance par pairs dans les jardins d'enfants: comment mesurer ces phénomènes et quelles en sont leurs conséquences [Isolation and maltreatment by peers in kindergarten: how to measure these phenomena and what are their consequences]? *Enfance, 47,* 241–260.

Alsaker, F. D. (2003). *Quälgeister und ihre Opfer. Mobbing unter Kindern — und wie man damit umgeht [Bullies and their victims. Bullying among children — and how to deal with it].* Bern: Verlag Hans Huber.

Alsaker, F. D. (2007). *Pathways to victimization and a multisetting intervention.* Unpublished Report. Swiss National Science Foundation, NFP52.

Alsaker, F. D., & Nägele, C. (2008). Bullying in kindergarten and prevention. In W. Craig, & D. Pepler (Eds.), *An international perspective on understanding and addressing bullying* (Vol. I, pp. 230–252). Kingston, Canada: PREVNet.

Alsaker, F. D., & Valkanover, S. (2001). Early diagnosis and prevention of victimization in kindergarten. In J. Juvonen, & S. Graham (Eds.), *Peer harassment in school: the plight of the vulnerable and victimized* (pp. 175–95). New York: Guilford.

Asendorpf, J. (1998). Die Entwicklung sozialer Kompetenzen, Motive und Verhaltensweisen [The development of social competence, motives, and behavior]. In F. E. Weinert (Ed.), *Entwicklung im Kindesalter* (pp. 155–176). Weinheim: Beltz.

Barr, D. (1997). Friendship and belonging. In R. L. Selman, C. L. Watts, & L. H. Schultz (Eds.), *Fostering friendship: Pair therapy for treatment and prevention* (pp. 19–30). New York: Aldine De Gruyter.

Baumgartner, A., & Alsaker, F. D. (2008). Mobbing unter Kindern und Jugendlichen: Die Rolle von individuellen sozialen Kompetenzen, Gruppenprozessen und sozialen Beziehungen [Bullying among children and adolescents: the role of individual and social competences, group processes, and social relationships]. In T. Malti & S. Perren (Eds.), *Entwicklung und Förderung sozialer Kompetenzen in Kindheit und Adoleszenz* (pp. 70–88). Stuttgart: Kohlhammer.

Boulton, M. J. (1999). Concurrent and longitudinal relations between children's playground behavior and social preference, victimization, and bullying. *Child Development, 70*, 944–954.

Boulton, M. J., & Smith, P. K. (1994). Bully/victim problems in middle-school children: stability, self-perceived competence, peer perceptions and peer acceptance. *British Journal of Developmental Psychology, 12*, 315–329.

Boulton, M. J., & Underwood, K. (1992). Bully/victim problems among middle school children. *British Journal of Educational Psychology, 62*, 73–87.

Bukowski, W. M. (2001). Friendship and the worlds of childhood. *New Directions for Child and Adolescent Development, 91*, 93–105.

Bukowski, W. M., & Hoza, B. (1989). Popularity and friendship. Issues in theory, measurement, and outcome. In T. J. Berndt & G. Ladd (Eds.), *Peer relationships in child development* (pp. 15–45). New York: Wiley.

Cairns, R. B., Cairns, B. D., Neckerman, H. J., Gest, S. D., & Gariépy, J. (1988). Social networks and aggressive behavior: Peer support or peer rejection? *Developmental Psychology, 24*, 815–823.

Champion, K., Vernberg, E., & Shipman, K. (2003). Nonbullying victims of bullies: Aggression, social skills, and friendship characteristics. *Applied Developmental Psychology, 24*, 535–551.

Crick, N. R., Ostrov, J. M., Burr, J. E., Cullerton-Sen, C., Jansen-Yeh, E., & Ralston, P. (2006). A longitudinal study of relational and physical aggression in preschool. *Journal of Applied Developmental Psychology, 27*, 254–268.

Egan, S. K., & Perry, D. G. (1998). Does low self-regard invite victimization? *Developmental Psychology, 34*, 299–309.

Erdley, C. A., Nangle, D. W., Newman, J. E., & Carpenter, E. M. (2001). Children's friendship experiences and psychological adjustment: theory and research. *New Directions for Child and Adolescent Development, 91*, 5–24.

Gifford-Smith, M. E., & Brownell, C. A. (2003). Childhood peer relationships: social acceptance, friendships, and peer networks. *Journal of School Psychology, 41*, 235–284.

Goldbaum, S., Craig, W. M., Pepler, D., & Connolly, J. (2003). Developmental trajectories of victimization: Identifying risk and protective factors. *Journal of Applied School Psychology, 19*(2), 139–156.

Griffin, R. S., & Gross, A. M. (2004). Childhood bullying: Current empirical findings and future directions for research. *Aggression and Violent Behavior, 4*, 379–400.

Hartup, W. W. (1992). Friendships and their developmental significance. In H. McGurk (Ed.), *Childhood social development: Contemporary perspectives* (pp. 175–205). Hove, UK: Erlbaum.

Hay, D. F., Payne, A., & Chadwick, A. (2004). Peer relations in childhood. *Journal of Child Psychology and Psychiatry, 45*(1), 84–108.

Hodges, E. V. E., Boivin, M., Vitaro, F., & Bukowski, W. M. (1999). The power of friendship: Protection against an escalating cycle of peer victimization. *Developmental Psychology, 35*, 94–101.

Hodges, E. V. E., Malone, M. J., & Perry, D. G. (1997). Individual risk and social risk as interacting determinants of victimization in the peer group. *Developmental Psychology, 33*, 1032–1039.

Howes, C. (1988). Peer interactions of young children. *Monographs of the Society for Research in Child Development, 53*(1), 1–87.

Howes, C. (1990). Social status and friendship from kindergarten to third grade. *Journal of Applied Developmental Psychology, 11*(3), 321–330.

Johnson, H. R., Thompson, M. J. J., Wilkinson, S., Walsh, L., Balding, J., & Wright, V. (2002). Vulnerability to bullying: Teacher-reported conduct and emotional problems, hyperactivity, peer relationship difficulties, and prosocial behaviours in primary school children. *Educational Psychology, 22*, 553–556.

Kochenderfer, B. J., & Ladd, G. W. (1996). Peer victimization: Manifestations and relations to school adjustment in kindergarten. *Journal of School Psychology, 34*, 267–283.

Kochenderfer, B. J., & Ladd, G. W. (1997). Victimized children's reponses to peers' aggression: Behaviors associated with reduced versus continued victimization. *Development and Psychopathology, 9*, 59–73.

Kokkinos, C., & Panayiotou, G. (2004). Predicting bullying and victimization among early adolescents: Associations with disruptive behaviors disorders. *Aggressive Behavior, 30*, 520–533.

Ladd, G. W., & Kochenderfer-Ladd, B. (2002). Identifying victims of peer aggression from early to middle childhood: analysis of cross-informant data for concordance, estimation of relational adjustment, prevalence of victimization, and characteristics of identified victims. *Psychological Assessment, 14*, 74–96.

Ladd, G. W., & Profilet, S. M. (1996). The Child Behavioral Scale: a teacher-report measure of young children's aggressive, withdrawn, and prosocial behaviors. *Developmental Psychology, 32*(6), 1008–1024.

Ladd, G. W., & Tropp-Gordon, W. (2003). The role of chronic peer difficulties in the development of children's psychological adjustment problems. *Child Development, 74*, 1344–1367.

Monks, C. P., Smith, P. K., & Swettenham, J. (2005). Psychological correlates of peer victimisation in preschool: Social cognitive skills, executive function and attachment profiles. *Aggressive Behavior, 31*, 571–588.

Newcomb, A. F., Bukowski, W. M., & Pattee, L. (1993). Children's peer relations: A meta-analytic review of popular, rejected, neglected, controversial, and average sociometric status. *Psychological Bulletin, 113*(1), 99–128.

Oden, S., & Asher, S. R. (1997). Coaching children in social skills for friendship making. *Child Development, 48*, 495–506.

Olweus, D. (1978). *Aggression in the schools: Bullies and whipping boys.* Washington DC: Hemisphere.

Olweus, D. (1993). *Bullying at school: What we know and what we can do.* Oxford, UK: Blackwell.

Pellegrini, A.D. (1993). Elementary-school children's rough-and-tumble play and social competence. *Developmental Psychology, 24,* 802–806.

Pellegrini, A. D., Bartini, M., & Brooks, F. (1999). School bullies, victims, and aggressive victims: factors relating to group affiliation and victimization in early adolescence. *Journal of Educational Psychology, 91*(2), 216–224.

Pepler, D., Craig, W. M., & O'Connell, P. (1999). Understanding bullying from a dynamic systems perspective. In A. Slater & D. Muir (Eds.), *The Blackwell Reader in Developmental Psychology* (pp. 440–451). London: Blackwell.

Perren, S., & Alsaker, F. D. (2006). Social Behaviour and Peer Relationships of Victims, Bully-victims, and Bullies in Kindergarten. *The Journal of Child Psychology and Psychiatry and Allied Disciplines, 47,* 45–57.

Perry, D., Hodges, V. E., & Egan, S. K. (2001). Determinants of chronic victimization by peers: A review and new model of family influence. In J. Juvonen & S. Graham (Eds.), *Peer harassment in school. The plight of the vulnerable and victimized* (pp. 73–104). New York: Guilford.

Perry, D. G., Perry, L. C., & Boldizar, J. P. (1990). Learning of aggression. In M. Lewis & S. Miller (Eds.), *Handbook of developmental psychopathology* (pp. 135–146). New York: Plenum.

Perry, D. G., Perry, L. C., & Kennedy, E. (1992). Conflict and the development of antisocial behavior. In C. U. Shantz & W. W. Hartup (Eds.), *Conflict in child and adolescent development* (pp. 301–329). New York: Cambridge University Press.

Perry, D. G., Willard, J. C., & Perry, L. C. (1990). Peers' perceptions of the consequences that victimized children provide aggressors. *Child Development, 61,* 1310–1325.

Ray, G. E., Cohen, R., Secrist, M. E., & Duncan, M. K. (1997). Relating aggressive and victimization behaviors to children's sociometric status and friendships. *Journal of Social and Personal Relationships, 14,* 95–108.

Rigby, K., Smith, P. K., & Pepler, D. (2004). Working to prevent school bullying: key issues. In P. K. Smith, D. Pepler, & K. Rigby (Eds.), *Bullying in schools. How successful can interventions be?* (pp. 1–12). Cambridge, UK: Cambridge University Press.

Rubin, K. H., LeMare, L. J., & Lollis, S. (1990). Social withdrawal in childhood: Developmental pathways to peer rejection. In S. R. Asher & J. D. Coie (Eds.), *Peer rejection in childhood* (pp. 217–249). New York: Cambridge University Press.

Salmivalli, C., & Isaacs, J. (2005). Prospective relations among victimization, rejection, friendlessness, and children's self- and peer-perceptions. *Child Development, 76,* 1161–1171.

Salmivalli, C., Lagerspetz, K., Björkqvist, K., Österman, K., & Kaukiainen, A. (1996). Bullying as a group process: participant roles and their relations to social status. *Aggressive Behavior, 22,* 1–15.

Salmivalli, C., & Nieminen, E. (2002). Proactive and reactive aggression among school bullies, victims, and bully-victims. *Aggressive Behavior, 28,* 30–44.

Schwartz, D., Dodge, K. A., & Coie, J. D. (1993). The emergence of chronic peer victimization in boys' play groups. *Child Development, 64,* 1755–1772.

Schwartz, D., Dodge, K. A., Pettit, G. S., & Bates, J. E. (1997). The early socialization of aggressive victims of bullying. *Child Development, 68,* 665–675.

Schwartz, D., Dodge, K. A., Pettit, G. S., & Bates, J. E. (2000). Friendship as a moderating factor in the pathway between early harsh home environment and later victimization in the peer group. *Developmental Psychology, 36,* 646–662.

Sullivan, H. S. (1953). The interpersonal theory of psychiatry. In H. S. Perry & M. L. Gawel (Eds.), *The collected works of Harry Stack Sullivan* (pp. 1–393). New York: Norton.

Sutton, J., Smith, P. K., & Swettenham, J. (1999). Bullying and 'theory of mind': a critique of the 'social skills deficit' view of antisocial behaviour. *Social Development, 8*(1), 117–134.

Toblin, R. L., Schwartz, D., Gorman, H., & Abou-ezzeddine, T. (2005). Social-cognitive and behavioral attributes of aggressive victims of bullying. *Journal of Applied Developmental Psychology, 26,* 329–346.

8

Bullying and Morality

Understanding How Good Kids Can Behave Badly

SHELLEY HYMEL, KIMBERLY A. SCHONERT-REICHL, RINA A. BONANNO,
TRACY VAILLANCOURT, AND NATALIE ROCKE HENDERSON

Bullying has long been considered a normal part of growing up. It has been featured in tales of youth by 19th-century authors like Charles Dickens (*Oliver Twist*, 1839; *The Life and Adventures of Nicholas Nickleby*, 1838) and Thomas Hughes (*Tom Brown's School Days*, 1857), and continues as a theme in Western literature over the past century, including Eleanor Estes' (1944) book, *The Hundred Dresses*, William G. Golding's (1959) classic, *The Lord of the Flies*, Margaret Atwood's (1998), *Cat's Eye,* and more recently, Nick Hornby's (2002) novel, *About a Boy*. Bullying is also a common theme in movies about children and youth (e.g., *Billy Madison, The Mighty, Bully, Ant Bully, Pay It Forward, Mean Girls*). Research attention to the topic of bullying, however, has only emerged in the past three decades, with early studies conducted by Scandinavian scholars like Dan Olweus (e.g., 1978) who remains a leader in the field today.

In some countries, serious attention to issues of school bullying has been borne of tragedy (e.g., Marr & Fields, 2000). In Norway, the suicide deaths of three boys (10–14 years old) in 1982 in response to peer bullying attracted media and public attention, and by 1983, the Norwegian Ministry of Education initiated a nationwide campaign against school bullying (Olweus, 1993, 1999). In Japan (Sugimori, 2002), the suicide death of a 13-year-old in 1986 in response to bullying drew public attention to the issue, leading to several published works on the topic, but it was not until the suicide death of another youth in 1994, a victim of peer extortion, that the Ministry of Education in Japan initiated its own efforts to address bullying in schools. In North America, public awareness and concern about bullying came closer to the turn of the century. In Canada, the brutal torture and murder of 14-year-old Reena Virk in 1997 at the hands of seven peers (6 girls and 1 boy, see Godfrey, 2005), followed by a series of suicide deaths by severely bullied youths thrust bullying into the media spotlight. In the United States, the Columbine massacre in 1999 rallied fear and outrage among the public, when secondary students Eric Harris and Dylan Klebold carried out a planned 3-hour revenge, killing a teacher and 12 students and wounding 20 others before taking their own lives.

The tragic deaths of students in countries around the world as a result of school bullying have lead many to consider the morality of such behavior, although research on bullying as a moral act has been very limited. If there is any "silver lining" to these tragedies, it is the fact that they have raised public awareness regarding the problems of school bullying and have stimulated a dramatic increase in empirical research on the issue. When we reviewed the number of published works on bullying through online databases,[1] we found no articles or books on the topic from 1961–1975. From 1976–1985, there were 15 publications (12 books, 3 articles), and from 1986–1995, the figure had jumped to 242 publications (67 articles, 175 books). From 1996 to 2005, this figure had skyrocketed to over 1,600 publications (609 articles, 1039 books; see also Berger, 2007). Despite this proliferation of research, we still do not understand the mechanisms that lead one child to dominate another, although we do more fully appreciate the complexity of this issue.

- We now recognize that bullying is a unique form of interpersonal aggression characterized by repeated efforts to intentionally harm another individual over whom the bully or bullies enjoy(s) the advantage of greater power. Although power can come in many forms (see Vaillancourt, Hymel, & McDougall, 2003; Vaillancourt, McDougall, Hymel, & Sunderani, this volume), it is the imbalance of power that distinguishes bullying from other forms of aggression, at least theoretically, and makes such behavior more reprehensible and unacceptable. In the real world, however, it is often difficult for adults as well as children to distinguish the two (Vaillancourt et al., 2008).
- We now know that bullying can take many forms—physical, verbal, social (relational), and electronic (cyber bullying), and that it overlaps substantially with interpersonal prejudices, including discrimination based on race, sex, disabilities, weight, sexual orientation, etc. (e.g., Darwich, Hymel, Pedrini, Sippel, & Waterhouse, 2008; Hymel, White, Ishiyama, Jones, & Vaillancourt, 2006; Kowalski, 2000; Pearce, Boergers, & Prinstein, 2002). At the same time, acts of bullying are often ambiguous, especially to outside observers. Physical bullying is often construed as "horsing around" or "rough and tumble play;" verbal bullying can be mistaken for playful teasing among friends that can be dismissed if the perpetrator was "just kidding."
- And, despite traditional stereotypes of bullies as social outcasts that resort to such behavior because they lack social competence, we now know that bullies are often high in social skill and social intelligence (Björkqvist, Österman, & Kaukiainen, 2000; Kaukiainen et al., 1999; Sutton, Smith, & Swettenham, 1999a, b). In fact, in one Canadian study, over half of the peer-identified bullies were viewed as powerful and as enjoying high social status (Vaillancourt et al., 2003).
- Sadly, we have also come to recognize that, although only a small number of students admit to regularly engaging in bullying (e.g., on a daily/weekly basis), a substantial proportion of our students admit to engaging in bullying at least occasionally. For example, in a study of bullying among 13-year-olds from 27 countries (Krug, Dahlberg, Mercy, Zwi, & Lozano, 2002), a small minority of students admitted to bullying others frequently (once a week or more), ranging from 1–10% across countries. However, another 12–64% of students across countries admitted that they "sometimes" engaged in bullying. How is it that so many of our children are willing to take advantage of others who have less power than they do, even if only "sometimes?"

In this chapter we explore the role of morality in understanding bullying behavior, reviewing research on the social cognitive underpinnings of bullying among children and youth. First, we consider research examining links between moral development and moral reasoning and aggressive behavior, including bullying, asking whether children who engage in bullying display systematic deficits in moral reasoning and/or bullying. Next, we consider research examining how attitudes and beliefs play a significant role in motivating and maintaining behavior, including peer bullying, and go on to consider the implications of Bandura's (1999, 2002) social cognitive theory of moral agency for bullying among children and youth. We examine the degree to which children are able to "morally disengage" from their bullying of others. Moral disengagement, however, is not only a characteristic of individuals. Following Bronfenbrenner's (1979) ecological model emphasizing the need to consider the child in the context of his/her social environment, we also consider moral disengagement as a characteristic of groups and how group, as well as individual levels of moral disengagement, impact the likelihood of bullying. Finally, we consider the implications of this work for prevention and intervention efforts addressing school bullying.

Moral Development and Bullying/Aggression

Are children who bully morally deficient? Do they lack empathy for other human beings? Firm answers to these questions are surprisingly elusive, as few published studies have directly addressed these issues. Accordingly, we first consider studies investigating the relation between moral development and aggression, a topic that has received a great deal of research attention over the years. The study of moral development has witnessed an expansive transformation over the last two decades, with research in the late 1960s-80s strongly influenced by Kohlberg's (1981, 1984) cognitive developmental approach, giving way to research considering a number of alternative theories of morality (Eisenberg & Fabes, 1998; Nucci, 2001; Turiel, 2002). What has remained constant across theoretical frameworks is interest in understanding how moral reasoning affects behavior, especially aggression (Berkowitz & Mueller, 1986; Tisak, Tisak, & Goldstein, 2006). Although debate continues regarding definitions of aggression (see Coie & Dodge, 1998), in this chapter we define aggression as "any form of behavior that is intended to injure someone physically or psychologically" (Berkowitz, 1993, p. 3). Morality, in turn, is defined in terms of "an act's harmful consequences" (Turiel, 1998, p. 904). Both definitions underscore the notion of creating intentional harm and victimization (Arsenio & Lemerise, 2004).

Although delinquency and aggression are not considered synonymous, some of the earliest empirical research on the relation between aggression and moral reasoning focused on juvenile delinquents. Harking back to Lawrence Kohlberg's dissertation research in 1958, the study of moral reasoning among delinquents has continued for decades, with several reviews and meta-analyses appearing in the last 15 years (e.g., Nelson, Smith, & Dodd, 1990; Smetana, 1990; Stams et al., 2006) and consistent findings emerging across studies. Simply put, juvenile delinquents generally reason at a lower moral stage than age-matched non-delinquents. As Stams et al. (p. 697) conclude: "developmentally delayed moral judgment is strongly associated with juvenile delinquency, even after controlling for socioeconomic status, gender, age, and intelligence."

The relation between aggression and moral reasoning within the normal population has not been studied extensively (Arsenio & Lemerise, 2004). Nevertheless, studies consistently demonstrate that social cognitive processes underlie children's social/moral reasoning, with research on social information processing (SIP) models of social adjustment (Crick & Dodge, 1994), and domain models of moral development (Nucci, 2001; Smetana, 1995), together providing a more coherent account of connections between children's social reasoning and intentional behaviors involving victimization. In the absence of research directly examining links between moral reasoning/development and children's aggressive behaviors, Arsenio and Lemerise (2004) speculate on how morality may be associated with different forms of aggression. Specifically, they argue that proactive aggression (instrumental aggression motivated by expectation of a reward rather than anger), which they consider to be synonymous with bullying, should be more directly linked to moral reasoning than reactive aggression (aggression motivated by frustration and anger) in part due to the implicit moral questions that are raised when attempting to understand the processes that underlie such behavior. That is, it appears that proactively aggressive children eschew moral norms in favor of instrumental goals (e.g., "I want his jacket"). Consistent with this hypothesis, research has shown that children identified as aggressive, relative to their non-aggressive peers, tend to utilize a hostile attribution style and perceive aggressive responses in a positive light (Crick, Grotpeter, & Bigbee, 2002). In contrast, children who are characterized as prosocial appear to adopt relational goals (e.g., "I want to be his friend.") as opposed to instrumental goals (Nelson & Crick, 1999).

Still, Arsenio and Lemerise (2004) caution us regarding the complexity of the relation between moral reasoning and proactive aggression, citing the paradox inherent in the mechanisms that seem to activate a proactively aggressive response. Specifically, although proactively aggressive children appear to intentionally violate moral standards by deliberately choosing to harm others for instrumental gains, they also demonstrate the ability to take the perspective of the other, albeit without empathy. Further complicating the picture are studies showing that, although many aggressive children display deficits and/or biases in social information processing (Crick & Dodge, 1999), other research indicates that some bullies demonstrate rather sophisticated social reasoning and higher levels of social intelligence (see Sutton et al., 1999a, c). Thus, the nature of the social cognitive roots of aggression and bullying remain unclear.

In one of the few studies examining links between aggression and moral reasoning, Schonert-Reichl (1999) considered a Canadian sample of 108 elementary children (grades 5–7) and found that the relation varied for boys and girls. For girls, peer-rated aggressive behavior was *not* significantly associated with moral reasoning. For boys, a significant and *positive* relation emerged between moral reasoning and peer-rated aggression; boys who displayed *higher* levels of moral reasoning were also viewed as more aggressive. In explaining this somewhat paradoxical finding, Schonert-Reichl suggested that boys might justify and sanction aggressive behavior, if it is done for the "right" reason. Another possibility is that adolescent boys may view aggression as acceptable due to their focus on instrumentality and physical play (Crick & Zahn-Waxler, 2003). Relatedly, Pepler and Craig (2005) suggest that physical aggression in early adolescent boys may be a normative extension of the rough-and-tumble play that characterizes elementary boys.

Murray-Close, Crick, and Galotti (2006) also examined the links between children's moral reasoning and peer and teacher assessments of physical and relational aggression in a U.S. sample of 639 students (grades 4–5). They found that students generally rated physical aggression as more wrong and more harmful than relational aggression, but after that, the pattern of results became more complex. Girls, for example, were more likely than boys to view aggressive behavior as wrong and as harmful. As well, although boys and girls did not differ in their judgments of the harmfulness of physical aggression, girls were more likely than boys to view relational aggression as harmful. With regard to links between moral reasoning and aggression, Murray-Close et al. found that children who peers viewed as relationally aggressive were *less* likely to view relational aggression as *wrong*, although they were *more* likely to view relational aggression as *harmful*.

Murray-Close and colleagues (2006) also examined whether students viewed physical and relational aggression as a moral issue (fundamental right and wrong), a social conventional issue (governed by social norms used to uphold social structure and order) or a personal issue (as issues of privacy and person choice—such as choosing how to dress). Girls were more likely to perceive relational and physical aggression as a moral issue. Boys, especially physically aggressive youth, were more likely to employ social conventional and/or personal reasoning when considering relational and physical aggression. A similar pattern was observed among girls with regard to relational aggression. That is, relationally aggressive girls were more likely to adopt a social conventional orientation regarding relational aggression. Gender differences notwithstanding, in both cases, more aggressive children appear to be less likely to view aggression as a moral issue.

Taken together, the research reviewed above indicates that, despite rather clear evidence that delinquent youth demonstrate lower levels of moral reasoning than non-delinquent youth, the links between moral reasoning and aggression are less clear and less well researched. Studies to date, however, suggest that these relationships are likely complex, varying as a function of the type of aggression considered and the sex of the individual. Unfortunately, research has not directly investigated whether deficits in moral reasoning characterize children who bully.

Empathy and Bullying

A critical feature of moral behavior is the capacity for empathy (e.g., Hoffman, 2000). Empathy is believed to play a vital role in all human interactions, underlying prosocial behavior and the development of social relationships as well as contributing to the desistance of aggression (Eisenberg & Miller, 1987; Schonert-Reichl, 1993). Although debates abound regarding definitions of empathy and its measurement (see Zhou, Valiente, & Eisenberg, 2003), it is generally agreed that empathy is a multidimensional construct including both cognitive and affective/emotional components (Davis, 1994). Research on the relation between empathy and aggressive behavior among children and youth has received considerable attention (Cohen & Strayer, 1996; Miller & Eisenberg, 1988), with studies demonstrating that empathy provides a buffer against aggressive tendencies and behaviors, in part due to the notion that highly empathic individuals can emotionally anticipate the harmful effects that their behavior might have on another (Hoffman, 2000). Moreover, both cognitive and emotional components of empathy have been found to play a mitigating role in interpersonal aggression and violence (Joliffe & Farrington, 2004; Kaukianen et al., 1999; Pedersen & Schonert-Reichl, forthcoming).

Given traditional stereotypes of a bully as a brutish oaf who is intellectually challenged, anxious, insecure, and prone to resolve conflicts through violence (Olweus, 1993), it not surprising that many assume that children who bully are deficient in their ability to empathize with the feelings of others. However, as noted previously, more recent research has shown that at least some bullies actually demonstrate high levels of social intelligence (e.g., Sutton et al., 1999). We could find only three studies to date that have empirically examined the empathy–bullying link. The first is a study conducted by Endresen and Olweus (2001) in a large sample of Norwegian adolescents (13–16 years of age). They found relatively weak correlations between self-reported empathic responsiveness and bullying ($rs = -.06$ to $-.17$ for boys, $-.02$ to $-.19$ for girls), although their measure of empathy did not taken into account the multidimensional nature of the construct. More recently, the empathy-bullying link has been examined by Espelage, Mebane, and Adams (2004) in a sample of 565 American middle school students (grades 6–8), and by Gini, Albiero, Benelli, and Altoe (2007) in a sample of 318 Italian adolescents (grades 7–8). Both studies used a well-established measure of empathy—the *Interpersonal Reactivity Index* (IRI; Davis, 1983)—tapping both empathic concern (i.e., the emotional dimension of empathy) and perspective-taking (i.e., the cognitive component of empathy). Espelage et al. reported significant negative relations overall between self-reported bullying and both perspective-taking ($r = -.44$) and empathic concern ($r = -.45$), although the relations for empathic concern were stronger for boys than for girls. Gini et al. also found significant negative relations between peer-assessed bullying and both empathic concern and perspective-taking, but only for boys ($r's = -.28, -.19$, respectively). Research linking empathy and aggression has also shown stronger relations for boys (see Miller & Eisenberg, 1988).

Taken together, studies to date generally support the notion that children who bully, especially boys, report lower levels of both cognitive and affective empathy. Interestingly, both Endreson and Olweus (2001) and Espelage et al. (2004) found evidence that students' attitudes toward bullying mediated the relationship between empathy and bullying. That is, students high in empathy reported negative attitudes toward bullying and therefore were less likely to engage in such behavior. Future research is needed to determine whether the low to modest correlations observed between empathy and bullying differ depending on the social intelligence and status of the bully (Sutton et al., 1999). As skilled manipulators, some bullies may be able to cognitively understand the perspective of others, but are deficient with regard to the emotional components of empathy, lacking the ability to anticipate the *emotional consequences* of their actions.

Beyond Deficits in Moral Reasoning

Given evidence that at least some of the students identified as bullies are at serious risk for juvenile delinquency and criminality (Farrington, 1993; Olweus, 1993), it may well be that some bullies demonstrate a limited capacity for moral reasoning and empathy. However, delays or deficits in moral reasoning do not appear to fully explain how or why most children are willing to abuse power in their interpersonal relations at least occasionally. As Menesini et al. (2003) suggest, deficit models may not be well suited to explaining bullying, especially given evidence reviewed above that many students who bully actually demonstrate high levels of social intelligence. A more useful perspective may be consideration of the adaptive motivation that underlies bullying behavior (see also Smith, 1991; Smith, Bowers, Binney, & Cowie, 1993).

Research has long demonstrated that an individual's attitudes and beliefs about aggression plays a significant role in supporting such behavior (see Vaillancourt & Hymel, 2004, for a review). Aggressive children espouse more positive attitudes about aggression and violence than their non aggressive peers, expecting that aggression can result in more positive rewards and reduce negative treatment by others (Perry, Perry, & Rasmussen, 1986), and can enhance self-esteem (Slaby & Guerra, 1988). Expectation that aggression will result in positive outcomes is especially evident among children who display proactive forms of aggression (Crick & Dodge, 1996). With regard to bullying behavior per se, we know that children who bully others endorse more positive beliefs about the use of aggression in addressing social conflicts (Bosworth, Espelage, & Simon, 1999; Olweus, 1997). Bentley and Li (1995), for example, found that students who admit to bullying others, as compared to students who are victimized and those who are neither bullies nor victims, expect bullying to yield positive outcomes, and view aggression as a legitimate response, sometimes the "only alternative." Pro-aggression attitudes, however, do not tell the entire story.

An alternative perspective comes from Albert Bandura's sociocognitive theory of moral agency (Bandura 1999, 2002; Bandura, Caprara, Barbaranelli, Pastorelli, & Regalia, 2001). In articulating his theory, Bandura critiques the literature on moral development and moral reasoning, arguing that these theories have focused primarily on moral *thought*, with insufficient attention given to how moral knowledge and reasoning are linked to moral *action*. In contrast, his theory of moral agency posits that moral reasoning is translated into actions through a number of self-regulatory mechanisms or self-sanctions which provide the motivation for and the cognitive regulation of moral behavior. Children gradually adopt the moral standards of the social groups to which they belong, and over time, these standards of right and wrong become internalized and come to serve as guides for behavior (see also Harris, 1995). However, people can selectively activate and disengage these self-sanctions. Whether and how these guides and standards impact actual behavior is determined by self-regulatory processes. Specifically, Bandura argues that the individual monitors his/her behavior and evaluates that behavior in terms of their adopted moral standards and the circumstances in which the behavior occurred, cognitively regulating that behavior through the consequences that the individual applies to him/herself, leading either to enhancement of self worth or to self condemnation. Thus, moral agency can either inhibit inhumane or immoral behavior or encourage behavior consistent with personal moral standards.

Importantly, Bandura's (1999, 2002) theory posits that these moral self-regulatory mechanisms are not always in operation, and can be selectively activated and even "disengaged" as a function of a number of social and psychological processes. In fact, Bandura argues that the relation between one's moral standards and actual behavior is mediated by moral disengagement. For example, in one study examining moral disengagement and support for the use of military force against others, McAlister, Bandura, and Owen (2006) found that, in the United States, adult's level of moral disengagement increased following the September 11, 2001, attack on the World Trade Center and the Pentagon and with it came stronger support for the use of military force, including retaliatory strikes against terrorist sanctuaries and aerial bombing of Iraq. Specifically, Bandura identifies eight distinct mechanisms, clustered within four broad strategies, through which individuals can "morally disengage" from conduct that may well be considered reprehensible.

The first three mechanisms proposed by Bandura (1999, 2002) serve to make harmful conduct look good through *cognitive restructuring*. This can be accomplished through several different mechanisms, including (a) moral justification, (b) euphemistic labeling, and (c) advantageous comparisons. Through *moral justification*, negative behavior is portrayed as serving a worthy social or moral function, thereby making it more acceptable. According to Bandura (1999), this form of moral disengagement is evident in military conduct, in that "over the centuries, much destructive conduct has been perpetrated by ordinary, decent people in the name of righteous ideologies, religious principles and nationalistic imperatives … Adversaries sanctify their own militant actions but condemn those of their antagonists as barbarity masquerading as outrageous moral reason. Each side feels morally superior to the other" (p. 195).

With regard to school bullying, social justification may be more likely than moral justification, as in the case of viewing bullying as "normal" and therefore socially acceptable. When adults and/or peers minimize or ignore bullying, or fail to intervene, such behavior can be interpreted as condoning bullying. Silence is complicity. Children might also justify bullying behavior as necessary to "toughen up" peers or as an effective means of communicating social norms and expectations. In our own survey of nearly 500 students in grades 8–10 (Hymel, Rocke Henderson, & Bonanno, 2005), we found that 64% of the students agreed that "Bullying is just a normal part of being a kid," and 28% agreed that "In my group of friends, bullying is okay."

Inhumane and negative behaviors such as bullying can also be restructured through *euphemistic labeling*, or using language that makes negative acts sound respectable. Bandura (1999) offers the military example of describing the civilians killed unintentionally by bombs as "collateral damage." With regard to school bullying, children and youth often minimize verbal harassment by saying it was "just a joke" or that they were "just kidding." Adults sometimes minimize bullying behavior by noting that "boys will be boys." The term bullying itself, given its overuse, can mask the severity of the behaviors involved.

The last cognitive restructuring mechanism proposed is *advantageous or exonerating comparison*, which refers to making a negative act seem less harmful by comparing it to a much worse act. Bandura (1999) offers several examples, including the perception of terrorist suicide attacks as acts of "selfless martyrdom" (p. 196), or minimizing the destruction of Vietnam by the US military as an intervention aimed at "saving the world from Communism." Children and youth who bully others also make advantageous comparisons, citing their behavior in reference to the behavior of others, most often notorious school bullies (termed social comparison; Festinger, 1954). As well, some youth fail to recognize that many bullying behaviors would be considered illegal acts (e.g., extortion, assault, etc.). In fact, when we surveyed Canadian students across a number of high schools, we found that only 62–75% of students across different high schools agreed that some bullying behaviors were in fact criminal offenses; 25–38% did not agree. For them, bullying seems far less reprehensible that criminal acts.

A second moral disengagement process involves *minimizing one's agentive role* in the harm that is caused, something that can be accomplished through two distinct mechanisms: *displacement of responsibility* and *diffusion of responsibility*. Decades ago, a famous (or infamous) series of "learning" experiments by Milgram (1974) demonstrated that individuals are capable of inflicting great harm to others if some legitimate authority accepts responsibility for such acts. In these experiments, adults were instructed to administer electric shocks to another individual (a confederate) whenever they got an answer wrong. Only about a third of the subjects refused to continue these shocks despite indications (staged) that they were extremely painful. Most followed directions and administered the shock as long as the experimenter said that he took full responsibility for the consequences. Viewing the experimenter as ultimately responsible allowed subjects to defer personal responsibility for their actions. Similar displacement of responsibility was evident among the commanders of Nazi concentration camps, and among soldiers involved in the MyLai massacre in Vietnam (Bandura, 1999). Such clear assumptions of responsibility by authorities is rarely seen in everyday life, however. With regard to school bullying, students often refuse to take responsibility for addressing bullying, arguing instead that it is the responsibility of adults. Hymel et al. (2005) found that in one school, about half of the grade 8-10 students *agreed* that adults at school should be responsible for protecting students against bullying and *disagreed* that it was their responsibility to intervene when they see bullying.

Minimizing one's agentive role in harmdoing can also be accomplished through *diffusion of responsibility*. Specifically, personal agency and responsibility for negative or harmful acts can be obscured and minimized when such responsibility is shared within a group. Social psychology research is replete with studies demonstrating the power of the group. Importantly, these studies have shown that, not only is the number of people in the group important, but also the nature of the group composition. Individuals are most likely to conform when there are three or more people in the group (e.g., Lantané, 1981), where there is unanimity (e.g., Ash, 1955) and group cohesion (e.g., Clark & Maass, 1988), and when the group includes high-status individuals (Driskell & Mullen, 1990). These studies have important implications for the study of bullying given that bullying is a group phenomenon (Lagerspetz, Björkqvist, Berts, & King, 1982; Olweus, 1993; Salmivalli, Lagerspetz, Björkqvist, Österman, & Kaukiainen, 1996) that is often charged by students who are powerful and visible in their school. Indeed, Craig and Pepler (1997; Hawkins, Pepler, & Craig, 2001) have shown that peer group members are present in over 85% of bullying incidents and Vaillancourt and colleagues (2003) have shown that popularity and bullying is the rule rather than the exception, with over half of students identified by schoolmates as bullies being considered high status peers and only 10% of bullies considered low in social power.

Of concern is the process of deindividuation, or the loss of self-awareness and apprehension that occurs in groups (Festinger, Pepitone, & Newcomb, 1952). Individuals often engage in behavior with others that alone they would not think of doing in part because groups offer a sense of anonymity and hence, reduce self-consciousness. In groups, minor indiscretions culminate into increasingly disinhibited behavior (e.g., Diener, 1976, 1979), transforming normally conscientious and prosocial individuals into people who ruthlessly cheer on a classmate who is torturing another student. Consistent with these arguments, observational research by Pepler and Craig (e.g., Atlas, Pepler, & Craig, 1998; Craig, Pepler, & Atlas, 2000; Hawkins, Pepler, & Craig, 2001; O'Connell, Pepler, & Craig, 1999) indicates that some peers actively reinforce the child who is bullying over 50% of the time. Thus, in most bullying incidents, personal accountability and responsibility can be minimized as it becomes diffused across participants.

The third broad strategy (and seventh mechanism) proposed for moral disengagement (Bandura, 1999) is the tendency to *disregard or distort the negative impact* of harmful behavior, allowing the individual to distance him/herself from the harm caused, or to emphasize positive rather than negative outcomes that result. For example, one high school coach recently argued that the practice of "hazing" in sports was typically not harmful and in fact serves to "build community." In our own surveys of students in grades 8–10 (Hymel et al., 2005), we found that a substantial number of students endorsed statements that effectively distorted the negative impact of bullying, focusing instead on its potential positive effects: 33% agreed that "Bullying gets kids to understand what is important to the group"; 44% agreed that "Bullying helps to make people tougher," and 21% agreed that "Bullying can be a good way to solve problems."

Bandura (1999, 2002) also notes that harmdoing is much easier when the suffering of the victim is not visible. If so, more indirect forms of bullying and especially cyberbullying, which affords greater distance between perpetrator and victim, may be far easier to rationalize. Ironically, the tendency for children who are victims of bullying to hide their discomfort and pain may inadvertently contribute to moral disengagement among those who bully. Indeed, in 1999, Hamed Nastoh committed suicide, a final act in response to ongoing taunting by peers regarding his sexuality. No one fully appreciated the pain this peer harassment caused him; even his friends said that he would just shrug off the teasing, not showing how much it bothered him.

The last mechanism proposed by Bandura (1999) involves efforts to *dehumanize and/or blame the victim*, seeing the victim as somehow deserving of bullying or partially responsible for their own maltreatment. Bandura (2002) points out that, in war, enemies are often dehumanized prior to battle, making it easier for soldiers to engage in combat. To illustrate, he described Pope Urbane's speech in 1095 to the Crusaders in which he described the Muslim enemies as "despicable" and "degenerate" "barbarians" who are "enslaved by demons" (p. 104). Today, Muslim extremists defend jihad as self-defense against "decadent infidels." Similarly, American soldiers referred to Japanese soldiers as "Nips" during WWII and referred to Vietcong soldiers as "Gooks" during the Vietnam War. Similarly, students who bully will often describe their victims as "losers" and "pathetic." In our own survey of secondary students (Hymel et al., 2005), we found that 56% of students agreed that "Most students who get bullied bring it on themselves," and 67% agreed that "Some kids get bullied because they deserve it." Most students (87%) agreed that "Kids get bullied because they are different." As well, 29% agreed with the rationalization that "It's okay to join in when someone you don't like is being bullied."

The idea that individuals can rationalize and justify their negative behavior towards other is not new. Psychologists have long recognized that most, if not all people justify their thoughts and behaviors in an attempt to convince others, and themselves, that their ideas and actions are rational. Self-justification is a powerful motivator, and one that occurs most often when a person simultaneously holds two competing cognitions. Festinger (1957) used the term *cognitive dissonance* to describe the tension that occurs when two inconsistent cognitions are held. His theory of cognitive dissonance has important implications for the study of bullying and has much in common with the tenets of moral disengagement. For example, cognitive dissonance theory would predict that almost all children and youth who engage in bullying behavior would try to justify their egregious acts to make them more palatable or more compatible with their self-image. Because most individuals perceive themselves to be good, moral citizens (self-serving bias; see Hoorens, 1996; Leary & Baumeister, 2000), engaging in behavior that challenges this positive self-perception would lead to tension and in turn the need to reduce dissonance. Said differently, those who bully others need to convince themselves and others that their behavior was justified. "I am a good and reasonable person who hurt someone. I hurt her because she was annoying to everyone. Had she not been so annoying, I would have never done what I did to her." In this example, dissonance is reduced by making the victim culpable. Aronson (1999) aptly clarified that the theory of cognitive dissonance does not picture people as rational beings; rather, it pictures them as rationalizing beings (p. 185). Justifying negative thoughts and behaviors makes people who bully others feel good about themselves, albeit at the cost of their victim (Vaillancourt et al., 2008). Although dissonance reduction is good for self-esteem maintenance, in the long-run, it is maladaptive because the individual avoids critically examining their negative thoughts and/or behaviors and hence continues to violate the rights of others. To date, most of the research on cognitive dissonance and moral disengagement has been conducted with adults. Within that literature, several studies have demonstrated significant positive relationships between moral disengagement and aggressive behavior (Bandura, 1999, 2001, 2002; Bandura, Barbaranelli, Caprara, & Pastorelli,, 1996). Of interest then is whether these theories are applicable to school bullying among children and youth. Only a handful of studies have examined this possibility (Barchia & Bussey, 2007; Gini, 2006; Hymel et al., 2005; Marini et al., 2008; Menesini et al., 2003; Paciello, Fida, Tramontano, Lupinetti, & Caprara, 2008), but collectively results of these studies suggest that moral disengagement may well be a key factor in bullying.

Menesini and colleagues (2003) were the first to examine the links between bullying and moral disengagement in 179 children (9–13 years of age) from Italy and Spain. Moral disengagement was assessed by evaluating the degree to which students attributed particular emotions to a hypothetical bully, with emotions of indifference and pride being associated with moral disengagement, and emotions of guilt and shame being associated with moral responsibility. They found that peer-identified bullies, relative to peer-nominated victims or outsiders, when asked to take the perspective of a hypothetical bully, reported more indifference and pride, suggesting greater moral disengagement. Bullies were also more likely than victims or outsiders to use egocentric reasoning to justify their attributions of emotions associated with disengagement, focusing on "positive consequences and personal advantages" or distorting consequences to the victim.

Gini (2006) investigated the social cognitions and moral emotions (guilt, shame) of 204 Italian children (aged 8–11 years) who were identified by peers as typically engaging in particular participant roles (bully, assistant to bully, reinforcer to bully, defender for victim, outsider, and victim) across a number of hypothetical scenarios that assessed children's social cognitions by asking them to put themselves in the role of the bully. Results indicated that peer-identified bullies did not demonstrate social cognitive deficits in theory of mind tasks nor did they perform more poorly in identifying others' emotions. However, compared with children who were viewed as defenders, willing to intercede on behalf of victims, children who bullied others as well as those who provided reinforcement and assistance to bullies, reported significantly higher levels of moral disengagement; defenders reported the lowest levels. Thus, bullies are not the only ones likely to morally disengage, those who assist in and reinforce bullying behavior also show such tendencies.

Canadian studies, examining student self-reports of moral disengagement, have yielded results similar to those of our European colleagues. For example, in a sample of 494 youth in grades 8–10, Hymel and colleagues (2005) found that the highest levels of moral disengagement were reported by students indicating that they frequently bullied others; the lowest levels were reported by those students who indicated that they had never bullied others. Results of regression analyses revealed moral disengagement accounted for 38% of the explained variance in self-reported bullying behavior. Beyond these overall main effects, however, the degree to which children were able to morally disengage from bullying varied significantly as a function of how much peer victimization they had experienced, at least for some students. Specifically, students who bullied frequently reported high levels of moral disengagement regardless of their victimization experiences and students who seldom or never bullied reported consistently low levels of moral disengagement, regardless of their victimization experiences. However, for students who reported bullying "a few times" or "once in a while," the more victimization they had experienced, the less likely they were able to morally disengage.

Subsequent research has served to replicate and extend these findings. Indeed, both Barchia and Bussey (2007) and Dane and colleagues (2008) found that the relations between moral disengagement and bullying may vary across physical, verbal, and relational forms of bullying, suggesting that different cognitive processes may be involved for different types of bullying. Barchia and Bussey examined self-reports of moral disengagement among 1285 Australian youth in grades 7–10 and found that greater moral disengagement was associated, not only with more reported bullying, but also with fewer efforts to intervene on behalf of victims (see also Gini, 2006). In a sample of 16,879 Canadian children and youth ranging in age from 8–20, Dane et al. found that, across different forms of bullying, bullies and bully-victims reported greater moral disengagement than victims and uninvolved youth, but that the differences between these two groups was much larger among secondary than elementary school students. Finally, in a recent dissertation, Barchia (2008) examined the relations between moral disengagement and aggressive behavior over the course of a school year. She found that high levels of moral disengagement predicted greater aggression 8 months later, even after accounting for initial levels of aggression.

Taken together, results of these studies demonstrate significant links between bullying behavior and moral disengagement, assessed in a variety of ways, across samples and countries. Of interest to developmentalists, as well as educators, is how and how early such behavior might begin. Moral disengagement is a very gradual process. As Bandura (2001) notes,

> Disengagement practise will not instantly transform considerate persons into cruel ones. Rather, the change is achieved by progressive disengagement of self-censure. Initially individuals perform mildly harmful acts they can tolerate with some discomfort. After their self-reproof has been diminished through repeated enactments, the level of ruthlessness increases, until eventually acts originally regarded as abhorrent can be performed with little anguish or self-censure. Inhumane practices become thoughtlessly routinized. The continuing interplay between moral thought, affect, action and its social reception is personally transformative. People not even recognize the changes they have undergone as a moral self.

Initial insights into the development of moral disengagement and its links to aggression and youth violence comes from two recent European studies. In a cross-sectional study, Ortega Ruiz, Sanchéz, and Menesini (2002) examined moral disengagement among samples of 9- and 13-year-olds in Spain ($n = 59$) and Italy ($n = 60$) who had been identified by peers/self as aggressors, victims and externals (outsiders to the interaction but present). They found that reported moral disengagement varied as a function of a number of factors, including age, country, and gender and how moral disengagement was assessed. For example, they found that moral disengagement increased with age among aggressors and victims, but decreased with age for those less directly involved (externals). However, moral disengagement was found to be generally higher (across groups) at age 9 among Spanish children, but generally higher at age 13 among Italian children. Age-related differences in moral disengagement, then, may reflect more than simple developmental changes.

More recently, longitudinal research by Paciello, Fida, Tramontano, Lupinetti, and Caprara (2008) investigated changes in moral disengagement among 366 Italian adolescents who completed self-report measures of moral disengagement at ages 12, 14, 16, 18 and 20. Overall, they found that males endorsed higher levels of moral disengagement than females. As well, moral disengagement decreased with age overall, with the largest drop observed among youth between the ages of 14 and 16, and with females displaying greater declines than males. The authors suggest that this general decline with age is not unexpected, given that individuals' capacity for self-regulation, perspective-taking and social adjustment generally improve with age (e.g., Eisenberg, 2000; Eisenberg, Fabes, & Spinrad, 2006), leading to enhanced moral reasoning and moral agency.

Replicating and extending previous research, Paciello et al. (2008) reported significant correlations, both concurrent and predictive, between moral disengagement and aggression/ violence, especially among boys. For example, peer evaluations of aggression predicted higher levels of moral disengagement at age 14, and also predicted physical and verbal aggression at age 20, but indirectly through reported moral disengagement at age 14. Violence at age 20 was also predicted from moral disengagement six years earlier. Using latent class growth analysis, Paciello and colleagues distinguished four developmental trajectories for moral disengagement:

1. a "nondisengaged group (19% of males, 55% of females) who initially scored low on moral disengagement and whose moral disengagement continued to drop over time,
2. a "normative group" (52% of males, 38% of females) who initially reported moderate levels of moral disengagement which also dropped over time,
3. a "later desister group" (8% of males, 5% of females) characterized by moderate to high levels of moral disengagement initially that *increased* between the ages of 14 to 16 years then dramatically *decreased* at ages 16 to 20, and
4. a "chronic group" reporting moderate to high levels of moral disengagement that remained constant across time (21% of males, 2% of females).

Not surprisingly, the latter two groups reported greater aggression and more problems with violence, with the desister group showing a decrease in aggression whereas the chronic group did not. Although students in the chronic group reported initial levels of need for reparation that were comparable to that of students in the normative and desister groups, their need for reparation decreased over time suggesting a decline in self-sanctioning behavior. As Bandura (1999) has suggested, moral disengagement appears to be a gradual process.

Beyond the Individual

The research reviewed thus far has focused primarily on morality as a characteristic of the individual. Until recently, bullying has also been considered a problem residing within the individual. However, research from around the world has acknowledged that bullying is a group phenomenon (e.g., Bukowski & Sippola, 2001; Morita & Kiyonaga, 1986; Salmivalli, Lagerspetx, Bjorkqvist, Österman, & Kaukiainen, 1996; Sutton & Smith, 1999). Similarly, moral disengagement can also be considered as a characteristic of the group. Indeed, our own research on secondary students' (grades 8–12) attitudes and beliefs about bullying (e.g., Hymel, Bonanno, & Rocke Henderson, 2002; Rocke Henderson, Hymel, Bonanno, & Davidson, 2002) suggests that student endorsement of particular beliefs about bullying varies considerably across schools. For example, student endorsement of the statement, "Some kids get bullied because they deserve it." ranged from 40% in one school to as many as 71% in another. Student endorsement of the statement "Most students who get bullied bring it on themselves." ranged from 37 to 58% across schools. Justifications for bullying also varied across schools, with 36 to 51% of students agreeing that "Some kids need to be picked on just to teach them a lesson," and 29 to 44% of students across schools agreeing that "Getting bullied helps to make people tougher." In light of such variation, it becomes important to determine whether moral disengagement at the group level also contributes to bullying behavior.

Relevant here is research on the impact of normative beliefs, reflecting an individual's "cognitive standard" about the (un)acceptability of particular behaviors (Huesmann & Guerra, 1997).

Several studies have shown that normative beliefs about aggression can impact individual normative beliefs and, in turn, actual aggressive behavior (Henry et al., 2000; Huesman & Guerra, 1997; Slaby & Guerra, 1988). Similarly, with regard to normative beliefs about bullying, Salmivallli and Voeten (2004) surveyed a sample of 1,220 Finnish students (grades 4–6) and found that classroom norms contributed significantly to the prediction of behavior over and above grade, gender, and individual attitudes about bullying.

Do normative or collective beliefs about moral disengagement similarly impact bullying? Bandura and colleagues (1996) also suggested that collective moral disengagement would likely contribute to "the perpetration of social injustices." In the only study to date to address this question, Vaillancourt et al. (2006) examined the extent to which attitudes about bullying at both the individual and group level were related to individuals' experiences as a bully, victim and witness, using multilevel linear modeling. Nearly 17,000 students in grades 4 to 12 from 116 schools completed surveys tapping both moral engagement and moral disengagement as well as experiences with different forms of bullying (physical, verbal, social) as bully, victim and witness. Of interest was whether collective, or group level attitudes reflecting the larger school context would predict reported bullying over and above individual attitudes and beliefs. In level 1 of the analysis, information about individuals was considered (sex, minority status, level of moral dis/engagement), and in level 2, information about collective or group attitudes was considered, including the average levels of reported dis/engagement for the entire school. Results indicated that greater collective moral disengagement was associated with student reports of greater involvement in bullying, as perpetrator and as witnesses. Importantly, however, higher collective (school) levels of moral disengagement contributed significantly to the prediction of bullying (but not victimization), over and above individual characteristics and beliefs. Collective levels of moral engagement *as well as* disengagement contributed significantly to reported witnessing of bullying. Thus, greater moral disengagement at the group level can also contribute to bullying behavior.

Implications and Future Directions

As the preceding review indicates, research on the morality of bullying behavior is limited, making conclusions about the moral underpinnings of bullying among children and youth difficult. Further research is clearly warranted. For example, it would be useful to know if childhood bullies, many of whom are at high risk for later criminality (Olweus, 1993), demonstrate deficits or delays in moral reasoning, as has been shown for juvenile delinquents (Stams et al., 2006). Is it possible that delayed moral development is a characteristic that can distinguish children who continue to bully and morally disengage from those who desist (e.g., Paciello et al.'s [2008] "chronic" versus "desister" groups). Longitudinal research would be particularly welcomed here.

However, for the larger majority of students who bully "sometimes," deficits in moral reasoning may not be evident, as has been the case in establishing links between moral reasoning and aggression generally. Similarly, deficits in empathy may or may not characterize students who bully, depending on gender and the ways in which empathy and bullying are measured. The present review indicates that the most promising area of research, demonstrating consistent findings across studies, is that linking bullying behavior to moral disengagement. Children and youth who bully (like adults who bully) appear to engage in high levels of moral disengagement. Future research is needed to explore this link further, in an effort to determine causal relationships.

Can levels of moral disengagement be reduced with concomitant reductions in bullying behavior? Definitive answers to this question are premature given the current state of research in this area. However, a recent study by Marini et al. (2008) provides some optimism in this regard. In a sample of almost 17,000 Canadian youth aged 8 to 20 years, they found that the more children were involved in anti-bullying practices (home-based and/or school-based), the lower their levels of moral disengagement, with stronger associations found for males. Although such associations do not demonstrate causal relationships, they do lend some encouragement to parent and teacher efforts to address the underlying social cognitions that are believed to motivate negative behaviors such as bullying. In this regard, school-based programs aimed at encouraging social and moral competence, as well as moral engagement rather than disengagement may be especially promising.

Within the literature on moral development, moral educators have long demonstrated the value of moral dilemma discussions in fostering positive moral growth (see Nucci & Narvaez, 2008; Solomon, Watson, & Battistich, 2001). For many years, school-based, universal prevention programs have been developed to foster empathic and social-emotional-moral growth in students. Such programs continue today, with demonstrated success. For example, in Italy, Renati and Zanetti (2008) have recently demonstrated that a teacher-administered, classroom-based program called The Moral Alphabet, involving a series of eight, 2-hour moral dilemma discussions over a 3-month period, lead to significant reductions in moral disengagement relative to controls.

Another example is a Canadian program called the Roots of Empathy (ROE; Gordon, 2005; see www.rootsofempathy.org). ROE is a theoretically-derived, universal preventive intervention that facilitates the development of children's social-emotional understanding in an effort to reduce aggression and promote prosocial behavior. The cornerstone of the program is monthly visits by an infant and his/her parent(s) that serves as a springboard for lessons on emotion knowledge, perspective-taking, and infant development. Research on the effectiveness of ROE has yielded consistent and highly promising findings regarding the impact of the program across age and sex (Schonert-Reichl, 2005; Schonert-Reichl, Smith, & Zaidman-Zait, forthcoming; Schonert-Reichl, Smith, & Hertzman, 2007). Children who have participated in ROE, compared to those who have not, demonstrate advanced emotional and social understanding, as well as reduced aggressive behavior (specifically proactive aggression) and increased prosocial behavior.

Although a great deal needs to be learned about the manner in which dimensions of morality, such as empathy, moral reasoning, and moral disengagement serve to inhibit or exacerbate bullying behaviors, the current state of the research supports that this area may prove to be fertile in shedding light on the underlying processes and mechanisms of bullying, and in turn, provide much needed direction for the design and implementation of prevention and intervention programs aimed at reducing bullying in schools. Surely, there is no single route to decreasing bullying behaviors in children and adolescents. Our review suggests that considering the moral dimensions of bullying can yield new insights into the ways in which we understand and address this complex phenomenon.

Note

1. Publication count was based on a keyword search ("*Bullying, or Bully, or Bullies, or Bullied*") of PsycINFO and WORLDCAT (duplicates omitted). PsycINFO, the online version of *Psychological Abstracts*, includes citations and summaries of journal articles (from 1887 to the present), book chapters, books, technical reports, and dissertations related to psychology and psychological aspects from more than 1,300 periodicals and more than 25 languages. WORLDCAT is the largest and richest bibliographic database in the world, consisting of the merged catalogues of thousands of the Online Computer Library Center's (OCLC) member university libraries and research institutions (http://www.oclc.org/worldcat/default.htm), including 57, 968, 788 bibliographic records of books, visual materials, computer files, Internet resources, and other various types of media resources.

References

Aronson, E. (1999). *The social animal*. New York: Worth.

Arsenio, W. F., & Lemerise, E. A. (2004). Aggression and moral development: Integrating social information processing and moral domain models. *Child Development, 75*, 987–1002.

Atlas, R., Pepler, D. J., & Craig, W. (1998). Observations of bullying in the classroom. *American Journal of Educational Research, 92*, 86–99.

Atwood, M. (1998). *Cat's eye*. Minneapolis, MN: Sagebrush Educational Resources.

Bandura, A. (1999). Moral disengagement in the perpetration of inhumanities. *Personality and Social Psychology Review, 3*, 193–209.

Bandura, A. (2001). *Selective moral disengagement in the exercise of moral agency*. Paper presented at the Association for Moral Education, Kohlberg Memorial Lecture, Vancouver, BC.

Bandura, A. (2002). Selective moral disengagement in the exercise of moral agency. *Journal of Moral Education, 31*, 101–119.

Bandura, A., Barbaranelli, C., Caprara, G. V., & Pastorelli, C. (1996). Mechanism of moral disengagement in the exercise of moral agency. *Journal of Personality and Social Psychology, 71*, 364–374.

Bandura, A., Caprara, V., Barbaranelli, C., Pastorelli, C., & Regalia, C. (2001). Sociocognitive self-regulatory mechanisms governing transgressive behavior. *Journal of Personality and Social Psychology, 80*, 125–135.

Barchia, K. & Bussey, K. (2007, March). *The role of moral disengagement in bullying and intervention: The development of a moral disengagement scale for bullying*. Paper presented at the biennial meeting of the Society for Research in Child Development, Boston, MA.

Bentley, K. M., & Li, A. K. F. (1995). Bully and victim problems in elementary schools and students' beliefs about aggression. *Canadian Journal of School Psychology, 11*, 153–165.

Berger, K. S. (2007). Update on bullying at school: Science forgotten? *Developmental Review, 27*, 90–126.

Berkowitz, L. (1993). Pain and aggression: Some findings and implications. *Motivation & Emotion, 17*, 277–293.

Berkowitz, M. W., & Mueller, C. W. (1986). Moral reasoning and judgments of aggression. *Journal of Personality and Social Psychology, 51*, 885–891.

Björkqvist, K., Österman, K., & Kaukiainen, A. (2000). Social intelligence – empathy = aggression? *Aggression and Violent Behavior, 5*, 191–200.

Bosworth, K., Espelage, D. L., & Simon, T. R. (1999). Factors associated with bullying behavior in middle school students. *Journal of Early Adolescence, 19*, 341–362.

Bronfenbrenner, U. (1979). *The ecology of human development*. Cambridge, MA: Harvard University Press.

Bukowski, W. M., & Sippola, L. K. (2001). Groups, individuals and victimization: A view of the peer system. In J. Juvonen & S. Graham (Eds.), *Peer harassment in school* (pp. 355–377). New York: Guilford.

Clark, R.D., III, & Maass, S. A. (1988). The effects of majority size on minority influence. *European Journal of Social Psychology, 18*, 381–394.

Cohen, D., & Strayer, J. (1996). Empathy in conduct disordered and comparison youth. *Developmental Psychology, 32*, 988–998.

Coie, J. D., & Dodge, K. A. (1998). Aggression and antisocial behavior. In W. Damon (Series Ed.) & N. Eisenberg (Vol. Ed.), *Handbook of child psychology, Vol. 3: Social, emotional, and personality development* (pp. 779–862). New York: Wiley.

Craig, W. M., & Pepler, D. (1997). Observations of bullying and victimization in the schoolyard. *Canadian Journal of School Psychology, 13*, 41–60.

Craig, W. M., Pepler, D. J., & Atlas, R. (2000). Observations of bullying on the playground and in the classroom. *International Journal of School Psychology, 21*, 22–36.

Crick, N. R., & Dodge, K. A. (1994). A review and reformulation of social-information-processing mechanisms in children's social adjustments. *Psychological Bulletin, 115*, 74–101.

Crick, N. R. & Dodge, K. A. (1996). Social information processing mechanisms in proactive and reactive aggression. *Child Development, 67*, 993–1002.

Crick, N. R., & Dodge, K. A. (1999). "Superiority" is in the eye of the beholder: A commentary on Sutton, Smith, and Swettenham. *Social Development, 8*, 128–131.

Crick, N. R., & Zahn-Waxler, C. (2003).The development of psychopathology in females and males: Current progress and future challenges. *Development and Psychopathology, 15*, 719–742.

Crick, N. R., Grotpeter, J. K., & Bigbee, M. A. (2002). Relationally and physically aggressive children's intent attributions and feelings of distress for relational and instrumental peer provocations. *Child Development, 73*, 1134–1142.

Dane, A., Marini, Z., Vaillancourt, T., Short, K., Cunningham, L., & Cura, M. (2008). *Moral disengagement in physical, verbal, social & cyber bullying: Relation to bully/victim status*. Poster presented at the International Society for the Study of Behavioral Development, Wurzburg, Germany.

Davis, M. H. (1983). Measuring individual differences in empathy: Evidence for a multidimensional approach. *Journal of Personality and Social Psychology, 44*, 113–126.

Davis, M. H. (1994). *Empathy: A social psychological approach*. Madison, WI: Brown & Benchmark.

Darwich, L., Hymel, S., Pedrini, L., Sippel, J., & Waterhouse, T. (2008, March). *Lesbian, gay, bisexual, and questionning adolescents: Their social experiences and the role of supportive adults in high school.* Paper presented at the biennial meeting of the Society for Reseearch in Adolescence, Chicago.

Dickens, C. (1838). *The Life and Adventures of Nicholas Nickleby.* London: Chapman & Hall.

Dickens, C. (1839). *Oliver Twist.* London: R. Bentley.

Diener, E. (1976). Effects of prior destructive behavior, anonymity, and group presence on deindividuation and aggression. *Journal of Personality and Social Psychology, 33,* 497–507.

Diener, E. (1979). Deindividuation, self-awareness, and disinhibition. *Journal of Personality and Social Psychology, 37,* 1160–1171.

Driskell, J. E. & Mullen, B. (1990). Status, expectations, and behavior: A meta-analytic review and test of the theory. *Personality and Social Psychology Bulletin, 16,* 541–553.

Eisenberg, N. (2000). Emotion, regulation, and moral development. *Annual Review of Psychology, 51,* 665–697.

Eisenberg, N., & Fabes, R. (1998). Prosocial development. In W. Damon & N. Eisenberg (Eds.), *Handbook of child psychology* (5th ed., Vol 3), *Social, emotional, and personality development* (pp. 701–778). Hoboken, NJ: Wiley.

Eisenberg, N., Fabes, R. A., & Spinrad, T. L. (2006). *Prosocial development.* Hoboken, NJ: Wiley.

Eisenberg, N., & Miller, P. A. (1987). The relation of empathy to prosocial and related behaviors. *Psychological Bulletin, 101,* 91–119.

Endresen, I. M., & Olweus, D. (2001). Self-reported empathy in Norwegian adolescents: Sex differences, age trends, and relationships to bullying. In A. C. Bohart, C. Arthurs, & D. J. Stipek (Eds.), *Constructive and destructive behavior: Implications for family, school, and society* (pp. 147–165). Washington, DC: American Psychological Association.

Espelage, D. L., Mebane, S. E., & Adams, R. S. (2004). Empathy, caring and bullying: Toward an understanding of complex associations. In D. L. Espelage & S. Swearer (Eds.), *Bullying in American Schools,* (pp. 37–61). Mahwah NJ: Erlbaum.

Estes, E. (1944). *The Hundred Dresses.* New York: Harcourt Brace.

Farrington, D. P. (1993). Understanding and preventing bullying. *Crime and Justice, 17,* 381–458.

Festinger, L. (1954). A theory of social comparison processes. *Human Relations, 7,* 117–140.

Festinger, L. (1957). *A theory of cognitive dissonance.* Stanford, CA: Stanford University Press.

Festinger, L., Pepitone, A., & Newcomb, T. (1952). Some consequences of deindividuation in a group. *Journal of Abnormal and Social Psychology, 47,* 382–389.

Gini, G. (2006). Social cognition and moral cognition in bullying: What's wrong? *Aggressive Behavior, 32,* 528–539.

Gini, G., Albiero, P., Benelli, B., & Altoe, G. (2007). Does empathy predict adolescents' bullying and defending behavior? *Aggressive Behavior, 33,* 467–476.

Golding, W. G. (1959). *Lord of the flies.* New York: Penguin.

Gordon, M. (2005). *Roots of empathy: Changing the world child by child.* Toronto: Thomas Allen.

Godfrey, R. (2005) *Under the bridge.* New York: Simon & Schuster.

Harris, J. R. (1995). Where is the child's environment? A group socialization theory of development. *Psychological Review, 102,* 458–489.

Hawkins, D. L., Pepler, D., & Craig, W. (2001). Naturalistic observations of peer interventions in bullying. *Social Development, 10,* 512–527.

Henry, D., Guerra, N., Huesmann, R., Tolan, P., VanAcker, R., & Eron, L. (2000). Normative influences on aggression in urban elementary school classrooms. *American Journal of Community Psychology, 28*(1), 60–81.

Hoffman, M. L. (2000). *Empathy and moral development: Implications for caring and justice.* New York: Cambridge University Press.

Hoorens, V. (1996). Self-favoring biases, self-presentation and the self-other asymmetry in social comparison. *Journal of Personality, 63,* 793–817.

Hornby, N. (2002), *About a boy.* New York: Penguin.

Huesmann, L. R., & Guerra, N. G. (1997). Children's normative beliefs about aggression and aggressive behavior. *Journal of Personality and Social Psychology, 72,* 408–419.

Hughes, T. (1857). *Tom Brown's school days.* London: Seeley Service.

Hymel, S., Rocke Henderson, N., & Bonanno, R. A. (2005). Moral disengagement: A framework for understanding bullying among adolescents. *Journal of Social Sciences, 8,* 1–11.

Hymel, S., White, A., Ishiyama, I., Jones, L., & Vaillancourt, T. (2006). *Bullying among Canadian secondary students: Links to racial discrimination and sexual harassment.* Paper presented to the International Society for the Study of Behavioral Development, Melbourne, Australia.

Joliffe, D., & Farrington, D. P. (2004). Empathy and offending: A systematic review and meta-analysis. *Aggression & Violent Behavior, 9,* 441–476.

Kaukiainen, A., Björkqvist, K., Lagerspetz, K., Österman, K., Salmivalli, C., Rothberg, S., et al. (1999). The relationships between social intelligence, empathy, and three types of aggression. *Aggressive Behavior, 25,* 81–89.

Kohlberg, L. (1981). *The philosophy of moral development: Essays on moral development* (Vol. I). New York: Harper & Row.

Kohlberg, L. (1984). *The philosophy of moral development: Essays on moral development* (Vol. II). New York: Harper & Row.

Kowalski, R. M. (2000). "I was only kidding!" Victims' and perpetrators' perceptions of teasing. *Personality and Social Psychology Bulletin, 26*, 231–241.

Krug, E. G., Dahlberg, L., Mercy, J.A., Zwi, A.B., & Lozano, R. (2002). *World report on violence and health*. Geneva: World Health Organization.

Lagerspetz, K., Björkqvist, K., Berts, M., & King, E. (1982). Group aggression among school children in three schools. *Scandinavian Journal of Psychology, 23*, 45–52.

Lantané, B. (1981).The psychology of social impact. *American Psychologist, 36*, 343–356.

Leary, M. R., & Baumeister, R. (2000). The nature and function of self-esteem: Sociometer theory. In M. Zanna (Ed.), *Advances in experimental social psychology* (Vol. 32, pp. 1–55). New York: Academic Press.

Marini, Z., Dane, A., Vaillancourt, T., Cunningham, L., Short, K., & Cura, M. (2008). *Anti-bullying practices and moral disengagement: Key gender differences*. Poster presented at the International Society for the Study of Behavioral Development, Wurzburg, Germany.

Marr, N. & Fields, T. (2000). *Bullycide: Death at playtime*. Oxfordshire, England: Success Unlimited.

McAlister, A. L., Bandura, A., & Owen, S. V. (2006). Mechanisms of moral disengagement in support of military force: The impact of Sept. 11. *Journal of Social and Clinical Psychology, 25*, 141–165.

Menesini, E., Sanchez, V., Fonzi, A., Ortega, R., Costabile, A., & Lo Feudo, G. (2003). Moral emotions and bullying: A cross-national comparison of differences between bullies, victims and outsiders. *Aggressive Behavior, 29*, 515–530.

Milgram, S. (1974). *Obedience to authority*. New York: Harper and Row.

Miller, P. A., & Eisenberg, N. (1988). The relationship of empathy to aggressive and externalizing/antisocial behavior. *Psychological Bulletin, 103*, 324–344.

Morita, Y., & Kiyonaga, K. (1986). *Bullying: The ailing classroom* [Ijime: Kyoshitsu no yamai]. Tokyo: Kaneko Syobo. [Revised Edition in 1994].

Murray-Close, D., Crick, N. R., & Galotti, K. M. (2006). Children's moral reasoning regarding physical and relational aggression. *Social Development, 15*, 345–372.

Nelson, D. A., & Crick, N. R. (1999). Rose-colored glasses: Examining the social information processing of prosocial young adults. *Journal of Early Adolescence, 19*, 17–38.

Nelson, J. R., Smith, D. J., & Dodd, J. (1990). The moral reasoning of juvenile delinquents: A meta-analysis. *Journal of Abnormal Child Psychology, 18*, 231–239.

Nucci, L. (2001). *Education in the moral domain*. New York: Cambridge University Press.

Nucci, L., & Narvaez, D. (Eds.). (2008). *Handbook of moral and character education*. New York: Routledge.

O'Connell, P., Pepler, D., & Craig, W. (1999), Peer involvement in bullying: Insights and challenges for intervention. *Journal of Adolescence, 22*, 437–452.

Olweus, D. (1978). *Aggression in the schools: Bullies and whipping boys*. Washington DC: Hemisphere Press: Wiley.

Olweus, D. (1993). *Bullying at school: What we know and what we can do*. Oxford, England: Blackwell.

Olweus, D. (1997). Tackling peer victimization with a school-based intervention program. In D. P. Fry & K. Bjorkqvist (Eds.), *Cultural variation in conflict resolution: Alternatives to Violence* (pp. 215–231). Hillsdale, NJ: Erlbaum.

Olweus, D. (1999). Sweden. In P. K. Smith, Y. Morita, Junger-Tas, D. Olweus, R. Catalano, & P. Slee (Eds.), *The nature of school bullying: A cross-national perspective* (pp. 7–27). London: Routledge.

Ortega Ruiz, R., Sánchez, V., & Menesini, E. (2002). Violencia entre iguales y desconexión moral: Un análisis transcultural [Bullying and moral disengagement: A cross-national comparison]. *Psicothema, 14*, 37–49.

Paciello, M., Fida, R., Tramontano, C., Lupinetti, C., & Caprara, G. V. (2008). Stability and change of moral disengagement and its impact on aggression and violence in late adolescence. *Child Development, 79*, 1288–1309.

Pearce, M. J., Boergers, J., & Prinstein, M. J. (2002). Adolescent obesity, overt and relational peer victimization and romantic relationships. *Obesity Research, 10*, 386–393.

Pedersen, C. L., & Schonert-Reichl, K. A. (forthcoming). *Prosocial moral reasoning and empathy-related responding: Relations to prosocial and aggressive behaviors in delinquent and comparison youth.*

Pepler, D. J., & Craig, W. (2005). Aggressive girls on troubled trajectories: A developmental perspective. In D. J. Pepler, K. C. Madsen, C. Webster, & K. S. Levene (Eds.), *The development and treatment of girlhood aggression* (pp. 3–28). Mahwah, NJ: Erlbaum.

Perry, D. G., Perry, L. C., & Rasmussen, P. (1986). Cognitive social learning mediators of aggression. *Child Development, 57*, 700–711.

Renati, R., & Zanetti, M.A. (2008). *The moral alphabet: A moral skills development training to prevent aggressive behavior in school*. Poster presented at the third annual meeting of PREVNet, a Canadian national organization aimed at Promoting Relationships and Eliminating Violence, Toronto, Ontario.

Salmivalli, C., Lagerspetz, K., Björkqvist, K., Österman, K., & Kaukiainen, A. (1996). Bullying as a group process: Participant roles and their relations to social status within the group. *Aggressive Behavior, 22*, 1–15.

Schonert-Reichl, K. A. (1993). Empathy and social relationships in adolescents with behavioral disorders. *Behavioral Disorders, 18,* 189–204.

Schonert-Reichl, K. A. (1999). Moral reasoning during early adolescence: Links with peer acceptance, friendship, and social behaviors. *Journal of Early Adolescence, 19,* 249–279.

Schonert-Reichl, K. A. (2005). Effectiveness of the Roots of Empathy program in promoting children's social and emotional competence. In M. Gordon, *The roots of empathy: Changing the world child by child* (pp. 239–252). Toronto, Ontario: Thomas Allen.

Schonert-Reichl, K. A., Smith, V., & Hertzman, C. (2007, March). *Promoting emotional competence in school-aged children: An experimental trial of the "Roots of Empathy" program.* Poster presented to the Society for Research in Child Development, Boston, MA.

Schonert-Reichl, K.A., Smith, V., & Zaidman-Zait, A. (forthcoming). *Impact of the "Roots of Empathy" program in fostering the social-emotional development of primary grade children.*

Slaby, R.G., & Guerra, N. G. (1988). Cognitive mediators of aggression in adolescent offenders: I. Assessment. *Developmental Psychology, 24,* 580–588.

Smetana, J. (1995). Morality in context: Abstractions, ambiguities, and applications. In R. Vasta (Ed.), *Annals of child development, Vol. 10* (pp. 83–130). London: Jessica Kingsley.

Smetana, J. G. (1990). Morality and conduct disorders. In M. Lewis & S. M. Miller (Eds.), *Handbook of developmental psychopathology* (pp. 157–179). New York: Plenum Press.

Smith, P. K. (1991). Hostile aggression as social skills deficit or evolutionary strategy? *Behavior and Brain Sciences, 14,* 315–316.

Smith, P. K., Bowers, L., Binney, V., & Cowie, H. (1993). Relationships of children involved in bully/victim problems at school. In S. Duck (Ed.), *Understanding relationship processes. Vol. 2: Learning about relationships* (pp. 184–212). Newbury Park, CA: Sage.

Solomon, D., Watson, M., & Battistich, V. (2001). Teaching and schooling effects on moral/prosocial development. In V. Richardson (Ed.), *Handbook of research on teaching* (pp. 566–603). Washington, DC: American Educational Research Association.

Stams, G. J., Brugman, D., Dekovic, M., van Rosmalen, L., van der Laan, P., & Gibbs, J. C. (2006). The moral judgment of juvenile delinquents: A meta-analysis. *Journal of Abnormal Child Psychology, 34,* 697–713.

Sugimori, S. (2002, November). Education, bullying, and school absenteeism: Changing individual-group relationships among Japanese youths after 1990's. Paper presented in the symposium, *Social and political change in the new millennium: Japan and Canada in comparative perspective,* organized by D. Edgington, M. Nakamura, M. Creighton, S. Orbaugh, S. Salsberg, S. Heine, and Y. Tiberghien for the UBC Year of Japan (2002–2003), Centre for Japanese Research, University of British Columbia, Vancouver, BC.

Sutton, J., & Smith, P. K. (1999). Bullying as a group Process: An adaptation of the participant role approach. *Aggressive Behavior, 25,* 97–111.

Sutton, J., Smith, P. K., & Swettenham, J. (1999a). Bullying and "theory of mind:" A critique of the social skills deficit view of anti-social behavior. *Social Development, 8,* 117–134.

Sutton, J., Smith, P. K., & Swettenham, J. (1999b). Social cognition and bullying: Social inadequacy or skilled manipulation? *British Journal of Developmental Psychology, 17,* 435–450.

Sutton, J., Smith, P. K., & Swettenham, J. (1999c). Socially undesirable need not be incompetent: A response to Crick and Dodge. *Social Development, 8,* 132–134.

Tisak, M. S., Tisak, J., & Goldstein, S. E. (2006). *Aggression, delinquency, and morality: A social cognitive perspective.* In M. Killen & J. Smetana (Eds.), *Handbook of moral development* (pp. 611–629). Mahwah, NJ: Erlbaum.

Turiel, E. (1998). Moral development. In W. Damon (Series Ed.) & N. Eisenberg (Vol. Ed.), *Handbook of child psychology: Vol. 3. Social, emotional, and personality development* (5th ed., pp. 863–932). New York: Wiley.

Turiel, E. (2002). *The culture of morality: Social development, context, and conflict.* Cambridge, England: Cambridge University Press.

Vaillancourt, T., & Hymel, S. (2004). *The social context of aggression.* In M. Moretti, M. Jackson, & C. Odgers (Eds.), *Girls and aggression: Contributing factors and intervention principles* (pp. 57–74). New York: Kluwer.

Vaillancourt, T., Hymel, S., & McDougall, P. (2003). Bullying is power: Implications for school-based intervention strategies. *Journal of Applied School Psychology, 19,* 157–176.

Vaillancourt, T., Hymel, S., Duku, E., Krygsman, A., Cunningham, L., Davis, C., et al. (2006). *Beyond the dyad: An analysis of the impact of group attitudes and behavior on bullying.* Paper presented at the 2006 International Society for the Study of Behavioral Development conference, Melbourne, Australia.

Vaillancourt, T., McDougall, P., Hymel, S., Krygsman, J., Miller, K., Stiver, M., et al. (2008). Bullying: Are researchers and children/youth talking about the same thing? *International Journal of Behavioral Development, 32,* 502–511.

Zhou, Q., Valiente, C., & Eisenberg, N. (2003). Empathy and its measurement. In S. J. Lopez & C. R. Snyder (Eds.), *Positive psychological assessment: A handbook of models and measures* (pp. 269–284). Washington, DC: American Psychological Association.

9

The Popularity of Elementary School Bullies in Gender and Racial Context

CLAIRE F. GARANDEAU, TRAVIS WILSON, AND PHILIP C. RODKIN

Whoever the perpetrator, the experience of being bullied at school is always painful. However, being bullied by a highly popular peer who enjoys the support of many classmates undoubtedly aggravates the victim's plight. When targeted by an influential peer, the victim's feelings of help-lessness, isolation, and low self-esteem may be exacerbated. The popularity of the bully may also contribute to the participation of the peer group in the harassment and rejection of the target child. In fact, numerous studies demonstrate that many school bullies are perceived as popular (e.g., Rodkin, Farmer, Pearl, & Van Acker, 2000) and central in their social network (Xie, Swift, Cairns, & Cairns, 2002). Although their sociometric status or level of social preference—the degree to which they are *liked*—remains low (e.g., LaFontana & Cillessen, 2002), they are fre-quently nominated by peers as "popular."

There is now considerable evidence that social status plays a crucial part in the issue of bul-lying. Surprisingly, the popularity and preference components of status tend to work in oppo-site directions with respect to concurrent and future aggressive behaviors. Longitudinal studies show that high perceived popularity in children and adolescents predicts an increase in both overt and relational aggression over time (Cillessen & Mayeux, 2004; Sandstrom & Cillessen, 2006), suggesting that the achievement of high popular status may facilitate future bullying. At the same time, the desire to maintain this status may serve as an important motive for peer harassment. In contrast, being liked has a buffering effect on aggression. Sandstrom and Cil-lessen (2006) showed that high likeability at the end of elementary school was linked to lower levels of overt and relational aggression at the end of middle school.

Children's social status is relative to the peer ecologies in which they develop. Within the survey tradition, social status has conventionally been determined by averaging nominations by peers, and children's behaviors can be valued or stigmatized depending on their group's social norms (Wright, Giammarino, & Parad, 1986). Group formation at school is largely influenced by gender and ethnicity, which are significant identity markers across the lifespan. Gender seg-regation is particularly pervasive in childhood. Same-gender interactions are more frequent than cross-gender interactions (Maccoby, 1998) and most aggression is directed against same-sex peers (Craig, Pepler, Connolly, & Henderson, 2001; Pellegrini, 2002; Russell & Owens, 1999). However, children frequently nominate opposite-gender peers for sentiments such as animosity (Rodkin, Pearl, Farmer, & Van Acker, 2003), attraction (Bukowski, Sippola, & Newcomb, 2000;

119

Rodkin, Farmer, Pearl, & Van Acker, 2006), and for girl nominees, bullying (Dijkstra, Lindenberg, & Veenstra, 2007; Olweus, this volume). Ethnicity is another segregation factor (Hallinan, 1982) that may engender negative and (ideally) positive intergroup sentiments (Rodkin, Wilson, & Ahn, 2007). The collective importance of gender and ethnicity to the peer ecology lies with respect to common points of cleavage (e.g., Criswell, 1937) together with potential hotspots—aggression and bullying—that may suggest negative intergroup relations.

Our goal in this chapter is to consider how aggressive behaviors are differentially rewarded or sanctioned in terms of peer status as a function of gender and ethnicity. We also discuss the impact of crossing gender and ethnic boundaries on bullies' popularity. For instance, are boys who harass girls more or less popular than boys who harass only other boys (Rodkin & Berger, 2008)? In the first part of the chapter, we open with an examination of gender differences in the relation between two subtypes of aggression and two subtypes of status. Next, we investigate the link between bullying and status in cross-gender relationships. In the second part, we turn to the role of ethnicity in the association between status and aggression using a person-in-context perspective. We conclude with implications for practice.

Gender, Social Status, and Aggression

Gender Differences in the Association between Forms of Aggression and Forms of Status

The question of interest in this section is whether boys' and girls' social status are similarly associated with aggressive behaviors. A common finding across studies is that aggressive children of both sexes tend to be disliked but popular. A closer examination of these associations separately for each type of aggression and each gender reveals a more intricate picture. While our focus is on children, we will pay attention to the development of these trends into adolescence.

Social Preference Physically aggressive boys and girls are generally disliked by their peers (LaFontana & Cillessen, 2002), but overtly aggressive girls tend to be even more disliked than their male counterparts (Cillessen & Mayeux, 2004). This discrepancy is particularly high among adolescents (Salmivalli, Kaukiainen, & Lagerspetz, 2000). A somewhat similar pattern emerges for relational aggression. Being relationally aggressive is linked to low social preference for both sexes in most studies. Findings are clear for females; relationally aggressive girls are consistently found to be disliked (LaFontana & Cillessen, 2002) and their decrease in likeability over time is stronger than it is for boys (Cillessen & Borch, 2006).

However, the association between relational aggression and social preference is harder to define for boys. Relationally aggressive boys are disliked in some studies (Cillessen & Mayeux, 2004) but not others (LaFontana & Cillessen, 2002). In later years, male relational aggression has been shown to be negatively correlated with social preference (Cillessen & Mayeux, 2004; Vaillancourt & Hymel, 2006) or positively correlated with their acceptance by other boys (Salmivalli et al., 2000). Overall, relationally aggressive boys are not as disliked as relationally aggressive girls. Whatever the form, aggression has a slightly more negative impact on girls' likeability than on boys' and this trend becomes more pronounced with age.

Perceived Popularity Among fourth- and fifth-grade boys and girls, physical aggression is negatively correlated with perceived popularity (LaFontana & Cillessen, 2002), although this negative association generally disappears in later grades (Cillessen & Mayeux, 2004) or becomes positive (Vaillancourt & Hymel, 2006). However, a study of Greek children from grade 4 to 6 found a positive correlation between overt aggression and perceived popularity for boys and not for girls (Andreou, 2006). One possible explanation for the lack of consistency in these findings lies in the overlap between overt and relational aggression. Rose, Swenson, and Waller (2004) found that a positive association between overt aggression and perceived popularity may not hold after controlling for the effect of relational aggression. There is no clear difference between boys and girls in elementary school, but gender differences appear in adolescence when physical aggression has no effect on boys' popularity but negatively predicts girls' popularity (Rose et al., 2004). Therefore, overt aggression seems to be increasingly detrimental to girls in regard to both sociometric and perceived popularity, although this is not always observed in early grades.

This pattern of associations somewhat differs when the influence of relational aggression on perceived popularity is considered. Relational aggression has been found to positively predict perceived popularity for both sexes in a sample of students from grade 4 through 6 (Andreou, 2006) and from grade 5 through 9 (Cillessen & Mayeux, 2004), although LaFontana and Cillessen (2002) found no association among fourth- and fifth-graders. The general trend is for relational aggression to become more strongly and positively associated with perceived popularity (Cillessen & Borch, 2006; Vaillancourt & Hymel, 2006). As early as sixth grade, relational aggression predicts high perceived popularity more strongly for girls than for boys. Regarding perceived popularity, relational aggression is overall more rewarding to girls. Nevertheless, aggressive boys are never as disliked by their peers as are aggressive girls.

In adolescence, the relation between aggression and status is moderated by certain peer-valued qualities such as attractiveness, athleticism, or stylishness (Vaillancourt & Hymel, 2006). The possession of such characteristics emphasizes the gender differences mentioned above. Overall, these characteristics have a more positive effect on aggressive boys' social status than on girls'. Thus, these findings demonstrate that the strong resentment toward relationally aggressive girls cannot be easily compensated. Further research is needed to determine if peer-valued characteristics have similar effects among younger children.

Possible Explanations

Which factors contribute to these gender differences in the costs and rewards of aggression? These findings may in part reflect disparities between boys' and girls' social aspirations and conceptions of popularity.

Gender Differences in Social Goals   Research on social goals supports the view that boys and girls pursue different things in their relationships with peers. In middle childhood, girls' goals are primarily oriented toward intimacy and the formation of friendships (see Rose & Rudolph, 2006). They are more likely than boys to endorse goals that involve supportiveness and the maintaining of relationships (Rose & Asher, 2004). In contrast, boys' goals tend to be more oriented toward competitiveness and the pursuit of high status (Maccoby, 1998). Rose and Asher (1999) found that boys endorsed revenge goals and sought to promote their self-interest more than did girls. Studies with early adolescents confirm girls' greater proclivity toward intimacy and boys' greater concern for dominance and popularity (Jarvinen & Nicholls, 1996; Kiefer & Ryan, 2008).

The strong value that girls attach to intimate bonds may account for their deep resentment toward relationally aggressive female peers who imperil their friendships. It may also explain why relationally aggressive girls, whose behaviors allow them to secure relationships for themselves, are often popular. They possess what is valued by the group. Similarly, relationally aggressive boys may not be as popular as their female counterparts due to the smaller importance that boys attach to relationships. Nevertheless, boys who adopt dominant behaviors—such as physical aggression—may not be as disliked as aggressive girls because the pursuit of dominance goals is more normative among males (see also Dijkstra et al., 2007).

Consistent with these discrepancies in social aspirations, research has shown that both types of status have different functions for boys and for girls. In a study of associations between status in fifth grade and emotional adjustment in middle school, Sandstrom and Cillessen (2006) found that perceived popularity tended to protect boys, not girls, from internalizing symptoms, while the reverse was true for likeability.

Different Conceptions of Popularity   The findings on gender differences in the association between status and aggression may also indicate that girls and boys differ in their conceptions of popularity. It is striking that relationally aggressive girls manage to combine very high levels of popularity with very low levels of social preference. For boys, the gap between status subtypes is more moderate. Studies consistently show that the relation between status subtypes is weaker for girls than it is for boys (LaFontana & Cillessen, 2002) and increasingly so over development (Cillessen & Mayeux, 2004; Vaillancourt & Hymel, 2006), suggesting that females make a clearer distinction between the two subtypes, popularity and preference, than do males. A study with fourth and fifth graders showed that boys had more extreme expectations concerning a popular or unpopular same-gender target than did girls (LaFontana & Cillessen, 1998). This suggests that girls' conceptions of social status may be more complex than boys'. For girls, someone's popularity is hardly predictive of the degree to which they will like that person.

Implications for Bullying Processes in Boys' and Girls' Groups

What do these findings tell us about the influence of bullies and the plight of victims in male and female networks in school? They demonstrate that aggressive children can gain high levels of perceived popularity no matter their gender. Even though boys generally tend to strive for dominant status more than girls (Maccoby, 1998), girls' social networks may be similar to that of boys with regard to hierarchical structure (Gest, Davidson, Rulison, Moody, & Welsh, 2007). Ethnographic studies have indeed revealed that aggressive youth of both sexes may be at the top of the hierarchy of highly stratified cliques (e.g., Adler & Adler, 1998).

Victims' Support   Victims may be more likely to receive peer support in girls' groups because aggressive girls are more disliked than aggressive boys. Despite their prestige, the strong resentment that aggressive girls elicit suggests that their victims may benefit from the compassion, even tacit, of the peer group. Actually, girls have been shown to be more sensitive to the distress of others compared to boys. Espelage, Mebane, and Adams (2004) demonstrated that girls scored higher than boys on several measures of empathy, such as caring and consideration of others, and that empathy tended to inhibit bullying mostly for girls. Nevertheless, the powerful status accorded to relationally aggressive girls suggests that girls' friendships must be fragile whenever the group includes a bully. Benenson and Christakos (2003) found that girls ended their close same-gender friendships more frequently and did more things to harm these friendships than boys. Therefore, the vulnerability of girls' relationships may actually foster bullying and rejection of victims in their groups, despite girls' greater empathy.

Aggressive boys' behaviors are usually less stigmatized than aggressive girls'. Studies have documented that boys' attitudes toward bullying are more positive (Crick & Werner, 1998), which indicates that boys' groups may be more promoting of bullying and less supportive of victims. However, other findings suggest a more nuanced view. As mentioned above, boys' friendships may be more stable and solid than girls', albeit less intimate. This has been shown to have a protective function against bullying (Hodges, Boivin, Vitaro, Bukowski, 1999).

Processes of Influence   The stronger distinction between social status subtypes among girls may have important implications for group processes at work in bullying situations. The popularity of bullies is a major concern because it is thought to give bullies power to influence their peers into harassing other classmates. If popular-aggressive children are highly disliked—as in the case of relationally aggressive girls—we may infer that the female peers who emulate them do so out of fear, without inner consent. If popular aggressive boys are not as disliked, it is possible that boys experience less inner dissonance when participating in bullying. They may be driven less by fear but more by a desire to maintain a dominant status (e.g., Pellegrini, 2002). More research is needed to clarify how the influence that bullies exert on their peers works and whether these mechanisms differ significantly between genders.

Due to the pervasiveness of gender segregation in school, we explored relations between status and aggression among boys and among girls, and compared them. We now examine these relations in cross-gender relationships.

Cross-Gender Perceptions of Status for Aggressive Peers

Although prepubescent boys and girls have starkly gender-segregated social networks, even strong boundaries are permeable (e.g., Maccoby, 1998). As two cultures living in close proximity within the confines of a larger social unit (i.e., the classroom or school), intergroup dynamics inevitably develop (Rodkin & Fischer, 2003). Unfortunately, intergroup dynamics between boys and girls are often overlooked due to the common processing of sociometric variables. Specifically, in most studies investigating linkages between aggression and status, children's levels of popularity and preference are determined by averaging nominations given by peers of both genders, or given only by same-gender peers. In these cases, the perception of each child by cross-gender peers is not possible to examine (see also Olweus, this volume).

However, some studies have disaggregated peer nominations in order to determine how boys and girls perceive one another (Card, Hodges, Little, & Hawley, 2005; Dijkstra et al., 2007). One finding from these studies is that girls may find some aggressive boys popular. This trend had first been observed among adolescents, and can be discerned in the context of the athletic jocks (and not academic elites) of Coleman's (1961) *Adolescent Society*. In more recent research, Pellegrini and Bartini (2001) found that aggression in adolescent boys predicted their being invited by girls to a date. This remained true even after controlling for the effect of physical attractiveness and peer affiliations. Bukowski and colleagues (2000) reported that girls started being attracted to aggressive boys after the transition to middle school, while they consistently disliked their aggressive female peers. In middle childhood, Rodkin et al. (2006) reported that, among fourth to sixth graders, girls disproportionately nominated aggressive boys as cool, but the reverse finding (boys nominating aggressive girls) did not hold.

These studies suggest that children and adolescents may not only tolerate aggression more from boys than girls, but girls may feel attracted to boys because of it. As any parent could guess, this is cause for concern. It implies that male bullies' high status relies on multiple sources of peer support (i.e., same-gender, other-gender) and therefore is not fragile. Even in cases when boys' bullying is met with disapproval by their same-gender peers, approbation by some girls may enable male bullies to maintain their social clout. These findings also raise important questions. First, does attraction to aggressive cross-gender peers lead to cross-gender bullying? Second, are bullies who target cross-gender peers as popular as bullies who engage only in same-sex bullying? In other words, do associations between aggression and status apply similarly to same- and cross-gender bullying? Finally, the influence of early pubertal timing on girls' attraction to older, delinquent peers (e.g., Caspi, Lynam, Moffitt, & Silva, 1993) should not be forgotten in future studies of gender, interpersonal attraction, and aggression.

Boys Bullying Girls

Coexisting with positive dynamics, such as nominations for being attractive, popular, and "cool," girls and boys get involved in negative dynamics that—as in the adult world—are loaded with implications for social status and aggression. Regrettably, little is known about boys bullying girls and vice versa, although Olweus (this volume) suggests that boys are more likely to be bullies, girls to be victims (see also Rodkin & Berger, 2008; Veenstra et al., 2007). Studies on the prevalence and specificity of cross-gender bully-victim dyads are scarce. One reason is that same-gender bullying is more frequent than cross-gender bullying (Craig et al., 2001; Pellegrini, 2001; Russell & Owens, 1999), but a second reason is methodological. Most research focuses on bullies and victims but rarely on bully-victim dyads. Extension of knowledge on cross-gender bullying requires analyses of, specifically, who bullies whom (Berger & Rodkin, 2009; Rodkin & Berger, 2008; Veenstra et al., 2007).

Prevalence of Cross-Gender Bullying   Cross-gender bullying is not rare. In a Norwegian study of fifth- to seventh-graders, Olweus (1993) found that more than 60% of victimized girls reported being bullied mainly by boys. In examining same and cross-gender victimization in a sample of fifth-to eighth- graders, Craig and colleagues (2001) found that at least part of all reported victimization was carried out by cross-gender peers. For verbal victimization in particular, girls were targeted by boys almost as frequently as they were by female peers.

Research on antipathies suggests that many young boys and girls, far from ignoring each other, report having a high number of enemies among cross-gender peers. In a large sample of sixth graders, 37% of participants had at least one cross-gender mutual antipathy (Witkow, Bellmore, Nishina, Juvonen, & Graham, 2005). Rodkin et al. (2003) assessed relationships of antipathy by identifying dyads of third and fourth grade children who nominated one another as "liked least." Over three assessment periods, between 40–50% of antipathy dyads included one boy and one girl. An implication of this finding is that boys' harassment of girls may emerge from a climate of tense social relations between groups of boys and groups of girls beginning in middle childhood. The prevalence of negative sentiments suggests that norms that support agonistic behavior can be pervasive. Growth in antipathy involvement predicts increases in relational aggression for girls and physical victimization for boys (Murray-Close & Crick, 2006), and thus may constitute fertile ground for peer harassment (Card & Hodges, 2007).

Bully and Victim Popularity by Gender   Being a target of aggression by cross-gender peers is a different experience from being victimized by a peer of the same gender. Gender segregation is so well-established among youth that any violation of it may make provocation even less acceptable. Sroufe, Bennett, Englund, Urban, and Schulman (1993) showed that young adolescents who frequently engaged in "borderwork" across gender were perceived as unpopular by peers and adults.

The typical case of a popular bully harassing a lower status peer may be questioned when bullies and their victims are of different genders. Rodkin and Berger (2008) reported that the popularity of the victim and the bully depended on the gender asymmetry of the bully-victim dyad. The unique aspect of the Rodkin and Berger (2008) *who bullies whom* survey measure is that children are asked to identify bullies together with the children whom each bully most often harasses. Virtually no female bullies were reported using this measure with a sample of European American fourth- and fifth-graders; therefore, comparisons were between boys bullying other boys and boys bullying girls. In male-male dyads, the bullies were popular and the victims were unpopular, reflecting the traditional imbalance of power in bully-victim relationships (Olweus, 1993). However, when a boy bullied a girl, the female victim was popular and the male bully unpopular. Regardless of victim gender, male bullies were highly aggressive (i.e., > +2 SD). These results challenge the notion that bullies are always more powerful than their victims, at least in terms of social power. In line with a prediction from evolutionary theory, when bullying crosses gender boundaries, aggression may lose its status-enhancing function (Bjorklund & Pellegrini, 2002).

A central issue with boys harassing girls is whether male aggressive behavior signifies acute, adaptive if immature social organizing functions that structure new development and interpersonal relationships (Berger, Karimpour, & Rodkin, 2008; Hawley, Little, & Rodkin, 2007), or whether cross-gender bullying is a real marker of later sexual harassment and psychopathology (Rodkin & Fischer, 2003). The study of cross-gender bullying is definitely complicated by boys and girls' engagement in romantically ambiguous interactions. In an attempt to make contact with the other sex, youngsters resort to secrecy and games that include provocation, pushing, chasing, and teasing where physicality is valued. It is necessary to distinguish cross-gender bullying with no sexual component from cross-gender harassment of a sexual nature. It may be difficult to make a clear distinction between playful behaviors and actual bullying, but this must be a challenge for future work.

Sexual Harassment

Who Is Involved in Sexual Harassment at School?   Sexual harassment is defined as unwanted behavior of a sexual nature perpetrated by one individual upon another. Among high-school students, more than 80% report that they experienced sexual harassment by peers at least once. Among them, 86% claimed that the harassment occurred for the first time before sixth-grade (AAUW, 2001), thus underscoring that sexual harassment becomes an issue early in development. Youth of both genders can be sexually harassed and adolescents with early pubertal maturity are at increased risk (Craig et al., 2001). Male perpetrators of sexual harassment at the end of middle school can be former elementary school bullies with an interest in heterosexual relationships (Pellegrini, 2001). An investigation of middle-school students by Eder, Evans, and Parker (1995) revealed that boys who become sexually aggressive are typically at the top, or at the bottom, of their peer hierarchy.

A Culture of Sexual Aggressiveness   Research on sexual harassment in school emphasizes that it is often fostered by dysfunctional beliefs about male-female relationships and emerges in a culture of gender inequality (Duncan, 1999). Eder and colleagues (1995) note that most boys' interest in girls is primarily based on sexuality. Boys who initially demonstrate sensitivity towards girls or admit to having affectionate feelings for them are openly ridiculed by their male peers. This results in heterosexual relationships being approached in an aggressive manner and sexual activity being envisioned as a form of contest in which "scoring" matters more than intimacy (Fine, 1987). Even girls may contribute to this climate by teasing boys with references to their sexual inadequacy, for instance. Targeting this whole culture of sexual aggressiveness should be a priority of prevention measures, but attempts at intervention are made difficult by the diversity of individual episodes of sexual harassment.

The Issue of Variability, Identification, and Report   Sexual harassment varies in its degree of seriousness from flipping a skirt and making lewd remarks to obscene gestures and physical assault. Some of these behaviors may seem like playful or harmless "borderwork" from an outer perspective, when it is in fact experienced as hurtful. One concern for intervention lies in the difficulty of assessing the level of hurtfulness. Moreover, sexual harassment can be ambiguous in its interpretation. What is actually a humiliating act of aggression may be dismissed by outsiders as a flattering demonstration of sexual interest. The popularity of some female victims of male harassment may lead some girls to appear to others to be well-adjusted and trouble-free despite harassment from an aggressive boy (Rodkin & Berger, 2008).

Accurate identification of sexual harassment is complicated by its lack of visibility, as it typically occurs outside the presence of adult authorities. Visibility may also be related to the context of sexual harassment. When harassment takes place within romantic relationships, challenges to intervention are numerous. Not only is the aggression rarely visible, but the victim may appear responsible for it due to his/her initial consent to be involved in the relationship. Research showing that adolescent girls may be attracted to aggressive boys (Bukowki et al., 2000; Rodkin et al., 2006) suggests that behaviors which would not be tolerated from a same-sex friend may be condoned when exhibited by a cross-gender romantic partner. Rodkin and Fischer (2003) emphasize the similarity between victims of sexual harassment at school and victims of domestic violence. Girls and women both may gradually internalize rules of power inequality within the relationship, which encourages women to censor their own behaviors and react passively to abuse. In such cases, the victim is unlikely to report being harassed to the school authorities.

In sum, a climate of unequal social relations between boys and girls and the pervasiveness of aggressive norms are major factors in sexual harassment at school (Rodkin & Fischer, 2003). Importantly, gender inequality in school may be a reflection of gender issues in the society at large. If one particular group enjoys greater power in the community, it may impact the peer ecology at school. This question is certainly not restricted to gender. Belonging to an ethnicity that is more or less dominant in the larger cultural context may influence children's social status at school, as well as the perception of their aggressive behaviors.

Social Status, Ethnicity, and Aggression

The United States boasts a panoply of ethnic minority groups that continues to increase in diversity. Amid these currents of change, efforts to capture simple snapshots of different ethnic groups belie demographic complexities. But one thing is certain—children usually lead ethnically segregated lives, even when they are nominally integrated in school settings (DuBois & Hirsch, 1990; Hallinan, 1982; Hallinan & Teixeira, 1987; Rodkin et al., 2007). Moreover, when children do form cross-ethnicity peer relationships, they tend to be less stable (Lee, Howe, & Chamberlain, 2007) and of lower quality (Hallinan & Teixeira, 1987) than same-ethnicity relationships. Nonetheless, when schools have some ethnic diversity, the social networks of elementary school children are much more likely to be integrated by ethnicity than by gender (e.g., Singleton & Asher, 1979).

In some ways, children within the United States share similar social preferences and demonstrate similar patterns of social status regardless of ethnicity. Black and White children alike tend to be popular when they are athletic, prosocial, bright, or "cool," but children are unpopular when they are shy or withdrawn (Meisinger, Blake, Lease, Palardy, & Olejnik, 2007). Likewise, almost all children prefer to play with peers who are helpful, nice, generous, and understanding (Kistner, Metzler, Gatlin, & Risi, 1993). In contrast to this invariance for prosocial behavior and popularity (Wright et al., 1986), how children perceive aggressive peers depends more on group norms (cf., Rodkin et al., 2006) that may vary with the ethnic context of school environments. For instance, African American children are often perceived as more aggressive (Graham & Juvonen, 2002) and less likely to be victimized than their peers (Hanish & Guerra, 2000). Substance abuse is linked to peer admiration among affluent White boys but not among African Americans (Becker & Luthar, 2007). Understanding how perceptions of aggressive children vary by ethnicity is difficult due to four reasons: (a) ethnicity and socioeconomic status are confounded; (b) individual ethnicity takes on different meanings in different ethnic contexts; (c) for different ethnic groups, aggression may serve adaptive and/or deleterious functions, again depending on context; and (d) despite growing ethnic diversity in the United States, most research continues to focus primarily on European American and, secondarily, African American children. We address these challenges and explain how links among ethnicity, aggression, and social status can be situated within a peer ecology framework.

Socioeconomic Status

Poor urban communities, the seat for a disproportionate number of U.S. ethnic minorities, are often viewed as hostile environments in which many children learn to be aggressive to survive in their daily lives. Indeed, children in disadvantaged urban settings are more likely to be victims and perpetrators of violence (National Center for Educational Statistics, 2003), have greater exposure to aggressive youth gangs (Stevenson, 1997), and have more life stressors. Most low-income minorities live in dense geographical areas marked by concentrated poverty. A student who attends a segregated minority school is 16 times more likely to be in a high-poverty school than a student in a segregated White school (Orfield, Bachmeier, James, & Eitle, 1997). Insofar as poverty begets violence, minority children in poor areas may be more likely to be aggressive as a normative, adaptive response to environmental risks and experienced racism (Stevenson, 1997). In addition, research has begun to consider individual ethnicity within the broader ethnic context of a classroom or school, assessing ethnic segregation while taking account of community residential patterns (Mouw & Entwisle, 2006).

Ethnic Context

From an early age, children learn to identify themselves as part of their ethnic group and adopt behavioral norms consistent with culturally valued beliefs and practices. There is reason to believe that the ethnic composition of the settings for peer interactions may impact children's aggression, along with what and whom children perceive to be popular.

Are aggressive children popular in some ethnic contexts more than in others? It is unclear whether having a particular classroom or school ethnic majority makes it easier or more difficult for aggressive children to be popular. Across most U.S. classrooms, whether there is a decisive ethnic majority or ethnic diversity, children perceive athletic, prosocial, bright, and cool children as popular, and they view shy, withdrawn children as unpopular (Becker & Luthar, 2007; Luthar & McMahon, 1996; Meisinger et al., 2007; Wright et al., 1986). The dark side of popularity is more difficult to pin down. Some research finds that aggressive children are popular when African Americans are a decisive majority in the classroom but are not popular when European Americans are in the majority (Meisinger et al., 2007). Other research shows that adolescents in predominantly White suburban schools, and Latino and African American students in urban schools, proportionately nominate aggressive peers as popular regardless of ethnicity (Luthar & McMahon, 1996). Given this ambiguity, it may be unwise to compare ethnic contexts in and of themselves. Such comparisons do not contrast how individual children and groups of children are embedded in their school-based social networks, nor do they reveal how different patterns of aggression and popularity can emerge within the same school for children of different ethnic backgrounds.

Minority vs. Majority Status

Two well-documented studies, when taken together, illustrate how children's social status may depend on whether they are among the ethnic majority or the ethnic minority in school. Coie, Dodge, and Coppotelli (1982), in their study of a largely European American sample, found that elementary school children viewed well-liked European American but not well-liked African American children as leaders in their classrooms. However, in their next study of an exclusively Black sample (Coie, Finn, & Krehbiel, 1984, as cited in Coie, Dodge, & Kupersmidt, 1990), socially preferred Black children were clearly viewed as leaders. The difference between the two studies suggests that whether African American children are perceived as leaders or as popular has less to do with their ethnicity per se than with their status as an ethnic minority or an ethnic majority group in a school. Other work has substantiated the view that children who are among the ethnic minority in the classroom tend to have lower social status and are less preferred as social partners (Kistner et al., 1993; Singleton & Asher, 1979).

It may be that a similar effect holds with regard to the link between aggression and popularity. Xie, Li, Boucher, Hutchins, and Cairns (2006), working with a sample of African American first, fourth, and seventh graders from an inner-city neighborhood, found that first and fourth graders associated popularity with prosocial behavior, appearance, and self-presentation, not aggression. It is when African Americans are a minority group (Rodkin et al., 2000) or are among a diverse school population (Ferguson, 2000; LaFontana & Cillessen, 2002; Luthar & McMahon, 1996) that the positive association between aggression and popularity seems to come into play for African American children.

A closer look at one study reveals how being the ethnic minority or majority in a classroom matters for African American children. Rodkin and colleagues (2000) used a person-oriented approach to examine subtypes of popular fourth to sixth grade boys. Their sample included 15 100% African American classrooms and 35 classrooms with European American pluralities. There were two popularity clusters: (a) model (popular-prosocial) and (b) tough (popular-antisocial). Most popular boys across ethnic backgrounds were model boys, but European American boys were disproportionately model and African American boys were disproportionately tough. Differences between African American and European American boys' popularity profiles were concentrated in classrooms in which African Americans were a numerical minority. African American boys in plurality White classrooms were highly overrepresented as tough, whereas African American boys in all-Black classrooms were represented as tough at rates similar to European American boys in plurality-White classrooms.

What accounts for variation in the popularity of aggression among African American boys in different contexts? Some posit that in response to the racism and inequalities in United States society, African American youth, especially young males, have fostered an "oppositional" peer culture that embraces antisocial norms—including aggression—and devalues school achievement (Fordham & Ogbu, 1986). Indeed, majority White classrooms can be unwelcome—if not hostile—environments for African American children (Rodkin et al., 2007), so oppositional stances in these classrooms may serve self-protective adaptive functions. Nevertheless, it is worrisome that such oppositional attitudes may be associated with poor academic outcomes, particularly for boys (see Graham & Juvonen, 1998), when these attitudes are conjoined with other economic and educational barriers (Mickelson, 1990).

The social-cultural perspective (Aboud, Mendelson, & Purdy, 2003; Brown & Bigler, 2005) contends that the larger cultural context influences how children perceive themselves as well as their own and other ethnic groups. But to Bronfenbrenner (1996), peer ecologies and other proximal microsystems are the contexts of paramount importance (cf., Rodkin & Wilson, 2007, p. 252). How might these views be reconciled? For example, do African American and European American children who are ethnic minorities in their respective schools experience similar social and behavioral outcomes? To address this question, Jackson, Barth, Powell, and Lochman (2006) investigated 57 diverse fifth-grade classrooms (ranging from 3% to 95% African American) and found that African Americans were more socially preferred, less aggressive, and attained more leadership roles as the percentage of African Americans in the classroom increased. In contrast, sociometric ratings for White children were less sensitive to classroom ethnic composition and more stable across classroom contexts.

The asymmetric findings for White and Black students reported by Jackson and colleagues (2006) may reflect concurrent proximal and distal environmental effects. As the authors speculate, "White children might be buffered from the effects of being a classroom minority by their relatively greater presence and dominance in the larger community" (p. 1333). In contrast to these recent findings, Kistner and colleagues (1993) reported that *both* White and Black children were less socially preferred when they were minorities in their classrooms, concluding that "it is being a racial minority within one's class, rather than race per se, that is associated with children's social standing among peers" (p. 451). Research using an individual-in-context framework and adapting a social-cultural perspective (see Aboud, et al., 2003; Brown & Bigler, 2005) could help evaluate the differential impacts of being a minority in the classroom versus being a cultural minority in society at large over the elementary and middle school years.

If ethnic (or ethnicity-in-context) differences in the aggression-popularity association do exist in childhood, might these differences attenuate in adolescence? Cillessen and Mayeux's (2004) 5-year longitudinal study revealed that peer approval of antisocial behavior, especially relational aggression, increased significantly from fifth grade into middle school; perhaps developmental effects eventually override any ethnic differences. Becker and Luthar's (2007) study of affluent, suburban (mostly White) and low-income, urban (mostly African American and Latina/o) seventh graders supports the view that ethnic differences do subside in adolescence. Becker and Luthar (2007) found that *regardless* of economic or ethnic background, adolescents like peers with prosocial, positive traits, but tend to admire those who act aggressively toward others. Becker and Luthar concluded that "adolescents in the low-income urban context appeared no more admiring of physically aggressive bullying behaviors than their counterparts at the very top of the socioeconomic ladder" (p. 135), although they cautioned that peer admiration of physical aggression may pose more long-term risks for urban youth than for suburban youth, who typically benefit from multiple economic and social safety nets.

Thus, it is possible that the popularity of aggression may be confined neither to small, deviant subpopulations, nor to an oppositional culture, but instead may reflect a broad trend among boys and girls, European and African American children, rich and poor (Rodkin et al., 2006). Children's social networks may perpetuate proximally adaptive aggressive norms in which aggression and possibly bullying is admired in ways that are complicated by ethnic differences and divisions when a harmonious classroom is not established.

Ethnic Identity and In-group Processes

Ethnic identity may be a link between ethnicity, aggression and bullying, and popularity. Although there is no single, widely agreed-upon definition of ethnic identity, ethnic identity can be understood to be one's identification with, attitudes towards, and sense of commitment to one's ethnic group (Phinney, 1990). But while there is a vast literature on aggressive behaviors and attitudes among minority youth, researchers have paid less attention to understanding the relationship between ethnic identity and aggression (McMahon & Watts, 2002).

However, two investigations have initiated the foray. In their study of 330 urban middle school Latina/o and African American preadolescents (10–13 years old), Arbona, Jackson, McCoy, and Blakely (1999) found that, for both groups, ethnic identity was significantly correlated with non-fighting attitudes. The authors concluded, "It seems that, together with other known predictors, feelings of pride and commitment to one's ethnicity are related to these adolescents' self-reported attitudes and skills in resolving conflicts with peers in non-violent ways" (p. 336). McMahon and Watts (2002) also found that, controlling for global self-worth, African American youth with a stronger sense of ethnic identity exhibit more active coping strategies and less aggressive beliefs and behaviors. A better understanding of how the ethnic compositions of schools and communities influence associations between children's ethnic identity development, popularity, and aggression will likely raise new questions. For example, when a group of children comprises an ethnic minority (or majority) in school, might they adopt aggressive attitudes and behaviors to achieve greater group solidarity and protect their emerging sense of ethnic identity? If such is the case, how might ethnic minority and majority children differentially perceive aggressive norms, and, in turn, how might differences in perception impact intergroup relations?

Closely related to ethnic identity, social network and peer group processes may provide mechanisms that reinforce or diminish the association between popularity and aggression. Children try to achieve a positive image of their own group, and to do so they make favorable social comparisons and reward peers who exemplify group norms (Abrams, Rutland, & Cameron, 2003). Children's groups can exhibit a "loyalty effect," where children prefer in-group members who favor the in-group over the out-group and may even reject in-group peers who associate with out-group members (Castelli, DeAmicis, & Sherman, 2007), often with the cost of being preferred less by out-group members (see Bellmore, Nishina, Witkow, Graham, & Juvonen, 2007). When aggression is the norm within a particular ethnic group, in-group processes such as the loyalty effect may perpetuate and even enhance exclusionary norms. Key aggressive individuals may be accorded high status, while orchestrating norms and serving as a symbol of group pride and cohesiveness.

Ethnicity and Victimization

Patterns of bullying and victimization may vary by ethnicity and school or classroom ethnic context. For example, although African American students may be less likely to be victimized in diverse school settings (Hanish & Guerra, 2000; Graham & Juvonen, 2002), African American children who are victimized may experience particularly poor psychological outcomes. This may be explained by the social misfit effect (Wright,et al., 1986), which posits that individuals who deviate from group norms are prone to rejection.

Graham and Juvonen (2002) explored the social misfit model in terms of ethnicity and aggression among early adolescents. Their diverse sample included 418 sixth and seventh graders, where African Americans and Latinos comprised the majority, and White, Asian, and Middle Eastern students were in the minority. Compared to the other ethnic groups, African American students were disproportionately nominated as aggressive and less often nominated as victims of harassment. However, African American children who were victims experienced higher levels of loneliness and anxiety, and lower levels of self-esteem than did Latino victims or victims who were among other minority ethnic groups. These results support the view that victims can be perceived by their own ethnic minority group as social misfits when their behavior deviates from group norms and that, in turn, these victims may bear a more severe psychological burden. Taking it one step further, one might speculate that in same-ethnicity cases when perpetrators are highly popular, the psychological impact of the social misfit phenomenon is exacerbated.

The Role of Teachers

Teachers have a profound influence on how children perceive their peers, in part by orchestrating classroom norms (Chang, 2004; Farmer, Xie, Cairns, & Hutchins, 2007), but also via their interpersonal contact with individual students. Teacher feedback alone is strongly related to children's preferences for and perceptions of their peers (White & Jones, 2000; White & Kistner, 1992) and can trump a child's prior beliefs about a peer (Costanzo & Dix, 1983). More germane to our present discussion, teachers' beliefs strongly affect how children accept or reject aggressive and withdrawn children. For example, aggressive children are less admired in classrooms led by teachers who advocate prosocial norms (Chang, 2003). And given the power of a teacher's evaluations and beliefs on children's social status and perceptions, a child's social status is sensitive to whether teachers and children have the same ethnic background. Jackson and colleagues (2006) found that both Black and White children enjoy higher social status and are more often perceived as leaders when they and their teachers have the same ethnic background, although this effect was stronger for Black than for White students. The congruency between teacher and student ethnicity has also been found to affect children's academic self-concept (Mpofu & Watkins, 1997).

Implications for Practice

How can schools and educators responsible for children's well-being intervene to help cultivate healthy social environments for the youth in their care? We advocate ecologically-based interventions that target school environments of unequal social relations between ethnicities and between genders (e.g., Cohen & Lotan, 1995). Berger, Karimpour, and Rodkin (2008) elaborate implications of bullying and victimization for primary prevention, and the need for all violence to be eradicated in the elementary schools of tomorrow. Many of their suggestions for primary prevention can be adapted to address the concerns we have outlined in this chapter.

Although we recommend that interventions be tailored to individual schools, successful interventions will share four essential characteristics. They must: (a) adhere to a common philosophy created by the constituents of the school; (b) attempt to create change via multiple dimensions of the school social ecology, including children's social networks, formal and informal relationships among faculty and staff, faculty-student relationships, and community-school liaisons; (c) enlist administrators, teachers, students, and parents to implement thoughtful school policies and classroom curricula; and (d) assess the progress of these interventions by taking frequent measurements of children's perceptions of the school's social climate, children's social networks and social status, as well as experiences regarding bullying, sexual harassment, and ethnic relations.

Designing meaningful interventions that will work in educational settings is challenging. In an effort to take on some of these difficulties, we elaborate in Table 9.1 on the objectives and intervention measures that comprise a multifaceted, ecological approach to intervention. Our proposals recommend the involvement of a wide range of stakeholders to implement school policies and curricula that promote children's welfare via character education; open, respectful channels of communication among children and adults; and an awareness of how children

Table 9.1 Objectives and Practices of Ecologically-Based School Interventions

Objectives	Intervention Measures
1. Measurement *Identify groups of children (gender or ethnic groups) who suffer the most from a climate of inequality and assess the frequency and seriousness of unfair treatments.*	Administer "school climate" surveys to all students about their experiences with bullying and various forms of prejudice, such as racism and sexism. Track changes in students' perceptions of the school climate over multiple years and use the results to tailor school and classroom policies. Assess children's social status and social networks to identify the popular children who likely influence social norms as well as isolated or rejected children who, along with popular girls, may be victims of bullying.
2. Encourage reporting and proactive measures through institutional changes *Increase the likelihood that children will report bullying and sexual harassment.* *Create organizational structures that encourage proactive measures to foster healthy social environments.*	Create a school-based philosophy to galvanize and coordinate initiatives at the classroom and individual levels. Implement policies for reporting harassment while educating children and adults about these procedures. Train school personnel to correctly identify forms of bullying, sexual harassment and ethnic victimization. Provide quality counseling to victims and perpetrators of bullying and sexual or ethnic harassment.
3. Change norms via teachers *Use teachers' power of influence to promote norms of equity and respect for diversity.*	Provide training to teachers to (a) increase their awareness that interactions with students can encourage an imbalance of power by conveying racial and gender stereotypes, and (b) encourage cooperative learning activities with students that emphasize the strengths of diversity. Develop learning communities among teachers where teachers and administrators read and discuss contemporary research related to how the social climate of school impacts children's social and academic welfare. Establish honest, trusting relationships between teachers and students.
4. Change norms via students *Use children's popularity to counteract aggressive norms.* *Develop empathy towards other ethnic groups and the other gender.*	Assess children's social status to identify students who are the most influential in promoting social norms. Through discussions and role-plays, increase children's knowledge of the opposite sex and other ethnic groups (to prevent tolerance of aggression from cross-gender peers or objectification of girls by boys).
5. Curricula interventions *Value character education as much as academic learning.*	Implement a character education curriculum that is substantively rich and intellectually challenging for students. Teach children how to be assertive (active and self-protective while not putting others in danger) rather than aggressive (endangering others) to achieve their goals. Teach children how to resolve conflicts peacefully.

are embedded in their peer groups and social networks. There is no substitute for experimental designs with randomized controls in school settings to evaluate the effects of an intervention on meaningful setting (e.g., classroom climate, normative beliefs) and individual (e.g., less harassment, greater learning) adjustment outcomes.

Dedication on the part of educators to understanding the relationships and sentiments within their social milieu may have lasting impact. Human social interactions are patterned by gender and ethnic background in countless ways in every culture around the world, for children and for adults. There is deep value in establishing positive cross-gender and cross-ethnicity interactions, but there are powerful countervailing forces that can at times make antagonistic interactions between genders and ethnicities a valuable commodity. These forces, abstracted from the daily life and play of children, become manifest in children's investment in *social status*, or who has disproportionate sway over others, and *social networks*, or who affiliates with whom. Educators with awareness of these common patterns of social cleavage and interaction within the peer ecology have an opportunity to manage childhood social dynamics (cf., Mulvey & Cauffman, 2001) towards the development of safe schools with engaged, connected children.

References

Aboud, F. E., Mendelson, M. J., & Purdy, K. T. (2003). Cross-race peer relations and friendship quality. *International Journal of Behavioral Development, 27,* 165–173.

Abrams, D., Rutland, A., & Cameron, L. (2003). The development of subjective group dynamics: Children's judgments of normative and deviant in-group and out-group individuals. *Child Development, 74,* 1840–1856.

Adler, P. A., & Adler, P. (1998). *Peer power: Preadolescent culture and identity.* New Brunswick, NJ: Rutgers University Press.

American Association of University Women Educational Foundation (2001). *Hostile hallways: Bullying, teasing, and sexual harassment in school.* Washington, DC: American Association of University Women.

Andreou, E. (2006). Social preference, perceived popularity and social intelligence. *School Psychology International, 27,* 339–351.

Arbona, C., Jackson, R. H., McCoy, A., & Blakely, C. (1999). Ethnic identity as a predictor of attitudes of adolescents toward fighting. *Journal of Early Adolescence, 19,* 323–340.

Becker, B., & Luthar S. S. (2007). Peer-perceived admiration and social preference: Contextual correlates of positive peer regard among suburban and urban adolescents. *Journal of Research on Adolescence, 17,* 117–144.

Bellmore, A. D., Nishina, A., Witkow, M., R., Graham, S., & Juvonen, J. (2007). The influence of classroom ethnic composition on same- and other ethnicity peer nominations in middle school. *Social Development, 16,* 720–740.

Benenson, J. F., & Christakos, A. (2003). The greater fragility of females' versus males' closest same-sex friendships. *Child Development, 74,* 1123–1129.

Berger, C., Karimpour, R., & Rodkin, P. C. (2008). Bullies and victims at school: Perspectives and strategies for primary prevention. In T. W. Miller (Ed.), *School violence and primary prevention* (pp. 287–314). New York: Springer.

Berger, C., & Rodkin, P. C. (2009). Male and female victims of male bullies: Social status differences by gender and informant source. *Sex Roles, 61,* 72–84.

Bjorklund, D. F., & Pellegrini, A. D. (2002). *The origins of human nature: Evolutionary developmental psychology.* Washington DC: American Psychological Association.

Bronfenbrenner, U. (1996). Foreword. In R. B. Cairns, G. H. Elder Jr., & E. J. Costello (Eds.), *Developmental science* (pp. ix–xvii). New York: Cambridge University Press.

Brown, C. S., & Bigler, R. S. (2005). Children's perception of discrimination: A developmental model. *Child Development, 76,* 533–553.

Bukowski, W. M., Sippola, L. K., & Newcomb, A. F. (2000). Variations in patterns of attraction to same and other-sex peers during early adolescence. *Developmental Psychology, 36,* 147–154.

Card, N. A., & Hodges, E. V. E. (2007). Victimization within mutually antipathetic peer relationships. *Social Development, 16,* 479–496.

Card, N. A., Hodges, E. V. E., Little, T. D., & Hawley, P. H. (2005). Gender effects in peer nominations for aggression and social status. *International Journal of Behavioral Development, 29,* 146–155.

Caspi, A., Lynam, D., Moffitt, T. E., & Silva, P. A. (1993). Unraveling girls' delinquency: Biological, dispositional, and contextual contributions to adolescent misbehavior. *Developmental Psychology, 29,* 19–30.

Castelli, L., DeAmicis, L., & Sherman, S. J. (2007). The loyal member effect: On the preference for ingroup members who engage in exclusive relations with the ingroup. *Developmental Psychology, 43,* 1347–1359.

Chang, L. (2003). Variable effects of children's aggression, social withdrawal, and prosocial leadership as functions of teacher beliefs and behaviors. *Child Development, 74,* 535–548.

Chang, L. (2004). The role of classroom norms in contextualizing the relations of children's social behaviors to peer acceptance. *Developmental Psychology, 40,* 691–702.

Cillessen, A. H. N., & Borch, C. (2006). Developmental trajectories of adolescent popularity: A growth curve modelling analysis. *Journal of Adolescence, 29,* 935–959.

Cillessen, A. H. N., & Mayeux, L. (2004). From censure to reinforcement: Developmental changes in the association between aggression and social status. *Child Development, 75,* 147–163.

Cohen, E. G., & Lotan, R. A. (1995). Producing equal-status interaction in the heterogeneous classroom. *American Educational Research Journal, 32*, 99–120.

Coie, J. D., Dodge, K. A., & Coppotelli, H. (1982). Dimensions and type of status: A cross age perspective. *Developmental Psychology, 18*, 557–570.

Coie, J. D., Dodge, K. A., & Kupersmidt, J. B. (1990). Peer group behavior and social status. In S. R. Asher & J. D. Coie (Eds.), *Peer rejection in childhood* (pp. 17–59). New York: Cambridge University Press.

Coie, J. D., Finn, M., & Krehbiel, G. (1984). *Controversial children: Peer assessment evidence for status category distinctiveness.* Paper presented at annual meeting of the American Psychological Association, Toronto.

Coleman, J. S. (1961). *The adolescent society: The social life of the teenager and its impact on education.* Glencoe, IL: Free Press.

Costanzo, P. R., & Dix, T. H. (1983). Beyond the information processed: Socialization in the development of attributional processes. In E. T. Higgins, D. N. Ruble, & W. W. Hartup (Eds.), *Social cognition and social development: A sociocultural perspective* (pp. 63–81). Cambridge, England: Cambridge University Press.

Craig, W. M., Pepler, D., Connolly, J., & Henderson, K. (2001). Developmental context of peer harassment in early adolescence. In J. Juvonen & S. Graham (Eds.), *Peer harassment in school: The plight of the vulnerable and the victimized* (pp. 242–261). New York: Guilford.

Crick, N. R., & Werner, N. E. (1998). Response decision processes in relational and overt aggression. *Child Development, 69*, 1630–1639.

Criswell, J. H. (1937). Racial cleavage in negro-white groups. *Sociometry, 1*, 81–89.

Dijkstra, J., Lindenberg, S., & Veenstra, R. (2007). Same-gender and cross-gender peer acceptance and peer rejection and their relation to bullying and helping among preadolescents: Comparing predictions from gender-homophily and goal-framing approaches. *Developmental Psychology, 43*, 1377–1389.

DuBois, D. L., & Hirsch, B. J. (1990). School and neighborhood friendship patterns of Blacks and Whites in early adolescence. *Child Development, 61*, 524–536.

Duncan, N. (1999). *Sexual bullying: Gender conflict and pupil culture in secondary schools.* New York: Routledge.

Eder, D., Evans, C., & Parker, S. (1995). *School talk: Gender and adolescent culture.* New Brunswick, NJ: Rutgers University Press.

Espelage, D. L., Mebane, S. E., & Adams, R. S. (2004). Empathy, caring, and bullying: Toward an understanding of complex associations. In D. L. Espelage & S. Swearer (Eds.), *Bullying in American schools: A social ecological perspective on prevention and intervention* (pp. 37–61). Mahwah, NJ: Erlbaum.

Farmer, T. W., Xie, H., Cairns, B. D., & Hutchins, B. C. (2007). Social synchrony, peer networks, and aggression in school. In P. H. Hawley, T. D. Little, & P. C. Rodkin (Eds.), *Aggression and adaptation: The bright side to bad behavior* (pp. 209–233). Mahwah, NJ: Erlbaum.

Ferguson, A. A. (2000). *Bad boys: Public schools in the making of black masculinity.* Ann Arbor: University of Michigan Press.

Fine, G. A. (1987). *With the boys: Little League baseball and preadolescent culture.* Chicago: University of Chicago Press.

Fordham, S., & Ogbu, J. U. (1986). Black students' school success: Coping with the "burden of 'acting White.'" *The Urban Review, 18*(3), 176–206.

Gest, S. D., Davidson, A. J., Rulison, K. L., Moody, J., & Welsh, J. A. (2007). Features of groups and status hierarchies in girls' and boys' early adolescent peer networks. In P. C. Rodkin & L. D. Hanish (Eds.), *Social network analysis and children's peer relationships* (pp. 43–60). San Francisco: Jossey Bass.

Graham, S., & Juvonen, J. (1998). Self-blame and peer victimization in middle school: An attributional analysis. *Developmental Psychology, 34*, 587–599.

Graham, S., & Juvonen, J. (2002). Ethnicity, peer harassment, and adjustment in middle school: An exploratory study. *Journal of Early Adolescence, 22*, 173–199.

Hallinan, M.T. (1982). The peer influence process. *Studies in Educational Evaluation, 7*, 285–306.

Hallinan, M. T., & Teixeira, R. A. (1987). Opportunities and constraints: Black-White differences in the formation of interracial friendships. *Child Development, 58*, 1358–1371.

Hanish, L. D., & Guerra, N. G. (2000). The roles of ethnicity and school context in predicting children's victimization by peers. *American Journal of Community Psychology, 28*, 201–223.

Hawley, P., Little, T. D., & Rodkin, P. C. (Eds.). (2007). *Aggression and adaptation: The bright side to bad behavior.* Mahwah, NJ: Erlbaum.

Hodges, E. V. E., Boivin, M., Vitaro, F., & Bukowski, W. M. (1999). The power of friendship: Protection against an escalating cycle of peer victimization. *Developmental Psychology, 35*, 94–101.

Jackson, M. F., Barth, J. M., Powell, N., & Lochman, J. E. (2006). Classroom contextual effects of race on children's peer nominations. *Child Development, 77*, 1325–1337.

Jarvinen, D. W., & Nicholls, J. G. (1996). Adolescents' social goals, beliefs about the causes of social success, and satisfaction in peer relations. *Developmental Psychology, 32*, 435–441.

Kiefer, S. M, & Ryan, A. M. (2008). Striving for social dominance over peers: The implications for academic adjustment during early adolescence. *Journal of Educational Psychology.*

Kistner, J., Metzler, A., Gatlin, D., & Risi, S. (1993). Classroom racial proportions and children's peer relations: Race and gender effects. *Journal of Educational Psychology, 85,* 446–452.

LaFontana, K., & Cillessen, A. H. N. (1998). The nature of children's stereotypes of popularity. *Social Development, 7,* 301–320.

LaFontana, K., & Cillessen, A. H. N. (2002). Children's perceptions of popular and unpopular peers: A multimethod assessment. *Developmental Psychology, 38,* 635–647.

Lee, L., Howe, C., & Chamberlain, B. (2007). Ethnic heterogeneity of social networks and cross-ethnic friendships of elementary school boys and girls. *Merrill-Palmer Quarterly, 53,* 325–346.

Luthar, S. S., & McMahon, T. J. (1996). Peer reputation among inner-city adolescents: Structure and correlates. *Journal of Research on Adolescents, 6,* 581–603.

Maccoby, E. E. (1998). *The two sexes: Growing up apart, coming together.* Cambridge, MA: Harvard University Press.

McMahon, S. D., & Watts, R. J. (2002). Ethnic identity in urban African American youth: Exploring links with self-worth, aggression, and other psychosocial variables. *Journal of Community Psychology, 30,* 411–431.

Meisinger, E. B., Blake, J. J., Lease, A. M., Palardy, G. J., & Olejnik, S. F. (2007). Variant and invariant predictors of perceived popularity across majority-Black and majority-White classrooms. *Journal of School Psychology, 45,* 21–44.

Mickelson, R. (1990). The attitude-achievement paradox among black adolescents. *Sociology of Education, 63,* 44–61.

Mouw, T., & Entwisle, B. (2006). Residential segregation and interracial friendship in schools. *American Journal of Sociology, 112,* 394–441.

Mpofu, E., & Watkins, D. (1997). Self-concept and social acceptance in multiracial African schools: A test of the insulation, subjective culture, and bicultural competence hypotheses. *Cross-Cultural Research, 31,* 331–355.

Mulvey, E. P., & Cauffman, E. (2001). The inherent limits of predicting school violence. *American Psychologist, 56,* 797–802.

Murray-Close, D., & Crick, N. R. (2006). Mutual antipathy involvement: Gender and associations with aggression and victimization. *School Psychology Review, 35,* 472–492.

National Center for Educational Statistics. (2003). *Violence in U.S. public schools: 2000 school survey on crime and safety* (NCES Publication No. 2004-314). Washington, DC: U.S. Department of Education.

Olweus, D. (1993). *Bullying at school.* Oxford, England: Blackwell.

Orfield, G., Bachmeier, M., James, D., & Eitle, T. (1997). Deepening segregation in American public schools: A special report from the Harvard project on school desegregation. *Equity and Excellence in Education, 30,* 5–23.

Pellegrini, A. D. (2001). A longitudinal study of heterosexual relationships, aggression, and sexual harassment during the transition from primary school through middle school. *Journal of Applied Developmental Psychology, 22,* 1–15.

Pellegrini, A. D. (2002). Bullying and victimization in middle school: A dominance relations perspective. *Educational Psychologist, 37,* 151–163.

Pellegrini, A. D., & Bartini, M. (2001). Dominance in early adolescent boys : Affiliative and aggressive dimensions and possible functions. *Merrill-Palmer Quarterly, 47,* 142–163.

Phinney, J. S. (1990). Ethnic identity in adolescents and adults: Review of research. *Psychological Bulletin, 108,* 499–514.

Rodkin, P., & Berger, C. (2008). Who bullies whom? Social status asymmetries by victim gender. *International Journal of Behavioral Development, 33,* 473–485.

Rodkin, P. C., Farmer, T. W., Pearl, R., & Van Acker, R. (2000). Heterogeneity of popular boys: Antisocial and prosocial configurations. *Developmental Psychology, 36,* 14–24.

Rodkin, P. C., Farmer, T. W., Pearl, R., & Van Acker, R. (2006). They're cool: Social status and peer group supports for aggressive boys and girls. *Social Development, 15,* 175–204.

Rodkin, P. C., & Fischer, K. (2003). Sexual harassment and the cultures of childhood: Developmental, domestic violence, and legal perspectives. *Journal of Applied School Psychology, 19,* 177–196.

Rodkin, P. C., Pearl, R., Farmer, T. W., & Van Acker, R. (2003). Enemies in the gendered societies of middle childhood: Prevalence, stability, association with social status, and aggression. In E. V. E. Hodges & N. Card (Eds), *Enemies and the darker side of peer relationships* (pp. 73–88). San Francisco: Jossey Bass.

Rodkin, P. C., & Wilson, T. (2007). Aggression and adaptation: Psychological record, educational promise. In P. H. Hawley, T. D. Little, & P. C. Rodkin (Eds.), *Aggression and adaptation: The bright side to bad behavior* (pp. 235–267). Mahwah, NJ: Erlbaum.

Rodkin, P. C., Wilson, T., & Ahn, H-J. (2007). Social integration between African American and European American children in majority Black, majority White, and multicultural elementary classrooms. In P. C. Rodkin & L. D. Hanish (Eds.), *Social network analysis and children's peer relationships* (pp. 25–42). San Francisco: Jossey-Bass.

Rose, A. J., & Asher, S. R. (1999). Children's goals and strategies in response to conflicts within a friendship. *Developmental Psychology, 35,* 69–79.

Rose, A. J., & Asher, S. R. (2004). Children's strategies and goals in response to help-giving and help-seeking tasks within a friendship. *Child Development, 75,* 749–763.

Rose, A. J., & Rudolph, K. D. (2006). A review of sex differences in peer relationship processes: Potential trade-offs for the emotional and behavioral development of girls and boys. *Psychological Bulletin, 132,* 98–131.

Rose, A. J., Swenson, L. P., & Waller, E. M. (2004). Overt and relational aggression and perceived popularity: Developmental differences in concurrent and prospective relations. *Developmental Psychology, 40,* 378–387.

Russell, A., & Owens, L. (1999). Peer estimates of school-aged boys' and girls' aggression to same- and cross-sex targets. *Social Development, 8,* 364–379.

Salmivalli, C., Kaukiainen, A., & Lagerspetz, K. (2000). Aggression and sociometric status among peers: Do gender and type of aggression matter? *Scandinavian Journal of Psychology, 41,* 17–24.

Sandstrom, M. J., & Cillessen, A. H. N. (2006). Likeable versus popular: Distinct implications for adolescent adjustment. *International Journal of Behavioral Development, 30,* 305–314.

Singleton, L. C., & Asher, S. R. (1979). Racial integration and children's peer preferences: An investigation of developmental and cohort differences. *Child Development, 50,* 936–941.

Sroufe, L. A., Bennett, C., Englund, M., Urban, G., & Schulman, S. (1993).The significance of gender boundaries in preadolescence: Contemporary correlates and antecedents of boundary violation and maintenance. *Child Development, 64,* 455–466.

Stevenson, H. C. (1997). "Missed, dissed, and pissed": Making meaning of neighborhood risk, fear and anger management in urban Black youth. *Cultural Diversity and Mental Health, 3,* 37–52.

Vaillancourt, T., & Hymel, S. (2006). Aggression and social status: The moderating roles of sex and peer-valued characteristics. *Aggressive Behavior, 32,* 396–408.

Veenstra, R., Lindenberg, S., Zijlstra, B., De Winter, A., Verhulst, F., & Ormel, J. (2007). The dyadic nature of bullying and victimization: Testing a dual-perspective theory. *Child Development, 78,* 1843–1854.

White, K. J., & Jones, K. (2000). Effects of teacher feedback on the reputations and peer perceptions of children with behavior problems. *Journal of Experimental Child Psychology, 76,* 302–326.

White, K. J. & Kistner, J. (1992). The influence of teacher feedback on young children's peer preferences and perceptions. *Developmental Psychology, 28,* 933–940.

Witkow, M. R., Bellmore, A. D., Nishina, A., Juvonen, J., & Graham, S. (2005). Mutual antipathies during early adolescence: More than just rejection. *International Journal of Behavioral Development, 29,* 209–218.

Wright, J. C., Giammarino, M., & Parad, H. W. (1986). Social status in small groups: Individual-group similarity and the social "misfit." *Journal of Personality and Social Psychology, 50,* 523–536.

Xie, H., Li, Y., Boucher, S. M., Hutchins, B. C., & Cairns, B. D. (2006). What makes a girl (or a boy) popular (or unpopular)? African-American children's perceptions and developmental differences. *Developmental Psychology, 42,* 599–612.

Xie, H., Swift, D. J., Cairns, B. D., & Cairns, R. B. (2002). Aggressive behaviors in social interaction and developmental adaptation: A narrative analysis of interpersonal conflicts during early adolescence. *Social Development, 11,* 205–224.

10

Bullying in Primary and Secondary Schools
Psychological and Organizational Comparisons

PETER K. SMITH

In this chapter I will compare bullying in primary and secondary schools, and especially what appears to be a difference in relative success rates of anti-bullying interventions, in these two sectors. In this connection I will briefly summarize the history of large-scale school-based anti-bullying interventions, starting with the Norwegian campaign in the 1980s, the Sheffield (UK) project in the early 1990s, and similar projects in Canada, Belgium, Finland, the United States, Germany, Spain, and elsewhere. I will overview the varying rates of success of these studies. I will then review the replicated finding that apparent reductions in bullying are generally less in the adolescent years. Finally, I will discuss possible reasons for the often lesser impact of anti-bullying programs in the adolescent years, focusing on two main areas: developmental changes in pupils, and organizational changes in schools. I will conclude by discussing the challenges this raises for improving the effectiveness of anti-bullying intervention work.

School-Based Anti-Bullying Interventions

Over the last 20 years, there have been an increasing number of school-based anti-bullying interventions, some quite large-scale (see e.g., Smith, Pepler, & Rigby, 2004). There have by now been several reviews of these projects (e.g., Rigby, 2002; Smith, Ananiadou, & Cowie, 2003; Smith, Schneider, Smith, & Ananiadou, 2004; Baldry & Farrington, 2007). The historically relatively new wave of these interventions, in many European countries, Australasia and North America, is probably due to a range of factors: the rapid increase in our knowledge base in this period, including the severe focused effects on victims and more diffusely on the school community; the publicity given to incidence rates, and to pupil suicides due to bullying; the resulting pressure from former victims and parents, and court cases against schools and education authorities; and in some countries, relatively new legal requirements (e.g., in England since 1999, it has been a legal requirement to have a school anti-bullying policy; a considerable number of European countries have some such requirement; Ananiadou & Smith, 2002).

It is worth noting that some relevant interventions would be beyond the scope of the school; for example, parent training, parental stress management, dealing with community violence, moderating effects of the mass media. Also, some researchers (e.g., Galloway & Roland, 2004) believe that broad interventions to improve school climate are more important than "bully-focused" interventions. Nevertheless, almost all intervention programs include some direct anti-bullying components. Direct interventions against bullying can be classified as responding to the main causes of bullying. Some focus on the bullying children: those who get particular satisfaction (and rewards) from bullying because of their temperament, home background, and peer group; some focus on those children who may be at greater risk of being a victim, because of their temperament, home background, lack of good friends, disability, or other kind of difference; and some focus on the school as providing greater or lesser opportunities for bullying to take place, through the physical environment and the school ethos, and sanctions policy. Such school-based interventions date back over 25 years, to the first nationwide Norwegian intervention campaign of 1982–84; since then there have been large-scale projects in England, Ireland, Germany, Belgium, Spain, Switzerland, Finland, Italy, Australia, Canada, and the United States.

These campaigns have had varying success rates. The evaluation of the first Norwegian campaign in Bergen, by Olweus (1993), produced reductions in bullying of around 50%. Subsequent work in Bergen has also produced encouraging results, of around 35–45% (Olweus, 2004). However, most other studies (including replications of the Olweus program in Schleswig-Holstein, and in South Carolina) have had more modest impacts. A few studies have reported some negative results (Smith, Pepler, & Rigby, 2004).

Some explanations for these varying success rates include the nature of intervention, the length of intervention, the extent of support by researchers promoting and evaluating the intervention, the extent of ownership by school and effective implementation, the age or grade of pupils, and the neighborhood, community, and national context (Smith et al., 2003). Here, we will focus on one of these—the age, or grade, of pupils.

How do primary and secondary schools compare, in the literature on anti-bullying interventions? Some projects are just at one school level, either primary or secondary (e.g., Cross, Hall, Hamilton, Pintabona & Erceg, 2004, in Australia; Rosenbluth, Whitaker, Sanchez, & Valle, 2004, in the United States; Alsaker, 2004, in Switzerland). In two such cases it was nevertheless reported that interventions had more effect with younger pupils. In Finland, Salmivalli, Kaukiainen, Voeten, and Sinisammal (2004) found that intervention effects were generally greater in Grade 4 (10–11 years) than Grade 5 (11–12 years). In Italy, Menesini, Codecasa, Benelli, and Cowie (2003) found that intervention effects were greater in 12- than 13- or 14-year-olds. Some other studies do not report age differences (e.g., Pepler, Craig, O'Connell, Atlas, & Charach, 2004, in Canada; Limber, Nation, Tracy, Melton, & Flerx, 2004, in the United States; Ortega, del Rey, & Mora-Merchan, 2004, in Spain; Koivisto, 2004, in Finland; O'Moore & Minton, 2004, in Ireland). However, some direct comparison of effects in primary and secondary schools is available in five studies. These will be reviewed in turn.

Olweus (Norway)

Olweus now has data on a number of large-scale evaluations of the Olweus Bullying Prevention Program in Bergen and Oslo, Norway; the first program was from 1983–85, with subsequent programs in the late 1990s and early 2000s. In a report on the findings from six projects, Olweus (2005, p. 4) writes (following a description of uniformly positive results in primary schools) that:

> Results in lower secondary schools have also been clearly positive in about half of our intervention projects, while the other projects have shown weaker effects....We have good reasons to believe that the more varied effects in the lower secondary schools are connected to how teaching is organized at this level and to the student' entry into puberty with its attendant increase in opposition to adult authorities. In addition we

have registered that important components of the program are not implemented to the same degree as in the primary schools.

Hanewinkel: Schleswig-Holstein Project (Germany)

Hanewinkel (2004) reported findings from use of the Olweus program in 37 primary and secondary schools, from grades 3 to 12 (ages 9–18 years), in 1994–96; grades 3 and 4 are (later) primary, grades 5 to 9 are Hauptschule or basic secondary, while grades 10 to 12 are higher grades for continuing students. The intervention was modeled after the Olweus program, with school-, class-, and individual-level interventions. Hanewinkel assessed both low-level (sometimes or more) and high-level (once a week or more) levels of victimization, and also separately for direct and indirect victimization. In fact, the program had no positive effects (some negative) for indirect victimization. Looking at the more positive findings for direct victimization, and averaging over grades at each level, there was not much difference by sector for low-level victimization: changes (reductions) of 12.4% in primary, 14.4% in secondary, or 11.9% in secondary through to Grade 12. However, for high-level victimization, the reduction in primary grades at 13.6% is much greater than that in secondary at 2.1%, or secondary through to Grade 12, which showed an increase of 10.6%. Hanewinkel comments of the intervention that the effects were most visible in younger grades but does not speculate further on why this might be so.

Smith and Sharp; Cowie, Boulton, Thompson: Sheffield Project (England)

In this project, 23 schools in Sheffield (16 primary schools, 8–11 years; 7 secondary, 11–16 years) undertook to develop a whole-school anti-bullying policy and to implement from a range of optional interventions, over four school terms from 1992–1993. The percentage changes in being bullied (decreases) averaged 14.1% in primary schools, considerably more than the 6.8% in secondary schools (see Smith & Sharp, 1994).

Pitts and Smith: Home Office Project (England)

In this Home Office funded project in Liverpool and London, England, four schools (1 primary and 1 secondary in each city), took part in interventions between 1991 and 1993. The percentage change in those never bullied (increases) averaged 35% in the primary schools, but only 4% in the secondary schools. Again, in neither of these English projects were possible reasons put forth for these differences in success (Pitts & Smith, 1995).

Stevens, van Oost, and de Bourdeaudhuij: Flanders Project (Belgium)

In this project (Stevens, van Oost, & de Bourdeaudhuij, 2004), 18 schools took part (9 primary and 9 secondary schools, pupils aged 10–16 years) in interventions modeled on the Bergen and Sheffield projects, between 1995 and 1997. There were three schools each in three conditions: (a) Treatment with Support, (b) Treatment without Support, and (c) Control. The percentage changes (decreases) in victim rates after 2 years were: for Treatment with Support, primary 3%, secondary 0%; for Treatment without Support, primary 6%, secondary 1%; for Control, primary 3%, secondary 1%. Changes are small, but in all conditions larger in the primary schools; as Stevens, de Bourdeaudhuij and van Oost (2000) comment, "The results revealed clear differences between the primary and secondary school level" (p. 206). The authors cite as possible reasons, developmental changes in conformity, and organizational differences between primary and secondary schools; within the latter category they cite more complex timetables and more difficulties for teachers to react (to bullying), in secondary schools, and more difficulty in program implementation.

Why Are Interventions Less Effective in Secondary Schools?

It does appear that when the success rates of interventions have been directly compared between primary and secondary schools, changes in secondary schools are smaller. Why should this be so? I reviewed some evidence concerning this at the National Coalition Against Bullying conference in Melbourne, Australia, in 2005, drawing on my own review material and the writings of Stevens and colleagues (2000). Subsequently, I have received comments on this issue from Olweus (personal communication, 2007; reproduced verbatim in appendix A). The main factors suggested are Developmental Changes, as children reach puberty and adolescence in secondary school, and Organizational Changes, related to the larger size and more complex organization of secondary (compared to primary) schools.

Developmental Changes   Adolescence has traditionally been seen as a period of turmoil and rebellion, initially based on psychoanalytic theorizing from the earlier twentieth century. While an over-emphasis on this was later put in perspective (e.g., Rutter, Graham, Chadwick, & Yule, 1976), nevertheless the distinctive nature of adolescence has been re-affirmed in much recent research. For example, Arnett (1999) contends that adolescence is characterized by conflict with parents, mood disruption, and risk behaviors; albeit moderated by cultural and socialization factors. Biological and cognitive changes in the adolescent years (such as neural and hormonal changes; sexual maturity; cognitive changes, adolescent egocentrism and the imaginary audience, the search for identity) result in changes in relationships. These can be readily understood from an evolutionary developmental psychology perspective, as broadly adaptive for many adolescents as they show their independence from parents and find and display their status in the peer group at a time when this is important for becoming attractive to the opposite sex (Bjorklund & Pellegrini, 2002; Weisfeld & Janisse, 2005). Particularly relevant in understanding bullying are:

1. Changes in pupil-pupil relationships
2. Changes in pupil attitudes to adults and school
3. Greater risk-taking and anti-social behavior generally
4. An increasing stability of victim and bullying tendencies, with age

Organizational Changes   Secondary schools are much larger than primary schools. In many countries and school systems, primary schools typically have around 100–200 pupils, whereas secondary schools may have 500–1,000 pupils. Inevitably secondary schools have a more complex organization, with more hierarchical layers and specialist roles in the teaching staff. In primary schools, most teaching is in one homeroom, so that the class-based peer group is rather constant and the class teacher has a formative influence. In secondary schools, with more specialist or optional subjects and more banding by ability according to subject, pupils often move to different classrooms and have varying class peers in different subjects; they may have their own tutor group, but there is likely no single teacher with the same influence as in the primary school. These could have implications for intervention programs as:

5. Change is more difficult in large organizations and intervention programs are less well-implemented.

6. The curriculum in secondary schools focuses more on traditional subject matter and examinations, and places less emphasis on personal and social education.
7. Teachers' roles may differ; specifically teachers in secondary schools may see responsibility for dealing with bullying as more diffused, and find it more difficult to react quickly to incidents.

These various explanations will be considered in turn, to assess what evidence may support them.

Developmental Changes

Pupils enter secondary school around age 11 years, shortly before or at the beginning of the period of puberty for most adolescents. The current age of menarche in Western societies is around 12–13 years (Hermann-Giddens, Slora, & Wasserman, 1997); with spermache for boys some 18 months later. Puberty is brought about by an increase in hormonal activity, specifically growth hormones, and adrenocorticotrophic and gonadotrophic hormones, which, in turn, bring about the growth spurt and changes in sexual characteristics and sexual maturity. These obviously affect behavior through the young person's awareness of these changes, and the fact that they are now able to have children themselves. There have been decades of debate about the extent to which these hormonal changes also have direct effects on behavior, with evidence, for example, that the onset of puberty increases parent-child distance and conflict, independent of chronological age (Steinberg, 1988). The pathways appear complicated, and Buchanan, Eccles, and Becker (1992, p. 101) concluded that "We have only begun to comprehend the many ways in which hormones affect and are affected by human emotions and behavior."

More recent work has placed greater emphasis on puberty and brain development (Blakemore & Choudhury, 2006; Romer & Walker, 2007). Just prior to puberty, there is an increase in grey matter, followed by a period of synaptic pruning after puberty which occurs mainly in the frontal cortex. It appears that a lot of remodeling of the brain is going on in areas that affect emotional regulation, response inhibition, planning, and executive functioning. There is some evidence that during this period the brain areas mediating emotional experience change more rapidly than those mediating cognitive regulation (Monk et al., 2003). These differential changes may well contribute to relevant aspects such as greater self-focus in adolescence and greater risk-taking.

Whether due to direct or indirect hormonal influences, neural developmental changes, or to more sociocultural factors such as expectations about and stereotypes of adolescence, this period is generally recognized as a time of turmoil, of increased peer pressure, and of strains on adult relationships, especially those in positions of authority (parents, teachers). A number of well-documented changes in adolescence could help understand why at least some adolescents become more resistant to anti-bullying interventions.

1. Changes in Pupil-Pupil Relationships

Characteristic changes in adolescence include more anxiety about friendships and more conformity to peer pressure, especially in anti-social situations; this increase in concern about peer relationships and status with same-sex and opposite-sex peers can lead to both bullying as an attempt to enhance status, and negative attitudes toward victims (and schemes to protect victims) as a way of protecting status.

More Anxiety about Friendships   Anxieties about friendships with peers appear to peak at early adolescence. For example Coleman (1980) asked adolescents to complete unfinished sentences about friendships in a small group, and analyzed the results for their emotional content. Themes of anxiety and fear of rejection by friends increased from 11 to 13 and then to 15 years, but declined by 17 years (the effect being stronger for girls than boys).

More Conformity to Peer Pressure, Especially in Anti-Social Situations   In a classic study, Berndt (1979) measured conformity to attitudes of peers, in hypothetical neutral (e.g., going to a film), prosocial (e.g., visiting a sick relative), and antisocial (e.g., stealing from shop) situations. Conformity to peers generally increased from 9 to 12 to peak at 15 years (then declined), but this increase was especially marked for conformity to peer pressure in antisocial situations.

Concern about Peer Group Status Can Be an Incentive to Bully Others   Rigby (1997), in a survey of Australian children, asked whether Bullying other students gets you admired by other children at this school. The percent agreeing with this was much greater in secondary school pupils: for boys, in primary schools 13.9%, in secondary schools 23.4%; for girls, in primary schools 9.5%, in secondary schools 14.5%.

Pellegrini and Bartini (2001) and Pellegrini and Long (2002, 2003) argue that aggression/bullying is used in early adolescence to enhance status, particularly with opposite-sex peers. This is particularly important in the first years of secondary school, as new status relationships are being established at an age when peer status issues are especially salient. Each sex uses preferred modes of aggression or bullying. Pellegrini and Long examined opposite-sex dating popularity in U.S. 12- to 13- year-olds. They found that for boys, physical aggression (but not relational aggression) correlates with opposite-sex dating popularity; for girls, it tended to be relational aggression (but not physical aggression) that did so.

More Negative Attitudes toward Victims   Rigby and Slee (1991) assessed attitudes toward victims in Australian students. In general, pupils express sympathetic attitudes toward victims, but a sizeable minority do not. The pro-victim attitudes are also greater in girls than boys. However, for both sexes (though more obviously for boys), these pro-victim attitudes are lowest at 14–6 years. Very similar age trends have been reported in Italian and English students by Menesini and colleagues (1997). These studies did not find strong interactions with gender, but Olweus and Endresen (1998), in a Norwegian sample, located the effect specifically in boys' attitudes toward boy victims. They found that (hypothetical) empathic concern for boys to boys *decreased* from 10 to 16, but *increased* for boys to girls, and for girls to either boys or girls.

More Skepticism about Peer Support Schemes in Secondary School Pupils, and Boys   Besides more negative attitudes toward victims in adolescence, there is also evidence that peer support schemes, which are designed to help victims by providing befriending, mentoring, or counseling from peer supporters, are viewed more negatively in secondary school, especially by boys. Smith and Watson (2004) reported findings from an evaluation of peer support schemes in 20 schools in England, including attitudinal responses from 834 pupils. When asked, "Is the peer support system in your school a good idea?", while the majority said "yes" and very few said "no," views are markedly (and significantly) more skeptical in secondary than primary school pupils, and especially in boys; see Table 10.1.

2. Changes in Pupil Attitudes to Adults and School

Besides increased peer pressure, it is well documented that parent-child relationships become less close in adolescence. For example, large-scale U. S. data from Rossi and Rossi (1991) gave

Table 10.1 Percentage Responses to 'Is the peer support system in your school a good idea?' in a Sample of English Primary (n = 455) and Secondary (n = 379) School Pupils (adapted from Smith & Watson, 2004)

	Yes	Not Sure	No
Primary boys	75	23	2
Primary girls	82	16	1
Secondary boys	59	35	7
Secondary girls	67	30	3

ratings for closeness to parents, at ages 10, 16, and 25; data was available for the four different parent-child dyads (mother-daughter, etc); and for two birth cohorts, those born in 1925–39 who were adolescents in the 1940s–50s, and those born during 1950–59 who were adolescents in the 1960s–70s. In every case, rated closeness is lower at 16 than at 10 years, recovering by 25. The dip in closeness is more pronounced in the later cohort, probably reflecting the turbulence and social protest of the 1960s, but to some extent is ubiquitous.

There appears to be little data on age-related changes in pupil attitudes toward teachers or other adults in school, and to schools themselves.

3. Greater Risk-Taking and Anti-Social Behavior Generally

Arnett (1992, 1999) sees reckless or risk-taking behaviors as characteristic of adolescence. These can include socially accepted behaviors, such as daring sporting activities; or less socially unacceptable behaviors and delinquent acts such as having unprotected sexual intercourse, drug-taking, shop-lifting, joy-riding, vandalism. In general, criminal offending rates are highest in the late teenage years (15–19 years; Farrington, 2005). The peer group is an important influence here; Berndt and Keefe (1995), in a study of U.S. 13- to 14-year-olds, found that those pupils with disruptive friends increased more in self-reported disruption; those with high quality friendships were generally less disruptive and more involved in school, but those whose friends were disruptive but also high quality were particularly likely to become more disruptive. Reputation enhancement theory (Emler et al., 1987; Carroll et al., 1999) suggests that 'deviant' adolescents and adolescent peer groups have different values concerning antisocial behavior; for non-deviant groups antisocial behavior might be a reason for exclusion, but for deviant groups it is a reason for inclusion. Bullying is clearly one form of antisocial behavior, which anti-bullying interventions generally highlight as being disapproved of by adults and the school; so opposition to such interventions may be especially likely in these deviant peer groups.

4. An Increasing Stability of Victim and Bullying Tendencies with Age

The incidence of self-reported victimization decreases with age (although with sometimes a temporary rise as pupils start secondary school); although the incidence of self-reported bullying others does not show such a decrease (Smith, Madsen, & Moody, 1999). However, even if victim rates fall with age, there is evidence that victims in secondary school are in more severe difficulties. They are less likely to seek help, and the stability of victim status is higher (Boulton & Smith, 1994; Card, 2003). Being labeled as a victim, and getting into a negative spiral of low self-esteem and lack of good friends, can make recovery more difficult (Graham & Juvonen, 2001). The stability of bullying roles also increases with age (Monks, Smith, & Swettenham,

2005; Boulton & Smith, 1994); besides developing characteristically aggressive behavior patterns, older bullying children may also get labeled as aggressive and bullying, which may in fact enhance their status in certain peer groups and again make change more difficult.

Organizational Changes

Secondary schools are different from primary schools, and their different characteristics might affect the success with which school-based anti-bullying interventions have impact, independent of any age-related changes in the pupils themselves. We will look at size and complexity and how this might effect implementation; changes in curricula; and changes in teacher's role.

5. Change Is More Difficult in Large Organizations

Secondary Schools Are Larger in Size Secondary schools are typically much larger in size than primary schools; but given that much anti-bullying prevention work is either class-based or individual-based, at least in terms of face-to-face interaction with pupils, it is not clear that school size in itself would be an important mediating factor. In fact, most evidence suggests that school size does not correlate significantly with rates of bullying or victimization (Olweus, 2004; Whitney & Smith, 1993), or school violence generally (Benbenishty & Astor, 2005).

More Complex Organizational Structure There are more levels of management in a typical secondary school. This might make the implementation of an anti-bullying program more difficult, or less effective, if for example there is a top-down approach from senior management. Although much intervention work is class-based, the homeroom class has less importance in secondary schools. Nevertheless, in an analysis of school-level predictors of implementation of classroom intervention measures (in schools in Norway using the Olweus Bullying Prevention program), Olweus (2004) found the most important predictors of implementation and effectiveness to be Openness in Communication and School Attention to Bullying Problems. Neither of these appear obviously related to size or complexity of organization, but rather to school climate and whether bullying is seen as a priority for teacher-based work.

6. The Curriculum in Secondary Schools Focuses More on Traditional Subject Matter

Lessons Are Less Class-Based In secondary schools it is not so easy for one class teacher to give a consistent message to influence pupils, as pupils will likely have quite a number of different teachers. This might particularly impact interventions centered on class-based rules, such as the Olweus program traditionally has been. However, most anti-bullying programs (e.g., the Sheffield, England, and Flanders projects mentioned above) use school-based rather than class-based policies. If these are implemented reasonably uniformly across the school, then the change in teaching and lesson structures might have little impact on the effectiveness of intervention.

Less Social Relationships Curriculum in Secondary Schools It is not clear whether this is the case. Personal and social education is a component of the school curriculum in many countries (e.g., it is a required component in both primary and secondary schools in England). A new curriculum in this area (SEAL: Social and Emotional Aspects of Learning) includes a module on bullying; it is currently being rolled out in primary schools and a version is being developed for secondary schools. Additionally, the larger size of secondary schools provides the opportunity for having specialized staff with responsibility for relationship issues. There may be a school counselor; or in English secondary schools, there will be a senior member of staff with responsibility for pastoral care of pupils. Such persons are generally less available or absent in primary schools.

7. Teacher's Roles May Differ

In the absence of a classroom teacher with very clear responsibility for pupils in their class, teachers in secondary schools might see responsibility for dealing with bullying as more diffused, and therefore might be less likely to take action. Stevens and colleagues (2000) suggest that they may find it more difficult to react quickly to incidents.

Diffusion of Responsibility   There appears to be little evidence to test these predictions, but Olweus (2004), in his study of predictors of implementation and effectiveness of class-based intervention measures, found the most important predictors at the teacher level were Perceived Staff Importance (influence and responsibility), Read Program Information, and Perceived Level of Bullying. The first of these might be influenced by the diffusion of responsibility that is argued to be more likely in secondary schools. The other two predictors appear to relate more to individual teacher commitment, and to how they evaluate the seriousness of the problem—issues not clearly related to school organization. Interestingly, two factors which Olweus found did not predict implementation effectiveness were measures of Teacher-Leadership Collaboration and Teacher-Teacher Collaboration (which, in fact, did predict weakly, but in a negative direction).

Teacher Involvement in Implementation of Anti-Bullying Programs   Some data on this can be found in the results from the Sheffield, England project (Smith & Sharp, 1994). Table 10.2 presents averaged data for the 16 primary and 7 secondary schools that took part, together with the range of scores across schools in each sector. Staff Involvement was based on interviews with participating staff in the schools, in which their involvement in policy development was coded on a 1 (low) to 4 (high) scale. Policy plus Options Input is a measure of the amount of time and effort (staff meetings, training sessions, classroom sessions, etc.) that each school put into preparing and implementing the whole school anti-bullying policy and associated interventions; the maximum score possible would have been 104. Perceived Action is a pupil-based measure, given at post-test, where pupils used a 5-point scale to indicate whether the school had done much to try and stop bullying.

The results do suggest that staff in primary schools were more involved in the development of the anti-bullying policy. However, there is no suggestion that primary schools put any more effort into the interventions. The difference in action as perceived by pupils is also quite slight. What is also noticeable in every measure is the large range of scores. Any between-sector differences are considerably less than within-sector differences.

Table 10.2 Means and Range of Scores by School for Anti-Bullying Implementation in Schools in the Sheffield Project (adapted from Smith & Sharp, 1994)

	Staff Involvement	Policy + Options Input	Perceived Action
Primary schools n = 16	2.68 (1.50–3.75)	45.5 (16–73)	1.17 (0.54–1.73)
Secondary schools n = 7	1.86 (1.10–3.13)	50.4 (20–79)	0.96 (0.58–1.39)

Discussion

This chapter has sought to find reasons for a well-replicated finding that anti-bullying interventions often have less success in secondary than in primary schools. Overall, there appears good reason from many decades of psychological research to suppose that individual developmental factors are important in this. As pupils enter puberty, they assert their independence, tend to conflict more with adults, and to engage in reckless or risk-taking behaviors. It becomes more important to impress peers and to seek status in the peer group. What form this takes will depend upon both the peer culture in the school and the wider society. However, in western societies the expectations of personal expression and autonomy, and the psychosocial moratorium—what Arnett (1992) terms "broad socialization"—will tend to facilitate such changes. Bullying weaker children can be a way of demonstrating power and status, and pupils who bully may appear cool and be thought of as popular (perceived popularity), even if many pupils may not like them personally. Helping victims runs a danger of being perceived as uncool and might lower the status of the defender. Of course, such trends are not inevitable. Older adolescent pupils are becoming more cognitively sophisticated, and able to understand others' feelings. Not all adolescents join deviant peer groups. Helping and defending behaviors can be seen as praiseworthy, and some adolescents will have a more mature and longer-term grasp of opportunities and will not reject school values. But generally, these risks appear greater in secondary schools due to the age of the pupils there.

Secondary schools are also larger. This will interact with peer group characteristics, in that the peer group will be larger. The referent peer group is likely to be a whole year group rather than a class. The peer group organization will itself be more complex, with different types of cliques as well as varying positions within cliques (Cairns, Leung, Buchanan, & Cairns, 1995). What impact does this have on bullying? There is certainly more opportunity for some deviant peer groups to arise; but there is also perhaps more opportunity for shy or victim-prone children to find other friends that they feel safe with. Overall, the variance of effectiveness of anti-bullying implementation programs might be increased, but it is not clear that the overall effectiveness would be greatly changed.

Other organizational factors may impact the success of anti-bullying interventions but the evidence is far from conclusive. Indeed, the evidence seems rather limited, but in general, it appears that school climate rather than school size (or organizational structure) is more important. Effective leadership and a climate of opinion in favor of intervention appear most important. There is some evidence (from Olweus' analyses and from the Sheffield project) that teachers in primary schools may feel more directly involved and responsible for anti-bullying work; but this does not necessarily translate into implementation, either as recorded by researchers or perceived by pupils. Clearly, organizational differences between primary and secondary sectors cannot be dismissed as an explanation of more limited intervention effectiveness in secondary schools, but developmental factors appear much better established. Moreover, the great within-sector school differences point to the importance of school factors related to leadership and school climate, rather than size and complexity of organization.

Summary of Implications for Practice

Many implications of this review simply reinforce existing good practice recommendations. It is clearly important to have good communication of school policy across the whole school, and a consistent response to bullying; to encourage good classroom climate and pupil-teacher relationships; and to involve parents and the community constructively (see Table 10.3).

Table 10.3 Implications for Practice

Be aware that bringing about changes in bullying behaviors in secondary schools is often more challenging than doing so in primary schools

In both sectors, effective leadership, commitment to anti-bullying work, and positive school climate are important factors for success

Especially in secondary schools, it will be important to involve pupils as much as possible in anti-bullying work—through policy development, and through peer support schemes, for example.

Peer group status is an especially important factor in secondary school pupils. Peer support schemes will benefit from having high status peer supporters. Victims of bullying will benefit from assertiveness training and development of friendship skills, to raise their status in the peer group

Although much of adolescent development is biologically primed, socialization does have an influence; in Western societies we will not wish to move to what Arnett (1992) terms "narrow socialization"—the kind of tight restrictions on adolescent development and self-expression found in many traditional societies. But it is legitimate for schools to develop effective anti-bullying policies and expect pupils to follow them; and this is likely to be more effective if pupils themselves are involved as much as possible, not only in developing the policy but also in implementing it. More pupil-led involvement may be crucial when teacher influence is relatively less.

Peer support schemes are an obvious avenue for this. The most successful peer support schemes are able to attract peer supporters (including enough boys) who are popular and of high standing in the peer group. Use of information technology (e.g., a school intranet referral system) can be useful here. More evidence is needed on the effectiveness of peer support schemes and they have a number of pitfalls, but an effective peer support scheme may enhance school climate and have a very positive effect on the ethos of peer groups, as well as having a more direct function of supporting victims.

Given the greater importance of status and power in adolescent peer groups, another important strand of intervention is going to be helping victims of peer bullying acquire more status and power themselves. Assertiveness training was for example used, with some success, in the Sheffield project (Smith & Sharp, 1994). A project in Kansas has used physical education and self-defense classes to teach self-regulation skills (Twemlow et al., 2001). Also important is to encourage friendship and social skills in victims and potential victims (Fox & Boulton, 2005). Ways in which potential victims can acquire status by providing a range of activities and opportunities to do well, can help break the cycle of despair that some pupils find themselves in.

References

Alsaker, F. D. (2004). Bernese programme against victimisation in kindergarten and elementary school. In P. K. Smith, D. Pepler, & K. Rigby (Eds.), *Bullying in schools: How successful can interventions be?* (pp. 289–306). Cambridge, UK: Cambridge University Press.

Ananiadou, K., & Smith, P. K. (2002). Legal requirements and nationally circulated materials against school bullying in European countries. *Criminal Justice, 2*, 471–491.

Arnett, J. (1992). Reckless behavior in adolescence: A developmental perspective. *Developmental Review, 12*, 339–373.

Arnett, J. (1999). Adolescent storm and stress, reconsidered. *American Psychologist, 54*, 317–326.

Baldry, A. C., & Farrington, D. P. (2007). Effectiveness of programs to prevent school bullying. *Victims and Offenders, 2*, 183–204.

Benbenishty, R., & Astor, R. A. (2005). *School violence in context: culture, neighborhood, family, school and gender.* Oxford, UK: Oxford University Press.

Berndt, T. J. (1979). Developmental changes in conformity to peers and parents. *Developmental Psychology, 15*, 608–616.

Bjorklund, D. F., & Pellegrini, A.D. (2000). *Evolutionary development psychology.* Washington, DC: American Psychological Association Press.

Blakemore, S. J., & Choudhury, S. (2006). Development of the adolescent brain: implications for executive function and social cognition. *Journal of Child Psychology and Psychiatry, 47,* 296–312.

Boulton, M. J., & Smith, P. K. (1994). Bully/victim problems in middle-school children: Stability, self-perceived competence, peer perceptions and peer acceptance. *British Journal of Developmental Psychology, 12,* 315–329.

Buchanan, C. M., Eccles, J. S., & Becker, J. B. (1992). Are adolescents the victims of raging hormones: evidence for activational effects of hormones on moods and behavior at adolescence. *Psychological Bulletin, 111,* 62–107.

Cairns, R. B., Leung, M-C., Buchanan, L., & Cairns, B. D. (1995). Friendships and social networks in childhood and adolescence: fluidity, reliability, and interrelations. *Child Development, 66,* 1330–1345.

Card, N. (2003, April). *Victims of peer aggression: A meta-analytic review.* Paper presented at Society for Research in Child Development biennial meeting, Tampa, Florida.

Carroll, A., Houghton, S., Hattie, J., Durkin, K., et al. (1999). Adolescent reputation enhancement: Differentiating delinquent, nondelinquent, and at-risk youths. *Journal of Child Psychology & Psychiatry, 40,* 593–606.

Coleman, J. C. (1980). *The nature of adolescence.* London: Methuen.

Cross, D., Hall, M., Hamilton, G., Pintabona, Y., & Erceg, E. (2004). Australia: The friendly schools project. In P. K. Smith, D. Pepler, & K. Rigby (Eds.), *Bullying in schools: How successful can interventions be?* (pp. 187–21). Cambridge, UK: Cambridge University Press.

Emler, N., Reicher, S., Ross, A., et al. (1987). The social context of delinquent conduct, *Journal of Child Psychology & Psychiatry, 28,* 99–109.

Farrington, D. P. (2005). Introduction to integrated developmental and life-course theories of offending. In D. P. Farrington (Ed.), Integrated developmental and life-course theories of offending. *Advances in criminological theory, Vol. 14* (pp 1–14). New Brunswick, NJ: Transaction

Fox, C. L., & Boulton, M. J. (2005). The social skills problems of victims of bullying: Self, peer and teacher perceptions. *British Journal of Educational Psychology, 75,* 313–328.

Galloway, D., & Roland, E. (2004). Is the direct approach to reducing bullying always the best? In P. K. Smith, D. Pepler, & K. Rigby (Eds.), *Bullying in schools: How successful can interventions be?* (pp. 37–53). Cambridge, UK: Cambridge University Press.

Graham, S., & Juvonen, J. (Eds.). (2001). An attributional approach to peer victimization. In J. Juvonen & S. Graham (Eds.), *Peer harassment in school: The plight of the vulnerable and victimised* (pp. 49–72). New York: Guildford.

Hanewinkel, R. (2004). Prevention of bullying in German schools: An evaluation of an anti-bullying approach. In P. K. Smith, D. Pepler, & K. Rigby (Eds.), *Bullying in schools: How successful can interventions be?* (pp. 81–97). Cambridge, UK: Cambridge University Press.

Hermann-Giddens, M., Slora, E., & Wasserman, R. (1997). Secondary sexual characteristics and menses in young girls. *Pediatrics, 99,* 505–512.

Koivisto, M. (2004). A follow-up survey of anti-bullying interventions in the comprehensive schools of Kempele in 1990–98. In P. K. Smith, D. Pepler, & K. Rigby (Eds.), *Bullying in schools: How successful can interventions be?* (pp. 235–249). Cambridge, UK: Cambridge University Press.

Limber, S. P., Nation, M., Tracy, A. J., Melton, G. B., & Flerx, V. (2004). Implementation of the Olweus Bullying Prevention programme in the southeastern United States. In P. K. Smith, D. Pepler, & K. Rigby (Eds.), *Bullying in schools: How successful can interventions be?* (pp. 55–79). Cambridge, UK: Cambridge University Press.

Menesini, E., Codecasa, E., Benelli, B., & Cowie, H. (2003). Enhancing children's responsibility to take action against bullying: evaluation of a befriending intervention in Italian middle schools. *Aggressive Behavior, 29,* 1–14.

Menesini, E., Eslea, M., Smith, P. K., Genta, M. L., Giannetti, E., Fonzi, A., & Costabile, A. (1997). A cross-national comparison of children's attitudes towards bully/victim problems in school. *Aggressive Behavior, 23,* 245–257.

Monk, C. M., McClure, E. B., Nelson, E. E., et al. (2003). Adolescent immaturity in attention-related brain engagement to emotional facial expression. *Neuroimage, 20,* 420–428.

Monks, C.P., Smith, P. K., & Swettenham, J. (2005). The psychological correlates of peer victimization in preschool: Social cognitive skills, executive function and attachment profiles. *Aggressive Behavior, 31,* 571–588.

Olweus, D. (1993). *Bullying in school: What we know and what we can do.* Oxford, UK: Blackwell.

Olweus, D. (2004). The Olweus Bullying Prevention program: Design and implementation issues and a new national initiative in Norway. In P. K. Smith, D. Pepler, & K. Rigby (Eds.), *Bullying in schools: How successful can interventions be?* (pp. 13–36). Cambridge, UK: Cambridge University Press.

Olweus, D. (2005). *New positive results with the Olweus Bullying Prevention Program in 37 Oslo schools.* Unpublished report. Bergen, Norway: HEMIL-Center.

Olweus, D., & Endresen, I. M. (1998). The importance of sex-of-stimulus object: Age trends and sex differences in empathic responsiveness. *Social Development, 3,* 370–388.

O'Moore, A. M., & Minton, S. J. (2004). Ireland: the Donegal Primary Schools' anti-bullying project. In P. K. Smith, D. Pepler, & K. Rigby (Eds.), *Bullying in schools: How successful can interventions be?* (pp. 275–287). Cambridge, UK: Cambridge University Press.

Ortega, R., Del Rey, R., & Mora-Merchan, J.A. (2004). SAVE model: An anti-bullying intervention in Spain. In P. K. Smith, D. Pepler, & K. Rigby (Eds.), *Bullying in schools: How successful can interventions be?* (pp. 167–185). Cambridge, UK: Cambridge University Press.

Pellegrini, A. D., & Bartini, M. (2001). Dominance in early adolescent boys: Affiliative and aggressive dimensions and possible functions. *Merrill-Palmer Quarterly, 47,* 142–163.

Pellegrini, A. D., & Long, J. D. (2002). A longitudinal study of bullying, dominance, and victimization during the transition from primary through secondary school. *British Journal of Developmental Psychology, 20,* 259–280.

Pellegrini, A. D., & Long, J. D. (2003). A sexual selection theory longitudinal analysis of sexual segregation and integration in early adolescence. *Journal of Experimental Child Psychology, 85,* 257–278.

Pepler, D. J., Craig, W. M., O'Connell, P., Atlas, R., & Charach, A. (2004). Making a difference in bullying: Evaluation of a systemic school-based programme in Canada.In P. K. Smith, D. Pepler, & K. Rigby (Eds.), *Bullying in schools: How successful can interventions be?* (pp. 125–139). Cambridge, UK: Cambridge University Press.

Pitts, J., & Smith, P. (1995). *Preventing school bullying.* London: Home Office Police Research Group.

Rigby, K. (1994). Attitudes and beliefs about bullying among Australian school children. The *Irish Journal of Psychology, 18,* 202–220.

Rigby, K. (2002). *A meta-evaluation of methods and approaches to reducing bullying in preschools and early primary schools in Australia.* Canberra: Attorney General's Department, Crime Prevention Branch.

Rigby, K., & Slee, P. T. (1991). Bullying among Australian schoolchildren: Reported behavior and attitudes to victims. *Journal of Social Psychology, 131,* 615–627.

Romer, D., & Walker, E. F. (Eds.). (2007). *Adolescent psychopathology and the developing brain.* Oxford, UK: Oxford University Press.

Rosenbluth, B., Whitaker, D. J., Sanchez, E., & Valle, L. A. (2004). The Expect Respect project: Preventing bullying and sexual harassment in US elementary schools. In P. K. Smith, D. Pepler, & K. Rigby (Eds.), *Bullying in schools: How successful can interventions be?* (pp. 211–233). Cambridge, UK: Cambridge University Press.

Rossi, A. H., & Rossi, P. H. (1991). *Of human bonding: Parent–child relations across the life course.* New York: de Gruyter.

Rutter, M., Graham, P., Chadwick, O., & Yule, W. (1976). Adolescent turmoil: fact or fiction? *Journal of Child Psychology and Psychiatry, 17,* 35–56.

Salmivalli, C., Kaukiainen, A., Voeten, M., & Sinisammal, M. (2004). Targeting the group as a whole: The Finnish anti-bullying intervention. In P. K. Smith, D. Pepler, & K. Rigby (Eds.), *Bullying in schools: How successful can interventions be?* (pp. 244–273). Cambridge, UK: Cambridge University Press.

Smith, D. J., Schneider, B. H., Smith, P. K., & Ananiadou, K. (2004). The effectiveness of whole-school antibullying programs: A synthesis of evaluation research. *School Psychology Review, 33,* 547–560

Smith, P. K., Ananiadou, K., & Cowie, H. (2003). Interventions to reduce school bullying. *Canadian Journal of Psychiatry, 48,* 591–599.

Smith, P. K., Pepler, D. K., & Rigby, K. (Eds.). (2004). *Bullying in schools: How successful can interventions be?* Cambridge: Cambridge University Press.

Smith, P. K., Madsen, K., & Moody, J. (1999). What causes the age decline in reports of being bullied in school? Towards a developmental analysis of risks of being bullied. *Educational Research, 41,* 267–285.

Smith, P. K., & Sharp, S. (Eds.). (1994). *School bullying: Insights and perspectives.* London: Routledge.

Smith, P. K., & Watson, D. (2004). *Evaluation of the CHIPS (ChildLine in Partnership with Schools) programme.* Research report RR570 to DfES. London: HMSO.

Steinberg, L. (1988). Reciprocal relation between parent-child distance and pubertal maturation. *Developmental Psychology, 24,* 122–128.

Stevens, V., de Bourdeaudhuij, I., & Van Oost, P. (2000). Bullying in Flemish schools: An evaluation of anti-bullying intervention in primary and secondary schools. *British Journal of Educational Psychology, 70,* 195–210.

Stevens, V., Van Oost, P., & de Bourdeaudhuij, I. (2004). Interventions against bullying in Flemish schools: Programme development and evaluation. In P. K. Smith, D. Pepler, & K. Rigby (Eds.), *Bullying in schools: How successful can interventions be?* (pp. 141–165). Cambridge, UK: Cambridge University Press.

Twemlow, S. W., Fonagy, P., Sacco, F. C., Gies, M. L., Evans, R., & Ewbank, R. (2001). Creating a peaceful school learning environment: A controlled study of an elementary school intervention to reduce violence. *American Journal of Psychiatry, 158,* 808–810.

Weisfeld, G. E., & Janisse, H. C. (2005). Some functional aspects of human adolescence. In B. J. Ellis & D. F. Bjorklund (Eds.), *Origins of the social mind: Evolutionary psychology and child development* (pp. 189–218). New York: Guilford.

Whitney, I., & Smith, P. K. (1993). A survey of the nature and extent of bullying in junior/middle and secondary schools. *Educational Research, 35,* 3–25.

Appendix A

Comments from Dan Olweus on why interventions may be less effective in older pupils (personal communication, May 16, 2007).

With regard to the issue of weaker results for students in junior high/lower secondary grades, I would like to say first that we obtained positive results also for what at that time was called the grade 7 cohort (the lowest grade in junior high; the grade system was later changed and the designation now is grade 8 in Norway) in the first Bergen Project. We also obtained clear reductions for the grade 9 cohort (+ for the younger cohorts; the grade 9 cohort was the only cohort from the junior high grades in this project) in the second Bergen Project, but these results have not been published in English journals (only a short report in Norwegian). But generally, I certainly agree that it is more difficult to get good results at these grade levels.

In talking about and presenting this issue I have usually invoked the following four factors as explanations (in brief):

- The organisation of the teaching is different in these grades and teaching focuses much more on subject matter than on social relations. The role of the homeroom/classroom teacher becomes less important (with fewer hours of teaching in the class) and the responsibility for the social relations among the students is "diffused" among the teachers (no one feels responsible).
- The teachers' definition of their own task as teachers (related to the first point) implies that they don't see it as their task to help solve or prevent bullying problems (and such responsibility was found to be an important factor in affecting degree of implementation of the program in the Kallestad and Olweus 2003 study) which in turn has the consequence that the program generally gets less well implemented in junior high school grades (documented in our internal analyses). Important components of the program such as class meetings, role playing, and introduction and enforcement of classroom/school rules against bullying, are less often/well implemented.
- Students enter puberty and tend to develop generally oppositional behaviour in response to adult views, values, and norms. Such behavior changes are also likely to come into play with regard to school efforts to change aggressive or generally acting out behavior. Many students don't want any longer to be "kind", "nice" and cooperative in relation to the adult world. They want to present themselves as independent, daring and oppositional.
- Many behavior tendencies tend to crystallize and be more automatized with increasing age. This is also likely to apply to aggressive/bullying tendencies and this will probably make the task of changing kids with such tendencies more difficult.

This is a quick summary of my key points on this issue.

11

Relations Among Bullying, Stresses, and Stressors
A Longitudinal and Comparative Survey Among Countries

MITSURU TAKI

Why Contextual Factors Are Needed in Explaining the Causality of Bullying

Some bullying literature published in Europe, in the late 1980s and early 1990s, emphasized the causality of bullying, and noted the family and/or personal innate factors as the main causes of bullying. Besag (1989) noted that research from the 1970s and 1980s found that family and personal temperamental factors were the main causes of bullying and victimization. Similarly, Smith and Thompson (1991) cited researchers during the same time period who argued that child characteristics, temperament, and family factors influence bullying behavior. Olweus (1993) discussed, on the basis of the research from the 1980s, that child rearing conditions could affect aggressive tendencies in children. These causality models have been extended to recent studies of bullying.

Such previous and recent bullying research share a common approach, including (a) using a single survey with children by a self-report questionnaire; (b) categorizing children as either a bully, victim, or bully/victim according to their reported bullying experiences; (c) comparing a number of factors regarding the category; (4) speculating on the causality of bullying on the basis of merely statistical significant differences; and (5) concluding that fixed factors like family, and/or personal innate factors as the main causes of bullying.

However, this author speculates that there is an implicit premise in such causality models and research approach, namely, the children who report the experience of victimizing others and/ or being victimized by others at a single time point are the particular children who are involved in bullying at any time point. In other words, the children who are categorized as bullies and/ or victims at one survey point should be bullies and/or victims in the past and also in future, because their experiences come from their extraordinary factors such as family and/or personal innate characteristics. As such characteristics are not changed easily, so their categorized bullying statuses are also stable. Only this premise makes it possible to postulate the stability of bullying status and justify the causality models and research approach that link the present status categorized by a single survey with the past family and/or personal innate factors. This author challenges this implicit premise, the causality models, and research approaches that have characterized much of the past research on bullying.

The truth of this implicit premise can be checked easily using longitudinal methodology.

Taki (1992) found on the basis of a Japanese longitudinal survey, conducted from 1985 to 1987, that there were few children who were consistently categorized as either bullies or victims through the duration of the study. These findings were replicated, surveying Japanese students twice each year, from 1998 to 2000 (Taki, 2001). Both studies revealed that: (a) bullying happens among all children, (b) bully and victim status changes over time, and (c) there is no evidence that bullying is consistently conducted only by particular individuals. These findings reject the implicit premise mentioned above that the children victimizing others and/or victimized are the extraordinary ones resulting from disadvantaged family and/or personal innate characteristics. Although the children who come from disadvantaged families and/or have personal innate characteristics might have a higher risk of involvement in bullying, more ordinary children are also involved. In other words, such extraordinary children are only a small part of the groups comprising all children who victimize others and/or are victimized. Therefore, the causality models and research approaches using these extraordinary children as playing a major role in bullying either as bullies or victims, cannot explain the whole bullying incident. Family and/or personal innate factors should merely be considered as risk factors but not main causal factors, even if they have a high correlation with bullying experiences. The causality models and research approach including these innate factors should be rejected.

However, in spite of the evidence shown above, such causality models and research approach with these innate factors have been supported strongly for a long time in European bullying research. This author suggests two main reasons for this support. First, there is no clear distinction between bullying and "mobbing" as defined in the early research by Dan Olweus. Thus, the explanation based on mobbing research was extrapolated to bullying research without actually studying bullying. Second, there is a dearth of longitudinal survey methodology in Europe and the truth of the implicit premise has not been evaluated by the empirical data. The details of these two reasons will be discussed.

Mobbing researchers were prominent in Scandinavian countries in the 1970s. Although mobbing is often understood to be equivalent to bullying, the findings of the 1970s were focused on aggressive behavior of boys, especially who were the high-risk children from disadvantaged families. Mobbing overlaps partly with bullying but the former findings should not be applied to the present bullying research. Nevertheless, some bullying researchers in 1980s, who were also mobbing researchers in 1970s, used the word bullying as equivalent to the word mobbing and unintentionally introduced the causality models and research approach of mobbing to bullying research. Olweus (1993), for instance, concluded that the causality of bullying was based chiefly on research with boys, but true for both boys and girls, though this citation should be written correctly as based chiefly on the mobbing research with boys in the 1970s but true for boys and girls in bullying in 1980s. However, he did not mention any differences between boys' mobbing and boys' and girls' bullying and treated the two as synonymous. Other literatures in the 1980s and 1990s on bullying also do not make a clear distinction between mobbing by the high-risk boys and bullying by ordinary boys and girls. Thus, the first reason why such causality models and research approaches have not been heretofore challenged underscores the blurry boundaries between bullying and mobbing.

The second reason for this confusion is the dearth of longitudinal survey methodology in Europe. If bullying is a problem of the extraordinary children from disadvantaged families as is mobbing, the same bullies and victims should appear repeatedly in longitudinal studies. In other words, conducting longitudinal research should easily provide answers to the question of whether or not bullying is the problem of the extraordinary children. However, traditional methodologies in European bullying research, as already discussed above, are based mostly on survey methodology given at just one point in time. So, the causality models and research approaches with innate factors have not been recognized as suspect for bullying research.

In the first part of this chapter, the findings from previous Japanese surveys (Taki, 1992, 2001) will be contrasted by recent surveys among Australia, Canada, Korea, and Japan. After rejecting the old causality models and research approaches with innate factors, a new causality model constructed by contextual factors to explain the temporary experiences and will be discussed.

The International Bullying Project

The data presented in this chapter are part of the International Bullying Survey Project (NIER project).[1] There are two parts to this project. The first part is that it was a longitudinal survey involving three waves of data collection. There is a strong policy regarding bullying in Japan which recognizes the seriousness of bullying stating, "It is possible that serious 'Ijime' [bullying] incidents may happen at any school, at any classroom and among any children" (Emergency Appeal by Minister of Education, 1996). This statement was made on the basis of evidence derived from a longitudinal survey (Taki, 1992), and it emphasizes the fact that bullying is the problem of not only extraordinary but also ordinary children. However, few longitudinal studies have been conducted in other countries and bullying has often been believed to be the problem of the extraordinary children, such as those involved in mobbing. Therefore, the three waves of data collection spanning 18 months was the minimum condition for the project that could illuminate whether bullies and victims are ordinary or extraordinary children across countries.

The second part is that the project involved a new definition of bullying and a new questionnaire where no direct words such as *bullying* in English, *Ijime* in Japanese and *Wang-ta* in Korean were used. A previous international comparative survey conducted in Japan, England, the Netherlands, and Norway with the questionnaire based on the Olweus study revealed that bullying in Japan is often less physical than other European countries (Morita, 2001). However, to ascertain whether the results of this study reflected the actual incident rates of bullying in these countries, further investigations are needed. Indeed, Kanetsuna and Smith (2002) pointed out that Japanese children generally have an image of less physical behavior from the word *Ijime*, whereas European and European American children often have a more direct and physical image from the word *bullying*.

There are two possible explanations for the differences among those countries. The first possibility is that there are differences in actual incidents among those countries. The second possible explanation is that there are biased images derived from the word bullying and the differences found among those countries come from such biased images of the word used in the questionnaire. The solution to this question for the current analysis was to utilize a questionnaire focusing on bullying but not directly using the word.

With the collaboration of other international researchers, the NIER project developed a new questionnaire without using the word bullying directly. The definition was based on the definition of Taki (2003):

> "Ijime bullying" is mean behavior or a negative attitude that has clear intention to embarrass or humiliate others who occupy weaker positions in a same group. It is assumed to be a dynamic used to keep or recover one's dignity by aggrieving others. Consequently, its main purpose is to inflict mental suffering on others, regardless of the form such as physical, verbal, psychological and social. The three conditions for serious "Ijime bullying" are: (1) membership, (2) the power of exchangeable status, and (3) frequency of victimization.

The word *Ijime-bullying* in the definition above is used for emphasizing the distinction between Ijime in Japan from bullying in European countries. The Japanese word Ijime is considered most similar to bullying, but typically refers to indirect behavior. The NIER project focused on the aspect of "indirect aggression" (see Lagerspets, Björkqvist, & Peltonen, 1988) in bullying. Therefore, students were provided with the following definition before completing the questionnaire:

> Students can be very mean to one another at school. Mean and negative behavior can be especially upsetting and embarrassing when it happens over and over again, either by one person or by many different people in the group. We want to know about times when students use mean behavior and take advantage of other students who cannot defend themselves easily.

Following the definition, students answered questions about experiences with victimizing others and being victimized by others. Examples of types of victimization were provided for the students so the extent of their victimization experience could be assessed through ratings from "never" to "'several a week" on a 5-point scale for the following forms of bullying: (a) physically (e.g., hitting, kicking, spitting, slapping, pushing you [them] or doing other physical harm, on purpose, jokingly); (b) physically (e.g., hitting, kicking, spitting, slapping, pushing you [them] or doing other physical harm, on purpose, harshly); (c) by taking things from you [them] or damaging your[their] property; (d) verbally (e.g., teasing, calling you [them] names, threatening, or saying mean things to you [them]); (e) socially (e.g., excluding or ignoring you [them], spreading rumors or saying mean things about you[them] to others or getting others not to like you [them]); and (f) by using computer, email or phone text messages to threaten you[them] or make you [them] look bad. The terms *jokingly* and harshly are used to capture the subtle difference between bullying that is masked by ambiguous action (e.g., bumping into someone) and bullying that is intentionally hurtful (e.g., a direct push).

Participants   The participants for the current study were fifth grade students from four countries, Japan, Australia, Canada, and South Korea. Data from 823 children in Japan, 103 in Australia, and 146 in South Korea were collected from spring of 2004 to spring of 2005 and 205 in Canada from fall of 2005 to fall of 2006.

First Study: Who Participates in Bullying? Extraordinary or Ordinary Children?

Tables 11.1 through 11.4 indicate the frequency in which children were involved in bullying during each time point. If the causality models based on the innate factors as mobbing research are correct and the extraordinary children who have family and/or personal innate problems become bullies and/or victims, their bullying status should be stable. In other words, the same children should appear as perpetrators and/or victims at every survey point in the longitudinal study. First, in Table 11.1 and Table 11.2, only the frequencies of children who report their bullying/victimization experiences as "more than once a week" are shown. They are named as the "frequent victims" and the "frequent perpetrators." If the existence of extraordinary children is the main cause of bullying, such children should report their experiences at least "more than once a week." Second, in Table 11.3 and Table 11.4, the children who report any bullying and victimization experiences are shown for comparison.

Table 11.1 shows those who reported being victimized "more than once a week." These descriptive results indicate that only a few (2–5%) children who are victimized "more than once a week" at every survey point report "teasing" across countries but few children (less than 2%) report other forms of bullying, with the exception of "exclusion" in Japan. In short, most of the frequent victims indicated a single experience across the three time points. It is hard to support the existence of stable victims from these results. Even if a few children across the three time

Table 11.1 The Rate of Frequent (more than once a week) Victimization

Country and repeat time	Victimized forms					
	Hit jokingly	Hit harshly	Taking property	Teasing	Excluding	E-mail
Japan						
3 times	0.9	0.2	0.1	2.1	2.2	0.1
Twice	4.3	1.2	1.4	6.7	6.3	0.2
Once	13.2	9.9	2.8	17.9	19.7	1.8
None	81.6	88.7	95.7	73.3	71.8	97.8
Australia						
3 times	1.0	0.0	0.0	4.9	1.0	0.0
Twice	4.9	5.0	1.0	5.9	2.0	0.0
Once	8.7	1.0	1.9	14.7	13.7	2.0
None	85.4	94.1	97.1	74.5	83.3	98.0
Canada						
3 times	1.5	0.5	0.0	2.0	1.0	0.0
Twice	7.3	4.9	3.4	6.4	6.8	2.4
Once	19.5	10.2	12.2	21.6	23.9	6.3
None	71.7	84.4	84.4	70.1	68.3	91.2
South Korea						
3 times	1.4	0.7	0.0	2.1	0.0	0.0
Twice	6.9	0.0	0.0	2.1	1.4	0.7
Once	18.1	7.6	2.1	14.1	4.9	2.1
None	73.6	91.7	97.9	81.7	93.8	97.2

points are treated as extraordinary, they alone cannot account for all the bullying incidents because they are only small proportion of the frequent victims.

Data from those who reported victimizing "more than once a week" are presented in Table 11.2. The results of this analysis indicate that few (less than 2%) children victimize others at any of the time points are across any forms in all countries. In short, most of the frequent perpetrators have only one experience across the three points. It is therefore equally difficult to support the existence of stable perpetrators, as it was for stable victims.

Table 11.3 shows all children who experienced victimization at any extent (i.e., "more than once in this term" rather than "more than once a week"). The results show that many (more than 20%) children victimized at any survey points are across some form of bullying in all countries. For instance, in Japan, 20–25% of children were victimized repeatedly by "teasing" and "excluding." However, in such forms of bullying, many other children (more than 70%) have been victimized at least once within the duration of the study. These results are similar to NIER and MEXT (Ministry of Education, Culture, Sports, Science and Technology, 2005). This research shows that repeated victims who report being "excluded" gradually reduces in number over time, while almost every child reports being victimized at least once time in 6 years. Although many repeated victims endorse the forms of "hit jokingly" and "teasing" in Australia, Canada, and South Korea, other children (more than 70%) also have been victimized at least once within a year-and-a-half. Even if the children who experienced bullying at all three time periods are treated as extraordinary, they can only

Table 11.2 The Rate of Frequent (more than once a week) Bullying

Country and repeat time	Victimizing forms					
	Hit jokingly	Hit harshly	Taking property	Teasing	Excluding	E-mail
Japan						
3 times	0.2	0.0	0.0	0.6	0.6	0.1
Twice	1.3	0.6	0.1	1.7	3.4	0.1
Once	6.1	3.3	1.3	.9.3	11.3	0.6
None	92.3	96.1	98.6	88.4	84.7	99.1
Australia						
3 times	1.0	0.0	0.0	1.0	0.0	0.0
Twice	1.0	0.0	1.0	1.0	1.0	0.0
Once	7.1	1.0	0.0	2.0	3.0	1.0
None	90.9	99.0	99.0	96.0	96.0	99.0
Canada						
3 times	1.5	0.0	0.1	0.5	0.0	0.0
Twice	2.9	2.0	0.2	2.5	1.5	0.5
Once	13.2	2.9	1.6	7.8	6.3	1.5
None	82.4	95.1	96.1	89.2	92.2	98.0
South Korea						
3 times	0.7	0.0	0.0	0.0	0.0	0.0
Twice	4.8	0.7	0.0	0.7	0.7	0.0
Once	19.9	2.8	1.4	8.4	1.4	2.1
None	74.7	96.6	98.6	90.9	97.9	97.9

account for part of the entire bullying incidents. These results do not support the causality models and research approaches with innate factors in the case of victimization.

Table 11.4 shows all children who experienced victimizing others at any frequency levels. The results show similar tendencies to that of victims. Although many repeated perpetrators can be found in the form of "excluding" in Japan and in the form of "hit jokingly" in the other countries, more than 70% have also victimized others at least once within a year-and-a-half. The causality models and research approach with innate factors are not supported in the case of all perpetrators in these data.

In conclusion, the causality models and research approach that assume that particular and extraordinary children who have family and/or personal innate problems are the main cause of bullying cannot be supported in this study. Even if there are repeated children involved in bullying and significant differences among family and/or personal innate factors were revealed, such factors should merely be considered as a risk factor. We should construct the causality with the premise that most of bullies and victims are ordinary children and the bullying statuses are not always stable.

Stress-Stressor Model with Contextual Factors for New Causality of Bullying

Taki (1996) claims that stress results in maladjustment in student's school experiences. Previous research has found a relationship between stress, stressors, and bullying (Taki, 1998). Based on findings from these studies, Taki (2001) developed the Stress-Stressor Model (see Figure 11.1).

Table 11.3 The Rate of Any Victimization

Country and repeat time	Victimized forms					
	Hit jokingly	Hit harshly	Taking property	Teasing	Excluding	E-mail
Japan						
3 times	11.9	4.3	3.1	19.9	24.3	0.5
Twice	16.8	11.7	8.5	23.8	26.8	2.6
Once	26.8	23.3	16.9	26.6	21.7	6.3
None	44.5	60.7	71.4	29.7	27.3	90.7
Australia						
3 times	22.3	5.0	6.8	19.6	12.7	1.0
Twice	21.4	4.0	12.6	26.5	19.6	4.9
Once	27.2	24.8	33.0	22.5	30.4	10.8
None	29.1	66.3	47.6	31.4	37.3	83.3
Canada						
3 times	33.2	7.8	9.8	16.2	20.0	3.9
Twice	27.3	23.9	21.0	19.0	29.3	7.8
Once	21.5	27.3	32.2	26.8	24.9	19.5
None	18.0	41.0	37.1	38.0	25.9	68.8
South Korea						
3 times	40.3	2.1	2.8	27.0	2.8	0.7
Twice	25.7	12.4	6.3	27.9	16.7	1.4
Once	18.8	17.9	20.8	24.0	26.4	11.1
None	15.3	67.6	70.1	21.1	54.2	86.8

Bullying Others   Among the six forms of victimizing, only "excluding," "teasing," and "hitting (jokingly)" were used for this scale. These items were categorized as one group through a factor analysis using data from the four countries.

Stress—Symptoms of Stress   Symptoms of stress is a concept based on Cooper (1981), meaning negative feelings and psychological symptoms and what we generally call stress. Lazarus and Folkman (1984) identified the same concept as "immediate effects of stress." When stress is treated as one series of symptoms in this study the internal correlation ratio is quite high. The components of the scale based on Okayasu (1997) are: (a) feel sick and tired, (b) get sick a lot, (c) get headaches, (d) get irritated, (e) get angry easily, (f) feel like shouting, (g) don't have much energy, (h) don't feel interested, (i) can't concentrate on school work, (j) worry about things, (k) feel very lonely, and (l) get depressed.

Stressor—Sources of Stress   Sources of stress are also a concept based on Cooper (1981). These are the causes of stress that can be seen as daily hassles (see Lazarus & Folkman, 1984) derived from school and family lives. "Stressor" here is the subjective perceptions of stressful experiences and not objective incidents. Consequently, they can be considered as the perceived sources of stress through cognitive appraisal, and thus there must also be an influence of social support from the external sources and one's sense of values. The components of stressors based on work by Okayasu (1997) are; (a) teachers ask me questions I can't answer, (b) can't understand my

Table 11.4 The Rate of Any Bullying

Country and repeat time	Victimizing forms					
	Hit jokingly	Hit harshly	Taking property	Teasing	Excluding	E-mail
Japan						
3 times	6.2	1.6	0.6	10.5	22.7	0.4
Twice	11.8	4.8	1.0	16.7	24.7	0.4
Once	20.9	15.6	7.2	27.3	19.8	3.5
None	61.1	78.0	91.2	45.6	32.8	95.7
Australia						
3 times	14.1	1.0	1.0	8.1	4.0	2.0
Twice	20.2	4.2	0.0	18.2	15.2	2.0
Once	31.3	14.6	10.1	28.3	22.2	9.1
None	34.3	80.2	88.9	45.5	58.6	86.9
Canada						
3 times	26.8	2.9	1.0	9.8	5.4	1.0
Twice	18.5	8.8	3.4	21.1	13.2	3.9
Once	25.4	22.0	16.6	23.0	21.0	12.2
None	29.3	66.3	79.0	46.1	60.5	82.9
South Korea						
3 times	34.2	3.4	0.0	9.8	1.4	0.7
Twice	26.0	9.7	2.1	21.0	16.4	0.7
Once	21.2	18.6	11.8	23.8	18.5	6.3
None	18.5	68.3	86.1	45.5	63.7	92.3

lessons, (c) get low test results, (d) teachers tell me off, (e) teachers take a personal interest, (f) teachers don't treat me fairly, (g) put me down because of my school marks, (h) put me down because of the way I look, (i) classmates call me names, (j) importance is put on doing well at school, (k) get nagged in my family, and (l) my family expects too much. Items a through c comprise the Study Stressor scale, items d though f comprise the Teacher Stressor scale, items g through i comprise the Peer Stressor scale, and items j through l comprise the Family Stressor scale.

Social Support Social support is characterized by positive relationships with others. The components are: (a) If I left out, I am encouraged; (b) If I express, I am listened; and (c) try to understand me. The same (a) to (c) are for Teacher Support, Peer Support, and Family Support.

Competitive View. Views are the personal and competitive views on "victory or defeat": (a) unhappy, if I not do better in my school-work; (b) unhappy, if I not look better than classmates; and (c) unhappy, if I not do better at a particular sport or hobby.

The Causality among Factors Various incidents in the daily lives of children are a source of stress such as academics, peer relationships, teachers, and families. These factors can increase levels of stress. However, if children perceive that they are the recipients of social support, they

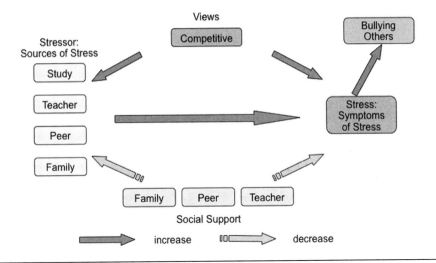

Figure 11.1

may not perceive their academics, peer relationships, teachers, and families as stressors. Further, social support may directly work to reduce stress. On the other hand, if children have a sense of competitive value, it increases the stressful feeling from the same incidents. Social support and competitive views that may work to reduce or increase stress are called "buffers." Finally, the high levels of stress may promote mean behavior or a negative attitude to bully weaker others. This may be especially true for children who lose their own dignity through various stressors and therefore try to relieve their stress and recover their dignity by bullying others who are weaker than themselves.

Participants and method.   Data from 400 boys and 414 girls in Grade 7 were collected in spring in 2004 in Japan. This survey was part of the NIER project mentioned above and utilized the same questionnaire. The statistical program, AMOS , was used to estimate the coefficients in this analysis.

Second Study: What Are the Main Causes of Bullying?

In Figure 11.2 for boys, the values of GFI, AGFI, CFI, and RMSEA indicate that this stress-stressor model robustly explains the process in which boys bully others. Although "competitive views," "social support," and "stressors" have high direct and indirect effects to "stress," only "peer stressor" has a direct effect (.51) to "bullying others." The results indicate that boys' victimizing behavior is mainly considered as a direct reaction from "peer stressor." However, "competitive views" and "study stressor" also show high indirect effects to "bullying others" via "peer stressor" (.22 and .24). Results are shown in Table 11.5.

In Figure 11.3 for girls, the values of GFI, AGFI, CFI, and RMSEA also indicate that this model robustly explains the process in which girls bully others. In girls, "stress" and "competitive views" have direct effects (.33 and .24) to "bullying others." These results indicate that girls' victimizing behavior mainly comes from a kind of coping with stress and jealousy. "Peer stressor" has no direct effect to bullying, but a high effect (.50) to "stress" and an indirect effect (.17) to "bullying others" via "stress." Both "study stressor" and "family stressor" also have indirect

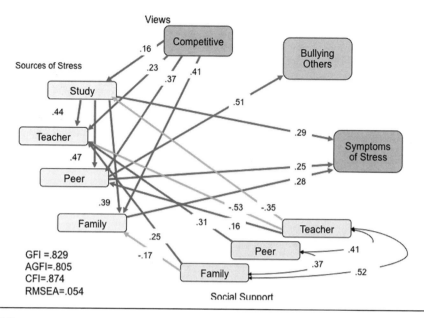

Figure 11.2

effects (.14 and .07). "Competitive views" not only have a direct effect but also an indirect effect (.12) to "bullying others," and finally its total effect (.36) is highest (see Table 11.5).

Conclusion: The Efficacy of the Stress-Stressor Model

A follow-up analysis of the same cohort 1 year later found that girls in Grade 8 showed almost the same causality as they did in Grade 7, although the participants who endorsed "bullying others" were not the same group from Grade 7 to Grade 8. However, boys in Grade 8 did not show the same causality as boys in Grade 7. Nevertheless, the coefficients changed according to the context of children, the causality can be explained by using same framework of the Stress-Stressor Model. Therefore, the coefficients in the model suggest which factors lead children to bullying behavior. According to the robust coefficients, the interventions to reduce the strength

Table 11.5 The Standardized Effect for Each Factor to Bullying Others: Boys and Girls in Grade 7

Factors	Boy			Girl		
	Total	Direct	Indirect	Total	Direct	Indirect
Stress	0.51	0.51	–	0.33	0.33	–
Study stressor	0.24	–	0.24	0.14	–	–
Teacher stressor	–	–	–	–	–	–
Peer stressor	–	–	–	0.17	–	0.17
Family stressor	–	–	–	0.07	–	0.07
Teacher support	–	–	–	−0.03	–	−0.03
Peer support	–	–	–	−0.06	–	−0.06
Family support	–	–	–	−0.02	–	−0.02
Competitive views	0.22	–	0.22	0.36	0.24	0.12

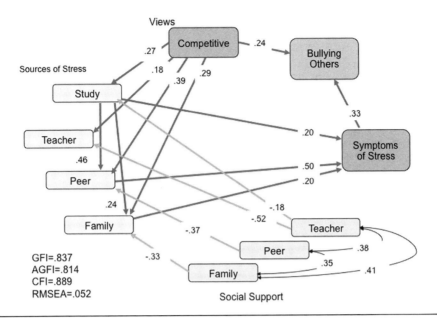

Figure 11.3

of factors or to break the strong relationships between factors should be utilized. The Stress-Stressor Model is useful to identify more effective interventions in reducing bullying behavior among students.

Implications for Practice

In this chapter I argue that it is not only the handful extraordinary children, but also the larger group of ordinary children, who are involved in bullying and victimization. Interventions focused on the extraordinary children with family difficulties and/or personal innate characteristics (i.e., impulsivity, depression, etc.) can reduce only a part of bullying incidents. To reduce bullying, interventions should be developed on the basis of the premise that anybody can be involved in bullying and/or victimization, depending upon contextual variables.

The Stress-Stressor Model described in this chapter shows the causality of bullying according to the contexts in which children function. This model helps us to understand which interventions are effective in each classroom, school, community, and country.

Note

1. This project started in 2003 and is lead by principal researcher Mitsuru Taki of the National Institute for Educational Research (NIER) in Japan. The first phase of the project includes researchers from Japan (Taki), Australia (Dr. Phillip Slee, Flinders University), Canada (Dr. Debra Pepler, York University and Dr. Shelley Hymmel, University of British Colombia) and Korea (Dr. Hee-og Sim, Kunsan University and Dr. Keum-Joo Kwak, Seoul Uuniversity). The second phase expands the collaboration to include United States (Dr. Susan Swearer, University of Nebraska) and China (Dr. Wai Ming, Tam, Chinese University of Hong Kong).

References

Besag, V. E. (1989). *Bullies and victims in schools*. Buckingham, UK: Open University Press.
Cooper, C. L. (1981). *The stress check: Coping with the stresses of life and work*. Englewood Cliffs, NJ: Prentice Hall.

Kanetsuna, T., & Smith, P. K. (2002). Pupil insights into bullying and coping with bullying: Abi-national study in Japan and England. *Journal of School Violence, 1,* 5–29.

Lagerspets, K. M. J., Björkqvist, K., & Peltonen, T. (1988). Is indirect aggression typical of females? Gender differences in aggressiveness in 11 to 12-year-old children. *Aggressive Behaviour, 14,* 403–414.

Lazarus, R. S., & Folkman, S. (1984). *Stress, appraisal, and coping.* New York: Springer.

Ministry of Education, Culture, Sports, Science and Technology (MEXT). (1997). *Seitosidou jou no Shomondai no Genjou to Monbusyou no Sesaku ni tuite* [Annual report of the actual conditions and the policy on student problems] (pp. 165–166). Tokyo: Author.

Morita, Y. (2001). *Ijime no Kokusai Hikaku Kenkyu* [International comparative survey on bullying: Japan, England, Netherlands and Norway]. Tokyo: Kaneko Shobo.

National Institute for Educational Policy Research (NIER) and Ministry of Education, Culture, Sports, Science and Technology (MEXT). (2006). *The Report of International Symposium on Education 2005: Save children from the risk of violence in school–based on the follow-up study and international comparison.* Tokyo: Author.

Okayasu, T. (1997). Mental health check list (simple version). In *Jidou-Seito no Mondaikoudou ni taisuru Jissenteki Taiouhou no Kaihatsu ni kansuru Kenkyuu* [A study of the development for practical interventions against problematic behaviours in school]. Miyazaki, Japan: Miyazaki University, Department of Education.

Olweus, D. (1993). *Bullying at school: What we know and what we can do.* Oxford, UK: Blackwell.

Smith, P. K., & Thompson, D. (1991). *Practical approaches to bullying.* London: David Fulton.

Taki, M. (1992). 'Ijime' Koui no Hassei Youin ni kansuru Jissyouteki Kenkyu [The empirical study of the occurrence of 'Ijime' behaviour]. *Kyouiku Sgakaigaku Kenkyuu* [The Journal of Educational Sociology], *50,* 366–388.

Taki, M. (1996). *'Ijime' wo Sodateru Gakkyu Tokusei* [Bullying and classroom management]. Tokyo: Meiji Tosho.

Taki, M. (1998). Kodomo no Stress to sono Youin [Child stress and the factors]. *Research Report, 36,* 1–11. Tokyo: The National Institute for Educational Research of Japan

Taki, M. (2001). Relation among bullying, stress and stressor: A follow-up survey using panel data and a comparative survey between Japan and Australia. *Japanese Society, 5,* 118–133.

Taki, M. (2003). 'Ijime bullying': Characteristics, causality and interventions. In St Catherine's College, University of Oxford, Kobe Institute (Ed.), *Oxford-Kobe seminars: Measures to reduce "bullying in schools"* (pp. 97–113). Oxford UK: University of Oxford.

12

Victimization and Exclusion

Links to Peer Rejection, Classroom Engagement, and Achievement

ERIC S. BUHS, GARY W. LADD, AND SARAH L. HERALD-BROWN

Peer Influences

This chapter describes a conceptual framework and empirical evidence linking peer rejection to children's school engagement and achievement via peer victimization and social exclusion. In addition to describing processes that contribute to our understanding of how peer rejection and subsequent victimization (including being bullied) may be linked to adjustment outcomes, one of the central contributions that this work makes to the literature is to describe more precisely the role that peer exclusion plays in children's school adjustment. While the constructs related to peer aggression included in this work were not explicitly linked to bullying (i.e., a specific subset of victimization behaviors), the peer victimization and exclusion described here are aggressive behaviors that have been consistently associated with bullying in child and adolescent contexts (e.g., Sandstrom & Cillessen, 2003; Espelage & Swearer, 2003; Underwood, Scott, Galperin, Bjornstad, & Sexton, 2004). As such, this model and the supporting evidence describe processes via which peer rejection and associated victimization consistent with aspects of bullying may impact adjustment in school contexts.

The premise that peer acceptance influences children's development and adjustment has driven developmental research since the 1930s (Ladd, 2003), and since that time a substantial body of findings has accumulated that is generally consistent with the premise that peer rejection is a cause of children's adjustment difficulties (see Ladd, Birch, & Buhs, 1999; Parker & Asher, 1987; MacDougall, Hymel, Vaillancourt, & Mercer, 2001; Vandell & Hembree, 1994). Recent longitudinal studies provided evidence that peer rejection predicts a range of adjustment problems independently from other risk factors such as aggressive or withdrawn behavior patterns (e.g., Coie, Lochman, Terry, & Hyman, 1992; Ladd & Burgess, 2001). Peer rejection/acceptance has, in contrast with dyadic relationships such as friendships, typically been defined as an attitudinal variable that indicates the level of peer sentiment (i.e., liking or disliking) directed toward group members. Measures of peer acceptance in school classrooms indicate how well liked a child is, on average, by classmates—low acceptance has been consistently linked with school disengagement and poorer academic readiness and achievement (Buhs & Ladd, 2001; Buhs, Ladd, & Herald, 2006; Ladd et al., 1999; Ladd, Kochenderfer, & Coleman, 1997; Vandell & Hembree, 1994).

Peer Rejection: How Is It Linked to Victimization, Exclusion, and Classroom Engagement?

Conceptual Framework   Findings from the peer relations literature have consistently linked peer rejection to school engagement and achievement, but there have not been as many studies that have attempted to provide descriptions of how peer sentiments (i.e., peer acceptance/rejection) might affect children's behaviors and attitudes, especially over time. The framework that guided our investigations of adjustment processes linked to peer rejection is based on propositions originally presented by Coie (1990) and hypothesizes that peer rejection affects achievement (and other aspects of adjustment) via two processes: (a) the negative behavioral treatment that rejected children receive from peers, and (b) the resulting changes this treatment causes in children's classroom participation (Figure 12.1—see also Buhs et al., 2006). Peers may first display their dislike for classmates by treating them more negatively than other peers (e.g., victimizing or bullying them)—this negative treatment then serves as a visible marker of peer rejection for the peer group. Second, once children are marked by this maltreatment they are more likely to be marginalized by peers and to move or be moved toward the periphery of classroom and peer activities. In other words, peers who become aware of children targeted for maltreatment are likely to avoid them or exclude them from activities and the targeted children themselves are also likely to disengage from peer activities as a means to avoid further abuse. Third, this disengagement from classroom activities will tend to have a negative impact on learning and ultimately will likely affect achievement.

A Unique Role for Exclusion?   Findings from an earlier empirical study that examined children's adjustment in kindergarten supported this model (Buhs & Ladd, 2001) and showed that rejected children tended to be victimized by classmates. Victimization, in turn, predicted lower levels of classroom participation over the course of the kindergarten year. Declining classroom participation and engagement was subsequently linked to poorer adjustment and achievement. What this earlier study did not examine, though, was whether or not different types of victimization might be independently linked to adjustment and/or have different pathways or processes via which they might affect adjustment. The earlier study relied on a conglomerate peer maltreatment variable that included peer exclusion as well as verbal and physical victimization—this did not allow an examination of potentially distinct relationships among these forms of victimization and subsequent disengagement or other adjustment outcomes. Because there was some evidence that peer exclusion was the strongest indicator of the victimization, we speculated that exclusion might play a more powerful role in predicting declines in engagement and achievement. This premise of a unique role for social exclusion is consistent with other recent conceptual and empirical work that proposes exclusion as a central construct in processes associated with peer maltreatment and victimization (Bukowski & Sippola, 2001; Sandstrom &

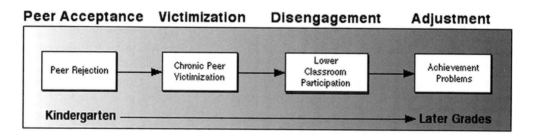

Figure 12.1 Hypothesized mediating process linkages. Adapted from Buhs et al., 2006.

Cillessen, 2003; Underwood et al., 2004). Bukowski and Sippola, in particular, suggested that active isolation (i.e., exclusion) of peers is a common means for groups to maintain identity and control access to social resources. The premises presented in this body of work, in general, are also consistent with our contentions that peer victimization and exclusion are likely to restrict children's access to social activities and resources within their peer group.

A Range of Outcomes   It is also important to note here that other, more broadly construed conceptual frameworks describing links between adjustment and other negative social and peer experiences (similar to and including bullying, victimization and exclusion) link these processes to psychological outcomes such as depression and anxiety (e.g., Lewinsohn, Hoberman, Teri, & Hautzinger, 1985). These researchers characterize aversive social experiences as stressful or unsupportive interactions and have presented frameworks that suggest a lack of support in a particular setting will lead to social and emotional disengagement from that context (see also Connell & Wellborn, 1991). Additionally, these models frequently suggest that the experience of social exclusion, victimization, and other stressful social interactions also likely create a greater risk for recurring adjustment problems and may play a role in long-term adjustment difficulties.

Exclusion and Victimization: A Study of Two Pathways to Disengagement and School Maladjustment

Testing a New Model   To further explore the role of exclusion in the processes linking rejection and victimization to classroom disengagement and achievement, we conducted a second study (described briefly below and in Buhs et al., 2006) that strengthened and expanded the examination of these processes. Note that prior work (Buhs & Ladd, 2001) implied that there were two pathways to disengagement. First, children are less able to participate actively in classroom activities because peer exclusion prevents them from doing so. Second, victimized children will tend to avoid the classroom or school setting as a means of escaping further maltreatment. Our design allowed us to test potentially independent contributions of both of these pathways to disengagement. Additional weakness also occurred due to limitations in the longitudinal design—the relatively short time span (the kindergarten school year) prevented us from determining whether early victimization patterns linked to peer rejection continued and whether or not chronic, long-term victimization (i.e., across multiple years) carried greater risk. Based on models of psychological risk, stress, and support (Dohrenwend & Dohrenwend, 1981; Ladd & Troop-Gordon, 2003), we hypothesized that more chronic, extended exposure to victimization would increase disengagement and decrease subsequent achievement. Following this logic, within this new study we decided to examine whether decreases in classroom engagement were better predicted by exclusion and decreases in avoidance were better predicted by general, physical and verbal victimization. We used a six-year prospective design that followed children from kindergarten through fifth grade, and our measures included indices of peer acceptance/rejection, peer exclusion, peer victimization/abuse, classroom engagement, school avoidance, and academic achievement.

Method   Peer group acceptance/rejection was defined here as the extent to which individuals were liked/disliked by classroom peers, and was measured with averaged sociometric ratings obtained from kindergarten classmates. One form of victimization, peer exclusion (teacher-rated), was defined as the extent to which children were the target of peer behaviors such as ignoring, avoiding, or refusing to associate with them in the classroom context. The other form of victimization, peer abuse (self-rated), was defined as the extent to which children were recipients of aggressive behaviors (i.e., verbal and physical victimization). Measures of both forms of victimization were obtained from kindergarten through grade five. Classroom disengagement was composed of classroom participation and school avoidance indices. Classroom participation (teacher-rated) included children's autonomous (e.g., starting activities, working independently, seeking challenges) and cooperative participation (i.e., adhering to classroom rules and role expectations; see Buhs & Ladd, 2001; Ford, 1985; Wentzel, 1991). School avoidance was defined as the degree to which children expressed a desire to avoid school and engaged in school-avoidant behaviors. Achievement was indicated by performance on individualized achievement tests. Children's classroom participation, school avoidance and achievement were measured in grades three and five, and earlier scores were partialled from later scores to create (residualized) indices that reflected change in children's performance (see Buhs et al., 2006, for complete descriptions of the method and measures). Additionally, we used teacher ratings of aggressive and withdrawn kindergarten behavior to control for antecedent behavioral styles previously linked to peer rejection and maltreatment.

The data used to examine this model were gathered from 380 children (190 girls) who were followed from age 5 (kindergarten) through age 11 (fifth grade) and were initially in 31 kinder-garten classrooms across 10 public schools. By the fifth grade, children were in 162 different classrooms across 32 schools. Children were dawn in nearly equal proportions from families from urban, suburban, or rural Midwestern communities and the sample's ethnic composition was 17.4% African American, 77.1% European American, 1.6% Hispanic, and 3.9% other. Family socioeconomic scores (socioeconomic index [SEI]; Entwisle & Astone, 1994) ranged from 0 (unemployed) to 97.16, with a mean of 49.14 (SEI scores of 50 are assigned to administrative support staff, health technicians, and electronic sales personnel).

Path Model and Results The structural model (see Figure 12.2) was constructed as follows (see Buhs et al., 2006, for a complete description of the model and analyses): First, paths were included

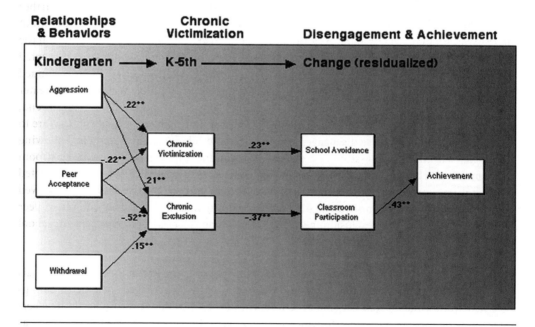

Figure 12.2 SEM Results (ns paths removed, other paths removed for clarity—see Buhs et al. 2006 for full model and detailed description). Notes: * p < .05, ** p < .01. x 2 (27, minimum n = 320) = 50.74, CFI=.97, RMSEA = .05. Adapted from Buhs et al., 2006.

to represent the hypothesis that early peer group rejection promotes chronic peer maltreatment (exclusion, abuse/victimization). Thus, lower levels of peer acceptance predict higher levels of chronic peer exclusion and chronic victimization. Because aggressive or withdrawn behavior with peers was likely to antecede peer rejection and peer maltreatment (for a review, see Ladd, 2003; MacDougall et al., 2001), these were included as potential predictors of chronic victimization and of changes in children's achievement. This made it possible to evaluate the paths from early rejection to chronic maltreatment in the context of other possible causes of chronic peer maltreatment, and to estimate the extent to which the hypothesized mediating pathways between acceptance/rejection, peer maltreatment, classroom disengagement accounted for changes in achievement independently of children's deviant behavioral styles. Next, paths from chronic exclusion to change in classroom participation, and from chronic abuse to change in school avoidance were created. Finally, we included paths from both indicators of classroom disengagement to changes in children's achievement so that it was possible to evaluate the hypothesis that declining classroom disengagement predicted lower achievement.

Our tests of this model (LISREL 8; Jöreskog & Sörbom, 2001) indicated that the model fit the data well (see Figure 12.2) and allowed us to interpret the results (note that the model fit data drawn from groups of boys and girls equally well). The results showed that peer rejection predicted chronic peer victimization and peer exclusion, independently of aggression and withdrawal. Victimization also predicted subsequent declines in school avoidance and peer exclusion predicted declines in classroom participation (additional estimates of paths from peer abuse to classroom participation and from peer exclusion to school avoidance were *not* significant). Only classroom participation, however, predicted declines in achievement (controlling for peer rejection effects on achievement). Additionally, indirect effects estimates indicated that chronic victimization, exclusion and disengagement were *independently* linked to achievement declines while controlling for peer rejection, aggression, and withdrawal. In total, the model tests suggested that chronic victimization and chronic peer exclusion mediated links between peer rejection and subsequent change in participation and achievement, and that classroom participation was the only independent mediator of links from chronic exclusion and abuse to achievement.

Conclusions

Attitudes to Behaviors   The findings discussed here supported and elaborated Coie's (1990) premises by showing that peer rejection is associated not only with concurrent victimization, but also with distinct forms of peer victimization that may endure over many school years, and with later, adverse adjustment outcomes. These links also support the view that early peer rejection is associated with at least two forms of chronic peer victimization (exclusion, physical/verbal abuse), that these types of victimization uniquely influence school engagement, and that chronic peer exclusion is likely to be more detrimental to children's academic success. No prior work presented support for this type of process within a single model or set of analyses.

Some of the findings discussed here also supported the premise that peers' dislike of classmates in kindergarten became a motive for victimization (i.e., the behavioral expression of peer rejection—see Buhs & Ladd, 2001; Connell & Wellborn, 1991; Ladd, 2003, for more detailed descriptions of similar conceptual frameworks). These findings were also consistent with the premise that victimization becomes more likely when a greater proportion of the peer group shares their dislike for a peer. In this study, children who were more rejected were, by definition, disliked by more of their classmates, and rejection predicted subsequent victimization. Perhaps, under these kinds of conditions, peers believe such treatment is justifiable because many peers harbor similar sentiments, or because disliked children lack allies and can thus be mistreated with impunity.

A Chronic Problem Recent findings have extended previous work by illustrating that children's dislike of peers in kindergarten predicts chronic victimization and other peer problems, including bullying. As Coie (1990) observed, early victimization may act as a visible sign of rejection for peer groups. These findings have also supported the contention that early patterns of rejection and victimization may become self-perpetuating or dynamic systems where peers' feelings of dislike toward individuals motivates more maltreatment, and displaying victimization in group contexts signals to others that victimized and excluded children are (or should be) disliked (i.e., a group contagion effect). Although this process may begin in kindergarten as children jockey for position in new peer groups, several mechanisms may play a role in the persistence of these patterns over time. First, peers' dislike toward particular classmates may persist from grade to grade via the social reputation that accompanies children, and promote continuity in victimization (see Hymel, Wagner, & Butler, 1990). Second, for these or other reasons (e.g., preferred cognitive scripts for social behavior, reinforcement histories, etc.), peers may continue their habitual interaction patterns when they encounter previously disliked children during later school years. Third, by re-establishing old behavior patterns at their new grade levels peers may signal to classmates that previously disliked and bullied or victimized children deserve further maltreatment.

Distinct Pathways for Long-Term Effects Our findings also showed that chronically excluded children tended to participate less in classrooms and that those who were chronically victimized were more likely to avoid school. This pattern is consistent with other findings discussed above and suggests that different forms of victimization might have distinct effects on children's school disengagement. Peer exclusion was linked to a type of disengagement that was, more than school avoidance, predictive of changes in achievement. Thus, although disliked children often become the targets of enduring victimization, the form of maltreatment that they experience may have different consequences for classroom engagement and achievement patterns (see also Fonagy, Twemlow, Vernberg, Sacco, & Little, 2005). Peer exclusion appears to be a stronger predictor of disengagement and subsequent declines in achievement. This is consistent with earlier models (Coie, 1990; Wentzel, 1991) that proposed that exclusion restricts children's access to social and instrumental resources that peers provide in the classroom and acts as a signal to classmates that some children are not integral members of the classroom group. Excluded children may then devalue their relationships with classroom peers and further withdraw from the classroom or school where the abuse occurred (see also Baumeister & Leary, 1995). This behavioral process probably contributes to serious school adjustment problems (i.e., lower achievement, internalizing problems). While peer victimization (e.g., physical and verbal abuse) was not independently predictive of achievement in our study, it may still play a role in children's emotional adjustment (e.g., internalizing problems; see Hawker & Boulton, 2000). This may also suggest that children victimized by this form of abuse may still be able to selectively participate (relative to more excluded children) in a subset of school activities that support learning and achievement. These and similar findings were also consistent with the contention that peer rejection and chronic maltreatment make independent contributions to changes in disengagement and achievement. While aggressive and withdrawn behavior patterns predicted later peer maltreatment, evidence of additive predictive links between rejection and peer maltreatment may also be viewed as consistent with contentions that many aggressive and withdrawn children (especially at early ages) are not rejected by their peers (e.g., Coie, 1990; Garandeau, Wilson, & Rodkin, this volume; Rodkin, Farmer, & Pearl, 2000; Younger, Gentile, & Burgess, 1993).

Evidence for an Expanded Role for Exclusion in Victimization Processes A number of other recent studies have also explored the role of exclusion in children's peer relationships, especially as a form of victimization (including within bullying relationships). Some of the findings presented in those studies also suggest that social exclusion may be central to more accurate conceptions of victimization, especially in school contexts, because it may be uniquely linked to later academic and social-emotional adjustment (e.g., Sandstrom & Cillessen, 2003; Underwood et al., 2004). Bukowski and Sippola's (2001) conceptual framework for understanding peer victimization contended that social exclusion/active isolation may be construed as victimization used to maintain group cohesion and homogeneity (i.e., a *function* of exclusion) and presented some supporting empirical evidence. Their suggestion of a central role for social exclusion in victimization processes is consistent with the contention that exclusion may be related to themes of membership to larger social groups or contexts and also with our hypothesis that denial of access to social groups significantly impairs individuals' attempts to access peer social and instrumental support within larger social groups (see also Asher, Rose, & Gabriel, 2001; Wentzel, 1991). Underwood and colleagues (Underwood et al., 2004) have also presented findings from an experimental study where their observations indicated that young adolescents consistently directed verbal and non-verbal social exclusion toward peers who were attempting to join an activity. Sandstrom and Cillessen also gathered self-reports, that indicated young adolescents, especially withdrawn children, reported exclusion by peers as a distinct facet of victimization in school contexts.

Taken together, a body of evidence appears to be emerging that suggests that peer exclusion is an aspect of maltreatment and victimization that warrants further attention as researchers examine processes linked to academic and psychosocial adjustment. While exclusion has previously been identified as an aspect of relational victimization (victimizing behaviors intended to damage relationships, distinct from physical and verbal aggression—see Crick & Grotpeter, 1996; Crick et al., 1999), it has not typically been operationalized or measured in a way that allows for an examination of potential independent effects or contributions to pathways to maladjustment. The study described above represents a step in that direction and suggests that future investigations should broaden conceptions of peer maltreatment, including bullying and victimization constructs, and examine the potential contributions of social exclusion to subsequent adjustment. Our findings illustrate the potential importance of peers' sustained acts of exclusion and although exclusion may not be as visibly harmful as verbal or physical abuse, it may be particularly detrimental to children's classroom participation, encourage disengagement from learning activities and may have a greater impact than verbal or physical victimization on academic progress.

Within a broader perspective, our results supported chronic stress models (Dohrenwend & Dohrenwend, 1981; Johnson, 1988) and indicated that chronic maltreatment may increase the risk for maladjustment, including school disengagement and achievement problems. As discussed above, findings from other studies of victimization effects suggest that the range of outcomes that are likely linked to these and similar processes also includes psychological outcomes such as internalizing problems (e.g., Buhs & Ladd, 2001; Ladd & Troop-Gordon, 2003; Lewinsohn et al., 1985). Taken in perspective, these findings support the broader premise that chronic, aversive peer interactions such as bullying and victimization play a role in a broad range of adjustment outcomes. In sum, chronic peer exclusion and victimization appear likely to alter the social context of the classroom and negatively impact adjustment across the elementary school years (see also Doll, Zucker, & Brehm, 2004, for an examination of related intervention strategies). The role of peer exclusion also appears central to descriptions of processes that

Table 12.1 Peer Rejection, Exclusion, and Victimization: Implications for Practice

Finding	Implication
Chronic victimization and exclusion predict disengagement and lower achievement	Children who experience higher levels of victimization across multiple years may be more at-risk (as compared to less frequently/infrequently victimized peers) and should be targeted for more consistent and long-term intervention and supports.
Exclusion is a form of victimization that predicts disengagement and lower achievement (independently and perhaps more strongly than physical or verbal victimization)	Although exclusion may be a more subtle form of victimization that is more difficult to observe, the long-term effects are potentially as damaging as forms more frequently targeted by adults for prevention/intervention (e.g. physical and verbal abuse). Practitioners need to be careful to detect and try to prevent these peer behaviors.
Disengagement linked to victimization likely plays a role in lower achievement	Victimized/bullied children may need to be provided with greater support in order to keep them engaged in school (e.g. alternate classroom activities or peer groups fostering more positive experiences in school).
Peer rejection and abuse contribute to disengagement and achievement problems over and above children's prior behavioral patterns	Rejection and victimization likely exacerbate aggressive or withdrawn children's peer problems—interventions likely need to target peer relationship problems in addition to individual behavioral patterns.

operate in the school context. More complete descriptions of these forms of maltreatment and victimization in school contexts, including those associated with bullying, is essential for the development of effective, empirically-based intervention programs.

Acknowledgment

Portions of the study discussed below were conducted as part of the Pathways Project, a longitudinal investigation of children's social/psychological/scholastic adjustment that is supported by the National Institutes of Health (1 & 2-RO1MH-49223; R01HD-045906 to Gary W. Ladd). Portions of the empirical data and analyses referred to in this chapter were originally published in the authors' 2006 article: Peer Exclusion and Victimization: Processes That Mediate the Relation Between Peer Group Rejection and Children's Classroom Engagement and Achievement. *Journal of Educational Psychology, 98*, 1–13.

References

Asher, S. R., Rose, A. J., & Gabriel, S. W. (2001). Peer rejection in everyday life. In M. R. Leary (Ed.), *Interpersonal rejection* (pp. 105–142). New York: Oxford University Press.

Baumeister, R. F., & Leary, M. R. (1995). The need to belong: Desire for interpersonal attachments as a fundamental human motivation. *Psychological Bulletin, 117,* 407–529.

Buhs, E. S., & Ladd, G. W. (2001). Peer rejection in kindergarten as an antecedent of young children's school adjustment: An examination of mediating processes. *Developmental Psychology, 37,* 550–560.

Buhs, E., Ladd, G., & Herald, S. (2006). Peer exclusion and victimization: Processes that mediate the relation between peer group rejection and children's classroom engagement and achievement? *Journal of Educational Psychology, 98,* 1–13.

Bukowski, W., & Sippola, L. (2001). Groups, individuals, and victimization: A view of the peer system. In J. Juvonen & S. Graham (Eds.), *Peer harassment in school: The plight of the vulnerable and victimized* in (pp. 355–377). New York: Guilford.

Connell, J. P., & Wellborn, J. G. (1991). Competence, autonomy, and relatedness: A motivational analysis of self-esteem processes. In M. R. Gunnar & L. A. Sroufe (Eds.), *The Minnesota Symposia on Child Development: Vol. 23. Self-processes and development* (pp. 43–77). Hillsdale, NJ: Erlbaum.

Coie, J. D. (1990). Towards a theory of peer rejection. In S. R. Asher & J. D. Coie (Eds.), *Peer rejection in childhood* (pp. 365–401). New York: Cambridge University Press.

Coie, J. D., Lochman, J. E., Terry, R., & Hyman, C. (1992). Predicting early adolescent disorder from childhood aggression and peer rejection. *Journal of Consulting and Clinical Psychology, 60,* 783–792.

Crick, N., & Grotpeter, J. (1996). Children's treatment by peers: Victims of relational and overt aggression. *Development and Psychopathology, 8,* 367–380.

Crick, N. R., Werner, N. E., Casas, J. F., O'Brien, K. M., Nelson, D. A., Grotpeter, J. K., et al. (1999). Childhood aggression and gender: A new look at an old problem. In D. Bernstein (Ed.), *45th Annual Symposium on Motivation: Gender and motivation* (pp. 75–141). Lincoln: University of Nebraska Press.

Dohrenwend, B. P., & Dohrenwend, B. S. (1981). Socioenvironmental factors, stress, and psychopathology. *American Journal of Community Psychology, 9,* 128–164.

Doll, B., Zucker, S., & Brehm, K. (2004). *Resilient classrooms: Creating healthy environments for learning.* New York: Guilford.

Entwisle, D. R., & Astone, N. M. (1994). Some practical guidelines for measuring youth's race/ethnicity and sociometric status. *Child Development, 65,* 1521–1540.

Espelage, D., & Swearer, S. (2003). Research on school bullying and victimization: What have we learned and where do we go from here? *School Psychology Review, 32,* 365–383.

Fonagy, P., Twemlow, S. W., Vernberg, E., Sacco, F. C., & Little, T. D. (2005). Creating a peaceful school learning environment: The impact of an antibullying program on educational attainment in elementary schools. *Medical Science Monitor, 11,* 317–325.

Ford, M. E. (1985). The concept of competence: Themes and variations. In H. A. Marlowe, Jr. & R. B. Weinberg (Eds.), *Competence development* (pp. 3–49). New York: Academic Press.

Hawker, D. S. J., & Boulton, M. J. (2000). Twenty years' research on peer victimization and psychosocial maladjustment: A meta-analytic review of cross-sectional studies. *Journal of Child Psychology and Psychiatry, 41,* 441–455.

Hymel, S., Wagner, E., & Butler, L. J. (1990). Reputational bias: View from the peer group. In S. R. Asher & J. D. Coie *Peer rejection in childhood* (pp. 156–186). New York: Cambridge University Press.

Johnson, J. H. (1988). *Life events as stressors in childhood and adolescence.* Newbury Park, CA: Sage.

Jöreskog, K., & Sörbom, D. (2001). *LISREL 8: Structural equation modeling with the SIMPLIS command language.* Hillsdale, NJ: Erlbaum.

Ladd, G. W. (2003). Probing the adaptive significance of children's behavior and relationships in the school context: A child by environment perspective. In R. Kail (Ed.), *Advances in child behavior and development* (pp. 43–104). New York: Wiley.

Ladd, G. W., Birch, S. H., & Buhs, E. S. (1999). Children's social and scholastic lives in kindergarten: Related spheres of influence? *Child Development, 70,* 1373–1400.

Ladd, G. W., & Burgess, K. B. (2001). Do relational risks and protective factors moderate the linkages between childhood aggression and early psychological and school adjustment? *Child Development, 72,* 1579–1601.

Ladd, G. W., & Troop-Gordon, W. (2003). The role of chronic peer difficulties in the development of children's psychological adjustment problems. *Child Development, 74,* 1344–1367.

Ladd, G. W., Kochenderfer, B. J., & Coleman, C. C. (1997). Classroom peer acceptance, friendship, and victimization: Distinct relational systems that contribute uniquely to children's school adjustment? *Child Development, 68,* 1181–1197.

Lewinsohn P. M., Hoberman, H., Teri, L., & Hautzinger, M. (1985). An integrative theory of depression. In S. Reiss & R. Bootzin (Eds.), *Theoretical issues in behavior therapy* (pp. 331–359). San Diego, CA: Academic Press.

MacDougall, P., Hymel, S., Vaillancourt, T., & Mercer, L. (2001). The consequences of childhood peer rejection. In M. R. Leary (Ed.), *Interpersonal rejection* (pp. 213–247). Oxford, UK: Oxford University Press.

Parker, J. G., & Asher, S. R. (1987). Peer relations and later personal adjustment: Are low-accepted children at risk? *Psychological Bulletin, 102,* 357–389.

Rodkin, P. C., Farmer, T. W., & Pearl, R. (2000). Heterogeneity of popular boys: Antisocial and prosocial configurations. *Developmental Psychology, 36,* 14–24.

Sandstrom, M., & Cillessen, A. (2003). Sociometric status and children's peer experiences: Use of the Daily Diary Method. *Merrill-Palmer Quarterly, 49,* 427–452.

Underwood, M., Scott, B., Galperin, M., Bjornstad, G., & Sexton, A. (2004). An observational study of social exclusion under varied conditions: Gender and developmental differences. *Child Development, 75,* 1538–1555.

Vandell, D. L., & Hembree, S. E. (1994). Peer social status and friendship: Independent contributors to children's social and academic adjustment. *Merrill-Palmer Quarterly, 40,* 461–470.

Wentzel, K. R. (1991). Social competence at school; Relation between social responsibility and academic achievement. *Review of Educational Research, 61,* 1–24.

Younger, A., Gentile, C., & Burgess, K. (1993). Children's perceptions of social withdrawal: Changes across age. In. K. E. Rubin & J. B. Asendorpf (Eds.), *Social withdrawal, inhibition, and shyness in childhood* (pp. 215–235). Hillsdale, NJ: Erlbaum.

13

Popular Girls and Brawny Boys

The Role of Gender in Bullying and Victimization Experiences

ERIKA D. FELIX AND JENNIFER GREIF GREEN

Gender differences are a hallmark of the popular perception of peer relationships and bullying. Consider the stereotypic illustration of a brawny boy physically pummeling a smaller peer while friends cheer in the background versus portrayals of girls using gossip, rumors, and backstabbing to victimize less-popular peers. Gender differences in bullying and victimization are not lost on young people. For example, in an anonymous school-based survey where we asked for comments about bullying experiences, one female student wrote:

> Teasing/harassment is different from females to males I think. Females are like vipers; they strike quickly and only the strongest can hold them off. Females exclude, tease and drop snide comments easily. Males, however…are like bears, using muscle and brawn over brain.

These polarized depictions of bullying among males and females raise questions about the extent to which gender-related differences are myth or reality. Either way, they underscore the need to consider school bullying in the context of gender[1] roles and the development of masculinity and femininity.

Further complicating the relationship between gender and bullying is the need to conceptualize this relationship in a cultural and developmental context. Just as pathways for developing gender-related identity reflect diverse cultural contexts, the dynamic peer relationships involved in bullying vary across sociocultural groups. Within an international framework it is particularly important to consider how gender and bullying are influenced by characteristics of the macrosystem (Bronfenbrenner, 1986).

In addressing gender differences, research often uses biological sex alone to divide their sample when reporting prevalence, social cognitive correlates and psychosocial adjustment differences. By dividing research samples by biological sex, researchers are conceptually using gender as a subject variable, which means that it is considered something implicit and static within the person that affects their behavior (Matlin, 2000). Considering gender this way is common, but masks the complexity of gender role development and the dynamic experience of gender-related bullying (Lagerspetz & Bjorkqvist, 1994).

This chapter presents research and theory on how gender interacts with bullying and bullying victimization experiences. The chapter will also describe a conceptual foundation for studying bullying and gender, address what we consider to be seven key questions about gender and bullying, and conclude with the evidence-based assertion that researchers need to actively consider gender-related findings when designing studies and interventions for bullying.

Conceptual Foundations for Studying Bullying and Gender

Although the study of the development of aggressive behavior traditionally focused on males, there has been growing interest in the development of aggression among females (Crick, Bigbee, & Howes, 1996; Lagerspetz & Bjorkqvist, 1994). Several extensive reviews of gender and the development of aggression have come out in recent years, and the reader is referred to these works for detailed information (e.g., Crick et al., 1999; Maccoby, 2004; Underwood, 2003). Here we summarize some of the conceptual issues cited by these authors that may be helpful in informing future studies on bullying and peer victimization.

Research studies differ in their findings as to how gender and aggression are related, with results indicating both marked differences and substantial similarities. For example, both males and females engage in physical and relational aggression; however they do so at different rates. To provide a framework for understanding these differences, gender-focused researchers (e.g., Maccoby, 1998; Maccoby & Jacklin, 1987; Maltz & Borker, 1982; Thorne & Luria, 1986) have developed "Two Cultures Theory." As summarized by Underwood (2003), this theory suggested that the gender segregation in young children's peer groups leads to such different experiences for males and females that it is as if they were operating within two distinct cultures. This theory garnered support from cross-cultural research on the early and middle childhood gender segregation in children's peer groups, as well as differences between girls' and boys' play and friendship patterns (Gottman & Mettetal, 1986; Maccoby & Jacklin, 1987; Serbin, Moller, Gulko, Powlishta, & Colburne, 1994). As Underwood (2003) wrote, "Two Cultures theorists consistently emphasize the importance of children's peer groups for the development of gender differences in social interaction" (p. 41). In the sections that follow, we discuss key questions in research on gender and bullying using a framework consistent with Two Cultures Theory. This theory is particularly appropriate in a handbook on international experiences with bullying, as it provides a conceptualization of bullying that incorporates cultural aspects of gender-identity development.

Key Questions

1. Are there Gender Differences in the Prevalence of Bullying and Bullying Victimization?

The answer to this question is largely dependent upon the way that bullying is defined and the type of bullying measured. For a long time researchers reported that males were more involved in aggression as both victims and perpetrators than were females. Evidence that males are more often bullies and/or victims than females has been reported from several countries including Brazil (DeSouza & Ribeiro, 2005), Germany (Scheithauer, Hayer, Petermann, & Jugert, 2006), Israel (Benbenishty & Astor, 2005), South Korea (Yang, Kim, Kim, Shin, & Yoon, 2006), Switzerland (Perren & Hornung, 2005), Turkey (Kepenekci & Çinkir, 2006), and the United States (Nansel et al., 2001). This finding has been consistent across studies using peer nomination methodologies (e.g., Espelage, Holt, & Henkel, 2003) and observational research (Craig & Pepler, 1997). A cross-national World Health Organization survey of bullying found that males reported that they were bullies more often than females in all countries surveyed; however females reported equal or sometimes more frequent victimization than males (Craig & Harel, 2004).

These differences in prevalence rates may not tell the whole story, as males and females may engage in and experience different forms of bullying (Crick & Grotpeter, 1995). A study of terms used to describe bullying in fourteen countries suggested that children (particularly younger children) more closely associated the word "bullying" with physical and verbal aggression than social exclusion (Smith et al., 2002). If this is the case, differences in rates of bullying and victimization among girls and boys found in studies may be methodological rather than substantive. Consistent with Two Cultures Theory, Lagerspetz and Bjorkqvist (1994) hypothesized that different social roles for males and females translate into differences in aggression. As much of the foundational research on bullying focused on predominantly male forms of victimization, such as physical victimization, the introduction of relational aggression as a form of aggression more often perpetrated by females was ground-breaking in promoting gender-sensitivity in aggression research (Crick et al., 1999).

Relational aggression refers to indirect victimization that involves harming others by hurting their relationships through lies, spreading rumors, and withdrawing friendship, (i.e., relational victimization; Crick et al., 1996). Some peer victimization research has suggested that girls more often experience relational victimization than boys, whereas boys are more likely to experience direct physical and verbal victimization than girls (Crick & Bigbee, 1998; Crick & Grotpeter, 1996; Rivers & Smith, 1994). Crick and Bigbee (1998) found that by including a measure of relational victimization in their studies, the number of identified victims increased, most of whom were girls. Students generally view relational aggression as a normative response to aggression, common among girls, and more common for girls than boys (Crick et al., 1996). With this new understanding of relational aggression came the recognition that previous studies of gender-related differences in the prevalence of bullying may have been influenced by the type of behavior studied and that female involvement in bullying was more prevalent than researchers originally recognized. As Smith and colleagues (2002) suggested, studies that ask whether children have experiences with "bullying" are more likely to elicit responses from boys who engage in overt aggressive behaviors, because many children do not consider indirect aggression to be "bullying."

In sum, variations in the expression of aggression suggest that the process of gender socialization impacts the development of peer dynamics. As suggested by the Two Cultures Theory, differences in societal constructions of masculinity, femininity, and bullying itself are likely to impact the way bullying is experienced (Gini & Pozzoli, 2006) and reported. Whereas boys are more likely to inflict harm using physical and verbal aggression, girls choose to use interpersonal aggression because they are more attuned to interpersonal dynamics (Crick & Grotpeter, 1995). In particular, the tendency for girls to have tighter friendship patterns than boys makes relational aggression a particularly powerful tool for aggression (Lagerspetz & Bjorkqvist, 1994). Interpreting gender differences in the prevalence of bullying behaviors requires that researchers are aware of the different types of aggression that are likely to be expressed by males and females, in order to describe an accurate picture of bullying and victimization.

2. How Do Bullying and Bullying Victimization Fit within the Context of Gender Socialization?

In many cultural contexts, power and control are linked to gender and gender roles. The way that children are socialized to perceive power, the type of power they seek, and the methods that they use to gain power are related to the development of masculinity and femininity (Gini & Pozzoli, 2006). Bullying, by definition, involves a disparity of power between people who bully and people being bullied, with a fundamental characteristic being that the victim cannot defend him or herself (Olweus, 1978). The person being bullied lacks the power to stop the bullying from occurring, and it is precisely this lack of power that is so harmful to children and adolescents who are chronically targeted. Power in the bullying relationship can come in many forms, and sources of power are not always evident to an outside observer (Rigby, 2002). The sources of power may include physical strength, popularity, belonging to a majority or privileged group, and possessing coveted skills (e.g., athletic or academic).

Power is often used in the bullying dynamic to enforce a form of social control, by demonstrating, negotiating, affirming, and defending existing status and social hierarchies (Mcallister, 2001). Observational and interview data in Mcallister's (2001) study suggested that status hierarchies are related to beliefs in socially scripted ideas of masculinity and femininity. For example, teasing and harassment can be used to reinforce what is considered acceptable behavior for each gender. Bullying exchanges may, in part, serve to reinforce socio-cultural scripts about how each gender should behave (Mcallister, 2001). Studies with youth and adults suggest that nonconforming or gender-atypical gender roles can be a factor in bullying victimization, especially for males (Friedman Koeske, Silvestre, Korr, & Sites, 2006; Erikson & Einarsen, 2004; Lee, 2002; Young & Sweeting, 2004). Gender-atypical behavior makes individuals different from their peers, which increases vulnerability to victimization (Young & Sweeting, 2004). Students who engage in gender-atypical behavior are also less likely to share common interests with same-sex peers, and thus may also struggle to develop friendships, which are protective against victimization. Young and Sweeting suggest that boys tend to experience stricter rules of gender conformity than do girls. They found that compared to boys with gender-typical leisure and sports interests, gender-atypical boys were twice as likely to be victimized. "Maleness" in boys protected against victimization, but for girls it increased their risk (suggesting that gender-atypical behaviors were also a risk factor for victimization in females; Young & Sweeting, 2004).

Research on adults mimics these findings in adolescents. In a retrospective study with gay male adults, Friedman and colleagues (2006) found that bullying mediated the relationship between gender-role nonconformity and suicidality. Also, being in a gender-atypical job was related to increased bullying victimization. Erikson and Einarsen (2004) studied assistant nurses in Norway and found that male assistant nurses were exposed to more workplace bullying than were their female counterparts. A qualitative study found workplace bullying for either sex was fueled in part by judgments of appropriate gender conduct and pressure to fulfill these social norms (Lee, 2002). Thus, this growing body of research supports exploring gender and gender roles as a factor in power imbalance in the bullying dynamic and risk for victimization.

Some discussions of gender-related victimization have led to questions about the overlap between bullying and sexual harassment (Stein, 2003). In particular, this question has been raised in the workplace where the term "sexual harassment" is more frequently used than the language of bullying, which is traditionally reserved for children. However, questions about experiences of sexual harassment in school-age children are important, just as the topic of bullying has received increased attention in adulthood and work settings.

3. Is it Bullying or Sexual Harassment?

There is growing awareness that the insults, lewd gestures, demeaning and sexist attitudes, cruel jokes, and sexual propositions are common among adolescents and similar to sexual harassment experienced by adults (Levesque, 1998). Adolescent peer sexual harassment is hypothesized to be based in a climate of unequal social relations between males and females during middle childhood and adolescence (Rodkin & Fischer, 2003). The emergence of sexual harassment is linked to adolescence, however, it is not typical or socially appropriate, thus should not be considered normative (McMaster, Connolly, Pepler, & Craig, 2002). Despite being a common problem among adolescents and conceptually similar to other forms of peer victimization, sexual harassment has traditionally been studied separately from these other forms of peer victimization or bullying.

Stein (2003) wrote that much of what researchers and educators consider bullying is actually sexual harassment. She asserted that labeling these behaviors "bullying" ignores the broader civil rights issues of victimization targeted at students because of their sex, and by extension, their race or sexual orientation. In the context of a work environment, Simpson and Cohen (2004) drew a distinction between bullying and harassment. They proposed that harassment is directed at a group feature (e.g., race, sex, sexual orientation), whereas bullying is typically directed at victims because of characteristics of the individual (e.g., personality, job-related competence).

By definition, sexual harassment is similar to bullying, in that it is a form of aggressive behavior in a relationship characterized by an imbalance of power; however, the content of the interaction is sexualized or related to the gender of the victim. Fitzgerald, Gelfand, and Drasgow (1995) have identified three types of sexual harassment. *Gender harassment* consists of behaviors that convey insulting, hostile, and degrading attitudes about a person's gender. Gender harassment closely resembles other forms of non-sexual verbal aggression, because it involves the intentional infliction of harm through verbal insults and name-calling. *Unwanted sexual attention* involves offensive, unwanted, and unreciprocated verbal and nonverbal behavior of a sexual nature. Physical gestures often associated with bullying, such as unwanted grabbing and touching, may also be considered unwanted sexual attention. *Sexual coercion* involves eliciting sexual cooperation through promise of reward or through force, which is similar to the intimidation often used by children who bully.

There is growing empirical evidence that the experience of sexual harassment overlaps substantially with other forms of direct and indirect bullying. For example, Felix and McMahon (2007) found that 49% of students reported experiencing all three types of victimization assessed (sexual harassment, relational victimization, and direct physical/verbal victimization) and 28% reported sexual harassment and at least one other form of victimization. This is consistent with other research showing a significant association between students who engage in bullying and those who engage in peer sexual harassment (DeSouza & Ribeiro, 2005; Pellegrini, 2001).

In their research on adolescents, McMaster and associates (2002) found that for both males and females, the three most common victimization behaviors they reported perpetrating were (a) homophobic name-calling; (b) sexual comments, jokes, gestures, or looks; and (c) making comments or rating sexual body parts. The most commonly experienced forms of sexual harassment were (a) homophobic name-calling, (b) sexual comments, and (c) being flashed. This indicates consistency in adolescent reports of perpetration and victimization of sexual harassment, which is unsurprising, as 78% of perpetrators also reported victimization and 56% of victims reported being perpetrators (McMaster et al., 2002).

In sum, bullying and sexual harassment can be conceptualized as a Venn diagram of two overlapping, but distinct experiences. Not all bullying is sexual harassment; many times bullying is directed at characteristics other than gender and does not involved sexualized comments or behaviors. In addition, not all sexual harassment is bullying. Sexual harassment does not necessarily have the hallmark characteristics of repetition and intentionality that define bullying. However, there is a fair amount of overlap between bullying and sexual harassment, particularly among older adolescents, indicating the importance of assessing these two constructs in tandem.

4. What Is the Difference between Cross-Gender and Same-Gender Bullying?

We earlier discussed how gender has been traditionally used as a subject variable in bullying and aggression research. Another conceptual viewpoint is to treat gender as a stimulus variable (Matlin, 2000). With this framework, a person's gender is viewed as something to which others react. For example, the content of a compliment in a social situation can depend on the gender of the recipient; it may be an appraisal of appearance for a female recipient, but an acknowledgement of achievement for a male. The gender-as-a-stimulus framework is perhaps more useful for understanding cross-gender peer victimization and forms of victimization like sexual harassment than the gender-as-a-subject variable framework.

When studying the bully-victim dyad or group, self-report research on school bullying has shown that boys were not commonly bullied by girls (Bentley & Li, 1995); however, girls were frequently bullied by boys at school. One study in Great Britain found that of victimized girls, 31% were being bullied only by boys, 36% by boys and girls, and 32.5% by girls only (Eslea & Smith, 1998). In comparison, boys reported that they were almost always bullied only by other boys (83.5%; Eslea & Smith). Olweus (1994) reported that in Norway, over 60% of victimized girls reported that their bullies were boys. Some boys reported being bullied by girls, but over 80% were mainly bullied by boys. In contrast, using naturalistic observation, a Canadian research team found that boys were the victims of girls' bullying in 52% of the observations (Craig & Pepler, 1997). They noted that boys were more likely to bully other boys than girls.

To assess which bullying behaviors were predominantly associated with cross-gender versus same-gender peer victimization, Felix and McMahon (2007) explored the rates of various forms of victimization for different gender-dyads among 111 urban, middle school students. They found that behaviors associated with teasing or gender harassment were more commonly same-gender victimization experiences for boys, but represented cross-gender victimization for girls. Girls did not report being hit, kicked, or pushed by boys. Students reported that other victimization behaviors, such as relational victimization, unwanted sexual attention, having property stolen or damaged, were perpetrated by both sexes.

The antecedents of cross-gender versus same-gender peer victimization may differ. For example, McMaster and colleagues (2002) noted that there are different motivational, behavioral, and contextual determinants in same-gender than in cross-gender sexual harassment. They found that cross-gender harassment was partially motivated by sexual interest, whereas same-gender harassment often took the form of verbal aggression (e.g., boys called other boys "gay" in an attempt to hurt them). Further, pubertal status and the gender composition of the peer network were independently associated with engaging in cross-gender harassment of others. Cross-gender harassment also increased with age, whereas same-gender sexual harassment did not. Finally, boys perpetrated and experienced more same-gender harassment than cross-gender harassment, but for girls it was the opposite. Taken together, these findings indicated that same- and cross-gender harassment were at least partially distinct and therefore the composition of the dyad should be considered in studies of bullying and victimization.

Overall, the previous sections on gender-related victimization lead to questions about the practical implications of attending to gender dynamics in bullying. The remaining sections of this chapter address the way that gender is related to the impact of bullying, how it affects the course and outcome of bullying, and how gender can be used to inform targeted interventions.

5. Is the Impact of Bullying Different for Boys than Girls?

There are many different ways bullying others and victimization affect student well-being, including having a negative impact on social cognitions, physical and mental health, peer and romantic relationships, school engagement, and academics. In this section we highlight some recent research on how the interaction of gender and victimization may influence social cognitions, mental health, and relationships.

Social Cognition   Victimization experience may be a factor affecting whether youth believe it is acceptable to behave aggressively. For example, Felix and McMahon (2007) found that males who experienced sexual harassment were more likely to believe that aggressive behaviors were acceptable (β = .48; R^2 = .36, $p < .01$), than females or males who experienced other forms of victimization. Sexual harassment may be an especially troubling form of victimization for middle school males as it targets their masculinity at a particularly vulnerable developmental period. As previously discussed, they may be targeted for displaying gender-atypical behavior (Young & Sweeting, 2004) and stronger beliefs supporting aggression may place them at higher risk for aggressing toward others in the future. Responding aggressively may actually serve to protect them from future victimization, as aggressive behavior may be considered gender-typical.

In another study on gender differences in the relation between aggression and social cognition, Musher-Eizenman and colleagues (2004) found different cognitive mediators of exposure to aggression and aggressive behavior for boys and girls. For girls, beliefs about retaliation were a strong mediator of the relations between exposure to aggression and aggressive behavior, whereas for boys, self evaluation was more important.

Mental Health   Research documents the harmful impact of chronic peer victimization on youth psychologically and academically (e.g., Craig, 1998, Kochenderfer & Ladd, 1996; Olweus, 1994; Schwartz, Gorman, Nakamoto, & Toblin, 2005). The role of gender in the relationship of peer victimization to psychosocial adjustment has recently been explored (Felix & McMahon, 2006). First, Felix and McMahon (2006) explored the relative relationship of multiple forms of victimization, including gender-related victimization such as sexual harassment and relational victimization, to internalizing and externalizing behavior. Sexual harassment (β = .29; $p < .01$) and overt physical and verbal victimization (β = .29; $p < .01$) were significantly related to internalizing behavior (R^2 = .27, $p < .01$), and sexual harassment had the only significant relation to externalizing behavior (β = .25; R^2 = .16, $p < .01$). This indicates that gender-related forms of victimization have a unique and significant relationship to adolescent well-being.

Felix and McMahon (2006) then assessed how being victimized by a boy compared to being victimized by a girl on psychosocial adjustment for both sexes. For both sexes, being victimized by a girl was not significantly related to internalizing or externalizing behavior. However, being victimized by a boy was related to these outcomes. For girls, experiencing sexual harassment (β = .28; $p < .05$) and direct verbal victimization (β = .34; $p < .05$) by a boy was significantly related to internalizing behavior problems (R^2 = .19, $p < .05$), but not to externalizing behaviors. For boys, being sexually harassed by a male peer was related to both internalizing (β = .56; R^2 = .21, $p < .05$) and externalizing behavior problems (β = .50; R^2 = .34, $p < .01$). Overall, this suggests that in this study being victimized by a boy had the strongest negative relationship to wellbeing for both boys and girls. Observational research conducted in Canada suggests boys may bully and harass more than girls (Craig & Pepler, 1997); the higher frequency of aggression may lead to increased risk for internalizing and externalizing problems for their victims.

For males, it appears that being sexually harassed by a male is particularly troubling. Although same-gender sexual harassment is receiving more attention, published reports tend to focus on legal issues surrounding it, and not its effect on the emotional wellbeing of male victims. It is unfortunate that most bullying prevention programs do not address sexual harassment. Rivers' (2004) research with adults who identify as lesbian, gay, and bisexual reveal that they recalled being bullied based on their sexual orientation as youth, and that for some this peer maltreatment is related to adult symptoms of posttraumatic stress. In another retrospective study, males who identified as gay as adults reported experiencing bullying and suicidal ideation in elementary, middle, and high school (Friedman et al., 2006). Friedman and colleagues found that bullying acted as a mediator between masculinity/femininity and suicidality. High levels of femininity predicted suicidality among bullied male students at the junior high level and a lack of masculinity increased suicide risk for students who were bullied in high school.

Dating Relationships   Youth who bully are at greater risk for unhealthy dating relationships than their non-bullying peers (Connolly, Pepler, Craig, & Taradash, 2000). Connolly and colleagues (2000) found that bullies perceive relationships with their boyfriends or girlfriends to be less intimate, less affectionate, and less durable than did comparison adolescents. Bullies were more likely to report that they would engage in undesirable activities to keep boyfriends/girlfriends and friends. Likewise, they perceived their dating relationships and friendships as less equitable in the relative power of each person than did the comparison adolescents. Bullies also perceived relationships with their friends to be less affectionate and less durable than did comparison adolescents. The authors did not find a gender difference in the report of romantic aggression. Given evidence that youth who are victimized often experience victimization in several different contexts (Finkelhor, Ormrod, & Turner, 2007), it is unsurprising that bullying may lead to unhealthy behaviors in dating relationships and that victims of bullying are more likely to also experience dating violence (Espelage & Holt, 2007). Future research should investigate the link between cross-gender sexual harassment and dating violence.

6. How Does Gender Affect Bullying Resolution?

Gender of the bystanders, the bully, and the victim may all influence the course of the bullying incident and how it is resolved. For example, in a study of kindergarten youth in the United States, Kochenderfer and Ladd (1997) found that boys in general (both in the victimized and larger groups) resorted to fighting back more than girls. In the larger group, girls reported walking away more often than boys. The authors hypothesized that girls may not fight back because their attackers are boys, and they may need to find alternate resolutions.

Likewise, research by Elliot and Faupel (1997) suggests boys and girls offer different solutions to bullying when presented with scenarios, and when asked for the best solution they choose different ones. Boys selected more punishment and victim action responses, in comparison girls recommended more whole school responses. Girls chose responses in all categories studied, whereas boys did not generate any "change bully" or "help victim" category responses.

In addition to gender, how a person copes with bullying may be influenced by how long it has been occurring. In a workplace study with adults, males were more likely than females to use assertive strategies and less likely to use avoidance or seek help (Ólafsson & Jóhannsdóttir, 2004). However, the more a person is targeted, the more likely they are to use avoidance and passive responses (doing nothing). This suggests that chronic victimization may diminish a person's ability to cope and respond to the point of becoming passive because strategies to directly deal with the bully have been unsuccessful.

Another factor to consider is the nature of the bullying dyad. In an observational study of peer interventions into bullying incidents, Hawkins, Pepler, and Craig (2001) noted that although boys and girls were equally likely to intervene in bullying overall, boys more often intervened when the bully and victim were male, and girls intervened more often when the bully and victim were female. Females who intervened were most likely to use verbal assertion compared with males who most frequently used physical assertion or a combination of physical and verbal assertion. This finding may reflect a greater skill or comfort among females in using verbal strategies compared to physical ones. However, boys and girls were equally effective in their interventions to stop the bullying incident. Findings regarding gender-related differences in intervention strategies can be useful for determining interventions that will be most effective for boys and girls.

7. How Can Awareness of Gender Issues Inform Intervention Success?

Given the negative influence of victimization on wellbeing, we must continue to develop and evaluate interventions. We have described how gender can affect bullying and victimization in many ways, including (a) the form that victimization takes, (b) the influence of gender role conformity versus non-conformity on the type of victimization experienced, (c) differences in aggressive behavior and the social cognitions that support aggression, (d) the psychological impact of bullying, and (e) gender differences in resolving and coping with bullying incidents. All of these factors should be considered when designing and implementing bullying prevention programs.

Historically, the greater attention paid to traditionally male forms of victimization may contribute to bullying prevention programs focusing more on overt forms of aggression, which are consequently more effective for males compared to females (e.g., Eslea & Smith, 1998; Frey et al., 2005). With the *Steps to Respect* prevention program (Committee for Children, 2001) effects were roughly comparable across gender; however, compared to girls, boys benefited more from program participation in terms of increases in prosocial behavior, and a greater decline in their difficulty responding assertively to bullying (Frey et al., 2005).

It could be that programs are not targeting relational (social) aggression as thoroughly as needed in order to have an impact on girls' victimization experiences. Cappella and Weinstein (2006) developed and evaluated a theory-based program targeting social aggression. This program was designed for a small group format and delivered to girls only. They found the program improved social problem-solving for all students. For students who teachers characterized as having high-levels of social problems at baseline, by the end of the program, teachers reported significant improvement in their prosocial behavior. This is a promising step towards adequately addressing relational victimization.

Intervention efforts also need to consider how gender influences other factors, including the likelihood of reporting bullying episodes, strategies for involving peers in interventions, and approaches to resolution. For example, Cowie (2000) evaluated a peer support intervention in primary and secondary schools. The intervention involved training peer supporters to befriend peers, engage in conflict resolution, and peer counseling. In student interviews, Cowie found that there was a marked gender imbalance with more females training to be peer supporters and seeking assistance from the peer supporters. In all stages of the intervention, female students were much more likely to use these services than their male counterparts. Furthermore, students reported that they preferred to seek peer assistance from same-sex classmates and peer supporters preferred to provide support to their same-sex peers.

Directions for Future Research

Throughout this chapter, we highlight the importance of considering gender-related research findings when designing studies and interventions. We are not the first to illuminate the importance of gender in understanding bullying (e.g., Crick et al., 1999; Lagerspetz & Bjorkqvist, 1994). One specific way that researchers can improve the gender sensitivity of their studies is by including a measure of sexual harassment when developmentally appropriate. By doing this, researchers can assess how victimization changes forms as children progress through puberty to adulthood. Eventually, it would be possible to assess how youth bullying and sexual harassment relates to workplace bullying and sexual harassment, as well as cross-gender sexual harassment and risk for dating and domestic violence. There has been a shift to routinely include measures of relational or social aggression in studies, which has greatly enhanced our understanding of the complexity of different forms of aggressive behavior. Now there is also a need to include measures of sexual harassment when studying adolescents so that the interrelationships among various forms of victimization can be elucidated.

We also need to consider in greater depth how gender influences intervention effectiveness. Researchers and educators have had a difficult time preventing relational or social aggression in current universal prevention programs. Indeed, research suggests that the social cognitions related to relational aggression may be distinct from those for physical aggression (Musher-Eizenmann et al., 2004). Hence, we need targeted intervention to address relational victimiza-

Table 13.1 Summary of Implications for Practice

Issue	Implications for Research and Practice
Assessments of bullying	• When developmentally appropriate, ask questions about sexual harassment • Include questions about the gender of people involved (bully, bully-victim, victim, bystanders, interveners) • Ask whether the bully and the victim are involved in a dating or sexual relationship • As appropriate, assess masculinity/ femininity, sexual orientation, and gender-typical/ atypical behaviors that may be related to victimization experiences • Ask about cultural and contextual factors that may be relevant to the development of gender-roles and relationships
For work with individual bullies and victims of bullying	• Look for gender-related patterns in selection of victims, or reports of bullies • Consider the source of the power disparity in the bullying relationship and whether it is related to gender or sexuality • Ask about the form of bullying and whether bullying includes relational aggression, indirect aggression, or sexual harassment • Ask about content of bullying episodes and indications of whether they are gender or gender-role related • Attend to presence of bystanders or multiple bullies, their gender, and their decisions regarding intervention • Consider whether the bullying episode is within the context of a dating relationship and select appropriate interventions • Recognize that it may be more difficult for males to report victimization, especially sexualized, and seek assistance than females
Prevention and Intervention Efforts	• Prevention and intervention efforts should include attention to relational aggression, indirect aggression, and sexual harassment, in addition to physical aggression • Schools can create a climate of tolerance by encouraging both male and female involvement in traditionally male and female activities, and promoting gender equity among students and staff. • Continue to develop and evaluate programs specifically targeting relational aggression and sexual harassment • Include gender-specific outcomes in program evaluation efforts, including attitudes about gender roles and sexual harassment, experiences with different forms of victimization, and experiences with bullying by members of the same and the other sex

tion. Some promising programs are beginning to emerge and we should continue to develop and evaluate efforts.

We also need to do this for sexual harassment. There is a dearth of programs on sexual harassment and modules within existing bullying prevention programs that address sexual harassment. *Expect Respect* is an exception, but the empirical support for this program has been disappointing thus far (Whitaker, Rosenbluth, Valle, & Sanchez, 2004). Some dating violence programs include a session on sexual harassment, but there is not empirical evidence that this dosage is adequate. Given that there is growing evidence that bullying is a risk-factor for sexual harassment (Pellegrini, 2001) and for coercive dating relationships (Connolly et al., 2000), researchers and interventionists from both the bullying and dating violence fields should consider explicitly addressing sexual harassment in their programs.

Conclusions

As long as there is gender inequity in society, power disparities in bullying will likely have a gendered component. When youth experience gender-related bullying it influences their understanding of themselves as developing men and women. In addition, these experiences provide a template for how young people begin to understand their role in intimate relationships. We echo the sentiment of Stein (2003) who expressed concern that when bullying is considered outside of the context of gender and sexual harassment these issues are not given the attention that they deserve.

Note

1. The term "gender" is typically used to refer to "masculinity/femininity rooted in sociocultural descriptions" (Lewine, Thurston-Snoha, & Ardery, 2006, p. 1362), as contrasted with "sex" which refers to "maleness/femaleness rooted in predominantly physical and biological characteristics" (Lewine et al., p. 1362). For the purposes of this chapter, we will primarily use the term "gender" and refer to masculinity and femininity roles that are socially constructed.

References

Benbenishty, R., & Astor, R. A. (2005). *School violence in context*. New York: Oxford University Press.

Bentley, K. M., & Li, A. K. F. (1995). Bully and victim problems in elementary schools and students' beliefs about aggression. *Canadian Journal of School Psychology, 11*, 153–165.

Bronfenbrenner, U. (1986). Ecology of the family as a context for human development: Research perspectives. *Developmental Psychology, 22*(6), 723–742.

Cappella, E., & Weinstein, R. (2006). The prevention of social aggression among girls. *Social Development, 15*(3), 434–462.

Committee for Children. (2001). *Steps to Respect: A bullying prevention program*. Seattle, WA: Author.

Connolly, J., Pepler, D., Craig, W., & Taradash, A. (2000). Dating experiences of bullies in early adolescence. *Child Maltreatment, 5*, 299–310.

Cowie, H. (2000). Bystanding or standing by: Gender issues in coping with bullying in English schools. *Aggressive Behavior, 26*, 85–97.

Craig, W. M. (1998). The relationship among bullying, victimization, depression, anxiety, and aggression in elementary school children. *Personality & Individual Differences, 24*, 123–130.

Craig W. M., & Harel, Y. (2004). Bullying, physical fighting and victimization. In C. Currie, C. Roberts, A. Morgan, R. Smith, W. Settertobulte, O. Samdal, et al. (Eds.), *Young people's health in context: International report from the HBSC 2001/02 survey. WHO policy series: Health policy for children and adolescents* (Issue 4, pp. 133–144). Denmark, Copenhagen: WHO Regional Office for Europe.

Craig, W. M., & Pepler, D. J. (1997). Observations of bullying and victimization in the schoolyard. *Canadian Journal of School Psychology, 13*, 41–60.

Crick, N. R., & Bigbee, M. A. (1998). Relational and overt forms of peer victimization: A multiinformant approach. *Journal of Consulting and Clinical Psychology, 66,* 337–347.

Crick, N. R., Bigbee, M. A., & Howes, C. (1996). Gender differences in children's normative beliefs about aggression: How do I hurt thee? Let me count the ways. *Child Development, 67,* 1003–1014.

Crick, N. R., & Grotpeter, J. K. (1995). Relational aggression, gender, and social-psychological adjustment. *Child Development, 66,* 710–722.

Crick, N. R., & Grotpeter, J. K. (1996). Children's treatment by peers: Victims of relational and overt aggression. *Development and Psychopathology, 8,* 367–380.

Crick, N. R., Werner, N. E., Casas, J. F., O'Brien, K. M., Nelson, D. A., Grotpeter, J. K., et al. (1999). Childhood aggression and gender: A new look at an old problem. In D. Bernstein (Ed.), *Nebraska symposium on motivation: Gender and motivation* (pp. 75–141). Lincoln: University of Nebraska Press.

DeSouza, E. R., & Ribeiro, J. (2005). Bullying and sexual harassment among Brazilian high school students. *Journal of Interpersonal Violence, 20,* 1018–1038.

Elliot, H., & Faupel, A. (1997). Children's solutions to bullying incidents: An interpersonal problem-solving approach. *Educational Psychology in Practice, 13,* 21–28.

Erikson, W., & Einarsen, S. (2004). Gender minority as a risk factor of exposure to bullying at work: The case of male assistant nurses. *European Journal of Work and Organizational Psychology, 13,* 473–492.

Eslea, M., & Smith, P. K. (1998). The long-term effectiveness of anti-bullying work in primary schools. *Educational Research, 40,* 203–218.

Espelage, D. L., & Holt, M. K. (2007). Dating violence and sexual harassment across the bully-victim continuum among middle and high school students. *Journal of Youth and Adolescence, 36,* 799–811.

Espelage, D. L., Holt, M. K., & Henkel, R. R. (2003). Examination of peer-group contextual effects on aggression during early adolescence. *Child Development, 74,* 205–220.

Felix, E. D., & McMahon, S. (2007). The role of gender in peer victimization among youth: A study of incidence, interrelations, and social cognitive correlates. *Journal of School Violence, 6,* 27–44.

Felix, E. D., & McMahon, S. D. (2006). Gender and multiple forms of peer victimization: How do they influence adolescent psychosocial adjustment? *Violence & Victims, 21,* 707–724.

Finkelhor, D., Ormrod, R. K., & Turner, H. A. (2007). Poly-victimization: A neglected component in child victimization. *Child Abuse & Neglect, 31,* 7–26.

Fitzgerald, L. F., Gelfand, M. J., & Drasgow, F. (1995). Measuring sexual harassment: Theoretical and psychometric advances. *Basic and Applied Social Psychology, 17,* 425–455.

Frey, K. S., Hirschstein, M. K., Snell, J. L., Van Schoiack Edstrom, L., MacKenzie, E. P., & Broderick, C. J. (2005). Reducing playground bullying and supporting beliefs: An experimental trial of the *Steps to Respect* program. *Developmental Psychology, 41,* 479–491.

Friedman, M. S., Koeske, G. F., Silvestre, A. J., Korr, W. S., & Sites, E. W. (2006). The impact of gender-role nonconforming behavior, bullying, and social support on suicidality among gay male youth. *Journal of Adolescent Health, 38,* 621–623.

Gini, G., & Pozzoli, T. (2006). The role of masculinity in children's bullying. *Sex Roles, 54,* 585–588.

Gottman, J. M., & Mettetal, G. (1986). Speculations about social and affective development: Friendship and acquaintanceship through adolescence. In J. M. Gottman & J. G. Parker (Eds.), *Conversations of friends: Speculations on affective development* (pp. 192–237). New York: Cambridge University Press.

Hawkins, D. L., Pepler, D. J., & Craig, W. M. (2001). Naturalistic observations of peer interventions in bullying. *Social Development, 10,* 512–527.

Kepenekci, Y. K., & Çinkir, Ş. (2006). Bullying among Turkish high school students. *Child Abuse and Neglect, 30,* 193–204.

Kochenderfer, B. J., & Ladd, G. W. (1996). Peer victimization: Cause or consequence of school maladjustment? *Child Development, 67,* 1305–1317.

Kochenderfer, B .J., & Ladd, G. W. (1997). Victimized children's responses to peers' aggression: Behaviors associated with reduced versus continued victimization. *Development and Psychopathology, 9,* 59–73.

Lagerspetz, K. M., & Bjorkqvist, K. (1994). Indirect aggression in boys and girls. In L. R. Huesmann (Ed.), *Aggressive behavior: Current perspectives* (pp. 131–150). New York: Plenum.

Lee, D. (2002). Gendered workplace bullying in the restructured UK civil service. *Personnel Review, 31,* 205–227.

Levesque, R. J. R. (1998). Emotional maltreatment in adolescents' everyday lives: Furthering sociolegal reforms & social service provisions. *Behavioral Sciences & the Law,16,* 237–263.

Lewine, R. R. J., Thurston-Snoha, B., & Ardery, R. (2006). Sex, gender, and neuropsyhological functioning in schizophrenia. *Journal of Clinical and Experimental Neuropsychology, 28,* 1362–1372.

Maccoby, E. E., (1998). *The two sexes: Growing up apart, coming together.* Cambridge, MA: Harvard University Press.

Maccoby, E. E. (2004). Aggression in the context of gender development. In M. Putallaz & K. L. Bierman (Eds.), *Aggression, antisocial behavior, and violence among girls: A developmental perspective* (pp. 3–20). New York: Guilford.

Maccoby, E. E., & Jacklin, C. N. (1987). Gender segregation in childhood. In H. W. Reese (Ed.), *Advances in child development and behavior* (pp. 239–287). San Diego: Academic Press.

Maltz, D. N., & Borker, R. A. (1982). A cultural approach to male-female miscommunication. In J. A. Gumperz (Ed.), *Language and social identity* (pp. 195–216). New York: Cambridge University Press.

Matlin, M. W. (2000). *The psychology of women, 4th edition*. New York: Harcourt Press.

Mcallister, L. (2001). Good kids, bad behavior: A study of bullying among fifth-grade school children. *Dissertation Abstracts International Section A: Humanities and Social Sciences, 16*(7-A), 2925.

McMaster, L. E., Connolly, J., Pepler, D., & Craig, W. M. (2002). Peer to peer sexual harassment in early adolescence: A developmental perspective. *Development and Psychopathology, 14*, 91–105.

Musher-Eizenmann, D. R., Boxer, P., Danner, S., Dubow, E. F., Goldstein, S. E., & Heretick, D. M. L. (2004). Social-cognitive mediators of the relation of environmental and emotional regulation factors to children's aggression. *Aggressive Behavior, 30*, 389–408.

Nansel, T. R., Overpeck, M., Pilla, R. S., Ruan, W. J., Simons-Morton, B., & Scheidt, P. (2001). Bullying behaviors among U.S. youth: Prevalence and association with psychosocial adjustment. *Journal of the American Medical Association, 285*, 2094–2100.

Ólafsson, R. F., & Jóhannsdóttir, H. L. (2004). Coping with bullying in the workplace: The effect of gender, age, and type of bullying. *British Journal of Guidance & Counseling, 32*, 319–333.

Olweus, D. (1978). *Aggression in the schools: Bullies and their whipping boys*. Washington, DC: Hemisphere.

Olweus, D. (1994). Annotation: Bullying at school: Basic facts and effects of a school based intervention program. *Journal of Child Psychology and Psychiatry, 35*, 1171–1190.

Pellegrini, A. D. (2001). A longitudinal study of heterosexual relationships, aggression, and sexual harassment during transition from primary school through middle school. *Applied Developmental Psychology, 22*, 119–133.

Perren, S., & Hornung, R. (2005). Bullying and delinquency in adolescence: Victims' and perpetrators' family and peer relations. *Swiss Journal of Psychology, 64*, 51–64.

Rigby, K. (2002). *New perspectives on bullying*. London: Jessica Kingsley.

Rivers, I. (2004). Recollections of bullying at school and their long-term implications for lesbians, gay men, and bisexuals. *Crisis, 25*, 169–175.

Rivers, I., & Smith, P. K. (1994). Types of bullying behavior and their correlates. *Aggressive Behavior, 20*, 359–368.

Rodkin, P. C., & Fischer, K. (2003). Sexual harassment and the cultures of childhood: Developmental, domestic violence, and legal perspectives. *Journal of Applied School Psychology, 19*, 177–196.

Scheithauer, H., Hayer, T., Petermann, F., & Jugert, G. (2006). Physical, verbal, and relational forms of bullying across German students: Age trends, gender differences, and correlates. *Aggressive Behavior, 32*, 261–275.

Schwartz, D., Gorman, A. H., Nakamoto, J., & Toblin, R. L. (2005). Victimization in the peer group and children's academic functioning. *Journal of Educational Psychology, 97*, 425–435.

Serbin, L. A., Moller, L. C., Gulko, J., Powlishta, K. K., & Coulburne, K. A. (1994). The emergence of gender segregation in toddler playgroups. In C. Leaper (Ed.), *Childhood gender segregation: Causes and consequences* (pp. 7–17). San Francisco: Jossey-Bass.

Simpson, R., & Cohen, C. (2004). Dangerous work: The gendered nature of bullying in the context of higher education. *Gender, Work and Organization, 11*, 163–186.

Smith, P. K., Cowie, H., Olafsson, R. F., Liefooghe, A. P. D., Almeida, A., Araki, H., et al. (2002). Definitions of bullying: A comparison of terms used, and age and gender differences, in a fourteen-country international comparison. *Child Development, 73*, 1119–1133.

Stein, N. (2003). Bullying or sexual harassment? The missing discourse of rights in an era of zero tolerance. *Arizona Law Review, 45*, 783–799.

Thorne, B., & Luria, Z. (1986). Sexuality and gender in children's daily worlds. *Social Problems, 33*, 176–190.

Underwood, M. (2003). Gender and peer relations: Separate worlds? In M. Underwood (Eds.), *Social aggression among girls* (pp. 35–53). New York: Guilford.

Whitaker, D. J., Rosenbluth, B., Valle, L. A., & Sanchez, E. (2004). Expect Respect: A school-based intervention to promote awareness and effective responses to bullying and sexual harassment. In D. L. Espelage & S. M. Swearer (Eds.), *Bullying in American schools* (pp. 327–350). Mahwah, NJ: Erlbaum.

Yang, S., Kim, J., Kim, S., Shin, I., & Yoon, J. (2006). Bullying and victimization behaviors in boys and girls at South Korean primary schools. *Journal of the American Academy of Child and Adolescent Psychiatry, 45*, 69–77.

Young, R., & Sweeting, H. (2004). Adolescent bullying, relationships, psychological well-being, and gender-atypical behavior: A gender diagnosticity approach. *Sex Roles, 50*, 525–537.

14
Parent-Child Relationships and Bullying

AMANDA B. NICKERSON, DANIELLE MELE,
AND KRISTINA M. OSBORNE-OLIVER

Introduction

Theorists and researchers from diverse orientations emphasize the importance of the parent-child relationship in facilitating healthy child development. Consistent with the growing recognition that bullying should be viewed from an ecological perspective that considers familial, peer, school, and community factors (Espelage & Swearer, 2003; Swearer & Espelage, 2004), this chapter explores the role of the parent-child relationship in bullying. We begin by providing an overview of different theoretical conceptualizations of the parent-child relationship, including relevant research on child outcomes. Next, research on the role of the parent-child relationship in bullying behavior for bullies, victims, and children who both bully others and are victimized by peers (i.e., bully-victims) is reviewed. We conclude with highlights of the major findings, implications for practice, and future research directions.

Theoretical Conceptualizations of Parent-Child Relationship

Parents play a pivotal role in children's cognitive, social, and emotional development. Attachment, social support, and family systems are three widely recognized theoretical conceptualizations of the parent-child relationship. In addition, disciplinary style and affective climate are constructs that have particular relevance for child behavior and bullying.

Attachment   The attachment bond between an infant and his or her primary caregiver is the earliest and most important bond in life, as it fosters the development of the internal working model and guides relationships throughout the lifespan (Bowlby, 1969). An infant's experience of a warm, intimate, and continuous relationship with his or her mother or attachment figure is important for healthy functioning (Bretherton, 1992). Mary Ainsworth's pioneering work with the "Strange Situation," in which she observed infant–parent interactions in several different scenarios revealed that infants could be categorized as securely or insecurely attached (Ainsworth, Blehar, Waters, & Wall, 1978). Securely attached infants cried when separated from their mother, but were easily consoled and happy to see her upon her return. Insecurely attached infants were noted to be either avoidant or ambivalent. Avoidant infants seemed not to notice when their mother left and they often "snubbed" her upon her return. Ambivalent infants clung to their mother, were afraid to explore their surroundings, became upset when their mother left, and were not easily consoled when she returned. These infant attachment styles are more strongly related to the mother's sensitivity and responsiveness than to individual child factors, such as temperament (Elicker, Englund, & Sroufe, 1992).

Securely attached infants are more readily socialized and competent than those with insecure attachment styles (Ainsworth & Bowlby, 1991; Elicker et al., 1992). The study of attachment has extended beyond the infant-mother dyad to close relationships throughout the lifespan, and attachment security has been correlated with positive outcomes such as social competence, interpersonal functioning, and subjective well-being for individuals in late childhood and adolescence (Nickerson & Nagle, 2004; Rice, 1990).

Social Support   Social support has been defined broadly as important interpersonal relationships that impact an individual's psychological and social functioning (Caplan, 1974). Social support is first derived from parents and subsequently from peers within a child's social network (Cobb, 1976). The content of support includes several dimensions: (a) emotional support, or feelings of love and trust; (b) informational support, or providing guidance or advice; (c) appraisal support, or providing evaluative feedback; and (d) instrumental support, such as providing an individual with materials and/or spending time with him or her (House, 1981).

Two hypotheses have been posited to explain how social support promotes a child's overall psychological health. The main effect hypothesis asserts that all children and adolescents, irrespective of the amount of stress they experience, benefit from social support provided by parents and others by fostering healthy psychological mental states, including feelings of security, belonging, stability, and a sense of self worth (Bal, Crombez, Van Oost, & Debourdeaudhuij, 2003; Cohen, Gottlieb, & Underwood, 2001; Cohen & Wills, 1985). In contrast, the stress-buffering hypothesis purports that social support serves as a buffer or coping mechanism, in which the perception of support might influence the child or adolescent to utilize positive coping strategies when stressful events occur, thus preventing the onset of maladjusted outcomes (Cohen et al., 2001; Cohen & Wills, 1985; Schreurs & de Ridder, 1997). Researchers have documented that parental social support is especially important when children are in crisis or experience high levels of stress (Frey & Rothlisberger, 1996; Furman & Buhrmester, 1985).

The relation between parental support and children's social and adjustment outcomes has been well-documented. Children who report high parental support are better adjusted in school and socially, have the resources to overcome stressful circumstances, and are less likely to experience stress (Demaray, Malecki, Davidson, Hodgson, & Rebus, 2005; Dubow & Tisak, 1989; Weigel, Devereux, Leigh, & Ballard-Reisch, 1998). Students with high levels of social support tend to have better interpersonal relationships and higher levels of self-esteem and self-reliance (Demaray et al., 2005). Furthermore, children and adolescents with parental support report higher levels of life satisfaction (Young, Miller, Norton, & Hill, 1995). Lack of parental social support has been associated with school failure, risky behaviors (e.g., smoking, drinking, drug use), anxiety, depression, withdrawal, and lower levels of life satisfaction (Domagala-Zysk, 2006; Kashani, Canfield, Borduin, Soltyz, & Reid, 1994; Piko, 2000).

Family Systems   Family systems theory rests upon three basic tenets: (a) relational patterns are learned and passed down through the generations (Klever, 2005); (b) current individual and family behavior is a result of these patterns; and (c) the family system is homeostatic, meaning that a change in one part of the system has an effect on the entire system (Prest & Protinsky, 1993). In family systems theory, problems are not conceptualized on the individual level, but instead are perceived as a dysfunction in the family as a whole.

Family members seek balance between individuality and connectedness to the family, which is known as differentiation. Differentiation of self is denoted by an individual's ability to maintain cognitive functioning when under pressure and to remain a distinctly separate person even within the context of an intimate relationship (Klever, 2005). Problems in the system can occur if family members are not adequately differentiated or if they are too disconnected or individuated (Charles, 2001). Two concepts of importance in family systems are cohesion and enmeshment. Cohesion refers to positive, supportive interactions within the family. In contrast, enmeshment is not an element of a supportive relationship; rather, it refers a controlling pattern that inhibits another family member's autonomy (Barber & Buehler, 1996).

Less research has been conducted on family systems than on attachment or social support, although the level of differentiation between family members has been found to have an impact upon mental health, with higher levels of differentiation associated with lower levels of psychological symptoms and perceived stress (Murdock & Gore, 2004). In addition, enmeshment is related to adolescents' externalizing and internalizing problems (Barber & Buehler, 1996). Enmeshment, or lack of differentiation from one's family is most related to increased risk for internalizing problems, such as social anxiety (Barber & Buehler; Peleg-Popko, 2002). It has been hypothesized that an enmeshed relationship where the parent controls the child's autonomy might undermine the child's sense of self-reliance, leading to a tendency to withdraw, particularly for boys (Barber & Buehler).

The Role of Parenting in Child Behavior

Although each of the aforementioned theoretical frameworks takes a unique perspective on the specific ways that parents influence children, each emphasizes the way in which aspects of the parent-child relationship contribute to the child's social, emotional, and behavioral development. Two other specific influences of parents on children that deserve mention are disciplinary style and affective climate.

Children whose parents adopt an authoritative style, which includes parental warmth and moderate control, experience better outcomes than those whose parents are authoritarian, characterized by high parental control and little warmth, or permissive, marked by low parental control and high warmth (Baumrind, 1980; Parke et al., 1998). In addition, an extensive body of research indicates that ineffective discipline (e.g., discipline that is not contingent on child behavior, harsh parental discipline) is related to children's aggressive and other aversive behaviors (e.g., Patterson, 1986; Vuchinich, Bank, & Patterson, 1992; Weiss, Dodge, Bates, & Pettit, 1992).

The affective climate within the family also influences child development. Higher levels of positive emotion expression in the home are related to children's positive perceptions of social situations (Nixon & Watson, 2001). Conversely, parents' depressed affect is associated with children's emotional dysregulation, insecure attachment, and risk for later academic, social, and psychological problems (Brennan et al., 2000; Carter, Garrity-Rokous, Chazan-Cohen, Little, & Briggs-Gowan, 2001; Parke et al., 1998).

Parent-Child Relationships and Bullying

Clearly, many facets of the parent-child relationship influence outcomes for children. A growing body of research has focused on the role of parent-child relationships in bullying. Because findings vary depending on the child's role in bullying, this section is separated by research regarding bullies, victims, and bully-victims. Whenever possible, we organize findings from this research as they relate to the aforementioned discussion of the theoretical conceptualizations of the parent-child relationship (i.e., attachment, social support, family systems) and specific influences (i.e., disciplinary style, affect) on child behavior.

Bullies According to attachment theory, the experience of a secure parent-child relationship is central for healthy functioning in other relationships, including those with peers. Indeed, research has indicated that the large majority of children who bully peers are insecurely attached (Monks, Smith, & Swettenham, 2005; Troy & Sroufe, 1987). In Troy and Sroufe's longitudinal study, all children who bullied peers had a history of an avoidant attachment style, indicating that the presence or absence of the mother seemed inconsequential to these infants. In addition, bullies often describe damaged relationships with their parents (Rigby, 1993).

Children who bully perceive lower levels of parental social support, particularly emotional support, than children in comparison groups (Demaray & Malecki, 2003; Rigby, 1994a). Moreover, a youth's perceived lack of parental social support predicts engagement in other violent activity, such as bringing a weapon to school (Malecki & Demaray, 2003). Despite a perceived lack of social support from parents, it should be noted that bullies report higher levels of social support from peers and classmates as compared to victims and bully-victims (Demaray & Malecki, 2003; Salmivalli, Huttunen, & Lagerspetz, 1997). Children and youth who self-report bullying behaviors tend to affiliate with peers who exhibit similar frequencies of low-level aggressive behaviors (Espelage, Holt, & Henkel, 2003). As such, bullies tend to be popular among their peers, especially when bullying is common in the context of their peer groups (Espelage & Holt, 2001; Espelage et al., 2003; Rodkin, Farmer, Pearl, & Van Acker, 2000; Salmivalli et al., 1997).

Similarly, research from a family systems framework indicates that bullies have lower family cohesion and more disengaged relationships with parents than do victims and controls (Berdondini & Smith, 1996; Bowers, Smith, & Binney, 1994). Bullies also are more likely than victims and children from control groups to not have a father at home (Berdondini & Smith, 1996; Bowers et al., 1994). Although not conducted from a family systems framework, relevant research indicates that in early to mid-adolescence, a lack of time spent with an adult and infrequent parent supervision is associated with a greater likelihood of bullying (Espelage, Bosworth, & Simon, 2000) and online harassment (Ybarra & Mitchell, 2004).

Parents' use of physical punishment and exertion of power have also been related to children's bullying behavior. Parents of children who bully tend to use physical punishment as the primary discipline strategy (Espelage et al., 2000; Schwartz, Dodge, Pettit, & Bates, 1997). An authoritarian parenting style and concern over exerting power has also been associated with bullying in children (Ahmed & Braithwaite, 2004; Cutner-Smith et al., 2006). The most extreme form of physical punishment and power exertion is child maltreatment. Children who have been maltreated, particularly those who have been physically or sexually abused, are more likely to bully others (Shields & Cicchetti, 2001).

The affective climate in the family, related to many of the aforementioned theories about the parent-child relationship, is also relevant for bullying behavior. In an examination of numerous structural, affective, and disciplinary variables, Rigby (1994b) found that negative affect in families had the strongest association with adolescents' tendency engage in bullying behavior. Bullies often come from families where a lack of empathy is displayed (Olweus, 1993) and where no effective model is provided for children to learn about dealing sensitively with others (Oliver & Oaks, 1994). For example, mothers with high empathy for their children have children who engage in less relational and overt bullying in preschool (Cutner-Smith et al., 2006). Lack of parental warmth, affection, or a weak emotional bond has been related to increased bullying behavior (Rigby, Slee, & Cunningham, 1999) and online harassment (Ybarra & Mitchell, 2004).

Marital discord is also associated with bullying, though child self-concept has been found to mediate this association (Christie-Mizell, 2003).

Victims   Research on victims of bullying has been conducted to examine several aspects of the parent-child relationship. Troy and Sroufe (1987) conducted a longitudinal study and found that all children observed to be victimized by peers had a history of being insecurely attached (i.e., avoidant or ambivalent). This is consistent with findings that parent responsiveness to children's needs is associated with decreased victimization (Ladd & Ladd, 1998).

Perhaps the most widely studied and consistent finding about parent-child relationships and victimization concerns enmeshment. Specifically, enmeshment with parents, characterized by emotionally intense, positive interactions, and overprotection on the part of the parent, has been associated with increased risk for victimization in studies using diverse methodologies, such as observations (Ladd & Ladd, 1998), child self-report (Bowers et al., 1994; Finnegan, Hodges, & Perry, 1998; Rigby et al., 1999), and interviews with parents of victimized boys (Olweus, 1991). In these families, victims report high and positive involvement with other family members when compared to non-victimized children (Bowers et al., 1994).

An examination of this research indicates that the enmeshment with parents may be specific to boys who meet the profile of a "passive" victim. It has been hypothesized that these emotionally intense parent-child relationships may encourage boys to display passive or dependent behaviors, which then place them at an increased risk for victimization (Ladd & Ladd, 1998). Further evidence to support the victimization cycle comes from Duncan's (1999) retrospective study of college freshmen, which found that those who had been physically or emotionally abused by parents were more likely to be victims of bullying than those who had not been abused. Additionally, maternal threat of rejection, coercion, and low encouragement of assertion have been associated with girls' risk for victimization (Finnegan et al., 1998).

Some research has suggested that attribution may play a central role both in terms of consequences and maintenance of victimization (Graham & Juvonen, 1998; Perry, Hodges, & Egan, 2001). Children who perceive themselves as victims tend to attribute this to internal, stable, and uncontrollable personal characteristics, which are, in turn, related to loneliness, anxiety, and low self-worth (Graham & Juvonen, 1998). Perry and colleagues (2001) suggest that boys who are enmeshed with their parents develop a "victim schema," with the parent as controlling and the self as helpless, which then contributes to peer victimization. Victims may view themselves as helpless either because they have been subordinated during parent-child conflicts or because they may have developed an over-dependent emotional attachment to a parent.

Research exploring victims' perceived levels of parental social support has yielded interesting findings. For example, Demaray and Malecki (2003) found that victims of bullying reported receiving the most parental support as compared to the students who were bullies, bully/victims, or in a comparison group. In addition, perceived paternal support is related to reduced victimization and rejection (Rubin et al., 2004), and positive father-son and daughter-son relationships serve as protective buffers for male and female adolescents experiencing peer bullying and physical dating violence, respectively (Flouri & Buchanan, 2002; Holt & Espelage, 2005). Similarly, research supports that maternal social support serves as a temporary moderator between other forms of peer victimization (e.g., physical dating violence and emotional abuse) and the likelihood of displaying symptoms of anxiety and depression (Holt & Espelage, 2005). The moderating relationship was particularly salient for African American males who reported experiencing low levels of physical violence and low to moderate levels of emotional abuse in dating relationships. This finding is noteworthy, considering that several studies have found Black students were more likely to be involved in bullying and victimization as compared to youth in other ethnic groups (Espelage & Holt, 2007; Juvonen, Graham, & Schuster, 2003; Peskin, Tortolero, & Markham, 2006). Native American youth also might be a vulnerable group for engagement in the bullying process, as they reportedly perceive the lowest levels of social support from their parents, teachers, and peers (Demaray & Malecki, 2003).

Bully-Victims   Interest has grown in the characteristics of students who assume the guise of both bully and victim in bullying situations. These youth have been referred to as provocative victims, aggressive victims, and bully-victims. Unlike victims who are more withdrawn and passive, they display anxious and aggressive reaction patterns that might actually make them more persistent targets of peer aggression (Schwartz, 2000) and other forms of victimization (e.g., physical and emotional dating violence and sexual harassment; Espelage & Holt, 2007).

Bully-victims have been shown to have high levels of avoidant attachment (Ireland & Power, 2004). Bully-victims have more troubled relationships with parents (Bowers et al., 1994) and report the lowest levels of parental support than children who are bullies, victims, or have no direct involvement in bullying (Demaray & Malecki, 2003). This is especially noteworthy considering that bully-victims and victims rated social support by parents and others as more important than did students in the bully and comparison groups (Demaray & Malecki). Thus, existing evidence suggests that bully-victims may be a particularly vulnerable group.

Aggressive victims are exposed to more marital conflict, maternal hostility, and aggressive punishments than passive victims and a normative group (Schwartz et al., 1997). Bully-victims indicate that their parents are low in accurate monitoring and warmth, yet high in overprotection and neglect, suggesting inconsistent discipline practices not tempered by warmth (Bowers et al., 1994). It has been theorized that the lack of affection and low monitoring by parents may leave bully-victims feeling like they have to fend for themselves; this, coupled with repeated exposure to violent and aggressive models of coping, may lead children to approach social situations in an ambivalent way, resulting in vacillation between aggressor, where they act out coercive behavior, and victim, where they feel helpless, physically weak, or emotionally dysregulated (Bowers et al., 1994; Perry et al., 2001).

Although this is a relatively new area of inquiry, the existing research concerning parent-child relationships and bullying reveals some consistent trends. Bullies are more likely to have avoidant attachment styles and distant, less supportive relationships with parents. In addition, parents of bullies are more likely than parents of other children to use physical means of discipline and to lack warmth and empathy. Victims also have insecure attachment styles, though they may be either avoidant or ambivalent. In contrast to bullies' distant relationships with parents, passive victims and boys, in particular, tend to have overly close and emotionally intense relationships with parents. The profile for children who are bully-victims, or provocative victims, reveals an avoidant attachment style with low perceived support from parents. The disciplinary style of their parents appears to be inconsistent, with features of hostility as well as neglect.

It is important to note that although research has revealed these trends, it would be remiss to interpret these findings as suggesting that blame be placed on parents for causing bullying and victimization. Social-ecological perspectives seek to understand the many complex influences and systems that contribute to behavior, including familial, peer, school, and community factors (Espelage & Swearer, 2003; Swearer & Espelage, 2004). For example, Brock, Nickerson, O'Malley, and Chang's (2006) theoretical model of peer victimization includes the pathways by which internal risk factors (e.g., withdrawn or irritable-inattentive behaviors), parenting style, poor relationships with teachers, lack of confidence in peer group standing, and absent or weak friendships interact to lead to an increased likelihood of being victimized. Therefore, although the parent-child relationship certainly plays an important role for child development, there are a host of other factors that influence relations with peers that need to be taken into account in research and practice. For example, an empirical study conducted by Ahmed and Braithwaite (2004) indicated that school variables were better at predicting children's roles as bullies, victims, or bully-victims than were family variables, though using both school and family variables resulted in the best predictions.

Implications for Practice

The link between the parent-child relationship and bullying has led researchers to assert the importance of involving parents in interventions for bullying (Nickerson, Brock, Chang, & O'Malley, 2006; Oliver & Oaks, 1994). An alternative perspective is that because parents are implicated in the behaviors of their children, it is all the more important for education to focus on the children themselves (Ybarra & Mitchell, 2004). We propose that both direct work with bullies and victims, and indirect interventions with parents, school staff, and peers are important for intervening with such a complex problem. A list of implications for practice is provided in Table 14.1.

A review of the aforementioned research findings regarding the parent-child relationship and bullying behavior suggest that parents of these children may benefit from interventions designed to: (a) increase their modeling of warm, empathic behavior; (b) promote the use of nonhostile discipline; and (c) increase monitoring and involvement. Although research has not been conducted assessing the effectiveness of these interventions for parents of bullies, teaching parents to manage child and adolescent behavior according to social learning principles (e.g., reinforcing prosocial behavior, problem solving, contingency contracting) has been shown to lead to reductions in aversive behavior (Dishion & Patterson, 1992; Kazdin, 1987).

Interventions for parents of victims may focus on having parents actively help children behave assertively and constructively in threatening or intimidating situations by teaching specific skills such as self defense, stress management, making assertive statements, responding to name-calling, and enlisting support from peers (Sharp, 1996). From a family systems perspective, it has been recommended that mental health professionals identify patterns that may contribute to victimization (e.g., maternal overprotection) and intervene accordingly by emphasizing differences between family members and encouraging children to become involved in

Table 14.1 Parent-Child Relationships and Bullying: Implications for Practice

Implications for Practice
• Recognize that bullying exists within a social-ecological framework, which includes the family context
• Educate parents about the variables associated with increased risk of bullying and victimization
• Inform parents of bullies about the importance of modeling warm, empathic responses
• Teach appropriate behavior management techniques to parents, including careful monitoring
• Work with parents of victims to understand how overly close, positive, and overprotective interactions may increase the likelihood of future peer victimization
• Encourage parents of victims to get children involved in activities that encourage independence, assertiveness, and healthy peer relationships (e.g., sports, clubs, acting)
• Provide opportunities for bullies and victims to have adult role models and sources of support in addition to parents
• Be alert for signs of child maltreatment when working with bullies and victims

extrafamilial structured activities with peers (Oliver & Oaks, 1994; Smith & Myron-Wilson, 1998). Findings indicating that parent-child relationships for bully-victims are inconsistent underscore the importance of tailoring interventions to the unique needs of bully-victims.

Furthermore, it is likely that intervening solely with the family will be insufficient to impact bullying at school (Ahmed & Braithwaite, 2004). This underscores the importance of intervening directly with bullies, victims, and indirectly with parents, peers, and school staff (Nickerson et al., 2006). For instance, children who bully who do not receive social support and effective discipline from parents may benefit from increase support and limit setting from teachers and school staff. Research finding that the association between marital discord and children's bullying behavior is mediated by child self-concept (Christie-Mizell, 2003) suggests that there are strengths that can be developed to buffer children from possible negative influences from the home environment.

Future Research Directions

Because this is a relatively new area of investigation, there are many possibilities for future research. More work is needed to better understand how attachment, family systems, and social support relate to bullying and victimization. Because research has suggested that the experiences of male and female bullies, victims, and bully-victims in families may differ, researchers should continue to explore the role of gender in these relationships. Although research has typically been conducted with mothers, it is possible the more distal father-child relationship has a closer resemblance and influence on extrafamilial relationships, such as interactions with peers (Ducharme, Doyle, & Markiewicz, 2002); therefore, more work is needed on the role of the father-child relationship in bullying and victimization. Similarly, research should expand to include children and adolescents from diverse family structures and different ethnic and cultural backgrounds to investigate how these variables influence the role of caregiver-child interactions and bullying. It is also important for research to use diverse methodologies to assess the extent to which children's self-report of their relationships with others may differ from observed behavior.

Future research should explore the parent-child relationships for children that play other roles in bullying, such as bystanders and defenders. Although bullying has typically been viewed as an interaction between two individuals (i.e., bully and victim), Christina Salmivalli and colleagues (Salmivalli, Lagerspetz, Bjorkqvist, Ostreman, & Kaukianien, 1996; Salmivalli et al., 1997) have identified other roles that peers play, such as reinforcer of the bully, assistant to the bully, defender of the victim, and outsider. Achieving a greater understanding of factors, including parent and family variables, which contribute to these different roles will more fully inform comprehensive bullying prevention and intervention efforts.

Finally, models that have been proposed for how parent-child relationships influence children's behavior and roles as bullies, victims, and bully-victims are in need of empirical testing. In addition, it will be important to test the effectiveness of various interventions, like the ones mentioned above, with parents and families of bullies and victims.

References

Ahmed, E., & Braithwaite, V. (2004). Bullying and victimization: Cause for concern for both families and schools. *Social Psychology of Education, 7*, 35–54.

Ainsworth, M. D. S., Blehar, M. C., Waters, E., & Wall, S. (1978). *Patterns of attachment*. Hillsdale, NJ: Erlbaum.

Ainsworth, M. D. S., & Bowlby, J. (1991). An ethological approach to personality development. *American Psychologist, 46*, 333–341.

Bal, S., Crombez, G., Van Oost, P., & Debourdeaudhuij, I. (2003). The role of social support in well-being and coping with self-reported stressful events in adolescents. *Child Abuse and Neglect, 27,* 1377–1395.

Barber, B. K., & Buehler, C. (1996). Family cohesion and enmeshment: Different constructs, different effects. *Journal of Marriage and the Family, 58,* 433–441.

Baumrind, D. (1980). New directions in socialization research. *American Psychologist, 35,* 639–652.

Berdondini, L., & Smith, P. K. (1996). Cohesion and power in the families of children involved in bully/victim problems of school: An Italian replication. *Journal of Family Therapy, 18,* 99–109.

Bowers, L., Smith, P. K., & Binney, V. (1994). Perceived family relationships of bullies, victims and bully/victims in middle childhood. *Journal of Social and Personal Relationships, 11,* 215–232.

Bowlby, J. (1969). *Attachment and loss.* New York: Basic Books.

Brennan, P. A., Hammen, C., Anderson, M. J., Bor, W., Najman, J. M., & Williams, G. M. (2000). Chronicity, severity, and timing of maternal depressive symptoms: Relationships with child outcomes at age 5. *Developmental Psychology, 36,* 759–766.

Bretherton, I. (1992). The origins of attachment theory: John Bowlby and Mary Ainsworth. *Developmental Psychology, 28,* 759–775.

Brock, S. E., Nickerson, A. B., O'Malley, M., & Chang, Y. (2006). Understanding children victimized by their peers. *Journal of School Violence, 5,* 3–18.

Caplan, G. (1974). *Support systems and community mental health: Lectures on concept development.* New York: Behavioral Publications.

Carter, A. S., Garrity-Rokous, F. E., Chazan-Cohen, R., Little, C., & Briggs-Gowan, J. (2001). Maternal depression and comorbidity: Predicting early parenting, attachment security, and toddler social-emotional problems and competencies. *Journal of the American Academy of Child and Adolescent Psychiatry, 40,* 18–26.

Charles, R. (2001). Is there any empirical support for Bowen's concepts of differentiation of self, triangulation, and fusion? *The American Journal of Family Therapy, 29,* 279–292.

Christie-Mizell, C. A. (2003). Bullying: The consequences of interparental discord and child's self-concept. *Family Process, 42,* 237–251.

Cobb, S. (1976). Social support as a moderator of life stress. *Psychosomatic Medicine, 38,* 300–314.

Cohen, S., Gottlieb, B. H., & Underwood, L. G. (2001). Social relationships and health: Challenges for measurement and intervention. *Advances in Mind-Body Medicine, 17,* 129–142.

Cohen, S., & Wills, T. A. (1985). Stress, social support, and the buffering hypothesis. *Psychological Bulletin, 98,* 310–357.

Cutner-Smith, M. E., Culp, A. M., Culp, R., Scheib, C., Owen, K., Tilley, A., et al. (2006). Mothers' parenting and young economically disadvantaged children's relational and overt bullying. *Journal of Child and Family Studies, 15,* 181–193.

Demaray, M. K., & Malecki, C. K. (2003). Perceptions of the frequency and importance of social support by students classified as victims, bullies, and bully/victims in an urban middle school. *School Psychology Review, 32,* 471–489.

Demaray, M. K., Malecki, C. K., Davidson, L. M., Hodgson, K. K., & Rebus, P. J. (2005). The relationship between social support and student adjustment: A longitudinal analysis. *Psychology in the Schools, 42,* 691–706.

Dishion, T. J., & Patterson (1992). Age effects in parent training outcome. *Behavior Therapy, 23,* 719–729.

Domagala-Zysk, E. (2006). The significance of adolescents' relationships with significant others and school failure. *School Psychology International, 27,* 232–247.

Dubow, E. F., & Tisak, J. (1989). The relation between stressful life events and adjustment in elementary school children: The role of social support and social problem-solving skills. *Child Development, 60,* 1412–1423.

Ducharme, J., Doyle, A. B., & Markiewicz, D. (2002). Attachment security with mother and father: Associations with adolescents' reports of interpersonal behavior with parents and peers. *Journal of Social and Personal Relationships, 19,* 203–231.

Duncan, R. D. (1999). Maltreatment by parents and peers: The relationship between child abuse, bully victimization, and psychological distress. *Child Maltreatment, 4,* 45–55.

Elicker, J., Englund, M., & Sroufe, L. A. (1992). Predicting peer competence and peer relationships in childhood from early parent-child relationships. In R. D. Parke & G. W. Ladd (Eds.), *Family-peer relationships: Modes of linkage* (pp. 77–106). Hillsdale, NJ: Erlbaum.

Espelage, D. L., Bosworth, K., & Simon, T. R. (2000). Examining the social context of bullying behaviors in early adolescence. *Journal of Counseling and Development, 78,* 326–333.

Espelage, D. L., & Holt, M. K. (2001). Bullying and victimization during early adolescence: Peer influences and psychosocial correlates. *Journal of Emotional Abuse, 2,* 123–142.

Espelage, D. L., & Holt, M. K. (2007). Dating violence and sexual harassment across the bully-victim continuum among middle and high school students. *Journal of Youth and Adolescence, 36,* 799–811.

Espelage, D. L., Holt, M. K., & Henkel, R. R. (2003). Examination of peer-group contextual effects on aggression during early adolescence. *Child Development, 74,* 205–220.

Espelage, D. L., & Swearer, S. M. (2003). Research on school bullying and victimization: What have we learned and where do we go from here? *School Psychology Review, 32*, 365–383.

Finnegan, R. A., Hodges, E. V. E., & Perry, D. G. (1998). Victimization by peers: Associations with children's reports of mother-child interaction. *Journal of Personality and Social Psychology, 75*, 1076–1086.

Flouri, E., & Buchanan, A. (2002). Life satisfaction in teenage boys: The moderating role of father involvement and bullying. *Aggressive Behavior, 28*, 126–133.

Frey, C. U., & Rothlisberger, C. (1996). Social support in healthy adolescents. *Journal of Youth and Adolescence, 25*, 17–31.

Furman, W., & Buhrmester, D. (1985). Children's perceptions of the personal relationships in their social networks. *Developmental Psychology, 21*, 1016–1024.

Graham, S., & Juvonen, J. (1998). Self-blame and peer victimization in middle school: An attributional analysis. *Developmental Psychology, 34*, 587–599.

Holt, M. K., & Espelage, D. L. (2005). Social support as a moderator between dating violence victimization and depression/anxiety among African American and Caucasian adolescents. *School Psychology Review, 34*, 309–328.

House, J. S. (1981). *Work stress and social support*. Reading, MA: Addison-Wesley.

Ireland, J. L., & Power, C. L. (2004). Attachment, emotional loneliness, and bullying behaviour: A study of adult and young offenders. *Aggressive Behavior, 30*, 298–312.

Juvonen, J., Graham, S., & Schuster, M. A. (2003). Bullying among young adolescents: The strong, the weak, and the troubled. *Pediatrics, 112*, 1231–1237.

Kashani, J. H., Canfield, L. A., Borduin, C. M., Soltyz, S. M., & Reid, J. C. (1994). Perceived family and social support: Impact on children. *The Journal of American Child and Adolescent Psychiatry, 33*, 819–823.

Kazdin, A. E. (1987). Treatment of antisocial behavior in children: Current status and future directions. *Psychological Bulletin, 102*, 187–203.

Klever, P. (2005). The multigenerational transmission of family unit functioning. *The American Journal of Family Therapy, 33*, 253–264.

Ladd, G. W., & Ladd, B. K. (1998). Parenting behaviors and parent-child relationships: Correlates of peer victimization in kindergarten? *Developmental Psychology, 34*, 1450–1458.

Malecki, C. K., & Demaray, M. K. (2003). Carrying a weapon to school and perceptions of social support in an urban middle school. *Journal of Educational and Behavioral Disorders, 11*, 169–178.

Monks, C. P., Smith, P. K., & Swettenham, J. (2005). The psychological correlates of peer victimization in preschool: Social cognitive skills, executive function and attachment profiles. *Aggressive Behavior, 31*, 571–588.

Murdock, M. L., & Gore, P. A. (2004). Stress, coping, and differentiation of self: A test of Bowen theory. *Contemporary Family Therapy, 26*, 319–335.

Nickerson, A. B., Brock, S. E., Chang, Y., & O'Malley, M. (2006). Responding to children victimized by their peers. *Journal of School Violence, 5*, 19–32.

Nickerson, A. B., & Nagle, R. J. (2004). The influence of parent and peer attachments on life satisfaction in middle childhood and early adolescence. *Social Indicators Research, 66*, 35–60.

Nixon, C. L., & Watson, A. C. (2001). Family experiences and early emotion understanding. *Merrill-Palmer Quarterly, 47*, 300–322.

Oliver, R., & Oaks, I. N. (1994). Family issues and interventions in bully and victim relationships. *School Counselor, 41*, 199–202.

Olweus, D. (1991). Victimization among school children. In R. Baenninger (Ed.), *Targets of violence and aggression* (pp. 45–102). Amsterdam: Elsevier Science.

Olweus, D. (1993). *Bullying at school: What we know and what we can do*. Malden, MA: Blackwell.

Parke, R. D., O'Neil, R., Isley, S., Spitzer, S., Welsh, M., Wang, S., et al. (1998). Family-peer relationships: Cognitive, emotional, and ecological determinants. In M. Lewis & C. Feiring (Eds.), *Families, risk, and competence* (pp. 89–112). Mahwah, NJ: Erlbaum.

Patterson, G. R. (1986). Performance models for antisocial boys. *American Psychologist, 41*, 432–444.

Peleg-Popko, O. (2002). Bowen theory: A study of differentiation of self, social anxiety, and physiological symptoms. *Contemporary Family Therapy, 24*, 355–369.

Perry, D. G., Hodges, E. V. E., & Egan, S. K. (2001). Determinants of chronic victimization by peers: A review and new model of family influence. In J. Juvonen & S. Graham (Eds.), *Peer harassment in school: The plight of the vulnerable and victimized* (pp. 73–104). New York: Guilford.

Peskin, M. F., Tortolero, S. R., & Markham, C. M. (2006). Bullying and victimization among Black and Hispanic adolescents. *Adolescence, 41*, 467–484.

Piko, B. (2000). Perceived social support from parents and peers: Which is the stronger predictor of adolescent substance use? *Substance Use and Misuse, 35*, 617–631.

Prest, L. A. & Protinsky, H. (1993). Family systems theory: A unifying framework for codependence. *The American Journal of Family Therapy, 21*, 352–360.

Rice, K. G. (1990). Attachment in adolescence: A narrative and meta-analytic review. *Journal of Youth and Adolescence, 19*, 511–538.

Rigby, K. (1993). School children's perceptions of their families and parents as a function of peer regulations. *The Journal of Genetic Psychology, 154*, 501–513.

Rigby, K. (1994a). Psychosocial functioning in families of Australian adolescent schoolchildren involved in bully/victim problems. *Journal of Family Therapy, 16*, 173–187.

Rigby, K. (1994b). Why do some children bully at school? The contributions of negative attitudes towards victims and the perceived expectations of friends, parents, and teachers. *School Psychology International, 26*, 147–161.

Rigby, K., Slee, P., & Cunningham, P. (1999). Effects of parenting on the peer relations of Australian adolescents. *The Journal of Social Psychology, 139*, 387–388.

Rodkin, P. C., Farmer, T. W., Pearl, R., & Van Acker, R. (2000). Heterogeneity of popular boys: Antisocial and prosocial configurations. *Developmental Psychology, 31*, 548–553.

Rubin, K. H., Dwyer, K. M., Booth-LaForce, C., Kim, A. H., Burgess, K. B., & Rose-Krasnor, L. (2004). Attachment, friendship, and psychosocial functioning in early adolescence. *Journal of Early Adolescence, 24*, 326–356.

Salmivalli, C., Huttunen, A., & Lagerspetz, K. M. J. (1997). Peer networks and bullying in schools. *Scandinavian Journal of Psychology, 38*, 305–312.

Salmivalli, C., Lagerspetz, K., Bjorkqvist, K., Ostreman, K., & Kaukianien, A. (1996). Bullying as a group process: Participant roles and their relations to social status within the group. *Aggressive Behavior, 22*, 1–15.

Schreurs, K. M. G., & de Ridder, D. T. D. (1997). Integration of coping and social support perspectives: Implications for the study of adaptation to chronic diseases. *Clinical Psychology Review, 17*, 89–112.

Schwartz, D. (2000). Subtypes of victims and aggressors in children's peer groups. *Journal of Abnormal Child Psychology, 28*, 181–192.

Schwartz, D., Dodge, K. A., Pettit, G. S., & Bates, J. E. (1997). The early socialization of aggressive victims of bullying. *Child Development, 68*, 665–675.

Sharp, S. (1996). Self-esteem, response style and victimization: Possible ways of preventing victimization through parenting and school based training programmes. *School Psychology International, 17*, 347–357.

Shields, A., & Cicchetti, D. (2001). Parental maltreatment and emotion dysregulation as risk factors for bullying and victimization in middle childhood. *Journal of Clinical Child Psychology, 30*, 349–363.

Smith, P. K., & Myron-Wilson, R. (1998). Parenting and school bullying. *Clinical Child Psychology and Psychiatry, 3*, 405–417.

Swearer, S. M., & Espelage, D. L. (2004). Introduction: A social-ecological framework of bullying among youth. In D. L. Espelage & S. M. Swearer (Eds.), *Bullying in American schools: A social-ecological perspective on prevention and intervention* (pp. 1–12). Mahwah, NJ: Erlbaum.

Troy, M., & Sroufe, L. A. (1987). Victimization among preschoolers: Role of attachment relationship history. *Journal of the American Academy of Child and Adolescent Psychiatry, 26*, 166–172.

Vuchinich, S., Bank, L., & Patterson, G. R. (1992). Parenting, peers, and the stability of antisocial behavior in preadolescent boys. *Developmental Psychology, 28*, 510–521.

Weigel, D. J., Devereux, P., Leigh, G. K., & Ballard-Reisch, D. (1998). A longitudinal study of adolescents' perceptions of support and stress: Stability and change. *Journal of Adolescent Research, 13*, 158–177.

Weiss, B., Dodge, K. A., Bates, J. E., & Pettit, G. S. (1992). Some consequences of early harsh discipline: Child aggression and a maladaptive social information processing style. *Child Development, 63*, 1321–1335.

Ybarra, M. C., & Mitchell, K. J. (2004). Youth engaging in online harassment: Associations with caregiver-child relationships, Internet use, and personal characteristics. *Journal of Adolescence, 27*, 319–336.

Young, M. H., Miller, B., Norton, M. C., & Hill, E. F. (1995). The effect of parental supportive behaviors on life satisfaction of adolescent offspring. *Journal of Marriage and the Family, 57*, 813–822.

15
Bullying and Social Status During School Transitions

ANTHONY D. PELLEGRINI, JEFFREY D. LONG, DAVID SOLBERG, CARY ROSETH, DANIELLE DUPUIS, CATHERINE BOHN, AND MEGHAN HICKEY

Aggression in schools in America and around the world is all too visible. The most visible variants of aggression are those presented on the evening news and on the front pages of newspapers. Instances of school shootings and suicides are the most horrendous variants of this problem. Indeed, many of the actors in these horrendous acts were victimized, or bullied, in school. Taking perhaps one of the most visible example, the "Jocks" in Littleton, Colorado, may have been targeted because they were perceived to have excluded and picked on specific youngsters. These victimized youngsters, in turn, massacred their victimizers.

Less noticeable forms of aggression, in the form of bullying, are observed across a variety of social settings, ranging from preschool classrooms (Smith & Thompson, 1991) to the adult workplace (Cowie, Naylor, Smith, Rivers, & Pereira, 2002). For example, young children have been observed systematically "picking on" peers or excluding a child from a peer group (e.g., Pellegrini et al., 2007). Adolescents too, victimize peers as they cut ahead in the lunch line or humiliate their classmates in the presence of opposite-sex peers (Pellegrini & Long, 2003). In many cases, the perpetrators of these aggressive acts are presented by some researchers as somehow lacking or deficient in appropriate social skills. From this view, the problem of bullying might be remediated if the perpetrators are taught a repertoire of appropriate social skills.

Bullying and Social Dominance

This chapter presents a model attempting to explain bullying and associated forms of aggression observed in a variety of school settings. Herein, we suggest that in many cases, though certainly not all, bullying is a form of proactive aggression, a type of aggression used to accomplish goals (i.e., instrumental), such as gaining access to toys or extorting a peer's lunch money. As in the examples cited above, some children and adolescents deliberately use this form of aggression to victimize their peers in the service of accessing resources, be they a place in line or a girl's attention. This view of bullying presented in this chapter is derived from our longitudinal research with preschoolers and adolescents, which reveals that bullying is used strategically to access some resources (Pellegrini, 2002). This view of bullying contrasts with considering bullies deficient in social skills. Individuals' "social dominance status" within a group is derived, in part, by their ability to defeat other individuals in dyadic contests for resources.

These sorts of contest competitions are typically conducted in places where the bullies' peers, but not teachers, can witness the results, resulting in bullies being viewed as socially dominant and central in their peer groups. Dyadic contests for resources and corresponding social dominance are especially prevalent when students make transitions from one school to another. During transitions, extant social hierarchies of groups are disturbed due to new students entering the group, some children leaving, and changes associated with physical maturity during adolescence. This chapter includes data supporting the hypothesis that bullying and other forms of proactive aggression used in dyadic contests with a peer are especially evident at school transition points such as the transition into preschool and the transition from primary to middle school. These two transition points mark the formation of new social groups where individuals typically sort out their social dominance status. We posit that some individuals use aggression and bullying tactics as strategies to establish social dominance in these new groups. In our view, bullying is a form of aggression used in the service of accomplishing some goal. Correspondingly, after one's goals are met and dominance status is established, we expect that rates of aggression should decrease. In short, aggression is used only to achieve a goal and once it is met, there's little profit in using aggression as individuals in the group recognize who is dominant and will typically cede contested resources to dominant peers.

From this perspective, proactive aggression and bullying are not used because youngsters have a deficient social problem solving repertoire. Aggressive children lacking social skills tend to be bully victims or provocative victims, and their aggression is reactive, not instrumental (Schwartz, Dodge, & Coie, 1993). Reactive aggression, or hostile aggression, typically occurs when the person is in a highly emotional state in response to a provocation (Pellegrini, Bartini, & Brooks, 1999; Schwartz et al., 1993). Consequently, these youngsters lack the requisite social skills to be socially dominant. In this chapter, bullying is defined, partially following Olweus (1993), as a deliberate and instrumental form of aggression that persists over time. Bullying can be either direct, based on physical intimidation (e.g., hitting or threatening to hit), or indirect, based on relational or social aggression (e.g., using rumors or innuendo to damage a peer's reputation). Bullying, then, is a form of proactive aggression that is motivated to achieve some outcome. Further, bullying is characterized by a power differential between the bully and the victim.

Correspondingly, we posit that bullying is used in the service of establishing social dominance, where social dominance is conceptualized as using physical or relational aggression in dyadic contests for resources. Dominant individuals are those who win resources more frequently than their peers (Hinde, 1976, 1980; McGrew, 1972; Pellegrini et al., 2007). This dyadic dimension of social dominance is the one most relevant to bullying. For example, two children may compete for a vacant swing seat where child A wins and child B loses, if this pattern persists over time, across activities, child A is in a dominant relationship with B. The second dimension of social dominance relates to the group. At this level a group is said to have a certain dominance structure, or hierarchy, such that individuals are hypothetically arranged from most dominant to least dominant. Such a hierarchy is based on the questionable assumption that all individuals in a group compete with each other at the dyadic level, and the result is a hierarchical arrangement of students from the most dominant to the least. Further, it is assumed that these relationships are transitive; for example if A defeats B and B defeats C, it is assumed that A will defeat C.

In practice, the assumption that all individuals in a classroom engage in aggressive contests with every other individual in that classroom has not, to our knowledge, been adequately tested, and it has not been supported where it has been tested (Pellegrini et al., 2007). Instead, individuals' aggressive interactions are not distributed across all individuals in a group, but rather aggressive interactions are selectively directed at certain individuals. For example, individuals only target peers with desired resources and those they think they can defeat (Archer, 1992). Examples of the selective uses of aggression can be found in preschoolers (Pellegrini et al., 2007) and adolescents (Pellegrini & Long, 2003) targeting select same-sex peers and primary school bullies who systematically direct aggression at vulnerable peers (Perry, Kusel, & Perry, 1988; Schwartz, Proctor, & Chen, 2001).

Most variants of social dominance theory posit that in new or emergent groups, such as pupils in a classroom at the start of a school year, aggression and bullying initially escalate and then stabilize after this period of initially high rates (e.g., Pellegrini & Long, 2003; Pellegrini et al., 2007; Strayer, 1980). Specifically, aggression in new groups is observed at relatively high rates as individuals sort out status, and rates of aggression should decrease with time. Social dominance structure in a group results from these dyadic contests (Bernstein, 1981; Hinde, 1978). Such trends have also been documented for early adolescents' aggression as they make the transition from primary to secondary school (Pellegrini & Long, 2003) and among preschoolers (Pellegrini et al., 2007). This sort of inverted-U trend in aggression and bullying frequencies (as displayed in Figure 15.1 and 15.3) is very different from the more general secular trends in aggression and bullying (see Figure 15.2), where aggression decreases monotonically with age (Olweus, 1978).

The inverted-U trends are probably due to subordinate individuals recognizing that the costs of challenging a more dominant individual outweigh the benefits because they are likely to be defeated. Similarly, high status individuals probably do not challenge subordinates because there is little to be gained (low benefits) while relatively high costs are likely to be incurred (e.g., social sanction, defeat). From this view, aggression should decrease with time after students make transitions into new schools. This chapter examines the extent to which instances of aggression and bullying vary as youngsters make two transitions: (a) into preschool and (b) from primary to middle school.

Decrements of Aggression and Bullying Across Time

Preschoolers' Aggression and Dominance Across the School Year.   First, the methods used with this nursery school sample are described. Briefly (for more detail see Pellegrini et al., 2007) this preschool study included 65 children (ranging in age from 3.2–5.2 years) enrolled in the Shirley G. Moore Nursery School of the University of Minnesota across a school year. Children's social behavior was directly observed by a team of observers who were graduate students in educational psychology. This chapter reports cooperative behavior and total number of wins: total number of aggressive behaviors ratios (total number of aggressive contests won to total number of aggressive contests). Teachers also rated children's proactive aggression (three items; e.g., starts fights, threatens or bullies, get others to gang up on peer), deception (four items, e.g., makes false statements, uses deception to manipulate peers, falsely accuses others), relational aggression (four items, e.g., tells peers not to play with other peer, gets others to dislike peers, keep others from joining play group), their social dominance (five items e.g., dominates classmates, tells others what to do, stands up for self), and bullying (one item, i.e., child threatens or bullies others in order to get his or her own way). Children were also asked to nominate three peers they like most and three they disliked.

The hypothesis that aggressive behavior would decrease across the school year was supported. As displayed in Figure 15.1, the trend showed significant decrease with time (each wave represents a 3-month interval). The decrease in aggression is consistent with social dominance theory, which posits that aggression decreases because individuals recognize, with time, that the

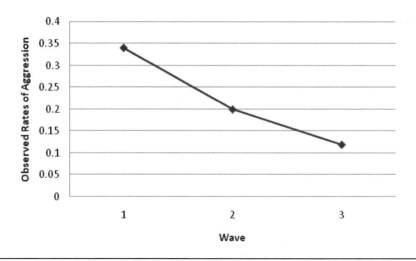

Figure 15.1 Preschoolers' decrement of aggression with time.

costs associated with aggressive contests outweigh the benefits. From this perspective, subordinate individuals may have recognized that the high costs (e.g., high likelihood of being defeated) associated with challenging more dominant individuals outweighed the relatively low benefits (access to abundant resources). Similarly, dominant individuals may also have recognized the low benefits (already being dominant over most individuals), relative to the high costs (e.g., teacher sanction) of aggressing against a subordinate peer.

The decrease in aggression may have been due to other factors as well. First, and related to the social dominance explanation, the social cohesion of these classrooms may have been partially responsible for the decrease. That is, the population of the school remained relatively stable across the year, with only four new children being added (a 6% change in the population). Such a minimal change in the classrooms' social structure may have helped to keep levels of aggression relatively low. Consistent with this interpretation, McGrew (1972) examined rates of aggression in preschool classrooms where new children were added to established classrooms and found low levels of aggression were aimed at the new children and that the new children's initiation of aggression was low. McGrew suggested that children's rates of aggression were related to the social norms of the classrooms.

A social norm related interpretation for the decrement in aggression may have been because children were being socialized over time to school rules encouraging cooperative behavior and discouraging contests and aggressive behavior. Teachers' actions are consistent with this interpretation;, a teacher intervened in many (41%) of all observed aggressive bouts. In further support of this socialization position, a positive and significant correlation was found between children's number of months in attendance at the school and observed cooperation ($r = 0.26$, $p < 0.05$). Further, if the socialization hypothesis is correct, then one would expect that decreases in aggression over time would only be observed in classrooms with clear social norms. Correspondingly, in schools with less clear social norms, one would expect prolonged aggression or even increased aggression until children learn this is how these schools are organized.

Thus, a combination of group cohesion and teacher socialization may explain the decrement of aggression across the school year. To more directly examine the mechanisms by which children are socialized to school rules, future research should document teachers' use of direct (e.g., reprimanding students for anti-social behavior and rewarding prosocial behavior) and indirect (modeling prosocial behavior) strategies for minimizing students' aggression and maximizing cooperation and how these strategies moderate children's aggressive and affiliative behaviors. The following section examines whether the same sort of trend was observed as youngsters made another transition, from primary to middle school.

Bullying Across the Transition from Primary to Middle School Year   The middle school data were collected across a 3-year period in Jackson County (GA) primary and middle schools. This longitudinal sample was comprised of predominately white, middle class youngsters attending primary and middle school in rural Georgia. Bullying was assessed using Olweus' (1989) self-report Senior Questionnaire during the spring of the fifth grade (final year of primary school) and the fall and spring of sixth and seventh grades (the first 2 years of middle school). A total of 70 males and 59 females were in the sample across the duration of the study.

Following the same logic articulated above, we posited uses of bullying would increase during the transition from the end of primary school, in fifth grade, to the start of middle school, in sixth grade, and then decrease again in seventh grade as social dominance is established. An alternative hypothesis to the transitional one is that decrements in aggression and bullying are due to the more general decreases in aggression with age, as displayed in Figure 15.2 below. These data come from English and Irish students who were otherwise similar to our sample except they stayed in the same schools from 12–14 years. Results from our middle school study showed a spike at the initial transition into middle school and then a decline, with time, similar to the preschool trends. Figure 15.3 shows this trend.

The message from the preschool and middle school data is quite clear; while aggression does decrease with age, brief spikes are evident when youngsters' social groups are disrupted. These disruptions can come in the form of long school holidays, moving from one school to another, or re-forming the composition classrooms yearly. As a result of such ruptures, youngsters use aggression to sort out their dominance status, and aggression decreases again as status is established. The following section discusses possible psychological processes associated with bullying, aggression, and social dominance during the preschool and middle school years.

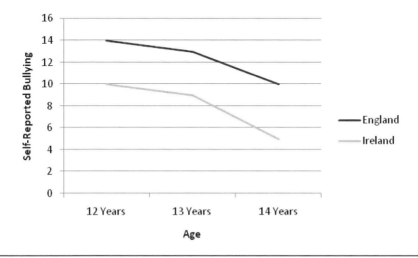

Figure 15.2 Decrement in bullying due to age.

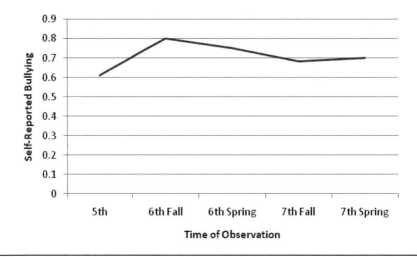

Figure 15.3 Decrement in bullying during the primary to middle school transition.

Forms of Aggression to Access Resources

This section examines the ways in which both preschool children and adolescents use different forms of aggression to achieve various goals. We argue that both preschool and middle school youngsters use aggression, including bullying, strategically to access various types of resources. From this view, these students are not using aggression in a reactive or provocative way, as is typified by socially inept children such as bully victims (Pellegrini, Bartini, & Brooks, 1999; Schwartz et al., 1993). Instead, they are using aggression proactively to accomplish goals and secure resources.

Preschoolers and middle schoolers compete for very different resources. In our observations of preschoolers, whenever two children were observed using aggression in a contest over a resource such as a treat, a place in line, or access to a computer or toy, we coded the identity of the children, the form of aggression used, and the winner of the contest.

Middle schoolers interactions are very different. These early adolescents have emerging interests in heterosexual relationships (Pellegrini & Long, in press); therefore access to opposite sex peers is an important resource. Further, the increasing importance of peer status during early adolescence, relative to childhood, should be implicated in the use of aggression and bullying in social dominance. From this perspective, one would expect adolescents' popularity to protect them from being victimized. That is, if bullying is used in the service of maximizing social status among their adolescent peers, we would not expect youngsters with relatively high social status to be victimized.

Preschoolers' Bullying, Aggression, and Social Dominance As noted above, we directly observed children's aggression and recorded the ratio of the number of wins to total number of aggressive dyadic contests, teachers' ratings, and peer nominations by classmates. More detail on the methods can be found in Pellegrini et al. (2007). Correlations between these measures are displayed in Table 15.1.

The correlations with the teacher rating of bullying were generally not consistent with our hypotheses. Using only one item to rate bullying probably was not adequate for a reliable and valid measure of this construct. However, other correlations that used broader dimensions of proactive aggression were closer to our predictions. Specifically, the measures of proactive and

Table 15.1 Correlations between Ratings[†] of Proactive Aggression, Bullying, Dominance, Winning Aggressive Bouts, Cooperative Behavior, and Like and Dislike Nominations

		Teacher Ratings				Observations		Peer Nominations	
		2	3	4	5	6	7	8	9
Deceptive	1	.48**	.39**	.07	.67**	.71**	.19	.11	.33**
Observed Wins	2		.51**	−.09	.59**	.43**	.31*	.39**	−.09
ProActAggres	3			−.23	.53**	.34**	.38**	.48**	−.18
RelAggress	4				−.10	.12	−.10	−.28	−.14
Dominance	5					.61**	.22	.33**	−.03
Bullying	6						.33**	.17	.41**
CooperBehav	7							.12	−.16
Likes	8								−.26*
Dislikes	9								

$p < 05$; ** $p < .01$. [†]Measures 1-5 are teacher ratings (1-7 Likert-type scale), measures 6 and 7 are directly observed behavior, and measures 8 and 9 are peer nomination.

relational aggression and winning aggressive bouts (which were significantly intercorrelated) were positively and significantly correlated with dominance. Correspondingly, winning aggressive bouts as well as relational aggression was related to teacher-rated dominance. The correlations between teacher rated dominance and winning aggressive bouts provides validity for our assumption that social dominance is, at root, a measure of resource-holding power. Perhaps most interestingly, relational aggression and social dominance were positively and significantly related to being liked by one's peers and the relations between deception and all measures of aggression and being liked by peers.

An important finding presented in this table is the inter-relation between all measures of aggression and the ability to act deceptively. In other words, aggressive children seem to have the social cognitive facility to use aggression in different forms, including getting what they want while at the same time being liked by their peers. This suggests that these children do not use aggression as a result of a deficit. Instead, they seem to be rather Machiavellian in their use of aggression to get things done for them.

Middle Schoolers' Bullying and Social Dominance   As noted above, adolescents compete for very different resources than preschoolers. During adolescence, peer relations generally, and heterosexual relationships, specifically, take on increased importance. The following section documents how early adolescents use aggression to access heterosexual contact in the context of monthly middle school dances.

In this work (Pellegrini & Long, in press), we directly observed youngsters' integration and use of aggression at monthly school dances held across the first full year of middle school. From a social dominance position, we expected boys' rates of aggression to predict their frequency of interaction with girls (i.e., gender integration) over time. For males, aggression should be a stronger predictor of integration than for females. We also examined the extent to which youngsters' popularity inhibited their being victimized, where victimization was defined using Olweus' (1989) self-report Senior Questionnaire.

Aggression and Gender Integration   Figure 15.4 shows the raw observed means over time for integration and aggression, where integration for males is defined as the ratio of boys / (boys + girls) and for girls as girls / (girls + boys) observed during school dances. Additionally, only

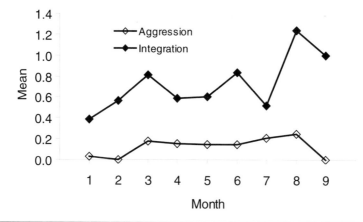

Figure 15.4 Aggression and integration observed means by month.

boys were observed using aggression, and only instances of physical aggression were observed. Specifically, during months 1, 3, 6, and 7 of the study, the percent of boys observed using physical aggression was, respectively, 6%, 7%, 11%, and 6%.

Table 15.2 lists the results for the unconditional regression models. The table indicates a significant positive slope coefficient (β_2) for both models. As illustrated in Figure15.4, the positive slope value indicated a tendency for the mean trend of aggression to have a similar shape as the mean trend of integration. The trends of both variables tended to increase in the early months, plateau in the intermediate months, and decrease at the latter months. Aggression models conditional on gender were also fit, but with the null hypothesis of no gender differences in the uses of aggression.

It was hypothesized that males' use of physical and verbal aggression at school dances and females' physical attractiveness would predict gender integration. While earlier work (Pellegrini & Long, 2003) did show that males' aggression predicted heterosexual interaction, heterosexual interaction in that study was assessed only indirectly, through peer nominations. In the current study this process was assessed more directly by observing both aggressive bouts and integration of peer groups at dances. The results suggest that aggression and peer group integration may affect each other, and counter to the hypothesis, similarly for both males and females across time. With this said, only physical aggression was actually observed and by boys only. Taken together with other results (Bukowski, Sipola, & Newcomb, 2000; Pellegrini & Long, 2003), these results point to the trend of youngsters using aggressive strategies to impress opposite sex

Table 15.2 Results for Aggression Predicting Integration

Effect	Marginal Model			Subject-Specific Model			Ratio[b]
	Estimate	SE	z-value	Estimate	SE	t-value[a]	
Intercept (β_1)	−.3953	.1309	−3.02**	−.8912	.1499	−5.94***	.44
Slope ($\beta2$)	.3144	.1405	2.24*	.4039	.2021	2.00*	.78
$Var(b_{1i})$	-	-	-	1.0895	.2720	4.01***	
$Var(b_{2i})$	-	-	-	.2797	.2301	1.22	
$Corr(b_{1i}, b_{2i})$	-	-	-	−.7667	.2392	−3.21**	

Note. [a]df = 117 for all t-tests; [b]Ratio = Marginal Estimate / Subject-Specific Estimate; *$p < .05$, **$p < .01$, ***$p < .001$.

peers. More troublesome is that girls want to affiliate with boys who use these aggressive strategies (Bukowski et al., 2000; Pellegrini, 2001; Pellegrini & Long, 2003).

Popularity as a Protective Factor in Middle School   As youngsters move from childhood to adolescence, the peer group takes on increased importance relative to the role of parents. Thus, youngsters' status in their peer groups becomes an increasing focus of attention. From a social dominance perspective, status within the peer group becomes an important resource. From this perspective, status within a group may act as either a protective or risk factor in being bullied. Recent research suggests that two dimensions of the peer experience, having friends and being liked by peers, serve as buffers against victimization (Hodges & Perry, 1999; Pellegrini et al., 1999).

Friends can protect each other from victimization, as demonstrated by the programmatic work of Perry and Hodges (Hodges & Perry, 1999), and others (Pellegrini, et al., 1999; Slee & Rigby, 1993). Additionally, being liked by a numbers of peers also seems to buffer victimization. Specifically, Pellegrini and colleagues (Pellegrini et al., 1999) found that the number of like-most nominations by peers was negatively related to victimization. Like-most nominations accounted for significant variance in victimization beyond that of reciprocal friend nominations. Pellegrini and colleagues argued that the number of like-most nominations may protect against bullying because peers represent possible social sanctions or allies against bullies. Perhaps more importantly, that bullies are concerned with social status among their peers would suggest that they would not target peers with allies or other forms of social affiliation, as bullies will not gain status with their peers if they victimize someone who is popular. Indeed, the opposite effect is more likely.

In a more rigorous test of the relative role of friends and like-most nominations as protective factors in victimization, we (Pellegrini & Long, 2002) tested these predictive relations longitudinally. The longitudinal design of this project enabled us to test the relative power of each construct to inhibit victimization. We predicted, based on earlier research (Hodges & Perry, 1999; Pellegrini et al., 1999), that one's reciprocal friendships as well as one's number of like-most nominations should relate negatively to victimization. However, based on earlier contemporaneous research (Pellegrini et al., 1999), it was posited that like-most nominations should be the more important of the two. Simply, being liked by a number of peers should moderate the stability of victimization, possibly because of resulting social disapproval for a large number of peers at a time when peer acceptance and status is especially important.

We used hierarchical regression analysis to test the hypothesis that victimization from primary to middle school was moderated by peer affiliation in middle school. The criterion variable, victimization at the end of seventh grade, was defined as the aggregate of self-report, peer nomination, direct observation, and diary measures collected in the second half of the seventh grade. The predictor variable was victimization in fifth grade and was measured with the Olweus (1989) self-report measure. The moderator variable was the sum of like most nominations at the start of seventh grade. The path from the predictor to the criterion variable was positive and significant ($R^2 = 0.03$, $\beta = 0.182$) and the moderation effect was significant and negative ($R^2 = 0.08$, $\beta = -0.28$). Thus, the moderation hypothesis for victimization was supported.

The moderation model predicting seventh grade victimization indicated that victimization was stable from the end of primary school to the end of seventh grade. This stability is consistent with other work (Olweus, 1993). That victimization is stable across this time span and across different peer groups and social institutions suggests there may be some personality-level variables at work. For example, cross-sectional work indicates that victimization is related to emotionality (Pellegrini et al., 1999).

Our results also suggest that peer status, in the form of most nominations, moderates victimization status. The role of peer popularity in inhibiting seventh grade victimization supports earlier contemporaneous research (Pellegrini et al., 1999). Peer disapproval for victimizing youngsters who are liked by their peers is probably an important deterrent for youngsters who are concerned with their emergent social status. This finding is consistent with the finding of Perry and colleagues (1990), who found that bullies tended to victimize youngsters who were held in low esteem by their peers. As a result, their aggression against these youngsters had few negative consequences for bullies.

Importance of Findings

The research outlined above has significant implications for policy makers, administrators, and teachers concerned with reducing the prevalence of bullying in schools. Our research indicates that two factors may contribute to a reduction in the frequency of bullying throughout the school year—social cohesion among students and teacher socialization.

The level of social cohesion among students is related to the frequency of aggression and bullying. When there is greater social cohesion among students, the frequency of bullying decreases. Schools with relatively stable populations are likely to see a reduction in bullying across the school year because students are able to maintain social cohesion. With fewer new students being added to the group, there are fewer disruptions to the social hierarchy and consequently fewer incidences of aggression and bullying. Therefore, teachers and administrators should pay particular attention to potential cases of bullying when new students are added to the school environment or following any event that may cause a disruption in social cohesion.

More concretely, cohesion can also be maximized by keeping cohorts of children intact as they progress across their educational experiences. When possible, children and adolescents should experience continuity in their peer groups across time. As in the case of English and Irish schools discussed above, bullying was minimized when youngsters did not change schools from primary to middle school. When they did change schools, as in American primary and middle schools, there was a spike in bullying at the transition.

In cases where it is necessary for children and adolescents to change schools, social cohesion can be maximized by keeping students in stable cohorts across an extended period of time. For example, some middle schools in Minneapolis place youngsters in a cohort of students when they enter school in the fifth grade, and the youngsters stay in that cohort for their entire 3-year middle school experience. In this model, group cohesion is sustained across time, and children not only form close relationships with peers, in the form of friendships, but also with teachers. These close relationships may minimize bullying by providing support and by providing an environment where children feel safe and secure in enlisting teachers' and peers' help if they are bullied. This environment is valuable because an important barrier to minimizing bullying in schools is children's reluctance to tell their teachers that they are being bullied (Eslea & Smith, 1998).

Our research also suggests that teachers need to take an active role in socializing children to recognize bullying and aggression as a problem, sanctioning children when they transgress, and modeling and suggesting alternative means of interaction.

Continuing in the socialization vein, many of the findings in our research are troubling, especially the finding that attitudes towards bullying become more positive with time across the middle school period and aggressive youngsters are popular with their peers, especially in adolescence. Because peer groups, schools, and families are major socialization agents of young adolescents, they should be made aware of these views. The negative consequences of these views

Table 15.3 Implications for Practice

Challenges

1) Contrary to traditional stereotypic portrayals of the bully as being maladjusted, most children who bully others enjoy high status among their peer group and display a host of positive characteristics such as leadership and athletic competence, and are quite socially-skilled.

2) Because bullies are often accepted by their peers, given positive social "feedback" , and afforded power and status within the peer group, attempts to alter or curtail their negative social behavior will be resistant to change.

3) It is socially advantageous for peers to support the powerful, high-status bully, making initiatives designed to encourage peer intervention difficult.

Recommendations

1) Peer-led interventions and peer-mediation need to be conducted by high status children who are not aggressive (prosocial-popular children). In fact, we would argue that such interventions are unlikely to be effective if not led (and perhaps initiated) by high-power prosocial children. Research by Cunningham and colleagues supports this hypothesis.

2) Interventions that take into account the nature of the power structure are needed.

3) Research that helps recognize the factors that distinguish children with or without implicit power who do or do not use explicit power is needed to help inform interventions.

for both victims and others should be presented to youngsters. Future research should also begin to search for possible origins of these views. Are there models for these sorts of behaviors in middle schools? Indeed, Olweus' (1993) seminal work revealed that school personnel sometimes model bullying behavior by belittling or threatening students.

Future research and policy should consider the role of school-level variables in bullying, victimization, and peer affiliation. Researchers should compile descriptions of school-level variables such as school policies toward bullying, access to counselors, adult supervision of peer interactions, and opportunities to affiliate with peers. It is important to derive these variables from the different perspectives of students, teachers, and neutral observers. This level of description could be useful in designing schools for young adolescents that support positive peer relationships and reduce victimization.

References

Archer, J. (1992). *Ethology and human development.* Hemel Hemstead, UK: Harvester Wheatsheaf.

Bernstein, I. S. (1981). Dominance: The baby and the bathwater. *Behavioral and Brain Sciences, 4,* 419–457.

Bukowski, W. M., Sipola, L. K., & Newcomb, A. F. (2000). Variations in patterns of attraction to same- and other-sex peers during early adolescence. *Developmental Psychology, 36,* 147–154.

Cowie, H., Naylor, P., Smith, P. K., Rivers, I., & Pereira, B. (2002). Measuring workplace bullying. *Aggression and Violent Behavior, 7,* 35–51.

Eslea, M., & Smith, P. K. (1998). The long-term effectiveness of anti-bullying work in primary schools. *Educational Research, 40,* 203–218.

Hinde, R. A. (1976). Interactions, relationships, and social structure. *Man, 11,* 1–17.

Hinde, R. A. (1978). Dominance and role. Two concepts with two meanings. *Journal of Social Biology Structure, 1,* 27–38.

Hinde, R. A. (1980). *Ethology.* London: Fontana.

Hodges, E. V., & Perry, D. G. (1999). Personal and interpersonal antecedents of victimization by peers. *Journal of Personality and Social Psychology, 76,* 677–685.

McGrew, W. C. (1972). *An ethological study of children's behaviour.* London: Metheun.

Olweus, D. (1978). *Aggression in schools: Bullies and whipping boys.* New York: Wiley.

Olweus, D. (1989). *The Senior Bully-Victim Questionnaire.* Unpublished manuscript.

Olweus, D. (1993). *Bullying at school.* Cambridge, MA: Blackwell.

Pellegrini, A. D. (2001). A longitudinal study of heterosexual relationships, aggression, and sexual harassment during the transition from primary school through middle school. *Journal of Applied Developmental Psychology, 22,* 119–133.

Pellegrini, A. D. (2002). Bullying, victimization, and sexual harassment during the transition to middle school. *Educational Psychologist, 37,* 151–163.

Pellegrini, A. D., Bartini, M., & Brooks, F. (1999). School bullies, victims, and aggressive victims: Factors relating top group affiliation and victimization in early adolescence. *Journal of Educational Psychology, 91,* 216–224.

Pellegrini, A. D., & Long, J. D. (2002). A longitudinal study of bullying, dominance, and victimization during the transition from primary through secondary school. *British Journal of Developmental Psychology, 20,* 259–280.

Pellegrini, A. D., & Long, J. D. (2003). A sexual selection theory longitudinal analysis of sexual segregation and integration in early adolescence. *Journal of Experimental Child Psychology, 85,* 257–278.

Pellegrini, A. D., & Long, J. D. (in press). An observational study of early heterosexual interaction at middle school dances. *Journal of Research in Adolescence.*

Pellegrini, A. D., Roseth, C., Mliner, S., C. Bohn, Van Ryzin, M., Vance, N., Cheatham, C. L., & Tarullo, A. (2007). Social dominance in preschool classrooms. *Journal of Comparative Psychology, 121,* 54–64.

Perry, D. G., Kusel, S. J., & Perry, L. C. (1988). Victims of peer aggression. *Developmental Psychology, 24,* 807–814.

Perry, D., Willard, J., & Perry, L. C. (1990). Peers' perceptions of the consequences that victimized children provide aggressors. *Child Development, 61,* 1289–1309.

Schwartz, D., Dodge, K. A., & Coie, J. D. (1993). The emergence of chronic peer victimization. *Child Development, 64,* 1755–1772.

Schwartz, D., Proctor, L., J., & Chen, D. H. (2001). The aggressive victim of bullying. In J. Juvonen & S. Graham (Eds.), *Peer harassment in school: The plight of the vulnerable and victimized* (pp. 147–174). New York: Guilford.

Slee, P. T., & Rigby, K. (1993), Australian school children's self appraisal of interpersonal relations: The bullying experience. *Child Psychiatry and Human Development, 23,* 273–287.

Smith, P. K., & Thompson, D. (Eds.). (1991). *Practical approaches to bullying.* London: David Fulton.

Strayer, F. F. (1980). Social ecology of the preschool peer group. In W. A. Collins (Ed.), *Minnesota symposium on child development, 13* (pp. 165–196). Hillsdale, NJ: Erlbaum.

16

Respect or Fear?

The Relationship Between Power and Bullying Behavior

TRACY VAILLANCOURT, PATRICIA MCDOUGALL,
SHELLEY HYMEL, AND SHAFIK SUNDERANI

Bullying is said to occur when a person is exposed to repeated intentional abuse on the part of one or more individuals who have more power than the person being victimized (Olweus, 1999). Central to the definition of bullying is the concept of asymmetrical power. Power is fundamental to all social relationships (Emerson, 1962; Russell, 1938), but its role in bully-victim relationships is a key factor distinguishing bullying from other forms of interpersonal aggression. Although it is impossible to bully others in *absence* of some form of power advantage, bullying may be best conceptualized as a "systematic abuse of power" (Smith & Sharp, 1994, p. 2). And it is precisely because they wield power that bullies are able to influence and change the behavior, attitudes, goals, and values of others. To fully unravel the complex nature of bullying, it is paramount that we begin to systematically delineate the ways in which bullying and power go hand in hand. In this chapter we explore the unique role of power in bully-victim relationships and its implications for addressing bullying in schools.

The Nature of Power

Power can be manifested in many different ways (French & Raven, 1959). A person can have power over another because he or she is older, stronger, or bigger (e.g., Olweus, 1993, 1999), because he or she is a majority member of a cohesive group (Clark & Maass, 1988; Gerard, Wilhelmy, & Conolley, 1968; Rosenberg, 1961), or because he or she is more socially competent, more popular, or more visible (Adler & Adler, 1998; Chance, 1967; Driskell & Mullen, 1990; Friske, 1993; Merten, 1997; Sutton, Smith, & Swettenham, 1999a, 1999b; Vaillancourt & Hymel, 2006; Vaillancourt, Hymel, & McDougall, 2003). These different forms of power are consistent with distinctions between more direct bullying through physical and verbal attacks, and more indirect bullying through social and relational forms of aggression. However, the forms in which bullying and power are manifested may be less important than the way in which such power has been achieved.

Power can be achieved in different ways and the type of power utilized has clear implications for the individual's status within the peer group (see Vaillancourt & Hymel, 2006; Vaillancourt et al., 2003). Decades ago, LaFreniere and Charlesworth (1983) distinguished between explicit and implicit power in social relationships. *Explicit power* is achieved forcefully through the use of aggression and coercion; *implicit power* is achieved by having competencies and assets (i.e., being attractive, rich, a good leader, socially skilled) that the peer group admires. *Explicit power* elicits fear, submission, and/or compliance from the peer group, regardless of one's acceptance by subordinates, whereas *implicit power* depends on the approval of peers (LaFreniere & Charlesworth, 1983). The distinction between explicit and implicit power is consistent with French and Raven's (1959) notions of *coercive power*, achieved by inspiring fear, and *referent power*, the ability to influence or change people's behavior and thinking simply by virtue of the fact that others want to be seen to be like the individual holding the power. In some cases, it can be difficult to discern whether the power wielded by young people who bully stems from *respect* or *fear,* or both.

Vaillancourt et al. (2003) used the constructs of explicit and implicit power to explain why it is that some children and youth who bully appear to enjoy considerable status within the peer group, while others do not. Over the past 5 years, there has been a virtual explosion of studies examining the link between the use of aggression and one's status within the peer group. Although research on peer rejection in children has traditionally emphasized evidence showing that aggressive behavior is associated with peer rejection and unpopularity (Rubin, Bukowski & Parker, 2006), more recent studies have demonstrated that in many cases, bullying and aggression are *not* perpetrated primarily by children and youth who are marginalized by the peer group, although some marginalized children do use aggression against their peers. Rather, it is often popular children and youth who are terrorizing their peers and these popular aggressors are often more aggressive than their unpopular counterparts (e.g., Cillessen & Borch, 2006; deBruyn & Cillessen, 2006a; Estell, Farmer, & Cairns, 2007; Lease, Kennedy, & Axelrod, 2002; Prinstein & Cillessen, 2003; Rodkin, Farmer, Pearl, & Van Acker, 2000; Rose, Swenson, & Waller, 2004; Vaillancourt & Hymel, 2006; Vaillancourt et al., 2003). Why might this be the case?

According to Vaillancourt and colleagues (2003, 2006), children and youth seek to achieve and maintain hegemony through the use of power (see also Adler, Kless & Adler, 1992; Bandura, 1973; Merten, 1997), but how that power is manifest will depend in part on how the power has been achieved. At one extreme is the traditional stereotype of bullies as socially inept, marginalized individuals who physically exploit others through their greater size, age and/or numbers and achieve their goals aggressively. For these children, bullying reflects the effective use of only explicit or coercive power. But power is not only attainable through aggressive means. At the other extreme are those students who rely solely on implicit or referent power. They are able to exert considerable influence on their peers, but they are more likely to be labeled *leaders*, not bullies, owing primarily to the fact that they do not rely on coercive or explicit power. Between these two extremes lies what Vaillancourt et al. (2003) believe to be the more common situation in which children and youth who bully rely on both implicit and explicit forms of power. Individuals are afforded some degree of power and/or status because they possess qualities and assets (implicit power) that other people would like to have or would like to be seen to be associated with (referent power) *and* they use aggression (explicit and/or coercive power) in concert with implicit power to attain and maintain status within the peer group. Although we certainly recognize that just about anyone can attempt to use explicit and/or coercive power, we do argue that it is very difficult to effectively use more relational and social forms of bullying without a foundation of status or peer acceptance within the group.

Hawley's research (2003a, 2003b) focuses on "bi-strategic controllers," children who effectively control resources through aggressive means, but who remain well-liked, central members of the peer group, presumably because in addition to their aggressive tendencies (explicit power), they are also socially skilled (implicit power). The combination of implicit and explicit power is illustrated in a study by Vaillancourt and Hymel (2006) who found that aggressive youth who were identified by peers as high on attractiveness, style, athleticism, etc. (thus *high* on *both* implicit and explicit power) were perceived by peers as the most popular and powerful adolescents in their school, whereas aggressors low on peer-valued characteristics (thus *low* on implicit and *high* on explicit power) were viewed as the least powerful, popular, and most highly disliked individuals in the school (see also Dijkstra, Lindenberg, Veenstra, Verhulst, & Ormel, 2007).

Rejected, unpopular aggressors low on peer-valued characteristics have been shown to be psychologically impaired and marginalized (Vaillancourt et al., 2003), and we suspect they represent the highly troubled yet underrepresented *bully-victim group* that is described in the literature (Batsche & Knoff, 1994; Hanish & Guerra, 2004; Kumpulainen & Rasanen, 2000; Nansel, Craig, Overpeck, Saluja & Ruan, 2004; Nansel et al., 2001; Schwartz, 2000). In Vaillancourt et al.'s (2003) study, less than 10% of bullies were classified as being low on power. These low-power bullies were rated by peers as being far less attractive and athletic than the high-power bullies. They also lacked the leadership skills that the high-power bullies possessed. Still, they wielded some form of explicit power, using aggression to intimidate and abuse their peers. However, as argued previously, this type of aggressor represents the minority in the peer group, with most aggressors being Machiavellian in their efforts to gain and maintain status (Hawley, 2003a, 2003b; Vaillancourt & Hymel, 2006; Vaillancourt et al., 2003).

Clearly, not all children and youth who possess implicit or referent power in the peer group will abuse this power (deBruyn & Cillessen, 2006b). We contend, however, that power afforded to persons with valued skills and assets, in no way guarantees that power is always used wisely and appropriately. What determines whether or not an individual who is afforded implicit power by the peer group will come to augment their power by relying additionally on use of explicit or coercive power? History is replete with examples of how power corrupts and there is no shortage of empirical studies of adults demonstrating "how the possession of power changes the power-holder" (Keltner, Gruenfeld, & Anderson, 2003, p. 266), often for the worse. Studies of adult males conducted over 30 years ago by Zimbardo (1971) and Kipnis (1972) clearly demonstrated the corrupting influence of power.

In the classic Zimbardo study, male undergraduate students were randomly assigned to the role of either prison guard or prisoner, given uniforms that corresponded to their assigned roles, and instructed to act out their parts. Although the first day proceeded without incident, the morale quickly changed thereafter. The "guards" disparaged the "prisoners" and began mistreating them by creating malicious and degrading routines. In fact, the atmosphere became so dreadful with the inhumane treatment of prisoners that Zimbardo (serving as the prison warden) was compelled to terminate the study after only 6 days, in what should have been a 2-week study.

Kipnis (1972) randomly assigned male participants to one of two conditions: one in which participants were afforded institutional power and the other in which participants were given no power. The results were striking. Those participants who maintained power were found to increase their attempts to influence the behavior of subordinates and view them as "objects of manipulation." As well, participants with power soon began to devalue the performance and worth of those over whom they wielded power and expressed a desire for distance from the less powerful. The title of Kipnis' paper asks, "Does power corrupt?" The answer was an emphatic yes. The question yet unanswered is to what degree the corrupting effect of power leads *children* to become bullies among their peers. Further research is needed to determine the developmental and group processes through which children learn to deal with power, either positively or negatively.

Taken together, developmental research on the complex links between popularity and aggression (e.g., Cillessen & Borch, 2006; deBruyn & Cillessen, 2006a; Estell et al., 2007; Olweus, 1977; Prinstein & Cillessen, 2003; Rose et al., 2004; Vaillancourt & Hymel, 2006; Vaillancourt et al., 2003) and the seminal social psychology studies of Zimbardo (1971) and Kipnis (1972) challenge the popular belief that meanness is typically inflicted by the mean at heart. Perhaps it is more accurate to say that *all* humans are *capable* of being aggressive and abusing their power. This may help to explain why bullying is so pervasive (Craig, 2004; Craig & Harel, 2004) and therefore could not possibly be accounted for by a minority of "mean" people. Rather, bullying may more accurately be characterized as part of the human condition in which most strive for superiority (Adler, 1930), popularity (Adler & Adler, 1998; Butcher & Pfeffer, 1986; Gavin & Furman, 1989; Jarvinen & Nicholls, 1996; Merten, 1997) or status (Barkow, 1975; Hogan & Hogan, 1991) in the hierarchically organized groups to which they belong (Bernstein, 1981; Buss, 1988; Mazur, 1985). The fact that bullying is often perpetrated by high status children (Cillessen & Borch, 2006; deBruyn & Cillessen, 2006a; Prinstein & Cillessen, 2003; Rodkin et al., 2000; Rose et al., 2004; Vaillancourt & Hymel, 2006; Vaillancourt et al., 2003) and adults (e.g., Baldwin, Daugherty, & Rowley, 1998; Quine, 2002; Manderino & Berkey, 1997; Sofield & Salmond, 2003) offers some insights into the individual and peer group processes that operate in the service of maintaining bullying behavior.

Why Is It so Difficult to Reduce Bullying?

Vaillancourt and Hymel (2004, 2006; see also Vaillancourt et al., 2003) suggest that bullying is difficult to eliminate because it "works"; children and youth who bully get what they want. However, bullying behavior is also promoted through biased self-perceptions and through both real and perceived support from both peers and adults. Much bullying behavior occurs "under the radar," without being caught or punished by adults. Observational research indicates that adults intervene on behalf of victims only 4% of the time (Craig & Pepler, 1995, 1997; see also Salmivalli & Voeten, 2004). And because "bullies are seldom punished for their aggressive behavior" (O'Connell, Pepler, & Craig, 1999, p. 439), their problematic behavior goes unimpeded, further devastating their victim(s).

Avoiding detection, however, is not the only problematic issue. Children who bully others are sometimes reinforced or even actively supported. Consistent with Olweus' (e.g., 1993) notion that bullying is a group phenomenon, seminal observational research by Craig and Pepler in Canada has shown that peer group members are present in over 85% of bullying incidents, yet only intervene on behalf of the victim about 11% of the time (Craig & Pepler, 1995, 1997; Hawkins, Pepler, & Craig, 2001). Extending this work, Salmivalli, Lagerspetz, Bjorkqvist, Osterman, and Kaukiainen (1996) demonstrated that children play different "participant roles" in bully-victim situations that go beyond the individual doing the bullying or the individual being victimized. Specifically, they found that 20% of students could be categorized as reinforcing the bullying (i.e., actively following) with an additional 7% serving as assistants (e.g., laughing or enticing the bullying; Salmivalli et al., 1996). Similarly, in their observational studies, O'Connell et al. (1999) found that peers reinforced the bully's behavior 54% of the time by passively watching and actively modeled the behavior 21% of the time (see also Salmivalli & Voeten, 2004). Thus, all too often children who bully receive feedback from both adults and the peer group that what they are doing is acceptable, if not sanctioned. The fact that aggression can be rewarded is not a new idea. In fact, over three decades ago Bandura (1973) suggested just that—aggression serves a utilitarian purpose in many social groups.

If one considers bullying from the perspective of the aggressor, it makes sense that bullying behavior persists despite our best efforts to reduce it (e.g., Smith, Schneider, Smith, & Ananaiadou, 2004). The children or youth who bully often enjoy considerable status and power within the peer group, are seldom admonished by either peers or adults for their negative behavior, and are sometimes actively encouraged by a small but significant number of peers when behaving inappropriately. Although their aggressive behavior may well reflect explicit or coercive power that evokes compliance through *fear*, such compliance may also be interpreted by aggressors as stemming from *respect*.

Research has shown that people with power are held in higher esteem (Barkow, 1975; Eibl-Eibesfeldt, 1989) and influence the group more than their less powerful peers (Bales, Strodtbeck, Mills, & Roseborough, 1951; Berger, Cohen, & Zelditch, 1972; Driskell & Mullen, 1990; French & Raven, 1959; Keltner et al., 2003). The powerful are looked at more, validated more, and respected more (Chance, 1967; Frisk, 1993) which translates into a perception of approval, perpetuating the erroneous belief that they are justified in their actions. Bullying is about power (Vaillancourt et al., 2003) in a society in which there is not enough power to go around and one person possessing power means that someone else has less power.

When we couple this with the natural human tendency to perceive ourselves favorably and to take from our environment information that is consistent with our self-schema it should not be particularly surprising why bullying has been so resistant to intervention efforts.

Biased self-perceptions, in turn, can exacerbate bullying behavior. There is a rich theoretical and empirical research history in social psychology documenting how people's perceptions of self affects the way they process information. For example, as human beings, we generally tend to think well of ourselves (see Myers & Spencer, 2004) and we process information more quickly and remember it more when it is consistent with our perception of how we are (see Higgins & Bargh, 1987; Symons & Johnson, 1997) We also have a tendency to think that most others share our opinions and act in similar ways, and therefore tend to find support for what we do and how we think (e.g., Krueger & Clement, 1994; Marks & Miller, 1987). We also tend to associate with people who act like us and think like us (see Myers & Spencer, 2004). The function of these types of self-serving biases is well established—they help maintain a positive view of self and protect us from depression (Snyder & Higgins, 1988). The problem, however, is that self-serving biases also tend to help people justify their egregious acts, morally disengaging from their negative impact on others, and making them more palatable and hence more likely to re-occur (Bandura, 1999, 2002; Bandura, Caprara, Barbaranelli, Pastorelli, & Regalia, 2001). Research has shown that children who are successful in their use of aggression are more likely to use aggression again in the future (Patterson, Littman, & Bricker, 1967). They also come to believe that their victims are deserving of the abuse they endure (e.g., Hymel, Rocke-Henderson, & Bonanno, 2005; Bandura, 1999, 2002; Bandura et al., 2001). Thus, children who bully others, especially high status bullies, can readily interpret their own social behavior as effective and others' compliance as warranted, confusing motivations of fear with respect. Such biased interpretations, when coupled with increased capacity for moral disengagement (see Hymel et al., this volume), make bullying behavior highly resistant to change.

The impact extends beyond the individual bully, however. What about the peer group who regularly witnesses these hostile exchanges? They are exposed to examples of aggression working effectively. Specifically, they see *powerful* individuals being reinforced for their use of aggression. This is problematic because children are more likely to imitate people who are powerful and rewarded for their behavior (Bandura, 1973). With respect to bullying, they see that the aggressor is rarely admonished by the peer group and rarely caught by adults (Craig & Pepler, 1995, 1997; see also Salmivalli & Voeten, 2004).

The Power of the Group

Why is it that members of the peer group fail to intervene on behalf of the victim or, worse yet, why does the peer group sometimes encourage the humiliation and oppression of another human being? The answer is at least three-fold. First, it is very risky to challenge a high status person. The risks include loss of status, friendship, and the increased likelihood of being bullied (e.g., retribution) for taking the appropriate steps. Because being popular is one of the most important pursuits for children and adolescents (Butcher & Pfeffer, 1986; Gavin & Furman, 1989; Jarvinen & Nicholls, 1996; Merten, 1997), the risk of status loss is not inconsequential. Even among adults, studies have shown that people will agree with something they do not believe in order to gain approval of others and avoid being rejected by the group (Miller & Anderson, 1979; Schachter, 1951), a phenomenon termed normative influence (Deutsch & Gerard, 1955).

Second, a powerful person can probably only be dissuaded by another powerful person (Salmivalli et al., 1996; Vaillancourt et al., 2003) or a group of individuals who are powerful because of their large numbers (Vaillancourt et al., 2003). Otherwise, if the "group" is seen as supporting the bully, the power of a group can alter the actions of a well-intended individual, as demonstrated in classic studies on conformity conducted by Solomon Asch (1952, 1955, 1957). These studies clearly showed that people are less likely to maintain a dissenting opinion in a large group even though their opinion is in fact correct. The implication is that group size can function as deterrent for a bystander who under a different set of circumstances would otherwise intervene. An aggressive mob victimizing an individual will reduce the likelihood of a bystander interfering because of the social costs he/she may endure for getting involved. In addition, the bystander may go along with the majority (i.e., the mob) and even encourage the mob because of passive social pressure placed on the individual to not dissent.

Third, the peer group itself can represent an influential, negative force beyond demands for conformity. Groups allow for diffusion of personal responsibility to occur and they tend to decrease both inhibition and apprehension among group members (Festinger, Pepitone, & Newcomb, 1952). This type of *deindividuation* may be why bullying behavior is often encouraged by the peer group (Craig & Pepler, 1995; O'Connell et al., 1999; Salmivalli & Voeten, 2004). Groups make people feel anonymous which decreases self-awareness and transforms the usually conscientious objector into the type of person who chants during a bullying episode. In 1967, a university student threatened to take his life by jumping from a tower while 200 students encouraged him to "Jump. Jump…", to which he complied (Myers & Spencer, 2004, p. 263). This was not an isolated incident. In a classic analysis of 21 occurrences in which a person threatened suicide by jumping from a large structure, Mann (1981) found that when the crowd was small and exposed by daylight they did not bait the jumper. However, when their identity was protected by the darkness of the night or by the larger size of the crowd, the group usually encouraged the suicidal person to jump (see Mullen, 1986 regarding lynch mobs).

In sum, members of a peer-group fail to intervene on behalf of an individual because the costs to the bystander may be too high, and social processes such as dissenting from the group and deindividuation are forces too strong for some individuals to combat and take a stance against an aggressor. The processes described thus far are most likely to operate in situations in which abuse of power occurs between individuals who are not part of the same social group. However, conflicts and instances of bullying often arise within groups or dyads of affiliated peers wherein members of the same group have been shown to jockeying for status within their close peer group (Savin-Williams, 1979). We turn next to consideration of the processes that may operate when more closely affiliated peers use and abuse power within relationships: youth gangs and friendships.

The Use of Power within Youth Gangs

In the adolescent context, augmenting group size in the form of recruiting gang members is an effective method of accruing power. Indeed, gangs can be an effective strategy (albeit an antisocial one) to combat victimization from more powerful individuals, although further empirical investigation is needed to confirm this association. In one Canadian study of gangs in a large city center, 78% of the urban youth sampled reported protection as being a major function of their gang involvement (Tanner & Wortley, 2002). Tanner and Wortley maintain that cultivating a reputation as a "gangster" may force a prospective bully to re-think his/her decision to choose a fellow gang member as a victim; the bully may incur the high cost of having to combat a group of individuals willing to stand up and/or to seek revenge should a member of its' own fall prey to the bully's aggressive attacks. In some cases however, powerful individuals can form coalitions with others to rival the power of a group/gang thereby fueling a sort of social "arms race."

Although gang membership can reduce victimization from powerful individuals, entering a gang is not a desirable (or feasible) option for most victimized young people. There is no guarantee a victim wanting to join a gang will be granted access into the social circle to reap the benefits of protection. Moreover, the victim may find the lifestyle of the social group/gang incongruent with his/her own lifestyle choices and may not want engage in activities often associated with gang involvement that pose a risk of legal consequences. Further research is needed to explore the processes underlying the use and abuse of power within youth gangs.

The Abuse of Power Within "Friendships"

The concept of friendship typically conjures images of all things wonderful, happy, and equitable: someone to trust, someone to care about, someone to share activities and personal information with, etc. Accordingly, it is sometimes difficult to contemplate that there can be a darker side of friendship (Berndt, 2004). Nevertheless, a significant portion of reported bullying occurs within friendship dyads. When Closson, Hymel, Konishi, and Darwich (2007) asked elementary school students (grades 4–7) to describe the last time they were bullied or harassed by peers, 35% reported that the perpetrator was someone within their own social group and 38% reported that the perpetrator was a friend. When asked about the last time they harassed or bullied others, 28% reported that the victim was within their social group and 29% indicated that the victim was a friend. How is it that friendships can in fact be unequal in power such that the lower status member of the friendship dyad becomes likely to tolerate and endure aggressive gestures initiated by a higher status member?

One fruitful perspective for understanding power dynamics among individuals within a friendship dyad is that of *social exchange theory* (see Homans, 1958; Thibaut & Kelley, 1959). Social exchange theorists posit that the key to understanding the intricate nature of human social relationships is to view them as an exchange of both goods and, more importantly, nonmaterial benefits such as approval and prestige. Ideally, the relationship should predicate itself on an equal transaction of assets. However, because no two people are identical, it is often the case that one individual within a dyadic relationship possesses more social assets (i.e., skills, popularity, etc.) than the other. This differential distribution of power can make the individual with fewer social assets vulnerable to victimization from the more dominant individual of the dyad, who assumes an advantageous position because of an inequity in the exchange.

In French and Raven (1959) terms, one friend may have "reward" power over another, controlling physical or emotional resources such that he or she is in a position to bestow (or remove) highly sought after outcomes (e.g., choosing to initiate, or not, the invitation to a key social gathering). The inequity in power means that the dominant individual is less dependent on the relationship and is more likely than the subordinate to withdraw from or terminate the relationship at any given time. In contrast, the subordinates' increased dependency on the relationship can lead him/her to compensate for his/her lack of contribution to the exchange by being willing to comply with the demands and/or to endure abuse (e.g., verbal derision) from the dominant individual. This form of power imbalance is known as the *principle of least interest* (Blau, 1964; Waller & Hill, 1951) and is likely a contributing factor in the abuse that occurs among supposed friends (e.g., Grotpeter & Crick, 1996).

Implications for Practice

There is a strange comfort felt in believing that aggression is maladaptive and committed by a small group of disturbed individuals. However, such beliefs have, in our opinion, led to a "psychopathology" bias in the field of bullying that ignores the fact that if most people are capable of perpetrating bullying behaviors then these behaviors must reward the user and serve some function (e.g., Archer, 1988; Daly & Wilson, 1988; Lorenz, 1966; Vaillancourt, 2005). We are not disputing that at least some bullying behavior by certain individuals can be linked to psychopathology. Rather, we suggest that the research reviewed herein challenges a singular focus on psychopathology by demonstrating that bullying is a human phenomenon and that the misuse of power is pervasive and universal.

Our review also highlights a "new" type of bully with important implications for prevention and interventions. This "new" type of bully, the Machiavellian bully, is perceived by peers as being popular, socially skilled and competent and uses aggression instrumentally to achieve power. He/she has high self-esteem (see Baumeister, Smart, & Boden, 1996), is low on psychopathology, and has many assets (e.g., attractiveness) for which he/she is importantly admired by peers. At least some of these young people who bully believe that their behaviors are entirely acceptable, even necessary to manipulate others in interpersonal situations for self-gain (Sutton & Keogh, 2000). The Machiavellian bully may well be a future CEO, professional athlete, or world leader and *represents the majority of children and youth who bully others* (e.g., Cillessen & Borch, 2006; deBruyn & Cillessen, 2006a; Estell et al., 2007; Lease et al., 2002; Olweus, 1977; Prinstein & Cillessen, 2003; Rodkin et al., 2000; Rose et al., 2004; Vaillancourt & Hymel, 2006; Vaillancourt et al., 2003). The Machiavellian bully stands in sharp contrast to the "classic," or more accurately, "stereotypical" bully, who is characterized as a highly aggressive, reactive, with poor self-esteem, poor social skills, and few assets and competencies. He/she is highly disliked by his/her peers and is not perceived as popular hence is not admired by peers (e.g., Vaillancourt et al., 2003). He/she is also high on psychopathology and is likely to persist in his/her use of aggression, placing him/her at risk for future incarceration; poorer academic achievement and the like (see Sourander et al., 2007). We suggest that this type of bully represents the minority of children who bully others. This type of bully may well be consistent with Moffitt's (1993) life-course persistent aggressor who is characterized by an entrenched pattern of aggression use, high psychopathology, poor neurological functioning and poor long-term social, academic and mental outcomes. Like the stereotypical bully, life-course persistent aggressors also represent the minority of aggressors, although they wreak the most havoc. Future research is needed to evaluate the validity of this hypothesis.

Although this dual taxonomy suggests a change in the way we view bullying, the outcomes for victims are the same—abuse at the hand of a peer. The implications for practice are admittedly complex. Because children and adolescents are concerned with social status and aspire to be popular among their peer group (Adler & Adler, 1998; Butcher & Pfeffer, 1986; Gavin & Furman, 1989; Jarvinen & Nicholls, 1996; Merten, 1997) and because aggression is often used by popular peers (Cillessen & Borch, 2006; deBruyn & Cillessen, 2006a; Estell et al., 2007; Lease et al., 2002; Olweus, 1977; Prinstein & Cillessen, 2003; Rodkin et al., 2000; Rose et al., 2004; Vaillancourt & Hymel, 2006; Vaillancourt et al., 2003) who are admired by classmates, it becomes difficult to dissuade children and youth from using aggression (Vaillancourt et al., 2003). How do you convince someone to change actions that are fundamental in the construction and maintenance of their power base? Complicating this further is the human tendency to "select" information from our environment that confirms or justifies our beliefs, attitudes and behaviors; and the powerful, often destructive influence of groups (see Myers & Spencer, 2004). The combination of all of these factors, coupled with our failure to appreciate heterogeneity among children and youth who bully others, has likely contributed to our poor performance on reducing bullying in schools (see Smith et al., 2004).

We think it quite possible that to shift the dynamics of power that are operational in sustaining bullying behavior we are going to have to empower the "group" to take action. Specifically, we are looking for young people to stand up within their school (and outside) settings and communicate to those who bully others that these behaviors will no longer be valued and will no longer be tolerated. Events on the eastern coast of Canada would suggest that this sort of shift may even be driven by students themselves (without direction from adults). After hearing about a ninth grade male who was being harassed for wearing a pink shirt to school, two seniors in a rural Nova Scotia high school staged a protest by creating a "sea of pink" among classmates. Purchasing pink shirts and spreading the word to everyone they could, these young men managed to motivate their peers to stand up in support of the victim. For these students, the answer did not appear to be the least bit complicated, "If you can get more people against them…to show we're not going to put up with it and support each other, then they're not as big a group as they think they are" (CBC News, 2007). More formally, efforts to address bullying through peer mediation may prove to be the most promising, especially when steps are taken to carefully select the peer mediators based on the nature of the power structure within a specific context. That is, peer-led interventions and peer-mediation need to be conducted by high status children who are not aggressive (prosocial-popular children). In fact, we would argue that such interventions are unlikely to be effective if not led (and perhaps initiated) by high-power prosocial children, a hypothesis supported by research by Cunningham and colleagues (Cunningham & Cunningham, 2006; Cunningham et al., 1998).

Acknowledgment

This chapter was supported by a Community-University Research Alliance grant from the Social Sciences and Humanities Research Council of Canada.

References

Adler, A. (1930). Individual psychology. In C. Murchison (Ed.), *Psychologies of 1930*. Worcester, MA: Clark University Press.

Adler, P. A., & Adler, P. (1998). *Peer power: Preadolescent culture and identity*. New York: Rutgers University Press.

Adler, P. A., Kless, S. J., Adler, P. (1992). Socialization to gender roles: Popularity among elementary school boys and girls. *Sociology of Education, 65,* 169–187.

Archer, J. (1988). *The behavioral biology of aggression*. Cambridge, UK: Cambridge University Press.

Asch, S. E. (1952). Social psychology. Englewood Cliffs, NJ: Prentice Hall.

Asch, S. E. (1955). Opinions and social pressure. *Scientific American, 193,* 31–35

Asch, S. E. (1957). An experimental investigation of group influence. In *Symposium on preventative and social psychiatry*. Symposium conducted at the Walter Reed Army Institute of Research, Washington, DC: U.S. Government Printing Office.

Bales, R. F., Strodtbeck, F. L., Mills, T. M., & Roseborough, M. E. (1951). Channels of communication in small groups. *American Sociological Review, 16,* 461–468.

Baldwin, D. C., Daugherty, S. R., & Rowley, B. D. (1998). Unethical and unprofessional conduct observed by residents during their first year of training. *Academy of Medicine, 73,* 1195–1200.

Bandura, A. (1973). *Aggression: A social learning analysis*. Englewood Cliffs, NJ: Prentice-Hall.

Bandura, A. (1999). Moral disengagement in the perpetration of inhumanities. *Personality and Social Psychology Review, 3,* 193–209.

Bandura, A. (2002). Selective moral disengagement in the exercise of moral agency. *Journal of Moral Education, 31,* 101–119.

Bandura, A., Caprara, G.V., Barbaranelli, C., Pastorelli, C., & Regalia, C. (2001). Sociocognitive self-regulatory mechanisms governing transgressive behavior, *Journal of Personality and Social Psychology, 80,* 125–135.

Baumeister, R., Smart, L., & Boden, J. (1996). Relation of threatened egotism to violence and aggression: The dark side of high self-esteem. *Psychological Review, 103,* 5–33.

Barkow, J. H. (1975). Prestige and culture: A biosocial interpretation. *Current Anthropology, 16*, 553–573.

Batsche, G. M., & Knoff, H. M. (1994). Bullies and their victims: Understanding a pervasive problem in the schools. *School Psychology Review, 23*, 165–174.

Berger, J., Cohen, B. P., & Zelditch, M. (1972). Status Characteristics and Social Interaction. *American Sociological Review, 37*, 241–255.

Berndt, T. J. (2004). Children's friendships: Shifts over a half-century in perspectives on their development and their effects. *Merrill-Palmer Quarterly, 50*, 206–222.

Bernstein, H. A. (1981). Survey of threats and assaults directed toward psychotherapists. *American Journal of Psychotherapy, 35*, 542–549.

Blau, P. M. (1964). *Exchange and power in social life*. New York: Wiley.

Buss, D. M. (1988). The evolution of human intrasexual competition: Tactics of mate attraction. *Journal of Personality and Social Psychology, 54*, 661–628.

Butcher, P., & Pfeffer, J. M. (1986). The behavioural approach in medical practice. *British Journal of Hospital Medicine, 36*, 209–215.

CBC News. (2007). Bullied student tickled pink by schoolmates t-shirt campaign. Retrieved October 8, 2007, from http://www.cbc.ca/canada/nova-scotia/story/2007/09/18/pink-tshirts-students.html?ref=rss

Chance, M. R. A. (1967). Attention structure as the basis of primate rank orders. *Man, 2*, 503–518.

Cillessen, A. H., & Borch, C. (2006). Developmental trajectories of adolescent popularity: a growth curve modelling analysis. *Journal of Adolescence, 29*, 935–959.

Clark, R. D., III, & Maass, S. A. (1988). The role of social categorization and perceived source credibility in minority influence. *European Journal of Social Psychology, 18*, 381–394.

Closson, L. M., Hymel, S., Konishi, C., & Darwich, L. (2007). *Bullying at School: Differences in Students' Personal and Academic Self-Perceptions*. Paper presented at the annual meeting of the "Investigating Our Practices" conference, Faculty of Education, University of British Columbia, Vancouver, BC, May, 2007.

Craig, W. (2004). Bullying and fighting. In *The Candian World Health Organization Report on the Health of Youth in Canada*. Canada: Health Canada.

Craig, W. M., & Harel, Y. (2004). Bullying and fighting. In *The World Health International Report*. Geneva: World Health Organization.

Craig, W. M., & Pepler, D. J. (1995). Peer processes in bullying and victimization: An observational study. *Exceptionality Education Canada, 5*, 81–95.

Craig, W. M., & Pepler, D. J. (1997). Observations of bullying and victimization in the school yard. *Canadian Journal of School Psychology, 13*, 41–59.

Cunningham, C. E., Cunningham, L., Martorelli, V., Tran, A., Young, J., & Zacharias, R. (1998). The effects of primary division, student-mediated conflict resolution programs on playground aggression. *Journal of Child Psychology and Psychiatry, 39*, 653–662.

Cunningham, C. E., & Cunningham, L. (2006). Student mediated conflict resolution programs. In R. A. Barkley (Ed.), *Attention-deficit hyperactivity disorder* (3rd ed., pp. 590–607). New York: Guilford.

Daly, M., & Wilson, M. (1988). *Homicide*. New York: Aldine de Gruyter.

Daugherty, S. R., Baldwin, D. C., & Rowley, B .D. (1998). Learning, satisfaction, and mistreatment during medical internship: A national survey of working conditions, *Journal of the American Medical Association, 279*, 1194–1199.

deBruyn, E. H., & Cillessen A. H. N. (2006a). Popularity in early adolescence: Prosocial and antisocial subtypes. *Journal of Adolescent Research, 21*, 607–627.

deBruyn, E. H., & Cillessen, A. H. N. (2006b). Heterogeneity of girls' consensual popularity: Academic and interpersonal behavioral profiles. *Journal of Youth and Adolescence, 35*, 412–422.

Deutsch, M., & Gerard, H. B. (1955). A study of normative and informational social influence upon individual judgment. *Journal of Abnormal and Social Psychology, 51*, 629–636.

Dijkstra, J. K., Lindenberg, S., Veenstra, R., Verhulst, F. C., & Ormel, J. (2007). The relation between popularity and aggressive, destructive, and normbreaking behaviors: Moderating effects of athletic abilities, physical attractiveness, and prosociality. *Journal of Research on Adolescence*.

Driskell, J. E., & Mullen, B. (1990). Status, expectations, and behavior: A meta-analytic review and test of the theory. *Personality and Social Psychology Bulletin, 16*, 541–553.

Eibl-Eibesfeldt, I. (1989) *Human ethology*. New York: Aldine de Gruyter.

Emerson, R. M. (1962). Power-dependence Relations. *American Sociological Review, 27*, 31–40.

Estell, D. B., Farmer, T. W., & Cairns, B. D. (2007). Bullies and victims in rural African American youth: behavioral characteristics and social network placement. *Aggressive Behavior, 33*, 145–159.

Festinger, L., Pepitone, A., & Newcomb, T. (1952). Some consequences of deindividuation in a group. *Journal of Abnormal and Social Psychology, 47*, 382–389.

French, J., & Raven, B. H. (1959). The bases of social power. In D. Cartwright (Ed.), *Studies in social power* (pp. 150–167). Ann Arbor, MI: Institute for Social Research.

Friske, M. (1993). School achievement and school adaptation in children in relation to CNS development as assessed by a complex reaction time. *Acta Paediatrica Scandinavica, 82*, 777–782.

Gavin, L., & Furman, W. (1989). Age difference in adolescents' perceptions of their peer groups. *Developmental Psychology, 25,* 827–843.

Gerard, H. B., Wilhelmy, R. A., & Conolley, E. S. (1968). Conformity and group size. *Journal of Personality and Social Psychology, 8,* 79–82.

Grotpeter, J. K., & Crick, N. R. (1996). Relational aggression, overt aggression, and friendship. *Child Development, 67,* 2328–2338.

Hanish, L. D., & Guerra, N. G. (2004). Aggressive victims, passive victims, and bullies: Developmental continuity or developmental change? *Merrill-Palmer Quarterly, 50,* 17–38.

Hawkins, D. L., Pepler, D. J., & Craig, W. M. (2001). Naturalistic observations of peer interventions in bullying. *Social Development, 10,* 512–527.

Hawley, P. H. (2003a). Prosocial and coercive configurations of resource control in early adolescence: A case for the well-adapted Machiavellian. *Merrill-Palmer Quarterly, 49,* 279–309.

Hawley, P. H. (2003b). Strategies of control, aggression, and morality in preschoolers: An evolutionary perspective. *Journal of Experimental Child Psychology, 85,* 213–235.

Higgins, E. T., & Bargh, J. A. (1987). Social cognition and social perception. *Annual Review of Psychology, 38,* 369–425.

Hogan, R., & Hogan, J. (1991). Personality and status. In D. G. Gilbert & J. J. Connolly (Eds.), *Personality, social skills, and psychopathology: An individual differences approach* (pp. 137–154). New York: Plenum.

Homans, G. C. (1958). Social behavior as exchange. *The American Journal of Sociology, 63,* 597–606.

Hymel, S., Rocke-Henderson, N., & Bonanno, R.A. (2005). Moral disengagement: A framework for understanding bullying among adolescents. Special issue: *Journal of Social Sciences, 8,* 1–11.

Jarvinen, D. W., & Nicholls, J. G. (1996). Adolescents' social goals, beliefs about the causes of social success, and satisfaction in peer relations. *Developmental Psychology, 32,* 435–441.

Keltner, D., Gruenfeld, D. H., & Anderson, C. (2003). Power, approach, and inhibition. *Psychological Review, 110,* 265–284.

Kipnis, D. (1972). Does power corrupt?, *Journal of Personality and Social Psychology, 24,* 33–41.

Krueger, J., & Clement, R. W. (1994). Memory-based judgments about multiple categories: A revision and extension of Tajfel's accentuation theory. *Journal of Personality and Social Psychology, 67,* 35–47.

Kumpulainen, K., & Rasanen, E. (2000). Children involved in bullying at elementary school age: their psychiatric symptoms and deviance in adolescence. An epidemiological sample. *Child Abuse Neglect, 24,* 1567–1577.

LaFreniere, P., & Charlesworth, W. R. (1983). Dominance, attention, and affiliation in a preschool group: A nine-month longitudinal study. *Ethology and Sociobiology, 4,* 55–67.

Lease, A. M., Kennedy, C. A., & Axelrod J. L. (2002). Children's social constructions of popularity. *Social Development, 11,* 87–109.

Lorenz, K. (1966). *On aggression.* New York: Harcourt, Brace and World.

Manderino, M.A. & Berkey, N. (1997). Verbal abuse of staff nurses by physicians. *Journal of Professional Nursing, 13,* 48–55.

Mann, L. (1981). The baiting crowd in episodes of threatened suicide. *Journal of Personality and Social Psychology, 41,* 703–709.

Marks, G., & Miller, N. (1987). Ten years of research on the false-consensus effect: An empirical and theoretical review. *Psychological Bulletin, 102,* 72–90.

Mazur, A. (1985). A biosocial model of status in face-to-face primate groups. *Social Forces, 64,* 377–402.

Merten, D. E. (1997). The meaning of meanness: Popularity, competition, and conflict among junior high school girls. *Sociology of Education, 40,* 175–191.

Miller, C. E., & Anderson, P. D. (1979). Group decision rules and the rejection of deviates. *Social Psychology Quarterly, 42,* 354–363.

Moffitt, T. E. (1993). Adolescence-limited and life-course-persistent antisocial behavior: A developmental taxonomy. *Psychology Review, 100,* 674–701.

Mullen, B. (1986). Atrocity as a function of lynch mob composition: A self-attention perspective. *Personality and Social Psychology Bulletin, 12,* 187–197.

Myers, D. G., & Spencer, S .J. (2004). *Social Psychology.* Toronto: McGraw-Hill Ryerson.

Nansel, T. R., Craig, W., Overpeck, M. D., Saluja, G., & Ruan, W. J. (2004). Cross-national consistency in the relationship between bullying behaviors and psychosocial adjustment. *Archives of Pediatric and Adolescent Medicine, 158,* 730–736.

Nansel, T. R., Overpeck, M., Pilla, R. S., Ruan, W. J., Simons-Morton, B., & Scheidt, P. (2001). Bullying behaviors among US youth: Prevalence and association with psychosocial adjustment. *Journal of the American Medical Association, 285,* 2094–2100.

O'Connell, P., Pepler, D., & Craig, W. (1999). Peer involvement in bullying: Insights and challenges for intervention. *Journal of Adolescence, 22,* 437–452.

Olweus, D. (1977). Aggression and peer acceptance in adolescent boys: Two short-term longitudinal studies of ratings. *Child Development, 48,* 1301–1313.

Olweus, D. (1993). *Bullying at school.* Cambridge, UK: Blackwell.

Olweus D. (1999). Sweden. In P. K. Smith, Y. Morita, J. Junger-Tas, D. Olweus, R. Catalano, & P. Slee (Eds.), *The nature of school bullying: A cross-national perspective* (pp. 7–27). London: Routledge.

Patterson, G. R., Littman, R. A., & Bricker, W. (1967). Assertive behavior in children: a step toward a theory of aggression. *Monographs of the Society for Research in Child Development, 32*, 1–43.

Prinstein, M. J., & Cillessen, A. H. N. (2003). Forms and functions of adolescent peer aggression associated with high levels of peer status. *Merrill-Palmer Quarterly, 49*, 310–342.

Quine, L. (2002). Workplace bullying in junior doctors: Questionnaire survey. *British Medical Journal, 324*, 878–879.

Rodkin, P. C., Farmer, T. W., Pearl, R., & Van Acker, R. (2000). Heterogeneity of popular boys: antisocial and prosocial configurations. *Developmental Psychology, 36*, 14–24.

Rosenberg, L. A. (1961). Group size, prior experience and conformity. *Journal of Abnormal and Social Psychology, 63*, 436–437.

Rose, A. J., Swenson, L. P., & Waller, E. M. (2004). Overt and relational aggression and perceived popularity: Developmental differences in concurrent and prospective relations. *Developmental Psychology, 40*, 378–387.

Rubin, K. H., Bukowski, W., & Parker, J. G. (2006). Peer interactions, relationships, and groups. In W. Damon (Series Ed.) & N. Eisenberg (Vol. Ed.), *Handbook of child psychology: Social, emotional, and personality development* (Vol. 3, 5th ed., pp. 619–700). New York: Wiley.

Russell, B. (1938). *Power: A social analysis*. London: Allen and Unwin.

Salmivalli, C., Lagerspetz, K., Bjorkqvist, K., Osterman, K., & Kaukiainen, A. (1996). Bullying as a group process: Participant roles and their relations to social status within the group. *Aggressive Behavior, 22*, 1–15.

Salmivalli, C., & Voeten, M. (2004). Connections between attitudes, group norms, and behaviour in bullying situations. *International Journal of Behavioral Development, 28*, 246–258.

Savin-Williams, R. C. (1979). Dominance hierarchies in groups of early adolescents. *Child Development, 50*, 923–935.

Schachter, S. (1951). Deviation, rejection and communication. *Journal of Abnormal and Social Psychology, 46*, 190–207.

Schwartz, D. (2000). Subtypes of victims and aggressors in children's peer groups. *Journal of Abnormal Child Psychology, 28*, 181–192.

Smith, J. D., Schneider, B. H., Smith, P. K., & Ananaiadou, K. (2004). The effectiveness of wholeschool antibullying programs: A synthesis of evaluation research. *School Psychology Review, 33*, 548–561.

Smith, P. K., & Sharp, S. (1994). The problem of school bullying. In P. K. Smith & S. Sharp (Eds.), *School bullying* (pp. 1–19). London: Routledge.

Snyder, C. R., & Higgins, R. L. (1988). Excuses: Their effective role in the negotiation of reality. *Psychological Bulletin, 104*, 23–35.

Sofield, L., & Salmond, S.W. (2003). Workplace violence: A focus on verbal abuse and intent to leave the organization. *Orthopaedic Nursing, 22*, 274–283.

Sourander, A., Jensen, P., Ronning, J. A., Elonheimo, H., Niemela, S., Helenius, H., et al. (2007). Childhood bullies and victims and their risk of criminality in late adolescence. *Archives of Pediatrics & Adolescent Medicine, 161*, 546–552.

Sutton, J., & Keogh, E. (2000). Social competition in school: Relationships with bullying, Machiavellianism and personality. *British Journal of Educational Psychology, 74*, 297–309.

Sutton J., Smith P. K., & Swettenham, J. (1999a). Bullying and theory of mind: A critique of the social skills deficit view of anti-social behaviour. *Social Development, 8*, 117–127.

Sutton, J., Smith, P. K., & Swettenham, J. (1999b). Social cognition and bullying: Social inadequacy or skilled manipulation? *British Journal of Developmental Psychology, 17*, 435–450.

Symons, C. S., & Johnson, B. T. (1997). The self-reference effect in memory: A meta-analysis. *Psychological Bulletin, 121*, 371–394.

Tanner, J., & Wortley, S. (2002). *The Toronto Youth Crime and Victimization Survey: Overview Report*. Centre of Criminology, University of Toronto, Toronto.

Thibaut, J. W., & Kelley, H. (1959). *The social psychology of groups*. New York: Wiley.

Waller, W., & Hill, R. (1951). *The family*. New York: Dryden.

Vaillancourt, T. (2005). Indirect aggression among humans: Social construct or evolutionary adaptation? In R. E. Tremblay, W. H. Hartup, & J. Archer (Eds.), *Developmental origins of aggression* (pp. 158–177). New York: Guilford.

Vaillancourt, T., & Hymel, S. (2004). The social context of children aggression. In M. Moretti, M. Jackson, & C. Odgers (Eds.), *Girls and aggression: Contributing factors and intervention principles* (pp. 57–69). New York: Kluwer.

Vaillancourt, T., & Hymel, S. (2006). Aggression, social status and the moderating role of sex and peer-valued characteristics. *Aggressive Behavior, 32*, 396–408.

Vaillancourt, T., Hymel, S., & McDougall, P. (2003). Bullying is power: Implications for school-based intervention strategies. *Journal of Applied School Psychology, 19*, 157–176.

Zimbardo, P. G. (1971). *The psychological power and pathology of imprisonment*. A statement prepared for the U.S. House of Representatives Committee on the Judiciary, Subcommittee No. 3: Hearings on Prison Reform, San Francisco, Calif., October 25.

17
Bullying Dynamics Associated with Race, Ethnicity, and Immigration Status

TRACEY G. SCHERR AND JIM LARSON

They call us names, like "ref" and say "Get back on the banana boat." (High school girl who emigrated from Guatemala to the United States)

They mostly don't say things to me, because I am big and my skin is light. (High school boy who emigrated from Cuba to the United States)

The Black kids all hang out by that door over there. I don't want no trouble, so I come in over at this one. They mostly don't come over here, either. (Latino high school student in the United States)

This chapter addresses the issue of bullying and bully victimization as a function of immigration status, ethnicity, and race. Although all bully victimization is distressing, there may be a special pain that accompanies victimization that is based upon a child's familial ethnic or racial identity. In such cases, the target is often not merely the individual child, but the entire group from which the child has developed belonging, identity, customs, and beliefs. Increases in global migration patterns have created parallel increases in the potential for clashes between groups. Efforts to scientifically examine the complex experiences of new arrivals to host countries relative to bully victimization are in their infancy, but patterns are starting to emerge. A more extensive body of research exists in the area of racial and ethnic bullying, some of which challenges common suppositions related to majority-minority bullying relationships. The chapter explores the theoretical explanations for between-group bullying and offers a hypothesis from the social cognitive (e.g., Aboud, 2003) and social identity (e.g., Nesdale, 2002) developmental literature.

Conceptual Foundations

Migration Patterns

People have migrated for different reasons and according to varying patterns throughout the world's history. Recent migration trends, however, reflect the more pervasive phenomenon of global migration. According to the United Nations' Global Commission on International

Migration (GCIM, 2005), estimates indicate approximately 200 million individuals have recently migrated internationally, double the number of immigrants of a quarter century ago.

Migration patterns vary from one global region to another. More specifically, Europe hosts the largest number of immigrants (56 million), followed by Asia (50 million), North America (41 million), Africa (16 million), Latin America (6 million), and Australia (6 million). Within these regions, the United States and the Russian Federation house the most immigrants. Australia, Canada, New Zealand, and the United States have traditionally granted residency or citizenship to large numbers of immigrants. Of those who migrate, most emigrate from China (35 million), India (20 million), and the Philippines (7 million; GCIM, 2005).

Not only do countries of origin and destination differ, but reasons for movement vary as well. Economic globalization and increased mobility have contributed much to this rise in migration. The potential for employment, wage increases, education, and improved public health lure many to move from their homelands to other countries (GCIM, 2005). Sometimes the impetus for migration has little to do with poverty. Movement can be prompted by more overt persecution or fear of it.

Of the present 200 million immigrants, over 9 million are refugees (GCIM, 2005). The United Nations defines a refugee as someone who has left the country of his or her nationality "owing to well-founded fear of being persecuted for reasons of race, religion, nationality, membership in a particular social group or political opinion" (United Nations High Commissioner for Refugees, [UNHCR], 2006). Of note, the past several years have brought a decrease in the number of refugees throughout the world (GCIM). However, 668,000 applications for asylum were filed in 2005 in Europe, Africa, Asia, and the Americas, respectively. The largest number of asylum applications in 2004–05 came from residents of Myanmar, Somalia, Serbia, Montenegro, the Russian Federation, the Democratic Republic of the Congo, and China. These applications for asylum were most frequently filed in France, the United States, Thailand, Kenya, the United Kingdom, and Germany (UNHCR, 2006).

Although world migration offers the potential for culturally rich economic and social development, difficulties also arise. The presence of migrants in a community can highlight perceived resource competition and differing value systems. Increased focus on security in response to terrorism has bred further suspicion of immigrants in many countries. Receiving countries may respond along a continuum from exclusionary policies to keep immigrants marginalized, or insistence on assimilation at the expense of migrants' cultures of origin, to allowing free expression of culture within legal parameters (GCIM, 2005). Not only is the receiving country affected by immigration, but those who emigrate from their countries of origin are also significantly impacted by the experience. Although complete demographic data are unavailable, the United Nations estimates 44% of those displaced persons for whom demographic information exists are children (UNHCR, 2006).

Migration of families and children throughout the world poses unique challenges for those who move and for education professionals responsible for assisting with their adjustment. The problem of bully victimization that attaches to immigration status is often entangled with and made potentially more injurious by ethnic differences in the bully-victim dyad. Professionals engaged in bully prevention efforts among populations of immigrant children need to be mindful of the risks associated with both.

Immigrant, Ethnic, and Racial Bullying

One of the challenges faced by immigrants and by non-immigrant students of various racial and ethnic backgrounds is the bullying that occurs between children on the basis of these differences. According to McKenney, Pepler, Craig, and Connolly (2006):

Bullying that targets another's ethnic background or cultural identity in any way is referred to as ethnic bullying. This form of bullying may include direct forms of aggression such as racial taunts and slurs, derogatory references to culturally-specific customs, foods, and costumes, as well as indirect forms of aggression, such as exclusion from a mainstream group of peers because of ethnic differences. (p. 242)

This definition subsumes racially-based harassment as a form of ethnic bullying. Although open to much social construction, race typically refers to shared ancestry (e.g., a person of Asian descent). Ethnicity relates to cultural origins and their corresponding beliefs and practices (e.g., a Chinese American). Despite their distinctions, "race" and "ethnicity" are frequently found to be used interchangeably in studies of school-based bullying. As a result, disentangling any unique effects of one over the other awaits the acceptance of more precise definitions. For purposes here, the term "ethnoracial" will be used.

Borrowing from McKenney et al.'s (2006) definition of ethnic bullying, "immigrant bullying" can be defined as bullying that targets another's immigrant status or family history of immigration in the form of taunts and slurs, derogatory references to the immigration process, physical aggression, social manipulation, or exclusion because of immigration status.

Commonly accepted definitions of bullying (e.g., McKenney et al., 2006; Olweus, 1993) include the presence of a power imbalance between the aggressor and victim. The terms "ethnoracial" and "immigrant" bullying describes bullying behavior directed at an individual because of his or her perceived membership in a situationally less powerful ethnic, racial, or immigrant group. The descriptor, "situationally less powerful" is critical because it is the qualitative composition of the greater socio-cultural context in which the bullying occurs that defines the power relationship (Schwartz, Proctor, & Chien, 2001).

Bully-related power imbalances along ethnoracial or immigrant lines can exist on a macro level school-wide or in smaller, more fluid micro levels. A particular group in a school building may be in a power position in one setting and in a more vulnerable position in another (e.g., the Latino lunch area, the Black entrance door). The fluidity of this relationship is such that students of any particular ethnic group may find themselves moving in and out of relative vulnerability even within a given day and within a single school setting.

The presence of diversity in a school building alone does not create an inevitable context for ethnoracial or immigrant bullying, but it can establish a prerequisite condition of asymmetrical power among the various groups of students in attendance. The commonly accepted definitions of bullying (e.g., McKenney et al., 2006; Olweus, 1993) include frequency and temporal components that require the negative interaction to be ongoing and predictable and not merely the result of impulse or occasional outbursts of temper. Similarly, ethnoracial and immigrant bullying are not defined by an occasional hurtful remark, but rather the existence of a systematic pattern of direct or indirect aggression over time. In a very real way, ethnoracial and immigrant bullying can become part of the peer culture in some school settings.

Example of Bullying Related to Immigration Status

To illustrate how bullying related to immigration status, race, and ethnicity may manifest, we solicited input from one of our graduate students. Sara's mother was born in the United States, and her father was born in Iran. As a result of educational and occupational pursuits, political upheaval, and personal circumstances, Sara's family has lived in several different countries. The following is a transcribed account of Sara's experiences and opinions related to ethnoracial and immigrant bullying.

Whatever is a characteristic that's different, that's a minority, those are the characteristics that are going to be made fun of and known as the odd or the weird because it's different. So, when I was in Iran, I was always called the American girl. Here, I'm mainly known as the foreign girl, the Iranian chick…just because over here that's what's different about me. I'm Iranian. No matter what country I went to it wasn't any different. Bullying towards minorities is always the same, even in Iran.

When I was in first grade and my brother was in second grade, we would take the bus to school. We would get made fun of so bad on the buses. We just hated going on there. Right after the revolution there would be riots all the time on the streets where people would say, "Death to America!" So, whenever we would go on the buses, they would make circles around us and be like, "Death to America! Death to America!" They always asked us questions like, "So, do you guys run around naked and do drugs?" because that's what they thought of Americans, sadly.

In America, I realized in Iran I had always been very comfortable talking to people. Over here, right away people started making fun of my accent because my English was so bad. They tried talking like that or just making fun of how I talked. I would go through so much anxiety when the teacher (called) on me and I had to talk in class because I didn't want people to hear…It was just like a popularity thing. The popular kids, that's how they got attention. They made fun of my accent, how I talked. People are not going to go against them. It was funny. It was like a joke to them. They walked by and tried to talk like me.

When I fasted, that was a big deal. Obviously, during lunch time, my brother and I were not eating. People would walk by, and they knew we were fasting. It was such a weird thing. They were like, "Oh, you want some of my food?" and making fun of us. They would laugh about it.

One of my friends was from Japan. She didn't know English at all. She was so scared of being in the lunchroom that she would somehow sneak in the bathroom and eat her lunch in a bathroom stall. Kids would bang her head into the locker as they walked by and laugh about her and say stuff about Japan. She couldn't speak any English at all, so that made it harder. When she tried to go talk to a teacher, the teacher got frustrated and told her to go find someone that can translate, or learn more English and then come, or some comment like that. I think that my brothers and I had it a little bit better because we did know some English. We were Americanized. Once I was Americanized, I became popular. But it had nothing to do with them accepting me. I just started doing more stuff like they did, or I learned more stuff. It just goes around all over the world. That's all I see. I don't see any difference in America or any other country.

After the whole incidents with terrorism and everything, my brothers and I, it's weekly that we got joked around, "Oh, you're gonna bomb us?" My brother has been called a "sand monkey." As a teenager, I was really emotionally hurt. Now we're just at a different stage that we don't take it seriously and we can joke back. But, as teenager, when people would say stuff like that, it's a more sensitive thing. You take it a different way, but that's just a different developmental level you're at yourself. So, it's a personal thing too, how you take it…Whatever the media portrays as a stereotype, that's what you're gonna be picked on for. For years I'm going to be picked on about bombing people. That's just how it's gonna be.

Research Examining Bullying

Sara's experiences with ethnoracial and immigrant bullying are both disconcerting and poignant. Stories like hers contain valuable qualitative information and offer windows into these forms of bullying. Unless qualitative data from multiple case studies are extracted and examined systematically, such individual accounts fail to provide sufficient data from which to develop evidence-based conclusions. There is, however, a relatively small but growing body of empirical research that examines issues associated with bullying and immigrant status and ethnoracial bullying that we will review next. Proposed theoretical explanations for development of the requisite prejudicial attitudes for bully perpetration will also be explored.

Bullying and Immigrant Status   Immigrant status as a mediator of bullying and bullying victimization has only recently begun to receive attention, and the data are mixed. McKenney and colleagues (2006) examined peer victimization of immigrant youth in urban Canada. The study included students in grades 7 through 11 and represented the following native Canadian and ethnic immigrant groups: European Canadian, Asian Canadian, African/Caribbean Canadian, South Asian Canadian, Latin American Canadian, Middle Eastern Canadian, and Other Ethnicities. This study found no significant differences in the level of victimization among the various immigrant groups. However, 14% of the sample reported having been victimized due to their ethnic status. This type of victimization was most prevalent among first generation Canadian students, those who were born in Canada but whose parents were born elsewhere. The authors posited that the greater visibility of ethnicity compared to immigration status contributed to these findings. The results of McKenney and colleagues' investigation indicated family immigration history, not just an individual student's immigration status, may relate to minority students experiencing ethnoracial bullying victimization.

It appears that some children of immigrants are not only victims of ethnic and immigrant bullying, but they also victimize others in similar ways. Pepler, Connolly, and Craig (1999) found approximately 10% of elementary and secondary students in Canada admitted to having perpetrated ethnic bullying. Interestingly, high school students whose parents were born outside of Canada reported more ethnic perpetration than did other groups of students. The authors suggested this pattern of change over time in ethnically-based perpetration from students with recent family immigration histories may reflect gradually increasing anger about previous or ongoing victimization related to ethnicity and family immigration status.

To further illustrate, bullying gangs among teens who immigrated to Israel from the former Soviet Union were studied (Tartakovsky & Mirsky, 2001). These immigrants settled in religious, secular, and collective boarding schools throughout Israel. Bullying behavior was but one of many delinquencies noted among these groups. Language barriers and ignorance regarding social norms, the authors suggested, aroused feelings of vulnerability and anxiety among immigrant youth. For these young people, forming gangs was done in an attempt to protect themselves against the uncertainties of their new environment.

In Austria, Strohmeier and Spiel (2007) implemented peer nominations and ratings of sixth and seventh grade students to uncover bullying relationships between native Austrian children and those who had emigrated from the former Yugoslavia, Turkish and Kurdish children, and a smaller number of youth from other nations. Analyses revealed native Austrian students were nominated as bullies and as victims more frequently than children in the various immigrant groups.

In addition, Strohmeier and Spiel (2007) investigated social risk factors such as social acceptance, number of friends, and cross-cultural friendship patterns to anticipate risk for social manipulation and exclusion within their sample. Of the Austrian sample studied, the Turkish-Kurdish immigrants were determined to be at risk socially due to less peer acceptance, most loneliness at school, and fewest friendships with classmates. Conversely, Yugoslavian children cultivated more cross-cultural friendships than all other groups of students studied. Explanatory hypotheses for the difficulty Turkish-Kurdish students experienced included lack of language proficiency and differing cultural norms related to behavior.

The complexity of immigrant bullying is apparent in the few existing studies of the phenomenon. Bully perpetration and victimization appear to exist in both native and immigrant populations. Children of particular immigrant groups may be at heightened risk for victimization as a function of the group's cultural similarities to or differences from the dominant group, their level of proficiency in the dominant language of the country, and a range of other yet elusive contributing variables. Similarly, immigrant students' likelihood to perpetrate bullying may also relate to situational and individual characteristics yet to be identified.

Ethnoracial Bullying   Research that examines bullying among and within racial and ethnic groups is emerging as well. In a study of Canadian students, Pepler and colleagues (1999) found that 17% of all elementary students and 17% of all high school students reported that they had been bullied by a student from another ethnic group. Within this sample, elementary students from ethnic minority groups were significantly more likely to report ethnic victimization.

In the Netherlands, Verkuyten and Thijs (2002) studied the extent of ethnic victimization among Dutch, Turkish, Moroccan, and Surinamese middle school-aged children. Surinamese, Moroccan, and Turkish individuals comprise the largest minority ethnic groups in the Netherlands. As such, Verkuyten and Thijs studied their experiences of bullying in comparison to those of majority Dutch students in more than 80 schools. As many as 42% of minority students reported having experienced racial name calling compared with 21% of Dutch majority students. A larger percentage of Turkish children, in particular, were taunted by racial name calling. Further, up to 30% of minority participants reported having suffered social exclusion from their peers in comparison to 21% of their majority classmates. Ethnic bullying of the three minority groups increased in schools with higher percentages of native Dutch students.

Similar to results of Verkuyten and Thijs's (2002) investigation in the Netherlands, several years earlier Siann, Callaghan, Glissov, Lockhart, and Rawson (1994) found ethnic minority students in a London and Glasgow sample believed their fellow minority peers were more likely to be bullied than were their schoolmates in the ethnic majority. This trend was recognized despite no significant differences between ethnic groups in self-reported bullying experiences or in perceptions of what behaviors can be considered bullying. However, differences emerged between schools related to bullying experiences and perceptions as a function of ethnicity. Interaction effects between gender and ethnicity in relation to bullying experiences surfaced as well. Hence, even when self-reports of bullying are similar across ethnic groups, minority students may perceive that their minority peers are victimized more frequently than their peers in the ethnic majority. Additionally, ethnic minority students' self-reports of bullying may differ as a function of school environment and/or gender in addition to ethnic group membership.

A survey of bullying experiences of teenage Hindu, Indian Muslim, and Pakistani youth in Britain uncovered some unique findings related to the interaction between ethnicity, religious affiliation, and bullying (Elsea & Mukhtar, 2000). Due to concerns cited by some schools about the sensitivity of the topic, the research team sought participants from temples and mosques in addition to schools. Each of the groups indicated they had been bullied by White students at roughly equivalent levels. However, higher rates of bullying were reportedly perpetrated by other Asian students of different religious or ethnic backgrounds from the victims. Hindu youth reported victimization by Pakistani youth, and Indian Muslim and Pakistani youth referenced victimization by Hindu youth. Further, Pakistani boys indicated they were most frequently targeted by Indian Muslim youth.

Additional analyses uncovered significant interactions between victim ethnicity and foci of bullying, including name, skin color, language, god(s), place of worship, religious festivals, food, and clothing. In particular, Hindu youth cited bullying victimization related to gods, name, and place of worship. Indian Muslims encountered bullying related to their clothing. Pakistani youth described bullying corresponding to language, food, and clothing (Elsea & Mukhtar, 2000). This research supported the findings heretofore seen with predominantly White populations that ethnic bullying can occur within racially similar groups as well as between racially and ethnically diverse groups.

The prevalence of racial name calling has been cited in additional literature on the topic. Mooney, Creeser, and Blatchford (1991) found 65% of a sample of elementary school students in London reported believing "racial teasing" occurred in schools. When asked how children were teased in their school, 17% referenced race, and 8% indicated they themselves were teased about their race. More Afro Caribbean Black students reported having been teased in general, and about their race specifically, than did White students.

In a more recent study in a large urban district in California, 26% of Hispanic minority students indicated they had been bullied because of race, ethnicity, or national origin along with 22% of Asian students, 18% of multiethnic students, and 7% of African American students (Lai & Tov, 2004). A survey of children in Australian schools also detected teasing as a result of race (Rigby, 2002). Aboriginal students comprised 2% of the sample, roughly representative of the proportion of all Aborigines in Australia. Nearly 16% of the minority Aboriginal students indicated they had been targeted for racial slurs frequently. This was a statistically significantly greater proportion than the 12.5% of non-Aboriginal students who reported similar experiences. Conversely, it should be noted that 36% of Caucasian majority students in Lai and Tov's investigation responded affirmatively to related questioning. Hence, this sort of victimization is not relegated solely to students from racial, ethnic, or immigrant minorities.

In some situations race may be used to predict who students will choose to bully and how they will victimize those students. Boulton (1995) studied elementary students in an urban area of the United Kingdom. More Asian than White students reported experiencing bullying on the basis of race, however, Asian and White students were nominated as bullies and as victims with similar frequencies when multiple types of bullying were considered. Further, these more general bully-victim relationships tended to be within the same race.

School context may interact with race and ethnicity in bullying situations. Hanish and Guerra (2000) acknowledged this relationship after they implemented peer nominations to estimate peer victimization in relation to race in two urban communities in the United States. Hispanic students received lower victimization scores than did African American or White students. The latter two student groups received similar victimization scores. However, school context differentiated victimization patterns. White children who attended predominantly non-White schools were at elevated victimization risk, and African American students who attended primarily African American schools were also at higher risk of being victimized by peers.

Within a particular school, minority and majority ethnic and racial statuses may play a role in bullying patterns. In Graham & Juvonen's (2002) sample of urban middle school students in the United States, African American and Latino students, both numerical majorities in the schools, were nominated most frequently as bullying perpetrators. The numerical minority students, who were White, Persian or Middle Eastern, Asian or Pacific Islander, or of another numerical minority, were most often nominated as victims of bullying.

Drawing definitive conclusions about racial and ethnic bullying is not possible given the limited and varying results from related studies. Trends are identifiable, however. Due to interactions with additional variables, isolating ethnicity or race to study bullying may limit understanding of this behavior. For example, Siann and colleagues (1994) found ethnic differences in bullying experiences only when interactions with school environment and gender were considered, respectively. Although racial and ethnic bullying seems to occur typically between bullies and victims of different racial and ethnic groups, examples of ethnic bullying within the same racial group have been cited (e.g., Elsea & Mukhtar, 2000). Some students, considered majority group members in the larger society, reported having been bullied about race (e.g., Lai & Tov, 2004). Across multiple studies, the racial and ethnic make-up of the schools the students attended contributed to differences in bullying experiences (e.g., Graham & Juvonen, 2002; Hanish & Guerra, 2000; Verkuyten & Thijs, 2002). In several investigations, students whose race or ethnic background was a numerical minority within their school building most frequently experienced bullying, especially ethnoracial bullying.

Theoretical Explanations   Bullying behavior that is directed against children because of their race, ethnicity, or because of their immigrant status may have its roots in normative processes of racial attitude and preferences development and group identification. Aboud and her colleagues (e.g., Aboud, 2003; Aboud & Doyle, 1996; Doyle & Aboud, 1995) have demonstrated that young children generally have more positive attitudes toward, and a greater preference for, members of their own racial group and tend to categorize others on the basis of race. Ethnic or racial prejudice in children or youth is defined as a predisposition to react unfavorably to members of another group because of their group affiliation (Aboud, 2003). Prejudice has been found to be high in children as young as 5 years old, but found to drop off significantly as children's cognitive processes emerge, and they are better able to understand the individual apart from his or her group-based identification (Doyle & Aboud, 1995). Brewer (1999) argued that among young children, what has been construed as negative attitudes toward members of different racial groups is in reality a preference for members of their own group. Aboud (2003) found evidence to support this conclusion and added that "out-group members suffer more from comparison than from outright hostility" (p. 56). Boulton (1995) concluded that this in-group and outgroup identification may be ultimately responsible for the development of negative attitudes and stereotyping toward outgroup members and lead to the avoidance of healthy between-group interactions. Graham and Juvonen (2002) acknowledged the development of group identification during the primary school years, but concluded that it becomes more solidified and takes on added significance with regard to bullying as children transition into adolescence in secondary school and seek to define their identities in the developmentally-salient peer culture.

If identification with one's own group is a normal developmental process, under what conditions and for what purposes does hostility toward other groups develop? Why does a student move from simple preference and comfort with others of his or her own group to the cognitive development of prejudice and then possibly to the subsequent behavioral perpetration of bullying?

Nesdale (2002) offered an explanation for the development of prejudice in children that incorporates the social cognitive theories of Aboud and others, and integrates social identity theory, or the desire of individuals to identify with those considered to have higher social status in order to bolster their own self-esteems. In Nesdale's construction, children who display ethnic prejudice pass through four developmental phases:

1. In the *Undifferentiated Phase*, racial cues are not salient with toddlers, and environmental stimuli are randomly responded to based upon what catches the child's attention. Color differentiation is acquired.

2. The *Ethnic Awareness Phase* emerges around 3 years of age and with greater saliency among children who reside in multi-ethnic communities. It is aided by labeling that the child is exposed to by adult identification of out-group members (e.g., "That man has dark skin. He is an African American."). It is at this time that the child develops the important sense of belonging to a particular group, and this is solidified by age 6 or 7.

3. In the *Ethnic Preference Phase*, children are found to show social preference for members of their own group, but this preference is mild and does not imply an accompanying hostility for other groups. Friendship and playmate preferences appear to be unrelated to ethnicity, and ethnicity pales in comparison with gender in this regard.

4. A child's emergence into the *Ethnic Prejudice Phase* depends upon three critical elements: (a) the acquisition of ethnic constancy, or the understanding that ethnicity is forever and people do not change with age; (b) the failure to acquire the ability to take the perspective or empathize with members of another group; and (c) the influence of the prevailing beliefs in the child's social environment.

Nesdale (2002) observed that a child's movement from ethnic preference to that of active ethnic prejudice is facilitated by how widely prejudicial views are expressed in the child's social environment, the level of extant competition and conflict among groups the child is witness to, and although the research to date is with adults, the level of threat to social standing perceived by the child's group. These influences notwithstanding, this model acknowledges that the ethnic views held by children reflect their own beliefs and attitudes and not necessarily or immutably those of parents or others in the social environment. Some children may simply choose not to go along with negative beliefs and behavior toward ethnic minority groups as a moral judgment.

The question of whether or not the majority of individuals who engage in ethnic bullying in the school context also hold prejudicial ethnic beliefs has not been empirically examined. Probabilities dictate that it is possible to hold prejudicial views but not engage in ethnic bullying behaviors and, conversely, to be unprejudiced but choose to bully members of other ethnic groups.

Need for Future Research

In the broadest sense, more research should be done on immigrant bullying and on ethnoracial bullying. More specifically, data need to be collected to firmly establish the prevalence of these forms of perpetration and victimization, which clearly exist, but have frequently eluded researchers' attention relative to other aspects of bullying behavior. In order for data to be gathered and analyzed systematically, definitions of immigrant bullying and ethnoracial bullying must be agreed upon. Further, group membership should be delineated as specifically as possible within this research. The authors of studies to date have frequently lamented the imprecise nature of participant identification.

Trends emerging from the available data indicate immigrant bullying and ethnoracial bullying result from a confluence of multiple, specific variables (e.g., size of majority and minority ethnicities within the school building, extent of language or cultural differences). The full array of contributing factors needs to be identified and their respective influences determined. In particular, the relationship between prejudices regarding immigrant status, race, and ethnicity and discriminatory bullying behavior should be explored. Theoretically, students' attitudes are influenced by their social environments. Several authors have noted that caste systems, racism, and religious and political tensions from the larger society are reflected in children's bullying behavior (Elsea & Mukhtar, 2000; Verkuyten & Thijs, 2002). Children can conform to prevailing social attitudes or take a moral stand against them. To what extent, then, does the larger socio-political context in which students live influence their prejudicial attitude formation and their participation in discriminatory bullying?

The school context has been identified as a potential variable affecting immigrant and ethnic bullying. School climate and student engagement need to be examined in relationship to the occurrence of these specific types bullying. In addition, the immigrant, racial, and ethnic compositions of a school or classroom may play roles in setting the stage for these types of bullying. Perhaps immigrant and ethnic bullying patterns differ between urban and rural schools as well. These possibilities warrant further scientific exploration.

Whether bullying directed at racial or ethnic identity or immigrant status precipitates outcomes that vary from that occasioned by more mutable or individualized qualities (e.g., small stature, perceived sexual orientation) remains unexplored. Although effects were somewhat small, McKenney et al. (2006) found ethnic victimization contributed to both internalizing and externalizing behavior. Perhaps the immutable nature of race or ethnicity contributes to its detrimental effects. Negative effects for perpetrators of ethnoracial bullying and for bully-victims have also been noted in terms of higher levels of internalizing and externalizing difficulties (Pepler et al., 1999). The effects of bullying on immigrant students may be even more pronounced. Their identity formation can be complicated by acculturation and intergenerational conflict in addition to the direct challenges of immigration.

Implications for Practice

School-based interventions for general bullying concerns have been developed and their effectiveness has been investigated (for reviews, see Limber, 2006; Rigby, 2006). However, the effect of these interventions specifically on immigrant or ethnoracial bullying has yet to be empirically demonstrated. Professionals charged with addressing the problems of immigrant and ethnoracial bullying are working with complex and comparatively not well understood bullying phenomena, but starting with research-supported bully prevention procedures and making adaptations to meet individual circumstances is recommended. Official descriptions of bullying in school conduct codes should contain references to the definitions of ethnoracial and immigrant bullying noted in this chapter. Incidence data should be maintained and monitored. Immigrant students and racial/ethnic minority students should have access to at least one trusted adult in the school who is fluent with regard to students' languages and familiar with their cultures of origin. Importantly, this person should be skilled in receiving and acting upon reports of bullying. Table 17.1 provides a summary of implications for practice.

The mere presence of immigrant, racial, and ethnic minority students does not in itself mean between-group bullying is manifest. Consequently, teachers and administrators should become aware of any local concerns through the use of specifically designed student surveys and student focus groups. Parents and selected community leaders with attachments to ethnic and racial minority students should be provided opportunities to collaborate with school personnel to foster a school climate that is safe and supportive for all groups. Increased recognition and affirmation of the customs, language, and traditions of local ethnic groups through multicultural education may assist in creating a greater climate of understanding and acceptance. Evidence-based practices in multicultural education should be adhered to and effects on ethnoracial and immigrant bullying monitored. Guidance in this endeavor may be obtained from respected organizations such as The National Council for the Social Studies (http://www.socialstudies.org/positions/multicultural/).

Table 17.1 Bullying Dynamics Associated with Race, Ethnicity, and Immigration Status: Implications for Practice

1. Assess for the prevalence of racial, ethnic, or immigrant bullying within the context of a well-designed process that may include student surveys and focus groups.
2. Include language in the school code that specifically prohibits bullying on the basis of race, ethnicity, and/or immigrant status.
3. Begin with bullying programs and procedures currently supported in the literature and make appropriate adaptations to local needs.
4. Provide opportunities to parents and community leaders for collaboration and input.
5. Identify adults in the school with requisite knowledge and skills as support persons to whom minority group students may turn for bullying concerns.
6. Assess current curriculum and provide increased multicultural education as needed.

Acknowledgments

The authors express their gratitude to the high school students in Miami, Florida, who willingly shared their observations for inclusion in this chapter. We also thank our graduate student, Sara, who candidly described her experiences with ethnoracial and immigrant bullying. Her honesty, bravery, and resilience are inspiring.

References

Aboud, F. E. (2003). The formation of in-group favoritism and out-group prejudice in young children: Are they distinct attitudes? *Developmental Psychology, 29*, 48–60.

Aboud, F. E., & Doyle, A. B. (1996). Does talk of race foster prejudice or tolerance in children? *Canadian Journal of Behavioral Sciences, 28*, 161–170.

Boulton, M. (1995). Patterns of bully/victim problems in mixed race groups of children. *Social Development, 4*, 277–293.

Brewer, M. B. (1999). The psychology of prejudice: In-group love or out-group hate? *Journal of Social Issues, 55*, 429–444.

Doyle, A. B., & Aboud, F. E. (1995). A longitudinal study of White children's racial prejudice as a social cognitive development. *Merrill-Palmer Quarterly, 41*, 210–229.

Elsea, M., & Mukhtar, K. (2000). Bullying and racism among Asian schoolchildren in Britain. *Educational Research, 42*(2), 207–217.

Global Commission on International Migration (GCIM). (2005, October). *Migration in an interconnected world: New directions for action.* Retrieved January 2, 2007, from http://www.gcim.org

Graham, S., & Juvonen, J. (2002). Ethnicity, peer harassment, and adjustment in middle school: An exploratory study. *Journal of Early Adolescence, 22*(2), 173–199.

Hanish, L. D., & Guerra, N. G. (2000). The roles of ethnicity and school context in predicting children's victimization by peers. *American Journal of Community Psychology, 28*, 201–223.

Lai, M., & Tov, W. (2004). *California Healthy Kids Survey 2002 Analysis.* Oakland, CA: Asian Pacific Islander Youth Violence Prevention Center, National Council on Crime and Delinquency.

Limber, S. P. (2006). The Olweus Bullying Prevention Program: An overview of its implementation and research base. In S. R. Jimerson & M. J. Furlong (Eds.), *Handbook of school violence and school safety* (pp. 293–307). Mahwah, NJ: Erlbaum.

McKenney, K. S., Pepler, D., Craig, W., & Connolly, J. (2006). Peer victimization and psychosocial adjustment: The experiences of Canadian immigrant youth. *Electronic Journal of Research in Educational Psychology, 9*(4), 239–264.

Mooney, A., Creeser, R., & Blatchford, P. (1991). Children's views on teasing and fighting in junior schools. *Educational Research, 33*(2), 103–112.

Nesdale, D. (2002). Social identity and ethnic prejudice in children. In D. Gabb & T. Miletic (Eds.), *Culture, race, and community: Making it work in the new millennium.* Retrieved January 17, 2007, from http://www.vtpu.org.au/resources/publications/ conferencepapers/crc.php

Olweus, D. (1993). *Bullying at school: What we know and what we can do.* Cambridge, MA: Blackwell.

Pepler, D., Connolly, J., & Craig, W. (1999). Bullying and harassment: Experiences of immigrant and minority youth. (CERIS Report). Retrieved January 11, 2007, from http://ceris.metropolis.net/Virtual%20Library/RFPReports/Pepler1997.pdf

Rigby, K. (2002). *New perspectives on bullying.* London: Jessica Kingsley.

Rigby, K. (2006). What we can learn from evaluated studies of school-based programs to reduce bullying in schools. In S. R. Jimerson & M. J. Furlong (Eds.), *Handbook of school violence and school safety* (pp. 325–337). Mahwah, NJ: Erlbaum.

Schwartz, D., Proctor, L. J., & Chien, D. H. (2001). The aggressive victim of bullying: Emotional and behavioral dysregulation as a pathway to victimization by peers. In J. Juvonen & S. Graham (Eds.), *Peer harassment in schools: The plight of the vulnerable and victimized* (pp. 147–174). New York: Guilford.

Siann, G., Callaghan, M., Glissov, P., Lockhart, R., & Rawson, L. (1994). Who gets bullied? The effect of school, gender and ethnic group. *Educational Research, 36*(2), 123–134.

Strohmeier, D., & Spiel, C. (2007). Immigrant children in Austria: Aggressive behavior and friendship patterns in multicultural school classes. In J. E. Zins, M. J. Elias, & C. A. Maher (Eds.), *Bullying, victimization, and peer harassment: A handbook of prevention and intervention* (pp. 103–120). New York: Haworth.

Tartakovsky, E., & Mirsky, J. (2001). Bullying gangs among immigrant adolescents from the former Soviet Union in Israel: A psych-culturally determined group defense. *Journal of Interpersonal Violence, 16*, 247–265.

United Nations High Commissioner for Refugees (UNHCR). (2006, June). *2005 Global Refugee trends.* Retrieved January 2, 2007, from http://www.unhcr.org/statistics

Verkuyten, M., & Thijs, J. (2002). Racist victimization among children in The Netherlands: The effect of ethnic group and schools. *Ethnic and Racial Studies, 25*, 310–331.

18

Bullying Beyond School
Examining the Role of Sports

ANNEMATT L. COLLOT D'ESCURY AND AD C. M. DUDINK

Children who are bullied at school often take part in sports as a protective factor against bullying. However, are they "safe" from bullying during their sports participation, or is it even worse? Judo is one sport that is supposed to stimulate the development of protective qualities. When a parent says, "Jim needs more self-confidence; judo might be a good thing," is it really a good thing or are the victims simply double targets? Are they victimized first at school and then again on the *tatami* mat in the judo class?

In this chapter we will question the value of sports as a protective value against bullying. Bullying has been studied in the context of sport (Endresen, & Olweus, 2005), and the results of these studies confirm our assertion that most of the children who are being bullied at school are also bullied during sports. Sports are not necessarily a booster against bullying. On the contrary, taking part in sports may be a risky context in respect to vulnerability to bullying behavior. This may be because coaches interfere less, children may communicate less with their coaches as compared to their teachers about bullying, children may experience their coaches as bullies, and coaches may be less aware of bullying (Endresen & Olweus, 2005). Teaching coaches the signs of bullying and victimization as well as teaching them interventions, should be an important component of sports. If coaches are not taught how to identify and respond to bullying, then advising a child who is being bullied to get involved in sports might be analogous to throwing a lamb in with the lions. Most importantly, advice about participation in sport should be related to the individual characteristics of the child.

Overview of Bullying

Bullying is not an unusual phenomenon, as reports of children being engaged in bullying range from 6% to 60% (Espelage & Swearer, 2003). This means that in virtually every school and classroom, at least two children have experienced bullying in one way or another.

Large differences in prevalence estimates suggest that researchers may have used different definitions, classification criteria, and measurement procedures (Solberg, Olweus, & Endresen, 2007) to assess bullying. Bullying is most often assessed using self-report. It has been defined according to the following definition: "a child is being bullied or victimized when he or she is exposed repeatedly and over time to negative actions on the part of one or more other children"

(Solberg et al., 2007). This definition means that one child is being bullied predominantly by the same individual or group of individuals a number of times over a period of time.

However, being bullied may also be a subjective experience as several components of bullying are open to an individual's interpretation, including "negative act" and "repeatedly." We contend that a one-time experience can have a very strong and maybe even chronic impact. In this chapter we will show that victims of bullying can experience very intense feelings that may persist over a number of years. Thus, they will report being bullied. In terms of their subjective experience, they may be right, for if they do feel that they have been bullied, if they do experience the fear, if they do experience the disturbance of normal social functioning, then the bullying does have a considerable effect over a considerable period of time (even though the bullying was not perpetrated by the same person over a number of times). The victim who is being bullied continuously over a certain amount of time, and the victim who experienced one traumatic bullying experience may experience the same consequences; however, they experience different types of bullying, which may be one reason for differing report rates. Also children who are victims of relational bullying may report different types and rates of bullying from children who are victims of overt (physical or verbal) bullying (Terranova, Sheffield Morris, & Boxer, 2008).

Teacher reports may be helpful in confirming child reports of bullying and victimization. However, teacher reports are not always accurate in reporting the feelings that victims experience. It is difficult for teachers to detect the subtle signs that encompass the bully/victim relationship. However, teachers are not to blame, for the social interaction only has meaning in the relation between the bully and the victim. Studies have found that teacher's reports are often more conservative than child self-reports, that is they underreport compared to children's reports. Thus, children's reports may be the most veridical reflection of bullying/victimization. Olweus (1989) reported that the shortcomings of self-report measures may be overcome by asking concrete questions about time, locations, persons, and situations increasing the objectivity of the information.

Overview of Bullying Programs

Programs against bullying are numerous, varying from websites where children can communicate and take part in "e-therapy" (www.pesten.nl; www.bullying.uk), to more structured intervention programs (Olweus, 2005). Many recommendations have been made with regard to how to approach the problem of bullying and most researchers agree that effective programs must be comprehensive (Espelage & Swearer, 2003). Programs should focus not only on the victim, but also on the bully, on the assistants or co-bullies, on the innocent bystanders and on the group of children who are aware of the bullying. Programs must include schools, families, and the communities.

While comprehensive programs are necessary, some interventions focus exclusively on bystanders. For example, television programs in the Netherlands (i.e., SIRE) and Japan (i.e., AC; Collot d'Escury, Wychel, & Driessen, 2002) have been developed to address the role of bystanders. The television spots have focused on waking up bystanders through presenting national heroes who have reported being victims of bullying. These have included individuals, from disc jockeys to elite sports heroes who discuss their victimization and the impact that the bullying had on their psychological functioning. The message is that anyone can be a victim, even individuals in positions of power or admiration, such as a disc jockey or a national sumo hero. These messages support the claims that victims of bullying can be hidden behind a most unlikely person. The aforementioned television programming examples has helped to increase the awareness of bullying in the Netherlands and in Japan. However, the claim that this awareness decreases bullying behavior is more difficult to prove.

As previously mentioned, bullying often happens in a subtle manner, which is difficult to detect. More importantly, even if children are able to detect subtle bullying behaviors and realize the harmful effects of bullying, it takes increased effort and often finances to implement interventions. Such interventions may include teaching youth how to intervene during a bullying situation and what to do to either to stop the bully or to support the victim. Other elements that may be important to consider through interventions include examining thoughts of self-preservation, such as "What will happen to me if I intervene?" and "Will I become the next victim?" While the television spots were appreciated by both children and adults, and may have helped increase general awareness of bullying, it takes increased effort and involvement to change behavior (Collot d'Escury et al., 2002). Thus, it is important to look to general educational programs, including Olweus' Bullying Prevention Program. This program is among the most well-known intervention efforts in schools and purports to reduce bully/victim problems. It is an active intervention aimed to increase the efforts from both teachers and peers in reducing bullying behavior (Olweus, 2005).

Programs directed specifically toward the bully and/or the victim usually are more direct than programs specifically designed to target bystanders. Programs targeting victims incorporate teaching communication, cooperation, confidence, and assertiveness. These programs teach students to communicate their wishes clearly; to be assertive; to practice effective communication skills; to practice good social skills; and to enhance self-efficacy (Milsom & Gallo, 2006; Olweus, 2005). Despite these coordinated efforts, the generalization of skills taught through intervention programs is more difficult. To be assertive in benign situations can be taught; but it is difficult for students to generalize these skills to the schoolyard, which is typically the domain of bullies (Camodeca & Goosens, 2005).

Programs directed at those who engage in bullying behavior often focus on cognitive distortions and on increasing cognitive skills. Training alternative social behaviors, teaching perspective taking, and focusing on cognitive restructuring are elements of interventions designed to work with students who are engaging in bullying behavior (Doll & Swearer, 2006). Additionally, increasing empathy, learning different social behaviors, increasing self-confidence and developing anger control strategies are incorporated in many bullying prevention and intervention programs (Espelage & Swearer, 2003).

Surprising few bullying prevention and intervention programs actively involve parents. Looking at interventions in the clinical field, which focus on behavior problems seen in children diagnosed with attention deficit-hyperactivity disorder (ADHD), conduct disorder (CD), and oppositional defiant disorder (ODD) provides evidence that non residential training which involves parents is most successful. These efforts will help to decrease impulsivity and increase positive parent-child relationships. They will also help reduce aggression and increase social skills, including communication, cooperation, and participation (Chronis, Jones, & Raggi, 2007; Pelham, Wheeler, & Chronis, 1998). Given the compatibility of the training goals between these clinical interventions and interventions for students who bully others, it is most probable that intervention programs focused to reduce bullying behavior may profit from parent support and parent training.

Bullying Beyond School: The Role of Sports

Often mentioned, but less studied in the bullying literature is the role of sports. Children participate in sports for many reasons. Additionally, sports are a major asset in health campaigns and the fight against obesity. Sports are important in physical and mental fitness as children who are involved in sports watch less television, drink less alcohol, smoke less, and use fewer drugs than those not involved in sports. On an individual basis, sports often are recommended as a means to increase psychological strength and resilience. Children who are shy, withdrawn, or low in the social hierarchy are thought to learn to overcome their shyness, raise their confidence, and increase their assertiveness through sports. In this way, sports may help serve as a protective factor against bullying.

Participation in sports has numerous benefits. Communication is used when players give each other feedback (e.g., "This pass was too slow," "This pass was too high," or "This pass was good"). In communicating with each other, players are aware of each other's presence to utilize teamwork and to increase the likelihood the team will be successful. Also important in sports are physical and mental resilience. This may include situations in which one team increases their mental toughness against a more skilled team to win or when an individual has to be physically strong in order to hold a position. These characteristics that are valuable in sports are similar to those mentioned in programs intended to reduce bullying and victimization (Olweus, 1994; Stevens, De Bourdeaudhuij, Van Oost, 2000).

Sports may also reduce or prevent bullying behavior. In team sports students have to work together and support their teammates. No matter how skilled an athlete, no one can win a game by themselves. Not even Michael Jordan could win a game on his own (though he presumably might have gotten close). By creating a team plan and working together, the opponent can be defeated. Every player is important in that goal. None of the players can be excluded or bullied into nonparticipation, because that will affect the quality of the whole team. In team sports players have to learn to control themselves and their anger. If a player kicks uncontrollably, it affects the quality of their game. If a player kicks towards another, no matter how irritating and frustrating the opponent may be, it's the player who is expelled. As a result, the team is penalized because of the negative actions of one player. If a player calls others bad names or argues with the referee, there are also negative consequences. Hence, team sports may offer a good context to learn to control frustration, to learn to cooperate and to become a team player, most of which are goals in bully prevention programs as well.

There are many reasons to focus on sports as a means of intervention, prevention, or remediation in bullying behavior. However, even though the reasons mentioned above may be helpful, there is another side that should be considered. Even though it is often hard to pinpoint why a child is bullied in the first place, characteristics of the child may be one of the reasons (Camodeca & Goossens, 2005). Being successful in sports is often protection against bullying. Sports are an important domain of competence among elementary and secondary school-age children. Research that has investigated the domains children value has found that sports are prominent (Harter, 2001). Being good at sports is highly valued among children and adolescents and relates to positive peer ratings. Individuals who are low on the social hierarchy may be viewed as clumsy and unathletic. The low status group they are placed in due to their low physical abilities in sports may be a factor in them becoming a victim or a bully-victim. Alternatively, these individuals may become a bully to obtain a higher level of social status.

In addition to the individual characteristics that may question the positive value of sports, the protective value of sports may also be questioned from a more general perspective. Sports may be stimulating competition rather than collaboration. For example, contact sports may actually induce aggression. Sports may increase or enhance the chances of engaging in bullying behaviors. Mostly the satisfaction in sports comes from winning. However, winning cannot exist without losing, which implies that the counterpart from the satisfaction and pleasure which results from winning is frustration due to losing. Sports may contain an intrinsic stimulating component (e.g., the sheer pleasure of hitting the ball in the middle of the racket, jumping a pole perfectly, or skating a fluent curve in a full speed short track race), but in the end winning is the main goal.

Many rules in sports offer ample opportunities for frustration. Decisions may be questionable due to their subjective interpretation. It is sometimes difficult to determine when one person is blocking another, preventing the other from reaching the ball, or attempting to make a play. Other complex and frustrating situations include starting procedures and penalties in athletic competitions such as skating or decisions based on judge's interpretations. Rules and decisions are often more complicated in youth sports. For instance, rules change as youth age (e.g., in basketball children under 8 years old are allowed to dribble three times whereas children over 8 are only allowed to dribble twice). Materials change, for example, from soft balls to harder balls, as youth age and the competitive level is higher. Courts become bigger when children get older and rules are applied differently. Many of these changes may result in insecurity and frustration for youth and may provide a perfect venue for aggression and bullying.

Another reason that may make those who participate in sports vulnerable to bullying and/or victimization is the fact that coaches are seldom trained in bullying prevention and intervention strategies. Their education is most likely in sports, including knowledge of the techniques and tactics that are required and may not be as well versed in social competence. In the Netherlands, even recent sports education does tend to pay more attention to youth social functioning; however, it is still a much undervalued aspect of the education of trainers and coaches.

On the one hand, bullying/victimization may occur less in sports as compared to school. Sports often require the players to work together for a common goal, whereas in school the emphasis is more focused on individual goals. On the other hand, sports possess many characteristics that increase the risk of bullying: sport is competitive by nature, rules are not always clear, selections can be horrendous, to name a few.

One of the sports often advised to young children who are vulnerable to bullying is Judo. Judo, as defined by its founders, has two principles: *seiyoku zeyo* and *jita kyoei*. The first principle is a technical one and refers to the techniques needed to reach maximum results with minimum effort. The second principle is a moral one which states that judo should help its players to become better human beings. These principles are contradictory to bullying behaviors and thus, less bullying is to be expected in judo as compared to bullying in school. In fact, these principles may even help children to become bully resistant. However, judo also is a highly physical and contact sport. Physical sports are reported to correlate negatively with moral judgment and positively with aggression, which would in contradiction, heighten the risk for bullying in judo (Bredemeier, Weiss, Shields, & Copper, 1986; Endresen & Olweus, 2005; Smulders, 2002). In addition, judo is not only often recommended to victims and potential victims of bullying in school but also to the bullies and potential bullies, which means that bullies and victims could be present together in judo. According to Olweus (1994), the mere presence of a potential bully and a potential victim may be sufficient to start the bullying dynamic; hence judo may offer profitable grounds for bullying. Bullying may be instigated through various group mechanisms, such as frustration, lack of control, or moral rules. It may be sustained through other mechanisms such as the conspiracy to remain silent, or diffusion of responsibility, but the presence of a potential bully and victim already form an important trigger. In addition, judo is an individual sport lacking the team mechanisms and the interdependence of players. Hence, although judo is advised as a positive means to deter bullying and victimization, a child who is advised to join judo may end up being a double target both at school and on the tatami mat.

One major difference between sports and school is the structure of a classroom as compared to the structure of sports settings. Additionally, in many countries, the education of a schoolteacher as compared to the education of soccer trainer or coach may be different. School is a fairly structured setting with regular hours and often stable classrooms and teachers, particularly at the elementary school level. On the other hand, sports are much more loosely structured with children participating in different sports, trainers changing, and opponents or teammates changing. This means that bullying may be even harder to recognize in sports than it is in school. Schoolteachers have an elaborate education in which social emotional development, including mechanisms such as bullying receive attention. Coaches and trainers have their education mainly built around various sports and the necessary technical and tactical aspects of it. Even though they most probably do pay attention to social interaction and are focused on positive interpersonal coaching within the team, they may not be trained to recognize bullying or trained to intervene when it occurs. Therefore, even though sports are considered to be highly important in contributing to a healthy life, including stimulating motor development, agility, general fitness, psychological fitness, teamwork, self-confidence, assertiveness, loyalty, and friendship, sports also contain a risk of bullying, which may decrease self-confidence, and increase submissive and dismissive behavior. However, more research is needed on bullying in sports in order to fully substantiate these claims.

The present study, therefore, intends to offer more information about bullying in sports. This study examined bullying in soccer, one of the most popular team sports in the Netherlands, as well as bullying in judo, a very popular individual sport particularly at elementary school age. Bullying was assessed through self-report measures using multiple informants (i.e., children and trainers).

Method

Participants

Participants were recruited from 14 soccer clubs and 12 judo clubs in the Netherlands. In Haarlem, Amsterdam, and Tilburg, reasonably big cities in the Netherlands; six clubs could not participate due to practical reasons. Participants were 441 children from 8 different soccer clubs and 481 children from 10 different judoka clubs. In addition, 15 judoka trainer questionnaires were collected.

Measures and Procedure

The questionnaire developed for this study was based on the original questionnaire of Olweus (1987), translated in Dutch and validated for the Dutch school population by Mooij (1992). The original questionnaire contained 39 questions in respect to bullying, including questions about being bullied, being a bully, bullying teachers, as well as questions about friends and friendships in the classroom. For example, participants responded items like this one: "How often do children say nasty and mean things to you in school" on a 5-point Likert-type scale from "never" to "several times a week." The original questionnaire from Olweus was adapted for this study to include questions about soccer and judo. Four questions were added that focus on specific dynamics in sports (e.g., "Have you ever been bullied by your trainer?" and "Who do you bully?"). The trainer questionnaire contained the same questions phrased from the perspective of the trainer. For example, trainers responded to items like this one: "What do you do when you notice bullying?" Responses included: "it never happens;" "I do nothing;" "I talk to the children that are involved;" "I talk to all the children;" and "Other."

Parental consent was obtained through the sport clubs. Clubs, parents, and children reacted very positively, which resulted in a 75–80% response rate. Questionnaires were filled in individually at the club, after training, in the *dojo* (training room), in the dressing room, or in the canteen belonging to the club. One of the researchers was present to answer individual questions.

Table 18.1 Participants Divided Over Sport and Age

Sports		Ages 7, 8, & 9	Ages 10, 11, & 12
Judo	481	215	266
Soccer	421	223	198

Questions that the participants asked were usually from the younger children, questioning time aspects, such as "What is meant by the previous year, the calendar year or the sports year?" or "What if I did not play judo last year?" Not all trainers were able to respond the questionnaires. Trainers often had to continue training other teams or had to train themselves after training the children. Fifteen trainer reports were included (see Table 18.1).

Results

Validity of the Bullying Questionnaire

To verify the validity of the adaptations of the original Olweus questionnaire, a principal components factor analysis (PCA) was conducted resulting in six factors closely resembling the factors reported by Olweus. The factor analyses done for the judo and soccer versions of the questionnaire resulted in similar findings. Coefficient alpha was calculated for each subscale (see Table 18.2). Apart from the scale, indirect bullying, all scales demonstrated at least the same or higher internal consistency compared with the school questionnaire. If bullying in the dressing room is deleted from the second subscale, alpha reaches .40. The reason for the comparatively low internal consistency on indirect bullying may be that indirect bullying is somewhat less easy to judge in the sport context.

Being Bullied in Sports

Results indicate that 25.5% of the children experienced bullying in sports as compared to 61% in school. When bullying is defined as at least regular, bullying in sport is reported by 10% of the children and bullying in school is reported by 23% (see Table 18.3).

Table 18.2 Cronbach's Alpha for the Subscales of the Questionnaires for Sport and School

Subscales	Sport	School
Direct bullying	.81	.82
Indirect bullying	.21 (.40)*	.60
Bullying	.85	.81
Position toward bullying	.54	.52
Bullying of the teacher/trainer	.82	.59
Intervention strategies	.62	.54

*Cronbach's alpha with item nr 9 'bullying in the dressing room' deleted.

Table 18.3 Percentage of Bullying in Sport and School

Bullying	Sport	School
Never	74.5 %	39%
1 or 2 times	16,6%	38%
Regularly	3,5%	15%
Once a/w	3,3%	4%
Several times a/w	2,1%	4%

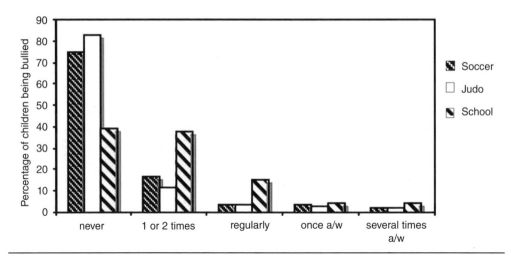

Figure 18.1 Bullying in soccer, judo, and school.

The prevalence of bullying in soccer and judo is almost equivalent. In Figure 18.1, results are reported for judo and soccer separately.

In the sports groups, children typically met only once or twice a week, in some cases time lapses between sessions were longer, and the younger children sometimes needed help with answering the questions. However, a more concrete question which focused on bullying over the last five weeks, resulted in 13% of the children reporting being bullied during sports.

Bullying in Sport

Six percent of the children reported that they were involved in bullying during sports. During school, 20% of the children reported to have been actively involved in bullying. When the two sports are separated, the amount of bullies in judo was different from that in both soccer and school. Although the percentage of children who reported to have been bullied is about the same, but the percentage of bullies in judo was somewhat lower (see Figure 18.2)

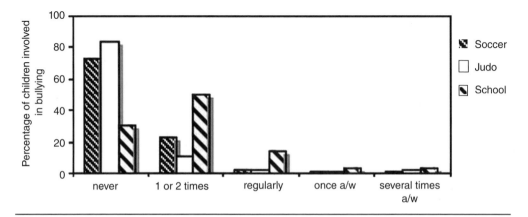

Figure 18.2 Bullies in soccer, judo, and school.

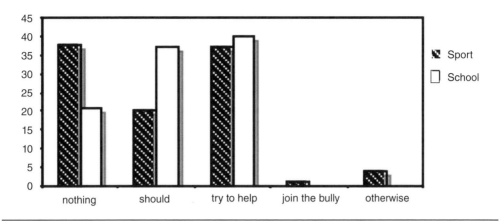

Figure 18.3 Characteristics of other children.

Bystander, Assistant, or Defender

In school settings, children can be classified as bullies, victims, bully/victims, and bystanders. Characteristics of bystanders range considerably, from children who do nothing; children who do nothing, but feel they should do something; children who interfere or intervene; and children who join in the bullying (see Figure 18.3).

Being Bullied in Places Other than Sports

The following question was asked to discern whether children were bullied in settings other than sports: "Are you being bullied elsewhere?" Participants could respond, "I am not bullied elsewhere," "Yes, in my neighborhood," "Yes, at school," and "Somewhere else."

Of the children who reported being bullied during sports, 65% reported being bullied elsewhere, 35.3% in school and 32.3% in their own neighborhood. The school questionnaire contained the question: "Are you being bullied elsewhere?" Fifty-four percent of the children who were bullied at school reported that they were also bullied elsewhere, e.g., 35% in the neighborhood and 18% "other" places. (Note that in the school questionnaire this question was asked of all the children, including the children who were not bullied at school. Hence the average percentage of children being bullied elsewhere may be somewhat higher for the children who are bullied in school.) Only 36% of children who were not bullied at either school or during sports, indicated that they were bullied elsewhere; 23 % indicated they were bullied in school; and 13% indicated they were bullied in the neighborhood (see Figure 18.4).

Involvement in Bullying and Impact on Friendships

Children who are bullied have less friends and report more feelings of loneliness as compared to children who are not bullied. Pearson correlations were significant for being bullied and feeling lonely ($p < .005$), being bullied and not having friends ($p < .005$), and being bullied and not being liked by your peers ($p < .005$).

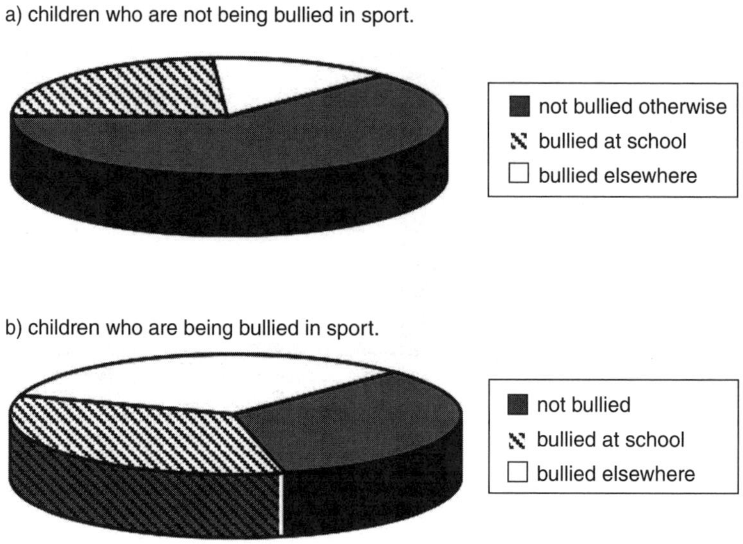

a) children who are not being bullied in sport.

not bullied otherwise
bullied at school
bullied elsewhere

b) children who are being bullied in sport.

not bullied
bullied at school
bullied elsewhere

Figure 18.4 Being bullied elsewhere.

Teachers and Trainers: Do they Intervene?

Twenty percent of the children reported that their teachers intervened in the bullying incident. Seventy percent of the children talked to their teachers and 60% of the children talked to their parents about the bullying in school. Further, 7.6% of the children reported that their trainers intervened, 14% percent of the children talked to their trainers, 21% of the children talked to their parents when bullied during sports (see Figure 18.5).

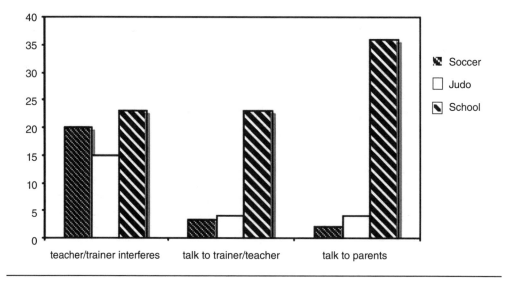

Figure 18.5 Interference of teachers and trainers, and communication with trainers/teachers and parents.

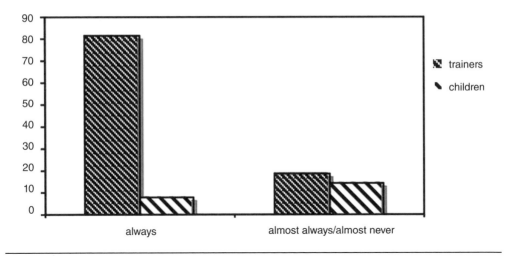

Figure 18.6 Intervention according to trainers and children.

Trainers

Trainers were asked how much they thought bullying occurred in sports and how often they intervened when they noticed bullying. Trainers reported that 20% of the children are bullied and that 81% of the time the trainers intervened (see Figure 18.6).

Discussion

The adapted questionnaire appears to be a valid measure of bullying during sports. Internal consistency was relatively equal for both the sports and school setting. This was consistent for sport in general as well as for judo and soccer separately. Therefore, the questionnaire appears to be a psychometrically sound measure of bullying behavior during sports.

Overall, the sports context and school context do not seem to differ greatly. In other words, the same percentages of children are identified as bullies and victims in both settings. However, these results may be misleading due to time constraints, including "Being bullied once a week in school" means one day out of five encounters per week (i.e., 20%), whereas "Being bullied once a week in sports" is close to 50% of the encounters each week. In younger children, who do not play matches yet, which is the case predominantly for judo, it may even be 100% of the encounters. However, the results do indicate that bullying certainly is no less in sports then in school.

Protection against bullying must come from teachers and trainers. However, the results indicated that children talked less to their trainers, only 14% of the children reported that they talk to their trainers, whereas 70% reported that they talked to their teachers. Children talk less to their parents when bullied in sports (i.e., 21% in sport vs. 60% in school). Children reported less intervention from trainers as compared to intervention from teachers. Twenty percent of the children reported their intervened, whereas 7.6% of the children reported that their trainers intervened. In contrast to the children, trainers reported that they always or almost always intervened when they noticed bullying (i.e., 81.7 % always and 17.3% almost always). A considerable number of children reported that their trainers bullied, a question not included in the school questionnaire. Therefore, it seems that sports do not seem to be able to offer protection against bullying.

Are children who participate in sports double targets? Children who are being bullied in one setting clearly are more vulnerable to bullying in another setting. Of the children who are being bullied in sports, 65% report being bullied elsewhere as opposed to only 36% of the children who are not being bullied. Being bullied in one place makes you vulnerable to bullying in another place. This is also true for the school setting; however, the percentages of being bullied elsewhere are considerably lower. This, at least, casts considerable doubt on the protective qualities of involvement in sports.

We did not distinguish the first teams, generally consisting of the best players, from the second teams. This might be important for a number of reasons. First, the first team often has a more professional trainer, who is at least educated in the aspects of bullying. The first team often has a larger staff consisting of a trainer, a coach, and a manager, as compared to the lower teams that generally have to manage with one trainer or coach. There may be more opportunities in lower teams for bullying since there are fewer adults to monitor the athletes. Second, the first team usually has higher competitive goals and more regulations. In the lower teams, rules are more loosely defined and differences between players can be larger. It stands to reason that the more undefined the rules, the higher the chances of bullying. Finally, one of the reasons for being bullied is not being good at sports, or to put it differently, one of the reasons for not being bullied is being good at sports. Often children who are referred to sports because of being bullied at school, are not good athletes. Chances that these children will end up in the lower teams are probably higher then chances that they get selected for the first team. Hence, the more vulnerable children (victims as well as bullies) end up in the teams that are less organized and possess less protection against bullying.

There may be different reasons for the assertion that students who are not good in sports may be more likely to get bullied. One reason is that children who are being bullied tend to be the unpopular children. On the other hand, being good at sports is an important asset and contributes to popularity (Harter, 1998). Children may not be good in sports because they are clumsy or not assertive enough and that again is one of the reasons for being bullied (Monks, Smith, & Swettenham, 2005). As far as the bullies are concerned, teachers may want to teach them cooperation and anger control, which are considered aspects that play a role in sports (Terranova et al., 2008).

Children want to participate in sports for many reasons. Sports are a major asset in health campaigns, including the fight against obesity. In the Netherlands, successful anti-obesity campaigns are based on contracts between overweight children and top sport players like the Dutch national soccer players and the Dutch world champions in skating. As previously stated, children, who are actively involved in sport watch less television, drink less alcohol, smoke less, and use fewer drugs. However, given the risk factors in sport, chances are high that the positive assets of sports only reach those who already are healthy, fit, and attracted to sports. If children who are clumsy and overweight go into sports, chances are high that they will experience the more detrimental aspects of sports. The fact that the amount of times you play judo correlates negatively with the amount of times a child is bullied suggests that the children who are being bullied tend to give up and disappear from the tatami mat.

Given the tremendous positive benefits of sports education for trainers, interpersonal factors such as bullying, should be a central issue for sport education. The questionnaire survey is an important vehicle for creating awareness and involvement among trainers. However, awareness is not enough; bullying in school can be hard to spot and bullying in sport can be even harder to spot. A training situation is much less controlled than a classroom situation, and sports contain many more uncontrolled elements. Surprisingly, in one of those uncontrolled elements, the dressing room, was not an important factor in bullying. This may be due to the age of the children. In soccer, showering and changing is uncommon for the D-players (10–12 years of age) and even C-players (12–14 years of age), who tend to come to the field in their sport outfit. In judo, changing is obligatory and bullying in the dressing room indeed was significantly higher as compared to soccer. In addition to raising awareness, trainers have to increase their specific knowledge about bullying during sports. The adopted questionnaire shows that bullying in sports equals bullying in school. The results also reveal that bullying in sports has somewhat different characteristics and even different sports seem to vary with respect to bullying.

Referring youth to play sports is a means to stimulate physical and mental assertiveness. The advice to join sports because of its qualities to increase confidence, resilience, cooperation, and frustration tolerance may be given without looking at the characteristics of the child. Soccer, for instance, is the main pastime activity among elementary school age children. Children who are not good at soccer often refrain from playing. The "mentally strong" ones become referee, goalie, or manage to remain somehow involved, whereas the more introverted children withdraw and tend to be lonely during breaks. For those children, soccer often is colored as "not my thing" and probably never will be "their thing," which is not to say that no sport will ever be "their thing." Compare, for instance, soccer and cricket. Soccer requires constant running and a lot of physical contact, while cricket requires a lot of patience and high concentration. Advising a child to go into sports, particularly as a therapeutic or helping mechanism, might require some thought as to which sports might be good for which particular child (Dudink, 1994).

Summary of Implications for Practice:

1. Heighten the bully-awareness" of trainers and of those involved in the management, and coaching of sports. Using the questionnaire might be a good start.
2. Heighten the knowledge of specific characteristics contributing to bullying in various sports. Increasing research on bullying in sport.
3. Increase intervention skills of trainers and coaches.
4. Heighten the awareness, knowledge, and mentality of bullying among those involved in sports; including teammates, peers, and parents. Adapting the Norwegian anti-bullying campaign to a sport setting might offer good opportunities.
5. More attention should be paid to characteristics of the child in relation to the requirements of the sport.

References

Bredemeier, B., Weiss, M., Shields, D., & Cooper, B. (1986). The relationship of sport involvement with children's moral reasoning and aggression tendencies. *Journal of Sport Psychology, 8*, 304–318.

Camodeca, M., & Goosens, F. A. (2005). Pesten op school: Recente ontwikkelinge en theoretische invalshoeken. [Bullying at school: recent developments and theoretical implications]. In A. Vuyt, M. v. Aken, J. Bosch, R.v.d. Gaag, & A. Ruijsenaars (Eds.), *Jaarboek ontwikkelingspsychologie, orthopedagogiek en kinderpsychiatrie* [Yearbook of psychology of development, psychology of education and child psychiatry] (pp. 82–97). Houten, The Netherlands: Editions Bohn Stafleu Van Loghum.

Chronis, A. M., Jones, H. A., & Raggi, V.L. (2007). Evidence based psychosocial treatment for children and adolescents with attention deficit hyperactivity. *Clinical Psychology Review, 26*(4), 486–502.

Collot d'Escury, A.M., Wychel, D., & Driessen, A. (2002). International research comparing non profit campaigns, AC in Japan and Sire in the Netherlands. Report published by the National Netherlands-Japan foundation.

Doll, B., & Swearer, S. M., (2006). Cognitive behavior interventions for participants in bullying and coercion. In R. B. Mennuti, A. Freeman, & R. Christner (Eds.), *Cognitive behavioral interventions in educational settings* (pp. 183–201). New York: Brunner-Routledge.

Dudink, A. C. M. (1994). Birth date and sporting success. *Nature, 368*, 592.

Endresen, I. M., & Olweus, D. (2005). Participation in power sports and antisocial involvement in preadolescent and adolescent boys. *Journal of Child Psychology and Psychiatry, 46*(5), 468–478.

Espelage, D. L., & Swearer, S. M. (2003). Research on school bullying and victimization: What have we learned and where do we go from here? *School Psychology Review, 32*, 365–384.

Harter, S. (1998). The development of self-representations. In W. Damon (Series ed.) & N. Eisenberg (Vol. Ed.), *Handbook of child psychology: Vol.3, Social emotional and personality development* (5th ed., pp. 553–557). New York: Wiley.

Harter, S. (2001). *The construction of the self: A developmental perspective.* New York: Guilford.

Milsom, A., & Gallo, L. L. (2006). Bullying in middle schools: Prevention and intervention. *Middle School Journal, 37*, 12–19.

Monks, C. P., Smith, P. K., & Swettenham, J. (2005). Psychological correlates of peer victimisation in preschool: Social cognitive skills, executive function and attachment profiles. *Aggressive Behavior, 31*, 571–588.

Mooij, T. (1992). *Pesten in het onderwijs* [Bullying in education]. Instituut voor Toegepaste Sociale Wetenschappen, Nijmegen.

Olweus, D. (1987). Bully/victim problems among schoolchildren in Scandinavia. In J. P. Myklebust & R. Omundsen (Eds.), *Psykologprofesjonen mor ar 2000* [Psychology towards the year 2000] (pp. 395–413). Bergen, Norway: Universitetsforlaget.

Olweus, D. (1989). Prevalence and incidence in the study of anti social behavior: Definitions and measurement. In M. Klein (Ed.), *Cross-national research in self-reported crime and delinqeuncy* (pp. 187–201). Dordrecht, The Netherlands: Kluwer.

Olweus, D. (1994). Bully/victim problems among Schoolchildren: Basic facts & effects of a school based intervention program. *Journal of Child Psychiatry & Allied Disciplines, 35*(7), 411–448.

Olweus, D. (2005). A useful evaluation design, and effects of the Olweus Bullying Prevention Program. *Psychology, Crime & Law, 11*(4), 389–402.

Pelham, W.E., Wheeler, T., & Chronis, A. (1998). Empirically supported psychosocial treatments for attention deficit hyperactivity disorder. *Journal of Clinical Child Psychology, 27*(2), 90–205.

Smulders, R. (2002). *Judo verpest.* [Judo sport]. Doctoral dissertation. Amsterdam: University of Amsterdam.

Solberg, M. E., Olweus, D., & Endresen, I. M. (2007). Bullies and victims at school: Are they the same pupils? *British Journal of Educational Psychology, 77*, 441–464.

Stevens V., De Bourdeaudhuij, I., & Van Oost, P. (2000). Bullying in Flemish schools: An evaluation of anti-bullying intervention in primary and secondary schools. *British Journal of Educational Psychology, 70*, 195–210.

Terranova, A. M., Sheffield Morris, A., & Boxer, P. (2008). Fear reactivity and effortful control in over and relational bullying: A six-month longitudinal study. *Aggressive Behavior, 34*, 104–115.

19

Cyberbullying
The Nature and Extent of a New Kind of Bullying, In and Out of School

PETER K. SMITH AND ROBERT SLONJE

Definition of Bullying and Cyberbullying

"Bullying" is often defined as being an aggressive, intentional act or behavior that is carried out by a group or an individual repeatedly and over time against a victim who can not easily defend him or herself (Olweus, 1999). Bullying is a form of abuse that is based on an imbalance of power; it can be defined as a systematic abuse of power (Smith & Sharp, 1994).

Most researchers in the area of bullying, and of aggression more generally, distinguish several main types. The most common categories are physical, verbal, and indirect or relational. Physical and verbal aggression are usually direct or face-to-face. During the 1990s, the scope broadened to include indirect aggression (done via a third party), and relational aggression (done to damage someone's peer relationships).

In recent years a new form of aggression or bullying has emerged, "cyberbullying," in which the aggression occurs through electronic means, and specifically mobile phones or the Internet. In this chapter we use the term "cyberbullying," which has come to be widely accepted in the literature. "Electronic bullying" has the same meaning but is less widely used. "Digital bullying" is restricted to bullying through digital means and would not include analog technology.

A corresponding definition of cyberbullying would be: An aggressive, intentional act carried out by a group or individual, *using electronic forms of contact*, repeatedly and over time against a victim who cannot easily defend him or herself.

There are numerous types of cyberbullying. Seven common at the time of writing (Smith et al., 2008) are:

1. via mobile phones:
   - Mobile phone call bullying (e.g., abusive or silent calls).
   - Text message bullying (via abusive text messages).
   - Picture/Video Clip bullying (via mobile phone cameras, includes taking a picture or clip of someone else in order to use it in an abusive manner; e.g., sending it to others or uploading it onto a website).

2. via the Internet:
  - E-mail bullying (sending or receiving abusive e-mails).
  - Chat-room bullying (being abusive or being abused whilst involved in chat room features).
  - Bullying through instant messaging (e.g., msn which is a form of a meeting community where others can see when you are logged in and send and receive instant messages).
  - Bullying via websites (e.g., create a website that is abusive towards a specific person; download information from an already existing website).

There is an important problem with defining cyberbullying as above. In traditional bullying, the acts or behaviors of the bully should be of a repetitive nature (more than just once). But due to the nature of cyberbullying, the act or behavior may repeat itself without the contribution of the cyberbully. For example, taking an abusive picture or video clip on a mobile phone may have occurred only once, but if the person receiving the image forwards it to anyone else, it could be argued that this falls under the category of repetition. Or, if something abusive is uploaded onto a webpage, every hit on that page could count as a repetition. Consequently, the use of repetition as a criterion for serious bullying (as often used traditionally, e.g., Olweus, 1999) may be less reliable for cyberbullying.

The Spread of Electronic Technology and of Cyberbullying

The use of mobile phones and of the Internet has increased very rapidly over the last 15 years. By now, a majority of the population in developed countries use both, frequently; and this includes young people. The U.S. Department of Commerce found that almost 90% of youth aged 12 to 17 years use computers, and by age 10 young people are more likely than adults to use the Internet (NTIA, 2002). According to Pew Internet and American Life Project (2001), about 74% of U.S. teenagers use instant messaging to communicate with friends. In the U.K., 60% of 16- to 24-year-olds use the Internet every day or almost every day, 26% at least once a week, 9% at least once a month, and only 5% less than that (ONS, 2007). The Mobile Life Report (2006) found that 51% of 10-year-olds and 91% of 12-year-olds in the U.K. now have a mobile phone.

With this spread has come the opportunity for cyberbullying. This use has appeared at different rates in different countries, although it has not been well-documented. Awareness of cyberbullying in the U.K. appears to have originated around 2001. The Department for Education and Science national anti-bullying pack, "Don't suffer in silence" (DfES, 2000), does not mention cyberbullying, but a revision published in 2002 mentions "sending malicious e-mails or text messages on mobile phones" (p. 9). Press reports on cyberbullying have since become quite frequent, and it has clearly diversified beyond bullying by text messages or e-mails.

Even if the phenomenon has only appeared a few years ago, it is clearly now significant in many countries, as our review will show. The research base is still limited, but expanding rapidly; here we review published and "in press" studies and data. The research so far suggests many similarities to traditional bullying, but also some important differences, and some continuing uncertainties in what is a rapidly changing and developing context of technological advance and social change. We first review some main research reports regarding types and incidence in different countries, then we will discuss some particular issues, notably age and gender differences, who is involved in the cyberbullying, the relative impact of types of cyberbullying on the victim, and possible characteristics found mainly in cyberbullying, notably breadth of audience, anonymity of the bully, and the difficulty of finding a safe haven when the bullying occurs in cyberspace. We then discuss what can be done; we give some student opinions on this, as well as mention some guidelines and advice sources. We conclude with some implications for research and for practice.

Some Main Research Studies: Types and Incidence

Here we mention data from the U.S., Canada, U.K., Norway, Sweden, Finland, Belgium, Netherlands, Greece, Australia, South Korea, and Japan. In general, studies have used anonymous self-report questionnaires assessing incidence of being victim and/or perpetrator of different types of cyberbullying; and other aspects (varying by study).

United States

Ybarra and Mitchell (2004) surveyed 1,501 youths aged 10–17 years who used the Internet regularly. Over the last year, 12% reported being aggressive to someone online, 4% were targets of aggression, and 3% were both aggressors and targets. The authors hypothesized that some victims of conventional bullying may use the Internet to attack others in a form of compensation. In a follow up study, these researchers and colleagues (Ybarra, Mitchell, Wolak, & Finkelhor, 2006) investigated 1,153 youths at the same age range. The figure for targets had risen to 9%, a 50% increase from the first study which collected data in 2000.

Raskauskas and Stoltz (2007) surveyed 84 students aged 13–18 years on three types of cyberbullying over the last school year; almost 49% reported being cybervictims (compared to 71% being traditional victims; these high figures stem from including "1–2 times" in the definition). The most common form of cyberbullying was by text messaging (experienced by 32%), followed by Internet/website (16%), and picture phone (10%). Additionally, about 21% reported being cyberbullies (compared to 64% traditional bullies). Many cyberbullied victims were also traditional victims, and most cyberbullies were also traditional bullies.

Canada

Li (2006) surveyed 264 students (grades 7–9 or ages 12–14 years) from three junior high schools in Canada. They were asked about being cyberbullied (e.g., via e-mail, chat room, cell phone) though without any further definition. About 25% reported being victims of cyberbullying; nearly two-thirds had been cyberbullied one to three times, the remainder more often. There was no gender difference here, but 17% reported they had cyberbullied others, with males twice as involved as females. In a later study with 432 students in grades 7–9, Beran and Li (2005) found that the incidence of cyberbullying had risen: 35% of the sample had experienced cyberbullying victimization once or twice, and 23% a few times or more. The figures for cyberbullying were 22% once or twice, and 4% a few times or more. No gender or grade differences were found.

U.K.

Oliver and Candappa (2003) briefly mentioned text message bullying in relation to a study on bullying generally in students aged 12–13 years; 4% had received nasty text messages, and 2% had received nasty e-mail messages. Similarly in a broad health-related questionnaire, Balding (2005) reported that just 1% out of some 5,000 pupils aged 10–11 years had been bullied in the last month through their mobile phone (compared to 22% who were called nasty names).

The NCH (formerly National Children's Home) has produced two surveys on cyberbullying in England. The first (NCH, 2002) reported that one quarter of 11- to 19-year-olds had been threatened or bullied via their mobile phone or personal computer, and 16% had received bullying or threatening text messages. Of those who had reported being bullied by text messages, 29% had not told anyone that they had been bullied. This was followed up by a more detailed survey of 770 young people aged 11–19 (NCH, 2005); 20% had been bullied or threatened by some sort of cyberbullying, 14% had been bullied or threatened through text messages, 5% through chat-rooms, and 4% through e-mail. In addition, 10% reported being photographed by a mobile phone camera and feeling threatened, and of these, 17% reported they felt the image had been sent to someone else. Also, 11% claimed to have sent a bullying or threatening message to someone else. Other main findings were that 26% of those bullied said it was a stranger bullying them, and 28% of those bullied told no one about the bullying. In both studies, the time frame is unspecified.

Noret and Rivers (2006) surveyed over 11,000 pupils from 2002 to 2005, asking: How often have you received any nasty or threatening text messages or e-mails? Altogether, 6.5% reported this at least "once in a while" (and 1.3% 'often'), and girls more than boys (7.6% vs. 5.1%). Over the 4-year period from 2002 to 2005, there was some increase: 5.8%, 5.9%, 7.4%, and 7.0% in successive years. This increase was confined to girls, such that in recent years cyber victimization was significantly higher in girls.

Smith and colleagues (2006) investigated 92 students aged 11–16 years, from 14 London schools. They reported that 22% of pupils had been victims of cyberbullying at least once, and about 7% more frequently than that, over the last couple of months. Most cyberbullying was done by one or a few students, usually from the same grade or year group. It often just lasted about a week, but sometimes much longer. Phone call, text messages and e-mail were the most common forms of cyberbullying, both inside and outside of school, while chat room bullying was the least common. Prevalence rates of cyberbullying were greater outside of school than inside.

Smith and colleagues (2008) also report data from a qualitative (focus group) study, and a further survey of 533 pupils aged 11–16 years from 5 schools in England. The latter study showed that 17% reported cyberbullying victimization; 5% in the last week or month, 5% this term, 4% the last school year, and 3% over a year ago. When asked how long ago they had taken part in cyberbullying others, 12% reported having done so in the last couple of months; 7% in the last week or month, 3% this term, 2% the last school year, and about 1% over a year ago. Few age or sex differences were found. This study compared cyberbullying directly with traditional bullying; whereas traditional bullying mainly occurred in school, cyberbullying mainly occurred outside school. Rates of victims telling an adult were less for cyber victims (59%) than traditional victims (70%).

The impact of cyberbullying was perceived as comparable to traditional bullying, except that mobile phone/video clip bullying had a much more negative impact. Being a cyber victim, but not a cyber bully, correlated with Internet use. Being a traditional victim, or bully, correlated with being a cyber victim, or bully; and in addition, many cyber victims were traditional bully-victims.

Norway

Olweus (personal communication, May 2007) has results for some 4,000 Oslo students, from 19 schools, obtained in 2005, with cyberbullying questions added to his bullying questionnaire. Looking at the results for two global questions, the percent being bullied electronically two or three times per month or more was 3.6%, for boys and 2.0% for girls; the percent bullying others electronically was 1.2% for boys and 0.4% for girls. Boys were thus more exposed and engaged in more cyberbullying. There appears to be a peak in incidence at grades 8 and 9 (14–15 years). In a follow-up question it was found that roughly 30–40% of electronic victims were bullied via mobile phone, 30–40% via the Internet, and some 20–30% via both. The correspondence between involvement on traditional bullying and cyber bullying was high: some 90% of cyberbullied children were bullied also in some other way; for bullying others the figure was 85%.

Sweden

Slonje and Smith (2008) investigated cyberbullying in 360 Swedish students aged 12–20 years. The most common forms of cyberbullying were e-mail and picture/video clip bullying, closely followed by phone call and text message bullying. Almost 12% of students were victimized by cyberbullying and 10% admitted cyberbullying others. The figures for victimization in lower secondary school (12–15 years) were almost 18%, but this fell to 3% in Sixth Form College (15–20 years). However, this decline with age was much less marked for being a cyberbully, 12% of lower secondary school pupils compared to 8% in Sixth Form College. A higher occurrence of cyberbullying took place outside of school compared to at school. The pupils also perceived that adults were not aware of electronic bullying to the same extent as traditional bullying.

Finland

Salmivalli and colleagues (personal communication, May 24, 2007) are collecting a large data set from schools across Finland that includes questions on cyberbullying. Respondents are from grades 3, 4, and 5; with some 6,500 respondents so far, the proportion of students exposed to cyberbullying "once or twice a month" or more often is 2.2% (girls 2.4%, boys 2.0%).

Belgium

Vandebosch and Van Cleemput (2009) surveyed 2,052 primary and secondary school pupils in Flanders. The most common forms of cyberbullying behavior were insults or threats, deception, spreading gossip, and breaking into someone's computer and changing their password. Over the past three months, 62% had experienced such victimization (experienced at least one form of potentially offensive behavior), 53% reported being perpetrators and 76% said they had been bystanders. These figures are high compared to other studies, perhaps because of differences in defining cyberbullying behaviour (e.g., including deception). The majority of pupils (64%) believed cyberbullying to be a "big problem."

Boys more often than girls tried out various deviant Internet and mobile phone activities. It was found that the more advanced Internet skills one had, the more likely one was to have experience with deviant Internet and mobile phone activities. The perpetrators had better self-image, and parents who were less involved with their computer and Internet use. Finally, there was a positive correlation between carrying out offensive behaviors in the offline and online world.

Some of the predictors for being a cybervictim were being a girl, and involvement in deviant Internet and mobile phone activities as perpetrator or bystander. There was also a positive correlation between social competence and victimization. As Vandebosch and Van Cleemput argue, this last predictor may seem unexpected, however, it may be that socially competent youth are more involved in online interactions and hence more exposed to cyberbullying behavior.

Netherlands

Van den Eijnden, Vermulst, Rooij, and Meerkerk (2006) surveyed 4,500 students aged 11–15 years in 2006. Negative online experiences were very common (e.g., 35% being insulted), and

17% reported being cyberbullied once a month or more, and 3% once a week or more. Boys, and students with a lower educational level, had a greater risk of being bullied, but the largest risk factors for being bullied on the Internet were being bullied in traditional ways, being a perpetrator of online bullying, and having online contacts with strangers.

Greece

Kapatzia and Syngollitou (2007) investigated cyberbullying in 544 Greek students aged 14–19 years, using an adaptation of the questionnaire from Smith and colleagues (2006). The prevalence rates for victims were: 15% once or twice, and 6% two or three times a month or more. The corresponding figures for being a cyberbully were 9% once or twice, and 7% two or three times a month or more. The occurrence of cyberbullying both for victims and bullies, and for both mobile phone and Internet bullying, was greater outside of school than in school.

There was only one age difference, younger pupils bullied others via mobile phones more outside of school. Boys more than girls admitted cyberbullying others using mobile phones, but girls were more often involved in Internet bullying, both as victims and perpetrators.

Australia

Campbell and Gardner (2005, cited in Campbell, 2005) reported that 14% of 120 eight grade students (aged 13) had been targeted by cyberbullying, and 11% had bullied others. The most prevalent method was bullying by text messaging, followed by chat room bullying and bullying through e-mail. Over half of the sample investigated thought cyberbullying was on the increase.

Cross-National

Three related studies have used Internet-based surveys including participants from a range of countries (although in these particular studies the majority of participants were from the United States) and backgrounds, who choose to respond. Patchin and Hinduja (2006) conducted a survey in 2004 (asking youths that visited a music artist's official website) and obtained participants aged 9 to 26 (and above). Out of these, 67% were younger then 18 and of these, three-quarters were female. Regarding ever having been involved in cyberbullying, almost 11% admitted being Internet bullies and about 30% reported Internet victimization.

With respect to the different forms of cyberbullying, the most prevalent were chat room bullying, and text messages via computers, closely followed by e-mail bullying; the least prevalent were in a newsgroup, text messaging via cell phone, bulletin board, and e-mail. The three most prevalent forms of bullying behavior were being ignored by others, disrespected by others, and being called names by others, even though threatening behaviors, rumor spreading, being picked on, and being made fun of were commonly prevalent forms in the victimization group, as well.

Hinduja and Patchin (2007a,b) collected data online from 1,388 frequent Internet users (18 hours/week average) between the ages of 6 and 17. About 34% (males 32%, females 36%) had been cyberbullied; by media, these were chat room 24%, computer text message 19%, e-mail 11%, bulletin board 8%, mobile phone text messaging 4%, and newsgroup 1%.

Burgess-Proctor, Patchin, and Hinduja (2008) investigated cyberbullying amongst 3,141 adolescent girls (age 8–17, data collected online). Thirty-eight percent reported victimization, with the most common media being chat rooms (26%), computer text messaging (22%) and e-mail (almost 14%). Common types of behavior included name-calling (e.g. fat, ugly) and spreading of gossip. When asked what kind of response to the bullying the victims took, almost 27% said they bullied the person back, 25% did nothing and 17% stayed offline.

A Cross-National Study in Four Countries

An International Symposium on Education Reform Report (NIER/MEXT, 2006) gives data from equivalent questionnaires for experiences of victimization by computer/e-mail, over specific time points during 2004–2005. Table 19.1 shows the findings (calculated from the original report) for primary and secondary age boys and girls, at three time points 6 months apart, and by two criteria (sometimes or more; and in brackets, once/week or more). Samples were not strictly comparable, but rates do appear higher in Australia and especially Canada, than in South Korea and Japan; although this is more marked for the lenient than the strict frequency criterion. The criterion also affects the age and gender differences found, which do also vary by country.

Summary of Prevalence Studies

A very wide range of incidence figures is available from the research reviewed. Ostensibly, reports of victimization of cyberbullying have varied from 1% (Balding, 2004) in the U.K., to 62% (Vandebosch & Van Cleemput, 2009) in Belgium, whilst frequencies for perpetrators range from 0.8% (Olweus, personal communication, May 2007) in Norway, to 53% in Belgium (Vandebosch & Van Cleemput, 2009). However since research on cyberbullying is a quite new area of investigation, research methods are even less standardized than in other areas.

One area of variation is the definition of cyberbullying. Some studies use an Olweus-type definition (as given at the start of this chapter), others essentially do not define it (Li, 2006), or measure Internet aggression more generally (Ybarra & Mitchell, 2004), or use a broader definition of cyberbullying (Vandebosch & Van Cleemput, 2009). Some studies have been limited to one or two media of cyberbullying (e.g., Noret & Rivers, 2006), others have used a more general term (cyberbullying, electronic bullying) or have separated mobile phone and Internet bullying (Kapatzia & Syngollitou, 2007) or have investigated a range of media (e.g., Smith et al., 2008).

Another area of variation is the time period used as a reference. This can be the last month (Balding, 2004) or last couple of months (e.g., Slonje & Smith, 2008), or if it ever happened (e.g. Li, 2006). In some cases the time period has been unspecified (e.g., NCH, 2002, 2005).

The nature of the sample will be an important factor. Some research such as Ybarra and Mitchell (2004) and Hinduja and Patchin (2007a,b) have investigated only Internet-using participants, whilst many others had samples from a number of schools and are more representative of the general population.

Finally, the date of a survey will be important in such a fast developing and changing area. For example the relatively low incidences in the U.K. reported by Oliver and Candappa (2003)

Table 19.1 Percentage of Pupils Victimised by Computer/email, Sometimes or More, and in Brackets, Once/Week or More, in Four Countries (adapted from NIER/MEXT, 2005)

	Primary boys	Primary girls	Secondary boys	Secondary girls
Japan	3.6 (1.1)	5.3 (0.9)	6.3 (1.2)	8.0 (1.0)
South Korea	4.8 (0.4)	5.9 (1.7)	4.2 (0.8)	6.0 (0.3)
Australia	6.9 (0.0)	10.1 (1.2)	7.8 (1.6)	7.1 (0.7)
Canada	13.0 (4.0)	17.4 (4.1)	20.7 (3.3)	20.5 (3.7)

and Balding (2004) may be because the incidence in the U.K. has increased over the last 5 years; there is direct evidence for this from Noret and Rivers (2006). The relative incidence of different media may be changing rapidly too; for example Smith and colleagues (2006, 2008) found a relative increase in bullying by instant messaging, which might reflect sample differences but also might genuinely reflect changes in the popularity of instant messaging from 2005 to 2006.

In and Out of School

Traditional bullying has mainly been studies in school, and indeed there is evidence that this is the most common venue for it (Olweus, 1999; Smith et al., 2008). However, it is clear that much cyberbullying takes place outside school. The venue of cyberbullying can be less clear-cut than for traditional bullying, as the act (e.g., sending an e-mail or text message) may be separated in time and/or place from where the act is received or noticed by the victim. Nevertheless, many pupils use mobile phones and the Internet more outside school (e.g., they will use Internet at home), and many schools place restrictions on mobile phone and Internet use within the school premises. When studies have asked this directly, it is clear that more cyberbullying is thought of as happening outside school (Smith et al., 2006, 2008; Kapatzia & Syngollitou, 2007; Slonje & Smith, 2008).

Age Differences

We know little about when children start cyberbullying. In the U.K. at the present time, mobile phone use is very slow in children 8 years and under, but rises rapidly from 9 to 12 years (Mobile Life Report, 2006). Most studies have been in the middle or secondary/high school age ranges. Some have found no age differences. For example, Patchin and Hinduja (2006) did not find any age differences in being a victim. Ybarra and Mitchell (2004) found that, in the United States, older students (15+ years) were more often Internet aggressors than were younger students (10–14 years); and Smith et al. (2008), in the U.K., found that older (14–16) students were often more involved in cyberbullying others compared to younger pupils (11–14). Slonje and Smith (2008) however, found that younger students (12–15) were victimized to a higher extent compared to older pupils (15–20), in Sweden, probably because the latter were a more selected group studying for university entrance.

Gender Differences

The area of gender differences is intriguing. In some respects cyberbullying is more like traditional indirect aggression or bullying (not done face-to-face), and thus one might look for more female involvement. Some studies have found this. Looking at victim rates, in the U.K. Noret and Rivers (2006) found their increase in text and e-mail victimization was limited to girls, while and Smith and colleagues (2006) found that girls were significantly more likely to be cyberbullied, especially by text messages and phone calls, than boys. Salmivalli (personal communication) reports higher cyber victimization of girls, in Finland; and Vandebosch and Van Cleemput (2000) in Belgium. Slonje and Smith (2008) found that girls more than boys were victims of e-mail bullying, in Sweden. Hinduja and Patchin (2007b) found that girls were more likely to be bullied by e-mails in comparison to boys. However, many studies report no differences (e.g., Smith et al., 2008; Li, 2006; Patchin & Hinduja, 2006; Ybarra & Mitchell, 2004). Olweus (personal communication) reports boys are more likely to be victims, in Norway; as does van der Eijnden and colleagues (2006) in the Netherlands.

Regarding doing the cyberbullying, many studies again report no gender differences; this in itself is interesting, given the usual preponderance of boys in traditional bullying. Some studies do report boys doing more cyberbullying. Li (2006) found that cyberbullying others was nearly twice as high in boys than girls; while in Norway, Olweus (personal communication) finds boys rates to be three times as high as girls. Slonje and Smith (2008) found boys more engaged in text message bullying, in Sweden; and Vandebosch and Van Cleemput (2009) found boys more at risk of deviant activities in Belgium.

It is likely that gender differences will vary by media of cyberbullying. Intriguingly, Kapatzia and Syngollitou (2007), in Greece, find more boys involvement in mobile phone bullying (bullying only), but girls more involved in Internet bullying (bully and victim). This is only partially consistent with other findings cited above; but there may well be appreciable cultural differences in use and practice in relation to electronic technologies, and also rapid historical changes as noted above.

Who Is Involved in the Cyberbullying

Sometimes victims of cyberbullying do not know who the perpetrator is. Smith and colleagues (2006) reported that about 1 in 5 of victims did not know who it was that bullied them. For Slonje and Smith (2008) this was about 1 in 3. However, when victims do know, it appears that often the perpetrators are from the same school as the victim (e.g., for 58% in Smith et al., 2006; 54% in Slonje & Smith, 2008). The bully may be one child or more. Smith and colleagues (2006) found that (when the victim knew the bully), this was often one person, with 24% reporting being bullied by one boy and 22% by one girl; but almost 1 in 4 reported being bullied by 2–3 students. Slonje and Smith (2008) found 36% of cyber victims reported being bullied by one boy and 12% by one girl; only 5% reported being bullied by more than one person.

These studies indicate that even though cyberbullying may escape school boundaries, it will often be students the victim knows at school who are involved in the bullying. However, some will be from outside school, e.g., 22% in Smith and colleagues (2006) findings. Vandebosch and Van Cleemput (2009) found that half of victims did not know who the bully was, 45% had been bullied from someone they knew from the offline world, while 14% had been bullied by somebody they knew only from the online world.

Correlates of Cyberbullying Involvement

There is evidence from several studies that involvement in cyberbullying correlates quite highly with involvement in traditional bullying (Raskauskas & Stoltz, 2007; Smith et al., 2008; Olweus, personal communication). Hinduja and Patchin (2007b) reported that youth engaged in offline bullying were more than five times likely to also engage in online bullying. However, the overlap is far from complete, and some studies have identified risk factors for involvement in cyberbullying.

One obvious factor is use of the Internet. Smith et al. (2008) found that high use of the Internet was a correlate of being a cyber victim. Hinduja and Patchin (2007b) also found that the more time one spends on the Internet, the more likely it was that one would experience cyberbullying. This study indicated other behaviors correlated to experiencing cyberbullying, including recent school problems, assaultive behaviors and substance use. Vandebosch and Van Cleemput (2009) found that victims of cyberbullying, compared to non-victims, did not estimate themselves highly regarding their social skills.

Ybarra and Mitchell (2004) reported that youth with problem behaviors (stealing, assault, vandalism, and police contact) were almost four times more likely to say they were Internet aggressor/target versus those who reported victimization only. They also suggested that traditional victims may be cyberbullies as a form of compensation; unable to retaliate face-to-face, they do so by electronic means. Neither Rauskauskas and Stoltz (2007) nor Slonje and Smith (2008) found support for this hypothesis; nor did Vandebosch and Van Cleemput (2009). Smith and colleagues (2008) did find a trend for traditional victims to also be cyberbullies; but out of 42 such cases, 30 were in fact traditional bully-victims. Perhaps rather than victims of traditional bullying becoming cyberbullies as a form of compensation, the status of bully (as a bully/victim) may have already been present prior to becoming a cyberbully, and traditional bully/victims are especially at risk of moving into the world of cyber bullying. However this hypothesis needs further testing.

The Impact of Cyberbullying on the Victim

Smith and colleagues (2006) investigated whether pupils in general perceived cyberbullying (and various media of cyberbullying) to have less, equal, or more of a negative impact compared to traditional bullying. The perceived impact was found to vary across media; picture/video clip bullying especially was perceived as having a greater negative impact than traditional bullying. Generally, there was a range of opinion, with some pupils replying that cyberbullying has the same effect on the victim ("I think they are equally as bad"; "they both can hurt"), could be worse ("loads of people can see it if it's on the Internet"; "it's constant all the time, really hard to escape"), or could be less harmful ("you can be more damaged by face-to-face bullying than cyber bullying, that's just words"; "a text is easier to ignore than something that happened in a specific place"; quotes from focus groups in Smith et al., 2008).

Using similar questions, Kapatzia and Syngollitou (2007) also found a range of responses, but with the mean impact for both mobile phone and Internet bullying being less than for traditional bullying. Slonje and Smith (2008 and personal data) found that not only does the perceived impact vary for different media, but perhaps also by status as victim/non-victim. Although samples of victims were relatively small, victims of cyberbullying usually perceived the impact to be more negative than the general sample of pupils.

A number of factors can affect impact. The nature of the hurtful material and the audience are obvious factors. The negative impact of picture/video clip bullying may be due to quite degrading material being circulated very widely (as can also happen in website bullying). Anonymity of the perpetrator can be important: "you don't know who it is, so more scared"; and also the possible isolation of the victim: "you haven't got friends around you to support you." Perceived planning/spontaneity and personal/impersonal intent of the bullying is another issue; an abusive comment on a website is clearly planned and personal in intent, whereas a nasty e-mail, for example, might be seen meant for anyone and not specifically for them.

Whatever the relative impact of cyberbullying compared to traditional bullying, it is certainly hurtful. Ybarra and colleagues (2006) found that 65% of the victims of cyberbullying felt worried or threatened by the incident, whilst 38% felt distressed. Patchin and Hinduja (2006) reported that although 43% of victims said that the cyberbullying did not affect them, common feelings associated with victimizations were frustration (43%), anger (40%) and sadness (27%). Hinduja and Patchin (2007a) found that while 35% of the victims answered that they were not bothered about the cyberbullying, 34% felt frustration, 31% anger, and 22% felt sadness. Burgess-Proctor et al. (2008) found that victims reported they felt frustrated (41%), angry (35%), sad (29%), or not bothered (32%). Beran and Li (2005) reported that 57% of victims felt angry, 36% felt sad and hurt.

Some Emerging Themes about Cyberbullying

Although overlapping with traditional bullying, cyberbullying clearly tends to have some particular distinguishing characteristics, that can influence aspects such as impact and coping strategies. One is "No place to hide." As one student put it, "You can't run or hide from cyberbullying." Unlike traditional forms of bullying, where once the victim gets home they are away from the bullying until the next day, cyberbullying is more difficult to escape from; the victim may continue to receive text messages or e-mails, or view nasty postings on a website, wherever they are. Another is "Breadth of audience." Cyberbullying can reach particularly large audiences in a peer group compared with the small groups that are the usual audience in traditional bullying. For example, when nasty comments are posted on a website, the audience that may see these comments is potentially very large. Third is "Invisibility of those doing the bullying." Cyberbullying is not normally a face-to-face experience, and (like rumor-spreading) provides those doing the bullying with some degree of 'invisibility' and at times anonymity. Online pseudonyms may be used on the Internet.

A fourth aspect is "Unawareness of consequences." Compared to most traditional bullying, the person carrying out cyberbullying may be less aware or even unaware of the consequences caused by his or her actions. This has particularly complex ramifications. On the one hand, it can enhance moral disengagement from the victim's plight (Hymel, Rocke Henderson, & Bonanno, 2005) and thus might make cyberbullying easier; without such direct feedback there may be fewer opportunities for empathy or remorse. There may also be less opportunity for bystander intervention to stop the bullying.

On the other hand, many bullying children enjoy the feedback of seeing the suffering of the victim. Additionally, one motive for bullying is thought to be the status gained by showing (abusive) power over others, in front of witnesses (Salmivalli et al., 1996; Pellegrini et al., this volume). The perpetrator will lack this in many cases of cyberbullying, unless steps are taken to tell others what has happened or publicly share the material. The nature of "witnessing" bullying, and of participant roles, appears more complex in cyberbullying and is in need of further investigation.

What Can Be Done: Student's Opinions, Some Guidelines, and Advice Sources

Victims often need to seek help in order to deal with bullying, and we know from studies of traditional bullying that many victims are reluctant to do this. This also appears true of cyberbullying. Indeed, Smith et al. (2008) found rates of victims telling someone to be lower for cyberbullying than traditional bullying. When victims of cyberbullying do tell someone, it appears to be most often friends, followed by parents, with teachers told rather infrequently (Smith et al., 2008; Slonje & Smith, 2008; Kapatzia & Syngollitou, 2007). Given the generational gap in use and awareness of new technologies, children and young people may feel that teachers and parents are less aware of the issues involved. Moreover, when much cyberbullying happens outside school, pupils may see less reason to tell teachers (even though the problem may often come back into the school, when the perpetrator is from the same school).

What actions do students think can be taken? Smith and colleagues (2008) found that in focus groups a common pessimistic theme was that little can be done to reduce cyberbullying: "I don't think you can ever stop cyber bullying at all because you'd basically have to get rid of all the communication things that we love and you can't do that." This pessimism was reinforced by frequent references to the anonymity in cyberbullying: "you can't report it because you don't know who they are," "bullies can hide themselves, change identity." The most common practical advice was to block or ignore it, both for mobile phones: "if you see a text from a random number, reject it," and for the Internet: "turn off your computer," "if harassment on the Internet, block them." In general, telling was often recommended: "get police to track down withheld number," "report abuse on message board." Responding to multiple choice items, a survey of 533 pupils aged 11–16 years found that the best ways to stop cyberbullying were regarded as "blocking messages/identities" (75%), "telling someone" (63%), "changing e-mail address/phone number" (57%), and "keeping a record of texts/e-mails" (47%), followed by "ignoring it" (41%), "reporting to authorities" (39%), "contact Internet service provider" (31%), and "asking them to stop" (21%), with the least popular advice being "fighting back" (20%).

Implications for Research

It is clearly important to include cyberbullying in current questionnaire and nomination instruments; for example the Olweus Bullying questionnaire now contains items on this. While some large surveys just assess cyberbullying as a global entity, it is apparent that different kinds of cyberbullying have some different characteristics (perhaps regarding age and sex differences, and very probably concerning impact, and coping strategies), so for many purposes it will be important to distinguish different types of cyberbullying

An interesting aspect is the importance of historical factors in work on cyberbullying. Awareness of cyberbullying in the media and in research studies is only some 5 years old. It is thus particularly important to know the dates of studies and surveys. The relevant technologies are still developing, and new forms of cyberbullying will undoubtedly emerge. Relatedly, it will be interesting to document the rise and transmission of existing and new forms of cyberbullying; for example the "happy slapping" or picture/video clip bullying has been described as spreading like a virus as the idea gets disseminated.

Implications for Practice

There are important implications for practice, if schools, parents, and others concerned with children and young people are to contain and reduce cyberbullying (see Table 19.2). An obvious first step is to raise awareness of the issue. Cyberbullying should be included explicitly in school anti-bullying policies (and indeed there may be a separate policy or policy section regarding appropriate use of mobile phones, and computers, within school). Anti-bullying materials used in the classroom need to embody examples of cyberbullying as well as traditional bullying. Teacher training materials for anti-bullying work should cover the issue. It is also vital to include information and guidance for parents; the older (parent, teacher) generation is generally less knowledgeable about new technological communication methods than the more recent generation—it is young people who are the experts.

Table 19.2 Implications for Practice

- Parents and teachers, as well as pupils, need to be aware of what is cyberbullying, its negative impact, and rights and responsibilities related to use of mobile phones and the internet. Cyberbullying needs to be included in school anti-bullying policies and intervention work.
- Some methods for reducing traditional bullying, will also be useful for cyberbullying; these include general education regarding relationships and respect for others, as well as bullying-focused interventions.
- In addition, some specific interventions for cyberbullying will be needed; including ways of contacting mobile phone companies and internet service providers, and information on legal rights in areas such as privacy and harassment on the internet.
- Researchers need to ensure that instrumentation is updated to include new forms of cyberbullying; and teacher training modules should cover the issue. Guidance for parents will also be helpful.

Some traditional methods for reducing bullying will be useful for cyberbullying, too. Besides bullying-focused interventions, this should include general relationships education, embodying respect for others, rights of others, asserting one's own rights in non-aggressive ways, and utilizing conflict management skills. In England the SEAL (Social and Emotional Aspects of Learning) program is being rolled in as part of the curriculum in primary schools, and this includes a module on bullying; there is no large scale formal evaluation but it has been well received by teachers, and a secondary school program is being developed.

But some more specific interventions will be helpful for cyberbullying—including guidance on liaison with mobile phone companies and Internet service providers, and the legal rights and responsibilities of all concerned (a relatively new issue where precedents are being set). Willard (2006) provides useful, general guidance. Many countries are now developing guidance on cyberbullying specifically, and/or Internet safety more generally. For example in England, the DfES (Department for Education and Skills) issued guidelines in late 2007 (http://www.teachernet.gov.uk/docbank/index.cfm?id=11910) In the Netherlands, there is a national campaign called Stop Digital Bullying (http://www.stopdigitaalpesten.nl).

While the challenges posed by cyberbullying are rather new, both researchers and practitioners are now becoming alerted to the issue, and, based on the previous experience of general anti-bullying work gathered over the last 10 or 20 years, it can be hoped that the response to cyberbullying will have positive effects.

Acknowledgments

Our thanks to Dan Olweus and Christina Salmivalli for sharing unpublished data for this chapter; to Neil Tippett for advice; and to Stan DePue for assisting with literature searches.

References

Balding, J. (2005). *Young People in 2004: The health-related behaviour questionnaire results for 40,430 young people between the ages of 10 and 15.* Exeter, UK: Schools Health Education Unit.

Beran, T., & Li, Q. (2005). Cyber-Harassment: A study of a new method for an old behaviour. *Journal of Educational Computing Research, 32,* 265–277.

Burgess-Proctor, A., Patchin, J. W., & Hinduja, S. (2008). Cyberbullying and online harassment: Reconceptualizing the victimization of adolescent girls. In V. Garcia & J. Clifford (Eds.), *Female victims of crime: Reality reconsidered* (pp. 162–176). Upper Saddle River, NJ: Prentice Hall.

Campbell, M. A. (2005). Cyber bullying: An old problem in a new guise? *Australian Journal of Guidance and Counselling, 15,* 68–76.

Department for Education and Skills. (2000). *Bullying: don't suffer in silence: An anti-bullying pack for schools* (second edition, revised 2002). London: HMSO

Hinduja, S., & Patchin, J.W. (2007a). Offline consequences of online victimization: School violence and delinquency. *Journal of School Violence, 6,* 89–112.

Hinduja, S., & Patchin, J.W. (2007b). Cyberbullying: An exploratory analysis of factors related to offending and victimization. *Deviant Behavior, 29,* 1–29.

Hymel, S., Rocke Henderson, N., & Bonanno, R. A. (2005). Moral disengagement: A framework for understanding bullying among adolescents. *Journal of Social Sciences, 8,* 1–11.

Kapatzia, A., & Syngollitou, E. (2007). *Cyberbullying in middle and high schools: Prevalence, gender and age differences.* Unpublished manuscript based on M.Sc. Thesis of A. Kapatzia, University of Thessaloniki.

Li, Q. (2006). Cyberbullying in schools: A research of gender differences. *School Psychology International, 27,* 157–170.

Mobile Life Youth Report. (2006). *The impact of the mobile phone on the lives of young people.* Carphone warehouse. Retrieved Augustsy 15, 2007, from http://www.yougov.com/archives/pdf/CPW060101004_2.pdf

NCH (2002). NCH National Survey 2002: Bullying. Retrieved from http://www.nch.org.uk

NCH (2005). Putting U in the picture - Mobile phone bullying survey 2005. Retrieved from http://www.nch.org.uk

NIER/MEXT (2006). *Save children from the risk of violence in school. Report of International Symposium on Educational Reform 2005.* Tokyo: National Institute for Educational Policy Research.

Noret, N., & Rivers, I. (2006, April). The prevalence of bullying by text message or email: results of a four year study. Poster presented at British Psychological Society Annual Conference, Cardiff, Scotland

NTIA (2002). A nation online: How Americans are expanding their use of the internet. Retrieved May 30, 2007, from http://www.ntia.doc.gov/ntiahome/dn/nationonline_020502.htm

Office of National Statistics (ONS). (2007). Retrieved July 24, 2009, from http://www.statistics.gov.uk/pdfdir/inta0807.pdf

Oliver, C., & Candappa, M. (2003). *Tackling bullying: Listening to the views of children and young people.* Nottingham, UK: Department for Education and Skills.

Olweus, D. (1999). Sweden. In Smith, P. K., Morita, Y., Junger-Tas, J., Olweus, D., Catalano, R. & Slee, P. (Eds.), *The nature of school bullying: A cross-national perspective* (pp. 7–27). London: Routledge.

Patchin, J. W., & Hinduja, S. (2006). Bullies move beyond the schoolyard: A preliminary look at cyberbullying. *Youth Violence and Juvenile Justice, 4,* 148–169.

Pew Internet and American Life Project. (2001). Teenage life online: The rise of the instant-messaging generation on the internet's impact on friendships and family relationships. Retrieved May 30, 2007, from http://www.pewinternet.org/report_display.asp?r=36

Raskauskas, J., & Stoltz, A. D. (2007). Involvement in traditional and electronic bullying among adolescents. *Developmental Psychology, 43,* 564–575.

Salmivalli, C., Lagerspetz, K. M. J., Bjorkqvist, K., Osterman, K., & Kaukiainen, A. (1996). Bullying as a group process: Participant roles and their relations to social status within the group. *Aggressive Behavior, 22,* 1–15.

Slonje, R., & Smith, P. K. (2008). Cyberbullying: Another main type of bullying? *Scandinavian Journal of Psychology, 49,* 147–154.

Smith, P. K., Mahdavi, J., Carvalho, M., Fisher, S., Russell, S., & Tippett, N. (2008). Cyberbullying, its forms and impact in secondary school pupils. *Journal of Child Psychology and Psychiatry.*

Smith, P. K., Mahdavi, J., Carvalho, M., & Tippett, N. (2006). An investigation into cyberbullying, its forms, awareness and impact, and the relationship between age and gender in cyberbullying. Research Brief No. RBX03-06. London: Department for Education and Skills.

Smith, P. K., & Sharp, S. (Eds.). (1994). *School bullying: Insights and perspectives.* London: Routledge.

Willard, N.E. (2006). *Cyberbullying and cyberthreats.* Eugene, OR: Center for Safe and Responsible Internet Use.

Vandebosch, H., & van Cleemput, K. (2009). Cyber bullying among youngsters: prevalence and profile of bullies and victims. *New Media & Society, 11,* 1–23.

Van den Eijnden, R. J. J. M., Vermulst, A., Van Rooij, T., & Meerkerk, G-J. (2006). *Monitor Internet en jongeren: Pesten op Internet en het psychosociale welbevinden van jongeren* [Cyberbullying and the psychosocial well-being of adolescents]. Rotterdam: IVO Factsheet.

Ybarra, M. L., & Mitchell, K. J. (2004). Online aggressor/targets, aggressors, and targets: a comparison of associated youth characteristics. *Journal of Child Psychology and Psychiatry, 45,* 1308–1316.

Ybarra, M. L., Mitchell, K. J., Wolak, J., & Finkelhor, D. (2006). Examining characteristics And associated distress related to Internet harassment: Findings from the Second Youth Internet Safety Survey. *Pediatrics, 18,* 1169–1171.

Section II

Assessment and Measurement of Bullying

20

The Assessment of Bullying

DEWEY G. CORNELL AND SHARMILA BANDYOPADHYAY

What is bullying? Bullying can generally be defined as the act of repeatedly humiliating a weaker person. Humiliation can be accomplished by physical intimidation or assault, or by verbal abuse that ridicules or demeans someone. A more subtle form of bullying involves excluding someone from social activities so that the person feels rejected and inferior to others. Thus bullying may be physical, verbal, or social.

A bully is in a position of dominance or superiority over the victim. Especially among boys, dominance might be achieved because one boy is larger or stronger than the other, or because several boys outnumber their victim. Among girls, physical size may not matter as much as social status and popularity. In all cases, the bully intimidates the victim, who is made to feel inferior. Bullying does not occur between equals, which distinguishes it from ordinary conflict between peers.

Because bullying is such a broad and abstract concept, it is difficult to distinguish from other forms of peer aggression and play. Consider the example of one boy who shoves another boy: If the aggressor is bigger than his victim, it might be bullying, but if the two boys are the same size, it is not bullying. If the action is done in a playful manner and the smaller boy is not hurt or distressed, the incident might be regarded as horseplay, but not bullying. And even when the bigger boy acts with malice, if the incident only happens once, the behavior might not be labeled bullying.

As evident in the example above, there are three essential criteria for bullying: peer dominance, harmfulness, and frequency (Olweus, 1999). First, bullying must be distinguished from ordinary conflict between peers of equal status. All peer conflict is not bullying, because a bully must have a position of dominance or superiority over the victim. Second, one student must inflict some kind of physical or emotional harm on the other. Mere teasing or horseplay that is not distressing would not be sufficient. Third, bullying is a repetitive, chronic activity, rather than a one-time event (Olweus, 1993a). A student who loses his or her temper and shoves a smaller child out of frustration would not be regarded as a bully unless he or she persisted in humiliating the child.

Despite the complexity of bullying as a construct, studies often rely on simpler definitions that may not conform to the three criteria of peer dominance, harmfulness, and frequency. A landmark national study of bullying (Nansel et al., 2001) by the National Institute of Child Health and Human Development (NICHD) in the United States, using a survey developed by the World Health Organization, presented students with the following definition:

> We say a student is BEING BULLIED when another student, or a group of students, say or do nasty and unpleasant things to him or her. It is also bullying when a student is teased repeatedly in a way he or she doesn't like. But it is NOT BULLYING when two students of about the same strength quarrel or fight. (Nansel et al., 2001, p. 2095)

This definition distinguishes bullying from other forms of peer conflict, but the criteria for harm—"nasty and unpleasant"—are ambiguous and could include peer interactions that do not rise to the level of harm associated with bullying.

The NICHD survey was administered in school classrooms to a nationally representative sample of 15,686 students in grades 6 through 10. Based on survey results, 29.9% of students in the United States—3 out of every 10 students—are either victims or perpetrators of bullying. Approximately 1 out of every 5 students—19.3%—was identified as a bully, and nearly 1 of every 6—16.9%—classified as a victim of bullying (6.3% of students fell into both bully and victim categories).

Alternatively, the Juvenile Victimization Questionnaire (JVQ; Finkelhor, Ormrod, Turner, & Hamby, 2005), developed by the Crimes Against Children Research Center of the University of New Hampshire, asked two questions to assess bullying:

> (1) In the last year, did any kid, even a brother or sister, pick on you by chasing you or grabbing your hair or clothes, or by making you do something you didn't want to do?

> (2) In the last year, did you get scared or feel really bad because kids were calling you names, saying mean things to you, or saying they didn't want you around?

The first question was designed to measure "bullying" and the second to measure "teasing or emotional bullying." These questions identify actions that are harmful, but do not clearly distinguish bullying from ordinary peer conflict and appear to include single events. This survey was administered by telephone interview to a nationally representative sample (Finkelhor et al., 2005) and found that 14.7% of 13- to 17-year-olds reported having been bullied according to the first question, and 20% reported having been victims of emotional bullying, as described in the second question, during the previous year. Methodological differences between the NICHD study and the JVQ study make direct comparisons impossible, but illustrate the diverse ways in which researchers can assess the prevalence of bullying.

The alternative to a simple—but potentially overly inclusive—definition is one that spells out the criteria for bullying in detail. For example, the most widely used student survey, the Olweus Bully/Victim Questionnaire (BVQ; Olweus, 1996; Solberg & Olweus, 2003), presents the following definition to students:

> We say a student is being bullied when another student or several other students
> - say mean and hurtful things or make fun of him or her or call him or her mean and hurtful names
> - completely ignore or exclude him or her from their group of friends or leave him or her out of things on purpose
> - hit, kick, push, shove around, or threaten him or her
> - tell lies or spread false rumors about him or her or send mean notes and try to make other students dislike him or her
> - and do other hurtful things like that.
> These things may take place frequently, and it is difficult for the student being bullied to defend himself or herself. It is also bullying when a student is teased repeatedly in a

mean and hurtful way. But we don't call it bullying when the teasing is done in a friendly and playful way. Also, it is not bullying when two students of about the same strength or power argue or fight. (Olweus, 1996, p. 2)

The BVQ asks students to report whether they have bullied others or been bullied by others "in the past couple of months." Using this definition, Solberg and Olweus (2003) calculated the prevalence of bullying among students in grades 5–9 in Bergen Norway, as 6.5% for bullies and 10.1% for victims.

Eslea et al. (2003) compared rates of bullying and victimization in seven countries, all using some form of the Olweus questionnaire. The differences across countries seemed much larger than could be explained by true national differences, and suggested the role of uncontrolled influences on survey responses. The percentage of students classified as bullies ranged from 2.0% in China to 16.9% in Spain. The percentage of students classified as victims ranged from 5.2% in Ireland to 25.6% in Italy. Similarly, the percentage of students who claimed no involvement in bullying ranged from 91% in Ireland to just 50.8% in Spain.

Accuracy of Student Self-report

Although student surveys are the principal means of measuring the prevalence of bullying, there has been insufficient attention to their reliability and validity (Cornell, 2006; Cornell, & Loper, 1998; Griffin & Gross, 2004; Leff, Power, & Goldstein, 2004; Rosenblatt & Furlong, 1997). Several bullying prevention programs provide student surveys, but report little or no information on their psychometric properties (Beane, 1999; Garrity, Jens, Porter, Sager, & Short-Camilli, 1994; Horne, Bartolomucci, & Newman-Carlson, 2003; Olweus, 2002).

The Olweus BVQ (Olweus, 2002) is the most important and widely used bullying survey worldwide, yet there is little published information about its reliability and validity. The package of materials that accompanies the BVQ states:

We have made lots of analyses on the internal consistency (reliability), the test-retest reliability and the validity of the Olweus Bully/Victim Questionnaire on large representative samples (more than 5000 students). The results are generally quite good. . . . Unfortunately, most of this psychometric information has not yet been published, due to lack of time. (Olweus, 2002, p. 1)[1]

A more recent report by Solberg and Olweus (2003) focused on the single questions used to identify bullies and victims of bullying. This study showed that endorsing either question with a frequency of "2 or 3 times a month" or more would distinguish victims from non-victims on measures of internalizing symptoms and distinguish bullies from non-bullies on measures of externalizing behaviors. The major weakness of these analyses is that all of the internalizing and externalizing measures were collected as part of the same survey process, so that the correlations were affected to an unknown degree by shared method variance. Moreover, there was no independent corroboration that the students were actually involved in bullying.

There are many reasons to be cautious about reliance on self-report (Cornell, 2006; Cornell & Loper, 1998; Cross & Newman-Gonchar, 2004; Furlong, Sharkey, Bates, & Smith, 2004; Griffin & Gross, 2004; Leff et al., 2004); self-report measures are dependent on the student's understanding of the survey questions and his or her memory for events that may be unpleasant to recall. Some students may be tempted to inflate accounts of their experiences, while others may minimize or deny their involvement in bullying.

Both careless and intentionally exaggerated responding could inflate estimates of bullying and bully victimization. Because these behaviors generally occur in a small percentage of students, careless marking by students will increase their frequency (e.g., random responses to a yes-no question will generate a 50% prevalence rate). Provocative adolescents will produce even higher rates if they systematically choose the most extreme answers. Furlong and colleagues (2004) identified a group of students who claimed to have carried a weapon 6 or more times in the past month (the most extreme response) on the Youth Risk Behavior Surveillance survey (YRBS). While this might be a credible response in some cases, these students also tended to give extreme responses indiscriminately on both healthy and high-risk items. A disproportionate number of these weapon-carrying students claimed to exercise every day, eat plenty of carrots, and drink lots of milk; they also claimed to make frequent suicide attempts, use heroin, sniff glue, and take steroids.

Validity screening procedures can substantially reduce estimates of the prevalence of high-risk behavior such as fighting, gang membership, and drug use. In a survey of 10,909 middle and high school students, Cornell and Loper (1998) found that one fourth of the surveys failed to meet validity screening criteria that included detection of students who omitted demographic information, marked a series of items all in the same way, or gave inappropriate answers to validity questions (e.g., answering "No" to "I am telling the truth on this survey"). The deletion of invalid self-report surveys reduced the estimated 30-day prevalence of fighting at school from 28.7% to 19.2%. Similarly, the estimated prevalence of self-reported drug use at school dropped from 25.1% to 14.8%, and carrying a knife at school dropped from 18.4% to 7.7%.

Cross and Newman-Gonchar (2004) screened three different school surveys for the presence of inconsistent responses to items with the same content (e.g., answering "never" when asked at what age they joined a gang and "yes" to the question, "Have you ever belonged to a gang?") and extreme responses (e.g., claiming to have used LSD 20 or more times in the past 30 days). Surveys with three or more inconsistent and/or extreme responses were identified as "suspect." Although only a small percentage of surveys were identified as suspect—2.7% in one sample and 4.4% in another sample using a different survey—including these suspect surveys dramatically affected the prevalence of high-risk behaviors. Estimates of the percentage of students carrying a handgun at school jumped by a magnitude of 30—from .1% to 3.2%—in one survey, and in another, reports of physically attacking or harming someone went from 9.9% to 15.8%. Reports of being physically attacked at school rose from 24.5% to 37.8%.

In one high school, the proportion of students who reported having been bullied was 45.7%, but after suspect surveys were removed from the sample, the proportion dropped to 25.0%, which is a reduction of more than 45% (Cross & Newman-Gonchar, 2004). In other words, the error in survey results that could be attributable to inconsistent and extreme responding—without considering other forms of error, such as limitations in memory or concentration—is larger than the typical reductions reported by many bully prevention programs (Smith & Ananiadou, 2003). Clearly, researchers should consider the implications of using a method to assess outcomes that is vulnerable to measurement errors which can be larger than the expected treatment effect.

Finally, Cross and Newman-Gonchar (2004) raised an important concern about the lack of standards for classroom administration of surveys. Teachers must be well-prepared and motivated to administer the survey and must be given clear instructions and adequate time. They must also be willing and able to engage students so that they take the survey seriously and attempt to complete it accurately. The survey should not be so laborious that students lose interest, fail to concentrate, or begin marking answers at random.

Cross and Newman-Gonchar (2004) observed striking differences in survey results between schools that used trained versus untrained survey administrators. In some cases the teachers were not given adequate instructions or advance notice that they would be administering a lengthy survey in their classroom. Although this was not a controlled study, the authors' post hoc observations were provocative; 28% of surveys obtained by untrained administrators failed to meet validity standards, whereas only 3% of those obtained by trained administrators were considered invalid. These findings raise concern that survey results are highly sensitive to the classroom environment and administratiion procedures.

Survey Anonymity

Even when a student survey uses a definition that clearly specifies the criteria of harm, dominance, and frequency, and students are properly motivated and willing to take the survey, there is the question of whether students can comprehend the complex concept of bullying and apply it appropriately. In any study where adult observers are asked to identify bullying behavior, it would be considered essential to train the observers and test them to make sure they were reliable and accurate in their ratings, yet studies of bullying that rely on student ratings do not present reliability data.

The primary reason why studies of bullying have not examined the accuracy of student self-report is that bullying surveys are usually administered on an anonymous basis, and anonymous self-reports cannot be validated against any external criterion of truth. Solberg and Olweus (2003) contend that anonymous surveys encourage more accurate reports of bullying because students are freed from concerns about revealing that they are bullies or victims of bullying. Although this is a plausible and widely held assumption, it must be empirically tested.

A recent study by Chan, Myron, and Crawshaw (2005) tested the assumption that anonymous survey administration results increased reports of bullying others and being the victim of bullying. These researchers administered the School Life Survey (Chan, 2002) to 562 students (ages 6 to 13) in 30 classrooms randomly assigned to two conditions: One group took the survey anonymously and the other was instructed to write their names on the survey. The two groups reported similar rates of bullying others and being the victim of bullying, with no statistically significant differences. It is noteworthy, however, that the study did not use the term "bullying" and instead asked students to endorse behaviors that reflected bullying, such as hitting, teasing, and lying about other students. A similar study using the BVQ or another survey that uses the term "bullying" is needed.

Another study examined the difference between anonymous and non-anonymous reports of drug use and illegal behavior such as stealing and weapon carrying (O'Malley, Johnston, Bachman, & Schulenberg, 2000). In this study, half of the national sample of adolescents taking the Monitoring the Future survey were assured that their answers were anonymous, while the other half were told that their answers would be held in confidence, but were required to report their names and addresses to the researchers. There was little or no difference in the reporting of sensitive information under the two conditions (O'Malley et al., 2000). This study suggests that the assurance of confidentiality may be sufficient to encourage reporting of sensitive and even illegal activity.

A study by Ahmad and Smith (1990) seems to support anonymous surveys. In this study, 93 students who had completed the Olweus survey then participated in an interview. Although 85% of the students who reported being victims of bullying were willing to admit this to the interviewers, only about half of the students who reported bullying others on the survey admitted to it in the interview. It might appear that students were more willing to admit involvement in bullying on the self-report survey than in a face-to-face interview, but Chan et al. (2005) astutely point out that the researchers did not determine which of the two reports were correct. It is possible that students responded carelessly or flippantly on the paper and pencil survey, but gave more carefully considered responses when interviewed. It is also possible that students did not fully recognize the restrictions in the Olweus definition of bullying and identified peer conflicts or disputes that were not bullying.

A recent examination of student responses to the School Climate Bullying Survey (SCBS; Cornell & Sheras, 2003) illustrates the variety of errors that can creep into student self-reports of bullying. This survey was administered on a confidential, non-anonymous basis using code numbers to protect student identity (Cornell, McDade, & Biasiolli, 2007). However, students were advised that if survey results indicated that they were victims of bullying, the researchers would notify one of the two school counselors to speak with them. A total of 19 students identified themselves as victims of bullying "about once a week" or "several times a week" in the past month. The students and counselors were familiar with the concept of bullying through the school's participation in the Olweus Bullying Prevention Program. After interviewing the students, the counselors concluded that only 10 of the 19 students were victims of bullying according to the Olweus definition. The responses of the nine students who reported bullying on the self-report survey, but did not appear to be victims of bullying, in the opinion of the counselor, are instructive:

• One said that he marked the form incorrectly as a joke;
• Two said that they had never been bullied, but evidently marked the survey by mistake;
• One said that some boys had bumped him in the hall early in the year, but had stopped;
• Two said that they had been bullied last year, but not this year;
• Three reported playful teasing among friends that did not appear to the meet the criteria for harmfulness or peer dominance.

The Problem of Shared Method Variance

There are strong practical reasons to rely on student self-report to assess bullying, since a large body of data can be collected from an entire school in a short period of time. If the survey is anonymous, then researchers may be freed of the problem of obtaining active parental consent and can achieve a less selective sample. Nevertheless, the use of anonymous self-report surveys places a severe limitation on research to identify causes and consequences of bullying, as self-reported bullying and victimization can only be correlated with characteristics that are measured at the same time. This design limitation has prevented researchers from investigating many aspects of bullying (e.g., developmental background, familial characteristics, school outcomes, effectiveness of individual interventions) that are important to understand and prevent bullying. It has also stymied efforts to understand why some prevention efforts have not been successful (Cornell, 2006; Cornell, Sheras, & Cole, 2006).

In addition to the limitations that reliance on anonymous self-report places on what researchers can measure, the results are confounded by shared method variance. Method variance refers to score differences produced by the measurement method rather than the construct of interest, and is widely recognized as one of the most common limitations in behavioral research (Podsakoff, MacKenzie, Lee, & Podsakoff, 2003). When two constructs are assessed by the same method (e.g., a pencil and paper self-report questionnaire, teacher ratings), the correlation between those constructs will be inflated or deflated to an unknown degree by shared method variance. Shared method variance is often overlooked or discounted in bullying research, but is widely recognized as a serious problem in other fields (Podsakoff et al., 2003). Cote and Buckley (1987) estimated that approximately one quarter of the variance in a typical research measure could be attributed to systematic sources of measurement error such as shared method variance, and that this problem was higher in the field of education than in other fields, such as marketing and sociology. The effects of shared method variance can be substantial. On average, the correlation between two attitude measures could be inflated to an observed correlation of .23 when the true correlation was zero, and deflated to .52 when the true correlation was 1.00 (Podsakoff et al., 2003).

Method effects for a self-report bullying survey can be produced by a variety of factors, including student reading level, mood, and attitude toward completing the survey. Social desirability effects are also important. A conforming-minded student who is reluctant to admit bullying behavior might be similarly reluctant to endorse hypothesized correlates of bullying, such as other forms of rule-breaking at school. Conversely, a student motivated to give flippant answers might endorse socially undesirable responses consistently across measures, particularly when the student has been assured that his or her answers are anonymous. The presence of students with both conforming and challenging attitudes would tend to inflate correlations in the hypothesized direction, creating the possibility of spurious findings.

A related problem is that students may respond to demand effects in denying bullying on a self-report survey. At the outset of a bullying prevention program, students might endorse some degree of involvement in bullying, but after being repeatedly lectured and reminded about the undesirability of bullying, students may learn to disavow and deny bullying on subsequent administrations of the survey, even if they have not changed their behavior with peers. If the self-report survey is the only source of information to indicate a reduction in bullying, it would not be possible to rule out that an apparent decline in bullying simply represents student acquiescence to an expected response pattern.

Peer Reports

Peer reports represent an alternative to self-report assessment of bullying. The peer report or nomination method usually involves asking students to identify classmates who match a descriptive statement or definition (Pakaslahti & Keltikangas-Jarvinen, 2000; Ladd & Kochenderfer-Ladd, 2002; Nabuzoka, 2003; Cornell & Brockenbrough, 2004). In variations of this method, students are asked to nominate a fixed number of classmates or to assign frequency ratings (e.g., never, sometimes, often) to each of their classmates.

Peer nominations have been found useful in assessing a wide variety of emotional and behavior problems, including peer aggression, delinquency, hyperactivity, anxiety, and depression (Huesmann, Eron, Guerra, & Crawshaw, 1994; Weiss, Harris, & Catron, 2004). Peer nomination studies have also been used to differentiate direct and indirect peer aggression, social exclusion, and interpersonal problems (Crick & Bigbee, 1998; Hill, Zrull, & McIntire, 1998; Pakaslahti & Keltikangas-Jarvinen, 2000). More recently, studies have shown the utility of peer-report measures of bullying and victimization (Chan, 2006; Kim, Leventhal, Koh, Hubbard, & Boyce, 2006; Ladd & Kochenderfer-Ladd, 2002). The value of peer nomination in research on bullying is illustrated in several studies that will be reviewed briefly here. These studies led to valuable insights into bullying that could not have been obtained from anonymous self-report surveys.

Olweus (1993b) used peer ratings (along with teacher ratings) to identify victims of bullying in a study of the influence of maternal and paternal relationships. He described a group of passive and unassertive boy victims who had close relationships with their mothers and poor identification with their father. In a follow-up study at age 23, these boys were no longer experiencing peer harassment or social isolation, but continued to display relatively high levels of depression and poor self-esteem.

A Korean study (Kim et al., 2006) using the Korean Peer Nomination Inventory (Kim, Koh, Noh, 2001; Kim, Koh, & Leventhal, 2004) examined the causal relationship between bullying and psychopathology as measured by the Korean Youth Self Report (Oh, Hong, & Lee, 1997), using data collected from seventh- and eighth-grade students on two occasions 10 months apart. An extensive series of logistic regression analyses tested competing models and found that symptoms of emotional and behavioral maladjustment were a consequence of being bullied (or bullying others) rather than a contributing factor.

A Canadian study by Chan (2006) asked victims of bullying to name their aggressors. In two schools spanning grades 1–8, 266 victims reported 435 names of bullies. Chan discovered patterns of bullying that have important implications for research and practice. Most notably, he identified 94 students who engaged in serial bullying, defined as bullying more than one victim. The serial bullies not only accounted for nearly 70% of the total victim population, they were also the most likely to engage in physical bullying. Concentrated efforts on these students would be critical to the success of a bullying prevention program.

Thunfors and Cornell (2008) investigated the peer popularity of American middle students identified as bullies or victims. In addition to completing the standard peer nomination form on the SCBS (Cornell & Sheras, 2003), the 379 students (grades 6–8) were asked to identify up to 10 of the most popular boys and girls in their grade. Over the course of the school year, the students identified as bullies by at least two classmates earned lower grades, accrued more discipline violations, and were more likely to be suspended from school than other students. However, bullies received substantially more endorsements as popular students (mean 20.6) than victims (3.6) or other students (12.8). These findings contradicted the stereotype that middle school bullies are social misfits lacking in popularity. In contrast, male and female bullies were among the most popular students at the middle school, despite the fact that the school had been engaged in a schoolwide bullying prevention effort for several years.

Limitations of Peer Reports

Peer reports, like all measures, have methodological strengths and weaknesses. As with self-reports, peer reports require that students understand and apply accurately the definition of bullying. However, the simple advantage of peer report over self-report is that scores are based on multiple informants, which tends to decrease measurement error and yield a more reliable result. Nevertheless, it would be useful to demonstrate that students comprehend the questions used in peer nominations.

Perhaps the most common reservation about peer nomination is concern over asking students to make judgments about one another. Teachers sometimes question whether such an exercise will stimulate teasing or cause anxiety. None of the studies of peer nomination reviewed in this chapter report such problems. There appears to be no published evidence that peer nominations have any harmful side-effects, although this issue may not have been sufficiently investigated.

A related concern is that students may object to reporting the names of classmates because they regard it as "snitching" or "tattling." In these cases, it may be useful to teach students the difference between seeking help to prevent someone from being hurt and informing on someone for personal gain. Student attitudes regarding a peer-report procedure and toward the school's bullying prevention efforts in general are likely an important factor in obtaining complete and accurate results. An evaluation of student reactions to peer nominations would be a useful contribution to the literature.

Solberg and Olweus (2003) objected to the use of peer reports in the assessment of bullying because of the arbitrariness in deciding on the number of nominations or cut-score needed to identify a student as a bully or victim of bullying. They pointed out that optimal cut-off points may differ according to classroom size, whether the survey uses one item or multiple items, and whether students systematically assign ratings to each classmate or nominate students from a list. These are all legitimate technical concerns, but can be addressed through systematic research. Many researchers have devised reliable and valid peer-report measures (Chan, 2006; Eron, Walder, & Lefkowitz, 1971; Kim et al., 2004; Pellegrini, 2001), although perhaps there is a need to compare measures and establish consensus on the most useful approach for assessing the prevalence of bullying.

Comparison of Self- and Peer Reports

There is only moderate correspondence between self- and peer reports, with correlations generally in the range of .14 to .42 (Achenbach, McConaughy, & Howell, 1987; Juvonen, Nishina, & Graham, 2001; Ladd & Kochenderfer-Ladd, 2002; Perry, Kusel, & Perry, 1988). Ladd and Kochenderfer-Ladd (2002) compared self- and peer reports of peer victimization among children in grades K-4, including physical, verbal, and social forms of aggression. They found that concordance between self- and peer reports was virtually 0 at the kindergarten level, but increased with age and reached .50 among fourth-grade students. In a follow-up study with children in grades 2–4, Ladd and Kochenderfer-Ladd (2002) examined the concordance among self, peer, and teacher report measures of child victimization. Once again, they observed increasing levels of concordance in higher grades. For fourth-grade students, self-reports correlated .47 with peer reports and .30 with teacher reports, while peer and teacher reports correlated .47.

Pellegrini (2001) assessed 367 sixth-graders with peer nominations and self-report rating scales (but not self-identification as a victim) from one of the earlier Olweus questionnaires. Trained observers conducted regular observations throughout an entire school year, and each month during the school year students wrote in a diary recounting any victim experiences in the previous 24 hours. The range of correlations among the four measures was .07 to .34. Peer nominations correlated significantly with all three of the other measures (.21 to .32, all $p < .05$), and the Olweus self-report scales correlated .34 with diary entries. Direct observation did not correlate significantly with self-report or the diary measure. This study clearly demonstrates the futility of relying on any single measure of bullying.

Juvonen et al. (2001) argued that self-report and peer-report methods are complementary and assess different constructs, because self-reports capture the student's self-perception—as distinguished from his or her social reputation, which is measured by peer report. Some studies have used both methods and identified students who perceive themselves to be (a) victims who are not perceived as victims by peers, (b) students who do not report themselves to be victims but are perceived as victims by peers, and (c) students who are identified as victims by both self-report and peer-report methods (Crick & Bigbee, 1998; Graham, Bellmore, & Juvonen, 2003; Pellegrini, Bartini, & Brooks, 1999).

Branson and Cornell (2007) compared self-reports with peer nominations in a sample of 355 middle school students. Self-report demonstrated low to moderate correspondence with peer nominations for bullying others ($r = .18$) and for victimization (.32). Despite their limited agreement, both self- and peer-reported bullying were associated with school maladjustment. Students identified as bullies by either method were more likely to endorse aggressive attitudes, make poorer grades in school, and be referred for disciplinary violations than other students. The correlation between peer-reported bullying and disciplinary violations (.52) was significantly larger than the correlation between self-reported bullying and disciplinary violations (.28). However, when both self-report and peer-report scores were entered into multiple regression analyses, both measures made independent, statistically significant contributions to the prediction of aggressive attitudes, grades, and disciplinary violations.

Both self- and peer reports of being a victim of bullying were correlated with self-reported depression, perceptions that school personnel were not responsive to bullying, and lower grades (Branson & Cornell, 2007). The corresponding correlations generated by self-report and peer report did not differ significantly from each other. Furthermore, both measures made independent, statistically significant contributions to the prediction of depression, perceptions of staff responsiveness to bullying, and grades. Branson and Cornell's findings support the use of both self-report and peer report to assess bullying.

Conclusions

The use of anonymous self-report surveys to assess bullying can have a powerful effect on the nature and course of both school interventions and research efforts. If school authorities or researchers choose to measure the baseline prevalence of bullying with an anonymous self-report measure, they may determine the prevalence of bullying, but they will not be able to verify the accuracy of their results because they will not know who is bullying whom. Furthermore, in the absence of knowing who the victims and bullies are, interventions will naturally focus on school rules and curriculum units on bullying. Meanwhile, counselors must wait for bullying to be reported before they can take action. Unfortunately, many students do not seek help for bullying, and teachers often do not detect it (Unnever & Cornell, 2003, 2004).

The peer-nomination method may be especially valuable for school prevention efforts because school personnel can interview specific students who are perceived to be victims and perpetrators of bullying, confirm their involvement, and then take appropriate steps to counsel the students and resolve the problem.

The research reviewed in this chapter raises concerns about the use of anonymous self-report to assess bullying, and recommends greater use of peer report methods. There is support for both methods, and some evidence that they may offer complementary—rather than redundant—information. The field is in need of further research on the accuracy of both methods, using independent criteria to validate reports that a student is a victim or perpetrator of bullying. Perhaps the most critical need is for a gold standard for determining whether a student is involved in bullying. Despite their convenience, neither self-report nor peer report is likely to be satisfactory, because there is no assurance that students are appropriately distinguishing bullying from other forms of peer conflict. Ultimately, self- and peer report must be confirmed by interviewing the participants and witnesses to determine whether actual bullying has occurred (Table 20.1 includes a summary of implications for practice).

Table 20.1 Implications for Practice: Recommendations for the Assessment of Bullying

1. Assessment measures should clearly distinguish bullying from other forms of peer aggression.
2. Instruments used to assess bullying should meet reasonable standards of reliability and validity.
3. Anonymous self report surveys yield limited information that cannot be verified as accurate. Confidential surveys may be adequate to protect student privacy, yet provide verifiable information.
4. Teachers should be well-prepared for survey administration and motivated to engage the students in taking the survey seriously.
5. Student surveys should be screened for careless or exaggerated responding.
6. Peer nominations can be a useful source of information in identifying bullies and victims.

Notes

1. In response to a request for additional information about the BVQ, Olweus replied, in part, "We have made a lot of analyses of the psychometric properties of the Questionnaire in addition to those specified in the 2003 Aggressive Behavior paper but relatively little of that has been published. We have so much involved in the large-scale, government-supported intervention project … that we have simply not had the time to publish but a small portion of our findings.…" (Dan Olweus, personal communication, March 16, 2007).

References

Achenbach, T. M., McConaughy, S. H., & Howell, C. T. (1987). Child/adolescent behavioral and emotional problems: Implications of cross-informant correlations for situational specificity. *Psychological Bulletin, 101,* 213–232.

Ahmad, Y., & Smith, P. K. (1990). Behavioral measures: Bullying in schools. *Newsletter of Association for Child Psychology and Psychiatry, 12,* 26–27.

Beane, A. (1999). *The bully-free classroom.* Minneapolis, MN: Free Spirit Publishing.

Branson, C., & Cornell, D. (2007). *A comparison of self and peer reports in the assessment of middle school bullying.* Unpublished report. University of Virginia, Charlottesville, Virginia.

Chan H. F. J. (2002). *The school life survey — A new instrument for measuring bullying and victimization.* Unpublished doctoral dissertation. University of Hull, UK.

Chan, H. F. J. (2006). Systemic patterns in bullying and victimization. *School Psychology International, 27,* 352–369.

Chan, H. F. J., Myron, R., & Crawshaw, M. (2005). The efficacy of non-anonymous measures of bullying. *School Psychology International, 26,* 443–458.

Cornell, D. G. (2006). *School violence: Fears versus facts.* Hillsdale, NJ: Erlbaum.

Cornell, D. G., & Brockenbrough, K. (2004). Identification of bullies and victims: A comparison of methods. *Journal of School Violence, 3,* 63–87.

Cornell, D. G., & Loper, A. B. (1998). Assessment of violence and other high-risk behaviors with a school survey. *School Psychology Review, 27,* 317–330.

Cornell, D., McDade, L., & Biasiolli, E. (2007). *A comparison of student self-report of bullying and counselor interviews.* Unpublished report. University of Virginia, Charlottesville, Virginia.

Cornell, D., & Sheras, P. (2003). School Climate Bullying Survey. Charlottesville: University of Virginia, Virginia Youth Violence Project.

Cornell, D., Sheras, P., & Cole, J. (2006). Assessment of bullying. In S. R. Jimerson & M. J. Furlong (Eds.), *The handbook of school violence and school safety: From research to practice* (pp. 191–210). Mahwah, NJ: Erlbaum.

Cote, J. A., & Buckley, M. R. (1987). Estimating trait, method, and error variance: Generalizing across seventy construct validation studies. *Journal of Marketing Research, 26,* 315–319.

Crick, N., & Bigbee, M. (1998). Relational and overt forms of peer victimization: A multi-informant approach. *Journal of Consulting and Clinical Psychology, 66,* 337–347.

Cross, J., & Newman-Gonchar, R. (2004). Data quality in student risk behavior surveys and administrator training. *Journal of School Violence, 3,* 89–108.

Eron, L. D., Walder, L. O., & Lefkowitz, M. M. (1971). *Learning of aggression in children.* Boston: Little, Brown.

Eslea, M., Menesini, E., Morita, Y., O'Moore, M., Mora-Merchan, J., Pereira, B., & Smith, P. (2003). Friendship and loneliness among bullies and victims: Data from seven countries. *Aggressive Behavior, 30,* 71–83.

Finkelhor, D., Ormrod, R., Turner, H., & Hamby, S. (2005). The victimization of children and youth: A comprehensive, national survey. *Child Maltreatment, 10,* 5–25.

Furlong, M., Sharkey, J., Bates, M. P., & Smith, D. (2004). An examination of reliability, data screening procedures, and extreme response patterns for the Youth Risk Behavior Surveillance Survey. *Journal of School Violence, 3,* 109–130.

Garrity, C., Jens, K., Porter, W., Sager, N., & Short-Camilli, C. (1994). *Bully-proofing your school.* Longmont, CO: Sopris West.

Graham, S., Bellmore, A., & Juvonen, J. (2003). Peer victimization in middle school: When self and peer views diverge. *Journal of Applied Psychology, 19,* 117–137.

Griffin, R. S., & Gross, A. M. (2004). Childhood bullying: Current empirical findings and future directions for research. *Aggression and Violent Behavior, 9,* 379–400.

Hill, R. W., Zrull, M. C., & McIntire, K. (1998). Differences between self- and peer ratings of interpersonal problems. *Assessment, 5,* 67–83.

Horne, A. M., Bartolomucci, C. L., & Newman-Carlson, D. (2003). *Bully Busters: A teacher's manual for helping bullies, victims, and bystanders* (Grades K-5). Champaign, IL: Research Press.

Huesmann, L., Eron, L., Guerra, N., & Crawshaw, B. (1994). Measuring children's aggression with teachers' predictions of peer nominations. *Psychological Assessment, 6,* 329–336.

Juvonen, J., Nishina, A., & Graham, S. (2001). Self-views versus peer perceptions of victim status among early adolescents. In J. Juvonen & S. Graham (Eds.), *Peer harassment in school: A plight of the vulnerable and victimized* (pp. 105–124). New York: Guilford.

Kim, Y. S., Koh, Y. J., & Leventhal, B.L. (2004). Prevalence of school bullying in Korean middle school students. *Arch Pediatric Adolescent Medicine, 158*, 737–741.

Kim, Y. S., Koh, Y. J., & Noh, J. S. (2001) Development of Korean-Peer Nomination Inventory (K-PNI): An inventory to evaluate school bullying. *Journal of Korean Neuropsychiatry Association, 40*, 867–875.

Kim, Y. S., Leventhal, B. L., Koh, Y. J., Hubbard, A., & Boyce, W. T. (2006). School bullying and youth violence: Causes or consequences of psychopathologic behavior. *Archives of General Psychiatry, 63*, 1035–1041.

Ladd, G. W., & Kochenderfer-Ladd, B. (2002). Identifying victims of peer aggression from early to middle childhood: Analysis of cross-informant data from concordance, estimation of relational adjustment, prevalence of victimization, and characteristics of identified victims. *Psychological Assessment, 14*, 74–96.

Leff, S., Power, T., & Goldstein, A. (2004). Outcome measures to assess the effectiveness of bullying prevention programs in the schools. In D. Espelage & S. Swearer (Eds.), *Bullying in American schools: A social-ecological perspective on prevention and intervention* (pp. 269–293). Mahwah, NJ: Erlbaum.

Nabuzoka, D. (2003). Teacher ratings and peer nominations of bullying and other behavior of children with and without learning difficulties. *Educational Psychology, 23*, 307–321.

Nansel, T., Overpeck, M., Pilla, R., Ruan, W., Simons-Morton, B., & Scheidt, P. (2001). Bullying behaviors among US youth: Prevalence and association with psychosocial adjustment. *American Medical Association, 285*, 2094–2100.

Oh, K. J., Hong, K. E., Lee, H. R. (1997). Korean-Youth Self Report (K-YSR). Seoul, Korea: Jungang Aptitude Research Center.

Olweus, D. (1993a). *Bullying at school: What we know and what we can do.* Oxford: Blackwell.

Olweus, D. (1993b). Victimization by peers: Antecedents and long-term outcomes. In K. H. Rubin & J. B. Asendorf (Eds.), *Social withdrawal, inhibition, and shyness in childhood* (pp. 315–341). Hillsdale, NJ: Erlbaum.

Olweus, D. (1996). The Revised Olweus Bully/Victim Questionnaire. Bergen, Norway: Mimeo, Research Center for Health Promotion (HEMIL), University of Bergen.

Olweus, D. (1999). Norway. In P. K. Smith, Y. Morita, J. Junger-Tas, D. Olweus, R. Catalano, & P. Slee (Eds.), *The nature of school bullying: A cross-national perspective* (pp. 28–48). New York: Routledge.

Olweus, D. (2002). *General information about the Revised Olweus Bully/Victim Questionnaire, PC program and teacher handbook* (pp. 1–12). Bergen, Norway: Mimeo, Research Center for Health Promotion (HEMIL), University of Bergen.

O'Malley, P. M., Johnston, L. D., Bachman, J. G., & Schulenberg, J. E. (2000). A comparison of confidential versus anonymous survey procedures: Effects on reporting of drug use and related attitudes and beliefs in a national study of students. *Journal of Drug Issues, 30*, 35–54.

Pakaslahti, L., & Keltikangas-Jarvinen, L. (2000). Comparison of peer, teacher and self-assessments on adolescent direct and indirect aggression. *Educational Psychology, 20*, 177–190

Pellegrini, A. D. (2001). Sampling instances of victimization in middle school: A methodological comparison. In J. Juvonen & S. Graham (Eds.), *Peer harassment in school: The plight of the vulnerable and victimized* (pp. 125–146). New York: Guilford.

Pellegrini, A. D., Bartini, M., & Brooks, F. (1999). School bullies, victims, and aggressive victims: Factors relating to group affiliation and victimization in early adolescence. *Journal of Educational Psychology, 91*, 216–224.

Perry, D., Kusel, S., & Perry, L. (1988). Victims of peer aggression. *Developmental Psychology, 24*, 807–814.

Podsakoff, P. M., MacKenzie, S. B., Lee, J. Y., & Podsakoff, N. P. (2003). Common method biases in behavioral research: A critical review of the literature and recommended remedies. *Journal of Applied Psychology, 88*, 879–903.

Rosenblatt, J. A., & Furlong, M. J. (1997). Assessing the reliability and validity of student self-reports of campus violence. *Journal of Youth and Adolescence, 26*, 187–202.

Smith, D., & Ananiadou, K. (2003). The nature of school bullying and the effectiveness of school-based interventions. *Journal of Applied Psychoanalytic Studies, 5*, 189–209.

Solberg, M., & Olweus, D. (2003). Prevalence estimation of school bullying with the Olweus Bully/Victim Questionnaire. *Aggressive Behavior, 29*, 239–268.

Thunfors, P., & Cornell, D. (2008). The popularity of middle school bullies. *Journal of School Violence, 7*, 65–82.

Unnever J., & Cornell, D. (2003). The culture of bullying in middle school. *Journal of School Violence, 2*, 5–27.

Unnever, J., & Cornell, D. (2004). Middle school victims of bullying: Who reports being bullied? *Aggressive Behavior, 30*, 373–388.

Weiss, B., Harris, V., & Catron, T. (2004). Development and initial validation of the peer-report measure of internalizing and externalizing behavior. *Journal of Abnormal Child Psychology, 30*, 285–294.

21

Scales and Surveys

Some Problems with Measuring Bullying Behavior

JAMES A. BOVAIRD

Bullying and associated behaviors are a growing problem at all levels of development. Typically, establishing whether or not an incidence of bullying or associated behavior (i.e., victimization, relational aggression, physical aggression, etc.) has occurred in a school setting is not inherently problematic, but once the behavior is detected, determining the level, severity, or prevalence of the behavior is not so straightforward. In addition, something must be done to change or eliminate the negative behaviors, resulting in the need to be able to accurately determine whether behavior has truly been changed. Thus, a considerable amount of research in school bullying involves determining the *level* of behavior and assessing *change* in behaviors at the individual student level. This can be as straightforward as determining that a student engaged in a pattern of negative behavior deemed to constitute bullying, and following corrective disciplinary action or re-education, the student's pattern of negative behavior was altered in a positive direction. In a broader prevention context, determining the level of and change in bullying behavior may involve a pre-post quasi-experimental design where the behavior is detected as generally present in a sample of students, some intervention is applied, and the level of the behavior is re-assessed. In other developmental contexts, researchers or practitioners may be interested in tracking changes in behavior over a period of time in order to determine the overall natural pattern of the behavior.

While conducting an intervention-based or observational longitudinal study may seem straightforward, the measurement properties of the assessment tools employed are often overlooked. Following the framework of the five W's and one H (i.e., who, what, where, when, how and, most importantly, why), this chapter will focus on the issues researchers and practitioners face in establishing measurement properties for measures of bullying and associated behaviors and their implications for the assessment of level and change in longitudinal contexts.

Who Is Conducting the Measurement?

Assessment of bullying behavior is typically conducted through the perspective of the self, peers, or persons in a position of authority such as parents, teachers, or administrators. However, measurement can vary as a function of who is doing the responding. Just as there is a degree of variability in the operational definition of bullying, there is variability in the measurement modality, where the results of the measurement process may vary as a function of who is doing the measuring. Shadish, Cook, and Campbell (2002) refer to this as a mono-method bias. As a threat to internal validity, mono-method bias suggests that all operationalizations that use the same method (peer or teacher nominations, self-report, etc.) risk that the method will become part of the construct being studied. So rather than the construct being operationalized as "bullying," it is more accurately operationalized as "peer perceptions of bullying," which may be distinct from "self-reported bullying." Several researchers have investigated the concordance between multiple informants, with varying degrees of agreement even among themselves (see Peets & Kikas, 2006; Graham, Bellmore, & Juvonen, 2003; Cornell & Brockenbrough, 2004; Tomada & Schneider, 1997; Swearer, Bovaird, Buhs, & Givens, 2007).

What Is Being Measured?

The first step in measuring any behavior is identifying a clear and implementable operational definition. A number of authors (e.g., Sveinsson & Morris, 2007; Tremblay, 2000; Underwood, 2003) have suggested that appropriately operationalizing bullying and related behaviors such as aggression is a fundamental problem in assessing such behaviors. Aggression itself is a multi-faceted construct with a long history and a broad set of subtypes that have at least two common features: (a) an intent to harm on the part of the aggressor and (b) a feeling of hurt on the part of the victim. As a subset of aggressive behavior, bullying is often used interchangeably with aggression, but is perhaps best viewed as proactive aggression (Espelage & Swearer, 2003).

While some researchers may argue that there is no clear operational definition of bullying (e.g., Rigby, Smith, & Pepler, 2004), other researchers (e.g., Espelage & Swearer, 2003) support Olweus' (1995) assertion that any definition of bullying consists of three primary components: behavior is aggressive and negative, it is carried out repeatedly, and the relationship is characterized by an imbalance of power. Olweus (1994) defined bullying as "a negative action when someone intentionally inflicts, or attempts to inflict, injury or discomfort upon another" (p. 1173). Olweus further stated that bullying involves an imbalance of strength and the behavior is repeated over time. There are more recent definitions that are also consistent with a three-component structure (see VandenBos, 2007). Discrepancies in the definition of bullying behavior and variability in the measurement methodologies used (including which or how many informants)—both major contributors to variability in how the latent construct is operationalized—can have profound effects on the perceived salience of the bullying phenomenon. For instance, Espelage and Swearer reported that prevalence rates of bullying vary depending on the definition of bullying and the researcher's methodology. While a thorough review of the relevant literature attempting to establish a strong operational definition of bullying or aggression is not intended, the following sections will discuss some of the measurement issues raised by the general two- (aggression) and three-component (bullying) operational definition structure.

Where Does the Measurement Occur?

A common modality for assessing bullying is the use of nomination inventories (see Perry, Williard, & Perry, 1990) where teachers or peers indicate who they perceive as engaging in bullying or victimization. Variations on the basic nomination procedure involve use of a roster where students or teachers are prompted to indicate which students from a list of students engaged in the behavior (see Perry et al., 1990), or the use of an open nomination process where students or teachers are asked to write down the names of any students they can think of that engaged in the behavior (see Swearer et al., 2007).

A common consideration in school-based research is the issue of nesting, most often in classrooms. For instance, students within the same classroom are more likely to be similar in their performance than students in different classrooms due to the hierarchical influence of the classroom context including teacher, social, and dynamic influences. While social and behavioral outcomes may be considered less-influenced by classroom nesting, the fundamental problem may still be a viable consideration. In the context of school-based bullying and related behaviors, such behaviors are most likely not influenced by teachers as much as they are social groupings. While the statistics vary in terms of the overall prevalence of bullying and victimization during the school years, at least one study suggests that up to 76.8% of students experience involvement in bullying at some point (Hoover, Oliver, & Hazler, 1992). However, bullying and victimization are behaviors engaged in or experienced by a minority (less than 50%) of students at a given period of time. For example, Nansel et al. (2001) found that 29.9% of the students reported moderate to frequent involvement in bullying behavior. Thirteen percent of students in the study reported involvement as a bully, 10.6% reported involvement as a victim, and 6.3% indicated they were both a perpetrator and victim of bullying behavior. When making nominations, whether of peers or of students, the ability to successfully designate a student as being engaged in a specific and relatively infrequent behavior will be influenced by which students the teacher/peer regularly comes into contact with.

In earlier grades, where the classroom provides a strong boundary to a student's school-based social context, nesting children within classrooms is likely an appropriate consideration. As students progress through the grades, however, the boundaries of their social groups expand and intermingle. With older school-aged children, it may be more appropriate to consider social cliques (Kwon & Lease, 2007, for example) or activity-based groupings (teams, clubs, music ensembles, etc.). A potential problem with nomination procedures with older children is that students who engage in bullying or victimization behaviors in more public forums (hallways, lunch room, recess, etc.) are more likely to be nominated than students who are equally engaged in the behaviors but are more subtle in the visibility of their expressions as in name-calling, gossiping, or exclusion from activities. In contrast, classroom rosters may limit the extent to which a student can be nominated, resulting in a type of ceiling effect.

When Does the Measurement Occur?

With the exception of direct observation by the researcher or interventionist who is collecting the data or is in a position to directly and immediately affect change in the offending individual's behavior, research into and reporting of bullying behavior requires retrospective measurement. That is, either the person who engaged in the negative behavior (self-reported bully) or someone who experienced or otherwise witnessed the behavior's occurrence (i.e., victim or bystander, respectively) must rely on a subjective autobiographical memory of the behavior's occurrence. Even an informant who did not directly witness or engage in the behavior first-hand but rather learned of the behavior's occurrence through a second-hand source must rely on an autobiographical memory to recall their knowledge of the behavior. Such memories are known to be unreliable and thus fallible to varying extents.

Autobiographical Memory

Cognitive psychology suggests that human memory is both *reconstructive* in that it involves using a variety of strategies for retrieving the original experiential memory traces to then rebuild, or reconstruct, the original experiences as a basis for the memory retrieval process (see

Kolodner, 1983), as well as *constructive* in that it allows for prior experiences to affect both how prior experiences are recalled and what can actually be recalled (Grant & Ceci, 2000).

Of particular relevance to school-based study of bullying and related behaviors is the reliance on *autobiographical memory*, or the memory of one's individual history, for measurement. Autobiographical memory is constructive in that individuals do not always remember exactly what has happened to them. Rather, people tend to remember their construction or reconstruction of what has happened in the past. More often than may be ideal, not all reported behaviors were directly observed by the person doing the reporting. Rather, reports are based on a combination of direct personal involvement as the bully, victim, bystander, etc. or through secondhand reports and even gossip. In the event that the person reporting the behavior did not personally experience the behavior, their memory of how they learned about the behavioral event becomes relevant. Generally speaking, though, autobiographical memory is considered to be quite accurate, but it is still subject to distortions.

Memory Distortions

Given the variability in serial positioning of time frames in independent studies and the length of the time frames used ("past 30 days," "this semester," etc.), it is plausible that a respondent's ability to reliably measure bullying is dependent upon distorted memories. Cognitive psychologists have repeatedly demonstrated a serial-position effect where the initial and most recent events are remembered most clearly. Given that bullying behaviors may have increased prevalence during certain phases of the school year as social networks develop and expand, the timing of the assessment relative to key temporal phases may capitalize on serial-position effects related to the timing of the school year. Some research even suggests that such phenomena may vary as a function of developmental phases (Rubin, 1996).

Roediger and McDermott (2000), among others, have found that people do tend to distort their memories. As an example, the simple act of verbalizing that something has happened to you, such as a student recounting a bullying occurrence to their friends, makes that student more likely to think it really did happen despite what the truth may be (Ackil & Zaragoza, 1998). Schacter (2001) presented "seven sins of memory," or ways in which memory distortions tend to occur. Five[1] of these distortions are decidedly relevant to the bullying construct. First, memories are *transient* in that the more time that has elapsed since the event in question, the more and faster the memory fades. The *blocking* distortion may be particularly relevant to the use of peer or teacher nominations to identify bullying behavior, as the respondent may know that a student did in fact engage in bullying-related behavior, but their ability to correctly recall who was the aggressor or the victim may be impaired or distorted.

Flash-bulb effects are another robust memory effect suggesting that people tend to better-remember events with personal significance or salience over less important events. If the student is currently experiencing a bullying event, he or she may be more likely to remember when they were bullied in the past, at the expense of when they may have been the aggressor; or memory of those relevant events may be magnified regardless of the salience of the actual experience (the *bias* distortion). Hearing through gossip or other second-hand reports of another student's participation in bullying may lead to incidence of the *suggestibility* distortion. Similarly, seeing a name listed on a nomination roster may lead respondents to think they directly saw or heard something, making them more likely to believe they actually did observe or experience it. Likewise, if someone thinks they saw or heard something, they are more susceptible to believing they actually did. Relatedly, according to the *misattribution* distortion, individuals cannot accurately remember the context where they experienced a particularly memory. Rather, they tend to remember what they think makes sense with what they remember experiencing rather than what was actually experienced. Misattribution, susceptibility, and suggestibility are particularly relevant to the reliability and validity of eyewitness memories.

Eyewitness Memory

Eyewitness memory research (e.g., Loftus, 1977) has shown that individuals have a great susceptibility to memory distortions in eyewitness accounts. People sometimes even think they remember things simply because they have imagined or thought about them (Garry & Loftus, 1994). Wells (1993) has shown how line-ups (similar to nomination rosters in the bullying context) can lead to faulty conclusions, because respondents assume that the perpetrator (bully) is in the line-up. Bothwell, Brigham, and Malpass (1989) have also shown that eyewitness memory is particularly weak when the witness is identifying a perpetrator who is of a different race or ethnicity.

While the validity of eyewitness memories at any age is debated in the cognitive literature, the eyewitness memories of children have been shown to be clearly suspect. Ceci and Bruck (1993) have shown that children are particularly susceptible to memory distortions, especially when asked leading questions. Ceci and Bruck have shown that the younger the children, the less reliable their testimony has been found to be. When the questioner is coercive or appears insistent on a particular answer, children of all ages are quite susceptible to providing answers the adult wants to hear.

How Is Bullying Being Measured?

In general, there are three basic formats for assessing bullying-related behavior. The first format is a rating scale, often said to be of the Likert type. This category also includes any other quantitative "continuous" measures of the relative degree of behavior that have a basic assumption of an underlying continuum most often referred to as the "normal" curve. The response set then represents a range of trait levels ordered from low to high where there always remains the conceptual potential for a score more extreme than the most extreme score observed (higher or lower). This format is consistent with determining the definitional component that a behavior is aggressive and negative in order to constitute bullying. This format would also be appropriate for assessing both the intent to harm and feeling hurt components of aggression definitions.

A second measurement format consists of a qualitative binary (two response options) response format such as true/false questions or checklists where an endorsement constitutes the presence of the behavior, trait, event, etc., and the absence of endorsement indicates the absence of the behavior. Examples of this type would include single direct observations or reports of behavior ("I bully others"—yes/no), or nomination forms where the respondent indicates whether or not they have observed the listed individuals engaging in the targeted behavior(s). This format might also be useful in determining the expression of specific bullying behaviors using a yes/no response as on a checklist (i.e., "they make fun of people," "they hit other kids," and "they get called names by other kids"). An extension of this format type would be polytomous (three or more response option) nominal structures that could be used in determining the student's role in bullying behavior (i.e., bully, victim, bystander, no involvement).

The third format consists of frequency counts of a target behavior. Whereas frequencies are considered continuous quantitative measures, they are distinct from rating scales in that they have a true lower limit at zero. Regardless of the actual incidence rates of bullying and victimization, a substantial portion of any population or sample does not exhibit the behavior, or rarely does so, thus the frequency is at or near zero. This type of data is non-normal by definition and subject to different statistical considerations. A frequency of occurrence format is appropriate for operationalizing the repeated nature of bullying behaviors and for counting either the number of individuals nominated or the number of times an individual is nominated.

Why Does Measurement Matter?

The choice of measurement format, complexity of the construct's operational definition, nature of the informant(s), and both internal (memory distortions) and external (classrooms or peer groups) contextual limitations interact to create a complicated set of methodological decisions that must be made by the researcher. As the following sections illustrate, such methodological decisions can have important measurement implications that, in turn, may have inadvertent effects upon the inference made from and ultimate generalizability of findings.

The observation of bullying and its associated behaviors is frequently discussed as *testing* or *assessment*, yet such actions refer to the process of sampling such behaviors. Behavioral sampling is usually accomplished by using an instrument such as a *scale, survey, test*, or *questionnaire* to obtain quantitative information about a set of related individual behaviors. While some bullying behaviors such as the act of striking the victim can be precisely measured with a single measurement if the action was directly observed or accurately reported, most bullying-related behaviors are much harder to directly observe or are much more complex, requiring multiple observations—often called *items, questions*, or *indicators*—to accurately triangulate, or capture, the level of the targeted behavior. This chapter will generically refer to behavioral observations as indicators inclusive of observations from peer or teacher nominations, self-report rating scales, or direct behavioral observations.

Quantification of multiple behaviors through use of an instrument requires the observation of multiple participants to determine the full range of behavior and requires a clear and definitive set of rules for associating numeric information with the actual observation. *Measurement* then is the means of assigning meaning to the numbers that are used to differentiate levels of behavior. A growing body of psychometric research suggests that assessment in general, and particularly the assessment of change, can be very susceptible to the measurement properties of the assessment tools used (e.g., Bovaird & Embretson, 2008; Embretson, 2007; Leite, 2007; Meade, Lautenschlager, & Hecht, 2005).

Scales of Measurement

The numerical representation of an observable behavior requires a clear and definitive rule for associating one and only one number with the magnitude of an individual's construct level. Given a sample O of N distinct participants, any participant can be assigned a true score $t(o_i)$. A procedure is then devised for pairing each participant o_i with its imprecise numerical measurement, $m(o_i)$. While the goal of measurement is to devise a procedure that minimizes the discrepancy between the true score $t(o_i)$ and the measurement $m(o_i)$, the potential for imprecision exists due to measurement error from both systematic (i.e., observer bias) and random (i.e., present emotional state) sources. Depending on the amount of information each contains relating the true score $t(o_i)$ and the measurement $m(o_i)$, measurement scales can be traditionally classified as one of four scales of measurement: nominal, ordinal, interval, or ratio (Stevens, 1946). As the names suggest, nominal scales contain only categorical information for distinguishing individuals from one another. Ordinal scales add a specific ordering to the discrete categorical information of a nominal variable, but it cannot be said by how much the categories truly differ.

Interval scales not only have distinct ordered categories, but the distances between categories have a metric and inherent meaning allowing arithmetic operations. Finally, ratio scales anchor the interval metric with a true zero point that indicates an absence of the characteristic. Interval and ratio scales are often classified as continuous data, and nominal and ordinal scales can be further classified as categorical data. Appropriate consideration of bullying data requires identification of the correct scale of measurement and the characteristics of the broader measurement context with which the measurement rules were derived.

Observed versus Latent

While bullying is an observable external behavior, more often than not, bullying is not directly observed. Instead, measurement relies on "direct" assessments such as questionnaires, scales, surveys, and self-reports or "indirect" assessments such as nominations or office referrals to both assess the degree of the behavior and even the identity of those exhibiting the behavior. In addition, bullying is not a single behavior, but rather a collection of three associated components—aggressive negative behavior, repetition, and involving a power imbalance—with temporal and frequency components that must be summarized. In addition, bullying is often assessed by more than one informant (peer, teacher, and/or self). Combining the difficulty of direct observation with its multi-component nature, bullying behavior can and must be considered a latent construct. The latent nature raises the issue of how bullying is scaled and how such behavior(s) is measured.

According to true score theory (Novick, 1966), given the assignment of an imprecise numerical measurement, $m(o_i)$, to each of N distinct participants of sample O, the deviation of the measurement from its true score, $t(o_i)$, can be attributed to measurement error, $e(o_i)$. The true score, $t(o_i)$, is assumed a fixed quantity, or constant, while the observable measurement, $m(o_i)$, and the imprecision of that measurement, $e(o_i)$, are assumed to be random values that vary from measurement occasion to measurement occasion. While the true score is assumed fixed, it is not directly observable, and so by definition is latent.

The Optimal Number of Indicators   The ability to adequately measure a latent variable depends on the number of behavioral observations that are made. In the event that only one measurement of a behavior occurs, it is impossible to separate out the relative contributions of true score and error to the observation, despite the fact that the existence (but not necessarily the extent) of measurement imprecision is often known and acknowledged. However, if there is more than one measurement of the same behavior, then there is the opportunity to begin to triangulate the relative contributions of true score and error by assuming that any variance shared between the two or more observations is attributable to the latent construct (true score) and the residual variance is measurement error. With three or more measurements of the same behavior it is then possible to distinguish the unobserved contributions of the latent construct, measurement error, and the relative quality of each individual measurement. For these reasons, the consensus among psychometricians is that a minimum of three observations is necessary to adequately measure a latent construct (see Little, Lindenberger, & Nesselroade, 1999). The top panels of Figure 21.1 illustrate these points. A more detailed explanation related to the identification of latent variables is available in Bollen (1989).

Formative versus Reflective Measurement   Once a set of representative behaviors has been identified, ideally three or more, the theoretical model underlying the nature of the latent construct must be considered. The bottom panels of Figure 21.1 pictorially represent the

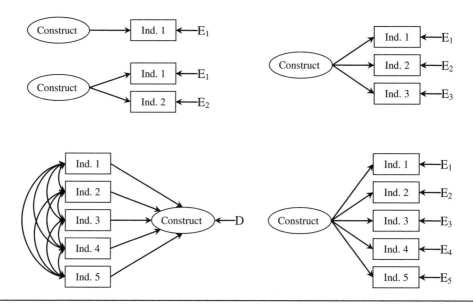

Figure 21.1 Five path diagrams illustrating the differences in available information based on the number of observations (i.e. indicators (Ind.)) measuring the latent construct and the causal directions involved in formative (bottom left) versus reflective (bottom right) measurement models. The construct reflects the true score, $t(o)$, and error terms (i.e. E_k) reflect the imprecision, $e(o)$, of a given measurement $m(o)$.

distinction between a formative measurement model and a reflective one. The bottom left panel demonstrates a construct that is "caused" by the measured variables. Since the measured behaviors are exogenous (external) to the factor, they are deemed cause or formative indicators. In formative measurement, any of a number of different combinations of behavior observations can lead to the same construct "score." There is no separation between true score and error for any of the measured variables, thus there is an assumption that all measurement has been accomplished with perfect reliability. All observations may be correlated, or they may not, but as exogenous predictors, the causal explanation for why they may be correlated is unanalyzed.

The bottom right-hand panel of Figure 21.1 demonstrates reflective measurement where the measured variable is assumed to be caused by the construct. Here the endogenous (internal) observations are referred to as effect or reflective indicators. Because the factor predicts the observed behavior, the model allows for imperfect prediction, or measurement error. In reflective measurement, the observable behaviors must be correlated as they are presumed to be manifestations of the same fundamental behavior, and the existence of the factor provides an explanatory mechanism for why the correlated behaviors occur. Reflective theories of measurement are very common in the social and behavioral sciences and education, especially in the context of ability or achievement testing.

A reflective operationalization of a latent bullying construct would require a presumption that bullying behavior does indeed exist, and therefore the ability to systematically observe its manifestations in terms of observable behavior as well. All individuals who have high levels of bullying behavior would be expected to manifest the same degree of aggression, engage in the negative behavior a similar number of times, and achieve a similarly superior position in terms of the power imbalance. Such behaviors should also be observable to similar degrees regardless of the informant (self, peer, or teacher). The degree to which multiple informants are non-congruous is then the extent to which a reflective operationalization may be less appropriate than a formative operationalization.

Formative measurement is also common in the social and behavioral sciences, but less frequently identified as such. A formative operationalization of bullying would allow for any two individuals to obtain the same level of the construct, but through different pathways or profiles. That is, one individual may be less aggressive, more repetitive, but achieve only a minor superior position, and do so in a very public forum like the school playground (i.e., repetitive name-calling); while another individual may be very aggressive, establishing a very dominant position, but engage in the behavior only a small number of times out of sight of the general populace (i.e., a fight away from school grounds). In both scenarios, the perpetrator may be measured equivalently in terms of the latent bully "score."

Classical versus Modern Test Theory

The theory of a common factor, or true score theory, is closely related to the framework for considering the psychometric properties of an instrument referred to as classical test[2] theory (CTT). CTT is often presented as in competition with another framework for considering the psychometric properties of instruments, item response theory (IRT), but both are most appropriate for use with a reflective measurement model and less so with a formative operationalization. The interested reader is referred to Bovaird and Embretson (2008) for an historical overview and contrasting of CTT and IRT.

The major hallmark of CTT is that as its name suggests, it is a test-level framework rather than one that focuses on individual examinee behavior. The only explicit assumptions made by the paradigm are that the distribution of measurement error is "normal" with a zero-mean and that measurement error has no relationship with any other variables, observed or latent. It's computational efficiency has made it extremely popular among applied researchers. In fact, anytime a scale score is constructed by summing or averaging responses, determining the number or proportion correct/endorsed/nominated, or otherwise comparing an obtained score to a set of reference norms, CTT is being utilized. The CTT index of score reliability—internal consistency (Cronbach, 1951)—is one of the most frequently reported statistics in support of the quality of testing outcomes.

CTT is considered to be fairly accurate when indicators provide continuous interval-level or Likert-type rating scale data, but is known to produce several shortcomings when applied to categorical (dichotomous or polytomous) or frequency count data. Three major problems arise from implementing a linear approximation appropriate for interval-level data on a non-linear system as with categorical and frequency count data. The first major problem introduced by applying CTT to categorical data is that the use of categorical outcomes requires the transition from thinking of the outcome as being measured on a continuous scale that extends infinitely in either direction to a system governed by the probability that a particular response will be made, and thus bounded by 0 and 1. With frequency counts, there is a fixed lower boundary of 0, but the upper boundary may be infinite. All the while, the latent construct is still considered to be latently measured on a continuous scale. CTT allows that respondents located towards the tails of the latent distribution may be predicted to have a probability that is out of bounds. The second major problem with CTT on categorical data is that the error variance cannot be considered independent of true score variance. This is especially the case with binary or dichotomous responses but also true for count outcomes and ordinal responses. Third, CTT makes the assumption that error variance is constant over all levels of the latent construct which is not a realistic assumption. In light of these limitations, item factor analysis (Bock, Gibbons, & Muraki, 1988) is one alternative, as is considering a nonlinear factor model such as IRT.

While CTT makes no explicit assumptions, IRT, sometimes referred to as modern test theory, makes two strong assumptions. First, local independence suggests that all respondents have a true score on at least one latent dimension that can explain performance resulting in independent observed responses. Second, the relationship between performance and the latent construct has a specific form. Most IRT models are generalizations of a fundamental generalized mixed model where the probability function is assumed to be logistic rather than normal due to the typical binary nature of the indicator data (see De Boeck & Wilson, 2004). Because IRT relies so strongly on modeling and the associated assumptions, IRT models are subject to model fit and are falsifiable (Embretson & Reise, 2000).

In contrast to CTT, IRT places the emphasis on individual behavior in the sense of the individual indicator response. Its purpose is to define an *item response function* based on a logistic function that maximizes the relationship between examinee and indicator characteristics (i.e., parameters) and the likelihood that a given response will be made. Behavior (response) then is a joint function of examinee location on the construct and indicator characteristics. By explicitly modeling indicator characteristics, indicators are allowed to vary in their centrality or typicality to the construct, usually referred to as difficulty in testing terms, and in their quality or relationship with the construct, referred to as discrimination. Ideally, an instrument has a set of indicators that broadly reflect the breadth of the construct, and all indicators provide strong discrimination in terms of being able to separate respondents.

The conceptual differences between CTT and IRT lead to a practical difference in terms of the frameworks' applicability to bullying research as well as all other areas of inquiry. CTT, by focusing on the test-level, implies that a researcher's explanatory ability is at the construct level since the focal point is the computed total score. That is, individual differences in the bullying construct can be explained, but not in terms of the expression or exhibition of individual behaviors that are presumed indicative of bullying behavior. In contrast, IRT, as an item-level framework, uses the presumption of the existence of a bullying construct as one means to help explain why certain bullying behaviors are exhibited but not others or exhibited to varying degrees of frequency. By disentangling the discrimination ability of construct indicators (i.e., the relationship between the indicator and the construct) from their "difficulty" or location on the trait (i.e., the relative frequency of expression or typicality), IRT allows that while all observable bullying behaviors may be equally important (or not) to the theoretical construction of the bullying construct (i.e., discrimination), some observable behaviors are more commonly expressed or more typical than others (i.e., difficulty or location). The following sections further illustrate the practical differences between IRT and CTT in terms of establishing the desirable properties of tests or measures of bullying, the implications to measuring change in a construct, and threats to the internal validity of inferences made about bullying behavior and its prevention.

Properties of Tests

Any measurement, whether scaled through CTT or IRT, should reflect four fundamental properties. A measure should be attainable through a *standardized* method of test administration, yielding scores with a *meaningful* metric that are both *reliable* and *valid*. Bovaird and Embretson (2008) present a number of benefits to considering IRT scaling in light of the four desirable properties of measures. For instance, IRT makes advanced testing modalities such as computer-based testing and computer-adaptive testing possible (Weiss, 1982). IRT also makes it possible for items to be generated on-the-fly and makes it possible to develop measures from cognitive principles (Embretson, 1998).

IRT is generally considered to have an *invariance* property whereas CTT scores are administration- and sample-specific. That is, CTT-derived summed scores can only be compared among respondents from the same sample who were given the same scale form. Under IRT, because the indicator characteristics are model parameters and thus considered population parameters (assuming calibration from a representative sample), different samples of respondents may be administered different forms of the instrument and their scores are directly comparable (see Embretson & Reise, 2000). The IRT invariance property makes comparing groups or subgroups much more meaningful through differential item functioning (DIF; Lord, 1980) and better facilitates the comparison of measures of the same trait and the measurement of change through linking and/or equating (Cook & Eignor, 1983).

The most compelling advantage of IRT over CTT is in regards to reliability. The most common CTT index of reliability—Cronbach's (1951) coefficient alpha—provides a single convenient index for all participants; however, its accuracy as a measure of reliability has been brought into question. If the construct space is multidimensional rather than unidimensional, Cronbach's alpha tends to be an overestimate of construct reliability, while the presence of non-parallel measures leads it to be an underestimate (Raykov, 1997). Alternatively, IRT focuses on indicator (and instrument) information, or how well an indicator (or instrument) differentiates among participants at a given level of the latent construct. This allows for error variances to vary as a function of the construct. This much more realistic scenario allows for different participants to be measured with differing levels of precision.

It is generally acknowledged that the correlation between an IRT-derived construct score and a CTT-derived summed score is usually very high ($r > .90$). IRT's allowance for differential precision across levels of the construct further allows IRT to provide better discrimination among participants in the extreme ranges of the construct. In addition, CTT has been shown to provide scaling problems for a number of fundamental research questions to be discussed in the next section.

Scaling's Impact on Change

Traditional statistical and modeling techniques that assess change in a construct over time such as ANOVA, regression, and path analysis suffer from restrictive assumptions, such as the sphericity of variances, independence of residuals, and the ever-present issue of unreliable measures (Rogosa & Willett, 1983). For these reasons, latent growth modeling tends to be the recommended framework (Little, Bovaird, & Slegers, 2006). While a thorough review of traditional methods or growth curve modeling is beyond the scope of this chapter, the interested reader is directed to Little and colleagues for a comprehensive review. Regardless of the analytic procedure used to determine the statistical robustness of observed behaviors or differences in behavior, the inference made depends on the framework used to scale the observations.

Bereiter (1963) indicated three basic problems with using a simple CTT-based difference score to indicate change: a paradoxical relationship between the test-retest correlation and the reliability of the change score, the initial score correlates negatively with the change score, and the lack of consistency in interpretability of the change score at different points in the distribution. A fourth problem is whether the change score actually reflects change due to a condition or is simple error (Embretson, 1998). All four problems can be addressed by a combination of IRT and the use of growth curve modeling (see Embretson & Reise, 2000).

Impact of Arbitrary Metrics

Blanton and Jaccard (2006) suggested that arbitrary metrics such as sample- and form-dependent CTT scores have little impact on research findings, yet this position is counter to a growing body of psychometric literature. In contrast, Embretson (2006) argues that research findings are not immune to scaling artifacts, and in fact are very susceptible to proper scaling through non-arbitrary metrics. The majority of the problems identified to date deal with the nature of the relationship between the latent construct and its observable measures. Maxwell and Delaney (1985) suggested that two groups with equal true/latent group means can differ significantly in observed means if observed scores are not linearly related to true scores. When outcome measures are inherently non-normal (i.e., Poisson, censored, binary, etc.)—this is violated by definition. Embretson (1996) found that a factorial ANOVA may yield a spurious interaction with raw CTT-derived summary scores when no latent interaction exists, due to a nonlinear relationship between raw and latent scores. Additionally, Embretson found the greatest accurate mean differences occur for populations for which scale-difficulty or centrality is most appropriate. That is, a scale containing indicators of bullying that are representative of individuals who are highly engaged in the behavior given to a sample who are highly engaged in bullying yields the greatest true comparison. Embretson (1994, 2007) also found that group comparisons of change and trend are impacted by a nonlinear relationship between observed and latent scores, where the group (gender designation, intervention group, etc.) that changes the most is the one for which the scale-sample match is most appropriate.

Embretson (2007) further looked at gain (change) scores, also finding that the largest accurate gains were observed for populations with best scale-sample match. Embretson moreover found through simulation methods that while there were also significant differences (and nontrivial effect sizes) observed between scales scores where there was not an adequate scale-sample match, the true/latent gains were in fact equal. Embretson also suggested that longitudinal trend studies will be negatively impacted by the mismatch between the examinee characteristics and the scale properties. That is, if the nature of the construct changes from grade to grade, even subtly in terms of which aspects of bullying behavior are more or less central to the latent construct, and the scale is constant, then the scale-sample match changes as well.

Davison and Sharma (1990) reported that relationships found for observed scores will also hold for latent variables, but both Type I and Type II error levels and power may not be so fortunate, indicating an impact on the inferential decision-making process. While not explicitly studied, this was also reflected in the reported research highlighting the dilemmas presented by nonlinear relationships between the latent and observed variables and the mismatch between scale properties and participant characteristics. In those cases where inflated mean differences were observed, the Type I error rate would be inflated, and underestimation of the true latent differences would result in Type II error inflation.

Threats to Internal Validity

While external validity is the aspect of validity most often associated with psychometrics, a number of measurement and research design characteristics can interact to have a significant impact on the internal validity of inferences or disciplinary actions taken as a result of a bullying investigation. Careful consideration of a number of the common threats to internal validity (see Shadish et al., 2002) is warranted when considering latent variable measurement models as the latent variable serves as an exogenous explanatory mechanism for observed behavior under the preferred reflective measurement model. Several threats to internal validity have been alluded to previously in this chapter, but this section will reinforce their relevance.

Longitudinal bullying research can be susceptible to *history effects* caused by an event outside the study that co-occurs with the construct rather than the construct itself. For instance, a number of longitudinal investigations rely upon cohort designs to maximize the amount of data collected, but cohort studies are particularly susceptible to school or district policies that change between academic years such as the implementation or re-emphasis of zero-tolerance policies. Interventions and other initiatives intended to curb the prevalence of bullying behavior also tend to occur in conjunction with the new school year, as do changes in school administrations. Significant fights or other notable widespread events can also tend to alter the within-year social dynamics but do not persist year-to-year. Additionally, just as the types of problems that exemplify math academic performance change from grade to grade, the types of behavior that exemplify bullying may also change based on age and grade. Certain manifestations of bullying behavior may change prevalence rates over the course of the academic year as well. Such *maturation effects* can be handled psychometrically through scale equating or linking made possible through IRT. General *attrition* obviously can also have significant impacts on the measurement of bullying behaviors. A loss of students engaging in negative behaviors can occur due to disciplinary actions (suspensions, etc.) or drop-out or transferring, all of which can produce artificially positive effects.

Scales can unfortunately lose their effectiveness as data collection mechanisms over time due to *testing* and *instrumentation* effects. Participants who have been previously assessed in repeated sampling paradigms are likely to affect the results of the next assessment. Interacting with the susceptibility and suggestibility distortions from memory research, having named someone on a previous nomination may make the respondent more likely to name that person again, regardless of whether the perpetrator is still engaged in the negative behavior. Thus the measurement mechanism becomes less accurate over time. Nominations in particular may also suffer from *regression towards the mean*. Students who are labeled as bullies will have an increased tendency to be watched by administrators and peers, increasing their chance for future nominations regardless of actual prevalence of behavior. Likewise, once attention is drawn to them as a bully either through notoriety or disciplinary action, students engaged in negative behaviors may consequently decrease their participation.

Finally, because engagement in bullying and related behaviors is self-initiated, *selection bias* cannot be avoided. Similarly, *interactive effects* due to classroom or social group nesting, which may serve as moderators that illustrate the conditions upon which a behavior is present or to what degree also cannot be manipulated in most school-based settings.

Conclusions and Implications for Practice

Bullying is a multifaceted phenomenon involving frequency, intent, and action which, when combined with a need for multiple measurement informants, results in the need for a complex measurement system for adequate operationalization. That is, a single observation may not be sufficient to reliably and validly determine that a bullying act has indeed occurred. Consequently, determining the level of bullying behavior and assessment of change in behavior as a result of prevention or intervention efforts depends upon a number of psychometric issues. Table 21.1 presents a summary table with implications for practice that summarize the key points of this chapter.

In addition to discussing the obvious decisions that must be made by researchers in terms of determining the appropriate level of measurement and the type of response format to be used, this chapter draws attention to a number of additional psychometric considerations. It is essential that the theoretical measurement model to be invoked in the ensuing data analysis appropriately considers the latent nature of the complex multi-faceted construct definition of bullying. Also of concern is the consistency and precision of observation, or lack thereof, due to multiple informants (peers, teachers, or self), contextual limitations (classrooms, peer

Table 21.1 Implications for Practice

	Recommendations for Practitioners and Researchers
Who	• Choose two or more informant modalities (self, peer, or teacher) to enable adequate triangulation of the behavior and minimization of mono-method bias in measuring the construct.
What	• Develop a clear operationalization of the bullying or aggression construct(s) that effectively capture either the three requisite components of bullying behavior [(1) behavior is aggressive and negative, (2) it is carried out repeatedly, and (3) the relationship is characterized by an imbalance of power] or the two components of aggression [(1) an intent to harm on the part of the aggressor, and (2) a feeling of hurt on the part of the victim].
Where	• Do not discount the potential influence of classroom or social group effects that may influence or limit the reliability and validity of nomination procedures. Homeroom effects should be ruled out in younger children, and social group effects should be ruled out with older children.
When	• Choose a consistent and recent period for retrospective reporting of bullying or related behaviors. Timing within a school term should be noted. • Assessment should be objective and standardized to minimize suggestion or susceptibility to eyewitness memory effects.
Why	• Choose between a formative or reflective model as the appropriate theoretical measurement model. • Measure at least three indicators of the construct. • Choose the scaling framework (CTT or IRT) that is most appropriate for the level of measurement (nominal, ordinal, interval, or ratio) of your indicators. • Careful consideration should be given to any potential threats to the internal validity of decisions.
How	• Determine the most appropriate indicator format or combination of indicator formats. • Realize that the choice of format has implications for how the data must be treated when using it to inform intervention or even disciplinary decisions.

groups, etc.), and the fallibility of human memory in accurately recalling both direct experience of bullying-related behavior and recollection of knowledge from second-hand sources. Finally, the decision to focus on the trait or its expression in terms of direct behavior and the selection of the appropriate measurement framework has a critical implication for the quality of scores from the assessment instrument and the inference and generalizability of the data to intervention or prevention efforts.

Notes

1. Schacter's (2001) "seven sins" are *transience, absent-mindedness, blocking, misattribution, suggestibility, bias*, and *persistence*. Five of the seven are relevant to recall of bullying behavior. *Absent-mindedness*, or the tendency to repeat a behavior only to realize that the behavior already occurred, and *persistence*, or remembering inconsequential details as more consequential than they really are, are of less relevance to recall of bullying behavior.
2. As both CTT and IRT have evolved from the academic testing context, the use of the term *test* can be generalized to any scale, survey, or inventory meant to collect observable manifestations of a latent construct.

References

Ackil, J. K., & Zaragoza, M. S. (1998). Memorial consequences of forced confabulation: Age differences in susceptibility to false memories. *Developmental Psychology, 34*, 1358–1372.

Bereiter, C. (1963). Some persisting dilemmas in the measurement of change. In C. Harris (Ed.), *Problems in measuring change* (pp. 3–20). Madison: University of Wisconsin Press.

Blanton, H., & Jaccard, J. (2006). Arbitrary metrics in psychology. *American Psychologist, 61*, 27–41.

Bock, R. D., Gibbons, R., & Muraki, E. (1988). Full-information item factor analysis. *Applied Psychological Measurement, 12*, 261–280.

Bollen, K. A. (1989). *Structural equations with latent variables*. New York: Wiley.

Bothwell, R. K., Brigham, J. C., & Malpass, R. S. (1989). Cross-racial identification. *Personality & Social Psychology Bulletin, 15*, 19–25.

Bovaird, J. A., & Embretson, S. E. (2008). Modern measurement in the social sciences. In P. Alasuutari, L. Bickman, & J. Brannen (Eds.), *Handbook of social research methods* (pp. 269–289). Los Angeles: Sage.

Ceci, S. J., & Bruck, M. (1993). Suggestibility of the child witness: A historical review and synthesis. *Psychological Bulletin, 113*, 403–439.

Cook, L. L., & Eignor, D. R. (1983). Practical considerations regarding the use of item response theory to equate tests. In R. K. Hambleton (Ed.), *Applications of item response theory* (pp. 175–195). Vancouver, BC: Educational Research Institute of British Columbia.

Cornell, D. G., & Brockenbrough, K. (2004). Identification of bullies and victims: A comparison of methods. *Journal of School Violence, 3*, 63–87.

Cronbach, L. J. (1951). Coefficient alpha and the internal structure of tests. *Psychometrika, 16*, 297–334.

Davison, M. L., & Sharma, A. R. (1990). Parametric statistics and levels of measurement: Factorial designs and multiple regressions. *Psychological Bulletin, 107*, 394–400.

De Boeck, P., & Wilson, M. (Eds.), (2004). *Explanatory item response models: A generalized linear and nonlinear approach*. New York: Springer-Verlag.

Embretson, S. E. (1994). Comparing changes between groups: Some perplexities arising from psychometrics. In D. Laveault, B. D. Zumbo, M. E. Gessaroli, & M. W. Boss (Eds.), *Modern theories of measurement: problems and issues* (pp. 211–248). Ottawa, Ontario, Canada: Edumetric Research Group, University of Ottawa.

Embretson, S. E. (1996). Item response theory models and spurious interaction effects in factorial ANOVA designs. *Applied Psychological Measurement, 20*, 201–212.

Embretson, S. E. (1998). A cognitive design system approach to generating valid tests: Application to abstract reasoning. *Psychological Methods, 3*, 300–396.

Embretson, S. E. (2006). The continued search for nonarbitrary metrics in psychology. *American Psychologist, 61*, 50–55.

Embretson, S. E. (2007). Impact of measurement scale in modeling developmental processes and ecological factors. In T. D. Little, J. A. Bovaird, & N. A. Card (Eds.), *Modeling contextual effects in longitudinal studies* (pp. 63–87). Mahwah, NJ: Erlbaum.

Embretson, S. E., & Reise, S. P. (2000). *Item response theory for psychologists*. Mahwah, NJ: Erlbaum.

Espelage, D. L., & Swearer, S. M. (2003). Research on school bullying and victimization: What have we learned and where do we go from here? *School Psychology Review, 32*, 365–383.

Garry, M., & Loftus, E. F. (1994). Pseudomemories without hypnosis. *International Journal of Clinical and Experimental Hypnosis, 42*, 363–378.

Graham, S., Bellmore, A., & Juvonen, J. (2003). Peer victimization in middle school: When self- and reer views diverge. *Journal of Applied School Psychology, 19*, 117–137.

Grant, E. R., & Ceci, S. J. (2000). Memory: Constructive processes. In A. E. Kazdin (Ed.), *Encyclopedia of psychology* (Vol. 5, pp. 166–169). Washington, DC: American Psychological Association.

Hoover, J. H., Oliver, R., & Hazler, R. J. (1992). Bullying: Perceptions of adolescent victims in the Midwestern USA. *School Psychology International, 13*, 5–16.

Kolodner, J. L. (1983). Reconstructive memory: A computer model. *Cognitive Science, 7*, 281–328.

Kwon, K., & Lease, A.M. (2007). Clique membership and social adjustment in children's same-gender cliques: The contribution of the type of clique to children's self-reported adjustment. *Merrill-Palmer Quarterly, 53*, 216–242.

Leite, W. L. (2007). A comparison of latent growth models for constructs measured by multiple items. *Structural Equation Modeling, 14*, 581–610.

Little, T. D., Bovaird, J. A., & Slegers, D. (2006). Methods for the analysis of change. In D. Mroczek & T. D. Little (Eds.), *Handbook of personality development* (pp. 181-211). Mahwah, NJ: Erlbaum.

Little, T. D., Lindenberger, U., & Nesselroade, J. R. (1999). On selecting indicators for multivariate measurement and modeling with latent variables: When "good" indicators are bad and "bad" indicators are good. *Psychological Methods, 4*, 192–211.

Loftus, E. F. (1977). Shifting human color memory. *Memory & Cognition, 5*, 696–699.

Lord, F. M. (1980). *Application of item response theory to practical testing problems*. Hillsdale, NJ: Erlbaum.

Maxwell, S. E., & Delaney, H. (1985). Measurement and statistics: An examination of construct validity. *Psychological Bulletin, 97*, 85–93.

Meade, A. W., Lautenschlager, G. J., & Hecht, J. E. (2005). Establishing measurement equivalence and invariance in longitudinal data with item response theory. *International Journal of Testing, 5*(3), 279–300.

Nansel, R. R., Overpeck, M., Pilla, R. S., Ruan, W. A. J., Simon-Morton, B., & Scheidt, P. (2001). Bullying behaviors among U.S. youth: Prevalence and association with psychosocial adjustment. *Journal of the American Medical Association, 285*, 2094–1200.

Novick, M. R. (1966). The axioms and principal results of classical test theory. *Journal of Mathematical Psychology, 3*, 1–18.

Olweus, D. (1994). Bullying at school: Basic facts and effects of a school based intervention program. *Journal of Child Psychology and Psychiatry, 35*, 1171–1190.

Olweus, D. (1995). Bullying or peer abuse at school: Facts and intervention. *Current Directions in Psychological Science, 4,* 196–200.

Peets, K., & Kikas, E. (2006). Aggressive strategies and victimization during adolescence: Grade and gender differences, and cross-informant agreement. *Aggressive Behavior, 32,* 68–79.

Perry, D. G., Williard, J. C., & Perry, L. C. (1990). Peers' perceptions of the consequences that victimized children provide aggressors. *Child Development, 61,* 1310–1325.

Raykov, T. (1997). Estimation of composite reliability for congeneric measures. *Applied Psychological Measurement, 21,* 173–184.

Rigby, K., Smith, P., & Pepler, D. (2004). *Bullying in schools: How successful can interventions be?* Cambridge, England: Cambridge University Press.

Roediger, H.L., III, & McDermott, K.B. (2000). Distortions of memory. In E. Tulving & F. I. M. Craik (Eds.), *The Oxford handbook of memory* (pp. 149–162). New York: Oxford University Press.

Rogosa, D. R., & Willett, J. B. (1983). Demonstrating the reliability of the difference score in the measurement of change. *Journal of Educational Measurement, 20,* 335–343.

Rubin, D. C. (Ed.). (1996). *Remembering our past: Studies in autobiographical memory.* New York: Cambridge University Press.

Schacter, D.L. (2001). *The seven sins of memory: How the mind forgets and remembers.* Boston: Houghton Mifflin.

Shadish, W. R., Cook, T. D., & Campbell, D. T. (2002). *Experimental and quasi-experimental designs for generalized causal inference.* Boston: Houghton Mifflin.

Stevens, S. S. (1946). On the theory of scales of measurement. *Science, 103,* 677–680.

Sveinsson, A. V., & Morris, R. J. (2007). Conceptual and methodological issues in assessment and intervention with school bullies. In J. E. Zins, M. J. Elias, & C. A. Maher (Eds.), *Bullying, victimization, and peer harassment: A handbook of prevention and intervention* (pp. 9–26). Binghamton, NY: Haworth.

Swearer, S. M., Bovaird, J. A., Buhs, E. S., & Givens, J. E. (2007, August). *Peer aggression and victimization: Patterns of change across middle school.* Paper presented at the American Psychological Association annual meeting. San Francisco, CA.

Tomada, G., & Schneider, B. (1997). Relational aggression, gender and peer acceptance: Invariance across culture, stability over time, and concordance among informants. *Developmental Psychology, 33,* 601–609.

Tremblay, R. E. (2000). The development of aggressive behavior during childhood: What have we learned in the past century? *International Journal of Behavioral Development, 24,* 129–141.

Underwood, M. K. (2003). *Social Aggression Among Girls.* New York: Guilford.

VandenBos, G. R. (2007). *APA Dictionary of psychology.* Washington, DC: American Psychological Association.

Weiss, D. J. (1982). Improving measurement quality and efficiency with adaptive testing. *Applied Psychological Measurement, 6,* 473–492.

Wells, G. L. (1993). What do we know about eyewitness identification? *American Psychologist, 48,* 553–571.

22

The Neurobiology of Peer Victimization and Rejection

TRACY VAILLANCOURT, JEAN CLINTON, PATRICIA MCDOUGALL,
LOUIS A. SCHMIDT, AND SHELLEY HYMEL

As a field of scientific inquiry, bullying has been studied since the 1970s (Olweus, 1999). Over the course of the last few decades, there has been a burgeoning interest in this topic. Indeed, this particular issue has given rise to an unprecedented international exchange of information, as well as collaborative cross-national investigations. Given such world-wide partnerships and attention to the issue, our understanding of the complexity of the problem of school bullying has increased dramatically in a short period of time. The bulk of this knowledge base has been primarily rooted in the disciplines of developmental psychology and education. This chapter expands our understanding of this phenomenon in light of established findings in the area of neuroscience, with the goal of providing an overview of applicable research to promote new ideas for scientific inquiry.

Although an understanding of the biological correlates of those who perpetrate the abuse of their peers is both interesting and important (see van Goozen, Snoek, Fairchild, & Harold, 2007, for review), this chapter focuses on the psychology and neurobiology of those who are victimized and rejected by their peers. Herein, particular emphasis is placed on studies that have linked changes in stress hormones and brain activity to peer victimization and peer rejection.

Peer Victimization and Peer Rejection

Peer victimization as a result of bullying is characterized by three critical components: intentionality, repetition, and power imbalance (Olweus, 1999). Thus, an occasional fight between two equals is not bullying. Rather, bullying is best conceptualized as repeated oppression and humiliation on the part of one or more person(s), with more power than the victim. Peer rejection refers to the active dislike of an individual on the part of their peers (Hymel, Vaillancourt, McDougall, & Renshaw, 2002; McDougall, Hymel, Vaillancourt, & Mercer, 2001). Peer rejection and peer victimization are not synonymous—although many bullied children are rejected by their peers such is not the case for all. Still, researchers have long demonstrated that peer victimization and peer rejection are correlated and are related to a similar constellation of negative outcomes. For example, both are related to increases in internalizing (e.g., depression, anxiety, and post-traumatic stress disorder) and externalizing problems (e.g., aggression, substance use and abuse; for reviews see Hawker & Boulton, 2000; Hymel et al., 2002; McDougall et al., 2001), greater physical health complaints (Rigby, 1998; Slee, 1995), and poorer school performance (Juvonen, Nishina, & Graham, 2000; Nansel, Haynie, & Simons-Morton, 2003; Schwartz, Gorman, Nakamoto, & Toblin, 2005). Recent longitudinal studies of peer victimized children suggest that peer abuse does not simply co-occur with other difficulties, but rather causes maladjustment (Arseneault et al., 2006; Kim, Leventhal, Koh, Hubbard, & Boyce, 2006; Kumpulainen & Rasanen, 2000; Sourander, Helstela, Helenius, & Piha, 2000). There is, in addition, evidence to suggest that peer rejection causes psychopathology (McDougall et al., 2001; Parker & Asher, 1987), although the nature of directionality in the latter case is less straightforward.

The link between problematic peer experiences and ensuing psychopathology should not be surprising considering that the need to belong is a fundamental human motivator (Baumeister & Leary, 1995) and the great importance that social bonding carries for human survival (e.g., Gilbert, 1992; MacDonald & Leary, 2005; Williams, 2007). The fact that positive social affiliation is firmly rooted in our evolutionary past may explain why it is that any form of social exclusion, ostracism, or rejection tends to be perceived as stressful (MacDonald & Leary, 2005; Williams, 2007). Interestingly, with theoretical and methodological advances in the field of neuroscience with respect to imaging techniques, researchers have been able to demonstrate that the pain of rejection extends beyond the psychological domain. These studies have shown that the pain experienced by social rejection is akin to the experiences of physical pain and that both physical and psychological pain are mediated by a similar physiological system (MacDonald & Leary, 2005, p. 210; see Herman & Panksepp, 1978; Nelson & Panksepp, 1998; Thornhill & Thornhill, 1989). For example, in a recent functional magnetic resonance imaging study, participants were scanned while playing a ball tossing game in which they were eventually excluded (Eisenberger, Liberman, & Williams, 2003, p. 290). Similar to what has been shown in physical pain studies, when participants were excluded from the game, the anterior cingulated cortex was more active and the right ventral prefrontal cortex, a brain region that has been linked to the regulation of pain distress and negative affect (Eisenberger et al., 2003). This work in and of itself suggests that we should be looking more closely at the neuroscience of peer relations because the role of the biological systems is not incidental but rather plays an important part in an individual's interpretation of, and experience with, social exclusion and peer abuse.

The Neurobiology Underlying Problematic Peer Relationship

Although the psychological sequela of peer victimization and rejection has been studied extensively, the neurobiological sequela of problematic peer relations has not. This paucity is especially intriguing given the decades of animal and human research linking early stress exposure to neurobiological alterations. In humans, physiological stress responses are under the direction of two distinct, albeit related systems: the sympathetic-adrenomedullary (SAM) system and the hypothalamic-pituatary-adrenocorticol (HPA) system (see Gunnar & Quevedo, 2007). The SAM system is associated with the release of epinephrine (adrenaline), while the HPA system (or axis) is associated with glucocorticoids (GCs) such as the stress hormone cortisol. Epinephrine is released quickly in times of stress whereas GCs take longer to develop and circulate for longer periods of time. In humans, most of the literature on the neurobiology of stress has focused on the HPA system, which is typically estimated through the non-invasive measurement of cortisol (saliva).

Cortisol is active in all individuals and shows a clear circadian rhythm, with levels being highest in the morning and declining progressively during waking hours (Kirschbaum & Hellhammer, 1989). In response to stress, corticotropin releasing factor (CRF) is released by the hypothalamus, which stimulates the synthesis and release of adrenocorticotropin hormone (ACTH) from the pituitary. ACTH causes the release of GCs from the adrenal cortex. There is a negative feedback system as CRF synthesis and release is inhibited by circulating levels of gluco-corticoids and mineralocorticoids mediated by GC receptors. In addition to other physiological responses, this neurochemical chain of reactions helps mobilize energy stores and facilitates behavioural responses to threat (e.g., flight or fight).

What is important to know about cortisol is that: (a) the brain is a "major target organ" (Gunnar & Quevedo, 2007, p.152) with many areas rich in GC receptors; and (b) excessive exposure to GCs has been shown to be harmful (Sapolsky, 1996, 2000; Sapolsky, Uno, Rebert, & Finch, 1990), potentially leading to neural cell death (see McEwen, 1998). In fact, unusually high levels of cortisol can change the response of the GCs receptors in the brain by either increasing or decreasing sensitivity, resulting in either an over-reaction (hyper-secretion) or under-reaction (hypo-secretion) of the HPA system to a new stressor (Dienstbier, 1989). Structural changes in the brain–in particular, the hippocampus–which is primarily associated with learning and memory (Squire, 1992), have been linked to excessive exposure to GCs (Sapolsky, 1996, 2000; Sapolsky et al., 1990). The hippocampus is especially vulnerable to elevated circulating cortisol levels because it has a high concentration of GCs receptors (e.g., McEwen, 1992). Ample evidence from animal and non-human primate models exists to support this association (e.g., Sapolsky, 1996; Sapolsky et al., 1990), along with a growing human literature (e.g., Lupien et al., 2005). For example, hippocampal volume reduction has been found among children and adults with post-traumatic stress disorder (PTSD) who were exposed to physical and sexual abuse (Bremner et al., 1997; Koverola et al., 2005; Stein, Koverola, Hanna, Torchia & McClarty, 1997). Note that, although this finding has been replicated extensively, it is not clear whether the hippocampal volume reduction is the result of exposure and subsequent cell death or whether a smaller hippocampus is a risk factor for the development of psychiatric complications following exposure (Stein et al., 1997). Lack of proof for this causal pathway in humans notwithstanding, the animal literature is clear on the directionality of these results—high circulating GCs damages the hippocampus (Sapolsky, 1996; Sapolsky et al., 1990).

Examining the HPA axis in reference to peer abuse and rejection is an important area of inquiry considering the extensive literature on child abuse which has demonstrated that exposure to stress (i.e., child maltreatment) is linked to persistent neuroendocrine changes. Specifically, children abused by their caregiver(s) show alterations to the HPA axis (see reviews by Bremner & Vermetten, 2001; DeBellis, 2001; Kaufman & Charney, 2001), measured primarily through changes in circulating GCs. There remains, however, much uncertainty in exactly how these changes come about, as there is no unidirectional impact. For example, whereas some have found that child abuse exposure is related to over activity of the HPA system (higher cortisol levels; Cicchetti & Rogosch, 2001), others have shown that under activity (lower cortisol levels) occurs in the case of chronic maltreatment (Hart, Gunnar, & Cicchetti, 1995; see Bremner & Vermetten, 2001). It may be that, for some, prolonged periods of hyperactivity of the HPA axis are followed by hyposecretion (i.e., reduction) as an adaptive process on the part of the organism (Bremner & Vermetten, 2001; Dienstbier, 1989). If true, then in some individuals, hyposecretion of cortisol in the face of stressors is likely the result of extreme or chronic stress, whereas in others hypersecretion of cortisol is associated with acute or less severe stress. This hypothesis is consistent with the literature on hypocortisolism, which is shown primarily among individuals who endure unremitting stress or have experienced an extreme traumatic event and then develop PTSD (Heim, Ehlert, & Hellhammer, 2000; Yehuda, 1997).

The experience of being maltreated by a caregiver is unquestionably stressful. Being abused and rejected by peers is also stressful and new studies examining the relation between HPA functioning and peer victimization and peer rejection have demonstrated similar results to those found with maltreated children (i.e., dysregulation of the HPA axis). For example, Gunnar and colleagues (Gunnar, Sebanc, Tout, Donzella, & van Dulmen, 2003) found that peer rejection was related to high cortisol levels in a preschool sample of 82 children. In their sample of 154 12-year-olds, Vaillancourt et al. (2008) found that peer victimization was related to hyposecretion of cortisol even after controlling for known confounds such as depression, anxiety, sex, age and pubertal status and after excluding children with a history of child maltreatment, foster care placement, psychotropic medication and oral contraception use, and aggression directed at peers or family members. When sex was examined as a possible moderator, the researchers found that, for boys, occasional exposure to peer victimization was associated with higher cortisol levels whereas for girls occasional exposure was associated with lower cortisol levels. Vaillancourt et al. argue that these sex differences may be related to sex differences in children's social goals. That is, because girls value being included more than boys, it may be that any form (or degree) of abuse or rejection is perceived as more stressful for girls than it is for boys. The assumption here is that hyposecretion of cortisol is indicative of exposure to more severe or chronic stress, a hypothesis that still requires validation.

These arguments are consistent with findings from several other investigations of bullying and cortisol production. In a study examining cortisol in relation to peer victimization, Kliewer (2006) found that bullied African American youth (age 11 years) living in high violence and low socioeconomic urban areas produced lower cortisol levels, after controlling for age, gender, internalizing symptoms and major life events. As well, Hansen et al. (2006) reported a significant relation between being bullied and decreased cortisol. In this study of 437 Swedish employees (mean age 45.5), bullied adult respondents (n = 22) had lower morning and afternoon cortisol concentration than their non-bullied counterparts. Similarly, within the broader literature on hypcortisolism, reduced levels of cortisol have been demonstrated primarily among individuals who had developed PTSD after experiencing an extreme traumatic event, and among individuals who endured incessant stress (Heim et al., 2000; Yehuda, 1997).

To date, the four studies examining links between poor peer experiences and cortisol have noted a pattern of HPA dysregulation. Such findings raise important new questions about the relation between poor health and peer abuse and rejection (Rigby, 1998; Slee, 1995; Wolke, Woods, Bloomfield, & Karstadt, 2001). Perhaps the poor health experienced by children who are bullied and or rejected is not psychosomatic, but rather reflects alterations in the immune pathways or "allostatic load" that has been linked to immunological deficits (McEwen, 1998). Allostasis is defined as "the ability to achieve [physiological] stability through change" (McEwen, 1998, p. 171; see also Schulkin, Gold, & McEwen, 1998). Allostatic load is the accumulation of stress responses (i.e., the environmental stressor is perceived, a physiologic and behavioral response ensues leading to allostasis and adaptation), which is linked to adverse health effects and pathological health outcomes (Heim et al., 2000; McEwen, 1998; Seyle, 1998). Studies examining this possibility among bullied and rejected children are clearly warranted, especially given established link between such negative social experiences and poor health.

The aforementioned studies also highlight the need to reconsider the robust finding of poor academic achievement among bullied and rejected children (Buhs, Ladd, & Herald, 2006; Juvonen et al., 2000; Nansel et al., 2003; Schwartz et al., 2005; Wentzel & Caldwell, 1997) from a neurobiological perspective. We know that the stress of being abused or rejected by peers is associated with alterations of the HPA axis (Gunnar et al., 2003; Hansen et al., 2006; Kliewer, 2006; Vaillancourt et al., 2007). We also know that persistent high levels of stress can lead to cell death in the hippocampus (via cortisol), which in turn can impair some types of new learning (e.g., Sapolsky, 1996). Despite this knowledge, the prevailing wisdom concerning the link between poor academic performance and peer abuse is that psychological difficulties mediate the relation between negative peer experiences and poor academic performance (Buhs et al., 2006; Juvonen, 2000; Schwartz et al., 2005; Wentzel & Caldwell, 1997). The neurobiological evidence reviewed here suggests an alternative explanatory mechanism may be operating. Perhaps bullied and rejected children do poorly in school because of a structural change to their brain that is associated with functional differences (i.e., poor memory) that are mediated through the repeated activation of the HPA axis. Studies considering this type of hypothesis are clearly needed.

The experience of being repeatedly oppressed, humiliated, ostracized, or rejected by peers is stressful and as such the observed links between neurobiological alterations and peer abuse and rejection should not be surprising. The current state of knowledge in the area of child abuse and neglect would contend that these early stressful life experiences get "under the skin" and are associated with neurological, structural and functional changes that go beyond those just described. For example, several researchers have found that maltreated children have abnormal brain-wave patterns (e.g., Ito, Teicher, Glod, & Ackerman, 1998; see also Teicher, Ito, Glod, Schiffer, & Gelbard, 1996, for review), patterns analogous to those observed in children and adults who are clinically depressed and anxious, as well as those at risk for such psychopathology (Davidson, 2000). These brain-wave differences are found in the frontal and temporal (cortical) regions of the brain. These cortical brain regions receive direct anatomical input from forebrain limbic areas known to be involved in the regulation and dysregulation of fear and stress (Rosen & Schulkin, 1998). Interestingly, shy children, who are likely to be rejected and victimized by their peers (Rubin, Stewart, & Coplan, 1995), also show greater relative right frontal electroencephalography activity (a marker of stress), high and stable heart rate at rest and in response to social stress, and exhibit high morning cortisol levels (see Kagan, 1994; Schmidt & Schulkin, 1999, for reviews). Although the causal relations among shyness, peer rejection, peer victimization, and psychophysiology have not been established, it seems plausible that there may be some children who are vulnerable to shyness and perhaps peer victimization and peer rejection, and this vulnerability manifests not only behaviourally but psychophysiologically as well. In other words, some children may be temperamentally vulnerable to peer rejection and/or peer victimization. Although research over the last two decades has sought to identify biological correlates that predict aggression (e.g., van Goozen et al., 2007, for review), what is also needed are longitudinal studies that track infants and children with particular psychophysiological profiles who might be at risk for peer victimization and/or peer rejection.

Beyond Stress-Reactivity: The Possible Buffering Effects of Oxytocin

In examining the potential neurobiological link between peer victimization/rejection and poor health and educational attainment, it may prove fruitful to extend the inquiry beyond cortisol to include the amino acid peptide oxytocin, given its connection to the HPA axis (Uvnäs-Moberg, 1998) as well as social affiliation and attachment behavior (Carter, 1998; Carter, Devries, & Gertrz, 1995; Insel & Young, 2001; MacDonald & Leary, 2005; Pedersen, 2004; Uvnäs-Moberg, 1998). Oxytocin is produced by the supraoptic (SON) and paraventricular (PVN) nuclei of the hypothalamus and is released into circulation from magnocellular neurons and from the parvocellular neurons in the PVN (Carter, 1998; Uväns-Moberg, 1998). Oxytocin is a very interesting peptide in that it acts both on certain targets of the body as a hormone (e.g., milk-ejection during lactation and the muscular contractions of the uterus during labour) as well as on brain regions associated with emotional and social behaviors. In short, this peptide serves as a kind of neurotransmitter and plays an important role in affiliative and maternal behavior.

In prairie voles (a small rodent that resembles a mouse), oxytocin has been shown to increase positive social behavior, and both oxytocin and social interactions have been shown to reduce the activity of the HPA axis (Carter, 1998). Similarly, Windle et al. (2004) reported that oxytocin attenuated the stress-induced HPA activity and anxious behavior by suppressing highly region-specific neural circuits. In a recent study of human males (Heinrichs, Baumgartner, Kirschbaum, & Ehlert, 2003), the intranasal administration of oxytocin was found to exhibit an anxiolytic effect (i.e., reduce anxiety). Moreover, the combination of oxytocin and the social support of a best friend before the introduction of a laboratory stressor were found to be associated with lower cortisol levels. Intranasal oxytocin has also been shown experimentally to increase trust among humans, suggesting that oxytocin helps to overcome the aversion of betrayal and enhances approach behavior (Kosfeld, Heinrichs, Zak, Fischbacher, & Fehr, 2005).

It has also been hypothesized that the anti-stress effects of social behavior may be mediated by oxytocin (Uvnäs-Moberg, 1998). That is, "socially-released oxytocin" is hypothesized to decrease the activity of the HPA axis (cortisol), thus promoting health (Carter et al., 1995; Heinrichs et al., 2003; Uvnäs-Moberg, 1998, p. 830). This hypothesis is interesting given the fact that social support and positive social experiences have been positively linked to health and well-being (Knox & Uvnäs-Moberg, 1998; Seeman & Syme, 1987). People with social support tend to feel better than people with few friends or relatives. In fact, isolated individuals tend to have a higher mortality rates than their better supported counterparts (e.g., Kaplan et al., 1994). Studies of bullied and or rejected children have demonstrated that these children often experience poor health (Rigby, 1998; Slee, 1995) and reduced cortisol secretion (e.g., Vaillancourt et al., 2008). Examining the role of oxytocin in these relations might yield important information about the biological mechanisms involved. For example, in a recent study, the link between peer victimization and stress symptoms was found to be moderated by isolation—participants who were bullied and isolated by their peers reported the highest level of stress symptoms (Newman, Holden, & Delville, 2005). Future research needs to address the role neurobiology plays in these relations. Do isolated victims show greater HPA activity and have lower oxytocin levels than non-isolated victims? Does this neurobiological difference uniquely contribute to their stress symptoms?

The Neurobiology of Peer Victimization and Rejection: A New Scientific Frontier

An abundance of knowledge has emerged in a relatively short period of time regarding the correlates of peer victimization and rejection. It is now known that children who are bullied/ rejected by their peers tend to suffer from a host of psychological issues, tend to do poorly at school and tend to feel unwell physically. Still, little is known about the causal processes and mechanisms associated with bullying and rejection, owing perhaps to the fact that we have begun only recently to empirically investigate the phenomenon of bullying. Humans are far too complex for subsequent science to be so narrow. What is needed is an integrated approach that gives consideration to both environment and biology. In doing so, it is imperative that scholars attend to the possible role neurobiology plays in the relation between adverse peer experiences and outcomes such as poor physical and mental health and educational attainment. However, it is also essential to acknowledge the importance of genes. Perhaps, in approaching the study of peer victimization/rejection from a more complex biopsychosocial perspective, we may better understand why it is that not all bullied or rejected children fare poorly and why for some the effects are disastrous.

Recent work in the area of gene-by-environment interactions highlights how much there is to consider and how far future research needs to go in order to truly understand the effects of bullying and peer rejection on the developing child. This point is best illustrated by Caspi and colleagues' (2003) longitudinal birth cohort study examining the interaction between early adverse life events (child maltreatment) and biological predisposition (serotonin) in predicting depression. Serotonin (5-HT) influences a variety of physiological and psychological processes, including, for example, cardiovascular function, respiration, appetite, sexual behavior, aggression, and learning (Lucki, 1998). Caspi et al. found that people who were maltreated in childhood and who had one or two of the short alleles of the serotonin transporter gene (5-HTT) were far more likely to be depressed than those with two long alleles. The vulnerability was especially pronounced for those with two short alleles. In fact, maltreated individuals with two long alleles were found to be no more likely to become depressed than individuals who were not maltreated. In biological terms, the functional polymorphism of the serotonin transporter gene (at the promoter region) moderates the relation between early adverse life events and depression at age 26. This study clearly illustrates a gene-by-environment interaction that may be critical with respect to peer abuse and rejection. Perhaps the impact of peer abuse and consequent difficulties are modulated through an underlying biological diathesis. Understanding that some individuals may be biologically vulnerable may lead to better and more meaningful and earlier treatment.

Biology is not necessarily destiny, however. In fact, recent work in epigenetics, the study of heritable changes in genome function that occur without a change in DNA sequence, actually points to the opposite conclusion. For example, researchers (Meaney and colleagues, see Weaver et al., 2005) have demonstrated that individual differences in the stress reactivity of adult rats are influenced by maternal behavior during infancy. Specifically, the environment (maternal pup licking/grooming and arched-back nursing or LG-ABN) triggers a group of molecules called methyl groups to attach itself to the control centre of the gene. Through a complex molecular and cellular process involving methylation (the process by which "a gene can be stably silenced" [Sapolsky, 2004, p. 791]), rat pups that are the offspring of less nurturing mothers (low LG-ABN) become adults who are predisposed to have higher stress release of glucocorticoids and display greater behavioral reactivity. However, cross fostering the biological offspring of low LG-ABN and high LG-ABN reverses the effect. That is, maternal behavior leads to life long changes of the stress response system that range from the "molecular to the behavioral level" (Sapolsky, 2004, p. 792). In experimental studies, researchers (see Weaver et al., 2005) have also shown that certain compounds can alter these otherwise permanent epigenetic changes, opening a whole world of possibilities for future intervention.

Meaney's work (Weaver et al., 2004, 2005) has important implications for humans because it demonstrates that social experiences have a significant impact on the developing person and may alter biology, which, in turn, may have a long-standing biological consequence at a level previously never contemplated (e.g., gene alterations). Although people may be born with similar genes, the environment can permanently alter the expression of the genes and consequently bring about differences in behavior. With respect to bullied or rejected children, the consequences extend beyond what has yet been imagined. We know these experiences are psychologically damaging, what we have failed to realize is just how brain altering and physiologically damaging these experiences may be.

Is it possible that the experience of being bullied is dissimilar for different children because their genes are more susceptible to environmental influence? Is it possible that some children are protected from the ill effects of peer victimization because of their gene expression? Two recent studies on the genetic and environmental influences on peer victimization provide contradictory evidence. In a recent study of 1,116 families with 10-year-old twins, Ball and colleagues (2008) found that the tendency for children to be bullied by peers was largely due to genetics (73% of variance) and to some extend, to the environmental factors that were unique to each twin. In this study, maternal reports were used to assess peer victimization. Conversely, in another large twin study of 506 6-year-old twins, Brendgen et al. (2008) found that peer-evaluated victimization was not related to a child's genetic disposition but rather was environmentally driven. Twenty-nine percent of the variance was accounted by shared environmental experiences and the remaining 71% of the variance was attributed to nonshared environmental sources. The striking differences between these two studies highlight an urgent need for more research in this area.

Implications for Practice

The present review underscores the pressing need to give due consideration to the neurobiology of peer victimization and rejection. The failure to turn our attention more fully to the neurobiological mechanisms and outcomes associated with peer victimization and rejection will perpetuate an incomplete picture of the impact of bullying. The findings reviewed herein are suggestive of more than just future directions for research. Indeed, the knowledge gained through work in this area also has strong implications for practice (discussed below and summarized in Table 22.1). For example, similar to what has been shown in the child maltreatment literature, if peer victimization and/or rejection does indeed change the structure and function of the developing child's brain, preventive efforts to end bullying in schools and communities must be accelerated. No longer should we accept the popular adage that peer victimization and/or rejection "builds character" or that it is a "rite of passage" to be tolerated. In fact, efforts to counter such stereotypes about bullying become imperative, given evidence that such negative peer experiences are associated with meaningful alterations to individual's capacity to handle stress (via alterations of the HPA), placing them at risk for psychopathology and ill health (McEwen, 1998). Such negative peer experiences may also alter gene expression (Weaver et al., 2004, 2005), reducing the chances of individuals reaching their fullest potential as well as compromising their health and well-being. The impact on the individual, in turn, becomes a cost borne by all of society, impacting health care and education and in turn productivity, citizenship and social capital.

A first step, then, is in educating people about the long-term consequences of peer victimization and rejection for the individual and the need to address these problems early on in the life of a child. Given increasing attention to problems of bullying in the worldwide media, the average parent, teacher, principal, and child care provider have only recently become aware of the fact that bullying and peer rejection are significant and indeed pervasive problems, with long term consequences for the individual. Yet, such awareness is necessary but not sufficient for long term changes in how we support our children. Within the field of education, for example, increasing attention to social and emotional functioning as a necessary focus within schools has begun to impact educational practice, not only because such skills are important considerations in their own right, but also because of recent evidence that they are foundational to academic learning (Hymel, Schonert-Reichl, & Miller, 2006; www.casel.org).

However, the more complex associations between peer victimization/rejection and neurobiological functioning (as reviewed in the present chapter) helps to provide a context for understanding why some children are differentially affected by their negative peer interactions. For some, the experience is quickly forgotten, while for others the experiences haunt them into adulthood and continues to compromise their sense of well-being years after the fact (Miller & Vaillancourt, 2007). A fuller understanding of the complex interplay between biology and life experience provides a foundation for understanding why these varying reactions may exist and their potential continuing negative impact for some individuals. Far too often people reflect back upon their own childhood and deduce that their experiences with bullying and/or rejection although unpleasant, did not substantially change their life for the worse. Such conclusions may

Table 21.1 Implications for Practice

	Recommendations for Practitioners and Researchers
Who	• Choose two or more informant modalities (self, peer, or teacher) to enable adequate triangulation of the behavior and minimization of mono-method bias in measuring the construct.
What	• Develop a clear operationalization of the bullying or aggression construct(s) that effectively capture either the three requisite components of bullying behavior [(1) behavior is aggressive and negative, (2) it is carried out repeatedly, and (3) the relationship is characterized by an imbalance of power] or the two components of aggression [(1) an intent to harm on the part of the aggressor, and (2) a feeling of hurt on the part of the victim].
Where	• Do not discount the potential influence of classroom or social group effects that may influence or limit the reliability and validity of nomination procedures. Homeroom effects should be ruled out in younger children, and social group effects should be ruled out with older children.
When	• Choose a consistent and recent period for retrospective reporting of bullying or related behaviors. Timing within a school term should be noted. • Assessment should be objective and standardized to minimize suggestion or susceptibility to eyewitness memory effects.
Why	• Choose between a formative or reflective model as the appropriate theoretical measurement model. • Measure at least three indicators of the construct. • Choose the scaling framework (CTT or IRT) that is most appropriate for the level of measurement (nominal, ordinal, interval, or ratio) of your indicators. • Careful consideration should be given to any potential threats to the internal validity of decisions.
How	• Determine the most appropriate indicator format or combination of indicator formats. • Realize that the choice of format has implications for how the data must be treated when using it to inform intervention or even disciplinary decisions.

lead to assumptions that victimization and rejection are normative experiences that inevitably lead to resilience and greater capacity to cope with social difficulties. They may also lead adults to conclude that some children's negative reactions to being bullied or rejected are an exaggeration, one to be countered with suggestions to "toughen up" or "learn to cope." However, a fuller appreciation of the ways in which biological function interacts with life experiences over time (biological embedding) allows one to understand that, although some children may be resilient, others are at greater risk as a function of biological vulnerability. Understanding this important interaction is critical to helping silence the skeptics and prompt people to be more proactive about the need intervene on behalf of bullied and rejected children (Hazler, Carney, & Granger, 2006). Although biology is not destiny, experiences with peer victimization and rejection can indeed get "under the skin" and significantly alter the individual's capacity to cope with stress, placing them further at risk for long-term maladjustment. Future research must also be directed toward consideration of how we might intervene to change neurobiological processes that have been set in motion. The bad news is that we know that the social communication systems of the brain are changed when children experience trauma. The good news is that the brain is a "use it or lose it" organ (use-dependent), and, while the stress system of the brain grows with negative experience, so can the relationship system of brain grow with appropriate interventions (Perry & Szalavitz, 2007).

Acknowledgments

This chapter was supported by a Community-University Research Alliance grant from the Social Sciences and Humanities Research Council of Canada. We thank Amanda Krygsman for her help with editing this chapter.

References

Arseneault, L., Walsh, E., Trzesniewski, K., Newcombe, R., Caspi, A., & Moffitt, T. E. (2006). Bullying victimization uniquely contributes to adjustment problems in young children: A nationally representative cohort study. *Pediatrics, 118*, 130–139.

Ball, H. A., Arseneault, L., Taylor, A., Maughan, B., Caspi, A., & Moffitt, T. E. (2008). Genetic and environmental influences on victims, bullies, and bully-victims in childhood. *Journal of Child Psychology and Psychiatry, 49*, 104–112.

Baumeister R. F., & Leary M. R. (1995).The need to belong: Desire for interpersonal attachment as a fundamental human motivation. *Psychological Bulletin, 117*, 497–529.

Bremner J. D., Randall, P., Vermetten, Staib, L., Bronen, R. A., Mazure, C., Capelli, S., McCarthy, G., Innis, R. B., & Charney, D. S. (1997). Magnetic Resonance Imaging-based measurement of hippocampal volume in posttraumatic stress disorder related to childhood physical and sexual abuse — A preliminary report. *Biological Psychiatry, 41*, 23–32.

Bremner J. D., & Vermetten, E. (2001). Stress and development: Behavioral and biological consequences. *Development and Psychopathology, 13*, 473–489.

Brendgen, M., Boivin, M., Vitaro, F., Girard, A., Dionne, G., & Pérusse, D. (2008). Gene-environment interaction between peer-victimization and child aggression. *Development and Psychopathology, 20*, 455–471.

Buhs, E. S., Ladd, G. W., & Herald, S. L. (2006). Peer exclusion and victimization: Processes that mediate the relation between peer group rejection and children's classroom engagement and achievement? *Journal of Educational Psychology, 98*, 1–13.

Carter, C. S. (1998). Neuroendocrine perspectives on social attachement and love. *Psychoneuroendrocrinology, 23*, 779–818.

Carter, C. S., Devries, A. C., & Gertrz, L. L. (1995). Physiological substrates of mammalian monogamy: The prairie vole model. *Neuroscience & Biobehavioural Reviews, 19*, 303–314.

Caspi, A., Sugden, K., Moffitt, T. E., Taylor, A., Craig, I. W., Harrington, H., et al. (2003). Influence of life stress on depression: Moderation by a polymorphism in the 5-HTT Gene. *Science, 301*, 386–389.

Cicchetti, D., & Rogosch, F.A. (2001). Diverse patterns of neuroendocrine activity in maltreated children. *Development and Psychopathology, 13*, 677–693.

Davidson, R. J. (2000). Affective style, psychopathology, and resilience: Brain mechanisms and plasticity. *American Psychologist, 55*, 1196–1214.

Debellis, M. D. (2001). Developmental traumatology: The psychobiological development of maltreated children and its implications for research, treatment and policy. *Development and Psychopathology, 13*, 539–564.

Dienstbier, R. (1989). Arousal and physiological toughness: Implications for mental and physical health. *Psychological Review, 96*, 84–100.

Eisenberger, N. I., Lieberman, M. D., & Williams, K. D. (2003). Does rejection hurt? An fMRI study of social exclusion. *Science, 302*, 290–292.

Gilbert, P. (1992). *Human nature and suffering.* Hillsdale, NJ: Erlbaum.

Gunnar, M. R., & Quevedo, K. (2007). The neurobiology of stress and development. *Annual Reviews of Psychology, 58*, 145–173.

Gunnar, M. R., Sebanc, A. M., Tout, K., Donzella, B., & van Dulmen, M. M. (2003). Peer rejection, temperament and cortisol activity in preschoolers. *Developmental Psychobiology, 43*, 346–358.

Hansen, A. M., Hogh, A., Persson, R., Karlson, B., Garde, A. H., & Orbaek, P. (2006). Bullying at work, health outcomes, and physiological stress response. *Journal of Psychosomatic Research, 60*, 63–72.

Hart, J., Gunnar, M., & Cicchetti, D. (1995). Salivary cortisol in maltreated children: Evidence of relations between neuroendocrine activity and social competence. *Development and Psychopathology, 7*, 11–26.

Hawker, D. S., & Boulton, M. J. (2000). Twenty years' research on peer victimization and psychological maladjustment: a meta-analytic review of cross-sectional studies. *Journal of Child Psychology & Psychiatry, 41*, 441–455.

Hazler, R. J., Carney, J. V., & Granger, D. A. (2006). Integrating biological measures into the study of bullying. *Journal of Counseling & Development, 84*, 298–307.

Heim, C., Ehlert, U., & Hellhammer, D. H. (2000). The potential role of hypocortisolism in the pathology of stress-related bodily disorders. *Psychoneuroendocrinology, 25*, 1–35.

Heinrichs, M., Baumgartner, T., Kirschbaum, C., & Ehlert, U. (2003). Social support and oxytocin interact to suppress cortisol and subjective responses to psychosocial stress. *Biological Psychiatry, 54*, 1389–1398.

Herman, B. H., & Panksepp, J. (1978). Effects of morphine and naloxone on separation distress and approach attachment: Evidence for opiate mediation of social affect. *Pharmacology Biochemistry and Behaviour, 9*, 213–220.

Hymel, S., Vaillancourt, T., McDougall, P., & Renshaw, P. D. (2002). Peer acceptance and rejection in childhood. In P. K. Smith & C. H. Hart (Eds.), *Blackwell Handbook of Childhood Social Development* (pp. 265–284). Oxford, UK: Blackwell.

Hymel, S., Schonert-Reichl, K., & Miller, L. D. (2006). Reading, 'riting, 'rithmetic and relationships: Considering the social side of education. *Exceptionality Education Canada, 16,* 149–192.

Insel, T. R., & Young, L. J. (2001). The neurobiology of attachment. *Neuroscience, 2,* 139–136.

Ito, Y., Teicher, M. H., Glod, C. S., & Ackerman, E. (1998). Preliminary evidence for aberrant corticol development in abused children: A quantitative EEG study. *Journal of Neuropsychiatry and Clinical Neurosciences, 10,* 298–307.

Juvonen, J. (2000). The social functions of attributional face-saving tactics among early adolescents. *Educational Psychology Review, 12,* 15–32.

Juvonen, J., Nishina, A., & Graham, S. (2000). Peer harassment, psychological adjustment, and school functioning in early adolescence. *Journal of Educational Psychology, 92,* 349–359.

Kagan, J. (1994). *Galen's prophecy: Temperament in human nature.* New York: Basic Books.

Kaplan G. A., Wilson T. W., Cohen R. D., Kauhanen J., Wu, M., & Salonen J. T. (1994). Social functioning and overall mortality: Prospective evidence from the Kuopio Ischemic Heart Disease Risk Factor Study. *Epidemiology, 5,* 495–500.

Kaufman, J., & Charney, D. (2001). Effects of early stress on brain structure and function: Implications for understanding the relationship between child maltreatment and depression. *Development and Psychopathology, 13,* 451–471.

Kim, Y. S., Leventhal, B. L., Koh, Y. J., Hubbard, A., & Boyce, W. T. (2006). School bullying and youth violence: Causes or consequences of psychopathologic behavior? *Archives of General Psychiatry, 63,* 1035–1041.

Kirschbaum, C., & Hellhammer, D. H. (1989). Response variability of salivary cortisol under psychological stimulation. *Journal of Clinical Chemistry & Clinical Biochemistry, 27,* 237.

Kliewer, W. (2006). Violence exposure and cortisol responses in urban youth. *International Journal of Behavioral Medicine, 13,* 109–120.

Knox, S. S., Uvnäs-Moberg, K. (1998). Social isolation and cardiovascular disease: An atherosclerotic Pathway? *Psychoneuroendocrinology, 23,* 877–890.

Kosfeld, M., Heinrichs, M., Zak, P.J., Fischbacher, U., & Fehr, E. (2005). Oxytocin increases trust in humans. *Nature, 435,* 673–676.

Koverola, C., Papas, M. A., Pitts, S., Murtaugh, C., Black, M. M., & Dubowitz, H. J. (2005). Longitudinal investigation of the relationship among maternal victimization, depressive symptoms, social support, and children's behavior and development. *Journal of Interpersonal Violence, 20,* 1523–1546.

Kumpulainen, K., & Rasanen, E. (2000). Children involved in bullying at elementary school age: Their psychiatric symptoms and deviance on adolescence. *Child Abuse & Neglect, 24,* 1567–1577.

Lucki, I. (1998). The spectrum of behaviors influenced by serotonin. *Biological Psychiatry, 44,* 151–162.

Lupien, S. J., Fiocco, A., Wan, N., Maheu, F., Lord, C., Schramek, T., & Tu, M. T. (2005). Stress hormones and human memory function across the lifespan. *Psychoneuroendicrinology, 30,* 225–242.

MacDonald, G., & Leary, M. (2005). Why does social exclusion hurt? The relationship between social and physical pain. *Psychological Bulletin, 131,* 202–223.

McDougall, P., Hymel, S., Vaillancourt, T., & Mercer, L. (2001). The consequences of childhood peer rejection. In M. Leary (Ed.), *Interpersonal rejection* (pp. 213–247). New York: Oxford University Press.

McEwen, B. S. (1992). Corticosteroids and hippocampal plasticity. *Annals of the New York Academy of Sciences, 746,* 134–142.

McEwen, B. S. (1998). Protective and damaging effects of stress mediators. *The New England Journal of Medicine, 338,* 171–179.

Miller, J., & Vaillancourt, T. (2007). Relation between childhood peer victimization and adult perfectionism: Are victims of indirect aggression more perfectionistic? *Aggressive Behavior, 33,* 230–241.

Nansel, T. R., Haynie, D. L., & Simons-Morton, B. G. (2003). The association of bullying and victimization with middle school adjustment. *Journal of Applied School Psychology, 19,* 45–61.

Nelson, E. E., & Panksepp, J. (1998). Brain substrates of infant–mother attachment: Contributions of opioids, oxytocin, and norepinephrine. *Neuroscience & Biobehavioural Reviews, 22,* 437–452.

Newman, M., Holden, G., & Delville, Y. (2005). Isolation and stress of being bullied. *Journal of Adolescence, 283,* 343–357.

Olweus D. (1999). Sweden. In P. K. Smith, Y. Morita, J. Junger-Tas, D. Olweus, R. Catalano, & P. Slee (Eds.), *The nature of school bullying: A cross-national perspective* (pp. 7–27). London: Routledge.

Parker, J. G., & Asher, S. R. (1987). Peer relations and later personal adjustment: Are low-accepted children at risk? *Psychological Bulletin, 102,* 357–389.

Pedersen, C. A. (2004). Biological aspects of social bonding and the roots of human violence. *Annals of the New York Academy of Sciences, 1036,* 106–127.

Perry, B.D. & Szalavitz, M. (2007). *The boy who was raised as a dog.* New York: Basic Books.

Rigby, K. (1998). The relationship between reported health and involvement in bully/victim problems among male and female secondary schoolchildren. *Journal of Health Psychology, 3,* 465–476.

Rosen, J. B., & Schulkin, J. (1998). From normal fear to pathological anxiety. *Psychological Review, 105,* 325–350.

Rubin, K. H., Stewart, S. L., & Coplan, R. J. (1995). Social withdrawal in childhood: Conceptual and empirical perspectives. In T. Ollendick & R. Prinz (Eds.), *Advances in clinical child psychology* (Vol. 17, pp. 157–196), New York: Plenum.

Sapolsky, R. M. (1996). Why stress is bad for your brain. *Science, 27,* 749–750.

Sapolsky, R. M. (2000). Glucocorticoids and hippocampal atrophy in neuropsychiatric disorders. *Archives of General Psychiatry, 57,* 925–935.

Sapolsky, R. M. (2004). Mothering style and methylation. *Nature Neuroscience, 7,* 791–792.

Sapolsky, R. M., Uno, H., Rebert, C. S., & Finch, C. E. (1990). Hippocampal damage associated with prolonged glucocorticoid exposure in primates. *Journal of Neuroscience, 10,* 2897–2902.

Schmidt, L. A., & Schulkin, J. (Eds.). (1999). *Extreme fear, shyness, and social phobia: Origins, biological mechanisms, and clinical outcomes.* New York: Oxford University Press.

Schulkin, J., Gold, P. W., & McEwen, B. S. (1998). Induction of corticotropin-releasing hormone gene expression by glucocorticoids: Implication for understanding the states of fear and anxiety and allostatic load. *Psychoneuroendocrinology, 23,* 219–243.

Schwartz, D., Gorman, A. H., Nakamoto, J., & Toblin, R. L. (2005). Victimization in the peer group and children's academic functioning. *Journal of Educational Psychology, 97,* 425–435.

Seeman, T. E., & Syme, S. L. (1987). Social networks and coronary artery disease: A comparison of the structure and function of social relations as predictors of disease. *Psychosomatic Medicine, 49,* 341–354.

Seyle, H. (1998). A syndrome produced by diverse nocuous agents. *Journal of Neuropsychiatry and Clinical Neurosciences, 10,* 230–231.

Slee, P. T. (1995). Bullying: Health concerns of Australian secondary school students. *International Journal of Adolescence & Youth, 5,* 215–224.

Sourander, A., Helstela, L., Helenius, H., & Piha, J. (2000). Persistence of bullying from childhood to adolescence- a longitudinal 8-year follow-up study. *Child Abuse & Neglect, 24,* 873–881.

Squire, L. R. (1992). Memory and the hippocampus: A synthesis from findings with rats, monkeys, and humans. *Psychological Review, 99,* 195–231.

Stein, M. B., Koverola, C., Hanna, C., Torchia, M. G., & McClarty, B. (1997). Hippocampal volume in women victimized by childhood sexual abuse. *Psychological Medicine, 27,* 951–959.

Teicher, M. H., Ito, Y., Glod, C. A., Schiffer, F., & Gelbard, H. A. (1996). Neurophysiological mechanisms of stress response in children. In C. R. Pfeffer (Ed.), *Severe stress and mental disturbances in children* (pp. 59–84). Washington, DC: American Psychiatric Press.

Thornhill, R., & Thornhill, N. W. (1989). The evolution of psychological pain. In R. W. Bell & N. J. Bell (Eds.), *Sociobiology and the Social Sciences* (pp.73–103). Lubbock: Texas Tech University Press.

Uvnäs-Moberg, K. (1998). Oxytocin may mediate the benefits of positive social interaction and emotions. *Psychoneuroendocrinology, 23,* 819–835.

Vaillancourt, T., Duku, E., deCatanzaro, D., MacMillan, H., Muir, C., & Schmidt, L. A. (2008). Variation in hypothalamic-pituitary-adrenal axis activity among bullied and non-bullied children. 294–305.

van Goozen, S. H. M., Snoek, H., Fairchild, G., & Harold, G. T. (2007). The evidence for a neurobiological model of childhood antisocial behavior. *Psychological Bulletin, 133,* 149–182.

Weaver, I. C. J., Cervoni, N., Champagne, F. A., D'Alessio, A. C., Sharma, S., Seckl, J. R., et al. (2004). Epigenetic programming by maternal behavior. *Nature Neuroscience, 7,* 847–854.

Weaver, I. C. J., Champagne, F. A., Brown, S. E., Dymov, S., Sharma, S., Meaney, M. J., et al. (2005). Reversal of maternal programming of stress responses in adult offspring through methyl supplementation: Altering epigenetic marking later in life. *Journal of Neuroscience, 25,* 11045–11054.

Wentzel, K. R., & Caldwell, K. (1997). Friendships, peer acceptance, and group membership: Relations to academic achievement in middle school. *Child Development, 68,* 1198–1209.

Williams, K. D. (2007). Ostracism. *Annual Review of Psychology, 58,* 425–452.

Windle, R. J., Kershaw, Y. M., Shanks, N., Wood, S. A., Lightman, S. L., & Ingram, C. D. (2004). Oxytocin attenuates stress-induced c-fos mRNA expression in specific forebrain regions associated with modulation of hypothalamo-pituitary-adrenal activity. *Journal of Neuroscience, 24,* 2974–2982.

Wolke, D., Woods, S., Bloomfield, L., & Karstadt, L. (2001). Bullying involvement in primary school and common health problems. *Archives of Disease in Childhood, 85,* 197–201.

Yehuda, R. (1997). Sensitization of the hypothalamic-pituitary-adrenal axis in posttraumatic stress disorder. *Annals of the New York Academy of Sciences, 821,* 57–75.

23

Assessment of Bullying/Victimization
The Problem of Comparability Across Studies and Across Methodologies

SUSAN M. SWEARER, AMANDA B. SIEBECKER,
LYNAE A. JOHNSEN-FRERICHS, AND CIXIN WANG

Bullying has become a ubiquitous problem for schools and communities over the past three decades. Initially, researchers focused on understanding bullying by investigating prevalence, risk factors, and psychological and behavioral correlates. More recently, the identification of effective prevention and intervention programs has become a primary focal point for researchers. However, to determine which interventions will effectively reduce bullying behaviors, it is imperative that researchers and educators start with accurately assessing involvement in bullying.

Considerable consensus has been reached in the extant bullying literature regarding the definition of bullying, involvement in bullying, and the psychological and social impact of involvement in bullying (Espelage & Swearer, 2004). However, less consensus has been reached regarding the most efficient, reliable, and valid methods for measuring bullying (Cornell, Sheras, & Cole, 2006; Swearer, Espelage, Vaillancourt, & Hymel, in press). There is significant variability in the methods utilized in the assessment of bullying. The majority of assessments are self-report questionnaires; however the question sets, definitions used, and cut-off points for determining involvement in bullying vary greatly. These inconsistencies may account for the variance in prevalence estimates of bullying across studies (Solberg & Olweus, 2003). This chapter investigates these issues in the extant bullying literature and examines data using different cut-off points to illustrate how these cut rates impact the assessment and correlates of bullying.

Overview of Bullying among School-Aged Youth

Researchers agree that the definition set forth by Olweus (1994) is the most widely accepted (e.g., Camodeca & Goossens, 2005; Espelage & Swearer, 2003; Griffin & Gross, 2004; Kokkinos & Panayiotou, 2004; Smith, 2004; Smith, Cowie, Olafsson, & Liefooghe, 2002; Unnever, 2005) definition of bullying. Olweus defines bullying as "a negative action when someone intentionally inflicts, or attempts to inflict, injury or discomfort upon another" in addition, he states there should be an imbalance of strength and the behavior is repeated over time (1994, p. 1173). Based upon this definition, researchers have acknowledged the importance of these three elements of bullying: (a) purposeful, (b) imbalance of power, and (c) continual.

There is also consensus regarding what is considered *involvement* in bullying. Specifically, involvement is considered by many to occur along a continuum, meaning that students can participate in multiple roles (Bosworth, Espelage, & Simon, 1999; Espelage & Swearer, 2003). In the general bullying literature, five roles have been identified: bully, victim, bully-victim, bystander, and uninvolved. Bullies are students who perpetrate the bullying behavior; victims are those students who are the targets of the bullying behavior; bully-victims are students who engage in both bullying others and being bullied themselves; bystanders are individual who observe bullying behavior; and finally, there are students who report no current involvement in bullying. This chapter will refer to involvement in "bullying/victimization" to indicate that these roles can be fluid and may fluctuate over time.

Definition of Bullying

There are three common components to all definitions of bullying (Olweus, 1994). Bullying is defined in the literature as an intentional negative action (including both verbal and physical) that occurs over time in a relationship characterized by an imbalance of strength and power (Olweus, 1994). Given this imbalance of strength and power, it is difficult for individuals being bullied to defend themselves. Some children may resort to bullying behaviors when they do not have other, more appropriate means of achieving their goals. Instead of developing positive means of interacting with and communicating their needs to others, these children learn to control others through manipulation and intimidation.

Purposeful Students who bully may use various means to hurt, harm, or damage their targets physically, socially, or emotionally. Specifically, their bullying actions are designed to intentionally cause harm. The harm endured by the victim can be physical, verbal, social, or relational in nature. Prior research on bullying has focused primarily upon understanding the characteristics and comorbidities associated with forms of bullying intended to hurt others through physical means (i.e., hitting, pushing, and fighting). Much of this research has been with boys who exhibited aggression in a direct and physical manner towards their peers. However, recent research has found that children can bully others in multiple ways (Crick & Grotpeter, 1995; Underwood, 2003). Girls have been found to be more likely to use relational aggression, defined as "harming others through purposeful manipulation and damage of their peer relationships" (Crick & Grotpeter, 1995, p. 711). This type of aggression takes the form of gossiping, leaving others out on purpose, or threatening to withdraw friendships. However, boys also engage in this form of bullying (Swearer, 2008). Therefore, the definition of bullying should be broad enough to incorporate both physical and relational forms of purposeful aggression.

Imbalance of Power Bullying behaviors occur to the extent that there is an imbalance of power between the bully and the victim (Smith & Sharp, 1994), such that the bully has more power and authority than the victim. An imbalance of power can be physical (i.e., the bully may be physically stronger or larger than the victim) or psychological (i.e., the bully may have higher social status than the victim or be able to readily damage the victim's social status). This imbalance of strength and power makes it difficult for victims to defend themselves. However, while researchers agree that an imbalance of power is a necessary condition for bullying, difficult questions arise regarding how to empirically assess differences in power that are inherent in the bullying dynamic.

Continual Bullying behavior happens repeatedly over time. Thus, it is not bullying when peers engage in an occasional argument or conflict (Olweus, 1984). However, there has been disagreement in the literature regarding the criteria for the frequency of aggressive acts as constituting bullying behavior. Some researchers include within the classification of bullying any and all aggressive behavior towards others. Other researchers specify that aggressive behavior directed toward others must meet a particular frequency cut-off or criteria in order to be classified as bullying. It can be argued that a less stringent definition of bullying may lead to over-identification of involvement in bullying/victimization and that a more stringent definition may lead to under-identification. It appears that much of the research conducted thus far has defined bullying inconsistently, often classifying singular acts of aggression as bullying instead of requiring repetition of the behaviors to denote bullying.

Increased understanding and awareness of bullying dynamics, as they typically occur in schools, provides staff and students with vital information about how to prevent future occurrences of bullying. School personnel who are informed about the essential components (i.e., purposeful, imbalance of power, continual) of bullying behavior may be more likely to accurately identify and more effectively respond to instances of bullying. Furthermore, an accurate method of measurement lends itself to data-based decision making, which helps to ensure that school personnel are addressing the relevant problems that the students are experiencing. With accurate assessment guiding data-based decision making, school personnel will be less likely to over- or underidentify bullying/victimization.

Measurement Issues

A primary concern in the bullying research is the lack of consistency in assessing bullying behaviors, which impacts the reported prevalence of bullying among youth. These different assessment strategies influence the ability to compare bullying involvement across studies. For example, a partial review of the literature found that the percentage of students involved in bullying ranged from 13% to 75% (Demaray & Malecki, 2003; Hoover, Olver, & Hazler, 1992; Kaltiala-Heino, Rimpela, Rantanen, & Rimpela, 2000; Nansel, Overpeck, & Pilla, 2001; Salmivalli, Lappalainen, & Lagerspetz, 1998; Seals & Young, 2003; Solberg & Olweus, 2003; Unnever, 2005; Woods & White, 2005). Implications for this wide range of prevalence rates may be partially explained by the methodologies in which bullying as assessed. Currently, there remains a lack of consistent and agreed upon methods for measuring bullying. Specifically, assessments vary in terms of whether a definition is used, the components of the definition, cut-off points for determining involvement, lack of reliability information, and the absence of validity studies.

The amount of information provided to participants concerning bullying varies across different bullying assessments. Some researchers argue that the word "bullying" itself should not be used in the assessment. For example, Espelage, Bosworth, and Simon (2001) suggest that using the word "bullying" and subsequently providing a definition may not be the best method for measuring bullying as there is no clear cut-off for what constitutes categorization along the bully/victim continuum. As such, some assessments query respondents regarding specific behaviors as their primary means to assess bullying, but do not provide a definition of bullying, (e.g., Bosworth et al., 1999; Chan, Myron, & Crawshaw, 2005; Espelage et al., 2001; Espelage, Holt, & Henkel, 2003; Kokkinos & Panayiotou, 2004). This creates a covert assessment of bullying, which may decrease the likelihood that respondents will "fake good" (Chan et al., p. 452). Students may be more likely to provide honest responses when they are unaware that the construct of bullying is being assessed.

On the other hand, Solberg and Olweus (2003) argue that to accurately assess bullying, the term "bullying" should be used and defined. Researchers are concerned that since bullying has become a commonly used descriptor among the general public, the term may not always be used accurately. Therefore, the provision of a definition may be necessary to ensure accurate reporting of one's own behavior or that of others. When the word "bullying" is used, some studies do not provide a definition. This may call into question the validity of such assessments that use the term without first defining it. Further research is necessary to determine whether providing a definition of bullying or not significantly affects accurate responding. Investigation regarding the reliability and validity in these instances is also needed.

There is little consensus regarding categorization of students along the bully/victim continuum (Espelage et al., 2001). There is a large amount of variability in terms of the cut-off points used to classify students as bullies, victims, bully-victims, or bystanders. Solberg and Olweus (2003) determined that students who reported being bullied "about once a week or more" reported more negative outcomes on various psychosocial adjustment variables compared to students who reported being bullied "2 or 3 times per month." However, the authors also found that there were significant differences between the students who were bullied "2 or 3 times a month" and those who reported being bullied "only once or twice." Based on the results of this study, Solberg and Olweus hypothesized that using "about once a week" as a cut-off point, there would be a large number of false positives. This would likely be the case since the "2 or 3 times a month" respondents also had clear bully/victim characteristics. Therefore, to capture all students who are affected by bully/victim interactions, the authors concluded that the cut-off point should include involvement of at least "two or three times per month." Some methods may be more restrictive in their interpretation of what constitutes repetition, while others may less restrictive, by including incidents that have only occurred "once or twice." Table 23.1 illustrates the variability in cut-off points across the extant bullying research. Studies included in this review were empirical studies that focused on bullying and included sufficient information to evaluate the measures and included middle-school aged students. Studies were excluded if they focused only on one group of students involved in bullying (e.g., bullies only) or if they used targeted populations such as a particular racial or ethnic group, one gender only, or juvenile offenders.

In addition to variability in terms of cut-off points and definition concerns, reliability data for bullying assessments is a topic of concern. Currently, there is relatively little reliability data available for most bullying assessments. Many bullying assessment materials were developed in response to the demand of school personnel and community members. As a result, the psychometric properties have not received adequate attention (Cornell et al., 2006). For example, the manual of one of the most widely used measures of bullying, the Olweus Bully/Victim Questionnaire (1986), reports that several analyses of reliability and validity have been conducted; however, none have been published (Furlong, Greif, & Sharkey, 2005). Furthermore, many assessments of bullying utilize a small question set which inhibits the analysis of internal consistency. The lack of reliability data currently available is an additional concern in the bullying research base.

The lack of concurrent and construct validity evidence is another troubling area for bullying researchers. Specifically, it is imperative that researchers begin to validate that their measures actually measure the construct of bullying and that those measures correlate with established measures. There are several methods that could be used to validate specific measures of bullying and victimization. Specifically, office referral data has been found to be a reliable method for identifying problem behaviors such as bullying (Loeber, Green, Lahey, Frick, & McBurnett, 2000; Sprague, Hill, Stieber, Simonsen, Nishioka, & Wagner, 2001; Swearer & Cary, 2003). As a result, office referrals may serve as validation for bullying assessments. Additional sources of

Table 23.1 Review of Bullying Involvement Assessment Strategies

Measure	Citation	Participant Age/Grade	Cut-Off Point	Definition Used	Components Assessed	Reported Prevalence Rate
Olweus Questionnaire (German version) Survey	Scheithaur et al., 2006	5th–10th grade	Involvement in a bullying/victimization at least "once per week" or "several times per week"	Yes	Continual Imbalance of Power Purposeful	12.1% bullies, 11.1% victims, 2.3% bully-victims 25.5% involvement
Olweus Questionnaire (adapted)	Unnever, 2005	7th–12th grade	Two or three times per month	Yes	Continual Imbalance of Power Purposeful	8.3% bullies 20.7 victims 8.2% aggressive-victims 37.2% involvement
Olweus Questionnaire (Italian version) Scale	Baldry & Farrington, 2004	11–15 years	At least sometimes in the last three months	Yes	Continual Imbalance of Power Purposeful	25.2% bullies 29.4% victims 54.6% involvement
Olweus Bullying Questionnaire	Collins et al., 2004	Post-Primary Students	Once or twice a term or two or three times per month	Yes	Continual Imbalance of Power Purposeful	26% bullies 24% victims 50% involvement
Olweus Bully/Victim Questionnaire	Solberg & Olweus, 2003	5th–9th grade; 11–15 years	Respond to one of seven items as occurring at least two to three times per month	Yes	Continual Imbalance of Power Purposeful	4.8% bullies 8.3% victims 1.6% bully-victims 14.7% involvement
Olweus Questionnaire (Italian version)	Baldry & Farrington, 1999	11–14 years	Sometimes or more	Yes	Continual Imbalance of Power Purposeful	25.2% bullies 29.4% victims 54.6% involvement
Two questions from the Olweus Questionnaire	Sutton & Keogh, 2000	8–12 years	"sometimes" or more	No	Continual	6% bullies 15% victims 4% bully-victims 25% involvement
WHO-HSBC Survey	Klomek et al., 2007	9th–12th grade	"Frequently"	Yes	Continual Imbalance of Power Purposeful	8% bullies 6.5% victims 14.5% involvement

(continued)

Table 23.1 Continued

Measure	Citation	Participant Age/Grade	Cut-Off Point	Definition Used	Components Assessed	Reported Prevalence Rate
WHO-HSBC Survey	Srabstein, McCarther, Shao, & Huang, 2006	6th–10th grade	"once a week" or more frequently	Yes	Continual / Purposeful / Imbalance of Power	6.4% bullies / 5.7% victims / 2.2% bully-victims / 14.3% involvement
WHO-HSBC Survey	Volk, Craig, Boyce, & King, 2006	12–19 years 6th–10th grade	"once a week" or more frequently	Yes	Continual / Purposeful / Imbalance of Power	6.1% bullies / 7.6% victims / 0.9% bully-victims / 14.6% involvement
WHO-HSBC Survey	Nansel et al., 2001	6th–10th grade	"once a week" or more	Yes	Continual / Imbalance of Power / Purposeful	8.8% bullies / 8.4% victims / 6.3% bully-victims / 23.6% involvement
Peer Victimization Scale & Bullying Behavior	Houbre et al., 2006	5th grade 9–12 years	2.5 out of 4	No	Purposeful	13% bullies / 18% victims / 10% bully-victims / 41% involvement
Unnamed Survey	Cassidy & Taylor, 2005	12–15 years	"persistent"	No	Continual	13% bullies / 16% victims / 9% bully-victims / 38% involvement
Status as a victim or bully	Ivarsson et al., 2005	14 years	"sometimes" "often" or "very often"	Mobbning	Purposeful	18% bullies / 10% victims / 9% bully-victims / 37% involvement
Bully Victim Questionnaire	Kokkinos & Panayiotou, 2004	11–15 years	75th Percentile	No	Continual	8.4% bullies / 21.5% victims / 15.3% bully-victims / 45.2% involvement

Bully Questionnaire	Demaray & Malecki, 2003	6th–8th grade	25th Percentile	No	Continual Purposeful	12% bullies 16% victims 13% bully-victims 41% involvement
Peer Relations Questionnaire	Seals & Young, 2003	7th–8th grade, 12–17 years	"often"	No	Continual Purposeful	10% bullies 13% victims 1% bully-victims 24% involvement
The Bully Survey	Swearer & Cary, 2003	6th–8th grade, 11–15 years	Yes to involvement as a bully, victim, or both during past year	Yes	Continual Imbalance of Power Purposeful	5% bullies 39% victims 30% bully-victims 74% involvement

validity may be found through correlating measures of aggression (e.g., Aggression Question-naire, Buss & Warren, 2000) with bullying assessments. Bullying is conceptualized as a subset of aggression; therefore measures of aggression, especially those with subscales relating to physi-cal, verbal, and indirect forms of aggression, can also provide evidence that bullying is being measured.

In addition to several other concerns in the bullying research base, there is variation in the type of self-report measures used for bullying assessment. Specifically, bullying self-report tends to be either scale or survey data. For example, Demaray and Malecki (2003); Houbre, Tarquinio, Thuillier, and Hergott (2006); and Kokkinos and Panayiotou (2004) utilize scales to determine involvement in bullying. On the other hand, Ivarsson, Broberg, Arvidsson, and Gillberg (2005); Seals and Young (2003); Scheithaur Hayer, Petermann, and Jugert (2006); and Swearer and Cary (2003), use survey data. Bullying scales focus on reporting frequency of behaviors to determine involvement in bullying whereas surveys focus on a broader picture of the bullying experience by querying about the location of the bullying, who responded and how (Espelage & Swearer, 2003). There are strengths and weaknesses associated with both methodologies. One must consider the purpose of the assessment to best determine which assessment will be the most useful.

Problems arise when there is a lack of consistency across research measures. Specifically, some bullying assessments do not provide a definition of bullying; yet assess bullying within the question set. However, using this procedure it is difficult to assess all three criteria set forth by Olweus (1993; e.g., purposeful, imbalance of power, and continual). For example, Kokkinos and Panayiotou (2004) assessed only the continual aspect, Houbre, Tarquinio, Thuillier, and Her-gott (2006) assessed only the purposeful behaviors, and Demaray and Malecki (2003) assessed continual behaviors and imbalance of power. As a result, it is difficult to determine whether any such bullying assessment *measures* bullying per se. Many of the assessments reviewed that do measure all three components do so by using a definition. Inclusion of a definition may ensure that respondents are in agreement regarding what bullying means. As a result, responses may be more likely to tap into actual bullying behavior, rather than relying on behavioral indicators of bullying. However, without validity studies it is unclear whether inclusion of a definition that incorporates all three components actually *measures* those aspects of bullying.

Solberg and Olweus (2003) are the only researchers who have systematically investigated the most accurate cut-off point for determining involvement in bullying based on frequency. While this is an important study, much more research is needed in terms of investigating the frequency of involvement in bullying and the associated consequences. In addition, there are no studies systematically investigating the impact of all three components of bullying. Specifically, it is imperative that we ensure that bullying assessments are accurately measuring bullying. There-fore, we must determine the appropriate cut-off points for determining involvement and the impact of imbalance of power and the purposeful intent of the behavior.

Consequences of Involvement in Bullying

The research in the area of bullying is replete with reports of the negative behavioral and psy-chological outcomes for students involved in bullying. Specifically, bullies have been found to be more angry (Bosworth et al., 1999), more depressed (Austin & Joseph, 1996; Bosworth et al., 1999; Slee, 1995), have poor self-concept (Houbre, Tarquinio, Thuillier, & Hergott, 2006), and higher incidence of conduct problems (Bosworth et al., 1999; Kokkinos & Panayiotou, 2004) compared to those not involved in bullying. Victims have been found to have higher incidences of depression (Craig, 1998; Hawker & Boulton, 2000; Seals & Young, 2003) and anxiety (Craig, 1998; Hawker & Boulton; Olweus, 1994; Rigby, 2003; Slee, 1994), cognitive problems (Houbre et al., 2006), friendship/social problems (Card, 2003; Ivarsson et al., 2005; Rigby; Storch, Brassard, & Masia-Warner, 2003 ; Rodkin, Farmer, & Pearl, 2006), and oppositional behavior (Kokkinos & Panayiotou, 2004). Furthermore, bully-victims have been found to be more depressed than bullies (Austin & Joseph, 1996; Ivarsson et al.) and victims (Swearer, Song, Cary, Eagle, & Mickelson, 2001; Kaltiala-Heino,et al., 2000), more anxious (Duncan, 1999; Swearer et al., 2001), exhibit problem behaviors (Ivarsson et al.; Kokkinos & Panayiotou) and experience more psychosomatic symptoms (Houbre et al., 2006) than others involved in bullying. Research on the negative effects of involvement as a bystander is relatively scarce. However, Nishina and Juvonen (2005) found that witnessing students being victimized is associated with increases in anxiety and school dislike. Based on this research, bullying appears to have a negative impact on the well-being of all students involved. However, considering the limitations of the bullying research base, these results must be investigated with a valid measure of bullying. In addition, it is unclear whether these psychosocial effects are more extreme for students who experience more frequent involvement in bullying/victimization and more severe imbalances in power.

Purpose of the Study

The purpose of this study was to examine different cut-off points for involvement in bullying and to derive involvement in bullying based on the classic elements of bullying: purposeful, imbalance of power, and continual. Based on responses to the Bully Survey (Swearer, 2001), five bully/victim involvement categories (BVIC) were derived by using different cut-off points as shown in Table 23.2. Table 23.3 shows the number of students involved in bullying based on the 14 different cut-off points. Using a large sample of students and different cut-off points for assessing bullying, the comparability of prevalence rates using different assessment methods was examined.

Specific research questions that guided this investigation were: (a) Which involvement status is most highly correlated with office referrals and does office referral data provide a validity check for self-reported involvement in bullying/victimization? (b) Which involvement status is most highly correlated with depression, anxiety, and aggression? (c) Is there a significant difference between students reporting infrequent involvement in bullying/victimization and frequent involvement in terms of severity and power imbalance?

Method

Participants

Data are presented from over 1,000 sixth-, seventh-, and eighth-grade students in five midwestern middle schools. Students in each cohort were administered a series of instruments during the spring of consecutive years, including 1999–2004. The following students participated in the study: 83 sixth-grade students (36 male and 47 female) in April 1999; 51 sixth-grade students (30 male and 21 female) in April 2000; 59 sixth-grade students (28 male and 31 female) in April 2001; 120 seventh-grade students (55 male and 65 female) in April 2001; 80 eighth-grade students (28 male and 52 female) in April 2001; 35 sixth-grade students (14 male and 21 female) in April 2002; 138 seventh-grade students (60 male and 78 female) in April 2002; 51 sixth-grade students (21 male and 30 female) in April 2003; 124 sixth-grade students in April 2004 (56 male and 68 female); 174 seventh-grade students (85 male and 89 female) in April 2004; 140 eighth-grade students (47 male and 93 female) in April 2004. The respective consent rates were: 42% in April 1999; 30% in April 2000; 41% in April 2001; 25% in April 2002; 33% in April 2003; and

Table 23.2 Bully/Victim Involvement Categories (BVIC)

	Bully Survey Criteria	Internal consistency
Bully status 1	Responded yes to the item, "Did you bully anyone this school year?"	n.a.
Bully status 2	Yes + indicated frequency by responding yes to "one or more times a day" or "one or more times a week."	n.a.
Bully status 3	Yes + frequency + "often happened" or "always happened" to a list of verbal and physical forms of bullying.	.85
Victim status 1	Responded yes to the item, "Have you been bullied this school year?"	n.a.
Victim status 2	Yes + indicated frequency by responding yes to "one or more times a day" or "one or more times a week."	n.a.
Victim status 3	Yes + frequency + "often happened" or "always happened" to a list of verbal and physical forms of bullying.	.89
Victim status 4	Yes + frequency + "often/always happened" + responded "often a problem" or "always a problem" to power differential items	.81
Bully-victim status 1	Bully status 1 + Victim status 2	n.a.
Bully-victim status 2	Bully status 2 + Victim status 2	n.a.
Bully-victim status 3	Bully status 3 + Victim status 3	n.a.
Bystander status 1	Responded yes to the item, "Did you ever see a student other than yourself who was bullied this school year?"	n.a.
Bystander status 2	Yes + indicated frequency by responding yes to "one or more times a day" or "one or more times a week."	n.a.
Bystander status 3	Yes + frequency + "often happened" or "always happened" to a list of verbal and physical forms of bullying.	.86
Not involved	Responded no to the items, "Have you been bullied this school year," "Did you ever see a student other than yourself who was bullied this school year, " and "Did you bully anyone this school year?'	n.a.

Note. n.a. = not applicable due to the dichotomous nature of the data.

24% in April 2004. Of the students having active parental consent to participate, 32 students dissented to participate in the study, 3 students relocated out of the school district, 2 students were expelled, and 1 student was unable to read due to language barriers. These figures are reflected in the participant rates reported. Thus, a total of 1,055 students, including 403 sixth-grade, 432 seventh-grade, and 220 eighth-grade students participated in the study.

Demographic characteristics for the participants across grades included, ages ranging from 11–13 years old (M = 11.67; SD = .55; n = 403) for the sixth-graders; 12–14 years old (M = 12.60; SD = .58; n = 432) for seventh-graders; and 13–15 years old (M = 13.54; SD = .54; n = 57) for the eighth-grade students. The racial distribution across cohorts was: 75% Caucasian, 6% African American, 6% Biracial, 5% Asian/Asian-American, 3% Latino, 1% Eastern European, and 1% Middle Eastern. These demographics are consistent with the overall school district population.

Measures

The Bully Survey (Swearer, 2001)   The Bully Survey is a three part, 31-question survey that queries students regarding their experiences with bullying, perceptions of bullying, and attitudes toward bullying. Bullying is defined in each section of the survey with the following definition: "Bullying is anything from teasing, saying mean things, or leaving someone out of a group to physical attacks (hitting, pushing, kicking) where one person or a group of people picks on

Table 23.3 Frequency, Percentage, Means, and SD of Different Measures Based on Different Involvement Cut-Offs

	Bully			Victim				Bully-victim			Bystander			Not involved
	s1	s2	s3	s1	s2	s3	s4	s1	s2	s3	s1	s2	s3	d
Frequency	84	26	60	361	47	248	146	296	39	145	214	77	193	98
%	8	2.5	5.7	34.3	4.5	23.5	13.8	28.1	3.7	13.7	20.3	7.3	18.3	9.3
Office referral	2.20	2.69	2.48	0.65	0.70	0.70	0.88	1.47	1.05	1.75	0.79	0.73	0.84	1.09
	(4.53)	(4.86)	(4.85)	(2.10)	(2.16)	(2.24)	(2.63)	(3.79)	(1.92)	(3.43)	(2.30)	(1.88)	(2.38)	(3.35)
N	84	26	60	361	47	248	146	293	39	145	214	77	193	96
Depression	10.56	8.50	10.96	9.38	12.75	11.01	12.76	11.49	16.00	13.71	5.51	3.00	5.43	5.48
	(7.74)	(6.36)	(7.66)	(7.51)	(8.33)	(7.84)	(7.91)	(8.66)	(11.31)	(9.68)	(4.96)	(3.29)	(5.03)	(6.65)
N	32	2	23	235	8	168	103	169	2	75	114	6	103	61
Anxiety	33.93	46.00	30.14	46.26	47.86	49.25	53.49	44.01	20.00	46.42	38.23	37.33	38.77	38.72
	(15.58)	(14.14)	(13.16)	(18.91)	(22.87)	(19.46)	(18.79)	(16.00)	1	(16.42)	(16.77)	(21.49)	(16.72)	(17.01)
N	30	2	21	227	7	164	103	162	1	72	113	6	103	60
Aggression total	95.69	88.50	96.21	79.64	88.14	84.00	86.18	89.35	117.00	95.45	69.13	70.33	69.80	69.09
	(23.82)	(28.99)	(26.14)	(21.35)	(15.49)	(21.80)	(22.17)	(20.76)	(4.24)	(19.65)	(17.97)	(14.54)	(18.28)	(19.38)
N	26	2	19	182	7	117	83	127	2	60	97	6	88	47
Physical aggression	22.12	16.00	22.84	15.60	20.13	16.52	16.52	19.07	24.50	20.58	13.85	10.50	13.88	14.45
	(10.19)	(11.31)	(11.11)	(6.85)	(6.17)	(7.19)	(7.43)	(7.53)	(6.36)	(7.87)	(6.40)	(2.74)	(6.57)	(5.91)
N	26	2	19	183	8	132	84	128	2	60	97	6	88	47
Verbal aggression	16.73	14.50	16.74	13.16	13.00	13.81	14.13	14.24	18.50	14.92	11.69	12.00	11.92	12.02
	(4.03)	(4.95)	(4.48)	(3.89)	(3.00)	(4.12)	(4.39)	(4.21)	(6.36)	(3.87)	(4.06)	(1.90)	(4.12)	(4.15)
N	26	2	19	182	7	131	83	128	2	61	97	6	88	47
Anger	19.62	18.00	19.95	15.88	15.00	16.76	17.08	17.98	24.50	19.23	13.46	14.00	13.46	13.66
	(6.11)	(5.66)	(6.70)	(5.51)	(7.60)	(5.74)	(6.04)	(5.30)	(0.71)	(5.06)	(4.70)	(5.96)	(4.78)	(4.78)
N	26	2	19	183	8	132	84	129	2	61	97	6	88	47
Hostility	20.58	28.50	20.00	21.20	21.50	22.46	23.70	21.90	26.50	23.67	17.53	19.50	17.72	17.60
	(6.08)	(3.54)	(6.23)	(6.22)	(5.58)	(6.26)	(5.88)	(5.76)	(2.12)	(5.50)	(5.16)	(4.46)	(5.24)	(5.23)
N	26	2	19	183	8	132	84	129	2	61	97	6	88	47
Indirect aggression	16.65	11.50	16.68	13.68	14.38	14.23	14.38	16.01	23.00	16.75	12.61	13.83	12.83	11.36
	(4.18)	(3.53)	(4.58)	(4.50)	(3.30)	(4.76)	(4.95)	(4.25)	(7.07)	(4.58)	(3.63)	(3.66)	(3.63)	(3.55)
N	26	2	19	183	8	132	84	129	2	61	97	6	88	47

Note. s1 = status by responding yes/no; s2 = status by responding yes/no + frequency; s3 = status by responding yes/no + frequency + behavioral descriptors; s4 = status by responding yes/no + frequency + behavioral descriptors + power imbalance.

another person over a long time. Bullying refers to things that happen in school but can also include things that happen on the school grounds or going to and from school." In Part A of the survey, students answer questions about when they were victims of bullying during the past year. If the participants report they have not been victims of bullying, they are instructed to skip Part A and begin at Part B. Part B of the survey addresses questions about the participants' observations of bullying behavior among their peers during the past year. If they report that they have not observed bullying behavior, the participants are instructed to skip Part B and resume completing the survey at Part C. Part C of the survey requests information from the participants about when they bullied other students. If the participants indicate that they have not bullied other students within the last year, they are instructed to skip Part C and complete the final section of the survey. The final section of the survey contains a scale that measures attitudes toward bullying. The current study examined 14 different cut-off points for involvement in bullying based on survey items from the Bully Survey (Swearer, 2001) querying dichotomous and continuous items.

Bully/victim involvement categories (BVIC) were derived by using different cut-off points for each category on the bully/victim continuum (i.e., bully, victim, bully/victim, bystander, and not involved). The cut-off points used were identical across each bully/victim category. To illustrate, Status 1 was derived by assessing involvement or no involvement based on responding yes/no to the item, "Have you been bullied this school year?" Status 2 was derived by assessing involvement or no involvement based on responding yes/no to the item, "Have you been bullied this school year?" and then indicating frequency by responding "yes" to "one or more times a day" or "one or more times a week." Status 3 was derived by assessing involvement or no involvement based on responding yes/no to the item, "Have you been bullied this school year?" and then indicating frequency by responding yes to "one or more times a day" or "one or more times a week" and then responding by checking "often happened" or "always happened" to a list of behavioral descriptors (i.e., nobody would talk to me; pushed or shoved me, etc.). Status 4 was derived by assessing involvement or no involvement based on responding yes/no to the item, "Have you been bullied this school year?" and then indicating frequency by responding yes to "one or more times a day" or "one or more times a week" and then responding by checking "often happened" or "always happened" to a list of behavioral descriptors (i.e., nobody would talk to me; pushed or shoved me, etc.) and then responding "often a problem" or "always a problem" to a list of psychosocial impact factors of the bullying (i.e., made me feel bad or sad; didn't come to school, etc.). Status 4 was the power imbalance status and as such, only applied to those students who were victims only.

Children's Depression Inventory (CDI; Kovacs, 1992)   This instrument is the most commonly used self-report measure of depression for children 7 to 17 years of age. The CDI consists of 27 items designed to assess symptoms of childhood depression. The CDI measures five highly-correlated factors: Negative Mood, Interpersonal Problems, Ineffectiveness, Anhedonia, and Negative Self-Esteem. These five factors are combined to yield one higher-order factor of childhood depression. Participants are asked to rate the severity of each item on a 3-point scale of 0 to 2 during the two weeks prior to testing. Total scores of 16 or greater are considered to indicate potential depression (Stark, Brookman, & Frazier, 1990). The CDI has demonstrated acceptable internal consistency and test-retest as well as convergent validity (Kovacs, 1992). In the present study, the internal consistency reliability using coefficient alpha was .89.

Multidimensional Anxiety Scale for Children (MASC; March, 1997)   This instrument is a self-report checklist assessing major dimensions of anxiety in children ages 8 to 19. The MASC consists of 39 items and covers 4 basic scales (Physical Symptoms, Harm Avoidance, Social Anxiety, and Separation/Panic), when combined these scales create a Total Anxiety Scale. Individuals are asked to rate the severity of each item based upon a 4-point Likert-type scale from "Never true about me" to "Often true about me." T-scores greater than 65 differentiate youth with an anxiety disorder diagnosis from youth without an anxiety disorder diagnosis (March, 1997). The MASC has demonstrated acceptable internal consistency reliability for all main factors and sub factors, including a total score coefficient alpha of .90 (March, Parker, Sullivan, Stallings, & Conners, 1997). In the present study, the internal consistency reliability using coefficient alpha was .91.

Aggression Questionnaire (AQ; Buss & Warren, 2000) This instrument is an updated version of the Buss-Durkee Hostility Inventory (Buss & Durkee, 1957), a standard measure for assessing anger and aggression. The AQ is a self-report measure, consisting of 34 items designed to assess anger and aggression in individuals ranging from 9 to 88 years old. The AQ has five subscales: Physical Aggression, Verbal Aggression, Anger, Hostility, and Indirect Aggression. A total aggression score (AQ Total) is also provided by summing the raw scores for the five subscales. Each item of the AQ describes a characteristic related to aggression. Participants are asked to read each item and rate how much each item is similar to themselves on a 5-point scale: 1 = "Not at all like me" to 5 = "Completely like me". AQ Total scores of 110 or greater (T-Score = 60) are considered to indicate high levels of aggression. In the present study, the internal consistency reliability using coefficient alpha was .91.

Office Referrals These data were collected by gathering school records and identifying the total number of referrals for each student. Information obtained from school records included: the number of referrals received; the type of referral (e.g., insubordination, physical aggression, verbal aggression, violation of the rules, etc.); and the administrative response (e.g., detention, suspension, expulsion, etc.). The type of incident was also recorded in qualitative format to assess a more thorough understanding of the nature of the referred behavior. These data were used to conduct an integrity check of the status groups (bully, victim, bully/victim, bystander, not involved) in order to validate participants' status as reported on the Bully Survey (Swearer, 2001) and are reported in Table 23.3.

Results

Participants were grouped according to status: (a) bully, (b) bully-victim, (c) victim, (d) bystander, and (e) not involved based on their responses to the Bully-Survey (Swearer, 2001). As described in the methods section, 14 different criteria were used to derive involvement in bullying/victimization behaviors.

Office Referrals and Involvement in Bullying/Victimization

Before we examined the differences in the number of office referral among the five different groups, Levene's test of homogeneity of variance was conducted and this assumption was violated, p < .001, and F_{max} >3. As a result, the non-parametric test Kruskal-Wallis was used instead of a one-way ANOVA. Results showed a significant overall difference in office referrals among the five groups when the first criteria was used (BVIC based on Yes/No), Chi-square (4, N = 1048) = 27.071, p < .001. A post-hoc analysis of the differences between mean rank pairs within the bully/victim continuum using a z statistic multiple comparison procedure indicated that bullies (mean rank = 603.51) obtained more office referrals than victims (mean rank = 494.52, p < .05) or bystanders (mean rank = 492.33, p < .05). Using equivalent methodology, bully-victims (mean rank = 562.63) also received more office referrals than victims (mean rank = 494.52, p < .05).

There were also significant overall differences in office referrals among the five groups when the second criteria was examined (BVIC based on frequency), Chi-square (4, N = 285) = 10.73, p = .03. However, follow up tests revealed no significant differences between the groups.

Significant overall differences in office referrals were found among groups when using the third criteria (BVIC based on frequency of specific behaviors), Chi-square (4, N = 742) = 33.56, p < .001. Follow up z-statistic multiple comparison procedures revealed that bullies (mean rank = 443.05) had more office referrals than victims (mean rank = 346.47, p < .05) and bystanders (mean rank = 346.45, p < .05). Likewise, bully-victims also had significantly more office referrals than both victims (mean rank = 346.47, p < .05) and bystanders (mean rank = 346.45, p < .05).

An independent sample t-test showed that when using the fourth criteria (BVIC based on power imbalance), victims and those not involved in bullying did not significantly differ in number of office referrals, t (240) = - 0.56, p = .58.

Anxiety and Involvement in Bullying/Victimization

Before examining the differences in anxiety scores among the five groups, Levene's test of homogeneity of variance was conducted and this assumption was met, ps > .05, and F_{max} < 3. One-way ANOVA tests were used to assess differences among groups. Results indicated significant group differences in anxiety scores between the groups when using the first criteria (BVIC based on yes/no), F (4, 591) = 7.17, p < .001. Tukey-Kramer post hoc tests showed that victims had significantly higher anxiety scores in comparison to bullies (mean difference = 12.33, p = .003), bystanders (mean difference = 8.03, p = .001), and not involved students (mean difference = 7.55, p = .02). Bully-victims also had significantly higher anxiety scores when compared to bullies (mean difference = 10.07, p = .03)

There were no significant group differences in anxiety when the second criteria was used (BVIC based on frequency), F (4, 75) = 0.80, p = .53.

When the third criteria (BVIC based on frequency of specific behavior) was used, significant differences in anxiety were found among groups, F (4, 419) = 10.73, p < .001. Tukey-Kramer post hoc tests showed that victims had significantly higher anxiety scores than bullies (mean difference = 19.11, p < .001), bystanders (mean difference = 10.48, p < .001), and not involved students (mean difference = 10.53, p = .001). Bully-victims also had significantly higher anxiety scores than bullies (mean difference = 16.27, p = .002) and bystanders (mean difference = 7.65, p = .04).

An independent samples t-test showed that victims (BVIC based on power imbalance) had significantly higher anxiety scores compared with not involved students, t (161) = 5.01, p < .001.

Aggression and Involvement in Bullying/Victimization

Having met the homogeneity of variance assumption through the use of Levene's test, ps > .05, and/or F_{max} < 3, two one-way ANOVAs were used to examine differences in aggression among groups. Overall significant group differences in aggression were found among the five groups using the first criteria (BVIC based on yes/no), F (4, 478) = 20.56, p < .001. Tukey-Kramer post hoc tests showed that victims had significantly lower aggression scores than bullies (mean difference = 16.05, p = .002), and bully-victims (mean difference = 9.71, p < .001), but significantly higher aggression scores than bystanders (mean difference = 10.51, p = .001), and not involved students (mean difference = 10.56, p = .02). Bullies had significantly higher aggression scores than bystanders (mean difference = 26.56, p < .001) and not involved students (mean difference = 26.61, p < .001). Bully-victims also had higher aggression scores than bystanders (mean difference = 20.22, p < .001) and not involved students (mean difference = 20.27, p < .001).

A significant overall group difference in aggression was detected among groups using the third criteria (BVIC based on frequency of behavior), F (4, 344) = 21.26, $p < .001$. Tukey-Kramer post hoc tests indicated that victims had significantly lower aggression scores than bully-victims (mean difference = 11.45, $p = .004$), but significantly higher aggression scores than bystanders (mean difference = 14.20, $p < .001$), as well as not involved students (mean difference = 14.91, $p < .001$). Bullies had significantly higher aggression scores than bystanders (mean difference = 26.42, $p < .001$) and not involved students (mean difference = 27.13, $p < .001$). Bully-victims also had significantly higher aggression scores than bystanders (mean difference = 25.66, $p < .001$) and not involved students (mean difference = 26.36, $p < .001$).

An independent samples t-test indicated that victims (BVIC based on power imbalance) had significantly higher aggression scores than not involved students, t (128) = 4.42, $p < .001$. Because the results with the victim group were unexpected, the five subscales in *Aggression Questionnaire*: physical aggression, verbal aggression, anger, hostility, and indirect aggression, were tested separately.

Physical Aggression Subscale   Levene's test of homogeneity of variance was conducted and this assumption was violated, $p < .001$, and $F_{max} > 3$. As a result, the non-parametric test Kruskal-Wallis was used instead of one-way ANOVA. Results showed a significant overall difference in physical aggression among the five groups when the first criteria was used (BVIC based on Yes/No), Chi-square (4, N = 481) = 46.60, $p < .001$. A post-hoc analysis of the differences between mean rank pairs within the five groups using a z statistic multiple comparison procedure indicated that bullies (mean rank = 319.54) had higher physical aggression scores than victims (mean rank = 227.02, $p < .05$), bystanders (mean rank = 189.11, $p < .05$) and not involved students (mean rank = 208.65, $p < .05$). Using equivalent methodology, bully-victims (mean rank = 296.23) also had higher physical aggression scores than victims (mean rank = 227.02, $p < .05$), bystanders (mean rank = 189.11, $p < .05$) and not involved students (mean rank = 208.65, $p < .05$). .

There were also significant overall differences in physical aggression among the five groups when the third criteria was examined (BVIC based on frequency of behavior), Chi-square (4, N = 346) = 39.71, $p < .001$. A post-hoc analysis of the differences between mean rank pairs within the five groups using a z statistic multiple comparison procedure indicated that bullies (mean rank = 226.21) had higher physical aggression scores than bystanders (mean rank = 135.03, $p < .05$) and not involved students (mean rank = 149.38, $p < .05$). Using equivalent methodology, bully-victims (mean rank = 229.06) also had higher physical aggression scores than bystanders (mean rank = 135.03, $p < .05$) and not involved students (mean rank = 149.38, $p < .05$).

An independent samples t-test indicated that victims (BVIC based on power imbalance) and those who were not involved in bullying were not significantly different in physical aggression, t (129) = 1.65, $p = 1.02$.

Verbal Aggression Subscale   Having met the homogeneity of variance assumption through the use of Levene's test, $ps > .05$, and/or $F_{max} < 3$, two one-way ANOVAs were used to examine differences in verbal aggression among groups. There was a significant group difference on verbal aggression scores among the five groups using the first criteria (BVIC based on yes/no), F (4,

480) = 13.43, $p < .001$. Tukey-Kramer post hoc test showed that bullies had significantly higher verbal aggression scores compared to victims (mean difference = 2.93, $p= .03$), bystanders (mean difference = 4.82, $p < .001$), and not involved students (mean difference = 4.72, $p < .001$). Victims had significantly higher verbal aggression scores than bystanders (mean difference = 1.89, $p = .008$). Bully-victims also had significantly higher verbal aggression score than bystanders (main difference = 3.00, $p < .001$), and not involved students (mean difference = 2.90, $p = .003$).

There were significant group differences on verbal aggression scores among the five groups using the third criteria (BVIC based on frequency of behavior), F (4, 345) = 9.74, $p < .001$. Tukey-Kramer post hoc test showed that bullies had significantly higher verbal aggression scores than victims (mean difference = 2.98, $p = .03$), bystanders (mean difference = 4.82, $p < .001$), and not involved students (mean difference = 4.72, $p < .001$). Victims had significantly higher verbal aggression scores than bystanders (mean difference = 1.84, $p = .01$). Bully-victims also had significantly higher verbal aggression scores than bystanders (main difference = 3.00, $p < .001$), and not involved students (mean difference = 2.90, $p = .003$).

An independent samples t-test indicated that victims (BVIC based on power imbalance) had significantly higher verbal aggression scores than those who were not involved in bullying, t(128) = 2.69, $p = .008$.

Anger Subscale   Having met the homogeneity of variance assumption through the use of Levene's test, $ps > .05$, and/or $F_{max} < 3$, two one-way ANOVAs were used to examine differences in anger among groups. There were significant group difference on anger scores among the five groups using the first criteria (BVIC based on yes/no), F (4, 481) = 15.56, $p < .001$. Tukey-Kramer post hoc test showed that bullies had significantly higher anger scores than victims (mean difference = 3.74, $p = .01$), bystanders (mean difference = 6.15, $p < .001$), and not involved students (mean difference = 5.96, $p < .001$). Victims had significantly higher anger scores than bystanders (mean difference = 2.42, $p = .003$). Bully-victims had significantly higher anger scores than victims (mean difference = 2.10, $p = .005$), bystanders (main difference = 4.51, $p < .001$), and not involved students (mean difference = 4.32, $p < .001$).

There were significant group differences on anger scores among the five groups using the third criteria (BVIC based on frequency of behavior), F (4, 346) = 16.14, $p < .001$. Tukey-Kramer post hoc tests showed that bullies had significantly higher anger scores than bystanders (mean difference = 6.49, $p < .001$), and not involved students (mean difference = 6.29, $p < .001$). Victims had significantly higher anger scores than bystanders (mean difference = 3.30, $p < .001$), and not involved students (mean difference = 3.10, $p = .006$). Bully-victims also had significantly higher anger scores than victims (mean difference = 2.47, $p = .02$), bystanders (main difference = 5.77, $p < .001$), and not involved students (mean difference = 5.57, $p < .001$).

An independent samples t-test indicated that victims (BVIC based on power imbalance) had significantly higher anger scores than those who were not involved in bullying, t (129) = 3.34, $p = .001$.

Hostility Subscale   Having met the homogeneity of variance assumption through the use of Levene's test, $ps > .05$, and/or $F_{max} < 3$, two one-way ANOVAs were used to examine differences in hostility among groups. There were significant group differences on the hostility scores among the five groups using the first criteria (BVIC based on yes/no), F (4, 481) = 11.66, $p < .001$. Tukey-Kramer post hoc test showed that victims had significantly higher hostility scores than bystanders (mean difference = 3.67, $p < .001$), and not involved students (mean difference = 3.60, $p = .002$). The bully-victims also had significantly higher hostility scores than bystanders (main difference = 4.37, $p < .001$), and not involved students (mean difference = 4.30, $p < .001$).

There were significant group differences on hostility scores among the five groups using the third criteria (BVIC based on frequency of behavior), F (4, 346) = 16.61, $p < .001$. Tukey-Kramer post hoc tests showed that victims had significantly higher hostility scores than bystanders (mean difference = 4.75, $p < .001$), and not involved students (mean difference = 4.87, $p < .001$). Bully-victims also had significantly higher hostility scores than bystanders (main difference = 5.96, $p < .001$), and not involved students (mean difference = 6.08, $p < .001$).

An independent samples t-test indicated that victims (BVIC based on power imbalance) had significantly higher hostility scores than those who were not involved in bullying, t (129) = 5.92, $p <.001$.

Indirect Aggression   Having met the homogeneity of variance assumption through the use of Levene's test, $ps > .05$, and/or $F_{max} < 3$, a one-way ANOVA was used to examine differences in indirect aggression among groups. There were significant group differences on indirect aggression scores among the five groups using the first criteria (BVIC based on yes/no), F (4, 481) = 17.82, $p < .001$. Tukey-Kramer post hoc test showed that bullies had significantly higher indirect aggression scores than victims (mean difference = 2.98, $p = .006$), bystanders (mean difference = 4.05, $p < .001$), and not involved students (mean difference = 5.29, $p < .001$). Victims had significantly higher indirect aggression scores than not involved students (mean difference = 2.32, $p = .007$). Bully-victims also had significantly higher indirect aggression scores than victims (mean difference = 2.33, $p < .001$), bystanders (mean difference = 3.40, $p < .001$), and not involved students (mean difference = 4.65, $p < .001$).

There were significant group difference on indirect aggression scores among the five groups using the third criteria (BVIC based on frequency of behavior), F (4, 346) = 14.22, $p < .001$. Tukey-Kramer post hoc tests showed that bullies had significantly higher indirect aggression scores than bystanders (mean difference = 3.85, $p = .004$), and not involved students (mean difference = 5.32, $p < .001$). Victims had significantly higher indirect aggression scores than not involved students (mean difference = 2.87, $p = .001$). Bully-victims also had significantly higher indirect aggression scores than victims (mean difference = 2.52, $p = .002$), bystanders (mean difference = 3.92, $p < .001$), and not involved students (mean difference = 5.39, $p < .001$).

An independent samples t-test indicated that victims (using the power imbalance criteria) had significantly higher indirect aggression scores than those who were not involved in bullying, t (129) = 3.68, $p < .001$.

Depression and Involvement in Bullying/Victimization

Before examining depression scores among groups, Levene's test of homogeneity of variance was conducted and this assumption was tenable only when using the second criteria (BVIC based on frequency) ($p > .05$). A one-way ANOVA test was used to explore differences in depression among groups using the second criteria. Significant overall differences in depression scores were found between groups using this criteria, F (4, 78) = 3.51, $p = .01$. Tukey-Kramer post hoc tests showed that victims reported significantly higher depression scores than not involved students (mean difference = 7.27, $p = .04$).

The non-parametric test Kruskal-Wallis was used instead of one-way ANOVA with the first and third criteria. Results showed significant differences in depression scores among groups when the first criteria was used (BVIC based on Yes/No), Chi-square (4, N = 611) = 66.51, $p < .001$. Follow up z-statistic multiple comparison procedures revealed that bullies (Mean Rank = 354.13), victims (Mean Rank = 320.26), and bully-victims (Mean Rank = 366.73) all reported higher levels of depression than bystanders (Mean Rank = 224.47, p <.05) and not involved students (Mean Rank = 209.93, p <.05).

Results also showed significant differences in depression scores among groups when the third criteria (BVIC based on frequency of behavior) was utilized, Chi-square (4, N = 430) = 81.76, p < .001. Follow up multiple comparison procedures indicated that again bullies (Mean Rank = 249.09), victims (Mean Rank = 247.33), and bully-victims (Mean Rank = 280.83) reported higher levels of depression than bystanders (Mean Rank = 151.12, p < .05) and not involved students (Mean Rank = 143.56, p < .05).

An independent samples t-test showed that victims (BVIC based on power imbalance) had significantly higher depression scores in comparison with not involved students, t (143.43) = 6.31, p < .001.

Discussion

One goal of this chapter was to add to the extant bullying literature base on measurement issues in bullying. Bullying is a subset of aggressive behavior; however, the three components of bullying: (a) purposeful; (b) imbalance of power; and (c) continual are not always assessed in the empirical literature base on bullying. The study presented in this chapter attempted to address this measurement conundrum by deriving bully/victim involvement categories based on these elements of the definition of bullying and then comparing the different involvement categories across office referrals, depression, anxiety, and aggression.

This study examined whether the different methods of defining involvement in bullying/victimization would be related to the frequency of office referrals across the groups and if office referral data were an accurate validity measure for involvement in bullying. Results from this study provide evidence that office referral data can be useful in validating involvement in bullying. Specifically, across all methodologies, bullies had more office referrals, followed by bully-victims, bystanders, victims, and not involved students. This indicates that office referrals are associated with bullying behavior and can provide concurrent validity for the assessment of bullying behaviors. These findings support previous research which has found that office referrals can be used as a validity tool for the measurement of bullying (Loeber et al., 2000; Sprague et al., 2001; Swearer & Cary, 2003). We advocate that at minimum, office referral data should be collected when studying bullying/victimization. This is especially important for studies that utilize self-report data in order to measure bullying/victimization.

Given that the extant bullying literature has found a link between involvement in bullying/victimization and psychological difficulties, this study sought to explore whether different involvement categories were associated with greater psychological difficulties. For example, would students who were involved in bullying/victimization less frequently (monthly) versus students who involved more frequently (daily or weekly) display less psychological difficulties? If we can determine the psychological impact of involvement in bullying/victimization, then we might be able to offer some suggestions as to the veracity of different cut-off points for determining involvement in bullying/victimization.

While intuitively obvious, when different cut-off points were used, the prevalence rates for the different involvement categories varied greatly (see Table 23.3). Specifically, the percentage of bullies identified ranged from 2.5% to 8%; victims ranged from 4.5% to 34.3%; bully-victims ranged from 3.7% to 28.1%; and bystanders ranged from 7.3% to 20.3%. Given this wide variability in this data set, it is clear that cut-off points matter and that the variability in the extant bullying literature is due to different methodologies used to assess bullying. Until a "gold-standard" for assessing bullying can be agreed upon by researchers, this problem will continue to plague the field.

Anxiety   Findings from this study provide further evidence that victims and bully-victims experience higher levels of anxiety than bullies, bystanders, and students who are not involved in bullying/victimization (Craig, 1998; Hawker & Boulton; Olweus, 1994; Rigby, 2003; Slee, 1994). These results were consistent across all measurement methodologies; and were particularly significant for those reporting involvement in bullying/victimization on a daily or weekly basis. Thus, adolescents who are victims or bully-victims on a frequent basis report significantly higher levels of anxiety. Furthermore, involvement even at a less frequent level is also associated with elevated anxiety scores indicating being bullied is significantly associated with anxiety.

Depression   The findings from this study also provide further evidence that depression is a pervasive psychological experience for those youth involved in bullying. Depression has been consistently linked to bullying others (Austin & Joseph, 1996; Bosworth et al., 1999; Slee, 1995), being victimized (Craig, 1998; Hawker & Boulton, 2000; Seals & Young, 2003), and both involvement in bullying/victimization (Austin & Joseph, 1996; Kaltiala-Heino et al., 2000; Swearer et al., 2001). The present results suggest that bullies, victims, and bully-victims all endorsed higher levels of depression than bystanders and students not involved in bullying. These results held across all four bully/victim involvement categories. Victims, in particular, were consistently identified as having significantly higher levels of depression across all four methodologies compared to bullies, bully-victims, bystanders, and not involved students. This finding further supports the connection between involvement in bullying/victimization and depression.

Aggression   As expected, bullies and bully-victims reported significantly higher aggression scores than victims, bystanders, and students not involved in bullying/victimization across all methodologies. However, in contrast to previous research, victims had significantly higher aggression scores than bystanders and not involved students. Therefore, the subscales of the Aggression Questionnaire (AQ; physical aggression, verbal aggression, anger, hostility, and indirect aggression) were investigated. As expected, bullies and bully-victims had significantly higher physical and verbal aggression scores than victims, bystanders, and those not involved in bullying. Victims reported significantly more hostility, anger, and indirect aggression than bystanders or students not involved in bullying. It could be that victims may experience elevated levels of hostility and anger because the imbalance of power involved in bullying likely inhibits the victim's ability to defend him or herself. As a result, they may internalize their frustration, leading to increased feelings of anger and hostility toward others. Interesting, data from this study suggest that victims do find an indirect outlet for their frustration. The indirect aggression subscale includes five items that appear to be methods victims can use to express their frustration (i.e., "I have been mad enough to slam a door when leaving someone behind in the room"; "when people are bossy, I take my time doing what they want, just to show them"; "when someone really irritates me, I might give him or her the silent treatment"; "I sometimes spread gossip about people I don't like"; and "I like to play practical jokes"). Thus, victims might use indirect aggression to express their frustration and anger in response to being bullied.

The goal in deriving 14 different bullying/victimization involvement categories was to determine whether or not this would reveal differences in terms of frequency, severity, and a power imbalance in the bullying/victimization dynamic. For example, if the criteria that included the power imbalance clearly identified the victimized students as more depressed or anxious, then one could conclude that the power imbalance is a crucial factor in the measurement of bullying/victimization behaviors. Interestingly, the use of frequency as an involvement category did not prove to be more effective in identifying involvement in bullying or group differences in terms of internalizing and externalizing problems. Specifically, there were no significant group differences when utilizing the continual restriction in terms of anxiety. However, with the more stringent cut-off, victims were found to have significantly higher levels of depression and anger than not involved students. This may indicate that a more restrictive cut-off is effective in identifying the small percentage of participants who are more significantly impaired.

The two methodologies that were equally effective in identifying within group differences were the dichotomous question (yes/no to involvement during the school year) and the higher frequency of bullying plus the behavioral indicators (list of physical and verbal forms of bullying). It was notable that a less stringent cut-off point appeared to be equally effective in identifying those students for whom involvement in bullying/victimization is particularly detrimental. However, it could be that providing the definition of bullying in a survey format "primes" the respondents to answer the questions, thinking about the definition of bullying that includes the three components.

This study is one step in attempting to parse out measurement issues facing the field. Specifically, the continued concern regarding the vast range in prevalence rates is an important issue for researchers to tackle. This chapter has revealed that different rates are clearly tied to different methodologies (i.e., cut-off points). This issue continues to plague the bullying research base in that depending on how bullying/victimization is measured, results will vary greatly. For example, by using different cut-off points, a study can report that that the majority of students are involved in bullying or that there are very few students involved in bullying. As a result, the accuracy of these prevalence rates and methodologies must continue to be investigated.

Finally, the methodology using higher frequency as a criterion was less effective in identifying within group differences except in terms of depression and aggression. It is unclear whether the significant findings were the result of more significant impairment as a result of repeated involvement. However, if students who are more frequently involved are more impaired, the most parsimonious method would be to use the dichotomous question as a screener and if they are, then look more closely at the students who report more frequent involvement.

Limitations and Directions for Future Research

This study was a cross-sectional analysis of involvement in bullying/victimization. As such, causation between the psychological variables and involvement in bullying/victimization was unable to be determined. Additionally, reasons for the office referrals were not coded, thus the reasons why the bullies and bully-victims were sent to the office were not unknown. Presumably, these are the students who are getting in trouble for their behavior; however, future research should assess the actual reasons for the office referrals. The format of survey used in this study limited analyses of several measurement issues facing the use of survey research. Specifically, all students were required to answer the dichotomous questions about involvement in bullying and as a result it was not possible to assess whether the use of behavioral indicators alone (i.e., scale data) or the yes/no response format was a more valid index of bullying/victimization. This assessment strategy also limited the ability to analyze the validity of utilizing a definition versus behavioral indicators which covertly assesses bullying since the two response formats were used simultaneously. Finally, the dichotomous question and frequency of involvement questions are comprised of only a few items and as a result, this limits the ability to calculate internal consistency reliability for some of the bully/victim categories. Despite these limitations, this study adds to our understanding of methodological issues in bullying research.

Future research is needed to empirically analyze the validity and reliability of the different assessment methodologies. Additional research should systematically test the validity and reliability of different assessments to determine which methodologies are the most accurate in the measurement of bullying/victimization. Future studies should also use multiple informants, behavioral observations, and should code office referrals more systematically in order to elucidate some of these reliability and validity issues. Finally, more rigorous psychometric analyses of bullying assessments are necessary. Test-retest reliability, internal consistency, and construct validity data are necessary to determine the quality and accuracy of our methodologies. Once an empirically-supported method for assessing bullying has been identified, researchers in the field should adhere to such guidelines to increase interpretability and comparisons across studies. Much of our knowledge regarding bullying may be inaccurate if previous assessments have not adequately measured the construct of bullying.

References

Austin, S., & Joseph, S. (1996). Assessment of bully/victim problems in 8- to 11-year-olds. *British Journal of Educational Psychology, 66,* 49–56.

Baldry, A. C., & Farrington, D. P. (1999). Brief report: Types of bullying among Italian school children. *Journal of Adolescence, 22*(3), 423, 426.

Baldry, A. C., & Farrington, D. P. (2004). Evaluation of an intervention for the reduction of bullying and victimization in schools. *Aggressive Behavior, 30*(1), 1–15.

Buss, A., & Durkee, A. (1957). An inventory for assessing different kinds of hostility. *Journal of Consulting Psychology, 21,* 343–349.

Buss, A. H., & Warren, W. L. (2000). *The Aggression Questionnaire.* Los Angeles: Western Psychological Services.

Bosworth, K., Espelage, D. L., & Simon, T. R. (1999). Factors associated with bullying behavior in middle school students. *Journal of Early Adolescence, 19*(3), 341–362.

Camodeca, M., & Goossens, F. A. (2005). Children's opinions on effective strategies to cope with bullying: The importance of bullying role and perspective. *Educational Research, 47,* 93–105.

Card, N. A. (2003, April). *Victims of peer aggression: A meta-analytic review.* Paper presented at Society for Research in Child Development biennial meeting, Tampa, Florida.

Cassidy, T., & Taylor, N. (2005). Bullying and victimisation in school children: The role of social identity, problem-solving style, and family and school context. *Social Psychology of Education, 12*(1), 63–76.

Chan, J. H., Myron, R., & Crawshaw, M. (2005). The efficacy of non-anonymous measures of bullying. *School Psychology International, 26,* 443–458.

Cornell, D. G., Sheras, P. L., & Cole, J. C. (2006). Assessment of bullying. In S. Jimerson & M. Furlong (Eds.), *Handbook of school violence and school safety: From research to practice* (pp. 191–210). Mahwah, NJ: Erlbaum.

Craig, W. M. (1998). The relationship among bullying, victimization, depression, anxiety, and aggression in elementary school children. *Personality and Individual Differences, 24,* 123–130.

Crick, N. R., & Grotpeter, J. K. (1995). Relational aggression, gender, and social-psychological adjustment. *Child Development, 66,* 710–722.

Demaray, K., & Malecki, C. (2003). Perceptions of the frequency and importance of social support by students classified as victims, bullies, and bully/victims in an urban middle school. *School Psychology Review, 32,* 471–489.

Duncan, R. (1999). Peer and sibling aggression: An investigation of intra- and extra-familial bullying. *Journal of Interpersonal Violence, 14,* 871–886.

Espelage, D. L., Bosworth, K., & Simon, T. R. (2001). Short-term stability and protective correlates of bullying in middle-school students: An examination of potential demographic, psychosocial, and environmental influences. *Violence and Victims, 16,* 411–426.

Espelage, D. L., Holt, M. K., & Henkel, R. R. (2003). Examination of peer group contextual effects on aggressive behavior during early adolescence. *Child Development, 74,* 205–220.

Espelage, D. L., & Swearer, S. M. (2003). Research on school bullying and victimization: What have we learned and where do we go from here? *School Psychology Review, 32,* 365–383.

Furlong, M. J., Greif, J. L., & Sharkey, J. D. (2005). *Assessing violence in our schools: Bullying.* Paper presented at the annual convention of the National Association of School Psychologists in Atlanta, GA.

Griffin, R. S., & Gross, A. M. (2004). Childhood bullying: Current empirical findings and future directions for research. *Aggression and Violent Behavior, 9,* 379–400.

Hawker, D. J., & Boulton, M. J. (2000). Twenty years' research on peer victimization and psychosocial maladjustment: A meta-analytic review of cross-sectional studies. *Journal of Child Psychology and Psychiatry, 41,* 441–455.

Hoover, J., Oliver, R., & Hazler, R. (1992). Bullying: Perceptions of adolescent victims in the Midwestern USA. *School Psychology International, 13,* 5–16.

Houbre, B., Tarquinio, C., & Hergott, E. (2006). Bullying among students and its consequences on health. *European Journal of Psychology of Education, 21,* 183–208.

Ivarsson, T., Broberg, A., Arvidsson, T., & Gillberg, C. (2005). Bullying in adolescence: Psychiatric problems in victims and bullies as measured by the youth self report (YSR) and the depression self-rating scale (DSRS). *Nordic Journal of Psychiatry, 59*(5), 365–373.

Kaltiala-Heino, R., Rimpela, M., Rantanen, P., & Rimpela, A. (2000). Bullying at school — and indicator of adolescents at risk for mental disorders. *Journal of Adolescence, 23,* 661–674.

Kokkinos, C. M., & Panayiotou, G. (2004). Predicting bullying and victimization among early adolescents: Associations with disruptive behavior disorders. *Aggressive Behavior, 30,* 520–533.

Kovacs, M. (1992). *Children's Depression Inventory.* Western Psychiatric Institute and Clinic: Pittsburgh PA.

Loeber, R., Green, S. M., Lahey, B. B., Frick, P. J., & McBurnett, K. (2000). Findings on disruptive behavior disorders from the first decade of the Developmental Trends Study. *Clinical Child and Family Psychology Review, 3,* 37–60.

March, J. (1997). *Anxiety disorders in children and adolescents.* New York: Guilford .

March, J., Parker, J., Sullivan, K., & Stallings, P. (1997). The Multidimensional Anxiety Scale for Children (MASC): Factor structure, reliability, and validity. *Journal of the American Academy of Child & Adolescent Psychiatry, 36,* 554–565.

Nansel, T. R., Overpeck, M., & Pilla, R. S. (2001). Bullying behaviors among US youth: Prevalence and association with psychosocial adjustment. *Journal of the American Medical Association, 285*(16), 2094–2100.

Nishina, A., & Juvonen, J. (2005). Daily reports of witnessing and experiencing peer harassment in middle school. *Child Development, 76,* 435–450.

Olweus, D. (1984). Aggressors and their victims: Bullying at school. In N. Frude & H. Gault (Eds.), *Disruptive behaviour in schools* (pp. 57–76). New York: Wiley.

Olweus, D. (1986). *The Olweus Bully/Victim Questionnaire.* Mimeo. Bergen, Norway: University of Bergen.

Olweus, D. (1993). *Bullying at school: What we know and what we can do.* Oxford, UK: Blackwell.

Olweus, D. (1994). Annotation: Bullying at school: Basic facts and effects of a school based intervention program. *Journal of Child Psychology and Psychiatry, 35,* 1171–1190.

Rigby, K. (2003). Consequences of bullying in schools. *Canadian Journal of Psychiatry, 48,* 583–590.

Rodkin, P. C., Farmer, T. W., & Pearl, R. (2006). They're cool: Social status and peer group supports for aggressive boys and girls. In J. E. Zins, M. J. Elias, & C. A. Maher (Eds.), *Bullying, victimization, and peer harassment: A handbook of prevention and intervention* (pp. 279–298). New York: Hawthorn Press.

Salmivalli, C., Lappalainen, M., & Lagerspetz, K. M. (1998). Stability and change of behavior in connection with bullying in schools. A two-year follow-up. *Aggressive Behavior, 24,* 205–218.

Scheithauer, H., Hayer, T., Petermann, F., & Jugert, G. (2006). Physical, verbal, and relational forms of bullying among German students: Age trends, gender differences, and correlates. *Aggressive Behavior, 32,* 261–275.

Seals, D., & Young, J. (2003). Bullying and victimization: Prevalence and relationship to gender, grade level, ethnicity, self-esteem, and depression. *Adolescence, 38,* 735–747.

Slee, P. T. (1994). Situational and interpersonal correlates of anxiety associated with peer victimization. *Child Psychiatry & Human Development, 25,* 91–107.

Slee, P. T. (1995). Peer victimization and its relationship to depression among Australian primary school students. *Personality and Individual Differences, 18,* 57–62.

Smith, P. K. (2004). Bullying: Recent Developments. *Child and Adolescent Mental Health, 9,* 98–103.

Smith, P. K., Cowie, H., Olafsson, R. F., & Liefooghe, A. P. (2002). Definitions of bullying: A comparison of terms used, and age and gender differences, in a fourteen-country international comparison. *Child Development, 73,* 1119–1133.

Smith, P. K., & Sharp, S. (1994). *School bullying: Insights and perspectives.* New York: Routledge.

Solberg, M. E., & Olweus, D. (2003). Prevalence estimation of school bullying with the Olweus Bully/Victim Questionnaire. *Aggressive Behavior, 29,* 239–268.

Sprague, J., Walker, H. M., Stieber, S., Simonsen, B., Nishioka, V., & Wagner, L. (2001). Exploring the relationship between school discipline referrals and delinquency. *Psychology in the Schools, 38,* 197–206.

Srabstein, J.C., McCarter, R. J., Shao, C., & Huang, Z. J. (2006). Morbidities associated with bullying behaviours in adolescents: School based study of American adolescents. *International Journal of Mental Health, 18*(4), 587–596.

Stark, K., Brookman, C., & Frazier, R. (1990). A comprehensive school-based treatment program for depressed children. *School Psychology Quarterly, 5,* 111–140.

Storch, E. A., Brassard, M. R., & Masia-Warner, C. L. (2003). The relationship of peer victimization to social anxiety and loneliness in adolescence. *Child Study Journal, 33,* 1–18.

Sutton, J., & Keogh, E. (2000). Social competition in school relationships with bullying, Machiavellianism and personality. *The British Journal of Educational Psychology, 70,* 443–456.

Swearer, S. M. (2001). *The bully survey.* Unpublished manuscript, University of Nebraska-Lincoln.

Swearer, S. M. (2008). Relational aggression: Not just a female issue. *Journal of School Psychology, 46,* 611–616.

Swearer, S. M., & Cary, P. T. (2003). Perceptions and attitudes toward bullying in middle school youth: A developmental examination across the bully/victim continuum. *Journal of Applied School Psychology, 19,* 63–79.

Swearer, S. M., & Espelage, D. L. (2004). A social-ecological framework of bullying among youth. In D. Espelage & S. Swearer (Eds.), *Bullying in American Schools: A social-ecological perspective on prevention and intervention* (pp. 1–12). Mahwah, NJ: Erlbaum.

Swearer, S. M., Espelage, D. L., Vaillancourt, T., & Hymel, S. (in press). What can be done about bullying?: The good, the bad, and the ugly realities of school-based bullying prevention and intervention. *Educational Researcher.*

Swearer, S. M., Song, S. Y., Cary, P. T., Eagle, J. W., & Mickelson, W. T. (2001). Psychosocial correlates in bullying and victimization: The relationship between depression, anxiety, and bully/victim status. In R. Geffner, M. Loring, & C. Young (Eds.), *Bullying behavior: Current issues, research, and interventions* (pp. 95–121). Binghamton, NY: Haworth Maltreatment and Trauma Press/The Haworth Press.

Underwood, M. K. (2003). *Social aggression among girls.* New York: Guilford.

Unnever, J. D. (2005). Bullies, aggressive victims, and victims: Are they distinct groups? *Aggressive Behavior, 31,* 153–171.

Volk, A. A., Craig, W., Boyce, W., & King, M. (2006). Adolescent risk correlates of bullying and different types of victimization. *International Journal of Adolescent Medicine and Health, 18*(4), 375–386.

Woods, S., & White, E. (2005). The association between bullying behaviour, arousal levels and behaviour problems. *Journal of Adolescence, 28,* 381–395.

24

Bullying Assessment

A Call for Increased Precision of Self-Reporting Procedures

MICHAEL J. FURLONG, JILL D. SHARKEY, ERIKA D. FELIX,
DIANE TANIGAWA, AND JENNIFER GREIF GREEN

Accurate assessment of bullying is essential to intervention planning and the evaluation of bullying prevention programs; however, assessment itself has been called the "Achilles' heel" of bullying research (Cornell, Sheras, & Cole, 2006). Researchers worldwide have long struggled to define and operationalize bullying in ways that facilitate cross-national comparisons and to accurately estimate the prevalence of bullying. These efforts have produced equivocal results with considerable differences in prevalence rates across studies (Smith et al., 1999), a finding that raises the issue of whether rates of bullying differ dramatically across samples or if differences reflect measurement imprecision. Other measurement concerns include variations in definitions and time frames used, whether or not to provide an a priori definition of bullying to respondents (Espelage & Swearer, 2003; Solberg & Olweus, 2003); whether to use self-report, peer nomination, or teacher report methods (Cornell et al. 2006; Solberg & Olweus, 2003); and whether currently used measures actually assess the subset of peer victimization that is intended to be captured by the scientific definition of bullying (Greif & Furlong, 2006).

Cornell and colleagues (2006) emphasize that bullying assessment has not been studied adequately and that this limits the reliability and validity of assessing aspects of bullying behavior. In addition, many self-report measures are designed to assess prevalence in schools and communities, and were not designed to gather information for intervention planning purposes with individual students who have been bullied and need assistance (Greif & Furlong, 2006). In the international context, considerable attention has been devoted to efforts to develop a consensus on how to define bullying (e.g., Arora, 1996; Naylor, Cowie, Cossin, de Bettencourt, & Lemme, 2006; Rigby, 2004; Smith, Cowie, Olafsson, & Liefooghe, 2002; Smith et al., 1999; Smorti, Menesini, & Smith, 2003). These substantial efforts have produced a consensus on the key elements of the scientific definition of bullying; however, no consensus has been reached on how to measure bullying across national and cultural divisions (Smith et al., 1999, 2002). The aim of this chapter is to examine persistently perplexing bullying definitional and measurement issues, to summarize the methodological and psychometric status of widely used self-report bullying assessment procedures, and to offer some perspectives on future directions for research and practice.

Definition of Bullying

The development and enhancement of any measurement procedure is based in the evolution of conceptual and operational definitions that have broad consensus among researchers. As reviewed by a number of bullying scholars (Arora, 1996; Rigby, 2004), the word "bullying" has obscure linguistic origins and has been used in various ways, even positively (as in "bully for you"), until the past century when it began to take on the connotation of excessive and unfair intimidation. As the term began to take on elements that reflected poorly on a person's behavior and personality, use of this term was adopted very early by psychologists (e.g., Calkins, 1916; Hall, 1904; Thorndike, 1919). Parten (1933) used the term to describe the aggressive "leadership" style of preschool-aged children. Subsequently, sporadic use of the term bullying appeared in research during the 1930s and 1940s, with studies examining its relationship to poor reading performance (Vauhgn, 1941), as a type of aggressive behavior (Pearce, 1948), and in the context of sociometric studies of best and least liked pupils (Smith, 1950).

It is notable that behaviors associated with bullying have occurred throughout human history in many cultures and the term was used in psychological research for decades without precise definition. It was not until the 1970s that researchers began to focus increasing attention on youth and school-related bullying. The early seminal research conducted in Scandinavian countries used the term "möbbning," which connotes group victimization (Heinemann, 1972; Pikas, 1975) of an individual "whipping boy" (Olweus, 1978, 1987), a term borrowed from biological sciences ("'Bullying' amongst birds," 1932). Simultaneously, Lowenstein in England began to examine school violence (1972, 1975) and expanded this work to include bullying. The first articles in the PsychInfo database to use the term "bully" (or bullying, bullies, or bullied) in the titles appeared in the late 1970s (Lowenstein, 1977, 1978; Olweus, 1978). Since that time, the term was slowly adopted and used, for example, in Australia (Rigby & Slee, 1991), Japan (Komiyama, 1986; Prewitt, 1988), Ireland (O'Moore & Hillery, 1989), the United Kingdom (Sharp & Smith, 1991), and the United States (Hoover & Hazler, 1991). Despite the increasing use of the term "bullying," developing a consensus on a word that captures this universal experience was elusive (Smith et al., 1999), with Schuster (1996) presenting a review of the research on mobbing (used more frequently now in work related contexts) and bullying (used in school and youth related contexts). Readers are referred to Arora's (1996) thoughtful and contemporary discussion of these definitional issues.

How researchers and practitioners define, and consequently measure, bullying has varied across studies (Espelage & Swearer, 2004). Students themselves have indicated that bullying is any unwanted act of verbal, physical, or social/relational aggression (LaFontaine, 1991; Smith & Levan, 1995). However, one of the pioneers and leading researchers in the area of bullying, Olweus (1993) suggests that bullying behaviors are those direct or indirect aggressive acts that have three qualities: (a) bullying behaviors are intentional, (b) repeated over time, and (c) between two parties where a power differential (e.g., in the form of physical strength or social status) exists. The most broadly used bullying definition is provided by Olweus:

> We say a student is being bullied when another student, or several students
> - say mean or hurtful things, make fun of him or her, or call him or her names; completely ignore or exclude him or her from their group of friends, or leave him or her out of things on purpose;
> - hit, kick, push, shove around, or lock him or her inside a room;
> - tell lies or spread false rumors about him or her, or send mean notes and try to make other students dislike him or her;
> - other hurtful things like that.

These things take place frequently, and it is difficult for the student being bullied to defend himself or herself.

But we do not call it bullying when students tease each other in a friendly, playful way. Also, it is not bullying when two students about the same strength or power argue or fight. (Solberg & Olweus, 2003, p. 246)

As apparent in this definition, bullying is a subset of the broader category of peer victimization (Björkvist, Ekman, & Lagerspetz, 1982); hence, it is not always easy to distinguish bullying from other victimization experiences with clear specificity and sensitivity. A challenge of bullying assessment methods is to distinguish bullying from other types of peer victimization including playful behavior (Cornell et al., 2006). As many have noted, friends or acquaintances can engage in teasing and horseplay that may look like bullying to an outside observer (Cornell et al., 2006; Rigby, 2004).

Recognizing the problems associated with establishing a viable, universal definition of bullying, Rigby (2004) expanded Olweus's definition to suggest that it includes seven essential elements: intentionality, a hurtful action, relative power imbalance, repetition, the perpetrator enjoys the experience, the act is unjust, and the victim feels oppressed. More generally, of these elements, researchers have broad consensus that bullying is a subset of all peer victimization that involves intentionality, repetition, and power imbalance (Greif & Furlong, 2006). Given the relatively recent intensive focus on bullying as a research topic and the still-yet settled matter of definition, researchers have used various strategies to measure this phenomenon.

Self-Report Bullying Measurement Approaches

Self-report assessments are the most commonly used method to measure bullying victimization, in part because they are easier for researchers and educators to implement than other methods such as intensive behavioral observations of schoolyard interactions. Researchers have debated the relative benefits of self-report versus other methods, such as reports from collateral informants or observations. Solberg and Olweus (2003) argue that self-report is the best method for ascertaining prevalence estimation, which is the type of information that educators and policy makers often need. On the other hand, Cornell and colleagues (2006) point out that many available measures do not report adequate reliability and validity information. They also state that self-reports are rooted solely in the student's perspective—some victims may exaggerate their experiences whereas others may minimize them—and peer nominations may provide more valid information. Another identified problem of self-reports is that careless and dishonest responding can inflate prevalence estimates (Cornell et al., 2006) and the response referent time frame may influence student responses in unexpected ways (Furlong & Sharkey, 2006).

Considering these limitations, there have been calls to use other assessment procedures, such as peer nominations (e.g., Chan, 2006; Chan, Myron, & Crawshaw, 2005) and behavioral observations (e.g., Cornell & Brockenbrough, 2004; Craig, Pepler, & Atlas, 2000; Craig & Pepler, 1997; Hawkins, Pepler, & Craig, 2001). Studies using these methodologies have provided valuable data that answered questions that could not be addressed by self-report data alone. However, as Espelage and Swearer (2003) point out, there are ethical and/or logistical problems with peer nominations and behavioral observations that make it difficult to obtain research review board approval and written guardian consent. Despite recognized limitations and calls to limit the use of self-report bullying measures (Cole, Cornell, & Sheras, 2006; Cornell et al., 2006), self-report has been and will undoubtedly continue to be the primary approach used by researchers across developmental, epidemiological, and intervention (prevention and treatment outcome measures) lines of research. Hence, it is critical to examine the status and quality of bullying self-report measures. The self-report measures used by researchers generally either (a) provide a working definition of bullying and ask a youth if they had experienced this type of victimization (or perpetrated such acts) or (b) present a list of victimization-related behaviors and ask how often the youth has experienced or committed them.

Definition-Based Self-Report Strategy

Assessments of bullying and bullying victimization often provide a definition of bullying to help students relate to the idea of bullying as defined by the researchers, with the intent of developing a shared meaning of the bullying experience across all study participants. These questionnaires use a definition of bullying to address the purposefulness of the aggressive acts, the power differential between the two parties, and a frequency response scale to assess the repetition of the behavior. Based on associations with poor mental health status variables, Solberg and Olweus (2003) argue that using a frequency criteria of "2–3 times per month" or more derives the best estimate of bullying victimization because it is easy to reproduce, interpret, and can "function reasonably well" (p. 242) when psychometric properties are tested for the purpose of prevalence estimation. Solberg and Olweus (2003) also suggest that providing a definition helps to separate acts of bullying from other forms of peer victimization by including the power imbalance characteristic of bullying, although Arora (1996) emphasizes that a definition that validly communicates cross-nationally is elusive. A description of research measures that use the definitional strategy follows.

Olweus Bully/Victim Questionnaires

The original Olweus Bully/Victim Questionnaire (OB/VQ; Olweus, 1986), a revised version (Olweus, 1996), and many other modified versions (e.g., Smith, 1991; Smith & Shu, 2000; Whitney & Smith, 1993) are the most widely used instruments in studies of bullying and bullying-victimization. There have been applications by researcher across many countries, including: Austria (Strohmeier & Spiel, 2003), China (Zhang, Gu, Wang, Wang, & Jones, 2000), Holland (Fekkes, Pijpers, & Verloove-Vanhorick, 2005), Ireland (O'Moore & Minton, 2005), Norway (Kristensen & Smith, 2003), and the United States (Dulmus, Theriot, Sowers, & Blackburn, 2004). The definition of bullying in the OB/VQ survey (presented in the introduction of this chapter) addresses the purposefulness, repetitiveness, and power imbalance aspects of bullying. Youth are presented with the definition and asked to keep it in mind as they respond to questions about their perceptions, observations, and participation (as bully or victim) in bully-related behavior. The original survey contained 56 items and the Revised OB/VQ has 36 primary items, with some supplemental questions. Both include questions about how often the students felt they had been bullied or had bullied others (as described in the definition provided) during the previous three months (1 = did not occur, 2 = occurred once or twice, 3 = occurred two or three times a month, 4 = occurred about once a week, 5 = occurred several times a week). The same response scale is used to ask about perpetration/victimization related to seven specific forms of bullying: verbal, exclusion, physical, spreading false rumors, personal items stolen/damaged, threats/coercion, and harassment related to one's race. Typically, responses to the perpetrator and victim items are used to classify youths into nonbully-nonvictim, victim, bully, and bully-victim groups (a June 1, 2007, PsychInfo search for these three terms located 164 entries; Solberg & Olweus, 2003; Solberg, Olweus, & Endresen, 2007). Solberg and Olweus (2003) suggest that youth who report being victimized or bullying others 2–3 times a month (during the previous three months) can be classified as chronic victims or bullies. They also present research showing that a smaller proportion of youth (10%–20% of victims) can be classified as both victims and bullies (bully-victims; Solberg et al., 2007).

Despite the prevalent use of the OB/VQ, there is surprisingly limited independent information about its psychometric properties, including both reliability and validity. Using Olweus's (1989) Senior Questionnaire (a version of the OB/VQ for 11- to 16-year-olds), Pellegrini, Bartini, and Brooks (1999) calculated alpha coefficients of .76 and .78 for bullying and bullying-victimization portions, respectively. Theriot, Dulmus, Sowers, and Johnson (2005) later reported alpha coefficients of .84 for the portions measuring experiencing bullying behaviors at least 2 or 3 times a month and .83 for experiencing bullying behaviors at least once a week for composites used in their analyses. Solberg and Olweus (2003) examined correlations between the dichotomized global scales and the specific bully behavior items and found correlations of .79 for being bullied and .77 for bullying, which, using a transformation, they claimed produce lower bound alpha estimates of .88 and .87 for bullied and bullying, respectively.

Evidence of validity was provided in a study with boys in school year levels 6–9, 60% of those identified as bullies were convicted of a crime by the time they were 24-years-old (Olweus, 1992). In another study, youth who were victimized at least 2–3 times a month differed significantly than their peers on measures of acceptance and belongingness with classmates, negative self-evaluations, and depression (Solberg & Olweus, 2003). In addition, bullies (victimized others at least 2–3 time a month) differed from non-bullies on measures of aggression and antisocial behavior (Solberg & Olweus, 2003).

More recently, Kyriakides, Kaloyirou, and Lindsay (2006) conducted the most sophisticated psychometric examination of the OB/VQ to date using a modified version with their sample of 335 Greek Cypriot 11- and 12-year-olds. Rasch analysis was used to examine reliability, model fit, meaning, and validity. This analysis found both good item fit, person fit, and range of item difficulty: –2.08 ("Bullied with mean names about my race or color") to 3.04 ("Hit, kicked, pushed, shoved around, or locked outdoors") for the victim items and –2.10 ("I bullied him or her with mean names with sexual meaning") to 3.03 ("I took money or other things from them or damaged their belongings") for perpetrator items. The analysis supported the contention that the OB/VQ measures one underlying construct and the authors concluded that construct validity was upheld.

Multidimensional Peer-Victimization

The Multidimensional Peer-Victimization (MPV scale) is another widely used research instrument. According to Mynard and Joseph (2000), "Bullying is the willful, conscious desire to hurt or frighten someone else. This might take the form of physical, verbal, or psychological bullying. There are many examples of bullying behavior. They all have as a common feature; the illegitimate use of power by one person over another. For example, bullying might comprise threats of violence or actual physical intimidation. It might comprise verbal malice or social ostracism" (pp. 170–171). Distilled from 45 original items, those with the highest factor loadings were retained to form four subscales: physical victimization (α = .85), verbal victimization (α = .75), social manipulation (α = .77), and attacks on property (α = .73; Mynard & Joseph, 2000). In one study, students were classified as "victims" or "non-victims" based on their response to a question on whether or not they were bullied. A series of *t*-tests revealed there were significant differences between the victims and the non-victims in their scores on the four subscales of the MPV, providing evidence for the validity of the measure (Mynard & Joseph, 2000).

Bully Survey

A revised version of the Bully Survey (Swearer, Turner, Givens, & Pollack, 2008) provides the following definition and examples of bullying, "Bullying happens when someone hurts or scares another person on purpose and the person being bullied has a hard time defending himself or herself. Usually, bullying happens over and over. [Examples are] punching, shoving and other acts that hurt people physically, spreading bad rumors about people; keeping certain people out of a 'group'; teasing people in a mean way; and getting certain people to 'gang up' on others" (p. 165). Following this definition are subscales of bullying and victimization experiences, observations of bullying, and attitudes towards bullying. Currently, most of the psychometric properties of the survey are for the subscales on attitudes towards bullying. According to Swearer, Song, Cary, Eagle, and Mickelson (2001), exploratory and confirmatory factor analyses on the attitude subscale support a one-factor solution. However, the RMSEA of .09 (Swearer et al., 2001) is generally considered marginal (McDonald & Ho, 2002) and the CFI of the model was low at .76 (Swearer et al., 2001). In another study, internal consistency for the attitude scale ranged from .55–.74 across three time periods, suggesting adequate internal consistency (Swearer & Cary, 2003). Few studies have investigated the construct validity of this survey and results thus far are not conclusive. Logistic regression analyses revealed significant relationships between scores on the attitude subscale and a measure of perception of school climate (Swearer et al., 2006). A study using an older version of the survey found significant differences between bullies, victims, bully-victims, and no-status students on a measure of anxiety (Swearer, Song, Cary, Eagle, & Mickelson, 2001). Also, Swearer and Cary (2003) suggest that the association between school office referrals for problem behaviors and bully status (more for bullies and less for victims) provides validity evidence. The Bully Survey provides a detailed assessment of students' bullying experiences that is ideally suited for large-scale campus surveys.

Limitations of the Definitional Approach

Researchers have debated the merits of defining bullying in surveys prior to asking students about their experiences. First and foremost, the definition of bullying has evolved over the past 20 years to include a broader range of victimization; thus, studies have varied in measurement practices. These practices have led to varying prevalence estimates and presumably have identified overlapping subsets of youths as bullies or victims of bullying—at the least, it is difficult to evaluate the nature and extent of cross-sample comparability. In addition, it has been suggested that even if definition consensus were possible, asking a youth to label himself or herself as a victim or a bully may provoke emotionally laden reactions and influence victims or bullies to not endorse experiences associated with the label (Cornell & Brockenbrough, 2004; Greif & Furlong, 2006; Hamby & Finkelhor, 2000). In this circumstance, bullying incidence would be underestimated and intervention outcomes would be affected by imprecise measurement.

Some have hypothesized that admitting to being a "bully" victim involves more than the mere recognition of specific victim events, but also implies that a youth has at some level accepted the psychological mantel of the defenseless victim (Greif & Furlong, 2006; Peskin, Tortolero, Markham, Addy, & Baumler, 2007). As a related example, research on adult victims of sexual harassment reveals that many participants endorsed experiencing all the behaviors and criteria associated with the legal definition of sexual harassment, but did not endorse the item at the end of the questionnaire asking whether they have experienced sexual harassment (Schneider, Swan, & Fitzgerald, 1997). A Danish study of workplace bullying found similar results with a definitional strategy of victimization producing prevalence estimates lower than when using a series of behavioral descriptions (Mikkelsen & Einarsen, 2001). This suggests that using a label may affect prevalence estimates because not all bully victims have internalized a self-image as being a "bully" victim. This is a particular problem for studies that do not provide a complex definition of bullying, but merely ask pupils how often they have been bullied, using the word without further clarification (e.g., Kshirsagar, Agarwal, & Bavdekar, 2007; Scholte, Engels, Overbeek, de Kemp, & Haselager, 2007).

Others argue that using a definitional strategy that includes multiple forms of aggression (e.g., presenting a definition listing various types of aggression and then asking the youth if he or she has been bullied) may produce heterogeneous data that mask trends and correlations among subtypes of bullying experiences (Cornell et al., 2006). Moreover, definitional measures may ask a single global question about bullying that includes a broad range of behaviors and does not allow for assessing the relative contribution of each form of bullying victimization to psychosocial adjustment (Cornell at al., 2006). It is important to distinguish among various forms of victimization when assessing psychosocial adjustment. For example, one study found that physical victimization and sexual harassment were more strongly related to psychosocial adjustment problems among urban middle school students than relational victimization (Felix & McMahon, 2006). Finally, researchers note that there is limited evidence that children can read and remember lengthy, grammatically complex definitions when responding to multiple questions about bullying experiences (Greif & Furlong, 2006).

Behavior-Based Self-Report Strategy

A second approach to bullying assessment emerged in the 1990s independently among several researchers. In this strategy, specific bully-related behaviors are presented and youth are asked to specify if they have committed them or experienced them as a victim. These behaviors typically include hitting, threatening, or spreading rumors, without specifically using the term bullying. Rather, the behavioral method breaks down the victimization experience into specific experiences in order to avoid stigma or bias associated with the term "bullying" and allows researchers to examine the frequency and type of victimization. These scales typically produce a summary score that provides a weighted index of victimization, with extreme responders being classified as bullies, victims, or both (e.g., DeSouza & Rineiro, 2005; Marini, Dane, Bosacki, & YLC-CURA, 2006).

Peer Victimization Scale

The Peer Victimization Scale developed by Neary and Joseph (1994) is a six-item survey that uses a forced-choice response format with students identifying whether a description (e.g., often teased or not teased) is "really true for me" or "sort of true for me." Good internal consistency has been reported in several studies (α =.82–.83; Austin & Joseph, 1996; Callaghan & Joseph, 1995; Neary & Joseph, 1994). Evidence of concurrent and construct validity was found in studies showing that students who reported they were "being bullied in this classroom" scored significantly higher than students who reported not being bullied (Callaghan & Joseph, 1995; Neary & Joseph, 1994). Also, significant correlations were found between scores on the Peer Victimization Scale and measures of depression, scholastic competence, social acceptance, physical appearance, behavioral conduct, global self-worth, and traumatic stress (Birleson, 1981; Callaghan & Joseph, 1995; Mynard & Joseph, 2000; Neary & Joseph, 1994).

Peer Relations Questionnaire

The Peer Relations Questionnaire (PRQ) uses a mixed strategy to assess bullying. First, it asks youths to respond to two items that inquire generally about bullying related behavior: (a) "How often have you been part of a group that bullied someone during the last year?" and (b) "How often have you, on your own, bullied someone during the last year?" The five-option response scale ranged from "never" (1) to "several times a week" (5). Second, it contains items describing behaviors that are associated with bullying (e.g., "enjoy upsetting wimps" and "like to make other kids scared"), victimization (e.g., "get picked on by others" and "get made fun of"), and prosocial behaviors (e.g., "enjoy helping others" and "help harassed children") (Rigby & Slee, 1993). A factor analysis found three subscales with four items in each: Bully, Victim, and Prosocial. Alpha coefficients for the subscales in two studies were all greater than .70 (Rigby, 1993; Rigby & Slee, 1993). Concurrent validity is evidenced by significant partial correlations between the three subscales and items taken from Smith's (1991) adaptation of the OB/VQ (Rigby, 1993). In addition, the partial correlation between the Prosocial Scale and the OB/VQ item assessing the degree to which a person would think or offer to help another peer was .42 for boys and .43 for girls (Rigby, 1993). Rigby and Slee (1993) report significant correlations between the three PRQ subscales and measures of self-esteem, happiness, school enjoyment, and family functioning, which supports its construct validity. The PRQ has been used in a number of studies of bullying and victimization (e.g., Morrison, 2006; Nguy & Hunt, 2004).

Illinois Aggression Scales

A recent addition to bullying measurement is a comprehensive instrument developed by Espelage and colleagues (Espelage & Holt, 2001; Espelage, Mebane, & Swearer, 2004). After interviewing students and conducting a literature review on bullying and victimization to obtain an initial set of items, principal-axis factoring was conducted on the original 21 items. Only items with factor loadings greater than .50 on their respective factor and less than .30 on the other factors were retained and included in the scales (Espelage & Holt, 2001; Espelage et al., 2004). The resulting Illinois Aggression Scales has three subscales: Bullying (e.g., "I teased other students" and "I upset students for the fun of it"); Fighting (e.g., "I got in a physical fight" and "I threatened to hit or hurt another student"); and Victimization (e.g., "Other students made fun of me" and "Other students picked on me") (Espelage & Holt, 2001). All three subscales possess good internal consistency (α = .83–.91; Espelage & Holt, 2001; Espelage, Mebane, & Adams, 2004). Evidence of content and construct validity is shown by the low correlation between the Bully and Victimization scales (r = .12) and a moderate correlation between the Bully and Fighting scales (r = .58; Espelage, Bosworth, & Simon, 2001; Espelage & Holt, 2001). A confirmatory factor analysis found that all three scales represented distinct factors (Espelage et al., 2001; Espelage & Holt, 2001). Furthermore, significant differences were found between bullies, victims, and no-status students on the aggressive behaviors, delinquent behaviors, anxiety/depression, and withdrawn behaviors of the Youth Self-Report (Achenbach, 1991) and measures of school connectedness, attitudes towards violence, and receipt of pro-violence messages from adults (Espelage & Holt, 2001). Significant differences were found between bullies, victims, bully-victims, and no-status students on two measures of empathy that assess for acts of caring and consideration towards others (Espelage et al., 2001) and significant differences were found between self-reported bullies and self-reported non-bullies on a peer-nominated bullying measure (Espelage & Holt, 2001; Espelage, Holt, & Henkel, 2003). The care of development and the evidence of validity are strengths of this measure.

Gatehouse Bullying Scale

The Gatehouse Bullying Scale measures how often respondents are victims of four forms of aggressive acts (e.g., teasing, rumors spread, left out, and threatened/hurt) and the amount of distress caused by the experience (Bond, Wolfe, Tollit, Butler, & Patton, 2007). Over a period of three weeks, test-retest stability was measured with kappa statistics between .36 and .63 and Spearman's rho between .44 and .65 (Bond et al., 2007). Scores on the Gatehouse Bullying Scale were compared to scores on the Peer Relations Questionnaire (Rigby, 1996) with a preceding definition of bullying to assess the concurrent validity of the Gatehouse Bullying Scale. Agreement between the two measures ranged from 75.6% to 90.1%, with kappa statistics between .42–.58 (Bond et al., 2007). Studies using the Gatehouse Bullying Scale found a significant relation between bully-victimization and symptoms of anxiety or depression among those who reported in the previous year that they had been victimized (Bond, Carlin, Thomas, Rubin, & Patton, 2001), and a significant relation between being bullied and substance abuse (Bond et al., 2004).

Limitations of the Behavior-Based Approach

Behavioral assessments of bullying created to date generally neglect to address all three aspects of the definition of bullying. These assessments often list behaviors and do not include information about context (De Los Reyes & Kazdin, 2005) and/or to explicitly assess power imbalance. To distinguish between bully and peer victims, behavioral strategies generally classify the group with the highest level of victimization experiences as "bullies" and those whose victimization reports fall below a set criteria as "victims" (Espelage & Swearer, 2003). Some issues associated with this approach are: (a) the criteria used to select extreme responders (e.g., one standard deviation above the mean, less, more) vary across studies (Solberg & Olweus, 2003); (b) educators conducting school-based surveys are unlikely to be able to complete the complex computations needed to classify students with statistical methods; and (c) unless additional items are co-administered, the behavioral method assesses only one aspect of the definition of bullying, which is the repetitive nature of the experience.

Advantages of Using Self-Report Strategies

Despite noted limitations, self-reports address many complex issues of understanding bullying behavior. First, self-report procedures are efficient and can be conducted in school, community, and laboratory settings with minimal cost, particularly if coupled with the use of web-based administration technology. Second, self-reports can assess the diverse and important subtypes of bullying behavior, including direct, indirect, and relational aggression. Third, they have the potential to assess the perceived power imbalance from the perspective of the bully, victim, or bully-victim. Fourth, they do not rely on consent from other participants (as in peer nomination procedures). Fifth, they assess the perspective of the participant (both bully and victim), which is critical when attempting to understand intentionality and impacts on psychosocial functioning. Finally, self-reporting can simultaneously assess and distinguish between different forms of bullying behavior to better understand differential impact.

Measurement Issues to Address

Although there are many advantages to using self-report, there are also unresolved issues to be addressed in order to move research and evaluation of prevention programs forward. There is a need to take a step back and examine some fundamental core measurement characteristics of bullying self-report instruments because few peer-reviewed, empirical articles detailing the psychometric properties of bullying instruments are available (Tarshis & Huffman, 2007).

Additional attention must be given to explore alternative strategies to assess power imbalance, one of the three key elements of bullying. Research has demonstrated the important distinction between the larger group of peer victims and the subset of bully victims (Furlong, Felix, Sharkey, Greif Green, & Tanigawa, 2006; Greif Green, Felix, Furlong, & Taylor, 2007). Namely, youth who have experienced repeated bullying have significantly poorer psychological health than youth who have experienced repeated peer victimization that was not bullying. Thus, relying solely on the repetitive nature of victimization may not be adequate for truly understanding the bully experience. Research needs to implement and test methods of assessing the power imbalance, a procedure that has been neglected up to this point, in order to further examine the importance of distinguishing peer victimization from bullying victimization.

Research is needed on the psychometric properties of available self-report bullying and bullying-victimization assessments. Scholars need to attain a more complete understanding of the impact of careless, dishonest, socially desirable, or otherwise invalid responses because there is very little empirical research addressing these influences on youth bully self-reports. The cognitive abilities of the responders should be taken into consideration. Reading levels, time frames, and response formats of these bullying and bullying-victimization assessments vary considerably. It is important to assure that the reading level of the instrument is appropriate for participants. Studies have also shown that the time frame (e.g., asking about bullying that has occurred in the past 30 days or in the past 12 months) used in questions may affect students' responses as well. It may be difficult for students to remember incidents of bullying and/or bullying-victimization when relying on long-term memory (Furlong & Sharkey, 2006; Hilton, Harris, & Rice, 1998). Furthermore, a response validity issue that warrants further examination is the possibility that questioning about bullying and victimization may elicit socially desirable responses (Espelage & Swearer, 2003), such that youth do not report bullying experiences because of the potential stigma associated with either victimization or perpetration. Validity checks within assessments and studies using a combination of self-report measures with peer nominations, teacher/parent-reports, and direct observation may elucidate these issues.

Before undertaking future studies on bullying and bullying-victimization, and in light of varying prevalence rates and contradictory findings, it may be wise to first reach a consensus among researchers on how to define bullying without ignoring the social context in which it occurs, and to also agree upon a criterion used to identify the four groups used predominately in research: bullies, victims, bully-victims, and no-status students. Many recent researchers cite the seminal study by Solberg and Olweus (2003) to support their use of this four-group classification. Although researchers do not always use the identical procedures or the same subset of specific bullying items, it is very common to form these four groups based on responses to a single victimization or bullying item from all those presented. Although this practice has been essentially unquestioned, the recent Rasch analysis of the Olweus victim and bullying items by Kyriakides et al. (2006) revealed that these items do not have the same level of item difficulty; hence, this classification scheme can place two pupils in a bully group when the behaviors they reported are at opposite ends of the bully behavior continuum, as suggested by the Rasch analysis. Further demonstrating this for victims, Greif Green et al. (2007) reported a strong positive association between the number of different types of victimization (e.g., verbal, physical, sexual) experienced in a month and the percentage of pupils scoring in the clinical range of a measure of posttraumatic stress (more than 50% of pupils reporting three or four types of frequent victimization were in the clinical posttraumatic stress range, compared to about 20% of pupils with one type of victimization).

For more than two decades researchers have typically relied on presenting a definition of bullying to youth and asking them to accept this definition and to map their personal experiences on to this definition. To be certain, this strategy has yielded important insights into the occurrence of bullying and its impacts on the development outcome of chronic bullies and victims. The use of a well-defined, single item, with specified response options may have the potential to ease interpretation and reproduction across the globe for the purpose of prevalence estimation given reasonable psychometrics for this purpose (Solberg & Olweus, 2003), which is the strategy used internationally via the World Health Organization Health Behavior in School-aged Children Survey (e.g., Nansel et al., 2004). Nonetheless, there is limited research evidence that youth are consistent enough in their responses to surveys designed merely to provide prevalence estimates when precise measurement is needed. There is a need to carefully assess short-tem stability of pupils' responses.

As an example, a series of ongoing validity studies related to the development of the California Bully Victimization Scale (CBVS; Furlong et al., 2006) are systematically investigating influences on bully victimization measurement to explore possible avenues to improve measurement precision. The CBVS uses a behavioral approach to assessing victimization experiences (the term bullying is not used) with questions about the types of victimization experiences scholars have identified (e.g., being threatened, excluded, sexually harassed). It also is designed to address intentionality and asks questions to gauge power imbalance and the relationship between bully and victim. Additional items query social support and assess the victim's emotional and psychological coping with the experience. In our initial analyses, the CBVS classifies a victim as experiencing bullying if the he or she reports frequently intentional victimization (i.e., 2–3 times per month or more) in one or more ways and the youth reports a disadvantageous power imbalance. The CBVS includes a multi-gating process designed to maximize sensitivity and specificity in an efficient matter. The second gate is more in-depth and conducted as a structured interview to allow for interviewer insight into the experience.

Preliminary findings of CBVS validity studies yield some insights into the methodological issues faced by bullying researchers and provide direction for additional research. For example, we co-administered the CBVS with the global bully victim item included in the Swearer (2001) Bully Survey. Furlong and colleagues (2006) found that the two-week victim classification stability of the CBVS (Kappa = .690) was superior to the definitional method (which used the word bullying; Kappa = .456). When comparing classification rates between the CBVS and definitional methods, 21.3% and 17.9% of students were classified as chronic victims, respectively. Even more significant than the difference in prevalence rates is the finding that there was only a partial overlap between the individual students who were identified as chronic victims using these two measures. Of the youth identified as chronic victims using the CBVS, only 44% were categorized as chronic victims using Swearer's Bully Survey. Likewise, of the youth identified by Swearer's definitional measure, only 37% were also considered chronic victims based on their responses to the CBVS.

This raises some rather intriguing methodological questions for researchers who use measures originally intended for prevalence estimation to compare and understand the bullying victimization experiences of specific youths. If the goal of bullying assessment is to classify bullies, victims, and bully-victims, it is crucial to understand the stability of classification and if changes do occur, why, given that bullying is by definition a stable experience (Scholte et al., 2007). If clinical outcome research is the goal, precision is needed when classifying pupils. As a second example, we co-administered the CBVS and the Bully Survey with several positive psychology scales, including a measure of children's hope. Results indicated significant differences between victims who did and did not report a power difference in the bully-victim relationship. In fact, on most measures, non-victims and victims were similar on measures of positive health, whereas chronic victims with a reported power imbalance scored markedly lower (You et al., 2008). Moreover, the distinction between outcomes for victims and chronic victims was

Table 24.1 Implications for Practice and Research: Issues in Bullying Assessment and Suggestions for Researchers and Practitioners

Issue	Suggestions for Research and Practice
Spend some time considering and developing a working definition of bullying	A first step is to look over the various definition of bullying that have been provided by researchers and to see which one best addresses your context. Are you interested primarily in knowing more about bullies, victims, or both? An often-ignored matter is your relative interest in group versus individual bullying behavior. Prior to conducting any survey or intervention project, settle on an operational definition of what it means to be bullied or to bully.
Consider the purpose in assessing bullying	The end-purpose of assessment data is very important to consider. If a school or community wants to initiate an on-going surveillance of bullying-related behaviors over time, then brief definition-based questionnaires are a good choice. As the depth of information need increases, then, of course, the questionnaire needs to be more detailed and provide information about when, where, and how bullying is occurring. If the goal is to develop group-level trends, then less precision is needed to distinguish between general peer victimization and bullying. In this circumstance, broad reduction in all type of victimization is sought. When the researcher or practitioner turns to administering questionnaires to asses the effectiveness of an intervention with a targeted group of victim or bullies, then the reliability and validity of the instrument should be examined very closely.
Examine the response time frame	Bullying questionnaires all ask about behaviors that occurred within a specific time. Researchers and practitioners are encouraged to examine these options in the context of the application. For example, are you interested in very recent experiences? Asking about past-year behaviors would not be a good choice for the evaluation of a school prevention program because it may not be responsive enough to recent changes. In our view, youth are better able to provide accurate information about recent (e.g., past month) then distant (e.g., past year) behaviors. In addition, frequent data gathering provides more corrective information than annual surveys.
Consider the types of bullying behaviors included in the questionnaire	Another key consideration is to examine which types of bullying behaviors are included in the survey, such as physical attacks, social isolation, etc. The items should describe behaviors in a way that is appropriate for the school social and cultural context and be aligned with the research, program, or intervention that is being implemented. Surveys should also address cultural and developmental influences.
Evaluate how the essential component of power imbalance is addressed	For general surveillance purposes, it is most practical to use one of the definition-based surveys to facilitate surveys of large numbers of students. These questionnaires address power imbalance; however, for local use, researchers and practitioners may want to augment information by holding focus groups with students to learn more about how they read and considered the definition provided. If there is an interest in understanding the bullying victim experience or providing targeted interventions for either victims or bullies, then consider conducting a more in-depth survey, structured interview, or both in a multi-tiered process.
Evaluate the function and purpose of bullying	Finally, when implementing or evaluating targeted intervention programs, consider using other known cross-informant assessment procedures to gather related clinical information, such as psychometrically sound measures of internalizing and externalizing problem behaviors. Also, particularly for bullies, completing a functional assessment of their behaviors may shed light on what is motivating and sustaining their mistreatment of their peers.

more powerful for the CBVS than the Bully Scale (Furlong et al., 2006). These results highlight the potential importance of including the power balance in a behavioral approach designed to understand the psychological functioning of the participant(s). Further research is needed to continue to clarify methodological issues in bullying research. Table 24.1 identifies issues in bullying assessment and provides suggestions for researchers and practitioners.

Conclusion

The term "bullying" has been defined as including three components, intentionality, repetition, and power imbalance; however, assessments of bullying do not often include all three components. Research suggests that all three components of bullying are important for understanding which students are most at-risk for negative psychosocial outcomes. However, bullying has not always been distinguished from victimization experiences across national studies. International consensus on the measurement of bullying components is needed to continue to move the field of bullying research forward from prevalence estimation to the measurement precision needed for use with individual students. More recent developments in bullying assessment (e.g., Bond et al., 2007; Tarshis & Huffman, 2007) have taken a classical test theory approach to this task by examining scale reliability, validity, and stability. Despite the psychometric advantages of new scales, these behavioral approaches do not specifically examine power imbalance. In developing a new scale, for example, Tarshis and Huffman (2007) concluded that most of the elementary school students in their scale development sample participated in bullying, which raises what appears to be the still unresolved issue in bullying assessment—How do researchers and practitioners accurately differentiate bullying from more normative, although still undesirable, peer victimization? If the act of bullying others or being chronically bullied by others (based in an abusive asymmetrical peer interaction) is known to have detrimental developmental outcomes for both parties, then it is essential that researchers and educational practitioners redouble their efforts to be able to accurately distinguish these youths from other youths involved in peer aggression. Although bullying research will continue to move forward, increased measurement precision will greatly facilitate and integrate knowledge across countries.

References

Achenbach, T. M. (1991). *Integrative guide for the 1991 CBCL/4-18, YSR and TRF Profiles*. Burlington: Department of Psychiatry, University of Vermont.

Arora, C. M. J. (1996). Defining bullying: Towards a clearer general understanding and more effective intervention strategies. *School Psychology International, 17*, 317–329.

Austin, S., & Joseph, S. (1996). Assessment of bully-victim problems in 8- to 11-year-olds. *British Journal of Educational Psychology, 66*, 447–456.

Birleson, P. (1981). The validity of depression disorder in childhood and the development of a self-rating scale: A research report. *Journal of Child Psychology and Psychiatry, 22*, 73–88.

Björkvist, K., Ekman, K., & Lagerspetz, K. (1982). Bullies and victims: Their ego picture, ideal ego picture and normative ego picture. *Scandinavian Journal of Psychology, 23*, 307–313.

Bond, L., Carlin, J. B., Thomas, L., Rubin, K., & Patton, G. (2001). Does bullying cause emotional problems? A prospective study of young teenagers. *British Medical Journal, 323*(7311), 480–484.

Bond, L., Patton, G., Glover, S., Carlin, J. B., Butler, H., & Thomas, L., & Bowes, G. (2004). The gatehouse project: Can a multilevel school intervention affect emotional wellbeing and health risk behaviours? *Journal of Epidemiology & Community Health, 58*, 997–1003.

Bond, L., Wolfe, S., Tollit, M., Butler, H., & Patton G. (2007). A comparison of the Gatehouse Bullying Scale and the peer relations questionnaire for students in secondary school. *Journal of School Health, 77*, 75–79.

"Bullying" amongst birds. (1932). *Nature, 129*, 395.

Calkins, M. W. (1916). *Volition and belief. Will and faith*. New York: MacMillan.

Callaghan, S., & Joseph, S. (1995). Self-concept and peer victimization among schoolchildren. *Personality and Individual Differences, 18,* 161–163.

Chan, J. H. F. (2006). Systemic patterns in bullying and victimization. *School Psychology International, 27,* 352–369.

Chan, J. H. F., Myron, R., & Crawshaw, M. (2005). The efficacy of non-anonymous measures of bullying. *School Psychology International, 26,* 443–458.

Cole, J. C. M., Cornell, D. G., & Sheras, P. (2006). Identification of school bullies by survey methods. *Professional School Counseling, 9,* 305–313.

Cornell, D. G., & Brockenbrough, K. (2004). Identification of bullies and victims: A comparison of methods. In M. J. Furlong, G. Morrison, R. Skiba, & D. Cornell (Eds.), *Issues in school violence research* (pp. 63–87). New York: Haworth Press.

Cornell, D. G., Sheras, P. L., & Cole, J. C. (2006). Assessment of bullying. In S. Jimerson & M. Furlong (Eds.), *Handbook of school violence and school safety* (pp. 191–210). Mahwah, NJ: Erlbaum.

Craig, W. M., & Pepler, D. J. (1997). Observations of bullying and victimization in the school yard. *Canadian Journal of School Psychology, 13,* 41–59.

Craig, W. M., Pepler, D., & Atlas, R. (2000). Observations of bullying in the playground and in the classroom. *School Psychology International, 21,* 22–36.

De Los Reyes, A., & Kazdin, A. E. (2005). Informant discrepancies in the assessment of childhood psychopathology: A critical review, theoretical framework, and recommendations for further study. *Psychological Bulletin, 131,* 483–509.

DeSouza, E. R., & Rineiro, J. (2005). Bullying and sexual harassment among Brazilian high school students. *Journal of Interpersonal Violence, 20,* 1018–1038.

Dulmus, C. N., Theriot, M. T., Sowers, K. M., & Blackburn, J. A. (2004). Student reports of peer bullying victimization in a rural school. *Stress, Trauma and Crisis: An International Journal, 7,* 1–16.

Espelage, D. L., Bosworth, K., & Simon, T. R. (2001). Short-term stability and prospective correlates of bullying in middle school: An examination of potential demographic, psychosocial, and environmental influences. *Violence & Victims, 16,* 411–426.

Espelage, D. L., & Holt, M. K. (2001). Bullying and victimization during early adolescence: Peer influences and psychosocial correlates. In R. A. Geffner, M. Loring, & C. Young (Eds.), *Bullying behavior: Current issues, research, and interventions* (pp. 123–142). Binghamton, NY: Haworth Maltreatment and Trauma Press/The Haworth Press.

Espelage, D. L., Holt, M. K., & Henkel, R. R. (2003). Examination of peer-group contextual effects on aggression during early adolescence. *Child Development, 74,* 205–220.

Espelage, D. L., Mebane, S. E., & Adams, R. S. (2004). Empathy, caring, and bullying: Toward an understanding of complex associations. In D. L. Espelage & S. M. Swearer (Eds.), *Bullying in American schools: A social-ecological perspective on prevention and intervention* (pp. 37–61). Mahwah, NJ: Erlbaum.

Espelage, D. L., Mebane, S. E., & Swearer, S. M. (2004). Gender differences in bullying: Moving beyond mean level differences. In D. L. Espelage & S. M. Swearer (Eds.), *Bullying in American schools: A social-ecological perspective on prevention and intervention* (pp. 15–35). Mahwah, NJ: Erlbaum.

Espelage, D. L., & Swearer, S. M. (2003). Research on school bullying and victimization: What have we learned and where do we go from here? *School Psychology Review, 32,* 365–383.

Espelage, D. L., & Swearer S. M. (Eds.). (2004). *Bullying in American schools: A social-ecological perspective on prevention and intervention.* Mahwah, NJ: Erlbaum.

Fekkes, M., Pijpers, F. I. M., & Verloove-Vanhorick, S. P. (2005). Bullying: Who does what, when and where? Involvement of children, teachers and parents in bullying behavior. *Health Education Research, 20,* 81–91.

Felix, E. D., & McMahon, S. D. (2006). Gender and multiple forms of peer victimization: How do they influence adolescent psychosocial adjustment? *Violence & Victims, 21,* 707–724.

Furlong, M. J., Felix, E. J., Sharkey, J. D., Greif Green, J., & Tanigawa, D. (2006). *Development of a multi-gating school bullying victimization assessment.* Paper presented at the Persistently Safe School Conference, Hamilton Fish Institute, George Washington University, Washington, DC, September.

Furlong, M. J., & Sharkey, J. D. (2006). A review of methods to assess student self-report of weapons on school campuses. In S. R. Jimerson & M. J. Furlong (Eds.), *Handbook of school violence and school safety* (pp. 235–253). Mahwah, NJ: Erlbaum.

Greif Green, J., Felix, E. D., Furlong, M. J., & Taylor, L. A. (2007, March). *The relationship between bullying and posttraumatic stress.* Paper presented at the Society for Research in Child Development, Boston.

Greif, J. L., & Furlong, M. J. (2006). The assessment of school bullying: Using theory to inform practice, *Journal of School Violence, 5,* 33–50.

Hall, G. S. (1904). *Juvenile faults, immoralities, and crimes.* New York: D. Appleton.

Hamby, S. L., & Finkelhor, D. (2000). The victimization of children: Recommendations for assessment and instrument development. *Journal of the American Academy of Child & Adolescent Psychiatry, 39,* 829–840.

Hawkins, D. L., Pepler, D. J., & Craig, W. M. (2001). Naturalistic observations of peer interventions in bullying. *Social Development, 10,* 512–527.

Heinemann, P. P. (1972) *Mobbning. Gruppvåld bland barn och vuxna* [Bullying. Group violence among children and grown ups]. Stockholm: Natur och Kultur.

Hilton, N. Z., Harris, G. T., & Rice, M. E. (1998). On the validity of self-reported rates of interpersonal violence. *Journal of Interpersonal Violence, 13,* 58–72.

Hoover, J. H., & Hazler, R. J. (1991). Bullies and victims. *Elementary School Guidance & Counseling, 25,* 212–219.

Komiyama, K. (1986). A study of the background factors related to bullying among junior high school students. *Reports of the National Research Institute of Police Science, 27,* 38–53.

Kristensen, S. M., & Smith, P. K. (2003). The use of coping strategies by Danish children classed as bullies, victims, bully/victims, and not involved, in response to different (hypothetical) types of bullying. *Scandinavian Journal of Psychology, 44,* 479–488.

Kshirsagar, V. Y., Agarwal, R., & Bavdekar, S. B. (2007). Bullying in schools: Prevalence and short-term impact. *Indian Pediatrics, 44,* 25–28.

Kyriakides, L., Kaloyirou, C., & Lindsay, G. (2006). An analysis of the Revised Olweus Bully/Victim Questionnaire using the Rasch measurement model. *British Journal of Educational Psychology, 76,* 781–801.

LaFontaine, J. (1991). *Bullying: The child's view.* London: Calouste Gulbenkian Found.

Lowenstein, L. F. (1972). *Violence in schools and its treatment.* Oxford, England: National Association of Schoolmasters.

Lowenstein, L. F. (1975). *Violent and disruptive behaviour in schools.* Oxford, England: National Association of Schoolmasters.

Lowenstein, L. F. (1977). Who is the bully? *Home & School, 11,* 3–4.

Lowenstein, L. F. (1978). The bullied and non bullied child: A contrast between the popular and unpopular child. *Home & School, 12,* 3–4.

Marini, Z., Dane, A., Bosacki, S., & YLC-CURA (2006). Direct and indirect bully-victims: Differential psychosocial risk factors associated with adolescents involved in bullying and victimization. *Aggressive Behaviour, 32,* 1–19.

McDonald, R. P., & Ho, M. R. (2002). Principles and practice in reporting structural equation analyses. *Psychological Methods, 7,* 64–82.

Mikkelsen, E. G., & Einarsen, S. (2001). Bullying in Danish work-life: Prevalence and health correlates. *European Journal of Work and Organizational Psychology. Special Issue: Bullying in the Workplace: Recent Trends in Research and Practice, 10,* 393–413.

Morrison, B. (2006). School bullying and restorative justice: Toward a theoretical understanding of the role of respect, pride, and shame. *Journal of Social Issues, 62,* 371–392.

Mynard, H., & Joseph, S. (2000). Development of the multidimensional peer-victimization scale. *Aggressive Behavior, 26,* 169–178.

Nansel, T. R., Craig, W., Overpeck, M. D., Saluja, G., Ruan, W. J., & Health Behaviour in School-aged Children Bullying Analyses Working Group. (2004). Cross-national consistency in the relationship between bullying behaviors and psychosocial adjustment. *Archieves Pediatriatric Adolescent Medicine, 158,* 730–736.

Naylor, P., Cowie, H., Cossin, F., de Bettencourt, R., & Lemme, F. (2006). Teachers' and pupils' definitions of bullying. *British Journal of Educational Psychology, 76,* 553–576.

Neary, A., & Joseph, S. (1994). Peer victimization and its relationship to self-concept and depression among schoolgirls. *Personality and Individual Differences, 16,* 183–186.

Nguy, L., & Hunt, C. J. (2004). Ethnicity and bullying: A study of Australian high-school students. *Educational and Child Psychology, 21,* 78–94.

Olweus, D. (1978). *Aggression in the schools: Bullies and whipping boys.* Oxford, England: Hemisphere.

Olweus, D. (1986). *The Olweus Bully/Victim Questionnaire.* Mimeo. Bergen, Norway: University of Bergen.

Olweus, D. (1987). Bully/victim problems among schoolchildren in Scandinavia. In J. P. Myklebust & R. Ommundsen (Eds.), *Psykologprofesjonen mot år 2000: Helsepsykologi, samfunnspsykologi og internasjonale perspektiver: Minneskrift til bjorn christiansen* [Psychology profession toward the year 2000] (pp. 395–413). Oslo, Norway: Universitetsforlaget AS.

Olweus, D. (1989). *Senior Questionnaire for Students.* Unpublished manuscript.

Olweus, D. (1992). Bullying among school children: Intervention and prevention. In R. D. Peters, R. J. McMahon, & V. L. Quiney (Eds.), *Aggression and violence through the life span* (pp. 100–125). Thousand Oaks, CA: Sage.

Olweus, D. (1993). *Bullying at school: What we know and what we can do.* Malden, MA: Blackwell.

Olweus, D. (1996). *The revised Olweus Bully/Victim Questionnaire.* Mimeo. Bergen, Norway: Research Center for Health Promotion (HEMIL Center), University of Bergen.

O'Moore, A. M., & Hillery, B. (1989). Bullying in Dublin schools. *Irish Journal of Psychology, 10,* 426–441.

O'Moore, A. M., & Minton, S. J. (2005). Evaluation of the effectiveness of an anti-bullying programme in primary schools. *Aggressive Behavior, 31,* 609–622.

Parten, M. B. (1933). Leadership among preschool children. *Journal of Abnormal & Social Psychology, 27,* 430–440.

Pearce, J. D. W. (1948). The community and the aggressive child. *Journal of Mental Science, 94,* 623–628.

Pellegrini, A. D., Bartini, M., & Brooks, F. (1999). School bullies, victims, and aggressive victims: Factors relating to group affiliation and victimization in early adolescence. *Journal of Educational Psychology, 91*, 216–224.

Peskin, M. F., Tortolero, S. R., Markham, C. M., Addy, R. C., & Baumler, E. R. (2007). Related bullying and victimization and internalizing symptoms among low-income Black and Hispanic students. *Journal of Adolescent Health, 40*, 372–375.

Pikas, A. (1975). Treatment of mobbing in school: Principles for and the results of the work of an anti-mobbing group. *Scandinavian Journal of Educational Research, 19*, 1–12.

Prewitt, P. W. (1988). Dealing with ijime (bullying) among Japanese students: Current approaches to the problem. *School Psychology International, 9*, 189–195.

Rigby, K. (1993). School children's perceptions of their families and parents as a function of peer relations. *The Journal of Genetic Psychology, 154*, 501–513.

Rigby, K. (1996). *Manual for the Peer Relations Questionnaire.* Underdale, Australia: University of South Australia.

Rigby, K. (2004). What it takes to stop bullying in schools: An examination of the rationale and effectiveness of school-based interventions. In M. J. Furlong, M. P. Bates, D. C. Smith, & P. Kingery (Eds.), *Appraisal and prediction of school violence* (pp. 165–191). Hauppauge, NY: Nova Science.

Rigby, K., & Slee, P. T. (1991). Bullying among Australian school children: Reported behavior and attitudes toward victims. *Journal of Social Psychology, 131*, 615–627.

Rigby, K., & Slee, P. T. (1993). Dimensions of interpersonal relation among Australian children and implications for psychological well-being. *Journal of Social Psychology, 133*, 33–42.

Schneider, K. T., Swan, S., & Fitzgerald, L. F. (1997). Job-related and psychological effects of sexual harassment in the workplace: Empirical evidence from two organizations. *Journal of Applied Psychology, 82*, 410–415.

Scholte, R. H., Engels, R. C., Overbeek, G., de Kemp, R. A., & Haselager, G. J. (2007). Stability in bullying and victimization and its association with social adjustment in childhood and adolescence. *Journal of Abnormal Child Psychology, 35*, 217–228.

Schuster, B. (1996). Rejection, exclusion, and harassment at work and in schools. *European Psychologist, 1*, 293–309.

Sharp, S., & Smith, P. K. (1991). Bullying in UK schools: The DES Sheffield bullying project. *Early Child Development and Care, 77*, 47–55.

Smith, G. H. (1950). Sociometric study of best-liked and least-liked children. *Elementary School Journal, 51*, 77–85.

Smith, P. K. (1991). The silent nightmare: Bullying and victimization in school peer-groups. *The Psychologist, 4*, 243–248.

Smith, P. K., Cowie, H., Olafsson, R. F., & Liefooghe, A. P. D. (2002). Definitions of bullying: A comparison of terms used, and age and gender differences, in a fourteen-country international comparison. *Child Development, 73*, 1119–1133.

Smith, P. K., & Levan, S. (1995). Perceptions and experiences of bullying in younger pupils. *British Journal of Educational Psychology, 65*, 489–500.

Smith, P. K., Morita, Y., Junger-Tas, J., Olweus, D., Catalano, R., & Slee, P. (Eds.). (1999). *The nature of bullying: A cross-national perspective.* New York: Routledge.

Smith, P. K., & Shu, S. (2000). What good schools can do about bullying: Findings from a survey in English schools after a decade of research and action. *Childhood, 7*, 193–212.

Smorti, A., Menesini, E., & Smith, P. K. (2003). Parents' definitions of children's bullying in a five-country comparison. *Journal of Cross-Cultural Psychology, 34*, 417–432.

Solberg, M. E., & Olweus, D. (2003). Prevalence estimation of school bullying with the Olweus Bully/Victim Questionnaire. *Aggressive Behavior, 29*, 239–268.

Solberg, M. E., Olweus, D., & Endresen, I. M. (2007). Bullies and victims at school: Are they the same pupils? *British Journal of Educational Psychology, 77*, 441–464.

Strohmeier, D., & Spiel, C. (2003). Immigrant children in Austria: Aggressive behavior and friendship patterns in multicultural school classes. *Journal of Applied School Psychology, 19*, 99–116.

Swearer, S. M. (2001). *Bully Survey.* Unpublished survey. Lincoln: University of Nebraska-Lincoln.

Swearer, S. M., & Cary, P. T. (2003). Perceptions and attitudes toward bullying in middle school youth: A developmental examination across the Bully/Victim continuum. *Journal of Applied School Psychology, 19*, 63–79.

Swearer, S. M., Peugh, J., Espelage, D. L., Siebecker, A. B., Kingsbury, W. L., & Bevins, K. S. (2006). A socioecological model for bullying prevention and intervention in early adolescence: An exploratory examination. In S. R. Jimerson & M. J. Furlong (Eds.), *Handbook of school violence and school safety: From research to practice* (pp. 257–273). Mahwah, NJ: Erlbaum.

Swearer, S. M., Song, S. Y., Cary, P. T., Eagle, J. W., & Mickelson, W. T. (2001). Psychosocial correlates in bullying and victimization: The relationship between depression, anxiety, and bully/victim status. In R. A. Geffner, M. Loring, & C. Young (Eds.), *Bullying behavior: Current issues, research, and interventions* (pp. 95–121). Binghamton, NY: Haworth Maltreatment and Trauma Press/The Haworth Press.

Swearer, S. M., Turner, R. K., Givens, J. E., & Pollack, W. S. (2008). "You're so gay!": Do different forms of bullying matter for adolescent males? *School Psychology Review, 37,* 160–173.

Tarshis, T. P., & Huffman, L. C. (2007). Psychometric properties of the Peer Interactions in Primary School (PIPS) Questionnaire. *Journal of Developmental & Behavioral Pediatrics, 28,* 125–132.

Theriot, M. T., Dulmus, C. N., Sowers, K. M., & Johnson, T. K. (2005). Factors relating to self-identification among bullying victims. *Children and Youth Services Review, 27,* 979–994.

Thorndike, E. L. (1919). *Man's equipment of instincts and capacities: Responses to the behavior of other human beings.* New York: Columbia University Press.

Vaughn, C. L. (1941). Classroom behavior problems encountered in attempting to teach illiterate defective boys how to read. *Journal of Educational Psychology, 32,* 339–350.

Whitney, I., & Smith, P. K. (1993). A survey of the nature and extent of bullying in junior/middle and secondary schools. *Educational Research, 35,* 3–25.

You, S., Furlong, M. J., Felix, E. D., Sharkey, J. D., Tanigawa, D., & Grief Green, J. (2008). Relations among school connectedness, hope, life satisfaction, and bullying victimization. *Psychology in the Schools, 45,* 446–460.

Zhang, W., Gu, C., Wang, M., Wang, Y., & Jones, K. (2000). Gender differences in the bully/victim problem among primary and junior middle school students. *Psychological Science, 23,* 435–439.

25

Variability in the Prevalence of Bullying and Victimization

A Cross-National and Methodological Analysis

CLAYTON R. COOK, KIRK R. WILLIAMS, NANCY G. GUERRA, AND TIA E. KIM

Bullying is not an isolated problem, occurring only in a particular country or social setting. Rather, it is a pervasive behavioral problem crossing national boundaries and penetrating virtually every social setting in which people have ongoing relationships with repeated interactions over time. Schools represent a social setting common to nearly every country throughout the world. As a result, researchers worldwide have devoted considerable attention to studying bullying in schools (Espelage & Swearer, 2004; Smith et al., 1999; Olweus, 1993; Rigby, 2002), as evident in the survey of bullying conducted by Smith and others (1999) involving 21 countries in America, Europe, Africa, Asia, and Australia.

Given the numerous studies of bullying in schools across and within countries, a comparative analysis of differences in the prevalence of bullying is warranted. For instance, research has not clearly determined the extent of variation among countries in the prevalence of bullying and victimization in schools. Moreover, little is known about the degree to which methodological aspects of these studies account for at least a portion of that variation, such as who reports bullying (e.g., self, peer, teacher, or parent), how bullying is measured (e.g., definition, label, or behavioral descriptor), and the temporal referent period used to elicit responses about involvement in this behavior as a bully, victim, or bully-victim (e.g., during the last week, the last 30 days, or last year).

Purpose of this Chapter

This chapter empirically explores these issues by performing a comparative analysis of school-based studies. More specifically, a meta-analysis is conducted to determine the variability of prevalence rates across those studies and whether their methodological features, in addition to geographic location, are related to this variability. The studies used were drawn from a larger meta-analytic investigation of the individual and contextual predictors of bullying and victimization in childhood and adolescence (Cook, Williams, Guerra, Kim, & Sadek, in press). That larger meta-analytic review included 128 independent studies, with samples of children and adolescents taken from 26 countries. A reduced sample of 82 studies involving 22 countries is analyzed in this chapter, given that some of the studies did not provide prevalence estimates.

Bullying Internationally

Bullying in schools is undoubtedly an international problem. However, contextual and cultural characteristics of countries are likely to influence bullying prevalence rates for instance to have meaning as a specific form of aggression. Bullying requires ongoing social relationships with repeated interactions over time, and the nature of those relationships and interactions are likely to differ from country to country and thus produce international variability in bullying prevalence rates.

Comparative research by Eslea et al. (2004) on prevalence rates and predictors of bullying and victimization across seven countries is instructive for the present analysis. These investigators found large differences in the percent of bullies and victims, using standardized versions of the Olweus Bullying Questionnaire. Prevalence rates of bullying perpetration ranged from 2% (China) to 17% (Spain), while the percent of students bullied ranged from 5% (Ireland) to a high of 26% (Italy). Besides differences in prevalence rates, Eslea and colleagues also found variation across countries by gender and social support. Although bullying was present in all countries, suggesting its universality, the reported findings showed that prevalence rates vary cross-nationally. This chapter does not specify and estimate the influence of contextual and cultural characteristics of countries on the prevalence of bullying and victimization. Rather, a preliminary analysis is conducted to determine how the proportion of children and youth identified as bullies, victims, or bully-victims differs by the geographic location of school-based studies.

Measurement of Bullying

Most researchers acknowledge that bullying is difficult to conceptualize and measure (Cornell, Sheras, & Cole, 2006; Griffin & Gross, 2004). Farrington's (1993) comments about bullying measurement are still suitable for present day bullying research. Specifically, he noted the insufficient concern paid to psychometric issues such as reliability and validity, as well as the need for more detailed comparisons between measurement methods. Although researchers have attempted to address the issues mentioned by Farrington (Chan, Myron, & Crawshaw, 2006), a limited understanding persists regarding the extent to which measurement methods influence the variability of bullying prevalence rates. This chapter does not directly assess issues of reliability and validity, but comparisons across different measurement methods are made. Specifically, three measurement issues are addressed.

First, studies differ on the specific time frame within which individuals are asked to recall how often they engaged in or were victimized by certain bullying behaviors (e.g., past week, past 30 days, past year). The measurement of bullying is time-sensitive since it involves repeated acts of aggression over time. The appropriate temporal referent period, however, is unclear. For example, it is not clear whether the prevalence rates of bullying will increase or decrease with a longer referent period; that is, as the time frame is lengthened (e.g., from past week to past year), does the percentage of students who bully or get bullied by others increase or decrease?

Second, the person reporting the behavior also remains a topic of debate. Self-reports are preferred by many researchers in measuring bullying (Espelage & Swearer, 2003); however, peer, teacher, and parent reports have also been used to identify incidents of bullying (Cornell et al., 2006). Self-report, such as the Olweus Bully/Victim Questionnaire (Olweus, 1996) and the Peer

Relations Questionnaire (Rigby & Slee, 1993), has been the predominant approach to measuring bullying because most acts are not known by adults or youth in general. However, self-reports are not free of limitations. For instance, the reliability of self-reports compared to other approaches has been questioned (Ladd & Kochenderfer-Ladd, 2002), with issues being raised such as memory decay, willingness to self-divulge, and honesty in reporting. As a result, some researchers have advocated the use of peer nomination procedures at the class level to measure bullying (Crick & Grotpeter, 1995; Pelligrini, Bartini, & Brooks, 1999), while others have recruited teachers and parents to report bullying. Again, little is known about the connection between who reports bullying and variation in prevalence rates. This connection is explored in the present study.

Third, measuring bullying apart from other forms of aggression involving children and adolescents is a difficult task (Cornell, Sheras, & Cole, 2006). Not all forms of fighting, name calling, and social exclusion constitute bullying. This specific form of aggressive behavior involves targeting particular individuals or groups of individuals with *repeated* acts of aggression over time to affirm power imbalances between "perpetrators" and "victims." Such repeated aggression can create or maintain status hierarchies or in-group, out-group distinctions within a school setting. To capture the nuances of this form of aggression, some researchers have measured bullying using a specific definition or label and asking respondents to report whether they have been involved as a perpetrator, victim, or both (bully-victim). Although some researchers contend that a definition is crucial for measuring bullying (e.g., Solberg & Olweus, 2003), others argue that a definition only serves to prime individuals unintentionally and thereby bias empirical results. Specific aggressive behaviors (e.g., "push, grab, or shove" "say mean things") are suggested as an alternative measurement approach. However, without explicit reference to bullying via a definition or label (e.g., do you bully other kids by calling them names?), the distinction between bullying and aggression more broadly defined may become blurred. The influence of this measurement issue on variation of prevalence rates remains an open question that the present analysis addresses.

Methods

Study Search and Selection Procedures

This chapter draws from the larger meta-analytic review of the individual and contextual predictors of bullying and victimization (Cook et al., in press). The population of studies analyzed included quantitative information about bullying and/or victimization occurring within a school setting and were published between 1999 and mid-2006. Two primary search methods were employed to ensure the location of a representative sample of published studies, including an electronic database search and bibliographic analysis of key review articles. These methods resulted in the retrieval of 1,197 potential studies for inclusion into the meta-analysis.

Selection Criteria   The 1,197 studies were closely examined to determine whether they met specific inclusion criteria. Four specific inclusion criteria were used for the present analysis: (a) quantitative data related to *prevalence* of school bullying and/or victimization, (b) victimization related to bullying and not general aggression, (c) non-intervention study, and (d) samples of children or adolescents (not adults). The application of these inclusion criteria reduced the number of articles from 1,197 to 82. See Cook et al. (in press) for a more detailed description of study search and inclusion methods.

Study Coding Scheme and Reliability of Coding Practices

A protocol was developed to guide the coding of primary study features relevant to the present analysis. Inter-rater reliability was determined by calculating Kappa statistics, with two independent researchers coding these study features. According to Landis and Koch (1977), Kappa values are categorized as low if .01–.20, fair if .21–.40, moderate if .41–.60, substantial if .61–.80, and perfect if .81–1.00. Kappa coefficients ranged from 0.81 (93% agreement) to 1.0 (100% agreement). The following is a brief description of each of the primary study features coded for this analysis.

Primary Study Features

Prevalence Rates   The definition of prevalence offered by Solberg and Olweus (2003) was used for this study: "prevalence usually refers to the number of persons with a defined disease relative to the total number of persons in the group or population exposed to risk" (p. 239). As such, data relating to proportion of children or youth who were identified as bullies, victims, or bully-victims from each sample were extracted from each study. For some studies, the authors reported multiple prevalence rates depending on the frequency of bullying behavior (e.g., "once or twice a month" and "about once a week"). In these cases, the average was taken and coded into the database.

Geographic Location of Study   To determine statistically whether geographic location of the study significantly influenced prevalence rates, studies were classified into one of three categories: United States, Europe, or Other Countries ($_K$ = 1.00). Granted, "Europe" and "Other Countries" are heterogeneous categories of nations, but these three geographic regions were used because only three or fewer studies were conducted within18 of the 22 countries represented in this sample (five had three, six had two, and seven had one), raising questions about the reliability of prevalence estimation in those countries.

Informant Source   The second variable coded to determine the influence of bullying measurement was the informant source (i.e., "who reported bullying"). Study information about the informant source was classified into one of four categories: self-report, peer-report, teacher-report, and parent-report. Since too few studies used parent-report, informant sources were limited to self, peer, and teacher ($_K$ = .92).

Bully Measurement Approach   Measurement approach (how bullying was measured) involved classifying studies into two groups: bullying or aggression. Studies were coded as measuring bullying if they made specific reference to bullying ("have you ever bullied someone" or "have you ever been bullied by someone") or provided a definition and asked participants to report related behaviors ("this is what bullying is, have you ever done that or has this ever happened to you"?). Studies were coded as measuring aggression if they used behavioral descriptors of aggressive acts ("do you tease others" "or "how often do you hit others") but did not make explicit reference to bullying ($_K$ = .87).

Temporal Referent Period   Studies were coded according to five categories of temporal referent periods used to obtain responses about involvement as a bully, victim, or bully-victim: past week, past 30-days, past 6-months, past year, or no referent period specified ($_K$ = 1.00).

Effect Size Adjustment and Tests of Heterogeneity

Prior to combining the proportions across studies, they were transformed using the Freeman-Tukey Double Arcsin Equation (Westfall & Young, 1993) to stabilize variances: $\hat{p} = 1/2 \left(\arcsin \left[\sqrt{\frac{p}{n+1}} \right] + \arcsin \left[\sqrt{\frac{p+1}{n+1}} \right] \right)$, where p hat is the transformed proportion, p is the number of individuals identified as bullies, victims, or bully-victims, and n is the total number of individuals in the study. These proportions were then used to compute weighted and un-weighted average estimates according to the three bully status groups (bullies, victims, and bully-victims) and different study features. All transformed proportions were weighted by their inverse variance: $w = \frac{1}{s_{\hat{p}}^2}$. Since prevalence rates represent the proportion of individuals within a given sample demonstrating a particular condition, statistical tests such as t-tests or analysis of variance procedures are inappropriate. Instead, pair-wise tests of proportional differences were used to examine differences between geographic location or measurement features of studies. The specific equations used were $z = \frac{p_1 - p_2}{s_{p1} - s_{p2}}$ and $s_{p1} - s_{p2} = \sqrt{\frac{p(1-p)}{n_1} + \frac{p(1-p)}{n_2}}$. The first equation is the actual test of difference between proportions, whereby p_1 and p_2 are the proportions for the different samples and s_{p1} and s_{p2} are the estimated standard errors between proportions. The resulting statistic is distributed as a z-score.

A random effect analysis approach was used, and the decision to do so was based on the following logic. Fixed effect models only account for the degree of uncertainty that comes from the specific samples included in specific studies for a specific meta-analysis. As a result, inference is conditional because it is based solely on the studies included in the meta-analysis. Random effects models make unconditional inferences about a population of study samples and characteristics that are more diverse than the finite number of studies included in a given meta-analysis. Given that the majority of Q statistics rejected the assumption of homogeneity and the desire to make inferences beyond the included studies, random effects analyses were conducted. Hence, generalization from the current findings can be made to other existing and future studies.

Homogeneity analyses using Conchran's Q were conducted for prevalence rates to determine whether they were estimating the same population mean (Hedges & Olkin, 1985): Cochran's $Q = \sum w_i (\hat{q}_i - q)^2$ A significant Q statistic indicates the prevalence rates are, in fact, heterogeneous, with other factors creating variability around the grand mean prevalence rate. These analyses also provided a basis for determining whether a random versus fixed effect analysis should be performed (Hedges & Vevea, 1998).

Results

Descriptive Statistics

Table 25.1 provides a summary of the descriptive information for the 82 included studies. As shown, study sample sizes varied widely, with a low of 44 and a high of 26,420. A total of 100,452 children and adolescents ages 3 to 18 years old were included in the 82 studies. Most studies included children ages 5 to 11 years old (35%). Moreover, over half of the studies were conducted in Europe (n = 45; 55%), with 26% (n = 21) conducted in the United States. The distribution of publication years indicated that the majority of studies were published in 2003 and 2004. The prevailing approach to measuring bullying was self-report (74%), with 16% relying on peers, and 10% using teachers to report bullying. The frequencies of studies using definition/labels or behavioral descriptors of aggression to measure bullying were nearly uniformly distributed, accounting for 46% and 54% of the studies, respectively. No temporal referent period was specified for a third of the studies, and the "past year" (18%) was the most frequently used time

Table 25.1 Descriptive Information of Studies Included in this Chapter

Descriptive Variables	Mean (Range)	Frequency	Percent
Sample Size	1607 (44 - 26,430)[a]		
Sample Age			
3 to 4 years (early childhood)		3	4
5 to 11 years (middle childhood)		29	35
12 to 14 years (early adolescence)		20	24
15 to 18 years (adolescence)		10	12
Mixed		20	24
Study Location			
United States		21	26
Europe		45	55
Other		16	20
Publication Year			
1999		5	6
2000		10	12
2001		11	13
2002		17	9
2003		9	11
2004		15	18
2005		15	18
2006		10	12
Informant Source			
Self-report		61	74
Peer-report		13	16
Teacher/Parent-report		8	10
Measurement approach			
Definition/Label		38	46
Behavioral descriptor of aggression		44	54
Time Referent Period			
Past week		7	9
Past 30-days		15	18
Past 6-months		15	18
Past year		18	22
Not reported		27	33

Note. [a] Two studies had sample sizes greater than 8,000. For purposes of aggregation and analysis, these values were winsorized to the next highest sample size value of 8000 participants.

referent period, followed by "past 30-days" and "past 6-months," each accounting for 15% of the studies.

Twenty-two countries were represented in this sample of studies (listed in order from most to least): United States (n = 21, 26%), England (n = 13, 16%), Australia (n = 7, 9%), Finland (n = 7, 9%), Ireland (n = 3, 4%), Scotland (n = 3, 4%), Italy (n = 3, 4%), Germany (n = 3, 4%), Netherlands (n = 3, 4%), Greece (n = 2, 2%), Canada (n = 2, 2%), Norway (n = 2, 2%), South Korea (n = 2, 2%), Switzerland (n = 2, 2%), New Zealand (n = 2, 2%), Japan (n = 1, 1%), Brazil (n = 1, 1%), Denmark (n = 1, 1%), France (n = 1, 1%), Portugal (n = 1, 1%), South Africa (n = 1, 1%), and Sweden (n = 1, 1%).

Prevalence Rates

As noted above, most countries had too few studies (three or less) to be analyzed separately, so three clusters of countries were created: United States, Europe, and Other Countries. Nonetheless, for descriptive purposes, Table 25.2 shows the prevalence rates for each of the 22 countries represented by the 82 included studies, with separate rates of bullies, victims, and bully-victims provided for boys and girls where possible. This table demonstrates the significant amount of variability between countries. Inspection of the combined prevalence rates indicated that they ranged from 5% (Sweden) to 44% (New Zealand) for bullies, 7% (Switzerland) to 43% (Italy) for victims, and 2% (Sweden) to 32 % (New Zealand) for bully-victims. For 16 countries, separate prevalence estimates were coded for boys and girls. Out of these 16 countries, 15 were associated with higher prevalence estimates of bullies for boys than girls. The one country with a higher prevalence of bullies for girls than boys was Italy. For prevalence estimates of victims, 15 countries had separate estimates for boys and girls, and of these 15, 11 had a higher prevalence of victims for boys than girls. The countries that had higher prevalence of victims for girls were Denmark, France, Italy, and Switzerland.

Table 25.3 presents the weighted and un-weighted average prevalence rates for gender, age range, and the combination of gender and age range by bully status group (bullies, victims, and bully-victims). The average weighted proportions of boys involved as bullies, victims, or bully-victims are greater than the proportions of girls in each of these groups. The odds ratio comparing these proportions is 2.5 suggesting that boys are 2.5 times more likely to be involved in bullying than girls. However, the odds ratios differed depending on the specific role along the bully-victim continuum (OR Bullies = 1.74; OR Victims = 1.1; OR Bully-Victims = 2.5). These results are largely consistent with prior research indicating a significant gender effect of bullying favoring boys. However, the small odds ratio for victims indicates that girls are as likely to be victims as boys. The prevalence rates by age ranges are consistent with prior research. Specifically, they show that bullying behaviors rise considerably from childhood (total = 41%) to early adolescence (total = 56%) and remain high during late adolescence (total = 59%). However, the pattern by age range differs slightly across the three bully status groups. The prevalence of bullies increases monotonically from the childhood to late adolescent years, whereas the prevalence rates for victims and bully-victims increases from childhood to early adolescence, but decreases slightly during the late adolescent years. The combined prevalence rates across gender and age ranges suggests that 53% of students on average are involved in bullying, with the greatest proportion of students involved as victims, followed by bullies and then bully-victims. This estimate is much larger than the commonly discussed prevalence rate of 30% of children and youth who are involved in bullying and victimization (Nansel et al., 2001; Solberg & Olweus, 2003). These finding suggest that bullying is actually a normative developmental experience for children and youth.

Accounting for the Variability of Prevalence Rates

The distribution of prevalence rates across studies was characterized by a high degree of variability. For example, the stem and leaf plot (Figure 25.1) depicting the distribution of prevalence rates for bullies demonstrates the variability in sample estimates. Indeed, all tests of heterogeneity for bullies [Cochran's Q (63) = 2,213], victims [Cochran's Q (71) = 1,890], and bully-victims [Cochran's Q (33) = 978] indicated significant heterogeneity. Four study characteristics were systematically tested to determine the extent to which they account for this variability. Given that

Table 25.2 Prevalence Rates for 22 Countries by Gender and Bully Status Group (Bullies, Victims, and Bully-Victims)

Geographic Location of Studies	Boys Prevalence			Girls Prevalence			Combined Prevalence		
	Bullies	Victims	B-V	Bullies	Victims	B-V	Bullies	Victims	B-V
European Countries									
Denmark	8.5 (1)	13.4 (1)	14.1 (1)	8.0 (1)	19.0 (1)	5.5 (1)	8.2 (1)	16.4 (1)	9.5 (1)
England	11.5 (3)	29.5 (6)	15.0 (1)	8.2 (3)	20.8 (6)	7.5 (1)	15.0 (9)	23.9 (12)	7.9 (6)
Finland	22.48 (6)	20.1 (5)	10.5 (4)	12.5 (6)	16.8 (5)	3.5 (4)	16.2 (7)	16.8 (6)	6.2 (4)
France	16.4 (1)	12.7 (1)	12.7 (1)	9.8 (1)	18.0 (1)	8.2 (1)	12.9 (1)	15.5 (1)	10.3 (1)
Germany	15.0 (1)	11.8 (1)	—	9.1 (1)	10.4 (1)	—	16.3 (3)	12.0 (2)	15.0 (1)
Greece	—	—	—	—	—	—	9.1 (2)	15.5 (2)	13.4 (2)
Ireland	—	—	—	—	—	—	6.0 (1)	26.2 (3)	—
Italy	34.4 (2)	53.1 (1)	—	38.6 (2)	64.6 (1)	—	43.0 (3)	42.9 (3)	7.4 (1)
Netherlands	45.1 (1)	45.8 (1)	—	29.9 (1)	43.5 (1)	—	18.8 (3)	22.9 (3)	7.6 (1)
Norway	9.8 (1)	8.1 (1)	4.5 (1)	3.7 (1)	6.7 (1)	1.8 (1)	6.0 (1)	11.3 (2)	7.2 (1)
Portugal	18.3 (1)	23.1 (1)	—	10.0 (1)	17.6 (1)	—	15.8 (1)	20.4 (1)	—
Scotland	—	24.0 (1)	—	—	12.5 (1)	—	20.3 (2)	16.4 (3)	6.1 (2)
Sweden	6.9 (1)	—	2.3 (1)	3.0 (1)	—	0.7 (1)	4.9 (1)	—	1.5 (1)
Switzerland	11.0 (2)	5.7 (2)	8.2 (2)	5.5 (2)	6.7 (2)	4.2 (2)	10.3 (2)	6.7 (2)	8.8 (2)
United States									
USA	22.1 (12)	23.7 (14)	10.6 (6)	15.1 (12)	18.8 (14)	4.9 (6)	17.9 (16)	21.5 (17)	7.7 (7)
Other Countries									
Australia	18.5 (2)	37.5 (4)	7 (1)	13.5 (2)	34.7 (4)	10.0 (1)	15.8 (2)	32.5 (3)	9.0 (1)
Brazil	—	—	—	—	—	—	14.0 (1)	—	—
Canada	—	—	—	—	—	—	33.0 (1)	31.5 (2)	—
Japan	—	—	—	—	—	—	16.5 (1)	10.4 (1)	—
New Zealand	49.0 (1)	—	—	39.0 (1)	—	—	44.0 (1)	42.5 (2)	32.0 (1)
South Africa	29.0 (1)	35.0 (1)	—	15.5 (1)	26.0 (1)	—	22.0 (1)	29.0 (1)	—
South Korea	14.7 (2)	9.7 (2)	8.6 (1)	8.1 (2)	6.2 (2)	5.7 (1)	11.3 (2)	7.9 (2)	7.2 (1)

Table 25.3 Weighted and Un-Weighted Prevalence Rates for Bullies, Victims, and Bully-Victims by Gender and Age Range

	Bullies			Victims			Bully-Victims			W Totals
	WX̄%	UWX̄%	95% C.I.	WX̄%	UWX̄%	95% C.I.	WX̄%	UWX̄%	95% C.I.	
Gender										
Boys	28.8	21.8	23.5 – 35.0	26.3	24.4	21.4 – 31.1	9.7	10.1	6.7 – 12.9	64.8
Girls	19.1	14.3	13.9 – 24.8	24.0	21.7	19.4 – 28.6	4.2	4.9	2.7 – 5.7	47.3
Age Range										
3 – 11 years	15.7	17.0	10.5 – 20.9	18.1	24.4	13.4 – 22.9	6.7	6.5	4.9 – 8.4	40.5
12 – 14 years	19.5	23.1	9.6 – 29.9	26.2	25.8	21.5 – 31.6	10.0	13.7	1.8 – 18.1	55.7
15 – 18 years	25.8	26.8	18.9 – 33.2	24.4	24.2	16.4 – 33.1	8.4	8.3	4.4 – 12.5	58.6
Combined	21.3a	18.7	17.3 – 25.3	23.7b	22.5	20.3 – 27.2	8.4c	8.4	6.4 – 10.4	53.4

a Prevalence rates from 64 studies used to compute average prevalence rate for bullies.
b Prevalence rates from 72 studies used to compute average prevalence rate for victims.
c Prevalence rates from 34 studies used to compute average prevalence rate for bully-victims.

random effects analyses are performed, only the combined prevalence rates for bullies, victims, and bully-victims were used to increase the statistical power of the following analyses.

Methodological Features of Studies   Recall that the three methodological features of the studies used in this analysis were the informant source, temporal referent period, and measurement method.

The informant reporting bullying behavior accounted for significant differences in the prevalence rates for bullies, victims, and bully-victims (See Table 25.4). Peer nomination approaches resulted in significantly smaller prevalence rates than both self-report and teacher-report for bullies and victims, while the opposite was true for the average weighted prevalence rates for

Stem	Leaf
8	0a
7	
6	7
5	8 8
4	3 4
3	2 3 3 7 8
2	0 0 2 4 5 8 Median ▼
1	0 0 0 1 1 2 2 2 2 2 3 3 3 4 4 4 4 4 4 5 5 5 6 7 7 9
0	1 4 4 5 5 5 5 6 6 6 7 8 8 8 8 9 9 9 9

Note: a this case was winsorized to the next value (0.67) when computing the average prevalence estimates.

Figure 25.1 Stem and leaf plot depicting the distribution of prevalence rates for bullies.

bully-victims. However, the difference in this latter case is not statistically significant, given the small number of studies in this category (n = 5).

The time referent period used to measure bullying also significantly accounted for variability in prevalence estimates (see Table 25.4). The expectation was that the longer the temporal referent period, the higher the estimated prevalence rate. Although generally supported, this expectation did not hold consistently for "past year." Prevalence rates did, in fact, increase with longer temporal referent periods up to and including the "past 6-months." However, the prevalence rates for studies using the "past year" were significantly lower than those of studies using "past 6-months," albeit significantly greater than studies using "past week."

The bullying measurement approach used in each study, or "how bullying was measured," significantly explained variation in prevalence rates for all three groups as well. Whereas studies that used a definition or label to measure bullying produced a higher weighted average prevalence rate of bullies than studies that used a behavioral descriptor of aggression, the reverse pattern was observed for victims and bully-victims. That is, studies that used behavioral descriptors of aggression to measure bullying produced higher average prevalence estimates of victims and bully-victims than studies that used a definition or label.

Geographic Location of Studies Besides methodological features, the geographic location of studies was examined as a potential factor accounting for differences in prevalence rates. Tests of heterogeneity indicated significant variability between countries. Concerning the groupings of countries by geographic location, the prevalence of bullies in studies conducted in the United States was significantly lower than those conducted in Europe or Other Countries throughout the world. As for the prevalence of victims, studies included in the Other Countries category had a significantly higher estimate than both the United States and Europe. No significant

Table 25.4 The Influence of Methodological Features and Geographic Location of Studies

	Bully Prevalence		Victim Prevalence		Bully-Victim Prevalence	
	Mean	z-test	Mean	z-test	Mean	z-test
Informant Source						
Self-report (a)	21.9	b	25.8	b	8.2	b
Peer nominations (b)	9.7	a, c	7.8	a, c	9.9	—
Teacher/Parent report (c)	21.2	b	25.3	b	7.3	—
Time Referent Period						
Past week (a)	14.5	b, c, d	17.9	c, d	5.2	c, d
Past 30-days (b)	17.3	a, c	18.8	c, d	6.1	c, d
Past 6-months (c)	31.3	a, b, d	30.9	a, b, d	10.0	a, b, d
Past year (d)	17.1	a, c	26.2	a, b, c	8.8	a, b, c
Bully Measurement						
Bully definition/label (a)	23.6	b	20.5	b	7.9	b
Aggression descriptors (b)	14.7	a	29.2	a	8.9	a
Geographic Location						
United States (a)	17.9	b, c	21.5	c	7.7	b, c
Europe (b)	20.9	a	20.7	c	6.4	a, c
Other Countries (c)	20.5	a	30.5	a, b	14.6	a, b

Note: Z-tests are pairwise comparisons testing the difference between two proportions. The letter corresponds to the level of the independent variable from which a particular level differs significantly.

difference was found between the prevalence estimates for the United States and Europe. For prevalence of bully-victims, all three geographic groupings of countries significantly differed from one another, with Other Countries associated with the highest prevalence rate, followed by the United States and then Europe (see Table 25.4).

Discussion

The aim of this chapter was to examine variability in prevalence rates of bullying and victimization across studies using meta-analytic procedures. The cross-national analysis of prevalence rates is particularly important in further understanding bullying around the world. Although the data supported the notion that bullying is a universal phenomenon, the extent to which children and youth were identified as bullies, victims, or bully victims varied significantly across countries. Two factors were examined to account for at least some of this variation: different methodological aspects of the studies analyzed and their geographic location. Both factors had statistically significant effects on the variability of prevalence rates. These findings have important implications for future research related to school bullying. Consider, first, the implications for measurement.

The widely disparate prevalence rates observed between informant sources highlighted the importance of selecting the optimal informant when reporting bullying behavior. Significantly lower prevalence rates were noted for peer nomination procedures than self-report and teacher-report methods. Interestingly, the latter method did not yield significantly different prevalence rates from those obtained for self-report. Although concerns have been raised that incidents of bullying go undetected by adults, these data suggest that peers may also miss incidents of this behavior. In fact, Solberg and Olweus (2003) argued that peer nomination or rating measures are not well suited and should not be used for estimating the prevalence of bullying due to the limited number of nominations and/or influence of class size. Instead, these authors suggest that self-report measures using some defined frequency within a specified time period be used. Self-report is the most widely accepted standard of measurement for bullying, but investigators should not ignore the limitations of this method, including issues such as positive illusory bias or socially desirable responding (see Gresham, MacMillan, Bocian, Ward, & Forness, 1998). Although different informants would likely produce different prevalence rates, accurate conclusions regarding the differences between informants cannot be made unless future research controls other aspects of measurement (e.g., temporal referent period, definition/label or behavioral descriptor, and response categories) across informant sources.

The present analysis also revealed that the temporal referent period and the measurement approach (the use of labels or definitions of bullying versus behavioral descriptors of aggression) were related to differences in bullying prevalence rates across school-based studies. Prior research has shown that these measurement distinctions do not appear to differentiate the predictors of bullying and other forms of aggression (Cook et al., in press), but the findings reported here suggest these distinctions do, in fact, influence the measurement of bullying prevalence rates.

It is important to also consider the implications of the findings on geographic location. From an international perspective, the degree to which bullying exists appears to vary depending on the countries being compared. For example, across countries, the highest prevalence rates were noted for New Zealand (44% bullies, 43% victims, and 32% bully-victims) and Italy (43% bullies, 43% victims, and 7% bully-victims), while the lowest prevalence rates were recorded for Sweden (5% bullies and 2% bully-victims) and Norway (6% bullies, 11% victims, and 7% bully-victims). The findings are consistent with prior research by Eslea et al. (2004) and Smith, Dowie,

Olafsson, and Liefooghe (2002), who also found country differences in prevalence rates; however, Eslea et al. (2004) held bully measurement methodology constant. Thus, despite the apparent international universality of bullying, the prevalence of this form of aggressive behavior is quite variable.

Future research should identify the contextual and cultural characteristics of nations that account for differences in bullying prevalence rates (e.g., gross domestic product, literacy rates, population mobility, political and economic instability). Moreover, future research should explore the empirical relations (if any) between bullying and other forms of aggression and violence. Such research would shed further light on whether bullying is a distinct form of aggression requiring separate theoretical explanation and preventive interventions or whether it is co-occurring with other types of aggression and violence. If so, a common etiology is implied, and thus, efforts to prevent or reduce any form of aggression and violence should also impact bullying.

However, no defensible conclusions can be drawn from cross-national research on bullying and victimization until investigators reach a consensus on the conceptualization and measurement of this behavior. Conceptual differentiation of bullying from other forms of aggression and violence is necessary for this behavior to be treated as a distinct behavioral phenomenon. Such differentiation is also a necessary starting point distinct, valid, and reliable measurement. As the present analysis demonstrated, instruments designed to measure bullying vary in terms of the informant source (e.g., self, peer, teacher/parent), measurement approach (e.g., definition, label, or behavioral descriptors), temporal referent period (e.g., past week, past 30-days, past 6-months, and past year), and the response categories for frequency of bullying or victimization (e.g., "bullied once a month," "two or three times a month," "four times or more," etc. compared to "never," "sometimes," "frequently," etc.). Moreover, each of these different features of measurement were empirically related to variability in the estimated prevalence rates across the school-based studies analyzed. The influence of different "response categories" was not empirically examined, but such categories are likely to produce variability in prevalence estimates, like the other measurement features addressed in this chapter. These issues should be addressed in future research on bullying because without some closure on the conceptualization and measurement of bullying, questions will continue to be raised about the "true" prevalence of bullying.

Conclusion

The key conclusion drawn from the findings reported in this chapter is that investigators must reach a consensus on the definition and measurement of bullying before valid and reliable comparisons of bullying and victimization prevalence rates can be made across countries. This conclusion does not discredit claims that contextual and cultural characteristics of counties account for variation in those rates. Such rates surely vary, and characteristics of countries undoubtedly have influence. Nonetheless, that influence must be distinguished empirically from variation generated by differences of definition and measurement. Until that is done, substantive accounts of cross-national differences in prevalence rates will be haunted by doubts about the meaning of bullying and the methods used to measure its occurrence.

References

Chan, H. F. John, Myron, R. R., & Crawshaw, C. M. (2006). The efficacy of non-anonymous measures of bullying. *School Psychology International 26*(4), 443–458.

Cook, C. R., Williams, K. R., Guerra, N. G., Kim, T. E., & Sadek, S. (in press). Predictors of bullying and victimization in childhood and adolescence: A meta-analytic investigation. *School Psychology Quarterly.*

Cornell, D., Sheras, P. L., & Cole, J. M. (2006). Assessment of bullying. In S. R. Jimerson & M. J. Furlong (Eds.), *Handbook of school violence and school safety: From research to practice* (pp. 191–209). Mahwah, NJ: Erlbaum.

Crick, N. R., & Grotpeter, J. (1995). Relational aggression, gender and social psychological adjustment. *Child Development, 66,* 710–722.

Eslea, M., Menesini, E., Morita, Y., O'Moore, M., Mora-Merchan, J. A., Pereira, B., et al. (2004). Friendship and loneliness among bullies and victims: Data from seven countries. *Aggressive Behavior, 30,* 71–83.

Espelage, D. L., & Swearer, S. M. (2003). Research on school bullying and victimization: What have we learned and where do we go from here? *School Psychology Review, 32,* 365–383.

Espelage, D. L., & Swearer, S. M. (2004). *Bullying in American schools.* Mahwah, NJ: Erlbaum.

Farrington, D. (1993). Understanding and Preventing Bullying. In M. Tonry (Ed.), *Crime and justice: A review of research* (p. 17). Chicago: University of Chicago Press.

Gresham, F. M., Macmillan, D. L., Bocian, K. M., Ward, S. L., & Forness, S. R. (1998). Comorbidity of hyperactivity-impulsivity inattention and conduct problems: Risk factors in social, affective, and academic domains. *Journal of Abnormal Child Psychology, 26,* 393–406.

Griffin, R. S., & Gross, A. M. (2004). Childhood bullying: Current empirical findings and future directions for research. *Aggression and Violent Behavior, 9,* 379–400.

Hedges, L. V., & Olkin, D. (1985). *Statistical methods for meta-analyses.* San Diego, CA: Academic.

Hedges, L. V., & Vevea, J. L. (1998). Fixed- and random-effects models in meta-analysis. *Psychological Methods, 3,* 486–504.

Ladd, G. W., & Kochenderfer-Ladd, B. (2002). Identifying victims of peer aggression from early to middle childhood: Analysis of cross-informant data for concordance, estimation of relational adjustment, revalence of victimization, and characteristics of identified victims. *Psychological Assessment, 14,* 74–96.

Landis, J. R., & Koch, G. G. (1977). The measurement of observer agreement for categorical data. *Biometrics, 33,* 159–174.

Nansel, T. R., Overpeck, M., Pilla, R. S., Ruan, J., Simons-Morton, B., & Scheidt, P. (2001). Bullying behaviors among U.S. youth: Prevalence and association with psychosocial adjustment. *The Journal of the American Medical Association, 285,* 2094–2100.

Olweus, D. (1993) Bullying at school: *What we know and what we can do.* Cambridge, MA: Blackwell.

Olweus, D. (1996). Bullying at school: knowledge base and an effective intervention program. *Annals of the New York Academy of Sciences, 74,* 265–276.

Pellegrini, A. D., Bartini, M., & Brooks, F. (1999). School bullies, victims, and aggressive victims: Factors relating to group affiliation and victimization in early adolescence. *Journal of Educational Psychology, 91,* 216–224.

Rigby, K. (2002). *New perspectives on bullying.* London: Jessica Kingsley.

Rigby, K., & Slee, P.T. (1993). Dimensions of interpersonal relating among Australian school children and their implications for psychological well-being. *Journal of Social Psychology, 133*(1), 33–42.

Smith, P., Dowie, H., Olafsson, R., & Liefooghe, A. (2002). Definitions of bullying: A comparison of terms used, and age and gender differences, in a fourteen-country international comparison. *Child Development, 73,* 1119–1133.

Smith, P. K., Morita, Y., Junger-Tas, J., Olweus, D., Catalano, R., & Slee, P. (Eds.). (1999). *The nature of school bullying: A cross-national perspective.* London: Routledge.

Solberg, M., & Olweus, D. (2003). Prevalence estimation of school bullying with the Olweus Bully/Victim Questionnaire. *Aggressive Behavior, 29,* 239–268.

Westfall, P. H., & Young, S. S. (1993). *Resampling-based multiple testing.* New York: Wiley.

Appendix A: Studies Included in Meta-Analysis

Adair, V. A., Dixon, R. S., Moore, D. W., & Sutherland, C. M. (2000). Ask your mother not to make yummy sandwiches: Bullying in New Zealand secondary schools. *New Zealand Journal of Educational Studies, 35,* 207–221.

Andershed, H., Kerr, M., & Stattin, H. (2001). Bullying in school and violence on the streets: Are the same people involved? *Journal of Scandinavian Studies in Criminology and Crime Prevention, 2,* 31–49.

Andreou, E. (2001). Bully/victim problems and their association with coping behaviour in conflictual peer interactions among school-age children. *Educational Psychology, 21,* 59–66.

Baldry, A. C. (2003). Bullying in schools and exposure to domestic violence. *Child Abuse and Neglect, 27,* 713–732.

Baldry, A. C., & Farrington, D. P. (1999). Types of bullying among Italian school children. *Journal of Adolescence, 22,* 423–426.

Baldry, A. C., & Farrington, D. P. (2005). Protective factors as moderators of risk factors in adolescence bullying. *Social Psychology of Education, 8,* 263–284.

Beran, T. N., & Tutty, L. (2002). Children's reports of bullying and safety at school. *Canadian Journal of School Psychology, 17,* 1–14.

Beran, T. N., & Violato, C. (2004). A model of childhood perceived peer harassment: Analyses of the Canadian National Longitudinal Survey of Children and Youth Data. *The Journal of Psychology, 138*, 129–147.

Berthold, K. A., & Hoover, J. H. (2000). Correlates of bullying and victimization among intermediate students in the Midwestern USA. *School Psychology International, 21*, 65–78.

Bond, L., Carlin, J. B., Thomas, L., Rubin, K., & Patton, G. (2006). Does bullying cause emotional problems? A prospective study of young teenagers. *British Medical Journal, 323*, 480–484.

Camodeca, M., & Goosens, F. A. (2005). Aggression, social cognitions, anger, and sadness in bullies and victims. *Journal of Child Psychology and Psychiatry, 46*, 186–197.

Camodeca, M., Goosens, F.A., Meerum-Terwogt, M., & Schuengel, C. (2002). Bullying and vicitimization among school-aged children: Stability and links to proactive and reactive aggression. *Social Development, 11*, 332–345.

Cassidy, T., & Taylor, L. (2005). Coping and psychological distress as a function of the bully victim dichotomy in older children. *Social Psychology of Education, 8*, 249–262.

Cerezo, F., & Ato, M. (2005). Bullying in Spanish and English pupils: A sociometric perspective using the BULL-S questionnaire. *Educational Psychology, 25*, 353–367.

Coggan, C., Bennett, S., Hooper, R., & Dickinson, P. (2003). Association between bullying and mental health status in New Zealand adolescents. *International Journal of Mental Health Promotion, 5*, 16–22.

Collins, K., McAleavy, G., & Adamson, G. (2004). Bullying in schools: A Northern Ireland study. *Educational Research, 46*, 55–71.

Curtner-Smith, M. E, Culp, A. M., Culp, R., Scheib, C., Owen, K., Tilley, A., et al. (2006). Mothers' parenting and young economically disadvantaged children's relational and overt bullying. *Journal of Child and Family Studies, 15*, 181–193.

Dao T. K., Kerbs, J. J., Rollin, S. A., Potts, I., Guitierrez, R., Choi, K., et al. (2006). The association between bullying dynamics and psychological distress. *Journal of Adolescent Health, 39*, 277–282.

DeSouza, E. R., & Ribeiro, J. (2005). Bullying and sexual harassment among Brazilian high school students. *Journal of Interpersonal Violence, 20*, 1018–1038.

Duncan, R. D. (1999). Peer and sibling aggression: An investigation of intra- and extra-familial bullying. *Journal of Interpersonal Violence, 14*, 871–886.

Eslea, M., & Mukhtar, K. (2000). Bullying and racism among Asian schoolchildren in Britain. *Educational Research, 42*, 207–217.

Espelage, D. L., Bosworth, K., & Simon, T. R. (2000). Examining the social context of bullying behaviors in early adolescence. *Journal of Counseling and Development, 78*, 326–333.

Espelage, D. L., & Holt, M. K. (2001). Bullying and victimization during early adolescence: Peer influences and psychosocial correlates. In R. A. Geffner, M. Loring, & C. Young (Eds.), *Bullying behavior: Current issues, research, and interventions* (pp. 123–142). New York: Haworth.

Fekkes, M., Pijpers, F. I. M., & Verloove-Vanhorick, S. P. (2005). Bullying: Who does what, when and where? Involvement of children, teachers, and parents in bullying behaviors. *Health Education Research: Theory & Practice, 20*, 81–91.

Flouri, E., & Buchanan, A. (2003). The role of mother involvement and father involvement in adolescent bullying behavior. *Journal of Interpersonal Violence, 18*, 634–644.

Fox, C. L., & Boulton, M. J. (2005). The social skills problems of victims of bullying: Self, peer and teacher perceptions. *British Journal of Educational Psychology, 75*, 313–328.

Glover, D., Gough, G., Johnson, M., & Cartwright, N. (2000). Bullying in 25 secondary schools: Incidence, impact, and intervention. *Educational Research, 42*, 141–156.

Hanish, L. D., & Guerra, N. G. (2004). Aggressive victims, passive victims, and bullies: Developmental continuity and developmental change? *Merrill-Palmer Quarterly, 50*, 17–38.

Hara, H. (2002). Justifications for bullying among Japanese schoolchildren. *Asian Journal of Social Psychology, 5*, 197–204.

Hunter, S. C., Boyle, J. M. E., & Warden, D. (2004). Help seeking amongst child and adolescent victims of peer-aggression and bullying: The influence of school-stage, gender, victimisation, appraisal, and emotion. *British Journal of Educational Psychology, 74*, 375–390.

Jeffrey, L. R., Miller, D., & Linn, M. (2001). Middle school bullying as a context for the development of passive observers to the victimization of others. In R. A. Geffner, M. Loring, & C. Young (Eds.), *Bullying behavior: Current issues, research, and interventions* (pp. 143–156). New York: Haworth.

Johnson H. R., Thompson, M. J. J., Wilkinson, S., Walsh L., Balding, J., & Wright, V. (2002). Vulnerability to bullying: Teacher-reported conduct and emotional problems, hyperactivity, peer relationship difficulties, and prosocial behaviour in primary school children. *Educational Psychology, 22*, 553–556.

Karatzais, A., Power, K. G., & Swanson, V. (2002). Bullying and victimization in Scottish secondary schools: Same or separate entities? *Aggressive Behavior, 28*, 45–61.

Kaukiainen, A., Salmivalli, C., Lagerspetz, K., Tamminen, M., Vauras, M., Maki, H., et al. (2002). Learning difficulties, social intelligence, and self-concept: Connects to bully-victim problems. *Scandinavian Journal of Psychology, 43,* 269–278.

Kim, Y. S., Leventhal, B. L., Koh, Y., Hubbard, A., & Boyce, T. (2006). School bullying and youth violence. *Archives of General Psychiatry, 63,* 1035–1041.

Kokkinos, C. M., & Panayiotou, G. (2004). Predicting bullying and victimization among early adolescents: Associations with disruptive behavior disorders. *Aggressive Behavior, 30,* 520–533.

Kristensen, S. M., & Smith, P. K. (2003). The use of coping strategies by Danish children classed as bullies, victims, bully/victims, and not involved in response to different (hypothetical) types of bullying. *Scandinavian Journal of Psychology, 44,* 479–488.

Kumpulainen, K., & Rasaen, E. (2000). Children involved in bullying at elementary school age: Their psychiatric symptoms and deviance in adolescence: An epidemiological sample. *Child Abuse and Neglect, 24,* 1567–1577.

Kumpulainen, K., Rasanen, E., & Puura, K. (2001). Psychiatric disorders and the use of mental health services among children involved in bullying. *Aggressive Behavior, 27,* 102–110.

Land, D. J. (2001). Teasing, bullying, and sexual harassment among adolescents. *Dissertation Abstracts International, 61,* 5029.

Landis, J R., & Koch, G. G. (1977). The measurement of observer agreement for categorical data. *Biometrics, 33,* 159–174.

Marsh, H. W., Parada, R. H., Craven, R. G., & Finger, L. (2004). In the looking glass: A reciprocal effects model elucidating the complex nature of bullying, psychological determinants, and the central role of self-concept. In C. E. Sanders & G. D. Phye (Eds.), *Bullying: Implications for the classroom* (pp. 63–109). New York: Elsevier.

Martin, J., & Gillies, R. M. (2004). How adolescents cope with bullying. *Australian Journal of Guidance and Counseling, 14,* 195–210.

Mills, C., Guerin, S., Lynch, F., Daly, I., & Fitzpatrick, C. (2004). The relationship between bullying, depression and suicidal thoughts/behaviours in Irish adolescents. *Irish Journal of Psychological Medicine, 21,* 12–116.

Monks, C. P., Smith, P. K., & Swettenham, J. (2005). Psychological correlates of peer victimization in preschool: Social cognitive skills, executive function and attachment problems. *Aggressive Behavior, 31,* 571–588.

Mouttapa, M., Valente, T., Gallaher, P., Rohrbach, L. A., & Unger, J. B. (2004). Social network predictors of bullying and victimization. *Adolescence, 38,* 315–335.

Nansel, T. R., Haynie, D. L., & Simons-Morton, B. G. (2003). The association of bullying and victimization with middle school adjustment. *Journal of Applied School Psychology, 19,* 45–61.

Natvig, G. K., Albrektsen, G., & Qvarnstrom, U. (2001). Psychosomatic symptoms among victims of school bullying. *Journal of Health Psychology, 6,* 365–377.

Nordhagen, R., Nielsen, A., Stigum, H., & Kohler, L. (2005). Parental reported bullying among Nordic children: A population-based study. *Child Care, Health and Development, 31,* 693–701.

Olafsen, R. N., & Viemero, V. (2000). Bully/victim problems and coping with stress in school among 10- to 12-year-old pupils in Aland, Finland. *Aggressive Behavior, 26,* 57–65.

Pereia, B., Mendonca, D., Neto, C., Valente, L., & Smith, P. K. (2004). Bullying in Portuguese schools. *School Psychology International, 25,* 241–254.

Perren, S., & Alsaker, D. (2006). Social behavior and peer relationships of victims, bully-victims, and bullies in kindergarten. *Journal of Child Psychology and Psychiatry, 47,* 45–57.

Perren, S., & Hornung, R. (2005). Bullying and delinquency in adolescence: Victims' and perpetrators' family and peer relations. *Swiss Journal of Psychology, 64,* 51–64.

Rigby, K. (2000). Effects of peer victimization in schools and perceived social support on adolescent well-being. *Journal of Adolescence, 23,* 57–68.

Rigby, K. (2005). Why do some children bully at school? The contributions of negative attitudes towards victims and the perceived expectations of friends, parents, and teachers. *School Psychology International, 2,* 147–161.

Salmivalli, C., & Nieminen, E. (2002). Proactive and reactive aggression among school bullies, victims, and bully-victims. *Aggressive Behavior, 28,* 30–44.

Schafer, M., Korn, S., Brodbeck, F. C., Wolke, D., & Schulz, H. (2005). Bullying roles in changing contexts: The stability of victim and bully roles from primary to secondary school. *International Journal of Behavioral Development, 29,* 323–335.

Scheithauer, H., Hayer, T., Petermann, F., & Jugert, G. (2006). Physical, verbal, and relational forms of bullying among German students: Age trends, gender differences, and correlates. *Aggressive Behavior, 32,* 261–275.

Schuster, B. (1999). Outsiders at school: The prevalence of bullying and its relation with social status. *Group Processes and Intergroup Relations, 2,* 175–190.

Seals, D., & Young, J. (2003). Bullying and victimization: Prevalence and relationship to gender, grade level, ethnicity, self-esteem, and depression. *Adolescence, 38,* 734–746.

Shields, A., & Cicchetti, D. (2001). Parental maltreatment and emotion dysregulation as risk factors for bullying and victimization in middle school. *Journal of Clinical Child Psychology, 30,* 349–363.

Smith, P. K., Talamelli, L., Cowie, H., Naylor, P., & Chauhan, P. (2004). Profiles of non-victims, escaped victims, continuing victims and new victims of school bullying. *British Journal of Educational Psychology, 74,* 565–581.

Sourander, A., Helstela, L., Helnius, H., & Piha, J. (2000). Persistence of bullying from childhood to adolescence—A longitudinal 8-year follow-up study. *Child Abuse and Neglect, 24,* 873–881.

Sullivan T. N., Farrell, A. D., & Kliewer, W. (2006). Peer victimization in early adolescence: Association between physical and relational vicitimization and drug use, aggression, and delinquent behaviors among urban middle school students. *Development and Psychopathology, 18,* 119–137.

Sutton, J., & Keogh, E. (2000). Social competition in schools: Relationships with bullying, Machiavellianism and personality. *British Journal of Educational Psychology, 70,* 443–456.

Sutton, J., Smith, P. K., & Swettenham, J. (1999). Social cognition and bullying: Social inadequacy or skilled manipulation? *British Journal of Developmental Psychology, 17,* 435–450.

Theriot, M. T., Dulmus, C. N., Sowers, K. M., & Johnson, T. K. (2005). Factors relating to self-identification among bully victims. *Children and Youth Services Review, 27,* 79–994.

Toblin, R. L., Schwartz, D., Hopmeyer-Gorman, A., & Abou-Ezzeddine, T. (2005). Social-cognitive and behavioral attributes of aggressive victims of bullying. *Applied Developmental Psychology, 26,* 329–346.

Unnever, J.D., & Cornell, D.G. (2004). Middle school victims of bullying: Who reports being bullied? *Aggressive Behavior, 30,* 373–388.

Vogel, S. W. (2006). The relationship between bullying and emotional intelligence. *Dissertation Abstracts International, 66,* 4311.

Warden, D., & MacKinnon (2003). Prosocial children, bullies and victims: An investigation of their sociometric status, empathy and social problem-solving strategies *British Journal of Developmental Psychology, 21,* 367–385.

Wild, L. G., Flisher, A. J., Bhana, A., & Lombard, C. (2004). Associations among adolescent risk behaviours and self-esteem in six domains. *Journal of Child Psychology and Psychiatry, 45,* 1454–1467.

Wilkins-Shurmer, A., O'Callaghanm M. J., Najmanm J. M., Bor, W., Williams, G. M., & Anderson, M. J. (2003). Association of bullying with adolescent health-related quality of life. *Journal of Pediatric Child Health, 39,* 436–441.

Wilson, C., Parry, L., Nettelbeck, T., & Bell, J. (2003). Conflict resolution tactics and bullying: The influence of social learning. *Youth Violence and Juvenile Justice: An Interdisciplinary Journal, 1,* 64–78.

Wolke, D., Woods, S., Stanfordm H., & Schulz, H. (2001). Bullying and vicitmization of primary school children in England and Germany: Prevalence and school factors. *British Journal of Psychology, 29,* 373–396.

Woods, S., & Wolke, D. (2004). Direct and indirect relational bullying among primary school children and academic achievement. *Journal of School Psychology, 42,* 135–155

Yang, S., Kim, J., Kim, S., Shin, I., & Yoon, J. (2006). Bullying and victimization behaviors in boys and girls at South Korea primary schools. *Journal of the American Academy Child and Adolescent Psychiatry, 45,* 69–78.

Section III

Research-Based Prevention and Intervention

26

A School Climate Intervention that Reduces Bullying by a Focus on the Bystander Audience Rather than the Bully and Victim

The Peaceful Schools Project of the Menninger Clinic and Baylor College of Medicine

STUART W. TWEMLOW, ERIC VERNBERG, PETER FONAGY, BRIDGET K. BIGGS, JENNIFER MIZE NELSON, TIMOTHY D. NELSON, AND FRANK C. SACCO

Bullying has broad effects on children's mental health, including early disruptive and aggressive behavior (Nansel, Overpeck, Hanie, Ruan, & Scheidt, 2003), school dropout, substance abuse (Kumplainen & Rasanen, 2000), depressed mood, anxiety, and social withdrawal (Dill, Vernberg, Fonagy, Twemlow, & Gamm, 2004; Swearer, Grills, Haye, & Cary, 2004). It also undermines educational achievement (Greenberg et al., 2003) and disrupts children's abilities to develop social relationships (Masten & Coatsworth, 1998).

Meta-analyses of 300 school-based violence intervention programs (Mytton, DiGuiseppi, Gough, Taylor, & Logan, 2002; Wilson, Gottfredson, & Najaka, 2001; Wilson, Lipsey, & Devzon, 2003) suggest that existing programs are effective (ES =.24–.36), but typically intervene with a small high-risk sample and involve single-group designs with highly-trained teachers and reactive measures such as therapy counseling, behavioral classroom management, and social competence enhancement. Programs directly targeting aggressive behavior are no more effective than those focusing on other aspects of social relations. Further, although there have been more individual-focused interventions than environmental-focused interventions (ratio of 4:1), both appear equally effective.

We have compared the effectiveness of a school climate focused approach, Creating a Peaceful School Learning Environment (CAPSLE), to a commonly used individually-focused approach and to a treatment-as-usual control group in a cluster-randomized longitudinal trial with one-year post-intervention follow-up. The individually-focused comparison condition, School Psychiatric Consultation (SPC), is a manualized protocol aimed at addressing mental health issues of children with disruptive behavioral problems, internalizing problems, or poor academic performance. The model has been used in school psychiatric consultation for several decades and involves assessment of children and observation of classroom behavior to create individually-tailored interventions targeting children with notable adjustment problems. Thirty-five consultation outcome studies utilizing programs similar to SPC showed improvement in academic performance (Berkovitz, 2001) and positive changes for children (Pearson, Jennings, & Norcross, 2001).

In this project, nine schools and over 3,600 students participated. Three schools were assigned to CAPSLE, three schools to SPC, and three schools to a delayed intervention condition. These latter schools received no intervention, but were promised the most effective of the other two interventions after a two-year period, if they desired it. This was an attempt to provide a motivated control group rather than a pure no-treatment group.

CAPSLE focused on the power dynamics of the bully-victim-bystander relationship in such a way that the prime focus, as detailed in this volume, was on the role of the bystander in the normalization of this dynamic to restore mentalizing. Mentalization is a term used to speak of the capacity to reflect, empathize, modulate affect, and set boundaries (Fonagy, Gergely, Jurist, & Target, 2002). Helpful bystanders are trained to function as natural leaders to assist other bystanders, bullies, and victims to realize and move out of pathological roles. The B-V-B dynamic is incompatible with mentalizing. So much of our work, as we detail later, encourages normalizing power dynamics with mentalization as the tool to achieve that end.

This program was instituted in elementary schools on the basis of the empirical hypothesis that beginning an intervention earlier in life is more likely to have a lasting effect than beginning later. The learning curve for children is especially influenced in the early years by complex psychological factors including identification with teachers as role models. One educator cogently noted that education is the cure only to the extent that ignorance is the disease. By overemphasizing intellectual and instructional approaches to problems in the learning environment, teachers, curriculum, and policy planners inadvertently occupy avoidant and abdicating bystander roles, thus undermining the potential value of their function as a psychological role model for children and exemplar of these critical factors which facilitate intellectual, social, and emotional learning.

The components of the program philosophy included the following:

1. Positive Climate Campaigns
   These campaigns use counselor led discussions, posters, magnets, bookmarks, and other devices to encourage a shift in language and thinking of all students and personnel in the school. These language tools help children identify and resolve problems that develop when coercive power dynamics dominate the school environment. Such effects are observed as children share playground equipment peacefully and do not push and jostle in the lunch line but talk about the b-v-b roles as options to understand the conflict. Positive climate campaigns repeatedly underscore for both students and teachers the dynamic that takes place between bully, victim, and bystander. This creates a context in which no participant can experience the situation without awareness of the mental state of the other and indeed without self-awareness.

   Rarely is the best way of achieving this done by drawing attention to the bully. Instead, the focus should be on the relationship between bully, victim, and bystander; this implicitly creates a demand on the child, the teacher and other staff to consider this interpersonal situation from a mentalizing perspective. It would be counterproductive to force students and teachers to explicitly describe the mental states of the participants. This might induce pseudo-mentalization, where mentalizing terms are used but the connection to the reality of the experience has been lost.

2. Classroom Management (Discipline plan)
   This aspect assists teachers' efforts at discipline by focusing on correcting root problems, instead of punishing and criticizing behaviors. A behavior problem in a single child is conceptualized as a problem for the whole class who participate in bully, victim, or bystander

roles. Scape-goating is reduced and insight into the meaning of the behavior becomes paramount. From this new perspective, a child's disruptive behavior is seen as an attempt to locate a valid social role within the group. At the point of disruption, the teacher would stop teaching and assign bully, victim, and bystander roles during class discussion. The bully being the child, the victim being the teacher and the bystanders would be the rest of the classroom, who may have laughed at the teacher's response to the disruptive student. If such a child repeatedly offends, the class would collectively fill out a power struggle referral alert. That is, every student would participate in determining and defining the bullying, victim, and bystander behavior according to a standardized form. At a later point, the children involved and sometimes even the parents of the child would be seen by the school counselor or social worker for a further understanding of the event. Punishment would not be invoked except as a very last resort when the disciplinary infractions were serious enough to require intervention by the school principal.

The child with a propensity to act violently is encouraged by this approach to develop a mental life representation of his experiences and adapt to it in a non-persecutory way (Fonagy, Gergely, Jurist, & Target, 2002). The essential component of this approach is that children do not experience themselves as having been punished, which would inhibit, rather than facilitate mentalization. Thus, the environment becomes conducive to thinking within the context of a counseling relationship that encourages mentalization. When a child is sent to the principal, the anxiety created by the system begins to inhibit any capacity to mentalize. This is so especially because principals are often quite defensive owing to school board and parental harassment, and their capacity to mentalize is often inhibited. Therefore, an encounter between a child and a principal in such a setting paradoxically cannot involve any reflecting from a mentalizing perspective. The pattern is to encourage the child to think about the perspective of others including his or her parents, as well as teachers and principals. Experience suggests that teachers who invoke punishment less frequently in response to classroom behaviors show classrooms with better academic performance and fewer disciplinary referrals.

3. Peer and Adult Mentorship

   Mentorship approaches are attempts to mirror outside the classroom what the classroom management plan does in the classroom, which involves getting all in the school system to understand the violent interaction, and to see if there is a way to resolve the problem collaboratively and without blame. Male mentors seem particularly helpful on the playground where much childhood aggression comes out. We have found that effective male mentors are rather relaxed older men of any race, often retired, non-competitive and who have children and grandchildren of their own. One particularly skilled mentor cleverly used magic tricks to distract children. He would make himself a buffer; for example, "Why don't you go first on the jungle gym, and I will try and catch each of you?" Thus, the fight becomes a game with him as the referee.

   Looking at mentoring from a mentalizing perspective requires the point of view of the "third," referred to as taking the problem out of a coercive dyad and bringing in a third party through which each person can perceive the other (Ogden, 1994). The mentor allows each party within the conflict to see through the eye of the mentor. The mentalizing action of the mentor and his magic trick creates a transitional space by this distraction in which the participants, the bully, the victim, and the bystander start thinking about a third thing, with a spontaneity essential for mentalizing.

4. The Gentle Warrior Physical Education Program

   This approach satisfies the physical education requirements in most school systems, using a combination of role-playing, relaxation, and defensive martial arts techniques. The approach helps children protect themselves and others with non-aggressive physical and cognitive strategies. For example, occupying bully, victim, and bystander roles provide students with alternatives to fighting. Learning ways to physically defend oneself when being grabbed, pushed, or shoved, combined with classroom discussion, teaches personal self control as well as respect and helpfulness towards others. These confidence-building skills support an essential component of the capacity to mentalize; that is, to allow children to feel confident enough and safe enough to be able to think. If a child is too frightened, the capacity to think is paralyzed and the victim mindset is adopted. A child experiencing an emergency mode of thinking is presented with simple-minded choices, running away or submitting. At the brain level, there is an inhibition of the frontal cortex in favor of the posterior parts of the brain, and the subcortex, that enables the fight-flight reaction to occur. Such a reaction is incompatible with mentalization (Frith & Frith, 2003). A safe environment from a mentalizing prospective has to be one in which a child experiences a situation that they can cope with (Twemlow, Fonagy, & Sacco, 2002).

5. Reflection Time

Adler (1958) pointed out that a natural social group has no right to exclude any member or, conversely, that every member of the group has a right to belong. From his point of view, narcissistic injury represented by bully, victim, and some bystander reactions are attempts by the child to regain entry into a social group and to be accepted by that social group. Although teachers may view the Peaceful Schools Program as training the child, the real aim is that the teachers actively become involved in mentalizing the child via the process of training. The serious problem of teachers who bully and are bullied by students and parents (Twemlow, Fonagy, Sacco & Brethour, 2006; Twemlow & Fonagy, 2005) is one example of how important the mentalizing function is for teachers impulsive stressed actions of teachers occur when mentalizing collapses under the influence of coercive and humiliating social pressures. As such, the system through its members becomes more psychologically aware and eventually the rules, regulations, and the policy of the system will embody mentalizing principles. Reflection time is one such method to encourage mentalizing in teachers and students; a period of 10 minutes or so at the end of each day when the classroom engages in a discussion of the day's activities from the point of view of bully, victim, and bystander behavior. After discussing this behavior, a decision is made about whether to display a banner outside the classroom indicating the class had a good day. Teachers note that the children are rather critical of themselves and do not put the banner up as much as the teachers might. The reflection time is a way of consolidating the day's activities and allowing the child and teacher to take a whole systems view of what is going on. In many ways the subject of the reflection matters less than that the reflection is taking place. If a system cannot be thought about in this way, then no mental representation of it can be created. Mentalization for its own sake is of no great value. The important thing is that it makes the system more peaceful.

The Importance of Mentalizing

A central aim of the CAPSLE program is to reduce bully-victim-bystander problems by promoting mentalizing. The complexities of mentalizing and the sense of self that emerges from this process are reflected in several conceptual difficulties in understanding how an individual is both part of a social system and, at the same time, an individual in that system, with their own will and sense of separateness. As interpersonal and current relational theories hold, the person feels defined by the social system, and their sense of reality is rooted in that reality being shared by others. We know that the world outside is real ultimately because others respond to us in ways that are consistent with our reactions.

The extraordinary impact of social responses on the developing individual is illustrated by experiments with six-month-old infants using the still-face paradigm (Weinberg & Tronick, 1996). In such research, a six-month-old infant is interacting with his mother, but by instruction the mother "freezes" her face for a minute or so during their interaction. After a few seconds of the mother not reacting, an infant tends to go into a state of despair. The infant recovers after normal interaction is resumed. The catastrophic effect on the infant is not just due to the loss of the care-giving object. Subsequent research with children of the same age has demonstrated that even if the person who "freezes" their interaction with the infant is a total stranger, the effect is so traumatic that a year later, at age 18 months, the picture of that stranger is avoided by the child (Weinberg & Tronick, 1996). The still-face paradigm is not a response unique to the mother-child relationship, but instead a response to the failure of the other to validate the infant's experience of the world outside.

The mirroring, understanding, and attuned social world is essential to us in early development not just to ensure that we acquire a sense of who we are, as Kohut (1984) and others have suggested, but also so that the child can develop an accurate appreciation of a shared external world. From this mentalizing perspective, the personal consensus between two people may be seen as creating an external (social) reality. When power dynamics influence that social reality, either through individual psychopathology or a social system that is disintegrating via use of coercion and punishment, then victim, victimizer, and bystander mindsets are created in members of the system, who then function in the robotic roles created by the non-mentalizing social system.

A helpful addition to these speculations is the notion of a chronic failure of mentalization in violent environments. We have found that a failure of mentalization creates for the witness to the power struggle (the bystander) an avenue to the pleasure of sadism. For the child to be able to enjoy being witness to the suffering of an other, he must be able to distance himself from the internal world of the other while benefiting from using the other as a vehicle for unwanted (usually frightened and disavowed) parts of their own self projected into the victim. Bystanders do not lack empathy, because it is precisely through projective identification with the victim (and or the bully) that the child is able to experience himself as more coherent and complete. Vicarious pleasure is gained by splitting and retaining the libidinal (pleasurable) aspect of aggression, and projecting the sadistic-aggressive aspect. Thus, affect inconsistent with a coherent sense of self is then seen as belonging to the victim of the vicious power dynamic.

However, the child's mentalizing is limited by the environment in that the suffering and pain of the victim need never be represented as mental states in one's consciousness. The fault is not in the child. Mentalizing is a fragile developmental function that is not acquired fully until early adulthood (if then). In most social contexts, it needs environmental support and requires a social system to scaffold it and ensure that reflection on the mental states of self and other is relatively comprehensive and covers painful as well as neutral mental states (Fonagy et al., 2002).

In contrast, a mentalizing interaction between individuals in the system allows for the individual to be both an individual and a member of the social system. From this synthesized perspective, the self in a mentalizing social system can be defined as the ongoing experience of otherness in the present, where the power dynamics are balanced and conducive to a full intellectual and emotional experience of self and other.

Results of the Peaceful Schools Project

The complex structured methodology and analytic strategy for this project is described in detail elsewhere. (Fonagy, Twemlow, Vernberg, Sacco, & Little, 2005; Fonagy, Twemlow, Vernberg, Mize, et al., 2009). The outcome of the interventions were measured with peer and self-reports of bullying and victimization, peer reports of aggressive and helpful bystanding, self-reports of empathy towards victims of bullying, self-reports of belief that aggression is legitimate, and classroom behavioral observation of disruptive and off-task behavior.

Compared to the other two conditions, results suggested that the experimental intervention showed a decrease in peer-reported victimization ($p < .01$), aggression ($p < .05$), and aggressive bystanding ($p < .05$), compared to control schools. The intervention showed less of a decline in empathy compared to psychiatric consultation ($p < .01$) and control conditions ($p < .01$).

Peaceful Schools also produced a significant decrease in off-task behavior ($p < .001$) and disruptive classroom behavior ($p < .001$), while behavioral change was not observed in the psychiatric consultation and control schools. The findings of reduced victimization ($p < .05$), aggression ($p < .01$) and aggressive bystanding ($p < .01$) were maintained in the follow-up year.

The major conclusion was that this program philosophy was effective in reducing children's experiences of aggressiveness and victimization. The strength of the study lay in its extraordinarily careful and detailed evaluation. The program showed that children did become more involved in helping to reduce aggressiveness, as suggested by the increasing engagement of Peaceful Schools children in non-aggressive and helpful bystanding behaviors. Such children help each other resist individual victimization by bullies in part by mentalizing a victim. This awareness allows children, teachers and other staff to take action to normalize power dynamics in the social system as a whole.

This intervention seems to reduce the natural tendency for children to harden their attitude to victimization over time, as other studies have shown (Vernberg et al., 2009) both girls and boys decide to not to get involved with dangerous situations at the high school level, presumably to reduce trouble for themselves.

The Gentle Warrior Program (GWP) and the Classroom Management component were examined separately. A total of 220 children in grades 3–5 were followed pre- to post-participation in GW booster sessions in year 3 of the intervention. Results indicated that higher participation was associated with lower levels of aggression for boys. No significant results were found for girls (Twemlow et al., 2007). Results of the Classroom Management evaluation indicated teachers' use of CAPSLE was related to improvement in student empathy, decreases in beliefs that aggression is legitimate, and increases in helpful bystanding behavior in year 2 of the intervention study (Biggs, Vernberg, Twemlow, Fonagy, & Dill, 2008).

Discussion

There are many elements of this intervention that need detailed discussion and we will outline some of these essential issues here:

Peaceful Schools was originally studied only in the United States and thus presumes certain culture-specific school structures, although the results of a study in Jamaica suggests that program content may be less important than how the program is implemented, especially considering teacher investment. In one K-6 school, poster contests, teacher essays, and Internet connection to the United States were tried and failed. The school did not buy into the program, primarily through insistence by the principal that baseline studies showing high levels of self-harming behavior were not true. The school used the internet resources provided by the program but devalued everything else.

Learning from this mistake, a different approach was tried in a new school in Jamaica with almost the same demographics. Both schools were administered the Peaceful Schools Victimization Scale. In the second attempt at implementation, the program developers spent more time observing and listening to teachers. A plan was drawn up using arts and crafts and a positive bystander pledge. The study is progressing and has attracted community support. A new craft center has been erected with funds from the program and community contributions. Measurements are in progress and the program is planning a more intensive Peaceful Schools intervention.

The program elements in the Peaceful School appear to be relevant across cultures and within language. The idea of the Gentle Warrior was changed to Bead Warriors to make the connection with bead making rather than martial arts but preserving the warrior concept depicted as strong courageous and kind. The program elements appear to be tools that are best used with teachers who buy into the program and will invest more than lip service into program implementation.

A similar replication was conducted in Aurora, Illinois, over the past 5 years. The annual questionnaires assessed change in the same way as in the peaceful school project. In this instance, the Positive Climate campaign was the focus, particularly using peace flags, lectures, and school projects, attuned to the Hispanic population of the school. Funding was from the Aurora Foundation, investing for the first time with the public school system. The foundation has since funded a local university to include training of teachers in developmental psychopathology and normal development in view of the large number of children traumatized by lethal violence against caregivers. The Gentle Warrior program was not used.

Overall, the program continued to demonstrate a high level of usefulness in spite of program modifications to suit the local conditions, highlighting once more the need to adapt programs to their local conditions. Other researchers (e.g., Rigby, 2006) highlight the importance of insisting on careful adherence to the protocol. Whereas treatment manuals are important for research and dissemination of effective treatments, we are skeptical that schools will follow an extensive program such as CAPSLE strictly by the manual and also believe that strict adherence without flexibility is not practical or necessary. Rather, our experiences with implementing CAPSLE in multiple schools in the United States and Jamaica speak to the need to adapt the program to the schools' unique needs and culture. Indeed, flexibility with implementation of manualized treatments has been emphasized by others (Kendall, 1998). In the case of CAPSLE, the major background framework for a successful school program is spelled out in Twemlow & Sacco (2008).

Given the lack of funding most public schools have to employ expensive consultants, a useful school intervention could be defined as one that teachers see as necessary and includes them in its design, is acceptable to existing values in the school, is low-cost, and is practical and realistic, aspects embodied in the pilot and experimental phase of the Peaceful Schools Project. During the pilot, the majority of the decisions made relating to defining bully, victim, and bystander roles and designing interventions were made by teachers, therefore their commitment and investment in the program was enormous from the beginning. In the three pilot schools used initially, teachers not only performed the necessary elements of the programs but also administered the testing, designed a number of the instruments, and several even scored the assessment measures. There was no problem in setting up this particular project because of the immense buy-in inaugurated by commitment to the project included from the teachers who designed it. If experts outside the system define the project and then "impose" it on the system as a whole, buy-in would have been compromised.

The intervention was also designed to not pathologize any children. A common circumstance concerns the use of Ritalin and other ADD compounds that create an automatic stigmatization of the child, since such compounds are delivered by school nurses and children are often bullied as "nut cases."

A program for public schools needs to be as low in cost as possible. This project cost virtually nothing, in terms of materials. The research piece of it was very expensive, but the actual money spent on the intervention procedures and professional consultation was less than $3,000 for the whole 3 years of the project.

Programs that will be effective approach the reality of the school itself. It must not interfere with the teaching process and involve too much curriculum add-on time, none of which CAPSLE does. In fact, CAPSLE involves no curriculum additions except the martial arts sessions conducted during physical education classes. As mentioned previously, this aspect of CAPSLE dovetails with typical physical education requirements. Further, physical education teachers generally have a less rigid curriculum than do classroom teachers and are more open to adopt new programs to the basic requirements for physical fitness. We had no problem in training physical education teachers to conduct these sessions because they require mostly skill with teaching children rather than skill in martial arts.

The program must be practical and realistic; that is, even after evidence for its effectiveness under controlled research conditions is established, it must be feasible and useful to schools. This is an aspect of the experimental programs that poses real challenges. If experimental programs become so focused on satisfying requirements for experimental design that they ignore the needs of the particular school, the interventions are at risk for losing their usefulness.

Issues relating to the choice of research instruments and methodologies to best explore school climate and what to do to reduce bullying were examined in some detail in this project over a period from 1992 to 2003 (Fonagy et al., 2009). In our experience, we have found it necessary to gather most evaluative information directly for the express purpose of measuring implementation and intervention outcomes. In particular, school records related to disciplinary actions proved to be of questionable value because of differences from school to school in the recording and reporting of infractions. For example, one of the schools in Peaceful Schools project recorded fewer than three disciplinary infractions for the entire school year whereas another school reported more than 380, even though data we gathered directly indicated similar levels of bullying in the two schools. On the other hand, school records were a useful source of demographic information and for scores on standardized achievement tests.

We also find value in gathering information from multiple sources. Self-reports of experiences with bullying and attitudes towards aggression proved to be the least controversial type of measurement and generally showed adequate psychometric properties in terms of reliability and convergence with more difficult-to-obtain measures such as peer nominations and teacher ratings of student behaviors. The usefulness of these measures for program evaluation is greatly enhanced if responses of individual students can be tracked over time rather than gathered anonymously. This allows for analysis of change over time for individual children (e.g., Dill et al., 2004) and the identification of developmental trends and variations in trajectories towards involvement in bullying and victimization (Biggs, Vernberg, Fonagy, Twemlow, Little, & Dill, in press).

Teacher reports have utility but may be problematic in some respects. For example, convergence between teacher-identified bullies and victims and self- or peer-identified bullies and victims is marginal and influenced by time of year. For example, of 12 third- through fifth-grade children identified in the fall semester as highly victimized and non-aggressive (i.e., submissive victims) on both peer nominations and self-reports, teachers identified only seven as frequently victimized (Wright, 2004). In the spring semester, 27 children were identified as submissive victims on both self-reports and peer nominations, and teachers identified 14 of these as frequent victims. Teacher and child characteristics may affect teacher reports of bully-victim problems. As one example using the Peaceful School dataset, teachers who reported that teachers in their school provided more positive support for their students over reported bully-victim behaviors relative to student reports (self-reports and peer nominations; Mize, Vernberg, Twemlow, Fonagy, & Little, 2006). Teachers who reported fewer negative student behavior problems and less concern about school safety underreported bully-victim problems compared to student reports.

Variability in reporter discrepancies was also related to student gender (teachers over-reported aggression among girls, compared to student reports) and ethnic minority status (teachers over-reported aggression among ethnic minority children, compared to student reports).

The importance of control conditions cannot be overstated. We, and others, find numerous age-related trends in bully-victim-bystander measurement (e.g., Salmivalli, 2002; Smith, Madsen, & Moody, 1999). For example, children tend to report less empathy towards targets of bullying, more approval of the use of aggression, and less victimization of themselves as they move into the higher elementary grades and into junior high school (Vernberg et al., 2009). These trends work against finding certain intervention effects (e.g., greater empathy and less positive views of aggression), but may exaggerate other effects (e.g., decreased victimization of self). Control conditions are essential to distinguish intervention effects from developmental trends.

Clearly, buy-in from the program participants—particularly teachers, superintendents, school districts, and the surrounding community—is a critical part of this program. With this importance in mind, we assessed teachers' attitudes toward CAPSLE and their relation to teachers' self-reported use of CAPSLE in classroom management. Results, (Biggs et al., 2008), indicated variability across schools and individual teachers in the degree to which teachers implemented the recommended practices. Teachers who followed CAPSLE principles and practices the most also tended to report seeing it as a helpful approach. These findings underscore the importance of buy-in for successful implementation.

The current political administration of the United States values academic performance as a primary index of how schools function. The "no child left behind" philosophy of schools highlights the importance of academic performance. There was a remarkable increase in academic performance in children who were active participants in the Peaceful Schools project for a period of 2 or more years. As part of the project, we looked at the impact of the Peaceful Schools program on education attainment in five elementary schools in one school district over a 5-year period (1994–1999; Fonagy et al., 2005). The program was rolled out in a step-wise fashion, starting in a single school, with an additional school incorporated in 1996 and three further schools in 1999.

The initial school was identified as a particular problem school and the second was a demographically matched school. The three schools included in 1999 were selected randomly from nine schools that volunteered for the program. The stepwise rollout presents multiple baselines because, other than the first school, program implementation was not contingent on school climate. Thus, changes associated with the timing of the program's introduction would not be confounded with changes caused by the program itself. Academic attainment test scores of 1,106 students were monitored before and after the introduction of the program across the school district. This sample was contrasted with an equivalent control sample of 1,100 students from the school district who attended schools that did not join the program. To increase the number of years on which comparisons could be based, any available test scores for the years of 1993, 1994, and 1995 were obtained both for students who participated in the program later and controls.

Children who participated in the Peaceful Schools program for two consecutive years performed better on standardized achievement tests than controls. Participation in the Peaceful Schools program was associated with pronounced improvements in the students' achievement test scores. These findings could not be accounted for by demographic factors, including age, gender, ethnicity, and low income or coincidental changes associated with a particular time period when the program was introduced. The use of a multiple baseline design further strengthens the claim that improvements in academic performance appear to coincide with the school implementing the Peaceful Schools program. Notable reductions in the scores of those students who left schools with active programs were also observed.

Concluding Comment

Schools have always been a captive community where young peoples' ways of thinking can be changed because of the way the state requires their attendance at school and allows their training to be structured. Whether this can be externalized into the adult community is an interesting question. There are few ways of studying complex social adult systems in ways that produce reliable and valid results, but certainly this work strongly suggests that if adults are open to such approaches (reflecting on the bystander role, mentalization, and power dynamics), then the possibility for large scale social change is clearly present.

References

Adler, A (1958). *What life should mean to you.* New York: Putnam Capricorn Books.

Berkovitz, I. (2001). Evaluations of outcome in mental health consultation in schools. *Child and Adolescent Psychiatric Clinics of North America, 10,* 93–103.

Biggs, B. K., Vernberg, E. M., Twemlow, S. W., Fonagy, P., & Dill, E. J. (2008). Teacher adherence and its relation to teacher attitudes and student outcomes In an elementary school based violence prevention program. *School Psychology Review, 237*(4), 533–549,

Biggs, B. K., Vernberg, E. M., Fonagy, P., Twemlow, S. W., Little, T. D., & Dill, E. J. (in press). Peer victimization trajectories and their association with children's affect in late elementary school. *International Journal of Behavioral Development.*

Dill, E., Vernberg, E., Fonagy, P., Twemlow, S., & Gamm, B. (2004). Negative affect in victimized children: The roles of social withdrawal, peer rejection, and attitudes to bullying. *Journal of Abnormal Child Psychology, 32,* 139–173.

Fonagy, P., Gergely, G., Jurist, E., & Target, M. (2002). *Affect regulation mentalization and the development of the self.* Other Press: New York.

Fonagy, P., Twemlow, S., Vernberg, E., Sacco, F., & Little, T. (2005). Creating a peaceful school learning environment: The impact of an anti-bullying program on educational attainment in elementary schools. *Medical Science Monitor, 11,* 317–325.

Fonagy, P., Twemlow, S., Vernberg, E, Mize, J., Dill, E., Little, T., & Sargent, A. J. (2009). A cluster randomized controlled trial of a child-focused psychiatric consultation and a school systems-focused intervention to reduce aggression. *Journal Child Psychology & Psychiatry, 50*(5), 607–616.

Frith, V., & Frith, C. (2003). Development and neurophysiology of mentalizing: Philosophical transactions of the royal society of London. *Biological Sciences, 358,* 459–473

Greenberg, M., Weissberg, R., O'Brien, M., Zins, J., Fredewricks, L., Resnik, H., & Elias, M. (2003). Enhancing school-based prevention and youth development through coordinated social, emotional and academic learning. *American Psychologist, 58,* 466–474.

Kendall, P. C. (1998). Directing misperceptions: Researching the issues facing manual-based treatments. *Clinical Psychology: Science and Practice, 5,* 396–399.

Kohut, H. (1984). *How does analysis cure?* A. Goldberg (Ed.). Chicago Ill., Chicago University.

Kumplainen, K., & Rasanen, E. (2000). Children involved in bullying at elementary school age: Their psychiatric symptoms and deviance in adolescence, an epidemiological sample. *Child Abuse Neglect, 24,* 1567–1577.

Masten, A., & Coatsworth, J. (1998). The development of competence in favorable and unfavorable environments. Lessons from research on successful children. *American Psychologist, 53,* 205–220.

Mize, J. A., Vernberg, E. M., Twemlow, S. W., Fonagy, P., & Little, T. D. (2006, March). *Victimization during preadolescence.* Paper presented at the Biennial Meeting of the Society for Research on Adolescence, K. S. Flanagan & S. A. Erath (chairs), Heterogeneity Among the Assessment and Experience of Peer Victimization and Aggression Throughout Adolescence.

Mytton, J., DiGuiseppi, C., Gough, D., Taylor, R., & Logan, S. (2002). School based violence prevention programs: Systematic review of secondary prevention trials. *Archives of Pediatrics & Adolescent Medicine, 156,* 752–762.

Nansel, T., Overpeck, M., Hanie, D., Ruan, W., & Scheidt, P. (2003). Relationship between bullying and violence in US youth. *Archives of Pediatrics & Adolescent Medicine, 157,* 348–353.

Ogden, T. (1994). *Subjects of analysis.* Northvale, NJ: Aronson.

Pearson, G., Jennings, J., & Norcross, J. (2001). A program of comprehensive school based mental health services in a large urban public school district: The Dallas model. *Child and Adolescent Psychiatric Clinics of North America, 10,* 207–231.

Rigby K. (2006). Ken Rigby interview. Retrieved from http://www.bullyingawarenessnetwork.ca/site.php?page=news, 53–54.

Salmivalli, C. (2002). Is there an age decline in victimization by peers at school? *Educational Research, 44,* 269–277.

Smith, P. K., Madsen, K. C., & Moody, K. C. (1999). What causes the age decline in reports of being bullied at school? Toward a developmental analysis of risks of being bullied. *Educational Research, 41,* 267–285.

Swearer, S., Grills, A., Haye, K., & Cary, P. (2004). Internalizing problems in students involved in bullying and victimization: Implications for intervention. In D. Espelage & S. Swearer (Eds.), *Bullying in American schools: A social-ecological perspective on prevention and intervention* (pp 63–83). Mahwah, NJ: Erlbaum.

Twemlow, S. W., Biggs, B. K., Nelson, T. D., Vernberg, E. M., Fonagy, P., & Twemlow S. (2009). Effects of participation in a martial arts based antibullying program on childrens aggression in elementary schools. *Psychology in the Schools,45*(10), 947–959.

Twemlow, S. W., Fonagy P, & Sacco, F. C. (2002). Feeling safe in school. *Smith College Studies in Social Work, 72*(2), 303–326.

Twemlow, S. W., Fonagy, P., & Sacco, F. (2004). The role of the bystander in the social architecture of bullying and violence in schools and communities. *Annals of New York Academy of Sciences, 1036,* 215–232.

Twemlow, S. W., & Fonagy, P. (2005). A note on teachers' who bully students in schools with differing levels of behavioral problems. *American Journal of Psychiatry, 163*(12), 2387–2389.

Twemlow, S. W., Fonagy, P., Sacco, F., & Brethour, Jr., J. R. (2006). Teachers who bully students: A hidden trauma. *International Journal of Social Psychology, 52*(3), 187–198.

Twemlow, S. W., & Sacco F. C. (2008). *Why school antibullying programs don't work.* New York: Jason Aronson imprint of Rowman & Littlefield.

Vernberg, E. M., Jacobs, A. K., Mize, J. A., Little, T. D., Twemlow, S. W., Fonagy, P., & Sacco, F. C. (2009). *Developmental trends in peer aggression, victimization, bystanding, and aggression-related attitudes.* Unpublished manuscript submitted for publication.

Weinberg, K. M., & Tronick, E. Z. (1996). Infant affective reactions to the resumption of maternal interaction after the still-face. *Child Development, 67,* 905–914.

Wilson, D., Gottfredson, D., & Najaka, S. (2001). School based prevention of problem behaviors: A meta analysis. *Journal of Quantitative Criminology, 17,* 247–272.

Wilson, S., Lipsey, M., & Devzon, J. (2003). The effects of school based intervention programs on aggressive behavior: A meta analysis. *Journal of Consulting & Clinical Psychology, 71,* 136-149.

Wright, M. P. (2004). *A longitudinal comparison of self- and other-identified submissive victims.* Unpublished doctoral dissertation, University of Kansas, Lawrence.

27

The Olweus Bullying Prevention Program
Implementation and Evaluation over Two Decades

DAN OLWEUS AND SUSAN P. LIMBER

In 1983, after three adolescent boys in Norway committed suicide, most likely as a consequence of severe bullying by peers, the Norwegian Ministry of Education initiated a nationwide campaign against bullying in schools. What has later become known as the Olweus Bullying Prevention Program (OBPP) was developed and initially evaluated within this context.

In this chapter, we will describe the conceptual basis for the program and summarize findings from the first evaluation. We then will describe in some detail the components of the program as typically used in the United States and summarize subsequent evaluations of the program, primarily in Norway and the United States.

Goals and Basic Principles of the OBPP

The main goals of the OBPP are to reduce existing bullying problems among students at school, prevent the development of new bullying problems, and more generally, achieve better peer relations at school (Olweus, 1993a; Olweus, Limber, & Mihalic, 1999; Olweus et al., 2007). These goals are met through a restructuring of the child's social environment at school. The restructuring is intended to reduce both opportunities and rewards for engaging in bullying behavior and to build a sense of community among students and adults within the school environment. Positive, pro-social behaviors are encouraged and rewarded (Olweus, 1993a, 2001a; Olweus et al., 2007).

The OBPP is based on four key principles: Adults at school should: (a) show warmth and positive interest and be involved in the students' lives; (b) set firm limits to unacceptable behavior; (c) consistently use nonphysical, nonhostile negative consequences when rules are broken; and (d) function as authorities and positive role models (Olweus, 1993a, 2001a; Olweus et al., 2007). These principles are derived chiefly from research on the development and modification of the implicated problem behaviors, in particular aggressive behavior (Baumrind, 1967; Loeber & Stouthamer-Loeber, 1986; Olweus, 1973, 1978, 1979, 1980). These listed principles have been translated into a number of specific measures to be used at the school, classroom, individual, and, in some contexts, the community level. These components will be described in some detail below.

Initial Evaluation of the OBPP

The OBPP was first implemented and evaluated in the First Bergen Project against Bullying, a longitudinal study that followed approximately 2,500 school children over a period of two-and-a-half years, from 1983 to 1985. Because the project was part of a nationwide campaign against bullying, it was not possible to conduct an experimental study with schools or classes randomly assigned to treatment and control conditions. Instead, an extended selection cohorts design (see below) was utilized in which same-aged students from the same schools were compared across three points in time (Olweus, 1991, 1993a. 1997, 2005). At Time 1, participants belonged to 112 classes in grades 5–8 from 28 elementary and 14 junior high schools in Bergen, Norway. The number of students participating in the 1983–84 evaluation (grades 6 through 8) was approximately 1,750 at each time point. The corresponding 1983–85 evaluation (grades 7 and 8) was based on approximately 1,210 students.

Results from the evaluation revealed marked (and statistically significant) reductions in self-report of bully/victim problems (based on an early version of the Olweus Bully/Victim Questionnaire, 1986). In the 1983–84 evaluation, the relative reduction for being bullied was 62.0% (from 10.0% to 3.8%) and 33.0% for bullying other students (from 7.6% to 5.1%). Corresponding results for the 1983–85 evaluation, involving the grade 7 and 8 students, were 64.0% (from 10.0% to 3.6%) and 52.6 % (from 7.6% to 3.6%) (Olweus, 1991, 1993a, 1997; Olweus & Alsaker, 1991). Similar results were obtained for two aggregated peer rating variables (class-aggregated peer estimates of "number of students being bullied in the class" and "number of students in the class bullying other students") and teacher ratings of bully/victim problems at the classroom level. With regard to the teacher data the effects were somewhat weaker. A marked "dosage-response" relationship ($r = .51$, $n = 80$) was observed, such that those classes in which essential components of the program (classroom rules against bullying, use of role playing, and classroom meetings) had been implemented experienced greater reductions in bullying problems (Olweus & Alsaker, 1991; Olweus & Kallestad, in press). Finally, the study also documented significant reductions in self-reports of general antisocial behavior, including vandalism, theft, and truancy, and improvements in aspects of the "social climate" of the class: Improvements were seen in students' self-reports of satisfaction with school life, improved order and discipline, more positive social relationships, and a more positive attitude toward school work and the school in general.

Detailed analyses of the quality of the data and the possibility of alternative interpretations of the findings led to the following general conclusions: It is very difficult to explain the results obtained as a consequence of (a) underreporting by the students; (b) gradual changes in the students' attitudes to bully/victim problems; (c) repeated measurement; or (d) concomitant changes in other factors, including general time trends (Olweus, 1991).

Factors Affecting Program Implementation

Research and experience indicate that implementation of the OBPP can vary substantially among teachers and schools (Kallestad & Olweus, 2003; Limber, 2006; Olweus, 2004). Systematic examinations of factors that affect implementation of prevention programs are relatively scarce but critical. As Biglan (1995) noted, "the adoption of an effective practice is itself a behavior in need of scientific research" (p. 51).

In an attempt to understand teacher- and school-level factors that affect implementation of the OBPP, Kallestad and Olweus (2003) analyzed responses of 89 teachers from 37 schools and assessed program implementation at two points in time in the First Bergen Project against Bullying. Although this multilevel study was not published until in 2003, the implications of the analyses were known and incorporated into the OBPP and its model of implementation long before publication of the paper. A detailed discussion of our findings and conclusions is beyond the scope of this chapter but can be found elsewhere (Kallestad & Olweus, 2003; Olweus, 2004). Here only a few general points will be emphasized.

The results from this study clearly indicated that the teachers were key agents of change with regard to adoption and implementation of the OBPP. Substantial amounts of variance in implementation could be predicted on the basis of teacher-level variables such as "perceived staff importance" (teacher efficacy), "having read (more of) the program materials," and "affective involvement" (empathic identification with victims of bullying). Also school-level variables such as "openness in communication among staff" (positive attitude to change) and the "school's attention to bullying problems" contributed substantially to prediction. This study shed light on several factors of importance and contributed to a better understanding of the process of program implementation. The results also suggested ways in which the program itself and its implementation could be improved.

Cultural Adaptation

Although the basic principles of the OBPP and its core components have remained largely unchanged, research and extensive experience from implementing the program in the field have naturally led to some adaptations of the program to different cultural contexts. The current employment conditions of teachers in the United States, for example, are such that less time can be devoted to staff discussion group meetings (below) than in Norway. As a consequence, the Bullying Prevention Coordinating Committee has been assigned a somewhat different role and greater responsibility for implementation of the program in the United States than in Norway (Limber, 2004). The organization of the training of trainers (named instructors in Scandinavia) also differs somewhat in the two countries (Olweus et al., 2007; Olweus, 2001a, 2004). Similarly, in line with much American tradition and recognizing the importance of community involvement in prevention efforts more generally and outside the school context, recent implementations of the program in the United States have encouraged schools also to include community-level components.

Table 27.1 summarizes the components of the OBPP at each of the four levels of focus as typically used in the United States the school, the classroom, the individual, and the community. Below, we will describe components at each of these levels of OBPP. Two recently published manuals, a *Teacher Guide* (Olweus & Limber, 2007) and a *Schoolwide Guide* (Olweus et al., 2007), provide much more detail about the program and its components for interested readers.

School-Level Components

Typically, the following eight program components are implemented schoolwide.

Bullying Prevention Coordinating Committee The Bullying Prevention Coordinating Committee (BPCC) is a building-level committee that is responsible for ensuring that all components of the OBPP are implemented in a school. The BPCC is a representative team from the school and broader community, which typically is comprised of 8 to 15 members, including a school administrator, a teacher from each grade level, a school counselor and/or school-based mental health professional, a representative of the non-teaching staff (such as a bus driver, custodian, or cafeteria worker), one or two parents, a representative from the community (such as staff from an after-school or youth organization or key representatives from the business or

Table 27.1 Components of the OBPP

School-Level Components
- Establish a Bullying Prevention Coordinating Committee.
- Conduct committee and staff trainings.
- Administer the Olweus Bullying Questionnaire schoolwide.
- Hold staff discussion group meetings.
- Introduce the school rules against bullying.
- Review and refine the school's supervisory system.
- Hold a school kick-off event to launch the program.
- Involve parents.

Classroom-Level Components
- Post and enforce schoolwide rules against bullying.
- Hold regular class meetings.
- Hold meetings with students' parents.

Individual-Level Components
- Supervise students' activities.
- Ensure that all staff intervene on the spot when bullying occurs.
- Conduct serious talks with students involved in bullying.
- Conduct serious talks with parents of involved students
- Develop individual intervention plans for involved students.

Community-Level Components
- Involve community members on the Bullying Prevention Coordinating Committee
- Develop partnerships with community members to support your school's program.
- Help to spread anti-bullying messages and principles of best practice in the community.

faith community), and other school personnel who may bring particular expertise (such as a nurse, school resource officer, Title IX representative). Where appropriate, one or two student representatives may also serve on the committee (typically middle, junior, or high school grades). As an alternative, a separate student advisory committee may be formed to help ensure meaningful participation by students in the planning and implementation of the program.

The responsibilities of the committee are to attend an intensive 2-day training by a certified OBPP trainer; develop a plan to implement the OBPP at their school; communicate the plan to staff, parents, and students; coordinate the program with other prevention/intervention efforts at the school; obtain ongoing feedback from staff, parents, and students about the implementation of the OBPP and make adjustments to the school plan as needed; and represent the program to the broader community (Olweus et al., 2007). The BPCC typically is chaired by an on-site OBPP coordinator, who may be a school counselor, administrator, prevention specialist, or a member of the non-teaching staff. The committee meets regularly throughout the life of the program (at least monthly for the first year of the program).

Training and Consultation In addition to the 2-day training provided to members of the BPCC, a certified Olweus trainer provides at least 1 year of in-person or telephone consultation to the school's on-site coordinator to help ensure fidelity to the model and to problem-solve as needed. Members of the BPCC (often with assistance from the trainer) provide a full day of training for all school staff prior to launching the program. Supplemental trainings that provide more intensive attention to particular topics (e.g., cyber bullying, classroom meetings) also may be held, as are yearly catch-up trainings for new staff.

Administration of the Olweus Bullying Questionnaire The Olweus Bullying Questionnaire is a validated, self-report survey that assesses students' experiences with and attitudes about bullying (Olweus, 2007; Solberg & Olweus, 2003). The questionnaire is administered (usually anonymously) to students in grades 3–12 prior to the implementation of the program and at regular (typically yearly) intervals thereafter. The questionnaire provides a detailed definition of bullying and, among other questions, asks students to disclose the frequency with which they have experienced and participated in various forms of bullying in the past couple of months. The current scannable questionnaire (for use in the United States, Olweus, 2007) has 40 standard questions, including some new questions about students' experiences with cyber bullying. A standard report of findings is produced for schools, which provides detailed information (in tables, graphs, and narrative) about the findings, frequently broken down by gender and grade. Schools use results from the survey to help raise awareness among students, staff, and parents about the problems of bullying; make specific plans for the implementation of the OBPP; and assess change over time (for girls and boys and across grade levels).

Staff Discussion Groups   Discussion groups of teachers and other school staff meet on a regular basis in order to learn about and have in-depth discussions about the OBPP and reflect on bullying and related prevention efforts at the school. These groups typically consist of no more that 15 personnel and are led by a member of the BPCC. It is recommended that they meet at least once per month for the first year of the program, and somewhat less frequently after that.

School Rules and Positive and Negative Consequences   Schools are asked to adopt four specific rules about bullying.
1. We will not bully others.
2. We will try to help students who are bullied.
3. We will try to include students who are left out.
4 If we know that somebody is being bullied, we will tell an adult at school and an adult at home.

The rules cover both direct and indirect forms of bullying, including social isolation and intentional exclusion from the peer group (Olweus & Limber, 2007). They are posted throughout the school and discussed with students and parents. Teachers and other staff are taught how to apply consistent positive and negative consequences to reinforce these rules.

Supervisory System   The BPCC in each school reviews and refines its supervisory system with the goal of reducing bullying behavior. This review includes determining "hot spots" for bullying based on results of the Olweus Bullying Questionnaire, developing strategies to increase supervision in common "hot spots," developing means of tracking and reporting bullying, assessing the attitudes and skills of supervising adults, and evaluating the school's physical design to reduce bullying.

School Kick-Off Event   Each school launches its program with students with an individually-designed event that is intended to increase awareness about bullying, introduce the OBPP to students, and clarify the school's rules and procedures relating to bullying. Schools are encouraged to hold a kick-off each subsequent year to introduce the program to new students and remind returning students about the school's efforts to prevent bullying.

Parent Involvement   Parents are viewed as important partners in preventing and intervening in bullying. They are involved in the OBPP in a number of ways, including serving on the school's coordinating committee, attending kick-off events and/or schoolwide parents meetings, and receiving regular information about bullying and the OBPP through brochures, newsletters, events, and online bulletin boards.

Classroom-Level Components

As illustrated in Table 27.1, there are three classroom-level components of the OBPP.

Post and Enforce School-Wide Rules Against Bullying   Teachers discuss in detail with their students (for example, in classroom meetings, below) the schoolwide rules about bullying to make sure the students have a clear understanding of what they are and mean. The rules are posted in every classroom for easy reference, and they are enforced using consistent positive and negative consequences. This common set of rules sends a signal to students, parents and others that the school has a unified and coordinated policy against bullying. These rules should be an independent part of the school's discipline policy (Olweus & Limber, 2007).

Classroom Meetings   Regular (weekly) class meetings in which teachers and students discuss bullying and related issues are important components of the OBPP. Purposes of the class meetings are to build class cohesion and community, discuss rules about bullying and positive and negative consequences for following or not following the rules, help students understand their roles in preventing and stopping bullying, and problem-solve strategies for addressing bullying. As part of these meetings, students engage in role-playing, which is intended to help build empathy and perspective-taking skills, generate possible solutions to bullying situations, and practice positive actions to take when confronted with bullying.

Classroom Meetings with Parents   Within the classroom setting, teachers are encouraged to hold several classroom-level meetings with parents about the OBPP. The purposes of these meetings are to help parents understand problems associated with bullying and ways that the school is addressing bullying through the OBPP, and to solicit parental input and involvement in the program (Olweus & Limber, 2007). Small, classroom-level meetings with parents also may help to build rapport with the teacher and build connections among parents of students in the class.

Finally, although not a core classroom-level component of the OBPP, schools are encouraged to integrate bullying prevention messages and strategies throughout the curriculum.

Individual-Level Components

As illustrated in Table 27.1, there are several individual-level components of the OBPP. First, staff are encouraged to increase supervision of students, particularly in known "hot spots" for bullying, and particularly of students who are known or suspected to be involved in bullying. Second, all staff are trained to intervene on-the-spot whenever they observe bullying. Specific procedures also have been developed to guide staff in how to react when a bully/victim problem has been identified or is suspected in a classroom. These procedures include serious talks with the child who is suspected of being bullied and his or her parents and after that, similar talks with the child who is suspected of bullying, and his or her parents. A clear message is communicated that the bullying will be stopped and that the situation will be closely monitored (see Olweus & Limber, 2007, pp. 87–106). In some schools, these meetings are conducted by counselors or administrators, but wherever possible, it is recommended that the meeting be led by the children's primary teacher or the staff member with the closest relationship with the student(s) involved. Finally, schools are encouraged to work with parents and mental health professionals to develop individualized plans, where appropriate, to provide support and other help for students who have been bullied and to correct the behavior of students who bully other students.

Community-Level Components

Recognizing that bullying does not stop at the doors of a school, committee members are encouraged to involve one or more community members on their BPCC, look for ways that community members can support the school's bullying prevention program, and collaborate to spread bullying prevention messages and strategies beyond the school into community settings where children and youth gather.

Subsequent Outcome Studies of the OBPP

Subsequent to the initial evaluation of the OBPP in the First Bergen Project against Bullying, six follow-up outcome evaluations of the OBPP have been conducted in Norway. The program has also been evaluated in several diverse communities in the United States, including rural South Carolina (Limber, Nation, Tracy, Melton, & Flerx, 2004; Melton et al., 1998), inner-city Philadelphia (Black & Jackson, 2007), suburban Chula Vista, California (Pagliocca, Limber, & Hashima, 2007), and Washington state (Bauer, Lozano, & Rivara, 2007).

In addition, several school-based anti-bullying programs inspired by the OBPP have been implemented and evaluated in various countries including Belgium (Stevens, de Bourdeaudhuij, & Van Oost, 2000; Stevens, Van Oost, & de Bourdeaudhuij, 2004), Canada (Pepler, Craig, Ziegler, & Charach, 1994; Pepler, Craig, O'Connell, Atlas, & Charach, 2004), Gemany (Hanewinkel, 2004), and the United Kingdom (Whitney, Rivers, Smith, & Sharp, 1994; Eslea & Smith, 1998; Smith, Sharp, Eslea, & Thompson, 2004). The results from these studies have been mixed, with both positive and negative (null) results, and it is important to emphasize that these studies cannot be seen as replications of the OBPP. The programs used in these interventions have deviated considerably, but to different degrees, from the OBPP model in terms of program content, implementation model, or actual implementation.

In this context, a study in the county of Rogaland, Norway, should be mentioned. In a short book chapter, Roland (1989) has claimed that an intervention study parallel to the one in Bergen was conducted in Rogaland with primarily negative results when outcome data were collected after 3 years, ending in 1986. In several respects, this account is grossly misleading. In summary, it has repeatedly been shown (e.g., Olweus, 1999a, 2004) that the studies in Bergen and Rogaland were two very different projects in terms of planning, data quality, times of measurement, and contact with the schools, and accordingly, also in terms of expected results. We find it necessary to point this out since several authors in the field still continue to erroneously present the Rogaland project as an (unsuccessful) evaluation of the OBPP.

Methodological Comments

Design Issues Before describing the individual outcome studies, some methodological comments are in order. With the exception of the New Bergen Project against Bullying (Olweus, 1999b, 2005), the South Carolina project (Melton et al., 1998), and the Washington state study (Bauer et al., 2007), which used a traditional (non-randomized) control group design, and the Philadelphia study (Black & Jackson, 2007), all evaluation studies have used the *extended version of the selection cohorts design* (Olweus, 2005; Cook & Campbell, 1979; sometimes called age-cohort design, Judd & Kenny, 1981). In this design, the data from two presumably equivalent (grade or school) cohorts of students are compared at two (or more) time points. One cohort provides data for Time 1 (before intervention) and the other data for Time 2, typically 1 year later and after approximately 8 months of intervention. In order to rule out explanations of the results in terms of differences in age or maturation, possible developmental changes are controlled by comparing age-equivalent groups/cohorts at the various time points. In our studies, for example, Grade 7 students at Time 2 (intervention group) are compared with same-aged Grade 7 students from the same schools at Time 1 (control condition, before intervention). Similar comparisons can be made for sets of grade cohorts such as grades 4 through 7 which cohorts have been the main target groups for the OBPP.

A strength of the design is that the majority of the members in the various grade cohorts have been recruited from the same, usually relatively stable populations and have been students in the same schools for several years. Consequently, there are often good grounds for assuming that a cohort measured at Time 1 differs only in minor ways from the adjacent cohort with which it is compared at Time 2. Another advantage is that several of the cohorts serve both as a baseline (Time 1) group in one set of comparisons and as an intervention (Time 2 or Time 3) group in another. This fact will serve as partial protection against selection bias (see Olweus, 2005).

In any study designed to evaluate the possible effects of an intervention program (or other similar factor), it is mandatory that the researcher examines and ideally is able to rule out most or all alternative explanations of the results in terms of possible confounding, "irrelevant" factors. This is true whether the study is experimental with randomization of subjects on conditions or quasi-experimental (Cook & Campbell, 1979).

The logic of the extended selection cohorts design (a quasi-experimental design) and possible threats to the "internal validity" of this design are discussed in considerable detail elsewhere (Olweus, 2005). One particular threat to consider in this design concerns the possibility that changes in the outcome variable at Time 2 (or Time 3) are a consequence of some irrelevant factor concomitant to the intervention, implying that obtained results can be given a "history interpretation." This threat may be difficult to completely rule out in a single study if little is known about results from studies with the same outcome variables without intervention. However, as regards the "being bullied" and "bullying other students" variables, which are regularly used in evaluations of the OBPP, there are now a number of large-scale Norwegian population studies without systematic intervention, which have shown very small or no changes for comparable cohorts in successive years (Furre, Danielsen, Stiberg-Jamt, & Skaalvik, 2006). Such findings certainly support an interpretation of positive intervention results in terms of effects of the intervention rather than of some other concomitant factor, including time trends and media attention.

Moreover, when positive results are repeatedly obtained in adequate replications, under somewhat varying conditions and in different time periods, this of course makes a history interpretation of the findings much more unlikely. In addition, the structure of the data obtained in the New National Initiative (described below) can shed a special light on the reasonableness of a history interpretation of our findings with the OBPP. This point will be discussed in a later section of the chapter.

Statistical Analyses and Effect Sizes   In all studies over which we have had some control, our statistical analyses have taken the hierarchical or nested structure of the data into account, with students nested within classrooms nested within schools. This is necessary to get correct (not too small) estimates of standard errors and thereby adequate tests of the significance of the intervention effects. One way of doing this is to adjust the magnitude of the standard errors (upwards) in a way that corresponds to the degree of dependence among the students (data) within the higher unit (by multiplication of the "ordinary" standard errors by the "design effect factor"; see Kish, 1987, p. 203, for example). In the more recent projects, we have used so called mixed models with the SPSS program or multilevel models with the HLM and/or Mlwin software packages. If the ordinary General Linear Model with standard t- or F-tests is used on nested data—a practice that is still quite common—the standard errors will be too small, resulting in too many significant findings. This problem has been pointed out in a number of publications over the past 10–15 years (e.g., Bryk & Raudenbush, 1992; Murray, 1998; Zucker, 1990) but many "interventionists" do not seem to be aware of this problem. As a consequence, many studies of intervention effects are incorrectly analyzed and may be considerably biased in a positive direction.

In several of our Norwegian evaluation studies, we have not provided much statistical detail with specified t- or F-tests and associated p-values. Although the standard alpha levels of .05, .01 may be considered a kind of benchmark against which the results obtained can be compared, such comparisons become less meaningful when the sizes of the samples involved are large or very large, which is the case with most of our studies. Under such conditions, even very small differences or changes become statistically significant. However, in various overview papers of our studies we have often noted that all main conclusions about the effects of the intervention program are based on results that are statistically significant or highly significant (e.g., Olweus, 1991, 2005).

Against this background, we have typically found it more meaningful to focus on some form of measure of the size of the intervention effects. A common effect size measure is Cohen's d (Cohen, 1988), the standardized mean difference, which is a useful measure for many purposes and situations. However, for universal intervention programs, which aim to target all students in a unit such as a school, a measure like Cohen's d (or a point biserial correlation or some variant of d) will be misleading, giving estimates that are too small, often much too small. The reason is that in most bullying intervention studies, a large proportion of the students, perhaps 60%–80%, are not directly involved in the problems (i.e., have a score of zero on relevant outcome variables such as being bullied or bullying other students) and thus cannot change to a lower score. Normally, the effect of an intervention is measured as the difference in proportions (or some similar measure) of "problem" students who have been exposed or not exposed to the intervention. With universal programs, however, the inclusion of a large group of "non-problem"/not-involved students (who cannot "improve") in the analyses will considerably "dilute" the effects of the program when effect is indexed by measures such as Cohen's d.

As a consequence, to estimate effects of the intervention, we have typically used a measure of Relative (percentage) Change which is calculated as the difference in percentages between the Control condition (the Time 1 measure in a selection cohorts design) and the Intervention condition 1 year later (the Time 2 measure for students in the same grades and schools as at Time 1 in a selection cohorts design) divided by the Control condition value. To express the value as a percentage, the difference in the numerator is multiplied by 100. To illustrate, if the percentage of bullied students in Grade 6 is 20% at Time 1 and there are 15% bullied students among the (former Grade 5, "now") Grade 6 students at Time 2 (after 8 months of intervention), the Relative Change score will be: (20-15)*100/20 = 25% reduction. However, if there are more bullied students at Time 2, this increase will come out as a negative Relative Change value. The relative change measure can also be used (with a slight modification) in a standard pre-post design with a control group and an intervention group measured at two time points. It is worth noting that the relative change measure is closely related to the measure of relative risk ratio (and Odds ratio when the relative risks are low) used in many epidemiological studies (Fleiss, 1994). These measures are not perfect with universal programs, but they give a better and more meaningful impression of what change has actually been achieved. It is often also useful to report or look at the absolute percentage change. In the example above, there would be a 20%–15% = 5% absolute reduction figure which can be used to estimate the number of students (in the school, school district, or larger unit) who have changed status from being bullied to not being bullied.

Outcome Variables, Gender Differences, and Grade Focus   For ease of understanding and convenience, most of our reports have used dichotomized versions of being bullied and bullying other students ("2 or 3 times a month" or more often) as outcome variables. There is a good deal of information about the psychometric properties of these variables (Solberg & Olweus, 2003; Olweus, 2007; Kyriakides, Kaloyirou, & Lindsay, 2006), and they have been found to function well for both prevalence estimation and the measurement of change (Olweus, this volume). However, as is well known, power is weakened when graded or continuous variables are dichotomized. Accordingly, when the statistical analyses have been conducted on the graded, non-dichotomized versions of these variables, the results in terms of statistical significance have typically been even stronger. The same is true when indexes of several related items such as the mean of all forms of being bullied (or bullying other students) have been used.

In addition, it should be mentioned that in a number of more detailed analyses we have usually also found changes in related variables reflecting increased intervention efforts on the part of the schools as viewed by the students. These data strongly support the interpretation that the positive results obtained are a consequence of the intervention. To illustrate, students at Time 2 (intervention) have typically reported more active intervention in bullying situations from both teachers and peers in comparison with reports from Time 1 students. Also, at Time 2 more students have responded that the homeroom/main classroom teacher had done "much" or "a good deal" to counter bullying in the classroom in the past few months. Due to space limitations, we will not focus on such results in this chapter.

In most of our evaluation studies in Norway, the registered relative changes in bully/victim problems have been relatively similar among boys and girls. Accordingly, not to overwhelm the reader with data, most of our results will be presented for boys and girls combined.

As mentioned, the main target groups of the OBPP have been students in grades 4 through 7 (which represent the elementary grades in Norway; modal ages 10 though 13), and most of the evaluation results in this chapter will concern students in these grades. The program has also been used with students in higher grades, although results for the typical junior high school grades (8 through 10) have been less consistent than for the lower grades. In a later section, we will also comment briefly on results for these grades.

The Nature of the Student Populations Studied   A brief comment on the nature of the populations of students studied in Norway is also in order. There seems to be a common view, in particular among U.S. researchers/readers, that Norwegian/Scandinavian students are more well-adjusted and less aggressive than their counterparts in American schools and, by implication, presumably easier to change with an anti-bullying program such as the OBPP. Such a view may not be unreasonable if comparison is made with American schools in very disadvantaged, inner city areas. However, if comparison is made between nationally representative samples of students in the United States and Norway, there is little support for such a view, with several empirical studies actually providing evidence to the contrary. For example, the international Program for International Student Assessment study from 2002 (PISA; conducted at 3-year intervals), which contains data from large, nationally representative samples of 15-year-old students from 29 OECD countries including the United States, contained a set of questions about noise and disruptive behavior in the classroom. Norway received a hardly flattering top ranking (worst of all countries) while U.S. students occupied rank number 24, close to the bottom-ranked (best) Japanese students. In the PISA study of 2000, the results were quite similar indicating that the measured characteristics are fairly stable over time (Kjærnsli, Lie, Olsen, Roe, & Turmo, 2004, 2006).

In the International Health and Behaviour of School Children study (HBSC; Craig & Harel, 2004, with data from 2001/2002), which contains the two global questions from the Olweus Bullying Questionnaire, the levels of problems were fairly similar for United States and Norwegian students in grades 6 and 8. The same was true of "having been involved in physical fighting three or more times in the previous 12 months." This study, which is carried out every 4 years, uses large nationally representative samples of students from selected grades. In the last two assessments (2001/2002 and 2005/2006), more than 30 countries participated in the study. All of these data clearly suggest that the common view of vast behavioral differences between Norwegian and "ordinary" U.S. students is greatly exaggerated and needs to be reconsidered.

In addition, it should be mentioned that the schools in Oslo, the capital of Norway, have an average of about 25% of students with an immigrant background, a considerable proportion of which come from non-Western countries. The OBPP has been implemented in some 40 Oslo schools with equally good results as in the rest of the country (see below).

Norwegian Outcome Studies with the OBPP 1997–2000

The New Bergen Project against Bullying   In this longitudinal project, Olweus (1999b, 2005) and members of the Olweus Bullying Prevention Research Group assessed approximately 2,400 students in grades 5, 6, and 7 from 11 intervention and 11 comparison schools. To make results comparable across studies in this chapter, the data for the two sets of schools were analyzed as two selection cohorts designs for two time points.

The schools were not randomized by conditions but had approximately the same levels of bully/victim problems at the start of the study (Time 1, May, 1997). One year later, a relative reduction of 23.6% in being bullied (from 12.7% to 9.7%) was registered for the fifth- to seventh-grade students in the intervention schools whereas comparable students in the comparison schools evidenced a small increase by 4.7% (from 10.6% to 11.1%). For bullying other students, the negative results for the comparison schools were more marked. These schools had a relative increase of 36.6% at Time 2 (from 4.1% to 5.6%) whereas the intervention schools showed a relative reduction of 21.4% (from 5.6% to 4.4%).

If one just looks at the results for the intervention schools, the results are less marked than in the First Bergen Project against Bullying. It is not unreasonable, however, to combine the results for the two sets of schools, subtracting the percentage Relative Change (keeping the sign) for the comparison schools from that of the intervention schools. If this strategy is followed, the Relative Change becomes 28.3% for being bullied (23.6 + 4.7) and 58% for bullying other students (21.4 + 36.6).

Considering the results for this study, it should also be emphasized that the OBPP had been in place for only 6 months or less when the second measurement took place. In addition, this particular year was a very turbulent one for all Norwegian teachers with the introduction of a new National Curriculum that made heavy demands on their time and emotional resources. This is likely to have reduced the quality of implementation of the program in this study.

The (First) Oslo Project against Bullying   This project (previously, in Olweus, 2004, called the Oslo Project against Bullying; Olweus, 2001b, 2005) used the ordinary extended selection cohorts design with two measurements, separated by a 1 year interval (November 1999–November 2000). For the approximately 900 students (at both time points) in grades 5 through 7, there were marked reductions in bully/victim problems: For girls and boys combined, the Relative Change (reduction) was 42.7 % (from 14.4% to 8.3%) for being bullied and 51.6% for bullying other students (from 66% to 3.1%). The results are shown in Figures 27.1 and 27.2.

The Need for Evidence-Based Intervention Programs

As bully/victim problems have gradually been placed on the official school agenda in many countries, a number of suggestions about their handling and prevention have been proposed. Some of these suggestions and approaches seem ill-conceived or maybe even counter-productive, others appear meaningful and potentially useful. A key problem, however, is that most of them have either failed to document positive results or have never been subjected to systematic research evaluation. Therefore it is difficult to know which programs or measures actually work and which do not.

The situation is well illustrated by the following facts. From the mid-1990s, a U.S. expert committee—the Blueprint Committee—has been engaged in systematically evaluating more than 600 presumably violence (or generally problem-behavior) preventing programs. For a program to be approved by the committee, it must fulfill certain minimum-level criteria (see Elliott, 1999):

• That the program had produced positive effects on relevant target groups (students in this case) in a relatively rigorous scientific evaluation.
• That the effects had lasted for at least 1 year.
• That the program had produced positive results in at least one site beyond the original one.

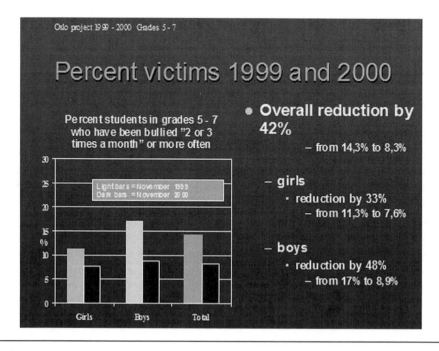

Figure 27.1

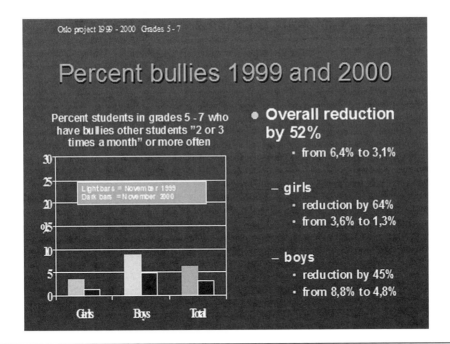

Figure 27.2

Up to 2008, only 11 of the evaluated programs (four of which are school-based and only one focusing on bullying) have satisfied the specified criteria and have been named "Blueprint Programs." A similar evaluation by an officially appointed, departmental committee was made in Norway in 2000. In this case, 25 programs designed to counteract and/or prevent "problem behavior" and in use in Norwegian schools were evaluated (Rapport, 2000). Only one program was recommended for further use in Norwegian schools without reservations.

The fact that the OBPP is one of the 11 Blueprint programs (Olweus et al., 1999) and, maybe in particular, was the program selected by the Norwegian departmental committee, is an important background for a government-funded national initiative in Norway.

A New National Initiative Against Bullying in Norway

In 2001, the Department of Education and Research (UFD) and the Department of Children and Family Affairs (BFD) decided that the OBPP was to be offered on a large-scale basis to Norwegian comprehensive schools over a period of years. In the period from 2001 to 2008, the program has been implemented in approximately 500 schools and more than 125 OBPP instructors have received thorough training in use of the program.

From an evaluation perspective, the new national initiative has provided a unique opportunity to examine the effects of the OBPP on very large samples of students and schools under ordinary conditions (i.e., without special efforts in terms of staff input or other resources) in the context of large-scale dissemination (Flay et al., 2005).

When a new school or group of schools adopt the OBPP, they regularly start by administering the Olweus Bullying Questionnaire (Olweus, 1996, 2007) some months before introduction of the program. One year after the initial measurement, the schools conduct a new survey with the same questionnaire to find out what results have been obtained and in what ways the individual school may need to increase its efforts. Many schools make new assessments after one, two, or more additional years.

By having data from several consecutive cohorts of schools entering the OBPP at half-year intervals, an excellent opportunity is provided to evaluate the reasonableness of a "history interpretation" of obtained intervention findings. As mentioned, such an interpretation implies that the results could be a consequence of general time trends, special media attention or some other "irrelevant" factor concomitant to the intervention rather than intervention. In particular, in September 2002, several important public actors including the Norwegian government, Children's Ombudsman, and the Teachers' Union officially signed a Manifesto against Bullying which gained a good deal of media attention. And at the end of 2002, both the King of Norway and the Prime Minister discussed the importance of counteracting bullying in schools in their traditional television and radio talks on New Year's Eve. In other phases of the evaluation period, there was only sporadic media attention to bully/victim problems in school. If such manifesto declarations and accompanying media attention had an effect on the amount of bully/victim problems in the country, this would be expected to show up in reduced levels of problems in schools entering the OBPP immediately or relatively shortly after the occurrence of these events. The extent to which empirical data support this assumption will be examined below.

In the research evaluations, we analyzed the data using the extended selection cohorts design, in which developmental or maturational effects are controlled, as described above. In addition, it is worth noting that the questionnaire data were collected by the schools themselves (following detailed written instructions about the administration procedures) and that the author of the OBPP did not participate other than sporadically in the training of instructors and had no contact whatsoever with the participating schools. Almost all of the training was undertaken by specially trained colleagues from the Olweus Group against Bullying at the Research Center for Health Promotion, University of Bergen.

Major Results from the New National Initiative Project.   Key results are shown in Figures 27.3 and 27.4. The upper curve of Figure 27.3 portrays the baseline percentages of bullied students in grades 4 through 7 from five different cohorts of schools which conducted their introductory surveys in the period from October 2001 to October 2003. As in earlier studies, to be classified as being bullied students had to respond to the global question in the Olweus Bullying Questionnaire that they had been bullied "2 or 3 times a month" or more in the past couple of months.

So far, we have mainly focused our evaluation analyses on the first three of these cohorts. The percentages of students (in the same grades and schools) who reported being bullied one year later, when the schools had used the OBPP for approximately 8 months, are shown in the lower curve of Figure 27.3. The two data points from each cohort of schools are connected with an arrow. To illustrate, the percentage of bullied students in the first cohort of schools ($n = 8,388$ students from 56 schools) was 15.2% while at follow-up 1 year later ($n = 8299$) this percentage had been reduced to 10.2%, a relative reduction of 33%. The relative reductions for the two consecutive cohorts of schools were almost identical, both amounting to approximately 34%, from 14.0% ($n = 4083$ students from 46 schools) to 9.2% ($n = 4,089$) for the second cohort, and from 13.2% ($n = 8,238$ students from 58 schools) to 8.7% ($n = 8,483$) for the third cohort. Absolute reductions for these three cohorts amounted to 4.9, 4.8, and 4.5 percentage points, respectively.

In Figure 27.4, the variable portrayed is bullying other students ("2 or 3 times a month" or more in the past couple of months). The general pattern of results is very similar to what was reported for being bullied in Figure 27.3, but at a lower level. The relative reductions for this variable for the three cohorts of schools were 37% (from 5.7% to 3.6%), 48% (from 5.9% to 3.1%),

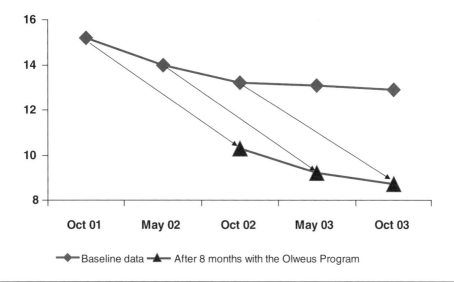

Figure 27.3 Percentage bullied students 2001–2003, elementary grades 4–7 before (upper curve) and after (lower curve) intervention. (Olweus, 2005, 11, 389-402). Reproduced with permission.

and 49% (from 5.1% to 2.6%), respectively. The absolute reductions amounted to 2.1., 2.8, and 2.5 percentage points.

Figures 27.3 and 27.4 show percentages for boys and girls combined for grades 4 through 7. Similar results were obtained when the data were analyzed separately for the two genders, the four grades, and when an even stricter criterion ("about once a week" or more often) was used in classifying students as being bullied or bullying other students. Marked improvements could thus be registered also for students who had been involved in more frequent and serious bully/ victim problems. (It should be noted that having been bullied/bullied other students "2 or 3

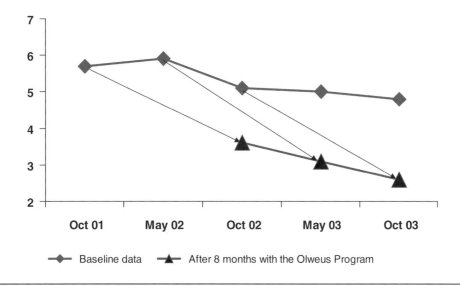

Figure 27.4 Percentage bullying students 2001–2003, elementary grades 4–7 before (upper curve) and after (lower curve) intervention. (Olweus, 2005, 11, 389-402). Reproduced with permission

times a month" by no means represents non-serious or trivial problems, as shown in Solberg and Olweus, 2003.) Similar positive results were also obtained with regard to the type of bullying that girls are often involved in—social isolation, rumour-spreading (relational bullying).

It is worth noting that the absolute percentage reductions in bully/victim problems in these analyses are roughly similar to those obtained in the First Bergen Project against Bullying (p. 378), although the relative reductions in the latter project are somewhat larger due to lower baseline (Time 1) values. Generally, it is important to emphasize that, although the results for the three cohorts of schools were strikingly similar, these studies are quite independent and are regarded as three separate evaluations/replications of the OBPP.

Is a "History Interpretation" Reasonable? As mentioned above, when using a selection cohorts design, a history interpretation of the results should be considered a possible threat to the validity of the conclusions and ideally be eliminated or made unlikely. Since the schools in our three studies came from many different parts of Norway, it is natural to look for general time trends or events with considerable media attention that might have an effect across the whole country as possible explanatory factors.

If we look at the upper curves in Figures 27.3 and 27.4 reflecting the levels of bully/victim problems in the five consecutive cohorts of schools that had not yet started with the OBPP, we can observe a slight decline over time. But there are no marked breaks in the curves around the time period—the latter half of 2002 and the beginning of 2003—when the Manifesto against Bullying was signed and the Prime Minister and the King held their official New Year's speeches. If these media events had had a clear general effect, we would have expected the levels of bully/victim problems of the schools administering the questionnaire in October 2002 and possibly May 2003 to have been considerably lower than those of the surrounding cohorts of schools.

Further, if there were such general effects, one would expect a relatively marked difference in the relative reductions in bully/victim problems for the various cohorts of schools. In particular, such possible effects would very likely have affected the levels of bully/victim problems of the first cohort of schools at the Time 2 assessment that was made in October 2002 (lower curve). One would thus have expected that the relative percentage reduction for this cohort would have been greater than for the other two consecutive cohorts. As can be seen in the figures, this was not the case. Accordingly, the pattern of data obtained certainly does not suggest that media attention and associated events had any observable effect on the levels of bully/victim problems of consideration here. However, the signing of the Manifesto and the related media attention seemed to have an effect on the schools/ communities' interest and willingness to apply for participation in the OBPP. The number of schools that took part in the OBPP training during the fall/spring period of 2002/2003 almost doubled ($n = 220$) compared to the corresponding period one year before ($n = 119$).

With regard to possible general time trends, the very similar results from successive, roughly comparable cohorts of schools (without intervention) indicate considerable stability over time in the average amount of bully/victim problems and do not suggest any marked time trend fluctuations in these levels. We have also found similar levels of stability when individual schools or groups of schools have been followed over time (typically at yearly intervals) without intervention.

In this context, it may be mentioned that the respected statistician Charles Reichardt in several places speaks quite favorably about the (simple) selection cohorts design for the evaluation of intervention effects in his chapter in Cook and Campbell's *Quasi-experimentation: Design and Analysis Issues for Field Settings* (1979, pp. 198–199). Also, in the new and revised edition of this book, Shadish, Cook and Campbell (2004, pp. 151–153) suggest certain ways of strengthening the (simple) selection cohorts design by including additional cohorts. This is clearly in line with the thinking behind use of the extended version of the selection cohorts design (above, and Olweus, 1991, 2005). In this form, the selection cohorts design with extensions both with regard to grade levels and number of consecutive cohorts is no doubt a quite strong design for effect evaluation.

A 5-Year Follow-Up Study in Oslo.   For 14 of the 24 Oslo schools from the first cohort, we have data for five assessments, from October 2001 to October 2006. The starting level for being bullied was 14.0%, which decreased to 9.8% the following year. The reduced level was retained and even further slightly reduced in the following years, reaching 8.4% in 2006. This change represents a 40% relative reduction from the starting value.

For bullying other students, the 2001 value was 5.5%, which declined to 2.8% in 2002 and to 2.7% in 2006, a relative reduction of 50.9%. The number of students participating in these analyses amounted to approximately 3,000 per assessment point. These results are important, since it has been shown (e.g., Beelman, Pfingstein, & Lösel, 1994) that many program effects are short-lived and are found to be considerably reduced when longer-term effects have been assessed (even after only 2 months after the end of the program phase). The reported results show that the effects of the OBPP can be quite long-term and suggest that the intervention schools had been able to change their "culture" and competence to counteract bullying in a more permanent way. It should also be noted that none of the students who took the questionnaire in 2001 participated in the 2006 assessment.

Norwegian Evaluation Studies Involving Grade 8–10 Students

Systematic use of the OBPP with students in grades 4 through 7 has consistently produced positive results and this record seems to be relatively unique in an international perspective (see Smith, Pepler, & Rigby, 1994; Ttofi & Farrington, 2009; Ttofi, Farrington, & Baldry, 2008). Positive results have also been obtained with students from junior high/lower secondary school grades (8 through 10), although less consistently and sometimes with weaker effects. For example, in the First Oslo Project, the OBPP was reasonably well implemented in Grade 8 and at Time 2 (in Grade 9) the percentage of bullied students was 6.3% compared with the 9.2% for the Grade 9 cohort 1 year earlier (at Time 1). This decrease represented a relative reduction by 32%. Also in the First Bergen Project, positive results were obtained for the junior high school cohort (Grade 8), after 8 and 20 months of intervention, respectively (see e.g., Olweus, 1991, 1997, where the designation Grade 7 corresponds to Grade 8 in the United States and today's Norwegian grade system). In the context of the New National Initiative, however, results for these grades at the 1-year follow-up (Time 2) have been more variable, sometimes producing positive results, at other times showing basically no difference between the Time 1 and Time 2 assessments.

However, in a recent study following 14 schools with grades 8 and 9 over a 2-year period from 2001 to 2003, the results at Time 3, after 20 months of intervention, were clearly different form those at Time 2 and Time 1. The percentage of bullied students had decreased from 8.0% at Time 1 to 5.8% at Time 3, a relative reduction of 27.5%. Similar results were obtained for bullying other students, with a relative reduction of 31%, from 6.1% at Time 1 to 4.2% at Time 3. The reductions from Time 1 to Time 2 were quite small for both variables. Although these results are based on a relatviely small number of schools, they suggest that it may take longer time to achieve consistently good results in grades 8–10 than in lower grades. Other researchers in the field also have had the experience that it is more difficult to reduce bully/victim problems in junior high/lower secondary grades (e.g., Smith & Sharp, 1994; Smith et al., this volume; Stevens et al., 2000; Salmivalli, Kaukiainen & Voeten, 2005).

We think there are several reasons for this state of affairs. Very briefly, one reason has to do with the individual development of the students, most of them entering puberty and a period of increasing liberation from parental influence and becoming more generally oppositional to authorities, including teachers (Arnett, 1992). Probably even more important, the organization of the teaching is different at this grade level (in Norway, and most Western countries as far as we know). The teachers become more subject oriented and many of the social functions that are typically taken care of by the homeroom teacher in lower grades are not fulfilled by anyone. In this way, the program can be expected to be less well implemented in these grades, which also has been documented in preliminary analyses in the New National Initiative Project (Olweus & Kallestad, in press). Accordingly, it is not unreasonable to expect weaker and less consistent results.

We are now in the process of planning a new intervention project in Norway with a special focus on schools with students in grades 8–10. A major task in that project will be to try to ensure that the various program components are implemented in a more systematic way.

Outcome Studies in the United States

South Carolina The first evaluation of the OBPP in the United States (Limber, Nation, Tracy, Melton, & Flerx, 2004; Melton et al., 1998) was conducted in the mid-1990s involving data from elementary and middle schools in six primarily rural school districts. The districts were organized into matched pairs based on geographic location and the demographics of the students. In each pair, the schools in one district were selected to receive the OBPP (Group A), while the schools in the other districts served as a comparison group for the first year of the project (Group B). During the first year of the project, there were 11 Group A (intervention) schools and 28 Group B (comparison) schools. Schools were not randomly assigned to groups. Although the project continued during a second year, it was found that implementation of the program in this period was inadequate (Limber et al, 2004). Accordingly, we restrict analyses here to the first year of the project. This decision is also motivated by the fact that only analyses involving the first two time points provide a clear-cut intervention vs. control comparison.

Although school-level demographic data were not available to researchers, district-wide demographic data indicated that the ethnicity of students ranged from 46% to 95% African American, and from 4% to 53% White. In all but one school district, the percentage of students receiving free or reduced lunches (a measure of poverty) ranged from 60% to 91%.

Data were analyzed as a pretest-posttest design with students in grades 4, 5, and 6 at Time 1 and followed up in grades 5, 6, and 7 one year later, at Time 2 (after 7 months of program implementation in Group A schools). It was not feasible to secure the identity of the individual students in the assessments which precluded adjustment of the outcome data for individual pretest values. Accordingly, the results reported are likely to be conservative due to less than maximum statistical power. At both Time 1 and Time 2, students completed an English-language version of the original Olweus Bullying Questionnaire (Olweus, 1986). They also completed a 42-question measure developed by Olweus to assess other antisocial behavior (Bendixen & Olweus, 1999). Students indicated the frequency with which they had engaged in a variety of antisocial behaviors (e.g., such as stealing money or other things, skipping school, and starting a fight with another student) within the past 3-month period. From these questions, we developed 8 scales:

theft (Cronbach's alpha = .81), vandalism (.72), violence (.69), delinquency (.90), substance abuse (.79), school misbehavior (.81), school sanctions (.74), and group delinquency (.70). (See Melton et al., 1998, for a more detailed description of the scales.)

Results indicated that the first year of the program affected students' engagement in bullying and other antisocial activities. There were consistent and significant ($p < .01$ or 001) Time (Time 1 vs. Time 2) × Group (A vs. B) interactions for several indices of bullying others (frequency of bullying other students in the last couple of months, frequency of bullying other students in the last week at school, frequency of participation in group bullying of others). At Time 1, 23.6% of students in Group A schools ($n = 2025$) indicated that they had bullied others several times or more. After 7 months of program implementation, this percentage dropped to 19.9%, a reduction of 15.7%. By comparison, at Time 1, 18.5% of students in Group B schools ($n = 4,229$) had bullied others several times or more often and after 7 months this percentage had risen to 20.7%, an increase of 11.9%. Thus, students in the intervention schools had an overall relative reduction in bullying others of 27.6%. However, no significant changes were observed in the frequency with which students reported being bullied

As expected, there was an increase over time in the frequency of self-reported antisocial behavior among control (Group B) students, while for the intervention students, there was either no increase or a slower rate of increase with regard to general delinquency ($p < .01$) and a number of the scales concerning vandalism ($p < .05$), school misbehavior ($p < .001$), and sanctions for school misbehavior ($p < .005$). The program thus seemed to slow the age-related rate of increase in students' involvement in antisocial behavior.

It should be noted that positive effects of the OBPP on antisocial behavior were also obtained in the First Bergen Project described above (Olweus, 1991). These results are not surprising given that one can easily see bullying as a form of antisocial behavior (Olweus, 1993b).

Philadelphia   Researchers have assessed the effectiveness of the OBPP in inner-city Philadelphia schools using the extended selection cohorts design. Black and Jackson (2007) examined the effectiveness of the program in six large public elementary and middle schools (enrollments of 456–1,295 students) over the course of 4 years of implementation. Students were primarily from low-income families (67%) and were predominantly African American (82%) and Latino (10%). The evaluation measures included an observation instrument to assess Bullying Incident Density (BID), the Olweus Bully/Victim Questionnaire (administered to students in grades 3–8), and a measure of fidelity of implementation.

The observation instrument consisted of a checklist of bullying behaviors that assessed physical, verbal, and emotional bullying (including name-calling, hitting, pushing, inappropriate touching, rumors, spitting, relational exclusion, teasing, taunting, cursing, raising voice in anger, and threatening gestures). Observations of middle school students took place during lunch, while observations of elementary students took place at recess. These areas were selected because they were identified through the anonymous questionnaire as being "hot spots" for bullying at the school. Fidelity of implementation was assessed yearly for each of 14 core components of the program (as identified by Olweus, Limber, & Mihalic, 1999). Implementation of each program component was dichotomous (positive or negative). Total fidelity scores for each school were calculated as the total number of core components implemented divided by the total number of components.

At baseline, incident density was 65 incidents per 100 student hours. After 4 years, BID had decreased 45% to 36 incidents per 100 student hours. There was no significant correlation between overall program fidelity of implementation and changes in BID. However, the authors reported that those program components that were most strongly associated with decreased BID included the posting of school rules about bullying, consistent enforcement of positive and negative consequences, and training adult monitors to engage students in activities. Anonymous self-reports of being bullied varied by school, but ranged from a decrease of 10% to an increase of 7% from Time 1 to Time 4. Unfortunately, at Time 4, only 1598 students completed the questionnaire, compared with 3,741 at baseline. Due to the great attrition, firm conclusions about students' self-reported victimization cannot be drawn in this study.

Washington   Bauer and colleagues (2007) assessed the effectiveness of the OBPP in Washington state, using a nonrandomized controlled trial with 10 public middle schools (grades 6–8, with 7 intervention and 3 control sites). White students represented the most prevalent ethnic group in intervention schools (40%), followed by Asian students (24%), African American students (12%), and Hispanic/Latino students (7%). Ethnic make-up of control schools was somewhat different, with significantly fewer White students (23%) and more African American students (28%). Researchers assessed relational and physical measures of victimization using four specific questions from the Olweus Bullying Questionnaire and found that relational victimization decreased by 28% among White students in intervention schools, relative to their peers in control schools, and physical victimization decreased by 37%. However, there were no similar effects for students of other races/ethnicities and no overall program effects regarding rates of victimization. Students in intervention schools were significantly more likely than those in control schools to perceive other students as actively intervening in bullying incidents. Similar analyses for student perceptions of teachers' or other adults' readiness to intervene were not statistically significant. The authors concluded that "implementation of the OBPP—may lead to variable differences in effectiveness based on factors related to culture, race, and the influence of the family/home environment" (p. 273) and recommended that school staff "should be aware of the influence that home, culture, and society have on student behavior, and tailor preventive measures accordingly" (p. 273).

In this context, it is worth noting that implementation of the OBPP has met with success in several ethnically diverse settings in the United States (e.g., Philadelphia, rural South Carolina, and southern California). Nevertheless, the authors' recommendations to carefully consider the unique setting of implementation and to make necessary cultural adaptations is important and is, in fact, encouraged by authors of the OBPP (Olweus et al., 2007).

Bauer and colleagues (2007) encourage continued use of the OBPP, as it "is the only bullying prevention program that is available that is comprehensive and that encompasses a whole-school approach" (p. 273). Further, they note that the program is an important vehicle for change because it helps to establish a common language about bullying and provides schools with the necessary framework to address bullying. They comment that the implementation of the OBPP in intervention schools was "broad and encompassed a significant regularity and consistency" (p. 273) that was lacking in comparison schools.

California   Pagliocca and colleagues (2007) evaluated the effectiveness of the OBPP in three elementary schools in a suburban southern California community over a 2-year period using a selection cohorts design. Outcome measures included student self-reports on the Olweus Bullying Questionnaire ($N = 1174$ at Time 1, $N = 1085$ at Time 2, and $N = 1119$ at Time 3), and anonymous reports by parents ($N = 761$ at Time 1, $N = 817$ at Time 2, and $N = 411$ at Time 3), and teachers ($N = 100$ at Time 1, $N = 72$ at Time 2, and $N = 78$ at Time 3). Overall, self-reported rates of being bullied among students decreased 21% after 1 year and 14% after 2 years. Decreases were particularly marked among fourth graders, where researchers observed a decrease of 32% after 1 year and 20% after 2 years of implementation. Researchers also observed decreases overall in students' reports of bullying others after 1 year (by 8%) and after 2 years (17%) of implementation.

Other findings of note included increases in bullied students' propensities to tell a teacher about their experiences (Time 1 vs. Time 3), students' perceptions that teachers or other adults at school try to stop bullying (Time 1 vs. Time 2), teachers' perceptions that there were clear rules about bullying (67% increase between Time 1 and Time 3), and teachers perceptions that they knew how to respond to bullying that they observed or heard about (78% increase between Time 1 and Time 3). There also were marked increases in teachers' beliefs that bullying policies had been fairly well or extremely well communicated to students (97% increase), parents (91% increase), teaching staff (72% increase), and non-teaching staff (79% increase) between Time 1 and Time 3. Finally, parents were more likely to believe that school administrators had done very much to stop bullying (18% increase between Time 1 and Time 2) but there were no differences in parents' perceptions of teacher activity to stop bullying.

Summary of U.S. Findings   To date, studies have evaluated the effectiveness of the OBPP in several diverse settings and elementary and middle school populations in the United States. Some have been conducted by authors of the OBPP (Limber et al., 2004; Pagliocca et al., 2007), while others have not (Bauer et al., 2007; Black & Jackson, 2007). The picture that emerges from these studies is that the OBPP has had a noticeable impact on students as well as adults. Clear decreases have been observed in students' self-reported bullying behavior, and antisocial involvement (Limber et al., 2004; Melton et al., 1998; Olweus, 1991), victimization (Bauer et al., 2007, for White students; Pagliocca et al., 2007), child victims' propensities to report bullying to adults at school (Pagliocca et al., 2007), and students' perceptions that students intervene to put a stop to bullying (Bauer et al., 2007). Observational measures of bullying among students (measured as Bulling Incident Density) also have shown significant decreases in relational and physical victimization (Black & Jackson, 2007) related to the implementation of the OBPP. Finally, in the one study to assess adults' perceptions of policies and practices related to bullying, teachers perceived clear improvements in schools that implemented the OBPP.

Although these findings are clearly encouraging, it should also be noted that the results from these studies have not been uniformly positive. Moreover, it would have been desirable to have somewhat more knowledge about and control over the fidelity of implementation of the program for some studies. Accordingly, current U.S. research (both planned and underway) will involve more detailed analyses of the effectiveness of the various program components and the conditions under which the program has the largest effects.

Conclusions and Practical Implications

The Olweus Bullying Prevention Program is built on the conviction that bullying need not and should not be a common or "natural" experience for children and youth. Results from more than 20 years of research, primarily in Scandinavia and the United States, confirm that bullying can, in fact, be considerably reduced through systematic school-wide efforts that reduce the opportunities and rewards for bullying and build a sense of community among students and adults. Such a restructuring of the school environment does not come without considerable commitment and effort on the part of administrators, staff, students, and parents. However, when one considers the numbers of students affected and the tremendous personal and economic costs of bullying—to involved students and their families, the broader school environment, and to society at large—these efforts are not only reasonable but quite necessary.

The numbers of students who may have avoided direct involvement in bullying (as victims or perpetrators of bullying) as a consequence of the OBPP is substantial. To illustrate, it may be useful to focus on the Norwegian findings. If we combine all six Norwegian large-scale evaluation studies presented in this chapter, there are some 25,000 students who have participated in the 1-year evaluations for grades 4–7 (taken the questionnaire at two time points separated by a year). If we assume conservatively, on the basis of our empirical results, that about 4% of the students in these grades have escaped being regularly bullied during the evaluation year, this means that a considerable number of students—approximately 1,000—have had safer and more positive school experiences for much of the evaluation period. We can also make the reasonable assumption that positive effects have been obtained for the approximately 25,000 students in grades K-3 who attended the same schools but did not participate in the questionnaire assessment. Assuming similar effects in these grades, the number of students who escaped bullying through the intervention program increases to approximately 2,000 students in these schools.

We can further assume that a certain proportion of the intervention schools have been able to maintain reduced levels of bully/victim problems also after the introductory implementation period is over, as was found in the 5-year follow-up Oslo project. In such a perspective, it becomes obvious that the effect of the intervention program in terms of numbers of students who have escaped bullying across multiple years, is quite substantial.

In suggesting an economic interpretation of these results, it is natural to point out that, with overwhelming probability, they represent very significant savings for society with respect to psychological/psychiatric treatment and health-related costs. There is ample documentation that a considerable proportion of victims of bullying suffer from depression, anxiety, poor self-esteem, and suicidal thoughts (e.g., Hawker & Boulton, 2000; Solberg & Olweus, 2003). A similar pattern of negative effects was also evident in a prospective follow-up study of two groups of boys aged 24 who had or had not been regularly bullied in school in grades 7 through 10, some 9 years earlier (Olweus, 1993b). A recent Norwegian thesis has further documented that among 160 young adults who sought psychiatric treatment for the first time (at an average age of 35 years), some 50% had been bullied during their school years, and the more they had been bullied, the greater their psychiatric symptoms (Fosse, 2006).

Although we have not (yet) assessed direct effects of the OBPP on academic achievement, it is very reasonable to assume that reductions in bullying would lead to increases in achievement, particularly for victims of bullying but also more generally, for classrooms with bully/victim problems. In the First Bergen Project, for example, the program effects included clear improvements in several "social climate" dimensions very likely related to academic achievement, as mentioned above. In a recent longitudinal study conducted in the United States, Buhs, Ladd, and Herald (2006) observed that peer rejection in kindergarten was associated with peer exclusion in grades K-5 (e.g., excluded from activities), which in turn was associated with decreased classroom participation, and ultimately lower academic achievement.

Although it has been found that former male school bullies are clearly overrepresented in the crime registers as young adults (Olweus, 1993; Sourander et al., 2007), it has not (yet) been documented that the OBPP directly leads to a reduction of adult criminality. However, in both the First Bergen Project and the South Carolina project, it was shown that the program also had clear effects on concurrent antisocial behaviors such as vandalism, theft, and truancy. Accordingly, it is very reasonable to assume that at least some proportion of the students who stop bullying in school as a consequence of the OBPP will be deflected from an antisocial trajectory. Considering the very major costs imposed by individuals with conduct problems or conduct disorder (e.g., Cohen, 1998; Scott, Knapp, Henderson, & Maughan, 2001), such a result would represent a very substantial saving to society, even if the number of "socialized" or averted bullies were quite small.

Ongoing evaluations of the OBPP in Norway, the United States, and elsewhere around the globe are being undertaken to assess the effectiveness of the program in diverse contexts and populations, which program components are particularly critical to program success, and which teacher-, school-, and community-level variables are particularly important with regard to program implementation. Assessing the general and differential effects of the OBPP on children's psychosocial well-being and mental health, academic achievement, and involvement with antisocial peers and the criminal justice system also will be very useful in order to estimate the potential savings that society can expect from the prevention of bully/victim problems in school and elsewhere.

References

Arnett, J. (1992). Reckless behavior in adolescence: A developmental perspective. *Developmental Review, 12*, 339–373.

Bauer, N., Lozano, P., & Rivara, F. P. (2007). The effectiveness of the Olweus Bullying Prevention Program in public middle schools: A controlled trial. *Journal of Adolescent Health, 40*, 266–274.

Baumrind, D. (1967). Child care practices anteceding three patterns of preschool behavior. *Genetic Psychology Monographs, 75*, 43–88.

Beelmann, A., Pfingsten, U., & Lösel, F. (1994). The effects of training social competence in children: A meta-analysis of recent evaluation studies. *Journal of Clinical Child Psychology, 23*, 260–271.

Bendixen, M., & Olweus, D. (1999). Measurement of antisocial behaviour in early adolescence: Psychometric properties and substantive findings. *Criminal Behaviour and Mental Health, 9*, 323–354.

Biglan, A. (1995). *Changing cultural practices: A contextualist framework for intervention research*. Reno, NV: Context Press.

Black, S. A., & Jackson, E. (2007). Using bullying incident density to evaluate the Olweus Bullying Prevention Programme. *School Psychology International, 28*, 623–638.

Bryk, A. S., & Raudenbush, S. W. (1992). *Hierarchical linear models: Applications and data analysis methods*. Newbury Park, CA: Sage.

Buhs, E. S., Ladd, G. W., & Herald, S. L. (2006). Peer exclusion and victimization: Processes that mediate the relation between peer group rejection and children's classroom engagement and achievement? *Journal of Educational Psychology, 98*, 1–13.

Cohen, J. (1988). *Statistical power analysis for the behavioral sciences* (2nd ed.). New York: Academic.

Cohen, M. A. (1998). The monetary value of saving a high-risk youth. *Journal of Quantitative Criminology, 14*, 5–33.

Cook, T. D., & Campbell, D. T. (1979). *Quasi-experimentation: Design and analysis issues for field settings*. Chicago: Rand McNally.

Craig, W. M., & Harel, Y. (2004). Bullying, fighting and victimization. In C. Curry, C. Roberts, A. Morgan, R. Smith, W. Settertobulte, O. Samdal, et al. (Eds.), *Young people's health in context*. WHO report no. 4, Health Policy for Children and Adolescents (pp. 133–144). Geneva: World Health Organization.

Elliott, D. S. (1999). Editor's introduction. In D. Olweus, S. P. Limber, & S. Mihalic, (1999). *The Bullying Prevention Program: Blueprints for Violence Prevention, 9* (pp. xi–xxiii). Boulder, CO: Center for the Study and Prevention of Violence.

Eslea, M., & Smith, P.K. (1998). The long-term effectiveness of ant-bullying work in primary schools. *Educational Research, 40*, 203–218.

Flay, B. R., Biglan, A., Gonzalez Castro, F., Gottfredson, D., Kellam, S., Moscicki, E. K., et al. (2005). Standards of evidence: Criteria for efficacy, effectiveness and dissemination. *Prevention Science, 6*, 151–175.

Fleiss, J. L. (1994). Measures of effect size for categorical data. In H. Cooper & L. V. Hedges (Eds.), *The Handbook of Research Synthesis* (pp. 245–260). New York: Russell Sage.

Fosse, G. K. (2006). *Mental health of psychiatric outpatients bullied in childhood*. Doctoral thesis, Department of Neuroscience, Faculty of Medicine, Norwegian University of Science and Technology, Trondheim.

Furre, H., Danielsen, I.-J., Stiberg-Jamt, R., & Skaalvik, E. M. (2006). *Analyse av den nasjonale undersøkelsen "Elevundersøkelsen"* [Analysis of the national study "The Student Investigation"]. Kristiansand, Norway: Oxford Research.

Hanewinkel, R. (2004). Prevention of bullying in German schools: An evaluation of an anti-bullying approach. In P. K. Smith, D. Pepler, & K. Rigby (Eds.), *Bullying in schools: How successful can interventions be?* (pp. 81–97). Cambridge, UK: Cambridge University Press.

Hawker, D. S. J., & Boulton, M. J. (2000). Twenty years' research on peer victimization and psychosocial maladjustment: A meta-analytic review of cross-sectional studies. *Journal of Child Psychology and Psychiatry and Allied Disciplines, 41*, 441–455.

Judd, C. M., & Kenny, D. A. (1981). *Estimating the effects of social interventions.* New York: Cambridge University Press.

Kallestad, J. H., & Olweus, D. (2003). Predicting teachers' and school's implementation of the Olweus Bullying Prevention Program: A multilevel study. *Prevention & Treatment, 6,* Article 21, posted October 1, 2003, at http://www. journals.apa.org/prevention

Kish, L. (1987). *Statistical design for research.* New York: Wiley.

Kjærnsli, M. Lie, S., Olsen, R. V., Roe, A., & Turmo, A. (2004). *Rett spor eller ville veier?* [On the right or the wrong track?]. Oslo: Universitetsforlaget.

Kjærnsli, M. Lie, S., Olsen, R. V., Roe, A., & Turmo, A. (2006). *Norwegian reports from TIMSS and PISA 2003: Summary and conclusions.* Oslo: Institute for Teacher Education and School Development, University of Oslo.

Kyriakides, L., Kaloyirou, C., & Lindsay, G. (2006). An analysis of the Revised Olweus Bully/Victim Questionnaire using the Rasch measurement model. *British Journal of Educational Psychology, 76*, 781–801.

Limber, S. P. (2004). Implementation of the Olweus Bullying Prevention Program in American Schools: Lessons learned in the field. In D. L. Espelage & S. M. Swearer (Eds.), *Bullying in American schools: A social-ecological perspective on prevention and intervention* (pp. 351–363). Mahwah, NJ: Erlbaum.

Limber, S. P. (2006). The Olweus Bullying Prevention Program: An overview of its implementation and research basis. In S. Jimerson & M. Furlong (Eds.), *Handbook of school violence and school safety: From research to practice* (pp. 293–307). Mahwah, NJ: Erlbaum.

Limber, S. P., Nation, M., Tracy, A. J., Melton, G. B., & Flerx, V. (2004). Implementation of the Oweus Bullying Prevention Program in the Southeastern United States. In P. K. Smith, D. Pepler, & K. Rigby (Eds.), *Bullying in schools: How successful can interventions be?* (pp. 55–79). Cambridge, UK: Cambridge University Press.

Loeber, R., & Stouthamer-Loeber, M. (1986). Family factors as correlates and predictors of conduct problems and juvenile delinquency. In M. Tonry & N. Morris (Eds.), *Crime and justice, 7* (pp. 219–339). Chicago: University of Chicago Press.

Melton, G. B., Limber, S. P. ,Cunningham, P., Osgood, D. W., Chambers, J. Flerx, V., et al. (1998). Violence among rural youth. Final Report. Washington, DC: U.S. Department of Justice, Office of Justice Programs, Office of Juvenile Justice and Delinquency Prevention.

Murray, D. (1998). *Design and analysis of group-randomized trials.* New York: Oxford University Press.

Olweus, D. (1973). Personality and aggression. I J. K. Cole, & D. D. Jensen (Eds.), *Nebraska Symposium on Motivation 1972* (pp. 261–321). Lincoln: University of Nebraska Press.

Olweus, D. (1978). *Aggression in the schools: Bullies and whipping boys.* Washington, DC: Hemisphere.

Olweus, D. (1979). Stability of aggressive reaction patterns in males: A review. *Psychological Bulletin, 86*, 852–875.

Olweus, D. (1980). Familial and temperamental determinants of aggressive behavior in adolescent boys: A causal analysis. *Developmental Psychology, 16*, 644–660.

Olweus, D. (1986). *The Olweus Bully/Victim Questionnaire.* Mimeo. Bergen, Norway: Research Center for Health Promotion, University of Bergen.

Olweus, D. (1991). Bully/victim problems among schoolchildren: Basic facts and effects of a school based intervention program. In D. J. Pepler & K. H. Rubin (Eds.), *The development and treatment of childhood aggression* (pp. 411–448). Hillsdale, NJ: Erlbaum.

Olweus, D. (1993a). *Bullying at school: What we know and what we can do.* New York: Blackwell.

Olweus, D. (1993b). Victimization by peers: Antecedents and long-term outcomes. In K. H. Rubin & J. H. Asendort (Eds.), *Social withdrawal, inhibition, and shyness* (pp. 315–341). Hillsdale, NJ: Erlbaum.

Olweus, D. (1996). *The Revised Olweus Bully/Victim Questionnaire.* Mimeo. Bergen, Norway: Research Center for Health Promotion, University of Bergen.

Olweus, D. (1997). Bully/victim problems in school: Facts and intervention. *European Journal of Psychology of Education, 12*, 495–510.

Olweus, D. (1999a). Norway. In P. K. Smith, Y. Morita, J. Junger-Tas, D. Olweus, R. Catalano, & P. Slee (Eds.), *The nature of school bullying: A cross-national perspective* (pp. 28–48). London: Routledge.

Olweus, D. (1999b). *Noen hovedresultater fra Det Nye Bergensprosjektet mot mobbing og antisosial atferd* [Some key results from The New Bergen Project against bullying and Antisocial Behavior]. Unpublished manuscript. Research Center for Health Promotion, University of Bergen, Norway.

Olweus, D. (2001a). *Olweus' core program against bullying and antisocial behavior: A teacher handbook.* Bergen, Norway: Author.

Olweus, D. (2001b). *Antimobbningprojekt i Oslo-skolor med meget gode resultater* [Anti-bullying project in Oslo schools with very good results]. Unpublished manuscript. Research Center for Health Promotion, University of Bergen, Norway.

Olweus, D. (2004). Bullying at school: Prevalence estimation, a useful evaluation design, and a new national initiative in Norway. *Association for Child Psychology and Psychiatry Occasional Papers, 23*, 5–17.

Olweus, D. (2005). A useful evaluation design, and effects of the Olweus Bullying Prevention Program. *Psychology, Crime & Law, 11*, 389–402

Olweus, D. (2007). *Olweus Bullying Questionnaire: Scannable paper version*. Center City, MN: Hazelden.

Olweus, D., & Alsaker, F. D. (1991). Assessing change in a cohort longitudinal study with heirarchical data. In D. Magnusson, L. R. Bergman, G. Rudinger, & B. Torestad (Eds.), *Problems and methods in longitudinal research* (pp. 107–132). New York: Cambridge University Press.

Olweus, D., & Kallestad, J. H. (in press). The Olweus Bullying Prevention Program: Effects of classroom components at different grad levels. In K. Osterman (Ed.), *Indirect and direct aggression*. New York: Peter Lang.

Olweus, D., & Limber, S. P. (2007). *Olweus Bullying Prevention Program Teacher Guide*. Center City, MN: Hazelden.

Olweus, D., Limber, S. P., Flerx, V., Mullin, N., Riese, J., & Snyder. M. (2007). *Olweus Bullying Prevention Program Schoolwide Guide*. Center City, MN: Hazelden.

Olweus, D., Limber, S. P., & Mihalic, S. (1999). *The Bullying Prevention Program: Blueprints for Violence Prevention, Vol.9*. Boulder, CO: Center for the Study and Prevention of Violence.

Pagliocca, P. M., Limber, S. P., & Hashima, P. (2007). Evaluation report for the Chula Vista Olweus Bullying Prevention Program. Chula Vista, CA: Chula Vista Police Department.

Pepler, D. J., Craig, W. M., O'Connell, P., Atlas, R., & Charach, A. (2004). Making a difference in bullying: Evaluation of a systemic school-based programme in Canada. In P. K. Smith, D. Pepler, & K. Rigby (Eds.), *Bullying in schools: How successful can interventions be?* (pp. 125–139). Cambridge, UK: Cambridge University Press.

Pepler, D. J., Craig, W., Ziegler, S., & Charach, A. (1994). An evaluation of an anti-bullying intervention in Toronto schools. *Canadian Journal of Community Mental Health, 13*, 95–110.

Rapport (2000). *Vurdering av program og tiltak for å redusere problematferd og utvikle sosial kompetanse* [Evaluation of programs and measures to reduce problem behaviour and develop social competence]. Oslo, Norway: Kirke-, undervisnings-, og forskningsdepartementet.

Roland, E. (1989). Bullying: The Scandinavian research tradition. In D. P. Tattum & D. A.Lane (Eds.), *Bullying in schools* (pp. 21–32). Stoke-on-Trent, UK: Trentham Books.

Salmivalli, C., Kaukiainen, A., & Voeten, M. (2005). Antibullying intervention: Implementation and outcome. *British Journal of Educational Psychology, 75*, 465–487.

Scott, S., Knapp, M., Henderson, J., & Maughan, B. (2001). Financial cost of social exclusion: follow up study of antisocial children in adulthood. *British Medical Journal, 323*, 191–194.

Shadish, W.R., Cook, T. D., & Campbell, D. T. (2002). *Experimental and quasi-experimental design for generalized causal inference*. Boston: Houghton-Mifflin.

Smith, P. K., Pepler, D., & Rigby, K. (1994). *Bullying in schools: How successful can interventions be?* New York: Cambridge University Press.

Smith, P. K., & Sharp, S. (Eds.). (1994). *School bullying: Insights and perspectives*. London: Routledge.

Smith, P. K., Sharp, S., Eslea, M., & Thompson, D. (2004). England: the Sheffield project. In P. K. Smith, D. Pepler, & K. Rigby (Eds.), *Bullying in schools: How successful can interventions be?* (pp. 99–123). Cambridge, UK: Cambridge University Press.

Solberg, M., & Olweus, D. (2003). Prevalence estimation of school bullying with the Olweus Bully/Victim Questionnaire. *Aggressive Behavior, 29*, 239–268.

Sourander, A., Jensen, P., Rönning, J. A., Elonheimo, H., Niemela, S., Helenius, H., et al. (2007). Childhood bullies and victims and their risk of criminality in late adolescence. *Archives of Pediatrics and Adolescent Medicine, 161*, 546–552.

Stevens, V., De Bourdeaudhuij, I., & Van Oost, P. (2000). Bullying in Flemish schools: an evaluation of anti-bullying intervention in primary and secondary schools. *British Journal of Educational Psychology, 70*, 195–210.

Stevens, V., Van Oost, P., & de Bourdeaudhuij, I. (2004). Interventions against bullying in Flemish schools: programme development and evaluation. In P. K. Smith, D. Pepler, & K. Rigby (Eds.), *Bullying in Schools: How Successful can Interventions be?* (pp. 141–165). New York: Cambridge University Press.

Ttofi, M. M., & Farrington, D. P. (2009). What works in preventing bullying: Effective elements of anti-bullying programmes. *Journal of Aggression, Conflict and Peace Research, 1*, 13–24.

Ttofi, M. M., Farrington, D. P., & Baldry, A. C. (2008). *Effectiveness of programmes to reduce bullying*. Stockholm: Swedish National Council for Crime Prevention.

Whitney, I., Rivers, I., Smith, P., & Sharp, S. (1994). The Sheffield project: methodology and findings. In P. Smith & S. Sharp (Eds.), *School bullying: Insights and perspectives* (pp. 20–56). London: Routledge.

Zucker, D. (1990). An analysis of variance pitfall: The fixed effect analysis in a nested design. *Educational and Psychological Measurement, 50*, 731–738.

28
School Bullying
A Crisis or an Opportunity?

KARIN S. FREY, LEIHUA V. EDSTROM, AND MIRIAM K. HIRSCHSTEIN

In 1999, a U.S. Supreme Court justice asked lawyers for a young woman who had endured years of peer sexual harassment, "Is this just kids being kids?" (Stein, 2003). In doing so, the justice posed a question that is often applied to bullying. Many adults view ostracism, demeaning behavior, even physical assaults among young people to be normal or "growth experiences" for the victims. Yet considerable evidence indicates that bullying can deny young people basic educational opportunities, as they attempt to escape daily harassment through truancy or dropping out (Slee, 1994), or develop maladaptive ways of coping with emotional trauma (e.g., Graham & Juvonen, 1998). Effects are not restricted to those actively bullied. Bystanders learn that aggression pays. They may experience a disturbing mix of feelings such as fear, pleasure, guilt, and moral confusion (O'Connell, Pepler, & Craig, 1999; Jeffrey, Miller, & Linn, 2001).

These and other serious consequences occur in the context of behavior that is, in fact, statistically normative, at least at low levels. Observations of third- to sixth-grade children on school playgrounds revealed that 77% were observed to bully or encourage bullying of school mates who were disadvantaged because of age, size, or peer support (Frey, Hirschstein, Snell, et al., 2005). Espelage, Bosworth, and Simon (2000) found that 80% of their middle school sample admitted bullying someone in the previous month.

In talking with parents, we sometimes compare schoolyard bullying to tantrums among 2-year-olds. While each behavior may reflect a developmentally typical way to exert influence, each may impede development if rewarded and habitual. Those who bully repeatedly may become reliant on coercion, and fail to develop positive relationship skills—a failure that may be played out in dating relationships (Connolly, Pepler, Craig, & Taradash, 2000), families (Duncan, 1999), and the workplace (Harvey, Heames, Richey, & Leonard, 2006). At the most severe end, bullying is associated with increased risk for substance use (Nansel et al., 2001) and involvement in street violence (Andershed, Kerr, & Stattin, 2001).

Since the Supreme Court case, the shock of repeated school shootings has stimulated the passage of state anti-bullying laws. These typically mandate zero tolerance policies in schools (Stein, 2003). Exclusionary measures, however, have not provided effective deterrence (Skiba et al., 2006). Just as bullying affects all within a school community, the conditions that foster or deter bullying are created by the actions of everyone in that community (Frey & Nolen, in press). Bystanders, for example, typically reward bullying with increased attention and friendly overtures (Craig & Pepler, 1995; Craig, Pepler, & Atlas, 2000; Salmivalli, 1999). Universal programs try to harness the power of educators, parents, and the peer group in order to effect constructive changes that benefit all. Positive changes in individuals are sustained when they occur in concert with supportive changes in the relationships they have with others. Thus, many researchers recommend systemic anti-bullying programs that target multiple levels and social mechanisms (e.g., Olweus, 1993; Pepler, Craig, & O'Connell, 1999; Swearer & Espelage, 2004).

This chapter describes the conceptual foundations and specific practices of the *Steps to Respect* program (Committee for Children, 2001) and summarizes evidence of effectiveness. We examine teacher implementation efforts, arguing that adult failure to exercise leadership and protect student well-being jeopardizes adult credibility and opportunities to mentor students.

Conceptual Foundations of the Steps to Respect Program

Frey and Nolen (in press) have outlined a transactional model of school-based prevention that describes processes that encourage systemic change or stasis. In successful interventions, social transactions reflect changes in social norms that have occurred throughout the school community and stimulate additional changes (such as improved social skills) within individuals. *Steps to Respect* is a multi-level program designed to interrupt vicious cycles (e.g., bullying- rewards from bystanders; bullying-revenge) that maintain aggression. The program coordinates a school-wide environmental intervention (Olweus, 1993), a cognitive-behavioral class curriculum (Kendall, 1993), and a selective intervention for those involved in bullying (Skiba et al., 2006).

A School-Wide Environmental Intervention

The purpose of the school-wide intervention is to lay the groundwork for an adult-student partnership and promote a civil, learning-conducive climate. Adults cannot deter bullying if young people do not entrust them with information about peer abuse. Conversely, such information will not be forthcoming unless adults demonstrate they are receptive (Unnever & Cornell, 2004). Consequently, administrators who introduce *Steps to Respect* at their school need to improve school infrastructure and staff capabilities prior to implementing lessons that encourage students to report bullying. The school-wide intervention also attempts to reduce the reinforcement students receive for bullying and increase systemic supports for prosocial alternatives. If adults can demonstrate effective leadership and supervision, students may be more likely to respond to adult guidance.

School Infrastructure   Teacher implementation is improved when it is accompanied by clearly defined roles and procedures, adequate training (Payne, Gottfredson, & Gottfredson, 2006), and a collegial peer network (Kallestad & Olweus, 2003). Group creation of policies and procedures promotes shared understanding of (a) school norms, (b) the consequences and sequence of events associated with violations of those norms, and (c) adult responsibilities. To accomplish program goals, administrators must lead the school in (a) planning and managing operational aspects of the programs; (b) inspiring and mentoring high quality classroom implementation; (c) documenting evidence of positive change; and (d) fostering cohesive and respectful peer relationships between staff members (Frey & Nolen, in press).

Staff Capabilities   Adults provide leadership to students by encouraging positive behaviors, redirecting negative ones, and providing models of empathic, effective, and responsible behavior. Many teachers report they are unprepared to deal with bullying problems (Boulton, 1997). They may underestimate the prevalence or potentially deleterious consequences (Hazler, Miller, Carney, & Green, 2001). Educators are not immune to ecological influences. Experiences with bully-conducive environments, for example, may predispose them to view annoying children as "deserving" of bullying. Such attitudes, coupled with inaction, may lead students to believe their teachers do not care about them (Astor, Meyer, & Behre, 1999). Perceptions that teachers care and that school is safe predict close teacher-student relationships, higher achievement, and fewer discipline problems (Crosnoe, Johnson, & Elder, 2004; Hamre & Pianta, 2001).

A Classroom Curriculum to Address Social Norms and Social-Emotional Skills

Classroom norm-building and instruction in responsible, effective social-emotional skills are crucial parts of an ecological and transactional approach to forging positive adult-student alliances. Students appear to view their teachers as better leaders (e.g., knowledgeable and effective) when their teachers actively promote respectful behavior and foster skills to avoid involvement in bullying (Frey, Hirschstein, Edstrom, & Snell, 2009). Equally crucial is the increased capability of students to handle their own problems or lead positive peer responses to bullying (Craig & Pepler, 1995). Programs attempt to improve behavior and the social-emotional skills believed to underlie behavior (Crick & Dodge, 1994; Huesmann, 1988; Kendall, 1993).

Goals and Beliefs Goals and beliefs are frequent targets of intervention due to their relative stability (Burks, Dodge, Price, & Laird, 1999) and power to motivate action. The unprovoked aggression typical of bullying occurs more frequently among youths that have dominance goals (Ojanen, Grönoos, & Salmivalli, 2005). They use fewer competent and more coercive strategies to resolve social conflicts than youths with egalitarian or prosocial goals (Frey, Nolen, Edstrom, & Hirschstein, 2005). Bullying is likely to increase when children believe it will bring rewards (Egan, Monson, & Perry, 1998), such as friendly overtures from bystanders (Craig & Pepler, 1995). More frequent intervention by educators combined with peer disapproval of aggression appears to be effective in changing norms about the acceptability of aggression (Henry et al., 2000).

Decision-Making Processes Children need to be effective decision makers in order to cope with bullying. During interactions, individuals construct specific goals, imagine possible actions, and evaluate the probability of success (Crick & Dodge, 1994). Decision making is itself shaped by beliefs about oneself and others. For example, practicing assertive responses to bullying may increase perceived competence and reduce reliance on aggressive retaliation (Egan & Perry, 1998).

Self-Regulation of Emotion and Behavior Bullying reduces the self-regulatory capacities of perpetrators and victims (see review by Vohs & Ciarocco, 2004). Witnessing bullying can also elicit strong emotions that interfere with competent decision making. Children who have difficulty regulating their emotions tend to respond in ways (e.g., visible fear, crying, ineffectual retaliation) that satisfy bullies' dominance goals and increase the risk of future victimization (Egan & Perry, 1998). Increased self-regulation on the part of victims may have a transactional effect if perceptions of these children as "easy marks" erode.

Individual Coaching for Children Involved in Bullying

Young people who are chronically victimized comprise a relatively small percentage (16.3%) of the student body (Nansel et al., 2001). Those who report bullying others frequently (15%) are also a small group (Espelage et al., 2000). Selected interventions (Skiba et al., 2006) provide timely assistance for those at-risk for future bullying and related adjustment problems.

Description of Steps to Respect School-Wide Environmental Intervention

Planning and Implementation   Manuals and training sessions for the Steps to Respect program help build an infrastructure that provides protection and ways for students to avoid future problems. This includes creation of an anti-bullying policy, disciplinary code, and reporting procedures; identification of campus areas requiring greater supervision; and assignment of adult roles. A two-day facilitator training guides strategic planning during the early phase of program adoption. Two training videos; safety guidelines for bus, lunchroom, and playground; and a lesson for children in kindergarten through grade 2 are included.

Training to Increase Adult Awareness and Effectiveness   Training and motivating supervisory adults to notice and intervene effectively are key program goals. The training manual provides written and video-based materials for a core instructional session for all school staff and two in-depth training sessions for teachers, administrators, psychologists and counselors. Part 1 provides a program overview, descriptions of direct and indirect bullying behaviors, and information that counters common myths (e.g., bullying is usually perpetrated by easily identified "problem" students). In part 2, educators practice strategies for responding to bullying reports and coaching students who are involved in bullying. Part 3 provides an orientation to the classroom curriculum. The administrator guide recommends school-wide procedures for increasing adult recognition of responsible social behavior. Materials for four "booster" staff trainings and parent-information nights are also included. Following training, teachers feel more prepared to deal with bullying than those in a control group (Hirschstein & Frey, 2006).

The Classroom Curricula

The classroom curricula focus primarily on the last 3 years of elementary school, a time when bullying and acceptance of bullying is on the rise (Frey & Nolen, in press; Hanish & Guerra, 2004; Swearer & Cary, 2003). Norms about aggression begin to stabilize in fourth grade, making subsequent change more challenging to effect (Huesmann & Guerra, 1997). The curricula are comprised of skill and literature lessons, developmentally sequenced into three grade levels. Videotapes, stories, and experiential activities serve as springboards for direct instruction, discussions, writing assignments, skill modeling and rehearsal—practices that support acquisition and generalization of skills and normative beliefs (Huesmann & Guerra, 1997).

Specific skills (e.g., recognition, refusal, and reporting of bullying behavior) are taught in the context of being part of the solution, versus part of the problem. Lessons provide examples of bystanders who display positive peer leadership or private support for bullied children. Following the 10 skill lessons is a literature unit based on children's novels (e.g., *The Well*, by Margaret Taylor). These lessons integrate social-emotional learning objectives (e.g., empathy) with language arts content, providing further opportunities to discuss issues related to healthy, egalitarian relationships. Letters to parents outline key concepts and home activities that reinforce skill acquisition.

Beliefs and Goals   *Steps to Respect* defines bullying as intentionally harmful behavior perpetrated by those who wield greater power (e.g., due to size, strength, social status, or weaponry). Teaching both students and teachers to distinguish tattling (trying to get people in trouble) from reporting (trying to keep people safe) is a key program element. Lessons encourage empathy and the pursuit of socially responsible goals. The program challenges the belief that bullying can be ethically justified (Gianluca, 2006; Rigby, 2005; Terasahjo & Salmivalli, 2003). Commitment to program goals may be heightened when children pledge to resist bullying, which links one morally relevant action to another: keeping one's promise (Panigua, 1992). Shifting social norms, combined with improved supervision, may encourage antisocial leaders (Rodkin, Farmer, Pearl, & Van Acker, 2006; Vaillancourt, Hymel, & McDougall, 2003) to reassess the rewards associated with bullying. Prosocial leaders may also increase their defense of those targeted for bullying as social responsibility norms and bystander options are discussed.

Decision-Making Processes   Victims of bullying are sometimes at risk of immediate harm. Lessons attempt to help children assess safety risks, identify responses they can use themselves, or seek assistance. Additional social problem-solving strategies are taught as a way to enhance friendship skills, as children with friends who support them encounter less bullying (Hodges & Perry, 1999; Kochenderfer & Ladd, 1997). Perspective-taking exercises encourage social inclusion within the peer system, increasing the likelihood that new friendship skills might be successful.

Self-Regulation of Emotion and Behavior   *Steps to Respect* teaches self-calming techniques and simple social scripts for responding assertively (e.g., calm, polite, and strong), a skill that discourages bullying (Espelage, Bosworth, & Simon, 2001) and provides a deterrent to victimization (Camodeca, 2005; Schwartz, Dodge, & Coie, 1993). Improving assertive and emotion regulation skills may also enable bystanders to manage emotional distress and channel their concern into socially responsible leadership (Eisenberg et al., 1996).

Those who bully vary in their level of social skill and self-regulatory capacity. Children who anger easily and lash out in a dysregulated fashion may become perpetrators and victims of aggression (Olweus, 1993; Toblin, Schwartz, Gorman, & Abou-ezzeddine, 2005). Thus, self-calming techniques may also reduce levels of bullying and retaliatory aggression.

Generalization Efforts   Because generalization is the ultimate goal of prevention, the program offers numerous activities and suggestions to generalize skills and beliefs to real life. Teachers are encouraged to model program skills, for example, by using audible self-talk when they become angry. Teachable moments offer opportunities for prompts, rehearsal, and feedback in the context of classroom social dynamics. Lessons provide extension activities that integrate social-emotional with academic content.

Coaching Selected Students

Steps to Respect prescribes brief individual coaching sessions with each participant in bullying episodes. These are intended to provide solution-oriented responses to immediate and long-term student needs. The coaching protocols (one for perpetrators, one for targets of bullying) provide strategies to establish facts, empower students to avoid future problems, and assess effectiveness. While not ignoring the need for sanctions, coaching sessions focus on empathy, problem-solving, and assertiveness skills. Educators help children practice social skills. They discuss school norms and collective responsibility for school safety. Some set up procedures to help children identify their own problem behaviors, and write a note to parents that describes a behavior-change plan. Besides setting up clear expectations, the note keeps the focus on behavior, rather than a pejorative label (see Frey, Edstrom, & Hirschstein, 2005, for more details).

Evaluation Research

Perhaps the most rigorous test of a program occurs in relatively unsupervised areas such as playgrounds. We had coders who were blind to condition make second-by-second observations of playground behavior in schools that had been randomly assigned to Steps to Respect or a control condition. We measured student attitudes and social skills with student surveys and teacher ratings (n = 1127). In keeping with the emphasis on adult roles in maintaining or changing the school's ecology, we also measured teachers' beliefs and classroom practices. Finally, we examined whether teacher coaching predicted later student beliefs and playground behavior.

Group Differences in Student Behavior after 6 Months   For 10 weeks in the fall and spring, coders observed playground behaviors of 544 students on at least 10 occasions (Frey, Hirschstein, et al., 2005). Multilevel analyses that controlled for the shared classroom environment examined changes from fall to spring (6-month posttest). Consistent with previous research showing elevated levels of playground aggression in the springtime (Grossman et al., 1997), bullying increased over the 6 months. A dramatic increase occurred in control schools (63.0%) as more students became involved as bullies. The corresponding increase in intervention schools was 14.1%. Overall, students were observed to bully another child about once an hour, but rates varied greatly between individuals. Group differences in bullying rates were largest among the students who had bullied in the fall. Fall perpetrators in the intervention group showed statistically significant declines in bullying rates (43.8%) compared to declines of 16.9% in the control group. Group differences in non-bullying aggression were not significant at the 6-month posttest, but argumentative behavior declined relative to the control group.

Behavior after 18 Months   Children in grades 3 and 4 were followed over 2 school years (*n* = 225). Students in both grades received Level 1 of the classroom curricula in the first year, and Level 2 in grades 4 and 5. Multilevel analyses showed substantial 18-month declines in antisocial playground behaviors. Bullying/victimization declined 34.5% and destructive bystander behaviors declined 78.0% (see Figure 28.1). Non-bullying aggression and argumentative behavior declined by 36.4% and 32.3%, respectively (Frey, Edstrom, et al., 2009). Depending on the individual, the program appeared to both reduce problem behaviors and prevent escalation. After 18 months of intervention, the problem behaviors of those involved in bullying events at pretest no longer differed from the level of non-involved peers. Non-involved peers showed no increase over time. In contrast, control-group students (*n* = 399) showed grade-related increases in problem behaviors (Frey, Hirschstein, et al., 2005).

Beliefs   Students were less accepting of bullying and aggression if they were in the intervention group, due to deterioration in the attitudes of control-group students across the school year (Frey, Hirschstein, et al., 2005). Fifth- and sixth-grade students, but not third- and fourth-grade students, responded to the intervention with increased confidence in their ability to respond assertively to bullying. However, student reports of aggression and victimization, and teacher reports of peer interaction skills, showed no significant group differences.

Teacher Attitudes and Behavior   Following staff training, intervention teachers reported feeling more prepared to deal with bullying than did control teachers. There were no group differences in teachers' beliefs that bullying is an important school problem (Hirschstein & Frey, 2006).

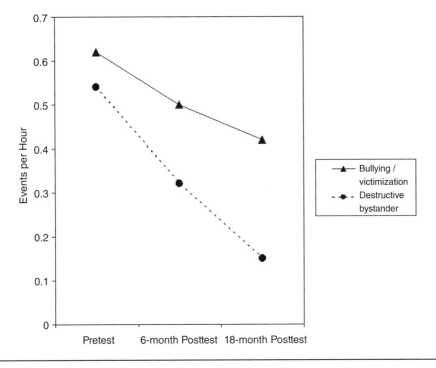

Figure 28.1 Playground behaviors at pretest and at 6- and 18-months after intervention (Adapted from Frey, Edstrom, et al., 2005).

Generalization Efforts and Coaching Teacher reports of their use of teachable moments to scaffold student behavior show moderate-to-strong correlations with observations of teacher behavior (Hirschstein, Van Schoiack Edstrom, Frey, & Nolen, 2001). Previous work suggests that teacher scaffolding of social-emotional skills may be differentially effective in intervention and control classrooms (Van Schoiack, 2000), perhaps because in-the-moment prompts that are not accompanied by formal instruction lack shared social norms and practice in pertinent skills.

Analyses undertaken within intervention classrooms indicate that in-the-moment prompts to use bullying coping skills predicted subsequent declines in playground aggression in fifth- and sixth-grade classrooms (Hirschstein, Edstrom, Frey, Snell, & MacKenzie, 2007). Springtime aggression was also lower in the higher grades if teachers coached students more frequently. Teacher efforts at coaching appeared especially important for children involved at pretest as victims and destructive bystanders. Victims were less likely to be targets of bullying during the spring (6-month posttest) with more frequent coaching (see Figure 28.2). Likewise, children who had encouraged bullying became less frequently involved as bystanders (Hirschstein et al., 2007).

Limitations and Future Research

A contribution of the Steps to Respect evaluation is the use of observational methods to assess changes in bullying and victimization. Additional work with larger school samples is needed to test effects on school social ecologies. We know of no evaluation research that examines changes in the peer social structure, for example. One possible result of a successful intervention is a shift to less hierarchical and more democratic interactions.

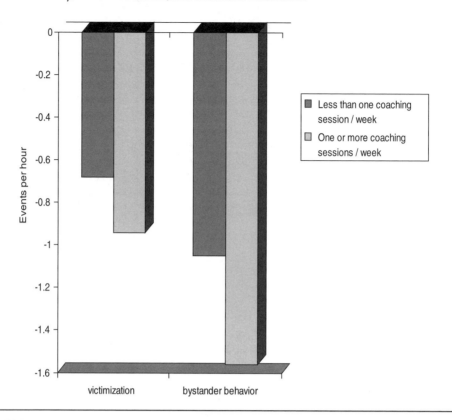

Figure 28.2 Weekly frequency of teacher coaching predicts fall-to-spring declines in victimization and destructive bystander behavior among children involved in those behaviors at pretest (adapted from Hirschstein et al., 2007).

There is also a need for longitudinal observations on the change process (Eddy, Dishion, & Stoolmiller, 1998). Even successful interventions may not proceed in a uniformly positive direction. The introduction of new ethical norms and environmental contingencies may stimulate push-back from students who stand to lose power (Frey & Nolen, in press). There may even be an exacerbation of tension between "early responders" and those determined to maintain their grip on power. Increasing our understanding of this process would greatly assist educators as they guide their students in a responsible, civil direction.

The dearth of research on implementation effects (Walker, 2004) is also a hindrance to establishing best practices. While our results argue for the importance of non-scripted program elements, experimental studies are needed to examine the larger classroom context. Such work could proceed, for example, by training randomly assigned teachers to (a) teach lessons, (b) coach individual students, or (c) teach and coach in the context of a school-wide program.

Such a study could also contribute to practice by examining teachers' decision making with respect to coaching. Educators underestimate the number of children who bully (Cornell & Brockenbrough, 2004). They may overlook students who appear well-behaved and socially powerful (Frey, 2005) compared to unskilled bully-victims, who react aggressively to provocations. Research (Leff, Kupersmidt, Patterson, & Power, 1999) and our own observations indicate that identification becomes more difficult with age and, presumably, skill of the child.

The greater responsiveness of older students to teacher coaching may simply reflect higher initial rates of aggression in fifth and sixth grades (Frey, Hirschstein, et al., 2005) or a greater focus on conflict resolution in the advanced program levels. Alternatively, more developmentally advanced students may be better able to enact skills they learn during coaching. Self-regulatory demands increase when individuals attempt unfamiliar social behaviors (Vohs, Baumeister, & Ciarocco, 2005), and younger children may require more practice. Finally, older students may simply be more sensitive to inconsistencies between teacher talk and action (Hirschstein et al., 2007). Teachers who make the effort to coach students provide a visible enactment of norms for caring and responsibility. Our data suggests that even small increases provide benefits that extend to bystanders, as well as victims and aggressors. Experimental designs can help ascertain the separate and joint influences of program content and developmental factors.

Another question for future research is the effect of low rates of adult intervention (Craig et al., 2000; Frey, Hirschstein, Snell, et al., 2005). We have previously suggested that apparent adult indifference to bullying may teach young people to tolerate coercive and abusive behavior (Frey & Hirschstein, 2008). Our playground observations showed that positive intervention on the part of peers or adults was extremely rare. Such consistency suggests powerful social norms that may interfere with the emergence of socially responsible leadership (Jeffrey et al., 2001).

What are the consequences of failures in adult leadership? Failure to provide specific guidance in the early school years may have unintended consequences later. Does adult enforcement of anti-tattling norms during elementary school help create the "code of silence" so disturbing to adults when weapons are brought to school? Failure of adults to provide protection may feed student perceptions that adults are incompetent (Hoover, Oliver, & Hazler, 1992) and uncaring (Astor et al., 1999). Do students in bully-conducive schools experience a crisis of confidence in adults? Our conversations with students indicate that they view bullying as an important issue. Are they less likely to trust and seek adult guidance if adults present themselves as irrelevant to young people's concerns? We need research that examines how adult leadership in the bullying arena might affect educators' ability to positively influence and mentor students.

Conclusions

Research has expanded our appreciation that bullying flourishes when social systems support it. Cross-national studies testify to the power of culture to influence bullying rates. Israel and the United States, for example, have high and moderately high rates of adolescent bullying relative to three Western European countries (Smith-Khuri et al., 2004). Because its frequency varies with culture, bullying may be more responsive to ecological interventions than adolescent problems that vary little across nations. We have argued that at some ages, experimentation with bullying is developmentally normal for American children. The United States may be unique in its attempt to deal with bullying through legal prohibitions. In the face of cultural supports for bullying, punitive frameworks are unlikely to foster the development of respectful means of influence.

In contrast, our work indicates that a multilevel intervention can yield substantial reductions in victimization, aggression, and argumentative and destructive bystander behavior. *Steps to Respect* combines a school-wide ecological intervention with overtly educational methods: classroom curricula and coaching of selected students.

Coaching provides a clear demonstration of teacher support for program norms. We believe that a disciplinary framework based on coaching offers three important advantages over well-intentioned zero tolerance policies (Frey, Edstrom, et al., 2005). First, it encourages reporting by demonstrating that adults are neither passive nor overly reactive in the face of bullying. Bystanders, and even victims, may subscribe to beliefs that bullying is inconsequential or deserved (Graham & Juvonen, 1998). Thus, expulsion may seem disproportionate and arouse student fears of a peer backlash, especially if the perpetrators have high status (Limber & Small, 2003).

Table 28.1 Implications for Practice: *Steps to Respect* Program Elements and Goals

Program Elements	Program Goals
Adult Leadership	Bolster adults' credibility as knowledgeable, caring, effective
	Foster ability to guide students, particularly in ethical matters
School-Wide Elements	Communicate policy and create supportive procedures
	Prepare adults to form student-adult partnerships
	Provide a practical demonstration of adult leadership
Classroom Curricula	Encourage personal link to norms via discussions and pledges
	Provide guidelines for bystander and victim responses to bullying
	Provide instruction, prompting, and practice in social-emotional skills
	Open teacher-student dialogue
Selected Intervention	Provide measured, consistent adult responses to bullying events
	Encourage student reporting
	Provide instruction and support to forestall future problems
	Enact norms of civility, justice, and respect

Second, the coaching model provides consistent, economical, and timely intervention. Inconsistencies in application of zero tolerance policies (Skiba et al., 2006) may be due in part to the number of young people involved in bullying—too many to be suspended. There is also the need to establish guilt beyond a reasonable doubt. Even with a considerable investment of time, the requisite proof may not be forthcoming, leaving adults in a relatively powerless position. Youngsters may develop entrenched bullying habits before clear evidence is available.

Third, coaching models provide important educational opportunities. Non-stigmatizing adult guidance exemplifies the values of anti-bullying programs. Students are expected to generate positive responses to bullying behavior, whether they are on the giving or receiving end. Students seem eager to understand and acquire a sense of power in their lives. Educators can help students learn requisite skills and communicate high standards of civility and responsibility. In sum, a coaching model provided in the context of a multilevel intervention enables adults to provide effective leadership, while scaffolding positive student development.

References

Andershed, H., Kerr, M., & Stattin, H. (2001). Bullying in school and violence on the streets: Are the same people involved? *Journal of Scandinavian Studies in Criminology and Crime Prevention, 2*, 31–49.

Astor, R. A., Meyer, H. A., & Behre, W. J. (1999). Unowned places and times: Maps and interviews about violence in high schools. *American Educational Research Journal, 36*, 3–42.

Boulton, M. J. (1997). Teachers' views on bullying: Definitions, attitudes, and ability to cope. *British Journal of Educational Psychology, 67*, 223–233.

Burks, V. S., Dodge, K. A., Price, J. M., & Laird, R. D. (1999). Internal representational models of peers: Implications for the development of problem behavior. *Developmental Psychology, 35*, 802–810.

Camodeca, M. (2005). Children's opinions on effective strategies to cope with bullying: The importance of bullying role and perspective. *Educational Research, 47*, 93–105.

Committee for Children. (2001). *Steps to Respect*: A bullying prevention program. Seattle, WA: Author.

Connolly, J., Pepler, D. J., Craig, W. M., & Taradash, A. (2000). Dating experiences of bullies in early adolescence. *Child Maltreatment: Journal of the American Professional Society on the Abuse of Children, 5*, 299–310.

Cornell, D. G., & Brockenbrough, K. (2004). Identification of bullies and victims: A comparison of methods. *Journal of School Violence, 3*, 63–87.

Craig, W. M., & Pepler, D. J. (1995). Peer processes in bullying and victimization in the schoolyard. *Exceptionality Education Canada, 5*, 81–95.

Craig, W. M., Pepler, D., & Atlas, R. (2000). Observations of bullying in the playground and the classroom. *School Psychology International, 21*, 22–36.

Crick, N. R., & Dodge, K. A. (1994). A review and reformulation of social information-processing mechanisms in children's social adjustment. *Psychological Bulletin, 115*, 74–101.

Crosnoe, R., Johnson, M., & Elder, G. (2004). Intergenerational bonding in school: Behavioral and contextual correlates of student-teacher relationships. *Sociology of Education, 77*, 60–81.

Duncan, R. D. (1999). Peer and sibling aggression: An investigation of intra- and extra-familial bullying. *Journal of Interpersonal Violence, 14*, 871–886.

Eddy, J. M., Dishion, T. J., & Stoolmiller, M. (1998). The analysis of intervention change in children and families: Methodological and conceptual issues embedded in intervention studies. *Journal of Abnormal Child Psychology, 26*, 53–69.

Egan, S. K., Monson, T. C., & Perry, D. G. (1998). Social-cognitive influences on change in aggression over time. *Developmental Psychology, 34*, 996–1006.

Egan, S. K. & Perry, D. G. (1998). Does low self-regard invite victimization? *Developmental Psychology, 34*, 299–309.

Eisenberg, N., Fabes, R. A., Karbon, M., Murphy, B. C., Carlo, G., & Wosinski, M. (1996). Relations of school children's comforting behavior to empathy-related reactions and shyness. *Social Development, 5*, 330–351.

Espelage, D. L., Bosworth, K., & Simon, T. R. (2000). Bullying and victimization during early adolescence: Peer influences and psychosocial correlates. *Journal of Counseling and Development, 78*, 326–332.

Espelage, D. L., Bosworth, K., & Simon, T. R. (2001). Short-term stability and prospective correlates of bullying in middle-school students: An examination of potential demographic, psychosocial, and environmental influences. *Violence and Victims, 16*, 411–426.

Frey, K. S. (2005). Gathering and communicating information about school bullying: Overcoming 'Secrets and Lies.' *Health Education, 105*, 409–414.

Frey, K. S., Edstrom, L. V., & Hirschstein, M. K. (2005). The *Steps to Respect* program uses a multilevel approach to reduce playground bullying and destructive bystander behaviors. In D. L. White, M. K. Faber, & B. C. Glenn (Eds.), *Persistently safe schools 2005* (pp. 47–56). Washington, DC: Hamilton Fish Institute, George Washington University.

Frey, K. S., & Hirschstein M. K. (2008). Preventing school bullying and confronting moral issues in the lives of young people. In M. J. Adams-Heggins, L. W. Rodney & C. J. Kowalski (Eds.), *Violence prevention: Diverse approaches to family and community* (pp. 266–279). Boston: McGraw-Hill.

Frey, K. S., Hirschstein, M. K., Edstrom, L. V. & Snell, J. L. (2009). Observed reductions in bullying, victimization and bystander encouragement: Longitudinal evaluation of a school-based intervention. *Journal of Educational Psychology, 101*, 466–481.

Frey, K. F., Hirschstein, M. K., Snell, J. L., Van Schoiack-Edstrom, L., MacKenzie, E. P., & Bruschi, C. J. (2005). Reducing playground bullying and supporting beliefs: An experimental trial of the *Steps to Respect* program. *Developmental Psychology, 41*, 479–491.

Frey, K. F., & Nolen, S. B. (in press). Taking "Steps" toward ecological change: A transactional model of school-wide social competence and bullying intervention. In J. Meece & J. Eccles (Eds.), *Schooling effects on children: Theory, methods, & applications*. Mahwah, NJ: Erlbaum.

Frey, K. S., Nolen, S. B., Edstrom, L. V., & Hirschstein, M. K. (2005). Effects of a school-based social-emotional competence program: Linking children's goals, attributions, and behavior. *Journal of Applied Developmental Psychology, 26*, 171–200.

Gianluca, G. (2006). Social cognition and moral cognition in bullying: What's wrong? *Aggressive Behavior, 32*, 528–539.

Graham, S., & Juvonen, J. (1998). Self-blame and peer victimization in middle school: An attributional analysis. *Developmental Psychology, 32*, 707–716.

Grossman, D. C., Neckerman, H. J., Koepsell, T. D., Liu, P. Y., Asher, K. N., Beland, K., et al. (1997). Effectiveness of a violence prevention program among children in elementary schools: A randomized controlled trial. *Journal of the American Medical Association, 277*, 1605–1611.

Hamre, B. K., & Pianta, R. C. (2001). Early teacher-child relationships and the trajectory of children's school outcomes through eighth grade. *Child Development, 72*, 625–638.

Hanish, L. D., & Guerra, N. G. (2004). Aggressive victims, passive victims, and bullies: Developmental continuity or developmental change? *Merrill-Palmer Quarterly, 50*, 17–38.

Harvey, M. G., Heames, J. T., Richey, R. G., & Leonard, N. (2006). Bullying: From the playground to the boardroom. *Journal of Leadership and Organizational Studies, 12*(4), 1–11.

Hazler, R., Miller, D., Carney, J., & Green, S. (2001). Adult recognition of school bullying situations. *Educational Research, 43*, 133–146.

Henry, D., Guerra, N. G., Huesmann, L. R., Tolan, P., VanAcker, R., & Eron, L. D. (2000). Normative influences on aggression in urban elementary school classrooms. *American Journal of Community Psychology, 28*, 59–81.

Hirschstein, M. K., Edstrom, L. V., Frey, K. S., Snell, J. L., & MacKenzie, E. P. (2007). Walking the talk in bullying prevention: Teacher implementation variables related to initial impact of the *Steps to Respect* program. *School Psychology Review, 36*, 3–21.

Hirschstein, M. K., & Frey, K. S. (2006). Promoting behavior and beliefs that reduce bullying: The *Steps to respect* program. In S. R. Jimerson & M. J. Furlong (Eds.), *The handbook of school violence and school safety: From research to practice* (pp. 309–324). Mahwah: Erlbaum.

Hirschstein, M. K., Van Schoiack Edstrom, L., Frey, K., & Nolen, S. B. (2001). The Social-Emotional Learning Checklist (SEL-C): Technical report. Committee for Children, Seattle, WA.

Hodges, E. V. E., & Perry, D. G. (1999). Personal and interpersonal antecedents and consequences of victimization by peers. *Journal of Personality and Social Psychology, 76*, 677–685.

Hoover, J. H., Oliver, R., & Hazler, R. J. (1992). Bullying: Perceptions of adolescent victims in the Midwestern USA. *School Psychology International, 13*, 5–16.

Huesmann, L. R. (1988). An information processing model for the development of aggression. *Aggressive Behavior, 14*, 13–24.

Huesmann, L. R., & Guerra, N. G. (1997). Children's normative beliefs about aggression and aggressive behavior. *Journal of Personality & Social Psychology, 72*, 408–419.

Jeffrey, L. R., Miller, D., & Linn, M. (2001). Middle school and bullying as a context for the development of passive observers for the victimization of others. In R. A. Geffner, M. Loring, & C. Young (Eds.), *Bullying behavior: Current issues, research, and interventions* (pp. 143–156). Binghamton, NY: The Haworth Maltreatment and Trauma Press.

Kallestad, J. H., & Olweus, D. (2003). Predicting teachers' and schools' implementation of the Olweus Bullying Prevention Program: A multilevel study. *Prevention and Treatment, 6*, Article 21. Retrieved March 4, 2004, from http://journals.apa.org/prevention/volume 6

Kendall, P. C. (1993). Cognitive-behavioral therapies with youth: Guiding theory, current status, and emerging developments. *Journal of Counseling and Clinical Psychology, 61*, 235–247.

Kochenderfer, B. J., & Ladd, G. W. (1997). Victimized children's responses to peers' aggression: Behaviors associated with reduced versus continued victimization. *Development & Psychopathology, 9*, 59–73.

Leff, S. S., Kupersmidt, J. B., Patterson, C. J., & Power, T. J. (1999). Factors influencing teacher identification of peer bullies and victims. *School Psychology Review, 28*, 505–517.

Limber, S. P., & Small, M. A. (2003). State laws and policies to address bullying in schools. *School Psychology Review, 32*, 445–455.

Nansel, T. R., Overpeck, M., Pilla, R. S., Ruan, W. J., Simons-Morton, B., & Scheidt, P. (2001). Bullying behaviors among US youth: Prevalence and association with psychosocial adjustment. *Journal of the American Medical Association, 285*, 2094–2100.

O'Connell, P., Pepler, D., & Craig, W. (1999). Peer involvement in bullying: insights and challenges for intervention. *Journal of Adolescence, 22*, 437 – 452.

Ojanen, T., Grönoos, M., & Salmivalli, C. (2005). An interpersonal circumplex model of children's social goals: Links with peer-reported behavior and sociometric status. *Developmental Psychology, 41*, 699–710.

Olweus, D. (1993). *Bullying at school: What we know and what we can do*. Cambridge, MA: Blackwell.

Panigua, F. A. (1992). Verbal-nonverbal correspondence training with ADHD children. *Behavior Modification, 16*, 226–252.

Payne, A. A., Gottfredson, D. C., & Gottfredson, G. D. (2006). School predictors of the intensity of implementation of school-based prevention programs: Results from a national study. *Prevention Science, 7*, 225–237.

Pepler, D. L., Craig, W. M., & O'Connell, P. (1999). Understanding bullying from a dynamic systems perspective. In A. Slater and D. Muir (Eds.), *The Blackwell reader in developmental psychology* (pp. 440–451). Malden, MA: Blackwell.

Rigby, K. (2005). Why do some children bully at school? The contributions of negative attitudes towards victims, and the perceived expectations of friends, parents, and teachers. *School Psychology International, 26*, 147–161.

Rodkin, P. C., Farmer, T. W., Pearl, R., & Van Acker, R. (2006). They're cool: Social status and peer group support for aggressive boys and girls. *Social Development, 15*, 175–204.

Salmivalli, C. (1999). Participant role approach to school bullying: Implications for intervention. *Journal of Adolescence, 22*, 453–459.

Schwartz, D., Dodge, K. A., & Coie, J. D. (1993). The emergence of chronic peer victimization in boys' play groups. *Child Development, 64*, 580–588.

Skiba, R., Reynolds, C. R., Graham, S., Sheras, P., Conoley, J. C., Garcia-Vazquez, E. (2006). Are zero tolerance policies effective in the schools? An evidentiary review and recommendations. Retrieved June 19, 2007, from http://www.apa.org/ed/cpse/zttreport.pfd

Slee, P. T. (1994). Situational and interpersonal correlates of anxiety associated with peer victimization. *Child Psychiatry and Human Development, 25*, 97–107.

Smith-Khuri, E., Iachan, R., Scheidt, P. C., Overpeck, M. D., Gabhainn, S. N., Pickett, W., et al. (2004). A cross-national study of violence-related behaviors in adolescents. *Archives of Pediatric and Adolescent Medicine, 158,* 539–544.

Stein, N. (2003). Bullying or sexual harassment? The missing discourse of rights in an era of zero tolerance. *Arizona Law Review, 453,* 783–799.

Swearer, S. M., & Cary, P. T. (2003). Perceptions and attitudes toward bullying in middle school youth: A developmental examination across the bully/victim continuum. In M. J. Elias & J. E. Zins (Eds.), *Bullying, peer harassment, and victimization in the schools: The next generation of prevention* (pp. 63–80). New York: Haworth.

Swearer, S. M., & Espelage, D. L. (2004). A social-ecological framework of bullying among youth. In D. L. Espelage & S. M. Swearer (Eds.), *Bullying in American schools: A social ecological perspective on prevention and intervention* (pp. 1–12). Mahwah, NJ: Erlbaum.

Terasahjo, T., & Salmivalli, C. (2003). "She is not actually bullied." The discourse of harassment in student groups. *Aggressive Behavior, 29,* 134–154.

Toblin, R. L., Schwartz, D., Gorman, A. H., & Abou-ezzeddine, T. (2005). Social-cognitive and behavioral attributes of aggressive victims of bullying. *Journal of Applied Developmental Psychology, 26,* 329–346.

Unnever, J. D., & Cornell, D. G. (2004). Middle school victims of bullying: Who reports being bullied? *Aggressive Behavior, 30,* 373–388.

Vaillancourt, T., Hymel, S., & McDougall, P. (2003). Bullying is power: Implications for school-based intervention strategies. In M. J. Elias & J. Zins (Eds.), *Bullying, peer harassment, and victimization in schools: The next generation of prevention* (pp. 157–177). New York: Haworth.

Van Schoiack, L. (2000). Promoting social-emotional competence: Effects of a social-emotional learning program and corresponding teaching practices in the schools (Doctoral dissertation, University of Washington, 2000). *Dissertation Abstracts International, 61,* 2689.

Vohs, K. D., Baumeister, R. F., & Ciarocco, N. J. (2005). Self-regulation and self-presentation: Regulatory resource depletion impairs impression management and effortful self-presentation depletes regulatory resources. *Journal of Personality and Social Psychology, 88,* 632–657.

Vohs, K., & Ciarocco, N. J. (2004). Interpersonal functioning requires self-regulation. In R. F. Baumeister & K. Vohs (Eds.), *Handbook of self-regulation* (pp. 392–410). New York: Guilford.

Walker, H. M. (2004). Commentary: Use of evidence-based intervention in schools: Where we've been, where we are, and where we need to go. *School Psychology Review, 33,* 398–407.

29

Cultural Variations in Characteristics of Effective Bullying Programs

RICHARD J. HAZLER AND JOLYNN V. CARNEY

People have abused their power over others throughout recorded history. Being physically, socially, emotionally, intellectually, or verbally more gifted than another can be used supportively or abused at the expense of others. Bullying has been one term used to conceptualize the abuse of power in ways that harm a weaker individual. Historically the term has been applied to youth, although it has gained additional use describing interactions between adults, businesses, and nations. The past 20 years of research has demonstrated that it is an international problem in scope to which no cultures are immune (McEachern, Kenny, Blake, Aluede, 2005). Attempts to prevent bullying or lessen its effects have likewise developed around the world, but with differences reflecting cultural variations (Smith, Morita, Junger-Tas, Olweus, Catalano & Slee, 1999).

Bullying prevention efforts have commonalties that are necessary for creating and maintaining success (Hazler & Carney, 2006), but these common factors do not exist in isolation. Culture provides a set of common experiences that create a context for how people interpret their environment and consequently how they interact with it (Cartledge & Johnson, 2004). Bullying takes one form in an individualistic society for example, and appears somewhat different in a more group oriented society. The generalities, however, of the bullying definition, problems that evolve from it, and general model of dealing with the issues remain similar across cultures (Rigby, 2002). What do vary are culturally influenced bullying circumstances, perceptions of the problems, the context in which bullying occurs, decision making on how to respond, and response styles (Smith, Morita, Junger-Tas, Olweus, Catalano & Slee, 1999).

Bullying prevention programs and published materials have multiplied many times since 1990 while being virtually non-existent in prior years (Hazler, Hoover, & Oliver, 1991). This growth of prevention efforts gained energy from increasing public recognition that youth suicides, shootings on school campuses, and other social and emotional problems had a significant portion of their origin in bullying contexts. Community after community, and nation after nation increasingly recognized that bullying, once thought of as child's play, could no longer be tolerated (Hazler & Carney, 2000; Smith et al., 1999). Many programs that came into use in the 1990s focused on strategies of teaching interpersonal skills and involving students in prevention efforts. These models augmented the more traditional emphases on discipline enforcement alone and full school assemblies that had been the primary tactics in the past (Scheckner & Rollin, 2003; Tolan & Guerra, 1994).

This chapter is designed to demonstrate how the general characteristics of bullying prevention programs need adaptations to be most effective within different cultures. This basic conceptual orientation section is followed by a set of broad internationally identified cultural differences (Hofstede & Hofstede, 2005) that offer a generalized way to examine cultural implications for bullying prevention programs. The final two sections offer examples of how these broad cultural differences can affect the design and implementation of basic bullying prevention program themes and implementation practices.

Conceptual Basis

Bullying has been confronted by local, state and national communities that have taken actions to set rules, regulations, and started prevention programs (Furlong, Morrison, & Greif, 2003). The evolution of bullying prevention in a given culture generally begins with an initial emphasis on developing rules, regulations, and even laws that target individuals or groups. Such programs are generally limited to involvement by select enforcement and support entities who work with bullies and victims to stop an abusive situation, prevent it from occurring again, and deal with the physical, mental, social, and emotional consequences for the individuals and groups involved. Actions generally include punishments, behavior change models, and social skill development for specific students without widespread involvement of others inside or outside the school system.

These first step initiatives were designed to deal with specific students were followed by universal bullying prevention programs that recognize the reality that virtually all youth are exposed to bullying as bystanders even if not as victims or bullies. Widespread exposure to bullying promotes a less-than-safe climate that impacts everyone, whether that exposure is as bully, victim, bystander, or some combinations of the three. Universal programs are the ones designed to produce the greatest amount of overall change for the most students. These programs have become the vast majority in use today and will therefore be given the focus of attention in this chapter.

The trend of starting from scratch within one's own culture has begun to alter as more programs have invested in quality evaluation efforts. Two programs have received particular attention in diverse countries with adaptations being made for translations and cultural variations. The Norway-based Olweus Bullying Prevention Program was one of the first comprehensive programs to be developed and has received the greatest use of any one program (Kallestad & Olweus, 2003; Olweus, 2005). It has received significant implementation in countries as diverse as Australia, Canada, Germany, Ireland, Japan, United Kingdom, and the United States (e.g., Limber, Nation, Tracy, Melton, & Flerx, 2004). The America-based Committee for Children has developed two programs that have also attracted attention from countries like Norway, Iceland, Japan, the Phillippines, Kurdistan, and Venezuela (Committee for Children, 1993, 2002; Grossman, Neckerman, Koepsell, & Liu, 1997; Samples & Aber, 1998). The two programs approach bullying in different ways, but each utilizes common theme and practice components that benefit from extensive theory and research.

International Cultural Differences

Any attempt at identifying all the cultural differences that influence programs around the world would require volumes of space not available here if it could be comprehensively done at all. Cultural differences clearly exist in areas of the world like Asia, Africa, Australia, Europe, North and South America. Moreover, additional wide variations exist within the different countries, communities, and subgroups that make up the larger culture. Geography, language, ethnic and religious affiliations, and families all produce cultural variations that have significant influence on what happens, how it is perceived, and how people react to those perceptions. The cultural variations are limitless so that any program seeking to help a given group of people must understand that group's worldview in order for the program to have culturally appropriate meaning.

This section highlights four broad areas of cultural differences that will influence the development, implementation, and evaluation of bullying prevention programs. Geert Hofstede (2001), and later with his son Gert Jan (Hofstede & Hofstede, 2005), have synthesized their own extensive international research in addition to that of others to demonstrate how the cultures of different nations effect organizations. Essential concepts from their work relate to how cultures affect organizations, schools, students, teachers, and why different approaches are needed for the cultural variations. Brief explanations of these differences are presented before demonstrating how they can influence the key themes, processes, and eventual outcomes of bullying prevention programs.

Readers are cautioned that the four broad cultural differences used here are not to be evaluated as one side of a continuum being better than the other. The caution is critical because reader views of which side of the continuum is more productive will vary depending on the reader's own cultural orientation. The continuums are important for those who want to successfully develop and implement such programs, since they must consciously put personal cultural preferences aside in favor of those from the culture in which the program is to be implemented. Programs are not culture neutral and must be adjusted in relation to specific cultural contexts.

Small versus Large Power Differences

The difference between those with formal power versus those without can be small or large depending on the culture. Where the difference in power is great, more authoritarian or dictatorial behaviors by governments, organizations, and individuals in power can be observed. People with formal power make decisions on their own and emotionally distance themselves from others seen as subordinates. Those out of power are highly dependent on the powerful and are likely to either go along with what they are told or fight against the system with little room for consultation and negotiation.

Cultures with smaller power differences allow more democratic behaviors and independence of actions by those with less formal power and influence. High and low power groups treat each other more as equals, which allows for greater variety of ideas and actions to surface. Those holding power in this situation must invest in the involvement of all groups to gain maximum success.

This power difference factor can be seen in schools and programming in numerous ways. Large power differences mean that decisions about if, when, where, and how bullying prevention programs will be implemented get determined by a few key people in power. Programs will be more leader-centered, because both leaders and followers are prepared to learn and behave in that way. Schools with less organizational power differences allow for greater active representation and involvement of all groups and individuals. There will be more negotiation and more variations in what people are allowed to do and to think.

Group Versus Individual Emphasis

A key issue in cultural variations is the degree to which individuals versus groups are seen as more or less important in how a system works. Individualistic societies have loose ties between individuals and everyone is expected to look out for oneself and secondly one's immediate family.

Independence and personal initiative are rewarded, creating a greater variety and extremes of outcomes both positive and negative. Group focused cultures place greater emphasis on integrating people into strong, cohesive groups. The value for individuals is that the group provides security and the value for the group benefits by getting unquestioning loyalty from members. More societies currently fit the group model better than the individual model although industrialized capitalistic Western societies tend to learn toward the individualistic side (Hofstede & Hofstede, 2005).

Bullying itself can be seen to take on different styles in these contexts. Individualistic cultures will tend to have more one-on-one bullying or one group versus another less powerful group. Expectations of help will emphasize the independence of individuals what they can do for themselves or others. Group oriented cultures have larger scale in-group versus out-group orientations and bullying is more likely to emphasize ostracism from the larger group and forms of abuse emphasizing how the individual does not fit. Supportive solutions in group-oriented cultures are more focused on how the group should behave toward the individual and how that person can better fit into the group.

Prevention programming in schools will be influenced by individualistic cultures expecting impartial treatment regardless of background, while group cultures may expect special treatment for the majority group. Individualistic cultures will focus learning on approaching new challenges and change, while the safety function of group cultures will give more emphasis on consistency of information and how to become a good group member. Gaining harmony through commonalties will be a key for group cultures whereas emphasizing the value of individual differences will have more power in individualistic cultures.

Masculine versus Feminine Approach

This factor is not males versus females, because the terms are not about sex or gender, but instead about sets of thinking and behaving. The terms "masculine" and "feminine" are used here to denote those perceptions and behaviors that have been more traditionally associated with either males or females. Some cultures emphasize these perceptions and behaviors as clearly being aligned with males and females. Other cultures attend to the differences, but presume people should have more or less components of both.

Degree of modesty is one concept that could come close to identifying many differences between masculine and feminine approaches. Whereas a feminine approach emphasizes self-modesty and caring for others, a more masculine approach highlights gaining personal success and making progress. Sympathy in the feminine model expresses the most concern for the weak, who may have never had strength and power, while the masculine model tends to first provide sympathy for the strong who are struggling. Expressing solidarity with others is common on the feminine end in comparison to making oneself visible and competitive on the masculine end.

Bullying programs generally emphasize gaining empathy as an important component and professionals need to take into consideration who it is that different cultures might see as needing such concern and how much concern those people should receive. Assumptions of who needs help, how much help is needed, and what type of help might be appropriate can vary greatly depending on whether one takes a help the weak first feminine approach or emphasizes a personal success first masculine model.

Uncertainty Avoidance versus Ambiguity Acceptance

Some cultures accept ambiguity as a normal or even exciting aspect of life. They view their experiences as open-ended and exciting because of potential unknown opportunities that may come their way. Others have strong needs to eliminate as much uncertainty as possible so that they can concentrate on specific life tasks with less concern about what is to happen. These cultural orientations also desire progress and advancement, but in a more controlled model that will help them plan and follow through in an orderly fashion.

Cultures with more ambiguity acceptance tend to limit the number of rules and allow for more variations in behavior. Higher uncertainty avoidance cultures have a greater emotional need for rules, even when the rules may not work. Just the fact that there are rules to follow, gives a sense of controlling ambiguity in day-to-day living. Thoughts and ideas follow in a similar pattern where more ambiguity acceptance tends to create more tolerance for new or different ideas. These same new or different ideas tend to be suppressed as deviant and therefore resisted when a culture emphasizes greater uncertainty avoidance. Even the relationship of relaxation to work is impacted by these differences. Cultures with high levels of uncertainty avoidance tend to have members who are more punctual with an inner urge to work hard and keep busy. People in cultures who are more comfortable with ambiguity, on the other hand, can enjoy a sense of feeling lazy and see punctuality as something that may or may not be necessary depending on the situation.

Expectations about participation in bullying prevention programs in schools will be particularly influenced by the level of uncertainty avoidance in a given culture. For example, expectations for how strict rules should be will initially vary, since cultures with lower levels of uncertainty avoidance will want comparatively lenient rules for children compared to the stricter and more rigid rules preferred by cultures with higher levels. Maximum acceptance and follow-through on those rules will be dependent upon how closely they match the general culture's orientation to ambiguity tolerance. The sense of pressure to get a program started with a clearly laid out plan of implementation will be more important to the high uncertainty intolerant while the more ambiguity tolerant culture will feel less pressure and more interest in exploring divergent ways of dealing with the problem.

Cultural Variations in Common Program Themes

There are three key questions that arise as awareness of bullying begins to grow in a community: (a) Do we have a bullying problem? (b) What is the nature of the problem and how bad is it? (c) How do we deal with the problem? People would like these three questions answered in straightforward ways so that preventions and interventions can be easily and directly established. But these answers do not lend themselves to such desires. The result is that there is no set of techniques that works uniformly in all cases. Techniques and programs most likely to succeed over time have been found to reflect critical program themes that include a social-ecological perspective model, empathic involvement, and reducing isolation of people and ideas (Hazler & Carney, 2006).

Social-Ecological Perspective

Bullying prevention programs are designed to unite as many people together in a community as possible to deal with the problem in coordinated ways. Cultural differences dictate the need for such programs to take into account the interactions between program characteristics and ecological contexts (Orpinas & Horne, 2006). This perspective has been the key difference in how bullying problems are approached in the past 20 years. It emphasizes that the culture of an environment can have a positive or negative influence on bullying so that no one individual or pair of individuals alone creates or maintains a bullying situation. Instead, it is the unique combination of individuals plus the ecological situation that will foster or discourage bullying over time (Espelage & Swearer, 2006; Swearer & Doll, 2001). This theme is the essential ingredient in considering the differing appearances that emerge in all the other aspects of bullying prevention programs when they are viewed by different cultures.

Where a school, community, or country has members of relatively similar cultural orientations, the task of uniting them is easier. They will have similar ways of approaching problems and solutions that will increase consensus on how to proceed. Entities with greater diversities of cultures will need to spend additional time and energy in the effort to bridge the differences. Diversity makes program development more complex and taxing, but it also increases the potential for revising ingrained ways of thinking and acting, thereby producing more creative mechanisms for change.

One particular problem that can arise is when one cultural orientation dominates others. This is likely to cause the development or programs and procedures to flow from one group while reducing or eliminating the views and involvement of other groups. The result is that those groups not involved are likely to either follow along with minimal commitment or fight the procedure either openly or in subversive ways. Many programs fail due to lack of commitment from one or more disaffected groups holding different views of the problem and solutions. It will take more time, energy, emotional investment, empathic understanding, and creative adaptations to deal with the more diverse group. Allowing for this time and energy is important, since ensuring investment from all concerned groups greatly increases the likelihood of success.

Empathic Involvement

Empathy is an essential ingredient in how people view and react to bullying (Espelage & Swearer, 2003). Personal identification with another individual or group promotes the personalized understanding that increases the likelihood that individuals or groups will reach out to help others. Abusive behaviors are also likely to decrease when empathy is developed for another. Gaining empathic understanding of others thus becomes a major theme in all phases of bullying prevention programs.

All cultural orientations express empathy, but they do it in different ways and to different groups. Some cultures will be less physically expressive and demonstrate their concern for others in quiet and reserved ways. Their demonstration could be in vague wording or actions that have culturally recognized meanings of understanding and support. Others will be physically demonstrative, loud, and direct in their approach to understanding. Cultures also vary in relationship to whom it is easier for them to acquire empathy for and how to communicate it. Where power differences are great and there is a more masculine approach, individuals tend to have understanding for and empathize with those like them, while those with less power and a more feminine approach will be more likely try to empathize with those who are in lesser positions. Bullying programs increase success potential by recognizing that success is dependent on implementation proceeding with a significant degree of empathic understanding for the various cultural orientations of everyone involved as well as for the individuals who are being harmed.

Isolation Reduction

Bullies as individuals or groups seek interactions with victims where their domination will go unquestioned. The last thing they want is for those who might shift the balance of power to become involved, so keeping victims isolated from intervention by others is essential. A key role for prevention programs is to increase social and emotional connections between people and groups in order to increase understanding and the likelihood of intervention.

Cultural differences on the group versus individual factor will have particularly obvious implications for perceptions of the problem and actions to be taken. Group-oriented cultures will have more bullying that relates to individuals being excluded from the primary large group, because the individual does not conform effectively to group norms. The strong sense of independence associated with more individualist cultures creates more situations where following norms is of less importance than demonstrating one's own strength. In this case, bullying is more likely to emphasize one person or subgroup bullying another.

Intervention is influenced because people in more individually oriented cultures will reason that individuals should provide support for others so that they will not struggle alone. In this case, intervention is seen as a personal decision to become involved or remain detached. Persons in the group orientation, on the other hand, will first seek some general group agreement on whether and how to take appropriate intervention action. Group consensus on what to do, rather than independent member decision making will be the expected norm in this case.

Well-conceived bullying prevention programs need to take into consideration how the different cultural orientations will play out in the standard bullying prevention program themes. While the themes remain for all cultures, people will relate to them differently in ways that affect their perceptions of the problems and adaptations that need to be made in development and implementation of a program.

Cultural Variations in Sequence of Program Practices

The three main themes of successful bullying prevention do not stand alone, but are instead integrated throughout a specific sequence of implementation progression that increases the likelihood of program success. The order of these sequential program stages flows from awareness building to policy development, skill development, continuing involvement, and assessment and adjustment. The stages are cyclical rather than a one-time-only means to an end. Success of the process leads to new growth and new issues to tackle, thereby producing the need for a cyclical process. Aspects of the stages will need attention at different times, so the sequence should not be taken as a lock-step procedure. Instead, the stages are a general order highlighting when each stage should be given greater emphasis.

Initial Awareness Building

People, organizations, and countries focus their attention first on following their traditional patterns of behaviors. They need a significant level of motivation to move beyond traditional patterns to initiate new prevention efforts. Bullying prevention programs get their start when a culture begins assigning significant importance to the issues that provides a push to reduce such behaviors. Bullying related suicides and shootings on school campuses among groups that have been previously thought to be safe from such harm have been primary motivators for action. The design of a program must therefore begin with gaining a personally significant awareness of the problem and communicating that to the larger community. Answering the questions of what individuals or groups in a culture feel threatened by bullying helps clarify how to best develop and implement awareness building for a specific culture.

The answer to the question of who feels threatened lies in recognizing where the threatened group falls on each of the four cultural difference continuums? For example, a culture with a high difference in who holds power would react to awareness building much differently if bullying problems were being observed in those with power versus those with minimal power. Those with great influence in this scenario would be more likely to create programs when they are directly suffering from problems with bullying and less likely to initiate programs when bullying is occurring with those in the low power category. If the power difference in the culture was small instead of large, those with more power would be more likely to attend to the problems of those with less power and those with less power would receive greater encouragement to assertively invest themselves in the process.

Awareness building in the first scenario would do best to provide empathy for the concerns of the high power people in order to help them understand the problems from a personalized perspective. This thinking might appear cold-hearted in relation to those without power, but may be necessary in order to motivate those who have the power to make things happen for everyone. The smaller power difference scenario could begin focusing awareness building more generally around all groups since they would be more likely to share decisions in what might be done.

The analysis above does not stand alone however, as other cultural factors will certainly interact. For example a highly feminine culture would give more attention to those who are weak. If this culture was also a high power difference culture, there would be competing influences on who would get attention that would be very different from a culture that was feminine and low power difference, or from a culture that was highly masculine and also high power. It is the interaction of the broad cultural differences that creates the unique characteristics around which awareness building activities are best built.

The specific vehicles used for creating awareness will also vary dependent on the how a culture receives different messages. Many forms of media are commonly used to provide initial information and encouragement for administrators, teachers, parents, and students to take part in additional awareness activities. Which forms of media and what people have the greatest influence will also vary from across cultures. What works well for adults will be different for children. What might be the best approach in a culture that desires clear and definitive answers will be different for a culture that thrives on exploration of issues. In all cases, activities are designed to increase personal recognition of how bullying is a clear and present danger to the well-being of students, the school, and community.

Policy Development

Examination and revision of current policies related to bullying is necessary to clearly demonstrate the official significance given to the problem and how that importance will translate into practical application (Limber & Small, 2003). Policies need to be developed early in programs and with the widest variety of individuals and groups represented who have significant influence over gaining the active involvement of others. How a given culture goes about this process will emphasize their unique aspects. Success will be dependent upon how wide the support is for the policies and how consistently they are implemented.

Differences in group versus individual orientation and high versus low power differentials can provide one example of the differing pressures on those trying to develop comprehensive policies. Group oriented cultures will immediately look to design policies that that everyone should follow, while individual focused cultures will struggle more with the rights of individuals. Adding a high power differential component to this equation expands the differences by deemphasizing the desired active involvement of all groups and putting the decisions in the hands of a few who see the task of creating policy as primarily their responsibility.

The ideal model might seem to be a moderately group-oriented culture with low power differences so that they would automatically work together to create policies that are best for the whole while also considering the individual. This would certainly fit the basic need to see all groups represented in policy development, but might not fit a culture that also emphasizes quick decisions to alleviate anxiety and definitive answers expected to remain constant. The reality is that professionals do not get to choose cultural combinations, but must work with what they are to develop policies in ways and with outcomes that can be supported by as many different orientations as possible.

Empathic Investment

Once a community is aware of the problem and involved enough to design a program and policies, the next step is to expand empathic understanding for those who are suffering from bullying. People can know enough to agree there needs to be a bullying prevention program, but still not choose to get involved in a personal way. Whether it is a nation, school, or individual, the press to step out of standard behaviors generally takes a major push from a personal connection to someone or something they can identify as being harmed. Before developing skills and implementing techniques, it is important for everyone, including students, to acquire a personalized empathy for others that provides the motivation for involvement.

First-hand experiences and current events are common ways of helping people identify with others in empathic ways. Newspaper stories of school violence receiving widespread attention or a suicide in a school, while horrific, are examples of teachable current events. They can draw people's attention to the feelings, trauma, and needs of others in ways to which everyone can relate. Videos, speakers, and group discussions can also focus student attention on the emotions and feelings of all participants in bullying situations and not just the victims.

Cultural interactions influence the degree to which empathy acquisition techniques will have the greatest effect. People may feel badly for those struggling with bullying in general, but they will be moved to action when they can also envision themselves as similarly vulnerable. The closer people's own situations feel to the situation of those suffering, the more empathy is raised and the greater the likelihood they will step out of their comfort zone to take meaningful action.

Whatever the vehicle for tapping empathic feelings, it must reflect the individual's culturally perceived environment to be successful. A more masculine perspective might better relate to someone failing in school or life, whereas a more feminine orientation might be emotionally moved more by someone who is socially isolated. Teachers in a large power difference culture might be better emotionally moved by realizing the struggle of another teacher who is bullied, or by a teacher who is hurting because of feeling inadequate to stop the bullying in a class. Students in a large power difference situation would not likely be significantly influenced by these teacher issues, but instead would be more likely to react to situations more specifically directed at them. Teachers and students in a small power difference culture, on the other hand, might well be moved by the other's situation, because they perceive a closer connection between the two groups.

Skill Development

Policies tend to first emphasize rules and punishments for bullying, but these do not provide the means for individuals to become involved except for those assigned to police abuses. Once members of the community have become empathically invested, they are more likely to begin seeking ways to take personal actions as individuals or groups. The focus of bullying prevention programs on everyone in an environment requires that once there becomes empathic motivation to act, then skills need to be taught so that individuals and groups can take appropriate actions. Cultural variations will emphasize some roles over others based on what is deemed assertive behavior, and who should use it under what circumstances.

The category of skills taught in prevention programs is generally termed social skills. These are skills that help people deal with themselves and others in ways that promote a safe and effectively functioning environment. Attending to one's own thoughts, emotions, situations along with those of others are the foundation skills. Learning socially appropriate ways to assertively and productively deal with these recognitions are the action steps that follow.

General definitions of the skills that are taught remain the same in different cultures, but how they can be implemented effectively will vary. Understanding of oneself and others for example, takes on different tones when one exists in a group culture versus a more individualistic culture. Persons in a more group-focused culture tend to see themselves in connection to the whole, whereas those in an individualistic culture will be more likely to see themselves as an independent entity. Understanding of the group culture will therefore need to give more emphasis to individual's place within groups as opposed to more self-only directed initial understanding for those in individualistic cultures. Learning to react to the understanding follows a similar path with the individualistic focus moving from individual efforts to group efforts. The group oriented society's training would move more smoothly from what groups can do to what individuals within groups can do.

People in large power difference cultures will not view their ability to interact with others in the same way as those in smaller power difference cultures. The larger the differences in power, the more prevention programs need to first give attention to individual groups before having them interact across groups. Asking teachers, parents, and students to work together where the power differences are great will be much more difficult than in a culture that sees everyone as more equal.

Programs will also see differences where societies differ on masculinity/femininity or willingness to deal with ambiguity. Assertiveness for example, looks different for a more social adaptation or feminine model than it does in a more competitive or masculine model. When uncertainty avoidance is higher in a culture, there will be more demand for specific skills that will clearly work even if not to the greatest degree. A more ambiguity accepting society, on the other hand, will be more willing to try a variety of skills, evaluate their success, and move on to other options.

On-Going Action Taking

Bullying is a behavior that evolves out of social interactions within a given environmental context. The interactions and context are continually present and always evolving as youth learn to deal with ever changing selves and others in a complex environment. Each new group of students needs initial direction and support while those who have been impacted by a prevention program need continuing involvement as they encounter new situations and stressors. Quality prevention programs maintain the involvement of participants in anti-bullying and associated relationship and climate issues by setting up vehicles for continuing awareness and action taking (Hazler, 1998). Such on-going activities may not always focus directly on bullying, but will connect bullying to broader issues of climate, safety, and personal relationships.

Continuous action taking for group oriented cultures or those with minimal power inequities are more likely to maintain involvement when they recognize everyone is working together on a regular basis. These programs would emphasize support for everyone and discussions will seek to reach working agreement on beliefs and actions. For cultures with more individual emphasis or greater power inequities, the motivation for continuing will likely be more about what benefits individuals see for themselves or their particular groups. Of course, no culture is perfectly dichotomous so prevention program implementers need to judge how much of each emphasis is appropriate for a given community.

Continuing investment in action taking is a difficult aspect to inspire in people as they generally want to fix a problem and be finished. This will be particularly true for a culture emphasizing avoidance of uncertainty or a more masculine culture. These orientations more than the ambiguity accepting or more feminine cultures will feel pressure to solve the problem and move on to other things. Unfortunately, social problems are just not amenable to being solved quickly and easily.

Prevention programs in the more masculine or uncertainty avoidant oriented cultures will likely need to set more specific, short range, achievable objectives so that success and confidence can be perceived in a time-frame that will keep people motivated. Attention will also need to be paid to then setting additional goals. This goal setting and achieving aspect can become very productive in the assessment and adjustment phase.

Assessment and Adjustment

Bullying prevention programs are designed to change situations in preferred directions that are more conducive to academic, personal, and social development. Whether and to what degree they are successful will be viewed differently by people with varied viewpoints. Only when the formal assessment of program activities and outcomes is formally planned and implemented on regular basis can programs objectively identify progress, adjust the focus of future attention, and revise programmatic efforts. Responsive and responsible ongoing activities are dependent upon formative and summative assessments on both the processes and products of prevention programs (Benkofske & Heppner, 1999).

Assessment procedures need to occur throughout the program in formative and summative forms, but their planning should take place early in program development when goals and objectives are set. Early development of assessment procedures will generally be welcomed by the masculine and uncertainty avoidance cultures in order to get goals and means of evaluating success clearly established. It may take more time to initially invest more feminine and ambiguity acceptance cultures in this process as they will likely feel less pressure to develop goals and assessment procedures and greater initial interest in discussing, gaining understanding, and taking initial actions. Prevention program developers must be cognitive of the differences so that they can both support the culture's needs and also find ways to guide them into actions for which they may have less motivation.

Assessment emphasis will also differ for group versus individual orientations, as it will for cultures with differing power inequalities. Individualistic oriented cultures will initially give attention to trying to evaluate individuals and their progress. They may look to mental and emotional diagnostic type of criteria in this case where as group oriented cultures will likely want to focus attention on how the overall community improves. Cultures with wider distances between groups because of power inequities will often want to see the other group evaluated for problems and themselves evaluated for how their situation is improved. Procedures and instrument design must take into account each of the cultural factors and their interactions in order to acquire reliable and valid data that will be accepted and used for further planning.

Conclusions

Bullying prevention programs have experienced an enormous expansion in the past two decades. The movement that began in the Scandinavian countries, expanded to Western countries, and is now growing rapidly around the world. A few programs that have demonstrated success and longevity are being adopted by cultures very different from the originating country. Success in these program adoptions is greatly influenced by the degree to which cultural variations can be integrated into the program. This chapter has discussed the basic program themes, sequential stages, and practices that are key parts of successful programs and how they are influenced by cultures variations. Table 29.1 outlines these factors.

Research has identified three themes that are the cornerstones of successful programs. These relate to taking a social-ecological perspective that integrates as wide a community involvement as possible rather than only focusing on bullies and victims themselves. They also emphasize the need to gain empathic involvement of people to create and maintain a personal and emotional connection to the problem. The third theme focuses on reducing the isolation of people and ideas in order to create greater exposure to the variations of ideas, information, and feelings of others.

Programs have also been shown to work best when they are implemented in specific sequential stages. Building knowledge and emotional awareness of the problem in all students and adults involved in the program is the essential beginning. Once awareness is raised and people begin to seek solutions there is a policy development stage focused on identifying and formalizing common values and behaviors. Skills to carry out support of the values and behaviors must

Table 29.1 Implications for Practice: Cultural Implications for Effective Bullying Prevention Programs and Implementation Practices

Program Themes	Implementation Practices	Cultural Implications
Social-Ecological Perspective	Integrate the fullest possible diversity of people and groups into community planning and implementation efforts	Greater diversity of cultures require additional inclusion efforts necessary for maximum program quality & success
Empathic Involvement	Create and maintain connections between people on the emotional level in addition to knowledge/information level	Expression of empathy ranges widely from physical to verbal, public to private, subtle to demonstrative
Reducing Isolation of People and Ideas	Reduce physical isolation opportunities and increase social, information, emotional, & ideological inclusion	Differing views of importance and implementation of connecting to others
Sequential Program Stages	**Implementation Practices**	**Cultural Implications**
Initial Awareness Building	Create both knowledge and emotional awareness that promotes understanding, a desire to help, and a press for timely action	Awareness must include how cultural influence interact with the type of bullying and emotional expression
Policy Development	Create common values, related rules of behavior, supportive activities, and enforcement procedures involving the fullest possible diversity of school/community participants	Values & rules of behavior should reflect the culture including the degree to which it tolerates ambiguity & human differences
Skill Development	Teach a wide variety of social skills that encourage abusers, victims, & bystanders alike to assertively implement social/behavioral values and policies	Different perceptions of self & others including what is viewed as socially appropriate assertive behaviors need consideration
Continuing Involvement	Provide regular time for discussions on the school's evolving climate, positive changes, problems, necessary actions, & how to use previously learned skills	Maintaining prevention program investment requires emphasizing unique motivation needs of a given culture
Assessment and Adjustment	Evaluate progress, identify changing needs, and direct adjustment of efforts	Cultures differ in when & how to evaluate, plus how to act on outcomes

be developed at a third stage. Bullying prevention programs cannot have lasting success when implemented for only a short period of time. It requires continuing involvement and regular attention to the climate that can support or reject bullying. Finally a program must be active in assessing the progress of the program and making changes to reflect those evaluations.

Cultures vary by the broad categories of continents, nations, or ethnicity, and also by many factors within those cultures. Research has identified four core differences between cultures that are offered in this chapter to assist program designer and/or implementer efforts to best fit a designated target population. Variations in how cultures deal with formal power differences will for example influence how much negotiation can be used, when, and by whom. Whether a program emphasizes more individual or more group decision making and actions relates to cultures that are more group oriented and others more individual focused. While traditional feminine versus masculine roles for individuals are being questioned to some degree in all cultures, group variations in traditional ways of thinking, feeling, and behaving need to be recognized and accounted for in programs. The fourth variation emphasized in this chapter is a culture's willingness to accept ambiguity versus investing more energy in gaining security and minimizing change. Taking these four cultural variations into account in the design and implementation of bullying prevention themes, stages, and practices will greatly increase the potential value of any program.

References

Benkofske, M., & Heppner, C. C. (1999). Program evaluation. In P. P. Heppner, D. M. Kivlighan, Jr., & B. E. Wampold (Eds.), *Research design in counseling* (2nd ed., pp. 488–515). Belmont, CA: Wadsworth.

Cartledge, G., & Johnson, C. T. (2004). School violence and cultural sensitivity. In J. C. Conoley & A. P. Goldstein (Eds.), *School violence intervention: A practical handbook* (2nd ed., pp. 441–482). New York: Guilford.

Committee for Children. (1993). *Second Step: A Violence Prevention Curriculum*. Seattle, WA: Author.

Committee for Children. (2002). *Steps to Respect: A Bullying Prevention Program*. Seattle, WA: Author.

Espelage, D. L., & Swearer, S. M. (2003). Research on school bullying and victimization: What have we learned and where do we go from here? *School Psychology Review, 32*, 365–383.

Espelage, D. L., & Swearer, S. M. (2006). *Bullying in American schools: A social-ecological perspective on prevention and intervention*. Mahwah, NJ: Erlbaum.

Furlong, M. J., Morrison, G. M., & Greif, J. L. (2003). Reaching an American consensus: Reactions to the special issue on school bullying. *School Psychology Review, 32*, 456–470.

Grossman, D. C., Neckerman, H. J., Koepsell, T. D., & Liu, P. (1997). Effectiveness of a violence prevention curriculum among children in elementary school. *Journal of the American Medical Association, 277*, 1605–1611.

Hazler, R. J. (1998). Promoting personal investment in systemic approaches to school violence. *Education, 119*, 222–231.

Hazler, R. J., & Carney, J. V. (2006). Critical characteristics of effective bullying prevention programs. In S. R. Jimerson & M. Furlong (Eds.), *Handbook of school violence and school safety: From research to practice* (pp. 275–292). Mahwah, NJ: Erlbaum.

Hazler, R. J., & Carney, J. V. (2000). When victims turn aggressors: Factors in the development of deadly school violence. *Professional School Counseling, 4*(2), 1–5, 112.

Hazler, R. J., Hoover, J., & Oliver, R. (1991). Student perceptions of victimization in schools. *Journal of Humanistic Education and Development, 29*(4), 5–15.

Hofstede, G. (2001). *Culture's consequences* (2nd ed.). Thousand Oaks, CA: Sage.

Hofstede, G., & Hofstede, G.J. (2005). *Cultures and organizations: Software of the mind*. New York: McGraw Hill.

Kallestad, J. H., & Olweus, D. (2003). Predicting teachers' and schools' implementation of the Olweus Bullying Prevention Program: A multilevel study. *Prevention and Treatment, 6*, Article 0021a. Retrieved January 3, 2005, from http://jounrals.apa.org/prevention/volume6/pre0060021a.html

Limber, S. P., Nation, M., Tracy, A. J., Melton, G. B., & Flerx, V. (2004). Implementation of the Olweus Bullying Prevention Program in the southeastern United States. In P. K. Smith, D. Pepler, & K. Rigby (Eds.), *Bullying in schools: How successful can interventions be?* (pp. 55–79). New York: Cambridge University Press.

Limber, S. P., & Small, M. A. (2003). State laws and policies to address bullying in schools. *School Psychology Review, 32*, 445–455.

McEachern, A. G., Kenny, M., Blake, E., & Aluede, O. (2005). Bullying in schools: International variations. *Journal of Social Sciences, 8,* 25–32.

Olweus, D. (2005). A useful evaluation design, and effects of the Olweus Bullying Prevention Program. *Psychology, Crime, & Law, 11,* 389–402.

Orpinas, P., & Horne, A. M. (2006). *Bullying prevention: Creating a positive school climate and developing social competence.* Washington, DC: American Psychological Association.

Rigby, K. (2002). *New perspectives on bullying.* Philadelphia: Jessica Kingsley.

Samples, F., & Aber, L. (1998). Evaluations of school-based violence prevention programs. In D. S. Elliott, B. A. Hamburg, & K. R. Williams (Eds.), *Violence in American schools* (pp. 217–252). Cambridge, UK: Cambridge University Press.

Scheckner, S. B., & Rollin, S. A. (2003). An elementary school violence prevention program. *Journal of school violence, 2,* 3–42.

Smith, P. K., Morita, Y., Junger-Tas, J., Olweus, D., Catalano, R., & Slee, P. (Eds.). (1999). *The nature of school bullying: A cross-national perspective* (pp. 1–4). New York: Routledge.

Swearer, S. M., & Doll, B. (2001). Bullying in schools: An ecological framework. *Journal of Emotional Abuse, 2,* 7–23.

Tolan, P., & Guerra, N. (1994). *What works in reducing adolescent violence: An empirical review of the field.* Boulder: University of Colorado Press.

30

Bully-Proofing Your Elementary School

Creating a Caring Community

WILLIAM PORTER, AMY PLOG, KATHRYN JENS,
CARLA GARRITY, AND NANCY SAGER

Overview

Bully-Proofing Your School (BPYS) was developed in 1994 as a comprehensive prevention program designed to reduce bullying at the elementary level. After recognizing that pull-out groups for bullies and victims were not effective, the authors researched what was known about effective bullying intervention in schools. Based on the pioneering ideas of Olweus (1991), a school-wide, systemic bullying intervention with teacher training and a student curriculum was developed. The focus of Bully-Proofing Your School is on creating a safer school environment for all by developing a culture within the school that is not conducive to acts of physical, verbal, or social aggression. This desired environment does not develop naturally; it must be created, nurtured, and sustained by the students, parents, teachers, and staff.

Although originally developed for elementary schools, Bully-Proofing Your School is now available across all age ranges from early childhood through high school. This chapter will focus on the elementary model as it has been implemented for over 13 years in schools throughout the United States and Canada. During these years, research on the dynamics of bullying, feedback from teachers and administrators, and most importantly feedback from students, have all contributed to an understanding of what are the key components of the BPYS program. Shifting power into the hands of what BPYS calls the "caring majority" of students and encouraging them to use pro-social interventions assertively and positively are thought to be critical features in the creation of a safe, supportive school environment where teachers can teach and students can learn. This cultural shift is most effective when implemented in the following way: First, the climate of the school is assessed, staff are trained and school-wide no-bullying rules are developed; then, students are taught protective strategies and the skills necessary to form a protective, caring group; finally, a positive climate throughout the school is developed by encouraging a shift of students from being a silent majority to being a caring majority, thereby developing a caring community. This chapter will provide more information on this process through discussion of the conceptual foundations, specific approaches, and research base of BPYS.

Conceptual Foundations

Development of a safe, inclusive, respectful environment where teachers can teach and students can learn is the ultimate goal of Bully-Proofing Your School. The intervention follows six guiding principles that will be summarized below. By following these principles, school staff, parents, and students work together to help make the above-stated goal a reality.

Principle 1: It is the responsibility of adults to ensure that school is a physically and psychologically safe environment in which children can learn. From this, it logically follows that full staff participation is an important element in the success of the program; this notion has been repeatedly supported by researchers who study successful implementation of prevention programs in schools (Elias, Zins, Graczyk, Weissberg, 2003; Michalic, Irwin, Elliott, Fagan, & Hansen, 2001; Nation et al., 2003; PPN, 2004). Full staff participation is much easier said than done. To achieve this, adults at school must believe that bullying is a problem at their school and falls within their role to intervene. Research has shown, however, that bullying is not seen by all staff to be an issue, particularly at the secondary level (O'Moore, 2000). Additionally, it has been found that teachers can feel unprepared to deal with bullying (Byrne, 1994) and would like to know more about how to do so effectively (Boulton, 1997). Appropriate adult responses to bullying are important to break the "code of silence" in which students do not tell adults about bullying. This occurs because children have been found to feel that adults do not listen or respond when they share concerns about bullying or if they do tell, the adults may intervene in a way that makes the situation worse (Bentley & Li, 1995; Hazler, 1996; Newman, Murray, & Lussier, 2001). Therefore, adult perceptions and skills must be considered as part of the process of adults ensuring that the school environment is a positive one.

Principle 2: Bullying is not synonymous with "conflict" or "aggression." Although bullying behaviors can be thought of as a subset of aggressive behavior, most definitions of bullying behavior make reference to the importance of a "power imbalance" between the bully and the victim (Espelage & Swearer, 2003; Furlong, Morrison, & Grief, 2003; Glew, Rivara, & Feudtener, 2000; Juvonen, 2001; Limber & Small, 2003; Nansel et al., 2001; Olweus, 1997; Pellegrini, 2002; Rigby, 2000; Smith et al., 2002). Because of this, it is thought that bullying does not respond to traditional conflict resolution interventions (Limber, Flerx, Nation, & Melton, 1998; Limber & Nation, 1991) and instead requires specific interventions, including adult intervention to impact the power differential. Further, as bullying takes many forms, it may require education for school staff so that they can discern between "bullying" and "normal conflict". This understanding is critical so that adults can intervene appropriately so the situation is not made worse for the victims and bystanders.

Principle 3: Bullies, when confronted with a caring community (a unified group of adults and students within a school), are defused. Research has consistently supported the importance of the bystanders to bullying (e.g., Craig, Pepler, & Atlas, 2000; Salmivalli, 1999). Student bystanders play an important role because: (a) adults are often only aware of a small amount of bullying that takes place at school (Cowie, 2000; Craig & Pepler, 1997; Gropper & Froschl, 1999); (b) students often do nothing or behave in ways that exacerbate bullying (Craig & Pepler, 1997; Craig et al., 2000; O'Connell, Pepler, & Craig, 1999; Salmivalli, 1999; Stevens, Van Oost, & De Bourdeaudhuij, 2000); and (c) the behavior of the bystanders may be more easily changed than that of the bully or the victim (Salmivalli, 1999). Even though the role of the students is important, enlisting the support of parents and the community at large is also a critical component of BPYS. Working together, *everyone* facilitates a shift of power away from the bullies and toward the caring community.

Principle 4: Punitive programs are only successful with bullying behavior to a point. O'Connell, Pepler, and Craig (1999) caution that intervention that just gives consequences to bullies is inadequate, and Limber and Small (2003) point out that punishments for bullying that are too severe may keep people from coming forward. It is a core belief of BPYS that the code of silence must be broken. Finally, so-called "zero-tolerance" policies (punishing major and minor disruptions relatively equally) have not been found to be effective means of creating a positive school climate (Furlong et al., 2003; Orpinas, Horne, & Staniszewski, 2003). BPYS is a no-nonsense program, not a punitive program. Rather than engaging in power struggles by attempting to discipline bully behavior as the sole intervention, this program focuses on shifting the power away from the bullies and teaching the bullies prosocial skills.

Principle 5: Bully-Proofing Your School will be most successful when implemented comprehensively. As Roland (2000) noted based on his observation of 15 years of bullying intervention in Norway, schools that implement bullying interventions in a more serious, complete, and systematic manner are those that are more likely to obtain positive results. Further, many researchers have discussed the importance of implementing an intervention with fidelity (Biglan, Mrazek, Carnine, & Flay, 2003; Blase & Fixsen, 2006; Kam, Greenberg, & Walls, 2003; Nation et al., 2003; Weissberg, 2004) or delivering the intervention as designed in a quality manner and at sufficient dosage (Elliott, 2006). While BPYS is flexible in embracing the various levels of resources from school to school, it is likely to have limited success if implemented piecemeal. Each component of the program is believed to be important; it is the presence of all the components within a school that will coalesce into a safe learning environment.

Principle 6: There are many means to an end. This program emphasizes the importance of recognizing and utilizing the different styles, strengths, and experiences of staff members. Some staff members are more comfortable and effective with bullies, others with victims. Each individual role is significant and each contributes to the successful implementation of the BPYS program. Similarly, due to the wide developmental spectrum in an elementary school, bullying itself along with the possible interventions is likely to look different depending on the grade of the students.

Being aware of how to best intervene and following the six guiding principles will help build the Caring Community—the foundation of the BPYS program. BPYS stresses modeling respect, building self-competence, and then nourishing the desire to care in children. The next section of this chapter describes the specific approaches recommended to "Bully-Proof" children most effectively.

Description of Specific Approaches

Bully-Proofing Your School was designed as a school-wide program that aims to train all staff who then instruct all students and to involve the parents and community in the program concepts and language. Schools are advised to go through a pre-implementation phase during which administration and staff acknowledge bullying as a problem, use needs-assessment to specifically identify areas of concern, and put behavioral expectations and discipline plans in place.

During the implementation phase, a staff committee (cadre) guides the components of the intervention described below.

1. Staff training, which is typically one day in length and covers the following essential information:
   - The definition of bullying and how it differs from normal peer conflict
   - Bully, victim, bystander roles and characteristics
   - Education on the dynamics of bullying, including the effect on learning and long-term consequences (e.g., depression and suicidality; Espelage & Swearer, 2003; Glew et al., 2000; Juvonen, Graham, & Schuster, 2003; Nansel et al., 2001; Solberg & Olweus, 2003; Rigby, 2000; O'Moore, 2000; Smith & Brain, 2000) in victims and later criminal behavior and domestic violence on the part of bullies (Colvin, Tobin, Beard, Hagan, & Sprague, 1998; Limber & Nation, 1991; Olweus, 1991, 1993; Smith, Bowers, Binney, & Cowie, 1993)
   - Adult conflict management styles which are most effective with bullies, victims, and bystanders (no-nonsense style for bullies and supportive style for victims)
   - Review of the curriculum and practice in teaching it
2. Student instruction, which consists of six lessons for the primary grades and six lessons for the intermediate grades. Essential concepts taught to the students include:
   - The definitions of bullying and bully, victim, and bystander roles
   - The three bully-proofing rules:
     - We will not bully other students
     - We will help others who are being bullied by speaking out and by getting adult help
     - We will use extra effort to include all students in activities at out school
   - HA HA SO (Help, Assert, Humor, Avoid, Self-talk, Own it); the six techniques students can use to decrease the emotionality of the situation and therefore protect themselves from bullying
   - CARES (Creative problem-solving, Adult help, Relate and join, Empathy, Stand up); the five techniques a student can use to help another student who is being bullied
   - The difference between tattling and telling
   - The importance of and ways of becoming part of a Caring Community; this includes discussion of that fact that caring behaviors will be recognized and rewarded
   - For primary students, instruction that focuses on friendship skills
3. Individualized interventions for victims
   - Instruction in friendship-making skills due to the strong relationship between social isolation, poor social skills, and being a victim (Demaray & Malecki, 2003; Juvonen et al., 2003; Nansel et al., 2001; Pellegrini, 2002; Solberg & Olweus, 2003)
   - Instruction about self-esteem and communication skills
4. Individualized interventions for bullies
   - Instruction about the thinking errors that cause antisocial behavior (Samenow, 1989), along with strategies to alter these thinking errors
   - Instruction in anger management and social problem-solving
5. Parent and community involvement, which can occur in a variety of ways (e.g., communication from the school via newsletters and family nights)
   - Education about the language and concepts of the program so that BPYS is supported not only at school, but also on the way to and from school; waiting at the bus stop and outside of school; and at youth sports, scouting, and other community activities

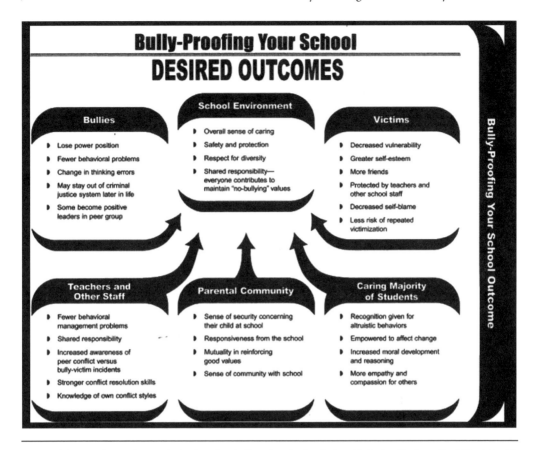

Figure 30.1 Reproduced with permission from Sopris West, Inc. Garrity, C., Jens, K., Porter, W., Sager, N., & Short-Camilli, C. (2004). *Bully-Proofing Your School: A comprehensive approach for elementary schools.* Second edition. Longmont, CO: Sopris West.

- Emphasis on the fact that bullying will not be tolerated and that kindness will be rewarded so that parents can help support this philosophy

The desired outcomes for these five program components and their impact on the school environment/climate are shown in Figure 30.1.

To ensure that these outcomes are achieved, evaluation is also an important aspect of effective implementation of the BPYS program. Evaluation is carried over into the final phase of BPYS, the sustained implementation phase. This phase occurs once BPYS is "up and running" and, in addition to ongoing evaluation, stresses the need for regular cadre meetings, efforts to keep the program visible and fresh, integration of BPYS with other programs and the stated goals of the school, empowerment of students, and continued technical assistance and financial resources.

Relevant Research

Bully-Proofing Your School includes components that have been consistently identified by research on bullying intervention as being necessary for positive climate changes/reductions in bullying to occur. Specifically, bullying intervention research typically points to the importance of assessment of bullying in the school paired with increased awareness of the dynamics of bullying (Eslea & Smith, 1998; Olweus, 1991, 1997; Orpinas et al., 2003; Peterson & Rigby,

1999; Smith, 1997; Whitney, Rivers, Smith, & Sharp, 1994). BYPS utilizes the Colorado School Climate Survey (CSCS). The CSCS was designed to assess bullying behaviors, perceptions of safety, and overall school climate, in order to provide schools with information on the degree of bullying within their school as well as factors that can help guide intervention (e.g., locations where bullying occurs, types of bullying behaviors, and student responses to experienced and observed bullying). Student, staff, and parent trainings all include information on the dynamics of bullying.

A second factor that has been identified as being important for effective bullying intervention is a school-wide, systemic approach (Arora, 1994; Eslea & Smith, 1998; Olweus, 1991, 1997; Orpinas et al., 2003; Peterson & Rigby, 1999; Pepler, Craig, Ziegler, & Charach, 1994; Smith, 1997; Stevens et al., 2000; Whitney et al., 1994). BPYS was designed as a systemic, comprehensive, climate change program. Establishment of rules and/or a policy regarding bullying (Arora, 1994; Eslea & Smith, 1998; Olweus, 1991, 1997; Orpinas et al., 2003; Pepler et al., 1994; Peterson & Rigby, 1999; Smith, 1997; Whitney et al., 1994) is also mentioned as a necessary (though not sufficient) component of effective bullying interventions. BPYS addresses this through the establishment of classroom rules paired with adoption of a school-wide discipline plan so that bullying behaviors are specifically addressed. Additionally, research points to the importance of interventions for bullies and victims (Eslea & Smith, 1998; Pepler et al., 1994; Sharp & Smith, 1991; Smith, 1997; Stevens et al., 2000; Whitney et al., 1994). The HA HA SO model described above provides tools for students to become less attractive as victims. Also, BPYS emphasizes no-nonsense staff strategies for responding to bullies and the importance of support for victims. BPYS provides supplemental interventions for victims and for bullies.

A final and critical component of effective bullying intervention is the involvement of peers (Cowie, 2000; Eslea & Smith, 1998; Naylor & Cowie, 1999; Orpinas et al., 2003; Pepler et al., 1994; Peterson & Rigby, 1999; Sharp & Smith, 1991; Smith, 1997; Stevens et al., 2000; Whitney et al., 1994). As stated above, peers are important for a number of reasons: generally, bullying is thought of as a problem that includes not just the bully and the victim, but also the social environment in which bullying occurs (Espelage & Swearer, 2003). Within this environment, adults are often unaware of the bullying, while other students are (Pepler et al., 1994). Moreover, though students typically report they do not condone bullying behavior, research has shown that students often behave in ways that exacerbate the bullying (Salmivalli, 1999). BPYS includes lessons that teach strategies to the bystander students. Further, the emphasis on Caring Community development—the core of Bully-Proofing Your School—stems from this research which has shown the importance of involving the entire peer community.

In addition to its solid foundation in research on effective implementation, some preliminary studies have been conducted that more directly assess the impact of Bully-Proofing Your School. Epstein, Plog, and Porter (2002) reported the results of a four-year longitudinal study of the impact of BPYS in a suburban elementary school. Significant decreases in bullying behaviors (physical, verbal, and exclusionary) and improved perceptions of safety across four school locations were found using time-lagged contrasts between equivalent groups (i.e., earlier time points served as controls for the later time points). Although this methodology is similar to that used in the original evaluation of the Olweus bullying prevention program (Olweus, 1991), the presence of a control school(s) would clearly allow for stronger conclusions about the impact of BPYS. A study by Beran and Tutty (2002) did include both an intervention (an adaptation of BPYS) and comparison school. They found decreased reports of witnessed bullying in an intervention school (t = 3.84, p = .001), but not in a comparison school (t =1 .45, n.s.). They also found decreased positive attitudes towards victims in a comparison school (t = 5.79, p < .001), but not in an intervention school.

Limitations and Future Research

Despite the preliminary studies that point to the effectiveness of BPYS, clearly more rigorous study of the impact of BPYS is needed. A multi-year, multi-site study of BPYS was conducted by the Center for the Study and Prevention of Violence and results are imminent. Following the results of this study, further research will be necessary to help identify which components of intervention are really important for positive change. This is particularly important given that, based on the over 13 years of experience the authors have had with implementation of BPYS in schools, it is evident there can be a sizable difference between the way a program is intended to be implemented and the way it actually is implemented. As stated previously, prevention researchers have stressed the importance of implementing an intervention with fidelity (Biglan, et al., 2003; Blase & Fixsen, 2006; Elliott, 2006; Kam et al., 2003; Nation et al., 2003; Weissberg, 2004). Clear understanding of what about a particular intervention makes it successful will be helpful in determining what components (e.g., anti-bullying rules, protective strategies, caring community) of an intervention are amenable to adaptation by a school and what components need to be implemented exactly as intended. Also based on the authors' applied experience, another issue that warrants further study is what factors allow for sustainability of the intervention. Schools are continually changing environments; changes in leadership, teachers, and program champions are common. As Elias and colleagues (2003) noted, turnover is a problematic feature of school settings. This turnover is just one contributing factor to the difficulty keeping a program fresh and alive in a school. Also, it is typical for a bullying prevention program to be implemented in a school that has other behavioral prevention programs in place. Further work is needed to better understand how to best integrate bullying prevention with other school-wide, systemic behavioral interventions.

Table 30.1 Implications for Practice

School Wide	Teachers/Staff	Student Instruction	Caring Community
• Program is school wide and systemic issues are considered prior to implementation • Clear behavioral expectations and discipline policy are in place • Administration is supportive of the intervention • There is a commitment for a number of years • A program cadre is chosen prior to implementation • All adults are included – staff, parents and community • Monitoring (use of data) and enlivening are ongoing • Program is integrated with other programs	• There is regular and consistent adult intervention • Staff is trained to recognize the power differential in bullying and to differentiate bullying from aggression and peer conflict • Intervention for bullies is no nonsense and usesprosocial consequences • Supportive intervention is used for victims • Teachable moments are regularly used	• All students are instructed in self protective skills and caring skills • Clear behavioral expectations are developed and consistently reinforced • The code of silence is broken • Bystanders are the critical change agent • Thinking errors for bullies are changed • Isolation is reduced for victims	• Caring community behaviors are identified • Caring community behaviors are acknowledged, rewarded, and celebrated

It is our belief that the context in which the implementation occurs may be as important as the particular intervention itself. Factors such as the reasons the intervention is put in place (e.g., a district-wide mandate, a response to an event in the school/community, etc.) can have a large impact on the implementation. Most implementations take place in "underresourced, overextended communities without the benefit of strong leadership and political advocacy at the highest levels" (Forgatch, 2003, p. 2). BPYS is a systemic, comprehensive climate change program that reduces bullying when implemented with fidelity. Sustaining the climate change from year to year is critical to its success and the tools for doing this will be addressed in a subsequent chapter.

References

Arora, C. M. J. (1994). Is there any point in trying to reduce bullying in secondary schools? A two year follow-up of a whole-school anti-bullying policy in one school. *Educational Psychology in Practice, 10*(3), 155–162.

Bentley, K. M., & Li, A. K. F. (1995). Bully and victim problems in elementary school and students' beliefs about aggression. *Canadian Journal of School Psychology, 11*(2), 153–165.

Beran, T. N., & Tutty, L. (2002). An evaluation of the Dare to Care: Bully Proofing Your School Program. Final report to RESOLVE Alberta, Canada: Author.

Biglan, A., Mrazek, P. J., Carnine, D., & Flay, B. R. (2003). The integration of research and practice in the prevention of youth behavior problems. *American Psychologist, 58*, 433–440.

Blase, K. A., & Fixsen, D. L. (2006, March). *Fidelity — why it matters and what research tells us.* Paper presentedat the Buleprints Conference, Denver, Colorado.

Boulton, M. J. (1997). Teachers' views on bullying: Definitions, attitudes and ability to cope. *British Journal of Educational Psychology, 67,* 223–233.

Byrne, B. J. (1994). Bullies and victims in a school setting with reference to some Dublin schools. *Irish Journal of Psychology, 15,* 574–586.

Colvin, G., Tobin, T., Beard, K., Hagan, S., & Sprague, J. (1998). The school bully: Assessing the problem, developing interventions, and future research directions. *Journal of Behavioral Education, 8*(3), 293–319.

Cowie, H. (2000). Bystanding or standing by: Gender issues in coping with bullying in English schools. *Aggressive Behavior, 26,* 85–97.

Craig, W. M., & Pepler, D. J. (1997). Observations of bullying and victimization in the schoolyard. *Canadian Journal of School Psychology, 13*(2), 41–60.

Craig, W. M., Pepler, D., & Atlas, R. (2000). Observations of bullying in the playground and in the classroom. *School Psychology International, 21*(1), 22–36.

Demaray, M. K., & Malecki, C. K. (2003). Perceptions of the frequency and importance of social support by students classified as victims, bullies, and bully/victims in an urban middle school. *School Psychology Review, 23,* 471–490.

Elias, M. J., Zins, J. E., Graczyk, P. A., & Weissberg, R. P. (2003). Implementation, sustainability, and scaling up of social-emotional and academic innovations in public schools, *School Psychology Review, 32,* 303–319.

Elliott, D. S. (2006, March). Improving the effectiveness of delinquency, drug and violence prevention efforts: Promise and practice. Paper presented at the Blueprints Conference, Denver, Colorado.

Epstein, L., Plog, A., and Porter, W. (2002, Summer). Bully-Proofing Your School: Results of a four-year intervention. *Emotional and Behavior Disorders in Youth,* 55–78.

Eslea, M. & Smith, P. K. (1998). The long-term effectiveness of anti-bullying work in primary schools. *Education Research, 40* (2), 203–218.

Espelage, D. L., & Swearer, S. (2003). Research on school bullying and victimization: What have we learned and where do we go from here? *School Psychology Review, 23,* 365–383.

Forgatch, M. S. (2003). Implementation as a second stage in prevention research. *Prevention & Treatment, 6* (Article 24). Retrieved February 5, 2004, from http://journals.apa.org/prevention/volume6/pre0060024c.html

Furlong, M. J., Morrison, G. M., & Grief, J. L. (2003). Reaching and American Consensus: Reactions to the special issue on school bullying. *School Psychology Review, 23,* 456–470.

Glew, G., Rivara, F., & Feudtner, C. (2000). Bullying: Children hurting children. *Pediatrics in Review, 21*(6), 183–189.

Gropper, N., & Froschl, M. (1999). *The role of gender in young children's teasing and bullying behavior.* Paper presented at the Annual Conference of the American Educational Research Association, Montreal, Canada, April 19–23.

Hazler, R. (1996). *Breaking the cycle of violence: Interventions for bullying and victimization.* Washington, DC: Accelerated Development.

Juvonen, J. (2001). Peer harassment as a personal plight and as a collective problem: Implications for intervention. *Psychological Science Agenda* (Sept./October), 6–7.

Juvonen, J., Graham, S, & Schuster, M. A. (2003). Bullying among young adolescents: The strong, the weak, and the troubled. *Pediatrics, 112,* 1231–1237.

Kam, C. M., Greenberg, M. T., & Walls, C. T. (2003). Examining the role of implementation quality in school-based prevention using the PATHS curriculum. *Prevention Science, 4,* 55–63.

Limber, S. P., Flerx, V. C., Nation, M. A., & Melton, G. B. (1998). Bullying among school children in the United States. In M. W. Watts (Ed.), *Crosscultural perspectives on youth and violence* (pp. 159–173). Stamford, CT: JAI Press .

Limber, S. P., & Nation, M. M. (1991). Bullying among children and youth, Juvenile Justice Bulletin. Retrieved from http://www.ojjdp.ncjrs.org/jjjbulletin/9804/bullying2.html

Limber, S., & Small, M. A. (2003). State laws and policies to address bullying in schools. *School Psychology Review, 23,* 445–455.

Michalic, S., Irwin, K., Elliott, D., Fagan, A., & Hansen, D. (2001, July). Blueprints for violence prevention. OJJDP juvenile justice bulletin. Retrieved February 27, 2004, from http://ncjrs.org/html/ojjdp/jjbul2001_7_3/contents.html

Nansel, T. R., Overpeck, M., Pilla, R. S., Ruan, W. J., Simons-Morton, B., Scheidt, P. (2001). Bullying behaviors among US youth: Prevalence and association with psychosocial adjustment. *Journal of the American Medical Association, 285,* 2094–2100.

Nation, M., Crusto, C., Wandersman, A., Kumpfer, K. L., Seybolt, D., Morrissey-Kane, E., & Davino, K. (2003). What works in prevention: Principles of effective prevention programs. *American Psychologist, 58,* 449–456.

Naylor, P., & Cowie, H. (1999). The effectiveness of peer support systems in challenging school bullying: the perspectives and experiences of teachers and pupils. *Journal of Adolescence, 22,* 467–479.

Newman, R. S., Murray, B., & Lussier, C. (2001). Confrontation with aggressive peers at school: Students' reluctance to seek help from the teacher. *Journal of Educational Psychology, 93,* 398–410.

O'Connell, P., Pepler, D., & Craig, W. (1999). Peer involvement in bullying: insights and challenges for intervention. *Journal of Adolescence, 22,* 437–452.

Olweus, D. (1991). Bully/victim problems among schoolchildren: Basic facts and effects of a school based intervention program. In K. Rubin & D. Pepler (Eds.), *The development and treatment of childhood aggression* (pp. 411–448). Hillsdale, NJ: Erlbaum.

Olweus, D. (1993). Bully/victim problems among schoolchildren: Long-term consequences and an effective intervention program. In S. Hodgins (Ed.), *Mental disorder and crime* (pp. 317–349). Sage: Newbury Park, CA.

Olweus, D. (1997). Bully/victim problems in school: Facts and intervention. *European Journal of Psychology of Education, 12,* 495–110.

O'Moore, M. (2000). Critical issues for teacher training to counter bullying and victimization in Ireland. *Aggressive Behavior, 26,* 99–111.

Orpinas, P., Horne, A. M., & Staniszewski, D. (2003). School bullying: Changing the problem by changing the school. *School Psychology Review, 23,* 431–444.

Pellegrini, A. D. (2002). Bullying, victimization, and sexual harassment during the transition to middle school. *Educational Psychologist, 37*(3), 151–163.

Pepler, D. J., Craig, W. M., Ziegler, S., & Charach, A. (1994). An evaluation of an anti-bullying intervention in Toronto schools. *Canadian Journal of Community Mental Health, 13*(2), 95–110.

Peterson, L., & Rigby, K. (1999). Countering bullying at an Australian secondary school with students as helpers. *Journal of Adolescence, 22,* 481–492.

Promising Practices Network (PPN). (2004). What are key ingredients in successful implementation? Retrieved February, 2004, from http://www.promisingpractices.net/ssd/ssd3b.asp

Rigby, K. (2000). Effects of peer victimization in school and perceived social support on adolescent well-being. *Journal of Adolescence, 23,* 57–68.

Roland, E. (2000). Bullying in school: Three national innovations in Norwegian schools in 15 years. *Aggressive Behavior, 26,* 135–143.

Salmivalli, C. (1999). Participant role approach to school bullying: Implications for interventions. *Journal of Adolescence, 22,* 453–459.

Samenow, S. (1989). *Before it's too late: Why some kids get into trouble and what parents can do about it.* New York.

Sharp, S., & Smith, P. K. (1991). Bullying in UK schools: The DES Sheffield Bullying Project. *Early Child Development and Care, 77,* 47–55.

Smith, P. K. (1997). Bullying in schools: The UK experiences and the Sheffield anti-bullying project. *Irish Journal of Psychology, 18*(2), 191–201.

Smith, P.K., Bowers, L., Binney, V., & Cowie, H. (1993). Relationships of children involved in bully/victim problems at school. In S. Duck (Ed.), *Understanding relationship processes: Vol. 2. Learning about relationships* (pp. 184–204). Newbury Park, CA: Sage.

Smith, P. K., & Brain, P. (2000). Bullying in schools: Lessons from two decades of research. *Aggressive Behavior, 26,* 1–9.

Smith, P. K., Cowie, H., Olafsson, R. F., Liefooghe, A. P. D. (with A. Almeida, H. Araki, et al.). (2002). Definitions of bullying: A comparison of terms used, and age and gender differences, in a fourteen-country international comparison. *Child Development, 73,* 1119–1133.

Solberg, M. E., & Olweus, D. (2003). Prevalence estimation of school bullying with the Olweus bully/victim questionnaire. *Aggressive Behavior, 29,* 239–268.

Stevens, V., Van Oost, P., & De Bourdeaudhuij, I. (2000). The effects of an anti-bullying intervention programme on peers' attitudes and behaviour. *Journal of Adolescence, 23,* 21–34.

Weissberg, R. P. (2004). Statement before the subcomittee on substance abuse and mental health services, U.S. Senate committee on health, education, labor and pensions. Retrieved March 2006, from www.k12coordinator.org/testimony.pdf

Whitney, I., Rivers, I., Smith, P. K., & Sharp, S. (1994). The Sheffield Project: Methodology and findings. In P. K. Smith & S. Sharp (Eds.), *School bullying insights and perspectives* (pp. 20–56). Routledge: London.

31

From Peer Putdowns to Peer Support

A Theoretical Model and How It Translated into a National Anti-Bullying Program

CHRISTINA SALMIVALLI, ANTTI KÄRNÄ, AND ELISA POSKIPARTA

Introduction

A glance at some titles of recent writings on school bullying or aggression, such as "Bullying Is Power" (Vaillancourt, Hymel, & McDougall, 2003; see also this volume), "It's Easy, It Works, and It Makes Me Feel Good" (Sutton, Smith, & Swettenham, 2001), or "The Allure of a Mean Friend" (Hawley, Little, & Card, 2007), reveals something about the relatively recent shift in the way bullying is perceived. No longer is it assumed to be driven by the bully's inability to engage in prosocial interaction with peers or to understand others' viewpoints. Bullying is rather seen as strategic, even skillful behavior that might help the bully to meet his or her needs and goals in the peer context. As bullying is often reinforced by group members, or at least appears as being accepted by the majority of peers (Salmivalli, Lagerspetz, Björkqvist, Österman, & Kaukiainen, 1996; Salmivalli & Voeten, 2004), it tends to endure and lead to the creation and sustaining of social norms that make it difficult even for the most prosocial children to take sides with the victim (Juvonen & Galvan, 2008).

The often introduced notion that prevention and intervention strategies addressing bullying should be research-based can be taken to mean two things. First, findings such as the ones above can help design effective methods to tackle bullying. In other words, research can inform us about the motivations and social dynamics that cause bullying and maintain it. These insights are needed to make hypotheses about the possible mechanisms of change and thus, about where and how the interventions should be targeted. On the other hand, the intervention programs themselves should be rigorously evaluated in studies meeting high scientific standards. This is important in order to ascertain that they have the hoped-for effects and are therefore worth investing in, but also in order to validate the theoretical model behind them. Intervention research is thus the final test for the hypothesized mechanisms behind bullying—as such it is not only "applied research" but becomes basic research itself.

In the current chapter, we present a view of bullying that is based on two lines of research: recent studies concerning the social standing of aggressive children in general and bullies in particular (Juvonen, Graham, & Schuster, 2003; Rodkin & Farmer, 2000) in classrooms, and the series of studies on participant roles in bullying that started a decade ago (e.g., Salmivalli et al., 1996; Salmivalli & Voeten, 2004). We move on to present a preliminary model for an anti-bullying program informed by this research, and describe the development and the core components of Finland's new national anti-bullying program, KiVa, which was piloted in Finnish comprehensive schools (2007–09). Finally, we will introduce the theory-based approach utilized in our evaluation of the KiVa program.

The Social Architecture of Bullying

Bullying behavior seems to be at least partly motivated by a pursuit of high status and a powerful position in the peer group. Both adolescent and adult bullies value dominance (Björkqvist, Ekman, & Lagerspetz, 1982) and social status (South & Wood, 2006). Having highly agentic goals, such as being respected and admired among peers, is associated with proactive aggression both concurrently (Salmivalli, Ojanen, Haanpää, & Peets, 2005) and longitudinally (Ojanen & Salmivalli, 2007). Bullying others is not a completely unsuccessful strategy to meet such goals, as studies have shown that even if bullies are not necessarily personally liked by many classmates, they are indeed perceived as popular and powerful (Caravita, DiBlasio, & Salmivalli, 2009; Vaillancourt, Hymel, & McDougall, 2003). There is also longitudinal evidence suggesting that aggression towards peers helps to maintain status (Juvonen & Galvan, 2008), even leading to increases in status over time (Cillessen & Borch, 2004).

How can someone who aggresses against others be popular in the group? Antisocial, tough behavior is often perceived as "cool" even in normative peer cultures (Rodkin, Farmer, Pearl, & Van Acker, 2006), and so is bullying (Juvonen & Galvan, in press). This is especially clear in adolescence, and it has been suggested that as antisocial and aggressive acts represent challenges to adult norms and values (Moffitt, 1993), they become more accepted (or at least less negatively viewed) when children approach adolescence.

Furthermore, as bullies do not target all, or even most of their classmates, but are often selective in their aggression (Troop-Gordon & Broch, 2005), many peers never come to experience personally the most harmful effects of their behavior. By choosing victims who are submissive (Schwartz et al., 1998), insecure of themselves (Salmivalli & Isaacs, 2005), physically weak (Hodges & Perry, 1999), and in a low-power, rejected position in the group (Hodges & Perry, 1999), the children who bully can repeatedly demonstrate their power to the rest of the group and thus renew their high-status position without the fear of being confronted.

The demonstrations of power need witnesses. It is no wonder that in most bullying incidents, a group of peers is present (Hawkins, Pepler, & Craig, 2001). Although it is possible that bullying incidents attract spectators, it is highly likely that the attacks are often initiated when a group of peers is already at the spot. The bystanders seldom intervene (O'Connell, Pepler, & Craig, 1999). Salmivalli et al. (1996) investigated the different participant roles children may have in bullying situations (victims, bullies, assistants of bullies, reinforcers of bullies, outsiders, and defenders of the victim) and found that rather than supporting the victim, many children acted in ways that encouraged and maintained bullying. For instance, relatively many bystanders reinforce the bully's behavior by laughing or cheering. Others might just silently witness what is happening, and such behavior might also be interpreted by the bully as approval of what he or she is doing.

Even if most children's attitudes are clearly against bullying (Rigby & Slee, 1991; Salmivalli, 2001), it seems that the presence and behavior of peers is more likely to maintain the resumption of bullying instead of finishing it. Fortunately, there are also students who defend and support the victim. Hawkins and colleagues (Hawkins et al., 2001) discovered that when peers intervened, 58% of their efforts were successful in stopping the bullying episode. In addition to direct intervention that was observed in the Hawkins et al. study, other kinds of support such as comforting the victim, or telling the teacher about bullying, might be helpful in other ways. If peers are part of the problem, they can also be part of the solution.

Why don't peers intervene and support the victim more often? It has been suggested (Juvonen & Galvan, 2008) that at least two motives might prevent children from taking sides with the victim. The first one is increasing one's own social standing by appearing more like the person in power (i.e., the bully). Not only do the group members want to side with the dominant one, they also have motivation to distance themselves from the low-status peers. As a consequence, little support of any kind is provided to the victim, who tends to get even more rejected as victimization continues (Hodges & Perry, 1999). The second motive is self-protection: by at least appearing to accept the bully's behavior, the child lowers—or believes to lower—his or her own risk of becoming the next victim (Juvonen & Galvan, 2008).

From the point of view of intervention, it is important to know which characteristics of bystanders should be influenced in order to increase their pro-victim behavior. What is known about these factors? Empathy is a characteristic often associated with prosocial, helping behavior (for a meta-analysis, see Eisenberg, 1987). Preliminary research done in our group (Caravita et al., 2009; Pöyhönen & Salmivalli, 2007) indicates that affective empathy, or the tendency to vicariously feel the affective state of the other, is indeed associated with supporting and defending the victims. However, the association is not very strong, indicating that empathy alone might not be sufficient to make a child take sides with the victimized student. This is understandable if we reconsider the nature of bullying incidents, including the powerful bully, the rejected victim, and the witnesses who are concerned about their own status and safety in the peer group.

Self-efficacy for defending refers to a child's perception of being able to engage in such behavior, knowing how it can be done, and finding it easy. Not surprisingly, we have found that after controlling for the effects of sex (girls typically defend more than boys) and empathy (girls scoring significantly higher), self-efficacy for defending has a unique *positive* association with supporting the victim. In the same time, it is *negatively* related to staying outside bullying incidents and not taking sides with anyone (Pöyhönen & Salmivalli, 2007).

Yet another correlate of defending behavior is a high status in the classroom (Salmivalli et al., 1996). Particularly in middle childhood, defending victims is related both to social preference (being well-liked) and to perceived popularity (Caravita et al., 2009). This suggests that a high status in the group enables an individual to take sides with the weak one. Perhaps socially preferred children are more ready to adopt defending behaviors than others due to their reduced risk of ending up as victims themselves, as well as their secure position in the group. Furthermore, children who support or defend the victim often believe that their parents and friends expect them to act so (Rigby & Johnson, 2006). Furthermore, they tend to have friends who also support the victim (Salmivalli, Huttunen, & Lagerspetz, 1997).

How peers behave in bullying situations is not only influenced by individual characteristics of the children, but also the norms of the whole classroom. A considerable amount of variation in participant role behaviors lies between classrooms (Salmivalli & Voeten, 2004), such that in some classes there is a stronger tendency to reinforce the bully whereas in others students tend to side with the victim or stay outside bullying situations. This variation can partly be explained by attitudes and norms at the classroom level. Similarly, classroom norms can be used to explain the acceptance of the bullies, which also varies significantly across classrooms (Sentse, Scholte, Salmivalli, & Voeten, 2007). Some intervention programs aiming to reduce problematic behaviors have utilized high-status children who get many sociometric choices in nomination tasks such as "persons who other kids listen to," or "these people set the trends for other kids" (Miller-

Johnson & Costanzo, 2004, p. 217) as models for others. The idea is that the best route to change the norms in the group is through its most influential members. We believe that high-status prosocial peers can be utilized in anti-bullying programs as well. When bullying goes on in a classroom, some such classmates could be specifically selected and mobilized to protect and support the particular victim. As high-status children and adolescents are often emulated by their peers, others might be more prone to take actions against bullying, and in support of the victim, when seeing the positive example provided by them.

Research Meets the Practice: A Preliminary Model for an Anti-bullying Program

According to us, the aim of an anti-bullying program should be threefold: first, it should attempt to put an end to ongoing bullying. Second, it should prevent the emergence of new bully-victim relationships. Last, but not least, it should aim at minimizing the consequences of victimization.

Children and adolescents facing bullying problems as bystanders are trapped in a social dilemma. On one hand, they understand that bullying is wrong and they would like to do something to stop it—on the other hand, they strive to secure their own status and safety in the peer group. A successful intervention would be one that helps them solve this social dilemma. This is not to say that specific bullies should not be targeted by adults. From our perspective, an anti-bullying program should include both universal and indicated actions.

The *universal* intervention refers to efforts made to influence the group norms and to build capacity in all children to behave in constructive ways, to take responsibility for not encouraging bullying, and to support the victims. The *indicated* intervention means that when bullying comes to the attention of school staff, that particular case needs to be handled in individual and group discussions between a teacher (or another adult) and the parties. Thus, the adults take the responsibility for putting an end to what is going on between the bully and the victim, and provide the necessary support for the victim. Additionally, selected group members (classmates) are utilized in effectuating the indicated intervention as well, challenging them to provide support for the victim.

The universal and indicated interventions included in our model are described in more detail in the following and displayed in Table 31.1.

Working with the Whole Class: The Universal Intervention

The anti-bullying program should raise the students' awareness of the role they play in the bullying process, as well as their empathic understanding of the victim's plight. It is imperative to help the students realize that their behavior is part of the problem as it maintains the negative behaviors that compromise the well-being of everyone and causes suffering to the victim. From the victim's perspective, it might actually be the impression that no one cares, rather than the bully's attacks as such, that cause the most negative feelings. Moreover, the students should be provided with safe strategies to support the victim. Supporting the victim can be safe when (a) it is based on common decisions and commitments done together in the group, and (b) it does not necessarily mean heroic acts of confronting the bullies, but can also consist of small things such as communicating understanding and support to the victim and befriending him or her. When the reward structure of the classroom changes, supporting and defending the victim might become behaviors that are reinforced by peers.

The main goals of the universal intervention are thus to reduce pro-bullying behaviors such as assisting or reinforcing the bully and to increase support for the victim. This can happen by raising awareness of the discrepancy between the attitudes children hold and their actual behavior as well as of the role the whole group often plays in maintaining bullying, enhancing empathy toward the victims and finally, learning and practicing safe strategies to intervene and support the victim (the left column of Table 31.1).

There are several reasons to believe that influencing bystanders (students who are neither bullies nor victims themselves) might lead to a more successful outcome than any attempts to change the bully's behavior alone. First, *if the motivation to bully is related to one's social standing in the group, then the group is in the key role of regulating bullying among its members.* For instance, if fewer children took on the role of reinforcer when witnessing bullying, and if the group refused to assign high status for those who bully, an important reward for bullying others would be lost.

Second, even if the change in bystanders' behavior would not lead (at least immediately) to changes in the bully's behavior, it is very likely to make a *difference in the victim's situation.* Mobilizing the classmates to support the victim is crucial in *minimizing the adverse effects for those who are victimized.* Studies interviewing former victims have indicated that the most traumatic memories from their schooldays include feelings of being excluded, along with the perception that others approve the bullying or at least did not care (Teräsahjo, 1997) rather than the negative behaviors of the bully as such. Victimization is an attack on the victim's status but also on his or her need to belong (Hawker & Boulton, 2001), and often a successful one. Furthermore, having protective friendships in the classroom has been shown to buffer against further victimization as well as the negative influences of victimization, such as internalizing problems (Boulton, Trueman, Chau, Whitehand, & Amatya, 1999; Hodges, Boivin, Vitaro, & Bukowski, 1999).

The third reason to influence the bystanders is a very pragmatic one: they might be *easier to influence* than the active, initiative-taking bullies. The bystanders have strong anti-bullying attitudes: they think that bullying is wrong, they feel bad for the victim, and they often express a wish to do something. Converting their already existing attitudes into behavior is a challenging task, but it might nevertheless be a more realistic goal than influencing an individual bully only by adult sanctions or rewards.

Putting an End to Bullying: The Indicated Intervention

The indicated part of the intervention (see the two right-side columns in Table 31.1) simply means that when bullying comes to the attention, the particular case is handled, not together in the classroom but by private, firm discussions (first separately with the bullying children and the victim), in which the adult makes it clear that bullying is not tolerated, challenging the students to change their behavior. Another function of the discussions is to let the victim know that the adult is aware of the bullying, understands how the victim feels, is on his or her side, and is going to do everything to make it stop. The discussions should be accompanied by follow-up meetings in which the adult makes sure that the bullying has stopped.

The peers should not be forgotten in effectuating the indicated intervention. They can be utilized by selecting some prosocial, preferably high-status children and challenging them to think of what they could do to support a particular victimized classmate. This might help the victims in two ways. First, high-status children are in the position of influencing others and setting the standards for acceptable and unacceptable behaviors (Juvonen & Galvan, 2008; Miller-Johnson & Costanzo, 2004). Their behavior is often emulated by other children in the classroom, so encouraged by their model the others might change their attitude toward the victim and start treating him or her more positively. On the other hand, being accepted and befriended by some classmates, and especially by high-status classmates, might significantly reduce the suffering of the victims and make them feel better about themselves. Third, the high-status prosocial classmates can function as protective factors against further victimization (cf., Hodges, Boivin, Vitaro, & Bukowski, 1999).

For high-status children, the risk of being victimized themselves is much lower than for other classmates, and therefore they might be more ready to support the victim(s). Our recent studies on the predictors of defending behavior support this view (Caravita et al., 2009; Pöyhönen & Salmivalli, 2007).

Translating the Model into Practice: The Development of a National Anti-bullying Program in Finland

Since the beginning of the 1990s, there has been a lot of public attention allocated to bully-victim problems in Finland. In the same time, changes in legislation concerning school safety and the development of anti-bullying policies have occurred. The Finnish Basic Education Act states (since 1999) that every student has the right to a safe school environment. Education providers have the responsibility of making sure that students do not experience acts of violence or bullying while at school. The Basic Education Act was further amended in 2003, stating that the education provider shall draw up a plan, in connection with curriculum design, for safeguarding pupils against violence, bullying and harassment, execute the plan and supervise adherence to it and its implementation. The legislation concerns all educational levels.

Despite the large attention to the problem and the legislative changes that have taken place, no changes can be observed in the frequencies of students being bullied during the past decade. Although Finland has been among the most active countries when it comes to research on bullying, no national large-scale interventions have been developed and put into practice. Among the few local initiatives that have been evaluated was the intervention study conducted in our group several years ago (Salmivalli, Kaukiainen, & Voeten, 2005; Salmivalli, Kaukiainen, Voeten, & Sinisammal, 2004). Although the intervention was based on the principles discussed above and presented in Table 31.1, all of the components (e.g., including selected classmates in the indicated part of the intervention, a clearly defined set of student lessons) were not present yet. The findings were very encouraging, however. For instance, self-reported victimization rates went down, even by 57% (Grade 4) and by 46% (Grade 5), expressed as a percentage of the baseline rate,

Table 31.1 A Model for an Anti-Bullying Program: Universal and Indicated Interventions

	Universal	Indicated	
Target	All children	Individual bully/ies and victim +	Selected (prosocial, high-status) classmates
Aim	Reducing pro-bullying behaviors Increasing peer support for victims Influencing classroom norms	Stopping the ongoing bullying Supporting the victim	Increasing peer support for the victim
	BY	BY	BY
	- increasing awareness, empathy, and efficacy to intervene	- making clear that bullying is not tolerated and has to stop immediately	- using high-status peers as protective friends and as models for others
Means	Student lessons	Individual & small group discussions & follow-up	Small-group discussion
Agent	Classroom teacher	School team member	Classroom teacher

in schools with a high degree of implementation of the program. In the low-implementation schools, the reductions were 29% and 15%, respectively, in grades 4 and 5. We also found hoped-for effects on self-reports of bullying others, students' beliefs and attitudes regarding bullying, and to some extent, in their participant role behaviors.

In 2006, the Finnish Ministry of Education launched a large project aiming to advance students' well-being at school. One part of the project is the development and evaluation of a national anti-bullying program, regarding which the Ministry signed a contract with the University of Turku. This work is being effectuated in the Department of Psychology and the Center for Learning Research and led by the first and the third author. This project gave us a chance to develop a comprehensive program with complete materials and manuals, plan the relevant teacher education, and to evaluate the effectiveness of the program in a large-scale study including the different provinces of Finland, with more than 100 schools and thousands of students from different grade levels.

KiVa: The New National Anti-Bullying Program in Finland

KiVa is an acronym of the expression Kiusaamista Vastaan, Against Bullying, but the word kiva also means in Finnish nice, good, and cute. KiVa (www.kivakoulu.fi) is a research-based program that provides schools with concrete materials for their anti-bullying work. The program focuses on the three aims described previously in this chapter. It attempts to put an end to ongoing bullying, to prevent the emergence of new bully-victim relationships, and finally, to minimize the negative consequences of victimization. KiVa involves both universal and indicated actions to meet these aims.

The unique features of the KiVa program include: (a) an exceptionally large variety of concrete materials for students, teachers, and parents; (b) utilization of the Internet and virtual learning environments, such as a computer game against bullying; and (c) emphasis on the bystanders, to encourage them to show that they are against bullying and support the victim, rather than encourage the bully.

The Student Lessons

The universal part of the program includes 20 hours of student lessons. The lessons are carried out by the classroom teacher, and they involve discussion, group work, short films about bullying, and role-play exercises. The topics of the lessons proceed from more general topics, such as the importance of respect in relationships and group communication and group pressure, to bullying and its mechanisms and consequences. In the short films that are viewed and discussed together, for instance, adults who were bullied as children tell about their schooldays and how their experiences have affected their life even later. Several lessons concern the role of the group in either maintaining bullying or putting an end to it. The group exercises involve, among other things, brainstorming different ways to support and help the bullied victims, and practicing them. After each lesson, a class rule is adopted, based on the central theme of the lesson. At the end of the school year the class rules are put together as the KiVa-contract, which is signed by everyone.

The central aims of the student lessons are to raise awareness of the role that group might play in maintaining bullying, to increase empathy towards victims, to promote children's strategies of supporting the victim and thus their self-efficacy to do so, and to increase children's coping skills when victimized. Essentially, the lessons try to help children resolve the social dilemma

Figure 31.1 Characters from the virtual school in the KiVa computer game. © Finnish ministry of education, reproduced by permission.

they are faced with (i.e., doing what they know is right or doing what seems to be normative in the group).

The Anti-Bullying Computer Game

One unique feature in the KiVa program is an anti-bullying computer game (see Figure 31.1), which the students play during the lessons described above. The game involves five levels, and the teacher always activates the next level of the game when a particular lesson has been gone through in the classroom. The game is started after lesson 3, the next level is played after lesson 5, and so forth, during the whole school year. Additionally, students can play the game in their free time at their homes. Each level of the KiVa game includes three components that have been named as I Know, I Can, and I Do.

In the "I Know" component, the students learn new facts about bullying but also examine what they have learnt from the lessons thus far. They are asked questions about the content of the lessons in game-like tasks, and they can test themselves with respect to different characteristics (e.g., how well you can resist the group pressure; what kind of classmate you are).

In the "I Can" component, the students move around in a virtual school and face different challenging situations in the corridors, playgrounds, and lunchrooms. They make decisions regarding how to respond in these situations, what to say and what to do, and get feedback based on the choices they make. They can also examine the feelings and thoughts of other characters in the game before and after their own actions.

The third component, "I do," is designed to encourage students to make use of their knowledge and skills in real life situations. This happens by asking them to report—at each level of the game—which ones of the learned skills they have put into practice, for instance, whether they have treated others with respect, whether they have resisted group pressure, or whether they have supported someone who was victimized. Again, the students get feedback based on their reports.

The KiVa program continues after the first year, and now the students themselves are even more actively involved. They have different class and school projects where they themselves create anti-bullying materials and plan and effectuate anti-bullying lessons for younger students. It should be noted that the version of KiVa described here is meant for students in grades 4–6. Modifications will be needed when we develop the version for the younger (grades 1–3) and older (grades 7–9) children.

To prevent bullying in the schoolyard, teachers supervising the recess are provided vests to enhance their visibility and to signal that bullying is taken seriously in the school. Parents are involved in the universal part of the program as well. A parents' guide is sent to each home that includes information about bullying and advice concerning the parents' possibilities to prevent and help reduce the problem. The schedule for program implementation during the first year is displayed in Table 31.2.

The Indicated Intervention: Tackling the Acute Cases

To effectuate the indicated part of the KiVa intervention program, there is a team of three teachers (or other school personnel) in each participating school that tackles, together with the classroom teacher, the acute cases of bullying that come to attention. This happens through a set of individual and group discussions that one or two team members go through with the victim and with the bullies, and systematic follow-up meetings. In addition to these discussions, the classroom teacher arranges a meeting with two to four classmates to encourage them to support the victimized child. The classroom teacher, who knows his or her own class best, selects classmates who are prosocial and preferably have a high-status position in the classroom. The team member(s) who have discussed with the victim have also asked him/her whether there are some

Table 31.2 The Shedule of Implementation of the KiVa-Program (Grades 4–6) during the School Year

Month	School Level	Classroom Level	Dyadic Level	Individual Level	Parents
August	Education for school teams & teachers Feedback from pretest	Lesson 1	**Immediate handling of the acute cases that come to attention + follow-ups**	**Support for individual victims/bullieswhen needed**	
September	Whole-school meeting	Lesson 2			Meeting with parents
October	School network meeting	Lesson 3 + KiVa game			Material sent to homes
November		Lesson 4			
December		Lesson 5 + KiVa game			
January	School network meeting	Lesson 6			
February		Lesson 7 +KiVa game			
March		Lesson 8			
April	School network meeting	Lesson 9 + KiVA game			
May	Whole-school meeting	Lesson 10 + KiVa game			Meeting with parents

friendly classmates who do not join in the bullying, and who might be able to provide support: also this information can be utilized when selecting the classmates. The teacher manuals and instruction provide detailed information about how the discussions are carried out.

As bullying often occurs when adults are not around and thus remains unnoticed by teachers and parents, it is important to encourage the students to report bullying. We believe that when children are told about the KiVa program, early in the first student lesson, and reminded about it throughout the school year (by the lessons, the computer game, the posters hanging on the school wall, etc.), they come to believe that adults at the school are serious about bullying and the victims are likely to get help. Consequently, both victims as well as onlookers who merely observe bullying will be more likely to report it. Furthermore, both school staff and parents are provided information about bullying and advice concerning how to detect it, which hopefully leads to more awareness and skills in identifying the bullying that is going on.

Support for the Implementation of KiVa

As studies have shown that implementation is a critical factor in the effectiveness of bullying interventions (Eslea & Smith, 1998; Olweus, 2004; Salmivalli, Kaukiainen, & Voeten, 2005), the teachers and the school teams are supported in the implementation of the KiVa program in several ways. The teacher's guide and all materials included in the program have been prepared to be as self-contained and ready-to-use as possible. Furthermore, all teachers carrying out the KiVa program in their classrooms are provided a web-based discussion forum where they can discuss and share experiences and ideas.

To support the indicated interventions, networks of school team members are created (each network consisting of three school teams (i.e., nine teachers or other adults working in the school) that meet three times during the school year in their own province with a key person trained to guide the networks. In the first phase, the program developers serve as the key persons themselves, in order to get the first-hand experience of the successes and possible difficulties in program implementation. In the dissemination phase of the KiVa program, new key persons will be trained.

Evaluation of KiVa

Aims of the Evaluation Study The evaluation study of the KiVa program has several interconnected objectives, which deal with investigating the program effects, providing information for further improvement of the program content and enabling high implementation fidelity in the schools adopting the program in the future.

The main objective is to evaluate how well the KiVa program can meet its aims: putting an end to ongoing bullying, preventing the emergence of new bullying cases, and minimizing the adverse consequences of victimization. The prevalence measurements of bullying and victimization will allow direct comparison of the effects of the program with the results of regular anti-bullying efforts already used in Finnish schools. Thus, the value of the program is put to a stringent test.

Another goal of the evaluation study is to examine *how* the program produces its positive effects and *when*. On the basis of varying results from previous research, not enough is known about these factors (Smith, Schneider, Smith, & Ananiadou, 2004). The evaluation of KiVa can provide some answers by correlating expected mechanisms of change with the outcome (i.e., actual change). For instance, the hypothesis regarding different participant role behaviors and their influence on ongoing bullying can be tested. If the behavior of students witnessing bullying actually has some effect on bullies, prevents the emergence of new bully-victim dyads, or eases the plight of the victims, this should be reflected in parallel changes in participant role behaviors and these phenomena. Similarly, we can test other assumptions regarding the factors that influence bully-victim problems at the individual, classroom, and school levels. This information can be used to target the program even more precisely at the most crucial factors. Moreover, we hope to be able to ascertain what are the minimum requirements (e.g., in terms of implementation), for successful bullying intervention and prevention, which students are most likely to be affected and under which circumstances, and so forth.

In the evaluation study, we will also investigate which factors predict the implementation of the KiVa program at teacher and school levels. Knowing the predictors of implementation allows one to estimate what kind of teachers and schools are likely to implement the program to a large extent and are thereby more probable to benefit from it. Conversely, by being able to identify schools likely to fall short of implementation, support can be tailored to the needs of the specific schools. Municipal educational administration and schools can then use this knowledge to make decisions about introducing the program and allocating resources to support its implementation.

Finally, we gather feedback from the participating students and teachers to further improve the quality of the program. The participants will evaluate the KiVa program by its components and as a whole. Knowledge about students' and teachers' experiences is valuable when refining the program to better suit the needs of its users. To accomplish all these four aims of evaluation, an extensive intervention study is being conducted with some of its features described below.

Sample, Design, and Assessments All Finnish comprehensive schools were invited to volunteer to pilot the KiVa program. From among the nearly 300 schools that announced their willingness to participate, a representative sample of 78 schools was chosen for the first phase of the evaluation (Table 31.3). Stratified random sampling was used to categorize the schools into 39 pilot and 39 control schools representing all provinces of Finland. In the first phase, the effectiveness of the program is investigated in grades 4, 5, and 6 of the pilot schools (the pre-test data collected in the spring, when they are finishing grades 3–5). The sample (pilot and control schools) consists of over 400 classes and more than 7,000 students. A parallel sampling procedure will be used in the second phase of the evaluation for grades 1–3 and 7–9. In this way, all grade levels in the Finnish comprehensive school are included in the study, and the total sample will amount to about 20,000 students.

Two designs are being used to evaluate the effects of KiVa program: a randomized experimental design and a cohort-longitudinal design with adjacent cohorts (Table 31.4). In this way it possible to have two separate control groups. This eliminates certain threats to validity, such as history effects in a cohort-longitudinal design.

Congruent with the goals of the evaluation study, a large number of factors are being assessed. The variables can generally be classified into six broad categories: background information (about school, students, etc.); bullying and victimization; potential precursors and consequences of bully/victim problems at individual, class, and school levels; implementation of the program

Table 31.3 The Two Phases of Program Evaluation

Phase	Year	Grades	Pilot schools (N)	Control schools (N)
1	2007–08	4–6	39	39
2	2008–09	1–3	39	39
		7–9	39	39

Table 31.4 The Cohort-Longitudinal Design, Arrows Indicating the Comparisons Made. Post-Test Data from Students in Each Cohort Are Compared with Baseline Data from Same-Aged Students from the Same Schools (i.e., in the previous cohort), Who Have Not Yet Been Exposed to the Intervention

Cohort	Pre-Test	Post-Test
1	—	grade 1
2	grade 1	grade 2
3	grade 2	grade 3
4	grade 3	grade 4
5	grade 4	grade 5
6	grade 5	grade 6
7	grade 6	grade 7
8	grade 7	grade 8
9	grade 8	grade 9

Note. The arrows indicate the comparisons made in the first phase of the evaluation study.

(universal and indicated interventions); factors predicting implementation of the program (such as teacher self-efficacy); and users' experiences of the program. Most of the data collection is web-based, and the data will include self-, peer- and teacher reports regarding the students' attributes and behaviors, as well as teachers' reports of their own beliefs and actions. All study participants receive their own personal user ID, which they use as a password for the questionnaires. Thus, individual participants can be identified at different time points while they remain in practice anonymous to the researchers. The bully-victim dyads will be identified by asking children questions such as "who do you bully?" or "who are the ones that bully you?" We will be able to follow the changes that take place in particular individuals, bully-victim dyads, and their contexts during the intervention.

The true longitudinal design is a significant improvement to the design of many earlier evaluation studies, which can be demonstrated with an example of students' outcome measures. Most of the previous bullying intervention studies have examined the levels of bullying and victimization, or the frequencies of bullies and victims, as their outcome variables. However, the designs have typically not allowed to find out whether possible *decreases in bullying others* are due to some of the bullies stopping/reducing bullying, or rather, some of the potential new bullies (children with risk factors for bullying) not starting to bully others in the first place. Similarly, we do not usually know whether *decreases in victimization* are caused by some of the victims escaping the victim role, or some of the potential victims (children with risk factors for victimization) not ending up as victims at all. Following particular individuals from pre- to post-test measurements will allow differentiating between these outcomes. The investigation of these alternative, but not mutually exclusive, processes will provide important information about whether the mechanisms of the KiVa program are mainly preventive or interceptive.

Conclusions

As bullying takes place in the context of a group of peers, and is often reinforced and maintained by peer processes, interventions are needed that target all students rather than just bullies and their victims. Students need to be provided with the sense of responsibility for everyone's well-being in the group, as well as safe strategies to support and help their fellow students who are victimized. However, when cases of bullying come to attention it is necessary to deal effectively with the individuals involved, ensuring that bullying stops. Moreover, selected high-status peers can be challenged to protect and support the victim in acute cases.

In our evaluation of KiVa, a new national anti-bullying program in Finland, we assess the prevalence of bullying and victimization in pilot and control schools at three time points during the In our evaluation study, we assess the prevalence of bullying and victimization in pilot and control schools at three time points during the school year, but also several risk factors and consequences of such problems. Moreover, a cohort-longitudinal design comparing adjacent cohorts can be utilized to verify the effects in another way. In addition to traditional self- and peer-report questions, we collect dyadic data which enables to identify the bully-victim dyads and follow them over time. Implementation of both universal and targeted interventions will be assessed in several ways, enabling to relate implementation to program effects. Importantly, we meet the school staff regularly and collect user experiences that further help us in refining our program. Although we cannot say anything about the program effects at this point, it has been received with enthusiasm by teachers and students in the pilot schools.

References

Björkqvist, K., Ekman, K., & Lagerspetz, K. (1982). Bullies and victims: Their ego picture, ideal ego picture and normative ego picture. *Scandinavian Journal of Psychology, 23*, 307–313.

Boulton, M., Trueman, M., Chau, C., Whitehand, C., & Amatya, K. (1999). Concurrent and longitudinal links between friendship and peer victimization: Implications for befriending interventions. *Journal of Adolescence, 22*, 461–466.

Caravita, S., DiBlasio, P., & Salmivalli, C. (2009). Unique and interactive effects of empathy and social status on inovlvement in bullying. *Social Development, 18*, 140–163.

Cillessen, A., & Borch, C. (2004). Developmental trajectories of adolescent popularity: A growth curve modeling analysis. *Journal of Adolescence, 29*, 935–959.

Eisenberg, N. (1987). The relation of empathy to prosocial and related behaviors. *Psychological Bulletin, 101*, 91–119.

Eslea, M., & Smith, P. (1998). The long-term effectiveness of anti-bullying work in primary schools. *Educational Research, 40*, 203–218.

Hawker, D., & Boulton, M. (2001). Subtypes of peer harassment and their correlates. In J. Juvonen & S. Graham (Eds.), *Peer harassment in school: The plight of the vulnerable and the victimized* (pp. 378–397). New York: Guilford.

Hawkins, D. L., Pepler, D. J., & Craig, W. M. (2001). Naturalistic observations of peer interventions in bullying. *Social Development, 10*, 512–527.

Hawley, P., Little, T., & Card, N. (2007). The allure of a mean friend: Relationship quality and processes of aggressive adolescents with prosocial skills. *International Journal of Behavioral Development, 31*, 170–180.

Hodges, E. V. E., Boivin, M., Vitaro, F., & Bukowski, W. (1999). The power of friendship: Protection against an escalating cycle of peer victimization. *Developmental Psychology, 35*, 94–101.

Hodges, E. V. E., & Perry, D. G. (1999). Personal and interpersonal antecedents and consequences of victimization by peers. *Journal of Personality and Social Psychology, 76*, 677–685.

Juvonen, J., & Galvan, A. (2008). Peer influence in involuntary social groups: Lessons from research on bullying. In M. Prinstein & K. Dodge (Eds.), *Peer influence processes among youth* (pp. 225–244). New York: Guilford.

Juvonen, J., Graham, S., & Schuster, M. (2003). Bullying among young adolescents: The strong, the weak, and troubled. *Pediatrics, 112*, 1231–1237.

Miller-Johnson, S., & Costanzo, P. (2004). If you can't beat 'em…induce them to join you: Peer-based interventions during adolescence. In J. Kupersmidt & K. Dodge (Eds.), *Children's peer relation: From development to intervention* (pp. 209–222). Washington, DC: American Psychological Association.

Moffitt, T. (1993). Adolescence-limited and life-course-persistent antisocial behavior: A developmental taxonomy. *Psychological Review, 100*, 674–701.

O'Connell, P., Pepler, D., & Craig, W., (1999). Peer involvement in bullying: Insights and challenges for intervention. *Journal of Adolescence, 22*, 437–452.

Ojanen, T., & Salmivalli, C. (2007). *Motivation matters: Social goals predict peer-reported social withdrawal, aggression, and sociometric status during early adolescence.* Paper presented in the SRCD biennial meeting, March 29–April 1, Boston.

Olweus, D. (2004). The Olweus Bullying Prevention Programme: Design and *implementation* issues and a new national initiative in Norway. In P. K. Smith, D. Pepler, & K. Rigby (Eds.), *Bullying in schools: How successful can interventions be?* (pp. 13–36). New York: Cambridge University Press.

Pöyhönen, V., & Salmivalli, C. (2007). *Cognitive and affective factors associated with defending the bullied victims.* Poster presented in the SRCD biennial meeting, March 29–April 1, Boston.

Rigby, K. & Johnson, B. (2006). Expressed readiness of Australian schoolchildren to act as bystanders in support of children who are being bullied. *Educational Psychology, 26,* 425–440.

Rigby, K., & Slee, P. T., (1991). Bullying among Australian school children: Reported behavior and attitudes toward victims. *Journal of Social Psychology, 131,* 615–627.

Rodkin, P., & Farmer, T. (2000). Heterogeneity of popular boys: Antisocial and prosocial configurations. *Developmental Psychology, 36,* 14–24.

Rodkin, P., Farmer, T., Pearl, R., & Van Acker, R. (2006). They're cool: Social status and peer group supports for aggressive boys and girls. *Social Development, 15,* 175–204.

Salmivalli, C. (2001). Peer-led intervention campaign against school bullying: Who considered it useful, who benefited? *Educational Research, 43,* 263–278.

Salmivalli, C., Huttunen, A., & Lagerspetz, K. (1997). Peer networks and bullying in schools. *Scandinavian Journal of Psychology, 38,* 305–312.

Salmivalli, C., & Isaacs, J. (2005). Prospective relations among victimization, rejection, friendlessness, and children's self- and peer-perceptions. *Child Development, 76,* 1161–1171.

Salmivalli, C., Kaukiainen, A., & Voeten, M. (2005). Anti-bullying intervention: Implementation and outcome. *British Journal of Educational Psychology, 75,* 465–487.

Salmivalli, C., Kaukiainen, A., Voeten, M., & Sinisammal, M. (2004). Targeting the group as a whole: The Finnish anti-bullying intervention. In P. K. Smith, D. Pepler, & K. Rigby (Eds.), *Bullying in schools: How successful can interventions be?* (pp. 251–273). New York: Cambridge University Press.

Salmivalli, C., Lagerspetz, K., Björkqvist, K., Österman, K. & Kaukiainen, A. (1996). Bullying as a group process: Participant roles and their relations to social status within the group. *Aggressive Behavior, 22,* 1–15.

Salmivalli, C., Ojanen, T., Haanpää, J., & Peets, K. (2005). "I'm O.K. but you're not" and other peer-relational schemas: Explaining individual differences in children's social goals. *Developmental Psychology, 41,* 363–375.

Salmivalli, C., & Voeten, M. (2004). Connections between attitudes, group norms, and behaviours associated with bullying in schools. *International Journal of Behavioral Development, 28,* 246–258.

Schwartz, D., Dodge, K., Hubbard, J., Cillessen, A., Lemerise, E., Bateman, H. (1998). Social-cognitive and behavioral correlates of aggression and victimization in boys' play groups. *Journal of Abnormal Child Psychology, 26,* 431–440.

Sentse, M., Scholte, R., Salmivalli, C., & Voeten, M. (2007). Person-group dissimilarity in involvement in bullying and its' relation with social status. *Journal of Abnormal Child Psychology, 35, 1009–1019.*

Smith, D., Schneider, B., Smith, P., & Ananiadou, K. (2004). The effectiveness of whole-school anti-bullying programs: A synthesis of evaluation research. *School Psychology Review, 33,* 547–560.

South, C., & Wood, J. (2006). Bullying in prisons: The importance of perceived social status, prisonization, and moral disengagement. *Aggressive Behavior, 32,* 490–501.

Sutton, J., Smith, P. K., & Swettenham, J. (2001). 'It's easy, it works, and it makes me feel good': A response to Arsenio and Lemerise. *Social Development, 10,* 74–78.

Teräshjo, T. (1997). *Mitä kuvaukset kertovat? Koulukiusaamisen pitkäaikaisseuraamuksien tutkimus esimerkkinä fenomenologisesta tutkimusotteesta* [A phenomenological sudy of the long-term consequences of victimization]. Unpublished master's thesis, University of Turku.

Troop-Gordon, W., & Broch, R. (2005). Peer-identified aggressor-victim dyads: Prevalence and associated adjustment outcomes. In N. Card & E. Hodges (Chairs), *Aggressor-victim relationships: Toward a dyadic perspective.* Symposium in the Biennial meeting of the Society for Research on Child Development, Atlanta, Ga.

Vaillancourt, T., Hymel, S., & McDougall, P. (2003). Bullying is power: Implications for school-based intervention strategies. *Journal of Applied School Psychology, 19,* 157–176.

32

How School Personnel Tackle Cases of Bullying

A Critical Examination

KEN RIGBY AND SHERI BAUMAN

School professionals around the world have learned a great deal about bullying over the last 10 years or so. They typically recognize that bullying is prevalent among boys and girls of all ages and that a substantial number of them are seriously harmed. They usually know that anti-bullying policies are generally expected of them. They are often well informed about what should be written down in the policy document. They are often aware of what can be done and said in classrooms to help prevent bullying. They generally agree that to tackle bullying effectively the school staff must all pull together, that is they recognize the value of a "whole school approach." All this is fine. However, when the question of what exactly is to be done when acts of bullying are discovered, more often than not, the confusion begins. This chapter reviews existing literature on how successful interventions to reduce bullying can be, and focuses especially on what schools are doing in addressing specific cases of bullying. It concludes with some suggestions about how such interventions can be more successful.

The Reported Effectiveness of Anti-Bullying Interventions

In appraising the evidence on the effectiveness of interventions, one should distinguish between (a) what schools do in applying anti-bullying programs that include preventative strategies, for example, the use of the school curriculum to educate children about bullying; and (b) what schools do in resolving particular cases of bullying that come to the attention of school staff. On the former there is now a limited but growing literature on the effectiveness of anti-bullying programs (see Baldry & Farrington, 2007; Smith, Pepler, & Rigby, 2004; Vreeman & Carroll, 2007). Outcomes from evaluated programs have been quite variable. Probably the best known anti-bullying program developed and evaluated by Olweus (1993) in Norway has provided evidence of between 30% and 50% reductions in reported bullying in schools. However, outside Norway the program's effectiveness has been minimal or unsustained, for example in Belgium, Germany and Southern Carolina (see Smith et al., 2004). On average, reductions in bullying in schools attributable to anti-bullying programs is around 15%. To some extent, the limited success of most of these programs could be due to a lack of thorough implementation. Several studies have shown that where implementation has been more thorough, significantly better results have been obtained (see, for example, Salmivalli, Kaukiainen, & Voeten, 2004).

On the question of central interest in this chapter, that is the success or otherwise of interventions with specific cases of bullying, there is comparatively little information. In part, this is because interventions have typically contained a number of diverse elements, for instance policy development, parental involvement, and work with children in classrooms to educate them about bullying. Hence the degree of success or otherwise of many of the evaluated programs cannot be attributed unambiguously to any specific component. Only a small number of studies have attempted to assess outcomes after specific cases of bullying have been addressed by the school.

Probably the most relevant indication of the effectiveness of such interventions comes from the children who have reported to teachers that they are being bullied at school and have subsequently reported on the outcome. These children comprise only in a minority of children who are bullied, as a good deal of bullying in schools is not reported and does not come to the attention of the school staff. According to surveys of schoolchildren (Smith & Shu, 2000; Rigby & Barnes, 2002) some 70% of children who are bullied do not report it to teachers. Hence, teachers can only respond to an unrepresentative sample of cases. Arguably these are cases that children feel desperate enough to seek help from teachers or perhaps have especially positive relations with teachers and believe they can help.

Two studies that provide estimates of how successful teachers are in dealing with cases of bullying that are reported to them by victims. This excludes cases that come to the attention of teachers in other ways, for example, through their own direct observations, reports from observers and reports from parents. The first of these studies was undertaken by Smith and Shu (2000) drawing upon findings taken from a survey conducted in England in 1996. Schoolchildren (N = 2,308) aged 10 to 14 from 19 schools in the London area were asked to indicate whether they had been bullied at school and, if so, whether they had told anyone about it. Among those who reported that they had been bullied, approximately 30% of them had told a teacher about it. Among these approximately 20% reported that the teachers had taken no action. For 80% or so of cases, teachers had taken some action to try to stop the bullying. Table 32.1 indicates the reported outcomes. From Figure 32.1 it is clear that the actions of teachers generally did not stop the bullying: this occurred in only about 27% of the reported cases, although the situation seems to have improved for the victim in a similar proportion of cases. Disconcertingly, in 28% of cases there was no change; that is the bullying continued at the same or similar intensity, and in 16% of cases the bullying actually got worse.

Smith and Shu (2000) also provide some interesting comparisons between outcomes when teachers are told about the bullying and outcomes when others are told. These are presented in Table 32.1. One should bear in mind that some students told more than one of these people or groups. However, the data does suggest that prospects of improving the situation for victims are not notably enhanced when teachers rather than parents were informed; indeed, it would appear that negative outcomes (i.e., the bullying getting worse) are more likely if teachers are told.

Table 32.1 Outcomes when Teachers, the Family, and Classmates Are Told (percentages reporting)

	Teachers	Family	Classmates
The bullying stopped	26.6	21.5	17.3
The bullying got less	28.7	33.9	25.6
Nothing changed	28.3	31.6	46.6
The bullying got worse	16.4	13.0	10.5

From Smith and Shu (2000)

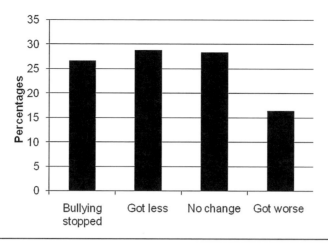

Figure 32.1 Effects of reported teacher interventions to stop bullying in schools.

A further study was undertaken in Australia by Rigby and Barnes (2002). From a large sample of Australian school children (N = 33, 236 aged 8 to 18 years (see Rigby, 1997), some 27% children reported that they had told a teacher about being bullied. Notably, the outcome from telling depended very much on the age of the child (see Figure 32.2). With increasing age, the likelihood of a positive outcome diminished. Whilst it was the case that for 8- and 9-year-olds teacher intervention appeared generally effective, by the time a student was 16 or 17 the most likely outcome of telling a teacher was "no change." Fairly consistently across the age range the proportion of children claiming that the intervention of teachers made matters worse is around 10%.

The results for the Australian sample are fairly similar to those obtained in England. Thus, it appears that teachers are generally not very effective in getting cases of bullying to stop. They quite often have a negligible effect and, according to reports from a not insignificant minority of children, may make matters worse.

What Schools Do About Bullying

Surprisingly, there is little known about what actions school personnel take when they are confronted with a case of school bullying. To provide some answers, Bauman and Rigby (2007)

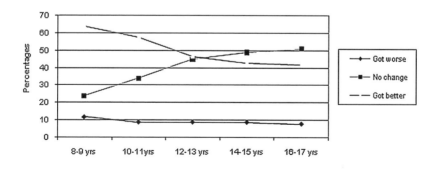

Figure 32.2 What happens when students tell about being bullied at school: Reports from Australian school children (From Rigby and Barnes, 2001).

recently conducted an anonymous online survey in a number of countries around the world, including the United States, Canada, Australia, and Norway. The responses to this survey were broadly similar in each country, suggesting that that how schools respond to cases of bullying are relatively unaffected by geography.

The largest sample obtained was from the United States (N = 715). Of these 61.6% reported that they were employed as school counselors. Mindful that responses could be influenced by the nature of the perceived bullying, especially its evident severity, a short description of a bullying incident was provided:

> A 12-year-old student is being repeatedly teased and called unpleasant names by another, more powerful, student who has successfully persuaded other students to avoid the targeted person as much as possible. As a result, the victim of this behaviour is feeling angry, miserable, and often isolated. (Bauman, Rigby, & Hoppa, 2008, p. 839)

This case may be viewed as an example of bullying of relatively low severity. Altogether, 24 possible responses to the case were listed and described. For each of these, respondents were asked to indicate how likely it was that they would respond in that way, using a five-point scale, from "definitely would" to "definitely would not" (A copy of the questionnaire can be viewed at http://www.ed.arizona.edu/bullying.) Principal components analyses were conducted on the scores from the responses, and five distinct factors were identified (Bauman & Rigby, 2007). These were (a) ignoring the incident, (b) disciplining the bully, (c) enlisting other adults, (d) working with victim, (e) working with the bully. (Here the emphasis was upon procedures designed to elicit constructive behavior on the part of the bully or bullies; responses for the United States are noted in Table 32.2.)

Levels of Agreement Among School Staff

The level of agreement among school staff depended very much on the approach in question. That something should be done about the case of bullying described above was generally not disputed. No more than 6% of all respondents thought that the matter should be ignored or that it should be left to the students to sort it out themselves. Remember that the bullying in question could be seen as relatively mild. One may conclude that in the United States the view that bullying incidents should be ignored is now probably held by very few educators in schools.

Disciplinary Action

The next highest level of agreement was over the use of disciplinary means of dealing with the case. Practically everyone (some 97%) believed that it should be made clear to the bully that the bullying behavior would not be tolerated, and some 71% believed that some form of punishment was justified. Less than 10% were opposed to this way of dealing with the problem. Clearly, a punitive approach to dealing with bullying—even with this comparatively mild case—is currently being endorsed by an overwhelmingly large proportion of school personnel and opposed by relatively few.

Enlisting Other Adults

Consistent with the philosophy of a whole-school approach, it was generally endorsed that responding to bullying required team work. Three quarters of the respondents were inclined to

Table 32.2 Percentages of US Respondents Providing Answers to Selected Questionnaire Items

	Agree Strongly	Agree	Unsure	Disagree	Disagree Strongly
Ignoring the incident					
I would ignore it	2	1	1	8	88
I would let the students sort it out themselves	1	2	4	35	58
Disciplining the bully					
I would make sure the bully was suitably punished	39	33	18	7	2
I would make it clear to the bully that his or her behaviour would not be tolerated	53	34	1	1	1
Enlisting other adults					
I would refer the matter to an administrator (e.g., principal, vice-principal, dean)	43	31	17	7	1
I would insist to the parent(s) or guardian(s) of the bully that the behaviour must stop	26	34	22	14	3
Working with the victim					
I would tell the victim to stand up to the bully	11	25	24	29	11
I would suggest that the victim act more assertively	18	41	18	17	5
Working with the bully					
I would convene a meeting of students, including the bully and tell them what was happening and ask them to suggest ways they could improve the situation	24	31	30	18	6
I would share my concern with the bully about what happened to the victim, and seek to get the bully to behave in a more caring and responsible manner.	42	37	10	8	2

report the incident to others in authority at the school, such as the principal or vice principal. Notably, a majority (60%) felt that parents or guardians should be contacted over the incident. Nevertheless, a substantial minority (17%) opposed this line of action.

Working with the Victim

Whether and how the victim should be worked with turned out to be highly contentious. There were those (46%) who felt that the victim should be told to stand up to the bully. Against these were (40%) of respondents who opposed this kind of action. Even on the matter of merely suggesting that the victim should act more assertively, there were a substantial proportion of dissenters (23%). Here then is an important issue over which members of a school staff are in serious disagreement.

Working with the Bully

Working with the bully, as distinct from applying an appropriate sanction, to achieve a constructive outcome was an approach that occasioned much disagreement among respondents. For example, 24% were strongly in favor of convening a meeting of students to work through the problem with the bully and 24% were opposed strongly or moderately to doing so. Here one should note the comparatively high proportion of educators who were simply "unsure."

Some 37% of respondents were unsure whether it was desirable to share one's concern about the victim's plight with the bully as a step towards resolving the problem. This suggests that a large proportion of staff members in schools are undecided or uninformed about methods such as the Method of Shared Concern and are reserving judgment.

Teachers and Counselors

The inclusion of a substantial proportion of counselors as well as teachers in the sample provided an opportunity to compare preferred ways of handling the incident of bullying. In relation to items given in Table 32.2, the two groups gave similar responses on the questions about whether the case of bullying should be ignored; that is, both groups on the whole believed that action should be taken. They held similar views on enlisting other adults and working with the bully. However, they differed significantly on the question of working with the victim, especially over encouraging the victim to act assertively. Some 61% of counselors and 39% of teachers favored this approach (chi square – 57.61, $p < .001$). They also differed significantly over the use of disciplinary means, especially on the desirability of making sure that the bully was suitably punished. Among teachers, 82% were prepared to use punishment, against 67% of counselors. This difference was statistically significant (chi square = 21.79, df = 2. $p < .001$).

Summary of Research Findings

The findings may be summarized as follows:

1. Published evaluation studies indicate that anti-bullying programs around the world have thus far had relatively little effect on the overall level of bullying.
2. To some extent, this lack of success is probably due to inadequate implementation of the programs.
3. A further explanation is that most bullying does not come to the attention of teachers.
4. When bullying is brought to the attention of teachers, typically they fail to stop it and, in some cases, make matters worse.
5. Difficulties in successfully dealing with cases of bullying increase as children get older.
6. Despite these difficulties, there is widespread recognition among school educators that something should be done to help, even in cases of relatively mild bullying.
7. When we examine closely how school educators think they should deal with cases of bullying, we find that the prevailing view endorsed by a large majority of teachers is that the right thing to do is to punish the bully.
8. School counselors are less inclined to adopt a punitive approach.
9. There is little agreement among teachers about the use of alternative non-punitive methods of dealing with cases of bullying, such as working with the victim and/or working with the bully.

Why School Personnel Respond as They Do to Cases of Bullying

First, there is almost unanimous acceptance that some action by school staff is needed to deal with relatively mild or moderately severe cases of bullying is almost certainly due to an increasing recognition in most countries that children have a basic human right to feel safe at school (Olweus, 1993). In addition, over the last 20 years there has been a rapidly growing body of research on its prevalence and the serious mental and physical damage to children that results from being repeatedly bullied at school (Rigby, 2003b). There is, however, still considerable disagreement over the employment of proposed non-punitive methods of resolving bully/victim problems in schools.

Focusing directly on changing the behavior of the bully by employing firm disciplinary means has long been the traditional way of dealing with bullying incidents. This approach has been reinforced by some influential educationalists, notably by Olweus (1993), through programs widely accepted in the United States endorsing the routine use of sanctions or penalties directed at those who have bullied someone; the aim being not only to punish the bully but also to deter others from engaging in bullying. Attractive to some is the practice of focusing primarily on the victim with the aim of strengthening his or her capacity to resist (see Field, 1999). This approach is appealing particularly to those who believe that everyone can learn how to stand up for themselves in any situation. Not surprisingly, given a recognition by educators that large imbalances of power between bullies and victims often exist, this view is unacceptable to many teachers and, to a lesser extent, by some counselors.

Non-punitive approaches that involve working on bully/victim problems have thus far gained comparatively little attention. Nevertheless, a substantial proportion of the respondents in the U.S. sample were supportive of measures that sought to work with the bully to bring about a positive change in behavior without coercion. For example, many endorsed the approach of convening a meeting of students, including the bully, to suggest ways they could improve the situation; or sharing one's concern with the bully (or bullies) about the welfare of the victim as a means of promoting more caring and responsible behavior. Increased knowledge of such alternatives may well result in a movement away from predominantly punitive approaches to handling cases of school bullying. It is noteworthy that school counselors tend to be more accepting of these alternative methods. This suggests that with further education in dealing with children's behavior problems, such strategies would gain greater credence and application.

Implications and Suggestions

Given the high level of acceptance among educators, both teachers and counselors, of the use of punitive methods as the stock response in dealing with cases of bullying, it appears that the acceptance of alternative methods could come about through a recognition of the limitations of the traditional way of dealing with bullies and an increasing awareness of the merits of alternative approaches.

Currently, there is little evidence available of the effectiveness of different kinds of treatments of bully/victim problems. Moreover, anti-bullying programs have invariably contained a variety of components and their outcomes cannot be attributed to any one of them. For example, the Olweus anti-bullying program included teacher education about bullying and classroom discussions with children about the rules that should govern their relations with each other, as well as advice on how cases of bullying should be dealt with. Whether dealing with cases of school bullying through the use of sanctions or penalties directed at the bully or at the bully's behavior is an effective way of dealing with cases has not been put to the test. It is based upon assumptions and these can and should be challenged. Evidence from studies of the effectiveness of punishment in reducing targeted behaviors does not appear supportive.

The Effectiveness of Punishment, as Applied to Children Accused of Bullying

Although it is generally agreed that there are times when some form of punishment is justified, as in the case of serious criminal behavior, and that in some cases it can be effective as a deterrent, there are limitations in its general effectiveness as a means of changing attitudes and

Table 32.3 Potential Limitations Regarding the Effectiveness of Punishment and Implications for Dealing with Bullying in Schools

---

- *Punishment tends to suppress the behaviour to which it directed, but typically only temporarily.* Long term solutions are preferable.
- *The effectiveness of punishment on the target depends in part on the degree of aversiveness of the punishment to the child and the likelihood of detection if the behaviour is repeated.* Punishments that can realistically be imposed by schools are generally fairly mild. Suspensions may be highly aversive for some students; for others they may even be desired.
- *Punishments imposed by schools are frequently of a generic nature, that is, unrelated to the specific offence, and do not draw the bully's attention to the harm caused by the bullying.*
- *The judgement made by the bully as to whether the punishment was deserved affects how he or she will react.* Attributing blame for bullying is often quite difficult as an element of provocation can be present. The punished child can feel resentful and motivated to act spitefully.
- *The reaction of the bully to being punished will be influenced by the degree of respect that is felt for the person or institution responsible for imposing the punishment.* Often children who behave anti-socially are not affected by being criticised by teachers.
- *How other students, especially friends react to what the bully has done and the punishment that the bully has received can greatly influence subsequent behaviour.* Approval by peers commonly outweighs disapproval by the school.
- *Whether the punishment deters others will depend in part on how likely it is that they will be caught.* In general, most bullying does not come to the attention of teachers, thus, strategies are needed to facilitate communication between students and teachers.
- *Having been punished, the bully will tend to employ more subtle ways of continuing the bullying in ways that are often difficult to detect.* Such indirect methods of bullying can be more harmful than more overt kinds, and beyond the capacity of the school to monitor effectively.

---

behaviors (Laslett, 1992). Table 32.3 contains hypotheses regarding the effectiveness of punishment that have a basis in psychological theory. In italics are some suggested implications for dealing with bullying in schools.

Suggestions for Improving the Means of Tackling Cases of Bullying in Schools

The most obvious and urgent need is to raise awareness of alternative methods of tackling cases of bullying in schools. This is despite the fact that numerous books and papers are available in which a range of alternative methods are described and discussed, for example, in Smith and Sharp (1994), Ross (2003), Rigby (1996, 2002, 2003a), Robinson and Maines (1997), Sullivan (2000), and McGrath and Noble (2005). Unfortunately, there is comparatively little information on tackling bullying in schools provided for teachers being trained in colleges and universities (see Bauman & Del Rio, 2005; Nicolaides, Toda, & Smith, 2002). Knowledge and training in alternative methods of intervention is typically being accessed by a limited number of schools that opt to make use of in-service seminars and workshops provided by experts who are able to provide the relevant service.

A Brief Outline of Alternative Methods of Tackling Cases of Bullying

Amongst the most promising alternative approaches are (a) Restorative Justice, (b) The Social Group Method (previously called the No-Blame Approach), and (c) the Method of Shared Concern. In the hands of trained practitioners, each of them has been shown to be effective in resolving some cases of bullying. Each appears to be more suited to some situations than others.

Restorative Justice   This term has been applied to describe ways of dealing with cases of unjust behavior including bullying in schools. It seeks to avoid the use of punishment in the sense of imposing penalties as a means of retribution or as a means of deterrence. Rather it seeks to provide conditions in which the offender will recognize the harm he or she has done and undertake actions to put things right, for example, through sincere apologies and reparations. The aim is to help mend damaged relationships rather than exact revenge.

Typically this requires a meeting involving the victim, the bully, and significant others (e.g., parents) at which point it is made clear that the bullying behavior is objectionable and not condoned by the community. The aim is to induce appropriate feelings of shame on the part of the bully. At the same time, the offender is treated with respect and offered the opportunity to become reintegrated into the community.

Under favorable circumstances, this approach has been shown to produce positive and lasting changes in individual bullies (Burssens & Vettenburg, 2006). Much depends on the readiness of the participants at the meeting to play their part. The victim is expected to describe the hurt that has been experienced, the bully to listen. People who care about either or both of them must be present and by their behavior show their concern and desire for a just outcome. The bully is expected to feel a sense of shame and a desire to put things right. The skill of the facilitator is crucial in bringing about a successful resolution to the problem that restores the fractured relationship and leads to an acceptance of the "reformed" bully by the school community.

This approach appeals strongly to those who recognize a need for a just resolution of bully/victim problems and the need for involvement on the part of all those who are affected by and care about what has happened. It recognizes that a crude punitive approach is likely to be ineffective or counter-productive, and that unless there is a change of heart on the part of the bully and sincere acceptance by the victim and the community that has been offended the bullying may well continue in more subtle and undetected ways. The desired changes are sometimes difficult to achieve. The shaming procedure can, on occasion, result in a child feeling stigmatized and resentful. The bully may "feel" punished, even if this is not intended. The bully may "fake" an apology. The supporters of the bully and the victim may not feel reconciled. The community may have reservations about accepting the bully back into the fold. Clearly the method, though appealing to many, requires considerable skill in its execution and the selection of appropriate cases.

For an account of the practical aspects of this approach, see Thorsborne and Vinegrad (2003). The effectiveness of the process has been comprehensively examined in the UK in a study reported by Bowles, Garcia Reyes, and Pradiptyo(2005). This latter study provides evidence of some successful applications, but does not claim that its use has reduced overall bullying in schools in which it has been applied.

The Support Group Approach   This approach was pioneered by two English educators, George Robinson and Barbara Maines (2007). It is a radical approach to dealing with cases of school bullying and has been adopted in a large number of schools, especially in the United Kingdom. Like the Restorative Justice approach, it is concerned with re-establishing good relations between individuals in conflict. It seeks to do so with the assistance of other members of the school community, especially other students. Unlike Restorative Justice, there is no implicit assumption that the bully needs to feel shame and act in a way to restore good relations with others before he or she can be accepted back into the school community.

The method requires first a gathering of information *directly* from the victim regarding the hurt he or she has suffered. A meeting is then convened with the identified bullies *plus* a number of other students who are expected to be to be helpful. The victim need not be present. Knowledge acquired about the plight of the victim is shared. Once positive suggestions on how to help solve the problem are forthcoming, the teacher leaves, confident that the victim will be helped. The situation is subsequently monitored carefully.

An important feature of the method is the use of pressure from the students present who are not involved in the bullying. It is assumed that these students will feel compassionate and supportive towards the victim and will be forthcoming in making suggestions about how the situation can be improved. Moreover, their presence will influence those responsible for the bullying to act more positively. By the teacher leaving the meeting when the students are working constructively on how the situation can be improved, the likelihood is that the emerging solution will be seen as "owned" by the students and not imposed by the teacher

It is sometimes argued that it is unreasonable and unrealistic to adopt the view that the bully is not to blame, as the original name of the method, No-Blame Approach, suggests. After all, commonsense suggests that the bully is responsible. Nevertheless, the *procedure* of avoiding direct blame can be justified if there is a real change in the desire for the bully to continue the bullying and a safe situation for the victim is thereby established. Less controversially, the method has more recently been termed the "Support Group Method." This draws attention to the vital contribution of the peer group in bringing about a sustainable solution.

A useful adaptation of this method has been proposed by Sue Young in 1989 called the Support Group Approach to Bullying in Schools. The extent of its use in schools in England and how well it is supported by teachers and local government authorities have recently been described by Smith and colleagues (2007). Notably, those who have applied the method, especially in primary schools have reported a high degree of satisfaction with outcomes.

The Method of Shared Concern   This method was devised by the Swedish psychologist, Anatol Pikas, and has been successfully applied in schools in many parts of the world including England, Australia, Canada, Finland, and Sweden. It has much in common with the No Blame Approach in that it does not seek to accuse and punish children who have bullied someone, but rather is concerned with establishing or re-establishing positive relations between those involved and more especially with developing a situation in which the victim feels safe. Unlike the No Blame Approach, it adopts a procedure that includes all the students who are thought to have been involved in the bullying, that is, the bully or bullies and the victim, and does so in a series of planned meetings with individuals and with groups.

First, information about the bullying incident is gathered indirectly, without interviewing the victim. The suspected bullies are then interviewed individually. No one is accused of bullying. The practitioner shares a concern about the plight of the victim and seeks to elicit (a) acknowledgement of the bad situation and (b) positive suggestions on how the matter can be resolved. Next the victim is interviewed to explain what is happening. Subsequently, other meetings with individual children are conducted to ascertain and reinforce progress. The next stage is to meet with all of them together. Finally, after talking with the victim, a meeting is held with the group with the victim present. Jointly, they work with the practitioner to reach a final and agreed solution.

Central to this approach is the recognition that bullying is typically a group phenomenon and can best be tackled by encountering members of the group individually and collectively. It is assumed that there is little value in blaming and punishing individuals, in part because they are likely to persist in bullying after they have been punished, and in part because the behavior of the students is largely under the influence or control of members of their group with whom they associate. Further, it is thought that by establishing a positive, respectful working relationship with the bullies individually then collectively, it is possible to make some progress towards a solution, especially if they can be brought to share a common concern for the plight of the victim. Once this has been achieved, it is possible to reach an acceptable solution to the problem through a joint meeting which involves the victim.

For a more detailed account, see Pikas (2002) and Rigby (2005). Smith and Sharp (1994)

have provided evidence of its effectiveness in a majority of cases. A training film for counselors and teachers in the application of the Method of Shared Concern is available from Chris Faull of Readymade Productions. It is described with video clips at http://www.readymade.com.au/method

On the Choice of Method

First, it should be recognized that dealing with cases of bullying when they occur is clearly not the only or the prime way of reducing bullying. In the long run especially, preventative and educational methods are more basic. Many schools have recognized this, though much more is needed in translating good intentions into good educational programs that promote positive and supportive relationships within the school community. Whilst this chapter deals with methods of dealing with cases, it must never be forgotten that what is done in tackling cases occurs within a social and educational context that needs to be supportive and consistent with how individuals are treated.

In the last analysis, what schools can do to tackle cases of bullying will be determined largely by the weight of opinion in a school about what should be done. However enlightened or evidence-based an approach may be, it is likely to be successful only when those who practice it are convinced that it is the best they can do. If there is marked division in a school about the use of a method or technique, its application is likely to be half-hearted or even counter productive. As noted, typically schools favor a strong disciplinary approach and the use of punishment even in cases of low or moderate severity. Hence, any introduction of alternative, non-punitive approaches will generally need to be accompanied by a relevant educational program and appropriate training. In short, educators in schools need to be presented with the evidence for and against a given approach; they need to discuss it; and they need to have a sound grasp of when and how it may best be used.

One stumbling block to innovation in the area of interventions against bullying lies in a tendency to treat all forms of bullying as equally severe and their perpetrators equally culpable and deserving of the same treatment. It is useful to consider the severity of bullying as occurring along a continuum, with extremely severe instances happening relatively infrequently and not very severe instances happening often, as depicted in Figure 32.3.

As an exercise, it is useful to ask the staff in a school to rate specific kinds of bullying in terms of severity from 1 to 10. These might include unpleasant name-calling, ignoring and isolating someone repeatedly, racist abuse, sexual coercion, offensive text messages, removing people's

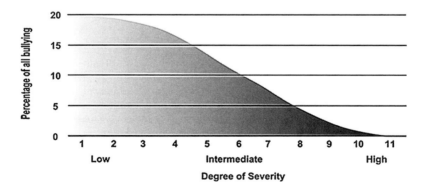

Figure 32.3 Continuum of bullying severity.

belongings, and spreading nasty rumors. One could ask also whether bullying by a group is more serious and deserving of attention compared with bullying by an individual, and how important repetition of an offence might be compared with a one-off offence. After learning to differentiate between different kinds of bullying, it becomes possible to discuss how different forms of intervention might be justified.

Our preference is generally for non-punitive responses to cases of bullying. However, where cases of very severe or criminal forms of bullying are concerned, strong action involving sanctions, in some cases, suspensions, are necessary. Parents must clearly be informed. In favorable circumstances (see above), Restorative Justice procedures may be necessary.

In addition, there are cases of quite low level severity which can be treated informally, for example, by a teacher pointing out that teasing or taunting someone is not the right thing to do. Ideally the child in question should be commended, if possible, for any positive acts. And the case discretely monitored.

For cases of moderate severity, there are alternatives to those noted above that could justify the use of either the Support Group Approach or the Method of Shared Concern. The first proviso is that the would-be practitioner is really familiar with how the method is implemented. A test is whether the potential user can make a clear distinction between each of these methods and Restorative Justice (often they are not differentiated). A second proviso is that the school be in agreement about the application of one or other of these methods, at least in defined circumstances. Generally speaking, conditions are favorable to their adoption when there is a strong commitment in the school to working with students to overcome problems, as is evident where there is an actively functioning student representative committee, peer support program, or student anti-bullying committee (see Petersen & Rigby, 1999).

Conclusion

Although many schools are now recognizing the importance of doing what they can to stop peer bullying, as yet schools have been only modestly and occasionally successful in addressing the problem. Nowhere is this more evident than in the area of interventions with cases of bullying that come to the attention of teachers. The most common response to bullying is to apply strong disciplinary and punitive action. There are grounds for supposing that this approach often does not work. Alternative non-punitive methods would appear to have at least an equal chance of success. These are not well understood, and a major challenge facing educators is to make these better known. Schools then can be sufficiently informed to choose what best suits their needs in particular circumstances.

References

Baldry, A. C., & Farrington, D. P. (2007). Effectiveness of programs to prevent school bullying. *Victims and Offenders, 2*, 183–204.

Bauman, S., & Del Rio, A. (2005). Knowledge and beliefs about bullying in schools: Comparing pre-service teachers in the United States and the United Kingdom. *School Psychology International, 26*, 428–442.

Bauman, S., & Rigby, K. (2007). *The handling bullying questionnaire: Insight into U.S teachers and school counselors' bullying interventions.* Manuscript submitted for publication.

Bauman, S., Rigby, K., & Hoppa, K. (2008). US teachers and school counsellors' strategies for handling school bullying incidents. *Educational Psychology, 28*, 837–856.

Bowles, R. A., Garcia Reyes M., & Pradiptyo R. (2005). *Monitoring and evaluation the safer school partnerships programme.* London: Youth Justice Board for England and Wales.

Burssens, D., & Vettenburg, N. (2006). Restorative group conferencing at school: A constructive response to serious incidents. *Journal of School Violence, 5*, 5–17.

Field, E. M. (1999). *Bully busting.* Lane Cove, New South Wales, Australia: Finch Publishing.

Laslett, R. (1992). *Effective classroom management.* Florence, KY: Routledge.

McGrath, H., & Noble, T. (Eds). (2005). *Bullying solutions.* Sydney, Australa: Pearson.

Nicolaides, S., Toda, Y., & Smith, P. K. (2002). Knowledge and attitudes about school bullying in trainee teachers. *British Journal of Educational Psychology, 72,* 105–118.

Olweus, D. (1993). Bullying at school. Oxford, UK: Blackwell.

Petersen, L., & Rigby, K. (1999). Countering bullying at an Australian secondary school. *Journal of Adolescence, 22*(4), 481–492.

Pikas, A. (2002). New developments in shared concern method. *School Psychology International, 23*(3), 307–326.

Rigby, K. (1996). *Bullying in schools and what to do about it.* Melbourne: Australian Council for Educational Research.

Rigby, K. (2002). *New perspectives on bullying.* London: Jessica Kingsley.

Rigby, K. (2003a). *Stop the bullying: A guide for teachers* (rev. ed.). Melbourne: Australian Council for Educational Research.

Rigby, K. (2003b). Consequences of bullying in schools. *The Canadian Journal of Psychiatry, 48,* 583– 590.

Rigby, K. (2005). The method of shared concern as an intervention technique to address bullying in schools: an overview and appraisal. *Australian Journal of Counselling and Guidance, 15,* 27–34.

Rigby, K., & Barnes, A. (2002). To tell or not to tell: the victimised student's dilemma *Youth Studies, 21*(3), 33–36.

Robinson, G., & Maines, B. (1997). *Crying for help: The no-blame approach to bullying.* Bristol, UK: Lucky Duck Publishing.

Robinson, G., & Maines, B. (2007). *Bullying: A complete guide to the support group method.* Bristol, UK: Lucky Duck Publishing.

Ross, D. M. (2003). *Childhood bullying, teasing and violence: What school personnel, other professionals and parents can do* (2nd ed.). Alexandria, VA: American Counseling Association.

Salmivalli, C., Kaukiainen, A., & Voeten, M. (2004). Targeting the group as a whole: the Finnish anti-bullying intervention. In P. K Smith, D. Pepler, & K. Rigby (Eds), *Bullying in schools: How successful can interventions be?* (pp. 251–273). New York: Cambridge University Press.

Smith, P. K., Pepler, D., & Rigby, K. (2004). *Bullying in schools: How successful can interventions be?* Cambridge, UK: Cambridge University Press.

Smith, P. K., & Sharp, S. (Eds.). (1994). *School bullying: Insights and perspectives.* London: Routledge.

Smith, P. K., & Shu, S. (2000). What good schools can do about bullying. *Childhood, 7,* 193–212.

Smith, P. K, Howard, S., & Thompson, F. (2007). Use of the support group method to tackle bullying, and evaluation from schools and local authorities in England. *Pastoral Care, 25*(2), 4–13.

Sullivan, K. (2000). *The anti-bullying handbook.* Oxford, UK: Oxford University Press.

Thorsborne, M., & Vinegrad, D. (2003). *Restorative practices in schools: Rethinking behaviour management.* Buderim, Queensland: Margaret Thorsborne and Associates.

Vreeman, R. C., & Carroll, A. E. (2007). A systematic review of school-based interventions to prevent bullying. *Archives of Pediatric Adolescent Medicine, 161,* 78–88.

Young, S. (1989). The support group approach to bullying in schools. *Educational Psychology in Practice, 14,* 32–39.

33

Peer Processes in Bullying

Informing Prevention and Intervention Strategies

DEBRA PEPLER, WENDY CRAIG, AND PAUL O'CONNELL

Through our research, we have come to understand bullying as a relationship problem that requires relationship solutions—because it is a form of aggression that unfolds in the context of relationships (Pepler, Craig, Yuile, & Connolly, 2004; Pepler, Jiang, Craig, & Connolly, 2008). A critical feature of the relationship dynamic in bullying is the power differential between the children who bully and the children who are victimized.[1] The repetitive nature of bullying serves to consolidate and increase the power differential in the relationship. Consequently, it is difficult for victimized children to extract themselves from a bullying relationship because they lack the power to shift the dynamics in the relationship and to put a stop to this form of abuse (Pepler, Craig, & O'Connell, 1999). Our observational studies and the research of many others now reveal that the problems of bullying encompass more than the child who is being aggressive and the child who is being victimized: the peer group provides the relational context for bullying (Craig & Pepler, 1995; Olweus, 1993; Salmivalli, Lagerspetz, Björkqvist, Österman, & Kaukiainen, 1996). If peer dynamics are essential to the processes in bullying, then interventions for bullying will have to focus on and shift these dynamics to promote positive interactions. In this chapter, we review research that highlights the peer context for bullying, describe the bi-directional processes that serve to sustain bullying dynamics and highlight research that reveals the potential of peer intervention. Based on this research, we draw implications for bullying prevention and intervention initiatives.

The developmental systemic perspective provides a framework for considering bullying in terms of individual characteristics and the relationship context of the peer group (Cairns & Cairns, 1991; Ford & Lerner, 1992; Magnusson, 1981, 1995). The developmental perspective directs us to consider children's strengths and challenges at different ages that might contribute to bullying problems. In the present consideration of the peer dynamics in bullying, the developmental perspective guides us to focus on the skills and attitudes required by peers to disengage from the natural peer processes that sustain bullying and to engage prosocially to put a stop to bullying. The systemic perspective guides us to focus on the relationship contexts for bullying to consider the norms and dynamics within the peer group that contribute to or discourage bullying, as well as the role of teachers in creating prosocial norms among classmates to support victimized children and to avoid reinforcing the aggressive behaviors of those who bully.

Peers Form the Relational Context of Bullying

Although there has been considerable attention paid to the roles that peers play both in research and in interventions (Cowie, 2004; Olweus, 1993; Salmivalli, Kaukiainen, Voeten, & Sinisammal, 2004), less is known about the potentially important peer processes in bullying episodes. With remote microphones and video cameras, we were able to step into children's interactions and observe the natural processes that unfold in bullying on the school playground and within the classroom (Pepler & Craig, 1995). Our observations reveal that peers play a crucial role in maintaining, exacerbating, and intervening in bullying episodes (O'Connell, Pepler, & Craig, 1999). Bullying is a social event in the classroom and on the playground: Peers were present in 85% to 88% of the episodes that we observed in these school settings (Atlas & Pepler, 1998; Craig & Pepler, 1995, 1997; O'Connell et al., 1999). Peers assumed many roles during observed bullying episodes: as bystanders, co-bullies, and interveners. Salmivalli and her colleagues have expanded our understanding of the roles that peers play in bullying. They have identified four roles played by peers in bullying episodes: assistants, reinforcers, defenders, and onlookers (Salmivalli et al., 1996). A substantial number of children are involved in bullying: the roles of bully, assistant, or reinforcer are assumed by up to 40% of school-aged children and the role of onlooker is played by up to 30% of school-aged children (Salmivalli, 2001). We will consider these various roles as part of the peer context of bullying.

Bullying is a form of social power that is exhibited and consolidated in the presence of a relevant social group. With an understanding of the power dynamics in bullying, it is not surprising to learn that peers quickly form an audience for bullying and contribute to the imbalance of power. On average, we observed 4.3 peers participating and watching a bullying episode, with a range of up to 14 children watching at a time (O'Connell et al., 1999). These children form the audience in the theatre of bullying. We found that the size of the audience for bullying matters: With more peers present, bullying episodes last longer—the show must go on. We observed young boys (grades 1 to 3; ages 6 to 8 years) to be most frequently present and young girls least frequently present in the peer audience. The attention of peers clearly reflected the power differential in the bully-victim relationship. Peers comprising the "audience" in bullying episodes spent about half their time passively watching the child who was bullying: These would be identified by Salmivalli and her colleagues (1996) as the onlookers. Peers spent about a quarter of their time actively engaged in the aggression and joining the bullying: these students would be identified as the assistants or reinforcers according to Salmivalli's categories. Peers spent only a quarter of their time attending to and intervening to support the victimized child: these students have the potential to fill Salmivalli's role of defenders.

Bullying often occurs within groups of familiar peers. Craig, Pepler, and Blais (2007) reported that both boys and girls were bullied by someone they knew a little or by someone in their peer group. The concern is twofold. First, peers who are familiar with one another are more aware of their friends' vulnerabilities, which can become the focus for bullying. When bullied by friends, it is challenging to escape the bullying, unless the peer dynamics of the peer group changes. In addition, as the closeness of the relationship between the children who bully and the child being victimized increases, it is less likely that the victimized child will do anything to stop the bullying. They fear losing their essential friendships or their connections within the peer group. Thus, interventions that include both familiar and unfamiliar peers are critical to change negative dynamics within peer networks and to provide alternative friendship groups that may be more supportive in developing healthy relationships.

There is a growing body of research on the negative aspects of peer dynamics. Dishion and his colleagues have shown how peers reinforce each other for negative behaviors, a dynamic that they have referred to as "deviancy training" (Dishion, Andrews, & Crosby, 1995; Dishion, McCord, & Poulin, 1999). These negative aspects of peer dynamics in bullying have received more attention than the prosocial aspects of peer intervention. Our observations, however, also reveal the potential of positive aspects of peer interaction to shift the dynamics in bullying. We observed that peers intervened more frequently than teachers (Craig & Pepler, 1997) and, as we discuss below, their interventions were effective in stopping bullying more than half the time (Hawkins, Pepler, & Craig, 2001).

The survey and observational research on peer involvement in bullying highlights the central role that peers play in this form of aggressive behavior. In considering peer interactions within bullying, it is important to examine the dynamics of bullying more closely to understand the multiple processes that maintain, exacerbate, and potentially terminate bullying episodes. In the next section, we consider not only the peers' influence on the child who initiated the bullying, but also the bullying child's influence on peers.

The Bi-Directional Processes in Bullying

Our observational research on the peer processes within bullying was based on a social interactional perspective (Cairns, 1979; Patterson, 1982; Patterson, Reid, & Dishion, 1992). From this perspective, children's behavioral patterns develop through the course of interactions in relationships within the family, peer group, school, and broader community. The influences are understood as bi-directional: children's behaviors are shaped by the social contexts in which they are consistently interacting and, at the same time, children's behaviors shape the behaviors of others. In considering the peer dynamics in bullying, therefore, we need to examine not only the processes that operate from peers to the bullying child, but also they ways in which the bullying child may promote peer involvement in this form of aggression. Our concern is that these bi-directional influences sustain the power differential and dynamics of bullying in the peer context.

Peer Support of Bullying   Peers who are present during a bullying episode can participate in multiple roles which may contribute to the maintenance and exacerbation of bullying episodes. A key feature of bullying is the use of power and aggression. If children who bully are motivated by the need to demonstrate power, then having an audience before whom to display the power may be motivating. The duration of bullying episodes is significantly correlated with the number of peers who form the audience for bullying (O'Connell et al., 1999). Some peers who are bystanders form a passive audience, but even these children provide positive feedback by attending, laughing, and making encouraging comments and gestures (Salmivalli et al., 2004). Other peers may actively contribute to bullying problems by taking the roles of assistants when they join with the child who is bullying (Salmivalli et al., 1996). Salmivalli and her colleagues (2004) note that these children eagerly join in bullying once it has started. In our observations, we found that peers' active joining of bullying shifted the bullying dynamics: when children actively joined in bullying, the child who had initiated the bullying became increasingly aggressive and aroused (O'Connell et al., 1999). Therefore, the active and passive involvement of peers who are standing by and watching bullying may serve to reinforce the dominance and aggression of the bullying child. Even peers' attention and lack of intervention may be interpreted as signs of support by those who are bullying.

Bullying Child's Engagement of Peers   The power dynamics within bullying are its defining feature. The child who bullies not only holds power over the child being victimized, but also holds power over the children who form the audience for bullying. Our videotapes reveal many situations in which the child who is bullying incites others to join in through taunts or direct requests. To examine the extent to which bullying children are able to engage others in the dynamics of bullying, we observed the reactions of peers to these directed comments or requests to join the aggression (O'Connell et al., 1999). We found that peers were significantly more likely to join in the bullying when the bullying child had made some form of request or instigating comment compared to the likelihood of joining spontaneously, without a request. Regardless of whether they were asked or not, boys, who were more frequently represented in the audience for bullying, were more likely than girls to join in bullying. This type of direct action on the part of the instigator of bullying is a clear example of deviancy training: Peers are being drawn in and potentially reinforced for their involvement in bullying.

Our observations confirm the students' own reports of peer participation in bullying from Salmivalli and colleagues' research (1996, 2004). In addition, they reveal the complex dynamics as this form of aggression unfolds. Even though a vast majority of children report that they find it unpleasant to observe bullying (Charach, Pepler, & Ziegler, 1995), the vast majority of bullying episodes have an audience. The peers who are watching seldom provide a neutral context for bullying: they are most often attentive and reinforcing of the child who is bullying and, therefore, contribute to the destructive dynamics of bullying.

Positive Peer Responses to Bullying

Although the majority of audience time during bullying episodes is spent attending to and supporting the child who initiated the bullying, 25% of the time peers are either attending to or actively intervening to support the victimized child.

This attention to the victimized child, together with the reports of a majority of children who find watching bullying upsetting, reveal the potential that peers have in reducing bullying problems. With our naturalistic observations, we were able to witness directly the efforts by peers to stop bullying (Hawkins et al., 2001). We observed children intervening in 19% of the episodes, which is in line with the research of Salmivalli and colleagues (1996) in which 17% of children reported that they were defenders and intervened to stop bullying. When children intervened, we observed that bullying stopped within 10 seconds in 57% of the episodes (Hawkins et al., 2001). One can speculate as to why bullying stops more than every other time within such a brief window. Because the defining feature of bullying is the exercise of power, it may be that the child who is bullying recognizes, at some level, the threat to his/her status when others stand up to defend the child being victimized and decides to stop using power aggressively at least in the moment. Regardless of the dynamics, our observations reveal that there is considerable potential to promote altruistic and supportive behaviors on the part of peers. The recommendation to include peers comes with a note of caution and highlights the need for specific training. In our naturalistic observations, peers were observed to intervene aggressively 47% of the time (Hawkins et al., 2001); therefore, there is a need for all children to be trained in appropriate conflict mediation and intervention skills.

The Challenge and Dilemma in Addressing Bullying Problems

Bullying is a complex problem which is challenging to address. Because of the destructive relationship dynamics and the serious consequences for those involved in bullying, these problems need to be constantly monitored and addressed to ensure healthy relationships and healthy development for all children and youth. The United Nations Convention on the Rights of the Child (UNCRC; United Nations, 1989), Article 29 specifies that education shall be directed to "[t]he preparation of the child for responsible life in a free society, in the spirit of understanding, peace, tolerance, equality of sexes, and friendship among all peoples, ethnic, national and religious groups and persons of indigenous origin." Therefore, it is the role of society to involve and educate youth to ensure they develop positive attitudes and behaviors and avoid using their power to bully or harass others. This societal function is the responsibility of parents, teachers, and other adults in the community who are in contact with children and youth.

The central dilemma in monitoring and addressing bullying problems is that the adults responsible for children's education and well being are seldom aware of bullying. Our observational research helps to clarify the dilemma and highlights the paradox: Adults are responsible, but are seldom present, during bullying; peers are present and without support may find it difficult to show social responsibility by intervening or alerting an adult about bullying. The situation is compounded by the finding that a majority of teachers report that they almost always intervene in bullying problems, whereas a minority of children report that teachers intervene to stop bullying (Charach et al., 1995). Our observations revealed that teachers intervened in only 4% and 18% of the bullying episodes on the playground and in the classroom, respectively, when there was no program in place (Atlas & Pepler, 1998; Craig & Pepler, 1997). This rate increased to 10%–11% on the playground and 14%–25% in the classroom when a bullying prevention program had been implemented (Pepler, Craig, O'Connell, Atlas, & Charach, 2004). If adults are not aware of the extent of bullying problems and of the discrepancy between their perceptions and children's reality, they will not be able to meet the challenge of eliminating the aggressive behaviors of children who bully, nor ensuring the safety of children who are victimized.

A consideration of the challenge and dilemma leads naturally to a focus on how adults can support peers to become their eyes and ears and to share in the important social responsibility to stop bullying.

What Is Needed to Meet the Challenge of Social Responsibility?

Adults are responsible for educating youth to ensure they develop positive attitudes and behaviors and avoid using their power to bully. To meet this responsibility, adults who live, work, and play with children and youth need an understanding of the complex peer dynamics that operate to exacerbate, maintain, and potentially terminate bullying interactions. With an understanding of these dynamics, adults will be able to consider a range of strategies that:

1. Address the needs of individual children involved in bullying as those who bully, those who are victimized, and those who are bystanders; and
2. Shift the social dynamics to (a) decrease the processes that reinforce children who bully and marginalize those who are victimized, and (b) increase the processes that promote prosocial interactions, social justice, and peer intervention.

Although children and youth are on the ground experiencing bullying on a daily basis, the changes necessary to meet the challenge of reducing bullying must be initiated and maintained by the adults in their lives. Given the focus of this chapter on the peer processes within bullying, we have limited our implications for prevention and intervention to those that pertain to building social skills, sensitivity, and responsibility among the peers who form the ever-present audience for bullying.

Prevention Through Creating Positive Peer Dynamics

Our understanding of bullying as a relationship problem that requires relationship solutions has guided our attention to intervention strategies that are formative. In other words, the interventions that we promote must teach children the skills, attitudes, and behaviors necessary for healthy relationships. Providing children with the behaviors and insights essential for skilled social interaction and positive relationships may be as or more complex and challenging than teaching them literacy or numeracy. Support for healthy social development, therefore, should begin early in children's lives and be consistently available as children meet new social challenges in each developmental stage and in diverse social contexts. The supports that children need are not a "one size fits all" solution: they must be tailored to children's different needs and capacities that vary by age, gender, skills, and backgrounds.

Regardless of how these supports are put in place, one overarching principle is clear: children depend on adults to help them understand bullying problems and to promote the development of essential social skills, social perceptions, and social responsibility. To create healthy relationships for all children and youth, adults must actively promote positive dynamics and reduce opportunities for negative dynamics among peers. From a developmental-systemic perspective, we understand that this task requires attention to both the development of many assets and attitudes within individual children, as well as attention to group norms, social processes, and power dynamics. In addressing the peer dynamics in bullying, the goal is to encourage altruistic behavior of peers and shift the power dynamics so those children who have a tendency to bully are discouraged from using power aggressively and those children who are victimized are supported, safe, and included in peer group.

Building Prosocial Assets and Attitudes Among Peers   Children need a range of explicit educational experiences to develop the skills and attitudes required to recognize the peer dynamics in bullying and to take action to address this form of abuse at the hands of peers. To promote social responsibility and peer intervention to stop bullying, children need support to develop an understanding of their own emotions and needs, perceptions of others' needs, and a range of skills together with values to enable them to feel confident in and responsible for taking a stand against bullying. Caprara and Steca (2007) have identified these characteristics as the foundation of prosociality.

When children are present during bullying episodes on the school playground, our observations indicate that many are not only attentive, but become actively involved in the interaction (Craig & Pepler, 1997; O'Connell et al., 1999). These data suggest that to promote prosocial behaviors and social responsibility, children first need to be aware of their own emotions and reactions. This type of self-awareness is not only the foundation of understanding others' emotions and developing empathy, but it is necessary to help children develop an awareness of how they respond to the dynamics within bullying. There is an opportunity to build on the finding that the vast majority of children find it unpleasant to watch bullying. Helping children recognize their own discomfort and giving them the opportunity to talk about their feelings will serve not only to motivate them to alleviate their discomfort, but also increase their sensitivity to others' distress. As Salmivalli and her colleagues (2004) suggest, change may come through making students aware of the discrepancy between their negative feelings and attitudes about bullying and their attention and behavior that may be contributing to bullying problems.

Children also need to develop empathy and concern for the well-being of others. These capacities rely on understanding one's own feelings and being able to recognize and interpret the feelings of others (Eisenberg et al., 1996). Many children have had the experience of being bullied at one time or another and can describe readily how it felt to be on the receiving end of this form of abuse. There are many avenues to develop empathy for victimized children through reading books (e.g., Committee for Children, 2001), watching films (e.g., Glazier, 2004), role plays, and drawing pictures or posters about the feelings associated with being bullied. Exploring feelings comprises an important component of restorative practices that have now emerged as an effective strategy to address bullying problems (Armstrong & Thorsborne, 2005; Morrison, 2007).

Understanding one's own feelings of discomfort and others' feelings associated with being bullied are necessary, but not sufficient in mobilizing children to lend support to victimized peers. It is also essential to provide them with the language, social skills, assertiveness skills, and sense of self efficacy to enable them to "support, console, persuade, and protect victimized children" (Caprara & Steca, 2007, p. 223). We cannot expect that children will spontaneously acquire the skills to intervene prosocially in bullying. In our observations of peer interventions, we found that the likelihood of prosocial or aggressive intervention strategies was about equal, as was the effectiveness of these two strategies (Hawkins et al., 2001). Children may need scripts for what to say and do to intervene in a positive way. Some children will have the social confidence to intervene directly, others will be concerned for their own safety and hesitate to take a stand on their own. Children need help understanding their social responsibility to do something when they know that bullying is going on. They can be coached to collectively take a stand and step in. When more than one child steps in, it helps to shift the power imbalance in bullying—reducing support for the child who is bullying and providing support to the victimized child. Even if children are not comfortable standing up themselves to those who bully, they must be encouraged to tell a responsible adult about this form of abuse at the hands of peers. It is essential that adults responsible for children in any context are ready to listen and respond constructively to address the bullying problem.

Building Blocks for Positive Peer Support   The key to creating conditions for positive peer dynamics is for adults to establish conditions in which children feel not only free, but responsible, to take the risk of speaking out about bullying dynamics they have observed, heard about, or experienced firsthand. Without a trusted adult who will listen respectfully and respond with relationship solutions, even those children with a deep sense of social justice and the social power to act will soon learn that telling is not worthwhile. In the Finnish bullying prevention program that focuses on the peer group as a whole, Salmivalli and her colleagues (2004) have put their efforts into training teachers. They argue that the majority of bullying episodes are unidentified by teachers because they are hidden, but also because teachers may not have a clear understanding of bullying. Salmivalli and her colleagues are also concerned that teachers may recognize and address bullying as a problem with an individual child (i.e., child who bullies or is victimized) and *a problem that arises from the dynamics within an extended group of children.*

From the research reviewed above, we can iterate the processes that lead peer dynamics awry as a basis to consider what is required to shift the peer dynamics and reduce bullying problems (see Table 33.1 for a summary of processes and implication for practice). Bullying seems to be maintained and exacerbated by the number of peers present, the imbalance of attention in favor of the child who is bullying rather than the victimized child, joining in bullying, emotions and arousal, pressure to participate in bullying, and hesitancy to intervene. Some of these peer group processes can be addressed in part through support for individual children's development of awareness, empathy, social concern, social skills, and social self efficacy. Others require a group-based approach: values, norms, and dynamics within the whole peer group need to be enhanced. There is emerging evidence that involvement in bullying is accounted for not only

Table 33.1 Peer Processes in Bullying and Implications for Practice

Peer Process	Prevention and Intervention Strategies
Many peers as bystanders	Adults aware of dynamics and ready to intervene Develop awareness of the discrepancy between negative feelings about bullying and their attention and behaviour Develop classroom rules with students Discussions, role-plays, drama exercises, and literature Pikas Method of Common Concern Support Group Approach (formerly No Blame Approach)
Imbalance of attention to child who is bullying	Adults aware of imbalance of power and alert to the subtle uses of power among peers Develop awareness of the discrepancy between negative feelings about bullying and their attention Restorative justice focusing on the dynamic of support Social architecture to create positive groupings and discourage negative groupings
Joining in bullying	Adults aware of group processes and prepared to intervene at group level Develop awareness of the discrepancy between negative feelings about bullying and their joining behaviour Discussions, role-plays, drama exercises, films, and literature Write poems, stories, drawing pictures or posters about the feelings associated with being bullied Pikas Method of Common Concern Support Group Approach (formerly No Blame Approach)
Emotions and arousal	Adults attending to children's emotions, labelling them, and promoting empathy Awareness of own emotions Awareness of emotions of others and especially of victimized children
Peer pressure to join	Adults aware of peer processes and ready to explore reasons that children join in Children's awareness promoted by discussions, role-plays, drama exercises, and literature
Hesitancy to intervene	Adults who listen and respond constructively Scripts, social skills, assertiveness skills, and sense of self efficacy and values to support others Discussions, role-plays, drama exercises, and literature Develop classroom rules with students Promote empathy and social responsibility Coached to collectively take a stand and step in Scripts for telling a trusted adult about bullying Restorative justice focusing on the dynamic of support

by individual factors, but also by the attitudes and behaviors within the broader social group (Hymel, Schonert-Reichl, & Miller, 2006; Salmivalli & Voeten, 2004).

The initial Norwegian bullying prevention program focused on classroom norms by having teachers work with the class to develop rules regarding bullying and interventions to support peers (Olweus, 1993). In more recent writing, Olweus (2004) also describes regular classroom meetings, role plays, and viewing a video about bullying followed by classroom discussions. Salmivalli and colleagues' (2004) program also focuses on involving the entire class to change attitudes and address the strong social pressure to join in bullying. Their approach was to educate the teachers in the participant roles in bullying and provide them with resources to for discussions, role-plays, drama exercises, and literature (Salmivalli et al., 2004). Some other programs have been developed to address the negative processes within a select group of peers actively involved or onlooking. The well-known Pikas Method of Common Concern (Pikas, 1989) and the Support Group Approach (formerly the No Blame Approach; Robinson & Maines, 1997) are two examples of bullying prevention strategies that focus on shifting peer attitudes and behaviors. Restorative justice practices are emerging as an effective intervention strategy for bullying problems. Restorative practices focus both on individual children's developmental needs and on the dynamics of support within the group in order to restore relationships (Morrison, 2007). These practices are ideal mechanisms to promote the relationship solutions required in bullying. "These practices, ranging from proactive to reactive, involve development and enhancement of relationships in schools and teaching of conflict resolution and problem-solving skills" (Armstrong & Thorsborne, 2005, p. 176).

These interventions are being demonstrated as effective in addressing bullying problems; however, the negative peer dynamics may require more focused attention to shift the power dynamics. We have proposed the metaphor of "social architecture" to refer to the opportunity for teachers and other adults involved with children to structure children's peer groups to promote positive peer experiences and to deconstruct negative peer experiences (Pepler, 2006; Pepler & Craig, 2007). Teachers can shift the dynamics and power imbalances in bullying by paying attention to peer relationships and taking responsibility for ensuring that all children are included and that troubling behaviors are not given a forum to flourish. For example, when teachers ask two children to be team leaders for baseball and to choose their teams, they allow the natural grouping processes to occur. Inevitably, this leaves less-skilled children in the humiliating position of not being chosen and then forced onto a team. With a social architecture approach, a teacher can choose a random or planned strategy to create balanced teams on which all children are included. In this way, teachers can engage children in positive interactions with a diverse mix of peers, providing the opportunity to promote the development of social skills, empathy, social responsibility, and positive group norms.

Within the framework of bullying interventions, social architecture can essentially function to reorganize children's group dynamics in three ways. First, it can be used to separate the child who is bullying from the victimized child and from the peers who reinforce the bullying behavior through their attention and joining. While separated, the children who bully require support to develop relationship skills, rather than exclusionary discipline that may promote hostility and frustration. Children who bully require support for positive relationship skills so that they can be quickly reintegrated into the peer group.

Second, social architecture can be used to embed victimized children within a positive peer context. These children often become isolated through the peer group dynamics of bullying. Through social architecture, teachers can ensure that marginalized children are embedded in a constructive, positive, peer context. The third process of social architecture is to promote a generally positive, respectful, accepting, and supportive climate within a social group. Within a supportive, collaborative climate and with expectations of respect and inclusion, children who are bystanders in bullying will recognize their responsibilities to intervene and will come to trust that adults will follow through with constructive responses to bullying problems. It is essential that adults find every opportunity to reinforce the children who intervene or report bullying, in order to increase the likelihood of this form of social responsibility. It is essential to work in partnership with children and youth to promote a positive climate. Children have a strong sense of social justice and what is fair—as it relates to themselves. There are opportunities to extend this sense of fairness to all those within the school community. Children see and hear about bullying long before the adults become aware of it; therefore, adults need to work collaboratively with children by learning from them and responding to their concerns. The leadership for this form of cultural change must come from the adults who are role models and who are responsible for promoting healthy relationships. Adults are responsible for restructuring the social context of the peer group to reduce the potential for negative dynamics for both the children who are bullying and for the children who are being victimized, as well as for bystanders.

Peer Processes in Bullying: Informing Prevention and Intervention

Research on the peer processes in bullying has advanced to the point at which we can no longer focus on individual children's developmental needs and behavior problems. All children are embedded within the social system of the peer group and without an understanding of and attention to the peer dynamics that maintain and exacerbate bullying, prevention and intervention efforts will fall short. To reduce bullying problems, adults need to take action to promote the development of healthy friendships and positive peer groups that will mobilize to support victimized peers. In addition, adults need to ensure that when bullying occurs, a large number of children do not gather to reinforce and join in with the child who initiated the bullying. Children need to be aware of and have skills and scripts to withstand the pressures to join in. They also need skills and scripts to meet their social responsibility to care for others within their school community. Adults must provide leadership and lessons for individuals and the collective of children in school or in other contexts such as at home, on sports teams, in recreation activities, and in the neighborhood. It is the adults' role to encourage peers' altruistic behaviors and shift the power dynamics so that children are discouraged from using power aggressively and those who are vulnerable are supported, safe, and included in the peer group.

Children involved in bullying are experiencing relationship problems that require relationship solutions. By supporting the development of relationship capacity and social responsibility for children and adolescents and by providing social contexts that promote healthy relationships, we can lay a foundation for healthy adaptation and positive relationships across the lifespan.

Note

1. Note that we avoid labeling children as "bullies" or "victims" because these labels constrain thinking of the problem as solely a characteristic of the individual, rather than emerging from complex social dynamics.

References

Armstrong, M., & Thorsborne, M. (2005). Restorative responses to bullying. In H. McGrath & T. Noble (Eds.), *Bullying Solutions: Evidence-based approaches to bullying in Australian schools* (pp. 175–188). Frenchs Forest, New South Wales, Australia: Pearson Longman.

Atlas, R., & Pepler, D. J. (1998). Observations of bullying in the classroom. *American Journal of Educational Research, 92,* 86–99.

Cairns, R. B. (1979). *Social development: The origins and plasticity of interchanges.* San Francisco: W. H. Freeman.

Cairns, R. B., & Cairns, B. D. (1991). Social cognition and social networks: A developmental perspective. In D. J. Pepler & K. H. Rubin (Eds.), *The development and treatment of childhood aggression* (pp. 411–448). Hillsdale NJ: Erlbaum.

Caprara, G. V., & Steca, P. (2007). Prosocial agency: The contribution of values and self-efficacy beliefs to prosocial behavior across ages. *Journal of Social & Clinical Psychology, 26,* 218–239.

Charach, A., Pepler, D., & Ziegler, S. (1995). Bullying at school: A Canadian perspective. *Education Canada, 35,* 12–18.

Committee for Children. (2001). *Steps to Respect: A Bullying Prevention Program.* Washington, DC: Author.

Cowie, H. (2004). Peer influences. In C. Sanders & G. Phye (Eds.), *Bullying: Implications for the classroom* (pp. 137–157). San Diego: Elsevier.

Craig, W., & Pepler, D. (1995). Peer processes in bullying and victimization: An observational study. *Exceptionality Education Canada, 5,* 81–95.

Craig, W., & Pepler, D. (1997). Observation of bullying and victimization in the schoolyard. *Canadian Journal of School Psychology, 13,* 41–59.

Craig, W., Pepler, D., & Blais, J. (2007). Responding to bullying: What works? *School Psychology International, 28,* 465–477.

Dishion, T. J., Andrews, D. W., & Crosby, L. (1995). Antisocial boys and their friends in early adolescence: Relationship characteristics, quality, and interactional process. *Child Development, 65,* 139–151.

Dishion, T., McCord, J., & Poulin, F. (1999). When interventions harm: Peer groups and problem behavior. *American Psychologist, 54,* 755–765.

Eisenberg, N., Fabes, R. A., Murphy, B., Karbon, M., Smith, M., & Maszk, P. (1996). The relations of children's dispositional empathy-related responding to their emotionality, regulation, and social functioning. *Developmental Psychology, 32,* 195–209.

Ford, D. H., & Lerner, R. M. (1992). *Developmental systems theory: An integrative approach.* Newbury Park, CA: Sage.

Glazier, L. (Writer/Producer), & Flahive, G. (Producer). (2004). *It's a girl's world: A documetary about social bullying* [Motion picture]. (Available from the National Film Board of Canada, 360 Albert Street, Suite 1005, Ottawa, Ontario, K1A 0M9)

Hawkins, D.L., Pepler, D., & Craig, W. (2001). Peer interventions in playground bullying. *Social Development, 10,* 512–527.

Hymel, S., Schonert-Reichl, K. A., & Miller, L. D. (2006). Reading, 'riting, 'rithmetic and relationships: Considering the social side of education. *Exceptionality Education Canada, 16,* 149–192.

Magnusson, D. (1981). *Toward a psychology of situations: An interactionist Perspective.* Hillsdale, NJ: Erlbaum.

Magnusson, D. (1995). Individual development: A holistic, integrated model. In P. Moen, G. Elder, & K. Lüscher (Eds.), *Examining lives in context: Perspectives on the ecology of human development* (pp. 19–60). Washington, DC: American Psychological Association.

Morrison, B. (2007). Schools and restorative justice. In G. Johnstone & D. Van Ness (Eds.), *Handbook of restorative justice* (pp. 325–250). Portland, OR: Willan Publishing.

O'Connell, P., Pepler, D., & Craig, W. (1999) Peer involvement in bullying: Issues and challenges for intervention. *Journal of Adolescence, 22,* 437–452.

Olweus, D. (1993). *Bullying at school: What we know and what we can do.* Oxford, UK: Blackwell.

Olweus, D. (2004). The Olweus Bullying Prevention Programme: Design and implementation issues and a new national initiative in Norway. In P. Smith, D. Pepler, & K. Rigby (Eds.), *Bullying in schools: How successful can interventions be?* (pp. 13–36). New York: Cambridge University Press.

Patterson, G. R., (1982). *Coercive family processes.* Eugene, OR: Castalia.

Patterson, G., Reid, J., & Dishion, T. (1992). *Antisocial boys.* Eugene, OR: Castalia.

Pepler, D. (2006). Bullying interventions: A binocular perspective. *Journal of the Canadian Academy of Child and Adolescent Psychiatry, 15,* 16–20.

Pepler, D., & Craig, W. (1995). A peek behind the fence: Naturalistic observations of aggressive children with remote audiovisual recording. *Developmental Psychology, 31,* 548–553.

Pepler, D., & Craig, W. (2007, February). Binoculars on bullying: A new solution to protect and connect children. *Voices for Children Report.* Retrieved from the PREVNet website http://prevnet.ca/Downloads/tabid/192/grm2id/57/Default.aspx

Pepler, D. J., Craig, W., & O'Connell, P. (1999.) Understanding bullying from a dynamic systems perspective. In A. Slater & D. Muir (Eds.), *Developmental Psychology: An Advanced Reader* (pp. 440–451). Malden, MA: Blackwell.

Pepler, D. J., Craig, W., O'Connell, P., Atlas, R., & Charach, A. (2004). Making a difference in bullying: Evaluation of a systemic school-based programme in Canada. In P. K. Simth, D. Pepler, & K. Rigby (Eds.), *Bullying in schools: How successful can interventions be?* (pp. 125–139). Cambridge, UK: Cambridge University Press.

Pepler, D., Craig, W., Yuile, A., & Connolly, J. (2004). Girls who bully: A developmental and relational perspective. In M. Putallaz & J. Kupersmidt (Eds.), *Aggression, antisocial behavior, and violence among girls* (pp. 90–109). New York: Guilford.

Pepler, D., Jiang, D., Craig, W., & Connolly, J. (2008). Developmental trajectories of bullying and associated factors. *Child Development, 79,* 325–338.

Pikas, A. (1989). A pure concept of mobbing gives the best results for treatment. *School Psychology International, 10,* 95–104.

Robinson, G., & Maines, B. (1997). *Crying for help: The no blame approach to bullying.* Bristol, UK: Lucky Duck Publishing.

Salmivalli, C. (2001). Group view on victimization: Empirical findings and their implications. In J. Juvonen & S. Graham (Eds.), *Peer harassment in school: The plight of the vulnerable and victimized* (pp. 398–419). New York: Guilford.

Salmivalli, C., Kaukiainen, A., Voeten, M., & Sinisammal, M. (2004). Targetting the group as a whole: The Finnish anti-bullying intervention. In P. K. Smith, D. J. Pepler, & K. Rigby (Eds.), *Bullying in schools: How successful can interventions be?* (pp. 251–274). New York: Cambridge University Press.

Salmivalli, C., Lagerspetz, K., Björkqvist, K., Österman, K., & Kaukiainen, A. (1996). Bullying as a group process: Participant roles and their relations to social status within the group. *Aggressive Behavior, 24,* 205–218.

Salmivalli, C., & Voeten, M. (2004). Connections between attitudes, group norms, and behaviour in bullying situations. *International Journal of Behavioral Development, 28,* 246–258.

United Nations. (1989, November). *The convention on the rights of the child NRC.* New York: Author.

34

The PEACE Pack

A Program for Reducing Bullying in Our Schools

PHILLIP T. SLEE

Overview

The international community is now expressing a significant concern with school bullying and violence (e.g., European Commission CONNECT project on Violence in Schools, http://www.gold.ac.uk/connect; International Observatory on School Violence, http://www.ijvs.com; Canada and North America, http://www.prevnet.ca). Recent Australian initiatives aimed at the issue of school bullying include nationally developed web sites (e.g., Bullying. No Way, http://www.bullyingnoway.com.au); national programs such as the "National Safe Schools Framework"; (http://www.nssf.com.au); and state funded school programs such as The South Australian, "Bullying, Out of Bounds" project (http://www.decs.sa.gov.au/schlstaff/pages/bullying). Bullying is recognized as an all too prevalent feature of Australian society that needs to be addressed.

Bullying: International Research

The pioneering research of Dan Olweus in Norway and Peter Smith in England and the outcomes of their successful practical intervention programs heralded an international focus on the problem of school bullying. Smith, Morita, et al. (1999) and Smith (2002) have edited and drawn together the findings from international research on bullying from a broad range of countries.

The Definition of School Bullying

In a special issue of *School Psychology Review*, Espelage and Swearer (2003) highlighted the significance of definitional issues. In their conclusion they noted that "This definitional issue is fundamentally related to accurate assessment of bullying and to conclusions researchers make about this complex dynamic" (p. 369). The nature of bullying is changing with the times. This is not to suggest that the forms of bullying first noted are no longer employed, but it does highlight that there have been shifts in the research foci and emphases over the last three decades as researchers have become more sophisticated in how they approach it. Therein, reviewing the literature it is proposed that there have been the following shifts in researching bullying: *direct* behaviors to *indirect*, *physical* to *verbal* to *psychological*, the *seen* to the *unseen*, and the *overt*

481

to the *covert*. The act of bullying is also moving to encompass the private worlds of technology generally known as cyber bullying. The changing foci on *developmental, cultural,* and *group dynamics* and *relational* aspects of the behaviors are also noted (Slee, 2001).

Variations in the definition of bullying exist (Slee, Hee-og, S., Taki, M., & Sullivan, 2003; Smith, Cowie, Olafsson, & Liefooghe, 2002). Whilst bullying has been defined in various ways over the last three decades, it is generally agreed that it is a particularly destructive form of aggression. It can be defined as physical, verbal, or psychological attack or intimidation that is intended to cause fear, distress, or harm to the victim, where the intimidation involves an imbalance of power in favor of the perpetrator. Taki, Slee, and Murray-Harvey (2002) assert in their definition that bullying is behavior characterized by a *power imbalance within a relationship context*, involving *repetition* of the bullying behavior, where the *deliberate intent* is to inflict *mental suffering* on the individual. Though school bullying can assume the form of physical, verbal, or indirect behavior, the significant focus in this definition is on the intention to *humiliate or embarrass* the other in a group context. Typically, there are repeated incidents over a period of time.

Research into Bullying in Australian Schools: Gender

The earliest published studies into school bullying in Australia were conducted by Rigby and Slee (1991, 1992, 1993). In 1994, an Australian Federal Senate inquiry into school bullying heralded a nationwide movement to address the issue of school violence, particularly bullying. As shown in Table 34.1, Australian research, based on a sample of 24,000 students from over 70 schools, indicates that over 20% of males and 15% of females report being bullied "once a week or more often" (Rigby & Slee, 1999a).

A further body of Australian research has focused on the relationship between bullying and gender (e.g., Owens, Daly, & Slee, 2005; Owens, Shute, & Slee, 2000, 2004; Shute, Owens & Slee, 2002). The general aim of this research is to better understand the extent and nature and the dynamics underpinning the nature of girls bullying behavior to better inform intervention programs. The research has highlighted some very particular features associated with girls and bullying (e.g., peer group acceptance).

Table 34.1 Incidence of Victimization According to Age; Students Reporting Being Victimized 'at Least Once a Week' in Co-Educational Schools in Australia

Age	Boys ($N = 13,977$)			Girls = ($N = 10,560$)		
	Schools	%	Students	Schools	%	Students
8	7	55.00	110	7	33.53	116
9	1 10	33.03	185	111	33.11	212
10	112	22.54	232	112	22.84	271
11	226	22.26	336	225	22.32	388
12	442	22.78	1193	442	22.21	1055
13	339	22.55	1807	440	22.09	1658
14	3 36	22.27	1675	335	11.32	1600
15	333	11.66	1510	332	11.22	1390
16	331	11.18	906	331	9.90	878
17	224	11.06	462	223	7.00	474
18	119	7.50	80	117	11.45	69

The Association of Bullying with Health and Psycho-Social Outcomes

In a study of the health of high school students (Slee, 1995), the students reported on their experience of school victimization and their level of physical health. The results showed that students who were most frequently bullied (once a week or more often) were significantly more likely to suffer poorer health (e.g., Espelage & Swearer, 2003; Davidson & Demaray, 2007). Indications of suicidal ideation and attempts at self-harm were significantly associated with self-reports and peer reports of school bullying (Rigby & Slee, 1999b). In a meta-analytic review of 20 years of research, Hawker and Boulton (2000) concluded that it was clear that victimization was positively associated with depression, loneliness, anxiety, low self-esteem, and poor social self-concept. Arising out of the recognition of the damaging effects of bullying on all those involved is the legal position in relation to bullying.

Bullying—The Law and Interventions

Over the past few years in Australia, the legal aspect of bullying has been increasingly referred to in the press and in research (Nicholson, 2006; Slee & Ford, 1999). A recent bullied student is set to receive approximately $Aus1m after successfully suing a state government over being bullied at a primary school (*The Advertiser*, 2007). As Fehring (1998, p. 9) notes, "teachers and schools are acting in locus parentis while a student is in their care. I believe that this requires teachers and schools to in fact actively intervene in any situation which comes to their knowledge which may involve significant risk of injury to a student in their care. This includes the risks of psychological injury so long as that injury is reasonably foreseeable." The Australian National SAFE Schools Framework has set in place procedures for providing a safe learning environment (http://www.dest.gov/archive/schools/publications/2004/resourcepack.pdf). Schools are now being asked to develop anti-bullying policies, grievance procedures, and intervention programs (Limber & Small, 2003; Slee & Ford, 1999).

Evaluations of School-Based Bullying Interventions

There is a body of evidence that school-based intervention programs can be effective in reducing the level of school bullying (Smith, Pepler, & Rigby, 2004). Widely known and well-documented evaluations include those by Olweus (1993), Smith and Pepler (1996), and Craig, Ziegler, and Charach (2004). Approximate effect sizes for intervention studies include a 50% reduction as reported by Olweus (1993), 17% reported by Smith and Sharp (1994), 30% reported by Pepler et. al (1994), and 30%–40% reported by Clearihan and colleagues (1999). Roland (1989) failed to find any reduction in the level of school bullying. However, one cannot easily compare the various intervention programs given the range and type of methods used, and the procedures employed (Stevens, Bourdeaudhuij, & Van Oost, 2000).

A key element of interventions is the adoption of an evidence-based approach. This approach warrants that rigorous evaluation be integrated into decisions about interventions by policy makers and practitioners (Commonwealth of Australia, 2000). Adapting a model described by Mrazek and Haggerty (1994), cited in Commonwealth of Australia (2000), interventions may be targeted: (a) universally at whole populations, (b) selectively at a population at risk, and (c) indicatively at "high-risk" individuals. Interventions (a) and (b) are usually identified in terms of "prevention," whereas (c) encompasses "early intervention." Developmental differences should also be taken into account in considering interventions, as knowledge about the specific ways in which children's understanding of violence changes as they mature is critical to designing effective programs for prevention and intervention (Smith, Madsen, & Moody, 1999).

Conceptual Foundations

Countering Bullying in the School Community: The PEACE Pack Program

A number of broad concepts underpin the PEACE Pack program including the idea that bullying is a wider community issue (Slee, 2001). The National Coalition Against Bullying (cited in McGrath & Noble, 2006) is just one example of where the issue of bullying has been addressed in the broader community context by interested groups. The movement toward the wider community initiative is underpinned by the writing of authors such as Etzioni (1995), who describes the social webs of communities as those which connect and bind individuals into groups of people who care for one another, which contribute to the maintenance of civic, social, and moral order. A related facet of communitarianism is that of "social capital."

Social Capital

Social capital refers to features in a social organization such as social networks, expectations, and trust, that facilitate coordination and cooperation for mutual benefit (Coleman, 1988; Putnam, 1993). It is derived from interpersonal relationships and an array of obligations, expectations, information channels and norms within families and communities. "Social capital resides in relationships and social organizations that individuals may use to achieve their interests and that promote positive adjustment" (Hetherington, 1999, p. 177). Emerging evidence exists for a link between social capital and factors such as school dropout and an increase in child behavior problems (Hetherington, 1999; Parcel & Menaghan, 1993; Runyan et al., 1998; Slee & Murray-Harvey, 2007).

Description of the Specific Approach: The PEACE Pack

The PEACE Pack is a systemically based intervention (Slee, 2001), with the acronym representing the orderly stages in the process for initiating, conducting, and evaluating a program for reducing school bullying (Preparation, Education, Action, Coping, and Evaluation). The program itself provides a framework for schools to assess the status of their anti-bullying policy in relation to policy and grievance procedures, curriculum initiatives, and student social support programs. The pack provides practical resources—such as examples of policy and lesson plans, as part of a comprehensive package to assist schools in developing their own intervention.

As described by Slee and Shute (2003), theoretically the program draws on essential principles of systems thinking (Dixon, Smith, & Jenks, 2004) whereby the issue of school bullying is nested within relationships and understood in terms of social constructivist thought. Broadly understood, interventions can involve "first-order" change whereby individuals caught up in the bully-victim cycle may need some assistance and strategies to deal with bullying. The school system remains the same with the bully viewed as the "bad" student in need of control and change and the victim viewed as an individual needing help and protection. If the view of the situation is accurate and constructive, and if, in fact, the students do simply need to acquire some new skills, then "first-order" interventions have a place in an intervention program (e.g., Owens, Shute, & Slee, 2004).

"Second-order" change will occur when the system itself begins to change, e.g., in reviewing policy and practice the school may gain some insight as to how the current procedures maintain and even amplify or encourage bullying. The school community in modifying attitudes, perceptions, and beliefs may choose to approach the issue of bullying from a very different perspective. By shifting focus and thinking in more systemic terms, change will resonate throughout the

The "P.E.A.C.E. " Process

Schematic representation of the P.E.A.C.E program to reduce bullying in our schools.

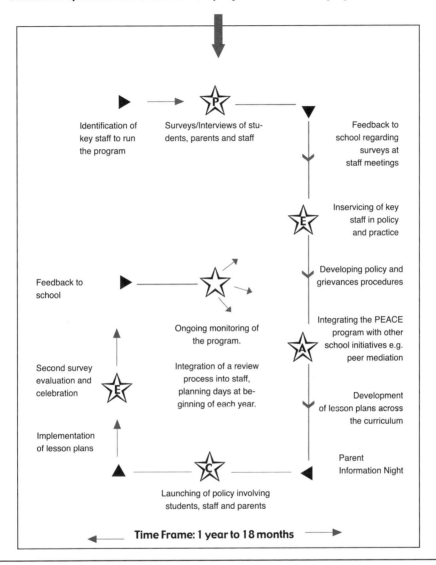

Figure 34.1 The PEACE Pack process. The frame-work for the interventions using the PEACE Pack is presented in the figure, and further details are available on the web site http://www.caper.com.au

school system. Instead of concentrating on changing the bad or problematic behavior of the bully and on helping the victim, consideration will be given to relationships, roles and interactions, and communication within the system which encourage or discourage bullying. When the system itself begins to change or realign, "second-order" change has occurred.

Systemic thinking is sharply at odds with more conventional, Western scientific thinking with its emphasis on remediation, deficits, and weaknesses in the individual (Slee & Shute, 2003). In contrast to such a deficit approach, systems-thinking emphasizes the active role of the individual in socially constructing meaning with a strong focus on competency, success, and individual strengths. It embraces the idea of the social, whereby meaning is constructed within the social setting of relationships, interactions and communication.

In its broad outlook, the PEACE Pack is directed universally at whole populations. It incorporates material such that consideration can be given selectively to a population at risk or indicatively at high-risk individuals. Research highlights that children with special needs (e.g., Aspergers) are particularly vulnerable to school bullying (Bottroff, 1998; Bottroff, Slee, & Michaelsen, 2007).

Preparation In the present study, all four schools desired to implement an anti-bullying program but each wanted to implement it in slightly different ways. In this first stage, the emphasis in the four schools was on gathering background information regarding the nature of school bullying to inform their interventions. Each school established a working party to address the issue of bullying which varied in nature across schools, e.g., in one school the working party comprised teachers from the curriculum group, while in another school the group comprised teachers, students, and community workers.

Education Data was gathered using an anonymous questionnaire before any details were provided to teachers, students, or parents about the issue of bullying. In one of the schools, the Student Representative Council (SRC) was very active in collecting information from students regarding their definition of bullying. The SRC took on the task of developing a school policy regarding bullying that was to be distributed to the community as part of the intervention program.

Action Each school used their established working party comprised of teachers, students, parents, and community workers to plan and implement their interventions. It was generally recognized that: (a) effective behavior support was needed that bases interventions on the identification of functional relationships between bullying and environmental events or contextual variables, rather than on punishment or aversive consequences; and (b) a graduated system of intervention was needed to meet the needs of all students. At the first level are universal interventions including the development of policy and grievance procedures and the use of effective teaching practices, such as creating "safe" play areas. At the next level, targeted interventions developed around students' unique strengths, needs, and behavior patterns were implemented (e.g., direct instruction in behavioral social skills).

Coping Following the collection, collation, and analysis of data from the school wide surveys various levels of intervention were initiated in each school in terms of the letters: A B C.

1. *Attitude.* The longer-term aim of all four schools was the development of an attitude/ethos within the school/community which openly and directly addressed the issue of bullying. The emphasis was on capturing a positive vision for the school focusing on creating a safe, caring community where bullying was sanctioned against because it detracts from the social capital of the community.
2. *Behaviors.* Schools focused on clear behavioral strategies put in place in terms o grievance procedures for recording, reporting on and following up incidents, clearly identified sanctions against bullying, and specific strategies for monitoring 'hotspots' where students felt 'unsafe' from bullying. The focus was on student relationships.
3. *Curriculum.* Schools developed lessons around language arts (e.g., designing posters, writing /reading stories), math (e.g., developing and evaluating school surveys), and health/ physical education (e.g., a play and dance about bullying performed at a school assembly).

Evaluating and Celebrating   At the completion of the interventions, schools celebrated in a variety of ways including: announcements of progress at school assemblies, class letters identifying ideas and accomplishments, school open days and displays at the school and local community shopping centers.

Relevant Research and Evidence of Effectiveness

A range of interventions using the PEACE Pack have been made in a number of schools in Australia and overseas at junior primary, primary, and secondary school level and evaluations reported (Slee, 1994, 1996; Slee & Mohyla, 2007). The following section will provide an overview of the findings from the most recent intervention program in four Australian primary schools using the PEACE Pack (Slee & Mohyla, 2007).

The research involved one- and two-year long school interventions involving 954 students comprising 458 males and 496 females ranging in age from 5 to 13 years old. The interventions involved four primary schools located in lower middle-class suburbs in metropolitan Adelaide in South Australia. The author had consulted extensively with the principals, teachers, and central education authorities in developing the interventions.

Measures

Subsequent to the administration of a school survey in the middle of term one, each school developed a common questionnaire. Data collected included: (a) demographic details, including gender and age; (b) questions related to students' experiences of school bullying (e.g., self-reported frequency of being bullied and bullying others, feelings of safety); (c) knowledge of school initiatives to address bullying; (d) confidence regarding addressing bullying themselves; and (e) whether in the last year there had been more or less bullying at their school. The questions are generally presented as descriptive Likert-type scales previously reported in various publications (see Slee, 2002). The questionnaire takes approximately 20 minutes or one school lesson to complete. Essentially the same questionnaire was repeated at yearly intervals across the four schools.

Design

The present study had a quasi-experimental field design with a pre- and post-test. As Grinnell (1981) has noted, when researchers cannot implement an experimental design involving the manipulation of an independent variable then a quasi-experimental design may be used. This procedure attempts to control for as many internal validity factors as possible, and, as Olweus (2005) has pointed out, there is a considerable literature on quasi-experimental designs documenting the strengths and weaknesses of this approach. A range of organizational imperatives meant that it was not possible to allocate schools to experimental and control groups or to randomly assign classes within schools to differential treatment effects.

Outcomes

As shown in Figure 34.2 for junior primary students (5–7 years old), 17% of boys and 19% of girls reported being bullied "less" after the year-long intervention. Gains were generally made across the junior primary population with an increase in young students reporting (a) they could not join in bullying others (+4%), (b) knowing more about how to stop bullying (+18%), (c) know-

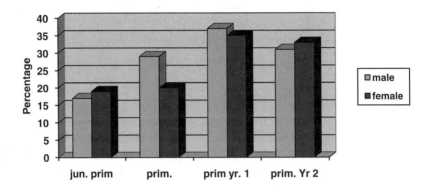

Figure 34.2 Percentages of junior primary and primary school students reporting they were 'bullied less' after one year and two year long interventions.

ing more about who to talk to if they were being bullied (+13%), and (d) feeling safer from being bullied (+22%).

Overall, for the primary school students (aged 8–12 years), 29% of boys and 20% of girls reported being bullied "less" after the year long interventions. Gains were generally made across the primary school population with, on average, students reporting they would know more about how to stop being bullied and who to talk to, with the gains being generally equivalent for males and females.

For one of the schools, the intervention was evaluated across a two-year period. In this school involving primary school students, on average 32% and 33% of students reported being 'bullied less' across the period, respectively. This school had entered the program because of specific concerns by teachers regarding the level of school bullying. The school had no policy or grievance procedure in place regarding school bullying. Students were actively involved by teachers in researching, developing, and launching policy and grievance procedures and the school adopted a community wide intervention program involving parents and community services such as the police (e.g., the police community liaison unit ran sessions for the students on protective behaviors). The school, in launching its policy to the community, had helium balloons released carrying anti-bullying messages far and wide. The symbolism of this particular component was that school bullying is indeed a community issue. As an interesting aside, several of the balloons were carried up to 100 kilometers and messages of support for the school's initiative were sent in by members of the public upon finding the balloon messages.

Students Bullied More or Less after the Interventions

One interesting aspect of the present study involving schools A, B, and C for which data was collected, concerned a small number of students across the junior primary and primary school age range who reported an 'increase' in the level of bullying following the year long intervention. In all, 98 students equating to 12% of the sample reported being bullied "more" and 21% reported being bullied "less" with the remainder "about the same" amount.

The highest frequency of students reporting they were being bullied "more" was in year one and two (21% compared to an average of 11% for years three to seven). Amongst the students reporting they were bullied "less," there was a sex difference with more males (57%) than females (43%) reporting being bullied "less" but with virtually no gender difference amongst the students reporting they were bullied "more."

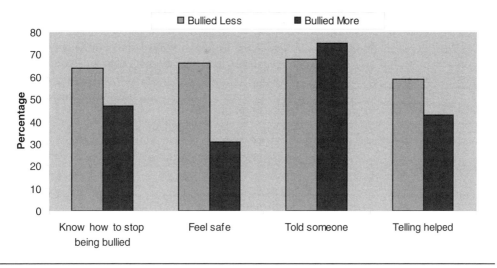

Figure 34.3 Students from schools A, B, & C reporting on their experiences of being bullied "less" or "more" after the year long interventions.

As shown in Figure 34.3, chi-square tests showed that those who reported they were bullied "less" after the intervention were significantly (p < .01) more likely than those who reported being bullied "more" to indicate that they knew how to stop being bullied (64% vs. 47%), to report feeling safe from bullying (66% vs. 31% p <.01) and to have told someone (63% vs. 75%, p < .03). There was no difference between the two groups in reporting that telling someone helped stop the bullying, although for those reporting being bullied less telling helped more (59% vs. 43%).

The present findings relating to the PEACE Pack interventions highlighted that the interventions resulted in a small group of students who reported being bullied "more" following intervention. These students were typically younger, female, knew less about stopping, felt less safe, had told someone, but reported that telling generally helped less. Pepler, Jiang, and Craig (2006) have highlighted the need to attend to particular groups of students in a school bullying intervention program because they may differentially benefit from such programs.

Internationally, aspects of the PEACE Pack have been translated into Japanese and the program implemented in a number of Japanese middle schools (Slee & Taki, 1999). In the Japanese year-long school-based interventions, the implementation of the program produced, amongst other findings, a reduction in bullying by exclusion of 13% in Grade 7 and 29% in Grade 8, respectively. The preliminary findings from the Japanese intervention study using the PEACE Pack suggest it is possible to adapt it cross-culturally to successfully intervene to reduce school bullying.

Limitations and Future Research

Overall, as noted by Stevens and colleagues (2000) and Vreeman and Carroll (2007), outcomes of school anti-bullying intervention programs have produced effects ranging from very strong to almost negligible. The PEACE Pack interventions resulted in approximately one-fifth of students in the overall sample reporting they were being bullied "less" as a result of year-long interventions, and this finding is broadly consistent with previous intervention studies. In developing the resource, the explicit intention was not to provide a rigid, lock-step process for addressing school bullying. Rather, the purpose was to provide a resource that was attuned to the sociocultural background of the school.

Limitations of the study include the quasi-experimental design lacking a control group for comparison, but this is largely due to the complex nature of schools which in the current climate in Australia are all required to be implementing the Safe Schools Frame-work. The data obviously relied on student's self reports and some triangulation of different data sources (e.g., teacher reports) is desirable. Much remains to be done in order to understand the dynamics underpinning a successful intervention program, particularly in a cross-cultural setting and in relation to students with special needs. Intervention programs should be contextualized and not simply replicated from one school or from one country to another (Oxford-Kobe Seminars, 2007).

Conclusion

School bullying is an issue that crosses individual, school, and community boundaries with effects that are indeed far-reaching, well-documented, and substantiated in psychological research. When individual and community concerns are frustrated and blocked, legal recourse is sought. In reviewing current literature, the weight of evidence is that those bullied have various legal remedies. In the light of available research the PEACE Pack, by acting in the best interests of those deemed to be most vulnerable, is seen to be fulfilling broader civic, social, and moral imperatives.

Summary Table of Implications for Practice

To conclude, the mother of a boy referred to me in my clinical practice by her doctor because of school bullying noted in one therapy session:

> I want change, I want to be part of the process in dealing with my son as a victim of harassment. I don't want to be told a policy is in place and we know best how to handle it. I want follow up. I want my anger acknowledged and valued. I especially don't want my present inability as a parent to participate, my silence to be seen as an acceptance of violence and harassment. I would like to see developed programs for children and programs for their parents and wider still, programs for our communities that deal with the issue of bullying.

Elements of this mother's story have implications for practice, some of which are highlighted in Table 34.2.

Table 34.2 Implications for Practice

Dixon et al., 2004; Pepler et al., 2006; Slee, 2001	School bullying is a systemic problem involving students, teachers, parents, and the broader community
Slee, 2001	School interventions are multi-layered involving short, medium, and long-terms goals
Vreeman & Carrol, 2007	The engagement of all school community members is crucial to the success of any intervention. 'Ownership' of the program by students appears particularly important. Interventions should involve the development and sustaining of 'genuine partnerships' between school and community systems
Bottroff et al., 2007	Consideration at whom the program is directed and whether there are some students who may need more intensive intervention
Smith, et al., 1999; Owens et al., 2000	Gender and developmental aspects should be considered in the implementation of a program

References

The Advertiser. (2007, May 15). Bullied student to get $1 million. *The Advertiser* (Adelaide. South Australia), pp.1–2.

Attorney-General's Department. (2002). *A meta-evaluation of methods and approaches to reducing bullying in preschools and early primary school in Australia* (K. Rigby, Ed.). Canberra: Commonwealth of Australia.

Bottroff, V. (1998). The development of friendship and the puzzle of autism. In P. T. Slee & K. Rigby (Eds.), *Children's peer relations* (pp. 91–10). Routledge: London.

Bottroff, V., Slee, P. T., & Michaelsen, K. (2007). *Perfect targets for bullying: Developing inclusive school communities by reducing bullying in mainstream education for students with autism spectrum disorders.* A keynote address for the biennial conference on Autismm Spectrum Disorders. Queensland, Australia, March 14–16.

Clearihan, S., Slee, P. T., Souter, M., Gascoign, Nichols, A., Burgan, M., et al. (1999). *Antiviolence bullying prevention project.* Victimology Conference Adelaide, May 25–26.

Coleman. J. S. (1988). Social capital in the creation of human capital. *American Journal of Sociology, 94,* 95–120.

Commonwealth Department of Health and Aged Care. (2000). *Promotion, prevention and early intervention for mental health — A monograph.* Mental health and special programs branch. Canberra, Australia: Commonwealth Department of Health and Aged Care.

Davidson, L. M., & Demaray, M. K. (2007). Social support as a moderator between Victimization and internalizing-externalizing distress from bullying. *School Review, 36*(3), 383–405.

Dixon, R., Smith, P. K., & Jenks, C (2004). Using systemic thinking to inform research on bullying. In K. Osterman & K. Bjorkqvist (Eds.), *Contemporary research on aggression.* Proceedings of the XVI World meeting of the International Society for Research on Aggression, Santorini, Greece.

Espelage, D., & Swearer, S. (2003). Research on School bullying and victimization. What have we learned and where do we go from here? *School Psychology Review, 32,* 365–385.

Etzioni, E. (1995). *New communitarian thinking, persons, virtues, institutions,and communities.* Charlottesville: University of Virginia Press.

Fehring, I. (1998). Responsibility for supervising students. *School Law.* Sydney: LAAMS Publications.

Grinnell, R.M. (1981). *Social work research and evaluation.* ITSACA, IL: Peacock

Hawker, S. J., & Boulton, M. (2000). Twenty years' research on peer victimisation and psychosocial maladjustment: A meta-analytic review of cross-sectional studies. *Journal Child Psychology & Psychiatry, 41*(4), 441–455.

Hetherington, M. (1999). Social capital and the development of youth from nondivorced, divorced, and remarried families. In W. A. Collins & B. Laursen (Eds.), *Relationships as developmental contexts* (part III, chapter 9). Mahwah, NJ: Erlbaum.

Keeves, J., & Watanabe, R. (Eds.). (2003). *The handbook on educational research in the Asia Pacific region.* Dordrecht, The Netherlands: Kluwer.

Limber, S. P., & Small, M. A. (2003). State laws and policies to address bullying in schools. *School Psychology Review, 32,* 445–455.

Ministerial Council on Education Training and Youth Affairs (MCEETYA). (2003). National Safe Schools Framework Report. URL. Retrieved from http://www.cecnsw.catholic.edu.au/National_Safe_Schools_Poster.pdf

Nicholson, A. (2006). Legal perspectives on bullying. In H. McGrath, & T. Noble, (Eds.), *Bullying solutions: Evidence-based approaches to bullying in Australian schools* (pp 17–45). Melbourne, Australia: Pearson Longman.

McGrath, H., & Noble, T. (Eds.). (2006). Bullying solutions: Evidence-based approaches to bullying in Australian schools. Melbourne, Australia: Pearson Longman.

Olweus D. (1993). *Bullying at school: What we know and what we can do.* Oxford, UK: Blackwell.

Olweus, D. (2005). A useful evaluation design, and the effects of the Olweus Bullying Prevention program. *Psychology, Crime, and Law, 11,* 389–402.

Owens, L., Daly, T., & Slee, P.T. (2005). Sex and age differences in victimization and conflict resolution among adolescents in a South Australian school. *Aggressive Behaviour,* 1–12.

Owens, L., Shute, R., & Slee, P. T. (2000). 'I'm in and you're out': Explanations for teenage girls' indirect aggression. *Psychology, Evolution & Gender, 2,* 19–46.

Owens, L., Shute, R., & Slee, P. T. (2004). Girls' aggressive behavior. *The Prevention Researcher, 11*(3), 9–12.

Oxford-Kobe Seminars. (2007). *Measures to reduce bullying in schools.* Kobe Institute, Kobe, Japan May 21–25.

Parcel, T. L., & Menaghan, E.G. (1993). Family social capital and children's behavior problems. *Social Psychology Quarterly. 56,* 120–135.

Pepler, D., Jiang., D., & Craig, W. (2006). *Who benefits from bullying prevention programmes?* Paper presented at International Society for the Study of Behavioral development Meeting. Melbourne, Australia, 2–6 July.

Putnam, R.D. (1993). Bowling alone: America's declining social capital. *Journal of Democracy, 6,* 65–78.

Rigby, K., & Slee, P. (1991). Bullying among Australian school children: Reported behavior and attitude towards victims. *Journal of Social Psychology, 131,* 615–627.

Rigby, K., & Slee, P. T. (1992). *Bullying in schools* [Video]. Melbourne. Australia: Australian Council for Educational Research.

Rigby, K., & Slee, P. T. (1993). Children's attitudes towards victims. In D. P. Tattum (Ed), *Understanding and managing bullying* (pp. 119–133). London: Heinemann Books.

Rigby, K., & Slee, P. T. (1999a). Suicidal ideation among adolescent schoolchildren, involvement in bully/victim problems and perceived low social support. *Suicide and Life-Threatening Behaviour, 29,* 119–130.

Rigby, K., & Slee, P. T. (1999b). In P. K. Smith, Y. Morita, J. Junger-tas, D. Olweus, R. Catalano, & P. Slee (Eds.), *The nature of school bullying. A cross-national perspective* (pp. 324–440). London: Routledge.

Rigby, K (2002). *New perspectives on bullying.* London: Jessica Kingsley.

Roland, E. (1989). Bullying: the Scandinavian tradition. In D. P. Tattum & D. A. Lane (Eds.), *Bullying in schools* (pp. 21–32). London: Trentham Books.

Runyan, D. K., Hunter, M. H., Socolar, R. R., Amaya-Jackson, L., English, D., Landsverk, J., et al. (1998). Children who prosper in unfavorable environments: The relationship to social capital. *Pediatrics, 101,* 12–18.

Shute, R., Owens, L., & Slee, P. T. (2002). 'You just look at them and give them daggers': Adolescent girls use of nonverbal aggression. *International Journal of Adolescence, 10,* 353–372.

Slee, P. T. (1994). I'm a victim — stop bullying. In K. Oxenberry, K. Rigby, & P. Slee (Eds.), *Childrens peer relations: Cooperation and conflict.* Children's Peer Relationships Conference Proceedings. Adelaide, Australia, January 19–22.

Slee, P. T. (1995). Bullying: Health concerns of Australian secondary school students. *International Journal of Adolescence & Youth, 5,* 215–224.

Slee, P. T. (1996). The PEACE Pack: A program for reducing bullying in our schools. *Australian Journal of Guidance and Counselling. 6,* 63–69.

Slee, P. T. (2001). *The PEACE Pack: A program for reducing bullying in our Schools.* Adelaide, Australia: Flinders University.

Slee, P. T. (2002). An Australian commentary on 'Violence in schools: The response from Europe." P. Smith (Ed.), *Violence in schools: An Australian commentary* (pp. 301–317). London: Routledge.

Slee, P. T., & Ford. D. (1999). Bullying is a serious issue – it is a crime! *Australian & New Zealand Journal of Law and Education, 4*(1), 23–39.

Slee, P. T., Ma, L., Hee-og, S., Taki, M., & Sullivan, K. (2003). *School bullying in five countries in the Asia-Pacific region.* In J. Keeves & R. Watanabe (Eds.), *The handbook on educational research in the Asia Pacific region.* Dordrecht, The Netherlands: Kluwer.

Slee, P. T., & Mohyla, J. (2007). The PEACE Pack: An evaluation of interventions to reduce bullying in four Australian primary schools. *Educational Research. 49,* 103–114.

Slee, P. T., & Murray-Harvey R. (2001). A comparative study of Australian and Japanese student's school lives. Unpublished manuscript.

Slee, P. T., & Murray-Harvey, R. (2007). Disadvantaged childrens' physical, developmental and behavioral health problems in an urban environment: Links with social capital. *Journal of Social Services Review , 14,* 371–373.

Slee. P. T., & Shute, R. (2003). Child development. Thinking about theories. London: Arnold.

Slee, P. T., & Taki, M. (1999). Interventions to reduce bullying in Japanese schools:The PEACE Pack. Society for Research in Child Development. Alberquerque, New Mexico, April. 16–22.

Smith, P. K. (2002). *Violence in schools. The response in Europe.* London: Routledge Falmer.

Smith, P. K., Morita, Y., Junger-tas, J., Olweus, D., Catalano, R., & Slee, P. (1999). *The nature of school bullying: A cross-national perspective.* London: Routledge.

Smith, P., Cowie, H., Olafsson, & Liefooghe, (2002). Definitions of bullying: A comparison of terms used, and age and gender differences, in a fourteen-country international comparison. *Child Development, 73,* 1119–1133.

Smith, P. K, Madsen, K. C., & Moody, J. C. (1999). What causes the age decline in reports of being bullied at school? Toward a developmental analysis of risks of being bullied. *Educational Research, 41,* 276–285.

Smith, P. K., Pepler, D., & Rigby, K. (2004). *Bullying in schools: How successful can interventions be?* Cambridge, UK: Cambridge University Press.

Smith, P. K., & Sharp, S. (Eds.). (1994). *School bullying: Insights and perspectives.* London. Routledge.

Stevens, V., Bourdeauhij, I. D., & Oost, P. V. (2000). Bullying in Flemish schools: An evaluation of anti-bullying interventions in primary and secondary schools. *British Journal of Educational Psychology, 70,* 195–210.

Taki, M., Slee, P. T., & Murray-Harvey, R. (2002). *Life at school in Australia and Japan: Modeling the impact of stress and support on school bullying amongst girls.* Symposium. Paper presented International Society Study of Behavioural Development, August 16–19, Quebec, Canada.

Vreeman, R., & Carroll, A. (2007). A systematic review of school-based interventions to Prevent bullying. *Archives of Pediatrics and Adolescent medicine, 161,* 78–88.

35

McKay School Safety Program (MSSP)

A Bilingual Bicultural Approach

REBECCA A. ROBLES-PIÑA, PAULETTE NORMAN,
AND CARRIE CAMPBELL-BISHOP

School prevention and intervention programs have been the standard for providing safety information regarding violence to all students (Samples, 2004), as schools provide the most logical setting for social development (Bronfenbrenner, 1979; Juvonen & Graham, 2004). However, there is little research indicating that school prevention programs affect all students equally, particularly those who are from non-majority groups. Programs that are equitable need to consider the following factors: (a) the school policy, No Child Left Behind Act of 2001 that emphasizes desegregation of data by ethnic groups and the use of empirically supported programs, and (b) an increasingly diverse Hispanic student population in our schools (U.S. Bureau of the Census, 2002). To date, there are no known U.S. school safety prevention programs that have been written about best practices for bilingual Hispanic children.

Questions about whether existing intervention programs address the needs of all children have been a most controversial topic. Earlier research by Tutty (1995) indicated an emphasis on cultural responsiveness to prevention programs by placing a stronger emphasis on race and cultural background when rating children's responses to certain issues related to sexual abuse. She wrote, "Questions about whether young children can actually learn concepts that may be counter to their developmental or cultural background remain important areas for continued investigation" (p. 2). Most recently, Ravitch had this to say about the mission of schools, "To be effective, schools must concentrate on their fundamental mission of teaching and learning. And they must do it for all children. That must be the overarching goal of schools in the twenty-first century" (2000, p. 467).

Curriculum-based school prevention and intervention programs are developed for elementary, middle/junior high, and high schools and some have determined effectiveness with moderate effect sizes (Wilson, Lipsey, & Derzon, 2003). However, there are many school-based violence prevention programs that have not been rigorously evaluated (Elliott & Tolan, 1999; Farrell, Meyer, Kung, & Sullivan, 2001; Juvonen & Graham, 2004; Powell et al., 1996; Samples & Aber, 1998), while others that have been evaluated yielded some disappointing results (Gottfredson, 2001).

The goal of all programs in prevention and intervention in schools is that programs be determined effective. Typically, effectiveness is based solely on measured outcomes; however, there are other variables to consider, such as developmental appropriateness, school transitions, and cost-effectiveness (Nation et al., 2003). Additionally, even when programs are developed for suitability of cultures that are distinct from the mainstream culture, it is important that evaluations go beyond surface structures such as language translation to include deep structures that are sensitive to cultural factors (Resnicow, Solar, Braithwaite, Ahluwalia, & Butler, 2000).

The U.S. Department of Education has suggested inclusion of several elements in effective school safety programs. One, various types of misconduct, such as aggression, bullying, and harassment need to be considered. Two, special attention is necessary to guard against discrimination on part of gender, race/ethnicity, religion, or sexual orientation differences. Three, programs need to change attitudes, willingness of children to report events, and a willingness of children to respect personal space (Glover, Gough, & Johnson, 2000).

The following is a review of specific school-wide prevention programs noting populations for which they were developed, goals, and effectiveness information. This is not an exhaustive list of all such programs.

Curriculum-Based School Prevention and Intervention Programs

The first school-wide curriculum-based school prevention program developed to prevent bullying was *The Bullying Prevention Program* for use in Norway in 1983–1985 by psychologist Dan Olweus (1991). The three primary goals of the program are: (a) increased awareness of bullying, (b) adult opposition to bullying behavior, and (c) protection and support of victims. It is intended that these goals be performed at multiple levels (community, school, classroom, and individual). In a sample of 2,500 students in the fourth through seventh grades taken from 42 schools and 112 classrooms, a 50% reduction of bullying behavior for boys and girls at all age levels was found.

The Bullying Prevention Program was replicated and evaluated for its effectiveness in two other international settings, the United Kingdom (Smith & Sharp, 1994) and Germany (Olweus, Limber, & Mihalic, 1999). The program in the United Kingdom identified as The Sheffield Project included a sample of 16 primary schools (N = 2,212) and 7 secondary schools (N = 4,256) with students ages 8 to 16. Results on effectiveness indicated that: (a) bully-victim problems decreased significantly, (b) student attitudes were positively impacted, and (c) rates of bullying incidents decreased. Similarly, The Bullying Prevention Program was replicated in Germany and produced comparable results with bullying victimization incidences being reduced from 18% to 15% over a two-year period.

The Flemish Antibullying Intervention Project was developed in Finland and the goals are: (a) a whole-school approach used for implementation, (b) emphasis of no-tolerance for bullying, and (c) provision of a supportive environment for bully and victim (Stevens, Van Oost, & Bourdeaudhuij, 2000). A sample of 728 primary school students ages 10-12 were taken from 55 classes in 11 schools and 1,456 secondary school students ages 13–6 from 136 classes. After two years, low mean scores from the intervention group versus high mean scores from the control group indicated an increase in rates of supporting victims and seeking teacher help.

The Lions-Quest Conflict Management Program was developed in Toronto, Canada, and had three major objectives: (a) changing attitudes about students' interactions, (b) increasing knowledge about non-violent techniques to be used with conflicts, and (c) fostering use of behaviors to use in conflict situations. Effectiveness data exists only for middle/junior high school students. The two-year program was evaluated using 1,900, seventh and eighth grade students using an intervention and non-intervention groups (Byrd, 1996). The results indicated that the intervention group made gains in: (a) increasing grade point ratios, (b) decreasing violence by 68%, and (c) increasing pro-social interactions among students.

A few school-wide prevention programs have cited using diverse ethnic groups in their study. One such program is *Cool Tools*, an adaptation of the original The Bullying Prevention Program that was developed in California (Nishina, Juvonen, & de la Sota, 2000). The goals of the program are to: (a) minimize the negative effects of bullying on children, and (b) learn coping strategies to use in mediating bullying incidents. An effectiveness pilot study was conducted on a group of African American boys in third through fifth grades; 31 were randomly assigned to the intervention and 35 assigned to a no-treatment control group (Graham, Taylor, & Hudley, 2003). Findings for this pilot study indicated modest effects and many limitations cited. The intervention was rated as more successful in increasing pro-social skills and motivations than with decreasing problem behaviors and negative social behaviors, as identified by teacher ratings.

One of the first bullying programs to be evaluated on a racially diverse sample was The Bullying Prevention Program (Sanchez et al., 2001) in Texas. The goal of the program was a whole-school approach to address bullying, sexual harassment, and gender violence. The sample included 740, fifth grade students whose ethnic composition was 16% (118) African American, 25% (185) Hispanic, and 59% (437) White. Of the students, 31.5% were on free and reduced lunches. Results indicated that the student experimental groups made gains over the control group in knowledge about sexual harassment. However, the researchers did not find differences between the experimental and control group on knowledge about bullying. Interestingly, during focus group discussions about 20% of the students reported that they had engaged in bullying someone in the past week. Further, a followup of students' self-report indicated that 37% of students had been bullied in the past three months. This is contradictory to the goal of the intervention, however, since baseline rates were not mentioned it is difficult to say whether there was an increase or decrease in bullying and victimization rates over the one-year project.

A qualitative study on the Expect Respect Program was conducted (Khosropour & Walsh, 2001) on fifth graders (N = 40) taken from four ethnically diverse elementary schools. Interview data indicated that students in the intervention group held adults at school rather than parents accountable for finding solutions to bullying and believed that nothing could be done about bullying.

A study including a Spanish-speaking group outside the United States is the Seville Antibullying in School (SAVE). This project was developed in Seville, Spain in response to an increase in bullying in Spanish schools (Ortega & Lera, 2000). The goals of the project are to: (a) test the fit of the conceptual model, (b) develop a questionnaire from the Olweus' questionnaire for use with the Spanish language and culture, and (c) develop an intervention program. The sample was composed of 4,914 students in 26 schools from elementary to high schools located in Seville. Data analyses are still pending.

In summary, most curriculum-based, school-wide bullying prevention programs have been developed around the original The Bullying Prevention Program developed by Olweus in Norway. Effectiveness data from programs evaluated in Norway, Finland, and England have proven satisfactory in decreasing bullying rates. A program developed in Spanish for the Hispanic population in Spain is still undergoing effectiveness results. A Texas study that did disaggregate data by ethnic groups did not find differences between groups on knowledge about bullying. Consequently, the above mentioned information provides a strong rationale for developing and evaluating a U. S. school prevention program that measures the effectiveness of increased knowledge with students whose culture and language are diverse.

Effective Characteristics of Coordinated Prevention Programs

Determining the effectiveness of school prevention programs is a major challenge and a suggested framework for the evaluation is one that includes the following six characteristics (Nation et al., 2003). The first characteristic is the use of a research-based risk and protective factor framework that involves families, peers, schools, and communities as partners to address multiple outcomes. In other words, it is best to examine problems from an ecological perspective that examines risk and protective factors (Bronfenbrenner & Morris, 1998). A second characteristic is that programs be long-term, age-specific, and culturally appropriate. Programs need to be designed so that they mirror the culture of the school and community and are inclusive of members from all cultures in the program planning, implementation, and evaluation (Schinke & Matthieu, 2003).

A third characteristic is the development of social-emotional skills in everyday life. Social, emotional, and ethical behavior are best developed through methods that include role plays, modeling, and applied practice (Bandura, 1995; Hawkins & Weis, 1985; Ladd & Mize, 1983). Further, use of problem-solving strategies in the community in which students live is necessary for developing social and emotional skills.

A fourth characteristic is the establishment of policies, institutional practices, and environments that nurture optimal development. The development of social supports such as those found in caring and nurturing adults are necessary to increase the protective factors that children need when faced with challenging or difficult times. Thus, it becomes necessary to include parents and members of the community as an integral part of the program.

A fifth characteristic is training of support staff on effective interpersonal skills so that they know how to implement the program effectively. It has been found that mediators to the success of any program are the trainers' interpersonal skills, knowledge of the program, warmth, empathy, humor, and knowledge of how young persons learn (Kumpfer & Alvarado, 2003).

A sixth characteristic is the adaptation of evidence-based programming to meet local community needs through strategic planning, ongoing evaluation, and continuous improvement. It is important that a "needs assessment" be conducted that identifies and addresses the school's problems, strengths, and concerns from a diverse group of individuals. Formative evaluation should be conducted to: (a) understand the strengths and areas of improvement for the program, (b) determine its cost-effectiveness, and (c) assess the benefits to all stakeholders (Tebes, Kaufman, & Connell, 2003; Wandersman & Florin, 2003).

Given the lack of school prevention programs that address the language and culture of Hispanic students, the purpose of this study is to address this gap by providing empirical evidence for a school safety prevention program that will increase the knowledge base of safety concepts for an at-risk, culturally diverse Hispanic population. This will be done by describing the development, implementation, and evaluation of the bilingual, bicultural McKay School Prevention Program (MSSP) from various stakeholders' perspectives including students, parents, and educators.

Methodology

Participants

Data were collected on 242 fourth graders from a large urban school district in Texas. Participants were composed of 106 (44%) males and 136 (56%) females; 184 (76%) Hispanic, 53 (22%) African American, and 5 (2%) Other. Over 70% of the students were on free and reduced lunch. There was a 92% student response rate to the pre- and post-tests, 52 out of 106 parents responded to the parent survey for a 49% response rate, and 15 school counselors and teachers were interviewed in focus groups.

Design

From 211 elementary schools, four schools were randomly selected to participate. Subsequently, 12, fourth grade classrooms were randomly assigned to 3 conditions: A (75), B (88), and C (67). Condition A received the MSSP pre-post tests, MSSP Curriculum, and video-tapes. Condition B did not receive the MSSP pre-test (this was done to assess whether the pre-test affected the post-test) but did receive the MSSP post-test, MSSP Curriculum, and video-tapes. Condition C, the control group, received MSSP pre- and post-tests and no treatment.

Curriculum Guide

The McKay School Safety Program (MSSP) (The McKay Foundation, 2004) is a bilingual, bicultural program (English and Spanish) developed for use with children ages 9–11. The goals of MSSP are to: (a) increase the knowledge of school safety concepts (bullying, self-esteem, respect of personal space, internet bullying, sexual exploitation) with bilingual Hispanic students, (b) teach students how to guard their personal space, (c) identify persons who wish to do them harm, and (d) teach students about how to report to trusted adults about person(s) who are bullying them, invading their personal space, and sexually abusing them.

An advisory council was formed to assure that MSSP goals were consistent with the language and cultural components of the community. The council was appointed by the superintendent of schools and was comprised of a project director, curriculum specialist, MSSP trainers, research director, administrative assistant of teachers, school counselors, school psychologist, co-principal investigators, a safe and drug free specialist, law enforcement officers, an accreditation specialist, and several parents. Six themes were identified from the needs-assessment conducted by the council and those led to the development of the six lessons included in MSSP.

These six lessons were developed to be used with third, fourth, and fifth grades and The MSSP Curriculum included activities around the following themes: (a) Self-Esteem (Auto Estima), (b) Internet Safety (Seguridad en el Internet), (c) Stranger Beware (Cuidado – Un Extraño), (d) When a Stranger Isn't So Strange (Cuando Un Extraño no es tan Extraño), (e) No Bullying Allowed (No Es Permitada Intimidación), and (f) Don't Invade My Space (No Invadas mi Espacio).

MSSP was also based on three theories for the development of the curriculum, videos, pre-post tests, and worksheets for the six lessons. Worksheets were developed to be sent home with the objective that parents assist children in filling out the worksheets while reinforcing concepts related to reading and school safety. Videos were developed to make the abstract concepts more concrete as actors demonstrated how to problem solve. Further, the videos provided open-ended questions that were used for student role playing.

Theories used were those that emphasized meeting student's social emotional needs while improving cognitive skills in culturally appropriate ways. Bloom's (1976) Taxonomy theory was used to assure that the materials developed increased higher critical thinking skills (knowledge, comprehension, application, analysis, synthesis, and evaluation). Maslow's theory of Hierarchy of Needs (Maslow, 1968) was used as a theoretical framework to assure that materials and training included aspects of safety, belongingness and love, esteem, and self-actualization. Sue, Arredondo, and McDavis' (1992) theory of multicultural counseling competencies was used for developing lessons and educating trainers in order to ensure culturally appropriate acquisition and dissemination of knowledge, skills, and dispositions.

Training was developed from the information provided by the needs assessment and advice provided by the advisory council. Three trainers were selected for their prior experience in working with children. One was a former police officer who had over 12 years experience working with youth, a second trainer had over 14 years working as an elementary teacher, and the third was a fluent English/Spanish speaker who worked in a children's museum and who attended one of the schools that was targeted for implementation of MSSP.

Two co-principal investigators were in charge of training and checking for treatment fidelity with the MSSP Curriculum. One co-principal investigator, a teacher with over 20 years experience working with at-risk populations was in charge of developing the lessons based on Maslow's and Bloom's theory, training and checking the trainers for treatment fidelity (assuring trainers were adhering equally to MSSP Curriculum). The second co-principal investigator, a bilingual psychologist with over 13 years experience in bilingual assessment and therapy, assured that the materials were translated appropriately and addressed the cultural needs of the community. Culturally sensitive meant that the materials, videos, and role-plays used names typically found in the neighborhood and were developed around themes selected by the council. Additionally, the second co-principal investigator conducted bi-monthly focus groups with trainers to assure they were processing their own biases in working with the target population.

Instrument

Pre- and post-tests were developed to gather information about knowledge of MSSP. The tests included 24 questions with four, multiple-choice responses for which there is a correct answer. An example of a question on internet safety was "What can I do if someone I do not know sends me a message on my computer asking me to meet them at the park?" In Spanish the question read "Que puedo hacer si alguien que yo no conozco me manda un mensaje a mi computadora, diciéndome que los encurentre en el parque?"

MSSP pre- and post-tests were found to be psychometrically sound. An estimate of reliability of .89 for internal consistency using a KR-20 formula (when questions have right and wrong answers; Drummond, 2000) was found for this sample. Validity was established in the following four ways: (a) taking the questions directly from the MSSP Curriculum, (b) submitting the survey to four different experts in the area of school safety for their feedback, (c) conducting a pilot study with a group of fourth grade students, and (d) developing the curriculum from a needs assessment conducted in the school district with the assistance of an advisory council. Recommendations from the community members and experts in the field of school safety were integrated into the survey.

Some of the recommendations made are noted. One, the advisory council and experts identified six themes for the curriculum based on the needs assessment. Two, some of the experts in school safety were concerned that the stem questions were too long and that perhaps reading ability was being assessed rather than knowledge of school safety. Three, experts recommended that more culturally based scenarios using visuals and hands on activities such as videos and role playing were needed in order for the students to take concepts from an abstract to a concrete level. Four, it was suggested that pre- and post-tests have a picture of the props used in the actual training so that the students could use these for memory recall. Fifth, it was suggested that Spanish words commonly used in the neighborhood be used in preparation of materials. All of these recommendations were made to the curriculum, video scripts, and tests.

Procedure

Permission was obtained from institutional review boards at the university and school district sites. Schools were involved in the study for 15 weeks with 2 weeks used for testing. For the remaining 13 weeks, 1 lesson was taught over a 2-week period, with two hours dedicated to each lesson per week. Worksheets were sent home with students and they were encouraged to work on them with their parents in order to reinforce the MSSP safety concepts as well as educating parents about what students were learning. Video tapes were used to model good problem solving skills as well as to provide scenarios for students to role play problem solving skills. Parents of students receiving MSSP were sent a survey to assess their perceptions about effectiveness. Moreover, focus groups were conducted every two weeks with teachers and school counselors to collect their perceptions of the effectiveness of MSSP. Co-principal investigators provided training and assured treatment fidelity, and cultural relevance of training.

Results

MSSP pre-post tests were prepared in English and Spanish, however, the majority of the students (97%) elected to take the English version and thus only the English versions of the tests were analyzed. Teachers, counselors, and trainers assisted students in reading questions when needed and pointed to the picture of the prop(s) on the tests to facilitate the student's memory recall of the lessons learned.

Several steps were followed to determine if the MSSP had increased the knowledge about safety topics for predominately Hispanic fourth grade, urban, at risk students. First, it was necessary to determine if there was a pre-test difference in knowledge between the experimental group A and control group C. A *t*-test of independent means indicated that there was a significant difference ($t(1, 141)$= -2.43, p = .01), with the control group having more knowledge (M = 73.45, SD = 14.57) by 5.61 points more than the experimental group (M = 67.84, SD = 13.55). This indicated that students in the control group who would not receive the MSSP treatment initially had more knowledge of MSSP school safety concepts than the experimental groups.

Second, to investigate if the pre-test had an effect on the post-test results, a *t*-test of independent means was conducted on the post-tests of the two experimental groups (A & B) and none was found. The respective means were (M = 81.76.45, SD = 14.57) and (M = 82.06, SD = 13.87). This indicated that the pre-test did not influence the knowledge of students on the post-test.

Third, to determine if there was a difference between experimental groups (Condition A and Condition B) and the control group (Condition C) on the MSSP post-test, an ANOVA was conducted. A statistically significant difference was found ($F (2,229)$ = 11.05, p < .01, d = .69, medium effect size). The mean scores for experimental groups, Condition A (M = 81.76, SD = 14.59) and Condition B (M = 82.06, SD = 13.87), were 10 points higher than the control group, Condition C (M = 72.06, SD = 15.05) (see Table 35.1). This difference should take into consideration that Condition C had scored close to 6 points higher on the pre-test.

To calculate effect size, the difference between scores of the experimental groups and the experimental group (numerator) was calculated (Baker, 1993). Subsequently, a weighted average of the two standard deviations was calculated (denominator) and divided into the numerator where a medium effect size of .69 was obtained (Cohen, 1988). An effect size of .69 indicates that the average student in the experimental group receiving MSSP (50th percentile of the score distribution for this group) would score at the 75th percentile of the score distributions of the control (not receiving MSSP) group.

Table 35.1 Effectiveness of McKay School Safety Program (MSSP) on Three Conditions (N = 242)

School and Condition	Pre-Mean (SD)	Post-Mean (SD)	Difference
A (Pre-Post Tests, MSSP Treatment)	67.84	81.76	13.92
	13.55	14.59	
B (Post-Test, MSSP Treatment)		82.06	No Pre-Test
		13.87	
C (Control, Pre-Post-Tests, No Treatment)	73.45	72.05	
	14.57	13.52	−1.40

Note: Statistically significant at < .01 Effect Size, d = .69 (MSSP) (N = 52) Mean (SD)

In summary, there are several indications for these findings. One, the control group initially indicated more knowledge about school safety concepts than the experimental groups. Two, the pre-test did not affect the post-test results. Three, the experimental groups demonstrated statistically significant more knowledge about school safety concepts than the control as well as more practical significance as evidenced by the medium effect size. Overall, the MSSP was found effective in improving the knowledge of school safety concepts for predominately Hispanic fourth grade, urban, at-risk students.

Parents' perceptions of the fourth graders receiving MSSP were assessed about their students' knowledge on school safety concepts. Out of 106 parents, 52 surveys were returned for a 49% response rate. The majority of the parents responded to the survey written in Spanish (see Table 35.2). Overall, parents reported that their children had learned the concepts taught in MSSP. Specific findings were that students: (a) were more comfortable and less scared after exposure to MSSP, (b) were most afraid of strangers and leaving the house than going to school and going to sleep, (c) knew the difference between a "good" and "bad" person, and (d) knew the difference between a "good" and "bad" touch.

Teachers and counselors of the fourth graders receiving MSSP were interviewed every two

Table 35.2 Parent Survey Responses to McKay School Safety Program (N = 52)

Question	Mean (SD)
What was your child's reaction to each of these feelings after the MSSP?	
Comfortable	3.95 (1.17)
Careful	3.80 (1.13)
Safe	3.69 (1.41)
Upset	2.50 (1.58)
Scared	2.49 (1.55)
Indicate how afraid you believe your child to be of the following after MSSP?	
Men strangers	3.38 (1.38)
Women strangers	2.87 (1.44)
Leaving the house	2.77 (1.43)
Going to school	2.45 (1.30)
Going to sleep	2.34 (1.07)
Do you believe your child knows the difference between a good person and a bad person?	41 (82%) Yes
	9 (8%) No
Do you believe your child knows the difference between a good touch and a bad touch?	43 (80%) Yes
	11 (20%) No

weeks during focus groups to evaluate their perceptions. They reported several findings. One, that MSSP students had increased knowledge about protecting their personal space (assessing their surroundings). Further, in protecting their personal space, students began questioning the motives of persons they loved and trusted in certain situations in which they felt uncomfortable. Two, students could identify safe adults and could communicate with safe adults about bullying practices, sexual offenses, and internet practices. Third, students made many more disclosures and reports to school personnel regarding bullying and sexual offenses after exposure to MSSP.

In summary, MSSP, a school safety prevention program that was based on a needs assessment of the community, written in Spanish and English and combining multiple school safety concepts (internet safety, sexual abuse, and bullying) for a predominately at-risk (70%), Hispanic, urban population was effective in increasing knowledge. Parents confirmed that students felt safer in the community and school after MSSP. Finally, counselors and teachers stated that MSSP had a positive influence on students and that disclosure about bullying and sexual abuse had increased. Implications of the findings are noted (see Table 35.3).

Discussion

The discussion section will be framed around the limitations, the theoretical framework of best practices for effective programs, and conclusion. The limitations are several. One, students had difficulty filling out the ethnic part of the demographic questions; students in the fourth grade seem confused by their ethnic identity. Fortunately, most of their teachers could assist in filling out this information on students' forms. Two, in order to avoid disrupting the academic time with students, we had to teach large classes of 40 and the role-playing activities and discussions were limited. Luckily, we had many bilingual teachers and counselors who volunteered to lead small groups and explain concepts in English. Three, due to funding of the grant, the training by the original trainers had to be discontinued. However, in order to provide for the sustainability of MSSP, materials were left behind with permission to make photocopies and school counselors and teachers were trained on how to implement MSSP.

The effectiveness of MSSP will be framed using the six characteristics of effective prevention programs (Nation et al., 2003). The first characteristic involves using research-based risk and protective factors framework to target multiple outcomes within a variety of stakeholders including students, parents, and community.

Evidence of an increase in protective factors while reducing risk factors was provided in multiple ways. One, protective factors were increased in the development of MSSP by community members that formed the council. Their role was to: (a) conduct a needs assessment, (b) review and make adjustments to curriculum guide, videos, and worksheets, and (c) monitor progress of

Table 35.3 Implications for Practice

1 The definitions of bullying, sexual abuse, self-esteem, and other concepts addressed in school bullying programs may vary depending on the language and culture of school and community.

2 A *needs assessment* developed and implemented by culturally aware school personnel and community is the first step in developing a school safety program including bullying.

3 A bullying program developed in Spanish will not have application to all Spanish-speaking populations due to the diversity of culture of the community and language. For example, the Spanish spoken in Spain is very different from that spoken in South Texas.

4 The particular language dialect; names of community centers, schools, and agencies; and names of community members need to be included in the development and implementation of a school bullying curriculum.

5 Evaluations of culturally and linguistically sensitive bullying programs need to assess all partners involved. Further, the program needs to be evaluated by someone understanding the culture and language.

MSSP and make recommendations for adjustments. Further, protective factors were increased by assessing various groups including students, parents, and community members regarding effectiveness.

Two, MSSP reduced the risk factors for students whose language and culture is diverse and who need to learn how to keep safe. MSSP was the first study that provided empirical support to suggest that bilingual, culturally diverse students in the U.S. can learn school safety concepts, a problem that was cited earlier in the research (Tutty, 1995). Three, MSSP increased the protective factors related to research design by using an experimental design and provided evidence of a rigorously evaluated school prevention program, a problem that was identified by several researchers (Elliott & Tolan, 1999; Farrell et al., 2001; Juvonen & Graham, 2004; Powell et al., 1996; Samples & Aber, 1998).

Four, this study's results add to the existing research on the effectiveness of school prevention programs for increasing knowledge gained by students, such as The Bullying Prevention Program implemented in European countries (Olweus, Limber, & Mihalic, 1999; Smith & Sharp, 1994; Stevens et al., 2000). Further, the results of this study add to the few U.S. curriculum-based school prevention programs that have attempted disaggregating data by ethnic groups (Nishina et al., 2000; Sanchez et al., 2001, Khospropour & Walsh, 2001). A caveat of this study is that it needs to be replicated with students of the same ethnic group as well as other ethnic groups to determine effectiveness.

The second characteristic highlights the importance of prevention programs being long-term, age specific, developmentally, and culturally appropriate. There were several ways in which this study addressed cultural and developmental appropriateness. First, MSSP was developed in Spanish and English since the population was predominately Hispanic and the six themes for study were those identified by the community in which the children lived, thus very culturally appropriate. Second, bilingual materials were developed to provide a school prevention program for children who are not only at a socioeconomic disadvantage but at a disadvantage of not understanding safety information needed for their own protection. Third, to address the developmental aspect of MSSP, Bloom's (1976) Taxonomy and cultural competencies (Sue et al., 1992) were used. Bloom's taxonomy was used primarily in formulating the type of questions that would promote critical thinking on the pre-post tests, worksheets, and videos. Sue and others' theory was used in the processing of cultural biases with trainers so that their dispositions would not affect their ability to impart knowledge and skills. Maslow's theory (Maslow, 1968) was used to assure that the developmental aspects of needs of safety, belongingness and love, esteem, and self-actualization were integrated with cognitive skills (Bloom, 1976) and cultural competencies of trainers (Sue et al., 1992).

A third characteristic of successful programs is that they be developed in a way that students can apply skills to daily life. There was one primary way this was achieved. Ample opportunities for role play were part of MSSP. Students observed problem solving scenarios on video and then they were requested to role play to unresolved dilemmas on the videos. Students used a variety of cultural responses such as: (a) speaking in English, Spanish, or a combination of English and Spanish, (b) using "made-up" settings such as traditional "hangouts" found in the community, (c) using the names of community members, (d) singing music that was heard in their community, and (e) using "made-up" props found in their community such as drinks like "agua fresca", discarded tires, bandanas, and crucifixes. Research indicates that when role playing is used in problem solving, students are more likely to internalize lessons learned and they are more apt to use the skills learned when needed (Bandura, 1995; Hawkins & Weis, 1985; Ladd & Mize, 1983).

A fourth characteristic of effective school prevention programs is that they provide data to establish policies, practices, and environmental supports. There were a couple pieces of evidence for this with MSSP. First, data analyzed provided initial support for the premise that bilingual students with diverse cultures can learn school safety concepts when the program is developed with the culture in mind. Second, data from parents indicated that they saw an improvement in their students as it related to less fears and more knowledge about keeping safe. Moreover, counselors reported that reports from students had increased after MSSP; a necessary element in children learning about safety (Glover et al, 2000). Based on the evidence provided, it is hoped that MSSP will be noted as an effective program that has the potential to be used with culturally diverse populations.

A fifth characteristic was the importance of training personnel with the kind of skills to implement the program effectively. All the trainers had many years of experience working with children and one trainer was completely bilingual. All trainers were animated, loved to sing, dance, and act, and knew the MSSP Curriculum. One of the co-principal investigators assured that they passed competencies for each of the six lessons. Trainers were also a part of the advisory council and took part in the development of the MSSP Curriculum and materials, even designing some of the props and developing songs and mimes to accompany the curriculum. The students evaluated the trainers very highly and frequently asked their teachers when they would return. Parents, teachers, and counselors made very positive comments about the high level of professionalism and commitment exhibited by the trainers.

A sixth characteristic is making sure that the program meets local community needs through strategic planning, ongoing evaluation, and continuous improvement. Evidence of this in MSSP was done in several ways. First, MSSP was developed from a needs-assessment conducted in the community by an advisory council that included diverse members of the community. Second, there were unannounced checks at schools to ensure treatment fidelity. Third, focus groups with educators were conducted every two weeks by the evaluator. Fourth, an external evaluator collected and analyzed the data about effectiveness. Information about the training and from school educators was reported to the council and MSSP co-principal investigators who made subsequent adjustments to MSSP based on information received.

In conclusion, much remains to be done in determining which school prevention programs will keep students safe and will fit certain populations. It is not the case that one program fits all; different school districts have different cultural and linguistic needs. By providing empirical support for school prevention programs such as MSSP, the door opens for further research that allows all children to learn safety concepts.

Acknowledgment

This study was funded by the Department of Education Safe and Drug Free Schools Grant.

References

Baker, D. P. (1993). Compared to Japan, the U.S. is a low achiever…really: New evidence and comment on Westbury. *Educational Researcher, 22*(3), 18–20.

Bandura, A. (1995). *Self-efficacy in changing societies.* New York: Cambridge University Press.

Bloom, B. S. (1976). *Human characteristics and school learning.* New York: McGraw-Hill.

Bronfenbrenner, U. (1979). *The ecology of human development: Experiments by nature and design.* Cambridge, MA: Harvard University Press.

Bronfenbrenner, U., & Morris, P. A. (1998). The ecology of developmental processes. In W. Damon (Series Ed.) & R. M. Lerner (Vol. Ed.), *Handbook of child psychology: Vol. I. Theoretical models of human development* (5th ed., pp. 993–1028). New York: Wiley.

Byrd, B. (1996). *A comparison of two school-based conflict management programs – Lions-Quest and Second Step.* Toronto, Ontario: Lions-Quest Canada.

Cohen, J. (1988). *Statistical power analysis for the behavioral sciences* (2nd ed.). New York: Academic Press.

Drummond, R. J. (2000). *Appraisal procedures for counselors and helping professionals* (4th ed.). Columbus, OH: Merrill.

Elliott, D. S., & Tolan, P. H. (1999). Youth violence prevention, intervention, and social policy: An overview. In D. J. Flannery & C. R. Hoff (Eds.), *Youth violence prevention, intervention, and social policy* (pp. 3–46). Washington, DC: American Psychiatric Press.

Farrell, A. D., Meyer, A. L., Kung, A. M., & Sullivan, T. N. (2001). Development and evaluation of school-based violence prevention programs. *Journal of Clinical Child Psychology, 30*(1), 207–220.

Gottfredson, D. C. (2001). *Delinquency and schools.* New York: Cambridge University.

Glover, D., Gough, G., & Johnson, M. (2000). Bullying in 25 secondary schools: Incidence, impact, and intervention. *Educational Research, 42*(2), 141–156.

Graham, S., Taylor, A., & Hudley, C. (2003). *Best foot Forward: A motivational intervention for at-risk youth.* Manuscript submitted for publication.

Hawkins, J.D., & Weis, J. G. (1985). The social development model: An integrated approach to delinquency prevention. *Journal of Primary Prevention, 6,* 73–97.

Juvonen, J., & Graham, S. (2004). Research-based interventions on bullying. In C. E. Sanders & G. D. Phye (Eds.), *Bullying: Implications for the classroom* (pp. 229– 255). San Diego, CA: Elsevier Academic Press.

Khosropour, S. C., & Walsh, J. (2001, April). *The effectiveness of a violence prevention program: did it influence how children conceptualize bullying?* Paper presented at the Annual Conference of the American Educational Research Association: Seattle, Washington.

Kumpfer, K. L., & Alvarado, R. (2003). Family-strengthening approaches for the prevention of youth problem behaviors. *American Psychologist, 58,* 457–465.

Ladd, G. W., & Mize, J. (1983). A cognitive-social learning model of social skill training. *Psychological Review, 90,* 127–157.

Maslow, A. H. (1968). *Toward a psychology of being* (2nd ed.). Princeton, NJ: Van Nostrand.

The McKay Foundation. (2004). *Curriculum Guide: A safer tomorrow begins with us today* Conroe, TX: McKay Publishing. The guide includes units on Self-esteem, Internet Safety, When a Stranger Isn't So Strange, No Bullying Allowed, Stranger Beware, and Don't Invade My Space.

Nation, M., Crusto, C., Wandersman, A., Kumpfer, K. L., Seybolt, D., Morissey-Kane, E., et al. (2003). What works in prevention: Principles of effective prevention programs? *American Psychologist, 58,* 449–456.

Nishina, A., Juvonen, J., & de la Sota, A. (2000, Spring). Violence prevention in elementary school: A systemic safe school approach. *Connections,* 3–8.

No Child Left Behind Act of 2001, Subpart 14 – Grants to improve the mental health of children, Sec 5541. Grants for the integration of schools and mental health systems of children, 20 U.S.C. § 6301 *et seq* (2001).

Olweus, D. (1991). Bully/victim problems among school children: Basic facts and a school based intervention program. In K. Rubin & D. J. Pepler (Eds.), *The development and treatment of childhood aggression* (pp. 411–448). Hillsdale, NJ: Erlbaum.

Olweus, D., Limber, S. P., & Mihalic, S. F. (1999). Bullying prevention program. In D. S. Elliot (Ed.), *Blueprints for violence prevention.* Book Nine. Boulder, CO: Center for the Study and Prevention of Violence.

Ortega, R., & Lera, M. J. (2000). The Seville Antibullying in School Project. *Aggressive Behavior, 26*(1), 113–123.

Powell, K. E., Dahlberg, L. L., Friday, I., Mercy, J. A., Thornton, T., & Crawford, S. (1996). Prevention of youth violence. Rationale and characteristics of 15 evaluation projects. *American Journal of Preventive Medicine, 12*(5, Suppl.), 3–12.

Ravitch, D. (2000). *Left behind: A century of failed school reforms.* New York: Simon & Schuster.

Resnicow, K., Solar, R., Braithwaite, R., Ahluwalia, J., Butler, J. (2000). Cultural sensitivity in substance abuse prevention. *Journal of Community Psychology, 28,* 271–290.

Samples, F. (2004). Evaluating curriculum-based intervention programs: An examination of preschool, primary, and elementary intervention programs. In C. E. Sanders & G. D. Phye (Eds.), *Bullying: Implications for the classroom* (pp. 203–227). San Diedo, CA: Elsevier.

Samples, F., & Aber, L. (1998). Evaluations of school-based violence prevention programs. In D. S. Elliott, B. A. Hamburg, & K. R. Williams (Eds.), *Violence in American schools: A new perspective* (pp. 217–252). Cambridge, UK: Cambridge University Press.

Sanchez, E., Robertson, T. R., Lewis, C. M., Rosenbluth, B., Bohman, T., & Casey, D. M. (2001). Preventing bullying and sexual harassment in elementary schools: The Expect Respect Model. *Journal of Emotional Abuse, 2*(2/3), 157–180.

Schinke, S. P., & Matthieu, M. (2003). Primary prevention with diverse population. In T. P. Gullotta & M. Bloom (Eds.), *Primary prevention and health promotion* (pp. 92–97). New York: Kluwer Academic/Plenum.

Smith, P. K., & Sharp, S. (Eds.). (1994). *School bullying: Insights and perspectives.* London: Routledge.

Stevens, V., Van Oost, P., & Bourdeaudhuji, I. de (2000). The effects of an anti-bullying intervention programme on peers' attitudes and behaviour. *Journal of Adolescence, 23*(1), 23–34.

Sue, D. W., Arredondo, P., & McDavis, R. J. (1992). Multicultural competencies/standards: A call to the profession. *Journal of Counseling and Development, 70*(4), 477–486.

Tebes, J. K., Kaufman, J.S., & Connell, C. M. (2003). The evaluation of prevention and health promotion programs. In T. P. Gullotta & M. Bloom (Eds.), *Primary prevention and health promotion* (pp. 42–61). New York: Kluwer Academic/Plenum.

Tutty, L.M. (1995). The revised Children's Knowledge of Abuse Questionnaire: Development of a measure of children's understanding of sexual abuse prevention concepts. *Social Work Research, 19*(2), 112–119.

U.S. Bureau of the Census. (2002). Table 1. *People and families in poverty by selected characteristics: 2000 and 2001.* Retrieved October 10, 2004, from http://www/census.gov/hhes/www/poverty/poverty01

Wandersman, A., & Florin, P. (2003). Community interventions and effective prevention. *American Psychologist, 58,* 441–448.

Wilson, S., Lipsey, M., & Derzon, J. (2003). The effects of school-based intervention programs on aggressive behavior: A meta-analysis. *Journal of Consulting and Clinical Psychology, 71,* 136–149.

36

Bully Busters

Reducing Bullying by Changing Teacher and Student Behavior

ARTHUR M. HORNE, SUSAN M. SWEARER, JAMI GIVENS, AND CHRISTINA MEINTS

Research and training focusing on the reduction of aggression and violence in schools and families has been a major focus within the United States and other countries for more than a half-century. During the 1960s and 1970s, extensive programs were developed and evaluated looking at the development of childhood aggression and violence and the most effective ways to reduce the problem in schools and families (Patterson, 1974; Reid, Patterson, & Snyder, 2002). Within the broad study of aggression, some researchers began focusing upon a more defined category of anti-social behavior: bullies, victims, and bystanders (Olweus, 1978).

A group of researchers at the University of Georgia had been examining effective programs for reducing classroom discipline problems and decided to apply a time-limited group intervention working with groups of students identified as engaging in bullying behavior, and other groups working with students who were the targets of the bullying (Horne, Glaser, & Sayger, 1994; Horne & Sayger, 1990; Horne & Socherman, 1996). The intervention, somewhat predictably in hindsight, did not work, and in fact led to students who bullied becoming more effective in their efforts, far from our desired goal (Turpeau, 1998). The bullying group members mentored one another on how to hone their aggressive skills; the students who had been the targets of bullying supported one another as being victims unable to do anything about their plight. The outcome of neither group approach was acceptable.

We then spent an academic year interviewing teachers and students to determine what they perceived as more effective methods of attending to the bullying problem. From those interviews, as well as bringing in the work we had done previously with oppositional defiant and conduct disordered youth (Fleischman, Horne, & Arthur, 1983; Horne & Sayger, 1990) and implementing concepts from other existing bully prevention programs, we developed the *Bully Busters* program. The term "Bully Busters" was selected by the teachers and students with whom we worked for the next two years implementing and evaluating the program. The middle school version of the Bully Busters program was published in 2000 (Newman, Horne, & Bartolomucci, 2000), the elementary version (Horne, Bartolomucci, & Newman-Carlson) in 2003, and the parent (Horne, Stoddard, & Bell) version in 2008.

The Bully Busters model was conceived to represent an ecological model in which the risk and protective factors of the individual child, the family, the school, the community, and societal events could be seen as influencing bullying behaviors. While all levels of influence are important, the focus of the model was upon those factors which teachers could impact: the child and the school. Bully Busters is a cognitive social learning model that emphasizes the importance of personal awareness, skills improvement, and moral development—empathic understanding, combined with background information for teachers and specific activities to foster greater understanding and skills on the part of students is at the core of the program. The full ecological model is described in detail in *Bullying Prevention: Creating a Positive School Climate and Developing Social Competence* (Orpinas & Horne, 2006).

A number of bully prevention or violence reduction programs require a school-wide commitment and often a major investment in resources in order to implement the program. In the schools in which we have worked, we have found that counselors, psychologists, and teachers request a program that is both affordable and that has a focused curriculum. Teachers have also expressed a desire to have a program that may be implemented in an individual classroom, by a particular teaching team, a specific grade level, or universally throughout the entire school. The Bully Busters program was developed so that it could be a school-wide intervention (preferable), but could also be implemented one classroom at a time, if individual teachers wanted to address the problem in their classrooms.

The Bully Busters middle school program is predicated on the assumption that aggression and bullying are behaviors borne of social skills deficits, lack of skills for taking others' perspective or a failure to empathically relate with others, and a moral or value system that denigrates others. In our experience, the most effective means of reducing aggression and bullying behaviors in the school is through a school-wide emphasis on helping teachers and students increase their awareness, knowledge, and efficacy regarding how they deal with school-based aggression and bullying (Newman-Carlson & Horne, 2004). This is accomplished by having school counselors, school psychologists, school social workers, or other trainers provide a psycho-educationally-based curriculum to the teachers, which the teachers then apply with their classrooms. Most commonly, this is done in a group format. The program has an emphasis on prevention, in that it challenges teachers, school administrators, and students to be proactive in developing initiatives in the school.

The Bully Busters program currently consists of three components (a high school version is in preparation):

- *Bully Busters: A Teacher's Manual for Helping Bullies, Victims, and Bystanders* — Grades 6–8 (Newman et al., 2000); a book developed for middle schools.
- *Bully Busters: A Teacher's Manual for Helping Bullies, Victims, and Bystanders* — Grades K–5 (Horne et al., 2003); a book developed for elementary schools.
- *Helping Bullies, Victims, and Bystanders: A Parent's Guide to Bully Busters* (Horne et al., 2008)

The Bully Busters program provides teachers with a written overview of specific areas of skills development related to students who bully others, followed by instructions for teachers on how to implement activities in the classrooms with students. The activities include specific processing questions to assist students in examining the impact of each activity, and evaluation instruments for each module and for overall program accomplishments.

To address issues of awareness and readiness for managing the problem of bullying in the school, the program implements two levels of assessment. The first level assesses teachers' sense of self-efficacy for working with problems of bullying. It also evaluates their classroom management skills and practices. The second level of assessment is completed by students and teachers and is used to examine the extent of bullying and aggression that students and teachers perceive occurs in the schools and to describe where the bullying problems occur. The results are then used to provide feedback to school personnel (teachers, administrators, support staff), to parents, and to other interested stake-holders (community agencies, religious/spiritual leaders).

Bully Busters includes seven modules, and every module provides several components: (a) the theoretical background for the module topic; (b) relevant research related to the topic; (c) guidelines for implementing activities with students; (d) a teacher goal form, in which the teacher defines her or his goals related to the module and identifies specific students in special need; (e) a final review of the content so that teachers may evaluate their knowledge of the topic and, following the implementation of the module, review their teacher goal form to assess the success of the implementation; (f) written guidelines for directing discussions related to the topic of the module; and (g) written activities for students; each activity is followed by questions that facilitate processing each of the activities with students.

Module One is designed to increase awareness of bullying and includes the following sections:

- The scope of the problem
- The "Double I/R" [Imbalance of power; Intentional, Repeated] criteria for bullying
- A personal definition of bullying for teachers and students
- The role of teachers in reducing bullying
- The core conditions for the prevention and reduction of bullying
- "Stop the bullying" activity

Students role-play constructive ways of interacting following scripts and scenarios provided in Module One, specifically focused on increasing awareness of the problem of bullying.

Module Two examines how bullying develops and the variety of forms it can take:

- The development of bullying behaviors
- The different forms of bullying
- The difference between male and female bullying
- The myths and misconceptions about bullying

Activities in this module include viewing films or movies in which characters are victims or bullies. This module ends with a guided discussion on common misconceptions about bullying.

Module Three focuses on recognizing the victim of bullying:

- The effects of victimization
- The myths and realities of victimization
- How to recognize victims and victimization
- The types of victims
- The differences and similarities between male and female victims
- How to break the code of silence which restricts victims from reporting incidents

A major emphasis of this module is on incorporating bystanders into the process of stopping bullying. Engaging bystanders receives considerable attention and is a major focus of the Bully Busters intervention. Teachers encourage students to break the "code of silence" that causes some students to withdraw from involvement. Involving bystanders helps create a safer climate for all students.

Module Four provides specific strategies to create a bully-free classroom:

- How to initiate and establish rapport
- The four "R's" of bully control

- General intervention strategies
- The principles of behavior change
- The specific areas of development for bullies
- Interventions for bullies and victims together
- Reputation changing for bullies

This module includes specific strategies related to classroom management (e.g., setting rules, acting quickly) and teachers also receive training in empathy skills education, social skills training, and anger control skills.

Module Five expands on students' skills development by providing specific strategies to implement with students who are victimized by bullies:

- Victim support
- General strategies for intervening with victims
- Teaching victims to change their behaviors
- Interventions for specific types of victims
- Assimilating victims into the group

These activities assist all students to become aware of their strengths, view themselves in a positive manner, and build skills and confidence in joining groups.

Module Six examines the role of prevention for helping teachers "set up for success" rather than have to address problems after they have developed. It is better to establish a classroom environment that prevents bullying problems than it is to have to solve problems after they develop. This module covers:

- Prevention issues and approaches
- School characteristics for peaceful schools
- Teacher characteristics that lead to reduced bullying
- Recommendations for preventing bullying and victimization: classroom, school
- Using your teacher and student support teams

Student activities focus on skills to prevent conflict from developing, such as problem solving, decision making, and social interaction skills. These skills build upon material from previous modules.

Module Seven addresses relaxation training, stress coping, and management of personal emotions. Teachers first learn to apply the skills to themselves and then teach the skills to their students:

- Stress awareness
- General recommendations for managing stress
- Steps for dealing with on-the-job stress
- Relaxation and coping techniques

The program finishes with a follow-up assessment of teachers' knowledge and self-efficacy, as well as a student and teacher survey of bullying in the school.

Program Evaluation

The Bully Busters program is under evaluation in a number of settings, and the results for teachers have generally been positive. For example, Newman-Carlson and Horne (2004) implemented the program to determine the efficacy of the model for reducing bullying behaviors at the middle school level. Results indicated that the program increased teachers' understanding and use of interventions, as well as self-efficacy as related to teachers' personal ability to deal effectively with bully-related situations. Furthermore, classroom incidences of bullying were reduced from their pre-intervention levels.

A second study conducted by Howard, Horne, and Jolliff (2002) found that the intervention program was effective in increasing teachers' knowledge of bullying intervention skills, teachers' use of bullying intervention skills, and teachers' general sense of self-efficacy in working with students, and reducing the rate of bullying incidents.

Other studies have found similar results, with teachers receiving the Bully Buster training reporting significantly higher levels of self efficacy for managing bullying behavior, greater knowledge of classroom behavior management, and fewer classroom behavior problems and office referrals than comparison teachers (Bell, 2007; Browning, Cooker & Sullivan, 2005; Howard et al., 2002; Newman-Carlson & Horne, 2004; Orpinas, Horne, & Staniszewski, 2003). An adaptation of the model has also been examined in a large federally funded project with promising results (Orpinas, Horne, & Multisite Violence Prevention Program, 2004). On the other hand, results from student evaluations have not been as positive in reporting reductions of aggression. In qualitative interviews with students they report becoming more aware of what bullying is and describe being more sensitized to aggressive events. Further they report more incidents as they become more experienced with the intervention. We have also found from interviews with students that they report aggression reduction in their classrooms and awareness of and sensitivity to bullying in other school settings, such as the cafeteria, playground, on the school bus, or in the neighborhood, as well as in their families from siblings or other family members. This supports the importance of a school-wide intervention that addresses the complexity of bullying across these settings.

Though the Bully Busters program has been to be an effective teacher-targeted awareness- and skills-based bullying reduction program, there is still a dearth of research examining the effectiveness of this program, and versions of it, in school systems across the globe.

Adaptations of the Program

In addition to the group implementation that has been conducted with classes and entire schools, Bully Busters has also been used as a part of an individual cognitive-behavioral intervention program for bully perpetrators (Swearer & Givens, 2006). The Bullying Intervention Program (BIP) has been described elsewhere (Espelage & Swearer, 2008), and in this chapter we will outline the rationale for the development of the BIP and report a case study of a student who participated in the BIP intervention.

Rationale for the Development of the Bullying Intervention Program

Group interventions for youth with similar behaviors and emotional issues is a widespread practice in child psychology and social work (Dishion & Stormshak, 2007). It is preferred to segregate deviant youth for group interventions because it makes logical and financial sense and because it reduces disruption in schools and communities (Dodge, Dishion, & Lansford, 2006). However, while government and school policies are well intentioned in their efforts to treat deviant youth by creating homogeneous groups, this actually exacerbates the problem (Dodge et al., 2006). Peer contagion and deviancy training may offset any potential benefits of treatment for aggressive youth.

Exposure and interactions with delinquent peers increase the likelihood that delinquency will take place during and outside treatment settings (Dodge et al., 2006; Gifford-Smith, Dodge, Dishion, & McCord, 2005). It also increases the likelihood that vulnerable adolescents will become deviant (Dodge et al., 2006). This has been described as "peer contagion," which hypothesizes that grouping antisocial youth for intervention activities encourages antisocial behavior. For example, one individual within the group may expose the group to new ideas and experiences (e.g., information about where to obtain drugs; Boxer, Guerra, Huesmann, & Morales, 2005).

Studies have found that grouping deviant peers together reduces any potential benefits of interventions and can lead to negative outcomes (see Dodge et al., 2006, for a review). Negative outcomes are increased when groups are under poor supervision and are poorly structured (Dodge et al., 2006). A study by Dishion, McCord, and Poulin (1999) examined individually based interventions for aggression. They found that systemic interventions aimed at reducing or preventing aggressive behavior in youth had adverse effects. These authors found that positive effects of interventions on youth may be offset when aggressive youth interact with other aggressive youth.

Deviant youth also seek out other deviant youth (Dodge et al., 2006), which may lead to deviancy training. The theory of deviancy training was established from the idea that deviant peers influence others to become more deviant. When antisocial behavior is displayed and reinforced by peers in a group (e.g., smiling, laughing), another peer observes that interaction and soon engages in similar behavior to receive the same reinforcement. Soon, the culture of the group is changed as there is more modeling and reinforcement of antisocial behavior than prosocial behavior (Dishion et al., 1999). Dodge and colleagues (2006) have recommended terminating programs that aggregate deviant youth. Programs that treat deviant youth as homogenous are problematic because they do not recognize the severity of individual problems.

Based on the concepts of peer contagion and deviancy training, an individualized intervention for working with youth who perpetrate bullying has been developed at the University of Nebraska (Swearer & Givens, 2006). Bloomquist and Schnell (2002) described best practices in implementing individual interventions to promote positive behavior in schools. The first step in implementing individual interventions is to accurately assess the severity of problem behavior. This includes defining the problem behavior in relation to the context in which it occurs. Then, an intervention can be chosen to target the problem behavior. When interventions are focused on the individual, they are specific and targeted to the individuals presenting problems and influencing contextual factors. This can be more beneficial than general school-wide and class-wide interventions, which do not consider each individual.

Following an assessment, an intervention (such as Bully Busters) is chosen based on the information obtained. An intervention can target a skill deficit, antecedents, consequences, beliefs, and family factors. During an assessment, consequences that the school believes are punitive may be identified as rewarding for the student. For example, the student is sent to in school suspension where several of his or her friends are also receiving an in school suspension, which reinforces their problem behavior. Reinforcing outcomes for positive behavior can be identified during the assessment instead. Interventions aimed at teaching replacement behaviors may also be identified. For example, interventions may teach children alternative behaviors to aggression or increase anger management skills (Bloomquist & Schnell, 2002).

Parent involvement is also an important component to individual interventions that reduce aggressive behavior (Bloomquist & Schnell, 2002; Dishion & Stormshak, 2007; Horne et al., 2008). For example, interventions that implement home-school notes that increase parent-teacher communication and the ability to manage problem behaviors at home at school. Factors more suitable for community agencies are also identified, including mentoring and psychotherapy. These services can supplement the services that the school is able to provide (Bloomquist & Schnell, 2002). These best practices guidelines were instrumental in the development of the Bullying Intervention Program.

Bullying Intervention Program Case Study

The BIP is a 3-hour individual intervention session between a therapist (school counselor, school psychologist, or school social worker) that adheres to a cognitive-behavioral focus. The first hour of the intervention session includes a comprehensive assessment that includes self-report measures of bullying and victimization, depression, anxiety, cognitive distortions, self-concept, and school climate. After the student completes the assessment measures (1 hour), he or she watches a 30-minute power-point presentation developed by the Target Bullying project, called "Bullying in Schools," and one of the videos, "Let's Get Real" (www.groundspark.org), "Stories of Us" (www.storiesofus.com), or "Bully Dance" (www.bullfrogfilms.org) with the therapist. A paper-and-pencil quiz over the presentation is given after the student views the power point presentation. Then the student completes the following worksheet activities from Bully Busters (Newman et al., 2000): Stop Rewind, Play it Again, Jump into My Shoes, Are you up to the Challenge?, Vacation Time, and Relaxation Time. This psychoeducational component of the BIP takes about two hours and is designed to educate the student about the nature of bullying and the detrimental effects that bullying has on everyone involved.

Upon completion of the intervention session, the therapist writes a three to five page bullying intervention treatment report that includes recommendations based on the data obtained from the questionnaires for the parent(s)/guardians, school, and student. The evaluation is shared with school personnel and parents during a face-to-face solution-oriented meeting that takes place one to two weeks after the intervention.

Ethan

Ethan was a 12-year-old biracial male student who was in the sixth grade at the time of his participation in BIP. He was referred to the BIP due to physical and verbal bullying of other students. Additionally, he had been in several physical fights that had escalated from his bullying behavior. During the assessment phase of the BIP, results from Ethan's self-report measures indicated that he was not experiencing depressive symptoms but he was experiencing some anxiety symptoms, specifically some separation anxiety and worry. Results from the How I Think Questionnaire (Barriga, Gibbs, Potter, & Liau, 2001) indicated significant cognitive distortions, specifically, minimizing/mislabeling; assuming the worst; and lying to others. In terms of self-concept, Ethan scored in the average range for global self worth, with his lowest scores on scholastic competence and behavioral conduct. On a survey about bullying and victimization, Ethan reported that he bullied others several times a day during the past school year. He endorsed both verbal and physical bullying. During the Bully Busters activities, Ethan completed the following worksheets: "Stop, rewind, play it again," "Proud to be me," "Ouch! That hurt," and "Stop the bullying." These worksheets were an important tool for helping the therapist and Ethan identify alternatives to bullying others.

Ethan completed the BIP intervention, which had a dramatic impact on his subsequent bullying behaviors. Figure 36.1 demonstrates the drop in his office referrals from 17 pre-intervention referrals compared to only one referral post-intervention. The pre-intervention period lasted nine months, from August to April, during which time Ethan was referred 17 times to the

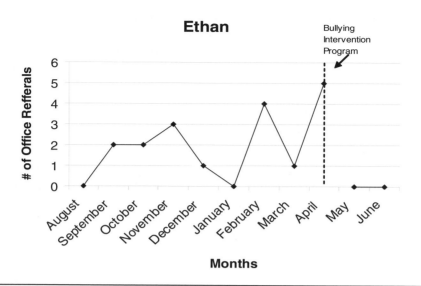

Figure 36.1 Number of office referrals pre- and post-intervention.

office for bullying behaviors. Ethan completed the Bullying Intervention Program in April. He received one office referral shortly after the intervention. During the remaining two months of school, Ethan received no office referrals. Specific recommendations for Ethan included individual cognitive-behavioral therapy to address his anxiety symptoms and to restructure his cognitive distortions. Additionally, since he reported bullying others in the cafeteria and hallways (which was also consistent with his office referrals), it was recommended that he be closely supervised during those times. During the solution-oriented meeting with Ethan, his parents, and the school, everyone agreed to help Ethan reduce his bullying behaviors.

Bully Busters Program: Worldwide Implementation

The Bully Busters Program has been implemented in some form in every state and several countries. Some have reported using it in conjunction with other programs. In a recent description of approaches to bullying reduction programs, Horne and colleagues (2008) described two approaches. The first emphasizes a model and the second a curriculum. The model approach provides a theoretically based approach that emphasizes creating a culture or climate that promotes a peaceful climate. The model approach often provides recommendations and suggestions for how the program may be implemented, but overall each school determines how the program will be implemented and conducted. The second approach, a curriculum based model, places an emphasis on activities and structured learning experiences, defining how the program should be conducted. Bully Busters has adhered more to the curriculum-based model. Given that there are specific learning objectives for the teachers and students, some schools that have adopted the first approach to reducing school bullying, the model approach, have incorporated the activities and materials from the Bully Busters program into their work, and have found the two models to be quite compatible.

Other variations have focused upon who delivers the program. We know that it has been implemented by teachers, counselors, school psychologists and school social workers, as well as some assistant principals. Some have implemented the program as a school-wide offering (which we recommend and prefer) and others have implemented the program by grade level, by teaching team, or sometimes by individual teachers taking the project on for their classrooms.

Implications for Practice

1. The Bully Busters Program is easily implemented in schools, classrooms, and can be modified for use in individual sessions.
2. Teachers are typically the front-line professionals in the schools who are dealing with bullying behaviors. Therefore, teacher buy-in is critical.
3. Bully Busters is an inexpensive and user-friendly program that can be tailored to meet the needs of different ecologies and cultures.
4. Bullying can be reduced when teachers, students, and parents work together.
5. Solution-oriented (versus punishment-oriented) approaches are the best way to reduce bullying in schools.

References

Barriga, A. Q., Gibbs, J. C., Potter, G. B., & Liau, A. K. (2001). *How I Think (HIT) Questionnaire Manual*. Campaign, IL: Research Press.

Bell, C. D. (2007). *Evaluation of an implementation of an abbreviated bully prevention program for reducing aggression in a middle school*. Unpublished doctoral dissertation, University of Georgia, Athens.

Bloomquist, M. L., & Schnell, S. V. (2002). *Helping children with aggression and conduct problems: Best practices for intervention*. New York: Guilford.

Boxer, P., Guerra, N. G., Rowell Huesmann, L., & Morales. (2005). Proximal peer-level effects of a small-group selected prevention on aggression in elementary school children: An investigation of the peer contagion hypothesis. *Journal of Abnormal Child Psychology, 33*(3), 325–338.

Browning, C. M., Cooker, P. G., & Sullivan, K. (2005). Help for the bully/peer abuse problem: Is bully busters in-service training effective? In G. R. Walz & R. K. Yep (Eds.), *Vistas: Compelling perspectives on counseling* (pp. 231–234). Alexandria, VA: American Counseling Association.

Dishion, T. J., McCord, J., & Poulin, F. (1999). When interventions harm—Peer groups and problem behavior. *American Psychologist, 54*, 755–764.

Dishion, T. J., & Stormshak, E. A. (2007). *Intervening in children's lives: An ecological, family-centered approach to mental health care*. Washington, DC: American Psychological Association.

Dodge, K. A., Dishion, T. J., & Lansford, J. E. (2006). Deviant peer influences in intervention and public policy for youth. *Social Policy Report: Giving Child and Youth Development Knowledge Away, XX*(1), 1–20.

Espelage, D. L., & Swearer, S. M. (2008). Current perspectives on linking school bullying research to effective prevention strategies. In T. W. Miller (Ed.), *School violence and primary prevention* (pp. 335–354). New York: Springer.

Fleischman, M. J., Horne, A. M., & Arthur, J. L. (1983). *Troubled families: A treatment program*. Champaign, IL: Research Press.

Gifford-Smith, M., Dodge, K.A., Dishion, T. J., & McCord, J. (2005). Peer influence in children and adolescents: Crossing the bridge from developmental to intervention science. *Journal of Abnormal Child Psychology, 33*(3), 255–265.

Horne, A. M., Bartolomucci, C. L., & Newman-Carlson, D. (2003). *Bully Busters: A teacher's manual for helping bullies, victims, and bystanders (grades K-5)*. Champaign, IL: Research Press.

Horne, A. M., Glaser, B., & Sayger, T. V. (1994). Bullies. *Counseling and Human Development, 27*, 1–12.

Horne, A. M., Raczynski, K., & Orpinas, P. (2008). A clinical laboratory approach to reducing bullying and aggression in schools and families. In L. L'Abate (Ed.), *Toward a science of clinical psychology: Laboratory evaluations and interventions* (pp. 117–131). Hauppauge, NY: Nova Science Publishers.

Horne, A. M., & Sayger, T. (1990). *Treating conduct and oppositional defiant disorders in children.*. New York: Pergamon.

Horne, A. M., & Socherman, R. (1996). Profile of a bully: Who would do such a thing? *Educational Horizons, 74*, 77–83.

Horne, A. M., Stoddard, J., & Bell, C. (2008). Helping bullies, victims, and bystanders: A parent's guide to bully busters. Champaign, IL: Research Press.

Howard, N., Horne, A., & Jolliff, D. (2002). Self-efficacy in a new training model for the prevention of bullying in schools. In R. Geffner, M. Loring, & C. Young (Eds.), *Bully behavior: Current issues, research, and interventions* (pp. 181–192). New York: Haworth Press.

Newman-Carlson, D., & Horne, A. (2004). Bully Busters: A psychoeducational intervention for reducing bullying behavior in middle school students. *Journal of Counseling and Development, 82,* 259–267.

Newman, D. A., Horne, A. M., & Bartolomucci, C. L. (2000). *Bully Busters: A teacher's manual for helping bullies, victims, and bystanders.* Champaign, IL: Research Press.

Olweus, D. (1978). *Aggression in the schools: Bullies and whipping boys.* Washington, DC: Hemisphere Press.

Orpinas, P., & Horne, A. M. (2006). *Bullying prevention: Creating a positive school climate and developing social competence.* Washington, DC: American Psychological Association.

Orpinas, P., Horne, A. M., & Multisite Violence Prevention Project. (2004). A teacher-focused approach to prevent and reduce students' aggressive behavior—The GREAT Teacher Program. *American Journal of Preventive Medicine, 26,* 29–38.

Orpinas, P., Horne, A. M., & Staniszewski, D. (2003). School bullying: Changing the problem by changing the school. *School Psychology Review, 32,* 431–444.

Patterson, G. R. (1974). Interventions for boys with conduct problems: Multiple settings, treatments, and criteria. *Journal of Consulting and Clinical Psychology, 42,* 471–481.

Reid, J. B., Patterson, G. R., & Snyder, J. (Eds.). (2002). *Antisocial behavior in children: Developmental theories and models for intervention.* Washington, DC: American Psychological Association.

Swearer, S. M., & Givens, J. E. (2006). Designing an alternative to suspension for middle school bullies. Paper presented at the annual convention of the National Association of School Psychologists, Anaheim, CA.

Turpeau, A. M. (1998). *Effectiveness of an anti-bullying classroom curriculum intervention on an American middle school.* Unpublished doctoral dissertation, University of Georgia, Athens.

37

Prevention of Bullying at a Systemic Level in Schools

Movement from Cognitive and Spatial Narratives of Diametric Opposition to Concentric Relation

PAUL E. DOWNES

Overview

Fromm (1973) observes that the easiest way to unite a group is to provide it with a common enemy, in other words to organize the group in diametric structured opposition to an external other. Conquergood (1994) portrays how male teenage street gangs in Chicago divide into diametric structured opposition even though there is no tangible reason for the content of these oppositions such as ethnic, socio-economic, racial, or regional differences. Based on his three-year ethnographic fieldwork, he observes that "there are hundreds of gangs in Chicago, but all of them align with one of two Nations: People or Folks" (p. 204), emphasizing that "the division between the two Nations, People and Folks, is absolutely arbitrary and constructed" (p. 207).

The diametric structure of the group relation portrayed by Conquergood (1994) ignored the contrasting structure to diametric relation observed cross-culturally by Levi-Strauss (1962, 1963), namely, concentric structures of relation. The interplay between diametric and concentric narratives of relation is developed in this chapter as a guiding framework for change to cognitive and spatial constructs in order to prevent bullying at the systemic level of the school and its interaction with its local communities. Child-centred qualitative research on school climate, curriculum, and bullying is focused upon, drawn from contexts of socio-economic disadvantage in elementary and high schools in different areas of Dublin, Ireland.

Cross-cultural research on bullying tends to highlight issues such as the need for comparability of prevalence figures for bullying, while being cognizant of the methodological difficulties of translating and ensuring common understandings of bullying across different cultures and languages (Solberg & Olweus, 2003). It is frequently difficult to make valid comparisons, especially as any understanding of bullying and measure of bully and victim problems reported in research depends on the definition used as well as the instrument employed to measure it (Kalliotis, 2000). A complementary cross-cultural focus with a holistic, relational emphasis adopts a guiding framework of change between diametric and concentric cross-cultural structures of relation.

Examining dimensions of a systems level focus for prevention of bullying in school takes curriculum as a key dimension in conjunction with other system level supports. According to Johnson and Johnson's (2000) review of Canadian research by Stevahn and colleagues (1997), integration of conflict resolution into academic units in middle and high school offered "frequent and continued practice of the conflict resolution procedures" so that they became "so over-learned that they become automatic patterns that guide behavior" (p. 704). Johnson and Johnson (2000) place some confidence in the results of these studies, as they had random assignment of students to conditions, rotation of teachers across conditions, clear definition of the training program and of the dependent variable etc. Yet, the focus of these studies was confined to the English literature curriculum, while later research by Stevahn and colleagues (2002) examined the Social Studies curriculum.

The New Revised Irish Primary School Curriculum (1999) offers a range of complementary opportunities to go beyond a simple program-based approach to prevention of bullying and towards making anti-bullying processes automatic patterns guiding behavior through integration of subjects across the broad curriculum. For example, the subject of drama offers opportunities for role-play around bullying and conflict resolution, English curricular goals include emotional expression and language, curricular goals in history include empathy and perspective-taking, approaches also relevant to the experience-based focus of the religion curriculum. This is in addition to the curricular subject of Social, Personal and Health Education (SPHE) where prevention of bullying is a core theme. Moreover, group work, informed by Vygotskyan theories of learning through social interaction, is a key teaching methodology in the Irish Primary School Curriculum (1999). The processes of interaction for group work such as developing agreed rules for communication and listening to others in the group, offer a potential to provide a classroom and school climate preventative of processes of bullying. The conclusions of Morgan's (2001) review of international research regarding drug prevention in schools also arguably apply to bullying prevention, namely, that effective interventions need to be of sufficient intensity and duration. An integrated curriculum for processes leading to prevention of bullying provides the opportunity for sufficient intensity and duration.

Johnson and Johnson (2000) conclude that

> The first and most important problem with the research is the lack of a theoretical base for most of the programs. The use of conflict resolution and peer mediation programs in the schools is a classic example of practice being developed and apart from the relevant theory and research. (p. 714)

In this chapter, it will be argued that movement from diametric constructs of opposition towards concentric structures of relation at a systemic level provides a theoretical base for developing bullying prevention approaches that incorporate the centrality of curricular approaches, while offering focus on wider systemic issues in contexts of socio-economically disadvantaged schools and communities in Ireland and beyond.

Conceptual Foundations

Diametric and Concentric Structures of Relation: Cross-Cultural Narratives of Relation

Drawing upon some Amerindian and Indonesian examples, structural anthropologist Levi-Strauss (1963) highlights two purportedly fundamental contrasting forms of binary opposition, namely diametric and concentric structures of binary opposition (see Figure 37.1 and Figure 37.2). A key feature of concentric and diametric dualism is that they are mutually interactive. They are

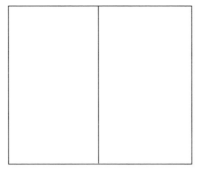

Figure 37.1 Diametric Dualism

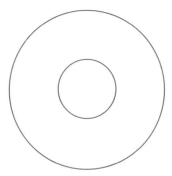

Figure 37.2 Concentric Dualism

structures of relation but also structures in relation—they are not simply separate individual structures but are fundamentally interlinked so that an increase in one is compensated for by a decrease in the other. Levi-Strauss (1973) himself emphasized that both dualisms tended to co-exist in "functional relation" (p. 73). This echoes the structuralist insight that meaning resides in relational difference rather than in a single term. As they are in mutual interactive tension, concentric and diametric dualisms are not just structures but are also fundamentally processes. The dynamic interplay between both allows for an explicit temporal dimension to their spatial relations, as change from one to the other is possible. Thus, they are not to be viewed as static images but more as opposing directions of spatial relation in dynamic tension with each other.

Levi-Strauss (1963) cites a range of examples of the concentric dualistic opposition observed by different anthropologists.[1] With regard to the Lower Mississippi Valley, Levi-Strauss (1963) emphasizes that concentric structures are genuinely ancient structures "which in America extends far back into antiquity, and whose later analogues were to be found in pre-Conquest Peru and Bolivia and in the social structure of the Sioux in North America and of the Ge and related tribes in South America" (p. 143). Other concentric structures can be found in Islamic, Russian, Chinese, Jewish, and East European contexts (see Downes, 2003a, for more information).

Conquergood (1994) cites Scholes' (1985) conception of the binary opposition of diametric dualism as a violence embedded within communication in Western culture:

> The most basic and most violent acts of differentiation are those that divide a field into two opposed units. This sort of 'binary opposition' is fundamental to the phonemic nature of speech and is deeply embedded in all Western thought. (p. 112)

Gilligan (1990) highlights the tensions between female adolescent experience and a Western logic based on rigid diametric dualisms:

> The either/or logic that Gail was learning as an adolescent, the straightline categories of Western thinking (self/other, mind/body, thoughts/feelings, past/present) and the if/then construction of linear reasoning threatened to undermine Gail's knowledge of human relationships by washing out the logic of feelings. (pp. 18–19)

There is a need to challenge a Western cultural priority for diametric oppositional structures over concentric structures of relation.

Jahoda's (1982) survey of anthropological research concludes that "the simplest and at the same time most common type of symbolic classification…is the dual one" (p. 251). As a functional compensatory interaction between concentric and diametric relations, recognized in rudimentary form by Levi-Strauss' structuralist anthropology, this framework provides systemic level goals to underpin causal interventions for prevention of bullying. Moreover, as *structures* of relation, they are pre-linguistic and thus are less culturally-bound than language reliant concepts.

Assumed Connection Rather than Assumed Separation Is a Feature of Concentric More than Diametric Dualism

Though Levi-Strauss (1962, 1963) did not explicitly highlight this difference, the inner and outer poles of concentric dualism are fundamentally attached to each other. Both poles coexist in the same space so that the outer circle overlaps the space of the inner one. The outer circle surrounds and contains the inner circle. The opposite that is within the outer circle or shape cannot detach itself from being within this outer shape. And though the outer circle or shape can move in the direction of greater detachment from the inner circle, it cannot itself fully detach from the inner circle (even if the inner circle becomes an increasingly smaller proportion of the outer). Full detachment could conceivably occur only through destroying or altering the form of the other pole; full detachment could occur only through destroying the very concentric nature of the whole opposition itself.

In contrast to this, with diametric dualism *both* oppositional realms *are basically detached and can be further smoothly detached* from the other. These conclusions operate for both dualisms whether they are viewed as being two-dimensional, or three-dimensional. A concentric dualism assumes connection between its parts and any separation is on the basis of assumed connection, whereas diametric dualism assumes separation and any connection between the parts is on the basis of this assumed separation.

A prima facie case for the psychological relevance of the contrast between assumed connection and separation occurs in Gilligan's (1982) qualitative research on relational states framing moral reasoning. One relational state is that of an assumed connection between self and other—an ethic of care. She contrasts this with an abstract, hierarchical, impersonal logic of justice approach based on a prior relational state of assumed separation between self and other. For example, Gilligan contrasts two children's modes of thought and relation:

> To Jake, responsibility means not doing what he wants because he is thinking of others; to Amy, it means doing what others are counting on her to do regardless of what she herself wants. she, assuming connection, begins to explore the parameters of separation, while he, assuming separation, begins to explore the parameters of connection. (Gilligan 1982, p. 38)

This distinction between assumed connection and separation holds even if one treats Gilligan's (1982) claim for an "association" (p. 2) between assumed connection and female experience as polemical.

Gergen (2000) envisages Gilligan's conception of a web of relationships and bonds of caring or assumed connection as being 'extended to form the basis for a postmodern, relational view of morality' (p.168). For Gergen, a relational self tends to replace essentialized versions of self; relationships create and recreate personal identity. The dynamic tension between assumed connection of concentric relation and assumed separation of diametric relation offer a conception of selves as a directional rather than merely static positional process. This allows for a multiplicity of positional states for selves and this multiplicity is not necessarily fragmentation as the relation between these multiple selves is the key. The key issue is the quality of relation, of concentric or diametric relation, as modes of assumed connection or assumed separation between these multiple and changing sites of selves.

Assumed connection requires a constant dynamic interplay of communication which resists the attribution of static labels such as the "bully" or the "victim" or the "rat" (i.e., the person who tells the teacher of the bullying problem) to the bullying context. Concentric and diametric relations offer not depth of core identities but offer core qualities of relation to and relational changes within a multiplicity of identities. It challenges cognitive constructs of children that facilitate bullying, namely, diametric constructs of assumed separation framing oppositional categories between self and other, such as those expressed in the following accounts of children in Downes (2004): "I would change all the bullies in my school to geeks" (6th class, F), "One of the biggest problems" in the school is bullying but "you don't wanna be a rat" (5th class, M), "If their hair is different or if they're smaller they would get called names" (5th class, M).[2]

Assumptions of connection treat connection as normalcy—connection between pupils themselves, between teacher and pupil, and between teachers. As Kutnick and Manson (1998) comment:

> Children who deviate from the expected norms of behaviour within the social system in which they participate (in the main, the school classroom) are the subjects of study … Within the literature, scant attention is paid to what constitutes normalcy, either in terms of its description or its development; it is taken for granted. (p. 167)

Children have often been regarded as "other" and adults as "norm." Concentric states of relation of assumed connection challenge traditional hierarchical relations between pupil and teacher, as hierarchy rests on a diametric mode of assumed separation.

Circle Time in SPHE involves both a spatial and relational change in the classroom. Pupils are not placed diametrically "side by side" in rows in the classroom, nor sitting at different tables. Rather they are seated alongside each other in a circle, whether sitting in chairs or on the ground. Similarly, the teacher is part of this circle, imminent within and not detached from this spatial arrangement. The relational state between pupils is a concentric mode of assumed connection, so that a trusting supportive environment is created. Moreover, the assumed connection between teacher and pupils challenges a traditional hierarchical relation of assumed separation, thereby bringing change from a diametric hierarchical relation towards a concentric relation of assumed connection. It is important to note that a concentric relation is not a monistic relation of identity so that the teacher would be the "same" as the pupils; rather as with the two poles of a concentric relation, allowance is made for a separation though this separation is on the basis of an assumed connection (see also Gilligan, 1982).

In contrast, diametric poles assume separation and any connection between diametric poles is based on the assumption of separation. As an expression of the assumed connection, the teacher may model a response him/herself before inviting responses from the circle of pupils. Circle Time challenges discourses providing a diametric split between adults and children, cognizant of Devine's (2001) indication of "particular power relation between adults and children, itself governed by discourses relating to the nature of children and childhood" (2001, p. 146). As Devine notes, "children are central actors within schools, yet they are frequently presumed not to have the capacity to reflect critically and constructively on their experience" (2001, p. 170). The New Revised Irish Primary School Curriculum (1999), including SPHE, places what Maxwell (1989) would term "self-regulation," in a central role. In other words, self-regulation is to be fostered in pupils by giving them the opportunity to participate in decision-making related to their own lives; involvement in decision-making develops responsibility, self-discipline, and self-directed behavior.

Interaction Between Foreground and Background Is a Feature of Concentric More than Diametric Dualism

Levi-Strauss (1963) makes another point, concerning observations of spatial modes of concentric dualism, which needs further development:

> The system is not self-sufficient, and its frame of reference is always the environment. The opposition between cleared ground (central circle) and waste land (peripheral circle) demands a third element, brush or forest—that is, virgin land—which circumscribes the binary whole while at the same time extending it, since cleared land is to waste land as waste land is to virgin land. (p. 152)

While this makes sense for the immediate example given, Levi-Strauss (1963) claims that nonself-sufficiency and orientation to the outside environment is a general quality of concentric as opposed to diametric dualism:

> In a diametric system, on the other hand, virgin land constitutes an irrelevant element; the moieties are defined by their opposition to each other, and the apparent symmetry of their closed structure creates the illusion of a closed system. (p. 152)

Levi-Strauss rejects closure for concentric dualism by implying that the relation of the background to both poles of the dualism is governed by *the relation within the dualism itself,* i.e., the mode of relation to the background is not extraneous to the respective modes of relation within the dualisms themselves. Thus, *as the concentric dualistic poles are in assumed connection to each other they are also in assumed connection to the background,* and this assumed connection to the background resists closure within the concentric dualism.

In contrast, *diametric dualism's relation to its own poles is one of assumed separation which then maintains an assumed separation with the background.* Moreover, diametric and concentric structures are dynamic processes as much as structures. Thus, a diametric structure tends to impose a diametric process in its interaction with the background, whereas a concentric structure initiates a concentric relation with the background. In this sense of involvement with the background, concentric dualism is not a self-contained structure. There is a closer proximity between background and foreground within concentric dualism relative to diametric dualism. In comparison, diametric dualism is a much more closed structure—closed off from the background.[3]

Focus on a dynamic concentric role for background factors with regard to bullying can be considered initially in relation to the issue of the passive bystander effect for bullying. Bjorkqvist and colleagues (1982) observed that the bully often gets support from other group members, while O'Moore, Kirkham, and Smith (1997) found from their nationwide study of Irish schools that 'Only half of the primary schoolchildren and less than half of the postprimary pupils reported that they had tried to help someone they saw being bullied' (p. 164). This attribution of a key background role to other pupils in the class is also echoed by Salmivalli and colleagues (2000) in their study of 573 sixth grade children in Finland, which concluded that "results support the notion that bullying may be regarded as a group phenomenon in which most children of a school class have a definable participant role" (p.586). Curricular approaches for bullying prevention offer the potential for involvement of previously passive bystanders in the class—for involvement of the whole class—in interventions to prevent bullying and for conceptualizing bullying taking place between members of the class as a whole class problem. Cognitions regarding the main protagonists in the bullying are constructed against the background of the need for the whole group to actively intervene.

A further focus on concentric interactive background issues, rather than a diametric passive relation between background and foreground, needs to be cognizant of conflicts taking place in the background in communities where students live. Community climate issues influence school climate. Byrne (1997) has highlighted the need for a community focus to include bullying "in the individual sports and youth clubs in the community" (p. 259), while noting that the Irish Department of Education Guidelines for Countering Bullying Behavior in Primary and Post-Primary Schools (1993) emphasized that "the issue of bullying behavior be placed in a general community context to ensure the cooperation of all local agencies in dealing appropriately with it." In research in designated disadvantaged schools[4] in Ballyfermot, Dublin (Downes, 2004), interviews with a small sample of local parents yielded the following observations:

> Some parents emphasize the problem of bullying on the streets as well as in school and suggest the need for some mediation involving the parents of the bully and the victim. It was suggested that some angry defensive parents tell children to hit back because they were bullied in school themselves. They highlight the need generally for support for parents in dealing with their children who have been bullied, though also noting an increasing willingness of children to admit that they have been bullied.

A background factors focus, challenging diametric relational assumptions of non-interactive background influences, highlights the issue of bullying outside school in contexts of socio-economically disadvantaged communities; it suggests the need for programs confronting bullying to be run both in a school context and also a community-based context, as bullying is not simply confined to school. Similarly, a report by the Irish Statutory Committee on Educational Disadvantage (2005) has highlighted the need to "make the school a focal point of community education." In other words, a concentric relation of interaction and assumed connection between school and community is needed to address background community factors affecting bullying in school, rather than a diametric relation of assumed separation and non-interaction between school and community.

Relevant Research and Evidence of Effectiveness (among Specific Populations, Who Provides Intervention)

Although a nationwide study of Irish schools found no statistically significant differences in the proportion of pupils bullied in designated disadvantaged schools compared to other schools

(O'Moore et al., 1997), significantly more pupils in designated disadvantaged schools reported that they bullied other pupils (O'Moore et al., 1997). In England, Whitney and Smith (1993) reported higher incidence of bullying problems in schools in disadvantaged areas, a finding which contrasted with the research in Sweden of Olweus (1980), which found no correlation between aggression levels of boys and the socio-economic conditions of their families measured in several different ways. These contrasts may be explained as being because relative deprivation may be less extreme in the context of Sweden, compared to England and Ireland.

In child-centered research on social climate factors and school supports in designated disadvantaged schools in Ballyfermot, Dublin, a notable minority of pupils drew an explicit link between not attending school and this being due to being bullied (Downes, 2004). In his review of school psychology in Ireland, Crowley (2006) observes that absenteeism is "significantly worse" (p. 179) in disadvantaged areas. There is evidence to suggest that the rate of behavioral and emotional difficulties is greater amongst children from lower socio-economic groups, who live in areas of social disadvantage, particularly those who live in poverty (Cooper, 2005, p. 75; Schneiders et al., 2003).

In 1998, the Education Act placed an obligation on Irish schools to "promote the ... social and personal development of students and provide health education for them" (p. 13). In response, SPHE became one of the six main subject areas of the new Primary School Curriculum in 1999. This was followed in 2000–2003 by the phased introduction of SPHE at high school level as part of the core curriculum for Junior Cycle. An international review of 207 school-based programs to prevent substance use found that interactive programs like SPHE, focusing on skills such as goal setting, assertiveness, communication, coping, and refusal skills, had a positive effect while the traditional didactic class format had minimal impact (Tobler et al., 2000). In Ireland, an evaluation of the *Mind Out* program which aims to promote positive mental health amongst 15–18 year olds (n = 693) demonstrated a number of positive short-term impacts, including raised levels of awareness of support services, greater compassion and understanding for a young person in distress, and more constructive action in seeking help for self and others (Byrne et al., 2004, 2005). In the school-based evaluation (*n* = 521), boys had expressed a strong preference for the activity-oriented exercises over the more discussion-based format; teachers (*n* = 33) also felt that these structured activities were more beneficial to students who might be less cognitively and emotionally well-developed (Byrne, 2007).

Curricular approaches to prevention of bullying in schools in socio-economically disadvantaged areas have been viewed as a key dimension in a sample of 12 teachers interviewed across four elementary schools in the Blanchardstown area of Dublin (Downes, Maunsell, & Ivers, 2006). Their responses in relation to whether bullying is a problem in their class included the following, which recognized the key role of SPHE and drama in their approaches, through their use of circle time and role play:

- Bullying "not a huge problem but has happened. Mostly happened outside school and not class time though i.e., on road at home. My strategy is no tolerance and children know and accept this, a lot of work done in 'circle time', role plays, etc."
- "No because children know of the serious consequences. We do a lot of 'circle time' type work on bullying and bullies in which the bully is painted as the coward/weak one."
- Bullying "not really, has happened over the years. SPHE lessons, circle time, role plays."

Another teacher response explicitly linked her bullying prevention response to the English curriculum: "bullying is not a major problem in my class. Our class often discuss the problem of bullying, especially as it arises a lot in the reader and other material."

It is notable that pupil questionnaire responses in these schools in Blanchardstown (Downes et al., 2006) did not raise the problem of bullying to the same extent as in a different socio-economically disadvantaged area, Ballyfermot, Dublin (Downes, 2004). Child-centered research involving 342 questionnaires across 6 elementary schools in Ballyfermot highlighted that pupils perceived bullying to be a major problem and frequently raised this issue in open questions in questionnaires, even when not directly asked about bullying itself (Downes, 2004). In contrast, bullying was very rarely raised without direct questioning by pupil responses to a similar questionnaire in a survey of 230 children across 4 comparable elementary schools in Blanchardstown (Downes et al., 2006). Whether there are different levels of implementation of the SPHE curriculum in relation to prevention of bullying in schools in the two areas is unclear.

Recent research in a third socio-economically disadvantaged area of Dublin, in its South West Inner City, has highlighted the stated reluctance of some teachers to engage with the SPHE curriculum (Downes & Maunsell, 2007). This may be due to more than simply time factors of teaching a wide curriculum. The SPHE curriculum presupposes that the teacher is in a concentric relational state of assumed connection with the pupils, and thereby challenges traditional conceptions of the teacher as being an authoritarian figure.[5] Assumed connection between teacher and pupils treats the teacher as a source of social and emotional support for socio-economically disadvantaged children (see Levitt, 1991; Rutter, 1985; Antonucci, 1990, on one significant other and benefits for mental health).

This broader view of the role of the teacher requires the teacher to overcome a Cartesian diametric split between reason and emotion (Downes, 2003b); it requires a teacher to view his/her role as not only an education professional but also as a health professional.[6] This has implications for pre-service teacher education and also professional development of teachers through inservice work. The class teacher is in a unique position to facilitate change in communicative relations between pupils given the duration and intensity of their interaction with the pupils. Recent Irish research regarding curricular implementation of Relationship and Sexuality Education (Mayock, Kitching, & Morgan, 2007) has also highlighted the reluctance of many teachers to implement curricular issues relevant to the emotional needs of their students. In a similar vein, Farrelly (2007) suggests that Irish teachers may not be aware that bullying prevention is a legal responsibility as a child protection issue (see also Olweus, 1997, on bullying prevention in schools as a fundamental democratic right).

In contrast to Solberg and Olweus' (2005, p. 256) observations in Norway of variance across different schools, Downes and colleagues (2006) found in Blanchardstown, Dublin, that a notable feature of pupil questionnaire responses was that "variation in levels of bullying was much more evident across 6th classes in the same school than variation across the four schools." Similarly in Ballyfermot primary schools, there was large variation in levels of bullying across the same class groupings (e.g., 5th class) in the same school—variation that was much more noticeable than that in levels of bullying across different schools (Downes, 2004). This common theme in both reports, of large variation in levels of bullying across classes of the same age in the same school, invites a further systemic level focus on moving from a diametric mode to a concentric mode of relation within the school.

Heidegger (1927) contrasts a mode of relation termed "side-by-side-ness" with a fundamental mode of "Being-alongside." This distinction echoes the side-by-side-ness of diametric dualism, in contrast to the assumed connection of the poles of concentric dualism, which are alongside each other. The Blanchardstown and Ballyfermot reports suggest that classroom approaches to the prevention of bullying are taking place side-by-side each other. Specifically, there is an assumed separation between curricular strategies for prevention of bullying in any given class and another class in the same school. There is a need to develop a systemic level focus on assumed connection between classroom approaches to prevention of bullying—in other words, movement from a diametric mode of relation of assumed separation between classroom approaches side-by-side each other. The Blanchardstown report (Downes et al., 2006) recommends that a staff member coordinate dissemination of good practice strategies for prevention and elimination of bullying within the school, and act as a support/mentor for other teachers in the school; while this staff member would liaise with the school principal in implementing the whole school anti-bullying policy, she or he would also serve as an intermediary between the class teacher and the principal. The class teacher may be more likely to approach another colleague—in this role as coordinator—for informal advice on intervention for bullying.

A whole school approach to prevention of bullying needs to include communication across classes with regard to contextually appropriate strategies for curricular implementation— something which may not frequently occur in Irish elementary schools where teachers can be isolated from each other. At the Irish National Forum on Ending Disadvantage (Gilligan, 2003), the key role of leadership training for school principals was recognized as being vital for contexts of socio-economic disadvantage. Principals potentially play a key role in overcoming a school climate of diametric relation between classes side by side to each other, in assumed separation regarding curriculum implementation for bullying prevention.

A focus on concentric interactive background factors in the community was highlighted in a recent survey in South Inner City "Old Dublin" (Downes & Maunsell, 2007) with regard to bullying experienced by a small minority of high school students, namely, through the phenomenon of "Gillying," or of "Being a gilly." According to focus group interviews with 17- to 18-year-olds in alternative forms of education, there are some young people in early secondary school who are engaged in gillying for older drug dealers. Specifically, they are keeping drugs in their possession for future selling by the dealers. The word "gilly" comes from the Irish "giolla" meaning servant and suggests an element of coercion in this process: "at 13 to 14 be a gilly, someone who keeps stuff for you, at 17 to 18 start selling, have people they're gillying for, younger than 15 to 16 if have an older fella [i.e. boyfriend], foreigners being forced into selling drugs to protect their families."

The theme of bullying was raised in these focus groups in relation to suicides of people under 18 who owed money for drugs and were coming under pressure to pay their drug debts (Downes & Maunsell, 2007). Intervention at a systemic level with regard to bullying in high school in contexts of socio-economic disadvantage needs to be cognizant of the background community factors which may impinge upon bullying in the school context. This requires funding for programs relevant to bullying prevention in the community, including regarding drug-related bullying. Sources of funding need to include a range of government departments including Education, Health, and Justice. Programs relevant to bullying prevention in communities with high levels of socio-economic disadvantage arguably need to be part of a state-level strategy for mental health promotion in education for contexts of disadvantage—a strategy that is wider than simply curriculum-based and school-based strategies (see also Downes & Gilligan, 2007).

Description of the Specific Approaches: SPHE Approaches

Focus group interviews with 4th class girls at St. Raphael's School, Ballyfermot (Downes, 2004b), a school which was not included in the first survey of Ballyfermot elementary schools (Downes, 2004a), provides an example of both the benefits of curricular-based interventions to prevent bullying—and also of the need for a wider systemic approach. Freiberg (1999) states in the U.S. context that "In practice, few climate measures tap students as a source of feedback" (p. 209). In contrast, the child-centered qualitative research relied on pupil feedback from focus groups in relation to a range of themes including classroom climate for bullying prevention. There was a consensus in the focus groups of girls from the same class that bullying had been a significant problem the previous year. Some attributed this to the fact that they had three substitute teachers that year (see also Morgan & Kitching 2007, on teacher turnover and retention in designated disadvantaged Irish elementary schools). All of the focus group respondents from this class stated that bullying was a very big problem the previous year but significant improvements had taken place, with sample answers including: "hasn't been bullying for a while," "all the bullying and fights last year…this year not as much," "a while ago there was fighting but as we grow up we have more sense, in circle time we put questions in a box." This latter response refers to the role of the new class teacher in employing the SPHE curriculum to prevent bullying attitudes and practices, both with circle time and with use of a box where pupils can tell their problems anonymously, a point reiterated by another respondent: "activity room, circle time, we speak any problems happening in school, have a suggestion box for problems if don't want to tell, only rule not allowed to say any people's names."

The SPHE curriculum also emphasizes issues around decision-making skills, and this was noted as being an important factor for bullying prevention by another respondent: "classes to help making decisions telling how to stop [being bullied]." Decision-making skills also require a supportive environment of trust between teacher and pupil, in other words, a concentric relation of assumed connection between teacher and pupil. Other pupil responses indicated that this relation was in place in order for them to confide in the teacher regarding bullying problems: "I told the teacher," "when you hold it in you don't know who is bullying," "if you are getting bullied you should tell." Another response indicated that the class teacher was, in practice, effectively integrating prevention of bullying themes within English lessons as well as SPHE: "bullying poems are helpful…."

It is important to note that while many of the focus group responses in St. Raphael's (Downes, 2004b) attributed improvements regarding the bullying situation to curricular interventions of the class teacher and to relational approaches which invited confiding in the teacher, two of the responses attributed improvements in the bullying situation to wider systemic issues: "it's getting better 'cos a lot of mothers came down to the school," "I think the school has got much better … two people on duty in the yard."

Parental involvement in bullying issues requires a bridge of communication between parent and school, in other words, development of an assumed connection between parent and school. A concentric more than diametric split relation between home and school cannot be presumed in contexts of socio-economic disadvantage where the parents' own experiences of school may have been very negative when they had been attending. Recognition of the need to overcome diametric relations of assumed separation between home and school has resulted in the Irish Home-School-Community-Liaison Scheme targeting designated disadvantaged schools. As Byrne (1997) notes, this scheme is "preventative rather than curative" (p. 263) in relation to problems such as bullying. This scheme is in place in St. Raphael's and arguably serves as a supporting condition for the mothers to come down to the school.

The locus of the yard as central to problems of bullying, raised by one of the respondents above, highlights a key limitation to curriculum-based approaches to prevention of bullying, in isolation from a wider systemic approach, including a whole school approach. O'Moore et al.'s (1997) nationwide study on bullying in Ireland revealed that playground or yard bullying is the most common place for bullying in elementary school, with 74% of those reporting being bullied stating that it took place in this location. This is in stark contrast with high school respondents in the same study where the most common location for bullying was the classroom itself, where 47% of those who reported being bullied stating that it was in the classroom.

A curricular approach to interventions for between class bullying has been developed in a designated disadvantaged elementary school in South Inner City Dublin (Hegarty, 2007). While this intervention was run during class time by a school psychologist, the approach taken could be adopted by class teachers as part of the SPHE curriculum, integrated with other parts of the Irish primary school curriculum. Hegarty (2007) provides an account of her intervention summarized in part here. Her goal was to change dominant narratives that children had about themselves, including reputations of being a bully: "Children, whose reputation in school does not sufficiently represent their lived experience, very rarely ask for therapy, but often act out or withdraw. A problem saturated story can then begin to dominate the conversations which take place about them in the school community."

She sought to challenge deficit descriptions of individual children through facilitating them in providing other ways of, in the words of White and Epson (1990, p. 14) "storying their experience." Hegarty's (2007) narrative approach worked to externalize problems on the assumption that the person is not the problem. The problem is the problem. In other words, she adopted an approach of assumed connection between pupils through a web of relationships in order to challenge static categories and labels such as being the bully or victim. In the language of Gilligan (1982), she implicitly moved away from a 'logic of justice' approach based on diametric relations of assumed separation between self and other and more towards a contextual ethic of care based on concentric models of assumed connection.

In developing an intervention to prevent bullying between two classes, she met with each class separately during class time and through Circle Time explored with them what sort of actions supported them in getting on with each other and what sort of actions undermined that "getting on." She asked them to "assess how well they got on together. Each class reported that they got on well within the classroom but could not get on with the other class. Neither class expressed a preference for this state of affairs continuing…Because I saw the feud as the problem, rather than the girls as the problem they were able to unite against it."

Circle Time permitted a concentric mode of relation of assumed connection between pupil and adult (whether teacher or psychologist), as well as between pupils themselves. She subsequently met with the classes together, paired them randomly with someone from the opposite class and asked them to compare lists of common interests made previously. In doing so, she was adopting standard approaches from social psychological research on prejudice, where prejudice is overcome not simply by contact but through cooperation on shared tasks. These shared tasks and areas of interest served the function of overcoming diametrically structured cognitions of 'us versus them' towards a focus on a concentric relation of assumed connection: "Children who had never spoken found themselves discussing sport and fashion and pop music and found much in common. They concluded that the battle zone had turned into a peace line. They ceremoniously shook hands." She then asked the children to write down the stories of what happened in order to help sustain the new peaceful situation: "Using language taken directly from the children's own writings I composed a certificate for them, which was given publicly at an event involving their parents. In this way the new story began to become embedded in a wider social domain."

Hegarty (2007) concludes that the feud and bullying did not take place again, and this was independently verified in the months subsequent to the intervention, through focus groups with the children (Downes & Maunsell, 2007). And to reiterate, every aspect of her approach can be viewed as a curricular approach to be employed by class teachers in giving expression to the SPHE curriculum, in conjunction with other curriculum areas such as English, in the New Revised Primary Curriculum (1999) in Ireland.

Limitations and Future Research

There were clear decreases in levels of bullying according to pupils in the classes described above in St. Raphael's, Ballyfermot (Downes, 2004b) and by Hegarty (2007). The benefits of curricular interventions were thus evident in these naturalistic settings, as part of retrospective evaluations of classroom and school climate for contexts of socio-economic disadvantage in Ireland. Nevertheless, obvious limitations of these examples of curricular type interventions are small sample size and the exclusively female gender of the pupils. Other limitations to examination of changes to concentric systemic and curricular approaches for bullying prevention include the need for more micro-level observational detail regarding the interface between community and school based interventions, and regarding the manner of implementation of the SPHE curriculum, integrated with other curricular subjects in relation to bullying. For contexts of educational disadvantage, future qualitative and quantitative studies on the effects of curricular and systemic approaches to prevention of bullying need more detailed accounts of the emotional and clinical disorders in the participating pupil population, the availability of social and emotional support services in the school and community, and their specific learning difficulties, if any.

A holistic, complex, systemic level focus on change from diametric to concentric relations needs to recognize that attempts at isolating a one-to-one correspondence between a prior intervention and a consequent change is vulnerable to criticisms of behavioristic reliance on one-to-one correspondences between antecedents and consequences. In the operant conditioning of Skinner's behaviorism, the operant is behavior defined by its consequences. Rachlin (1984) suggests that the pattern of determination by conditioning is more complex than a single one-to-one-to-one correspondence between a behavior and a consequence[7]:

> It would seem to be an important task for psychology to determine what the (overt behavioral) criteria are for the use of mental terms, how they change with circumstances, how they interact with one another. Before doing this job, it may be necessary to widen the conception of the operant, as originally advanced by Skinner, from a single discrete event (such as a lever press) to a complex pattern of events that may occur over days and weeks and (consequently) to alter the notion of reinforcement from contiguity between a pair of discrete events (response and reward) to more complex correlations that have meaning only over an extended period. (p. 567)

As holistic interventions to prevent bullying at a systemic level of school and community require a complex pattern of events, it becomes harder to isolate a one-to-one correspondence between the systems level interventions and the outcome of decreased bullying or low initial levels of bullying. The UN Special Rapporteur on the international right to health distinguishes between structural, process, and outcome indicators of the right to health, including—significantly for issues of bullying—mental health. The Special Rapporteur (UN, 2006) notes that the right to health is subject to progressive realization and that this requires development of indicators and benchmarks. Curricular and systemic level interventions for bullying are structural indicators. A framework for evaluation of structural indicators needs to be developed that is broader than simply outcome indicators, which tend to rely more on correspondence between one prior antecedent and the consequent outcome (see also Downes, 2007). A preventative approach to bullying at a systemic level focuses on a range of processes that need to be built up at a classroom and school climate level as supporting conditions to prevent bullying, though these are not of themselves isolated "magic bullet" causes (see also Downes, 2007) to prevent bullying.

Table 37.1 Dimensions of a Concentric Relational and Integrated Curriculum for Bullying Prevention

- Curriculum approaches to bullying prevention potentially offer sufficient intensity and duration to bring habitual change to the system of relations in the class and school.
- The Irish Primary School Curriculum (1999) offers a model of how to integrate anti-bullying approaches with developing social, emotional and cognitive skills across the elementary school curriculum in subjects such as Drama, English, History, and Religion as well as Social, Personal, and Health Education.
- A curricular approach provides the opportunity for a concentric mode of relation between the foreground protagonists in the bullying within the class and the background group that constitutes the rest of the class – to ensure that the potentially active background role of the rest of the class group can be activated so that they see a bullying problem in the class as a class problem.
- Professional development of teachers and teacher pre-service education needs to challenge teachers to go beyond a Cartesian diametric split between reason and emotion, in order to make promotion of a positive class and school climate a priority to prevent bullying.
- Concentric relations of assumed connection between teachers are needed, regarding mutual dialogue to ensure consistent curricular implementation across classes in the same school in relation to prevention of bullying strategies. This requires change to the more prevailing diametric mode of relations of assumed separation between teachers 'side by side' in the same school regarding curricular implementation.
- Leadership training for school principals is needed, especially in socio-economically disadvantaged areas, to develop concentric school climate relations to overcome the Cartesian diametric split between reason and emotion in the role of the class teacher — and to facilitate curricular implementation of bullying prevention strategies across classes so that that implementation is not *ad hoc* in classes 'side by side' to each other.
- There is a systemic level need for specific designated teachers to offer a supportive role to facilitate this concentric mode of assumed connection between teachers at a systemic level in order to provide consistent curricular implementation of anti-bullying strategies
- Diametric modes of relation leading to 'us versus them' labels in bullying between classes can also be challenged through a coordinated curricular approach to bullying prevention between classes where the bullying problem is viewed as the problem rather than the children themselves being seen as the problem. The challenge is to develop concentric narratives of assumed connection between classes through cooperative tasks leading to reframing of existing diametric narratives in a public manner.
- Concentric relations of assumed connection challenge traditional hierarchical relations between teacher and students, as well as attribution of static labels to children as 'bully' or 'victim'. There is a need for professional development of teachers to move from a diametric structured logic of justice apportioning blame and towards a concentric structured ethic of care which treats bullying as problems of relation requiring construction of new narratives of identity for individuals and relationships between individuals and groups in the school.

In addition to developing broader evaluation frameworks for structural indicators, future research needs to identify other dimensions where diametric relations (of assumed separation and a passive role for background factors) need to be changed to concentric relations (of assumed connection and an interactive role for background factors) as part of a systemic focus on the school and its local community regarding bullying. The framework of compensatory relation between concentric and diametric dualisms invites further applications across different cultural contexts for prevention of bullying.

Table 37.2 A Wider Concentric Systemic Focus for Bullying Prevention: Complementary to Curricular Approaches

- In contexts of socio-economic disadvantage in particular, there is a need for a wider systemic approach than simply a curriculum based approach in order to develop concentric relations of assumed connection between parents and the school to facilitate interventions regarding bullying. Diametric relations of assumed separation between home and school often occur in contexts of high levels of socio-economic disadvantage, and there is a need for programs to overcome such diametric relations.
- Especially in contexts of socio-economic disadvantage, there is a need to develop concentric relations of assumed connection between the school and the local community to acknowledge the potentially active background role community factors may be having on bullying within the school system. This requires funding for programs relevant to bullying prevention in the community, including regarding drug related bullying, from a range of Government Departments including Education, Health, and Justice.

Notes

1. These include the village plan of Omarakana in the Trobriand Islands (Malinowski), the Baduj of western Java and the Negri-Sembilan of the Malay peninsula (de Jong), the village of the Winnebago tribe (Radin).
2. Sixth class pupils in Ireland are usually aged 11–12, 5th class are aged 10–11.
3. See Nisbett, Peng, Choi, and Norenzayan (2001), Downes (2003, 2006) for examples of meaning dependent on the background in cognitive psychology with regard to language, perception, attribution, and thinking.
4. Schools in Ireland are designated as disadvantaged on the basis of socio-economic and educational indicators such as unemployment levels, housing, medical card holders, and information on basic literacy and numeracy. See also Downes & Gilligan (2007) for a critique of the negative labeling effects of terming schools "disadvantaged," while maintaining the need for positive discrimination for these schools regarding resource allocation.
5. Corporal punishment in schools was made illegal in Ireland in 1981.
6. See also the Irish *Quality Development of Out of School Services* (QDOSS) network report on bridging health and education needs in out of school services and a role for bullying prevention for out of school services in contexts of socio-economic disadvantage (Downes, 2006).
7. This widening of the operant to a complex pattern of events echoes Quine's (1961) critique of a discrete event falsification in science that ignored the complex systemic interaction of observations and theory.

References

Antonucci, T. C. (1990). Social supports and social relationships. In R. H. Binstock & L. K. George (Eds.), *Handbook of aging and the social sciences* (4th ed., pp. 205–226). Burlington, MA: Academic Press.

Bjorkqvist, K., Ekman, K., & Lagerspetz, K. M. J. (1982). Bullies and victims: The ego picture, ideal picture and normative ego picture. *Scandinavian Journal of Psychology, 23,* 307–313.

Byrne, B. J. (1997). Bullying: A community approach. *Irish Journal of Psychology, 18,* 258–266.

Byrne, M. (2007). Health for all. In P. Downes & A. L. Gilligan (Eds.), *Beyond educational disadvantage* (pp. 343–353). Dublin: Institute of Public Administration.

Byrne, M., Barry, M. M., Nic Gabhainn, S., & Newell, J. (2005). The development and evaluation of a mental health promotion programme for post-primary schools in Ireland. In B. B. Jensen & S. Clift (Eds.), *The health promoting school: International advances in theory, evaluation and practice* (pp. 383–408). Copenhagen: Danish University of Education Press.

Byrne, M., Barry, M. M., & Sheridan, A. (2004). Implementation of a school-based mental Health promotion programme in Ireland. *International Journal of Mental Health Promotion, 6,* 17–25.

Conquergood, D. (1994). For the nation: How street gangs problematize patriotism. In H. W. Simons & M. Billig, (Eds.), *After postmodernism: Reconstructing ideology critique* (pp. 200–221). London: Sage.

Cooper, P. (2005). Social, emotional and behavioural difficulties, social class and educational attainment: Which are the chickens and which are the eggs? *Emotional and Behavioural Difficulties, 10,* 75–77.

Crowley, P. P. (2006). School psychology in Ireland. In S. R. Jimerson, T. D. Oakland, & P. T. Farrell (Eds.), *The handbook of international school psychology* (pp. 177–188). London: Sage.

Devine, D. (2001). *Locating the child's voice in Irish primary education.* In A. Cleary & M. Nic Ghiolla Phadraig (Eds.), *Understanding children* (Vol. 1, pp. 145–174). Cork, Ireland: Oak Tree Press.

Downes, P. (2003a). Cross-cultural structures of concentric and diametric dualism in Levi-Strauss' structural anthropology: Structures of relation underlying the self and ego relation? *Journal of Analytical Psychology, 48,* 47–81.

Downes, P. (2003b). The new curriculum of social, personal and health education in Irish primary schools: Self-awareness, introversion and the role of the teacher. *Kwartalnik Padagogiczny* [Journal of Education, Poland], *190,* 93–112.

Downes, P. (2004a). *Psychological support services for Ballyfermot: Present and future.* Dublin: Commissioned Research Report for URBAN, Ballyfermot, in conjunction with Ballyfermot Drugs Task Force.

Downes, P. (2004b). *Voices from children: St. Raphaels Primary School Ballyfermot.* Dublin: Commissioned Research Report for URBAN, Ballyfermot.

Downes, P. (2006). Newtonian space: The 'blind spot' in Newell and Simon's information processing paradigm. *Journal of Cybernetics and Human Knowing, 13,* 25–55.

Downes, P. (2007). Why SMART outcomes ain't always so smart. In P. Downes & A.-L. Gilligan (Eds.), *Beyond educational disadvantage* (pp. 57–69). Dublin: Institute of Public Administration.

Downes, P., & Gilligan, A.-L. (2007). Beyond disadvantage: Some conclusions. In P. Downes & A-L. Gilligan (Eds.), *Beyond educational disadvantage* (pp. 463–491). Dublin: Institute of Public Administration.

Downes, P., & Maunsell, C. (2007). *Count us in: Tackling early school leaving in South West Inner City Dublin, An integrated response.* Dublin: South Inner City Community Development Association (SICCDA).

Downes, P., Maunsell, C., & Ivers, J. (2006). *A holistic approach to early school leaving and school retention in Blanchardstown: Current issues and future steps for services and schools.* Dublin: Commissioned Research Report for Blanchardstown Area Partnership.

Educational Disadvantage Committee. (2005*). Moving beyond educational disadvantage 2002–2005.* Dublin: Department of Education and Science.

Farrelly, G. (2007). Bullying and social context: Challenges for schools. In P. Downes & A.-L. L. Gilligan (Eds.), *Beyond educational disadvantage* (pp. 429–440). Dublin: Institute of Public Administration.

Freiberg, H. J. (1999). Three creative ways to measure school climate and next steps. In H. J. Freiberg (Ed.), *School climate: Measuring, improving and sustaining healthy learning environments* (pp. 208–218). London: Falmer Press.

Fromm, E. (1973). *The anatomy of human destructiveness.* Harmondsworth, England: Penguin

Gergen, K. J. (2000). *The saturated self: Dilemmas of identity in contemporary life.* New York: Basic Books.

Gilligan, A. L. (Ed.) (2003). *Primary education: Ending disadvantage, Proceedings and Action Plan of National Forum.* Dublin: Educational Disadvantage Centre, St. Patrick's College, Drumcondra.

Gilligan, C. (1982). *In a different voice.* Cambridge MA: Harvard University Press.

Gilligan, C. (1990). Preface. In C. Gilligan, N.P Lyons, & T. J. Hanmer (Eds.), *Making connections: The relational worlds of adolescent girls at Emma Willard School* (pp. 6–29). Cambridge, MA: Harvard University Press.

Hegarty, T. (2007). Towards a narrative practice: Conversations in a city centre school. In P. Downes & A.-L. Gilligan (Eds.), *Beyond educational disadvantage* (pp. 441–450). Dublin: Institute of Public Administration.

Heidegger, M. (1927). *Being and time* (J. MacQuarrie & E. Robinson, Trans.). Oxford, England: Basil Blackwell.

Irish Department of Education. (1993). *Guidelines on countering bullying behaviour in schools.* Dublin: The Stationery Office.

Irish Department of Education and Science. (1999). *The New Revised Primary School Curriculum.* Dublin: The Stationery Office.

Jahoda, G. (1982). *Psychology and anthropology: A psychological perspective.* London: Academic Press.

Johnson, D. W., & Johnson, R. T. (2000). Conflict resolution and peer mediation programs in elementary and secondary schools: A review of the research. In P. K. Smith & A. D. Pellegrini (Eds.), *Psychology of education: Major themes* (Vol. IV, pp. 671–727). London: Routledge.

Kalliotis, P. (2000). Bullying as a special case of aggression: Procedures for cross-cultural assessment. *School Psychology International, 27,* 47–64.

Kutnick, P., & Manson, I. (1998). Social life in the classroom: Towards a relational concept of social skills for use in the classroom. In A. Campbell & S. Muncer (Eds.), *The social child* (pp. 165–188). Hove, England: The Psychology Press.

Levi-Strauss, C. (1962). *The savage mind* (Trans. G. Weidenfeld 1966 Nicolson Ltd.). Chicago: Chicago University Press.

Levi-Strauss, C. (1963). *Structural anthropology vol. 1* (C. Jacobsen & B. Grundfest Schoepf, Trans.). London: Allen Lane. The Penguin Press.

Levi-Strauss, C. (1973). *Structural anthropology vol. 2* (M. Layton, Trans.). London: Allen Lane. Penguin Books.

Levitt. M. J. (1991). Attachment and close relationships: A life-span perspective. In J. L. Gewirtz & W. M. Kurtines (Eds.), *Intersections with attachment* (pp. 183–205). Hillsdale, NJ: Erlbaum.

Maxwell, J. (1989). Mediation in the schools: Self-regulation, self-esteem and self-discipline. *Mediation Quarterly, 7,* 149–155.

Mayock, P., Kitching, K., & Morgan, M. (2007). *Relationships and sexuality education in the context of social, personal and health education: An assessment of the challenges to full implementation of the programme in post-primary schools.* Dublin: Department of Education and Science.

Morgan, M. (2001). *Drug use prevention: Overview of research.* Dublin: National Advisory Committee on Drugs.

Morgan, M., & Kitching, K. (2007). Job satisfaction of beginning teachers. In P. Downes & A.-L. Gilligan (Eds.), *Beyond educational disadvantage* (pp. 367–378). Dublin: Institute of Public Administration.

Nisbett, R. E., Peng, K., Choi, I., & Norenzayan, A. (2001). Culture and systems of thought: Holistic versus analytic cognition. *Psychological Review, 108,* 291–310.

O'Moore, A. M., Kirkham, C., & Smith, M. (1997). Bullying behaviour in Irish schools: A nationwide study. *Irish Journal of Psychology, 18,* 141–169.

Olweus, D. (1980). Familial and temperamental determinants of aggressive behavior in adolescent boys: A causal analysis. *Developmental Psychology, 16,* 644–660.

Olweus, D. (1997). Bully/Victim problems in school: Knowledge base and an effective intervention program. *Irish Journal of Psychology, 18,* 170–190.

Quine, W. V. O. (1961). *From a logical point of view* (2nd ed.). New York: Harper

Rachlin, H. (1984). Mental yes. Private no. *Behavioral and Brain Sciences, 7,* 566–567.

Rutter, M. (1985). Resilience in the face of adversity: Protective factors and resistance to psychiatric disorder. *British Journal of Psychiatry, 147,* 598–611.

Salmivalli, C., Lagerspetz, K., Bjorkqvist, K., Osterman, K., & Kaukiainen, A. (2000). Bullying as a group process: Participant roles and their relations to social status within the group. In P. K. Smith & A. D. Pellegrini (Eds.), *Psychology of education: Major themes* (Vol. IV, pp. 574–592). London: Routledge

Schneiders, J., Drukker, M., Van der Ende, J., Verhulst, F. C., Van Os, J., & Nicolson, N. A. (2003). Neighbourhood socioeconomic disadvantage and behavioural problems from late childhood into early adolescence. *Journal of Epidemiology and Community Health, 57,* 699–703.

Scholes, R. (1985). *Textual power.* New Haven, CT: Yale University Press.

Solberg, M. E., & Olweus, D. (2003). Prevalence estimation of school bullying within the Olweus Bully/Victim Questionnaire. *Aggressive Behavior, 29,* 239–268.

Stevahn, L., Johnson, D. W., Johnson, R. T., Green, K., & Laginski, A. M. (1997). Effects on high school students of conflict resolution training integrated into English literature. *Journal of Social Psychology, 137,* 302–316.

Stevahn, L., Johnson, D. W., Johnson, R. T., & Schultz, R. (2002). Effects of conflict resolution training integrated into a high school social studies curriculum. *Journal of Social Psychology, 142,* 305–333.

Tobler, N. S., Roona, M. R., Ochshorn, P., Marshall, D. G., Streke, A. V., & Stackpole, K. M. (2000). School-based adolescent drug prevention programs: 1998 meta-analysis. *Journal of Primary Prevention, 20,* 275–337.

United Nations Economic and Social Council. (2006, March 3). Commission on Human Rights, Economic, Social and Cultural Rights. *Report of the Special Rapporteur on the right of everyone to the enjoyment of the highest attainable standard of physical and mental health, Paul Hunt.* New York: Author.

White, M., & Epson, D. (1990). *Narrative means to therapeutic ends.* New York: Norton.

Whitney, I., & Smith, P. K. (1993). A survey of the nature and extent of bullying in junior/middle and secondary schools in English schools. *Education Research, 35,* 3–25.

38

Teachers' Management of Student Bullying in the Classroom

LAURA M. CROTHERS AND JERED B. KOLBERT

Overview

Classroom teachers may benefit from perceiving peer victimization among students as a behavior management issue that can be prevented or addressed through authoritative discipline, guidance curricular approaches, and teacher-parent partnerships, among other methods.

Conceptual Foundations

Successful management of student behavior in the classroom is a necessary condition of an environment in which all children can learn. Interestingly, although student misbehavior has historically been a concern of teachers, the issue of lack of discipline has reached heightened proportions, being seen as one of the most problematic of school systems in the United States (Bear, 1998). In particular, externalizing behavior problems exhibited by children, including antisocial conduct, impulsivity, aggression, defiance, and overactivity can be disruptive and stressful for both students and educators (Hinshaw, 1992).

Child bullying is an externalizing behavior that troubles both teachers and students in the classroom, although there may be different beliefs among such individuals regarding the most effective means of addressing peer victimization at school. In a study investigating teachers' and students' perceptions of anti-bullying interventions, researchers noted that while students tended to endorse strategies in which adults take responsibility for handling student bullying, such as creating a structured classroom environment inhospitable to peer victimization, educators endorsed solutions such as children learning to ward off bullies by themselves through assertiveness training (Crothers & Kolbert, 2004). The problem suggested by this disparity is that while children look to educators to ensure their safety in instances of peer victimization, teachers may feel as though this is not within their power or responsibility to address.

Even when educators are empowered to intervene in childhood bullying, they may not do so effectively. In a national study conducted by Dake, Price, Telljohann, and Funk (2003) investigating the perceptions and practices of classroom teachers in bullying prevention and intervention, researchers found that while 86.3% of the teachers in the sample reported using serious talks with the bully and victim to intervene in instances of bullying, less than one third of the educators set aside classroom time to discuss bullying (31.7%) or involved students in creating classroom rules against bullying (31.2%), suggesting that teachers may not use all of the tools available to them in intervening when bullying occurs.

Teachers seem also to have different attitudes and respond differentially to instances of bullying based upon the type of victimization (physical, verbal, or relational). Relational bullying tends to be viewed less seriously by teachers, who are then less likely to use immediate intervention with this behavior, in comparison to their responses to verbal or physical bullying (Yoon & Kerber, 2003). Yoon (2004) notes that teachers' self-efficacy in behavior management, empathy toward victims, and perceptions of the seriousness of bullying incidents are important factors in predicting the likelihood of intervention by teachers in child bully-victim problems. Because classroom educators are often the primary responders in addressing bullying among students, the following strategies are suggested to assist teachers in preventing and responding to bullying as it occurs.

Specific Interventions

Guidance Curricular Approaches

Whole-school anti-bullying intervention programs typically include psychoeducational techniques designed to teach children about bullying and its negative effects upon both perpetrators and victims. Teachers can employ similar methods to either present or reinforce information about bullying in their individual classrooms even in the absence of such school-wide programs. Traditionally, although guidance lessons are delivered by school-based mental health professionals, teachers can easily integrate activities such as reading and discussing books, art projects, creative story writing, journal writing, role-playing bullying scenarios and developing appropriate solutions, and watching videos and debating the messages contained therein into regular education curricula (Foschl, Sprung, & Mullin-Rindler, 1998; Whitted & Dupper, 2005).

Classroom guidance has been found to be effective in improving students' behavior and attitudes (Gerler & Anderson, 1986). However, it is important that activities designed to enhance the social-emotional skills of children be both comprehensive and developmentally-based (Nicoll, 1994). One such lesson that teachers can use in helping students identify bullying and develop options for response is: "Bullies and Bullying: Deconstructing Events," published by a collaborative effort of the National Football League, the publisher, Scholastic, and the nonprofit educational organization, Facing History and Ourselves. This lesson is part of the curriculum, "One World: Connecting Communities, Cultures, and Classrooms," which is free of charge and may be downloaded from http://scholastic.com/oneworld (Curriculum Review, 2004).

Researchers have noted that bibliotherapy helps children to experience emotional release through abreaction and catharsis as well as to gain insight into solutions for problems they might be experiencing (Nicholson & Pearson, 2003). Especially for young children, drama, art projects, videos, books, and discussions about bullying can help give children the symbolism and language to identify and talk about the experience of bullying. Teachers of young children can act out bullying scenarios using puppets to play the roles of victim and bully. As children mature into adolescence, teachers can ask them to write about bullying in their journals or to develop a script for a depiction of bullying, and encourage the children themselves or have the students use puppets to act out the scenario.

Videos and books can also be a helpful medium in assisting educators in introducing awareness of the problem of bullying in their students. Books can be used to aid children in understanding that bullying is a common problem, highlighting the negative effects of bullying upon individuals, emphasizing to them the need to seek help from adults. Teachers can use these materials and experiences as a catalyst for discussions about bullying in their classrooms. Audiovisual materials may also bring realism to bullying scenarios, and allow youngsters to imagine themselves in the roles of bully and victim, possibly encouraging empathy and understanding.

Classroom Management Techniques

Effective teachers have been found to exhibit an authoritative disciplinary style that integrates the use of three types of strategies, "classroom management and positive climate strategies for preventing behavior problems, operant learning strategies for the short-term management and control of behavior problems, and decision-making and social problem-solving strategies for achieving the long-term goal of self-discipline" (Bear, 1998, p. 23).

In explanation, teachers who are adept at managing student behavior in the classroom work to prevent student bullying through creating a classroom climate incompatible with peer victimization, respond quickly and appropriately using behavioral strategies to address bullying as it occurs, and work to improve children's social skills and conflict management skills so that future bullying is less likely. While the first two authoritative disciplinary style techniques will be described in this section, the last method will be explored later in this chapter.

Teachers may find it helpful to consider classroom management as an aspect of school climate, instruction, and curriculum rather than one of control (Levin & Nolan, 2004). Teachers should recognize that they are leaders in creating a caring classroom environment in which all children are valued and appreciated, and no child is marginalized or excluded from play or instructional activities (Gottfredson, 2001; Greene, 2006). In reviewing the Peaceable Classroom model, Stomfay-Stitz and Wheeler (2006) state that this is a program in which issues of violence and bullying can be addressed and reduced through a classroom climate in which children are taught peaceful alternatives to the antisocial behaviors modeled by society (Levin, 1994). One of the first strategies in addressing bullying in the classroom is to establish rules prohibiting it. At the beginning of the year, teachers can sit down with their class and collaboratively develop the list of rules for the classroom, including prohibition of bullying. As children suggest rules, educators can take the opportunity to discuss feelings children might have when they are the victims of aggressive behavior. The rules should be posted and reviewed periodically throughout the year to ascertain whether there is a need for modification or addition of behavior guidelines.

Students also need to be provided with information that instructs them in the way in which they should handle bullying behavior, as well as identifying the differences between appropriate and inappropriate relationships between and among children and teachers (Boulton & Underwood, 1992). This information can be discussed when reviewing the school and classroom code of conduct, or as a part of a social skills training curriculum. As part of a general classroom management strategy, teachers can also implement incentive systems for all students that encourage children to control their aggressive behavior and demonstrate pro-social behavior. Peer-mediated positive behavior support programs, which include positive reinforcement in the form of token economies and praise, as well as self-monitoring and teacher and peer monitoring, have been found to have positive effects upon students' socially-appropriate classroom behavior (Christensen, Young, & Marchant, 2004). Behavioral contracts can be used with bullies, in which children are asked to sign a form guaranteeing they will not prey upon other students (Smokowski & Kopasz, 2005).

Effective instruction is a powerful form of classroom management, since children who are actively engaged in learning are less likely to have the time and inclination to engage in bullying. Curriculum that encourages children to question their own assumptions and participate in critical thinking reduces boredom and opportunities to bully for entertainment purposes. Katz and Chard (2000) encourage the use of project work that encourages children to engage in in-depth investigations of topics that are of interest to them and exploring events and objects in their classrooms and communities by cooperating, collaborating, and sharing responsibilities (Bullock, 2002). Additionally, overlapping activities so that students are continuously busy on learning tasks diminishes the opportunity that children have to assert power over one another.

Another means of addressing bullying in the classroom is teacher vigilance about students' behavior in the classroom and throughout the school in general. Teachers need to be omniscient regarding student conduct and activities, since bullying often occurs in the classroom without educators' knowledge. Behavior problems such as bullying are also as likely to occur during unstructured times, such as transitioning from one class or activity to the next, in the gym, in the cafeteria, on the bus, and so forth. Consequently, adults responsible for supervising children's conduct during those times need to be instructed of the signs of bullying behavior, and given the authority to intervene when they suspect bullying is occurring.

Cooperative Learning Activities

One of the ways that teachers can increase students' familiarity and acceptance of others is to use cooperative learning activities in the classroom. In particular, students across various disability categories, including students with learning disabilities, students with behavioral and emotional disorders, children with traumatic brain injury diagnoses, and students who have visual impairments, are at risk for social skill deficits and an increased risk of victimization by peers (Praeter, Bruhl, & Serna, 1998). Cooperative learning is an approach that can be used in strengthening students' social skills and acceptance of students with disabilities, and has been shown to be effective in improving attitudes and relationships among children in ethnically-diverse and special education inclusion classrooms (Boulton & Underwood, 1992; Cowie, Smith, Boulton, & Laver, 1994; Johnson & Johnson, 1994; Praeter et al., 1998; Vaughan, 2002).

Teachers can develop cooperative learning groups and offer group rewards to enhance social integration and pro-social mixing among students which would not ordinarily occur (Hoover & Hazler, 1991; Johnson & Johnson, 1994). Educators should strive to balance competitive activities, which focus upon individual achievement, with cooperative goals that emphasize group achievement (Hazler, 1996). Foschl and Gropper (1999) suggest an activity in which teachers have students build a wall from blocks that represent the reasons preventing children from being friends with one another, and then engage in problem-solving to suggest ways to reduce these impediments (focusing on teasing, bullying, and divisive social attitudes).

However, teachers should consider power differentials between children when planning for groups of students to work collaboratively in the classroom. Since bullying is associated with both implicit (wealth, attractiveness, and athletic competence) and explicit (physical and relational aggression) forms of power, educators need to make sure that groups are not vastly different in their power status (Vaillancourt, Hymel, & McDougall, 2003). Additionally, because teachers may be naturally inclined to group bullies and victims together, they may wish instead to consider forming groups with individuals who have only slight differences in social power. Alternately, since bullies tend to be of high social status and power, educators can appeal to high-status non-bullies to intervene on victims' behalf when they are being victimized by peers. When assured that a high-status child would be amenable to advocating for another child, a teacher might then feel comfortable assembling these individuals together (Vaillancourt et al., 2003).

Assertiveness, Self-Esteem, and Social Skills Training for Victims of Bullying

Bullying prevention programs often include long-term interventions that address common deficits among victims of bullying. Social skills training appears indicated since research suggests that a child's poor social skills are a major risk factor for victimization (Boulton, Trueman, Chau, Whitehand, & Amataya, 1999; Hodges, Boivin, Vitaro, & Bukowski, 1999), and because perpetrators may regard social isolates as attractive targets given the unlikelihood of assistance from other peers. Furthermore, the development of friendships may provide the isolated student with the emotional support to reduce the pain of low social status. Teachers can promote victims' self-efficacy by helping these children to recognize the strengths they possess that may be attractive to potential friends.

First, teachers can instruct students to replace negative self-statements with more positive or realistic ones to increase children's confidence and reduce social anxiety. Bullied students are often realistically pessimistic about the likelihood of success in developing friendships, as research suggests that the social status of victimized students is both negative and fairly stable (Boulton & Smith, 1994; Salmivalli, Lappalainen, & Lagerspetz, 1998). Thus, victimized children and adolescents may require encouragement to attempt the risk-taking essential for establishing social connections. Teachers may encourage victimized students to focus on their effort in making friends, rather than on the results, which rarely lead to immediate success, since friendships often take time to develop. Further, some victimized students' lack of social intelligence interferes with their pursuit of friendship. For example, victimized children or adolescents may fail to understand the social status of other students, and thus, may seek to befriend the most popular students, who are unlikely to reciprocate the desire for friendship. In such cases, the teacher can ask victimized students to think about who seems to want or need a friend, explaining that since popular students have many friends, they may not have enough time for additional friendships.

An example of a long-term intervention to assist victimized students is Fox and Boulton's (2003) study of the effects of an 8-session social skills/assertiveness training program which was provided through a group format. The social skills component of the program was used to teach students a variety of skills, including listening, having conversations, and asking to join in peer groups, while the assertiveness component of the program was employed to instruct students in the use of more confident body language, relaxation skills, cognitive strategies, and verbal strategies for dealing with bullying. The researchers found that the program led to a significant increase in victims' self-esteem, which was maintained at a 3-month follow-up, but noted that the program did not have a significant impact upon victims' number of friends, peer acceptance, depression, and anxiety. Additionally, group interventions for victimized students may result in greater success when role-playing is utilized, in which specific behaviors modeled for students are followed by supervised practice with peers.

Training in social skills has long been the standard approach for increasing the quality and repertoire of social skills of students with learning, emotional, and behavioral disabilities (Lewandrowski & Barlow, 2000). Recently, there have been directives within the field of special education to emphasize the acquisition of skills that protect students with disabilities against peer victimization, given that the limited research on the issue is suggestive of a positive relationship between learning, emotional, and behavioral disabilities and being bullied by peers (Flynt & Morton, 2004; Nabuzoka, 2003). Mishna (2003), in her recommendations for working with students with learning disabilities who are involved in bullying, implied that although special educators have the resources and training to provide social skills training to address specific behavioral deficits, these individuals must collaborate with general education teachers to help them understand how they can reinforce social skills training, since students with learning disabilities often fail to generalize newly acquired behaviors to other contexts (e.g., Kavale & Forness, 1996).

Constructive Conversations with Victims of Bullying

When asked about what teachers do to put a stop to bullying, students report that educators intervene in bullying scenarios less often than children would prefer (Crothers & Kolbert, 2004). Victims may feel that bullies are actually receiving more teacher attention than do those who are being harassed by peers. Characteristics associated with students who are frequently victimized include anxiety and social isolation (Goldbaum, Craig, Pepler, & Connolly, 2003; Hodges et al., 1999; Olweus, 1993), depression and low self-esteem (Boivin & Hymel, 1997; Egan & Perry, 1998; Olweus, 1993), and poor academic performance (Olweus, 1993).

Assisting the student who is frequently bullied may require both short- and long-term intervention. Short-term interventions refer to addressing specific incidents of bullying, while long-term interventions involve building confidence and avoiding the probability of future victimization. Since victims are unlikely to report bullying because they fear exacerbation of the problem or retribution, it is essential that during an investigation of peer aggression teachers attempt to alleviate the high levels of anxiety often experienced by victims (e.g., Goldbaum et al., 2003). Educators should inform the child that whatever he or she decides to reveal will be held in confidence, while simultaneously building rapport and educating the victim in identifying what emotions he or she is likely to be experiencing. Additionally, the teacher can instill hope in the youngster by sharing that he or she has had success in dealing with such incidents in the past. Victims often internalize bullying, attributing the unwanted behaviors evidenced by peers to characteristics of themselves (Hodges et al., 1999). Thus, it is important to help the victim to realize that he or she has done nothing to provoke the bullying behavior, as well as emphasizing that his or her anger or fear regarding the experience is normal and justified.

Once information about the bullying behavior has been gathered, it is important to explain to the victim what the teacher will do with the information, which may include talking with "witnesses" and the alleged perpetrator(s), assigning a negative consequence to the perpetrator, and informing other teachers of the behavior so that they more closely observe the involved students. If the alleged incident is either severe or is indicative of an ongoing pattern, the teacher can gather additional data by interviewing other students who may have witnessed such incidents. Educators can ask the victim to identify other students who are not friends of the victim or the perpetrator who may have observed such events, explaining to the victim that these "witnesses" will not be informed of how they were recognized as being involved. In many cases, the victimization has been occurring for several months and thus the victim can readily identify other students who may have observed such events. Furthermore, victims should be encouraged to approach the teacher if bullying incidents reoccur.

Constructive Conversations with Students Who Frequently Bully

Research on students who frequently bully reveals some common characteristics of such children and adolescents. Perpetrators of bullying behavior tend to lack empathy (Maeda, 2004; Olweus, 1993; Warden & Mackinnon, 2003), misattribute their peers' actions as being the result of hostile intentions, demonstrate impulsivity, perceive aggression as an acceptable way to resolve conflict, and exhibit a high need for dominance (Graham & Juvonen, 1998; Olweus, 1993; Ross, 1996). Whereas students who are frequently victimized are generally unpopular with peers, perpetrators of bullying tend to have above-average popularity (Vaillancourt et al., 2003), although there is some evidence to suggest that their popularity declines in high school (Olweus, 1993).

When first meeting with a student who appears to be bullying peers, the teacher should be firm, immediately indicating that he or she is speaking with the student because of his or her inappropriate behavior. The educator should also then explain which classroom or school rule has been violated as well as describing the corresponding consequence. To gain the trust of the bully, it is probably best to begin the conversation with the identification of the bullying behavior and the consequence for this behavior, since a straightforward delivery assures the student that he or she will not be "trapped" into a lie by asking him or her for his or her version of events. Thus, it is important that teachers collect evidence from other student witnesses prior to meeting with the perpetrator. The teacher should also inform the bully that other teachers and school staff will be made aware of the incident to prevent such behaviors from occurring in the future.

Next, the teacher should shift into using more of a concerned and caring tone, as the objective is to enable the perpetrator to non-defensively evaluate whether his or her behavior is meeting his or her goals. A common misperception among adults is that students who bully have low self-esteem and are motivated to bully others in an attempt to feel better about themselves (Olweus, 1993). Rather than attempting to increase perpetrators' self-esteem, teachers can affirm the student's strengths and popularity. Since research has been suggestive of bullies' need for dominance, a discussion of the student's high social status may be appealing to students who frequently bully (Graham & Juvonen, 1998; Olweus, 1993; Ross, 1996).

Ideally, this tactic will enable the perpetrator to realize that victimization of peers is unnecessary to the achievement of his or her desire for social status. It also serves to help build the teacher-student relationship, increasing the likelihood that the student will engage in self-evaluation. As the student begins to develop trust in the educator, the teacher can more assertively raise the value of concern for others, encouraging the student to consider what the victim was feeling, and what restitution may be owed, in an attempt to address perpetrators' frequent lack of empathy (e.g., Warden & Mackinnon, 2003). It may be helpful to engage early adolescent perpetrators in discussions regarding the potential ramifications of bullying, such as the negative impact upon friendships in later grades, explaining that the popularity of students who use aggression typically decreases when they enter high school (Olweus, 1993).

Although there is limited research concerning long-term individual interventions for perpetrators, one promising intervention involves strategies to increase the empathy of perpetrators. Perpetrators may be assigned to help younger students or students with disabilities under the supervision of an adult who provides praise and other forms of reinforcement for exhibiting helping behaviors. Research has found that such role-taking experiences can promote empathy levels of adult helpers (Reiman, 1998). Furthermore, providing perpetrators with such a valued role may appeal to their attraction to status (e.g., Graham & Juvonen, 1998).

Parent-Teacher Collaboration

Although many interventions can be successfully undertaken at school, it is often important and necessary to work with the families of bullies and victims. In fact, research suggests there is a significant relationship between parenting style and bullying. Baldry and Farrington (2000) found that middle school students categorized as bullies were both more likely to have authoritarian parents and to have frequent disagreements with their parents. Additionally, Flouri and

Buchanan (2003) found both low mother and father involvement to be significantly correlated with bullying behavior in adolescence. Myron-Wilson (1999) studied the relationship between parenting style and participant roles involved in bullying, which included the following: (a) bully, (b) reinforcer, (c) assistant, (d) defender, (e) outsider, and (f) victim. The results revealed that reinforcer bullies reported receiving less parental warmth and more punitive parenting, while assistant bullies were more likely to perceive their parents as being neglectful. Parents of perpetrating children may not regard bullying as a concern, possibly because such a strong power differential is demonstrated in their own family system. In other words, such behavior may appear to parents of bullies as normal and effective. Thus, it is important for teachers to recognize that parents of bullies may become emotionally reactive when school official raise concerns about their children's victimizing behavior.

Best practice in addressing bullying includes involving the parents of perpetrators in the identification and resolution of such a problem. However, parents of perpetrators may question the need to conference with school personnel given that such individuals often use power-oriented strategies themselves in relating to their children (e.g., Baldry & Farrington, 2000), and thus fail to regard the issue as a problem. In such cases, teachers are encouraged to notify the parent, possibly through an e-mail or telephone contact, if incidents of bullying continue. A realistic objective in conferencing with parents of perpetrators is to gain at least enough of their support so that they will not undermine teachers or administrators by directly or indirectly implying to their children that they do not need to adhere to the school rules regarding bullying.

In conferencing with parents of perpetrators, teachers should use a no-nonsense factual presentation, and avoid engaging in questioning, long discussions, or using a tone that invites blame upon the parents of the bully. Similar to student perpetrators of bullying, it is not uncommon for parents to minimize or deny the bullying incident. For such situations, it is best that the school staff be prepared to offer a narrative description of the incidents. Furthermore, the teacher may present to the parents of the bully, in a respectful and non-emotional manner, the possible consequences if their child continues such behaviors, which may include further school sanctions, and eventually decreased popularity among peers (Olweus, 1993). Another effective technique is for the teacher to share with the parents what they regard as some of their child's strengths, invite the parents to do so as well, and then ask the parents what they believe their child needs to learn at this point in his or her development.

Victims who require long-term intervention may also benefit from parental involvement, since there is some research suggesting that victims may either have punitive, authoritarian parents (Baldry & Farrington, 2000; Myron-Wilson, 1999), or enmeshed, overprotective parents (Olweus, 1993; Smith & Myron-Wilson, 1998). Overprotective parents may become more so when made aware of their child's victimization. For example, they may attempt to become their child's best friend, engaging in many social activities that may temporarily satisfy the youngster's need for companionship but might paradoxically interfere with the child's acquisition of friends. In such cases, teachers can help the parent(s) acquire a more developmentally-appropriate response to their child's need for friends. Teachers can share how parents play a vital role in children's social development, and encourage the parents of the victimized child to explore how they might help to promote their child's social development. This may involve helping parents to recognize their child's resources for attracting peers, or having parents identify what might be several relationship skills that the child could realistically acquire at this juncture in development.

Parents can encourage their child to invite peers to their home or to become involved in social organizations that relate to their child's strengths. Since encouraging non-athletic victimized children to become involved in team sports may lead to further social isolation or rejection,

Table 38.1 Summary Table of Implications for Practice

Guidance curricular approaches	Curriculum Review (2004)
Art projects	Foschl, Sprung, & Mullin-Rindler (1998)
Classroom guidance lessons	Gerler & Anderson (1985)
Creative writing	Nicholson & Pearson (2003)
Drama	Nicoll (1994)
Journal writing	Whitted & Dupper (2005)
Reading and discussing books	
Watching videos	
Classroom management techniques	Bear (1998)
Classroom climate	Boulton & Underwood (1992)
Classroom rules	Bullock (2002)
Effective instruction	Christensen, Young, & Marchant (2004)
Lesson overlapping	Gottfredson (2001)
Positive behavior support	Greene (2006)
Teacher vigilance and supervision	Katz & Chard (2000)
	Levin (1994)
	Levin & Nolan (2004)
	Smokowski & Kopasz (2005)
	Stomfay-Stitz & Wheeler (2006)
Cooperative learning activities	Boulton & Underwood (1992)
	Cowie, Smith, Boulton, & Laver (1994)
	Foschl & Gropper (1999)
	Hazler (1996)
	Honma (2003)
	Hoover & Hazler (1991)
	Johnson & Johnson (1994)
	Pink & Brownlee (1988)
	Praeter, Bruhl, & Serna (1998)
	Vaillancourt, Hymel, & McDougall (2003)
	Vaughan (2002)
Assertiveness training, self-esteem training, and social skills training for victims of bullying	Boulton & Smith (1994)
	Boulton, Trueman, Chau, Whitehand, & Amataya (1999)
	Flynt & Morton (2004)
	Fox & Boulton (2003)
	Hodges, Boivin, Vitaro, & Bukowski (1999)
	Kavale & Forness (1996)
	Lewandrowski & Barlow (2000)
	Mishna (2003)
	Nabuzoka (2003)
	Salmivalli, Lappalainen, & Lagerspetz (1998)
Constructive conversations with victims of bullying	Boivin & Hymel (1997)
	Crothers & Kolbert (2004)
	Egan & Perry (1998)
	Goldbaum, Craig, Pepler, & Connolly (2003)
	Hodges et al. (1999)
	Olweus (1993)
Constructive conversations with children who frequently bully	Graham & Juvonen (1998)
	Maeda (2004)
	Olweus (1993)
	Reiman (1998)
	Ross (1996)
	Vaillancourt et al. (2003)
	Warden & Mackinnon (2003)
Parent-teacher collaboration	Baldry & Farrington (2000)
	Bowers, Smith, & Binney (1994)
	Flouri & Buchanan (2003)
	Myron-Wilson (1999)
	Olweus (1993)
	Smith & Myron-Wilson (1998)

parents of victims can be encouraged to consider enhancing their child's physical development through supporting participation in individual sports such as karate, bicycling, swimming, and running. Parents can promote their child's social cognition by helping them to analyze social interactions, encouraging their child to hypothesize about what the facial gestures, statements, and behaviors might indicate about the perspectives of their peers. Parents can also use role-playing to help their child with a variety of social situations, including handling bullying, seeking others for friendship, or managing conflict within friendships.

Discussion and Future Research

Teachers are a very important part of the solution to childhood bullying. It is important to recognize, however, that teachers can also undermine bullying prevention and intervention techniques through uninformed, incomplete or less-than-enthusiastic implementation (Vernberg & Gamm, 2003). Because of this, Espelage (2004) notes that "interventions need to include an assessment of teachers' attitudes toward bullying and how it [sic] relates to their in-classroom behavior toward students" (p. 5). Thus, it is essential that educators be trained in bullying prevention and intervention in order to increase both their confidence and skills in addressing peer victimization in the classroom (Bauman & Del Rio, 2006; Espelage, 2004). Ultimately, it is necessary that educators are empowered to play a pivotal role in solving the peer victimization problems that occur among children to ensure both their psychological and physical safety at school.

References

Baldry, A. C., & Farrington, D. P. (2000). Bullies and delinquents: Personal characteristics and parental styles. *Journal of Community and Applied Social Psychology, 10,* 17–31.

Bauman, S., & Del Rio, A. (2006). Preservice teachers' responses to bullying scenarios: Comparing physical, verbal, and relational bullying. *Journal of Educational Psychology, 98,* 219–231.

Bear, G. G. (1998). School discipline in the United States: Prevention, correction, and long-term social development. *School Psychology Review, 27,* 14–32.

Boivin, M., & Hymel, S. (1997). Peer experiences and social self-perceptions: A sequential model. *Developmental Psychology, 33,* 135–145.

Boulton, M. J., & Smith, P. K. (1994). Bully/victim problems in middle school children: stability, self-perceived competence, peer-perceptions and peer acceptance. *British Journal of Developmental Psychology, 12,* 315–329.

Boulton, M. J., Trueman, M., Chau, C., Whitehand, C., & Amataya, K. (1999). Concurrent and longitudinal links between friendship and peer victimization: Implications for befriending interventions. *Journal of Adolescence, 22,* 461–466.

Boulton, M. J., & Underwood, K. (1992). Bully victim problems among middle school children. *British Journal of Educational Psychology, 62,* 73–87.

Bowers, L., Smith, P. K., & Binney, V. (1994). Perceived family relationships of bullies, victims, and bully/victims in middle childhood. *Journal of Social and Personal Relationships, 11,* 215–232.

Bullock, J. R. (2002). Bullying among children. *Childhood Education, 78,* 130–133.

Christensen, L., Young, K. R., & Marchant, M. (2004). The effects of a peer-mediated positive behavior support program on socially appropriate classroom behavior. *Education and Treatment of Children, 27,* 199–234.

Cowie, H., Smith, P., Boulton, M., & Laver, R. (1994). *Cooperation in the multi-ethnic classroom.* London: David Fulton.

Crothers, L. M., & Kolbert, J. B. (2004). Comparing middle school teachers' and students' views on bullying and anti-bullying interventions. *Journal of School Violence, 3,* 17–32.

Curriculum Review. (2004). Get the drop on bullying. *Curriculum Review, 44,* 7–8.

Dake, J. A., Price, J. H., Telljohann, S. K., & Funk, J. B. (2003). Teacher perceptions and practices regarding school bullying prevention. *Journal of School Health, 73,* 347–355.

Egan, S. K., & Perry, D. G. (1998). Does low self-regard invite victimization? *Developmental Psychology, 34,* 299–309.

Espelage, D. L. (2004). An ecological perspective to school-based bullying prevention. *The Prevention Researcher, 11,* 3–6.

Flynt, S. W., & Morton, R. C. (2004). Bullying and children with disabilities. *Journal of Instructional Psychology, 31,* 330–333.

Flouri, E., & Buchanan, A. (2003). The role of mother involvement and father involvement in adolescent bullying behavior. *Journal of Interpersonal Violence, 18,* 634–644.

Foschl, M., & Gropper, N. (1999). Fostering friendships, curbing bullying. *Educational Leadership,* 72–75.

Foschl, M., Sprung, B., & Mullin-Rindler, N. (1998). *Quit it! A teacher's guide on teasing and bullying for use with students in grades K-3.* New York: Educational Equity Concepts, Inc., Wellesley College Center for Research on Women, and NEA Professional Library.

Fox, C. L., & Boulton, M. J. (2003). Evaluating the effectiveness of a social skills training programme for victims of bullying. *Educational Research, 45,* 231–247.

Gerler, E. R., & Anderson, R. F. (1986). The effects of classroom guidance on children's success in school. *Journal of Counseling and Development, 65,* 78–88.

Goldbaum, S., Craig, W. M., Pepler, D., & Connolly, J. (2003). Developmental trajectories of victimization: Identifying risk and protective factors. In M. J. Elias & J. E. Zins (Eds.), *Bullying, peer harassment, and victimization in the schools: The next generation of prevention* (pp. 139–156). New York: Haworth.

Gottfredson, D. C. (2001). *Schools and delinquency.* New York: Cambridge.

Graham, S., & Juvonen, J. (1998). A social cognitive perspective on peer aggression and victimization. *Annals Child Development, 12,* 21–66.

Greene, M. B. (2006). Bullying in schools: A plea for measure of human rights. *Journal of Social Issues, 62,* 63–79.

Hazler, R. J. (1996). *Breaking the cycle of violence: Interventions for bullying and victimization.* Bristol, PA: Accelerated Development.

Hinshaw, S. P. (1992). Externalizing behavior problems and academic underachievement in childhood and adolescence: Causal relationships and underlying mechanisms. *Psychological Bulletin, 111,* 127–155.

Hodges, E. V. E., Boivin, M., Vitaro, F., & Bukowski, W. M. (1999). The power of friendship: Protection against an escalating cycle of peer victimization. *Developmental Psychology, 35,* 94–101.

Hoover, J. H., & Hazler, R. J. (1991). Bullies and victims. *Elementary School Guidance and Counseling, 25,* 212–219.

Johnson, R. T., & Johnson, D. W., (1994). An overview of cooperative learning. In J. S. Thousand, R. A. Villa, & A. I. Nevin (Eds.), *Creativity and collaborative learning: A practical guide to empowering students and teachers* (pp. 31–44). Baltimore: Brookes.

Katz, L., & Chard, S. (2000). *Engaging children's minds: The project approach* (2nd ed.). Stamford, CT: Ablex.

Kavale, K. A., & Forness, S. R. (1996). Social skills deficits and learning disabilities: A meta-analysis. *Journal of Learning Disabilities, 29,* 226–237.

Levin, D. E. (1994). *Teaching young children in violent times: Building a peaceable classroom. Preschool-grade 3 violence prevention and conflict resolution guide.* Cambridge, MA: Educators for Social Responsibility.

Levin, J., & Nolan, J. F. (2004). *Principles of classroom management: A professional decision-making model.* New York: Pearson.

Lewandrowski, L. J., & Barlow, J. R. (2000). Social cognition and verbal learning disabilities. *Journal of Psychotherapy in Independent Practice 4,* 35–47.

Maeda, R. (2004). Empathy, emotion regulation, and perspective taking as predictors of children's participation in bullying. *Dissertation Abstracts International Section A: Humanities and Social Sciences, 64,* 3957.

Mishna, F. (2003). Learning disabilities and bullying: Double jeopardy. *Journal of Learning Disabilities, 36,* 336–347.

Myron-Wilson, R. (1999). *Parenting style: And how it may influence a child's role in bullying.* ERIC (No. ED429731).

Nabuzoka, D. (2003). Teacher ratings and peer nominations of bullying and other behaviour of children with and without learning difficulties. *Educational Psychology, 23,* 307–321.

Nicholson, J. I., & Pearson, Q. M. (2003). Helping children cope with fears: Using children's literature in classroom guidance. *Professional School Counseling, 7,* 15–21.

Nicoll, W. G. (1994). Developing effective classroom guidance programs: An integrative framework. *School Counselor, 41,* 360–364.

Olweus, D. (1993). *Bullying at school: What we know and what we can do.* Cambridge, MA: Blackwell.

Praeter, M. A., Bruhl, S., & Serna, L. A. (1998). Acquiring social skills through cooperative learning and teacher-directed instruction. *Remedial and Special Education, 19,* 160–172.

Reiman, A. J. (1998). The evolution of social role-taking and guided reflection framework in teacher education: Recent theory and quantitative synthesis of research. *Teaching and Teacher Education, 15,* 597–612.

Ross, D. (1996). *Childhood bullying and teasing.* Alexandria, VA: American Counseling Association.

Salmivalli, C., Lappalainen, M., & Lagerspetz, M. J. (1998). Stability and change of behavior in connection with bullying in schools: A two-year follow-up. *Aggressive Behavior, 24,* 205–218.

Smith, P. K., & Myron-Wilson, R. (1998). Parenting and school bullying. *Clinical Child Psychology and Psychiatry, 3,* 405–417.

Smokowski, P. R., & Kopasz, K. H. (2005). Bullying in school: An overview of types, effects, family characteristics, and intervention strategies. *Children in Schools, 27,* 101–110.

Stomfay-Stitz, A., & Wheeler, E. (2006). Welcome again to the peaceable classroom. *Childhood Education, 83,* 32E–33E.

Vaillancourt, T., Hymel, S., & McDougall, P. (2003). Bullying is power: Implications for school-based intervention strategies. *Journal of Applied School Psychology, 19,* 157–176.

Vaughan, W. (2002). Effects of cooperative learning on achievement and attitude among students of color. *The Journal of Educational Research, 95,* 359–364.

Vernberg, E. M., & Gamm, B. K. (2003). Resistance to violence prevention interventions in schools: Barriers and solutions. *Journal of Applied Psychoanalytic Studies, 5,* 125–138.

Warden, D., & Mackinnon, S. (2003). Prosocial children, bullies and victims: An investigation of their sociometric status, empathy and social problem-solving strategies. *British Journal of Developmental Psychology, 21,* 367–385.

Whitted, K. S., & Dupper, D. R. (2005). Best practices for preventing or reducing bullying in schools. *Children and Schools, 27,* 167–175.

Yoon, J. S. (2004). Predicting t*eacher* interventions in bullying situations. *Education and Treatment of Children, 27,* 37–45.

Yoon, J. S., & Kerber, K. (2003). Bullying. *Research in Education, 69,* 27–35.

39

School Bullying and the Case for the Method of Shared Concern

KEN RIGBY

Probably the most common way of responding to bullying in schools is to assert the importance of certain values or ideals that should govern interpersonal relationships between students. These include making statements about treating people as ends and not as means, that individuals are infinitely precious, and that they deserve respect and acceptance, whoever they are. Consistent with this approach, in 2005 the Australian Federal Government produced a list of values to be taught in Australian schools. Of these, some are concerned with interpersonal relations: Care and Compassion, Respect, Fair Go, Responsibility, Understanding, Tolerance, and Inclusion. Currently, there is no evidence that the teaching of such values has led to an improvement in interpersonal relationships among Australian students. In the United States it has been suggested that the key to the improvement in student relationships lies in the assertion of the value reflected in students bonding with the school (Cunningham, 2007). In Spain the value of convivencia has been seen as vital. This has been translated as including "a spirit of solidarity, fraternity, co-operation, harmony, a desire for mutual understanding and the desire to get on well with others" (Ortega, Del Rey, & Mora-Merchan, 2004, p. 169). The question seldom addressed by idealists is how can a program based upon recognition of such virtues be implemented.

Sometimes we come across programs that appear to be implementable, that is associated with a technology that might work. The best known are programs that begin by asking us to identify the kinds of behaviors that we want to stop and which can be reinforced negatively and incur punishment and those we would like to promote which can be reinforced positively and rewarded. This line of thinking has a long history, coming into prominence through the pioneering work of Watson in the 1920s, advanced further by Skinner in the 1950s. Essentially it underpins the proposals for countering school bullying promoted by Olweus (1994) and his numerous followers, more especially in the United States. Perhaps in its purest form we find it illustrated in a program implemented and evaluated in Oregon. Middle school students were taught appropriate social behaviors. They were commended and reinforced for observing these rules; certain mildly negative consequences were applied when rules were violated. Following a careful evaluation of outcomes, it was concluded that there were no significant reductions reported by students for physical or verbal attacks (Metzler, Biglan, & Rusby, 2001).

The limitations of an approach to stopping school bullying through staff members providing appropriate contingencies of reinforcement have become increasingly evident. For one thing, much bullying is, so to say, invisible (i.e., indirect or covert and hardly detectable). Most bullying does not come to the attention of teachers, however insistently schools exhort students to tell if they are being bullied. Hence a good deal of bullying cannot be negatively reinforced. Furthermore, it is often the case that teachers are unable to administer sufficiently effective reinforcers to control aberrant behavior. The satisfaction on the part of those who are able to dominate another student and the admiration that comes from a significant group of supporters may well outweigh the influence of school authorities who have quite limited means of punishing an offender. Given such dissatisfaction with the punitive approach of reducing bullying, many educators have sought to develop more effective ways in which the problem can be addressed.

Rightly, many educators have begun to stress the importance of promoting among students more positive relationships towards each other. There is evidence that children who are frequently involved in bully/victim problems at school tend to be deficient in co-operativeness (Rigby, Cox, & Black, 1997). It has been argued that this deficiency can be overcome by introducing co-operative learning in the classroom (Cowie, Smith, Boulton, & Laver, 1994). This can lead such students to realize that they can achieve their own personal ends more effectively if the work with others and maintain good relationships with them. The training of selected students as peer-supporters or befrienders to help others who are experiencing difficulties at school can also contribute to a more caring school environment (Menesini, Codecasa, & Benelli, 2003). Bystanders witnessing children who are being bullied can be trained to mediate effectively (see Rigby & Johnson, 2006; Rigby, 2008). Such strategies as these are being employed in some schools to improve student interpersonal relationships.

However, despite a range of thoughtful educational and preventive steps being taken to reduce bullying, it is known that what teachers do when cases of bullying come before them is quite often ineffective and sometimes counterproductive. According to students in England who have reported to teachers that they were being bullied, as many as 45% of them have claimed that the bullying did not diminish; in 16% of cases the bullying got worse (Smith & Shu, 2000). A similar study conducted in Australia revealed that outcomes were much less positive in secondary schools than in primary schools (Rigby & Barnes, 2002). As children become older, it becomes more and more difficult for teachers to help them if they are being bullied.

The question of what teachers should do when they are confronted with a case of bullying remains unresolved. To summarize: It is obvious that the assertion of values and ideals does not, of itself, provide the answer. The most widely used "technology," that of rewarding and punishing according to stipulated rules, in many cases makes little or no difference. Promoting pro-social behavior through cooperative leaning, the training of peer supporters, buddies and bystanders may have only a limited effect on how some students relate to each other. So what is the teacher or counselor to do when, despite such strategies being implemented, a child is being bullied and action needs to be taken by a school authority?

The Psychology of Children Who Bully

In order to tackle cases of bullying, we need to have a realistic conception of what the perpetrators are like. Views on what bullies are like vary a good deal, some being extremely simplistic and misguided. A common view is that they are vicious and hateful, lacking in social skills, low in self-esteem, lacking in empathy, cowardly, incapable of remorse, and needing to be controlled by the threat of punishment. The view of the bully as an unredeemable demon is easily discounted. Some children actually quit bullying others. Less obviously untrue is the view that those who bully lack social skills and are incapable of behaving appropriately, and therefore need to be instructed or skilled. While this may sometimes be so, a great deal of bullying, especially bullying of a subtle and indirect kind, demands a high level of social skill. The belief that bullies have low self-esteem is held by many teachers and other professional educators, but is, as a generalization, probably untrue, as many research studies have shown, e.g., Slee and Rigby (1993) and Callaghan and Joseph (1995). Seeking to reduce the motivation to bully others by bolstering up the bully by flattery is, as a rule, a quite mistaken strategy. Granted that the quality of empathy often appears to be low in bullies, especially in relation to the person being victimized, it is by no means absent and should not be assumed. Finally, we have seen that managing bullies exclusively through the use of punishment tends to be ineffective.

Arguably, when a teacher meets an individual child who has bullied someone, statistical generalizations about the nature of bullies derived from psychological studies are of limited value and in some cases likely to be misleading. It is better to think that under some circumstances any child may engage in bullying someone. Although some children appear to be more genetically predisposed to engage in bullying than others (see Ball et al., 2008), social, cultural, or peer group influences may actually incline children who are not so predisposed to engage in acts of bullying. This is to face facts; not to prepare one to excuse the child, but rather to make it possible for the teacher or counselor to understand the perspective of the individual child.

A further consideration is that the attitude the bully hold towards the child being bullied is unlikely to remain settled and always the same. It is likely to fluctuate according to mood and circumstances. This is true of all of us. As Ouspensky (1950) argued, it is best to consider each person as having a variable self-concept, or as he put it, to constitute a large number of "I" states which are activated selectively at different times. This is particularly true of adolescents. As Logan Pearsall Smith (1931) put it: Don't laugh at a youth for his affectation; he is only trying on one face after another to find a face of his own.

It is tempting to form a fixed impression of the villainous bully before us and to believe that we have him or her summed up. However perspicacious we may be, this is rarely the case, if only because he or she may be constantly changing. Perhaps the most important factor to such change is the presence, physically present or imagined, of the bully's friendship or support group. We are prone to see, erroneously, the bully as a detached individual, rather than one who is part of a group that helps to form and maintain his identity. To understand the bully one must strive to understand that person's relationship with significant others—friends, the more distant peer-group, family, community and school; for to a large extent it is their influence that accounts for what he or she thinks and does. Notice though that the bully is influenced by what he or she conceives as the expectations of others; not necessarily what others actually believe. Many people suffer what has been termed "pluralistic ignorance" that is they attribute to others beliefs that they do not really have (Miller, 1987) and are influenced by these false norms. To understand anyone, including the bully, we need to know what he or she believes others think.

It can be misleading to think that children who engage in bullying cease to do so for a single reason. In fact motives may be mixed. Commonly it is assumed that students quit bullying because they have been forced to comply, especially when the perceived negative consequences of continuing outweigh any positives. The process of compliance may, of course, be involved in changes in behavior as Kelman (1958) clearly demonstrated as occurring under conditions of close surveillance; however, this is commonly difficult to achieve in the school environment. A further process may occur: that of identification with another person whose attitudes and/or behavior preclude one acting as a bully. Thus a child whose empathy has been aroused by a recognition of the plight of a victim may feel unable to continue to bully that person. Alternatively, that child may identify strongly with a person he or she greatly admires who is acting in a way to support victims. The moratorium on bullying may last as long as the admiration lasts. Finally, a child may stop bullying because he or she has internalized values that are incompatible with bullying, such as tolerance and acceptance of differences in others.

Relating to Children Who Bully

One may distinguish several ways in which one confronts the child who has bullied. For generations the most common way is to investigate what has happened, apportion blame and guilt and deliver a stern judgment and an appropriate sentence. It is still not uncommon to see teachers trying to dominate and intimidate children who bully others so that they dare not continue to do so. That approach is sometimes commended on the mistaken grounds that it is expeditious and generally effective. As we have seen, it is often not effective, especially with older students, and is likely to require considerable surveillance of those punished and sometimes repeated and time consuming meetings. A second way is to convey to the bully that he or she has done something wrong and elicit an admission to that effect and insist upon some form of restitution, for example an apology or reparation to whatever has been damaged. It is emphasized that the aim of the interaction here is to restore damaged relationships rather than to inflict any suffering on the part of the bully. This so-called restorative justice approach seems to me an advance of the traditional approach. However, it is typically the case that the admission of guilt and associated feelings of shame is deliberately induced by the teacher and may not be genuine or sustained. Although the teacher commonly does not intend a punishment, it may be conceived as such by the recipient. Above all, the teacher has not in any real sense met with the bully and has failed to gain an understanding of the forces that are motivating the behavior.

Listening

Teachers and instructors are programmed, to a large extent, to tell others what they should know and what they must do. Unfortunately, this orientation acts so as to prevent understanding, a necessary prerequisite to helping someone, for instance to help a child to stop being a bully. Long ago the 19th century existential writer Kierkegaard (Bretall, 1973, pp. 333–334) said what was needed if we want to help anyone.

> If real success is to attend the effort to bring a man [or boy] to a definite position, one must first of all take pains to find him where he is and begin there.

This is rarely done. The starting point with the bully is typically "Look, see what you have done wrong! What are you going to do about it?" Kierkegaard goes on:

> In order to help another effectively I must understand more than he—yet first of all surely I must understand what he understands. If I do not know that, my greater understanding will be of no help to him. If however, I am disposed to plume myself on my greater understanding it is because I am vain or proud, so that at bottom, instead of benefitting him, I want to be admired. But all true effort to help begins with self-humiliation: the helper must first humble himself under him he would help, and therewith must understand that to help does not mean to be sovereign but to be a servant, that to help does not mean to be ambitious but to be patient, that to help means to endure for the time being the imputation that one is in the wrong and does not understand what the other understands.

Finally the writer turns to the case of someone who is angry and is really in the wrong—the typical bully.

> Take the case of a man [or child] who is passionately angry, and let us assume that he really is in the wrong. Unless you can begin with him by making it seem as if it were he that had to instruct you, and unless you can do it in such a way that the angry man, who was too impatient to listen to a word of yours, is glad to discover in you a complaisant and attentive listener—if you cannot do that, you cannot help him at all.

It must be emphasized that the aim of the teacher is not to find reasons for excusing the bully, but rather that unless the art of listening is practiced in the course of talking with a bully the teacher will not be dealing with the actual person before him, but rather with an abstraction that bears little relation to reality.

A Technology to Deal with School Bullying: The Method of Shared Concern

A technology that is consistent with the assumptions outlined above about the nature of children who bully and the probable effects of alternative approaches is the Method of Shared Concern. This method originated in the work of Anatol Pikas (1989, 2002). Further explanations of the method can be found in Smith and Sharp (1994) and in Rigby (2002, 2005).

In summary, the Method of Shared Concern operates as follows. A case of bullying is identified as one of intermediate severity, that is, one that is not regarded as relatively mild, nor one that is viewed as involving serious or criminal behavior. On the basis of reports and/or direct observations of student bullying behavior, a number of students who are believed to have participated in the bullying are interviewed individually by the practitioner of the method, commonly the school counselor or psychologist.. The practitioner shares his or her concern over the reported distress of the target of the bullying and invites the interviewee to describe what he or she knows or has noticed about the situation. Importantly, no accusations are made. Once some knowledge of the situation has been acknowledged, attention turns to what can be done to help the person who has become distressed. Suggestions are elicited and warmly received by the interviewer. A further meeting is arranged to monitor what happens. The target of the bullying is subsequently interviewed and informed about what has been happening. The practitioner listens carefully and supportively to the victim's account, noting whether he or she has in any way provoked the conflict. Further individual meetings with the suspected bullies are conducted to ascertain progress. When the practitioner is satisfied that sufficient progress has been paid, a group meeting is convened with the suspected bullies. They are complimented for their positive actions and prepared for a final meeting involving the person they have bullied. With their approval, the student who has been bullied is invited to a final meeting with others to bring about a final solution to end the bullying.

An Illustration of the Method

The following is an account of the application of the method in a hypothetical case in which someone (we will call him Tom) is being bullied by several boys. This account includes some comments and observations on the process.

> It had become apparent to a practitioner of the method that an adolescent student, Tom, was being bullied and a number of students had been identified as probably involved as perpetrators or as bystanders. It was thought that they could help in resolving the problem.

Each of the students was interviewed in turn, starting with the student who was thought to be the ringleader. The meetings took place in private where there could be no interruptions. To maintain good contact and to allay any suspicions, no notes were taken during the interview.

Practitioner (P): I understand that Tom has been having a hard time of it lately and I am quite concerned about him. [P went on to explain why she thought that this was so; then asked the student directly: I wonder what you have noticed? There was not the slightest suggestion of an accusation].

Student (S): [Long pause—P can wait !] He's mostly on his own. Seems a bit down these days. [There may sometimes be a flat denial of there being anything at all wrong with Tom. It this happens, P must start exploring the circumstances or situations in which S sees Tom, how he is getting on with Tom and how they usually interact together. Commonly S will reveal that things aren't so good between them—and that the victim, in this case Tom, could in fact feel unhappy about what has been happening to him. Importantly this should emerge naturally in the course of the interview and not a result of pressure being applied.]

P: It mustn't feel too good, being Tom.

S: I suppose so. [S may go on to justify his/her actions in relation to Tom—in which case P simply listens]

Once there was an acknowledgement of Tom's plight, P moved on to the next stage. (Co-operation with S is likely to be better if it is made clear that the practitioner is not out to punish anyone.)

P: I am wondering what you and I can do to make things a bit better for Tom.

S: [Long pause] Well, I guess I could chat with him and ask him how he is … [Pause] Maybe I could have a word with one of my mates who has been teasing him a bit—makes him a bit miserable at times. [Often at this stage the S will not personally acknowledge bullying anyone—and should not be pushed to do so]

P: [Enthusiastically—not grudgingly] That would be excellent. I will be talking to some other students who may also be able to help. And I would like to talk with you again to see how things go with Tom [An appointment was made to see the student again one or two days later]

Some Variations

Of course, the interaction may take a different turn. For instance, the suspected bully may deny knowledge of Tom's distress or refuse to discuss his relationship with Tom This may be due to genuine ignorance, or, more commonly, a reluctance to cooperate, even after it is made clear that no punishment is intended. On occasions one may need to repeat one's concern and say: Well, it seems like you don't want to talk about it today. We will talk later. And one must arrange do so.

Sometimes the student may expressly deny any personal involvement and say somebody else is upsetting Tom. One might say: Well, you have some influence with X (the other person). I wonder if you could have a word with him. I guess he would listen to what you might say.

In some cases, the student may question how he or she has been chosen to be interviewed. Here the P needs to make it clear to S that the choice was *not* based on what the Tom had disclosed, but rather because it was thought that he or she, knowing Tom, would be able to provide more relevant information and help to solve the problem.

Subsequently each member of the group of students who were thought to be involved in the bullying was interviewed along the same lines.

Interview with Victim   The victim was seen *after* all the suspected bullies had been interviewed. It is essential that the interviewer begins by expressing concern, sympathy and support over what has been happening. The victim is typically reluctant to make any accusations against the bullies because that could lead to them treating him or her even worse. This reluctance can be overcome once the victim understands that nobody will be punished. Questions need to be asked to find out whether the victim has been doing anything to bring on the bullying—that is by acting as *a provocative victim*. But, as before, no blame should be directed at the student. The interviewer discloses that he or she has actually talked with the bullies individually and that each of them agreed to cooperate.

Further Meetings with Individual Bullies   As previously arranged, meetings were carried out to ascertain progress. When P was satisfied that progress had been made, a further meeting was arranged with the group of suspected bullies.

The Meeting with the Whole Group   At this meeting it was possible to (a) compliment the members on the progress that has been made and (b) to respond to a suggestion from members of the group that *the* victim be invited to join them for a final meeting. (If this had **not** happened, P would have made the suggestion.) It was intended that this final meeting would resolve the problem with the students' active cooperation. Reassurances were elicited from group members that they would act positively towards the victim at that meeting.

Further Meeting with the Victim   Tom was invited to join the group for a final meeting, with assurances that there would be no unpleasantness at the meeting and that the group would be working towards resolving the problem. (The victim should never be forced to come to such a meeting but will do so if a trusting relationship has been developed with the practitioner.)

Final Group Meeting   At this meeting the conflict was finally resolved and each member of the group recognized that this had been achieved. (Notice that sometimes at this final meeting, P needs to facilitate adjustments in the behavior of *both sides*, especially if it is thought that the victim has behaved provocatively. In short, P must play the role of mediator and help (not force) the students to reach an agreement—sometimes, if warranted, in writing and as a contract—about how they will treat each other in the future).

Assumptions Underlying the Method

The application of the Method of Shared Concern makes a number of assumptions which are thought to justify this approach.

1. Children who bully are similar to other children in having fluid views on the significance of what they are doing. At different times and in different situations, bullying someone may be viewed by students in quite different ways; for instance, as justified because the victim was "asking for it" or as an act of cruelty, as a fun or as something that is seriously wrong. In the course of a therapeutic interview, one can help children to reflect on what they are thinking and doing in a more stable, realistic, and socially desirable way.
2. Children who bully can be influenced more readily in a one-to-one encounter with a practitioner of the method. When members of the child's group are physically present, the

pressure to conform to the perceived norms of their group is difficult for them to resist. The method therefore begins with one to one interviews with individual members of a group who are thought to be involved in the bullying or to have an understanding of what has been happening.

3. When students are accused of bullying they typically become defensive and are unable or unwilling to think constructively. Consistent with the need to understand the perspective of the interviewees, no accusations are made by the practitioner. After conveying a sincere concern for the well-being of a student who has become the target of bullying, the practitioner's role is to listen non-judgmentally.

4. Punishment or the threat of punishment is unlikely to produce a comprehensive and lasting solution. The desire to continue the bullying often remains and the bullying is carried out in subtle and indirect ways that are very difficult to monitor. Shared Concern aims at producing an agreed and enduring. solution to the problem

5. Students are rarely devoid of empathy, even those who engage in acts of bullying. Assuming some, albeit possibly limited potential for empathy on the part of the interviewee, the practitioner focuses upon the distressing condition of the person being targeted, and looks for—and generally receives—an acknowledgement of that person's plight.

6. Students have internal conflicts about what they are doing. Not uncommonly, students involved in bullying feel at times uncomfortable, experiencing pressure from their friends to conform to group norms by engaging in or supporting the bullying. Helping students to see where their best interest lies can occur in the course of an interview.

7. When a person's distress is acknowledged, there is a natural reaction to want to see it overcome Attention then turns to how the practitioner and the interviewee can work together to alleviate the distress. Suggestions are commonly forthcoming and can be reinforced.

8. Reluctance to help may persist if it is thought the person being targeted has informed against the group. Hence it is important to avoid this happening by collecting information about what has happened without seeing the victim first. (The victim is seen later to further clarify the situation.)

9. Convincing evidence of actual helpful behavior on the part of those who have been interviewed is needed before progress can be acknowledged. The situation must be carefully monitored. Once progress has clearly been made a group meeting can be convened.

10. Bullying occurs mainly in a group context and is sustained through the influence of the group. Consistent with the need to involve the group of students in reaching an agreed solution, group meetings are held, first with the suspected perpetrators and then with all the students including the victim.

11. Positive reinforcement is commonly more effective than punishment as well as being more socially acceptable. The giving of reinforcement of actions that are positive, that is involving constructive action directed towards the cessation of the bullying, can encourage students further to reach an agreed and enduring solution.

12. Conflicts commonly require adjustments in the behavior of all parties. A mediated solution to the problem is often necessary to remove any bases for the resumption of the bullying. Once agreement has been reached by the entire group regarding future conduct, the bullying is likely to cease.

Evaluating the Method

As we have seen, the Method of Shared Concern makes significant assumptions about the nature of bullies and the consequences of treating children involved in bullying in a particular way.

This is also true of other approaches. For instance, disciplinary methods which apply punishment or consequences assume that children who are treated in this way will be less likely to continue bullying others. Restorative Justice assumes that once children can be induced to feel ashamed of their behavior and say they are sorry for what they have done the bullying will cease. No conclusive evidence has been provided to support either of these propositions. By contrast, applications of Shared Concern have been evaluated in two studies in the United Kingdom and shown to have been effective in the treatment of most, if not all cases (Smith & Sharp, 1994; Duncan, 1996). The approach has been incorporated in a number of programs that have significantly reduced bullying in selected schools in Australia, Spain (Ortega & Lera, 2000), and Finland (Salmivalli, Kaukiainen, Voetin, & Sinasammal, 2004). Nevertheless, more research is needed. I am currently evaluating the effectiveness of the method in 20 schools in Australia in a project supported by the Australian Federal Government.

Implications for School Practice

There has been accumulating evidence, cited above, that the Method of Shared Concern has been used effectively in dealing with cases of bullying in schools. However, certain conditions that should be met before the method is employed (see Table 39.1 for a summary of implications for practice).

First, the practitioner should be thoroughly conversant with the procedures involved in implementing the method. Because the notion of sharing one's concern about a problem is intuitively appealing to many teachers and counselors, it is sometimes assumed that little more than such sharing is required. In fact, a great deal more needs to be done. The steps taken in implementing the method follow a logical sequence and some training is needed. Ideally, this should be acquired through those that have received instruction from trainers who have successful used the method in schools. A number of such trainers have received appropriate training from the originator of the Method of Shared Concern, Anatol Pikas, or from those trained by him in workshops conducted for instance, in Sweden, England, and Australia. A useful DVD and booklet providing training in a version of the Method of Shared Concern is now available (Readymade Productions, 2005).

Basic to the method is that attitude of the practitioner. If the practitioner is angry and prone to act vindictively, the method cannot be successfully applied. Uppermost must be a feeling of genuine concern for the victim and a desire to convey that concern. This must be clearly conveyed. At the same time, the suspected bully must be listened to as a person whose perception of the situation needs to be understood and not condemned. The practitioner must resist any impulses to be judgmental and be prepared to mediate between the students to reach an acceptable solution.

Although some variations in how the method is implemented will inevitably occur between practitioners, there are some clear limitations on what can be incorporated into the method and remain consistent with the approach. Most obviously, accusing students of having bullied someone or stating that he or she has behaved inappropriately is contrary to its basic rationale. Any threats as to what will happen to the student suspected of bullying someone if he or she does not desist is counterproductive.

It follows that bullying of a kind that the school believes *must* be punished cannot be dealt with using the Method of Shared Concern. Bullying that involves extreme or repeated acts of violence or criminal behavior will normally require a punitive response. Judgments may, of course, differ as to where the line should be drawn between acts of bullying which must incur penalties or sanctions and acts of bullying which do not necessarily do so. Before the Method of

Shared Concern can be used, a broad consensus is needed among a school staff on the circumstances that justify its use. If the application of the method fails to result in the victim becoming safe from peer abuse, a more disciplinary approach is required.

It is a requirement that, as far as possible, information about the bullying should not be obtained directly from the victim. This is to prevent the victim being further victimized for having informed on fellow students. It follows that a school using the Method should be highly sensitive to what is happening between students. Careful surveillance of student behavior is needed. In addition, it is suggested that students be invited to talk confidentially to staff when they believe that a particular student is having a hard time with peers and needs help. This is more likely to happen in schools where peer support groups are formed and utilized (Rigby, 2007) or anti-bullying committees of students are instituted and, most importantly, it is understood that helping a student will not lead to anyone being punished.

Adopting the Method of Shared Concern does not imply that other ways of helping students can be neglected. Highly compatible with the method is the use of Quality Circles (Sharp, 1996). This involves a series of meetings of students convened by a teacher to enable students to raise and explore issues that concern them, individually and collectively and to research and suggest ways in which problems may be overcome. Class activities that aim at developing pro-social attitudes, conflict resolution skills and assertiveness, as opposed to either aggressive or submissive behavior, can also help, especially when students meet in the final stage of the application of the method to work out an enduring solution to the conflict.

The Method of Shared Concern should be viewed essentially as a means by which students can solve a problem of peer relations that is causing distress to one of their members. It is an educational, problem-solving activity. Since no accusations are being made, the school can legitimately promote this activity without requiring parental approval. Nevertheless, parental involvement over cases may occur, especially if the issue of bullying is brought to the attention of the school by a parent or if the nature of the bullying is so severe that parental involvement is required.

In some cases of bullying, parents are understandably angry about how their child has been treated by peers at school and may demand that the offenders be punished. How the school responds will depend upon its agreed policy and will usually take into account a number of factors, including the severity and repetitiveness of the bullying. Where it is thought that the Method of Shared Concern is appropriate, the question may be raised with the parents as to whether they would prefer to have the perpetrators punished or the child be safe from further bullying. Parents commonly prefer the latter and can usually see that punishment may fail to achieve that end. They need nevertheless to be convinced that the method will lead to a genuine agreement being reached among the perpetrators and that the bullying will cease and their child will be safe. Hence using the Method of Shared Concern implies a role for teachers in educating parents about the nature and efficacy of the approach.

It follows that the school adopting the method should be up front about that adoption. Its nature and rationale need to be explained. It should be made clear that it is an educational, problem-solving approach that will be used under certain clearly defined circumstances. Meetings with parents should be convened to discuss the approach and appropriate literature distributed.

The school must be prepared to allocate the necessary resources for the application of the method. This should include time for the training of potential practitioners and a discussion of the approach with the rest of the school staff. There needs to be general support for the use of the method under agreed conditions. In allocating resources the time taken for its application must be taken into account, bearing in mind that a series of meetings with the relevant students will

Table 39.1 Implications for Practice: Conditions That Should Be Met Before the Method of Shared Concern is Employed (Discussed in detail within the Chapter)

- Practitioners must fully understand the procedures involved in implementing the Method. *The steps taken in implementing the Method follow a logical sequence and some training is needed. A training DVD for the Method of Shared Concern is available (see www.readymade.com.au/method).*
- The attitude of the practitioner is important. *It is essential that a feeling of genuine concern for the victim is conveyed and the suspected bully must be listened to as a person whose perception of the situation needs to be understood and not condemned.*
- There are clear limitations on what can be incorporated into the method and remain consistent with the approach. *For instance, accusations of bullying or or stating that a student has behaved 'inappropriately' is contrary to its basic rationale.*
- Bullying that the school believes *must* be punished cannot be dealt with using the Method of Shared Concern. *Consensus is needed among a school staff on the circumstances when the method will be used.*
- As much as possible, information about the bullying should not be obtained directly from the victim. *This is important to prevent the victim being further victimised for having informed on fellow students.*
- Adopting the Method of Shared Concern does not imply that other ways of helping students can be neglected. *Class activities to develop pro-social attitudes, conflict resolution skills and assertiveness, can be helpful.*
- The Method of Shared Concern should be viewed as a means by which students can solve a problem of peer relations. *It is an educational, problem-solving activity.*
- The Method of Shared Concern implies a role for teachers in educating parents about the nature and efficacy of the approach. *Parents may be angry about how their child has been treated by peers at school and may demand that the offenders be punished, however, some parents may understand that the Method will lead to a genuine agreement being reached among the perpetrators and that the bullying will cease and their child will be safe.*
- Schools adopting the method should be 'up front' about its adoption of the Method of Shared Concern. *It must be made clear that it is an educational, problem-solving approach that will be used under certain clearly defined circumstances.*
- The school must be prepared to allocate the necessary resources for the application of the Method. *The time for training, application, and evaluation of outcomes must be taken into account.*

be required. Outcomes from the use of the method should be periodically assessed. These should include the extent to which the primary aim of the intervention has been successful, namely the cessation of the bullying and the sense of safety on the part of the person who was victimized.

References

Australian Commonwealth Government. (2005). *National Framework for Values Education in Australian Schools.* Canberra: Australian Commonwealth Government.

Ball, H. A, Arseneault, L., Taylor,A., Maughan,B., Caspi, A., & Moffitt, T.E. (2008). Genetic and environmental influences on victims, bullies and bully-victims in childhood. *Journal of Child Psychology and Psychiatry, 49,* 104–111.

Bretall, R. (Ed). (1973). *A Kierkegaard anthology* (R. Bretall, Trans.). Princeton, NJ: Princeton University Press.

Callaghan, S., & Joseph, S. (1995). Self-concept and peer victimisation among school children. *Personality and Individual Differences, 18,* 161–163.

Cowie, H, Smith, P., Boulton, M., & Laver, R. (1994). *Cooperation in the multi-ethnic classroom.* London: David Fulton.

Cunningham, J. (2007). Level of bonding to school and perception of the school environment by bullies, victims, and bully victims. *The Journal of Early Adolescence, 27,* 457–478.

Duncan, A. (1996). The shared concern method of resolving group bullying in schools. *Educational Psychology in Practice, 12*(2), 94–98.

Kelman, H. C. (1958) Compliance, identification, and internalization: Three processes of attitude change. *Journal of Conflict Resolution, 2,* 51–60.

Menesini, E., Codecasa, E., & Benelli, B. (2003). Added Enhancing children's responsibility to take action against bullying: Evaluation of a befriending intervention in Italian middle schools. *Aggressive Behavior,* 10–14.

Metzler, C. W., Biglan, A., & Rusby, J. C. (2001). Evaluation of a comprehensive behavior management program to improve school-wide positive behavioral support. *Education and Treatment of Children, 24,* 448–479.

Miller, D. T. (1987). Pluralistic ignorance: When similarity is interpreted as dissimilarity. *Journal of Personality and Social Psychology, 53*(2), 541–550.

Olweus, D. (1994). *Bullying in schools.* Boston: Blackwell.

Ortega, R., Del Rey, R., & Mora-Merchan, J. A. (2004). SAVE Model: An antibullying intervention in Spain. In P. K. Smith, D. Pepler, & K. Rigby (Eds.), *Bullying in schools: How successful can interventions be?* (pp. 167–186). Cambridge, UK: Cambridge University Press.

Ortega, R., & Lera, M. J. (2000). Seville anti-bullying school project. *Aggressive Behaviour, 26,* 113–123.

Ouspensky, P. (1950). *The psychology of man's possible evolution.*New York: Hedgehog Press.

Pikas, A. (1989). The Common Concern Method for the treatment of mobbing. In E. Roland & E. Munthe (Eds.), *Bullying: an international perspective* (pp. 91–104). London: David Fulton in association with the Professional Development Foundation.

Pikas, A. (2002). New developments in Shared Concern Method. *School Psychology International, 23*(3), 307–326.

Readymade Productions. (2005). The Method of Shared Concern: A staff training resource for schools. Retrieved from http://www.readymade.com.au/method

Rigby, K. (2005). The Method of Shared Concern as an intervention technique to address bullying in schools: An overview and appraisal. *Australian Journal of Counselling and Guidance, 15,* 27–34.

Rigby, K. (2007). *Bullying in schools and what to do about it* (rev. ed.). Melbourne, Australia: ACER.

Rigby, K (2008). *Children and bullying: How parents and teachers can reduce bullying in schools.* Boston: Blackwell-Wiley.

Rigby, K., & Barnes, A. (2002). To tell or not to tell: the victimised student's dilemma. *Youth Studies, Australia, 21*(3), 33–36.

Rigby, K., Cox, I. K., & Black, G. (1997). Cooperativeness and bully/victim problems among Australian schoolchildren. *Journal of Social Psychology, 137*(3), 357–368.

Rigby, K., & Johnson, B. (2006). Expressed readiness of Australian school children to act as bystanders in support of children who are being bullied. *Educational Psychology, 26,* 425–440.

Salmivalli, C., Kaukiainen, A., Voetin, M., & Sinasammal, M. (2004). Targeting the group as a whole: The Finish anti-bullying intervention. In P. K. Smith, D. Pepler, & K. Rigby (Eds.), *Bullying in schools: How successful can interventions be?* (pp. 251–275). Cambridge, UK: Cambridge University Press.

Sharp, S. (1996). The role of peers in tackling bullying in schools. *Educational Psychology in Practice, 11,* 17–22.

Slee, P. T,. & Rigby, K. (1993). The relationship of Eysenck's personality factors and self-esteem to bully/victim behaviour in Australian school boys. *Personality and Individual Differences, 14,* 371–373.

Smith, L. P. (1931). *Afterthoughts.* London: Constable and Company.

Smith, P. K., & Shu, S. (2000). *What good schools can do about bullying. Childhood, 7,* 193–212.

Smith, P. K., & Sharp, S. (Eds.).(1994). *School bullying: Insights and perspectives.* London: Routledge.

40

Sustainability of Bullying Intervention and Prevention Programs

AMY PLOG, LAWRENCE EPSTEIN, KATHRYN JENS, AND WILLIAM PORTER

Introduction

Throughout this book, it is clear that considerable effort has gone into bullying prevention research and program development around the world. The mere existence of effective bullying prevention programs, however, is not sufficient for ensuring positive outcomes. Once such programs have been developed, the next step is for them to be put into practice and sustained over time. This can prove difficult given that in schools interventions are often implemented reactively; "programs du jour" are a potential response to the frequently changing behavioral and academic priorities with which schools are entrusted. This is particularly problematic given that research (e.g., Limber & Nation, 1991; Roland, 2000; Whitney, Rivers, Smith, & Sharp, 1994) has shown that the longer and more thoroughly a bullying prevention program is employed, the more likely are positive changes in student behavior and school climate.

The authors of this chapter were involved in the development of the Bully-Proofing Your School (BPYS) program. Observations following trainings in schools across the country revealed a great deal of variation in the degree of fidelity with which each school implemented the program and with the schools' ability to sustain the program over time. Some schools put BPYS into practice and were still using it enthusiastically five years after they had started. Other schools successfully started the program, but had staff changes and then stopped using it, while others never fully put the program into action. From these experiences and a review of research on variables related to successful implementation of prevention programs, the four-stage model presented below was developed. Based on this research, it appears that the variability with which schools were observed to implement BPYS is not unique to this particular program, or to implementation of bullying prevention programs in general. Rather, these factors can be said to guide any preventive intervention in schools, regardless of the content of that program.

While the term "implementation" has been used more generally above, the following chapter breaks down implementation into a four-stage model. The model begins with the Pre-implementation stage and factors that occur prior to intervention efforts. The second stage is the Program Selection stage, with a focus on characteristics of the program to be chosen that might impact successful outcome. Stage 3, the Implementation phase, encompasses the steps necessary for high-quality implementation of the intervention. Finally, Stage 4, the Sustained

Implementation phase, includes factors that are important for ensuring that the intervention continues over time.

Bully prevention programs are only as effective as the manner in which they are implemented. Effective implementation is dependent not only on the program itself, but also on consideration of variables such as staff, time, and financial resources. There are no known training materials that will achieve their goals in the absence of committed staff with adequate resources and administrative support (McGuire, 2001). These circumstances, though, are likely to be the exception rather than the rule (Forgatch, 2003). Further, under those conditions, one could argue that the need for intervention itself is minimized; instead, "it is precisely those schools whose populations are most in need of prevention and intervention services that are least able to provide those services" (Gottfredson, 1997). Given this, the goal of the current model is to delineate the critical factors for successful implementation given the limited resources with which schools often must operate. It should be noted that others have also suggested multiple phase models of intervention (see, for example, Graczyk, Domitrovitch, Small, and Zins, 2006, or the National Implementation Research Network website). The current model is a merger of this research and the authors' experience with implementation of BPYS in schools.

Stage 1: Pre-Implementation

The pre-implementation phase includes largely systemic factors that warrant consideration prior to selection or execution of a particular intervention. As Elliott and colleagues (2003) stated, the adoption of evidence based interventions in schools requires attention to the context of schools. Specific pre-implementation factors include:

- Administrative support
- Staff buy-in
- Needs assessment
- School-wide discipline/academic plan

One of the most universally discussed contextual factors that needs to be present if an intervention is to be successful is *administrative support* (Elliott, 2006; Gottfredson & Gottfredson, 2002; Kam, Greenberg, & Walls, 2003). In a school, the support of the principal is thought to be important for many reasons. Specifically, principals control the resources (e.g., money, staff, time; Elias, Zins, Graczyk, & Weissberg, 2003), their attitudes can influence the staff's likelihood to support the intervention, and they serve encouraging and monitoring roles (Han & Weiss, 2005). A second level of administrative support is from district-level administration. Though it is certainly beneficial for school boards and superintendents to support the intervention, it is our experience that, due to schools' desire for site-based control, district "mandates" can prove ineffective. When "support" from administration is seen as coercive and directive, it may be more difficult to adequately achieve the second goal of the pre-implementation phase.

The second component of the pre-implementation phase is *staff buy-in*. The crucial nature of staff ownership, consensus, and support of stakeholders are all discussed in the prevention literature (D'Andrea, 2004; Elias et al., 2003; Fixsen, Naoom, Blase, Friedman, & Wallace, 2005; Weissberg, 2004). Despite the importance of having teachers in a school lend their support prior to beginning an intervention, teachers might be resistant to change (Elias et al., 2003; Elliott, Kratochwill, & Roach, 2003). Fortunately, research also suggests factors that are linked to greater acceptance of a new intervention (Flannery et al., 2003; Gottfredson, 1997; Han & Weiss, 2005; Kallstead & Olweus, 2003; Rogers, 2003). These include the severity of the problem such that the more severe the problem, the more likely teachers will support intervention; the characteristics of the proposed intervention itself, for example the length and complexity of the program; teacher familiarity with the program's underlying principles; teacher perceptions of competency in the role they will play in the intervention; and general staff morale. Based on our observation of the schools with which we have worked, a final factor that can increase the potential for teacher buy-in is the extent to which teachers perceive that the intervention will make their job easier and/or help them be more successful.

The next pre-implementation factor, a *needs assessment*, can provide information that leads to staff "buy-in." Data can be used to clearly identify the problem and help demonstrate that intervention is necessary (Kallstead & Olweus, 2003; Promising Practices Network [PPN], 2004). Needs assessment is also important to identify measurable targets for change. As Fixsen and colleagues (2005) note, the needs and strengths of a community must be known before an attempt is made to implement an innovation (Fixsen et al., 2005). Data from the needs assessment can also be used to more effectively guide the intervention.

The last component of pre-implementation is a *school-wide discipline/academic plan*. A clear, consistent plan for what is taught and how learning is evaluated is important. Additionally, expectations for student behavior, acknowledgments and celebrations of pro-social behavior, and consequences for behavioral violations should be formally delineated. Visible and directly-stated discipline and academic plans provide organizational stability, which is said to be a factor in high-quality program implementation (Elliott, 2006).

Stage 2: Program Selection

The program selection phase considers characteristics of the program itself that have been linked to successful outcome. Generally, the more clearly core (essential/ indispensable) elements are defined, the more readily the intervention can be successfully put into practice (Fixsen et al., 2005). Related to this, standardization of methods and materials improves the quality of implementation (Elliott, 2006; Gottfredson & Gottfredson, 2002). In addition to these general considerations, specific characteristics of successful prevention programs that are factors in this stage include:

- Preventive, theory and evidence based
- Developmentally appropriate and engaging
- System-wide
- Adaptable
- Connected to goals /mission of school

Effective programs need to be *preventive*. By definition, prevention programs have maximum impact when they occur at an age before children struggle with the issue (Greenberg et al., 2003; Leadbeater, Hoglund, & Woods, 2003; Nation et al., 2003). In addition, good programs are *theory and evidence based*. Effective programs have scientific justification and a sound theoretical rationale (Elliott, 2006; Nation et al., 2003). For example, bullying research has consistently demonstrated the importance of peer observers in the dynamic of bullying behavior (Cowie, 2000; O'Connell, Pepler, & Craig, 1999; Orpinas, Horne, & Staniszewski, 2003; Stevens, Van Oost, & De Bourdeaudhuij, 2000). Successful bullying prevention program, therefore, would include a component to impact peer observers. A program's basis in theory alone is not sufficient; theoretical soundness must be matched with evidence that the program impacts the variables it is designed to impact. Clearly, whenever possible, it is preferable to implement programs with empirical support (Elliott, 2006).

A second factor for consideration in selecting a program is whether it is *developmentally appropriate and engaging.* Effective prevention programming is age specific and culturally appropriate (Weissberg, 2004). Programs that cover a wide age range should have different materials and curriculum for each level with developmentally appropriate language and concepts. For example, children have been found to be less likely to report bullying to an adult as they progress into adolescence (Newman, Murray, & Lussier, 2001; Whitney & Smith, 1993). While encouraging younger students to tell an adult when they experience bullying might be a successful strategy, with older students a more successful strategy might be to involve peers in the bullying intervention because older students are more likely to go to their peers than adults for help (Peterson & Rigby, 1999). It is important that materials be culturally sensitive and relevant. For example, inner city students will have difficulty relating to a curriculum with scenarios and photos of exclusively suburban students. Regardless of the program content, sound programs use varied, engaging, interactive instructional approaches that allow for application of skills (Elias et al., 2003; Greenberg et al., 2003; Nation et al., 2003).

Choosing a program that is *system-wide* is the third program selection recommendation. Skill building interventions have been found to be more effective when they are accompanied by environmental change (Elliott, 2006; Gottfredson, 1997; Greenberg et al., 2003; Weissberg, 2004). Environmental change can be achieved through coordination of the intervention with interventions already in place and through attention to the context in which the intervention will occur, with efforts such as training teachers, clarifying rules (or what not to do), and posting expectations (what to do) throughout the school. System-wide interventions also involve parents, all school staff, and the community in intervention. Inclusion of all key members of the school community has been noted to be part of effective programming (Greenberg et al., 2003).

The fourth factor in program selection is *program adaptability.* Programs need to address the unique needs of a school. Adaptation of an intervention to the needs of the community requires balance with assurance of treatment integrity (Elias et al., 2003; Elliott, 2006; Nation et al., 2003; Weissberg, 2004; Weisz, Sandler, Durlak, & Anton, 2005). For fidelity of implementation, one must stick to core components of the selected program. Knowing the conditions under which the intervention works and with which populations allows for strategic planning of adaptations. Examples of potentially important adaptations are translation of materials into another language in a community with many non-English speakers or emphasis on relational aggression in an all-girls school given the significance of this form of bullying with girls (Crick & Bigbee, 1998).

The fifth and final factor for this stage is that the intervention should be *connected to goals/ mission of the school.* Effective interventions are linked to the goals of the district, school improvement efforts, and existing curriculum (Elias et al., 2003; Han & Weiss, 2005; Leadbeater et al., 2003). Because the primary mission of schools is academic learning, it will be important that a program, directly or indirectly, be linked to improved academics. In the absence of direct evidence of this, it might be helpful to highlight the growing body of research that demonstrates the connection between social emotional learning and academics (Graczyk et al., 2000; Weissberg, 2004). Programs that have clear goals and goals that are stated in observable/measurable terms will be best for matching to a school's goals. Clarity of these goals is also important so that schools can hold the program accountable for the anticipated changes. Consideration of all of these factors is important in the selection of a prevention program that is likely to be effective.

Stage 3: Implementation

Once pre-implementation factors have been addressed and the program has been selected, the intervention can begin. As mentioned previously, school personnel often tire of implementing fad programs and become skeptical when they are asked to initiate the latest in a long line of prevention programs that are seen as unsuccessful. Programs can appear ineffective and be prematurely abandoned not because the intervention itself is ineffective, but rather because school personnel failed to proactively address situational factors that could maximize the potential for success. A combination of experience and research has identified several such factors necessary for successful program implementation. Those factors include:

- Program champion/cadre
- Long-term (three to five years) focus
- Adequate staff and students training
- Communication with the parent community
- Implementation fidelity
- Ongoing evaluation

At the beginning of an intervention, a committee (*cadre*) of dedicated, enthusiastic people should be established. They are typically the group that is trained by experts with the intervention, who then subsequently train the rest of the staff. The cadre meets on a regular basis (at least monthly). This group serves several functions: overseeing implementation, problem solving, and maintaining momentum (Elias et al., 2003; PPN, 2004). Because of the potential likelihood of staff turnover, it has been suggested that there are several program champions on this committee (Elliott et al., 2003). Our experience has been that programs often start off strong when there is a single, passionate advocate (or program champion) for a program, but frequently the program will fade away if that person leaves. By having several committed staff members, the risk of losing a key person is reduced. It is wise for schools to carefully select and plan for their cadre given that staff turnover will occur.

The second factor for this stage is a *long-term focus*. Prevention programming is effective when it is long term (Weissberg, 2004). Maintaining momentum is a key task for the cadre (this will be discussed further in Stage 4). Climate change programs can typically take as long as three to five years for the program to become fully integrated into the school culture (Elliott et al., 2003). Because of this, the planning committee needs to have a long-term plan/time table. With competing initiatives and scarce resources, schools run the risk of stopping a program before it has had a chance to fully take effect. In addition, because time is often a limited commodity in schools, staff members often rush the implementation process. The notion of "go slow to go fast" is an important one. If a school spends sufficient time and thought in their initial planning of the program, there is a greater chance that the program will be successful. In contrast, if a school rushes through the initial planning, they will likely begin the implementation with a shaky foundation, all but guaranteeing that problems will occur and that staff will not see the program as being worthy of continuing.

Adequate *training of staff and of students* is the next important component when implementing any program (Elias et al., 2003; Leadbeater et al., 2003; Wiessberg, 2004). Programs that have been shown to be effective, have been ones that have been put into action with fidelity (Biglan, Mrazek, Carnine, & Flay, 2003; Blase & Fixsen, 2006; Kam et al., 2003; Nation et al., 2003; Wiessberg, 2004). If the staff does not understand the basic underpinnings of the program, they may leave out key components that they see as cumbersome or time-consuming, in other words, not implement the intervention as it was designed (Leadbeater et al., 2003). Staff needs to be trained not only in the specific procedures and logistical aspects of the program, but in the background and philosophy as well. This can help them understand all the "when, where, how, and with whom" of using the new approach (Fixsen et al., 2005). Successful programs frequently involve approaches or strategies that are counter-intuitive or outside of the staff's current skill set or comfort zone. Adequate staff training helps address this along with the issues of low morale, staff buy in, and support for the program (D'Andrea, 2004; Nation et al., 2003).

Once staff has been trained, students then need to be trained. As with academic instruction, behavioral instruction typically involves a skill set that must be directly taught. Students need to learn these skills, as they are a crucial element in insuring the program will be successful. For example, with bully prevention, bystanders are crucial in stopping the spread of bullying behaviors (Cowie, 2000; Craig & Pepler, 1997; Gropper & Froschl, 1999; O'Connell et al., 1999; Salmivalli, 1999; Stevens, et al., 2000). Students must learn the key role that bystanders play in bully prevention as well as specific strategies for *how* to intervene when they witness a bullying situation. Students also need repeated opportunities to practice these skills and opportunities to discuss how they were able to use them in everyday situations. Social emotional skills are most effective when children are taught how to apply the skills in their everyday life (Leadbeater et al., 2003; Weissberg, 2004).

Another important component of successful climate change is the *involvement of parents and the community* (Leadbeater et al., 2003; Weissberg, 2004). Parents are more likely to support a program if they understand the underlying philosophy/purpose of the program. Their support can reinforce at home the skills that are learned at school. Also, parent involvement allows them to hold the school accountable for implementation of the program. Parents desire safe and caring school environments for their children and therefore can be the driving force behind the intervention. Potentially the most important component of the implementation phase is making sure that that program is *implemented with high fidelity* (Biglan et al. 2003; Blase & Fixsen, 2006; Kam et al., 2003; Nation et al., 2003; Weissberg, 2004). Logically, in order to replicate the positive impact of programs that have been proven to be effective, these programs need to be implemented as designed in a quality manner (Elliott, 2006). Sometimes, schools will modify the programs. Some modifications are acceptable, particularly those that make the materials culturally relevant to the students in a particular community. However, often schools will modify or scale down the intervention because of time constraints. Schools that do this run the risk of reducing the effectiveness of the intervention; higher implementation fidelity has been found to be associated with better outcomes across a wide range of prevention programs and practices (Blase & Fixsen, 2006; Kam et al., 2003). It is important that the implementation be monitored by observation and the use of implementation checklists to insure that the program is being executed faithfully and fully (Biglan et al., 2003; Blase & Fixsen, 2006; Elias et al., 2003). In order to differentiate between implementation and effectiveness problems, it is important to know what people are doing and how they are doing it (Blase & Fixsen, 2006).

Ongoing *evaluation* of the program, the final implementation component, is important for a variety of reasons. First, school staff must see that the program is having a positive impact on their school. Seeing positive effects help motivate schools to continue with the program. In addition, ongoing evaluation helps schools adjust the implementation to meet the needs of the school and improve the effectiveness of the implementation. For example, schools implementing the Bully-Proofing Your School program might find that students are reporting feeling safer in certain areas of the school (e.g., classroom, cafeteria) but not others (e.g., playground). In this situation, the staff could increase their teaching of bystander skills, particularly as they relate to reducing bullying incidences on the playground. Evaluation is also important to clearly demonstrate the impact of the program; anecdotal information is not sufficient to show that a program is working, particularly for a program that does not have an evidence base (Elliott, 2006). As mentioned above, both process and outcome data should be collected to assess both effectiveness and implementation fidelity. Generally, effective prevention programs include an evaluation component to ensure decision making is based on data (Leadbeater et al., 2003).

For bullying prevention programs, assessment of bullying behaviors in a school is critical. While schools might be tempted to rely on discipline referrals, these reports are not likely to provide a complete assessment of bullying in the school given than research has suggested that children do not always seek adult help (Newman et al., 2001) and that adults typically are only aware of a small amount of bullying that takes place at school (Cowie, 2000). Though some disagreement exists as to the best way to assess bullying behavior, for example whether to rely on peer or self-report (Juvonen, Graham, & Schuster, 2003; Solberg & Olweus, 2003) or whether or not to include a definition of bullying (Austin & Joseph, 1996; Bosworth, Espelage, & Simon, 1999; Smith et al., 2002), an anonymous survey of student perceptions of bullying behavior provides necessary information to help the school to determine the impact of the intervention.

Stage 4: Sustaining Implementation

Stage 4 includes those factors that need to be considered to have the prevention effort sustained and incorporated into the culture of the school. During this period, the belief in and the practice of the program become part of the foundation of the school. The three preceding stages aim for a sustainable program so that initial efforts are not wasted. Sustainability should be considered when laying the groundwork for, selecting, and implementing a bullying prevention program. After a program has begun, further attention will need to be paid to variables that allow the intervention to be sustained over time. The program must adapt and the cadre must continue to meet in order to develop institutional rituals, and become proactive rather than reactive to problems.

The different factors of the sustaining implementation stage are:

• Accommodation of teacher, principal, or cadre/program champion change
• Integration of the intervention
• Ongoing needs assessment and evaluation—needs to be used to celebrate change and/or modify the program
• Ongoing cadre meetings that occur on a regular basis
• Ongoing technical support/training
• Empowerment of students

The most basic step in sustainability of the program over time is accommodation of staff changes (Elias et al., 2003). School staff and administration turn over annually. Therefore, planning in the spring for the *orientation and training of new personnel* in the fall is important; related to this, ensuring that the administration continues to be supportive is fundamental. It is also important that program champions are still in place and that there are regularly scheduled times for the cadre to meet.

One factor that is often over-looked, but is necessary to address at this point, is the staff who are operating out of their comfort zone. Though understanding of the underlying principles of the intervention should initially be considered in the program selection stage, it is possible that staff's underlying beliefs will not become apparent until the intervention has begun. Staff members' underlying assumptions about child development or human behavior may conflict with what they are asked to do as part of the intervention. For example, the fourth author of this chapter worked with a school that had implemented Bully-Proofing Your School and found that the expectation of BPYS that children take responsibility for their behavior was difficult for several members of the staff who believed that fear and punishment were necessary to keep students in place. Actively attending to staff and attempting to resolve such conflictual beliefs is important for the intervention to continue to operate in the school.

The next aspect of this phase is the active *integration of the intervention* plan with the practices of the school and with other intervention programs that are in place (Elliott, 2006; Gottfredson & Gottfredson, 2002; Greenberg et al., 2003; Weissberg, 2004). As new programs are introduced in the school, staff can be overwhelmed with "one more thing" being added to their role. In fact, uncoordinated prevention efforts can be disruptive and are not likely to show their intended effects (Greenberg et al., 2003; Weissberg, 2004). When multiple programs are in place, time spent discerning what are the common features of the interventions will ensure that staff are not doing the same tasks multiple times. Sugai (2006) suggests that school committees working toward similar goals, e.g., safety, bullying, character education, be combined. This combined group can ensure that efforts are coordinated and executed in an efficient manner. In addition to integration of the program with other intervention efforts, the more that a prevention program fits into what school staff do on a day to day basis, the easier it will be for them to sustain the prevention efforts. This task will require attention both at the outset of the intervention and over time as specific strategies become more apparent. Examples of ways to do this are: posting rules, expectations, and strategies throughout the school building; including the code of conduct in the school newsletter; stating the plan as part of the school mission; developing and using common language; printing language logos on t-shirts, back packs, book markers, planners; and noting dates for community meetings and tips for parents and community members on the school calendar. These types of endorsements will institutionalize the school-wide effort to develop a common language and become an integral part of the practices and belief of the school and community. Integration of an intervention into normal school operations is also predictive of quality of implementation (Elliott, 2006; Gottfredson & Gottfredson, 2002).

The third factor of this stage is the use of *data and evaluation* not only to validate the outcome of the effort but also to acknowledge the effort and celebrate the gains, both small and large. Continued teacher support follows from a connection between what they do and positive changes that result from the program (Han & Weiss, 2005). It is important for the staff to realize the results of their effort in a fun, positive, and regular manner. Too often data and evaluation are not used in a timely, practical manner. Regular data collection such as student, staff, and/or parent surveys and review of discipline and attendance records paired with discussion of the results can help to maintain momentum. Use of data also guides ongoing adaptation to the changing needs of the school and directs problem-solving as the need arises.

The fourth sustaining implementation component is ongoing *cadre meetings*. A committee of sustainers has the charge of keeping the program fresh and trouble-shooting any barriers that emerge. This cadre or committee needs to be identified and have high visibility and administrative support. They will need to meet regularly and also as problems arise. As mentioned above, it continues to be good to have co-leaders to help sustain the program during time of transitions and staff changes. Multiple leaders also serve to bring twice the energy and ideas to the effort.

The fifth factor is the use of on-going *technical assistance*. This can be done by an outside individual who has expertise with the program. This person's role can include assessing implementation fidelity, developing strategies to effectively overcome barriers, and identifying and assisting with training needs. Ongoing technical assistance has been linked to improved implementation fidelity (Blasé & Fixsen, 2006). Technical assistance should be scheduled in a regular, proactive manner. For maximum effectiveness, training needs to be continuous (Biglan et al., 2003). Technical assistance can also be done collaboratively by having cadres and champions from different schools meet together to share success and problems. This colleague-type interaction capitalizes on the collective knowledge and expertise of individuals implementing the program and can be not only informative but also energizing.

Finally, the general theme of sustained prevention programming is *empowerment of students* to make their school a more positive place. Fostering respectful, supportive relationships is critical for successful intervention and positive outcomes (Greenberg et al., 2003; Leadbeater et al., 2003; Nation et al., 2003). Systematic support for and reward of positive behaviors are also an important part of this process (Greenberg et al., 2003). With these in place, students are more likely to act on their desire for their school to be a safe environment. Students are a powerful resource in several ways. Their knowledge of what occurs in the school can help guide the intervention. In addition, all students have been said to play a role in the dynamic of bullying behavior (Cowie, 2000; O'Connell et al., 1999; Orpinas, et al., 2003; Stevens et al., 2000) and their ability to take a stand can be an essential component for creating a caring school climate where teachers can teach and students can learn.

Conclusion

A four-stage model that identifies factors a school will need to address in selecting, beginning, and sustaining a prevention or climate change program has been presented. The goal of identifying these factors is to maximize the likelihood of effective and lasting bullying prevention program implementation. This is particularly important given that schools that are in greatest need of these programs often operate in environments of limited resources (Forgatch, 2003). Knowledge of these factors that, when not addressed, may impede effective implementation can

Table 40.1 Summary of Implications for Practice

	Systemic Considerations	Staff	Students	Community	Data Collection
Stage 1 Pre-Implementation	• School-wide discipline/academic plan	• Administrative support • Staff buy-in			• Needs assessment
Stage 2 Program Selection	• Preventive • Developmentally appropriate and engaging • System-wide • Connected to goals/mission	• Adaptable to the needs of the students, staff, and community			• Evidence and theory based
Stage 3 Implementation	• Long-term focus • Fidelity of Implementation	• Program champion/ cadre • Adequate staff training	• Adequate student training	• Involve parents/ community	• Fidelity (what is done by whom) • Evaluation
Stage 4 Sustained Implementation	• Integration with school and other programs • Ongoing technical assistance	• Accommodate staff changes • Regular cadre meetings	• Students empowered		• Ongoing evaluation

help schools to target their efforts and to ensure a positive impact on the school and its students. In addition, awareness that implementation is an ongoing, complex, multi-stage process and not a time-limited, circumscribed event should maximize the positive potential impact of bullying prevention programs in schools.

References

Austin, S., & Joseph, S. (1996). Assessment of bully/victim problems in 8 to 11 year-olds. *British Journal of Educational Psychology, 66,* 447–456.

Biglan, A., Mrazek, P. J., Carnine, D., & Flay, B. R. (2003). The integration of research and practice in the prevention of youth behavior problems. *American Psychologist, 58,* 433–440.

Blase, K. A., & Fixsen, D. L. (2006, March). *Fidelity — Why it matters and what research tells us.* Presentation at the Blueprints Conference, Denver, Colorado.

Bosworth, K. Espelage, D. L., & Simon, T. R. (1999). Factors associated with bullying behavior in middle school students. *Journal of Early Adolescence, 19,* 341–362.

Cowie, H. (2000). Bystanding or standing by: Gender issues in coping with bullying in English schools. *Aggressive Behavior, 26,* 85–97.

Craig, W. M., & Pepler, D. J. (1997). Observations of bullying and victimization in the schoolyard. *Canadian Journal of School Psychology, 13*(2), 41–60.

Crick, N. R., & Bigbee, M. A. (1998). Relational and overt forms of peer victimization: A multiinformant approach. *Journal of Consulting and Clinical Psychology, 66,* 337–347.

D'Andrea, M. (2004). Comprehensive school-based violence prevention training: A developmental ecological training model. *Journal of Counseling & Development, 82,* 277–286.

Elias, M. J., Zins, J. E., Graczyk, P. A., & Weissberg, R. P. (2003). Implementation, sustainability, and scaling up of social emotional and academic innovations in public schools. *School Psychology Review, 32,* 303–319.

Elliott, D. S. (2006, March). *Improving the effectiveness of delinquency, drug and violence prevention efforts: Promise and practice.* Presentation at the Blueprints Conference, Denver, Colorado.

Elliott, S. N., Kratochwill, T. R., & Roach, A. T., (2003). Commentary: Implementing social-emotional and academic innovations: Reflections, reactions, and research. *School Psychology Review, 32,* 320–326.

Fixsen, D. L., Naoom, S. F., Blase, K. A., Friedman, R. M., Wallace, F. (2005). *Implementation Research: A Synthesis of the Literature.* Tampa, FL: University of South Florida, Louis de la Parte, Florida Mental Health Institute, The National Implementation Research Network (FMHI Publication # 231).

Flannery, D. J., Vazsonyi, A. T., Liau, A. K., Guo, S., Powell, K. E., Atha, H., Vesterdal, W., & Embry, D. (2003). Initial behavior outcomes for the PeaceBuilders universal school-based violence prevention program. *Developmental Psychology, 39,* 292–308.

Forgatch, M. S. (2003). Implementation as a second stage in prevention research. *Prevention & Treatment, 6* (Article 24). Retrieved February 2004, from http://journals.apa.org/prevention/volume6/pre0060024c.html

Gottfredson, D. (1997). School-based crime prevention. In L. W. Sherman, D. Gottfredson, D. Mackenzie, J. Ect, P. Reuter, & S. Bushway (Eds.), *Preventing Crime: What Works, What Doesn't, and What's Promising.* Retrieved March 2006 from http://www.ncjrs.gov/works/chapter5.htm

Gottfredson, D. C., & Gottfredson, G. D. (2002). Quality of school-based prevention programs: Results from a national survey. *Journal of Research in Crime & Delinquency, 39*(1), 3–35.

Graczyk, P. A., Matjasko, J. L., Weissberg, R. P., Greenberg, M. T., Elias, M. J., & Zins, J. E. (2000). The role of the Collaborative to Advance Social and Emotional Learning (CASEL) in supporting the implementation of quality school-based prevention programs. *Journal of Educational and Psychological Consultation, 11*(1), 3–6.

Graczyk, P. A., Domitrovitch, C. E., Small, M., & Zins, J. E. (2006). Serving all children: An implementation model framework. *School Psychology Review, 35,* 266–274.

Greenberg, M. T., Weissberg, R. P., O'Brien, M. U., Zins, J. E., Fredricks, L., Resnick, H., et al. (2003). Enhancing school-based prevention and youth development through coordinated social, emotional, and academic learning. *American Psychologist, 58,* 466–474.

Gropper, N., & Froschl, M. (1999). The role of gender in young children's teasing and bullying behavior. Paper presented at the Annual Conference of the American Educational Research Association (Montreal, Canada, April 19–23).

Han, S. S., & Weiss, B. (2005). Sustainability of teacher implementation of school-based mental health programs. *Journal of Abnormal Child Psychology, 33,* 665–679.

Juvonen, J., Graham, S., & Schuster, M. A. (2003). Bullying among young adolescents: The strong, the weak, and the troubled. *Pediatrics, 112,* 1231–1237.

Kallstead, J. H., & Olweus, D. (2003). Predicting teachers' and schools' implementation of the Olweus Bullying Prevention Program. *Prevention & Treatment*, 6 (Article 21). Retrieved February 2005, from http://journals.apa.org/prevention/volume6/pre0060021a.html

Kam, C-M., Greenberg, M. T., & Walls, C. T. (2003). Examining the role of implementation quality in school-based prevention using the PATHS curriculum. *Prevention Science, 4*, 55–63.

Leadbeater, B., Hoglund, W., & Woods, T. (2003). Changing context? The effects of a primary prevention program on classroom levels of peer relational and physical victimization. *Journal of Community Psychology, 31*, 397–418.

Limber, S. P., & Nation, M. M. (1991). Bullying among children and youth, Juvenile Justice Bulletin. Retreived from http://www.ojjdp.ncjrs.org/jjjbulletin/9804/bullying2.html

McGuire, J. (2001). What works in correctional intervention? Evidence and practical implications. In G. A. Bernfield, D. P. Farrington, & W. Lescheid (Eds.), *Offender rehabilitation in practice: Implementing and evaluating effective programs* (pp. 25–43).

Nation, M., Crusto, C., Wandersman, A., Kumpfer, K. L., Seybolt, Morrisey-Kane, E., et al. (2003). What works in prevention: Principles of effective programs. *American Psychologist, 58*, 449–456. National Implementation Research Network. Retrieved from http://nirn.fmhi.usf.edu/

Newman, R. S., Murray, B., & Lussier, C. (2001). Confrontation with aggressive peers at school: Students' reluctance to seek help from the teacher. *Journal of Educational Psychology, 93*, 398–410.

O'Connell, P., Pepler, D., & Craig, W. (1999). Peer involvement in bullying: insights and challenges for intervention. *Journal of Adolescence, 22*, 437–452.

Orpinas, P., Horne, A. M., & Staniszewski, D. (2003). School bullying: Changing the problem by changing the school. *School Psychology Review, 23*, 431–444.

Peterson, L., & Rigby, K. (1999). Countering bullying at an Australian secondary school with students as helpers. *Journal of Adolescence, 22*, 481–492.

Promising Practices Network (PPN). (2004). What are key ingredients in successful implementation? Retrieved February 2004, from http://www.promisingpractices.net/ssd/ssd3b.asp

Rogers, E. M. (2003). *Diffusion of Innovations* (5th ed.). New York: Free Press.

Roland, E. (2000). Bullying in school: Three national innovations in Norwegian schools in 15 years. *Aggressive Behavior, 26*, 135–143.

Salmivalli, C. (1999). Participant role approach to school bullying: Implications for interventions. *Journal of Adolescence, 22*, 453–459.

Smith, P. K., Cowie, H., Olafsson, R. F., Liefooghe, A. P. D. (with A. Almeida, H. Araki, et al.). (2002). Definitions of bullying: A comparison of terms used, and age and gender differences, in a fourteen-country international comparison. *Child Development, 73*, 1119–1133.

Solberg, M. E., & Olweus, D. (2003). Prevalence estimation of school bullying with the Olweus bully/victim questionnaire. *Aggressive Behavior, 29*, 239–268.

Stevens, V., Van Oost, P., & De Bourdeaudhuij, I. (2000). The effects of an anti-bullying intervention programme on peers' attitudes and behaviour. *Journal of Adolescence, 23*, 21–34.

Sugai, G. (2006). *School-wide Positive Behavior Support: Getting started*. Retrieved November 2007, from http://www.pbis.org/pastconferencepresentations.htm

Wiessberg, R. P. (2004). Statement before the subcommittee on substance abuse and mental health services, U.S. Senate committee on health, education, labor and pensions. Retrieved March 2006, from http://www.k12coordinator.org/testimony.pdf

Weisz, J. R., Sandler, I. N., Durlak, J. A., & Anton, B. S. (2005). Promoting and protecting youth mental health through evidence-based prevention and treatment. *American Psychologist, 60*, 628–648.

Whitney, I., Rivers, I., Smith, P. K., & Sharp, S. (1994). The Sheffield Project: Methodology and findings. In P. K. Smith & S. Sharp (Eds.), *School bullying insights and perspectives* (pp. 20–56). London: Routledge.

Whitney, I., & Smith, P. K. (1993). A survey of the nature and extent of bullying in junior/middle and secondary schools. *Educational Research, 35*(1), 3–25.

41

International Perspectives on Bullying Prevention and Intervention

SHANE R. JIMERSON AND NAN HUAI

Scholars around the world have been working diligently to better understand antecedents and outcomes associated with bullying behaviors, as well as developing and implementing prevention and intervention programs to reduce bullying behaviors (see, for instance, recent international volumes, e.g., Jimerson, Swearer, & Espelage, 2009; Smith, Pepler, & Rigby, 2004). These international efforts have advanced our collective understanding of bullying behaviors. For instance, the prevailing international definition of bullying is—repeated aggressive behavior in which there is an imbalance of power or strength between the two parties (e.g., physical size, psychological/social power, or other factors that result in a power differential). Furthermore, it is generally agreed that bullying behaviors may be direct or overt (e.g., hitting, kicking, name-calling, or taunting) or more subtle or indirect in nature (e.g., rumor-spreading, social exclusion, friendship manipulation, or cyber-bullying). Considering that bullying has been documented among youth in many countries around the world (e.g., Australia, Brazil, Canada, Denmark, England, Finland, France, Germany, Greece, Ireland, Italy, Japan, Netherlands, New Zealand, Norway, Portugal, Scotland, South Africa, South Korea, Sweden, Switzerland, and the United States), the central premise of this chapter is that this international phenomenon affords an opportunity to learn from colleagues throughout the world.

The primary purpose of this chapter is to share a summary and synthesis of bullying prevention and intervention programs around the world, to glean further insights and identify implications for practice. Cultural and contextual considerations are also discussed. The first section offers a brief overview of prevention and intervention programs to address bullying, which have been implemented in various countries around the world. The second section, explores themes that emerge from reports of international bullying prevention and intervention programs, including: (a) contextual considerations shared among programs, (b) outcome evaluation common to programs, and (c) implications based on the lessons and challenges learned through these programs.

Examples of International Bullying Prevention and Intervention Programs

This section provides a brief overview of prevention and intervention programs to address school bullying from numerous countries around the world. These brief descriptions include information regarding the years when the program was initiated, core components of each program and relevant publications for further consideration. An exhaustive review of all programs in all countries is beyond the scope of this chapter. However, those included below are provided as examples for further consideration. Over the past three decades, researchers and practitioners in Europe, Canada, and Australia have been leaders in research to understand antecedents and outcomes of bullying, as well as develop and implement prevention and intervention programs. Programs discussed below include those from Australia, Canada, England, Flemish, Finland, Germany, Ireland, Norway, Spain, Switzerland, and the United States.

The Olweus Bullying Prevention Program

Among the most widely recognized school-based bullying prevention programs around the world, is the Olweus Bullying Prevention Program developed in Norway (Olweus, 1991, 1993a, 1993b; Olweus, Limber, & Mihalic, 1999). Following his related scholarship during the 1970s, Olweus' prevention projects in the 1980s were among the first to emerge around the world. The Olweus program has been implemented in numerous locations in Norway, including the Bergen Project Against Bullying 1983–1985 (42 intervention schools), the New Bergen Project Against Bullying 1997–1998 (14 intervention schools), the Oslo Project Against Bullying 1999–2000 (10 intervention schools), and a recent national initiative against bullying in Norway initiated in 2000. The Olweus program emphasizes that it is critical to develop a school environment (a) that is characterized by warmth and involvement on the part of adults, (b) where there are clear rules for behavior, (c) where there are consistent and non-hostile sanctions that are consistently applied when rules or norms are violated, and (d) where adults act as authorities and positive role models (Olweus, 1993b; Olweus et al., 1999). The Olweus program includes strategies that are implemented at the school-wide level, within the classroom, and at the individual level. The Olweus program has also been used more recently in the United States (Limber, 2006). A brief description of the Olweus Bullying Prevention Program as implemented in Norway is offered below, as well as international modifications and implementation projects.

The Norwegian Model   The following provides a brief summary of intervention at the school-wide level, within the classroom, and at the individual level (Olweus et al., 1999). Core school-wide interventions include: (a) administering an anonymous questionnaire to provide student perspective regarding the extent of bull /victim problems, locations of bullying, and attitudes toward bullying behaviors within the school; (b) establishing a Bullying Prevention Coordinating Committee to meet periodically and oversee information, prevention, and intervention activities; (c) placing adult supervision of students in areas where bullying is reported to occur most frequently; (d) organizing a school meeting day so that school staff may review the results of the survey, become familiar with the Olweus program, and make specific plans for implementation; (e) conducting meetings with parents to inform them of the results of the survey, discuss plans for intervention, and involve parents in all aspects of the implementation; and (f) developing staff discussion groups who meet regularly for an opportunity to learn more about the program and to share successes and challenges (Olweus, 2004). Key elements of the classroom interventions include: (a) establishing and enforcing rules about bullying; (b) holding regularly-scheduled classroom meetings with students to discuss bullying, relations, and the relevant class/school rules, as well as engage students in role-plays and other activities designed to help them understand the consequences of bullying and effective strategies to reduce bullying; and (c) conducting classroom-level meetings with parents to present information regarding bullying and strategies to reduce bullying behaviors (Olweus, 1993b; Olweus et al., 1999). Core elements of individual interventions include: (a) meetings with students who bully and with students who are bullied (separately), to help to ensure that bullying stops and that children get additional support and/or guidance they may need, and (b) meetings with school staff, and parents of affected students are also encouraged to help inform parents and involve them in stopping the bullying behavior. Multiple publications describe the outcomes associated with implementing the Olweus program in Norway (e.g., Olweus, 1993b, 1994, 2004).

International Implementation of the Olweus Bullying Prevention Program There are numerous adaptations, implementations, and evaluations of the Olweus bully prevention program internationally. An adapted version of the Olweus program was implemented and investigated in 37 schools in Germany 1994–1996 including several key components: (a) survey of bullying behaviors among students, (b) coordinating group to conduct leadership activities, (c) restructuring the school yard, (d) establishing classroom rules against bullying, (e) teacher training courses, (f) communications between victims and bullies, (g) regular classroom discussions about bullying, (h) increased supervisions during recess, (i) talks with parents of involved students, (j) cooperative learning experiences, (k) common class activities, and (l) cooperation among teachers and parents (see Hanewinkel, 2004, for further details and outcomes associated with these efforts). An adapted version of the Olweus program was implemented and investigated in three elementary schools in Canada 1992–1995 including three critical elements: (a) staff training, (b) codes of conduct, and (c) improved playground supervision. With specific interventions at the school level, parent level, classroom level, and with individual children (i.e., bullies or victims; see Pepler, Craig, Ziegler, & Charach, 1994; Pepler, Craig, O'Connell, Atlas, & Charach, 2004, for further details and outcomes associated with these efforts).

Implementation in the United States During the most recent decade, Limber, Nation, Tracy, Melton, and Flerx (2004) conducted the first wide-scale implementation and evaluation of the Olweus program in the United States. Implementation in the United Sates included modifications to address some of the unique challenges of implementation in American school systems (Limber, 2006). Modifications included: (a) developing school-wide rules against bullying (as opposed to classroom rules) to ensure consistency of rules across classrooms; (b) Intensive training of committee members and school staff and ongoing consultation to on-site coordinators in each school for at least one year; (c) adapting materials and developing new supportive materials, (e.g., suggested topics/lesson plans for classroom meetings); and (d) involving community members to address bullying problems within the school and within the broader community. See Limber (2006) for further discussion of the use of the Olweus Bullying Prevention Program in the United States.

The PEACE Pack Bullying Intervention Program

The PEACE (Preparation, Education, Action, Coping, and Evaluation) Pack (Slee, 1994. 2001, this volume) provides a system level framework for schools to assess the status of their anti-bullying policy in relation to policy and grievance procedures, curriculum initiatives, and student social support programs. The PEACE Pack also provides practical resources (e.g., examples of policy and lesson plans, as part of a comprehensive package to assist schools in developing their own intervention). With an emphasis on system level influences, the PEACE Pack process includes: (a) Preparation and consideration of the nature of the bullying (e.g., establishing a working committee of stakeholders); (b) Education and understanding of the issues (e.g., gathering information, collecting surveys); (c) Action taken and strategies developed to reduce bullying (e.g., developing policies, developing grievance procedures, developing a graduated system of intervention); (d) Coping strategies for staff, students and parents (e.g., curriculum development to influence attitudes and behaviors); and (e) Evaluation, review and celebration of the program (e.g., sharing accomplishments in students assemblies, class letters, and with local groups and media). In this model, the interventions selected are those consistent with the needs of the particular school system. Slee (this volume), emphasizes that through focusing in more systemic terms (in contrast to focusing on changing "bad" or problematic behavior of the bully and on "helping" the victim), consideration will be given to relationships, roles and interactions, and communication within the system which encourage or discourage bullying. Slee and colleagues (Slee, 1996, 2001, 2005, this volume; Slee & Mohyla, 2007) offer a description of the project, implementation details, as well as related outcome analyses.

The Method of Shared Concern to Prevent Bullying

This method was originally developed by the Swedish psychologist, Anatol Pikas (1989, 2002). Initial applications to address bullying appear to have emerged in the 1990s, further discussion of the Method is provided by Smith and Sharp of England (1994) and by Rigby of Australia (2002, 2005, this volume). The method has been applied in schools in many parts of the world including England, Australia, Canada, Finland, and Sweden (Rigby, 2009). The Method of Shared Concern does not seek to accuse and punish children who have bullied someone, but rather emphasizes establishing or re-establishing positive relations between those involved and more especially with developing a situation in which the victim feels safe. A key component of this approach is the recognition that bullying is typically a group phenomenon and can best be addressed by communicating with members of the group individually and collectively. The Method of Shared Concern uses a procedure that includes all students who are believed to have been involved in the bullying to participate in a series of planned meetings with individuals and with groups. As described by Rigby (2009), the following procedures would be used: (a) information about the bullying incident is gathered indirectly, without interviewing the victim; (b) suspected bullies are then interviewed individually (to establish a positive, respectful, working relationship, prior to meeting collectively), wherein, the practitioner shares a concern about the plight of the victim and seeks to elicit acknowledgement of the bad situation and discuss positive suggestions on how to resolve the situation; (c) the victim is interviewed next, to obtain their perspective on what is happening; (d) subsequently other meetings with the children (i.e., suspected bullies and victim) are conducted to reinforce progress; (e) the next meeting is with the victim and suspected bullies together to work with the practitioner to reach a final and agreed solution. A training film regarding the application of the Method of Shared Concern is available from Readymade Productions (http://www.readymade.com.au/method).

The Sheffield Bullying Prevention Project

The Sheffield Project in England emerged in 1991 following administration of the Olweus questionnaire in 1990 (Smith, Sharp, Elsea, & Thompson, 2004). In the Sheffield Project, all participating schools (23) were asked to include the "core intervention," which was comprised of a basic "whole school policy" on bullying. The school policy emphasized: (a) raising awareness about bullying, (b) consultation through the school, (c) developing the policy content, (d) disseminating the policy widely, (e) implementing the policy, and (f) evaluating the effectiveness of the policy. In addition, optional interventions were made available, including (a) curriculum-based strategies (i.e., video, drama, literature, quality circles; 15 schools); (b) direct work with students (i.e., assertiveness training for victims, direct work with bullies using the Method of Shared Concern, school tribunals or bully courts, peer counseling; 12 schools); and (c) making changes to playgrounds and lunch breaks (i.e., working with lunchtime supervisors, redesigning playground environment; 18 schools). Smith and colleagues (2004) offer a description of the project, implementation details, as well as related outcome analyses.

Bully-Proofing Your School Prevention Program

The Bully-Proofing Your School (Garrity, Jens, Porter, Sager, & Short-Camilli, 1994, 2000) prevention program was developed in the United States and published in 1994. The Bully-Proofing Your School program is a bully prevention program designed for elementary and middle school students that offers a systems-wide approach for handling bully/victim problems. The focus of the program is on creating a caring majority of students who take the lead in establishing and maintaining a safe school community. The program includes classroom curriculum, staff training, interventions for working with bullies, victims, and bystanders, and strategies for the ongoing development of the schools' caring community. Implementation involves three phases: (a) creating an awareness of the bullying problem in the school following an assessment of the climate of the school, providing information about bullying through staff training, and developing school-wide rules and bullying policies; (b) teaching protective skills to help students learn strategies for dealing with bullying behaviors and to increase resistance to victimization; and (c) enhancing the school climate by promoting the development of a caring majority of students who are encouraged to stand up for the victims with the promise of adult support and acknowledgment. Several studies (e.g., Epstein, Plog, & Porter, 2002; Menard, Grotpeter, Gianola, & O'Neal, 2008) report results of the effectiveness of the program.

The Flemish Anti-Bullying Intervention Program

The Flemish Anti-Bullying Intervention program (Stevens & Van Oost, 1994) was inspired by the Norwegian model program and the Sheffield Project. Implementation and evaluation of the Flemish Anti-Bullying Intervention program in 24 schools was completed between 1995 and 1997. The core components of the intervention program included: (a) intervention in the school environment (e.g., whole-school policy towards bullying, awareness, consultation with school and community members, and developing the policy, informing all about the policy, and providing training sessions for targeted groups); (b) intervention with the peer group (e.g., four groups sessions directed at students who are not actively involved in bullying, to increase positive attitudes toward victims and encouraging peer involvement to reduce bully behaviors); and (c) support for bullies and victims (e.g., strategies for teachers and for others to address bullying behaviors, intensive support for victims to help enhance social skills and develop assertive behaviors in peer conflict situations). Stevens, Van Oost, and de Bourdeaudhuij (2004) offer a description of the project, implementation details, as well as related outcome studies.

The Sevilla Anti-Violencia Escolar (SAVE) Anti-Bullying Intervention Program

The SAVE anti-bullying intervention program (Ortega, 1997; Ortega & Leer, 2000) was implemented in 5 schools in Spain during the 1995–1996 academic year. A key principle underlying this project was that of *convivencia* (a spirit of solidarity, co-operation, harmony, a desire for mutual understanding, the desire to get on well with others, and the resolution of conflict through dialogue or other nonviolent means), wherein, the different persons who participate in school (teachers, students, and families) are linked together (Ortega, Del Rey, & Mora-Merchan, 2004). The key components that the SAVE program offered were: (a) democratic management of interpersonal relationships; (b) cooperative group work; (c) education of feelings, attitudes, and values; (d) direct interventions with students at risk or involved in bullying; (e) working with families; and (f) teacher training. Ortega and colleagues (2004) provide a description of the project and implementation details, as well as related outcome studies.

The Bernese Program Against Victimization

The Bernese program against victimization in Kindergarten was implemented in 8 Kindergarten classrooms in Switzerland during the 1997–1998 academic year. The key principle for this program was to enhance teachers' capability of handling bully/victim problems. Thus, teachers were offered intensive supervision for about 4 months. During each meeting with a participating teacher, a common schedule was followed: (a) information regarding specific topics regarding victimization and its prevention, (b) implications of the information regarding victimization and its prevention, (c) introduction to specific implementation tasks, (d) then teachers worked in small groups on the preparation of practical implementation strategies, (e) between meetings teachers were encouraged to carry out some specific preventative strategies, and (f) the next meeting then began with a discussion of the teachers' experiences with implementing the task. Four additional key aspects were (a) flexibility in implementation; (b) cooperation between the consultants and the teachers, as well as teachers and parents; (c) realistic intermediate objectives; and (d) the usefulness of group discussions and mutual support. Alsaker (2004) offers a description of the project and implementation details, as well as related outcome studies.

The Donegal Primary Schools Anti-Bullying Intervention Project

The Donegal Primary Schools anti-bullying intervention project was implemented in 1998, following a 1993 nationwide survey of bullying in Ireland and 1993 publication of the Ireland Department of Education Guidelines for preventing and countering bullying in primary and post-primary schools. The Donegal Primary Schools project was implemented in 42 schools between 1998 and 2000. The Irish national schools program implemented, was based on four key elements of the 1996 Norwegian program: (a) training of a network of professionals who would then provide leadership in their schools and communities; (b) teacher's resource pack with information about bullying, classroom management, development of a positive atmosphere, and cooperation among staff, leadership, parents, and teachers; (c) parent's resource pack with information about the prevalence, types, causes, and effects of bullying behaviors, as well as intervention support strategies; and (d) work with students to create an environment that did not accept bullying, including awareness-raising and strategies for preventing and countering bullying behaviors. O'Moore and Minton (2004) offer a description of the project and implementation details, as well as related outcome information.

The Finnish Anti-Bullying Intervention Program

The Finnish anti-bullying intervention was implemented in 16 schools in Finland between 1999 and 2000. The focus of this program is on teacher training, providing teachers with: (a) feedback about the situation in their class (based on information from a pre-intervention survey); (b) facts about bullying research; (c) alternative methods of intervening in bullying (i.e., individual, class, and school levels), with an emphasis on classroom level interventions; (d) an opportunity to share their experiences regarding effective interventions; and (e) consultation on individual cases that teachers found difficult. In contrast to a clearly defined standard intervention, the aim was to provide general information, research findings, and ideas about bullying prevention and intervention strategies, and then have the teachers adapt and develop plans to meet their needs. Three general principles were emphasized for the classroom plans: (a) awareness building, (b) self-reflection regarding one's behavior related to bullying situations, and (c) commitment to anti-bullying behavior (including class-rules). Individual-level intervention that were discussed during the training included, the No Blame Approach (see Smith & Sharp, 1994), the Farsta method (Ljungström, 2000), and the importance of systematic follow-up was emphasized, as well as the importance of cooperation with parents. At the school-level, training included an emphasis on the importance of a school-policy against bullying behaviors. Salmivalli, Kaukiainen, Voeten, and Sinisammal (2004) provide a description of the project and implementation details, as well as related outcome studies.

The Friendly Schools Project

The Friendly Schools project was implemented in 15 schools (focusing on fourth and fifth grade students) in Australia 2000–2003. The project used the *Principles of Successful Practice for Bullying Reduction in Schools* (Pintabona, Cross, Hamilton, & Hall, 2000) to design and implement multi-level, multi-component, whole-school bullying reduction intervention. The core components of the Friendly Schools project targeted: (a) the whole-school community (e.g., establishment of a committee to build their commitment, through policy and capacity to address bullying); (b) students' families (e.g., awareness raising and skill-based self-efficacy activities); and (c) grade 4 and 5 students and their teachers (e.g., through teacher training and comprehensive teaching and learning support materials). The Friendly Schools classroom curriculum activities included 9 sessions designed to promote: (a) an understanding of bullying behaviors and why it is unacceptable, (b) students' ability to discuss bullying with peers and adults, (c) adaptive responses to being bullied, (d) peer and adult support for student who are being bullied, and (e) discouragement of bullying behaviors. Cross, Hall, Hamilton, Pintabona, and Erceg (2004) offer a description of the project and implementation details, as well as related outcome studies.

The Steps to Respect Bullying Prevention Program

The Steps to Respect program (Committee for Children, 2001) is a universal, multi-level program published in 2001, which aims to reduce bullying problems in elementary school. This program involves coordinating a school-wide environmental intervention with social-cognitive curricula. The environmental intervention aims to provide adults and children with systemic support, procedures, and guidance to impede bullying and motivate prosocial behavior throughout a school. Classroom lessons and instructional practices (designed for use in grades 3 through 6) target children's normative beliefs related to bullying as well as social-emotional skills to counter bullying and promote healthy relationships. The environmental intervention includes: (a) developing and communicating clear school-wide anti-bullying policy and procedures; (b) increasing adult awareness, responsiveness, and guidance in relation to bullying events; and (c) increasing systemic supports for prosocial behavior (Hirschtein & Frey, 2006). The social-cognitive classroom curricula provide multiple pathways to influence behavior: (a) building specific bullying prevention skills, (b) fostering general social-emotional skills, and

(c) addressing beliefs and peer group norms related to bullying and promoting socially responsible beliefs among students (Hirschtein & Frey, 2006). The program guide presents an overview of goals, content, and the research foundation, as well as a blueprint for developing anti-bullying policies and procedures (Committee for Children, 2001).

A related program, Student Success Through Prevention (Second Step; Committee for Children, 2008), was originally developed as a social-emotional skills development and violence prevention program (Fitzgerald & Van Schoiack Edstrom, 2006). The curriculum for grades 6–8 was recently revised. As part of that revision, the program was expanded in scope to include a focus on bullying prevention and substance abuse prevention. The current middle school program, including its effects on bullying, has not been evaluated.

Expect Respect—Bullyproof Prevention Program

The Expect Respect program was implemented in 6 elementary schools (focusing on fifth grade classrooms) in the United States between 1998 and 2000. The Bullyproof program (Sjostrom & Stein, 1996) was used as the core classroom resource. The Bullyproof teacher's guide aims to address teasing and bullying among fourth and fifth grade students. The teacher's guide provides 11 lessons, incorporating class discussion, role plays, case studies, writing exercises, reading assignments, art activities, and homework. The core components of the Bullyproof program include (a) providing children a conceptual framework and a common vocabulary that helps them to explore the links between teasing and bullying, and (b) increasing the ability and willingness of bystanders to intervene when bullying occurs, thus, reducing the social acceptance of bullying behaviors. Additional components of the Expect Respect program included: (a) staff training to raise awareness and prepare school personnel to respond effectively to bullying behaviors (e.g., 6 initial professional development hours for all administrators, counselors, and teacher, and then 3 hours each semester); (b) policy development to ensure consistent reports for bullying behaviors (e.g., statement of philosophy, definition of bullying, expectations for actions in response to incidents, and a commitment to maintaining confidentiality of targets, witnesses, and students accused of bullying); (c) parent education to build support and involve parents in the project (e.g., 2 presentations each year providing information about the project, common vocabulary to discuss the issues, and strategies for helping children who are bullying or being bullied); and (d) support services from school counselors to help support both victims and bullies. Rosenbluth, Whitaker, Sanchez, and Valle (2004) provide a description of the project and implementation details, as well as related outcome studies.

Bully Busters Bullying Prevention Program

The Bully Busters program was developed in the United States and published by Newman, Horne, and Bartolomucci (2000; grades 6–8) and by Horne, Bartolomucci, and Newman-Carlson (2003; grades K–5). Bully Busters is a psychoeducational program designed to help teachers increase their awareness, knowledge, and intervention strategies for bullying behavior. Recognizing the important role that teachers may play in changing the behaviors of children at school, the Bully Busters program focuses on helping teachers to address bullying and victimization behaviors (Newman-Carlson & Horne, 2004). Two Bully Busters manuals address implementation in grades K–5 and grades 6–8, respectively. Each manual is organized into learning modules, including a teacher information component and a series of classroom activities. The classroom activities are designed to increase student participation in reducing and preventing bullying, increase teachers' self-efficacy for addressing bullying and victimization behaviors, as well as to strengthen the teacher-student relationship. For instance, the 7 modules of the Bully Busters grades 6–8 manual (Newman, Horne, & Bartolomucci, 2000) address: (a) increasing awareness of bullying, (b) recognizing the bully, (c) recognizing the victim, (d) interventions for bullying behavior, (e) recommendations and interventions to assist victims, (f) the role of prevention, and (g) relaxation and coping skills. A Bully Busters parent's guide was also recently developed (Horne, 2008). Newman-Carlson and Horne (2004) provide a description of the project and implementation details, as well as related outcome studies.

A Synthesis of Bullying Prevention and Intervention Programs

In the past two decades, researchers in countries around the world have conducted various investigations of bullying prevention and intervention programs (Smith, Pepler, & Rigby, 2004). After the success of the Bergen bullying intervention project spearheaded by Norwegian researcher, Dan Olweus, adapted versions of the original Olweus bullying intervention program have been used in the United States (Limber et al., 2004), Germany (Hanewinkel, 2004), Belgium (Stevens, De Bourdeaudhuij, & Van Oost, 2000), England (Smith, Sharp, Eslea, & Thompson, 2004), Australia (Cross, Hall, Hamilton, Pintabona, & Erceg, 2004), Canada (Pepler et al., 1994), Finland (Salmivalli, Kaukiainen, & Voeten, 2005), and Ireland (O'Moore & Minton, 2004). There are also other programs that bear less resemblance to the Norwegian model, albeit embracing some core components included in the Olweus program, such as, the SAVE program in Spain (Ortega et al., 2004), the Australia PEACE Pack (Slee, 2005), the USA Steps to Respect Program (Frey et al., 2005), the USA Bully-Proofing Your School (Garrity et al., 2000), the USA Bully Busters program (Newman-Carlson & Horne, 2004), and the USA Expect Respect and Bully-proof programs (Rosenbluth et al., 2004; Sjostrom & Stein, 1996). In the next section, we discuss several emerging themes from various programs implemented in different social-cultural environments. The following provides a discussion of program philosophies, contents, evaluation outcomes, and challenges.

Themes of Bullying Prevention and Intervention

Olweus' bullying prevention and intervention program (Olweus, 1993b) has served as a blueprint for various adaptations across nations. Its influence on other programs is also evident. For instance, the definition of bullying with the three key characteristics (frequency, duration, and intentional harm) by Olweus is widely accepted and used in all studies. It is not surprising that the systematic prevention and intervention programs embrace several fundamental principles established in the original model. On the other hand, some variations are noted in the framework and component of the bullying prevention/ intervention programs. In the following section, we discuss: (a) the contextual model of bullying intervention/prevention as a shared feature among programs, (b) outcome evaluation issues common to programs reviewed, and (c) implications based on the lessons and challenges learned through these programs. To keep the discussion coherent, for the first and second issues, we first present the shared themes or principles, followed by the notable variations among programs.

Contextual Factors: Some Shared Features

School-wide and Classroom Policies: Setting the Stage   First and foremost, all of the reviewed programs recognize that bullying phenomenon occurs in a social environment that involves the interplay among peers, school personnel, parents, and physical environment. Swearer and

Espelage (2004) further defined a social-ecological framework of bullying that extends to the community and broader cultural system, which are in addition to the components such as peer dynamics, adult-children interaction, and parental education identified by the Olweus program and most of its adapted versions. By acknowledging the contextual and interactive nature of bullying phenomenon, researchers precluded simplistic and isolated solutions such as merely "talking down a bully," or punishing bullying behaviors. Instead, changes are effected through restructuring of social environment (Stevens, De Bourdeaudhuij, & Van Oost, 2001; Swearer & Espelage, 2004). The Olweus Bullying Prevention Program and its adapted versions in England, Canada, Australia, Germany, and Belgium consist of a whole-school policy as an overarching umbrella that sets the broad backdrop for the bullying prevention and intervention. In some cases, even though structured whole-school policy was not mandated component of the program due to the organization style of the school, class-wide rules and codes of conduct are in place to set clear expectations for behaviors (e.g., Salmivalli et al., 2005)

Teachers and Staff: Managing Behavioral Changes Contingency-based behavioral modification is applied to shape and manage interpersonal behaviors. In the school setting, teachers, staff, and other adult personnel naturally are considered enforcers of the rules. However, are the school personnel equipped with accurate and in-depth understanding and perceptions of school bullying to assume the responsibility of intervention? Previous research revealed that teachers had reported fewer bullying incidents than students did (Stockdale, Hangaduambo, Duys, Larson, & Sarvela, 2002). They also tended to only recognize overt physical and verbal bullying but not covert relational aggression (Bauman & Del Rio, 2005). Given these findings, researchers of bullying prevention and intervention emphasized the importance of educating school personnel as an essential precursor to the implementation of the programs. Various programs used the results from the bullying questionnaire completed by students to educate teachers about the prevalence of bullying/victimization. Additional training materials and/or workshops were provided to increase teachers' capacity to establish and reinforce class rules, and handle bullying incidents. It is also noted that some programs provided on-going consultation support for teachers to sustain the implementation of programs (Hanewinkel, 2004; Limber et al., 2004).

Peers: The Active Participants Peers are the essential participants in the phenomenon of bullying. Peer dynamics are the most important and immediate influence on children's behavior (Bronfenbrenner, 1979; Lewin, 1943). Bullying prevention and intervention programs reviewed above all targeted peer ecology as a major component of intervention. Closer examinations of these components further revealed that education, or raising awareness about bullying and victimization, again was the precursor to changing behaviors. In addition, empowering student groups to handle bullying appear to be another goal of the programs. A variety of materials and activities, such as videos, novels, drama, group discussion, and role plays were included in prevention and intervention programs (Stevens et al., 2001). Notably, programs have placed emphasis on somewhat different aspects of peer relationships and dynamic. For example, the Steps to Respect Program (Frey et al., 2005) aimed at fostering socially responsible beliefs and building social skills. The Finnish and Flemish anti-bullying programs (Salmivalli et al., 2005; Stevens et al., 2004), on the other hand, emphasized changing by-standers' behavior. These programs sought to mobilize by-standers—the majority of children who are not directly involved in bullying incidents—to withdraw support from bullying perpetrators, extend empathy towards victims, and develop skills to intervene with bullying (directly and/or by enlisting help from adults). Other programs appear to embrace a combination of social skill instruction and by-stander behavior change (e.g., Cross et al., 2004; Ortega et al., 2004). Another prominent similarity shared by the reviewed programs is the use of multiple pedagogical modalities to address the peer factors in bullying prevention/ intervention. Specifically, videos and group discussions based on videos, dramas, and role plays are widely used to stimulate children's interest in the topic and facilitate effective acquisition of skills.

Parents: The Influence Beyond Schools Developmental and ecological studies have revealed the connection between family dynamic and children's social behaviors, including bullying and victimization (Franz & Gross, 1996). Most of the programs reviewed, with the exception of the Finnish (Salmivalli et al., 2005) and English (Smith, Sharp, et al., 2004) programs included parental involvement. Parental involvement in these programs was typically imbedded in the education/awareness raising component (e.g., (Frey et al., 2005; Hanewinkel, 2004; Olweus, 1993a; Pepler et al., 1994; Stevens et al., 2004). Also, parents of bullies and victims who were targeted in individual-level interventions were often contacted. The Friendly School in Australia (Cross et al., 2004) and Steps to Respect (Frey et al., 2005) provided on-going informational materials for parents during the program implementation. For these two projects, the materials included activities or suggestions that coincided with program content implemented at school. Parental application of the materials was expected to reinforce skill acquisition and behavioral change.

Other Contextual Factors: Variations among Programs

Individuals Coinciding with a mutli-tier prevention and intervention framework, the original Bergen Project (Olweus, 1993b) and several of its adaptations (Hanewinkel, 2004; Pepler et al., 1994; Stevens, De Bourdeaudhuij, et al., 2000) included an element of individual intervention. In addition to the participation in group activities within the program (e.g., anti-bullying curriculum, discussions, and role-plays), bullies and victims were individually targeted through in-person meeting with teachers and/ or parents to specifically address their challenges. Some programs, however, accomplished student-level activities only through group-based activities (e.g., Frey et al., 2005; Smith, Sharp, et al., 2004).

The Physical Environment and Adult Supervisions In several programs (Limber et al., 2004; Olweus, 1993b; Pepler et al., 1994; Smith, Sharp, et al., 2004), policies effecting whole-school climate change were accompanied by modifications of physical environment, especially environments where unstructured activities take place (e.g., playgrounds and lunchroom). These modifications include rearrangement of furniture or equipment and increase of adult supervisions. In other programs (Hanewinkel, 2004; Salmivalli et al., 2005; Stevens, De Bourdeaudhuij et al., 2000), the modifications of environmental factors primarily focused on the social aspects such as school policies and behavioral codes. Such variation may be partially due to the specific existing conditions, resources, schedule, or organization of schools and activities. For instance, The Sheffield Project in England was able to enlist local government agencies to re-landscape schools' playground while constraint of resources preclude other projects from effecting similar changes in the physical environment (e.g., Hanewinkel, 2004).

Program Evaluation

A component of outcome evaluation has been present in bullying prevention/intervention programs since the implementation and investigation of Olweus' original program (Olweus, 1993b).

A thorough discussion of the program evaluation methodology is beyond the scope of this chapter. Interested readers may refer to Section II Assessment and Measurement of Bullying for more information. In the present section, we summarize common issues in study design, data analyses, and results among the bullying prevention/ intervention programs.

Research Design   Regarding to research design, a shared feature among different programs is the multi-level analyses of outcome variables. As the systematic bullying intervention/ prevention programs consist of components at different ecological levels, the evaluation of outcomes are conducted on several levels, namely, individual level, classroom level, and school level.

The cross-cohort design and the mixed design (with both between group and pre- and post-intervention tests) have been used in outcome evaluations of the various programs. The nature of bullying behaviors and the practical factors that affect empirical research are the two major determinants that influence researchers' selection of research design. For instance, Olweus (1993a, 1993b), Smith et al. (2004), Pepler et al. (1994), and Salmivalli et al. (2005) adopted the cross-cohort design to control for the developmental change of bullying behaviors. This design allows comparison of same-age children in adjacent cohorts with intervals between measurements. The "within child" developmental changes that may confound the intervention effects are controlled as each time point comparison is carried out between comparable children with and without intervention at a specific age. Because of the involvement of several adjacent cohorts of children, this design is feasible in the practical circumstances. On the other hand, some researchers (Cross et al., 2004; Frey et al., 2005) examined both the "within child" changes across time intervals (i.e., pre- and post-intervention), and the control vs. experimental groups. Studies with intervention/experiment and control groups are deemed the most rigorous in the examination of anti-bullying program effectiveness (Smith, Schneider, Smith, & Ananiadou, 2004). However, practical challenges sometimes hinder implementation of this type of design. For instance, Pepler et al. (1994) found the initially intended "waiting-list control" design ineffective, as schools are too different to achieve "true control." In addition, the pre-intervention data gathering in "control group" also tends to sensitize participants and even mobilize them to act on bullying issues, thus invalidating the "control" condition.

Sources of Outcome Variables   Outcome evaluations of bullying prevention/intervention programs routinely utilize results from children's self-report questionnaires and surveys as outcome measures (D. J. Smith et al., 2004). The fact that bullying and victimization are individual experiences that often occur beyond adults' oversight and/ or awareness makes self-report an essential component of the data. There is, however, a problem that underlies the self-report measures (D. J. Smith et al., 2004). Self-report measures of bullying/ victimization are often not significantly correlated with other types of measures, including independent observations and teacher ratings (Hirschstein, Van Schoiack Edstrom, Frey, Snell, & MacKenzie, 2007; Pellegrini & Bartini, 2000). Children's subjectivity and social and cognitive developmental stages greatly influence their self-report perception and experience with bullying. Multi-source and multi-method data gathering is essential in helping researchers understand the impact of anti-bullying programs.

Coded observation data by trained professionals stands out as a valuable information source. The cost and resources involved in the observation approach makes it unlikely to be adopted on a large scale in practical implementation of anti-bullying programs. However, adequately devised and conducted observations complement subjective self-report with more objective information. It yields powerful data that help researchers understand the complex processes and aspects involved in bullying prevention and intervention. For instance, with observation data in addition to children's self-report, Pepler et al. (1994) was able to detect a decline in the rate of bullying observed by trained professionals, whereas children's self-report actually demonstrated an increase. Hirschstein et al. (2007) did not observe a rise in victimization, which was reported by the child participants. Taking into consideration of multiple data sources, these researchers speculated an artificial sensitization effect induced by the anti-bullying programs.

Implementation Factors As systematic prevention/ intervention programs that involve the participation of various parties and implementation at different levels, it is important to examine how the implementation variables influence the outcomes (Hirschstein et al., 2007; Kallestad & Olweus, 2003; Salmivalli et al., 2004; Smith, Sharp, et al., 2004; Stevens et al., 2000). These variables primarily concern the adherence and/ or quality of program implementation. The addition of implementation integrity data in the multi-level regression analyses has shed lights on the relationship between the implementation integrity and/or quality and outcomes. For instance, Smith, Sharp, and colleagues (2004) reported significant positive relationship between overall program implementation quality and children's perception about schools' actions towards bullying and positive changes in their schools. In addition, school staff's involvement in the program implementation is significantly correlated with the changes in children's self-report experience of bullying and being bullied. Salmivalli et al. (2004) concluded that intervention effects were more often found in schools with higher degree of implementation. It is noted, however, the significant and positive association between high level of implementation and desirable outcomes is not universal among different investigations. Non-significant findings and findings that contradict predicted relationship have emerged. In the Hirschstein et al. (2007) study, while the quality of the program implementation was positively related to teachers' ratings of social skills, it actually corresponded to higher level self-reported victimization and more children perceived difficulty responding assertively to bullying. The researchers speculated several possible explanations for the surprising findings. First, it is possible that pre-test self-report victimization was depressed due to the social stigma attached to victimization, which was in turn reduced by high quality instruction of the Steps to Respect lessons, thus resulting in elevated post-test victimization report. Second, the lessons may have sensitized students to report victimization. Finally, from a methodological point of view, the focus on adherence and quality of lesson implementation may have restricted the data range, making it difficult to detect intervention effects.

When Hirschstein et al. (2007) made further distinction between "talking the talk" implementation (i.e., adherence and quality of teaching the lessons involved in the Steps to Respect Program) vs. "walking the walk" practice (i.e., teachers' generalized support outside of anti-bullying lessons). They found different results of the two levels of implementation. Specifically, while "talking to talk" is associated with mixed outcomes (see above), the "walking the walk" practice—generalizing support in contexts beyond program lessons was associated with reduction in observed antisocial behaviors, victimization, and destructive by-stander behaviors.

Outcomes The Olweus' original anti-bullying program reported successful outcomes. For instance, outcomes for intervention studies include a 50% reduction (Olweus, 1993b), 17% reduction (Smith & Sharp, 1994), 30% reduction (Pepler et. al., 1994), and 30%–40% reduction (Clearihan et al., 1999). However, the majority of subsequent programs evaluated so far rarely found outcomes that approximate the dramatic success of the Norwegian program (Smith, Schneider, et al., 2004). In general, the outcomes were mixed. For example, in Canada, Pepler et al. (1994) found steady decrease of self-reported bullying and victimization in some schools but not the others. In the United States, Frey et al. (2005) found no significant change in self-report bullying and aggression, but significant decrease in self-report victimization. Employing a rigorous observation and coding method, however, Frey et al. (2005) did not find significant decrease in observed victimization. On the contrary, they observed significant reduction of bullying and aggression among children who were perpetrators in the pretest phase. Regarding by-standers behaviors Stevens and De Bourdeaudhuij et al. (2000), found that among primary school students, there was a small decrease of by-standers intervening with bullying in the experiment group. Secondary students in the experiment group, however, reported improved by-stander attitudes, self-efficacy, and actions regarding bullying. In Australia, Cross et al. (2004) reported largely non-significant change between experiment and control groups across time intervals in terms of perceptions of social support and attitudes towards victims.

On one hand, the mixed pattern of results in part reflects the complexity of school-wide prevention and intervention programs. Socio-cultural factors and political climate affect the implementation of anti-bullying programs. Even though the adaptations of the original Olweus program reviewed above embraced the theoretical framework and "active ingredients" of the Norwegian program (Smith, Schneider, et al., 2004; Stevens et al., 2001), the different social, political, and organizational features in different countries may have played an important role in the implementation process. Smith, Schneider, et al. (2004) speculated that the timing of the intervention in relation to significant incidence (e.g., national news on student suicides related to victimization), small class size, quality teacher training, and a strong tradition of nation-wide mandated intervention may have contributed to the significant success of the Olweus program. Socio-cultural and political factors (at society level and school/ organization level) obviously influence how school administrators and staff perceive the anti-bullying programs, which may have direct implications on the quality and integrity of implementation (Hanewinkel, 2004; Smith, Sharp, et al., 2004; Stevens et al., 2004). Financially, socio-cultural and political factors also affect funding and resources invested in anti-bullying programs. The longitudinal nature of bullying prevention/ intervention programs requires sustained support (grant monies and policies) and efforts, without which, the effects of anti-bullying programs are likely to diminish (Limber et al., 2004).

On the other hand, methodological issues complicate the investigations of anti-bullying program outcomes. First, the adoption of multiple types of data is imperative to understanding the program effects. Due to the lack of relationship among observation data, children's self-report and adult ratings, the integrated use of at 2 or more measures is more likely to reveal the impact of the bullying prevention/ intervention programs from various perspectives. Second, qualitative data and analyses are needed for in-depth understanding of the program impact. Currently, Outcome variables and analyses are predominantly quantitative. In the few studies where qualitative data was collected through teacher report and interviews (Salmivalli et al., 2005; Smith, Sharp et al., 2004), the focus of the data was on implementation integrity and quality. And these data were coded and entered into quantitative analyses. Quantitative analyses answer questions such as "is it effective?" and "is there a significant change?" In light of the mixed findings to these questions, however, qualitative studies such as in-depth interviews are needed to answer "why is it effective (or not effective)?" and "how does the change happen?" In another word, rigorous qualitative analyses may unveil the processes and mechanisms, through which anti-bullying programs influence children's and adults' experience, perceptions, and actions related to bullying.

Finally, the validity of the self-report questionnaire/survey in terms of measuring bullying-related behavior warrants further investigation. The validity issue has more to do with the wording of items and questions on instruments than the statistical property. Greif and Furlong (2006) discussed the mismatch between bullying surveys/ questionnaires and the definition of bullying. According to Olweus (1993b), power differentiation between perpetrators and victims, frequency (repetition), duration, and intention to harm are the defining characteristics of bullying. However, most of the questionnaires used in the evaluations only probe the frequency of behaviors over a period of time (e.g., "How many times were you called names since Christmas?"). They do not, however, address whether the behaviors are intended to harm or hurt and whether there is power differentiation between the individuals involved. Teasing and rough-and-tumble play can be developmentally appropriate and functional social interaction among children (Schwartz, Dodge, Pettit, & Bates, 1997). These behaviors indeed should be differentiated from bullying. Greif and Furlong (2006) incorporated questions regarding the intention of behaviors and whether the person involved is perceived to be stronger, smarter, or more popular than the respondent. Davidson and Demaray (2007) revised the Greif and Furlong (2006) survey by simultaneously measuring intention and power difference involved in each of the behaviors that may be involved in bullying. For instance, the respondent was asked to rate the frequency of being called names in school. Additionally, the child was to indicate whether the name-calling was "just joking" or "meant to be mean." Next, the child chose his/her emotional response to the name calling among "Not Bad," "Kinda Bad," and "Really Bad." The child also select "Yes" or "No" responses respectively to questions "Was the person who was mean to you more popular? Stronger? And/or smarter?" Finally, the child responds whether the name calling makes him/her worried or scared. Using the revised survey, Davidson and Demaray (2007) compared the prevalence of bullying and victimization measured by behaviors that are (a) frequent only, (b) frequent and intentional, (c) frequent and with power difference, and (d) frequent, intentional, and with power difference. In addition, the percentage of children's emotional responses to these behaviors (e.g., feeling bad, scared and worried) were also calculated. Highly variable prevalence rates were identified for most of the behaviors. For example, using the frequency only criteria, 51% of the children reported being called names 2 or 3 times a month. The prevalence sharply dropped to 14% when "intention" is added (i.e., it is done to be mean, not joking). When using all three criteria (frequency, intention, and power difference), the prevalence was 9%. These emerging investigations on the measurement issues highlight the needs for the refinement of instrument validity, which may enhance the sensitivity of detecting changes effected by programs on "true" bullying and victimization.

Results of Meta-Analyses   Two recent meta-analyses review the effectiveness of bullying interventions (Smith, Schneider, et al., 2004; Merrell, Guelder, Ross, & Isava, 2008). Smith, Schneider, and colleagues (2004) completed a meta-analysis of 14 studies, published between 1989 and 2003, which included data from whole-school anti-bullying programs. The 14 studies were from projects in 10 countries (i.e., Australia, Belgium, Canada, England, Finland, Germany, Italy, Norway, Switzerland, and the United States). The authors concluded that the majority of programs yielded non-significant outcomes when considering student self-report measures of bullying and victimization. Merrell and colleagues (2008) completed a meta-analysis of 16 studies, published between 1994 and 2003, including studies focusing on the broad range of interventions (e.g., small group, classroom, as well as whole-school interventions). The 16 studies were from 6 countries (e.g., Belgium, Canada, Italy, Norway, the United Kingdom, and the United States). The majority of the outcomes revealed no meaningful change, either positive or negative. The authors concluded that the majority of outcome variables in school bullying intervention studies are not meaningfully impacted. Furthermore, the authors highlighted that school bullying intervention programs are more likely to influence knowledge, attitudes, and self-perceptions, rather than actual bullying behaviors. The results of these recent meta-analyses offer sobering information for those engaged in efforts to develop and implement bullying prevention and intervention programs around the world.

Conclusions and Implications

School bullying is a prevalent phenomenon across different countries and cultures (Nishina, 2004). It has various short- and long-term negative consequences on both the victims and the perpetrators. The success of Olweus bullying prevention/ intervention program has served as a model for programs in different countries. Other systematic anti-bullying programs embraced the ecological perspective (e.g., school and classroom environment) to address bullying reduction (common elements and implications for practice are identified in Table 41.1). However, most of the existing evaluations yielded either non-significant or mixed results on program effectiveness (Galloway & Roland, 2004; Smith, Schneider, et al., 2004).

Some researchers attempted to explain the mixed results and lack of positive outcomes among anti-bullying programs partially through a social-biological/ evolution perspective (see Nishina, 2004, for a comprehensive review). This perspective maintains that peer aggression is a form of common socialization process, which sometimes serves adaptive social functioning among humans and other primates through offering evolutionary advantages to the group. For instance, peer aggression can be a means of delineating social hierarchy, which stabilizes the peer group, enhances within-group cohesion, and creates a sense of affiliation among members. The social hierarchy (e.g., aggressors receiving admiration, acceptance, and support from group members), in turn reinforces the aggression. Nishina (2004) argues that "… it is difficult, if not impossible, to *completely* eliminate peer harassment" (p. 50). However, "[b]ully/victim problems have broader implications… They really concern some of our fundamental democratic principles: Every individual should have the right to be spared oppression and repeated, intentional humiliation, in school as in society at large" (p. 48; Olweus, 1993b). Despite the possible inherent nature of bullying (i.e., human nature) and mixed findings of program effectiveness, the study of anti-bullying program should continue.

In light of the limited effectiveness reported by the majority of existing studies, Smith, Schneider, and colleagues (2004) asserted that "… only a cautious recommendation can be made that whole-school anti-bullying interventions be continued until they are evaluated further" (p. 558). With regard to outcome evaluations, there has been mounting evidence that data collection from multiple sources (e.g., teacher ratings, children's self-report, observations, peer nominations) is vitally important to the detection of program effects. Another aspect of data collection concerns the wording of self-report surveys/ questionnaires, a most frequently used approach in bullying measure. Instruments with more fine-grained wording that probe the occurrence of behaviors with the defining features of "true" bullying and victimization may be more sensitive to detect program effects. Furthermore, implementation integrity and quality are variables that significantly influence outcomes. Therefore, they are essential in both research data analyses and empirical practice. It is also imperative that future research collect and analyze qualitative data on the process through which the programs affect the interaction among students and between teachers and students. The process-oriented data reveals the mechanisms that cause or inhibit behavioral changes. Finally, from a perspective of program design, Galloway and Roland (2004) proposed that bullying behaviors are highly correlated with other problem behaviors in general. Given the constraint in the resources available to teachers and schools, a broader behavioral management program, rather than a program specifically and explicitly focus on bullying may produce more significant and sustainable positive effects. In the future, it would be beneficial to examine the effect of broad-band school-based behavioral programs on students' peer interaction, including bullying and victimization.

This volume intends to review the research and knowledge base across different countries. It is noted, however, that most of the studies discussed were conducted in industrialized Western

Table 41.1 Implications for Practice Considering International Perspectives on Bullying Prevention and Intervention

Implications for Infrastructure to Promote Bullying Prevention and Intervention Activities
- Efforts should begin early and continue through the school-age years
- Strong leadership is required (e.g., administration and committee members)
- Parent and community involvement is critical in the planning process and implementation of programs
- An ongoing commitment from school personnel is essential (e.g., teachers, student support professionals)
- Ongoing staff development and training are necessary to refine and sustain programs
- Programs must be culturally sensitive to student diversity issues (e.g., contextual considerations)
- Programs must be developmentally appropriate (e.g., considering the social, emotional, and cognitive development of the students)

Implications for School-Level Bullying Prevention and Intervention Activities
- Beginning with administration of a student questionnaire is valuable to determine the nature and extent of bullying problems at school, these data may also be used as a base-line, to examine change following implementation of programs
- Establishing a bullying prevention and intervention coordinating committee is important to provide ongoing leadership (e.g., a small group of teachers, administrators, counselors, parent representative, relevant community leaders/experts, and other school staff, to plan, facilitate implementation, monitor, and evaluate efforts).
- Organizing professional development or in-service days to review findings from the questionnaire, discuss problems of bullying at the school, and solicit input to develop bullying prevention and intervention activities
- Coordinating school-wide events to launch the program (e.g., assemblies, parent information sessions)
- Providing increased supervision in areas that are hot spots for bullying and violence at the school
- Establishing and disseminating of school-wide rules and sanctions against bullying
- Developing a school context focused on promoting and reinforcing positive and prosocial peer behaviors (e.g., school-wide positive behavioral support strategies)
- Promoting parent involvement in school activities (e.g., highlighting the program at parent meetings, school open houses, and special violence prevention programs; encouraging parents' participation in planning activities and school events)
- Establishing regularly scheduled classroom meetings, so that teachers may engage students in discussion, role-playing, and creative activities related to preventing bullying

Implications for Individual-Level Bullying Prevention and Intervention Activities
- Responding to all bullying incidents to provide immediate intervention by school staff (e.g., appropriate student support service professionals, meet with victims and bullies)
- Involving parents of bullies and victims of bullying, to help problem solve and reduce conflict, where appropriate.
- Formating "friendship groups" or other supports for students who are victims of bullying, in an effort to promote positive peer relationships and prosocial skills
- Involving school counselors or mental health professionals, where appropriate.

Implications for Community-Level Bullying Prevention and Intervention Activities
- Convening meetings with leaders of the community to make the program known among a wide range of residents in the local community, also may include encouraging local media coverage of the school's efforts
- Involving community members in the school's anti-bullying activities (e.g., soliciting assistance from local business to support aspects of the program, involving community members in school district-wide events)
- Engaging community members, students, and school personnel in anti-bullying efforts within the community (e.g., introducing core program elements into summer church school classes).

Implications for School Administrators — Bullying Prevention and Intervention Activities
- Assess the awareness and the scope of the bullying problem at your school through student and staff surveys.
- Closely supervise children on the playgrounds and in classrooms, hallways, restrooms, cafeterias and other areas where bullying occurs in your school.
- Conduct school-wide assemblies and teacher/staff in-service training to raise awareness regarding the problem of bullying and to denounce tolerance for such behavior.
- Post and publicize clear behavior standards, including rules against bullying, for all students. Consistently and fairly enforce such standards.
- Encourage parent participation by establishing on-campus parents' centers that recruit, coordinate and encourage parents to take part in the educational process and in volunteering to assist in school activities and projects.
- Establish a confidential reporting system that allows children to report victimization and that records the details of bullying incidents.

(continued)

Table 41.1 Continued

- Ensure that your school has all legally required policies and grievance procedures for sexual discrimination. Make these procedures known to parents and students.
- Receive and listen receptively to parents who report bullying. Establish procedures whereby such reports are investigated and resolved expeditiously at the school level in order to avoid perpetuating bullying.
- Develop strategies to reward students for positive, and prosocial behavior.
- Provide school-wide and classroom activities that are designed to build self-esteem by spotlighting special talents, hobbies, interests and abilities of all students and that foster mutual understanding of and appreciation for differences in others.

Implications for Teachers—Bullying Prevention and Intervention Activities

- Provide students with opportunities to talk about bullying and enlist their support in defining bullying as unacceptable behavior.
- Involve students in establishing classroom rules against bullying. Such rules may include a commitment from the teacher to not "look the other way" when incidents involving bullying occur.
- Provide classroom activities and discussions related to bullying and violence, including the harm that they cause and strategies to reduce them.
- Develop a classroom action plan to ensure that students know what to do when they observe a bully/ victim confrontation.
- Teach cooperation by assigning projects that require collaboration. Such cooperation teaches students how to compromise and how to assert without demanding. Take care to vary grouping of participants and to monitor the treatment of participants in each group.
- Take immediate action when bullying is observed. All teachers and school staff must let children know that they care and will not allow anyone to be mistreated. By taking immediate action and dealing directly with the bully, adults support both the victim and the witnesses.
- Confront bullies in private. Challenging a bully in front of his/her peers may actually enhance his/her status and lead to further aggression.
- Notify the parents of both victims and bullies when a confrontation occurs, and seek to resolve the problem expeditiously at school.
- Refer both victims and aggressors to counseling whenever appropriate.
- Provide protection for bullying victims, whenever necessary. Such protection may include creating a buddy system whereby students have a particular friend or older buddy on whom they can depend and with whom they share class schedule information and plans for the school day.
- Listen receptively to parents who report bullying and investigate reported circumstances so that immediate and appropriate school action may be taken.
- Avoid attempts to mediate a bullying situation. The difference in power between victims and bullies may cause victims to feel further victimized by the process or believe that they are somehow at fault.

Implications for Students—Bullying Prevention and Intervention Activities
Depending on the situation and their own level of comfort, students can:
- seek immediate help from an adult;
- report bullying/victimization incidents to school personnel;
- speak up and/or offer support to the victim when they see him/her being bullied—for example, picking up the victim's books and handing them to him or her;
- privately support those being hurt with words of kindness or condolence;
- express disapproval of bullying behavior by not joining in the laughter, teasing or spreading of rumors or gossip; and
- attempt to defuse problem situations either single handedly or in a group—for example, by taking the bully aside and asking him/her to "cool it."

Implications for Parents—Bullying Prevention and Intervention Activities
- The best protection parents can offer their children who are involved in a bully/victim conflict is to foster their child's confidence and independence and to be willing to take action when needed.
- Be careful not to convey to a child who is being victimized that something is wrong with him/her or that he/she deserves such treatment. When a child is subjected to abuse from his or her peers, it is not fair to fault the child's social skills. Respect is a basic right: All children are entitled to courteous and respectful treatment. Communicate to your child that he or she is not at fault and that the bully's behavior is the source of the problem.
- It is appropriate to communicate with the school if your child is involved in a conflict as either a victim or a bully. Work collaboratively with school personnel to address the problem. Keep records of incidents so that you can be specific in your discussion with school personnel about your child's experiences at school.

(continued)

Table 41.1 Continued

- You may arrange a conference with a teacher, principal or counselor. School personnel may be able to offer some practical advice to help you and your child. They may also be able to intervene directly with each of the participants. School personnel may have observed the conflict firsthand and may be able to corroborate your child's version of the incident, making it harder for the bully or the bully's parents to deny its authenticity.
- While it is often important to talk with the bully or his/ her parents, be careful in your approach. Speaking directly to the bully may signal to the bully that your child is a weakling. Speaking with the parents of a bully may not accomplish anything since lack of parental involvement in the child's life is a typical characteristic of parents of bullies. Parents of bullies may also fail to see anything wrong with bullying, equating it to "standing up for oneself."
- Offer support to your child but do not encourage dependence on you. Rescuing your child from challenges or assuming responsibility yourself when things are not going well does not teach your child independence. The more choices a child has to make, the more he or she develops independence, and independence can contribute to self-confidence.
- Do not encourage your child to be aggressive or to strike back. Chances are that it is not his or her nature to do so. Rather, teach your child to be assertive. A bully often is looking for an indication that his/her threats and intimidation are working. Tears or passive acceptance only reinforces the bully's behavior. A child who does not respond as the bully desires is not likely to be chosen as a victim. For example, children can be taught to respond to aggression with humor and assertions rather than acquiescence.
- Be patient. Conflict between children more than likely will not be resolved overnight. Be prepared to spend time with your child, encouraging your child to develop new interests or strengthen existing talents and skills that will help develop and improve his/her selfesteem. Also help your child to develop new or bolster existing friendships. Friends often serve as buffers to bullying.
- If the problem persists or escalates, you may need to seek professional or legal help or contact local law enforcement officials. Bullying or acts of bullying should not be tolerated in the school or the community. Students should not have to tolerate bullying at school any more than adults would tolerate such situations at work.

Sources: The implications noted above were adapted from the bullying prevention and intervention programs reviewed in this chapter, as well as the information available in the public domain through the United States Department of Education (2008). Exploring the Nature and Prevention of Bullying. Available on-line at http://www.ed.gov/admins/lead/safety/training/bullying/index.html

countries. Relatively little is known about school bullying prevention/intervention in Asia, Africa, and Eastern Europe. Socio-cultural and political factors have a strong influence on resources, organizational characteristic, and climate of schools. The design and implementation of anti-bullying program may vary greatly. Nonetheless, the comparative examination of programs among different nations may advance the understanding of bullying/victimization issues in various contexts.

References

Alsaker, F. D. (2004). Bernese programme against victimization in kindergarten elementary school. In P. K. Smith, D. Pepler, & K. Rigby (Eds), *Bullying in schools: How successful can interventions be?* (pp. 289–306). Cambridge, England: Cambridge University Press.

Bauman, S., & Del Rio, A. (2005). Knowledge and beliefs about bullying in schools: Comparing pre-service teachers in the United States and the United Kingdom. *School Psychology International, 26*(4), 428–442.

Bronfenbrenner, U. (1979). *The ecology of human development: Experiments by nature and design.* Cambridge, MA: Harvard University Press.

Clearihan, S, Slee, P. T., Souter, M., Gascoign, Nichols, A., Burgan, M., & Gee, J. (1999, May). *Antiviolence bullying prevention project.* Paper presented at the Victimology Conference, Adelaide, Australia.

Committee for Children. (2001). *Steps to Respect: A bullying prevention program.* Seattle, WA: Author.

Committee for Children. (2008). *Second Step: Student Success Through Prevention.* Seattle, WA: Author.

Cross, D., Hall, M., Hamilton, G., Pintabona, Y., & Erceg, E. (2004). Australia: The Friendly Schools project. In P. K. Smith, D. Pepler, & K. Rigby (Eds), *Bullying in schools: How successful can interventions be?* (pp. 187–210). Cambridge, England: Cambridge University Press.

Davidson, L., & Demaray, M. (2007). *The "My Experiences with Classmates at School" Bullying Survey Revision.* Paper presented at the National Association of School Psychologists Annual Convention, New York.

Epstein, L., Plog, A., & Porter, W. (2002). Bully proofing your school: Results of a four-year intervention. *Emotional and Behavioral Disorders in Youth, 2*(3), 55–56, 73–77.

Fitzgerald, P., & Van Schoiack Edstrom, L. (2006). Second Step: A violence prevention curriculum. In S. R. Jimerson, & M. J. Furlong, *The handbook of school violence and school safety: From research to practice* (pp. 383–394) Mahwah, NJ: Erlbaum.

Franz, D. Z., & Gross, A. M. (1996). Parental correlates of socially neglected, rejected, and average children: A laboratory study. *Behavior Modification, 20*(2), 170–182.

Frey, K. S., Hirschstein, M. K., Snell, J. L., Van Schoiack Edstrom, L., MacKenzie, E. P., & Broderick, C. J. (2005). Reducing playground bullying and supporting beliefs: An experimental trial of the Steps to Respect Program. *Developmental Psychology, 41*(3), 479–491.

Galloway, D., & Roland, E. (2004). Is the direct approach to reducing bullying always the best? In K. Rigby (Ed.), *Bullying in schools: How successful can intervention be?* (pp. 37–54). Cambridge, England: Cambridge University Press.

Garrity, C., Jens, K., Porter, W., Sager, N., & Short-Camilli, C. (1994). *Bully-Proofing Your School: A comprehensive approach for elementary schools.* Longmont, CO: Sopris West.

Garrity, C., Jens, K., Porter, W., Sager, N., & Short-Camilli, C. (2000). *Bully-Proofing Your School: A comprehensive approach for elementary schools* (2nd ed.). Longmont, CO: Sopris West.

Greif, J. L., & Furlong, M. J. (2006). The assessment of school bullying: Using theory to inform practice. *Journal of School Violence, 5,* 33–50.

Hanewinkel, R. (2004). Prevention of bullying in German schools: an evaluation of an anti-bullying approach. In K. Rigby (Ed.), *Bullying in schools: How successful can interventions be?* (pp. 81–97). Cambridge, England: Cambridge University Press.

Hirschstein, M. K., Van Schoaick Edstrom, L., Frey, K. S., Snell, J. L., & MacKenzie, E. P. (2007). Walking the talk in bullying prevention: Teacher implementation variables related to initial impact of the Steps to Respect Program. *School Psychology Review, 36*(1), 3–21.

Hirschtein, M. K., & Frey, K. S. (2006). Promoting behavior and beliefs that reduce bullying: The *Steps to Respect* Program. In S. R. Jimerson & M. J. Furlong, *The handbook of school violence and school safety: From research to practice* (pp. 309–324). Mahwah, NJ: Erlbaum.

Horne, A. M. (2008). *A parent's guide to understanding and responding to bullying: The Bully Busters approach.* Champaign, IL: Research Press.

Horne, A. M., Bartolomucci, C. L., & Newman-Carlson, D. (2003). *Bully Busters: A teacher's manual for helping bullies, victims, and bystanders (grades K-5).* Champaign, IL: Research Press.

Kallestad, J. H., & Olweus, D. (2003). Predicting teachers' and schools' implementation of the Olweus Bullying Prevention Program: A Multilevel Study. *Prevention & Treatment, 6* (1).

Lewin, K. (1943). Psychology and the process of group living. *Journal of Social Psychology, 17,* 113–131.

Limber, S. P. (2006). The Olweus bullying prevention program: An overview of its implementation and research basis. In S. R. Jimerson & M. J. Furlong (Eds.), *The handbook of school violence and school safety: From research to practice* (pp. 3–19). Mahwah, NJ: Erlbaum.

Limber, S. P., Nation, M., Tracy, A. J., Melton, G. B., & Flerx, V. (2004). Implementation of the Olweus Bullying Prevention programme in the Southeastern United States. In K. Rigby (Ed.), *Bullying in schools: How successful can interventions be?* (pp. 55–79). Cambridge, England: Cambridge University Press.

Ljungström, K. (2000). *Mobbing i skolan* [Bullying in Schools]. Ordkällan, Sweden: Pedaktiv.

Menard, S., Grotpeter, J., Gianola, D., & O'Neal, M. (2008). *Evaluation of Bullyproofing Your School: Final report.* U.S. Department of Justice Document 221078. Retrieved October 1, 2008, from http://www.ncjrs.gov/pdffiles1/nij/grants/221078.pdf

Merrell, K. W., Guelder, B. A., Ross, S. W., & Isava, D. M. (2008). How effective are school bullying intervention programs? A meta-analysis of intervention research. *School Psychology Quarterly, 23,* 26–42.

Newman-Carlson, D., & Horne, A. M. (2004). Bully Busters: A psychoeducational intervention for reducing bullying behavior in middle school students. *Journal of counseling and development, 82* (3), 259–267.

Newman, D. A., Horne, A. M., & Bartolomucci, C. L. (2000). *Bully Busters: A teacher's manual for helping bullies, victims, and bystanders.* Champaign, IL: Research Press.

Nishina, A. (2004). A theoretical review of bullying: Can it be eliminated? In G. D. Phye (Ed.), *Bullying: Implications for the classroom* (pp. 35–62). New York: Elsevier.

Olweus, D. (1991). Bully/victim problems among schoolchildren: Basic facts and effects of a school based intervention program. In D. J. Pepler & K. H. Rubin (Eds.), *The development and treatment of childhood aggression* (pp. 411–448). Hillsdale, NJ: Erlbaum.

Olweus, D. (1993a). Bully/victim problems among schoolchildren: Long-term consequences and an effective intervention program. In S. Hodgins (Ed.), *Mental disorder and crime* (pp. 317–349). Thousand Oaks, CA: Sage.

Olweus, D. (1993b). *Bullying at school: What we know and what we can do.* Cambridge, MA: Blackwell.

Olweus, D. (1994). Annotation: Bullying at school: Basic facts and effects of a school based intervention program. *Journal of Child Psychology and Psychiatry, 35,* 1171–1190.

Olweus, D. (2004). Bullying at school: Prevalence estimation, a useful evaluation design, and a new national initiative in Norway. *Association for Child Psychology and Psychiatry Occasional Papers No. 23*, 5–17.

Olweus, D., Limber, S. P., & Mihalic, S. (1999). *The Bullying Prevention Program: Blueprints for violence prevention, Vol. 10.* Boulder, CO: Center for the Study and Prevention of Violence. .

O'Moore, A. M., & Minton, S. J. (2004). Ireland: The Donegal Primary Schools anti-bullying project. In P. K. Smith, D. Pepler, & K. Rigby (Eds), *Bullying in Schools: How successful can interventions be?* (pp. 275–288). Cambridge, England: Cambridge University Press.

Ortega, R. (1997). El proyecto Sevilla Antiviolencia Escolar. Un modelo d intervencion preventiva contra los malos tratos entre inguales [The Seville school antiviolence project: A model intervention and prevention program to prevent abuse among youth]. *Revista de Educacion, 313*, 143–160.

Ortega, R., & Leer, M. J. (2000). Seville anti-bullying school project. *Aggressive Behavior, 26*, 13–123.

Ortega, R., Del Rey, R., & Mora-Merchan, J. A. (2004). SAVE model: An anti-bullying intervention in Spain. In P. K. Smith, D. Pepler, & K. Rigby (Eds.), *Bullying in Schools: How successful can interventions be?* (pp. 167–186). Cambridge, England: Cambridge University Press.

Pellegrini, A. D., & Bartini, M. (2000). An empirical comparison of methods of sampling aggression and victimization in school settings. *Journal of Educational Psychology, 92*, 360–366.

Pepler, D. J., Craig, W. M., O'Connell, P., Atlas, R., & Charach, A. (2004). Making a difference in bullying: Evaluation of a systemic school-based program in Canada. In P. K. Smith, D. J. Pepler, & K. Rigby (Eds.), *Bullying in Schools: How successful can interventions be?* (pp. 125–140). Cambridge, England: Cambridge University Press.

Pepler, D. J., Craig, W. M., Ziegler, S., & Charach, A. (1994). An evaluation of an anti-bullying intervention in Toronto schools. *Canadian Journal of Community Mental Health, 13*(2), 95–110.

Pikas, A. (1989). The Common Concern Method for the treatment of mobbing. In E. Roland & E. Munthe (Eds.), *Bullying: an international perspective* (pp. 91–104). London: David Fulton in association with the Professional Development Foundation.

Pikas, A. (2002). New developments in shared concern method. *School Psychology International, 23*(3), 307–326.

Pintabona, Y., Cross D., Hamilton, G., & Hall, M. (2000). *A Delphi study of successful practice in the prevention, reduction and management of bullying in schools.* Bentley, Western Australia: Curtin University of Technology, Western Australian Centre for Health Promotion Research.

Rigby, K. (2002). *New perspectives on bullying.* London: Jessica Kingsley.

Rigby, K. (2005). The method of shared concern as an intervention technique to address bullying in schools: an overview and appraisal. *Australian Journal of Counselling and Guidance, 15*, 27–34.

Rosenbluth, B., Whitaker, D. J., Sanchez, E., & Valle, L. A. (2004). The Expect Respect project: preventing bullying and sexual harassment in US elementary schools. In P. K. Smith, D. Pepler, & K. Rigby (Eds), *Bullying in Schools: How successful can interventions be?* (pp. 211–250). Cambridge, England: Cambridge University Press.

Salmivalli, C., Kaukiainen, A., & Voeten, M. (2005). Anti-bullying intervention: Implementation and outcome. *British Journal of Educational Psychology, 75*(3), 465–487.

Salmivalli, C., Kaukiainen, A., Voeten, M., & Sinisammal M. (2004). Targeting the group as a whole: The Finnish anti-bullying intervention. In P. K. Smith, D. Pepler, & K. Rigby (Eds.), *Bullying in Schools: How successful can interventions be?* (pp. 251–274). Cambridge, England: Cambridge University Press.

Schwartz, D., Dodge, K. A., Pettit, G. S., & Bates, J. E. (1997). The early socialization of aggressive victims of bullying. *Child Development, 68*(4), 665–675.

Sjostrom, L. & Stein, N. (1996). *Bullyproof: A teacher's guide on teasing and bullying for use with fourth & fifth grade students.* Wellesley, MA: Center for Research on Women.

Slee, P. T. (1994, January). I'm a victim — stop bullying. In K. Oxenberry, K. Rigby, & P. Slee (Eds), *Childrens peer relations: Cooperation and conflict.* Conference proceedings (pp. 19–22). Adelaide, Australia.

Slee, P. T. (1996). The P.E.A.C.E. Pack: A program for reducing bullying in our schools. *Australian Journal of Guidance and Counselling, 6*, 63–69.

Slee, P. T. (2001). *The PEACE Pack: A program for reducing bullying in our Schools (3rd ed.).* Adelaide, Australia: Flinders University.

Slee, P. T. (2005). The P.E.A.C.E. Pack: Evaluation of a program for the successful reduction of school bullying. In H. McGrath & T. Noble (Eds.), *Bullying solutions. Evidence-based approaches to bullying in Australian schools.* Sydney: Pearson.

Slee, P. T., & Mohyla, J. (2007). The PEACE Pack: An evaluation of interventions to reduce bullying in four Australian primary schools. *Educational Research, 49*, 103–114.

Smith, P. K., Pepler, D., & Rigby, K. (Eds.). (2004). *Bullying in schools: How successful can interventions be?* New York: Cambridge University Press.

Smith, D. J., Schneider, B. H., Smith, P. K., & Ananiadou, K. (2004). The effectiveness of whole-school antibullying programs: A synthesis of evaluation research. *School Psychology Review, 33*(4), 547–560.

Smith, P. K., & Sharp, S. (Eds.). (1994). *School bullying: Insights and perspectives.* London: Routledge.

Smith, P. K., Sharp, S., Eslea, M., & Thompson, D. (2004). England: The Sheffield project. In P. K. Smith, D. Pepler, & K. Rigby (Eds.), *Bullying in Schools: How successful can interventions be?* (pp. 99–124). Cambridge, England: Cambridge University Press.

Stevens, V., De Bourdeaudhuij, I., & Van Oost, P. (2000). Bullying in Flemish schools: An evaluation of anti-bullying intervention in primary and secondary schools. *British Journal of Educational Psychology, 70*(2), 195–210.

Stevens, V., De Bourdeaudhuij, I., & Van Oost, P. (2001). Anti-bullying interventions at school: Aspects of programme adaptation and critical issues for further programme development. *Health Promotion International, 16*(2), 155–167.

Stevens, V., & Van Oost, P. (1994). *Pesten op School: Een actieprogramma* [Bullying at school: An action program]. Kessel-Lo, The Netherlands: Garant Uitgevers.

Stevens, V., Van Oost, P., & de Bourdeaudhuij, I. (2000). The effects of an anti-bullying intervention programme on peers' attitudes and behavior. *Journal of Adolescence, 23*(1), 21–34.

Stevens, V., Van Oost, P., & de Bourdeaudhuij, I. (2004). Interventions against bullying in Flemish schools: Programme development and evaluation. In P. K. Smith, D. Pepler, and K. Rigby (Eds), *Bullying in Schools: How successful can interventions be?* (pp. 141–166). Cambridge, England: Cambridge University Press.

Stockdale, M. S., Hangaduambo, S., Duys, D., Larson, K., & Sarvela, P. D. (2002). Rural elementary students', parents', and teachers' perceptions of bullying. *American Journal of Health Behavior, 26*(4), 266–277.

Swearer, S. M., & Espelage, D. L. (2004). A social-ecological framework of bullying among youth. In S. M. Swearer & D. L. Espelage (Eds.), *Bullying in American schools: A social-ecological perspective on prevention and intervention* (pp. 1–12). Mahwah, NJ: Erlbaum.

Editors' Biographies

Shane R. Jimerson, **PhD**, is a Professor at the University of California, Santa Barbara. His international appointments have included: The University of Hong Kong; Tallinn University, Estonia; Sri Venkateswara University, Tirupati India; Massey University, New Zealand; Bahria University, Islamabad Pakistan; and The University of Manchester, England. Dr. Jimerson is the co-founder of the International Institute of School Psychology (http://education.ucsb.edu/jimerson/IISP). His scholarly publications and presentations have provided insights regarding; school violence and school safety, school crisis prevention and intervention, developmental pathways of school success and failure, the efficacy of early prevention and intervention programs, school psychology internationally, and developmental psychopathology. Among numerous publications, he is the lead-editor of *The Handbook of School Violence and School Safety: From Research to Practice* (2006, Erlbaum), a co-editor of *Best Practices in School Crisis Prevention and Intervention* (2002, National Association of School Psychologists), the lead editor of *The Handbook of International School Psychology* (2007, Sage), and the lead editor of *The Handbook of Response to Intervention: The Science and Practice of Assessment and Intervention* (2007, Springer Science). He is also co-author of *School Crisis Prevention and Intervention: The PREPaRE Model* (2009, National Association of School Psychologists), a co-author of a five-book grief support group curriculum series *The Mourning Child Grief Support Group Curriculum* (2001, Taylor and Francis), co-author of *Identifying, Assessing, and Treating Autism at School* (2006, Springer Science), co-author of *Identifying, Assessing, and Treating Conduct Disorder at School* (2008, Springer Science), co-author of *Identifying, Assessing, and Treating PTSD at School* (2008, Springer Science), co-author of *Identifying, Assessing, and Treating ADHD at School* (2009, Springer Science), and co-author of the *Promoting Positive Peer Relationships (P3R): Bullying Prevention Program* (2008, Stories of Us). He serves as the Editor of *The California School Psychologist* journal, Associate Editor of *School Psychology Review*, and has served on the editorial boards of numerous journals including, the *Journal of School Psychology and School Psychology Quarterly*. Dr. Jimerson has chaired and served on numerous boards and advisory committees at the state, national, and international levels, including; Vice President for Convention Affairs and Public Relations of Division 16 (School Psychology) American Psychological Association, Chair of the Research Committee of the International School Psychology Association, Chair of the Division 16 (School Psychology) conference proceedings for the American Psychological Association conference, and Chair of the School Psychology Research Collaboration Conference. The quality and contributions of his scholarship are reflected in the numerous awards and recognition that he has received, including the Best Research Article of the year award from the Society for the Study of School Psychology, the Outstanding Article of the Year Award from the National Association of School Psychologists', *School Psychology Review,* the *American* Educational Research Association Early Career Award in Human Development, the Outstanding Research Award from the California Association of School Psychologists, membership in the Society for the Study of School Psychology, the Lightner Witmer Early Career Contributions Award from Division 16 (School Psychology) of the American Psychological Association, and Fellow of the American Psychological Association, Division 16 (School Psychology). His scholarship continues to highlight the importance of early experiences on subsequent development and emphasize the importance of research informing professional practice to promote the social and cognitive competence of children.

Susan M. Swearer, PhD, is an Associate Professor of School Psychology at the University of Nebraska, Lincoln. She is the author of over 50 publications, most of which are about bullying and victimization among school-aged youth. She is the co-editor of the book, *Bullying in American Schools: A Social-Ecological Perspective on Prevention and Intervention* (2004, Routledge), co-author of the recent book, *Bullying Prevention and Intervention: Realistic Strategies for Schools* (2009, Guilford), and co-author of the *Promoting Positive Peer Relationships (P3R): Bullying Prevention Program* (2008, Stories of Us). She is on the editorial review boards of the *Journal of Anxiety Disorders, School Psychology Review, Journal of School Violence,* and *Journal of School Psychology.* Dr. Swearer is a supervising psychologist in the Counseling and School Psychology Clinic at the University of Nebraska, Lincoln, is the Director of the APA-approved Nebraska Internship Consortium in Professional Psychology (NICPP), and the co-director of the "Bullying Research Network" (http://brnet.unl.edu). She has conducted research on the relationship between depression, anxiety, and externalizing problems for over a decade. Her research and clinical foci are interrelated and include the examination of the comorbidity of psychological disorders in children and adolescents; the relationship of internalizing psychopathology on externalizing behavior; and cognitive-behavioral interventions for youth and their families. Current research projects include a longitudinal investigation of bullying and victimization in school-age youth; an international comparative study on bullying and victimization; and the evaluation of an individually-based intervention for bullying behaviors. Dr. Swearer has taught high school special education students (behavioral and emotional disabilities) and has worked as a licensed professional counselor with children, adolescents, and families in residential treatment, inpatient, and outpatient settings.

Dorothy L. Espelage, PhD, is a Professor of Child Development and Associate Chair in the Department of Educational Psychology at the University of Illinois, Urbana-Champaign. She is a University Scholar and has fellow status in Division 17 (Counseling Psychology) of the American Psychological Association. She earned her PhD in Counseling Psychology from Indiana University in 1997. She has conducted research on bullying for the last sixteen years. As a result, she presents regularly at national conferences and is author on over 70 professional publications. She is co-editor of *Bullying in American Schools: A Social-Ecological Perspective on Prevention and Intervention* (Routledge), co-author of *Bullying Prevention and Intervention: Realistic Strategies for Schools* (Guilford), and co-author of the *Promoting Positive Peer Relationships (P3R): Bullying Prevention Program* (2008, Stories of Us). She is on the editorial board for *Journal of Counseling and Development, Journal of Counseling Psychology, Journal of Educational Psychology,* and *Journal of Youth and Adolescence.* She has presented hundreds of workshops and in-service training seminars for teachers, administrators, counselors, and social workers across the United States. Her research focuses on translating empirical findings into prevention and intervention programming. Dr. Espelage has appeared on many television news and talk shows, including *The Today Show, CNN, CBS Evening News,* and *The Oprah Winfrey Show* and has been quoted in the national print press, including *Time Magazine, USA Today,* and *People* magazine.

Contributors

Francoise D. Alsaker, Ph.D., is a Professor of Developmental Psychology at the University of Bern, Switzerland. alsaker@psy.unibe.ch

Sharmila Bandyopadhyay is a doctoral student in the Curry Programs in Clinical and School Psychology at the University of Virginia. sharmila@virginia.edu

Sheri Bauman, Ph.D., is an Associate Professor, Department of Educational Psychology, University of Arizona, Tucson. sherib@u.arizona.edu

Bridget K. Biggs, Ph.D., is an Assistant Professor in the Clinical Child Psychology Program at the University of Kansas. biggsbk@ku.edu

Catherine Bohn is an Assistant Professor of Educational Psychology at the Wichita State University. bohn0066@umn.edu

Rina A. Bonanno, Ph.D., School of Education, Dowling College. BonannoR@Dowling.edu

James A. Bovaird, Ph.D., is an Assistant Professor of Educational Psychology at the University of Nebraska-Lincoln. jbovaird2@unl.edu

Eric S. Buhs, Ph.D., is an Associate Professor of Educational Psychology at the University of Nebraska – Lincoln. ebuhs2@unl.edu

Carrie Campbell-Bishop, M.A., School Counselor, Barbara Bush Elementary, Woodlands, Texas. cbishop@conroeisd.net

JoLynn V. Carney, Ph.D., is an Associate Professor of Counselor Education at The Pennsylvania State University. jcarney@psu.edu

Jean Clinton, M.D., Department of Psychiatry and Behavioural Neurosciences, McMaster University. clintonj@mcmaster.ca

Annematt L. Collot d'Escury, Ph.D., is an Associate Professor Clinical Developmental Psychology at the University of Amsterdam, The Netherlands. acollotdescury@fmg.uva.nl

Clayton R. Cook, M.A., is a pre-doctoral intern at Girls and Boys Town in Omaha, Nebraska. He is completing his Ph.D. in school psychology at the University of California, Riverside. clayton.cook@email.ucr.edu

Dewey G. Cornell, Ph.D., is Professor of Education in the Curry Programs in Clinical and School Psychology at the University of Virginia. dcornell@virginia.edu

Wendy Craig, Ph.D., is Professor of Psychology, Queen's University, and Scientific Co-Director of PREVNet, Kingston Canada. wendy.craig@queensu.ca

Laura M. Crothers, D.Ed., is an Assistant Professor in the Department of Counseling, Psychology, and Special Education at Duquesne University. crothersl@duq.edu

Paul E. Downes, Ph.D., is Director of the Educational Disadvantage Centre and Senior Lecturer in Psychology in the Education Department at St. Patrick's College, Drumcondra, (A College of Dublin City University), Dublin, Ireland. paul.downes@spd.dcu.ie

Ad C.M. Dudink, Ph.D., is an Associate Professor Developmental Psychology at the University of Amsterdam, The Netherlands. A.C.M.Dudink@uva.nl

Danielle Dupuis is a Ph.D. student in Educational Psychology at the University of Minnesota, Twin Cities Campus. dupui004@umn.edu

Leihua V. Edstrom, Ph.D., School Psychologist, Bellevue School District, Washington. leihuave@yahoo.com

Lawrence Epstein, Ph.D., is trainer and researcher with Creating Caring Communities, creators of the Bully-Proofing Your School program, and a School Psychologist with the Cherry Creek School District in Greenwood Village, Colorado. lepstein@cherrycreekschools.org

Dorothy L. Espelage, Ph.D., is a Professor of Educational Psychology at the University of Illinois, Urbana-Champaign. espelage@illinois.edu

Erika D. Felix, Ph.D., is an Assistant Researcher in the Counseling, Clinical, and School Psychology Department of the Gevirtz Graduate School of Education at the University of California, Santa Barbara. efelix@education.ucsb.edu

Peter Fonagy, Ph.D., FBA., is Freud Memorial Professor of Psychoanalysis, UCL, London, England; Director, The Anna Freud Centre, London, England. PFonagy@compuserve.com

Karin S. Frey, Ph.D., Research Associate Professor, Educational Psychology, University of Washington. karinf@u.washington.edu

Michael J. Furlong, Ph.D., is a Professor of Counseling, Clinical, and School Psychology at the University of California, Santa Barbara. mfurlong@education.ucsb.edu

Claire F. Garandeau, M.A., is a doctoral candidate in the Department of Educational Psychology at the University of Illinois, Urbana-Champaign. cgarand2@uiuc.edu

Carla Garrity, Ph.D., is an author with Creating Caring Communities, creators of the Bully-Proofing Your School Program, and a child psychologist in independent practice with The Neuro-Developmental Center in Denver, Colorado. Carla_Garrity@hotmail.com

Jami Givens, M.A., is a doctoral candidate in School Psychology at the University of Nebraska – Lincoln in Lincoln, NE. jamigivens@yahoo.com.

Jennifer Greif Green, Ph.D., is a Postdoctoral Research Fellow in the Department of Health Care Policy at Harvard Medical School. green@hcp.med.harvard.edu

Nancy G. Guerra, Ed.D., is a Professor of Psychology at the University of California, Riverside. nancy.guerra@ucr.edu

Eveline Gutzwiller-Helfenfinger, Ph.D., is a Lecturer and Researcher at the Teacher Training University of Central Switzerland, Lucerne. eveline.gutzwiller@phz.ch

Richard J. Hazler, Ph.D., is a Professor of Counselor Education at The Pennsylvania State University. hazler@psu.edu

Natalie Rocke Henderson, Ph.D. candidate, Department of Educational and Counselling Psychology, and Special Education, University of British Columbia. rocke1@telus.net

Sarah L. Herald-Brown, Ph.D., is an Assistant Professor of Human Development and Environmental Studies at Indiana University of Pennsylvania. Sarah.Brown@iup.edu

Meghan Hickey is a Ph.D. student in Educational Psychology at the University of Minnesota, Twin Cities Campus. hick0146@umn.edu

Miriam K. Hirschstein, Ph.D., Research Scientist, Center on Infant Mental Health and Development, University of Washington. mir@u.washington.edu

Arthur M. Horne, Ph.D., is Dean of the College of Education and Distinguished Research Professor of Counseling Psychology at the University of Georgia, Athens, GA. ahorne@uga.edu

Nan Huai, Ph.D., is a Researcher at the University of Wisconsin, Madison. nhuai@wisc.edu

Shelley Hymel, Ph.D., Department of Educational and Counseling Psychology and Special Education, University of British Columbia. shelley.hymel@ubc.ca

Kathryn Jens, Ph.D., is an author, trainer, and researcher with Creating Caring Communities, creators of the Bully-Proofing Your School program, and a school psychologist with the Cherry Creek School District in Greenwood Village, Colorado. kjens@cherrycreekschools.org

Shane R. Jimerson, Ph.D., is a Professor at the University of California, Santa Barbara. jimerson@education.ucsb.edu

Lynae A. Johnsen-Frerichs, M.A., Doctoral Candidate at the University of Nebraska – Lincoln. lynae.frerichs@gmail.com.

Antti Kärnä, M.A., Department of Psychology, University of Turku, Finland. antti.karna@utu.fi

Tia E. Kim, Ph.D., is a Post-Doctoral Fellow with the Southern California Academic Center for Excellence in Youth Violence Prevention. tia.kim@ucr.edu

Jered B. Kolbert, Ph.D., is an Associate Professor in the Department of Counseling and Development at Slippery Rock University. jered.kolbert@sru.edu

Gary W. Ladd, Ed.D., is a Full Professor of Psychology and Family and Human Development at Arizona State University. Gary.Ladd@asu.edu

Jim Larson, Ph.D., is a Professor of Psychology and Coordinator of the School Psychology Program at the University of Wisconsin-Whitewater. larsonj@uww.edu

Susan P. Limber, Ph. D., is Professor at the Institute on Family and Neighborhood Life, Clemson University. slimber@clemson.edu.

Jeffrey D. Long, Ph.D., is an Associate Professor of Educational Statistics at the University of Minnesota, Twin Cities Campus. longj@umn.edu

Patricia McDougall, Ph.D., Department of Psychology, St. Thomas More College, University of Saskatchewan. patti.mcdougall@usask.ca

Christina Meints, Ed.S., is a school psychologist with the Omaha Public Schools in Omaha, NE. christina_meints@hotmail.com

Danielle Mele, M.S., is a doctoral student in School Psychology at the University at Albany, State University of New York. Meled15@yahoo.com

Rosalind Murray-Harvey, Ph.D., is a Professor in Education at Flinders University, Adelaide, Australia. rosalind.murray-harvey@flinders.edu.au

Timothy D. Nelson, M.A., is a graduate student in the Clinical Child Psychology Program at the University of Kansas. tdnelson@ku.edu

Jennifer Mize Nelson, M.A., is a graduate student in the Clinical Child Psychology Program at the University of Kansas. jmize@ku.edu

Amanda B. Nickerson, Ph.D., is an Assistant Professor of School Psychology in the Department of Educational and Counseling Psychology at the University at Albany, State University of New York. anickerson@uamail.albany.edu

Paulette Norman, M.A., President, The McKay Foundation Conroe, Texas. mpme5095@yahoo.com

Paul O'Connell Ph.D., C.Psych. is a Psychologist with the Toronto District School Board, Toronto Canada.

Dan Olweus, Ph.D., is a Research Professor of Psychology at the University of Bergen, Bergen, Norway. olweus@psyhp.uib.no.

Pamela Orpinas, Ph.D., is a Professor in the Department of Health Promotion and Behavior at the University of Georgia, Athens, GA. porpinas@uga.edu

Kristina M. Osborne-Oliver, C.A.S., is a doctoral student in School Psychology at the University at Albany, State University of New York. Surrealist326@yahoo.com

Anthony D. Pellegrini, Ph.D., Professor of Educational Psychology at the University of Minnesota, Twin Cities Campus. pelle013@umn.edu

Debra Pepler, Ph.D., C. Psych. is Professor of Psychology, York University, Senior Associate Scientist at The Hospital for Sick Children, and Scientific Co-Director of PREVNet, Toronto Canada. pepler@yorku.ca

Amy Plog, Ph.D., is Director of Research for Creating Caring Communities, creators of the Bully-Proofing Your School Program, and a research psychologist with the Cherry Creek School District in Greenwood Village, Colorado. aplog@cherrycreekschools.org

William Porter, Ph.D., is Director of Creating Caring Communities, creators of the Bully-Proofing Your School Program. williamporter@creatingcaringcommunities.org

Elisa Poskiparta, Ph.D., Head of the Center for Learning Research, University of Turku, Finland. elisa.poskiparta@utu.fi

Ken Rigby, Ph.D., is an Adjunct Professor in the School of Education at the University of South Australia, Adelaide, South Australia. Ken.rigby@unisa.edu.au

Rebecca A. Robles-Piña, Ph.D. Associate Professor in the Department of Educational Leadership & Counseling at the Sam Houston State University, Huntsville, Texas. edu_rar@shsu.edu

Philip C. Rodkin, Ph.D., is an Associate Professor of child development in the Departments of Educational Psychology and Psychology at the University of Illinois, Urbana-Champaign. rodkin@uiuc.edu

Cary Roseth, Ph.D., is an Assistant Professor of Educational Psychology at Michigan State University. Rose0528@umn.edu

Frank C. Sacco, Ph.D., President, Community Services Institute, Boston & Springfield, Massachusetts; Adjunct Professor at Western New England College, Springfield, Massachusetts. FCSacco@aol.com

Nancy Sager, M.A., is an author, consultant, and trainer for Creating Caring Communities, creators of the Bully-Proofing Your School Program. nancy4848@mac.com

Christina Salmivalli, Ph.D, Professor of Psychology, University of Turku, Finland, and Center for Behavioural Research, University of Stavanger, Norway. tiina.salmivalli@utu.fi

Tracey G. Scherr, Ph.D., is an Assistant Professor of Psychology at the University of Wisconsin-Whitewater. scherrt@uww.edu

Louis A. Schmidt, Ph.D., Department of Psychology, Neuroscience & Behaviour, McMaster University. schmidtl@mcmaster.ca

Kimberly A. Schonert-Reichl, Ph.D., Department of Educational and Counselling Psychology, and Special Education, University of British Columbia. kimschon@interchange.ubc.ca

Jill D. Sharkey, Ph.D., is an Academic Coordinator in the Counseling, Clinical, and School Psychology Department at the University of California, Santa Barbara. jsharkey@education.ucsb.edu

Amanda B. Siebecker, M.A., Doctoral Candidate at the University of Nebraska – Lincoln. mandasiebecker@yahoo.com

Phillip T. Slee, Ph.D., is a Professor in Human Development at Flinders University, Adelaide, Australia. phillip.slee@flinders.edu.au

Robert Slonje is a doctoral student of Psychology, University of London, England.

Peter K. Smith, Ph.D., is Professor of Psychology and Head of the Unit for School and Family Studies, Goldsmiths College, University of London, England. p.smith@gold.ac.uk

David Solberg is a Ph.D. student in Educational Psychology at the University of Minnesota, Twin Cities Campus. solb0031@umn.edu

Shafik Sunderani, Hons. B.A., Department of Psychology, Neuroscience & Behaviour, McMaster University. sundersa@mcmaster.ca

Susan M. Swearer, Ph.D. is an Associate Professor of School Psychology at the University of Nebraska – Lincoln. sswearer@unlserve.unl.edu

Mitsuru Taki, M.A., is a principal researcher, guidance and counseling research centre, National Institute for Educational Policy Research, Tokyo, Japan. a000110@nier.go.jp

Diane Tanigawa, is a doctoral student in the Counseling, Clinical, and School Psychology Department at the University of California, Santa Barbara. dtanigaw@education.ucsb.edu

Stuart W. Twemlow, M.D., Professor of Psychiatry, Menninger Department of Psychiatry, Baylor College of Medicine. Houston, Director Peaceful Schools and Communities Project and Medical Director HOPE unit, The Menninger Clinic, Houston Texas. stwemlow@menninger.edu

Tracy Vaillancourt, Ph.D., Faculty of Education and School of Psychology, University of Ottawa and Department of Psychology, Neuroscience & Behaviour, McMaster University. tracy.vaillancourt@uottawa.ca

Eric Vernberg, Ph.D., is a Professor of Clinical Child Psychology at the University of Kansas. vernberg@ku.edu

Cixin Wang, M.S., Doctoral Student at the University of Nebraska – Lincoln. cixinwang@gmail.com

Kirk R. Williams, Ph.D., is a Professor of Sociology and Co-Director of the Presley Center for Crime and Justice Studies at the University of California, Riverside. kirk.williams@ucr.edu

Travis Wilson is a doctoral candidate in the Department of Educational Psychology at the University of Illinois, Urbana-Champaign. wilson2@uiuc.edu

Index

Page numbers in italics refer to Figures or Tables.